ISBN 978-1-5283-3341-2
PIBN 10919436

1 MONTH OF
FREE
READING

at

www.ForgottenBooks.com

By purchasing this book you are eligible for one month membership to ForgottenBooks.com, giving you unlimited access to our entire collection of over 1,000,000 titles via our web site and mobile apps.

To claim your free month visit:
www.forgottenbooks.com/free919436

English
Français
Deutsche
Italiano
Español
Português

www.forgottenbooks.com

Mythology Photography **Fiction**
Fishing Christianity **Art** Cooking
Essays Buddhism Freemasonry
Medicine **Biology** Music **Ancient**
Egypt Evolution Carpentry Physics
Dance Geology **Mathematics** Fitness
Shakespeare **Folklore** Yoga Marketing
Confidence Immortality Biographies
Poetry **Psychology** Witchcraft
Electronics Chemistry History **Law**
Accounting **Philosophy** Anthropology
Alchemy Drama Quantum Mechanics
Atheism Sexual Health **Ancient History**
Entrepreneurship Languages Sport
Paleontology Needlework Islam
Metaphysics Investment Archaeology
Parenting Statistics Criminology
Motivational

REPORT OF THE
NATIONAL ACADEMY
OF SCIENCES

FISCAL YEAR
1933–1934

REPORT OF THE
NATIONAL ACADEMY
OF SCIENCES

FISCAL YEAR
1933–1934

UNITED STATES
GOVERNMENT PRINTING OFFICE
WASHINGTON : 1935

LETTER OF TRANSMITTAL

. ———

NATIONAL ACADEMY OF SCIENCES,
January 30, 1935.

Hon. JOHN N. GARNER,
President of the United States Senate.

SIR: I have the honor to transmit to you herewith the report of the president of the National Academy of Sciences for the fiscal year ended June 30, 1934.

Yours respectfully,

W. W. CAMPBELL, *President.*

CONTENTS

CONTENTS

ACT OF INCORPORATION

AN ACT To incorporate the National Academy of Sciences

Be it enacted by the Senate and House of Representatives of the United States of America in Congress assembled, That Louis Agassiz, Massachusetts; J. H. Alexander, Maryland; S. Alexander, New Jersey; A. D. Bache, at large; F. B. Barnard,[1] at large; J. G. Barnard, United States Army, Massachusetts; W. H. C. Bartlett, United States Military Academy, Missouri; U. A. Boyden,[2] Massachusetts; Alexis Caswell, Rhode Island; William Chauvenet, Missouri; J. H. C. Coffin, United States Naval Academy, Maine; J. A. Dahlgren,[2] United States Navy, Pennsylvania; J. D. Dana, Connecticut; Charles H. Davis, United States Navy, Massachusetts; George Englemann, Saint Louis, Missouri; J. F. Frazer, Pennsylvania; Wolcott Gibbs, New York; J. M. Giles,[3] United States Navy, District of Columbia; A. A. Gould, Massachusetts; B. A. Gould, Massachusetts; Asa Gray, Massachusetts; A. Guyot, New Jersey; James Hall, New York; Joseph Henry, at large; J. E. Hilgard, at large, Illinois; Edward Hitchcock, Massachusetts; J. S. Hubbard, United States Naval Observatory, Connecticut; A. A. Humphreys, United States Army, Pennsylvania; J. L. Le Conte, United States Army, Pennsylvania; J. Leidy, Pennsylvania; J. P. Lesley, Pennsylvania; M. F. Longstreth, Pennsylvania; D. H. Mahan, United States Military Academy, Virginia; J. S. Newberry, Ohio; H. A. Newton, Connecticut; Benjamin Peirce, Massachusetts; John Rodgers, United States Navy, Indiana; Fairman Rogers, Pennsylvania; R. E. Rogers, Pennsylvania; W. B. Rogers, Massachusetts; L. M. Rutherfurd, New York; Joseph Saxton, at large; Benjamin Silliman, Connecticut; Benjamin Silliman, junior, Connecticut; Theodore Strong, New Jersey; John Torrey, New York; J. G. Totten, United States Army, Connecticut; Joseph Winlock, United States Nautical Almanac, Kentucky; Jeffries Wyman, Massachusetts; J. D. Whitney, California; their associates and successors duly chosen, are hereby incorporated, constituted, and declared to be a body corporate, by the name of the National Academy of Sciences.

Sec. 2. *And be it further enacted,* That the National Academy of Sciences shall consist of not more than fifty ordinary members, and the said corporation hereby constituted shall have power to make its own organization, including its constitution, bylaws, and rules and regulations; to fill all vacancies created by death, resignation, or otherwise; to provide for the election of foreign and domestic members, the division into classes, and all other matters needful or usual in such institution, and to report the same to Congress.

Sec. 3. *And be it further enacted,* That the National Academy of Sciences shall hold an annual meeting at such place in the United States as may be designated, and the academy shall, whenever called upon by any department of the Government, investigate, examine, experiment, and report upon any subject of science or art, the actual expense of such investigations, examinations, experiments, and reports to be paid from appropriations which may be made for the purpose, but the academy shall receive no compensation whatever for any services to the Government of the United States.

GALUSHA A. GROW,
Speaker of the House of Representatives.
SOLOMON FOOTE,
President of the Senate pro tempore.

Approved, March 3, 1863.
ABRAHAM LINCOLN, *President.*

---

[1] The correct name of this charter member was F. A. P. Barnard.
[2] Declined.
[3] The correct name of this charter member was J. M. Gillis.

AMENDMENTS

AN ACT To amend the act to incorporate the National Academy of Sciences

Be it enacted by the Senate and House of Representatives of the United States of America in Congress assembled, That the act to incorporate the National Academy of Sciences, approved March third, eighteen hundred and sixty-three, be, and the same is hereby, so amended as to remove the limitation of the number of ordinary members of said academy as provided in said act.

Approved, July 14, 1870.

_____

AN ACT To authorize the National Academy of Sciences to receive and hold trust funds for the promotion of science, and for other purposes

Be it enacted by the Senate and House of Representatives of the United States of America in Congress assembled, That the National Academy of Sciences, incorporated by the act of Congress approved March third, eighteen hundred and sixty-three, and its several supplements be, and the same is hereby, authorized and empowered to receive bequests and donations and hold the same in trust, to be applied by the said academy in aid of scientific investigations and according to the will of the donors.

Approved, June 20, 1884.

_____

AN ACT To amend the act authorizing the National Academy of Sciences to receive and hold trust funds for the promotion of science, and for other purposes

Be it enacted by the Senate and House of Representatives of the United States of America in Congress assembled, That the act to authorize the National Academy of Sciences to receive and hold trust funds for the promotion of science, and for other purposes, approved June twentieth, eighteen hundred and eighty-four, be, and the same is hereby, amended to read as follows:

"That the National Academy of Sciences, incorporated by the act of Congress approved March third, eighteen hundred and sixty-three, be, and the same is hereby, authorized and empowered to receive by devise, bequest, donation, or otherwise, either real or personal property, and to hold the same absolutely or in trust, and to invest, reinvest, and manage the same in accordance with the provisions of its constitution, and to apply said property and the income arising therefrom to the objects of its creation and according to the instructions of the donors: *Provided, however,* That the Congress may at any time limit the amount of real estate which may be acquired and the length of time the same may be held by said National Academy of Sciences."

SEC. 2. That the right to alter, amend, or repeal this act is hereby expressly reserved.

Approved, May 27, 1914.

ANNUAL REPORT OF THE NATIONAL ACADEMY OF SCIENCES

REVIEW OF THE YEAR 1933-34

Several subjects of special interest to the academy in the current year were described briefly in the address made by the president of the academy at the annual spring meeting held in the period April 22–25, 1934, from which the quoted paragraphs below are taken:

At a time of great national stress and strain, in the middle year of the Civil War, 1863, the Congress of the United States, desiring to have a definite organization of men learned and experienced in the physical and biological sciences to which it could go for knowledge and advice on scientific subjects, gave charter to such an organization, through the adoption of an act to incorporate the National Academy of Sciences; and to said act President Lincoln attached his signature in approval. The one and only purpose of the academy in the eyes of the Congress was that it should be the adviser of the Government in scientific matters, as expressed in the charter, thus: "* * * the academy shall, whenever called upon by any department of the Government, investigate, examine, experiment, and report upon any subject in science or art (meaning not the esthetic arts, but the practical arts), the actual expense of such investigations, examinations, experiments, and reports to be paid from appropriations which may be made for the purpose, but the academy shall receive no compensation whatever for any services to the Government of the United States."

When an American citizen, necessarily a contributor to knowledge, accepts election to membership in the academy, he tacitly agrees to heed every such summons, and to serve his Government to the best of his ability, in the manner described, without expectation of receiving compensation. In the 71 years of its life, the academy has responded many times to the Government's call, on the terms prescribed in the charter, and gladly.

The charter condition, "that the academy shall receive no compensation whatever for any services to the Government of the United States", exemplifies the correct and only wise policy. The academy, in providing knowledge and in giving advice, must be wholly disinterested in the financial or material sense. The academy is interested in the truth, in its origins and causes, and especially when giving advice, in the consequences of the truth; and it must not compromise with expediency.

    *   *   *   *   *   *   *

This beautiful and interesting building, the home of the academy, was completed and occupied just 10 years ago. Previously, and during the first 61 years of its life, the academy had no home it could call its own. Administrative headquarters and rooms and other facilities for the successive April meetings were most generously made available by the secretary and regents of the Smithsonian Institution. The long delay in securing an abiding place had one valued advantage: the legal title to this building and to its grounds rests with the National Academy of Sciences. The land was provided by gifts to the academy made by many public-spirited citizens; and the building, and an endowment fund to cover the costs of the building's maintenance and administration for the use of the National Academy of Sciences and the National Research Council, were the exceedingly generous gift of the Carnegie Corporation.

There are some unfortunate consequences of the long delay in finding a permanent home. Ever since 1863, countless publications on scientific subjects have been coming to the academy, by gift and exchange. There are many tens of thousands of books, pamphlets, journals, etc., in the large basement room that was planned and constructed to receive book shelves, and there are the library room fitted to receive the six or seven thousand volumes most in demand, and the beautiful reading room to the west of the library room; but until 2 days ago there had been no positive and material action taken to provide a working library or even an orderly arrangement of the books. A little over a year ago I appointed a committee to study and consider our library problem, and to formulate a definite library policy, under the able chairmanship of David White, for recommendation to the academy's council; and some very desirable decisions concerning a library policy have this week been made. (The committee's findings, and its recommendations concerning policies for the library as approved by the council of the academy on Apr. 22, 1934, are as published on pp. 20 of this report.)

Secondly, the walls of our rooms are in the main bare and monotonous. We have no portraits, busts, tablets, or other works of art in commemoration of our deceased members. Those of us who have been privileged to visit the rooms of the Royal Society, of the colleges in Oxford and Cambridge, and of similar institutions in Great Britain and on the European Continent, know how vitally such memorials contribute to the attractiveness and the spiritual effectiveness of those institutions. In recent months the council of the academy has considered this subject, in relation to the academy's rooms, and a committee is in process of appointment, with duty to formulate a policy for submission to the council.

The academy has been exceedingly fortunate, uniquely fortunate, in view of its comparative youth, in its receipt of gifts and bequests to serve as foundations for the awarding of medals and prizes of money, and the making of grants in aid of research. We have nine medal funds, not counting the Barnard gold medal (for which a committee of the academy selects the recipient for recommendation to Columbia University in New York, the university making the actual award once in 5 years, in recognition of meritorious services to science). Six of the academy's medals and likewise the Barnard medal bear the honored names of deceased academy members; and eight foundations providing grants for aid in research projects also bear the names of deceased members. For these valued provisions the academy is deeply grateful. The awards and grants are made in recognition of noteworthy accomplishments in research, and for the encouragement of research activity and discovery in the future. More briefly, they are to be interpreted as honors conferred by the National Academy of Sciences upon their recipients, but in this connection I should like to repeat a statement in my address of 2 years ago: the academy's ability to confer honor upon its members and others of high achievement proceeds from the honors conferred upon the academy by its members through their accomplishments in the advancement of knowledge.

In the current academic year the academy is awarding 5 medals and 4 honoraria. * * * One of the awards, that of the Charles Doolittle Walcott Medal and Honorarium for stimulation of research in pre-Cambrian and Cambrian life, we make this year for the first time.

In the course of the year many requests have come to the academy from the Executive branch of the Government for information, recommendation, and service in the domain of the physical and biological sciences. These requests have been complied with, in every case, as fully and promptly as the nature of the subject involved would permit.

On April 24, 1934, the president of the academy received a formal communication from the National Planning Board, Hon. Frederic A. Delano, chairman, requesting "the advice of the National Academy of Sciences regarding the role of science in national planning", accompanied by the specification that the academy's report on the subject be available for the use of the board some time before July 1, 1934. Accordingly, only 8 weeks, as a maximum, remained for the work of preparing the report. Fortunately, there was in existence, and subject to immediate call, the academy's standing committee on Government relations, consisting of John C. Merriam, chairman, 15 other members of the academy, and 1 non-academy member, to which the request could be referred. The duty of compliance with the request was assigned to said committee, on April 25. The committee met 3 days later in the academy building for the preliminary study of the subject, and the planning of the work. Members in attendance had come from as far as Harvard University and the University of Wisconsin. With the assistance of 30 contributing colleagues in the many divisions of science, more especially of 3 colleagues, E. D. Merrill, R. S. Woodworth, and F. E. Wright, who composed a small subcommittee on the subject, Chairman Merriam brought the report to completion on June 18, 1934, on which date the document was transmitted, through the office of the president of the academy, by air mail to the National Planning Board, then in session at Newburgh-on-the-Hudson. The committee's report is published on pages 25 to 43, of this annual report of the academy.

The work of the special committee on funds for publication of research, extending over the 9-year period, 1925-34, came to a close on June 30, 1934. The personnel of the committee—Raymond Pearl, chairman, E. G. Conklin, Arthur L. Day, and Oswald Veblen—continued unchanged through the full period; an obvious and significant advantage in the administration of the important subject involved. In 1925 the General Education Board had generously granted to the academy the sum of $30,000, expendable in the 3 fiscal years, 1925-28, for the publication of such results of scientific research as could not well be otherwise accomplished. In 1928 the Education Board continued their support of this activity by appropriating the further sum of $75,000, or $25,000 for each year of the second triennial period, 1928-31. Early in 1931 the Rockefeller Foundation provided the funds for this special publication service for the third triennial period, 1931-34, in amount $60,000. Inasmuch as the work was to terminate at the close of this period, the grant specified that the sums available for the 3 years would be $25,000, $20,000, and $15,000, respectively. The total sum made available by the two organizations was $165,000. The academy's appreciation of the generous provisions made by the board and by the foundation was formally expressed at the appropriate times.

The sum available for the publication of research results in the years 1933-34 was distributed, in 24 grants, as follows: 3 in astronomy, 2 in physics, 1 in geophysics, 1 in palaeontology, 1 in seismology, 1 in geography, 2 in zoology, 1 in genetics, 1 in entomology, 3 in medicine, 5 in botany, 2 in anthropology, and 1 general.

The dues of the United States as an adhering member of the International Council of Scientific Unions and of the several affiliated unions for the calendar years 1920 to 1931, inclusive, were paid almost entirely from United States Government funds appropriated by the Congress specifically for this purpose, said funds to be expended under the direction of the Secretary of State; the amounts to be paid to the several international organizations being certified to the Secretary of State by the National Academy of Sciences at the request of the National Research Council, the research council being the representative of the United States in the International Council of Scientific Unions. For reasons associated with the economic state of the Nation, the Congress made no appropriations to pay the adherence dues for the calendar years 1932 and 1933. In the emergency, the research council, at very considerable sacrifice, paid the dues of these 2 years from funds available for its own support, in amounts approximating $6,000 per annum. Before the close of the year 1933 the research council, in view of its reduced annual income, recognized that, unless the Congress due to assemble in early December 1933, should make an appropriation for this purpose, the research council could not and would not assume an obligation to continue the payments essential to the adherence of the United States after December 31, 1933. Notice to that effect was sent to the appropriate officers of the international organizations, at the request of the National Research Council, by the president of the National Academy of Sciences on December 18, 1933. ·

Through the kind offices of Hon. Sol Bloom, Member of the House of Representatives and of the House Committee on Foreign Affairs, an enabling act (House bill No. 6781) was introduced in the Congress, passed by "the House and by the Senate, and approved by the President of the United States on June 16, 1934, authorizing the making of appropriations to pay the annual share of the United States as an adhering member of the International Council of Scientific Unions and associated Unions, * * * (in) the sum of $9,000 for the fiscal year ending June 30, 1935." Unfortunately, the enabling act could not be succeeded by a positive item of appropriation, because of the pressure of business in the closing days of the session, but it is hoped that the actual appropriation will be made in the next session of the Congress as a deficiency measure. A more comprehensive treatment of this subject may be found in the report of the foreign secretary on pages 12 and 13.

From the income of the academy's trust funds available for aid in research activities, 26 grants were made within the year: 8 in astronomy, 5 in physics, 2 in geology, 4 in palaeontology, 1 in oceanography, 3 in zoology, and 3 on the subject of meteors. The largest grant was $800, and the smallest $75. The total allotment for the year was $8,450.

The papers on the scientific program for the autumn meeting of 1933 numbered 46. Their distribution among the fields of science was as follows: mathematics 2, astronomy 6, physics 10, chemistry 4, geology 4, meteorology 1, botany 1, zoology 1, physiology 7, pathology 3, medicine 1, psychology 3, anthropology 1, engineering 1, general science 1.

At the annual meeting in April 1934, 55 papers were presented: in mathematics 1, astronomy 5, physics 13, chemistry 3, geology 8, meteorology 2, botany 7, zoology 4, physiology 3, pathology 2, medicine 3, genetics 1, psychology 1, anthropology 1, general science 1.

Fifteen new members of the academy were elected at this year's annual meeting, bringing the total membership to 282. The limiting number of members now specified by the academy's constitution is 300. There is one member emeritus. Two foreign associates were elected in 1934, making the present number 45 * * *. The constitution limits the number to 50.

MEETINGS OF THE NATIONAL ACADEMY

AUTUMN MEETING, 1933

The 1933 autumn meeting of the National Academy of Sciences was held at Cambridge, Mass., upon invitation by the Massachusetts Institute of Technology, on November 20, 21, and 22, 1933.

BUSINESS SESSION

Sixty-six members responded to roll call, as follows:

Abbot, C. G.
Adams, C. A.
Adams, Roger
Bailey, I. W.
Barbour, Thomas
Benedict, F. G.
Birkhoff, G. D.
Blakeslee, A. F.
Boring, E. G.
Bowman, Isaiah
Bridgman, P. W.
Brown, E. W.
Calkins, G. N.
Campbell, W. W.
Cannon, W. B.
Castle, W. E.
Cattell, J. McKeen
Clinton, G. P.
Compton, K. T.
Conant, J. B.
Daly, R. A.
Davisson, C. J.

Dodge, Raymond
DuBois, E. F.
East, E. M.
Flexner, Simon
Folin, Otto
Gregory, W. K.
Hall, E. H.
Harrison, R. G.
Henderson, Yandell
Hovgaard, William
Hulett, G. A.
Hull, A. W.
Hunt, Reid
Johnson, Douglas
Keith, Arthur
Kemble, E. C.
Kennelly, A. E.
Keyes, F. G.
Kraus, C. A.
Lamb, A. B.
Langmuir, Irving
Lefschetz, Solomon

Lindgren, Waldemar
Lyman, Theodore
Mark, E. L.
Miles, W. R.
Millikan, R. A.
Morse, Marston
Parker, G. H.
Richtmyer, F. K.
Robinson, B. L.
Saunders, F. A.
Sauveur, Albert
Shapley, Harlow
Sherman, H. C.
Slater, J. C.
Smith, Theobald
Squier, G. O.
Veblen, Oswald
White, H. S.
Wilson, Edwin B.
Woodworth, R. S.
Wright, F. E.
Zinsser, Hans

PRESIDENT'S ANNOUNCEMENTS

The president of the academy made the following announcements:

DEATHS SINCE THE APRIL MEETING

Members.—William Thomas Councilman, born January 1, 1854, elected to the academy in 1904, transferred to the roll of members emeriti in November 1929, died May 27, 1933.

William Lewis Elkin, born April 29, 1855, elected to the academy in 1895, died May 30, 1933.

DELEGATES APPOINTED SINCE THE APRIL MEETING

To the Fifth General Assembly of the International Union of Geodesy and Geophysics, held at Lisbon, Portugal, September 17-24, 1933: William Bowie, Capt. H. N. Heck, William H. Hobbs, R. E. Horton, John A. Fleming, Harry D. Harradon, Walter D. Lambert, James B. Macelwane, Thomas G. Thompson, Capt. David McD. LeBreton.

TEMPORARY CHAIRMAN OF SECTION OF ZOOLOGY AND ANATOMY

C. A. Kofoid appointed to conduct the nominating balloting of the section during the absence of Chairman McClung in Japan.

5

TRUST FUND COMMITTEES

Joseph Henry Fund, D. L. Webster appointed chairman, to succeed W. F. Durand; term 5 years ending with the annual meeting in April 1933.

Charles Doolittle Walcott Fund, the Institut de France has renominated Charles Barrois as its representative on the board of trustees of the Walcott Fund for a further term of 4 years.

MARINE BIOLOGICAL LABORATORY

The recommendation by the council that Thomas Barbour be appointed representative of the National Academy of Sciences on the committee of review of the Marine Biological Laboratory was approved by the academy.

HIGHWAY RESEARCH BOARD

In order to carry on the work of the highway research board of the division of engineering and industrial research of the National Research Council effectively, it is necessary that there be a close affiliation and cooperation between that board and the United States Department of Agriculture. To bring this about, the Bureau of Public Roads shares with the National Research Council the expenses of the committees' work. This year, as in previous years, the contract was renewed for the year 1933–34. The amount involved was the payment by the Department of Agriculture to the treasurer of the National Academy of Sciences of the sum of $15,000 in installments. The money is used in connection with the research work of the committees.

REPORTS OF THE TREASURER AND AUDITING COMMITTEE

The annual report of the treasurer of the academy covering the fiscal year 1932–33 was presented, and upon recommendation by the council of the academy was accepted for inclusion in the printed annual report of the National Academy of Sciences for that period.

The report of the auditing committee was presented, and upon recommendation by the council of the academy was accepted for inclusion in the printed annual report of the National Academy of Sciences for the fiscal year 1932–33.

These reports appeared on pages 67–100 of the annual report of the National Academy of Sciences for the fiscal year 1932–33.

TRANSFER TO ROLL OF MEMBERS EMERITI

Charles Loring Jackson, elected to the academy in 1883, was transferred to the roll of members emeriti upon his request and with the unanimous recommendation of the council of the academy.

AMENDMENTS TO THE BYLAWS

The bylaws of the academy were amended as indicated below, upon the suggestion of two members and with the approval and recommendation of the council of the academy:

VI.1 (Property). The first sentence to read: "All apparatus and other materials of permanent value purchased with money from any grant from a trust fund shall be the property of the academy unless specific exception is made in the grant or by subsequent action of the council." (This reading removes the last eight words of the sentence: "or the directors of the trust fund concerned.")

III.5 which read: "A local committee of five members, appointed for each meeting, and the home secretary shall together constitute the committee of arrangements, of which the home secretary shall be chairman." This section was recast to read as follows: "For the annual meeting a local committee of five members, appointed for each meeting, and the home secretary shall constitute the committee of arrangements, of which the home secretary shall be chairman.

For the autumn meeting a member of the local group shall be chairman of the local committee, of which the home secretary shall be a member ex officio."

II.3 which read: "The assistant secretary, who may be a nonmember of the academy, shall receive a salary to be fixed by the council." This section was recast to read: "The executive secretary, who may be a nonmember of the academy, shall receive a salary to be fixed by the council."

Amendments approved.

JAMES CRAIG WATSON FUND

Consideration was given to the election of a successor to W. L. Elkin (deceased) as one of the three members of the board of trustees of the James Craig Watson fund. The recommendation of the council that Frank Elmore Ross, of Yerkes Observatory, be made trustee was approved by the academy.

J. LAWRENCE SMITH FUND

The committee unanimously recommends that a grant of $250 be made to Prof. C. C. Wylie of the University of Iowa on the understanding that $200 will be contributed by the graduate college of that university in aid of Professor Wylie's proposed researches on meteors.

The committee unanimously recommends that a grant of $175 be made to Mr. Shapley of the Harvard College Observatory to aid in the construction of a meteor spectrograph.

· FRANK SCHLESINGER, *Chairman.*

Recommendations approved.

CHARLES DOOLITTLE WALCOTT FUND

The request of Mrs. Mary Vaux Walcott that the scope of the Charles Doolittle Walcott award be amended to include recognition of work concerning pre-Cambrian life as well as that of the Cambrian, was approved upon recommendation by the council of the academy.

REPORT OF THE COMMITTEE ON CONSERVATION

The Committee on Conservation of Natural Resources has continued to discuss certain of the greater scientific problems which relate to national interest. Effort has been made to obtain such understanding of these questions as would, if required by special conditions, permit the academy to give its aid in the discussion.

JOHN C. MERRIAM, *Chairman.*

Report accepted.

REPORT OF THE COMMITTEE ON LONG-RANGE WEATHER FORECASTING

The committee on long-range weather forecasting has not been called together since the meeting upon which report was made to the last meeting of the academy. There has, however, been continued concentrated effort on the part of members of the committee and of the institutions concerned with this question with a view to securing additional data upon interpretation of long-range forecast of weather or climatic conditions.

Without considering these investigations as related to the academy, recognition must be given to Dr. C. G. Abbot for his work on solar radiation and its relation to climate.

In the Carnegie Institution of Washington there has been continued study from many angles on the type of problem set up by Dr. A. E. Douglass on relation between changes in weather, or climate, and variations in nature and rate of growth in trees. There has also been careful study of this problem in its relation to solar phenomena as illustrated by work of Dr. Abbot and studies at Mount Wilson Observatory.

Continued refinement of methods, both by conference and by study of particular points in this program, has meant continuing advance toward better understanding of these extremely difficult but fundamental problems.

JOHN C. MERRIAM, *Chairman.*

Report accepted.

COMMITTEE ON SCIENTIFIC PROBLEMS OF NATIONAL PARKS

The committee on scientific problems of national parks has continued its study of two main projects, namely those at Grand Canyon and at Crater Lake National Park. At both places there is now in operation an extremely interesting program offering easy opportunity to visitors to see those natural features which are considered by leading students to have the largest significance from the point of view of science and education.

The program at Grand Canyon has reached a stage at which it functions in a fully satisfactory way. It gives opportunity to study specifically each one of a number of the principal scientific elements of the Grand Canyon. At the same time the problem is so stated that the relation between these elements is also evident.

At Crater Lake the plan of the new station has just been put in operation, but it has demonstrated the effectiveness of a program through which the natural features of greatest interest are pointed out with a view to giving through them an interpretation of the principal scientific problems of the area. At Crater Lake the aesthetic element is also related to the picture.

JOHN C. MERRIAM, *Chairman.*

Report accepted.

PRESENTATION OF THE COMSTOCK PRIZE

At the dinner of the academy held on November 21, 1933, the Comstock Prize, consisting of $2,500, was presented to Percy Williams Bridgman. The award had been approved at the preceding April meeting, in recognition of Dr. Bridgman's investigations leading to the increased understanding of the electrical constitution of matter. The presentation address was made by Dr. Max Mason, chairman of the committee on the Cyrus B. Comstock Fund.

SCIENTIFIC SESSIONS

The following papers were presented at the scientific sessions by members of the academy or persons introduced by members:

MONDAY, NOVEMBER 20, 1933

Carl Anderson and Seth Neddermeyer (introduced by Robert A. Millikan): Relation between positron electron pairs and single positives resulting from gamma ray collisions with atomic nuclei.

Robley Evans, Robert A. Millikan, and Victor Neher: Cosmic ray fluctuations and their interpretations.

G. LeMaitre (introduced by Harlow Shapley): Evolution of the expanding universe.

H. P. Robertson (introduced by Harlow Shapley): The physical background of relativistic cosmology.

Henry Norris Russell and Donald H. Menzel: The terrestrial abundance of the permanent gases.

T. E. Sterne (introduced by Harlow Shapley): Radial stellar pulsations of appreciable amplitude.

Cecilia H. Payne (introduced by Harlow Shapley): Discussion of magnitudes and colors from the Harvard photographic photometry.

D. H. Menzel and T. E. Sterne (introduced by Harlow Shapley): The necessity for the existence of magnetic fields associated with sun-spot vortices.

F. E. Wright: Polarization of sun's rays reflected by the moon. Illustrated.

C. G. Abbot: Sun spots and weather.

Gibbs and R. C. Williams (introduced by F. K. Richtmyer): A direct ...tion of the atomic weight of the electron.

Albert W. Hull: Limiting current density in ionized gases.

Carl Anderson, Robert A. Millikan, Seth Neddermeyer, and William Pickering: The mechanism of cosmic ray counter action.

Irving Langmuir: The evaporation and sputtering of thorium from thoriated filaments.

F. K. Richtmyer and F. W. Barnes: The use of ground and etched crystals in X-ray spectrometry.

T. R. Cuykendall and S. W. Barnes (introduced by F. K. Richtmyer): Rocking curves obtained by transmission of the X-ray beam through calcite crystals.

Arthur E. Morgan (by invitation): Muscle Shoals and the Tennessee Valley problem.

TUESDAY, NOVEMBER 21, 1933

Thorne M. Carpenter (introduced by Francis G. Benedict): Biological variations in sugar utilization.

Allan Winter Rowe (introduced by Francis G. Benedict): The gaseous metabolism of some dwarfs and giants. Illustrated.

H. C. Sherman and L. N. Ellis: Necessary vs. optimal intake of vitamin G (B_2).

Cyrus H. Fiske (introduced by O. Folin): The nature of the depressor substance of the blood.

Simon Flexner: The nerve path of infection in poliomyelitis and its significance. Illustrated.

James B. Murphy (introduced by Simon Flexner): Tumor inhibiting factors extractable from tissues. Illustrated.

L. T. Bullock, R. Kinney, and M. I. Gregersen (introduced by Walter B. Cannon): The use of hypertonic sucrose solution to reduce cerebrospinal fluid pressure without a secondary rise.

Arturo Rosenblueth (introduced by Walter B. Cannon): Central excitation and inhibition in reflex changes of heart rate.

H. Davis, A. Forbes, and A. J. Derbyshire (introduced by Walter B. Cannon): The recovery period of the auditory nerve and its significance for the theory of hearing.

J. F. Fulton (introduced by Raymond Dodge): The functions of the premotor area of the cerebral cortex.

Walter R. Miles: Ocular-rotation centers for the two primary axes. Illustrated.

Ernest E. Tyzzer (introduced by E. B. Wilson): Loss of virulence in the protozoön of "blackhead," a fatal disease of turkeys, and the immunizing properties of attenuated strains.

Hans Zinsser and M. Ruiz Castañeda: Active and passive immunization in typhus fever. Illustrated.

R. G. Hoskins (introduced by E. B. Wilson): The schizophrenic psychosis with special reference to homeostasis.

William K. Gregory: Polyisomerism and anisomerism in cranial and dental evolution among vertebrates.

J. L. Cartledge and A. F. Blakeslee: Mutation rate increased by ageing seeds as shown by pollen abortion.

WEDNESDAY, NOVEMBER 22, 1933

George O. Squier: Combined sound and light distributor.

Charles P. Berkey and Frank E. Fahlquist: A geologic section of the Quabbin Aqueduct in central Massachusetts. Illustrated.

Chester Stock (introduced by John C. Merriam): Eocene primates from California. Illustrated.

John C. Merriam: Present status of the problem of the antiquity of man in North America.

Edgar B. Howard (introduced by John C. Merriam): Association of artifacts with mammoth and bison in eastern New Mexico. Illustrated.

William Hovgaard: An investigation of the stresses in longitudinal welds.

Hans Müller (introduced by J. C. Slater): Dielectric properties of crystals.

P. A. Levene and Alexandre Rothen: Chemical structure and optical activity. (Read by title.)

· Edwin J. Cohn (introduced by J. B. Conant): Contrasting properties of ions, zwitterions and uncharged molecules.

Evald L. Skau and Wendell H. Langdon (introduced by F. G. Keyes): A development of a theoretical basis for the behavior of controlled time-temperature curves.

H. E. Edgerton and K. J. Germeshausen (introduced by K. T. Compton): Demonstration of high-speed photography of motions of animals and insects.

Marston Morse: A solution of the Poincaré continuation problem.

Marshall H. Stone (introduced by G. D. Birkhoff): Boolian algebras and their applications to topology.

ANNUAL MEETING, 1934

The National Academy of Sciences held its annual spring meeting, 1934, in the academy building, Washington, D. C., on April 23, 24, and 25, 1934.

BUSINESS SESSION

One hundred and twenty-seven members were present, as follows:

Abbot, C. G.	Hall, E. H.	Morgan, T. H.
Adams, Roger	Harper, R. A.	Noyes, W. A.
Aitken, R. G.	Harrison, R. G.	Osborn, H. F.
Allen, E. T.	Hektoen, Ludvig	Osterhout, W. J. V.
Bancroft, W. D.	Henderson, L. J.	Parker, G. H.
Benedict, F. G.	Henderson, Yandell	Pearl, Raymond
Berkey, C. P.	Hildebrand, J. H.	Pillsbury, W. B.
Berry, E. W.	Howard, L. O.	Reid, H. F.
Bigelow, H. B.	Howe, M. A.	Richtmyer, F. K.
Birge, R. T.	Howell, W. H.	Ritt, J. F.
Blakeslee, A. F.	Hrdlicka, Ales	Rous, Peyton
Bowman, Isaiah	Hubble, Edwin	Ruedemann, Rudolf
Bridgman, P. W.	Hudson, C. S.	Russell, H. N.
Campbell, D. H.	Hulett, G. A.	Schuchert, Charles
Campbell, W. W.	Hull, A. W.	Scott, W. B.
Cannon, W. B.	Ives, H. E.	Seashore, C. E.
Cattell, J. McKeen	Jewett, Frank B.	Shapley, Harlow
Clinton, G. P.	Johnson, Douglas	Sherman, H. C.
Coble, A. B.	Jones, L. R.	Stebbins, Joel
Coblentz, W. W.	Keith, Arthur	Stejneger, Leonhard
Compton, A. H.	Kennelly, A. E.	Streeter, G. L.
Compton, K. T.	Keyes, F. G.	Swanton, John R.
Conant, J. B.	Knopf, Adolph	Swasey, Ambrose
Conklin, E. G.	Kofoid, C. A.	Tennent, D. H.
Crew, Henry	Kraus, C. A.	Ulrich, E. O.
Cross, Whitman	Kunkel, L. O.	Vaughan, T. W.
Davenport, C. B.	Lefschetz, Solomon	Veblen, Oswald
Davis, Bergen	Leith, C. K.	Washburn, Margaret F.
Davisson, C. J.	Levene, P. A.	Wheeler, W. M.
Day, A. L.	Lillie, F. R.	Whipple, G. H.
Detweiler, S. R.	Lindgren, Waldemar	White, David
Dodge, B. O.	Lyman, Theodore	White, H. S.
Dodge, Raymond	McCollum, E. V.	Whitehead, J. B.
Donaldson, H. H.	Mendell, L. B.	Willis, Bailey
DuBois, E. F.	Mendenhall, C. E.	Wilson, Edmund B.
Duggar, B. M.	Mendenhall, W. C.	Wilson, Edwin B.
East, E. M.	Merriam, J. C.	Wissler, Clark
Eisenhart, L. P.	Merrill, E. D.	Wood, R. W.
Emerson, R. A.	Merritt, Ernest	Woodruff, L. L.
Erlanger, Joseph	Miller, D. C.	Woodworth, R. S.
Flexner, Simon	Millikan, R. A.	Wright, F. E.
Fred, E. B.	Mitchell, S. A.	
Gherardi, Bancroft	Modjeski, Ralph	

PRESIDENT'S ANNOUNCEMENTS

The president of the academy made the following announcements:

DEATHS SINCE THE AUTUMN MEETING

Members.—Henry Stephens Washington, born January 15, 1867, elected to the academy in 1921, died January 7, 1934.

William Morris Davis, born February 12, 1850, elected to the academy in 1904, died February 5, 1934.

Edward Wight Washburn, born May 10, 1881, elected to the academy in 1932, died February 6, 1934.

Augustus Trowbridge, born January 2, 1870, elected to the academy in 1919, died March 14, 1934.

George Owen Squier, born March 21, 1865, elected to the academy in 1919, died March 24, 1934.

Foreign associate.—Fritz Haber, of the University of Berlin, elected a foreign associate in 1932, died February 1, 1934.

ASSIGNMENT OF BIOGRAPHICAL MEMOIRS

Edward Sylvester Morse, assigned to L. O. Howard.
Samuel Wesley Stratton, assigned to A. E. Kennelly.
Ernest Julius Wilczynski, assigned to Ernest P. Lane, nonmember.
John Joseph Carty, assigned to Frank B. Jewett.
Henry Stephens Washington, assigned to Whitman Cross.
William Morris Davis, assigned to Douglas W. Johnson.

SECTION CHAIRMEN

New chairmen of sections, elected by the sections, for a term of 3 years, commencing at the close of the present annual meeting:

Section of mathematics.—A. B. Coble to succeed L. P. Eisenhart.
Section of zoology and anatomy.—F. R. Lillie to succeed C. A. Kofoid (acting chairman).

DELEGATES APPOINTED SINCE THE AUTUMN MEETING

To the inauguration of Bessie Carter Randolph as president of Hollins College, Hollins, Va., February 21, 1934: S. A. Mitchell.

To the inauguration of Joseph M. M. Gray as chancellor of the American University, Washington, D. C., March 3, 1934: W. W. Campbell.

To the Eleventh Conference of the International Union of Chemistry and the Ninth International Congress of Pure and Applied Chemistry, Madrid, Spain, April 5 to 11, 1934: Arnold K. Balls, Edward Bartow, John Van N. Dorr, Raleigh Gilchrist, Harry N. Holmes, Lauder W. Jones, Gilbert N. Lewis, Atherton Seidell, Alexander Silverman, Robert E. Swain, and John W. Turrentine.

To the Congress of Mathematicians of the Slav Countries, Prague, Czechoslovakia, September 23 to 28, 1934: Solomon Lefschetz.

STANDING COMMITTEE APPOINTMENTS

Auditing committee.—J. R. Swanton, chairman; W. C. Mendenhall, E. O. Ulrich.

Finance committee.—C. G. Abbot and Gano Dunn reappointed as members, to serve with the president and treasurer of the academy and the chairman of the research council, the treasurer being chairman of the committee.

TRUST FUND COMMITTEE APPOINTMENTS

Henry Draper fund.—V. M. Slipher, to succeed H. N. Russell as chairman, for the period ending in 1937; P. W. Merrill, to succeed H. N. Russell as member. Term, 5 years.

J. Lawrence Smith fund.—F. L. Ransome, to succeed A. O. Leuschner as member. Term, 5 years.

Cyrus B. Comstock fund.—W. D. Coolidge, to succeed William Duane as member. Term, 5 years.

Marsh fund.—H. F. Reid to succeed David White as member. Term, 5 years.

Murray fund.—C. A. Kofoid to succeed William Bowie as member. Term, 3 years.

Marcellus Hartley fund.—Harvey Cushing, to succeed Gano Dunn as member and chairman. Term, 3 years; Herbert Hoover, reappointed as member. Term, 3 years.

Mary Clark Thompson fund.—Waldemar Lindgren, to succeed F. L. Ransome as member. Term, 3 years.

Joseph Henry fund.—D. L. Webster's term as chairman extended 1 year, to terminate in 1939.

John J. Carty fund.—H. J. Muller, to succeed R. A. Millikan as member. Term, 5 years.

BOARD OF TRUSTEES OF SCIENCE SERVICE

William H. Howell was elected by the executive committee of the council of the academy to succeed himself as one of the three representatives of the academy on the Board of Trustees of Science Service, Inc.; the others being R. A. Millikan (1935) and David White (1936).

JOSEPH A. HOLMES SAFETY ASSOCIATION

David White was reappointed as the academy representative for the year beginning July 1, 1934, on the Joseph A. Holmes Safety Association.

CHARLES A. COFFIN FOUNDATION

Bergen Davis was appointed as the academy representative on the Charles A. Coffin Foundation, succeeding Gano Dunn.

PROCEEDINGS, MANAGING EDITOR

Announcement was made of the election, by the council of the academy on the preceding evening, of Edwin B. Wilson as managing editor of the Proceedings of the National Academy of Sciences, to succeed himself, for the period ending with the autumn meeting in 1935.

DUES

The recommendation of the council that dues for membership in the academy for the year ending with the annual meeting in 1935 be $10, of which $5 shall be for the Proceedings, was approved.

REPORT OF THE FOREIGN SECRETARY

The foreign secretary of the National Academy of Sciences presented at the annual meeting of the academy held on April 23, 1934, an oral report, with the understanding that it would be followed later by a written report covering the fiscal year from July 1, 1933, to June 30, 1934.

In honoring men in foreign countries who have contributed to world knowledge the academy from year to year elects a few foreign associates; and while the nominations are made by the council of the academy, the foreign secretary is constantly reviewing the work of those abroad engaged in research in the natural sciences for suggestions for consideration by the council. The constitutional limit of the number of foreign associates in the academy at any one time is 50, and at the present there are 45. The distribution of this group on a percentage basis in the fields represented in the academy is as follows: Mathematics, 18 percent; astronomy, 11; physics, 15; engineering, 7; chemistry, 11; geology and paleontology, 15; botany, 7; zoology and anatomy, 7; physiology and biochemistry, 7; pathology and bacteriology, 0; anthropology and psychology, 2. In the academy the membership in the same fields is distributed on a percentage basis as follows: Mathematics, 8 percent; astronomy, 10; physics, 12; engineering, 6; chemistry, 11; geology, 10; botany, 8; zoology and anatomy, 12; physiology and biochemistry, 8; pathology and bacteriology, 6; anthropology and psychology, 9.

This year the academy on nomination of the council of the academy conferred its highest honor for a foreigner on two men—V. Bjerknes of the University of Oslo, Norway, for his outstanding work in oceanography and meteorology, and Robert Robinson, Dyson Perrins Laboratory, South Parks Road, Oxford, England, for his exceptional work in organic chemistry—by electing them foreign associates of the academy.

On the recommendation of the academy to the Department of State, the United States was represented by 6 delegates at the Fifth General Assembly of the International Union of Geodesy and Geophysics held at Lisbon, Portugal, September 17–24, 1933, and by 12 delegates at the Eleventh Conference of the International Union of Chemistry, and the Ninth International Congress of Pure and Applied Chemistry, held at Madrid, Spain, April 5–11, 1934. Through the division of foreign relations of its National Research Council the academy was represented by 8 delegates at the meeting of the Fifth Pacific Science Congress held in Victoria and Vancouver, B. C., from June 1 to 14, 1934.

Perhaps the matter of greatest importance in the foreign secretary's office this year has been the continuation of the support of the National Academy of Sciences in the adherence of the National Research Council to the International Council of Scientific Unions and its affiliated unions. During the years 1920–31 the United States Government has paid the American share of the expenses of the unions, through the Department of State, from an appropriation made by Congress for the purpose. This appropriation was omitted by the Congress for economic reasons during the depression, 1932–33. At this time, however, the amount needed was paid by the National Research Council. The research council has found itself unable to continue such payments and in the interest of American science and of American prestige the president of the academy and the chairman of the National Research Council joined in an effort to restore these governmental appropriations. Through the interest and kindness of Congressman Sol Bloom, a bill was introduced in the House of Representatives, to enable the United States, as a Government, to renew and continue adherence to the council and affiliated unions. In connection with a hearing arranged for by Congressman Bloom before the Committee on Foreign Affairs of the House of Representatives, it became possible to consolidate the sentiment of some of the representative men of the country in support of this move. The president of the academy, being in Washington at the time, devoted the necessary time to sending out requests to the organizations and scientific men of the United States interested in the work of the International Council of Scientific Unions, with the result that when the hearing was called there was overwhelming evidence in the form of letters and statements showing that it was desirable on the part of Congress to approve, by passage of the act, authorization for the adherence of the United States. The bill (H. R. 6781) which it was hoped would become a continuing enabling act, was acted and reported on favorably by the Committee on Foreign Affairs of the House, but received on the floor of the House an objection on account of the continuing-from-year-to-year phase. In order that the measure might not be defeated entirely, Congressman Bloom accepted an amendment limiting payment to 1 year, thus establishing a precedent for its authorization. This bill is called an enabling act and constitutes an authorization for an appropriation to be made for payment of the share of the United States for the year 1934. It is necessary that the actual appropriation be considered by the Committee on Appropriations on an estimate submitted by the Secretary of State through the Bureau of the Budget. The authorization bill as amended passed the Senate during the closing hours of the last session and was signed by the President of the United States too late, however, for the item making the appropriation to be included in the deficiency bill passed a few hours later. Nevertheless this item will be included by the State Department and the Bureau of the Budget in the next deficiency bill to be considered at the session of Congress opening January 1935.[1]

ROBERT A. MILLIKAN,
Foreign Secretary.

Reported accepted.

REPORT OF THE HOME SECRETARY

For the year elapsing since the date of the last annual meeting no scientific Memoirs of the National Academy of Sciences have been issued. Of the Biographical Memoirs, two are in press: the eleventh and last memoir of volume 15 and the first memoir of volume 16. Three manuscripts are in hand awaiting printing.

Since the last annual meeting 1 member emeritus and 6 members have died:

William Thomas Councilman, born January 1, 1854, elected to the academy in 1904, transferred to the roll of members emeriti in November 1929, died May 27, 1933.

William Lewis Elkin, born April 29, 1855, elected to the academy in 1895, died May 30, 1933.

Henry Stephens Washington, born January 15, 1867, elected to the academy in 1921, died January 7, 1934.

William Morris Davis, born February 12, 1850, elected to the academy in 1904, died February 5, 1934.

---

[1] See introductory reference to the subject on p. 4, this annual report of the academy.

Edward Wight Washburn, born May 10, 1881, elected to the academy in 1932, died February 6, 1934.

Augustus Trowbridge, born January 2, 1870, elected to the academy in 1919, died March 14, 1934.

George Owen Squier, born March 21, 1865, elected to the academy in 1919, died March 24, 1934.

One foreign associate has died since the annual meeting: Fritz Haber, of the University of Berlin, elected a foreign associate in 1932, died February 1, 1934.

One member, Charles Loring Jackson, was transferred to the roll of members emeriti upon his request at the last autumn meeting.

There are now 271 members, 1 member emeritus, and 43 foreign associates.

FRED. E. WRIGHT, *Home Secretary.*

Report accepted.

REPORT OF THE TREASURER

Attention was called to the annual report of the treasurer of the academy for the period July 1, 1932, to June 30, 1933, contained on pages 67–100 of the annual report of the academy for the fiscal year 1932–33, which had just been distributed to the members.

The semiannual, supplementary statement of the treasurer as of December 31, 1933, was presented and accepted as a matter of record.

REPORTS OF TRUST FUNDS

ALEXANDER DALLAS BACHE FUND

At the meetings of the academy held in April and November 1933, the board of directors of the Bache fund of the National Academy of Sciences made the following grants:

No. 336, for $400, to Miss Cecilia H. Payne, Harvard College Observatory, for the determination of photographic magnitudes of southern hemisphere stars.

No. 337, for $400, to Mr. Robert R. McMath, McMath-Hulbert Observatory, for motion-picture researches on the solar prominences.

No. 338, for $100, to Dr. Graham Edwards, School of Medicine, University of Buffalo, for renal researches.

No. 339, for $400, to Dr. O. J. Lee, Dearborn Observatory, for investigations of the spectra of faint stars.

No. 340, for $200, to Dr. J. Elery Becker, Iowa State College, for researches on the protozoal parasites of ground squirrels.

No. 341, for $500, to Dr. Michael Heidelberger, Presbyterian Hospital, New York, for the purchase of an interferometer for the study of precipitin reactions.

No. 342, for $500, to Dr. H. M. Randall, University of Michigan, for the construction and improvement of apparatus for infra-red spectroscopy.

No. 343, for $400, to Dr. H. S. Jennings, Johns Hopkins University, for researches in protozoal genetics.

No. 344, for $400, to Dr. Eric Ponder, New York University, for researches on the narcosis of cardiac muscles.

EDWIN B. WILSON,
W. J. V. OSTERHOUT,
HEBER D. CURTIS, *Chairman.*

Report accepted.

JAMES CRAIG WATSON FUND

Your board of trustees of the Watson fund unanimously recommends as follows:

No. 49.—A grant of $100 to Dr. Dirk Brouwer, Yale University Observatory, to pay the incidental expenses in connection with the reduction, compilation, discussion, and publication of occultations of stars by the moon. This amount will suffice to carry on this work until June 1935.

G. C. COMSTOCK,
F. E. ROSS,
A. O. LEUSCHNER, *Chairman.*

Report accepted and recommendation approved.

HENRY DRAPER FUND

The chairman of the committee on the Henry Draper fund, Mr. H. N. Russell, presented an oral statement regarding the financial condition of that fund.

Report accepted.

J. LAWRENCE SMITH FUND

The committee now recommends to the academy that a grant of $400 be made to Messrs. H. Shapley and E. Öpik of Harvard College Observatory to aid the discussion of some 28,000 observations of meteors made in Arizona last year.

FRANK SCHLESINGER, *Chairman.*

Report accepted and recommendation approved.

BENJAMIN APTHORP GOULD FUND

The directors of the Gould fund of the National Academy of Sciences have the honor to report as follows:

Grants made during the year April 1, 1933, to March 31, 1934:

Oct. 23, 1933, to Harlan T. Stetson for investigations of correlation between variations in latitude and positions of the moon_____ $400
Dec. 7, 1933, to Benjamin Boss for support of the Astronomical Journal_____ 800
Feb. 19, 1934, to J. S. Plaskett, Dominion Astrophysical Observatory, for work on variable stars_____ 300
Mar. 15, 1934, to Frank C. Jordan, Allegheny Observatory, for the measurement of parallax plates_____ 500

HEBER D. CURTIS,
F. R. MOULTON, *Chairman.*

(The third member of the board of directors, Dr. E. W. Brown, is absent from the country.)

Report accepted.

WOLCOTT GIBBS FUND

No awards were made from the Wolcott Gibbs fund during the past year.

E. P. KOHLER, *Chairman.*

Report accepted.

CYRUS B. COMSTOCK FUND

The chairman of the committee on the Cyrus B. Comstock fund reported on the financial condition of that fund.

Report accepted.

MARSH FUND

The chairman of the committee on the Marsh fund, Mr. T. Wayland Vaughan, presented an oral report concerning grants made from the Marsh fund last year, supplemented by the following recommendations from the committee for new grants:

To Prof. Douglas W. Johnson, Columbia University, for the employment of assistance in preparing projected profiles for southern Wisconsin for use in a study of the correlation of Appalachian erosion surfaces_____ $100
To Dr. C. B. Read, United States Geological Survey, to defray field expenses in collecting fossil plants in the coal fields of Belgium and nearby regions_____ 225
To Mr. Albert E. Wood, Long Island University, for the study of Geomyidae, pocket gophers, of Long Island, mostly to pay for illustrations__ 100
To Rear Admiral J. D. Nares, chairman, International Hydrographic Bureau, Monaco, toward expenses of the employment of additional assistance in plotting data on ocean depths in charts to be used in a new edition of the General Bathymetric Chart of the Oceans_____ 125

T. WAYLAND VAUGHAN, *Chairman.*

Report accepted and recommendations approved.

MURRAY FUND

The committee on the Murray fund unanimously recommends that the Agassiz medal for the year 1934 be awarded to Dr. Haakon H. Gran, professor of botany, University of Oslo, for his contributions to knowledge of the factors controlling organic production in the sea.

HENRY B. BIGELOW, *Chairman.*

Report accepted and recommendation approved.

MARCELLUS HARTLEY FUND

On behalf of the committee on the award of the public welfare medal from the Marcellus Hartley fund, I have the honor to report that the committee has given careful consideration to a number of names and that by the requisite vote of two-thirds of its members,. the committee hereby formally recommends to the National Academy of Sciences for the award of the medal in 1935, for eminence in the application of science to the public welfare, the name of Mr. August Vollmer, for his application in police administration, of scientific methods to crime detection and to crime prevention.

HERBERT HOOVER,
WILLIAM H. WELCH,
MAX MASON,
JOSEPH S. AMES,
HENRY H. DONALDSON,
GANO DUNN, *Chairman.*

Report accepted and recommendation approved.

DANIEL GIRAUD ELLIOT FUND

The chairman of the committee on the Daniel Giraud Elliot fund, Mr. Ross G. Harrison, presented an oral recommendation from that committee to the effect that the Elliot Medal and Honorarium for 1932 should be awarded to James P. Chapin, of the American Museum of Natural History for his work entitled "The Birds of the Belgian Congo." (Pt. I, Bull. Amer. Mus. Nat. Hist., vol. 65, 1932, pp. 1–x+, 756, 10 pls., 208 figs. and map.)

Report accepted and recommendation approved.

MARY CLARK THOMPSON FUND

The committee of the National Academy for the Mary Clark Thompson fund unanimously recommends that the Mary Clark Thompson medal be awarded to Charles Schuchert, New Haven, Conn., professor emeritus of paleontology, Yale University, and of historical geology in the Sheffield Scientific School, and emeritus curator of invertebrate paleontology in the Peabody Museum, for his important work in the classification and distribution of paleozoic invertebrates, for the broad perspective, originality, faithfulness of detail, and stimulating philosophy of his contributions to historical geology, and for his outstanding accomplishments in the field of paleogeography;

And further, that an honorarium in the sum of $250 accompany the medal.

W. C. MENDENHALL,
F. L. RANSOME,
DAVID WHITE, *Chairman.*

Report accepted and recommendations approved.

JOSEPH HENRY FUND

Mr. L. P. Eisenhart, acting as chairman of the committee on the Joseph Henry fund in the absence of Mr. Webster, presented the mimeographed report of that committee, supplemented by recommendations.

The following are abstracts of reports received covering the work done during the past year under the grants from the Joseph Henry fund.

52. Professor Ralph E. Cleland, Goucher College, Baltimore, Md., $400, for the continuance of studies on the cytology and genetics of Oenothera. This grant has proved of inestimable value to Professor Cleland in providing technical assistance in the growth of crosses and the collection of cytological material. The material studied within this year sheds light on numerous relationships between species, notably: (1) Between those from California and certain forms from the East; (2) Between a species from Iowa and others previously analyzed; (3) Between Cockerelli and certain other species. Two manuscripts have been completed, much other material has been collected for study, and some progress has been made on a monograph summarizing the whole cyto-genetical situation in Oenothera.

53. Prof. Fred Allison, Alabama Polytechnic Institute, Auburn, Ala., $750, for the continuance of studies with his magneto-optic effect. This effect has been used as heretofore for a great variety of researches, summarized in the following papers:

Magneto-Optic Nicol Rotation Method for Quantitative Analysis of Calcium, by Bishop, Dollins, and Otto.

Manganese Isotopes, by Otto and Bishop.

Isotopes of Sodium and Cesium, by Dollins and Bishop.

Isotopes of Chlorine, by Bishop and Allison.

Some Further Remarks on the Use of the Magneto-Optic Method, by Jones and Goslin.

Some Quantitative Studies of the Localization of Uranium in the Principal Organs of Rabbits During the Course of Uranium Intoxication by Use of the Magneto-Optic Method, by Jones and Goslin.

Detection and Estimation of Formaldehyde Within the Cell of a Green Plant by the Allison Apparatus, by Sommer, Bishop, and Otto.

The Formation of Formaldehyde by the Action of Ultra-violet Light on Carbon Dioxide and Water: An Application of the Allison Magneto-Optic Apparatus, by Yoe and Wingard.

In addition to the work described in these papers, researches have been started on several other lines, as follows:

(1) A cooperative program with Prof. Arthur Holmes of the University of Durham, England, on the analysis of rocks for their content of calcium[41] isotope for the purpose of studying the origins and ages of geologic formations.

(2) Investigations whose aim is to find a satisfactory theory of the physical phenomena underlying the magneto-optic method.

(3) Improvements in the apparatus and technique which, it is hoped, will tend to bring the method into more general use as a tool in research.

(4) Efforts are being made to adapt a photographic method to the detection of the minima.

(5) The work continues in progress on the so-called "isotopic influence", the studies thus far having been confined to the isotopes of calcium, scandium, and hydrogen.

(6) Further investigations on the isotopes of hydrogen.

(7) Additional studies on certain radio-derived materials.

(8) Continuation of the studies on the isotopic constitution of the metallic elements.

54. Dr. C. E. McClung, University of Pennsylvania, $700, to aid in the collection of Orthopteran material in Japan and elsewhere. Dr. McClung is now.in Japan and no report has been received from him.

55. Dr. Ales Hrdlicka, of the United States National Museum, $500, to aid in the collection of anthropological material in Alaska. Owing to necessary curtailments in the field work at the beginning of May 1933, the proposed work had to be delayed until this year, and with the permission of the secretary of the academy, the grant has been held over for this use. It is now being expended on an expedition to Kodiak Island to continue excavations begun there in 1932.

On behalf of the Joseph Henry fund, the following recommendations for grants under this fund are hereby presented to the academy:

(1) Five hundred dollars to Prof. Edward L. Bowles and Mr. Ellis A. Johnson, of the Massachusetts Institute of Technology, for expenses in connection with their research on fluctuation noise in circuits and amplifiers. (This research has been in progress since 1929 and additional funds are necessary to continue it at this time.)

(2) Seventy-five dollars to Prof. T. Wayland Vaughan, of Scripps Institution of Oceanography of the University of California, for collecting biological material in order to complete his work on a treatise to be entitled: "Handbuch der Paleozoologie."

(3) Three hundred dollars to Prof. F. A. Jenkins, of the University of California, to assist him toward the purchase of a 30,000-line diffraction grating to be used in connection with his researches on band spectra.

(4) Four hundred dollars to Prof. Simon Freed, of the department of chemistry, University of Chicago, toward the construction of an electro-magnet to be used in his researches on magnetic susceptibility of metals dissolved in liquid ammonia.

(5) Four hundred dollars to Prof. Ernest O. Lawrence, of the University of California, toward the purchase of a cathode ray oscillograph with accessory apparatus to be used for the detection and measurement of various nuclear radiations.

D. W. TAYLOR,
L. R. JONES,
L. P. EISENHART, *Acting Chairman.*

Report accepted and recommendations approved.

JOHN J. CARTY FUND

Under the terms of the deed of gift of the John J. Carty fund designations for award cannot be made oftener than once in 2 years. In view of this limitation and the fact that the medal was awarded last year, the committee has no recommendation to make to the academy this year.

F. B. JEWETT, *Chairman.*

Report accepted.

CHARLES DOOLITTLE WALCOTT FUND

After much correspondence the board of directors of the Charles Doolittle Walcott fund, consisting of G. G. Abbot, Charles Barrois, F. A. Bather, E. O. Ulrich, and the chairman, recommends Dr. David White for the Walcott medal and financial honorarium in consideration of his excellent work, published and unpublished, on the Precambrian algae life of the Grand Canyon of Arizona. The medal and honorarium is especially awarded because of Dr. White's new methods of preparing the fossil material for study revealing the microstructure of these early evidences of plant life, and further that the rocks entombing their life are of marine origin.

CHARLES SCHUCHERT, *Chairman.*

Report accepted and recommendation approved. The Walcott medal and honorarium were presented to Dr. White at the dinner of the academy on the following evening, in compliance with a special request by the council of the academy. This was the first time the Walcott medal had been presented.

REPORT ON THE PROCEEDINGS

It is customary at this time to make a report on the Proceedings of the National Academy of Sciences. With the close of the calendar year of 1933 we completed the nineteenth volume of the Proceedings. There were 200 contributions making 1,069 pages. The average length of the contributions was 5.3 pages. The distribution was as follows:

Mathematics	47	Botany	5
Astronomy	19	Genetics	27
Physics	13	Physiology and biochemistry	17
Chemistry	18	Pathology and bacteriology	3
Geology and paleontology	22	Anthropology and psychology	10
Zoology and anatomy	19		

Of the 200 contributions 65 were members of the academy and 4 were by National Research Fellows and 39 were read before the academy.

E. B. WILSON, *Managing Editor.*

Report accepted.

REPORT OF COMMITTEE ON OCEANOGRAPHY

The committee on oceanography begs to state that the reports of Dr. T. Wayland Vaughan on the interpational status of oceanography, and of Dr. T. G. Thompson on the subject of oceanography in universities, referred to in the last annual report of the committee, while in an advanced stage of preparation, are not yet completed. Funds have been reserved for publication of these reports subject to approval of the academy. It is recommended that the committee be continued pending completion of these reports, reserving decision as to the future status of the committee.

FRANK R. LILLIE, *Chairman.*

Report accepted and recommendation approved.

REPORT ON FUNDS FOR PUBLICATION OF RESEARCH

The following grants were made in aid of the publication of scientific research during the year 1933–34 upon recommendation by the academy committee on funds for publication of research, approved by the council of the academy:

A grant of $600 to the Lowell Observatory, Flagstaff, Ariz., to assist in the publication of a memoir on the Spectrum of the Night Sky, by V. M. Slipher; conditional upon an equal amount being secured from other sources.

A grant of $300 to the Yerkes Observatory, Williams Bay, Wis., to aid in the completion of Ross's series of photographs of the Milky Way, in continuation of a previous grant.

A grant of $900 to the American Journal of Science, to help toward the more prompt publication of accumulated manuscripts, for the present academic year only, and not renewable.

A grant of $1,000 to the Bulletin of the Seismological Society of America, to aid in the publication of 10 manuscripts specifically named; for the present academic year only, and not renewable.

A grant of $750 to "Phytopathology" to aid in the more prompt publication of accumulated manuscripts; for the present academic year only, and not renewable.

A grant of $500 to "Genetics" to aid in the more prompt publication of accumulated manuscripts; for the present academic year only, and not renewable.

A grant of $500 to the International Journal of American Linguistics to aid in the publication of accumulated manuscripts, particularly a grammar of the Yuchi language and of the Zuni language; for the present academic year only, and not renewable.

A grant of $600 to Dr. George R. Cowgill, Yale University, New Haven, Conn., to assist in the publication of a monograph entitled "The Vitamin B Requirement of Man in Health and Disease"; conditional upon the remaining funds being obtained from other sources.

A grant of $750 to the Journal of Paleontology, to aid in the more prompt publication of accumulated manuscripts.

A grant of $300 to Dr. N. W. Popoff, Highland Hospital, Rochester, N. Y., to make possible the adequate illustration of a memoir on digital vascular mechanism in relation to glomic tumors.

A grant of $160 to Dr. William Henry Burt, California Institute of Technology, Pasadena, Calif., to aid in the publication of a report on "The Mammals of Southern Nevada", the remaining funds having been provided from other sources.

A grant of $500 to be administered by the Astrophysical Journal to aid in the publication of articles where the authors do not have the funds available to meet the regular charges. This is not a subsidy to the Astrophysical Journal as such. It will enable a submitted and approved list of papers to be published where the extra cost has to be met by the individual or his institution.

A grant of $500 to the American Folklore Society, to aid in the publication of a monograph for which the remaining funds will be obtained from other sources.

A grant of $500 to "Ecology", to aid in the more prompt publication of accumulated manuscripts.

A grant of $400 to Prof. Thorndike Saville, New York University, College of Engineering, New York City, to assist in the publication of the Transactions of the Section of Hydrology of the American Geophysical Union.

A grant of $1,000 to the Institute of the History of Medicine, Johns Hopkins University, Baltimore, Md., to aid in the more prompt publication and more adequate illustration of accumulated manuscripts in the bulletin of the institute.

A grant of $500 to "Isis", to aid in the more prompt publication of worthy material.

A grant of $1,500 to the American Institute of Physics, to help in initiating a portion of their general publication program which is designed to place the whole assembly of physics journals on a self-supporting basis.

A grant of $600 to the Annals of the Association of American Geographers, to aid in the more prompt publication of worthy material.

A grant of $1,000 to the American Journal of Botany, to aid in the more prompt publication of worthy material.

A grant of $500 to "Rhodora", to aid in the more prompt publication of worthy material.

A grant of $500 to the bulletin and memoirs of the Torrey Botanical Club, to aid in the more prompt publication of worthy material.

A grant of $500 to "Physiological Zoology", to aid in the more prompt publication of worthy material.

A grant of $500 to "Psyche" to aid in the more prompt publication of worthy material.

RAYMOND PEARL, *Chairman.*

Report accepted.

PROGRESS REPORT OF THE COMMITTEE ON LIBRARY

To the President and Council of the National Academy:

Your committee appointed to report a plan with recommendations covering the library problem of the academy submits the following progress report:

On recommendation of the committee a grant of $250 was made by the executive committee to cover the cost of unwrapping and roughly surveying, without attempt to catalog or list, the accumulation of publications in the basement of the academy building.

The remaining bundles have been opened and publications unwrapped.

The entire accumulation has been sorted by countries, and the publications of scientific societies have been grouped under the respective issuing institutions.

Periodicals are segregated by series.

A visual inventory is now possible.

A preliminary survey shows regrettable incompleteness of sets, general deficiency as to publications antedating the academy, and lack of many of the more important issues of leading scientific societies of the world. A number of high-rank institutions are wholly unrepresented. Several post-war research organizations are well represented.

Some of the leading periodicals covering science in general published in other countries are entirely wanting. Some rare and important independent works are present. On the other hand, many very important specialistic series are wholly or largely lacking.

The recommendations now submitted relate primarily to questions of policy to be considered by the academy in regard not only to books now on hand, but books to come.

The further steps in the procedure of the committee, including the preparation of a budget to accompany its final recommendations, depend, naturally, on the approval or rejection by the council of these recommendations.

1. It is the unanimous recommendation of your committee that the academy do not attempt to organize, maintain, and operate a general consulting scientific library in its building. The academy has not room (as well as need) for such a library.

2. The committee recommends that space in our library room be given: Firstly, to the leading and most dignified publications of other national academies of the world—peers of our own academy; secondly, to the leading scientific periodicals of the world covering the field of general science; thirdly, to the most important publications relating to the history of science, the histories of the leading learned societies, records of the life work achievements of the most outstanding men of science, centenary, semicentennial, and similar publications covering progress in the different fields of natural science; fourthly, antiquarian works (now on hand or to be received as gifts) of especial interest or importance relating to early science or the history of science; and fifthly, a limited number of reference works, including bibliographies, dictionaries, catalogs, scientific directories, etc., together with the International Critical Tables and other important publications issued under the auspices of our academy.

3. The committee recommends that such portions of our accumulated publications as are not selected for conservation in the building be disposed of to some outside institution or agency.

4. A majority of the committee favors treatment of the library problem on a permanent basis and from the standpoint only of the broad interests and welfare of the National Academy.

5. The committee recommends the appointment of a subcommittee of 3 or 5 members who, if the foregoing recommendations are approved by the council, will be charged with the duty of final decision of many questions relating to the choice of publications of other national academies, of leading scientific periodicals, of antiquarian and other historical records of special importance, of de luxe publications of especial interest and attractiveness or value, and of reference books, catalogs, etc., to be finally bound and installed in the library room.

Such a small subcommittee should be composed of men easily accessible to Washington who may meet in the stack room and examine and differentiate publications as to whose inclusion or rejection the chairman or a minority of the present committee may have doubt.

The subcommittee should have power of final action, subject to advance instructions by the library committee and authorization by the council if such authorization is to be made.

DAVID WHITE,
Chairman of the Committee.

The recommendations of the committee were approved by the council on April 22, 1934.

The subcommittee of the library committee has been constituted, as follows: Dr. Claude S. Hudson, chairman; Dr. W. W. Coblentz, Dr. Raymond Pearl, Dr. George L. Streeter, Dr. John R. Swanton.

REPORT OF COMMITTEE ON BIOGRAPHICAL MEMOIRS

The committee on Biographical Memoirs has considered the serious problem of arrears in preparation of the memoirs. An interval of 15 to 30 years after the death of a member before publication of the memoir relating to that member is common. Just now there are 15 memoirs delayed over 15 years; and about 60 memoirs altogether remain unprepared. It is concluded that part of the trouble lies in the extension of the ideal of long memoirs. A number of biographies over 100 pages in length have been prepared. The higher the ideal of length of a memoir the smaller the chances of its eventual preparation. To remedy this situation your committee recommends:

1. That the memoirs ordinarily should not exceed 16 octavo pages or 6,000 words, not including the bibliography. The bibliography, it is believed, should be complete for the scientific papers published.

2. In cases where no biography has been prepared after the lapse of 10 years, and if in the meantime satisfactory memoirs have appeared from other sources than the academy series, such existing biography may be accepted in lieu of a new one; or an abstract of such existing biography, not to exceed 15 pages, should be prepared and printed in the academy series of Biographical Memoirs.

The records of members of the academy who are still active are very incomplete. Less than two-thirds of the members have sent in photographs of themselves. Members are requested to deposit recent photographs of themselves at least once in 25 years. About one-third of the members have furnished family histories on the schedules that are provided. We urge that members send in these schedules even though they may not have been able to complete them fully. Other personal biographical material is solicited for the secretary's files.

To facilitate the work of the eventual biographer it is requested that each member of the academy deposit with the secretary a list of titles of his published books and papers, or at least a statement of where such a list may be found.

CHARLES B. DAVENPORT, *Chairman.*

Report accepted.

REPORT ON BUILDINGS AND GROUNDS

The building for the National Academy of Sciences and the National Research Council celebrates this year its tenth birthday; it was dedicated during the April meeting in 1924. The 10 years that have passed have left no scars, and there have been no major repairs, and, so far as can be ascertained, it is in as good a condition as when turned over by the contractor.

In a brief annual report it is difficult to picture all the activities in the maintenance of a building and the ground surrounding it for there is a routine in cleaning and keeping things in order that must go on from day to day. Perhaps of equal importance is the continued watchfulness to prevent deterioration, and the small repairs which, in the aggregate, take up time but save much in the way of large expenses later.

The joints in the marble require continual inspection as the expansion and contraction open them during the warm and cold weather. Each year, as funds will allow, the pointing of a portion of the building is taken care of, and this year it was the east end from the roof down to the second-floor windows that received attention. Copper, when used in gutters and similar places, notwithstanding expansion joints, will, under extreme heat and cold, wrinkle, and the continued wrinkling and straightening out eventually causes a break.

In connection with the compensation insurance for the employees, which is required by law, it was necessary to erect safety guards over the belts and pulleys in the machine shop. In every other respect the building was reported in excellent condition by the inspectors.

Many of the exhibits, not to mention the white marble, have suffered from coal smoke. To remedy this, methods of heating have been investigated and estimates for oil burners and automatic stokers have been secured. The question of securing steam from the Government central heating plant is still under consideration. It would cost in the neighborhood of five or six thousand dollars to make the necessary stepdown valve connections with the building, and in addition an act of Congress may be necessary.

Immediately after taking out the lombardy poplars consideration was given to a rearrangement of cedars. This was done, and it was found that it would be necessary to secure about 18 new cedars of uniform size to replace some of those which had suffered through being overshadowed by the poplars.

A study has been made of the lighting system in the board room which has been felt at times inadequate. The experiment of using three or four movable indirect lighting standards will, it is hoped, improve the situation.

Part of the equipment of the building for use in connection with lectures and scientific papers is the picture screen in the auditorium. The old one had been in use for a number of years and had become so discolored that it gave distortion to the picture. It was replaced by one of the latest type.

The painting of the rooms, corridors, and other parts of the building has been continued, looking toward the completion of the entire building.

Constitution Avenue (formerly B Street), upon which the Academy-Research Council Building faces, has been scheduled for improvement by widening and repaving for a number of years. Early in the fall money became available from some of the emergency funds which made it possible for the Bureau of Public Roads to reconstruct the street from foundation to surface. It is now practically completed. The laying of a cement sidewalk in front of the building was included.

PAUL BROCKETT,
Custodian, Buildings and Grounds.

Report accepted.

REPORT ON EXHIBITS

Continued study of the methods of showing the apparatus and other exhibits so that they will be better understood has resulted in many improvements, and a meeting of the joint committee of the National Academy of Sciences and National Research Council on exhibits added further suggestions which are being carried out.

One of the most striking of the new exhibits is an unique group of photographs of the moon assembled by the Committee on Study of Surface Features of the Moon of the Carnegie Institution of Washington. It consists of a large mosaic photograph and of transparencies showing a portion of the surface of the moon at the last quarter projected on a plane and on a sphere. The two transparencies bear the same relation to each other that a school geography map of a hemisphere of the earth bears to a terrestrial globe. On the globe the surface features are shown in correct relations while on the plane the features near the margin are greatly foreshortened and distorted. The outer surface of the globe was coated with photographic emulsion by the research laboratory of the Eastman Kodak Co.

To the exhibit of the General Electric Co. there has been added a complete new series of tubes and transparencies showing the developments that have taken place in the field of X-ray apparatus. There is exhibited the C A crystallographic Coolidge X-ray tube which is used for crystal analysis by X-ray diffraction and is operated at 42,000 volts and 25 milliamperes continuously. The molybdenum target is cooled by water. There is also included the new cathode ray tube and the X P 3 diagnostic Coolidge X-ray tube. It is not possible to operate these because of danger to the public, but the method of construction is given in detail, and this together with the descriptive labels makes it possible to study and to see how they work when in operation.

Dr. Warren H. Lewis and P. W. Gregory, of the Department of Embryology of the Carnegie Institution of Washington, are originators of a very interesting film made during their studies on the rabbit ovum; they have kindly supplied the academy with a copy of this film which attracts a great deal of interest.

Small repairs are attended to daily, and at intervals a thorough overhauling is given each instrument. The Michelson interferometers (a) showing small displacement made visible by light waves, and (b) the Michelson interferometer for measuring linear distances were taken apart, cleaned, bolts tightened, and the mirrors recoated. The result is that the lines, as seen by the visitor, are steady and more distinct.

The Wilson Cloud Chamber, constructed and deposited by the Bureau of Standards, was overhauled by that Bureau, and, in the reconstruction, all the new developments were included. It is now possible for the observer to repeat the ray tracts continuously after pressing the button and waiting about 60 seconds.

The larger part of the material from the laboratory of the National Advisory Committee for Aeronautics remains in Chicago for the continuation of the Century of Progress Exposition this year.

Visitors to the exhibition, both young and old, take something away with them. Parents often come in and state that their children have asked them to come to see the exhibits and press the buttons. Classes from schools and colleges from all parts of the East come to study the experiments in actual operation. Rarely has a day passed when we have not had two or three. The number of visitors during the last year was 37,286.

PAUL BROCKETT, Secretary.
Joint Committee on Exhibits.

Report accepted.

REPORT ON THE ROLE OF SCIENCE IN NATIONAL PLANNING

Prepared by the academy's standing committee on Government relations, Dr. John Campbell Merriam, chairman, in response to the request of the Honorable Frederic A. Delano, chairman of the National Planning Board, Federal Emergency Administration of Public Works, addressed to the president of the National Academy of Sciences on April 24, 1934. This report was completed and transmitted to the National Planning Board on June 18, 1934.[1]

FEDERAL EMERGENCY ADMINISTRATION OF PUBLIC WORKS,
NATIONAL PLANNING BOARD,
Washington, April 24, 1934.

Dr. W. W. CAMPBELL,
  President of the National Academy of Sciences,
            Washington, D. C.

DEAR DR. CAMPBELL: On behalf of the National Planning Board I am writing to request the advice of the National Academy of Sciences regarding the role of science in national planning. The National Planning Board consisting of Mr.

[1] See introductory reference to the subject on p. 2, this annual report of the academy.

Frederic A. Delano, chairman, Dr. Wesley C. Mitchell, Dr. Charles E. Merriam, is engaged in the preparation of a memorandum on the subject of national planning, considering the historical development of national planning in the United States, various types of planning now under way, alternative suggestions regarding the scope, method organization and types of national planning; all with a view to making recommendations on this subject by July 1, 1934. We should very greatly appreciate the advice and counsel of the National Academy of Sciences in this undertaking.

Sincerely yours,

FREDERIC A. DELANO, *Chairman.*
By CHARLES W. ELIOT, 2D.,
Executive Officer National Planning Board,
For the Administrator.

NATIONAL ACADEMY OF SCIENCES,
April 25, 1934.

Hon. FREDERIC A. DELANO,
Chairman National Planning Board,
Washington, D. C.

DEAR MR. DELANO: I yesterday received your letter of April 24, requesting the advice and counsel of the National Academy of Sciences on the subject of national planning, as described in the second sentence of your valued communication. Duly appreciating the potential opportunity of rendering valuable service to the National Planning Board, and fully realizing the great responsibility involved, the academy accepts the commission, and will endeavor to present to you its report on the subject in advance of the date, July 1, 1934, set for the making of the board's recommendations. After considering the apparent elements of our problem, I have today entrusted and charged the academy's standing committee on Government relations, of which Dr. John C. Merriam has during many years been the chairman, with the duty of studying the problem systematically and intensively, and of preparing the committee's report; and I have urged that the first meeting of the committee be held not later than Monday, April 30, or if possible on April 28.

Doubtless Dr. Merriam, quite likely accompanied by one or two of his colleagues on the committee, will desire the privilege of conferring with you, or with one or both of your colleagues on the board, to make certain that our first vision of the problem's elements is correct in all essentials.

Assuring you of the desire of the officers and members of the academy to be helpful to the National Planning Board in its important undertaking, I am

Yours sincerely,

(Signed) W. W. CAMPBELL,
President.

THE ROLE OF SCIENCE IN NATIONAL PLANNING

1. DEFINITION OF SCIENCE IN RELATION TO PLANNING

In the following discussion science is assumed to represent materials obtained through investigation in the natural sciences; it represents

25

also the attitude of mind or method of approach used in study of these fields. It may include such extension of these investigations as naturally reaches into consideration of the nature of human beings and of their activities.

Both point of view and convenience of classification make important the recognition of a grouping of activities under the head of social and humanistic studies as contrasted with those commonly grouped under natural sciences. There must be wide overlap and close interlock of these subjects, and it is important that there be recognition of need for unity in effort along all lines of investigation. At the same time it is desirable to keep in mind the requirement for specialized study in different fields if intensive work is to be done.

Viewing the problem of science in another way, we appreciate the fact that objectives of the student of natural science are quite different from those of the sociologist, of the student of economics, or of the student of government. The scientist is concerned with securing information relating to materials and the situations which obtain in the world about us, as also with reference to the nature and activities of human beings. This search involves not only definition of what we call facts, but must include the relations between these facts. In ultimate analysis it is essential that we know also the significance of the materials gathered with reference to human interests. In this last type of activity work of the scientist examining nature overlaps that of the student of social sciences, engineering, economics, and government. It is difficult to determine what properly belongs in each field, but greater difficulty for mankind would be encountered if there were no overlap or interlock among these subjects.

Responsibility for determination of what constitutes national planning is presumably not a part of the obligation involved in preparation of this statement regarding the role of science further than is implied in recognition of the idea that planning means a forward look for the purpose of securing the most effective type of organization based upon obtainable knowledge. In the statement which follows it is assumed that the role of science concerns essentially the presentation of facts and the relations between facts arising out of science, all being so stated as to aid in consideration of any planned program.

2. Role of Science in Adjustment to Changing Conditions

In considering the type of forward look which may be represented by planning, science will naturally be considered as having a significant role by reason of the fact that through development of new materials and new knowledge it makes possible the adjustment to new types of situations. If we were known to be dealing with a static world in which the materials available, and our knowledge regarding these materials and of man were approximately complete, it would be possible to formulate plans which, with slight variation, might operate almost indefinitely. By whatever means we use for viewing the history of the world, it is clear that we are dealing with almost continuously changing conditions to which adjustment must be made. With these modifications must also be taken into consideration the fact that human nature seems to demand continuing variation of

conditions and, if possible, continuing improvement.   In this varying
program contributions of constructive thought arising from all fields
of science have important part by giving opportunity on the one hand
for adjustment to new situations and, in another direction, for continuing development in response to the desire for advance made
possible by the vision of human intelligence.

In the history of civilization the urge for development of new
interests and new activities has been satisfied in many ways.   This
has been done through certain aspects of the arts, philosophy, religion,
new types of business organization, military activities—all have contributed to the human desire for change and what we call advance.
The last century seems to have shown less marked advance in certain aspects of life important to man than occurred in the previous 2,000 years.
But activities coming out of the growth of science have given us means
for new developments of transportation, geographic discovery, communication, and a multitude of other things, perhaps culminating in
the automobile and the radio of the present day.   A relatively large
percentage of these recent advances have arisen from the activities
science carried to application by engineering.   The extent to which
these things have satisfied the human craving for change and growth
it will remain for history to determine, but it would seem that for the
immediate future the type of change in the new worlds of activity,.
and even of thought, made possible by science will have an important
place in satisfying certain of the intellectual and spiritual interests of
mankind.

3. Extent to which Development of Science May Make Further Contribution to Understanding of Materials and
Conditions in the World of Things, Physical, Biological,
and Human

One of the most important contributions of modern science and
research is the indication that we are very far from having a complete
knowledge of anything in the. world of the physical, biological, or
human values.   Within the physical universe alone very great advances have been made within the last generation in our knowledge
of materials, forces, and conditions encountered on all sides in everyday
life.   In biology the degree of complication is still greater, and investigators generally hold the view that we are just beginning to
understand fundamental life conditions and processes.

Although the realm of human values is at times assumed to represent a category within which the method of approach of science has
relatively little importance, intensive study continues to uncover relationships in which factors developed by science are seen to have
large significance.   The enormous complication of human values has
made the subject almost infinitely difficult.   It is also true that those
factors comprised in what is known as freedom of judgment introduce
an element making the situation vastly difficult.   Nevertheless, it is
to be recognized that even within the field of human values increase
of knowledge and its better interpretation tend continuously to
introduce new features of the scientific type which must be taken into
consideration in any planning program.

To those acquainted with the development of science there is little
difficulty in accepting the suggestion that our knowledge of nature

and man will increase greatly with the coming centuries. It is also to be expected that human constructive activity will bring about the creation of conditions and relationships which have not existed previously. If this suggestion be accepted, development of any planning program of national scope must take into consideration the significance of these new factors in bringing about readjustments. While it is not possible to predict the direction which such changes will take, or the specific fields in which discoveries, inventions, or new creative activities may express themselves, it would be unfortunate if these possibilities were neglected in a general planning program.

4. NEED FOR BALANCED PROGRAM OF RESEARCH, INTERPRETATION AND APPLICATION

Importance of the role which science should have in national planning depends in a measure upon the extent to which proper balance can be maintained among factors relating to origin, interpretation, and application of scientific knowledge. Upon the adequacy of guidance for growth of this knowledge and its use will depend the possibilities for securing new data needed for adjustment or for creative activity, as also the formulating of an adequate program through which scientific information may be interpreted and so placed as to make possible engineering or economic or social application. Up to the present time, in general, relation among these three phases of development of science has been allowed to proceed in accordance with interests of the agencies concerned. Exceptions to this procedure are found in the industries where research is developed for the specific purposes of application, and in some measure in educational institutions where interpretation of the contribution of science constitutes a primary function. Recent activities, especially in the field of adult education and through the public press, have tended to give relatively high value to the interpretation aspect of development in science.

Any long-range planning program of local, national, or international scope will naturally put definite stress upon advance of fundamental research as a means of contributing toward improvement of the condition of mankind. So important is this idea that its consideration should be emphasized regardless of the specific means for carrying out such a program, whether by private institutions or through public support.

It is also important that in any program of planning, consideration be given to the extent of interpretation or of educational effort devoted to making clear the significance of science and research.

It is essential also that a national planning program give attention to study of the actual application values deriving from research in its various forms. Organization of means by which results of science already available or arising through new discoveries could come into human use may mean an enormous contribution to betterment of conditions for life. Organized effort for such study may well arise through support of the Government, as well as naturally through all private institutions concerned with such activities.

As a part of the idea of a maintenance of balance in development of science through research activities it is essential that attention be given to the manner of development and use of new materials, principles, conditions, or relations such as may be discovered by scientific effort. The present widespread interest in what has been looked upon as the disturbing influence of scientific discovery is an indication that attention should be given to control of the new instruments and ideas as they appear, whether this be in the field of the physical sciences or in the region of scientific discussion or economic and political ideas.

The law of survival of the fittest would ultimately care for new materials and new ideas. But our knowledge of evolutionary processes over the ages indicates clearly that intelligent grouping or cooperation or guidance, without the necessity of absolute restraint, may bring about relatively favorable conditions and in a shorter time than is possible through influence of the law of survival of the fittest or the fight for existence. It is a part of the responsibility of an intelligent people to consider values which it creates and their relation to other values. It is doubtful whether long-range planning activity can perform a more important service than that which may be contributed through study of possible situations in this field. Further study of all programs relating to protection given by patents may aid in discussion of this question.

In connection with examination of this problem it is important to note that science is international in its scope. No planning program can be effective which neglects consideration of this situation. There are many fields of science, such, for example, as geology, oceanography, and meteorology, in which international cooperation is essential for advance. Consideration of this situation is also important in the study of a balanced program for use of scientific knowledge in the most favorable ways. ·

5. RELATION OF SCIENCE TO EDUCATION IN A NATIONAL PLANNING PROGRAM

Although relation of science to education will probably be stressed in consideration of activities in the field of the social sciences or education, it may be important to emphasize certain aspects of this relationship under the discussion of the role of science as such. Modern thought has tended toward development of the idea that science is one of the most important ways of expression for creative thought or activity. Actually science is more largely discoverer and interpreter, and only in part concerned with creative interests. Constructive or creative thought or activities may be shown more largely through the arts and engineering, and yet it is not possible to avoid recognition of the idea of creative work as connected with the development of scientific thought. Without pressing to a conclusion the question of relation of science to creative work, it is important to call attention to the fact that science stands specifically for search after facts and principles, and for the necessity of judgments based upon realities considered by logical processes.

The idea of inquiry and research dominant in the field of science has extended itself with increasing emphasis into all subjects and interests represented in everyday life. Through its relation to present-day thought, science has certainly exerted a very important influence concerning the need for facts and for recognition of realities as the basis for judgment. If this principle could be extended widely into education, the influence would be very great. Especially important might it

be in the effect upon citizenship as defined in the form of democratic
government under which we live.

If, in any program of national planning, consideration is given to
continuing development of the ideas upon which the present form of
government rests, the scientific attitude toward knowledge and toward
life should be emphasized as a part of the educational system.

6. The Role of Special Fields in Science as Related to National Planning

In considering the role of science with relation to a national plan, it
is assumed that there is recognition if distinct difference between
judgments in planning activities looking a considerable distance into
the future as contrasted with decisions often made in business or
governmental operations where it is not possible to secure complete
data. It is assumed that the idea of planning involves consideration
of those fundamental features which may have importance in the
longer look ahead.

The judgment of science would be distinctly unfavorable to the
basing of plans for the future upon materials imperfectly understood,
or upon information which cannot be given adequate statement. At
the same time it would be unwise to develop great projects on the
basis of specific data merely because they have long been accepted,
when there is evidence that wholly new points of view may be developed by research. Considering the subject of planning from this
point of view, the role of various subjects in science has been examined
in the light of developments which may be expected to take place.

MATHEMATICS

Although the role of mathematics as related to planning does not
need discussion, it is important to consider the state of development
of this subject. The situation can best be defined by quotation from
a memorandum by Arthur B. Coble, a member of the National
Academy and of the committee to which study of this problem was
referred. This statement reads as follows:

During the last half century pure mathematics in America has reached a
position comparable to that in any European country. This growth has been
steady and well maintained. There is every reason to expect it to continue and
no reason at present to stimulate it to increased activity. We now have the
leadership to develop as large a number of well-trained mathematicians as the
country is likely to need. Of these we may expect a reasonable proportion to
become really expert in advancing the bounds of the pure science, and in satisfying
the demands of other sciences.

As knowledge in any field of thought tends to become more exact, so also does
it tend to seek expression in mathematical, or at least in statistical, terms. Thus
we must expect to find an increasing use of mathematical terminology, of the
mathematical formulation of ideas, and eventually of mathematical deduction.
When this expectation is realized the necessity for broader and sounder training
in mathematics in our schools and colleges will become urgent. There is particular need both for more expert instruction in, and for revaluation of the content of,
elementary mathematics.

In general it may be said that the progress of applied mathematics in America
has not kept pace with that of pure mathematics. There is present need for a
well-supported journal in this field to serve as a concentration point for a number
of interests which at present are too scattered to become potent. Such a medium
would facilitate the interaction between pure and applied mathematics and would
stimulate the growth of an American school of applied mathematicians. Achievement in this field would seem to be a quite normal expression of American genius.

Every general scientific program should make provision for the support of well ordered progress in pure and applied mathematical research and instruction. This is particularly necessary because the science itself has little popular appeal and must make its contribution to the general welfare through the medium of other sciences.

With the certainty of greatly increased use of mathematics in an infinite number of ways in every field of science, and especially in application of science through engineering and in the field of economics there could be no greater contribution toward assurance of accuracy and toward constructive development in planning than would be found in guaranteeing the best development of mathematics and its application.

PHYSICS AND CHEMISTRY

While physics and chemistry commonly occupy independent fields, these two phases of science may be considered together as representing broadly the physical basis of the world and of life. Advances have proceeded so rapidly in recent years that in many instances there has been almost complete reorganization of large divisions of these subjects within a decade. In a great variety of planning activities both physics and chemistry represent an important part of the foundation upon which the program is built.

In the present emergency a large percentage of special activities developed are either physical or chemical, or illustrate both subjects. The great power projects involve not only engineering but new aspects of physical application. The production of synthetic ammonia and nitrates which may make this country independent of Chile for saltpeter is related to a great engineering project. Problems of land use, so far as they concern soils, involve chemistry and physics to an extent which we have only recently come to appreciate.

The number of industries which are largely founded upon chemical processes is so great that the list would cover many pages. The rate of change in these activities, not only in development of technique but in appreciation of the underlying principles, is so rapid that a student leaving college educated in the principles of the science up to the time of his graduation may find difficulty in proceeding with the practical application in an industrial laboratory. Development of such industries as that related to the production of rayon, or modern methods for production of high-grade paper pulp illustrate processes which have attained importance in the life of the people and show very rapid change from year to year.

Production of new materials by synthetic processes, such as camphor and synthetic ammonia, means a readjustment to the problem of production which requires careful handling in business and in international trade.

The contribution of chemistry as an aid to the agriculturist in soil fertilization, eradication of pests, and in connection with the biological study of the whole problem of crop production, represents a new era in cultivation of crops.

The aid of chemistry in study of life processes, including the nature and method of operation of the constituents of living organisms, represents one of the greatest advances of modern times. So in other directions the contribution to the possibilities of medical treatment, either by introduction of substances into the intestinal tract, or by injection of substances such as insulin, or by isolation of important elements such as the vitamins, means enormous advance from conditions of the last century.

Perhaps the most important suggestion that can be made regarding the role of physics and chemistry in national planning is that it is no longer possible to take up any great project in the field of engineering, power, agriculture, food, or even the study of biology in its application to medicine and the normal processes in the human being, without calling into consultation leading experts in these fields.

In connection with discussion of these subjects it is important to emphasize again the fact that, with the rapid advance which has been made, and which may be predicted for the future, it is important to look into any great planning project through the eyes of those who are acquainted with the developments which are likely to produce great changes within years or decades.

Illustration of the type of change which may take place in a great program through application of both physics and chemistry is found in examination of the history of the oil industry in America for the past 25 years. We note on one hand the enormous change in the nature and use of the products from the oil fields through the advances of chemistry. On the other hand, one appreciates the significance of advance in location and recovery of oil through application of combined contributions from research in geology and physics.

While it is not always possible to predict the direction in which contribution of science may turn in the field of physics and chemistry, there may be no doubt that all planning operations in anyway related to physics or chemistry should be examined from the point of view of those who are most fully acquainted with the fundamental aspects of these subjects, as they may touch great programs in the fields of engineering and economics.

ASTRONOMY

The contributions of astronomy have had exceptional value from the earliest known periods of history. Heavenly bodies have furnished the chart and the means of guidance for travelers in space moving over the earth's surface, and have also given us milestones for the journey of mankind through time. In another direction the materials of astronomy have contributed in an extremely important manner to the deepening of thought, and have stimulated spiritual life through the ages.

The fact that interest of man in the heavenly bodies has tended to develop a shroud of mystery over everything that touches the outside world of space should not deceive us into assuming that elements of reality have been absent from human conceptions of the heavens and what they contain. There should be no doubt that the influence of astronomy, even in its more fundamental aspects, has been extremely important upon the development of human thought in many fields including even what we call the practical features of everyday life.

At the present time interest concerning what lies in the outside world of space tends, not less than in earlier ages, to develop appreciation of the vastness and orderliness of the universe.

From another point of view certain aspects of astronomical research are considered by some to have significance relative to practical planning problems as they touch the history and changes of climate on the earth. Should the investigations of certain astronomers and physicists make it clear that the earth's intake of energy from the sun varies to such an extent as to produce difference in climatic states, an extremely important contribution would be made.

While a national planning program may not concern itself specifically with problems in the field of astronomy, it is essential that in any forward looking plan there be continuing consideration and intensive investigation on the greater questions of astronomical research. Such support may touch what we consider the essentials for maintenance and normal development of life. It would also concern those fields of thought which influence the intellectual and spiritual aspects of life which are, after all, the basic elements in human living.

METEOROLOGY

Determination of nature and extent of changes in temperature, climate, and weather over the earth at varying latitudes and through time represents one of the most interesting possibilities related to a planning program. Developments of weather prediction in recent years have been among the most important contributions of science. Thus far forecasting has been limited to short periods. In various fields of science there is under consideration the possibility of longer range in prediction involving weeks, months, or years.

Advance in weather prediction has in part been based upon purely geographical changes observed in temperature, humidity, and other details of atmospheric condition. But out of the most fundamental aspects of science there has come, in considerable part through the work of Dr. V. Bjerknes, of Norway, the theoretical studies on circulation of water and air which have brought a new point of view regarding the conditions of our environment. They have also brought methods of application of these ideas which have largely revolutionized our understanding of weather changes. Developing out of theoretical studies in the field of mathematics, and then in mathematics and physics, and finally out of application of the results to discussion of physical conditions of the atmosphere, quiet, persistent, intellectual inquiry and scientific vision have made a great contribution to understanding of our physical surroundings. There has been no more important addition to knowledge in the planning sense than what has grown out of these investigations and their application.

In any long-range planning program it is important that consideration be given to the practical aspects of the general problem of meteorology, and also to the further deveolpment of those theoretical, mathematical, physical, and in some measure geographical, conditions upon which further advances in knowledge will be based. It is also important that support be given to such well founded studies as have bearing upon the larger program of long-range prediction. In study of these questions it is important again to recognize that progress can be made only on the basis of the most fundamental researches and through use of elements obtained from the whole world. Without international cooperation advance is almost impossible. Incidentally, the common interests of various countries in study of meteorological and oceanographical problems have brought about cooperation, the development of mutual interests, and international friendships.

BIOLOGY AND AGRICULTURE

In spite of the almost infinite complication of elements involved in life processes, modern developments in biology have equalled if not exceeded in importance those in physics, chemistry, astronomy, and mathematics. Recent advances made possible by the microscope, the techniques of chemistry and physics, and the contribution of new theories or modes of interpretation such as that presented by the general law of evolution, have permitted us to look into a wholly new world of life. Relations of life phenomena to behavior like those represented in studies of endocrine glands, hormones, and other controlling or stimulating agents have furnished a new view of life processes.

Application of the fundamental principles derived from studies in structure, physiology, and genetics to problems of agriculture and medicine has brought practically a new agriculture, a new medicine, and a new approach to the study of normal processes of life.

In agriculture there is practically no phase of the entire field which does not now rest upon basic biological knowledge, or upon biology coupled with physics, chemistry, meteorology, or other fundamental scientific subjects. But it is probable that in this field application of results has not in all areas kept pace with discoveries. Materials accumulated have often remained merely as facts without application. The commendable efforts of government and of private institutions to bring biological science into practical use have gone far to facilitate advance in use of scientific data. There can be no doubt that any future planning program must involve consideration of aspects of education which not only give us further development of biological science but may also bring better appreciation of its values in the affairs of everyday life. This means extension of education and also simplification of the materials which enter into the educational program.

At the moment there seems a tendency to assume that because research has been taken up in certain fields of agricultural application, and is recognized as important, therefore the problems are solved. As a matter of fact, in many instances we have hardly reached the stage at which inadequacies of our machinery have become apparent.

The results of agricultural overproduction have in some measure tended to lessen the pressure to place this and related subjects on the most satisfactory basis. Possibly the present situation teaches us the need for having considerable range in the types of control over the processes of agriculture. We realize now that this control should relate not merely to quantity, but also to variation in kind and in quality of product, so that application of science to agriculture in the future may increase the opportunities and the requirement of personnel.

In the field of animal biology the problems have proved even more complicated and more difficult than in study of plant life. The element of behavior, resting as it does upon nervous organization, physiology, and intricate patterns of little-known relations, has opened a field of study so significant that we are hardly able as yet to appreciate its ultimate value. In last analysis application of results from these behavior studies to man himself may be looked upon as one of the goals. It has become clear that instead of knowing man fully, we are ly beginning to understand his basic nature and his capacities.

With special reference to significance of these subjects of plant and animal biology in planning studies, it is important, as in other subjects, to emphasize particularly the fact that we only begin now to understand the fundamental elements of life processes. Study of the methods by which recent advances have been made leads one to accept the view that there is before us an enormous field of opportunity for advance in knowledge in nearly every subject under discussion. It is probably not too much to say that a vast bulk of knowledge to be obtained lies just beyond the field of the known, but may be secured in large part by careful development of methods of research now in use.

BIOLOGY AND LAND USE

Recent extensive and intensive studies on the general problem of land use have been intimately related to many aspects of biological research, but have involved also a wide variety of problems ranging through physics, chemistry, geology, meteorology, climatology, and even certain subjects having intimate relation to astronomical research. The biological aspect of land-use research involves the relations of animals and plants to their environment, which is in turn only a form of statement regarding processes of evolution through which existing situations have developed. We realize that variations of land types, and of the plant crops and animals which live upon them, can be understood only if we have acquaintance with the whole range of biological variation and the story of geological evolution with relation to the life world.

From another point of view it is important to realize that the problem of land use requires for its solution on one side an intimate study of geological processes as they determine land forms and land structure. In another direction the nature and development of land use is dependent upon climatic and meteorological conditions. The geological phase of the land problem viewed as a question in planning must be interpreted to some extent in terms of fundamental geological phenomena such as those which control the forming of the Mississippi delta, or such as are expressed in erosion processes complicating the problem of water storage behind the Boulder Dam.

The meteorological and climatic aspects of land use are again dependent upon the study of basic phenomena which require for their interpretation understanding of the almost infinitely difficult questions arising out of study of dynamics of the atmosphere, and the little understood basic factors which have to do with climatic changes. We have also still to learn whether climatic variation relates itself to influences arising outside the earth.

It is assumed that consideration of a national plan will ultimately find necessity for study of the land-use program in its broader phases. Much of what needs to be done concerns organization and administration, which will in part be guided by principles outside the field of the natural sciences. Among other factors it will be recognized that land use does not relate solely to the nature of the land and what grows on it, or the location according to latitude or climate. It involves also practical human conditions concerning maintenance of life, and with them recognition of the desires, purposes, and ideals of the people involved.

So far as the role of science is concerned, it is important to note that the carrying out of any important land-use program will involve intensive research in many fields of science in which we recognize the need for much knowledge not yet available. It will also be necessary to bring about a correlation of the results from various widely separated research fields, such as those involving biological process, climatic change, ecological relations, and evolutionary history and adaptation of life forms. The problem presents an extremely interesting challenge. But the fact that effort is made to organize the details in a program does not mean that the results will be available immediately. Among the great needs will be the planning of research of the most fundamental type in the fields involved, and the securing of cooperation between investigators in these critical regions of study.

BIOLOGY AND MEDICINE

The spur of demand arising out of human suffering has through the ages held attention continuously upon the basic problems of medicine. The greatest advances in this field have come in recent centuries, and perhaps one should say within the last few decades. Beginning with bettered knowledge of the human body and its functioning presented in anatomy and physiology, modern science has brought to medicine a wealth of information from every field of science as represented through biology. While it is difficult to make comparisons, it may be that medicine stands today as the best organized and most effective of all disciplines resting upon science.

Among the great questions faced in study of a national plan one must recognize consideration of medical aid as among the most significant. The requirements should not be looked upon as wholly concerning curative measures. The tendency of modern medicine and science looks rather to preventive medicine. In a sense we shift from study of the pathological to requirements for maintenance of normal conditions.

No better statement of this problem can be made than is presented by Dr. William H. Howell, a distinguished physiologist and member of the National Academy, who has studied this problem as chairman of the division of medicine of the National Research Council and as chairman of the research council. Dr. Howell's statement follows:

The future developments of medicine, so far as they may be directed intelligently by foresight and deliberate planning, are more evident on the preventive than on the curative side. It is scarcely necessary to say that our knowledge of the cause and treatment of human diseases is far from being complete. The only rational hope that we can entertain of making this knowledge more satisfactory lies in the encouragement of further research. Anything that can be done to increase the facilities for medical research will unquestionably contribute to the advancement of medicine, yet everyone who is familiar with the subject is aware that greater progress is frequently made by indirect rather than by direct methods of approach. In such matters definite planning for concrete ends may bring only negative results. Experience teaches us that the wise procedure is to make provision for the widest possible encouragement of fundamental research, under the belief that in this way no really significant and profitable line of development will be overlooked.

On the preventive side, however, especially in the great field of public health, we possess now much knowledge that is applicable to the relief of human suffering but which is not being used in the most effective way. In this field intelligent planning is feasible, and there is practical certainty that immense good will result as regards improvement in the health, vitality, and efficiency of the people, and in the reduction of the economic burden due to illness. The public health work that comes closest to the great bulk of our people is that of the county health units.   These units safeguard the health of the inhabitants of our rural districts and small towns.   Their activities take various forms, such as protection against the spread of infectious diseases, the medical, surgical, and obstetrical care of those who cannot afford the services of a private physician, the discovery and eradication of unsanitary conditions, the diagnosis of physical and mental ailments and provision for their treatment, the dissemination of a knowledge of personal and public hygiene in the homes and especially in the school, the isolation and care of the tuberculous poor, etc.   In some of the more prosperous parts of the country these health units are well organized and well supported, but in many regions the population is too poor or too ill-informed to make full use of this means of protection.   They need both instruction and financial assistance. Some of the private foundations, and the Federal Public Health Service as well, have made systematic efforts from time to time to educate backward communities to a recognition of the necessity of establishing such local health units, but the field is so large and is so vitally important to the prosperity of the Nation as a whole, that it would seem to be desirable for the Government to take cognizance of the opportunity and to develop in a large way plans for the adequate support of a Nation-wide system of county health units.   As these units are now organized or may be organized they do not infringe upon the traditional rights of the private practitioner, and do not involve the troublesome question of State medicine.   This latter problem has been discussed in detail by the National Committee on the Cost of Medical Care.   Its recommendations in regard to lines of future development go as far, perhaps, in this direction as is possible at present in view of the generally antagonistic attitude of the medical profession.

Attention should also be called to a valuable statement by Dr. Herbert M. Evans, a member of the National Academy, who has interested himself in this problem.   A part of the statement from Dr. Evans' paper is represented in the following quotation:

What is not generally understood is that the distinction between health and disease is often not clearly marked, but that one condition gradually grades into the other.   The slight derangement of a physiochemical mechanism like that of sugar control in the body exists for a comparatively long time before inevitable disorder supervenes.   The discovery of insulin may be stated to be the outstanding therapeutic achievement of our century, but the best possible sermon on the critical need for more biological research can be preached on the subject of insulin. Although 12 years have elapsed since this discovery, we do not yet know the chemical nature of insulin nor the mechanism of its marvelous control of carbohydrate metabolism.   There seems little doubt but that our knowledge of the participation of many internal secretions in the bodily mechanism will be enormously extended by future research and, in particular, that these researches will confer upon us the power to improve normal life, that is, to render more effective enormous numbers of individuals not afflicted by outspoken diseases.   It is an amazing thing that the medical research institutions of the world have paid relatively little attention to such studies, most of them being still concerned predominantly with bacteriology and still in the epoch of Pasteur and Koch.

The heights to which mankind may thus climb in control over its own destinies and capacities are certainly great even if at present only vaguely known.   No conceivable sinking fund will create future dividends in human welfare comparable to a reasonably liberal provision for steadily continued scientific research.

In considering that forward look involved in a national planning program it will be important, as in discussion of the role of other sciences, to recognize the continuing need for intensive study of the most fundamental questions relating to biology as they may be required in medicine.   It is essential also that any broad plan include the relation of medicine to the education of the people up to such a stage as will permit the highest use of data derived from medicine.

It is essential, further, that problems of medicine be considered in relation to public-health administration, and that means be devised by which the contribution of science and of medicine as an art be fitted into an administrative program which will bring the benefits of the most advanced knowledge for aid in maintenance of health for the people as a whole.

EARTH SCIENCES

Contribution of the earth sciences to scientific knowledge represents, on the one hand, all that we know regarding natural resources derived from the inorganic earth and, from another side, it furnishes the most fundamental and perhaps most significant aspect of historical science. From another angle of vision the earth sciences give us one of the most interesting illustrations of need for cooperative study representing the whole earth. From one country alone it is not possible to secure an adequate account of the history of the earth or its structure.

Closely related to geology in the limited sense is the record of life seen in palaeontology and extending upward into early human history as represented by archaeology. From another point of view geography represents the distribution of features on the face of the earth. According to point of view, geography may be absorbed in part into geology, or some of its critical features may be included in the field of social and governmental problems.

The mineral resources of the earth have drawn attention of human kind from the dawn of history. The effort to develop the most favorable conditions for discovery and extraction of mineral products has in recent years attracted interest of geologists, palaeontologists, geographers, physicists, chemists, and engineers. The purely commercial enterprise set up for profit may extend itself, on the one hand, into a palaeontological study involving evolution of species of the horse or various types of mollusks, or in another direction it may concern itself with physical data regarding the innermost regions of the earth. Knowledge derived from these basic scientific studies has increased greatly our acquaintance with materials available within the earth, of the means by which they have been accumulated, and of the ways by which we may take up exploitation of such deposits.

Consideration of the problem of mineral resources has been discussed by Dr. C. K. Leith, a member of the National Academy and of the committee charged with the preparation of this report, and the following extract from Dr. Leith's memorandum presents an important point of view:

The problem of intelligent use of mineral resources is illustrative of the kind of contribution geologic science can make to national planning. A geologist studies the origin of mineral resources and their stratigraphic and geologic distribution. He knows the present and potential resource of each mineral for each country and for each locality. He knows better than anyone else their irregularity of distribution and the limited possibilities of correction of these irregularities by human effort. To him it is a scientific reality that some countries and some localities have abundant supplies of essential minerals and that other less-favored parts of the world do not have them and cannot possibly develop them. He knows that mineral supplies in different parts of the world are complementary; that nations are interdependent in regard to them; that international movement of certain minerals is decreed by nature and not by human law; that as regards mineral resources there is no such thing as equality of economic opportunity among nations or equal capacity for self-determination. He knows what minerals are possessed in adequate quantity for national defense, what minerals are lacking, and where else they may be obtained. He knows the needs of conservation of the various minerals.

It seems too obvious for argument that all of these facts must be taken into account in framing an intelligent national policy for the use and conservation of mineral resources, and that such a policy should be one of the important components in broader national planning. Nevertheless this simple conclusion is not generally recognized by geologists, by the mineral industry, nor by the public. The problem is approached piecemeal from the standpoint of tariffs, treaties, taxes, codes, and many local State conservation laws. Geologic science has not only the opportunity but the duty to introduce the perspective it alone can supply and to aid in national planning for the effective and conservational use of mineral resources.

One of the critical questions in geology at the present time concerns conservation or the highest use of mineral supplies available to mankind. This problem relates itself intimately to the whole field of synthetic chemistry and artificial production of new supplies, if and when, in future milleniums the quantity of most valuable minerals in the earth may diminish to the vanishing point.

Another aspect of geological science which will concern mankind critically in the future touches significance of studies on the forms of the land and characters of superficial earth strata in relation to questions concerning land use. Cooperation between the geologist, the climatologist, and the student of agriculture, is essential for maintenance of conditions most favorable for utilization of the earth's surface.

From the point of view of one concerned with a record of events, geology, paleontology, and archeology present the most extensive and elaborate statement of history that we shall obtain in the universe. Significant as the element of time appears in the field of astronomy, it is from the geological record that we have the fullest evidence and, in a sense, the clearest reality of time with a specific delineation of events in the order in which they have occurred. Against this background there will be projected the various aspects of historical study as we approach the point at which historical science will take rank as one of the important phases of knowledge. Attention may be called to the fact that planning in the national or international sense, representing as it does a forward look, will have increasing justification from the evidence of historical science interpreted at the same time in the light of science and of human experience.

Striking illustration of influence exerted by fundamental research upon planning is furnished by the present status of protection against earthquake risk. The result coming out of long and intensive studies of geological structure, combined with investigation of earthquake vibrations through the medium of geology and physics, is giving us now for the first time an understanding of what actually takes place in movements of the earth's crust. We are today not only in a position to understand the geological structure, and the history of development of structures in much of the earth, but seismology has brought study of earth movement to a point at which we see the process in operation. Earth science has also furnished a satisfactory interpretation of the influence of geological movements upon man-made structures. While it is not possible to eliminate or to divert crustal movements, it is now feasible to determine the nature of activity to be expected in a given region. Through this information we have learned the nature of precautions which must be taken in building construction, and in the engineering sense have developed a program for construction which is adequate under most conditions.

In the sense of planning we begin now to see the extent of earthquake risk over wide areas. We appreciate also the nature of the precautions which must be taken, together with costs involved in guaranteeing a reasonable security. Up to the present time no general plan concerning handling of these risks has been prepared for this country. While the dangers might be extremely small in certain areas, there will ultimately be advantage in bringing together the data from all phases of science including seismology, geology, and related subjects in order to give some idea of the approximate risks encountered and to insist upon safeguards necessary for all structures in public use. Such a plan worked out with care would ultimately have value for the whole of the United States.

ANTHROPOLOGY, PSYCHOLOGY, AND HUMAN BEHAVIOR

The elements of anthropology may be grouped under the headings of human biology, culture, and language. Psychology, representing interpretation of states of mind, along with human behavior considered both from the point of view of the individual and of the mass, brings scientific examination of man into the field covered by sociology and government. It is difficult to draw sharp lines among these various subjects. If one were sure that mind separates itself wholly from the physical foundation or background, classification would be relatively easy, although interpretation of existing phenomena might be relatively difficult.

If it should become possible to place the study of man, from the point of view of his physical background and his mental development, on such a basis that we could secure a clear view over structure, activities, and interests of human beings, the application of anthropology to national planning would have enormous significance.

At the moment, we are just beginning to understand the underlying phenomena of human life, and question frequently arises regarding extent to which data derived from the study of so-called "primitive human types", or of human history broadly, can be applied to problems concerning planning of economic organization and other aspects of human interests and occupations.

It is doubtless true that as studies of sociology and government advance, and as anthropology, psychology, and human behavior proceed we shall find the overlap widening, and the mutual support of these subjects increasing in significance.

If the most important study of mankind is man, and if anthropology, psychology, and human behavior represent application of scientific methods to these investigations they should have great value in all aspects of planning in which human problems are significant. It is interesting to note that where the application of anthropology and psychology has been developed, as in the contacts with native peoples through colonial policy of England and Holland, the relation has proved of real importance.

Within the field of planning programs of the United States at the moment, questions relative to present and future opportunities of the Indian or native American are perhaps to be handled up to a certain point in terms of anthropology, psychology, and archeology as they relate to development of the characteristics and culture of these peoples. Whether development in other types of peoples is on a plan so different from that of the native American that it may not be considered satisfactorily by the anthropologist, historian, anp psychologist remains to be seen. It is interesting to note that in Mexico machinery set up for examination of problems relating to crime has included representation of the legal profession, of the profession of anthropology, and of medicine. It is believed that this arrangement has contributed toward solution of urgent questions.

Study of problems relating either to increase or limitation of population, or population migrations, involves fundamental anthropological concepts, and should in large measure be guided by scientific principles. The importance of such problems in any planning program will be very large. In the same way all types of questions which have to do with crime, or physical or mental deterioration, or the betterment of stock by use of scientific eugenics, will come within the field of science as it touches anthropology and psychology.

In any plan looking over the whole field of human activities for this country it will be important to give definite emphasis to aspects of psychology, anthropology, and cultural history which can furnish interpretation of conditions and states of mind of the people individually and in groups. There can be little doubt that emphasis upon common-sense or factual determination of anthropological conditions, and application of the data to planning problems in sociology and government, will, in the future, have vastly greater importance than has been recognized heretofore in use of these subjects. The extent to which government can, or should, control such activities is itself a planning problem. Up to the present time the research undertakings of universities and scientific institutions have been the main source of knowledge in these fields. It may be wise to limit in some measure the control of such activities through governmental agencies. In the long run it may appear that understanding cooperation through private agencies represents one important means of bringing the scientific study of man into effective touch with administrative and planning programs.

7. Consideration of Balance Between Science and Administration in National Planning

Assuming that the contribution of science toward materials and points of view may be large in any planning program, it is important to realize that much of the value of science depends upon intensity of concentration on specific subjects, while planning must be comprehensive and expressed in terms of administration. Administration in itself should be recognized as not merely organization. It is a program which must fit to the needs of human beings, and for which there should be satisfactory responses in human life. In a planning program arranged to utilize the values of science, consideration will naturally be given to means of organization, and there must be such interchange of ideas as will make it possible to utilize the maximum values in science to meet real human needs under an adequate human administration.

It must be recognized that neither government nor central organization of any type can exercise complete control over development of science and research. The initiative which makes discovery and invention possible arises out of individual interest, and this is an element not subject to complete control. It becomes necessary, therefore, to arrive at an understanding of means by which the constructive elements in science can grow to the highest degree out of individual interest, and at the same time leave possibility for utilization of such data in an administrative plan which will depend for its control in large measure upon recognition of mutual interests. If the Government of this country maintains approximately its present form, the need for careful planning of such relationship as has been discussed will be increasingly important.

Without reference to governmental problems, the balance between scientific development and planning activities must be considered with relation to all of the industries ranging from mechanical to agricultural, in studies of land use, transportation, finance, planning for organization of cities and States, and education. It is desirable also to emphasize the fact that such a balance is essential in development of the most favorable conditions for the enjoyment of life and even for growth in spiritual values. Too largely do we seem to accept the idea that for those features which represent the highest elements of life, carefully defined and guided thought for the morrow has relatively little significance.

The means by which balance can be defined as among the interests and contributions of science, the elements arising out of studies of social, economic, and governmental questions, and those features which have to do with the values of life cannot be determined through the thought of a moment only. These questions represent one of the most difficult of all problems in the advance of civilization. They involve on one hand the possibility of high development of specialized knowledge for the benefit of mankind and, on the other, advantages in organization of society for mutual benefit. The spread between the highest expression of these two types of interests is wide. There is, nevertheless, an intermediate position which must be found in order to secure the benefits of both.

INDIVIDUAL DOCUMENTS CONSTITUTING BASIC MATERIALS FOR REPORT ON ROLE OF SCIENCE IN NATIONAL PLANNING PREPARED FOR THE NATIONAL PLANNING BOARD

In preparation of the report a considerable group of documents was assembled by members of the committee and by others invited to present special statements, and by still others who were invited by those who had been requested to prepare statements. After the general problem and the materials available had been examined by the chairman of the committee and the three members of the academy whom the chairman had been authorized to call together, an outline of the report was prepared and a group of 30 documents was selected covering the general field of science. These 30 documents, constituting the basic materials of the report, were made available to the National Planning Board with the understanding that the individual documents, as personal reports, would be considered as confidential. The summary under the heading "The Role of Science in National Planning" was then brought together for use of the National Planning Board in the broad study of this problem.

The documents transmitted to the National Planning Board are listed as follows:

Number	Title	Contributor	Pages
1	The Role of Science in National Planning	F. E. Wright	1–6
2	....do	R. S. Woodworth	7–9
3	Mathematics	A. B. Coble	10–11
4	Place of Chemistry in Consideration of the Role of Science in National Planning.	Roger Adams	12–15
5	Physiology, Biochemistry, and Point of View Relative to Planning.	L. J. Henderson	16–17
6	Physics in National Planning	K. T. Compton	18–22
7	Astronomy	W. W. Campbell	23–26
8	Meteorology	J. A. Fleming	27–29
9	Planning and Engineering Science	A. E. Kennelly	30–32
10	Plant Biology and Policy	E. D. Merrill	33–36
11	Plant Biology	A. F. Blakeslee	37–38
12	....do	R. A. Harper	39–40
13	....do	White & Lipman	41–43
14	....do	G. W. Field	44–53
15	Forest Research	E. A. Sherman	54–58
16	Relation of Science to Land Utilization	David Weeks	59–62
17	Relation of Biological Sciences to Problems of the Government.	C. A. Kofoid	63–68
18	Biological Survey Research	J. N. Darling	69–78
19	Medicine	W. H. Howell	79–81
20	Fundamental Research in Physiology	H. M. Evans	82–84
21	Bacteriology	K. F. Meyer	85–86
22	Geological Science in National Planning	C. K. Leith	87–90
23	Earthquakes in National Planning	J. P. Buwalda	91–97
24	Geographical Research	W. W. Atwood	98–100
25	Psychology	R. S. Woodworth	101–104
26	Anthropology	Clark Wissler	105–107
26a	....do	A. L. Kroeber	107a
27	....do	Fay-Cooper Cole	108–109
28	Eugenics	C. B. Davenport	110–112
29	Migration Studies	H. H. Laughlin	113–116

ELECTIONS

The elections at the annual meeting resulted as follows:

Foreign secretary: T. H. Morgan (succeeding R. A. Millikan) for a term of 4 years commencing July 1, 1934.

Members of the council of the academy: H. S. Jennings (succeeding W. B. Cannon), and Roger Adams (reelected), for a term of 3 years commencing July 1, 1934.

Foreign associates: V. F. K. Bjerknes, Oslo, Norway; Robert Robinson, Oxford, England.

Members: Vannevar Bush, Massachusetts Institute of Technology, Cambridge, Mass.; Herbert Spencer Gasser, Cornell University Medical School, New York City; Edmund Newton Harvey, Princeton University, Princeton, N. J.; Dennis Robert Hoagland, University of California, Berkeley, Calif.; Ernest Orlando Lawrence, University of California, Berkeley, Calif.; James Flack Norris, Massachusetts Institute of Technology, Cambridge, Mass.; John Howard Northrop, Rockefeller Institute for Medical Research, Princeton, N. J.; Charles Palache, Harvard University, Cambridge, Mass.; Thomas Milton Rivers, Rockefeller Institute for Medical Research, New York City; Edward Sapir, Yale University New Haven, Conn.; Elvin Charles Stakman, University of Minnesota, Minneapolis, Minn.; Harry Shultz Vandiver, University of Texas, Austin, Texas; Norbert Wiener, Massachusetts Institute of Technology, Cambridge, Mass.; Sewall Green Wright, University of Chicago, Chicago, Ill.

PRESENTATION OF MEDALS

Five gold medals were presented at the dinner on Tuesday evening April 24, 1934, as follows:

Agassiz medal for oceanography, to Bjorn Helland-Hansen, of the Geofysiske Institutt, Bergen, Norway, in recognition of his work in physical oceanography and especially for his contributions to knowledge of the dynamic circulation of the ocean. In the absence of Dr. Helland-Hansen the medal was received for him by the Honorable Halvard H. Bachke, Minister of Norway. The presentation address was made by Dr. Henry B. Bigelow, chairman of the committee on the Agassiz medal award.

Daniel Giraud Elliot medal and honorarium of $200 for 1930, to George Ellett Coghill, Wistar Institute of Anatomy and Biology, Philadelphia, Pa., in recognition of his work: "Correlated anatomical and physiological studies of the growth of the nervous system in Amphibia." The presentation address was made by Dr. Ross G. Harrison, chairman of the committee on the Elliot medal.

Daniel Giraud Elliot medal and honorarium of $200 for 1931, to Davidson Black, a native of Canada, who was professor of anatomy at the Peiping Union Medical College, Peking, China, at the time of his death in Peking on March 15, 1934. This award had been approved before the death of Dr. Black, in recognition of his work on an adolescent skull of Sinanthropus Pekinensis in comparison with an adult skull of the same species and with other hominid skulls, recent and fossil. The medal and honorarium were received by Dr. Frank Dawson Adams, foreign associate of the academy, from Canada, on behalf of the legal representatives of Dr. Black. The presentation address was made by Dr. Henry Fairfield Osborn, a member of the committee on the Elliot Fund.

Public Welfare medal, to David Fairchild, formerly of the United States Department of Agriculture, Washington, D. C., for his exceptional accomplishments in the development and promotion of plant exploration and the introduction of new plants, shrubs, and trees into the United States. Doctor Fairchild, being unable to attend the dinner, designated Mr. K. A. Ryerson, Chief of the Bureau of Plant Industry, of the United States Department of Agriculture, to receive the medal in his behalf. The presentation address was made by Dr. Henry H. Donaldson, a member of the committee on the Public Welfare medal award.

Charles Doolittle Walcott medal and honorarium of $1,350, to David White, of the United States Geological Survey, Washington, D. C., in recognition of his work, published and unpublished, on the Precambrian algae life of the Grand Canyon of Arizona. The presentation address was made by Dr. Charles Schuchert, chairman of the board of directors of the Walcott Fund.

SCIENTIFIC SESSIONS

The scientific sessions for the presentation of papers by members of the academy or persons introduced by them were well attended. The papers presented were as follows:

MONDAY, APRIL 23, 1934

J. L. Cartledge, A. D. Shamel, and A. F. Blakeslee: Two large-fruited bud sports of Bartlett pear identified as tetraploids by pollen size (illustrated).

B. O. Dodge: A lethal for ascus abortion in neurospora (illustrated).

W. J. V. Osterhout and S. E. Hill: Anesthesia produced by distilled water (illustrated).

W. A. Setchell: Thermal overflows, thallophytes, and rock building (illustrated).

B. M. Duggar, J. R. Stauffer, and Farrington Daniels: Quantum relations in photosynthesis with chlorella (illustrated).

Francis O. Holmes (introduced by L. O. Kunkel): A genetic factor for localization of tobacco-mosaic virus in *Capsicum* (illustrated).

E. B. Fred and P. W. Wilson: On photosynthesis and free nitrogen fixation by leguminous plants (illustrated).

A. J. Riker (introduced by L. R. Jones): Some problems in cellular pathology as approached through studies both of crown gall and related pathological growths of plants and of cell-stimulating bacteria (illustrated).

Joseph Hall Bodine (introduced by C. E. Seashore): Cellular oxidations—Some phases of the respiratory activity of normal and blocked embryonic cells (illustrated).

G. H. Parker: The prolonged activity of momentarily stimulated nerves (illustrated).

Charles B. Davenport: Ontogeny and phylogeny of man's appendages (illustrated).

C. A. Kofoid: An interpretation of the conflicting views as to the life cycle of the foraminifera.

Earl H. Myers (introduced by C. A. Kofoid): The life history of *Patellina corrugata* a foraminifera (illustrated).

Ales Hrdlicka: The life history of an anatomical feature (illustrated).

Henry Fairfield Osborn: Senescent hypotheses as to the nature and causes of evolution (illustrated).

A. M. Skellett (introduced by Herbert E. Ives): A method for observing the solar corona without an eclipse (illustrated).

Edwin Hubble and Milton L. Humason: The velocity-distance relation for isolated extra-galactic nebulæ (illustrated).

Joel Stebbins and Albert E. Whitford: An application of the photoelectric amplifier to the photometry of faint stars and nebulae (illustrated).

John Strong (introduced by R. A. Millikan): Aluminizing process for coating telescope mirrors (illustrated).

C. G. Abbot: Studies of weather periodicities (illustrated).

Harvey Fletcher (introduced by F. B. Jewett): Loudness and pitch of musical tones and their relation to intensity and frequency (illustrated).

C. E. Seashore: The quality of sound (illustrated).

Edwin Hubble: The realm of the nebulæ (illustrated).

TUESDAY, APRIL 24, 1934

Edward Kasner: Transformations in optics (illustrated).

C. C. Lauritsen and H. R. Crane (introduced by R. A. Millikan): Transmutations by artificially accelerated particles (illustrated).

John Strong (introduced by R. A. Millikan): Pure rotation emission spectrum of HC_1 flame (illustrated).

Carl D. Anderson and Seth Neddermeyer (introduced by R. A. Millikan): The distribution of energies among the positive electrons ejected from some artificially produced radio-active bodies (illustrated).

B. F. J. Schonland (by invitation): Lightning and the development of its discharge.

P. I. Wold (introduced by F. K. Richtmyer): On the implications of a variable velocity of light.

Sir Arthur Stanley Eddington: The unification of relativity theory and quantum theory.

R. A. Millikan, I. S. Bowen, and Victor Neher: Cosmic ray energies at very high altitudes (illustrated).

Arthur H. Compton: Interpretation of data from world cosmic ray survey (illustrated).

R. W. Wood: A direct-vision objective grating for Döppler effect in star clusters (illustrated).

V. M. Slipher and Arthur Adel: Studies of the spectral atmospheric absorptions observed at the Lowell Observatory in the spectra of the giant planets.

W. D. Bancroft and J. E. Rutzler, Jr.: Sodium rhodanate and anesthesia.

Yandell Henderson, A. W. Oughterson, L. A. Greenberg, and C. P. Searle: The third major mechanical factor in the circulation of the blood.

Eugene F. DuBois and James D. Hardy: Surface temperature and radiation of heat from the human body (illustrated).

Francis G. Benedict and Howard F. Root: The potentialities of extreme old age (illustrated).

Simon Flexner: Source and mode of infection in poliomyelitis.

Peyton Rous and J. W. Beard: The neoplastic traits of a mammalian growth due to a filterable virus—the Shope rabbit papilloma (illustrated).

John C. Merriam: Science and conservation.

Raymond T. Birge: The present status of the values of e, h, and e/m (illustrated).

F. K. Richtmyer and S. W. Barnes: On the natural widths of the L-series X-ray spectrum of gold (illustrated).

Arthur H. Compton and E. O. Wollan: "Appearance" of atoms as observed with X-rays (illustrated).

Frederick D. Rossini (introduced by W. W. Coblentz): The energies of the atomic linkages in the normal paraffin hydrocarbons (illustrated).

Arthur W. Thomas (introduced by H. C. Sherman): A new conception of metallic oxide hydrosols (illustrated).

P. A. Levene and Albert L. Raymond: Thio sugars.

E. T. Allen: Neglected factors in the development of thermal springs.

Douglas Johnson: Supposed meteorite scars of South Carolina (illustrated).

Douglas Johnson, J. H. Mackin, and Arthur Howard: Geomorphic researches in the Yellowstone Park and Big Horn Basins, Wyoming (illustrated).

Richard J. Lougee (introduced by Charles P. Berkey): Time measurements of an ice readvance at Littleton, N. H. (illustrated).

W. B. Scott: The fauna of the White River Oligocene (illustrated).

David White: The seeds of *Supaia*, a Permian Pteridosperm (illustrated).

Bailey Willis: African Rift Valleys (illustrated).

Bailey Willis: Isostasy and the eruptive crust.

Florence R. Sabin: Biographical memoir of Franklin Paine Mall. (Read by title.)

REPORT OF THE NATIONAL RESEARCH COUNCIL

FOR THE YEAR JULY 1, 1933, TO JUNE 30, 1934

(Prepared in the office of the chairman of the council with the assistance of the chairmen of divisions of the council)

The following report is presented to the National Academy of Sciences concerning the activities of the National Research Council for the fiscal year, July 1, 1933, to June 30, 1934, the eighteenth year of the existence of the council.

ORGANIZATION OF THE NATIONAL RESEARCH COUNCIL

Officers of the council for 1934-35.—The officers of the council for the year July 1, 1934, to June 30, 1935, as duly elected, are as follows:

GENERAL OFFICERS

Honorary chairman: George E. Hale, honorary director, Mount Wilson Observatory, Carnegie Institution of Washington, Pasadena, Calif.

Secretary emeritus: Vernon Kellogg, National Research Council, Washington, D. C.

Chairman: Isaiah Bowman, director, American Geographical Society; National Research Council, Washington, D. C.

Treasurer: Arthur Keith, treasurer, National Academy of Sciences, Washington, D. C.

CHAIRMEN OF THE DIVISIONS OF GENERAL RELATIONS

Federal relations: George R. Putnam, commissioner, Bureau of Lighthouses, Department of Commerce, Washington, D. C.

Foreign relations: T. H. Morgan, chairman of the division of biology, William G. Kerckhoff laboratories of the biological sciences, California Institute of Technology, Pasadena, Calif.

States relations: Raymond A. Pearson, president, University of Maryland, College Park, Md.

Educational relations: William Charles White, chairman, medical research committee, National Tuberculosis Association; pathologist in charge of tuberculosis research, National Institute of Health, Washington, D. C.

CHAIRMEN OF THE DIVISIONS OF SCIENCE AND TECHNOLOGY

Physical sciences: F. K. Richtmyer, professor of physics and dean of the graduate school, Cornell University, Ithaca, N. Y.

Engineering and industrial research: Charles F. Kettering, vice president and director, General Motors Corporation; president, General Motors Research Corporation, Detroit, Mich.

47

Chemistry and chemical technology: F. W. Willard, executive vice president, Nassau Smelting & Refining Co., 50 Church Street, New York City.

Geology and geography: Edson S. Bastin, professor of petrology; chairman of the department of geology and paleontology, University of Chicago, Chicago, Ill.

Medical sciences: Francis G. Blake, Sterling professor of medicine, School of Medicine, Yale University, New Haven, Conn.

Biology and agriculture: I. F. Lewis, dean of the university and professor of biology and agriculture, University of Virginia, Charlottesville, Va.

Anthropology and psychology: Edward Sapir, Sterling professor of anthropology and linguistics, and fellow of Trumbull College, Yale University, New Haven, Conn.

(The organization of the National Research Council for 1933-34, including its members and committees, is given in appendix 4.)

New organization of the council.—This is the first year in which the new organization of the National Research Council, authorized in the spring of 1933, has been in effect. Under the new organization the affairs of the council have been conducted mainly by the administrative committee (composed of 12 members, including 4 officers of the National Academy of Sciences, the chairman of the council, and the chairmen of the 7 divisions of science and technology). This committee has held seven meetings during the year: October 6, November 17, December 22, 1933; February 10, March 29, May 20, and June 2, 1934. The executive board of the council held its annual meeting on April 25, 1934.

The financial situation of the council has permitted the retention of chairmen for its divisions of science and technology only on a part-time basis, for which the council has paid but a modest honorarium. Whatever usefulness the council may have rendered to American science during the past year has been due in large part to the unselfish and enthusiastic services rendered by the division chairmen who have made frequent journeys to Washington and have conducted much additional council business in residence at their respective institutions. It is evident that the leadership of the division chairmen is one of the most important features of the organization.

Under the new plan of organization the membership of the National Research Council has been materially reduced as the following table indicates:

	1932-33	1933-34
Executive board	46	38
Division of—		
Federal Relations	44	43
Foreign Relations	47	47
States Relations	21	21
Educational Relations	20	21
Physical Sciences	26	22
Engineering and Industrial Research	44	38
Chemistry and Chemical Technology	23	13
Geology and Geography	19	12
Medical Sciences	25	21
Biology and Agriculture	18	12
Anthropology and Psychology	21	17
Total	354	305

Through a certain duplication of membership the total number of individual members of the council this year is 241. The number of scientific societies represented in the membership is 76, approximately the same as heretofore. There are now about 135 committees of the executive board and of the divisions of the council comprising a total membership of about 900 in addition to the members of the council itself.

(The Executive order, issued by President Wilson in 1918, requesting the National Academy of Sciences to perpetuate the National Research Council, is given in appendix 1; and the new articles of organization of the council and bylaws of the council, adopted in 1933, are given in appendices 2 and 3.)

Retirement of Chairman Howell.—Upon the completion of the term of office of Dr. William H. Howell as chairman of the Research Council for the year 1932–33, the executive board of the council took the following action at its meeting on June 13, 1933:

Moved, that the executive board of the National Research Council expresses its grateful appreciation to its retiring chairman, Dr. W. H. Howell, for his untiring efforts in the successful administration of the council's affairs during the past year. Adopted unanimously.

The council is under great obligation to Dr. Howell for the year which he gave to its affairs. It was during his incumbency that the council revised its plan of organization, Dr. Howell taking the principal part.

Honorary vice chairman.—It is with deepest regret that the death is recorded of Dr. William H. Welch, honorary vice chairman of the National Research Council, on April 30, 1934. Dr. Welch was president of the National Academy of Sciences from 1913 to his resignation in April, 1917, and in that capacity, in company with Messrs. Edwin G. Conklin, George E. Hale, Charles D. Walcott, and Robert S. Woodward, presented to President Wilson the offer of the academy of any service within its scope in the event of the emergency of war which was then seen to be imminent. Dr. Welch participated actively in the subsequent organization of the National Research Council which was set up by the academy in order to meet President Wilson's acceptance of this offer. Dr. Welch was a member of the first executive committee of the National Research Council and as such took part in the operations of the council during the period of the war. With the reorganization of the council on a peace-time footing, Dr. Welch served continuously as a member-at-large of the executive board of the council from 1919 until his death. The National Research Council is deeply indebted to Dr. Welch for his wise counsel and for his clear vision of the most effective way in which to utilize the scientific resources of the country in time of emergency and in the further development of these resources for the general welfare.

GENERAL ACTIVITIES OF THE COUNCIL

Two of the major enterprises upon which the council has been engaged are its post-doctorate fellowships and a system of grants-in-aid of research. These have been the subject of special consideration during the past year because they bear rather directly upon the advance of science in the United States in so far as such advance depends upon the selection and encouragement of talented young scholars and upon special support for projects that are of exceptional promise and that require only moderate assistance for their completion. Special reports on these two enterprises present the results of a comprehensive study of procedures and accomplishments. A third statement was prepared for early publication,[1] presenting a brief summary of certain major activities of the Research Council on which the scientific public may desire information with the least possible delay.

National research fellowships.—In making a fresh study of the results of its three fellowship systems (a) in physics, chemistry, and mathematics, (b) in the medical sciences, and (c) in the biological sciences, the advisory committee on fellowships sought to estimate the value of such fellowships in the development of American science and to examine closely alternative procedures for their administration. This study has been directed by an advisory committee on fellowships which gives general attention to the work of the three boards.

Two of the boards have maintained field secretaries who have spent several months visiting institutions at which fellows are located as one means of obtaining intimate knowledge of the qualifications of applicants for fellowships, of the work of the fellows appointed, of the facilities available for their work at institutions in which they are located, and especially of the relationships of these post-doctorate fellowship systems to the social and educational needs of the country.

A meeting of the three fellowship boards was held in Washington on April 26, 1934, for the open discussion of questions pertaining to the fellowship administration, and a report upon conclusions arising from the study was prepared for the Rockefeller Foundation from which the fellowship funds were derived.

The fellowship program of the National Research Council was launched after the World War because a certain group of men had a vision of high possibilities. In the interests of our welfare as a people it was sought to raise the standards of scholarship and accomplishment in the fundamental sciences and place American science at least on a par with European science. To do this it was thought necessary to increase the opportunities for exceptionally gifted students. The first group of fellowships was established in 1919 in physics and chemistry for the main purpose of increasing the resources of the basic sciences which contribute to the advancement of medicine. Advancement in the fundamentals of physics and chemistry was regarded as prerequisite to a desirable further advance in medical research. This first group of fellowships was later extended to include mathematics and astronomy.

In 1922 a second group of fellowships was founded to include the medical sciences, and in 1923 a third group was provided for the biological sciences, including botany, zoology, anthropology, psychology, and the fundamental aspects of agriculture and forestry.

During subsequent years up to June 30, 1934, a total of $3,461,374.25 has been expended on these fellowships. Taking into account selections in the spring of 1934, 1,006 fellows have been appointed for periods of 1 year, 2 years, and occasionally 3 years, of whom 166 have had active status during the greater part of the past year. It is to be noted that the National Research fellows do not increase the number of doctorates in science given by American universities each year, but

---

[1] Isaiah Bowman. Summary Statement of the Work of the National Research Council, 1933–34. (Science, vol. 80, no. 2078, pp. 368–373; Oct. 26, 1934.)

rather that they serve as a means of providing a selected number of picked men who have recently received their doctor's degree with a period of additional training and experience.

With the coming into maturity of this younger group of scientists, a considerable number, ranging from about 39 percent of all past fellows in the biological sciences to about 49 percent in the physical sciences, are found to be occupying positions of professorial grade in colleges and universities. Most of the past fellows of the council have remained in academic work and are assuming positions of prominence in the scientific world. The effect of these fellowships upon the development of physics in the United States has been especially marked. The four annual awards in pure chemistry thus far made by the American Chemical Society upon the foundation established in 1930 by Dr. A. C. Langmuir have been given to past fellows of the council.

These results seem to indicate either that the selections made by the board in the appointment of fellows have for the most part been sound in their recognition of research ability or that the added years of research experience furnished by the fellowships have been particularly beneficial to the men appointed. On either basis the expenditure of a certain amount of money in the development of scientific leadership would seem to have been justified, for it is the leaders in the forefront of their professions who set the pace of progress.

A close relation is beginning to be seen also between these fellowship systems and the regime of preparation of students for the doctor's degree, since it is apparent that students trained under a liberal system in the methods of research during their predoctorate years will presumably be in preferred positions to benefit from their work as fellows.

The total expenditures of the three fellowships boards since their organization is shown in the following table:

Board	Year of organization	Years in operation	Total expenditures
Physics, chemistry, and mathematics	1919	15	$1,615,320.97
Medical sciences	1922	12	744,158.38
Biological sciences	1923	11	1,101,894.90
Total			3,461,374.25

Summary of National Research Fellowships, Jan. 1, 1934

	Active			Under appointment	Past fellows	Total number of fellowships
	United States	Abroad	Total			
I. Physical sciences:						
Physics	29	1	30	0	135	165
Chemistry	27	3	30	0	137	167
Mathematics	14	1	15	0	80	95
Total	70	5	75	0	352	427
II. Medical sciences	25	3	28	3	192	223
III. Biological sciences:						
Agriculture	7	3	10	0	22	32
Anthropology	4	0	4	0	14	18
Botany	12	2	14	0	60	74
Forestry	0	2	2	0	2	4
Psychology	14	0	14	0	59	73
Zoology	16	3	19	0	83	102
Total	53	10	63	0	240	303
Grand total	148	18	166	3	784	953

Grants-in-aid.—For the past 5 years the National Research Council has administered a research aid fund provided by the Rockefeller Foundation. This fund, lately on the order of $50,000 a year, has been allocated in comparatively small grants, averaging less than $600 each, for the aid of individual investigators. It is used for the purchase of instruments, equipment, supplies, and the materials of research, for technical and mechanical assistance, and for field expenses. A smaller additional sum has been used for the expenses of conferences upon special problems or occasionally for the support of particular programs of coordinated research.

The awarding of research grants is not made as special relief during lean financial years. It is intended to supply a constant and legitimate need among research workers for resources which they urgently require but which their institutions cannot for the moment provide. For over 50 years educational and philanthropic institutions have been making grants on an increasing scale for the promotion of research. It is now a recognized procedure. This means of fostering research has the advantage not only of providing support for scientific work, but also of recognizing merit. It often unlocks resources in the individual and in his institution which could hardly have been realized without this additional aid. Rightly applied, it cannot but increase the productivity of the investigator and quicken the research life of the institution. The making of research grants has therefore come to be an established method for advancing knowledge.

During the 5-year period, 1929–34, 552 grants have been made to 421 individual investigators located in 120 universities and colleges and in a limited number of other educational and research institutions of the United States; $296,714.82 has been distributed in this way. In addition, $20,036.79 has been used for conferences (of which 26 have been held during this period) and 5 grants totaling $15,500 have been applied to the support of several programs of coordinated investigations under the sponsorship of the divisions of the Research Council. Altogether $35,536.79 has been used through 31 appropriations for grants for these general purposes. Trends in research have been reflected in certain groups of grants. Six grants, totaling $3,768.80, were made for work on problems relating to the isotopes of hydrogen; a group of 16 grants totaling $11,150 for research in the field of endocrinology; 9 grants totaling $6,150 for the support of the excavation of selected archaeological sites; and a special grant for a conference on the southeastern archaeology of the United States, for the purpose of promoting high standards of field work in American archaeology and the preservation of archaeological materials for systematic and well-directed study.

The total number of grants given during the past 5-year period are grouped below according to fields of application.

	Number of grants	Amount granted		Number of grants	Amount granted
Conferences	26	$20,036.79	Biological sciences	115	$54,446.00
Cooperative projects	5	15,500.00	Anthropology	45	23,509.75
Physics	79	45,895.06	Psychology	40	19,535.00
Engineering	17	11,560.00			
Chemistry	64	37,980.50	Total	583	332,251.60
Geology and geography	95	48,871.00			
Medical sciences	97	54,917.50			

International Critical Tables.—With the publication last year of the index to the International Critical Tables of Numerical Data, Physics, Chemistry, and Technology, as the eighth volume in the series, this enterprise is regarded as completed. The publishers reported in September 1933, that the total sales of the tables had been as follows: Volume I, 7263; volume II, 7087; volume III, 6943; volume IV, 6801; volume V, 6644; volume VI, 5707; volume VII, 5396; index, 3859.

Certain surplus funds resulting from royalties on the sale of the tables have been invested pending a possible revision of the tables, but the income therefrom will be used meanwhile for the purchase of books, subscriptions to scientific publications, and other source material for the Research Information Service of the council. This fund amounted on June 30, 1934, to $6,299.63.

Annual tables.—The National Research Council has received and transmitted to the officers of the Annual Tables of Constants and Numerical Data in Chemistry, Physics, Biology, and Technology in Paris, the sums contributed annually by the Rockefeller Foundation under a 5-year appropriation of $18,000 toward the support of the tables. The allotment available under this appropriation for the calendar year 1934 is $3,000, and the allotments for the two succeeding years are $2,000 and $1,000.

Committees on instruments and methods of research.—The executive committee of the International Council of Scientific Unions at its meeting in London on May 18, 1932, appointed an international committee on instruments and methods of research, composed of one member from each of the affiliated international unions and certain additional members, to consider the possibility of extending the use of instruments and research methods to other fields of investigation than those in which these instruments and methods might have been first developed; and also to study the opportunities for the advancement of scientific work through the construction of instruments for the development of methods upon which the next immediate steps of advancement seem to depend.

To cooperate in this country with the international committee the National Research Council has appointed an advisory committee on instruments and methods of research to suggest to the Research Council what steps could be taken to contribute to the advancement of these objectives in the United States. The committee has rendered a preliminary report and is carrying its consideration of the matter forward into next year.

Scientific publications.—In view of the increasing amount of scientific material offered for publication and the reduced resources at the command of scientific journals, attention has been drawn in many quarters to the present financial condition of scientific publications. A committee of the division of biology and agriculture of the Research Council has been reviewing the situation of biological journals, and a general committee of the council has been appointed to study the conditions of research publications in all fields of science in consultation with editors and other advisers. Two years ago a committee of the division of chemistry and chemical technology gave special attention (through a conference held on Jan. 29 and 30, 1932) to the conditions of publication of the several types of chemical literature, and the divisions of chemistry and chemical technology and of physical sciences jointly discussed this matter further at a conference on April

6, 1934 (see pp. 67 and 72). In 1928 the division of anthropology and psychology held two conferences (Mar. 30 and 31, and Nov. 30 and Dec. 1, 1928) to discuss the publication situation in psychology upon the basis of an exhaustive analysis of the material published in American psychological journals and of the facilities of those journals.

Last year the Research Information Service of the council made a survey of the amount of material (totaling 47,218 pages) published during 1932 in 51 representative scientific journals of the United States. With respect to the sources of the articles printed this analysis shows that about 65 percent of the pages contributed to these journals during the period examined came from authors located in educational institutions, that 5 percent were contributed by authors in endowed research institutions, 9 percent from hospitals, 8 percent from officials in governmental agencies (mainly of the Federal Government) and 13 percent from scientific men in industrial laboratories. Data were also obtained concerning the publication costs of 37 of these publications. The results of this inquiry showed that few of these journals are adequately supported financially in the sense of being able to print promptly all of the acceptable manuscripts offered for publication.

The present stringency of funds under which many scientific journals are laboring has brought forward the suggestion that costs of publication should be regarded as an integral part of research programs and that allowances should be made in the budgets of such programs for publication costs. Certain journals have also proposed that research and educational institutions contribute regularly to the support of scientific journals or meet a page cost to cover articles offered by their staff or faculty members.

Cooperation with the Bureau of Standards.—The National Research Council has continued to act as fiscal agent for the administration of funds contributed from nongovernmental sources, mainly in the industries, for the support of investigations carried on at the National Bureau of Standards on problems relating to industrial development. The projects to which these funds have been directed during the past year have included investigations upon methods of locking screw threads; the fabrication of the structural steel work of buildings; the fire resistance of various building materials; the acoustic properties of material used in building; the corrosion resistance of iron pipes; the testing of special chemical reagents; the thermal properties of liquids used as antifreezing compounds in automobiles; the characteristics of chromel-alumel thermocouples; the rating of water-current meters; and the durability of paper and the preservation of records. A total of $12,990.17 has been expended during the year on these 10 projects.

Relations with the War and Navy Departments.—Arising out of an exchange of views which had been carried on during the previous year between officials of the Navy Department and of the National Research Council relating to technical problems of the Department, a conference was held in Washington on January 2, 1934, between representatives of the Navy Department, of the Science Advisory Board, and of the National Research Council for a discussion of means by which the scientific resources of the country might be made the more readily available to the Navy Department through an agency such as the National Research Council. A similar conference was held with representatives of the War Department.

Patent policy.—The present patent policy of the National Research Council is based upon a resolution adopted by the executive board on February 13, 1924, as follows:

Moved, that in the event patentable discoveries are made in the course of work carried on under the auspices of the National Research Council it is expected that the fellows or others, on the approval of the Research Council which will defray the cost, will apply for patents on such discoveries as should be protected in the interests of the public and that such patents will be assigned to the National Research Council; and, further

That the National Research Council hereby declares its intention to dedicate to the use of the public, in such manner as the Research Council may deem most effective, the results of such discoveries as are made in the course of investigations conducted under the auspices of the Research Council. Adopted.

In each of the patent cases considered by the council during the past year, consideration has been given to the contributions which other institutions had made toward the investigations involved and the responsibilities of the council for administering the funds entrusted to it in the interests of the public. The council is, however, continuing the study of its patent policy in the light of such cases as they occur and is also interested in a comparative study of the patent policies which are being developed in other educational and research institutions and which register advance in the formulation of sound opinion.

The proper disposition of rights to the results of research is recognized as a problem of great complexity, involving among other factors the following: The suggestions which have been made abroad through the International Institute of Intellectual Cooperation for the extension of the principle on which patent rights are based at present into the realm of intangible scientific property; the increasing complexity of our own patent system; the legitimate rights of the public, of the inventor, and of the sponsoring institution or institutions, all of which need to be evaluated and harmonized; the growing use of patents for the control of standardized and reliable products, particularly those used in medicine; the high ethical standards of certain professions invoked against the exploitation of the results of scientific work at the expense of the public; the reiteration of suggestions that additional scientific work be supported from the commercial proceeds of initial investigations; and the relation of patents to industrial development and particularly to the growth of new industries.

The administration of the results of scientific work on a basis at once ethical, just to all concerned, and practical, obviously demands deep and constant study. Each case which can be thoroughly considered from all points of view throws light upon certain aspects of the general problem, and the council intends to integrate these case studies through its committee on patent policy in the further development of its own policy and procedures.

SCIENCE ADVISORY BOARD

In order to meet special needs of the Government arising from the rapid expansion of governmental organization and activities under the economic emergency of the past 2 or 3 years, President Roosevelt appointed a Science Advisory Board in the summer of 1933. The initial Executive order appointing this Board and a subsequent order enlarging its membership are as follows:

ESTABLISHMENT OF SCIENCE ADVISORY BOARD UNDER THE NATIONAL RESEARCH
COUNCIL

The National Research Council was created at the request of President Wilson
in 1916 and perpetuated by Executive Order No. 2859, signed by President
Wilson on May 11, 1918. In order to carry out to the fullest extent the intent
of the above Executive order there is hereby created a Science Advisory Board
with authority, acting through the machinery and under the jurisdiction of the
National Academy of Sciences and the National Research Council, to appoint
committees to deal with specific problems in the various departments.

The Science Advisory Board of the National Research Council will consist of
the following members who are hereby appointed for a period of two years:

Karl T. Compton, chairman, president, Massachusetts Institute of Technology, Cambridge, Massachusetts.

W. W. Campbell, president, National Academy of Sciences, Washington, D. C.

Isaiah Bowman, chairman, National Research Council; director, American
Geographical Society, New York City.

Gano Dunn, president, J. G. White Engineering Corporation, New York City.

Frank B. Jewett, vice president, American Telephone & Telegraph Co.;
president, Bell Telephone Laboratories, Inc., New York City.

Charles F. Kettering, vice president, General Motors Corporation; president,
General Motors Research Corporation, Detroit, Michigan.

C. K. Leith, professor of geology, University of Wisconsin, Madison, Wisconsin.

John C. Merriam, president, Carnegie Institution of Washington, Washington,
D. C.

R. A. Millikan, director, Norman Bridge Laboratory of Physics, and chairman of the executive council, California Institute of Technology, Pasadena,
California.

FRANKLIN D. ROOSEVELT.

THE WHITE HOUSE, *July 31, 1933.*
[No. 6238]

APPOINTMENT OF ADDITIONAL MEMBERS TO THE SCIENCE ADVISORY BOARD

The following-named persons are hereby appointed as additional members of
the Science Advisory Board established by Executive Order No. 6238, of July
31, 1933:

Roger Adams, professor of organic chemistry and chairman of the department of chemistry, University of Illinois, Urbana, Illinois (president-elect of the
American Chemical Society).

Simon Flexner, director of the laboratories of the Rockefeller Institute for
Medical Research, New York City.

Lewis R. Jones, professor emeritus of plant pathology, University of Wisconsin, Madison, Wisconsin.

Frank R. Lillie, Andrew MacLeish distinguished service professor of zoology
and embryology, and dean of the division of the biological sciences, University
of Chicago, Chicago, Illinois.

Milton J. Rosenau, professor of epidemiology, Harvard School of Public
Health, Boston, Massachusetts.

Thomas Parran, State commissioner of health of New York, Albany, New York.

The term of office of the persons herein appointed shall terminate on July 31,
1935.

FRANKLIN D. ROOSEVELT.

THE WHITE HOUSE,
May 28, 1934.
[No. 6725]

The Executive order creating the Science Advisory Board was at
once recognized by the National Research Council and the facilities
of the council were made available to the Board. During the past
year each of the divisions of the council has cooperated directly with

the Board on matters of common interest. The first meeting of the Board was held in Washington on August 21 and 23, 1933. Five other meetings of the Board have been held this year and one special meeting of its executive committee.

The Board has received a number of requests for advice from departments of the Government. To these it has replied with written reports among which are the following:

1. Preliminary report of the special committee on the Weather Bureau.
2. Report of joint committee on the National Bureau of Standards.
3. Technical supplement to the manual of instructions for foreign commerce service officers.
4. First report of the committee on the Geological Survey and the Bureau of Mines.
5. Report on a proposed bureau of mineral economics and statistics.
6. Report on the Geological Survey.
7. Report on the Bureau of Mines.
8. Preliminary recommendations of the land-use committee relating to soil erosion.
9. Preliminary report of the land-use committee on land resource and land use in relation to public policy.

In addition the Board has itself given consideration to several other matters and has referred still others to the National Research Council or other bodies. Among matters which have been referred to the National Research Council are:

1. Plans for the excavation of prehistoric village sites in the area to be inundated by the building of the Norris Dam in the Tennessee Valley: to the division of anthropology and psychology, for consideration by the committee on State archaeological surveys.
2. A plan for obtaining systematic biological and psychological ratings for men employed in the Civilian Conservation camps and under the Civil Works Administration: to the divisions of biology and agriculture and of anthropology and psychology.
3. Advice to the Navy Department on technical problems.
4. The Science Advisory Board has also noted with interest the cooperative studies of occupational standards sponsored by the division of anthropology and psychology and the United States Employment Service.

The Board has received much assistance throughout the year from the staff of the division of engineering and industrial research of the council, particularly in the establishment of relationships between the Board and agencies of the Federal Government which are concerned with industrial research (see p. 70).

In turn the administrative committee of the National Research Council has referred the following matters to the Science Advisory Board:

1. Means by which the subscription of the United States to the annual expenses of the International Council of Scientific Unions and six affiliated unions can be paid.
2. Means by which the travel expenses can be paid for official delegates from the United States attending international scientific congresses.

The Science Advisory Board has also invited the attention of other organizations to certain matters which have come to its notice as follows:

1. The utilization of unemployed scientific personnel in the relief plans of the Civil Works Administration: to the American Association for the Advancement of Science.
2. Advice in the establishment of consumers' standards for common commodities: to the visiting committee of the National Bureau of Standards.

The Board has been financed from three sources during the year. The travel expenses of members attending its first meeting August 21 and 23, 1933, amounting to $759.11, were paid by the National Academy of Sciences. Subsequently the Public Administration Clearing House appropriated the sum of $2,075 for expenses of the Board. During August, September, October, and November the Board utilized $1,293.99 of this sum and returned to the clearing house early in November the balance of $781.01. The main financial resources of the Board, however, have come from an appropriation of $50,000 made by the Rockefeller Foundation for the expenses of the Board during the year beginning November 1, 1933. This sum has been used by the Board for general clerical and travel expenses and for making special investigations required to meet specific requests for advice from the Government. Up to June 30, 1934, expenses totaled $18,992.10.

Detailed information in regard to the activities of the Science Advisory Board will be found in its first report (published in December, 1934).

BIOLOGICAL ABSTRACTS

The year 1934 marks volume VIII of the Biological Abstracts which has been supported by appropriations from the Rockefeller Foundation of $75,000 for editorial expenses in the calendar year 1933, of $20,000 for indexing (available during 1932 and 1933), and $65,000 for editorial expenses for 1934 in addition to $20,000 for printing and editing indexes (available during 1934 and 1935).

Beginning with volume I in December, 1926, as an expansion of Botanical Abstracts, which had been published for 8 years previously, to include the fields of zoology and, subsequently, incorporating Abstracts of Bacteriology, this journal now publishes annually from 20,000 to 30,000 abstracts of papers in all fields of biology taken from a total reading list of about 5,000 scientific periodicals. The cost of printing the Abstracts is met from subscriptions and from a limited amount of advertising. The editorship of the Abstracts is under independent management, sponsored by the Union of American Biological Societies; but the editorial funds are administered by the National Research Council.

With the increasing interdependence of science which is indicated by the multiplication of problems in the borderlands involving two or more of the classical disciplines, the need for a systematic review of related literature is becoming more and more apparent. The use of biological literature extends far beyond the limits of the special fields of zoology and botany. It is resorted to by both physicists and chemists working upon problems relating to biology, and it is, of course, fundamental in the application of biological knowledge to all fields of medicine and public health. Over 25 percent of the institutional subscriptions to the Abstracts are for medical establishments, and over 16 percent of the individual subscribers are engaged in medical research. The organization of the great mass of literature annually produced in all the fields of biology bears rather directly on the welfare of society.

Biological Abstracts provides, in fact, more than a mere directory of current biological publications. The Abstracts assist also in the coordination of the basic sciences of biology with a number of other related sciences. The maintenance of a research tool of this nature thus becomes a matter of great importance in raising the general level of scientific competence.

AMERICAN GEOPHYSICAL UNION

The fifteenth annual meeting of the American Geophysical Union was held in Washington, D. C., on April 26, 27, and 28, 1934, and was attended by a number of geophysicists from Canada and Mexico, in addition to those from the United States. An adjourned meeting of the union was held in Berkeley, June 20 and 21. The papers presented at these two meetings were unusually large in number and were published in the Transactions of the Union in two volumes (June, 1934).

The program of the meeting included a discussion of the development of meteorology in the United States in connection with the recent recommendations of the Science Advisory Board concerning studies of the upper air and movements of major air masses; mountain meteorology; the determination of longitude at Honolulu as part of an international program for 1933; gravimetric work in the North American continent; the recent installation of tilt meters and progress in first order leveling as aids in seismological research; reports upon recent earthquakes; studies of the propagation of artificially produced seismic waves; the organization of ocean weather records for new applications and the analysis of climatological, aerological, and river-gage data obtained through operations of the Civil Works Administration and Public Works Administration; aerological results obtained under the program for the International Polar Year of 1932–33; studies of atmospheric electricity in the United States and also in South Africa; the results of radio transmission studies in geophysical investigations and in geological mapping; and the relation of radio waves to earth potential; reports from several oceanographic agencies; a number of papers dealing with special problems of volcanology and hydrology; and reports of the Western Interstate Snow Survey Conference held at Berkeley.

The United States was represented at the Fifth General Assembly of the International Union of Geodesy and Geophysics which was held at Lisbon, Portugal, between the dates September 17 and 24, 1933, by the five following delegates:

John A. Fleming, acting director, department of terrestrial magnetism, Carnegie Institution of Washington, Washington, D. C.

Harry D. Harradon, librarian, department of terrestrial magnetism, Carnegie Institution of Washington, Washington, D. C.

Walter D. Lambert, senior mathematician, U. S. Coast and Geodetic Survey, Washington, D. C.

James B. Macelwane, S. J., director, department of geophysics, St. Louis University, St. Louis, Mo.

Thomas G. Thompson, director, oceanographic laboratories, University of Washington, Seattle, Wash.

Captain David McD. LeBreton, naval attaché at the American Embassy in Paris, attended as the representative of the United States Hydrographic Office. The assembly was attended by over 200 delegates and guests representing 25 of the 37 adhering countries. Dr. William Bowie, chief of the division of geodesy of the United States Coast and Geodetic Survey, was elected president of the International

Union for the ensuing 3-year period. At this meeting action was taken reducing temporarily, until the next general assembly in 1936, the amount of the dues payable by member countries in the union to three-fourths of the amount (in Swiss gold francs) agreed upon in the revision of the statutes of the union effected at the Stockholm meeting in 1930. For the United States the annual dues are thus reduced from 16,000 Swiss francs ($3,088 at par) to 12,000 Swiss francs ($2,316 at par). The sixth meeting of the union will be held in Edinburgh in the fall of 1936.

The total membership of the American Geophysical Union is now 379, which represents a gain of 24 members during the past year.

PUBLICATIONS OF THE NATIONAL RESEARCH COUNCIL

During the past fiscal year the National Research Council has published six volumes in its Bulletin series (major and technical papers, usually of considerable length) and two numbers in its Reprint and Circular series (shorter and usually more general papers). The total number in the Bulletin series is now 95, and in the Reprint and Circular series the number is 106. Several additional publications are now in press. A number of miscellaneous papers have also been issued. (For a list of the titles of all publications of the research council issued prior to January 1928 see No. 73 of the Reprint and Circular series.) More recent titles are given in the subsequent annual reports of the council.

The publications issued in the two series during the year July 1, 1933, to June 30, 1934, are as follows:

BULLETIN SERIES

No. 90. Physics of the Earth. VI. Seismology. By the committee on seismology, division of physical sciences, James B. Macelwane, chairman. October 1933. Pages, 223. Price, paper $2, cloth $2.50.

No. 91. Industrial Research Laboratories of the United States. By Clarence J. West and Callie Hull. August 1933. Pages, 223. Price $2.

No. 92. Numerical Integration of Differential Equations. By A. A. Bennett, William E. Milne, and Harry Bateman. November 1933. Pages, 108. Price $1.

No. 93. Systems of Electrical and Magnetic Units, by Sir R. T. Glazebrook, Henri Abraham, Leigh Page, G. A. Campbell, H. L. Curtis and Arthur E. Kennelly. December 1933. Pages, 112. Price $1.

No. 94. Fellowships and Scholarships for Graduate Work in Science and Technology. Third edition. By Callie Hull and Clarence J. West. June 1934. Pages, 194. Price $1.

No. 95. Funds Available in the United States for the Encouragement of Research in Science and Technology. Third edition. By Callie Hull and Clarence J. West. Pages, 162. Price $1.

REPRINT AND CIRCULAR SERIES

No. 105. Doctorates Conferred in the Sciences by American Universities, 1932–33. By Callie Hull and Clarence J. West. 1933. Pages, 63. Price $0.50.

No. 106. History of the National Research Council, 1919–33. (Ten articles by several authors, reprinted from Science, vols. 77 and 78). January 1934. Pages, 61. Price $0.50.

MISCELLANEOUS PUBLICATIONS

Among its miscellaneous publications the council has published the following papers during the past year:

Organization and Members, National Research Council, 1933–34. April 1934. Pages, 69.

Annual Report, National Research Council, 1932–33. Separate reprint from the Annual Report of the National Academy of Sciences, 1932–33. Pages, 85.

Index to Proceedings of the Highway Research Board, volumes 1–12, inclusive (1921–32), including abstracts of the papers and reports published in these Proceedings. November 1933. Pages, 108.

SALES

The total amount received from sales of council publications from July 1, 1933, to June 30, 1934, is $4,204.69, of which $2,028.56 has been credited to the rotating fund for the publication of monographs of the division of physical sciences.

FINANCES

The total amount of money expended through the National Research Council during the fiscal year 1933–34 was $811,578.31. The distribution of these expenditures among the major types of activities of the council, together with a comparison with similar expenditures of the previous year, is shown as follows:

	1932–33		1933–34	
	Amount	Percentage	Amount	Percentage
Fellowships	$313,904.70	37.7	$360,238.74	44.4
Designated projects	286,743.45	34.4	240,775.48	29.7
Administered funds	89,224.44	10.7	112,770.61	13.9
General maintenance	144,041.01	17.2	97,793.48	12.0
Total	833,913.60	100.0	811,578.31	100.0

The funds disbursed for fellowships during 1933–34 were expended by the several fellowships boards and committees of the council as follows:

	Stipends and travel expenses of—		Administrative expenses	Total expenditures
	Fellows in the United States	Fellows abroad [1]		
Physics, chemistry, and mathematics	$137,746.87	$11,876.59	$7,153.98	$156,777.44
Medical sciences	48,313.05	6,612.86	2,658.77	57,584.68
Biological sciences	103,736.94	25,383.83	8,838.62	137,959.39
National Live Stock and Meat Board	4,375.00			4,375.00
Drug addiction	3,042.23			3,042.23
Magneto-optical analysis	500.00			500.00
Total	297,714.09	43,873.28	18,651.37	360,238.74

[1] Expenditures made by the Paris office of the Rockefeller Foundation for American fellows abroad are reported for the period from June 1, 1933, to May 31, 1934, rather than for the fiscal year.

Of these fellowship funds, $7,917.23 (2.19 percent) was contributed from industrial sources. The funds for the three groups of postdoctorate fellowships were contributed by the Rockefeller Foundation.

Funds for specially designated projects, amounting to $240,775.48 (29.7 percent of the total expenditures of the council) were contributed from outside sources for the support of research mainly of a cooperative nature and were expended under the direction of boards or committees of the council or cooperating agencies. Of this sum $7,300.22 (3 percent) was contributed from technical or industrial agencies. The following tabulation indicates the amounts expended upon certain of these projects during the years 1932–33 and 1933–34:

	1932–33	1933–34
Grants-in-aid	$60,725.39	$52,171.55
Highway research	23,417.12	17,115.37
Welding research	2,201.31	2,093.74
Research in problems of sex	73,237.50	74,717.42
Research on drug addiction	51,802.56	49,434.46
Effects of radition on living organisms	17,954.84	21,034.46
Child development investigations	7,096.46	7,005.40
Other projects	27,993.08	17,203.08
Total	270,428.26	240,775.48

The funds administered by the council as fiscal agent for other organizations, $112,770.61 (13.9 percent of the total disbursements of the council for the year), included $79,556.43 for Biological Abstracts; $12,990.17 for 10 projects of investigation conducted at the National Bureau of Standards; and $18,922.10 for the Science Advisory Board.

The sums expended through the council in 1933–34, aside from its own funds, for fellowships, for designated research projects, and as fiscal agent, amounted to $713,784.83 (87.9 percent of the operating expenditures of the council). This represents an increase of $23,912.24 over the total of similar expenditures for the previous year. Of the sums expended during the current year, $20,790.39 (2.9 percent) was contributed by industrial agencies.

The remaining portion of the year's operating expenditures ($97,793.48) was derived chiefly from the income from the endowment provided by the Carnegie Corporation for the council. Of this sum $95,339.32 was disbursed under provisions of the general administrative budget of the council for the current year, and $2,454.16 to meet obligations incurred under previous budgets and for miscellaneous minor purposes. These sums were expended for the general maintenance of the council, and constitute about one-eighth (12 percent) of the total operating expenditures of the council for the year. They were used for the general expenses of the divisions and committees of the council, for salaries, publications, supplies, service charges (exclusive of the general maintenance of the building and grounds) and for similar expenses. The proportion of funds spent for general maintenance of the council in 1933–34 is less than this proportion for last year (one-eighth against one-sixth) of the total expenditures of the council, the actual amount expended for this purpose this year ($97,793.48) being distinctly less (by 32.1 percent) than the expenditures for similar purposes last year ($144,041.01). These decreases were due in part to savings made possible through the reorganization of the council last year, but they were effected mainly by a reduction of the council's staff, by salary reductions and by other economies necessitated by the decreased funds available for maintenance purposes this year.

A detailed statement of the finances of the National Research Council will be found in the report of the treasurer of the National Academy of Sciences and the National Research Council (pp. 118 to 124).

DIVISION OF FEDERAL RELATIONS

The resignation is recorded with regret of the chairman of the division of Federal relations of the council, Dr. George Otis Smith, who has long been connected with the council and has served as chairman of this division since 1927. The succeeding chairman of the division is Dr. George R. Putnam, Commissioner of the Bureau of Lighthouses, United States Department of Commerce, who has been employed in governmental work since 1890.

DIVISION OF FOREIGN RELATIONS

R. A. MILLIKAN, Chairman

International dues.—The National Research Council at present adheres to the International Council of Scientific Unions, formerly known as the "International Research Council", and to six of the international scientific unions, as follows:

	Statutory amount of dues	Equivalent in United States currency at par for 1932
International Council of Scientific Unions	100 pre-war gold francs	$19.30
International Astronomical Union	3,200 pre-war gold francs	617.60
International Union of Chemistry	$675	675.00
International Union of Geodesy and Geophysics	16,000 Swiss francs	3,088.00
International Scientific Radio Union	800 pre-war gold francs	154.40
International Union of Pure and Applied Physics	1,600 French francs	62.72
International Geographical Union	40 pounds sterling	194.66
Total		4,811.08

The council formerly adhered to the International Mathematical Union, until the expiration in 1931 of the convention establishing that union.

During the greater part of the past 15 years the share of the United States in the annual expenses of these international organizations has been paid through governmental appropriations. For the first year or two of the relationships of the National Research Council to these organizations and occasionally in subsequent years in which, by reason of change in the basis of assessment, the governmental appropriation was not sufficient to meet at once the increased dues of certain unions, the council has made payments toward dues from the William Ellery Hale fund or from its own general funds. In addition, because of the failure of the Seventy-second Congress to continue the payment of these dues after 1931, the National Research Council met the obligations in full by payments totaling $5,637.19 for 1932 and $6,142.62 for 1933. The National Research Council made dues payments to prevent a lapse in relationships of the United States with these important international scientific organizations. It was recognized by the administrative committee of the council, however, that the Research Council could not continue to carry the responsibility for the payment of such dues indefinitely and at a meeting of the committee on November 17, 1933, action was taken directing that information be sent to the officers of the appropriate organizations "that unless arrangements can be made to pay these dues through Government appropriation it will be necessary for the National Reesarch Council to withdraw its support of these organizations as of December 31, 1933." Notification to this effect was sent to the corresponding officers at the request of the council by the president of the National Academy of Sciences in December, 1933.

Almost coincidently with the taking of this action, a measure to provide regularly for the payment by the Government of dues in the international scientific unions was introduced in the House of Representatives by Representative Sol Bloom (through bill H. R. 6781). A hearing upon the bill was held on March 6, 1934, by the House Committee on Foreign Affairs, which was attended by about 25 scientific men who spoke or contributed written statements in favor of the bill. The bill, amended to authorize the making of an appropriation later to pay the dues for the calendar year 1934, was passed by Congress and became a law (June 16, 1934) as follows:

[H. R. 6781, Public—No. 371—73d Cong.]

AN ACT To authorize appropriations to pay the annual share of the United States as an adhering member of the International Council of Scientific Unions and associated unions

Be it enacted by the Senate and House of Representatives of the United States of America in Congress assembled, That there is hereby authorized to be appropriated, to be expended under the direction of the Secretary of State, in paying the annual share of the United States as an adhering member of the International Council of Scientific Unions and associated unions, including the International Astronomical Union, International Union of Chemistry, International Union of Geodesy and Geophysics, International Union of Mathematics, International Scientific Radio Union, International Union of Physics, and International Geographical Union, and such other international scientific unions as the Secretary of State may designate, the sum of $9,000 for the fiscal year ending June 30, 1935.

Approved, June 16, 1934.

International scientific meetings abroad.—The National Research Council has been represented at international scientific meetings abroad during the past year as follows:

> International Union of Geodesy and Geophysics, Lisbon, Portugal, September 17–24, 1933, by six representatives (see p. 59).
> Third International Technical and Chemical Congress of Agricultural Industries, Paris, March 26–31, 1934, by three representatives.   (See p. 70.)
> Ninth International Congress of Pure and Applied Chemistry and Twelfth Conference of the International Union of Chemistry, Madrid, Spain, April 5–11, 1934, by 6 councilors and 4 additional delegates.   (See p. 70.)
> Dr. Edwin P. Hubble, astronomer of the Mount Wilson Observatory of the Carnegie Institution of Washington, Pasadena, has been appointed to represent the National Research Council at the Second General Assembly of the International Council of Scientific Unions which will be held in Brussels between the dates July 9 and 11, 1934.
> The council will also be represented at the International Geographical Congress which will be held at Warsaw, Poland, during the period August 23–31, 1934, at the Sixth General Assembly of the International Scientific Radio Union, London, September 12–19, 1934, and at the meeting of the International Union of Pure and Applied Physics, which will be held in Paris between the dates October 1 and 6, 1934.

Fifth Pacific Science Congress.—The National Research Council has received, among reports of the Fifth Pacific Science Congress which was held in Victoria and Vancouver, B. C., between the dates June 1 and 14, 1933, a number of resolutions adopted by the Congress, recommending for early investigation certain problems bearing currently upon the development of scientific knowledge of the Pacific region. These resolutions are being brought to the attention of organizations in the United States which may be interested in them.

The place for holding the next Congress in this series has been left to the decision of a general hold-over committee appointed by the Fifth Pacific Science Congress. This committee is composed of Dr. Henry M. Tory as chairman, director of laboratories in the Canadian National Research Council, Ottawa, and of one representative from each of the countries of the Pacific area which have been actively concerned in the work of the Pacific Science Association.

DIVISIONS OF STATES AND EDUCATIONAL RELATIONS

While in its earlier years the National Research Council gave consideration to the study of types of scientific organization in educational and governmental institutions, the attention of the council during recent years has been turned largely to other problems related directly to programs of scientific research. Less attention has therefore been given recently to the considerations which had formerly occupied the divisions of States relations and of educational relations of the council.

It is believed in the council that many matters concerning the relationships of various types of scientific institutions should be carefully studied and that new problems of organization of science in education and in government are constantly arising which should be considered from both the philosophical and the practical points of view. With the present trends of attention in the council the divisions of educational relations and of States relations and also the division of Federal relations have been quiescent. It is felt, however, that a place should be retained in the council for the divisions in view of the rapid changes now in progress in the educational field, changes which are even now affecting to an important degree the types of training in science which future citizens are to receive.

DIVISION OF PHYSICAL SCIENCES

F. K. RICHTMYER, Chairman

With the publication this year of three reports, the present program of the division of physical sciences for the publication of a series of research monographs has been brought nearly to completion. The papers recently published are—

(a) Part VI, Seismology, of a comprehensive treatise upon The Physics of the Earth, by J. B. Macelwane, H. O. Wood, H. F. Reid, J. A. Anderson, and P. Byerly. (N. R. C. Bulletin 90, October 1933.)

(b) The report of the committee on numerical integration entitled, "Numerical Integration of Differential Equations", by Albert A. Bennett, William E. Milne, and Harry Bateman. (N. R. C. Bulletin 92, November 1933.)

(c) A series of papers presented at the meeting of the American section of the International Union of Pure and Applied Physics, which was held in Chicago on June 24, 1933, entitled "Systems of Electrical and Magnetic Units", by R. T. Glazebrook, H. Abraham, L. Page, G. A. Campbell, H. L. Curtis, and A. E. Kennelly. (N. R. C. Bulletin 93, December 1933.)

Other bulletins in preparation include two contributions to the treatise on The Physics of the Earth which will deal with terrestrial magnetism and electricity, and with the internal constitution of the earth. Much of the material assembled for a section of this treatise upon field methods for detecting unhomogeneities in the earth's crust has been published during the year in the journal Physics. The material for a monograph on Line Spectra of the Elements is now in preparation, and the second report from the committee on rational transformations, Selected Topics in Algebraic Geometry, II, is now in press.

Mathematical books.—A fourth book has just been published through the use of the revolving fund for the publication of mathematical books, which was established in 1920. This latest volume, entitled "Algebraic Functions", prepared by Prof. G. A. Bliss, of the University of Chicago, was published in December 1933 in cooperation with the American Mathematical Society. Previous books published by means of this fund are:

The Theory of Transformation of Surfaces, by Luther P. Eisenhart, Princeton University, 1922.
Plane Cubic Curves, by Henry S. White, Vassar, 1925.
Linear Difference Equations, by P. M. Batchelder, University of Texas, 1928.

Glossary of physical terms.—The division of physical sciences has undertaken the preparation and publication of a descriptive glossary of physical terms, including marginal terms used in allied fields which are likely to occur also in physical literature. It is estimated that the list will eventually contain some 5,000 items, and it is planned to prepare the list first in preliminary mimeographed form subject to revision before its final printing.

Magneto-optical method of chemical analysis.—The division has sponsored the testing of the value of a highly sensitive method for the analysis of chemical solutions by magneto-optical means, which has been proposed by Prof. Fred Allison, of the Alabama Polytechnic Institute. Upon recommendation of the Research Council and with the endorsement also of the American Physical Society, the Rockefeller Foundation made a grant of $2,500 to the University of Virginia, to be used by Prof. J. W. Beams in carrying out test studies of this method. The division also has administered funds of $500 contributed by the Research Corporation of New York toward the stipend of an assistant to Professor Beams, and the Council has made a grant from its research aid fund of $665 for technical assistance, equipment, and other expenses.

Service institute for biophysics.—Growing out of the division's interest in borderland problems between physics and other sciences, the division has encouraged the preparation of plans for the establishment of a Washington Biophysical Laboratory "to undertake fundamental investigations in quantitative biology and to collaborate with other scientific organizations in the development of instruments and methods of measurement and in such other ways as will promote research in the fields of quantitative biology." A board of directors has been formed to take charge of the Institute and to solicit funds for its support, as follows:

Lyman J. Briggs, Director, National Bureau of Standards.
F. K. Richtmyer, professor of physics, Cornell University.
Vincent DuVigneaud, professor of biochemistry, George Washington University.
George W. McCoy, Director, National Institute of Health.
James W. Jobling, professor of pathology, College of Physicians and Surgeons, Columbia University.
Frederick S. Brackett, secretary of the board of directors and director of the Washington Biophysical Laboratory.

Research committees.—Research committees of the division are engaged upon the preparation of a bibliography of orthogonal polynominals, a bibliography of mathematical tables and aids to computers, investigations upon methods of measurement of radiation and of the determination of physical constants, the development of exhibition methods and technique, and the relation between physics and the medical sciences with special reference to the receptor organs. Several of these committees now have reports in process of preparation.

Cooperation between physics and chemistry.—In the interest of increasingly effective work in borderlands of science, the divisions of physical sciences and of chemistry and chemical technology held a joint conference in New York on April 5, 1934. Two special topics were discussed at this conference, (*a*) cooperation in the publication of abstracts of scientific articles, and (*b*) plans for holding a roundtable conference for the discussion of research upon the isotopes of hydrogen. In the development of the latter topic a committee was subsequently authorized to be composed of a physicist, a chemist, and a biologist, to plan for the development of coordinated investigations upon these problems.

International Scientific Radio Union.—The American section of the International Scientific Radio Union functions continuously as an organization in the United States for the exchange of research information in this field and for the encouragement of investigations upon radio communication, as well as to relate American interests in the subject to developments abroad through the International Scientific Radio Union. The American section holds an annual meeting in Washington at about the time of the April meeting of the National Academy of Sciences. These annual meetings, which are attended by several score of radio engineers and investigators, have become significant occasions for the exchange of information in this field in the United States. The last meeting in this series was held in Washington on April 27, 1934, jointly with the Institute of Radio Engineers. Over 20 papers were presented at the meeting upon fundamental aspects of radio problems.

DIVISION OF ENGINEERING AND INDUSTRIAL RESEARCH

CHARLES F. KETTERING, Chairman

The division of engineering and industrial research represents the principal relationship of the National Research Council to practical applications of scientific knowledge in industrial development. This relationship and the means for maintaining it have been regarded as highly important for the National Research Council in carrying out its purposes and this importance is enhanced by the ever-increasing utilization of scientific and technical discoveries in industry and the dependence of industrial and social progress upon the continuing development of basic scientific knowledge. The new industries especially, of which several have appeared during the current generation and which have come to occupy major positions in the industrial world, were based upon the new developments of scientific knowledge, and still depend upon the continuation of such developments. The division of engineering and industrial research is charged with the duty of relating the pure sciences to industrial progress as a contribution toward commerical prosperity and the public welfare. It therefore stands very close to the main purposes of the National Research Council. With these considerations in view, the contributions of this division of the council during the past year have a peculiar significance.

Annual meeting.—The annual meeting of the division of engineering and industrial research which was held in New York City on the evening of November 23, 1933, was utilized by the committee of the Department of Commerce on decentralization of industry to place before a representative group of industrialists, engineers, and others the plans and program of this committee. The decentralization of industry is considered to be most important by the Business Advisory and Planning Council. The meeting was addressed by Mr. W. A. Julian, Treasurer of the United States and chairman of the Committee on the Decentralization of Industry of the Business Advisory and Planning Council; also by Dr. Willard L. Thorpe, Director of the Bureau of Foreign and Domestic Commerce, and by several other representatives of the Government.

The committee considers decentralization of industry as meaning the shift in location of manufacturing establishments from highly congested urban areas to suburban and rural areas, with some reduction in the average size of manufacturing establishments. The objectives of the committee were announced as follows:

1. To constitute itself the agency to centralize and consolidate all information on the subject, stimulate action, and coordinate all efforts directed toward a socially better and more economic distribution of industry and population.

2. To determine the present movement—whether toward centralization or decentralization, the rate of movement, and the factors responsible.

3. To determine whether or not decentralization of industry is socially desirable and economically desirable.

4. To determine whether or not the Government should attempt to accelerate or retard the movement and to recommend the methods which should be employed.

5. To determine the needs of temporary agencies, such as the Subsistence Homestead Division of the Department of the Interior, the Tennessee Valley Authority, and the Emergency Relief Administration, and the assistance which the committee should render to these agencies.

While the division took no position on these questions it was glad to afford the opportunity to this committee of the Government to present its views to representative business and industrial leaders.

Highway Research Board.—The thirteenth annual meeting of the Highway Research Board was held in Washington on December 7 and 8, 1933. The registered attendance, 314, was larger than at any previous meeting of the Board and included representatives from 26 States and from Canada, besides a considerable local attendance. Special attention was given in this meeting to matters of highway economics, to highway financing, and to traffic surveys, in addition to the consideration of technical problems of the materials and methods of construction of highways, of air resistance on vehicles, of friction resistance of highway surfaces, and of the design and maintenance of highways of different types.

The report of the twelfth annual meeting of the Highway Research Board (Dec. 1–2, 1932) was distributed in the summer of 1933 as a volume of 412 pages in an edition of 1,900 copies. The board has also published a subject and author index to the first 12 volumes of its proceedings, together with an abstract of the 281 papers contained in these proceedings. Beginning with September, 1933 .the board has issued its Highway Research Abstracts (in mimeographed form) monthly on a schedule of 10 numbers per year. These abstracts present a synopsis of the more important current contributions in the literature of the field of highway development and also much laboratory information not otherwise published.

Among other projects of investigation the board is supporting studies of the use of steel of high elastic limit for concrete reinforcement in highways in cooperation with the Iowa State College, Ames, Iowa.

Welding research.—The committee on fundamental research in welding held its fourth annual conference in Detroit, October 3, 1933, in conjunction with the meeting of the American Welding Society and the Metal Congress Exposition. The attendance at this conference numbered about 40, of whom many were university men interested in the fundamental aspects of the physical and chemical problems of welding practice. Papers were presented at this conference dealing with the tensile tests of welds, fatigue and strains in welded metals, internal stresses and stress distribution in welds, and magnetic characteristics of deposited metal. The committee has been in touch with about 50 basic projects of investigation during the past year relating to the welding arts which are being studied in university laboratories.

The annual meeting of the American Bureau of Welding, which is sponsored jointly by the American Welding Society and the division of engineering and industrial research of the National Research Council, was held in New York City on April 26, 1934, with an attendance of about 60. In addition to progress reports upon the several research projects sponsored by the bureau, special consideration was given at the meeting to the planning of a program of investigations upon the ductility of welded joints. The committee of the bureau on structural steel welding has established a research fellowship at Lehigh University for the purpose of conducting a series of investigations on welded connections commonly used in structural work. These investigations will parallel photoelastic studies being conducted at the university upon welded seat angles.

Electrical insulation.—The committee on electrical insulation held its sixth annual meeting in Philadelphia on November 14–15, 1933, at the Moore School of Electrical Engineering of the University of Pennsylvania in conjunction with the meeting of the Philadelphia section of the American Institute of Electrical Engineers. Special attention was given in the program of this meeting to the correlation of theoretical physics with engineering and to the coordination of chemical and electrical research on dielectrics. The report of this meeting has been issued (in photolithographed form), presenting abstracts of the eighteen papers on the program and a bibliography on liquid dielectrics.

Two monographs have recently been published (John Wiley and Sons, Inc.) in the series which is being sponsored by the committee on electrical insulation, the full series being composed as follows:

No. 1. The Nature of a Gas, by Leonard B. Loeb; 153 pages, 1931.
No. 2. The Electrical Properties of Glass, by J. T. Littleton and G. W. Morey; 184 pages, 1933.
No. 3. Liquid Dielectrics, by Andeas Gemant; 185 pages, 1933.

Heat transmission.—The committee on heat transmission has sponsored the publication of two monographs which have been completed during the past year, as follows:

The Measurement of the Total Radiation of Carbon Dioxide Gas and Water Vapor, by Charles H. Gilmorer, Massachusetts Institute of Technology.
The Transmission of Heat between Flowing Oils and a Metal Tube, by J. F. D. Smith.

Cooperation with the Science Advisory Board.—A part of the time of the staff of the division of engineering and industrial research has been devoted this year to the Science Advisory Board in establishing relationships with governmental agencies, particularly in the Department of Commerce, which are concerned with research in industry. The division was enabled to suggest a standard paragraph concerning research to be included as a part of the model industrial code of the National Recovery Administration; it also called attention to important information contained in the reports upon hearings which have been held on the large number of industrial codes that have been examined; it has facilitated the announcement of the movement for the decentralization of industry, and has given consideration to means for the encouragement of new industries; and it has proposed that analytical studies be made of the causes of mechanical failure of airplanes in flight whether of a destructive nature or not, in order that steps may be taken to provide the type of meteorological data which in most cases it is believed would have obviated these failures. The division has also called the attention of the Bureau of Foreign and Domestic Commerce to the importance of obtaining information in regard to technical advances abroad through the foreign commerce service officers, and has prepared a set of instructions for these officers with this in view. The division has also cooperated with the committee on railway research appointed by the Science Advisory Board at the request of the Federal Coordinator of Transportation.

DIVISION OF CHEMISTRY AND CHEMICAL TECHNOLOGY

F. W. WILLARD, Chairman

International Union of Chemistry.—At a conference of chemists held at the University of Santander, Spain, between the dates August 8 and 17, 1933, plans were made for holding the Eleventh Conference of the International Union of Chemistry in Madrid between the dates April 5 and 11, 1934, and for holding the Ninth International Congress of Pure and Applied Chemistry in association with the conference of the union at the same time.

The National Research Council was represented on this occasion by 6 councilors and 4 additional delegates to the union, and all of these representatives were also accredited to the International Congress of Pure and Applied Chemistry, as follows:

COUNCILORS

Edward Bartow, chairman of the delegation, professor of chemistry and head of the department of chemistry and chemical engineering, University of Iowa, Iowa City, Iowa.
Lauder W. Jones, professor of chemistry, Princeton University, Princeton, N. J.
Gilbert N. Lewis, professor of chemistry and dean of the College of Chemistry, University of California, Berkeley, Calif.

Alexander Silverman, professor of chemistry and head of the department of chemistry, University of Pittsburgh, Pittsburgh, Pa.

Robert E. Swain, professor of chemistry, Stanford University, Stanford University, Calif.

John W. Turrentine, research chemist, United States Bureau of Chemistry and Soils, Washington, D. C.

Arnold K. Balls, senior chemist, United States Bureau of Chemistry and Soils, Washington, D. C.

John Van Nostrand Dorr, president of the Dorr Co., 247 Park Avenue, New York City.

Raleigh Gilchrist, associate and research chemist, National Bureau of Standards, Washington, D. C.

Atherton Seidell, chemist, National Institute of Health, Treasury Department, Washington, D. C.

The following appointments were also made among members of this delegation to represent the National Research Council at meetings of committees of the union on this occasion:

Committee for the reform of the nomenclature of biological chemistry, Robert E. Swain.

Committee on the reform of the nomenclature of inorganic chemistry, Alexander Silverman.

Committee on the coordination of scientific terminology, John W. Turrentine.

Committee on annual table of constants and numerical data, Edward W. Bartow; Atherton Seidell, alternate.

Committee on thermochemistry, Raleigh Gilchrist.

Committee on physical chemical standards, Gilbert N. Lewis; Arnold K. Balls, alternate.

The conference of the union was attended by representatives from 15 of the 26 countries adhering to the union and by several American chemists in addition to those appointed by the Research Council as its representatives. The work of the union is carried on through commissions appointed to deal with important current topics in chemistry. The International Congress of Pure and Applied Chemistry, on the other hand, is organized into groups according to subdivisions of the field, and its sessions are held for the presentation of papers in these groups, over 250 papers having been contributed at the Madrid meeting. The attendance at the congress was about 1,200. The last international congress was held in New York in 1912. The next conference of the International Union of Chemistry will be held in Lucerne in 1936, and the next Congress of Pure and Applied Chemistry in Rome in 1938. Dr. N. Parravano, president of the National Chemistry Commission of Italy and professor of chemistry, University of Rome, was elected president of the union for the ensuing 4-year period. Prof. Edward Bartow was elected a vice president of the union and thus becomes ex officio the chairman of the American section of the union, which is composed of the membership of the division of chemistry and chemical technology of the National Research Council.

Other international chemical meetings.—The National Research Council was also represented by Prof. Edward Bartow and Dr. Atherton Seidell at a conference on chemical documentation which was held in the International Office of Chemistry in Paris on March 27 and 28, 1934.

The Research Council was represented at the Third International Technical and Chemical Congress of the Agricultural Industries, which was held in Paris between the dates March 26 and 31, 1934, by Dr. Arnold K. Balls, Dr. Raleigh Gilchrist, and Dr. John W. Turrentine.

On account of delay in receiving information about the Thirteenth Congress of Industrial Chemistry, which was held at Lille, France, on September 24, 1933, it was unfortunately impossible for the National Research Council to arrange to be represented.

Chemical literature.—The double problem of providing facilities for the initial publication of the large volume of results of chemical research each year and also of making this literature generally and systematically available to chemists has been before the council's division of chemistry and chemical technology for some time. During the past year this matter was made a subject for special discussion at the joint conference of the divisions of chemistry and chemical technology and of physical sciences, which was held at the Chemists Club in New York City on April 6, 1934. The value of abstracting journals is recognized both as a means for distributing news of current work and also as an organized directory for reference. On an international scale, the problem has also been discussed by the International Union of Chemistry, the conference which was held in Paris on March 26–31 being the second formal occasion for the discussion of these matters. At this conference it was proposed to develop a system of national centers of documentation for the registering, abstracting, and distributing of chemical literature in the several countries participating. The International Office of Chemistry in Paris has also proposed to establish an international catalog of periodicals in the field of chemistry. Approximately 3,500 are already known to be published in 58 countries. Chemical Abstracts, published in the United States, has published a list of 1,996 of the principal chemical periodicals of the world. It has also been suggested that libraries themselves undertake to furnish photographic film reproductions of articles in chemistry desired by individual investigators.

Annual Survey of American Chemistry.—The eighth volume of the Annual Survey of American Chemistry, prepared jointly by the division of chemistry and chemical technology and the Research Information Service of the council, was published in May 1934, as a book of 408 pages containing 25 articles contributed by 27 authors, together with an author and subject index. The plan for the ninth volume in this series, reviewing American contributions during the calendar year 1934, has been approved and provides for 25 chapters. According to the editorial plan for this series of volumes, such subjects as the kinetics of homogeneous gas reactions, subatomic phenomena and thermodynamics and thermochemistry, colloids, contact catalysis, aliphatic, carbocyclic, and heterocyclic compounds, biochemistry and petroleum rubber chemistry will be discussed in each volume. In the forthcoming volume the subjects of photochemistry, industrial application of X-rays, nonferrous metals, food chemistry, fermentation chemistry, trade wastes, soil fertilizers, the processing of coal and synthetic textiles, which are reported every 2 years, will be included. Other subjects, reported less frequently, will also be added to the ninth volume, as follows: Theories of solutions, radioactivity, alcoholic beverages, processing of natural fibers, the chemistry of solvent utilization and chemical engineering unit processes.

At its meeting on May 11, 1934, the division of chemistry and chemical technology took action to discharge its committee on the publication of the annual survey of American chemistry and to transfer the future preparation of the survey to the Research Information Service.

Preservation of records.—For the past 3 years the division has maintained an advisory committee to the National Bureau of Standards to counsel with the bureau in regard to its investigations upon the durability of paper and the preservation of records. These investigations have been supported by contributions from the Carnegie Corporation of New York City totaling $30,000, in addition to the facilities provided by the bureau. The bureau has been enabled to recommend (1) certain minimum conditions for the preservation of records and (2) certain minimum specification requirements for papers of different grades for permanent, semipermanent, and current records. A report has recently been prepared especially for the attention of librarians upon the optimum conditions for the storage of records (B. W. Scribner, Preservation of Records in Libraries, Library Quarterly, vol. IV, no. 3, pp. 371–383; July 1934).

Corrosion of iron pipe.—In the fall of 1933 the division also appointed an advisory committee to the National Bureau of Standards on the corrosion of ferrous pipe material, in response to a request from the director of the bureau, to advise the bureau in regard to planning tests on the corrosion of iron pipe and to cooperate in the preparation of a final report. These investigations during the coming year will be supported in part by funds contributed by certain steel corporations and administered through the National Research Council.

Chemistry of colloids.—The colloid symposium, which it had been proposed to hold last year in cooperation with the division of colloids of the American Chemical Society at the University of Wisconsin, in commemoration of the closing of the first 10-year series of these symposia, was necessarily postponed for a year, but was held at Madison, Wis., on June 14, 15, and 16, 1934, as the eleventh symposium in this series. The program provided for the presentation of about 25 papers in addition to the discussion of matters of nomenclature.

An index to the monographs previously published representing the first 10 of these symposia, has been published (in mimeographed form) by the division of chemistry and chemical technology. The papers presented at the recent symposium are being prepared for publication commercially by Prof. Harry B. Weiser of the Rice Institute, chairman of the committee, in the usual monograph form. The twelfth symposium in this series will be held at Cornell University, Ithaca, N. Y., June, 1935.

Contact catalysis.—The tenth annual report of the committee on contact catalysis, reviewing advancements in this field of heterogeneous catalysis during the approximate academic year 1932–33, was prepared by Dr. Guy B. Taylor, of E. I. du Pont de Nemours & Co., Wilmington, Del. Because of the reduced facilities of the Journal of Physical Chemistry, it has not been possible to publish Dr. Taylor's report in that journal as have been the previous reports in this series. The division of chemistry and chemical technology is therefore planning to publish Dr. Taylor's report in mimeographed form in the fall of 1934, together with the eleventh report in this series for 1933–34, which has been prepared by Prof. R. E. Burk, of Western Reserve University.

Laboratory construction and equipment.—The committee on laboratory construction and equipment has distributed an extensive questionnaire covering matters relating to the designing and building of scientific laboratories in order to assemble information on recent developments. The results of this inquiry, when tabulated, will be available for those requesting information concerning laboratory construction and will be made the basis of a supplementary report on laboratory materials and planning now under consideration. Reference material has been accumulated in the files of the chairman of the committee, Prof. C. R. Hoover, professor of chemistry, Wesleyan University, Middletown, Conn., and has been augmented recently by the addition of a set of standard plans and specifications for the laboratories of high schools of science.

Ring systems.—Difficulties have been encountered by the committee on the preparation and publication of a list of ring systems in organic chemistry, which has arranged jointly with the American Chemical Society for the publication of an extensive list of ring systems now known. A year ago the manuscript of this catalog was estimated to be about one-half completed. Notes in regard to new ring systems are being added as these are reported with view to keeping the list up to date for possible publication later.

Hydrogen isotopes.—At a joint conference of physicists and chemists in New York City on April 6, 1934, it was recognized that, on account of the very rapid development of knowledge of the isotopes of hydrogen, a committee to effect a certain coordination of research in this field was desirable. This committee was appointed by the division of chemistry and chemical technology in the spring of 1934 with representation upon it of chemists, physicists, and biologists. The committee held a general conference at Cleveland, Ohio, in the fall of 1934 and discussed the present status of researches in this field, arriving at certain agreements as to bases of cooperation. Another meeting is scheduled for April, 1935 at New York.

DIVISION OF GEOLOGY AND GEOGRAPHY

W. H. TWENHOFEL, Chairman

Accessory minerals of crystalline rocks.—The committee on accessory minerals of crystalline rocks has prepared a report reviewing the progress of recent research in this field and giving an abstract of contributions made to the literature of crystalline rocks during the past year both in the United States and abroad. A special section of the report reviews recent contributions upon the accessory minerals of sedimentary rocks as related to crystalline rocks from which these sediments may have been derived.

Batholiths.—The second edition of the report (mimeographed) of the committee on batholithic problems, which was issued in the summer of 1933 in preparation for the Sixteenth International Geological Congress, has been issued to meet continued demands for this review of recent progress in this field. An annotated list of papers selected from the papers mentioned in the Bibliographic List of Papers on Batholiths and the Mechanics of Igneous Intrusions (issued by the division of geology and geography in 1931) is now in preparation.

Bibliography of Economic Geology.—The Annotated Bibliography of Economic Geology has been published semiannually since 1928, presenting each year from 2,000 to 2,500 annotated references to world literature of economic geology and including technical papers relating to the geological and mineralogical aspects of rocks and soils and to the examination and discovery of ore deposits by geophysical methods.

Of the total amount contributed for this bibliography ($19,509.78), there remains a sufficient sum to carry on the editorial preparation of this journal until June 30, 1936, the editorial expense ranging from $2,000 to $3,000 per year. The bibliography is published by special arrangement with the Economic Geology Publishing Co. Subscriptions in early years fully paid the publication expense but of late years they have fallen off heavily.

Cooperation with the Bureau of the Census.—During the past year two projects in which the council has been cooperating with the Bureau of the Census have been brought to completion. Manuscript maps were completed in 1933 for most of the States showing boundaries of minor civil divisions (townships, boroughs, etc.) on a scale of 1:500,000. These maps will be republished on a scale of 16 miles to an inch (approximately 1:1,000,000) and will be used as bases to show the distribution of population, farm acreage, etc. A report upon "Types of Farming in the United States", published by the Bureau of the Census during 1933, is organized upon a principle proposed by the committee in earlier cooperative work with the bureau. According to this principle State maps are made that show minor civil divisions which can be grouped in major physiographic provinces. This makes it possible to assemble statistical material according to natural geographic units.

A third undertaking of the committee has been to aid the Bureau of the Census in obtaining assistance for the preservation of its early records. The matter was presented to the Forty-second Annual Conference of the Daughters of the American Revolution (in Washington, Apr. 17–21, 1933), which adopted a resolution calling the attention of Congress to the importance of preserving these early records. Funds made available to the Bureau of the Census through the Civil Works Administration have made it possible to undertake the systematic restoration and the photostatic copying of 221 volumes containing population reports for 1800, 1810, 1820, and comprising over 100,000 pages.

International Geographical Union.—The United States national committee of the International Geographical Union distributed information to all geographers in this country concerning the International Geographical Congress held in Warsaw, Poland, August 23 to 31, 1934, and arranged for the assembling and shipping of a collection of maps for exhibition at the congress. The exhibit included contributions from Government bureaus, university departments of geography, and geographical societies, and was planned to show the types of American maps issued for various purposes and the historical development of methods of cartography in the United States. The materials comprising the exhibit were designed for later distribution to various organizations in Poland. Among some 20 American geographers who had planned to attend the congress, the National Research Council was represented by the following American geographers:

S. W. Boggs, geographer, Department of State, Washington, D. C.

Isaiah Bowman, chairman, National Research Council, and director, American Geographical Society, New York City.

Louise A. Boyd, Arctic explorer, San Francisco, Calif.
Gen. J. G. Steese, United States Army (retired), Tulsa, Okla.
John K. Wright, librarian, American Geographical Society, New York City.

Isostasy.—The committee on isostasy has continued to assemble and exchange information in regard to investigations bearing upon the theory of isostasy. Gravity observations which are being made continually by the United States Coast and Geodetic Survey provide basic data. From oil production and mining operations and from the work of certain research institutions concerned with seismological studies, data are also gathered which are analyzed by the members of the committee, and other students of geodesy, with view to effecting a better understanding of the relative effect of vertical or radial forces and of horizontal or tangential forces in the deformation of the earth's crust, and of the conditions under which an isostatic balance between units or blocks in the earth's crust may be acquired in certain regions. Two groups of data particularly are needed to test fully the cause and process of isostatic adjustment: (a) "Many more gravity observations made at locations where the structure and density of the superficial rocks are definitely known"; and (b) "corresponding determinations of the structure, density and thickness of the underlying rocks between depths of 2 and 10 miles obtainable only by seismic methods." The practical value of these studies in oil prospecting, for example, is increasingly appreciated and the committee recommends that surveys should be extended and correlated with seismological investigations.

Land classification.—The committee on land classification was organized in the spring of 1933 to direct attention to basic problems of land classification which are involved in Federal and State land administration. The interest of the National Research Council in these studies, the importance of which is being recognized to an increasing degree, is represented also by cooperation with the committee on land use of the Science Advisory Board, and with a standing committee on land classification and utilization of the Pacific Science Association, appointed in response to a recommendation adopted at the Fifth Pacific Science Congress to promote coordinated investigation upon problems of land use in various countries of the Pacific region. Members of these committees have also maintained relations with geographers and economists interested in land problems. and with investigators in various branches of the Federal Government and with several State groups engaged in the study of land problems. The main purpose of the Research Council's committee has been to develop standard methods for the classification of land types.

Measurement of geological time.—The committee on the measurement of geological time has sponsored investigations of the problem of determining the age of geological units by chemical means. Atomic disintegration has come to be regarded as an acceptable method for such age determinations. The chemistry of isotopes of pure lead and their exact rate of decay, and the analysis of such minerals as allamite, monazite, titanite, and samarskite have provided the main lines of approach. The annual report of the committee (issued in mimeographed form) reviews the contribution of a number of workers in this field.

Micropaleontology.—The annual report of the committee on micropaleontology again presents a review of the current trends of research on this subject. Early work in micropaleontology was based principally upon a study of the foraminifera and ostracoda. Micropaleontologic methods have now been extended so as to become adaptable to several other groups of organisms, including fossil diatoms, which broaden the scope of this study particularly in its application to petroleum geology. Members of the committee have contributed to the report summaries of current research in micropaleontology for particular sections of the United States or for special geological horizons.

Ore deposition.—The committee on ore deposition has concentrated its attention upon two general problems: (1) the genesis of the lead-zinc-copper deposits of the Mississippi Valley, and (2) the zoning of ore deposits as exemplified by occurrences in the United States. In the encouragement and coordination of these investigations the committee has held two meetings during the past year, the first at the University of Chicago on December 30, 1933, and the other at Baxter Springs, Kans., on March 26, 1934. The problems discussed by the committee include the mode of occurrence and origin of cherts of the Boone—the ore-bearing formation of the Tri-State district, the proportion of silica, limestone, and dolomite in deep-well cuttings in the Boone, the occurrence of intrusive igneous rocks of Paleozoic age or younger in the central part of the Mississippi Valley, the ores of the old Cornwall copper mine in Missouri, the occurrence of tourmaline in minute crystals in the Tri-State ores, and certain structural features of the Missourian lead-zinc district.

Paleobotany.—Through the series of annual reports of the committee on paleobotany, reviewing the progress of research in this field from year to year, a notable feature has been the increasing attention which many workers have been giving to studies of ancient climate based upon remains of plant material. Such material seems to lend itself more readily to interpretation in terms of climate and ecology than animal material on account of the (1) structure and cuticular adaptations of plants; (2) geographic distribution; and (3) relations of plant remains to the sediments in which they are found. For the coming year the committee has been largely reorganized. An annotated bibliography of 57 papers on the paleobotany of North America is appended to the annual report of the committee.

Petroleum geology.—The committee on petroleum geology has encouraged studies upon the origin, migration, transformation, and accumulation of petroleum and natural gas and upon methods of exploration and recovery of oil and gas in the reservoir rocks. Among recent developments may be mentioned the preparation of a glossary of structural terms used in petroleum geology, a review of the knowledge of reservoir rocks, an analysis and mapping of particular formations in oil fields, the interpretation of geological structure and stratigraphy characteristic of oil areas, and a study of temperatures in deep wells.

The present trends in petroleum geology seem to be toward the increased employment of aerial photography in mapping, the use of micropaleontology for correlation purposes, the development of geophysical instruments for oil exploration, and the perfection of equipment for observing pressures and temperatures at the bottoms of deep wells. The comparatively frequent drilling of wells in recent years to depths greater than 10,000 feet is expected to contribute much to the knowledge of the outer layers of the earth's crust.

Scientific results of drilling.—The committee on scientific results of drilling has continued to assemble information concerning sources from which drilling records and specimens may be obtained. It endeavors to provide for the exchange of information and to arrange for the preservation of well-drilling samples and records at suitable centers for geological research. The committee has recognized several institutions as depositories of well cores and logs with the understanding that materials donated to these institutions will be permanently preserved. These institutions now include Pennsylvania State College, the Illinois State Geological Survey, the University of Wichita, University of Kansas, West Virginia University, Princeton University, and the Corps of Engineers of the United States Army.

When it is recalled that the only information available concerning the precise materials of which the earth's crust is composed at depths below ordinary mining operations must come from the drilling of wells and occasionally from deep mines, the importance of the systematic preservation of drilling records and well cores becomes obvious.

Sedimentation.—The committee on sedimentation has prepared a special report containing about 20 papers appearing during the years 1932 to 1934 which contribute to knowledge of the processes of sedimentation and of sedimentary deposits in geology. The committee has at its disposal for the support of research the royalties from the sale of the "Treatise on Sedimentation", first and second editions, and from the sale of geologic color charts prepared in 1928. These funds have amounted altogether to $2,385.87. A certain amount has already been used by the committee for the support of investigations, leaving a balance as of June 30, 1934, of $1,524.83. A grant from this fund was made toward the support of the Journal of Sedimentary Petrology in 1933, which is now in its fourth volume.

State geological surveys.—The committee on State geological surveys is engaged in the preparation of a model plan for a State geological survey. For such a survey, whether termed a State geological survey or a State bureau of mines or a State division of mineral resources, the following functions among others are recognized:

1. To investigate and report upon the basic geological structure of the State.
2. To determine the mineral resources of the region.
3. To develop the information necessary to exploit these resources properly.
4. To find new or improved uses for mineral resources.
5. To provide reliable maps and geological engineering data for the State.
6. To survey the water resources and soils of the State.
7. To collect statistics of the production and consumption of the State's mineral resources and competitive market conditions.
8. To furnish instructional information for the State's public schools, normal schools, and colleges.
9. To provide information concerning the State's mineral resources for the use of the public.
10. To assemble the data necessary as the basis for a State policy of conservation and development.

In the preparation of this plan the committee has appointed a number of subcommittees to deal with various phases of the work of a typical State geological survey.

Stratigraphy.—The committee on stratigraphy is organized for the promotion of a critical study of general problems encountered in stratigraphic classification and description. The enormous increase in the amount of current literature on stratigraphy and the rapid advancement of the past few decades indicate to the committee that its major objective should be the synthesis and coordination of present knowledge of the stratigraphy of North America with view to the establishment of a more satisfactory basis for the correlation of these units within the geologic time scale. At the request of the committee on principles of stratigraphic nomenclature of the Association of State Geologists, the division's committee on stratigraphy has agreed to respond to specific questions of interpretation of the rules of nomenclature which may be raised by geologists from time to time.

Members of the committee have undertaken the responsibility for the coordination of present stratigraphic knowledge at first in regard to 10 early geological systems, including the Cambrian, Ordovician, Silurian, Devonian, Mississippian, Pennsylvanian, Permian, Triassic and Jurassic, Cretaceous, Tertiary. A handbook has been planned which will include graphic key sections for each of these systems, synthetic diagrams, and correlation charts.

Tectonics.—The committee on tectonics calls special attention to the publication this year of a volume entitled the "Deformation of the Earth's Crust", by Prof. Walter H. Bucher, of the University of Cincinnati (Princeton University Press, 1933), to the preparation of which the committee has lent encouragement. In addition the committee has endorsed a number of other research projects which are of a continuing nature, including a large-scale tectonic map of the United States and an accompanying treatise, an earthquake map of New England, an index of geological maps for Europe, Asia, and Africa (the index for North America and the West Indies having been issued last summer in advance of the Sixteenth International Geographical Congress), a transcontinental geological cross section, a geophysical survey of the southwestern extension of the Appalachian folds, the tectonics of the sea bottom, especially in the region of the Bartlett Trough south of Cuba, a list of State geological maps, a glossary of structural tectonic terms in geology, and a compilation of geologic laws affecting world tectonics. The committee is also in touch through its members with much of the other work in progress in the United States pertaining to the structure and deformation of the earth's crust, and in the annual report of the committee reviews of this work are given, making the report a research directory in this field for the United States.

Representation of the division.—The division is represented in the board of directors of the American Association of Water Well Drillers, which has been concerned mainly during the past year with formulating the National Recovery Administration code for the well-drilling industry; and also on the technical committee on scientific classification of coal of the American Society of Testing Materials. The latter committee has devoted its attention this year to specifications for the classification of coal according to its rank (or degree of metamorphosis), taking cognizance also of calorific value, fixed carbon, ash and sulphur content and temperature of softening of the ash. Mr. Arthur Keith represents the division on the advisory council of the Board of Surveys and Maps of the Federal Government.

DIVISION OF MEDICAL SCIENCES

FRANCIS G. BLAKE, Chairman

Animal parasitology.—A final report was published during the year by Dr. W. W. Cort jointly with Dr. G. F. Otto, of Johns Hopkins University, upon the results of the field and laboratory studies sponsored by the committee on medical problems of animal parasitology of the division of medical sciences and conducted under the supervision of Dr. Cort between the years 1927 and 1932 on the occurrence of ascariasis in children in the Southern States. This study was supported by grants totaling $27,850 from the American Child Health Association and by cooperative contributions from health departments of a number of States in which these studies were carried on. The study was begun in Virginia and Tennessee and was extended eventually into Kentucky, North Carolina, Louisiana, Florida, and Arkansas.

G. F. Otto and W. W. Cort. Distribution and epidemiology of human ascariasis in the United States. American Journal of Hygiene, vol. 19, pp. 651–712, May 1934.

The work of Dr. Henry E. Meleny, of the school of medicine of Vanderbilt University on *Endamoeba histolytica*, which was instigated as one of the results of the studies on ascariasis and which has been supported mainly by an appropriation of $16,200 to Vanderbilt University from the Rockefeller Foundation, has proceeded with valuable results as far as is possible with the funds available. The committee on animal parasitology has also sponsored a study of Manson's blood fluke, *Schistosoma mansoni*, in Puerto Rico by Dr. E. C. Faust, of the school of medicine of Tulane University. In this study the school of tropical medicine of the University of Puerto Rico has also generously cooperated. Two papers have been published upon the results of this study:

E. C. Faust. Studies on schistosomiasis mansoni in Puerto Rico; history of schistosomiasis in Puerto Rico. Puerto Rico J. Pub. Health & Trop. Med., vol. 9, pp. 154–161, December 1933.
E. C. Faust, W. A. Hoffman, C. A. Jones, J. L. Janner. Studies on schistosomiasis mansoni in Puerto Rico; epidemiology and geographical distribution of schistosomiasis mansoni in Puerto Rico; survey of intestinal parasites in endemic schistosomiasis areas in Puerto Rico. Puerto Rico J. Pub. Health & Trop. Med., vol. 9, pp. 447–471, June 1934.

Climate and health.—It has not been possible to carry out the program proposed last year by the committee on climate and health for a study of the effects of tropical climate upon the health of human beings because of the difficulty in obtaining research funds for this project. However, with the aid of a special grant of $400 from the Research Council a compilation and analysis have been undertaken of published data derived from many parts of the world on heat effects in the tropics.

Gonococcus and gonococcal infections.—The committee on the gonococcus and gonococcal infections was appointed in April, 1933, to take charge cooperatively for the division of medical sciences of the Research Council and the American Social Hygiene Association of a survey of the facilities for research on the gonococcus and of investigations which are in progress in the United States relating to gonococcal infections. During the past year a review has been made by the collaborator for the committee, Dr. Ruth Boring Thomas, of the staff of the American Social Hygiene Association, of all of the important literature on this subject which has been published in the last 5 years, and much information has been assembled concerning investigations on problems relating to the gonococcus both in the United States and abroad.   This material will be prepared for publication during the coming year.

Infectious abortion.—The joint committee of the divisions of medical sciences and of biology and agriculture on infectious abortion, appointed in 1922, has been primarily concerned with the veterinary, agricultural, and bacteriological aspects of infectious abortion in farm animals, especially cattle and swine.   It was under the auspices of this committee that the Central Brucella Station was established in 1929 at the Michigan State College of Agriculture and Applied Science for the collection and preservation for study of strains received from many parts of the world of the bacillus causing the disease of infectious abortion in animals and undulant fever in man.   During the past year the committee has determined to expand its field of work to include all aspects of brucella infections both in animal and in man. The name of the committee has accordingly been changed to the committee on brucella infections, and because of the increased interest in the human phase of the problems involved it has been agreed to relate the committee in the council wholly to the division of medical sciences.

Microbiology of the soil.—Sponsored by the committee on the microbiology of the soil, work has been carried on for the past 2 years at the New Jersey State Agricultural Experiment Station upon the fate in the soil of certain strains of tubercle bacilli from birds, cattle, and man, and also of certain acid-fast bacteria the chemistry and economic relations of which are fairly well known.   The immediate program for these investigations will be completed in the fall of 1934.

"The committee looks upon the cyclic recurrence of epidemics as one of the most important problems of infectious diseases and regards the earth as a great reservoir" for the life of infectious organisms outside the human body.   "Not only can the soil serve as a medium where various causative agents of plant and animal diseases are able to survive for varying periods of time but also a number of organisms become normal inhabitants of the soil.   This is true of numerous plant diseases, and of various anaerobic bacteria which cause human and animal diseases . . ."   Lack of funds, however, will not permit the continuation of these studies beyond the preparation of a report upon the work carried on thus far.

Narcotics.—Within the past year significant results have begun to appear from the 5 years of work sponsored by the council's committee on drug addiction upon the chemistry and the physiological properties of narcotic drugs.   During these years two strong research teams of 10 or 12 members each have been organized—one at the University of Virginia for a study of the chemistry of narcotic alkaloids, and one at the University of Michigan for the investigation of the physiological effects of narcotics.   These research centers have made themselves highly specialized and efficient agencies of experimentation in their respective fields.   Knowledge of the chemistry of narcotic alkaloids and of the pharmacological effects of these substances has been organized, and this field of chemistry has been developed so as to make this country competent to sustain itself in this regard.   It is felt that much has been accomplished in advancing knowledge of the analytical and synthetic chemistry of narcotic alkaloids and in the development of substances without habit-forming properties which may be used for the replacement of opium derivatives in medical practice. A high degree of cooperation, also, has been built up between these two university laboratories, two Bureaus of the Federal Government—the United States Public Health Service and the Bureau of Narcotics—and three commercial drug manufacturing concerns.

The group of collaborators located in the department of chemistry at the University of Virginia has produced 264 substances, of which 120 are phenanthrene derivatives (several of which are similar in their chemical formulation to vitamin D and the carcinogenic factor of tar) and 144 are morphine derivatives. Seventy-one of these substances had been previously prepared by others but 93 of them are entirely new. All of these 264 substances have been tested for their physiological properties by the group working at the University of Michigan and the committee is now making clinical studies of a selected group of five substances which seem to have definite value to determine their addiction liability.

One of these substances (dihydrodesoxymorphine-D) seems to possess definite advantages over morphine and has been patented by the discoverer and presented, with the consent of the National Research Council, to the Secretary of the Treasury of the United States to insure its reaching its maximum usefulness if its value seems borne out, or to insure its control with further study if it should prove to be an addiction drug.

The committee in cooperation with the United States Public Health Service and the Department of Health of Massachusetts is now undertaking the study of the use of certain other of the new drugs which have been developed and tested in its previous work for application in the treatment of drug addicts with the intention of later extending these studies, if successful, to the use of these drugs as narcotics and analgesics in general medical practice when more has been learned of their physiological and medical properties.

Registry of pathology.—The American Dental Association has recently approved the addition of a registry of dental and oral pathology as a division of the American Registry of Pathology at the Army Medical Museum, Washington, D. C. This registry was established in 1931 with the sponsorship of the division of medical sciences of the council for the assembling of data, including detailed case records, pathological specimens, etc., concerning certain diseases and their response to various types of treatment. The diseases for which material has at first been assembled are certain forms of malignant tumors, particularly those of the eye and of the bladder, and lymphatic tumors. The registry now has the endorsement and support of the American Association of Pathologists and Bacteriologists, the American Association for Cancer Research, and the American Academy of Ophthalmology and Otolaryngology. The total number of cases recorded in the registry (on Dec. 31, 1933) was as follows: Ophthalmic pathology 368, bladder tumors 896, lymphatic tumors 386. The materials of the collection are being constantly increased and carefully studied. Twelve sets of specimens of ophthalmic pathology have been prepared during the year upon materials in the collection, and two papers have been published as follows:

Callender, G. R. Tumors and tumorlike conditions of lymphocyte, myclocyte, erythrocyte, and reticulum cell. American Journ. Path., vol. 10, pp. 443–466, July 1934.

[Ferguson, R. S.] Cancer of the bladder: study based on 902 epithelial tumors of the bladder in the Carcinoma Registry of the American Urological Association. J. Urology, vol. 31, pp. 423–472, April 1934.

Research in problems of sex.—The program of the committee for research in problems of sex during the past year has included the allocation of grants to 20 collaborators located at 14 institutions from funds provided for this purpose by the Rockefeller Foundation. The projects on which these investigators have been engaged may be grouped as follows: 9 relating to the hormonal or endocrinal aspects of sex; 7 relating to other features of the reproductive process or to factors influencing it; 1 concerning the relation of the nervous system to sexual behavior and reproduction; and 2 relating to sexual behavior in the primates. This distribution reflects the dominance recently of current research interest in the hormonal and related physiological aspects of the problem of sex over the neurological, the psychobiological, and sociological phases of these problems. Expenditures upon these projects during the past year have totaled $70,859.04, slightly more than the expenditures of the previous year. During the year 69 papers have been published by the collaborators with the committee.

While the contributions to knowledge of the phenomena of sex coming from the work sponsored by this committee have been numerous, over 700 articles having been published by collaborators with the committee during the 13 years of its work, the most important results of this work for the future of science are regarded as the development during the past decade at a score of institutions of laboratories competent in personnel and equipment to carry these and related investigations further. Upon the establishment at these institutions of certain of the more extensive investigations which have comprised the committee's general program and which are now going forward independently of assistance from funds of the committee, the committee now proposes to turn its attention mainly to two groups of problems relating to the psychobiology and psychophysiology of sex, through the support (a) of well-developed projects requiring moderate assistance and (b) of a larger group of problems which may be of a developmental or exploratory nature, some of which may ultimately be continued if found to be productive of results useful in the development of knowledge in this particular field. With fairly comprehensive knowledge now at hand concerning the medical phases of this subject, it is becoming increasingly important, also, from the point of view of medical practice to be able to produce the hormones of sex synthetically by inexpensive methods in order to permit their application in connection with the process of growth and disease. For the coming year the committee has provided grants totaling $59,380 allotted to 21 investigators located at 17 institutions from a further appropriation made by the Rockefeller Foundation. Most of these investigators are among those who have been cooperating with the committee for several years.

Tropical medicine.—On the basis of the survey of world facilities for the study of tropical medicine, which has been sponsored by the division of medical sciences, the committee in charge of this survey sent an extensive questionnaire in the fall of 1933 to 123 Government representatives throughout the world who are in position to furnish the desired information in regard to facilities available at various medical centers, and the particular diseases which these centers are so located as to be able to study effectively. About 60 replies to the questionnaire have been received. The results will be compiled and published later. The expenses of the survey are met from an appropriation of $2,500 provided by the Leonard Wood Memorial for the Eradication of Leprosy.

On February 5 and 6, 1934, a conference was held in Washington, D. C., under the auspices of the committee on survey of tropical diseases to consider the establishment of an organization for the promotion of research in this field. This conference was attended by about 30 representatives of various institutions in the United States engaged in research upon tropical diseases. As a result an American Academy of Tropical Medicine has been formed and incorporated under the laws of the District of Columbia with a charter membership of 50, for the purpose of increasing knowledge of the prevention of human and animal diseases of warm climates and of the distribution, cause, nature, treatment, and control of these diseases. The academy is empowered to receive and administer funds for this purpose.

DIVISION OF BIOLOGY AND AGRICULTURE

Ivey F. Lewis, Chairman

Aquiculture.—The committee on hydrobiology and aquiculture of the division of biology and agriculture has submitted a memorandum to the Tennessee Valley Authority with the support of the American Fisheries Society concerning aquiculture and the encouragement of the fisheries resources of the Tennessee Valley area. The memorandum suggests making an exemplary development of inland fish culture in the Tennessee Valley as a means for supplementing the agricultural productivity of the region.

Barro Colorado Island Laboratory.—The Barro Colorado Island Laboratory in the Panama Canal Zone continues to serve as an outpost for biological field work in the tropics despite much reduced income this year. The tenth annual report of the laboratory for the operating year closing February 8, 1934, lists 37 scientists who visited the island during the year for study purposes and 29 papers published during the year upon work which had been carried on from the laboratory as a base. The total number of such papers is now 239. A fireproof building of brick and concrete has been added to the establishment on the island and now houses the library, the herbarium, the species index to local fauna and flora, and special instruments of the station. The laboratory is supported mainly by subscriptions from American educational and research institutions.

Biological Abstracts.—The division of biology and agriculture, through which Biological Abstracts (see also p. 58) is related to the National Research Council, has supported the Abstracts in its efforts to obtain editorial funds. This year, after 7 years of operation of the Abstracts, the division has undertaken for the Rockefeller Foundation to make an evaluation of the services of this journal to the advancement of biology and other sciences and to problems relating to biology in other basic sciences.

Bibliography of North American Forestry.—The "Bibliography of North American Forestry", which has been in preparation by the

Forestry Service since 1929, has been completed for the literature since 1930. The division of biology and agriculture has contributed certain funds for the early expenses of this bibliography from a fund provided by the Southern Pine Association some years ago for forestry research. It is planned to continue the compilation of the bibliography to include literature for the year 1933 before it is published.

Grasslands.—The committee on the ecology of grasslands has sought to encourage the study of grasslands of the various types found on the North American continent by the preparation of a plan for the systematic study over a period of years of natural grass areas in several typical localities in Arizona, Texas, Oklahoma, Nebraska, North Dakota, Illinois, and Saskatchewan. These studies would include investigations of the animals as well as the plants peculiar to these regions. The ownership of considerable areas of grassland by the research and educational institutions conducting the proposed investigations is believed to be essential for the stability of this program of observation and study in order to provide uninterrupted control of these lands. The recommended studies, while proposed from a purely biological standpoint, have an important bearing upon studies of land classification which are sponsored by a committee of the division of geology and geography, upon studies of land use made by a committee of the Science Advisory Board, and upon other studies of pioneer and marginal regions in which the council has long been interested.

Human heredity.—The committee on human heredity has undertaken the encouragement of research on two projects: (*a*) A study of the inheritance of degenerative diseases, especially those of the circulatory system; and (*b*) a study of hereditary crebellar ataxia. With the publication of a book entitled "After Three Centuries: A New England Family", prepared by Dr. Ellsworth Huntington, of Yale University, the specific purpose of the subcommittee on family records has been completed.

National Live Stock and Meat Board fund.—The National Live Stock and Meat Board has continued to provide funds for the support of investigations upon the place of meat in the human diet by an appropriation of $3,750 available for the past year. This sum makes a total of $52,750 which this board has made available for these purposes during the past 10 years. These funds have been used this year for the support of investigations conducted by Dr. George O. Burr, associate professor of botany at the University of Minnesota, upon the value of different kinds of dietary supplements in infant eczema; of an investigation by Dr. H. H. Mattill, professor of biochemistry at the University of Iowa, upon the nutritive value of animal tissues for growth, reproduction and lactation; and of an investigation by Dr. Alfred Chanutin, professor of biochemistry at the University of Virginia, upon the relation of protein to the diet in diseases of the kidney.

Effects of radiation on living organisms.—The committee on effects of radiation on living organisms has continued its program of support of investigations upon the effects of light, ultraviolet rays, X-ray radiation, and radium emanations upon living plant and animal material during the past year through 22 research grants totaling $20,185 from funds provided from appropriations of $12,500 a year each for a period of 5 years from both the General Education Board and the Commonwealth Fund. This is the last year of the period for which these two organizations have made these annual appropriations. A balance of about $8,500 remaining from these funds will be available until December 31, 1934, from which the committee plans to make 17 allotments of a few hundred dollars each to 15 of its previous collaborators and to 2 additional investigators. In addition, several commercial corporations have made loans of apparatus and of radio-active materials upon recommendations from the committee. Eleven publications have resulted from the year's work.

The committee has recommended that future work in the study of the effects of radiation include the effects of ultraviolet rays and of other radiations, not only on protoplasm in general, but especially on certain important substances associated with protoplasm such as viruses, both plant and animal, and also bacteriophage, hormones, and antibodies. The committee has in preparation through a subcommittee a survey of present knowledge of the biological effects of radiation which will be published as a two-volume treatise during the coming year.

The committee on effects of radiation has also undertaken the administration of a fund of $10,000 made available by the Rockefeller Foundation in December, 1933 for a survey of the field of mitogenetic radiation, and for the support of investigations upon this subject. On March 17, 1934, a conference was held in New York attended by some 20 biologists and physicists for the purpose of advising the committee in the initiation of critical studies of mitogenetic radiation. A program was subsequently drawn up of research to be undertaken at the University of Wisconsin in cooperation with investigations to be carried on also in the University of Rochester and at Cornell University, beginning in the summer of 1934.

Scientific publications.—The attention which the division of biology and agriculture gave to matters of scientific publications by organizing a conference of editors of biological journals which was held on January 16, 1932, has been continued during the past year through two subcommittees of the committee which had charge of this conference for the purposes (a) of ascertaining what steps might be taken to effect a certain degree of cooperation among editors of biological journals, and (b) of considering problems of financing and producing journals of biology. In connection with the latter subject two reports have been prepared—one upon means for the preservation of the original data of research, and the other upon lithoprinting as adapted to biological documentation.

DIVISION OF ANTHROPOLOGY AND PSYCHOLOGY

A. T. POFFENBERGER, Chairman

Archaeological surveys.—The committee on State archaeological surveys has published its eleventh compilation of brief reports on archaeological field work conducted by various agencies of the United States during the year 1932 as Archaeological Field Work in North America During 1932, by Carl E. Guthe (American Anthropologist, vol. 35, no. 3, pp. 483–511; July 1933). The manuscript of a similar report covering the year 1933 and listing about 70 field projects has been prepared for subsequent publication in mimeographed form.

Two numbers in the Circular series maintained by the committee on State archaeological surveys have been issued during the past year. The first of these (No. 15, Aug. 5, 1933) was the Fourth Annual Statement of Institutional Plans for Field Investigations for the Summer of 1933. The second (No. 16, May 8, 1934) related to dendrochronology in the Mississippi Valley, and gave instructions for the preservation of remains of wood as found, for instance, in structures of the mound builders for study under the Douglass system of tree-ring dating.

The office of the committee on State archaeological surveys is located at the University of Michigan and is supported in part by the university and in part (since 1929) by annual appropriations from the Carnegie Institution of Washington, which for the past 2 years has been $2,250 per year. The committee, which has been in existence for 14 years, now has under consideration the formation of a society of American archaeology to meet three purposes: (1) To give each student of American archaeology a proprietary interest in the activities of the organization; (2) to extend the contacts of the organization to include all those who are interested in American archaeology either professionally or as amateurs; (3) to provide a stable self-supporting organization as a security for the continuation of the work which the committee has been sponsoring.

Archaeology of the Tennessee Valley.—Early in the fall of 1933 the chairman of the Tennessee Valley Authority called the attention of the National Research Council to the prospective loss of important archaeological material in the Tennessee Valley when certain dams then projected should have been completed with the consequent inundation of valley areas. In cooperation with the Science Advisory Board and with the Smithsonian Institution a subcommittee of the committee of the division of anthropology and psychology on State archaeological surveys formulated a plan for a local archaeological survey. Support was obtained from the Carnegie Corporation to the extent of two appropriations totaling $2,000, which have been used mainly for travel expenses of supervisors of the survey and for the purchase of equipment and supplies. The work was organized under the immediate supervision of Prof. William S. Webb, of the University of Kentucky, who was also appointed as archaeologist in charge by the Tennessee Valley Authority. With the aid of personnel furnished by the Civil Works Administration and by State relief organizations, including at one time (in March 1934) 19 assistant supervisors and over 1,000 laborers, two sites were thoughly explored during the winter and spring of 1934. At one of these sites, that of the Norris Basin, a large number of domiciliary mounds were found. At the other site, that of the Wheeler Basin, where certain work had already been done by the Alabama Museum of Natural History, several large shell mounds were excavated on islands in the Tennessee River. The movable relics of these ancient habitations are to be transferred for preservation and study to suitable centers of archaeological research. The chairman of the division of anthropology and psychology has made the following statement concerning the significance of this work:

The areas included in the archaeological investigations of the Tennessee Valley Authority were known to have been occupied by the Cherokee Indians as well as by many migrating groups. Research of a reconnaissance nature carried on in the past had indicated the presence of a mass of material of great historical value. It was imperative, therefore, that trained archaeologists be given an opportunity to preserve the data before they were forever obliterated.

The body of archaeological information yielded by the investigation is greater than that secured by any other expedition in this general area. A complete photographic series comprising many hundreds of pictures is an important part of the record. Voluminous field notes covering thousands of pages supplement the photographs and furnish the necessary data on the collections of material objects of stone, shell, bone, pottery, and wood. These notes and photographs contain invaluable records of methods of construction and of details of architectural features exposed by the examination of village sites and domiciliary mounds. Long series of fragments of pottery, one of the best criteria for determining cultural changes, have been saved for examination by specialists. The human skeletons found in the graves will be studied by pathologists and physical anthropologists. Wood samples have been gathered from the area, which may prove to be a means of determining the ages of the many sites through an interpretation of the record in the growth rings of trees. This huge quantity of archaeological material in the form of photographs, notes, and specimens will be of great value to the students of American Indian history for many years to come, provided it is properly preserved. It will furnish many details of the extinct cultures of the region, which heretofore could be described in only vague and indefinite terms. It will permit the recognition of cultural relationships which have been unknown because of lack of data. Some evidence already seems to indicate the existence of early undescribed cultures. Again, certain architectural details appear to have a definite cultural significance. Finally, the progress and results of this investigation should help to acquaint the general public with the soundness of modern archaeological research methods, and with the historical significance of the tangible remains of the Indian occupation of our country.

Child development.—The work of the committee on child development has been continued through appropriations from the General Education Board of $6,300 for each of the 2 years 1933-34 and 1934-35. During this period it is expected that the Society for Research in Child Development, organized at Chicago in June 24, 1933, will take over most of the functions of the present committee of the division of anthropology and psychology. The society now has a membership of about 175, and the first regular meeting of the society has been announced to be held in Washington on November 3 and 4, 1934. The committee on child development continues to publish Child Development Abstracts (in planograph form), now in its eighth volume, and with the current year has added to the bimonthly issues of the Abstracts brief résumés of work in progress. There are now about 240 subscribers to the Abstracts in addition to the members of the Society for Research in Child Development, who receive the Abstracts as one of the perquisites of membership.

Directory of American anthropology.—As a step toward the possible preparation later of a full directory of American anthropology, the office of the division of anthropology and psychology has compiled (in mimeographed form) a list of anthropologists in the United States who have received their graduate degrees in this field during the past 5 years. The list includes 144 names.

Occupational standards.—For over a year the division of anthropology and psychology has been concerned with the planning of an extensive study of standards of occupational fitness, including "the discovery of those patterns of human ability, attitudes, aptitudes, and interests which make for success and happiness in the various occupations and the construction of practical testing instruments for the measurement of these traits." In regard to this undertaking, the chairman of the division states:

This study was prompted by the passage of the Wagner bill at the close of the last session of Congress, which provided for the establishment of a system of United States employment offices and placed upon the United States Department of Labor the responsibility for an adequate and scientifically sound program of vocational adjustment. Two needs emerged at once, namely, the need for analysis and classification of occupations and the need for means of specifying the functions which each job called for, as well as means for discovering the ability of people to perform these functions. The Social Science Research Council volunteered to attack the first of these needs and the Secretary of Labor called upon the Science Advisory Board for help in solving the second. This board consulted with the division of anthropology and psychology of the National Research Council and provided funds for a conference of specialists on the problems of vocational selection. A plan of attack was evolved which gave promise of financial support from one of the large foundations.

As the plans have matured, the two projects of job specification and the determination of standards have been merged under the direction of one committee to which members are nominated by both the Social Science Research Council and the National Research Council. This joint committee is actively at work, a staff has been engaged and investigators are already making an attack in a way never previously attempted on more than a very restricted scale. There are good prospects of securing the funds necessary for the long-term project which the solution of these large problems demands.

The series of researches when completed will have far-reaching practical applications. It will provide a system for occupational census-taking which for the first time will be based on something more than superficial resemblance among jobs; it will facilitate the transfer of workers among occupations, as levels of need rise and fall, on the basis of functional similarities and differences among them, and will furnish a proper foundation for the measurement of fitness to succeed in the various occupations. If applied in the life-period of occupation-choosing, it should prevent maladjustments and the consequent dissatisfactions that arise therefrom. The less direct consequences of the fulfillment of such a program cannot even be envisioned at present.

Psychology of the highway.—The work of the committee on the psychology of the highway has been carried on during the past 4 years from the Iowa State College of Agriculture and Mechanic Arts as headquarters, and in order to provide a group of advisers for this work so located as to be able to keep in touch with it readily, a special subcommittee for the midwestern area has been appointed. One of the major undertakings of the committee is the development of reliable tests for automobile drivers. Work on this problem has required the construction of a transportable experimental laboratory in order to make it possible to test a sufficient number of drivers to furnish observational material for the committee's research program. The committee has therefore equipped a special truck and a trailer with testing apparatus for this purpose. Tests with experienced commercial drivers were made possible through the cooperation of the Chrysler Corporation at Detroit and of the United Motor Coach Co. at Chicago and at Des Plaines, Illinois; 132 skilled drivers having been tested during the past year. A large number of tests of other drivers were obtained at the clinic of the committee at the Iowa State College and also by means of the transportable laboratory which was taken to a number of towns in Midwestern States.

A study of the records of one of the corporations cooperating with the committee indicates that "accidents are primarily the faults of the driving habits of the man at the wheel." They are not due to chance. Most accidents are caused by accident-prone individuals. These individuals come into difficulty not only in automobile driving but in other work in which they may be engaged. An important part of the problem of testing commercial drivers seems therefore to be to ascertain those traits which constitute accident-prone individuals in order to relieve these individuals of the responsibility of driving company machines.

Problems in which other members of the committee are engaged include studies of reaction time as applied to automobile drivers, methods of road lighting, a study of particularly reckless driving, and the relation of visual acuity and other factors to driving ability.

In a monograph on license plates, which has been completed and now awaits publication, nine ideal color combinations are discussed as suitable for use in the United States.

Two papers on color discrimination are being submitted for publication, one discussing a modification of Helmholtz's apparatus for studying color discrimination; and the other discussing the effects of intensity changes on color discrimination.

Papers published this year which have resulted from these studies are as follows:

A. R. Lauer; Discrimination of Relatively Pure Spectral Colors by Normal and Color-blind Subjects. Psychological Bulletin, 1933, vol. 30, p. 687, November 1933.

- A. R. Lauer; Lighting Conditions and Other Factors to be Considered in the Use of the Clason Acuity Meter. American Journal of Optometry, vol. 10, no. 6, p. 194, June 1933.

A. R. Lauer and H. L. Kotvis; Automotive Manipulation in Relation to Vision. Journal of Applied Psychology, 1934, vol. 18, pp. 422-31, June 1933.

In addition to contributions from a number of universities the work of the committee on the psychology of the highway has been specially supported in the past by appropriations from the American Optometric Association. With an appropriation of $1,000 for the current year, these have now totaled $5,662.93.

The chairman of the committee on the psychology of the highway represents the division of anthropology and psychology in the public-safety advisory committee of the National Safety Council. This advisory committee has been giving special attention to bases for the examination of applicants for automobile driving licenses, to a movement for the rigid enforcement of traffic laws, and to a campaign for the reduction of traffic accidents by sponsoring safety contests throughout the United States. These contests were held in 441 cities during 1932 and in 287 cities in 44 States during 1933.

Psychiatric investigations.—A survey has been in progress for the past 3 years under the direction of the committee on psychiatric investigations upon the status of research in the field of psychiatry. This committee has just brought to completion a comprehensive summarization of the bases of research in this field. The report consists of statements from some 25 recognized authorities upon the fundamental contributions which can be made to psychiatry from such underlying fields as neurology, pharmacology, endocrinology, serology, general and experimental psychology, clinical psychology, cultural anthropology, and heredity. The survey has been supported by a grant of $10,000 from the Carnegie Corporation of New York. The report upon the survey (published in the fall of 1934) bears the title "Problems of Mental Disorder", and is edited by Prof. Madison Bentley, of Cornell University.

Survey of South American Indians.—It has been possible this year for the division of anthropology and psychology to revive plans suggested by the division 2 years ago for the preparation of a Handbook of South American Indians in the form of a companion volume to the Handbook of American Indians North of Mexico issued by the Bureau of American Ethnology of the Smithsonian Institution in 1907. Following conferences in Washington on December 13, 1933, and in Philadelphia on January 2, 1934, for the discussion of this project, an advisory committee of 19 members with a working committee of 3 members has been appointed and plans are now in process of development with a view to making a survey of the materials relating to the Indians of South America and the West Indies under the auspices of the Smithsonian Institution, and to the subsequent publication of a descriptive handbook of these native tribes.

It is intended that the proposed handbook should fill three fundamental needs in American anthropology: (1) it will bring together in an accessible and orderly form the now widely scattered data on the aboriginal people of South America; (2) it will contribute toward the knowledge of culture sequences found on the American continents; and (3) it should indicate clearly the nature of additional field investigations needed to complete this knowledge of the rapidly vanishing South American native cultures. The enterprise will be international in scope in that it will call for cooperation of Americanist scholars in both North and South America and also in Europe.

RESEARCH INFORMATION SERVICE

C. J. WEST. Director

The Research Information Service of the council has compiled a number of general directories and data lists during the past year, in addition to taking charge of the editing and administration of the council's publications, and providing informational services for the divisions and other offices of the council and for the Science Advisory Board.

Census of graduate students in chemistry.—The tenth compilation of the Census of Graduate Students in Chemistry will be published in the Journal of Chemical Education for August 1934. The data for the academic year 1933–34 shows, for the first time during the past decade, a decrease in the number of research students reported in comparision with the previous year. For the current year there were 278 fewer candidates for the master's degree, and 47 fewer candidates studying for the doctor's degree than in 1932–33 in the 141 institutions which have made returns. The total numbers of research students in chemistry for these years are:

	For master's degrees	For doctor's degrees
1932–33	1,580	1,768
1933–34	1,302	1,721

There was also a decrease of 65 in the number of faculty members from the preceding year; i. e., 1,421 members of teaching departments of chemistry in 1933–34, against 1,486 in 1932–33.

Doctorates in the sciences.—The annual summary of Doctorates Conferred in the Natural Sciences in American Universities was published in August 1933 (Reprint and Circular Series No. 105, 63 pp.). This compilation shows that during 1932–33, 1,343 doctorates were conferred in the sciences by 62 universities in the United States as compared with 1,241 doctorates conferred in the sciences by 65 universities in 1931–32, an increase of 102. Of the 1,341 degrees recently conferred the four leading sciences were: Chemistry, 417; physics, 123; zoology, 115; psychology, 101. An extract of this compilation was published in Science (vol. 78, p. 241, Sept. 15, 1933); the data for chemistry and related fields were published in the Journal of Chemical Education (vol. 10, pp. 679–703, November 1933); and those for bacteriology and human pathology in the Archives of Pathology (vol. 16, p. 403, September 1933).

Cooperative arrangements have recently been completed with the Association of Research Libraries for the publication of a joint list of all doctorates conferred by American universities. This list will include for the current year data concerning doctorates in the sciences in the same form in which these data have been prepared by the Research Information Service during the past 14 years.

Industrial scholarships.—The résumé of Research Scholarships and Fellowships Supported by Industry, made by the Research Information Service in alternate years, was also issued this year (Industrial and Engineering Chemistry, News Edition, vol. 12, pp. 191–194, May 20, 1934). This compilation shows about 200 scholarships and fellowships supported by 115 corporations at 60 American educational institutions.

Fellowships and scholarships.—The third edition of the list of Fellowships and Scholarships for Graduate Work in Science and Technology was issued in June 1934 (as National Research Council Bulletin No. 94, 194 pp., replacing Bulletin No. 72, August 1929). This list gives details as supplied by 190 American universities and other organizations in this country regarding the fellowships and scholarships open to graduate students for study in the United States and abroad. A number of fellowships and scholarships have been discontinued permanently or temporarily since the last bulletin was issued. However, many new sources have been included.

Research funds in the United States.—A third edition of the previously issued list of Funds Available in the United States for the Support and Encouragement of Research in Sciences and its Technologies was issued this year as Bulletin No. 95, June 1934, 162 pages. This list gives information supplied by 276 universities, societies, and other research and scientific institutions in regard to funds, medals, and prizes available for the support of scientific investigations and for the recognition of research achievement in the sciences in the United States.

Industrial Research Laboratories.—The fifth edition of Industrial Research Laboratories of the United States, including Consulting Research Laboratories, was issued in August 1933 (as Bulletin No. 91, 223 pp.) The bulletin lists 1,562 laboratories, 58 less than were given in the last edition (Bulletin No. 81, January 1931). An analysis of the data of the current edition, showing particularly changes in the general situation of the employment of research men in industry during the past 3 years, was published as a Survey of Personnel Changes in Industrial Research Laboratories, 1930–33, in the Industrial Laboratory Record (vol. 2, pp. 154–159, September 1933). This survey showed that in 1933 there were 23,742 scientifically trained employees, as against 36,212 such employees listed in these laboratories in 1930, a decrease of about 34.4 percent.

Other activities.—The Research Information Service is also collecting material for the third supplement to the Bibliography of Bibliographies in Chemistry and Chemical Technology, covering bibliographies which have appeared since the last supplement was issued as National Research Council Bulletin No. 86, March 1932. The service has cooperated with the division of chemistry and chemical technology in the issuing of the Annual Survey of American Chemistry (see p. 72), assuming the whole responsibility for the preparation of this volume. The service also made a special summarization in the fall of 1933 of the publications of the International Council of Scientific Unions and of the six international unions to which the National Research Council adheres and of the attendance from the United States at meetings of these organizations. The service has compiled a list of over 200 major projects in which the council as a whole or through its divisions or committees has been engaged since its reorganization after the war period in 1919, and is now engaged in expanding this list into a complete historical description of the activities of the council. In addition, a number of indexes have been prepared in connection with editing publications of the council, and the service has made an analysis of publication facilities and costs for 51 typical scientific periodicals (see p. 56).

ANNUAL REPORT OF THE TREASURER

July 1, 1933, to June 30, 1934

To the PRESIDENT OF THE NATIONAL ACADEMY OF SCIENCES:

I have the honor to submit the following report as treasurer of the Academy for the year from July 1, 1933, to June 30, 1934, and as treasurer of the National Research Council for the same period. As is customary, the first part of this report concerns the transactions of the National Academy of Sciences, including the general fund and the appropriations under the custodian of buildings and grounds, while the second part covers the accounts of the National Research Council.

NATIONAL ACADEMY OF SCIENCES

The contract with the Bank of New York & Trust Co., dated June 29, 1933, provides that the bank shall be custodian of securities of the academy. This contract has been in operation during the past year.

On June 30, 1934, the securities held by the academy and by the research council were distributed among seven different classes as follows:

	Book value			
	Held by academy	Held by research council	Total held	Percent of total
I. Bonds of railroads	$596,793.00		$596,793.00	17.6
II. Bonds of public utility corporations	521,715.00	$15,400.00	537,115.00	15.9
III. Bonds of industrial corporations	493,804.15		493,804.15	14.6
IV. Bonds of United States, States, counties, and municipalities	149,907.50	26,000.00	175,907.50	5.3
V. Bonds and notes secured by first mortgage on real estate	534,900.00	35,333.00	570,233.00	16.9
VI. Bonds of foreign governments	310,883.50	15,412.50	326,296.00	9.7
VII. Common stocks of companies	686,264.80		686,264.80	20.0
Total	3,294,267.95	92,145.50	3,386,413.45	100.0

The firm of Loomis, Sayles & Co. has continued to act as financial advisers to the National Academy of Sciences during the year just closed.

The following table indicates the current interest yield on the bonds and other securities, except common stocks, held by the academy, according to the valuation used:

	Amount	Yield, percent
Face value of bonds held	$2,698,600.00	4.93
Book value of bonds held	2,608,003.15	5.10
Market value, June 30, 1934	2,395,750.88	5.55

On June 30, 1934, the purchases of common stocks were distributed among 42 different companies, and the total cost of these common stocks was $686,264.80. The market value of these stocks on June 30, 1934, was $719,317.50.

During the year the Rockefeller Foundation made three contributions totaling $14,860 to aid in the publication of scientific research material in accordance with grants approved by the academy. A detailed list of the payments made to the scientific journals and institutions participating in these grants is presented elsewhere in this report.

The investment reserve fund was designed to absorb losses sustained by the academy in the sale of bonds. The following shows the operation of this fund during the year just closed:

Overdraft on July 1, 1933		$367,022.52
Losses sustained:		
On sale of bonds	$228,657.35	
Fees to financial advisers	19.04	
Payment of back taxes, advertising, and legal fees on real estate	6,726.04	
Gross loss for year	235,402.43	
Profits experienced:		
On sale of bonds	$39,539.69	
Transferred from various funds, 5 percent of income from investments	8,397.05	
Refund	.81	
Gross profit for year	47,937.55	
Net loss for year		187,464.88
Overdraft on June 30, 1934		554,487.40

The total receipts of the academy during the year from all sources amounted to $496,887.18.

The miscellaneous disbursements amounted to $542,645.45, and payments on grants and medals and honoraria amounted to $13,778.08; total disbursements for the year $556,423.53.

The consolidated investment fund stands at $252,777.94, the same as shown in the last annual report. Of this amount, the sum of $206,611.25 was invested, and the sum of $46,166.69 was uninvested as of June 30, 1934.

The total expenditures up to June 30, 1934, for acquisition of site amounted to $185,764.50, and for erection and equipment of building for the use of the National Academy of Sciences and the National Research Council, paid from funds received from the Carnegie Corporation of New York, $1,446,879.82, and paid from separate Academy funds, $1,765, making a total for building and site, $1,634,409.32. In addition to these the sum of $925.22 was expended from academy funds during the year for equipment of the building, making a total of $9,383.48 for this purpose, the sum of $8,458.26 having been previously spent. The sum of $3,120.18 is held in the building construction fund as of June 30, 1934.

Below is found a list of bonds, now held by the National Academy of Sciences, which are in default:

$50,000 International Match Corporation 5-percent 20-year sinking-fund debentures, due Nov. 1, 1947; last interest paid was Nov. 1, 1931; represented by certificates of deposit of Bank of New York & Trust Co.

136,000 Kansas City, Fort Scott & Memphis Ry. Co. 4-percent refunding-mortgage fully guaranteed bonds, due Oct. 1, 1936; last interest paid was Oct. 1, 1932.

50,000 Lackawanna & Wyoming Valley R. R. Co. 5-percent first-mortgage bonds, due Aug. 1, 1951; last interest paid was Feb. 1, 1933.

50,000 Missouri Pacific R. R. Co. 5-percent first and refunding mortgage bonds, series G, due Nov. 1, 1978; last interest paid was Nov. 1, 1932.

60,000 Missouri Pacific R. R. Co. 5-percent first and refunding mortgage bonds, series I, due Feb. 1, 1981; last interest paid was Feb. 1, 1933.

50,000 New Orleans, Texas & Mexico Ry. Co. 5½-percent first-mortgage bonds, series A, due Apr. 1, 1954; last interest paid was Oct. 1, 1932.

25,000 Raleigh & Augusta Air Line R. R. Co.-Seaboard Air Line Railway Co., 5-percent first-mortgage, guaranteed, due Jan. 1, 1931; bonds represented by certificate of deposit of the Mercantile Trust Co. of Baltimore; last interest paid was July 1, 1931.

50,000 St. Louis-San Francisco Ry. Co., 4½-percent consolidated mortgage bonds, series A, due Mar. 1, 1978; last interest paid was Sept. 1, 1932.

Some years ago efforts were made to constitute a fund known as "National Research Fund", the intention being to raise $1,000,000 a year for a period of 10 years, such fund to be used for research. Due to a variety of causes, most of which were influenced by the economic depression through which the entire country has passed during the last 5 years, the fund was never completed although more than one-third of the pledges made for the first year were actually paid in cash to the academy. After holding such contributions for more than 3 years in the expectation of completing the financing of this fund, it was decided to return a pro rata share to the contributors, and to cancel their pledges for the subsequent years. Accordingly, the bonds held for the National Research Fund were converted into cash, and, with the consent of every donor except one, refunds were made to the original contributors, such refunds amounting to $356,402.48. This practically has wound up the fund, only the sum of $46.94 remaining in the fund, and it is expected that within the near future this amount will be refunded to the one remaining contributor. While the academy regrets it was unable to complete the financing of this project, it desires here to record its deep appreciation of the generous response made by the various donors, many of whom had paid the first year's pledge in full.

The mortgages on real estate held by the academy have caused much concern during the year. Owners of such property have found it difficult, and sometimes impossible, to obtain sufficient rentals to cover carrying charges including interest. Most of the mortgages held by the academy were on New York city real estate and were guaranteed as to the payment of principal and interest by mortgage and title companies, such guaranteed mortgages being held in good esteem at the time of their acquisition. Payment of interest continued to be made until practically all of the mortgage and title companies became insolvent and were taken over by the New York State superintendent of insurance in rehabilitation, thus rendering the guaranty worthless. Whereupon, the finance committee of the academy voted to release the mortgage and title company from its guaranty in each case as rapidly as this could be accomplished. During the year it was necessary to foreclose the mortgages on two pieces of property in New York and on one piece in Washington, D. C., the academy taking title in each case on bids less than the amount of the mortgage. Such foreclosures have burdened the academy with the payment of back taxes, water rents, legal fees, and necessary repairs. One mortgage on property in Washington, D. C., was paid off in full in cash.

TRUST FUNDS OF THE ACADEMY

The trust funds of the academy, the income of which is administered for specific purposes, are enumerated below. The capital of certain funds has been increased beyond the original gift or bequest by the transfer of accumulated income at the request of the donors or by action of the academy.

Bache fund: Bequest of Alexander Dallas Bache, a member of the academy, 1870, to aid researches in physical and natural sciences_____ $60, 000. 00

Watson fund: Bequest of James C. Watson, a member of the academy, 1874, for the promotion of astronomical science through the award of the Watson gold medal and grants of money in aid of research_____ 25, 000. 00

Draper fund: Gift of Mrs. Henry Draper, 1883, in memory of her husband, a former member of the academy, to found the Henry Draper medal, to be awarded for notable investigations in astronomical physics; the balance of income is applied to aid research in the same science_____ 10, 000. 00

Smith fund: Gift of Mrs. J. Lawrence Smith, 1884, in memory of her husband, a former member of the academy, to found the J. Lawrence Smith gold medal, to be awarded for important investigations of meteoric bodies and to assist, by grants of money, researches concerning such objects_____ 10, 000. 00

Gibbs fund: Established by gift of Wolcott Gibbs, a member of the academy, 1892, and increased by a bequest of the late Morris Loeb, 1914, for the promotion of researches in chemistry_____ 5, 545. 50

Gould fund: Gift of Miss Alice Bache Gould, 1897, in memory of her father, a former member of the academy, for the promotion of researches in astronomy_____ 20, 000. 00

Comstock fund: Gift of Gen. Cyrus B. Comstock, a member of the academy, 1907, to promote researches in electricity, magnetism, or radiant energy through the Comstock prize money, to be awarded once in 5 years for notable investigations; the fund is to be increased ultimately to $15,000_____ 12, 406. 02

Marsh fund: Bequest of Othniel Charles Marsh, a member of the academy, 1909, to promote original research in the natural sciences; to the original bequest of $10,000 the academy has added interest received from the estate and has authorized the increase of the fund to $20,000 by annual additions from income___ 20, 000. 00

Murray fund: A gift from the late Sir John Murray, 1911, to found the Alexander Agassiz gold medal, in honor of a former member and president of the academy, to be awarded for original contribution to the science of oceanography_____ 6, 000. 00

Hartley fund: A gift from Mrs. Helen Hartley Jenkins, 1913–14, in memory of her father, Marcellus Hartley, to found the medal of the academy awarded for eminence in the application of science to public welfare_____ 1, 200. 00

Billings fund: Established by the bequest of Mrs. Mary Anna Palmer Draper (Mrs. Henry Draper) of $25,000, in 1915, to support the publication of the Proceedings of the academy or for other purposes to be determined by the academy, 7 installments_ 22, 313. 39

Elliot fund: Gift of Margaret Henderson Elliot, to found the Daniel Giraud Elliot gold medal and honorarium for the most meritorious work in zoology or paleontology published in each year_____ 8, 000. 00

Thompson fund: Gift of Mrs. Mary Clark Thompson, 1919, the income thereof to be applied for a gold medal of appropriate design to be awarded annually by the academy for the most important services to geology and paleontology, the medal to be known as the Mary Clark Thompson gold medal_____ 10, 000. 00

Joseph Henry fund: The sum of $40,000 was contributed by Fairman Rogers, Joseph Patterson, George W. Childs, and others, as an expression of their respect and esteem for Prof. Joseph Henry. This amount was deposited with the Pennsylvania Co. for Insurance of Lives and Granting Annuities in trust, with authorization to collect the income thereon and to pay over the same to Prof. Joseph Henry during his natural life, and after his death to his wife and daughters, and after the death of the last survivor to "deliver the said fund and the securities in which it shall then be invested to the National Academy of Sciences, to be thenceforward forever held in trust under the name and title of the 'Joseph Henry fund.'" The death of Miss Caroline Henry on Nov. 10, 1920, has removed the last surviving heir of Joseph Henry to the income of the Joseph Henry fund. To assist meritorious investigators, especially in the direction of original research. Amount received by the academy from the Pennsylvania Co. for Insurance of Lives and Granting Annuities, $39,739.57 to which was added $423.93 from income........... $40,163.50

Walcott fund: Gift of Mrs. Mary Vaux Walcott, 1928, in honor of her husband, a former member and president of the academy, the income to be used for the award of medals and honoraria to persons, the results of whose published researches, explorations, and discoveries in pre-Cambrian or Cambrian life and history shall be judged most meritorious, the award to be made every 5 years, to be known as the "Charles Doolittle Walcott fund"_ 5,000.00

Carnegie endowment fund: By resolution voted Mar. 28, 1919, and amended several times since, the Carnegie Corporation of New York pledged $5,000,000 to the National Academy of Sciences for the purposes of the academy and the National Research Council, of which $1,450,000 was reserved and paid for the erection of a building, and the remainder, $3,550,000, to be capitalized at such times as the corporation finds convenient in view of its other obligations, the amount remaining in the hands of the corporation to bear interest at the rate of 5 percent per annum; seven installments completing capitalization........... 3,550,000.00

John J. Carty Medal and Award for the advancement of science: Gift of American Telephone & Telegraph Co., Nov. 13, 1930, in recognition of the distinguished achievements of John J. Carty as a scientist and engineer, and his noteworthy contributions to the advancement of fundamental and applied science, and in appreciation of his great services for many years in developing the art of electrical communication and as a lasting testimonial of the love and esteem in which he is held by his many thousand associates in the Bell System; the income thereof to be used for a gold medal and award, not oftener than once in 2 years, by vote of the National Academy of Sciences, to an individual for noteworthy and distinguished accomplishment in any field of science coming within the scope of the charter of the National Academy of Sciences_____ 25,000.00

In addition to the above-named funds, the academy holds the following:

Agassiz fund, bequest of Alexander Agassiz, a member of the academy, 1910, for the general uses of the academy_____ 50,000.00

Nealley fund, bequest of George True Nealley, 1925, for the general purposes of the academy, $20,896.01, less refund November 1926, $1,500, to a creditor of the estate; supplemented by additional sum from the estate, March 1931, $159.54_____ 19,555.55

Total_____ 3,900,183.96

Accounts with individual funds July 1, 1933, to June 30, 1934

	General fund		Agassiz fund	
	Income	Capital	Income	Capital
Balance July 1, 1933:				
Cash	$8,971.19			
Invested	8,967.00			$50,000.00
Receipts:				
Interest on investments:				
Agassiz fund	4,389.84			
Nealley fund	971.48			
Annual dues from members	1,375.00			
Total	24,674.51			50,000.00
Disbursements:				
General expenses	5,301.66			
Transfer to investment reserve fund	268.07			
Fees to financial advisers	114.22			
Balance June 30, 1934:				
Cash	10,748.06			
Invested	8,242.50			50,000.00
Total	24,674.51			50,000.00

	Bache fund		Billings fund	
	Income	Capital	Income	Capital
Balance July 1, 1933:				
Cash	$573.26			
Invested		$60,000.00		$22,313.39
Receipts: Interest on investments	2,979.69		$1,108.29	
Total	3,552.95	60,000.00	1,108.29	22,313.39
Disbursements:				
Grants	2,300.00			
Office expenses	5.00			
Transfer to investment reserve fund	148.98		55.41	
Fees to financial advisers	61.87		19.04	
Transfer to academy proceedings			1,033.84	
Balance June 30, 1934:				
Cash	1,037.10			
Invested		60,000.00		22,313.39
Total	3,552.95	60,000.00	1,108.29	22,313.39

	Building construction		Building site	
	Income	Capital	Income	Capital
Balance July 1, 1933:				
Cash	$120.18		$4,862.67	
Invested	3,000.00		13,093.00	
Receipts:				
Interest on investments			528.54	
Bonds sold			5,549.75	
Total	3,120.18		24,033.96	
Disbursements:				
Transfer to investment reserve fund			26.43	
Fees to financial advisers			19.04	
Bonds bought			5,549.75	
Balance June 30, 1934:				
Cash	120.18		10,805.49	
Invested	3,000.00		7,543.25	
Total	3,120.18		24,033.96	

Accounts with individual funds July 1, 1933, to June 30, 1934—Continued

	Carnegie endowment fund		Carnegie Corporation special	
	Income	Capital	Income	Capital
Balance July 1, 1933:				
Cash		$371,092.70	$9,903.73	
Invested		3,178,907.30		
Receipts:				
Interest on investments	$138,859.80			
Interest on deposits	197.32			
Bonds sold		1,452,029.60		
Total	139,057.12	5,002,029.60	9,903.73	
Disbursements:				
Bonds bought		1,452,029.60		
Accrued interest on bonds bought	4,039.80			
Commission on stock dividends	3.53			
Transfer to investment reserve fund	6,938.12			
Taxes, fire and liability insurance, etc., on real estate	2,640.71			
Fees to financial advisers	3,678.98			
Transferred to Carnegie endowment fund, income account, N. R. C., 1934	81,579.61			
Transferred to Carnegie endowment fund, income account, N. A. S., 1934	40,176.37			
Committee on the library			400.00	
Travel, National Research Fund			137.66	
Science Advisory Board, travel			744.82	
Government relations allotment			444.71	
Clerical expenses			50.00	
Balance June 30, 1934:				
Cash		577,825.55	8,126.54	
Invested		2,972,174.45		
Total	139,057.12	5,002,029.60	9,903.73	

	John J. Carty Medal and Award		Comstock fund	
	Income	Capital	Income	Capital
Balance July 1, 1933:				
Cash	$495.61	$337.50	$3,668.11	$660.77
Invested		24,662.50	3,000.00	11,745.25
Receipts:				
Interest on investments	1,093.97		768.98	
Bonds sold		7,220.00	1,000.00	6,676.50
Total	1,589.58	32,220.00	8,437.09	19,082.52
Disbursements:				
Bonds bought		7,220.00	1,000.00	6,676.50
Transferred to investment reserve fund	54.70		38.45	
Fees to financial advisers	23.80		19.04	
Honorarium			2,500.00	
Engrossing			20.00	
Balance June 30, 1934:				
Cash	1,511.08	391.25	2,859.60	7,337.27
Invested		24,608.75	2,000.00	5,068.75
Total	1,589.58	32,220.00	8,437.09	19,082.52

Accounts with individual funds July 1, 1933, to June 30, 1934—Continued

	Consolidated fund		Draper fund	
	Income	Capital	Income	Capital
Balance July 1, 1933:				
Cash	$1,159.58	$2,241.19	$761.27	----------
Invested		250,536.75		$10,000.00
Receipts:				
Interest on investments	12,771.37		497.04	
Bonds sold		115,736.75		
Total	13,930.95	368,514.69	1,258.31	10,000.00
Disbursements:				
Bonds bought		115,736.75		
Accrued interest on bonds bought	166.50			
Distribution of consolidated fund	12,551.36			
Transferred to investment reserve fund			24.85	
Fees to financial advisers			9.52	
Balance June 30, 1934:				
Cash	1,213.09	46,166.69	1,223.94	
Invested		206,611.25		10,000.00
Total	13,930.95	368,514.69	1,256.31	10,000.00

	Elliot fund		Fees to financial advisers	
	Income	Capital	Income	Capital
Balance July 1, 1933:				
Cash	$1,485.37			
Invested	942.00	$8,000.00		
Receipts:				
Interest on investments	454.18			
Bonds sold	942.00			
Transferred from various funds			$4,369.10	
Received from National Research fund			390.26	
Total	3,823.55	8,000.00	4,759.36	
Disbursements:				
Transfer to investment reserve fund	22.71			
Fees to financial advisers	9.52			
Medals and medal boxes	504.40			
Engrossing	25.00			
Honoraria	400.00			
Payment to Loomis, Sayles & Co.			4,759.36	
Bonds bought	942.00			
Balance June 30, 1934:				
Cash	1,919.92			
Invested		8,000.00		
Total	3,823.55	8,000.00	4,759.36	

	Fund for oceanographic research		Gibbs fund	
	Income	Capital	Income	Capital
Balance July 1, 1933:				
Cash	$5,190.43		$1,396.94	
Invested			1,023.75	$5,545.50
Receipts:				
General Education Board	7,455.17			
Interest on investments			324.38	
Refunds from T. Wayland Vaughan	630.60			
Royalties	3.50			
Total	13,279.70		2,745.07	5,545.50
Disbursements:				
Salary, T. Wayland Vaughan	3,675.00			
Clerical expenses	1,927.50			
Traveling expenses	1,702.71			
Miscellaneous expenses	86.17			
Transfer to scientific publication fund	5.75			
Transfer to investment reserve fund			16.22	
Fees to financial advisers			4.76	
Balance June 30, 1934:				
Cash	5,882.57		1,700.34	
Invested			1,023.75	5,545.50
Total	13,279.70		2,745.07	5,545.50

Accounts with individual funds July 1, 1933, to June 30, 1934—Continued

| | Gould fund | | Grand Canyon project | |
	Income	Capital	Income	Capital
Balance July 1, 1933:				
Cash	$2,743.44	$415.00	$24.19	
Invested	14,438.25	19,585.00		
Receipts:				
Interest on investments	1,534.60			
Bonds sold	10,945.75	4,382.50		
Total	29,662.04	24,382.50	24.19	
Disbursements:				
Grants	1,350.00			
Bonds bought	10,945.75	4,382.50		
Transfer to investment reserve fund	76.73			
Fees to financial advisers	38.06			
Balance June 30, 1934:				
Cash	13,258.98	4,797.50	24.19	
Invested	3,992.50	15,202.50		
Total	29,662.04	24,382.50	24.19	

| | Hale lectureship | | Hartley fund | |
	Income	Capital	Income	Capital
Balance July 1, 1933:				
Cash	$82.89		$607.28	
Invested	291.00			$1,200.00
Receipts:				
Interest on investments	12.27		58.99	
Bonds sold	291.00			
Total	677.16		666.27	1,200.00
Disbursements:				
Medal and medal box			99.55	
Transfer to investment reserve fund	.61		2.95	
Bonds bought	291.00			
Balance June 30, 1934:				
Cash	385.55		563.77	
Invested				1,200.00
Total	677.16		666.27	1,200.00

| | Joseph Henry fund | | Investment reserve fund | |
	Income	Capital	Income	Capital
Balance July 1, 1933:				
Cash	$653.46			
Invested	1,023.75	$40,163.50		
Receipts:				
Interest on investments	2,043.90			
Refund			$0.81	
Profit on sale of bonds			39,539.69	
Transferred from various funds			8,397.05	
Overdraft June 30, 1934			554,487.40	
Total	3,721.11	40,163.50	602,424.95	
Disbursements:				
Grants	2,550.00			
Transfer to investment reserve fund	102.20			
Fees to financial advisers	42.83		19.04	
Loss on sale of bonds			228,657.35	
Taxes, advertising, and legal fees on real estate			6,726.04	
Overdraft July 1, 1933			367,022.52	
Balance June 30, 1934:				
Cash	2.83			
Invested	1,023.75	40,163.50		
Total	3,721.11	40,163.50	602,424.95	

Accounts with individual funds July 1, 1933, to June 30, 1934—Continued

	Marsh fund		Murray fund	
	Income	Capital	Income	Capital
Balance July 1, 1933:				
Cash			$2,279.36	
Invested		$20,000.00	2,039.00	$6,000.00
Receipts:				
Interest on investments	$992.81		413.97	
Refund from M. K. Elias	1.50			
Bonds sold			1,039.00	
Total	994.31	20,000.00	5,771.33	6,000.00
Disbursements:				
Grants	550.00			
Medal and medal box			368.50	
Transfer to investment reserve fund	51.20		20.70	
Fees to financial advisers	19.04		9.52	
Bonds bought			1,039.00	
Balance June 30, 1934:				
Cash	374.07		3,333.61	
Invested		20,000.00	1,000.00	6,000.00
Total	994.31	20,000.00	5,771.33	6,000.00

	National Academy of Sciences, special		National Parks problems	
	Income	Capital	Income	Capital
Balance July 1, 1933, cash			$3,156.87	
Receipts:				
Reimbursements	$89,824.04			
Due from National Research Council July 1, 1933	2,000.00			
Total	91,824.04		3,156.87	
Disbursements:				
Expenses of academy	89,824.04			
Crater Lake painting, booklets, and studies			551.60	
Balance June 30, 1934:				
Cash			2,605.27	
Due from National Research Council June 30, 1934	2,000.00			
Total	91,824.04		3,156.87	

	National Research fund		Nealley fund	
	Income	Capital	Income	Capital
Balance July 1, 1933:				
Cash	$138,420.59	$50.00		
Invested	193,188.75			$19,555.55
Receipts:				
Interest on investments	7,783.40			
Interest on deposits	146.90			
Profit on sale of bonds	17,967.00			
Bonds sold	466,207.50			
Total	823,714.14	50.00		19,555.55
Disbursements:				
Bonds bought	466,207.50			
Accrued interest on bonds bought	207.88			
Loss on sale of bonds	508.80			
Postage and insurance on bonds	.28			
Fees to financial advisers	390.26			
Refunds to contributors	356,399.42	3.06		
Balance June 30, 1934:				
Cash		46.94		
Invested				19,555.55
Total	823,714.14	50.00		19,555.55

Accounts with individual funds July 1, 1933, to June 30, 1934—Continued

	Organization expenses, National Research fund		Emergency fund Proceedings	
	Income	Capital	Income	Capital
Balance July 1, 1933:				
Cash	$31.33		$378.13	
Invested			2,917.50	
Receipts:				
Interest on investments			38.86	
Bonds sold			2,917.50	
Total	31.33		6,251.99	
Disbursements:				
Organization expenses	31.33			
Transfer to investment reserve fund			1.94	
Fees to financial advisers			4.76	
Bonds bought			2,917.50	
Balance June 30, 1934, cash			3,327.79	
Total	31.33		6,251.99	

	Academy Proceedings		Joint Proceedings	
	Income	Capital	Income	Capital
Balance July 1, 1933:				
Cash	$2,725.84		$5,740.75	
Invested	1,995.75		2,910.00	
Receipts:				
Interest on investments	113.84		65.59	
Annual dues	1,375.00			
Subscriptions			1,886.53	
Reprints and separates	107.45		1,908.14	
Bonds sold			2,910.00	
Transfer from Billings fund	1,033.84			
Contribution by National Research Council			2,500.00	
Transfer from academy Proceedings representing contribution by National Academy of Sciences			2,500.00	
Total	7,351.72		20,421.01	
Disbursements:				
Salary of managing editor			1,200.00	
Printing and distributing			8,463.79	
Bonds bought			2,910.00	
Expenses:				
Boston office			475.00	
Washington office			294.65	
Transfer from academy Proceedings representing contribution by National Academy of Sciences	2,500.00			
Transfer to investment reserve fund	5.69		3.28	
Fees to financial advisers			4.76	
Balance June 30, 1934:				
Cash	2,850.28		7,069.53	
Invested	1,995.75			
Total	7,351.72		20,421.01	

Accounts with individual funds July 1, 1933, to June 30, 1934—Continued

	Publication fund for research		Scientific publication fund	
	Income	Capital	Income	Capital
Balance July 1, 1933, cash	$1,735.82		$1,624.16	
Receipts:				
Rockefeller Foundation	14,860.00			
Royalties			1.37	
Transferred from fund for oceanographic research			5.75	
Total	16,595.82		1,631.28	
Disbursements:				
Grants	15,735.00			
Traveling expenses	121.16			
Balance June 30, 1934, cash	739.66		1,631.28	
Total	16,595.82		1,631.28	

	Smith fund		Thompson fund	
	Income	Capital	Income	Capital
Balance July 1, 1933:				
Cash	$2,791.50		$1,422.50	$200.00
Invested	3,970.75	$10,000.00	932.50	9,800.00
Receipts:				
Interest on investments	679.72		403.50	
Bonds sold	2,492.50		932.50	9,800.00
Total	9,934.47	10,000.00	3,691.00	19,800.00
Disbursements:				
Grants	825.00			
Bonds bought	2,492.50		932.50	9,800.00
Transfer to investment reserve fund	33.99		20.18	
Fees to financial advisers	19.04		9.52	
Telegram			.63	
Balance June 30, 1934:				
Cash	5,065.69		2,728.17	1,037.50
Invested	1,478.25	10,000.00		8,962.50
Total	9,934.47	10,000.00	3,691.00	19,800.00

	Walcott fund		Watson fund	
	Income	Capital	Income	Capital
Balance July 1, 1933:				
Cash	$505.10	$362.50	$1,062.46	$1,876.25
Invested	700.00	4,637.50	5,496.50	23,123.75
Receipts:				
Interest on investments	312.22		1,205.85	
Bonds sold	2,100.00	4,637.50	5,496.50	11,055.00
Special contribution	20.00			
Total	3,637.32	9,637.50	13,281.31	36,055.00
Disbursements:				
Honorarium	1,350.00			
Bonds bought	2,100.00	4,637.50	5,496.50	11,055.00
Accrued interest on bonds bought	38.38			
Grants			900.00	
Transfer to investment reserve fund	15.61		60.29	
Fees to financial advisers	4.76		33.31	
Medal	30.00			
Balance June 30, 1934:				
Cash	98.57	135.00	5,791.21	525.00
Invested		4,865.00	1,000.00	24,475.00
Total	3,637.32	9,637.50	13,281.31	36,055.00

Statement of assets and liabilities, June 30, 1934

ASSETS

[Securities purchased during the fiscal year 1933-34 are indicated thus (*)]

	Face value	Book value	Market value June 30, 1934
Real estate owned	$128,500.00	$128,500.00	$128,500.00
Mortgage notes, secured by first mortgage on real estate	398,400.00	398,400.00	398,400.00
SECURITIES			
American Telephone & Telegraph Co. 5-percent 30-year collateral trust gold, due Dec. 1, 1946; nos. 640, 4604, *10927, 29245, 29246, 41419, *42526, *43733, *43734, *45849, *47282-*47284, *49576, *53149, *58466, *64235-*64247, *66042, *67397, *74425, *74513, *74630, *74633; 35 at $1,000 each	35,000.00	37,065.00	38,150.00
American Telephone & Telegraph Co. 5-percent 35-year debenture bonds due Feb. 1, 1965; nos. M17-939, M19-041, M64-124-M64-135, M64-519, M72-201-M72-203, M72-311-M72-316, M72-324, M75-045-M75-050, M91-899, M91-900, M106-560-M108-562, M115-287-M115-289, M131-196-M131-200, M144-885, M145-413, M145-414; 47 at $1,000 each	47,000.00	51,208.75	51,758.75
Argentine Government loan 1926 6-percent external sinking fund gold, public works issue of Oct. 1, 1926, due Oct. 1, 1960; nos. M1211-M1213, M1255, M1981, M2342, M3255, M3356, M3816, M3818, M6183, M6537, M8435, M8436, M8605, M10423-M10437, M10902, M10904, M10905, M12793, M15271; 25 at $1,000 each	25,000.00	24,936.25	20,500.00
Armour & Co. 4½-percent 30-year real estate first mortgage gold bonds, due June 1, 1939; nos. 33346, 35056-35058, 35340, 37700, 37912, 39066, 39644, 40771, 41261, 41767, 41768, 41906, 43315; 15 at $1,000 each	15,000.00	13,935.40	14,868.75
Baltimore & Ohio Railroad Co., Southwestern Division, 5-percent first-mortgage gold, due July 1, 1950; nos. M15352, M18188, M18189, M20332-M20337, M20639-M20643, M23191, M27436, M27437, M29334, M35855, M40090-M40092; 22 at $1,000 each; nos. D395, D396; 2 at $500 each	23,000.00	22,515.00	22,827.50
Baltimore & Ohio Railroad Co. 5-percent refunding and general mortgage, series A, due Dec. 1, 1995; nos. M30222, M33708, M37053, M58345; 4 at $1,000 each; nos. D1256, D1298; 2 at $500 each	5,000.00	4,526.25	4,061.25
Baltimore & Ohio Railroad Co. 5-percent refunding and general mortgage, series D, due Mar. 1, 2000; nos. M4863-M4892; 30 at $1,000 each	30,000.00	28,650.00	24,450.00
Bell Telephone Co. of Canada 5-percent first mortgage, series C, bonds, due May 1, 1960; nos. CM00084, CM00085, CM00277-CM00279, CM00397, CM00527-CM00529, CM00628, CM00629, CM00719, CM00720, CM00750, CM01453-CM01458, CM02295-CM02296, CM02827, CM03184, CM03192, CM03193, CM06441-CM06445, CM06449, CM06450; 35 at $1,000 each	35,000.00	36,488.75	38,500.00
Carolina, Clinchfield & Ohio Ry. 6-percent first and consolidated mortgage gold bonds, series A, due Dec. 15, 1952; nos. M652, M908, M933, M1907, M2231, M2434, M2482, M2483, M2609-M2613, M2732, M2864, M2885, M3731-M3733, M3955, M4052-M4054, M4362, M4436-M4440, M5223, M5804, M5902, M5906, M6349, M6818-M6822, M7031; 40 at $1,000 each; nos. D91, D92, D130-D133, D159, D240-D250, D797, D796; 20 at $500 each	50,000.00	54,210.00	54,000.00
City of Brisbane, Australia, 5-percent 30-year sinking fund gold bonds, due Mar. 1, 1957; nos. 3368, 3360, 3418-3422, 3789-3793, 3926-3932, 4400-4402, 4630, 4720, 5376, 5975, 6634, 6638, 7341, 7425, 7472, 7487; 30 at $1,000 each	30,000.00	27,670.00	25,200.00
City of Tacoma, Green River special water fund no. 2, 5-percent, due Oct. 1, 1939; nos. 1508-1511; 4 at $1,000 each	4,000.00	4,140.00	3,970.00
Columbia Gas & Electric Corporation 5-percent debenture bonds, due Jan. 15, 1961; nos. A9157-A9181; 25 at $1,000 each	25,000.00	24,437.50	21,625.00
Commonwealth of Australia 5-percent external loan of 1925, 30-year gold bonds, due July 15, 1955; nos. M11659-11661, M34201, M34552-M34556, 'M51712' M51713, M54872, M60000, M71394, M73402; 15 at $1,000 each	15,000.00	14,662.50	14,100.00
Commonwealth of Australia 5-percent 30-year external loan of 1927, due Sept. 1, 1957; nos. 34384-34406; 25 at $1,000 each	25,000.00	24,425.00	23,531.25
Consolidated Gas Co. of N. Y. 5½-percent 20-year debenture bonds, due Feb. 1, 1945; nos. M318, M319, M3214, M3317-M3326, M5235-M5245, M5738-M5740, M9598-M9601, M11397-M11399, M11643-M11646, M15509, M15654, M16671-M16680, M21938, M21940, M22190, M22374-M22376, M23870, M23871, M26142, M27181, M27182, M28852, M28905, M28906, M34787, M35519, M38629, M38630, M40419, M44300, M44803, M47911, M48338; 72 at $1,000 each; nos. D1530, D1531; 2 at $500 each	73,000.00	75,200.00	78,383.75
Cosmos Club, Washington, D. C., 4½-percent bonds, due July 1, 1949; nos. 288, 289, 291, 292, 294, 299, 305, 350; 8 at $1,000 each	8,000.00	8,000.00	6,400.00

Statement of assets and liabilities, June 30, 1934—Continued

ASSETS—Continued

[Securities purchased during the fiscal year 1933–34 are indicated thus (*)]

	Face value	Book value	Market value June 30, 1934
SECURITIES—continued			
Denver & Salt Lake Railway Co., Moffat Road, 6-percent first mortgage gold bonds, series A, due Jan. 1, 1950; nos. M1460–M1464, M1467–M1478, M1489, M1490, M1495, M1510, M1779, M1828, M1829, M2463; 25 at $1,000 each	$25,000.00	$26,250.00	$25,250.00
Dominion of Canada 5-percent third war loan 20-year bonds due Mar. 1, 1937; nos. E02374–E02376, E05443, E05444, E19151, E23763–E23765, E40822, E40823, E178424, E178425, E201852–E201854, E204857–E204863; 23 at $1,000 each	23,000.00	22,108.75	24,782.50
Edison Electric Illuminating Co. of Boston 5-percent 2-year notes, due July 16, 1934; nos. 477, 833–837, 1436–1460, 10251–10269; 50 at $1,000 each	50,000.00	51,568.75	50,062.50
Federal Land Bank of Columbia, S. C., 5-percent Federal Farm Loan, due May 1, 1941; nos. M122955–M122957, M122967–M122975; 12 at $1,000 each	12,000.00	11,280.00	12,150.00
General Motors Acceptance Corporation 5-percent serial gold notes, series J, due Mar. 1, 1936; nos. M46824–M46827, M47517, M47518, M48044, M48206, M48207, M48243, M48634, M49469; 12 at $1,000 each	12,000.00	11,797.50	12,495.00
Goodyear Tire & Rubber Co. 5-percent first mortgage and collateral trust bonds due May 1, 1957; nos. M2001, M2766, M2779, M2780, M3573, M5965, M12741, M15293, M17623, M19518–M19521, M20721, M23021, M24476, M25063, M25475–M25479, M26848, M30598, M34067, M38695–M38699, M39056–M39068, M42907, M43357, M48568, M48569, M54288–M54297, M54551, M56107; 59 at $1,000 each; nos. D129, D702; 2 at $500 each	60,000.00	56,102.50	60,150.00
Government of the Argentine Nation 6-percent external sinking fund gold bonds, due Oct. 1, 1959; nos. M5611, M10464, M10470, M18165, M18363–M18365, M19643, M20578, M23810; 10 at $1,000 each	10,000.00	9,957.50	8,187.50
Grand Trunk Ry. Co. of Canada, Canadian National Railways, 6-percent 15-year sinking fund gold debenture bonds, guaranteed, due Sept. 1, 1936; nos. M00976–M00978, M01129, M01762, M02855, M03925, M04011, M04589, M09544, M10380, M14578–M14592, M14803, M18462–M18471, M19390, M19391, M19530, M19765, M19801, M20542, M21487, M21539, M22610, M23600, M23699; 48 at $1,000 each; nos. D0139–D0142; 4 at $500 each	50,000.00	53,600.00	53,812.50
Grand Trunk Western Ry. Co. first-mortgage 50-year 4-percent gold, due July 1, 1950; nos. 346, 1141, 1584, 1613, 3060, 3061, 3888, 4304, 5025, 5605, 5606; 11 at $1,000 each; nos. 15, 265, 774, 781, 839, 994, 1019, 1055, 1059, 1104, 1189, 1378, 2141, 2143, 2738, 2884, 2942, 2970, 2976, 3220; 20 at $500 each	21,000.00	16,215.00	18,007.50
Great Northern Ry. Co. 7-percent 15-year general mortgage, series A, due July 1, 1936; no. M61777–M61782; 6 at $1,000 each; no. D3241; 1 at $500; nos. C3291, C3536; 2 at $100 each	6,700.00	6,465.50	6,415.25
Humble Oil & Refining Co. 5-percent 10-year gold debenture bonds, due Apr. 1, 1937; nos. *5736, *5737, *6410, *6546, *7567–*7572, *10006, *10317, *12290–*12297, *14025–*14029, *14033, *14034, 16195–16204, 16311–16325, *17676–*17681, *18269, *18270, *18285–*18287, *19104, *19405, *19520, *19521, *19552, *19553, *19619, *19637–*19639, *19949, *20301; 75 at $1,000 each	75,000.00	77,268.75	78,468.75
Inland Steel Co. 4½-percent first-mortgage sinking fund, series A, bonds, due Apr. 1, 1978; nos. 10843, 10844, 11422–11427, 11993, 11994, 12708, 12709, 13051, 15938–15942, 15945–15949, 17002, 17003, 19753, 19754, 22395, 22396, 23426–23428, 25336–25342, 28968; 40 at $1,000 each	40,000.00	34,785.00	39,650.00
International Match Corporation 5-percent 20-year sinking fund gold debenture bonds, due Nov. 1, 1947; nos. M17061–M17070, M21205, M21206, M22101–M22108, M22111–M22115, M22131–M22135, M23277–M23281, M36988–M37002; 50 at $1,000 each	50,000.00	49,100.00	5,250.00
Kansas City, Fort Scott & Memphis Ry. Co. 4-percent refunding mortgage, fully guaranteed bonds, due Oct. 1, 1936; nos. 32, 756, 1013, 1093, 1418–1421, 1447, 1660, 2326, 2593, 2898, 3546, 4196, 4312, 4348, 4468–4472, 4610, 4621, 4787, 4944, 5096, 5447, 5728, 5930, 5932, 6224–6227, 6802, 6811, 6812, 6906, 7191, 7444, 7449, 7475, 7612, 7640, 7641, 7662, 7933, 7934, 8023–8025, 8027, 8028, 8062, 8222, 8624, 8739, 8880, 8970, 9486, 10036, 11733, 11742, 13062–13064, 13483, 13484, 14113, 14256, 14561, 14562, 14651, 14952, 15186, 15187, 15226, 15946, 16079, 16081–16085, 16207, 16276, 16767, 17281, 18104, 18173, 18177, 18453, 18782, 18783, 18806, 18856, 18947, 19069, 19154, 19655, 19893, 19911, 20178, 20235, 20694, 20891, 21065, 21345, 21346, 21387, 21730, 21880–21889, 22822, 22935, 23065, 23124, 23271, 24023, 24188, 24206, 24221, 24542, 24650, 25215, 25499, 25500; 136 at $1,000 each	136,000.00	79,096.25	66,130.00

ASSETS—Continued

[Securities purchased during the fiscal year 1933-34 are indicated thus (*)]

	Face value	Book value	Market value June 30, 1934
SECURITIES—continued			
Kansas City Southern Ry. Co. 5-percent refunding and improvement mortgage bonds, due Apr. 1, 1950; nos. M464, M827, M1139–M1141, M1576, M2142, M4310, M4840, M4861, M7091, M7208, M7902, M9833, M10769, M11350, M12276, M12997, M13816, M14505, M14950, M18955–M18957, M19213, M20178, M20242–M20244, M20401; 30 at $1,000 each	$30,000.00	$15,721.25	$22,650.00
Kingdom of Norway 6-percent 20-year external loan sinking fund gold bonds, due Aug. 1, 1944; nos. 1620-1624, 3665, 3855, 5317, 5925, 6458–6461, 6532, 6557–6559, 6611, 6612, 6614, 8803, 8804, 8880, 11125–11129, 13165, 13166, 14085, 14812, 14818–14820, 15531, 15532, 15703, 13756, 17285, 17286, 17311, 17771, 19312, 19896, 20871, 22047, 22048, 22112, 23338, 23344; 51 at $1,000 each	$51,000.00	53,880.75	50,745.00
Kingdom of Sweden 5 1/2-percent 30-year gold bonds, due Nov. 1, 1954; nos. M518–M523, M1531–M1533, M1551–M1561, M8700, M8748, M8749, M8899, M9972, M12400, M12401, M12730–M12734, M14392, M14647, M18418, M21321, M21322, M23418, M23506, M24917; 40 at $1,000 each	40,000.00	41,630.00	41,200.00
Lackawanna & Wyoming Valley R. R. Co. 5-percent first-mortgage gold bonds, dated July 1, 1913, due Aug. 1, 1951; nos. M853–M905; 50 at $1,000 each	50,000.00	48,750.00	11,500.00
*Liggett & Myers Tobacco Co. 7-percent bonds due Oct. 1, 1944; nos. 448, 3124–3126, 3957–3959, 4697–4701, 5366–5369, 6701, 6702, 7201, 7218, 7228–7231, 7241, 7242, 7251, 7252, 7294–7300, 7348–7350, 8007, 9195, 9196, 9964, 10285, 11219, 13573, 13763–13766, 15135; 50 at $1,000 each	50,000.00	51,845.00	53,750.00
Missouri Pacific Railroad Co. 5-percent first and refunding mortgage gold bonds, series G, dated Nov. 1, 1928, due Nov. 1, 1978; nos. M20326–M20375; 50 at $1,000 each	50,000.00	48,712.50	15,000.00
Missouri Pacific Railroad Co. 5-percent first and refunding mortgage, series I, due Feb. 1, 1981; nos. T252–T256, T7644–T7647, T39855–T39859, T39861–T39863, T43949–T43954; 23 at $1,000 each; nos. M9994, M10757, M10758, M16440–M16442, M18265, M18828, M18829, M23249, M30095, M30444, M30546, M30901–M30905, M30908–M30915, M31587, M33255, M38252, M38253, M39860, M39861, M40437–M40440, M46664; 37 at $1,000 each	60,000.00	31,983.75	17,700.00
National Dairy Products Corporation 5 1/4-percent gold debenture bonds due Feb. 1, 1948; nos. M3002, M5146–M5191, M16029, M22546, M33198, M46795, M46796, M67999, M71719, M71720, M72246, M75482, M76648–M76658, M76700, M76701; 70 at $1,000 each	70,000.00	69,171.25	68,425.0
New Orleans, Texas & Mexico Railway Co. 5 1/2-percent first-mortgage gold bonds, series A, due Apr. 1, 1954; nos. M439–M448, M647, M1610, M1765–M1767, M1808–M1810, M3396, M6873, M6874, M6896, M6897, M7099, M8135, M8207, M9643, M9950, M9996, M11059–M11063, M11944–M11948, M12486, M12487, M14131–M14133, M14417, M14418, M16406–M16408; 49 at $1,000 each; nos. D200, D201; 2 at $500 each	50,000.00	51,763.75	11,000.00
Niagara Falls Power Co. 5-percent first and consolidation mortgage bonds, series A, due July 1, 1959; nos. M4994–M4997, M6157–M6162; 10 at $1,000 each	10,000.00	9,860.00	10,750.00
Niagara Falls Power Co. 6-percent first and consolidation mortgage gold bonds, series AA, due Nov. 1, 1950; nos. M388, M571, M608, M740, M741, M775, M1129, M1843, M2412, M2561, M2808, M3072, M4269, M4371, M4501, M4502, M4608, M4682, M4696, M5001, M5007, M5008, M5545, M5796, M5881, M6050, M6143, M6855, M6881, M6882, M6907, M6978, M7343, M7359, M7422, M7494, M7542, M7745, M8156, M8157, M8274, M8276, M8335–M8341, M8360, M8689, M8690; 52 at $1,000 each; nos. D161, D162, D180, D200, D378, D1220, D1221, D1229, D1465, D1542, D1701, D1838, D1839, D1853, D1854; 15 at $500 each	59,500.00	63,748.75	64,855.00
North American Co. 5-percent debentures, due Feb. 1, 1961; nos. M505, M1404, M1839–M1847, M3951–M3953, M5801–M5810, M5991, M5992, M7712–M7714, M8286, M11067, M13856, M13996, M14009, M14209, M15222, M15223, M15855, M17286, M17527, M17769, M17770, M17964, M18532, M18571, M19074, M19288, M23252–M23256, M23701, M23730, M23954, M24316, M24317, M24704, M24705, M24943; 60 at $1,000 each	60,000.00	49,750.00	53,400.00
Northern Pacific Railway Co. 6-percent refunding and improvement mortgage, series B, due July 1, 2047; nos. M3544–M3547, M26853, M26854, M27750–M27754, M84522–M84525, M103231–M103245; 30 at $1,000 each	30,000.00	30,912.50	29,850.00
*Ohio Power Co. 4 1/2-percent first and refunding mortgage, series D, bonds due June 1, 1956; nos. M3248–M3251, M10226–M10230, M10300, M10301, M12400, M12929, M13457, M13696, M13697, M13754, M20986–M20989, M22690, M22691, M25016–M25020, M25569, M28196, M28197; 31 at $1,000 each	31,000.00	30,293.75	31,813.75

Statement of assets and liabilities, June 30, 1934—continued

ASSETS—Continued

[Securities purchased during the fiscal year 1933–34 are indicated thus (*)]

	Face value	Book value	Market value June 30, 1934
SECURITIES—continued			
Pacific Telephone & Telegraph Co. 5-percent first mortgage and collateral trust sinking fund 30-year bonds, stamped, due Jan. 2, 1937; nos. M8660, M9559, M10461–M10465, M10619, M10700, M10824, M11130, M11403, M11404, M11954, M11955, M12083, M12156, M12519; 18 at $1,000 each	$18,000.00	$18,850.00	$19,327.50
Pennsylvania Power & Light Co. 4½-percent first-mortgage bonds due Apr. 1, 1981; nos. 50380–50383; 4 at $1,000 each	4,000.00	3,850.00	3,960.00
Pillsbury Flour Mills Co. 6-percent first-mortgage 20-year bonds, due Oct. 1, 1943; nos. M91, M92, M993, M994, *M1062, M1295, M2098, M2403, *M2898, M3503, M4033, M4351, M4581, M4894, M5486; 15 at $1,000 each; nos. D94, D480; 2 at $500 each	16,000.00	16,885.00	17,240.00
Raleigh & Augusta Air Line Railroad Co., Seaboard Air Line Railway Co., guaranteed first-mortgage 5-percent due Jan. 1, 1931; nos. 701–725; 25 at $1,000 each	25,000.00	25,000.00	16,500.00
Republic of Finland 5½-percent external loan sinking fund gold bonds, due Feb. 1, 1958; nos. M3263–M3268, M3440, M3441, M3580, M6960–M6964, M6966, M6967, M6969, M8040, M8552, M9179, M9233, M9234, M9835–M9839, M10250, M10326, M10329, M10774, M11267–M11270, M11416–M11419, M12189–M12196, M12657, M12658, M12660–M12663, M12754, M13030, M14358, M14461; 57 at $1,000 each; no. D819; 1 at $500	57,500.00	50,153.75	53,403.13
St. Louis-San Francisco Railway Co. 4½-percent consolidated mortgage gold bonds, series A, due Mar. 1, 1978; nos. M7881–M7895, M14120–M14134, M17108, M17963, M17964, M19029, M25732–M25737, M41182, M41183, M41216, M62420–M62424, M91633, M91634; 50 at $1,000 each	50,000.00	43,850.00	8,875.00
Southern Bell Telephone & Telegraph Co. 30-year first-mortgage 5-percent sinking fund gold, due Jan. 1, 1941; nos. M5845, M6230, M9739, M10618, M11576–M11579, M12369, M13965, M15568–M15570, M19695–M19697, M27301, M30234–M30236; 20 at $1,000 each	20,000.00	20,643.75	21,600.00
Standard Oil Co. of New Jersey 5-percent 20-year gold debentures due Dec. 15, 1946; nos. *3312, *42396, 46490–46499, 46501–46505, 46507, 46509–46513, 46515, *108011, *108012, *108014, *108016, *108018, *118958, *118960–*118965, *118967–*118969, *119001–*119007, *119009–*119012, *119016–*119024, *119027; 60 at $1,000 each	60,000.00	62,563.75	63,375.00
State of New South Wales, Australia, 5-percent external 30-year sinking fund gold bonds, due Feb. 1, 1957; nos. M9770, M9771, M9775, M17979, M17980, M21242–M21248, M21356–M21358, M22163, M22164, M23024–M23026; 20 at $1,000 each	20,000.00	19,127.50	18,450.00
State of Queensland, Australia, 20-year 7-percent sinking fund external loan gold, due Oct. 1, 1941; nos. M8229–M8231, M8289, M8801, M8898, M9250, M9367, M9378, M9647, M9648, M9725, M9777–M9779, M9929, M10131, M10158, M10610, M10611; 20 at $1,000 each	20,000.00	22,331.50	20,700.00
Texarkana & Fort Smith Railway Co. 5½-percent first-mortgage guaranteed gold bonds, series A, due Aug. 1, 1950; nos. M101, M102, M754–M763, M1593–M1595, M1739, M1742, M1777–M1779, M2014–M2018, M3001, M3002, M3908–M3910, M5767, M6078, M6482, M6757–M6760, M6912, M8341–M8343, M9299, M9472, M9473, M9029–M9631; 47 at $1,000 each; nos. D102, D103, D186, D202, D237, D264; 6 at $500 each	50,000.00	52,271.25	47,062.50
*Texas Corporation 5-percent convertible sinking fund debentures, due Oct. 1, 1944; nos. 553–556, 2682, 2683, 20333, 20834, 27996, 31044, 31137, 31138, 46340, 67358, 77518, 77525, 77526, 78560, 78561, 93936, 95491–95494; 24 at $1,000 each	24,000.00	24,720.00	24,840.00
Union Oil Co. of California 6-percent 20-year, series A, gold, due May 1, 1942; nos. M140–M142, M661, M662, M1733–M1735, M5231, M6140–M6143, M8726; 14 at $1,000 each; nos. D1026, D1027; 2 at $500 each	15,000.00	15,630.00	17,137.50
U. S. of America 4¼-percent Liberty loan, due Oct. 15, 1938; nos. B–00408452-H58, B–00408462-H68, B–00408472-H78, B–00408482-H88, B–00408492-F96, B–00494892; 34 at $1,000 each	34,000.00	35,275.00	35,296.25
*U. S. of America 4¼-percent–3¼-percent Treasury bonds, due Oct. 15, 1945; nos. 67226F–67229K, 67230L, 67231A–67239K, 67240L, 67241A; 16 at $1,000 each	16,000.00	16,600.00	16,600.00
*U. S. of America 3-percent Treasury notes, series A–1935, due June 15, 1935; nos. 19644-D, 19645-E; 2 at $10,000 each	20,000.00	20,587.50	20,562.50
*U. S. of America 3¼-percent Treasury notes, series A–1936, due Aug. 1, 1936; nos. 20965-E, 21121-A/21126-F, 21127-H, 21128-J/21130-L, 21131-A/21136-F, 21137-H, 21138-J/21140-L, 21198-J/21200-L, 21201-A/21206-F; 30 at $1,000 each; nos. 2994-D, 6859-K; 2 at $5,000 each; nos. 15093-O, 18288-J; 2 at $10,000 each	60,000.00	62,025.00	63,075.00
Vicksburg, Shreveport & Pacific R. R. Co. prior lien mortgage 6-percent renewed at 5 percent, gold, due Nov. 1, 1915, extended to Nov. 1, 1940; nos. 561, 661, 794, 962, 1323; 5 at $1,000 each	5,000.00	5,050.00	5,050.00
Total	2,698,600.00	2,608,003.15	2,395,750.88

Statement of assets and liabilities, June 30, 1934—Continued

ASSETS—Continued

[Securities purchased during the fiscal year 1933–34 are indicated thus (*)]

	Face value	Book value	Market value June 30, 1934
COMMON STOCKS			
*American Can Co. common, par $25, 200 shares	$5,000.00	$18,515.00	$19,250.00
*Atchison, Topeka & Santa Fe Ry. Co. common, par $100, 300 shares	30,000.00	18,102.50	17,850.00
Atlantic Refining Co. common, par $25, 500 shares (*400 shares purchased during 1933–34)	12,500.00	13,272.50	12,375.00
*Continental Can Co. common, par $20, 200 shares	4,000.00	13,335.00	15,900.00
Corn Products Refining Co. common, par $25, 250 shares (*200 shares purchased during 1933–34)	6,250.00	21,368.67	16,250.00
*E. I. du Pont de Nemours & Co. common, par $20, 300 shares	6,000.00	23,507.50	26,587.50
General Motors Corporation common, par $10, 700 shares (*600 shares purchased during 1933–34)	7,000.00	21,227.50	21,612.50
*Liggett & Myers Tobacco Co. common B, par $25, 100 shares	2,500.00	9,595.00	9,550.00
National Biscuit Co. common, par $10, 500 shares (*430 shares purchased during 1933–34)	5,000.00	27,106.98	17,625.00
*Norfolk & Western Ry. Co. common, par $100, 160 shares	16,000.00	26,876.90	29,080.00
Northern Pacific Ry. Co. common, par $100, 400 shares (*300 shares purchased during 1933–34)	40,000.00	9,650.00	9,500.00
*Pennsylvania Railroad Co. common, par $50, 500 shares	25,000.00	15,887.50	15,375.00
*Socony-Vacuum Oil Co., Inc., common, par $15, 1,000 shares	15,000.00	12,525.00	15,750.00
Standard Oil Co. of New Jersey common, par $25, 600 shares (*500 shares purchased during 1933–34)	15,000.00	24,077.50	26,325.00
*Union Oil Co. of California common, par $25, 500 shares	12,500.00	10,625.00	8,000.00
*United States Gypsum Co. common, par $20, 400 shares	8,000.00	17,572.50	17,400.00
United States Smelting, Refining & Mining Co. common, par $50, 200 shares (*100 shares purchased during 1933–34)	10,000.00	14,285.00	25,600.00
United States Steel Corporation common, par $100, 400 shares (*300 shares purchased during 1933–34)	40,000.00	18,002.50	15,450.00
Westinghouse Electric & Manufacturing Co. common, par $50, 160 shares	5,000.00	4,365.00	3,612.50
*F. W. Woolworth Co. common, par $10, 600 shares	6,000.00	26,402.50	29,775.00
	270,750.00	346,300.05	352,867.50
Air Reduction Co., Inc., common, no par, 200 shares		20,825.00	19,700.00
*American Cyanamid Co. B common, no par, 200 shares		2,587.50	3,650.00
*American Radiator & Standard Sanitary Corporation common, no par, 1,000 shares		15,462.50	14,250.00
Bethlehem Steel Corporation common, no par, 500 shares (*400 shares purchased during 1933–34)		16,937.50	16,500.00
*Burroughs Adding Machine Co. common, no par, 800 shares		12,675.00	11,300.00
*Caterpillar Tractor Co. common, no par, 800 shares		17,337.50	22,200.00
*Columbia Gas & Electric Corporation common, no par, 200 shares		4,100.00	2,750.00
First National Stores, Inc., common, no par, 300 shares (*250 shares purchased during 1933–34)		17,236.50	19,050.00
General Electric Co. common, no par, 900 shares (*800 shares purchased during 1933–34)		21,055.00	17,887.50
*W. T. Grant Co., no par, 500 shares		16,575.00	15,500.00
Hercules Powder Co. common, no par, 500 shares (*400 shares purchased during 1933–34)		24,290.00	36,000.00
*International Business Machines Corporation common, no par, 200 shares		26,471.50	27,600.00
*International Nickel Co. of Canada, Ltd., common, no par, 1,000 shares		19,275.00	26,000.00
*Johns-Manville Corporation common, no par, 300 shares		14,530.25	15,600.00
*Libbey-Owens-Ford Glass Co. common, no par, 700 shares		21,092.50	22,050.00
*Otis Elevator Co. common, no par, 100 shares		2,062.50	1,562.50
J. C. Penney Co. common, no par, 600 shares (*500 shares purchased during 1933–34)		27,165.00	34,500.00
*Republic Steel Corporation common, no par, 200 shares		3,562.50	3,125.00
*Sears, Roebuck & Co. common, no par, 500 shares		20,250.00	20,875.00
Standard Oil Co. of California common, no par, 200 shares (*150 shares purchased during 1933–34)		7,926.50	6,900.00
Timken Roller Bearing Co. common, no par, 700 shares (*600 shares purchased during 1933–34)		20,092.50	21,000.00
Union Carbide & Carbon Corporation common, no par, 200 shares (*100 shares purchased during 1933–34)		8,455.00	8,450.00
		339,964.75	366,450.00
Total par and no par		686,264.80	719,317.50
Total securities, including common stocks		3,294,267.95	3,115,068.38

Statement of assets and liabilities, June 30, 1934—Continued

SUMMARY

Book value of securities as above, including common stocks		$3, 294, 267. 95
Bank balance June 30, 1934:		
American Security & Trust Co.:		
National Academy of Sciences	$22, 107. 96	
National Research fund	46. 94	
		22, 154. 90
Bank of New York & Trust Co		143, 483. 15
Advanced to National Academy of Sciences, special		2, 000. 00
Income receivable:		
Carnegie endowment fund income account, N. A. S., 1934		3, 716. 28
Carnegie endowment fund income account, N. R. C., 1934		10, 000. 00
Property account (buildings and grounds at cost):		
Building	$1, 448, 644. 82	
Grounds	185, 764. 50	
		1, 634, 409. 32
Property account (equipment at cost)		9, 383. 48
Total assets		5, 119, 415. 08

LIABILITIES

	Income	Capital		Income	Capital
General fund:			Murray fund:		
Invested	$8, 242. 50		Invested	$1, 000. 00	$6, 000. 00
Uninvested	10, 748. 06		Uninvested	3, 333. 61	
Agassiz fund, invested		$50, 000. 00	National Parks problems, uninvested	2, 605. 27	
Bache fund:			National research fund, uninvested		46. 94
Invested		60, 000. 00	Nealley fund, invested		19, 555. 55
Uninvested	1, 037. 10		Proceedings:		
Billings fund, invested		22, 313. 39	Academy account:		
Building construction fund:			Invested	1, 995. 75	
Invested	3, 000. 00		Uninvested	2, 850. 28	
Uninvested	120. 18		Joint account, uninvested	7, 069. 53	
Building site fund:			Emergency fund, uninvested	3, 327. 79	
Invested	7, 543. 25		Publication fund for research, uninvested	739. 66	
Uninvested	10, 895. 49		Scientific publication fund, uninvested	1, 631. 28	
Carnegie Corporation, special, uninvested	8, 126. 54		Smith fund:		
Carnegie endowment fund:			Invested	1, 478. 25	10, 000. 00
Invested		2, 972, 174. 45	Uninvested	5, 085. 69	
Uninvested		577, 825. 55	Thompson fund:		
John J. Carty Medal and Award:			Invested		8, 962. 50
Invested		24, 608. 75	Uninvested	2, 728. 17	1, 037. 50
Uninvested	1, 511. 08	391. 25	Walcott fund:		
Comstock fund:			Invested		4, 865. 00
Invested	2, 000. 00	5, 068. 75	Uninvested	98. 57	135. 00
Uninvested	2, 859. 60	7, 337. 27	Watson fund:		
Consolidated fund, uninvested	1, 213. 09		Invested	1, 000. 00	24, 475. 00
Draper fund:			Uninvested	5, 791. 21	525. 00
Invested		10, 000. 00	Appropriations under custodian of buildings and grounds, uninvested	471. 17	
Uninvested	1, 223. 94				
Elliot fund:			Total (dr.)	424, 608. 62	3, 900, 230. 90
Invested		8, 000. 00			
Uninvested	1, 919. 92		Total income (dr.)	424, 608. 62	
Fund for oceanographic research, uninvested	5, 882. 57		Total capital	3, 900, 230. 90	
Gibbs fund:			Total income and capital	3, 475, 622. 28	
Invested	1, 023. 75	5, 545. 50	Capital invested in property	1, 634, 409. 32	
Uninvested	1, 700. 34		Capital invested in equipment	9, 383. 48	
Gould fund:					
Invested	3, 992. 50	15, 202. 50	Total liabilities	5, 119, 415. 08	
Uninvested	13, 258. 98	4, 797. 50			
Grand Canyon project, uninvested	24. 19		Consolidated investment fund:		
Hale lectureship, uninvested	385. 55		Invested		206, 611. 25
Hartley fund:			Uninvested	1, 213. 09	46, 166. 69
Invested		1, 200. 00			
Uninvested	563. 77			1, 213. 09	252, 777. 94
Joseph Henry fund:					
Invested	1, 023. 75	40, 163. 50			
Uninvested	2. 33				
Investment reserve fund:					
Uninvested (dr.)	554, 487. 40				
Marsh fund:					
Invested		20, 000. 00			
Uninvested	374. 07				

General fund, National Academy of Sciences, from July 1, 1933, to June 30, 1934

RECEIPTS

	Budget July 1, 1933, to June 30, 1934	Actually received July 1, 1933, to June 30, 1934	Budget balance, June 30, 1934
Interest on investments:			
Agassiz fund	$4,700.00	$4,389.84	$310.16
Nealley fund	1,000.00	971.48	28.52
Annual dues from members	1,200.00	1,375.00	[1] 175.00
	6,900.00	6,736.32	163.68
Balance from previous year	16,000.00	17,938.19	[1] 1,938.19
	22,900.00	24,674.51	[1] 1,774.51

DISBURSEMENTS

	Budget July 1, 1933, to June 30, 1934	Actually disbursed, July 1, 1933, to June 30, 1934	Budget balance June 30, 1934
Treasurer's office:			
Auditor's fees	$200.00	$200.00	....
Bond of treasurer	25.00	25.00	....
Miscellaneous expenses	300.00	239.21	$60.79
Transfer to investment reserve fund, 5 percent of income	375.00	268.07	106.93
	900.00	732.28	167.72
Home secretary's office:			
Assistant secretary's salary	600.00	600.00	....
Stationery and miscellaneous office expenses	400.00	399.61	.39
Reference books	50.00	46.90	3.10
Binding	50.00	....	50.00
Printing, multigraphing and engraving	250.00	240.17	9.83
Express and telegrams	250.00	204.09	45.91
	1,600.00	1,490.77	109.23
Annual meeting	900.00	734.37	165.63
Autumn meeting	500.00	500.00	....
	1,400.00	1,234.37	165.63
Election of members	350.00	344.44	5.56
Memoirs, editorial	150.00	66.50	83.50
Printing of Biographical Memoirs	1,200.00	770.50	429.50
Current publications, preparation for distribution	100.00	69.40	30.60
Postage, regular	250.00	168.50	81.50
Contingent fund	400.00	371.10	28.90
Library binding	800.00	180.75	619.25
Expenses of members attending executive meetings of council of the academy	300.00	255.34	44.66
	3,550.00	2,226.53	1,323.47
Total for all	7,450.00	5,683.95	1,766.05
Surplus	15,450.00	18,990.56	....
Grand total	22,900.00	24,674.51	....

[1] In excess of budget.

Appropriations under custodian of buildings and grounds, July, 1, 1933, to June 30, 1934

RECEIPTS

	Budget July 1, 1933, to June 30, 1934	Actually received July 1, 1933, to June 30, 1934	Budget balance, June 30, 1934
From Carnegie endowment fund	$44,122.98	$40,176.37	$3,946.61
From reversions from previous year	544.02	544.02	
Reimbursement	1.35	1.35	
	44,668.35	40,721.74	3,946.61

DISBURSEMENTS

	Budget July 1, 1933, to June 30, 1934	Actually disbursed, July 1, 1933, to June 30, 1934	Budget balance, June 30, 1934
Salaries, office of custodian of buildings and grounds	$6,780.00	$6,780.00	
Salaries, employees, building	23,611.00	23,591.46	$19.54
Coal	1,500.00	1,381.00	119.00
Electricity	1,815.00	1,815.00	
Gas	20.00	8.25	11.75
Contingent fund, maintenance of building	5,923.57	5,887.92	35.65
Maintenance of exhibits	3,525.00	3,480.61	44.39
	43,174.57	42,944.24	**230.33**
Insurance, 1933–37	2,493.78	2,022.61	471.17

Balance July 1, 1933 .... $691.45
Appropriated July 1, 1933 .... 1,493.78

2,185.23
:,. Expended July 1, 1933 to June 30, 1934 .... 1,714.06

Balance June 30, 1934 .... 471.17

	45,668.35	44,966.85	701.50

Reversions June 30, 1934, amounting to $230.33 have been credited to "Carnegie Endowment Fund, income account, N. A. S., 1934".

Condensed statement of receipts and disbursements, National Academy of Sciences, July 1, 1933, to June 30, 1934

RECEIPTS

Balance July 1, 1933, as per last report $81,691.25
Cash receipts:
    Academy Proceedings:
        Annual dues $1,375.00
        Reprints and separates 107.45
                         $1,482.45
    Joint Proceedings:
        Subscriptions 1,886.53
        Reprints and separates 1,908.14
        National Research Council 2,500.00
                         6,294.67
General fund, annual dues 1,375.00
Publication fund for research, contributions by the
    Rockefeller Foundation 14,860.00
Scientific publication fund, royalties 1.37

Condensed statement of receipts and disbursements, National Academy of Sciences, July 1, 1933, to June 30, 1934—Continued

RECEIPTS—continued

Cash receipts—Continued.
　Fund for oceanographic research:
　　Contribution by the General
　　　Education Board_____ $7,455.17
　　T. Wayland Vaughan, refunds___ 630.60
　　Royalties_____ 3.50
　　　　　　　　　　　　　　　　　　　 ――――――― $8,089.27
　Total income from investments_____ 167,463.05
　National Research fund:
　　Sale of bonds_____ $291,284.79
　　Reimbursement for interest on
　　　bonds_____ 278.44
　　　　　　　　　　　　　　　　　　　 ――――――― 291,563.23
　Interest allowed on bank deposit:
　　Bank of New York & Trust Co.:
　　　National Research fund_____ 146.90
　　　Carnegie endowment fund___ 197.32
　　　　　　　　　　　　　　　　　　　 ――――――― 344.22
　Walcott fund, special contribution_____ 20.00
　Investment reserve fund, reimbursement_____ .81
　Fees to financial advisers, received from National
　　Research fund_____ 390.26
　Marsh fund, M. K. Elias, refund_____ 1.50
　Contingent fund, maintenance of building, reim-
　　bursement_____ 1.35
　Consolidated fund, real estate mortgage paid in
　　full_____ 5,000.00
　　　　　　　　　　　　　　　　　　　 ―――――――$496,887.18

　　　　Total_____ 578,578.43

DISBURSEMENTS

General fund:
　Treasurer's office:
　　Auditor's fees_____ $200.00
　　Bond of treasurer_____ 25.00
　　Miscellaneous expenses (not including
　　　$114.22, fees to financial advisers;
　　　and $2.52, charges by Bank of New
　　　York & Trust Co.)_____ 122.47
　　　　　　　　　　　　　　　　　　　 ――――――― $347.47
　Home secretary's office:
　　Assistant secretary's salary_____ 600.00
　　Stationery and miscellaneous office
　　　expenses_____ 399.61
　　Reference books_____ 46.90
　　Printing, multigraphing, and engrav-
　　　ing_____ 240.17
　　Express and telegrams_____ 204.09
　　　　　　　　　　　　　　　　　　　 ――――――― 1,490.77
　Annual meeting_____ 734.37
　Autumn meeting_____ 500.00
　Election of members_____ 344.44
　Memoirs, editorial_____ 66.50
　Printing of Biographical Memoirs_____ 770.50
　Current publications, preparation for distribution 69.40
　Postage, regular_____ 168.50
　Contingent fund_____ 371.10
　Library binding_____ 180.75
　Expenses of members attending executive meetings
　　of council of the academy_____ 255.34
　　　　　　　　　　　　　　　　　　　 ――――――― $5,299.14

Condensed statement of receipts and disbursements, National Academy of Sciences, July 1, 1933, to June 80, 1934—Continued

DISBURSEMENTS—continued

Appropriations for maintenance of buildings and grounds under custodian of buildings and grounds:

Salaries, office of custodian of buildings and grounds	$6, 780. 00	
Salaries, employees, building	23, 591. 46	
Coal	1, 381. 00	
Electricity	1, 815. 00	
Gas	8. 25	
Contingent fund, maintenance of building	5, 887. 92	
Maintenance of exhibits	3, 480. 61	
Insurance, 1933–37	1, 714. 06	
		$44, 658. 30
Fees to financial advisers		4, 759. 36
To National Research Council for general maintenance expenses		91, 374. 96
Joint Proceedings:		
Salary, managing editor	$1, 200. 00	
Printing and distributing	8, 463. 79	
Expenses:		
Boston office	475. 00	
Washington office	294. 65	
		10, 433. 44
Fund for oceanographic research:		
Salary, T. Wayland Vaughan	3, 675. 00	
Clerical expenses	1, 927. 50	
Traveling expenses	1, 702. 71	
Miscellaneous expenses	86. 17	
		7, 391. 38
Carnegie Corporation special:		
Travel, National Research fund	137. 66	
Travel, Science Advisory Board	744. 82	
Committee on the library	400. 00	
Government relations allotment	444. 71	
Clerical expenses	50. 00	
		1, 777. 19
National Parks problems:		
Crater Lake painting, booklets and studies		551. 60
Publication fund for research:		
Traveling expenses of committee members	121. 16	
Genetics	500. 00	
The Torrey Botanical Club	1, 000. 00	
Yerkes Observatory	300. 00	
Seismological Society of America	1, 000. 00	
American Journal of Science	900. 00	
Yale University Observatory	375. 00	
Ecology	500. 00	
Phytopathology	750. 00	
American Folk-Lore Society	500. 00	
Astrophysical Journal	500. 00	
International Journal of American Linguistics	500. 00	
Journal of Paleontology	750. 00	
American Institute of Physics, Inc	1, 500. 00	
Institute of History of Medicine	1, 000. 00	
N. W. Popoff	300. 00	
The New England Botanical Club, Inc	500. 00	
American Journal of Botany	1, 000. 00	
Association of American Geographers	600. 00	
Isis	500. 00	
Psyche	500. 00	
Lowell Observatory	600. 00	

DISBURSEMENTS—continued

Publication fund for research—Continued.

Physiological Zoology	$500. 00	
William Henry Burtt	160. 00	
American Geophysical Union	400. 00	
George R. Cowgill	600. 00	
		$15, 856. 16

Carnegie endowment fund:

Refund of interest on bonds	278. 44	
Real-estate taxes, water rents, commissions	1, 958. 06	
		2, 236. 50

National Research fund:

Postage and insurance	.28	
Refunds to contributors	356, 402. 48	
Fees to financial advisers	390. 26	
		356, 793. 02

Investment reserve fund, real-estate taxes, water rents, advertising, recording		1, 483. 07
Organization expenses, National Research fund, organization expenses		31. 33

Payments from trust and other funds:

Bache fund:

Office expenses	$5. 00	
H. M. Randall, grant	500. 00	
H. S. Jennings, grant	400. 00	
Eric Ponder, grant	400. 00	
Henry B. Ward, grant	500. 00	
H. T. Stetson, grant	250. 00	
Cecilia Payne Gaposchkin, grant	250. 00	
		$2, 305. 00

Comstock fund:

Percy W. Bridgman, honorarium	2, 500. 00	
Engrossing	20. 00	
		2, 520. 00

Elliot fund:

George Ellet Coghill, honorarium	200. 00	
Estate of Davidson Black, honorarium	200. 00	
Medals and medal boxes	504. 40	
Engrossing	25. 00	
		929. 40

Gould fund:

Frank Schlesinger, grant	300. 00	
J. S. Plaskett, grant	300. 00	
Frank C. Jordan, grant	500. 00	
W. J. Luyten, grant	250. 00	
		1, 350. 00

Hartley fund, medal and medal box		99. 55

Joseph Henry fund:

Ralph E. Cleland, grant	200. 00	
Fred Allison, grant	550. 00	
Ales Hrdlicka, grant	500. 00	
Simon Freed, grant	400. 00	
Edward L. Bowles, grant	500. 00	
Ernest O. Laurence, grant	400. 00	
		2, 550. 00

Marsh fund:

Eleanora Bliss Knopf, grant	125. 00	
Albert Elmer Wood, grant	200. 00	
International Hydrographic Bureau, grant	125. 00	
Douglas Johnson, grant	100. 00	
		550. 00

Murray fund, medal and medal box		368. 50

Condensed statement of receipts and disbursements, National Academy of Sciences,
July 1, 1933, to June 30, 1934—Continued

DISBURSEMENTS—continued

Payments from trust and other funds—Continued.
Smith fund:

Harlow Shapley, grant	$575.00	
C. C. Wylie, grant	250.00	
		$825.00
Thompson fund, telegram		.63

Walcott fund:

David White, honorarium	1,350.00	
Medal	30.00	
		1,380.00

Watson fund:

A. Kopff, grant	800.00	
Dick Brouwer, grant	100.00	
		900.00

Total payments from trust and other funds	$13,778.08
Total disbursements	556,423.53
Balance June 30, 1934	22,154.90
Grand total	578,578.43

NATIONAL RESEARCH COUNCIL

The disbursements of the National Research Council, under the authority of the National Academy of Sciences during the year ended June 30, 1934, amounted to $811,676.79. Sales of bonds held for temporary investment amounted to $25,014.10. Interest received on temporary investment amounted to $6,453.85, of which $6,151.34 was credited to National Research Council, and $302.51 to Bibliography of Economic Geology.

The investment reserve fund on June 30, 1933, stood at $382.02, a decrease for the year of $7,036.93. This fund operates to prevent the council suffering a loss on the selling or calling of bonds.

The book value of securities held by the council on June 30, 1934, was $92,145.50. The following shows the current interest yield on these bonds, according to the valuation used:

	Amount	Yield
		Percent
Face value of bonds held	$92,333.00	5.18
Book value of bonds held	92,145.50	5.19
Market value, June 30, 1934, of bonds held	91,548.00	5.23

The receipts from various organizations during the year for investigations to be made in cooperation with the United States Bureau of Standards amounted to $11,375, as compared with $6,245 for similar purposes last year.

During the fiscal year ended June 30, 1934, the activities of the council were supported by funds from various sources, of which the principal are listed as follows:

(1) From the Carnegie endowment fund: For general maintenance expenses of the National Research Council. This contribution represents the only money available for general maintenance expenses. The research council has disbursed in addition other funds contributed by a large number of organizations and individuals for specific purposes named by the donors. The diversity of these researches is indicated by the following list of receipts, and the disbursements for these purposes are several times larger than the expenditures for general maintenance____ $91, 374. 96

(2) From the Rockefeller Foundation:

For National Research fellowships in physics, chemistry, and mathematics, year 1933 (R. F. 29131)_____	85, 091. 40
For the same purpose, year 1934 ·(R. F. 29131 and R. F. 31052)_____	73, 946. 13
For fellowships in medicine, year 1933 (R. F. 29060)_____	35, 611. 61
For the same purpose, year 1934 (R. F. 29060 and R. F. 31054)_____	19, 983. 44
For fellowships in the biological sciences, year 1933 (R. F. 29004 and R. F. 29005)_____	95, 541. 69
For the same purpose, year 1934 (R. F. 29004, R. F. 29005, and R. F. 31053)_____	22, 119. 74
For international biological abstracts, year 1933 (R. F. 33022)_____	43, 355. 72
For the same purpose, year 1934 (R. F. 34005)_____	26, 092. 82
For indices of Biological Abstracts (without year)_____	5, 000. 00
For the same purpose, year 1934–35 (R. F. 34005)_____	1, 314. 99
For sex research fund, year 1934_____	72, 811. 59
For committee on drug addiction, Rockefeller Foundation, year 1933_____	23, 189. 05
For the same purpose, year 1934_____	25, 864. 66
For research aid fund, year 1933_____	30, 000. 00
For the same purpose, year 1934_____	20, 000. 00
For fellowships in the biological sciences, studying abroad, year 1933 (R. F. 29132)_____	9, 268. 93
For the same purpose, year 1934 (R. F. 29132)_____	9, 750. 20
For mitogenetic radiation_____	2, 500. 00
Total from the Rockefeller Foundation_____	601, 441. 97

(3) From the General Education Board, for committee on child development, year 1934_____ 6, 300. 00
(4) From Research Corporation, for the magneto-optical process of chemical analysis_____ 500. 00
(5) From various organizations for the highway research board_____ 17, 578. 94

(6) From various organizations for work to be conducted in cooperation with United States Bureau of Standards:

For methods of locking screw threads_____	600. 00
For thermal investigations_____	1, 025. 00
For investigations on steel structures_____	170. 00
For acoustic properties of materials_____	1, 150. 00
For thermal properties of liquids_____	1, 330. 00
For corrosion-resistance of pipe materials_____	2, 400. 00
For testing chemical reagents_____	2, 000. 00
For fire resistance of materials_____	500. 00
For current meter investigations_____	2, 200. 00
Total_____	11, 375. 00

(7) From various organizations:

For American Bureau of Welding_____	1, 012. 50
For welding wire specifications_____	50. 00
For heat transmission_____	9. 60
For Science Advisory Board_____	32, 000. 00
For bibliography of economic geology_____	5, 647. 51
For research fund, committee on sedimentation_____	174. 70
For committee on drug addiction, Squibb fellowships_____	1, 400. 00

(7) From various organizations—Continued.

For committee on drug addiction, Merck fellowship	$700. 00
For committee on drug addiction, Mallinckrodt fellowship	1, 000. 00
For National Live Stock and Meat Board fellowships	3, 750. 00
For effects of radiation on living organisms	25, 000. 00
For Tennessee Valley Archeology	2, 000. 00
For visual limitations for motorists	1, 000. 00
For child development abstracts	1, 153. 45
For annual tables	3, 050. 00
For royalties, international critical tables	537. 81

Total receipts during the year from all sources _____ 850, 740. 25

Receipts and disbursements, National Research Council, from July 1, 1933, to June 30, 1934

RECEIPTS

Appropriation	Received during year	Previously reported	Transfers and other credits	Budget	Budget balance
Rockefeller Foundation:					
National Research fellowships (R. F. 29131) 1933	$85, 091. 40	$69, 908. 60		$155, 000. 00	
National Research fellowships (R. F. 29131 and R. F. 31052) 1934	73, 946. 13			115, 000. 00	$41, 053. 87
Research fellowships in medicine (R. F. 29060) 1933	35, 611. 61	14, 388. 39		50, 000. 00	
Research fellowships in medicine (R. F. 29060 and R. F. 31054) 1934	19, 983. 44			40, 000. 00	20, 016. 56
Fellowships in the biological sciences (R. F. 29004 and R. F. 29005) 1933	95, 541. 69	29, 458. 31		125, 000. 00	
Fellowships in the biological sciences (R. F. 29004, R. F. 29005, R. F. 31053) 1934	22, 119. 74			100, 000. 00	77, 880. 26
International biological abstracts (R. F. 33022) 1933	43, 355. 72	31, 643. 89	$0. 39	75, 000. 00	
International biological abstracts (R. F. 34005) 1934	26, 092. 82			65, 000. 00	38, 907. 18
Indices of Biological Abstracts	5, 000. 00	15, 000. 00		20, 000. 00	
Indices of Biological Abstracts (R. F. 34005) 1934–35	1, 314. 99			20, 000. 00	18, 685. 01
Sex research fund, 1933		74, 210. 43	926. 64	75, 137. 07	
Sex research fund, 1934	72, 811. 59		1, 494. 02	74, 305. 61	
Committee on drug addiction, Rockefeller Foundation, 1933	23, 189. 05	26, 810. 95		50, 000. 00	
Committee on drug addiction, Rockefeller Foundation, 1934	25, 864. 66			25, 864. 66	
Research aid fund, 1932–33		60, 400. 00	3. 22	60, 403. 22	
Research aid fund, 1933	30, 000. 00	20, 000. 00	8. 40	50, 008. 40	
Research aid fund, 1934	20, 000. 00			20, 000. 00	
Fellowships in the biological sciences, studying abroad (R. F. 29132) 1933	9, 268. 93	10, 731. 07		20, 000. 00	
Fellowships in the biological sciences, studying abroad (R. F. 29132) 1934	9, 750. 20			10, 000. 00	249. 80
Mitogenetic radiation	2, 500. 00			2, 500. 00	
Leonard Wood Memorial for the Eradication of Leprosy, survey of tropical diseases		2, 500. 60	3. 00	2, 503. 60	
Rotating fund, physics committees	2, 028. 56	11, 513. 54		13, 542. 10	
Research Corporation, special	500. 00			500. 00	
General Education Board, committee on child development, 1934	6, 300. 00			6, 300. 00	
Highway research board, 1933	1, 250. 00	22, 807. 41		24, 057. 41	
Highway research board, 1934	16, 328. 94	4, 343. 35		20, 672. 29	
American Bureau of Welding	1, 012. 50	15, 110. 63		16, 123. 13	
Welding wire specifications	50. 00	235. 00		285. 00	
Heat transmission	9. 60	43, 145. 17		43, 154. 77	
Science Advisory Board	32, 000. 00			32, 000. 00	
Bibliography of Economic Geology	5, 647. 51	26, 154. 71		31, 802. 22	
Research fund, committee on sedimentation	174. 70	2, 151. 17		2, 325. 87	
Committee on drug addiction, Squibb fellowships	1, 400. 00	1, 400. 00		2, 800. 00	
Committee on drug addiction, Merck fellowship	700. 00			700. 00	
Committee on drug addiction, Mallinckrodt fellowship	1, 000. 00			1, 000. 00	
National Live Stock and Meat Board fellowships	3, 750. 00	43, 038. 87		46, 788. 87	
Effects of radiation on living organisms	25, 000. 00	106, 365. 39		131, 365. 39	
Tennessee Valley Archaeology	2, 000. 00			2, 000. 00	
Visual limitations for motorists	1, 000. 00	4, 662. 93		5, 662. 93	

Receipts and disbursements, National Research Council, from July 1, 1933, to June 30, 1934—Continued

RECEIPTS—Continued

Appropriation	Received during year	Previously reported	Transfers and other credits	Budget	Budget balance
Child-development abstracts	$1,153.45	$10,859.94		$12,013.39	
National intelligence tests, 1921	978.87	22,372.77		23,351.64	
International Critical Tables		333,441.34	$537.81	333,979.15	
Royalty account, International Critical Tables	537.81	50,742.93		51,280.74	
Annual tables	3,050.00	48,697.61		51,747.61	
Methods of locking screw threads	600.00	45,315.00		45,915.00	
Thermal investigations	1,025.00	800.00	77.91	1,902.91	
Investigations on steel structures	170.00	15,725.00		15,895.00	
Acoustic properties of materials	1,150.00	20,511.31	1.68	21,662.99	
Thermal properties of liquids	1,330.00	4,325.00	8.75	5,663.75	
Corrosion-resistance of pipe materials	2,400.00			2,400.00	
Testing chemical reagents	2,000.00			2,000.00	
Fire resistance of materials	500.00	11,190.00		11,690.00	
Current meter investigations	2,200.00	1,000.00		3,200.00	
Carnegie Endowment Fund	91,374.96		204.65	91,579.61	
Total	810,063.87	1,200,950.71	3,266.47	2,211,083.73	$196,792.68
Sale of bonds	25,014.10				
Interest on bonds	6,151.34				
Miscellaneous receipts	4,233.27				
Reimbursements	5,277.67				
Total receipts	850,740.25				
July 1, 1933, cash in banks	27,518.35				
Grand total	878,258.60				

DISBURSEMENTS

Division	Disbursed during year	Previously reported	Reversions and other charges	Budget	Budget balance
I. Federal Relations:					
General maintenance, 1934			$100.00	$100.00	
II. Foreign relations:					
General maintenance, 1934	$2.00		58.00	100.00	$40.00
Division of foreign relations, William Ellery Hale Fund, 1921	1,301.91	$761.52		2,063.43	
Annual dues to international unions, 1934	6,268.78		126.16	6,394.94	
III. States relations:					
General maintenance, 1934	7.50		92.50	100.00	
IV. Educational relations:					
General maintenance, 1934	23.00		77.00	100.00	
Division of educational relations, Commonwealth Fund		7,304.01		8,051.55	747.54
V. Physical sciences:					
General maintenance, 1931		1,517.81	232.19	1,750.00	
General maintenance, 1933		963.31	36.69	1,000.00	
General maintenance, 1934	708.83		291.17	1,000.00	
Revolving fund for publication of mathematical books	1,188.10	2,992.71		4,902.16	721.35
Physics committees, 1932		912.50		1,500.00	587.50
Rotating fund, physics committees	3,317.15	5,614.60		13,542.10	4,610.63
Research Corporation, special	500.00			500.00	
Research fellowships (R. F. 29131) 1933	116,100.95	39,021.45		155,122.40	
Research fellowships (R. F. 29131 and R. F. 31052) 1934	40,676.49			115,000.00	74,323.51
VI. Engineering and industrial research:					
General maintenance, 1933	49.14	1,454.86		1,504.00	
General maintenance, 1934	1,283.14			1,299.00	15.86
Highway research board, 1933		19,714.06	4,343.35	24,057.41	
Highway research board, 1934	17,115.37			20,672.29	3,556.92
American Bureau of Welding	1,063.13	15,060.00		16,123.13	
Structural steel investigation	900.46	14,833.02		22,526.68	6,793.20
Heat transmission	703.67	41,270.87		43,154.77	1,180.23
Fundamental research in welding	42.08	1,783.91		1,950.00	124.01
Welding wire specifications	88.07	196.93		285.00	

*Receipts and disbursements, National Research Council, from July 1, 1933, to June 30, 1934—*Continued

DISBURSEMENTS—Continued

Division	Disbursed during year	Previously reported	Reversions and other charges	Budget	Budget balance
VII. Chemistry and chemical technology:					
General maintenance, 1934	$779.51	....	$512.49	$1,300.00	$8.00
Travel, chairman, division of chemistry and chemical technology, 1933	123.95	$626.05	....	750.00	....
VIII. Geology and geography:					
General maintenance, 1934	1,434.02	....	9.98	1,500.00	56.00
Committee on measurement of geologic time	21.55	128.45	....	**150.00**	....
Committee on measurement of geologic time, 1929–30	60.00	1,940.00	....	2,000.00	....
Bibliography of economic geology	2,046.12	24,516.02	....	31,802.22	5,240.08
Research fund, committee on sedimentation	465.58	335.46	....	2,325.87	1,524.83
International cartographic **exhibit**, Warsaw	17.93	....	....	150.00	132.07
IX. Medical sciences:					
General maintenance, 1934	614.68	792.48	....	1,407.16	....
Sex research fund, 1933	926.64	74,210.43	....	75,137.07	....
Sex research fund, 1934	73,790.78	....	....	74,305.61	514.83
Fellowships in medicine (**R. F.** 29060), 1933	33,072.47	16,927.53	....	50,000.00	....
Fellowships in medicine (R. F. 29060 and R. F. 31054), 1934	24,512.21	....	....	40,000.00	15,487.79
Committee on drug addiction, Squibb fellowships	1,342.23	806.69	....	2,800.00	651.08
Committee on drug addiction, Rockefeller Foundation, 1933	26,317.96	23,682.04	....	50,000.00	....
Committee on drug addiction, Rockefeller Foundation, 1934	23,116.50	....	....	25,864.66	2,748.16
Survey of tropical diseases	196.36	1,705.36	....	2,503.00	601.28
Committee on drug addiction, Merck fellowship	700.00	....	....	700.00	....
Committee on drug addiction, Mallinckrodt fellowship	1,000.00	....	....	1,000.00	....
X. Biology and agriculture:					
General maintenance, 1933	7.84	1,210.32	....	1,318.16	100.00
General maintenance, 1934	1,061.46	....	138.54	1,200.00	....
Committee on forestry	....	7,295.43	....	10,029.99	2,734.56
Food and nutrition committee	....	9,219.18	....	9,675.00	455.82
Fellowships in the biological sciences (R. F. 29004 and R. F. 29005), 1933	87,783.22	37,507.03	....	125,290.25	....
Fellowships in the biological sciences (R. F. 29004, R. F. 29005, and R. F. 31053), 1934	31,157.04	....	....	100,000.00	68,842.96
National Live Stock and Meat Board fellowships	4,375.00	41,513.03	....	46,788.87	900.84
International biological abstracts (R. F. 33022), 1933	36,863.40	38,136.21	.39	75,000.00	....
International biological abstracts (R. F. 34005), 1934	31,958.95	....	....	65,000.00	33,041.05
Committee on infectious abortion, 1929–30	205.66	119.22	....	350.00	25.12
National committee on botanical nomenclature	50.00	2,923.25	....	3,060.85	87.60
Pharmaceutical researches	....	265.16	....	560.00	294.84
Effects of radiation on living organisms	21,034.46	98,408.34	....	131,365.39	11,922.59
Biological abstracts, 1929	....	4,992.10	....	5,000.00	7.90
Committee on infectious abortion, Certified Milk Producers' Association	....	1,499.92	....	1,500.00	.08
Committee on infectious abortion, Commonwealth Fund, 1931	....	6,599.64	....	6,600.00	.36
Committee on research publications, 1932	....	393.92	....	600.00	206.08
Fellowships in the biological sciences, studying abroad (R. F. 29132), 1933	9,268.93	10,731.07	....	20,000.00	....
Fellowships in the biological sciences, studying abroad (R. F. 29132), 1934	9,750.20	....	....	10,000.00	249.80
Indices of biological abstracts	7,810.35	12,189.65	....	20,000.00	....
Indices of biological abstracts (R. F. 34005), 1934	2,923.73	....	....	20,000.00	17,076.27
Mitogenetic radiation	705.20	....	....	2,500.00	1,794.80

Receipts and disbursements, National Research Council, from July 1, 1933, to June 30, 1934—Continued

DISBURSEMENTS—Continued

Division	Disbursed during year	Previously reported	Reversions and other charges	Budget	Budget balance
XI. Anthropology and psychology:					
General maintenance, 1933	$27.61	$968.99	$3.40	$1,000.00	
General maintenance, 1934	1,053.17		205.37	1,303.26	$44.72
National intelligence tests, 1921	823.50	16,019.14		23,351.64	6,509.00
Visual limitations for motorists	1,036.06	4,249.92		5,662.93	376.95
Child development abstracts	705.40	7,262.46		12,013.39	4,045.53
Committee on child development, Spelman Fund, 1933		7,096.46		7,096.46	
Psychiatric investigations	1,679.91	5,052.80		10,000.00	3,267.29
Committee on child development, General Education Board, 1934	6,300.00			6,300.00	
Tennessee Valley Archaeology	1,735.61			2,000.00	264.39
Expenses and supplies, 1933	223.37	4,532.61	459.71	5,215.69	
Expenses and supplies, 1934	3,834.93		29.87	3,900.70	35.90
New equipment, general, 1933		705.68	44.32	750.00	
New equipment, general, 1934	159.98		48.79	300.00	91.23
Salaries, 1934	69,489.34		1,080.66	70,570.00	
Telephone and telegraph, 1933	143.86	2,178.26	123.72	2,445.84	
Telephone and telegraph, 1934	2,277.38			2,489.91	212.53
Executive board:					
General maintenance, 1934	920.91		579.09	1,500.00	
American Geophysical Union, general maintenance, 1934	350.00			350.00	
Publications and publicity:					
General maintenance, 1932		10,600.00		12,100.00	1,500.00
General maintenance, 1933	1,965.87	8,012.76	121.37	10,100.00	
General maintenance, 1934	1,283.88		807.88	4,305.05	2,213.29
National Academy proceedings and subscriptions, 1934	2,500.00			2,500.00	
International auxiliary language		9,630.02		10,065.00	434.98
International Critical Tables		327,679.52		333,979.15	6,299.63
Royalty account, International Critical Tables		50,742.93	537.81	51,280.74	
Annual tables	2,968.61	48,691.29		51,747.61	87.71
Auditor's fees, 1933	300.00			300.00	
Grants in aid (R. F. 29061)	417.82	100,221.46		100,639.28	
Research aid fund (R. F. 30105)	1,946.18	96,385.25		101,120.28	2,788.85
Research aid fund (R. F. 32010), 1932–33	2,836.22	51,107.83		60,403.22	6,459.17
Research aid fund (R. F. 32109), 1933	28,111.33	19,362.43		50,008.40	2,534.64
Research aid fund (R. F. 33121), 1934	18,860.00			20,000.00	1,140.00
Attorney's fees, 1934	200.00		50.00	250.00	
Science Advisory Board	18,922.10			32,000.00	13,077.90
Problems of refrigeration				984.19	984.19
Methods of locking screw threads	40.00	45,240.32		45,915.00	634.68
Investigations on steel structures	1,030.00	14,683.09		15,895.00	181.91
Fatigue properties of Alclad aluminum		1,452.85		1,500.00	47.15
Investigation of propeller fans		1,231.27		1,241.00	9.73
Concrete and clay investigations		7,006.12		7,100.00	93.88
Brick work		459.18		1,000.00	540.82
Gumming characteristics of motor fuels	169.58	3,338.00	7.93	3,345.93	
Impermanency of records		29,830.42		30,000.00	
Acoustic properties of materials	4,283.47	17,193.74		21,662.99	185.78
Investigation of physics of plumbing systems		2,719.10		3,200.00	480.90
Properties of gaseous mixtures		2,999.18	.82	3,000.00	
Thermal properties of liquids	1,469.74	4,078.34		5,663.75	115.67
Fire resistance of materials	1,193.16	10,337.23		11,690.00	159.61
Properties of volatile liquid fuels		2,796.68		2,800.00	3.32
Current meter investigations	42.89	309.77		3,200.00	2,847.34
Thermal investigations	729.44	712.60		1,902.91	460.87
Corrosion-resistance of pipe materials	2,031.89			2,400.00	368.11
Testing chemical reagents	2,000.00			2,000.00	
Research information service:					
General maintenance, 1933	36.47	11,273.53		11,310.00	
General maintenance, 1934	644.93		8,942.57	9,590.00	2.50
Total	811,678.31	1,498,236.77	19,061.77	2,644,782.28	315,905.43
Investment reserve fund	98.48				
Purchase of bonds					
Total disbursements	811,676.79				
June 30, 1934, cash in banks	66,581.81				
Grand total	878,258.60				

National Research Council condensed balance sheet as of June 30, 1934

ASSETS

	Face value	Book value	Market value June 30, 1934
SECURITIES			
General maintenance fund:			
Mortgage notes secured by first mortgage on real estate	$35,333.00	$35,333.00	$35,333.00
Federal Land Bank bonds 5 percent 1941/1931, Wichita, due May 1, 1941, nos. M125427, M125428, 2 at $1,000 each; Columbia, due May 1, 1941, nos. M122976–M122978, 3 at $1,000 each; Spokane, due Nov. 1, 1941, nos. M131444–M131447, 4 at $1,000 each; Wichita, due Nov. 1, 1941, nos. M130002–M130004, M130027, M130029, M130030–M130033, M130036, M130039–M130045; 17 at $1,000 each	26,000.00	26,000.00	26,325.00
Government of the Argentine Nation 6-percent external sinking-fund gold bonds, due June 1, 1959; nos. M16652, M33319–M33322; 5 at $1,000 each	5,000.00	5,017.50	4,100.00
Kingdom of Norway 6-percent 20-year external loan sinking-fund gold bonds, due Aug. 1, 1944; nos. 621, 1361, 1362, 16940–16944, 21025, 24896; 10 at $1,000 each	10,000.00	10,395.00	9,950.00
Pennsylvania Power & Light Co. 4½-percent first-mortgage bonds, due Apr. 1, 1981; nos. 50364–50379; 16 at $1,000 each	16,000.00	15,400.00	15,840.00
Total	92,333.00	92,145.50	91,548.00

SUMMARY

Book value of securities as above	$92,145.50
Cash in banks June 30, 1934	66,581.81
Bank of New York & Trust Co.	16,442.00
Income receivable as shown under column "Budget balance", receipts, page 121	196,792.08
National Academy of Sciences, special, advances from various funds	8,000.00
Property account, equipment at cost	33,151.18
Total assets	413,112.17

LIABILITIES

Capital invested in property	33,151.18
Current liabilities:	
Division appropriations as shown under column "Budget balance", disbursements, page 123	315,905.43
Unappropriated fund, general	53,674.54
National Academy of Sciences, special	10,000.00
Investment reserve fund	382.02
Contingent expenses, 1934	
Total liabilities	413,112.17

July 31, 1934.

ARTHUR KEITH, *Treasurer.*

REPORT OF THE AUDITING COMMITTEE

NATIONAL ACADEMY OF SCIENCES,
August 13, 1934.

Dr. W. W. CAMPBELL,
President National Academy of Sciences,
2101 Constitution Avenue, Washington, D. C.

DEAR PRESIDENT CAMPBELL: Availing itself of the provisions of section 5, article V, of the bylaws of the academy, the auditing committee engaged the services of the firm of William L. Yaeger & Co., public accountants, to audit the treasurer's accounts. This firm, after a systematic examination of the records of the treasurer and of the securities of the academy and the research council, has submitted a detailed report of its findings with exhibits attached. The committee has compared this report with that of the treasurer and adopts as its own the opinion of the accountants that the treasurer's report correctly presents the financial condition of the academy and the National Research Council and is an accurate statement of operations for the fiscal year ending June 30, 1934.

In compliance with the instructions to auditing committees contained in the bylaws of the academy, the accountants report that they have verified the record of receipts and disbursements maintained by the treasurer and the agreement of book and bank balances; examined all securities in the custody of the treasurer and the trustee of securities and found them to agree with the book records; examined all vouchers covering disbursements for the account of the academy, including the National Research Council, and the authority therefor, and compared them with the treasurer's record of expenditures, and examined and verified the account of the academy with each trust fund. The accountants furthermore state that they found the books of account well and securely kept and the securities in charge of the trustee conveniently filed as well as securely cared for.

The auditor's report is transmitted herewith to become a part of the records of the treasurer's office.

Very respectfully yours,

JOHN R. SWANTON, *Chairman.*
E. O. ULRICH.
W. C. MENDENHALL.
Auditing Committee, National Academy of Sciences, 1934.

NATIONAL ACADEMY OF SCIENCES

1. CONSTITUTION

[As amended and adopted Apr. 17, 1872, and further amended Apr. 20, 1875; Apr. 21, 1881; Apr. 19, 1882; Apr. 18, 1883; Apr. 19, 1888; Apr. 18, 1895; Apr. 20, 1899; Apr. 17, 1902; Apr. 18, 1906; Nov. 20, 1906; Apr. 17, 1907; Nov. 20, 1907; Apr. 20, 1911; Apr. 16, 1912; Apr. 21, 1915; Nov. 11, 1924; Nov. 9, 1925; Oct. 18, 1927; Nov. 18, 1929; Sept. 18, 1930; Apr. 24, 1933]

PREAMBLE

Empowered by the act of incorporation enacted by Congress, and approved by the President of the United States on the 3d day of March, A. D. 1863, and in conformity with amendments to said act approved July 14, 1870, June 20, 1884, and May 27, 1914, the National Academy of Sciences adopts the following amended constitution and bylaws:

ARTICLE I.—OF MEMBERS

SECTION 1. The academy shall consist of members, members emeriti, and foreign associates. Members must be citizens of the United States.

SEC. 2. Members who, from age or inability to attend the meetings of the academy, wish to resign the duties of active membership may, at their own request, be transferred to the roll of members emeriti by a vote of the academy.

SEC. 3. The academy may elect 50 foreign associates.

SEC. 4. Members emeriti and foreign associates shall have the privilege of attending the meetings and of reading and communicating papers to the academy, but shall take no part in its business, shall not be subject to its assessments, and shall be entitled to a copy of the publications of the academy.

ARTICLE II.—OF THE OFFICERS

SECTION 1. The officers of the academy shall be a president, a vice president, a foreign secretary, a home secretary, and a treasurer, all of whom shall be elected for a term of 4 years, by a majority of votes present, at the annual meeting of the year in which the current terms expire. The date of expiration of the terms of office shall be June 30. In case of a vacancy the election shall be held in the same manner at the meeting when such vacancy occurs or at the next stated meeting thereafter, as the academy may direct, and shall be for a term expiring on June 30 of the fourth year after that in which the election takes place. A vacancy in the office of treasurer or home secretary may, however, be filled by appointment of the president of the academy until the next stated meeting of the academy.

126

COUNCIL

SEC. 2. The officers of the academy, together with six members to be elected by the academy, and the chief executive officer of the National Research Council (provided he be a member of the academy), shall constitute a council for the transaction of such business as may be assigned to them by the constitution or the academy.

EXECUTIVE COMMITTEE

SEC. 3. There shall be an executive committee of the council of the academy, composed of seven members, consisting of the president and vice president of the academy, the chief executive officer of the National Research Council (provided he be a member of the academy), the home secretary of the academy, the treasurer of the academy, and additional members of the council of the academy appointed by the president.

Their term as members of the executive committee shall be coterminous with the term of their other office.

Except those powers dealing with nominations to membership in the academy, the executive committee between the meetings of the council shall have all the powers of the council of the academy, unless otherwise ordered by the council.

The members of the executive committee of the academy shall by virtue of their office be members of the executive board of the National Research Council and shall represent the academy at all its meetings.

The president and home secretary of the academy shall, respectively, be chairman and secretary of the executive committee.

In the absence of the president and the vice president or home secretary the executive committee may select from among its members a chairman or a secretary pro tem.

The executive committee shall keep regular minutes and shall report all of its proceedings to the council of the academy for their information.

Unless otherwise ordered by the council of the academy or the executive committee, the executive committee shall meet once in each calendar month, and a special meeting may be called at any time by authority of the chairman, on reasonable notice.

Four members of the executive committee shall constitute a quorum. Letter ballots shall not be valid unless ratified at a meeting.

CUSTODIAN OF BUILDINGS AND GROUNDS

SEC. 4. On recommendation of the president, the council of the academy shall appoint a "custodian of buildings and grounds", who, except where otherwise provided in the constitution and bylaws, shall have custody of all buildings, grounds, furniture, and other physical property belonging to the National Academy of Sciences or the National Research Council, or entrusted to their care.

He shall be responsible for and shall manage and administer these under such generic rules as the council of the academy may make, and shall approve all vouchers for pay rolls and disbursements that come under authorized budget items or are specifically authorized by the council of the academy for the maintenance and operation of the academy's and the research council's physical property.

He shall hold office at the pleasure of the council of the academy and shall receive such salary as it may agree and shall give such bond for the faithful performance of his duties as it may require.

He shall prepare and present to the finance committee of the academy the buildings and grounds division of the general budget.

ADVISORY COMMITTEE ON BUILDINGS AND GROUNDS

He shall be chairman of a joint advisory committee of five on buildings and grounds, of which two members shall be appointed by the president of the academy from the academy council, and two from the executive board of the National Research Council, which committee shall decide, subject to the approval of the council of the academy, all questions of allocation of space and use of public rooms.

FINANCE COMMITTEE

SEC. 5. There shall be a finance committee, of which the treasurer shall be chairman, consisting of the president of the academy (or in his absence the vice president), the treasurer, the chief executive officer of the National Research Council (provided he be a member of the academy), and two other members of the academy appointed by the president, one of whom shall be a member of the executive board of the National Research Council.

It shall be the duty of the finance committee to provide for the safe custody of all financial resources of the academy and to determine all matters relating to the purchase and sale of its securities.

It shall be the further duty of the finance committee to prepare and present to the council of the academy for adoption the "general budget", made up of the three "divisional budgets", of the academy proper, of the research council, and of buildings and grounds, which divisional budgets shall be presented to the finance committee, respectively, by the treasurer, the chief executive officer of the National Research Council, and the custodian of buildings and grounds.

The finance committee shall be empowered to employ competent investment counsel (hereinafter called the financial adviser) to advise with the committee upon the purchase and sale of all securities, mortgages or other investments.

PRESIDENT

SEC. 6. The president of the academy, or, in case of his absence or inability to act, the vice president, shall preside at the meetings of the academy, of the academy council, and of the executive board of the National Research Council; shall name all committees except such as are otherwise especially provided for; shall refer investigations required by the Government of the United States to members especially conversant with the subjects, and report thereon to the academy at its meeting next ensuing; and, with the council, shall direct the general business of the academy.

EXPERTS ON COMMITTEES

It shall be competent for the president, in special cases, to call in the aid, upon committees, of experts or men of special attainments not members of the academy.

GOVERNMENT REQUESTS

The president shall be ex-officio a member of all committees empowered to consider questions referred to the academy by the Government of the United States.

SECRETARIES

SEC. 7. The foreign and home secretaries shall conduct the correspondence proper to their respective departments, advising with the president and council in cases of doubt, and reporting their action to the academy at one of the stated meetings in each year.

It shall be the duty of the home secretary to give notice to the members of the place and time of all meetings, of all nominations for membership, and of all proposed amendments to the constitution.

It shall be the duty of the home secretary to keep the minutes of each business and scientific session and after approval to enter these upon the permanent records of the academy.

TREASURER

SEC. 8. The treasurer shall attend to all receipts and disbursements of the academy, giving such bond and furnishing such vouchers as the council may require. He shall collect all dues, assessments, and subscriptions, and keep a set of books showing a full account of receipts and disbursements and the condition of all funds of the academy. He shall be the custodian of the corporate seal of the academy.

ADMINISTRATIVE COMMITTEE, NATIONAL RESEARCH COUNCIL

SEC. 9. The president, vice president, home secretary, and treasurer shall be members of the administrative committee of the National Research Council and shall represent the academy at all its meetings.

ARTICLE III.—OF THE MEETINGS

ACADEMY

SECTION 1. The academy shall hold one stated meeting, called the annual meeting, in April of each year in the city of Washington, and another stated meeting, called the autumn meeting, at a place to be determined by the council. The council shall also have power to fix the date of each meeting.

Special business meetings of the academy may be called, by order of eight members of the council, at such place and time as may be designated in the call.

Special scientific meetings of the academy may be held at times and places to be designated by a majority of the council.

SEC. 2. The names of the members present at each session of a meeting shall be recorded in the minutes, and 20 members shall constitute a quorum for the transaction of business.

SEC. 3. Scientific sessions of the academy, unless otherwise ordered by a majority of the members present, shall be open to the public; sessions for the transaction of business shall be closed.

COUNCIL OF THE ACADEMY

SEC. 4. Stated meetings of the council shall be held during the stated or special meetings of the academy, and four members shall constitute a quorum for the transaction of business. Special meetings of the council may be convened at the call of the president and 2 members of the council or of 4 members of the council.

DUES IN ARREARS

SEC. 5. No member whose dues are in arrears shall vote at any business meeting of the academy.

ARTICLE IV.—OF ELECTIONS AND REGULATIONS

SECTION 1. All elections of officers and members shall be by ballot, and each election shall be held separately.

SEC. 2. The time for holding an election of officers shall be fixed by the academy at least 1 day before the election is held.

COUNCIL OF THE ACADEMY

SEC. 3. The election of six members of the council shall be as follows:

At the annual meeting in April 1907, 6 members of the council to be elected, of whom 2 shall serve for 3 years, 2 for 2 years, and 2 for 1 year, their respective terms to be determined by lot. Each year thereafter the terms of 2 members shall expire and their successors, to serve for 3 years, shall be elected at the annual meeting in each year. The date of expiration of the terms shall be June 30.

SECTIONS

SEC. 4. The academy shall be divided by the council into sections representing the principal branches of scientific research. Each section shall elect its own chairman to serve for 3 years. The chairman shall be responsible to the academy for the work of his section.

NOMINATIONS

Proposals for nomination to membership may be made in writing by any five members of the academy and addressed to the home secretary; each such proposal shall be accompanied by a record of the scientific activities of the person proposed and a list of his principal contributions to science, in triplicate; and with a statement as to the sections to which the name proposed shall be submitted for consideration. Such proposals as have been received by the home secretary prior to October 15 shall upon that date be sent by him to the chair-

man of the sections designated, with a copy of the record and list
of contributions.

· Nominations to membership in the academy shall be made in writing and approved by two-thirds of the members voting in a section
on the branch of research in which the person nominated is eminent;
or by a majority of the council in case there is no section on the subject, or by a majority (however distributed) of the members voting
in any two sections. The nomination shall be sent to the home
secretary by the chairman of the section before January 1 of the year
in which the election is to be held, and each nomination shall be
accompanied by a list of the principal contributions of the nominee
to science. This list shall be printed by the home secretary for
distribution among the members of the academy.

ELECTION PROCEDURE

SEC. 5. Election of members shall be held at the annual meeting
in Washington in the following manner: There shall be two ballots—
a preference ballot, which must be transmitted to the home secretary
in advance of the annual meeting, and a final ballot, to be taken at
the meeting.

PREFERENCE BALLOT

Preference ballot.—From the list of nominees submitted by the
home secretary, each member shall select and inscribe on a ballot,
to an extent not greater than one-half, nor less than one-third the
list, those names which he prefers, as these limits shall be interpreted
by the home secretary in his discretion, and announced by him, no
weight being attached to the order of the names, and ballots not
complying with these requirements being discarded. A list or the
nominees shall then be prepared, on which the names shall be entered
in the order of the number of votes received by each. In case two
or more nominees have the same number of votes on this preference
list, the order in which they shall be placed on the list shall be determined by a majority vote of members present.

After the preference list has been made up in the manner stated,
the chairman of any section having two or more nominees on the
list may, when its first nominee is reached, request the permission
of the academy to interchange the positions (on the preference list)
of the nominees of his section, without altering in any way the positions of nominees from other sections. If a majority of the members
of the academy present favor permitting a section to make such interchange of its own nominees, it shall be done before proceeding further
with the election.

FINAL BALLOT

A vote shall be taken on the nominee who appears first on the
preference list, and he shall be declared elected if he receive two-
thirds of the votes cast and not less than 30 votes in all. A vote
shall then be taken in similar manner on the nominee standing second
on the preference list, and so on until all the nominees on the preference list shall have been acted on, or until 15 nominees shall have
been elected, or until the total membership of the academy shall have
reached 300.

ELECTION

. Not more than 15 members shall be elected at one annual meeting.

It shall be in order at any point in the course of an election to move that the election be closed. If two-thirds of those present vote in favor of such motion, it shall prevail and the election shall thereupon terminate.

Before and during elections a discussion of the merits of nominees will be in order.

SEC. 6. Every member elected shall accept his membership, personally or in writing, before the close of the next stated meeting after the date of his election. Otherwise, on proof that the secretary has formally notified him of his election, his name shall not be entered on the roll of members.

FOREIGN ASSOCIATES

SEC. 7. Foreign associates may be nominated by the council and may be elected at the annual meeting by a two-thirds vote of the members present.

CERTIFICATES OF ELECTION

SEC. 8. A diploma, with the corporate seal of the academy and the signatures of the officers, shall be sent by the appropriate secretary to each member on his acceptance of membership, and to foreign associates on their election.

RESIGNATIONS

SEC. 9. Resignations shall be addressed to the president and acted on by the academy.

DUES, NONPAYMENT

SEC. 10. Whenever a member has not paid his dues for 4 successive years, the treasurer shall report the fact to the council, which may report the case to the academy with the recommendation that the person thus in arrears be declared to have forfeited his membership. If this recommendation be approved by two-thirds of the members present, the said person shall no longer be a member of the academy, and his name shall be dropped from the roll.

ARTICLE V.—OF SCIENTIFIC COMMUNICATIONS, PUBLICATIONS, AND REPORTS

SCIENTIFIC SESSIONS

SECTION 1. Communications on scientific subjects shall be read at scientific sessions of the academy, and papers by any member may be read by the author or by any other member, notice of the same having been previously given to the secretary.

SEC. 2. Any member of the academy may read a paper from a person who is not a member and shall not be considered responsible for the facts or opinions expressed by the author, but shall be held responsible for the propriety of the paper.

Persons who are not members may read papers on invitation of the council or of the committee of arrangements.

PUBLICATIONS

SEC. 3. The academy may provide for the publication, under the direction of the council, of Proceedings, scientific Memoirs, Biographical Memoirs, and reports.

PROCEEDINGS

The Proceedings shall be primarily a medium of first publication for original articles in brief form of permanent scientific value.

MEMOIRS

. The scientific Memoirs shall provide opportunity for the publication of longer and more detailed scientific investigations.

The Biographical Memoirs shall contain an appropriate record of the life and work of the deceased members of the academy.

ANNUAL REPORT

. An annual report shall be presented to Congress by the president and shall contain the annual reports of the treasurer and the auditing committee, a suitable summary of the reports of the committees in charge of trust funds, and a record of the activities of the academy. for the fiscal year immediately preceding, and other appropriate matter. This report shall be presented to Congress by the president after authorization by the council. It shall also be presented to the academy at the annual meeting next following.

TREASURER'S REPORT

The treasurer shall prepare a full report of the financial affairs of the academy at the end of the fiscal year. This report shall be submitted to the council for approval and afterwards presented to the academy at the next stated meeting. He shall also prepare a supplementary financial statement to December 31 of the ensuing fiscal year for presentation at the annual meeting.

GOVERNMENT REQUESTS

. SEC. 4. Propositions for investigations or reports by the academy shall be submitted to the council for approval, except those requested by the Government of the United States, which shall be acted on by the president, who will in such cases report their results to the Government as soon as obtained and to the academy at its next following stated meeting.

SEC. 5. The advice of the academy shall be at all times at the disposition of the Government upon any matter of science or art within its scope.

ARTICLE VI.—OF TRUST FUNDS AND THEIR ADMINISTRATION

TRUSTS

SECTION 1. Devises, bequests, donations, or gifts having for their object the promotion of science or the welfare of the academy may be accepted by the council for the academy.   Before the acceptance of any such trust the council shall consider the object of the trust and all conditions or specifications attaching thereto.   The council shall make a report of its action to the academy.

MEDALS

SEC. 2. Medals and prizes may be established in accordance with the provisions of trusts or by action of the academy.

TRUST FUND COMMITTEES

SEC. 3. Unless otherwise provided by the deed of gift, the income of each trust fund shall be applied to the objects of that trust by the action of the academy on the recommendation of a standing committee on that fund.

ARTICLE VII.—OF ADDITIONS AND AMENDMENTS

Additions and amendments to the constitution shall be made only at a stated meeting of the academy.   Notice of a proposition for such a change must be submitted to the council, which may amend the proposition, and shall report thereon to the academy.   Its report shall be considered by the academy in committee of the whole for amendment.

The proposition as amended, if adopted in committee of the whole, shall be voted on at the next stated meeting, and if it receives two-thirds of the votes cast it shall be declared adopted.

Absent members may send their votes on pending changes in the constitution to the home secretary in writing, and such votes shall be counted as if the members were present.

2. BYLAWS

[In accordance with a resolution of the academy, taken at its meeting on Apr. 21, 1915, the bylaws are arranged in groups, and each group is numbered to correspond with the article of the constitution to which it relates]

I

1. The holders of the medal for eminence in the application of science to the public welfare shall be notified, like members, of the meetings of the academy, and invited to participate in its scientific sessions.

II

1. The proper secretary shall acknowledge all donations made to the academy, and shall at once report them to the council for its consideration.

2. The home secretary shall keep a record of all grants of money or awards of prizes or medals made from trust funds of the academy. The record for each grant of money shall include the following items: Name of fund, date and number of the grant, name and address of recipient, amount of grant and date or dates of payment, purpose of grant, record of report of progress, and resulting publications.

3. The executive secretary, who may be a nonmember of the academy, shall receive a salary to be fixed by the council.

· 4. The treasurer shall keep the home secretary informed of all warrants received from directors of trust funds not controlled by the academy and of the date or dates of payment of all warrants.

GOVERNMENT REQUESTS

5. The treasurer is authorized to defray, when approved by the president, all the proper expenses of committees appointed to make scientific investigations at the request of departments of the Government, and in each case to look to the department requesting the investigation for reimbursement to the academy.

TREASURER, NATIONAL RESEARCH COUNCIL

· 6. The treasurer is authorized to act as the treasurer ex officio of the National Research Council.

BURSAR

· 7. The treasurer shall have the assistance of a salaried and bonded officer, the bursar, who shall be chosen by the finance committee and be directly responsible to the treasurer.

INVESTMENTS

8. All investments and reinvestments of either principal or accumulations of income of the trust and other funds of the academy shall be made by the treasurer, in accordance with the decisions of the finance committee, in the corporate name of the academy, in the manner and in the securities designated or specified in the instruments creating the several funds, or, in the absence of such designation or specification, in bonds of the United States or of the several States, or in bonds or notes secured by first mortgages on real estate, in investments legal for savings banks under the laws of Massachusetts or New York, or in other securities recommended by the financial adviser.

The treasurer may invest the capital of all trust funds of the academy which are not required by the instruments creating such funds to be kept separate and distinct, in a consolidated fund, and shall apportion the income received from such consolidated fund among the various funds composing the same in the proportion that each of said funds shall bear to the total amount of funds so invested: *Provided, however,* That the treasurer shall at all times keep accurate accounts showing the amount of each trust fund, the proportion of the income from the consolidated fund to which it is entitled, and the expenses and disbursements properly chargeable to such fund.

The treasurer shall have authority, with the approval of the finance committee, to sell, transfer, convey, and deliver in the corporate name and for the benefit of the academy any stocks, bonds, or other securities standing in the corporate name.

CUSTODIAN OF SECURITIES

9. On the recommendation of the finance committee, the council shall contract with a bank, trust company, or corresponding fiduciary institution to serve as the custodian of securities, including all of the

academy's personal property in the form of bonds, mortgages, and other securities, to collect the income from them, to protect the academy in respect to expirations, reissues, and notifications, and to buy or sell securities on the order of the treasurer, as approved by the finance committee.

CONTRACTS

10. No contract shall be binding upon the academy which has not been first approved by the council.

DUES

11. The assessments required for the support of the academy shall be fixed by the academy on the recommendation of the council and shall be payable within the calendar year for which they are assessed.

FINANCE COMMITTEE MEETINGS

12. The finance committee may invite to be present at any of its meetings the chief executive officer of the research council, the custodian of buildings and grounds, and the bursar, but they shall not vote.

III

ANNUAL MEETING—DATES AND PROCEDURES

1. The annual meeting of the academy shall begin on the fourth Monday of April.[1] At the business sessions of the academy the order of procedure shall be as follows:
(1) Chair taken by the president, or, in his absence, by the vice president.
(2) Roll of members called by home secretary (first session of the meeting only).
(3) Minutes of the preceding session read and approved.
(4) Stated business.
(5) Reports of president, secretaries, treasurer, and committees.
(6) Business from council.
(7) Other business.

RULES OF ORDER

2. The rules of order of the academy shall be those of the Senate of the United States, unless otherwise provided by the constitution or bylaws of the academy.
3. In the absence of any officer, a member shall be chosen to perform his duties temporarily, by a plurality of viva voce votes, upon open nomination.

DEATHS

4. At each meeting the president shall announce the death of any members since the preceding meeting. As soon as practicable thereafter he shall designate a member to write—or to secure from some other source, approved by the president—a biographical notice of each deceased member.

---

[1] The first sentence of bylaw III;1 was deleted by action of the academy in business session on November 19, 1934.

LOCAL COMMITTEE

5. For the annual meeting a local committee of five members, appointed for each meeting, and the home secretary shall constitute the committee of arrangements, of which the home secretary shall be chairman. For the autumn meeting a member of the local group shall be chairman of the local committee, of which the home secretary shall be a member ex officio.

SCIENTIFIC PROGRAM

It shall be the duty of the committee of arrangements to prepare the scientific program for the annual meeting, and for this purpose it shall be empowered to solicit papers from members or others. It shall also be empowered to ascertain the length of time required for reading papers to be presented at the scientific sessions of the academy and, when it appears advisable, to limit the time to be occupied in their presentation or discussion.

The committee of arrangements shall meet not less than 2 months previous to each meeting. It shall prepare the detailed program of each day and in general shall have charge of all business and scientific arrangements for the meeting for which it is appointed.

PAPERS—TIME LIMIT

6. No paper requiring more than 15 minutes for its presentation shall be accepted unless by invitation of the committee of arrangements.

No speaker shall occupy more than 30 minutes for presentation of papers during the scientific sessions of a single meeting of the academy, except by invitation of the committee of arrangements.

Time shall not be extended except by vote of the academy, and then not to exceed 5 minutes. The presiding officer shall warn speakers 2 minutes before the expiration of their time.

The discussion of individual papers shall be limited not to exceed 5 minutes, and the total time for discussion by any one speaker for all scientific sessions in any one meeting shall not exceed 15 minutes, unless approved by the academy.

In order that adequate opportunity be given for the discussion of papers on the program the committee of arrangements shall, in making up the program for the scientific sessions, allot not more than 80 percent of the available time of each session to the actual reading of papers.

If the number of papers accepted is too large to be presented in the scientific sessions, provision shall be made for holding two or more sessions simultaneously.

In arranging the program the committee of arrangements shall group the papers as nearly as practicable according to subject.

No paper shall be entered upon the printed program of scientific sessions unless the title is in the hands of the committee of arrangements at least 2 weeks in advance of the meeting. In the event that titles are received later, they shall be placed in order of receipt at the end of the list and read, if there is time. Such supplementary titles shall be conspicuously posted.

IV

SECTIONS

1. The term of service of each chairman of a section shall be 3 years, to date from the closing session of the April meeting next following his election. Chairmen of sections shall be chosen by mail ballot, the member receiving the highest number of votes cast to be deemed elected. It shall be the duty of each retiring chairman to conduct the election of his successor, and to report the results of the election to the home secretary before the April meeting at which his term of service expires. Should any section fail to elect a chairman before November 1, the president is empowered to appoint a temporary chairman to serve until the April meeting next following. No chairman shall be eligible for reelection for two consecutive terms.

NOMINATION BALLOTS

2. The chairman of each section of the academy shall submit to the members of his section, not later than November 1 of each year, a ballot containing the names of all those persons who received not less than two votes in the nominating ballot of the preceding year, or have been submitted to the chairman by the home secretary, and of any other persons who were newly proposed for consideration on the nominating ballots of the preceding year. Each member of the section shall be expected to return this ballot to the chairman within 2 weeks with his signature and with crosses against the names of those persons whom he is prepared to endorse for nomination. Each member may also write upon the ballot in a place provided for the purpose any new names he desires to have included in the ballot to be submitted to the section in the following years. The vote resulting from this ballot shall be regarded as informal.

The chairman shall then submit to the members of his section a new ballot showing the results of the informal vote; and each member shall be expected to return this ballot to the chairman with his signature and with crosses placed against the names of three persons whom he judges to be most worthy of nomination. In order to secure an adequate number of nominations, the chairman, when necessary, shall obtain by personal solicitation a fuller vote of his section or shall submit to the section a supplementary formal ballot.

The chairman shall then certify to the home secretary, prior to January 1, the names of all persons who have been voted for on the formal ballots, together with a statement of the number of votes each received and of the number of members voting. Of these, all persons who receive the votes of two-thirds of the members voting in the section in cases voted upon by one section only, or the votes of one-half (however distributed) of the members voting in any two sections in cases voted upon by more than one section, shall be considered nominated.

3. Nominations for membership shall give the full name, residence, and the official positions successively held by the candidate, in addition to the list of his contributions to science required by the constitution.

PREFERENCE BALLOT

4. Preference ballots for the election of members shall be sealed in a blank envelope, which shall be enclosed in another bearing the name of the sender, and which shall be addressed to the home secretary, who shall cause the ballots to be tabulated for use at the election. If in any case it is impossible to determine who cast the ballot, or if the latter contain more or fewer than the number of names provided for in article IV, section 5, of the constitution, the ballot shall be rejected, but minor defects in a ballot shall be disregarded when the intent of the voter is obvious.

5. All discussions of the claims and qualifications of nominees at meetings of the academy shall be held strictly confidential, and remarks and criticisms then made may be communicated to no person who was not a member of the academy at the time of the discussion.

V

PROCEEDINGS

1. The publication of the Proceedings shall be under the general charge of the council, which shall have final jurisdiction upon all questions of policy relating thereto.

The National Academy of Sciences and the National Research Council shall cooperate in the publication of the Proceedings, beginning with volume VII.

MEMOIRS

2. Memoirs may be presented at any time to the home secretary, who shall report the date of their reception at the next session; but no Memoir shall be published unless it has been read or presented by title before the academy.

Before publication all Biographical and scientific Memoirs must be referred to the committee on publication, who may, if they deem best, refer any Memoir to a special committee, appointed by the president, to determine whether the same should be published by the academy.

3. Memoirs shall date, in the records of the academy, from the date of their presentation to the academy, and the order of their presentation shall be so arranged by the secretary that, so far as may be convenient, those upon kindred topics shall follow one another.

TREASURER'S REPORT

4. The annual report of the treasurer shall contain—

(1) A concise statement of the source, object, and amount of all trust funds of the academy.

(2) A condensed statement of receipts and expenditures.

(3) A statement of assets and liabilities.

(4) Accounts with individual funds.

(5) Such other matter as he considers appropriate.

AUDITING COMMITTEE

5. The accounts of the treasurer shall, between July 1 and August 1 of each year, be audited under the direction of a committee of three members to be appointed by the president at the annual meeting of the academy. It shall be the duty of the auditing committee to verify the record of receipts and disbursements maintained by the treasurer and the agreement of book and bank balances; to examine all securities in the custody of the treasurer and the custodian of securities and to compare the stated income of such securities with the receipts of record; to examine all vouchers covering disbursements for account of the academy, including the National Research Council, and the authority therefor, and to compare them with the treasurer's record of expenditures; to examine and verify the account of the academy with each trust fund. The auditing committee may employ an expert accountant to assist the committee. The reports of the treasurer and auditing committee shall be presented to the academy at the autumn meeting and shall be published with that of the president to Congress. They shall be distributed to the members in printed form at the annual meeting.

VI

PROPERTY

1. All apparatus and other materials of permanent value purchased with money from any grant from a trust fund shall be the property of the academy unless specific exception is made in the grant or by subsequent action of the council. Receipts for all such property shall be signed by the grantee and shall be forwarded to the home secretary, who shall file them with the custodian of buildings and grounds. All apparatus and unused material of value acquired in this way shall be delivered to the custodian of buildings and grounds on completion of the investigation for which the grant was made, or at any time on demand of the council, and the custodian of buildings and grounds shall give an appropriate release therefor.

2. A stamp corresponding to the corporate seal of the academy shall be kept by the secretaries, who shall be responsible for the due markings of all books and other objects to which it is applicable.

Labels or other proper marks of similar device shall be placed upon objects not admitting of the stamp.

3. The fiscal year of the academy shall end on June 30 of each year.

VII

STANDING COMMITTEES—RESEARCH FUNDS

1. Standing committees of the academy on trust funds, the income of which is applied to the promotion of research, shall consist of 3 or 5 members. In order to secure rotation in office in such committees, when not in conflict with the provisions of the deeds of gift, the term of service on a committee of 3 members shall be 3 years; on a committee of 5 members the term shall be 5 years.

2. The annual reports of the committees on research funds shall, so far as the academy has authority to determine their form, give a current number to each award, stating the name, position, and address of the recipient; the subject of research for which the award

is made and the sum awarded; and in later annual reports the status of the work accomplished under each award previously made shall be announced, until the research is completed, when announcement of its completion, and, if published, the title and place of publication shall be stated, and the record of the award shall be reported as closed.

VIII

AMENDMENTS

1. Any bylaw of the academy may be amended, suspended, or repealed on the written motion of any two members, signed by them, and presented at a stated meeting of the academy, provided the same shall be approved by a majority of the members present.

3. ORGANIZATION OF THE ACADEMY

JULY 1, 1934 — *Expiration of term*

Campbell, W. W., president	June 30, 1935
Day, A. L., vice president	June 30, 1937
Morgan, T. H., foreign secretary	June 30, 1936
Wright, F. E., home secretary	June 30, 1935
Keith, Arthur, treasurer	June 30, 1936

ADDITIONAL MEMBERS OF THE COUNCIL

1932–35:	1933–36:	1934–37:
Harrison, R. G.	Compton, K. T.	Adams, Roger
Russell, H. N.	Cattell, J. McKeen	Jennings, H. S.

1933–35:
Bowman, Isaiah, ex officio, as chairman of the National Research Council [1]

EXECUTIVE COMMITTEE OF THE COUNCIL

Campbell, W. W. (chairman)	Day, A. L.	Russell, H. N.
Bowman, Isaiah [1]	Harrison, R. G.	Wright, F. E.
	Keith, Arthur	

SECTIONS

1. *Mathematics*

Coble, A. B. (chairman), 1937	Dickson, L. E.	Osgood, W. F.
Alexander, J. W.	Eisenhart, L. P.	Ritt, J. F.
Bateman, Harry	Evans, G. C.	Vandiver, H. S.
Bell, E. T.	Kasner, Edward	Van Vleck, E. B.
Birkhoff, G. D.	Lefschetz, Solomon	Veblen, Oswald
Blichfeldt, H. F.	Miller, G. A.	White, H. S.
Bliss, G. A.	Moore, R. L.	Wiener, Norbert
	Morse, Marston	

2. *Astronomy*

Stebbins, Joel (chairman), 1935	Curtis, H. D.	Russell, H. N.
Abbot, C. G.	Frost, E. B.	St. John, C. E.
Adams, W. S.	Hale, G. E.	Schlesinger, F.
Aitken, R. G.	Hubble, E. P.	Seares, F. H.
Anderson, J. A.	Leuschner, A. O.	Shapley, Harlow
Babcock, H. D.	Merrill, P. W.	Slipher, V. M.
Bowie, William	Mitchell, S. A.	Trumpler, R. J.
Brown, E. W.	Moore, J. H.	Wright, W. H.
Campbell, W. W.	Moulton, F. R.	
	Ross, F. E.	

---

[1] The constitution of the academy specifies that the chairman of the National Research Council be a member of the council of the academy and a member of the executive committee of the council of the academy, provided he be a member of the academy.

3. Physics

Hull, A. W. (chairman), 1936.
Ames, J. S.
Barus, Carl.
Birge, R. T.
Bridgman, P. W.
Coblentz, W. W.
Compton, A. H.
Compton, K. T.
Coolidge, W. D.
Crew, Henry
Davis, Bergen

Davisson, C. J.
Duane, William
Epstein, P. S.
Hall, E. H.
Ives, H. E.
Kemble, E. C.
Lawrence, E. O.
Lyman, Theodore
Mason, Max
Mendenhall, C. E.
Merritt, Ernest
Miller, D. C.

Millikan, R. A.
Nichols, E. L.
Pierce, G. W.
Pupin, M. I.
Richtmyer, F. K.
Saunders, F. A.
Slater, J. C.
Thomson, Elihu
Webster, D. L.
Wilson, Edwin B.
Wood, R. W.

4. Engineering

Durand, W. F. (temporary chairman), 1935
Adams, C. A.
Bush, Vannevar
Dunn, Gano
Emmet, W. L. R.
Gherardi, Bancroft

Hoover, Herbert
Hovgaard, William
Jewett, F. B.
Kennelly, A. E.
Kettering, C. F.
Modjeski, Ralph
Ryan, H. J.

Sauveur, Albert
Stillwell, L. B.
Swasey, Ambrose
Taylor, D. W.
Whitehead, J. B.

5. Chemistry

Kohler, E. P. (chairman), 1935
Adams, Roger
Bancroft, W. D.
Baxter, G. P.
Bogert, Marston T.
Bray, W. C.
Conant, J. B.
Franklin, E. C.
Gomberg, Moses
Harkins, W. D.

Hildebrand, J. H.
Hudson, C. S.
Hulett, G. A.
Jacobs, W. A.
Johnson, T. B.
Keyes, F. G.
Kraus, C. A.
Lamb, A. B.
Langmuir, Irving.
Levene, P. A. T.
Lewis, G. N.

Lind, S. C.
Michael, Arthur
Norris, J. F.
Noyes, A. A.
Noyes, W. A.
Pauling, Linus
Stieglitz, Julius
Tolman, R. C.
Whitney, W. R.

6. Geology and Paleontology

Leith, C. K. (chairman), 1936
Allen, E. T.
Berkey, C. P.
Berry, E. W.
Bowman, Isaiah
Cross, Whitman
Daly, R. A.
Dana, E. S.
Day, A. L.

Johnson, D. W.
Keith, Arthur
Knopf, Adolph
Lawson, A. C.
Leverett, Frank
Lindgren, Waldemar
Mendenhall, W. C.
Merriam, J. C.
Osborn, H. F.
Palache, Charles

Ransome, F. L.
Reid, H. F.
Ruedemann, Rudolf
Schuchert, Charles
Scott, W. B.
Ulrich, E. O.
Vaughan, T. W.
White, David
Willis, Bailey
Wright, F. E.

7. Botany

Merrill, E. D. (chairman), 1935
Allen, C. E.
Bailey, I. W.
Bailey, L. H.
Blakeslee, A. F.
Campbell, D. H.
Clinton, G. P.

Dodge, B. O.
Duggar, B. M.
East, E. M.
Emerson, R. A.
Fred, E. B.
Harper, R. A.
Hoagland, D. R.
Howe, M. A.

Jones, L. R.
Kunkel, L. O.
Osterhout, W. J. V.
Robinson, B. L.
Setchell, W. A.
Stakman, E. C.
Trelease, William

8. Zoology and Anatomy

Lillie, F. R. (chairman), 1937
Barbour, Thomas
Bigelow, H. B.
Calkins, G. N.
Castle, W. E.
Chapman, F. M.
Conklin, E. G.
Davenport, C. B.
Detwiler, S. R.
Donaldson, H. H.
Gregory, W. K.

Harrison, R. G.
Harvey, E. N.
Herrick, C. J.
Howard, L. O.
Jennings, H. S.
Kellogg, Vernon
Kofoid, C. A.
McClung, C. E.
Mark, E. L.
Morgan, T. H.
Muller, H. J.
Parker, G. H.

Pearl, Raymond
Stejneger, Leonhard
Stockard, C. R.
Streeter, G. L.
Sturtevant, A. H.
Tennent, D. H.
Wheeler, W. M.
Wilson, Edmund B.
Wilson, H. V. P.
Woodruff, L. L.
Wright, S. G.

9. Physiology and Biochemistry

Henderson, L. J. (chairman), 1936
Abel, J. J.
Benedict, F. G.
Benedict, S. R.
Cannon, W. B.
Carlson, A. J.
Chittenden, R. H.

Clark, W. M.
DuBois, E. F.
Erlanger, Joseph
Evans, H. M.
Folin, Otto
Gasser, H. S.
Henderson, Yandell
Howell, W. H.

Hunt, Reid
Jones, Walter
McCollum, E. V.
Mendel, L. B.
Richards, A. N.
Shaffer, P. A.
Sherman, H. C.
Van Slyke, D. D.

10. Pathology and Bacteriology

Hektoen, Ludvig (chairman), 1936
Avery, O. T.
Cole, Rufus
Cushing, Harvey
Dochez, A. R.
Flexner, Simon

Landsteiner, Karl
MacCallum, W. G.
Northrop, J. H.
Novy, F. G.
Opie, E. L.
Rivers, T. M.
Rous, Peyton

Sabin, Florence R.
Smith, Theobald
Wells, H. Gideon
Whipple, G. H.
Zinsser, Hans

11. Anthropology and Psychology

Woodworth, R. S. (chairman), 1935
Angell, J. R.
Boas, Franz
Boring, E. G.
Breasted, J. H.
Cattell, J. McKeen
Dewey, John
Dodge, Raymond

Hrdlicka, Ales
Kroeber, A. L.
Lashley, K. S.
Laufer, Berthold
Lowie, R. H.
Merriam, C. H.
Miles, W. R.
Pillsbury, W. B.
Sapir, Edward

Seashore, C. E.
Stratton, G. M.
Swanton, J. R.
Terman, L. M.
Thorndike, E. L.
Washburn, Margaret F.
Wissler, Clark
Yerkes, R. M.

4. STANDING COMMITTEES OF THE ACADEMY

ALBERT NATIONAL PARK

Yerkes, R. M. (chairman)
Chapman, F. M.
Wissler, Clark

AUDITING COMMITTEE

Swanton, J. R. (chairman)
Mendenhall, W. C.
Ulrich, E. O.

BIOGRAPHICAL MEMOIRS

Davenport, C. B. (chairman)
Hrdlicka, Ales.
Thorndike, E. L.
White, David
Wright, F. E.

BUILDING COMMITTEE (ORIGINAL JOINT COMMITTEE OF ACADEMY AND RESEARCH COUNCIL ON CONSTRUCTION)

Dunn, Gano (chairman)
Brockett, Paul (secretary)
Hale, G. E.
Howe, H. E.
Kello, Vernon
Merriam, J. C.
Millikan, R. A.
No__ A. A.

BUILDINGS AND GROUNDS ADVISORY COMMITTEE (JOINT COMMITTEE OF ACADEMY AND RESEARCH COUNCIL)

Brockett, Paul (chairman)

Day, A. L.
Kellogg, Vernon

White, David
Wright, F. E.

CALENDAR

Wright, F. E. (chairman)
Campbell, W. W.

Dunn, Gano
Millikan, R. A.

Russell, H. N.

CONSERVATION OF NATIONAL RESOURCES

Merriam, J. C. (chairman
Bowman, Isaiah

Cattell, J. McKeen
Merrill, E. D.
White, David

Wissler, Clark
Wright, F. E.

EXHIBITS (JOINT COMMITTEE OF ACADEMY AND RESEARCH COUNCIL)

Wright, F. E. (chairman)
Brockett, Paul (secretary)
Hale, G. E. (member at large)

Shapley, Harlow (member at large)
The chairman of each of the sections of the academy

The chairman of each of the divisions of the research council

Executive Committee on Exhibits

Wright, F. E. (chairman)
Brockett, Paul (secretary)

Day, A. L.
Hale, G. E.
Kellogg, Vernon

Merriam, J. C.

FINANCE COMMITTEE

The treasurer of the academy, chairman ex officio

The president of the academy, ex officio (or in his absence, the vice president)

The chairman of the National Research Council, ex officio
Abbot, C. G.
Dunn, Gano

FUNDS FOR ACADEMY PURPOSES

Flexner, Simon (chairman)

Kellogg, Vernon
Shapley, Harlow

White, David

FUNDS FOR PUBLICATION OF RESEARCH

Pearl, Raymond (chairman)

Conklin, E. G.
Day, A. L.

Veblen, Oswald.

GOVERNMENT RELATIONS

Merriam, J. C. (chairman)
The president of the academy
The vice president of the academy

The chairman of the research council
The chairman of the division of Federal relations of the research council

The chairman of each of the sections of the academy
Wright, F. E.

Subcommittee A (Physical Sciences)

Merriam, J. C. (chairman)
Hull, A. W.
Kohler, E. P.
Leith, C. K.

Stebbins, Joel
Wilson, Edwin B.
The president of the academy

The home secretary of the academy

Subcommittee B (Biological Sciences).

Merriam, J. C. (chairman)
Angell, J. R.
Hektoen, Ludvig
Lillie, F. R.

Merrill, E. D.
Woodworth, R. S.
The president of the academy

The home secretary of the academy

LIBRARY

White, David (chairman)
Adams, W. S.
Cattell, J. McK.

Compton, K. T.
Henderson, Yandell
Lillie, F. R.

Parker, G. H.
Scott, W. B.
Brockett, Paul

Subcommittee

Hudson, C. S. (chairman), 1937
Coblentz, W. W. (vice chairman), 1937

Pearl, Raymond, 1936.
Streeter, G. S., 1936

Swanton, John R., 1935

LONG-RANGE WEATHER FORECASTING

Merriam, John C. (chairman
Abbot, C. G.
Bigelow, H. B.

Bowman, Isaiah
Compton, Karl T.
Kennelly, A. E.
Marvin, C. F.

Taylor, D. W.
Vaughan, T. W.
Willis, Bailey
Wilson, Edwin B.

OCEANOGRAPHY

Lillie, F. R. (chairman)
Bigelow, H. B. (secretary)

Bowie, William
Conklin, E. G.
Day, A. L.

Duggar, B. M.
Merriam, J. C.
Vaughan, T. W.

PROCEEDINGS, EDITORIAL BOARD

Blake, F. G.
Bowman, Isaiah
Day, A. L.
Duane, William
Dunn, Gano
Eisenhart, L. P.
Harrison, R. G.

Henderson, L. J.
Jewett, F. B.
Kettering, C. F.
Lewis, I. F.
Millikan, R. A.
Osterhout, W. J. V.
Poffenberger, A. T.

Richtmyer, F. K.
Schlesinger, Frank
Twenhofel, W. H.
Washington, H. S.
Wheeler, W. M.
Willard, F. W.
Wright, F. E.

PUBLICATIONS OF THE ACADEMY

The president

The home secretary

Conklin, E. G.

REVISION OF THE CONSTITUTION

Wilson, Edwin B. (chairman)

Day, A. L.
Dunn, Gano.

Merriam, J. C.
Morgan, T. H.

SCIENTIFIC PROBLEMS OF NATIONAL PARKS

Merriam, J. C. (chairman)

White, David
Whiting, Frederic Allen

Wright, F. E.

WEIGHTS, MEASURES, AND COINAGE

Kennelly, A. E. (chairman)
Ames, J. S.

Baxter, G. P.
Bowie, William

Mendenhall, C. E.
Wood, R. W.

5. TRUST FUNDS OF THE ACADEMY

ALEXANDER DALLAS BACHE FUND

[$60,000]

Researches in physical and natural science

Board of directors

Curtis, Heber D. (chair- Osterhout, W. J. V.   Wilson, Edwin B.
man)

JAMES CRAIG WATSON FUND

[$25,000]

Watson medal and the promotion of astronomical research

Trustees

Leuschner, A. O. (chairman)   Ross, F. E.

WATSON MEDAL AWARDS

Gould, B. A., 1887	Chandler, S. C., 1894	Leuschner, A. O., 1915
Schoenfeld, Ed., 1889	Gill, Sir David, 1899	Charlier, C. V. L., 1924
Auwers, Arthur, 1891	Kapteyn, J. C., 1913	de Sitter, Willem, 1929

HENRY DRAPER FUND

[$10,000]

Draper medal and investigations in astronomical physics

Members of the committee

Slipher, V. M. (chairman), 1937	Aitken, R. G., 1935	Shapley, Harlow, 1936
	Merrill, P. W., 1939	Stebbins, Joel, 1938

HENRY DRAPER MEDAL AWARDS

Langley, S. P., 1886	Abbot, C. G., 1910	Russell, H. N., 1922
Pickering, E. C., 1888	Deslandres, H., 1913	Eddington, A. S., 1924
Rowland, H. A., 1890	Stebbins, Joel, 1915	Shapley, Harlow, 1926
Vogel, H. K., 1893	Michelson, A. A., 1916	Wright, William Hammond, 1928
Keeler, J. E., 1899	Adams, W. S., 1918	
Huggins, Sir Wm., 1901	Fabry, Charles, 1919	Cannon, Annie Jump, 1931
Hale, George E., 1904	Fowler, Alfred, 1920	
Campbell, W. W., 1906	Zeeman, Pieter, 1921	Slipher, V. M., 1932

J. LAWRENCE SMITH FUND

[$10,000]

J. Lawrence Smith medal and investigations of meteoric bodies

Members of the committee

Schlesinger, F. (chairman, 1935	Abbot, C. G., 1936	Moulton, F. R., 1937
	Allen, E. T., 1938	Ransome, F. L., 1939

J. LAWRENCE SMITH MEDAL AWARDS

Newton, H. A., 1888   Merrill, George P., 1922

BARNARD MEDAL FOR MERITORIOUS SERVICES TO SCIENCE [1]

Discoveries in physical or astronomical science or novel application of science to purposes beneficial to the human race

---

[1] Every 5 years the committee recommends the person whom they consider most deserving of the medal, and upon approval by the academy the name of the nominee is forwarded to the trustees of Columbia University, who administer the Barnard medal fund.

Members of the committee

Day, Arthur L. (chair- Campbell, W. W. Noyes, A. A.
man)   Davis, Bergen   Tolman, R. C.

BARNARD MEDAL AWARDS

Rutherford, (Lord) Ernest, Bragg, (Sir) William H., Bohr, Niels, 1925
1909   1914   Heisenberg, Werner, 1930
       Einstein, Albert, 1921

BENJAMIN APTHORP GOULD FUND

[$20,000]

Researches in astronomy

Board of directors

Moulton, F. R. (chair- Brown, E. W.   Curtis, H. D.
man)

WOLCOTT GIBBS FUND

[$5,545.50]

Chemical research

Board of directors

Kohler, E. P. (chairman) Baxter, G. P.   Franklin, E. C.

CYRUS B. COMSTOCK FUND

[$12,406.02]

Prize awarded every 5 years for most important discovery or investigation in electricity, magnetism, and radiant energy, or to aid worthy investigations in those subjects

Members of the committee

Mason, Max (chairman), Coolidge, W. D., 1939 Compton, A. H., 1938
1935   Crew, Henry, 1937 Miller, D. C., 1936

COMSTOCK PRIZE AWARDS

Millikan, R. A., 1913 Duane, William, 1923. Davisson, C. J., 1928
Barnett, S. J., 1918   Bridgman, P. W., 1933

MARSH FUND

[$20,000]

Original research in the natural sciences

Members of the committee

Vaughan, T. W. (chair- Berry, E. W., 1938 Merrill, E. D., 1935
man), 1936   Gregory, W. K., 1937 Reid, H. F., 1939

AGASSIZ FUND

[$50,000]

General uses of the academy

MURRAY FUND

[$6,000]

Agassiz medal for contributions to oceanography

Members of the committee

Bigelow, H. B. (chair- Johnson, Douglas, 1936 Kofoid, C. A., 1937
man), 1935

AGASSIZ MEDAL AWARDS

Hjort, Johan, 1913
Albert I, Prince of Monaco, 1918
Sigsbee, C. D., 1920
Pettersson, Otto Sven, 1924
Bjerknes, Vilhelm, 1926

Weber, Max, 1927
Ekman, Vagn Walfrid, 1928
Gardiner, J. Stanley, 1929
Schmidt, Johannes, 1930
Bigelow, Henry Bryant, 1931

Defant, Albert, 1932
Helland - Hansen, Bjorn, 1933
Gran, Haakon Hasberg, 1934

MARCELLUS HARTLEY FUND

[$1, 200]

Medal for eminence in the application of science to the public welfare

Members of the committee

Cushing, Harvey (chairman), 1937
Ames, J. S., 1936

Hoover, Herbert, 1937
Mason, Max, 1935

Donaldson, H. H., 1936

PUBLIC WELFARE MEDAL AWARDS

(In memory of Marcellus Hartley)

Goethals, G. W., 1914
Gorgas, W. C., 1914
Abbe, Cleveland, 1916
Pinchot, Gifford, 1916
Stratton, S. W., 1917

Hoover, Herbert, 1920
Stiles, C. W., 1921
Chapin, Charles V., 1928
Mather, Stephen Tyng, 1930

Rose, Wickliffe, 1931
Park, William Hallock, 1932
Fairchild, David, 1933
Vollmer, August, 1934

DANIEL GIRAUD ELLIOT FUND

[$8,000]

Medal and honorarium for most meritorious work in zoology or paleontology published each year

Members of the committee

Harrison, Ross G. (chairman)

Osborn, H. F.

Wheeler, W. M.

DANIEL GIRAUD ELLIOT MEDAL AWARDS

Chapman, F. M., 1917
Beebe, William, 1918
Ridgway, Robert, 1919
Abel, Othenio, 1920
Dean, Bashford, 1921
Wheeler, Wm. Morton, 1922

Canu, Ferdinand, 1923
Breuil, Henri, 1924
Wilson, Edmund B., 1925
Son Stensio, Erik A., 1927
Seton, Ernest Thompson, 1928

Osborn, Henry Fairfield, 1929
Coghill, George Ellett, 1930
Black, Davidson, 1931
Chapin, James P., 1932

BILLINGS FUND

[$22,313.39]

For partial support of the Proceedings, or for such other purposes as the academy may select

MARY CLARK THOMPSON FUND

[$10,000]

Medal for most important services to geology and paleontology

Members of the committee

White, David (chairman), 1935

Lindgren, Waldemar, 1937

Mendenhall, W. C., 1936

MARY CLARK THOMPSON MEDAL AWARDS

Walcott, Charles Doolittle, 1921
Margerie, Emm. de, 1923
Clarke, John Mason, 1925
Smith, James Perrin, 1928

Scott, William Berryman, 1930
Ulrich, Edward Oscar, 1930
White, David, 1931

Bather, Francis Arthur, 1932
Schuchert, Charles, 1934

JOSEPH HENRY FUND

[$40,163.50]

To assist meritorious investigators, especially in the direction of original research

Members of the committee

Webster, D. L. (chairman), 1939

Jones, L. R., 1938
Taylor, D. W., 1936

Thorndike, E. L., 1935
Wilson, H. V., 1937

GEORGE TRUE NEALLEY FUND

[$19,555.55]

For the general purposes of the academy

CHARLES DOOLITTLE WALCOTT FUND

[$5,000]

For stimulation of research in pre-Cambrian or Cambrian life by award of a medal and honorarium

Board of directors

Schuchert, Charles (temporary chairman)

Abbot, C. G.[3]
Barrois, Charles [4]

Lang, W. D.[5]
Ulrich, E. O.

CHARLES DOOLITTLE WALCOTT MEDAL AWARD

White, David, 1934

JOHN J. CARTY FUND

[$25,000]

Medal and monetary award, not oftener than once in every 2 years, to an individual for noteworthy and distinguished accomplishment in any field of science coming within the scope of the charter of the academy

Members of the committee

Jewett, F. B. (chairman), 1936

Bancroft, W. D., 1937
Howell, W. H., 1938

Jennings, H. S., 1939
Osterhout, W. J. V., 1935

JOHN J. CARTY MEDAL AWARD

Carty, John J., 1932

CARNEGIE ENDOWMENT FUND

[$3,550,000]

For the purposes of the National Academy of Sciences and National Research Council

[3] Representing the Smithsonian Institution.
[4] Representing the Institut de France.
[5] Representing the Royal Society of London.

6. MEMBERS OF THE NATIONAL ACADEMY OF SCIENCES

JULY 1, 1934

Elected

Abbot, Charles Greeley, Smithsonian Institution, Washington, D. C_____ 1915
Abel, John Jacob, Department of Pharmacology, Johns Hopkins Medical
School, Baltimore, Md_____ 1912
Adams, Comfort Avery, Harvard Engineering School, Cambridge, Mass_ 1930
Adams, Roger, University of Illinois, Urbana, Ill_____ 1929
Adams, Walter Sydney, Mount Wilson Observatory, Pasadena, Calif____ 1917
Aitken, Robert Grant, Lick Observatory, Mount Hamilton, Calif_____ 1918
Alexander, James Waddell, Princeton, N. J_____ 1930
Allen, Charles Elmer, University of Wisconsin, Madison, Wis_____ 1924
Allen, Eugene Thomas, 1862 Mintwood Place, Washington, D. C_____ 1930
Ames, Joseph Sweetman, Johns Hopkins University, Baltimore, Md____ 1909
Anderson, John August, Mount Wilson Observatory, Pasadena, Calif____ 1928
Angell, James Rowland, Yale University, New Haven, Conn_____ 1920
Avery, Oswald Theodore, Rockefeller Institute for Medical Research,
Sixty-sixth Street and York Avenue, New York City_____ 1933
Babcock, Harold Delos, Mount Wilson Observatory, Pasadena, Calif____ 1933
Bailey, Irving Widmer, Bussey Institution, Forest Hills, Boston 30, Mass_ 1929
Bailey, Liberty Hyde, Ithaca, N. Y_____ 1917
Bancroft, Wilder Dwight, 7 East Avenue, Ithaca, N. Y_____ 1920
Barbour, Thomas, Museum of Comparative Zoology, Cambridge, Mass__ 1933
Barus, Carl, Brown University, Providence, R. I_____ 1892
Bateman, Harry, California Institute of Technology, Pasadena, Calif____ 1930
Baxter, Gregory Paul, T. Jefferson Coolidge Jr. Memorial Laboratory,
Cambridge, Mass_____ 1916
Bell, Eric Temple, California Institute of Technology, Pasadena, Calif__ 1927
Benedict, Francis Gano, Nutrition Laboratory, 29 Vila Street, Boston,
Mass_____ 1914
Benedict, Stanley Rossiter, Cornell University Medical College, 1300 York
Avenue, New York City_____ 1924
Berkey, Charles Peter, Department of Geology and Mineralogy, Columbia
University, New York City_____ 1927
Berry, Edward Wilber, Johns Hopkins University, Baltimore, Md_____ 1922
Bigelow, Henry Bryant, Museum of Comparative Zoology, Harvard Uni-
versity, Cambridge, Mass_____ 1931
Birge, Raymond Thayer, University of California, Berkeley, Calif_____ 1932
Birkhoff, George David, 948 Memorial Drive, Cambridge, Mass_____ 1918
Blakeslee, Albert Francis, Carnegie Station for Experimental Evolution,
Cold Spring Harbor, Long Island, N. Y_____ 1929
Blichfeldt, Hans Frederik, Stanford University, Stanford University, Calif_ 1920
Bliss, Gilbert Ames, University of Chicago, Chicago, Ill_____ 1916
Boas, Franz, Columbia University, New York City_____ 1900
Bogert, Marston Taylor, 566 Chandler Laboratories, Columbia University,
New York City_____ 1916
Boring, Edwin Garrigues, Harvard University, Cambridge, Mass_____ 1932
Bowie, William, U. S. Coast and Geodetic Survey, Washington, D. C____ 1927
Bowman, Isaiah, American Geographical Society, Broadway at One Hun-
dred and Fifty-sixth Street, New York City_____ 1930
Bray, William Crowell, Department of Chemistry, University of California,
Berkeley, Calif_____ 1924
Breasted, James Henry, The Oriental Institute, University of Chicago,
Chicago, Ill_____ 1923
Bridgman, Percy Williams, Jefferson Physical Laboratory, Cambridge,
Mass_____ 1918
Brown, Ernest William, 116 Everit Street, New Haven, Conn_____ 1923
Bush, Vannevar, Massachusetts Institute of Technology, Cambridge,
Mass_____ 1934
Calkins, Gary Nathan, Columbia University, New York City_____ 1919
Campbell, Douglas Houghton, Stanford University, Stanford University,
Calif_____ 1910
Campbell, William Wallace, Lick Observatory, Mount Hamilton, Calif__ 1902
Cannon, Walter Bradford, Harvard Medical School, 240 Longwood Ave-
nue, Boston 17, Mass_____ 1914
Carlson, Anton Julius, University of Chicago, Chicago, Ill_____ 1920
Castle, William Ernest, 186 Payson Road, Belmont, Mass_____ 1915

6. Members of the National Academy of Sciences—Continued

Elected

Cattell, James McKeen, Garrison, N. Y_____ 1901

Chapman, Frank Michler, American Museum of Natural History, Seventy-
seventh Street and Central Park West, New York City_____ 1921

Chittenden, Russell Henry, Sheffield Scientific School, New Haven, Conn__ 1890

Clark, William Mansfield, Johns Hopkins Medical School, Washington and
Monument Streets, Baltimore, Md_____ 1928

Clinton, George Perkins, Connecticut Agricultural Experiment Station,
New Haven, Conn_____ 1930

Coble, Arthur Byron, University of Illinois, Urbana, Ill_____ 1924

Coblentz, William Weber, Bureau of Standards, Washington, D. C_____ 1930

Cole, Rufus, Hospital of the Rockefeller Institute, Sixty-sixth Street and
York Avenue, New York City_____ 1922

Compton, Arthur Holly, University of Chicago, Chicago, Ill_____ 1927

Compton, Karl Taylor, 111 Charles River Road, Cambridge, Mass_____ 1924

Conant, James Bryant, Harvard University, Cambridge 38, Mass_____ 1929

Conklin, Edwin Grant, Princeton University, Princeton, N. J_____ 1908

Coolidge, William David, General Electric Co., Schenectady, N. Y_____ 1925

Crew, Henry, 620 Library Place, Evanston, Ill_____ 1909

Cross, Charles Whitman, 101 East Kirke Street, Chevy Chase, Md_____ 1908

Curtis, Heber Doust, Detroit Observatory, Ann Arbor, Mich_____ 1919

Cushing, Harvey Williams, Yale Medical School, New Haven, Conn_____ 1917

Daly, Reginald Aldworth, Geological Museum, Harvard University, Cambridge, Mass_____ 1925

Dana, Edward Salisbury, 24 Hillhouse Avenue, New Haven, Conn_____ 1884

Davenport, Charles Benedict, Carnegie Institution of Washington, Cold
Spring Harbor, Long Island, N. Y_____ 1912

Davis, Bergen, Columbia University, New York City_____ 1929

Davisson, Clinton Joseph, Bell Telephone Laboratories, 463 West Street,
New York City_____ 1929

Day, Arthur Louis, Geophysical Laboratory, 2801 Upton Street, Washington, D. C_____ 1911

Detwiler, Samuel Randall, College of Physicians and Surgeons, 630 West
One Hundred and Sixty-eighth Street, New York City_____ 1932

Dewey, John, Columbia University, New York City_____ 1910

Dickson, Leonard Eugene, University of Chicago, Chicago, Ill_____ 1913

Doches, Alphonse Raymond, Columbia University, Presbyterian Hospital,
620 West One Hundred and Sixty-eighth Street, New York City_____ 1933

Dodge, Bernard Ogilvie, New York Botanical Garden, Bronx Park (Fordham Station), New York City_____ 1933

Dodge, Raymond, Institute of Human Relations, Yale University, New
Haven, Conn_____ 1924

Donaldson, Henry Herbert, Wistar Institute of Anatomy, Philadelphia,
Pa_____ 1914

Duane, William, 695 Huntington Avenue, Boston, Mass_____ 1920

DuBois, Eugene Floyd, New York Hospital, 525 East Sixty-eighth Street,
New York City_____ 1933

Duggar, Benjamin Minge, Biology Building, University of Wisconsin,
Madison, Wis_____ 1927

Dunn, Gano, 43 Exchange Place, New York City_____ 1919

Durand, William Frederick, Stanford University, Stanford University,
Calif_____ 1917

East, Edward Murray, Bussey Institution, Forest Hills, Boston 30, Mass__ 1925

Eisenhart, Luther Pfahler, Princeton, N. J_____ 1922

Emerson, Rollins Adams, Cornell University, Ithaca, N. Y_____ 1927

Emmet, William Le Roy, General Electric Co., Schenectady, N. Y_____ 1921

Epstein, Paul Sophus, California Institute of Technology, Pasadena, Calif_ 1930

Erlanger, Joseph, Washington University School of Medicine, 4580 Scott
Avenue, St. Louis, Mo_____ 1922

Evans, Griffith Conrad, Department of Mathematics, University of California, Berkeley, Calif_____ 1933

Evans, Herbert McLean, Anatomical Laboratory, University of California, Berkeley, Calif_____ 1927

Flexner, Simon, Rockefeller Institute for Medical Research, Sixty-sixth
Street and York Avenue, New York City_____ 1908

6. Members of the National Academy of Sciences—Continued

Elected

Folin, Otto Knut Olof, Department of Biological Chemistry, Harvard Medical School, Boston, Mass_____ 1915
Franklin, Edward Curtis, Stanford University, Stanford University, Calif. 1914
Fred, Edwin Broun, College of Agriculture, University of Wisconsin, Madison, Wis_____ 1931
Frost, Edwin Brant, Yerkes Observatory, Williams Bay, Wis_____ 1908
Gasser, Herbert Spencer, Cornell University Medical College, 1300 York Avenue, New York City_____ 1934
Gherardi, Bancroft, 195 Broadway, New York City_____ 1933
Gomberg, Moses, University of Michigan, Ann Arbor, Mich_____ 1914
Gregory, William King, American Museum of Natural History, Seventy-seventh Street and Central Park West, New York City_____ 1927
Hale, George Ellery, Mount Wilson Observatory, Pasadena, Calif_____ 1902
Hall, Edwin Herbert, 39 Garden Street, Cambridge, Mass_____ 1911
Harkins, William Draper, University of Chicago, Chicago Ill_____ 1921
Harper, Robert Almer, Columbia University, New York City_____ 1911
Harrison, Ross Granville, Yale University, Osborn Zoological Laboratory, New Haven, Conn_____ 1913
Harvey, Edmund Newton, Princeton University, Princeton, N. J_____ 1934
Hektoen, Ludvig, 637 South Wood Street, Chicago, Ill_____ 1918
Henderson, Lawrence Joseph, 4 Willard Street, Cambridge, Mass_____ 1919
Henderson, Yandell, Yale University, New Haven, Conn_____ 1923
Herrick, Charles Judson, Department of Anatomy, University of Chicago, Chicago, Ill_____ 1918
Hildebrand, Joel Henry, University of California, Berkeley, Calif_____ 1929
Hoagland, Dennis Robert, University of California, Berkeley, Calif_____ 1934
Hoover, Herbert Clark, Palo Alto, Calif_____ 1922
Hovgaard, William, Hotel Margaret, Columbia Heights, Brooklyn, N. Y. 1929
Howard, Leland Ossian, Bureau of Entomology, U. S. Department of Agriculture, Washington D. C_____ 1916
Howe, Marshall Avery, New York Botanical Garden, Bronx Park, New York City_____ 1923
Howell, William Henry, 232 West Lanvale Street, Baltimore, Md_____ 1905
Hrdlicka, Ales, U. S. National Museum, Washington, D. C_____ 1921
Hubble, Edwin Powell, Mount Wilson Observatory, Pasadena, Calif____ 1927
Hudson, Claude Silbert, National Institute of Health, Twenty-fifth and E Streets, Washington, D. C_____ 1927
Hulett, George Augustus, Princeton University, Princeton, N. J_____ 1922
Hull, Albert Wallace, Research Laboratory, General Electric Co., Schenectady, N. Y_____ 1929
Hunt, Reid, Harvard Medical School, Boston, Mass_____ 1919
Ives, Herbert Eugene, Bell Telephone Laboratories, 463 West Street, New York City_____ 1933
Jacobs, Walter Abraham, Rockefeller Institute for Medical Research, Sixty-sixth Street and York Avenue, New York City_____ 1932
Jennings, Herbert Spencer, Johns Hopkins University, Baltimore, Md___ 1914
Jewett, Frank Baldwin, American Telephone & Telegraph Co., 195 Broadway, New York City_____ 1918
Johnson, Douglas Wilson, Columbia University, New York City_____ 1932
Johnson, Treat Baldwin, Bethwood, Amity Road, Bethany, Conn_____ 1919
Jones, Lewis Ralph, University of Wisconsin, Madison, Wis_____ 1920
Jones, Walter, Hopkins Apartments, Baltimore, Md_____ 1918
Kasner, Edward, Columbia University, New York City_____ 1917
Keith, Arthur, U. S. Geological Survey, Washington, D. C_____ 1928
Kellogg, Vernon Lyman, 2305 Bancroft Place, Washington, D. C_____ 1930
Kemble, Edwin Crawford, Jefferson Physical Laboratory, Harvard University, Cambridge, Mass_____ 1931
Kennelly, Arthur Edwin, Harvard University, Cambridge, Mass_____ 1921
Kettering, Charles Franklin, General Motors Corporation, Detroit, Mich. 1928
Keyes, Frederick George, Massachusetts Institute of Technology, Cambridge, Mass_____ 1930
Knopf, Adolph, Yale University, New Haven, Conn_____ 1931
Kofoid, Charles Atwood, University of California, Berkeley, Calif_____ 1922
Kohler, Elmer Peter, Converse Laboratory, Harvard University, Cambridge, Mass_____ 1920

6. Members of the National Academy of Sciences—Continued

Elected

Kraus, Charles August, Brown University, Providence, R. I_____ 1925
Kroeber, Alfred L., University of California, Berkeley, Calif_____ 1928
Kunkel, Louis Otto, Boyce Thompson Institute for Plant Research, Inc., Yonkers, N. Y_____ 1932
Lamb, Arthur Becket, Chemical Laboratory, Harvard University, Cambridge, Mass_____ 1924
Landsteiner, Karl, Rockefeller Institute for Medical Research, Sixty-sixth Street and York Avenue, New York City_____ 1932
Langmuir, Irving, General Electric Co., Schenectady, N. Y_____ 1918
Lashley, Karl Spencer, University of Chicago, Chicago, Ill____ _____ 1930
Laufer, Berthold, Field Museum of Natural History, Chicago, Ill_____ 1930
Lawrence, Ernest Orlando, University of California, Berkeley, Calif_____ 1934
Lawson, Andrew Cowper, University of California, Berkeley, Calif_____ 1924
Lefschetz, Solomon, 190 Prospect Street, Princeton, N. J_____ 1925
Leith, Charles Kenneth, University of Wisconsin, Madison, Wis_____ 1920
Leuschner, Armin Otto, Students' Observatory, University of California, Berkeley, Calif_____ 1913
Levene, Phoebus Aaron Theodore, Rockefeller Institute for Medical Research, Sixty-sixth Street and York Avenue, New York City_____ 1916
Leverett, Frank, 1724 South University Avenue, Ann Arbor, Mich_____ 1929
Lewis, Gilbert Newton, University of California, Berkeley, Calif_____ 1913
Lillie, Frank Rattray, University of Chicago, Chicago, Ill_____ 1915
Lind, Samuel Colville, School of Chemistry, University of Minnesota, Minneapolis, Minn_____ 1930
Lindgren, Waldemar, Massachusetts Institute of Technology, Cambridge, Mass_____ 1909
Lowie, Robert Harry, University of California, Berkeley, Calif_____ 1931
Lyman, Theodore, Jefferson Laboratory, Harvard University, Cambridge, Mass_____ 1917
Mac Callum, William George, Johns Hopkins Medical School, Baltimore, Md_____ 1921
McClung, Clarence Erwin, University of Pennsylvania, Philadelphia, Pa_ 1920
McCollum, Elmer Verner, School of Hygiene and Public Health, 615 North Wolfe Street, Baltimore, Md_____ 1920
Mark, Edward Laurens, 109 Irving Street, Cambridge, Mass_____ 1903
Mason, Max, Rockefeller Foundation, 49 West Forty-ninth Street, New York City_____ 1923
Mendel, Lafayette Benedict, Sterling Hall of Medicine, Yale University, 333 Cedar Street, New Haven, Conn_____ 1913
Mendenhall, Charles Elwood, Sterling Hall, University of Wisconsin, Madison, Wis_____ 1918
Mendenhall, Walter Curran, U. S. Geological Survey, Washington, D. C_ 1932
Merriam, Clinton Hart, 1919 Sixteenth Street, Washington, D. C_____ 1902
Merriam, John Campbell, Carnegie Institution of Washington, Washington, D. C_____ 1918
Merrill, Elmer Drew, New York Botanical Garden, Bronx Park (Fordham Station), New York City_____ 1923
Merrill, Paul Willard, Mount Wilson Observatory, Pasadena, Calif_____ 1929
Merritt, Ernest George, Rockefeller Hall, Ithaca, N. Y_____ 1914
Michael, Arthur, 219 Parker Street, Newton Center, Mass_____ 1889
Miles, Walter Richard, Institute of Human Relations, 333 Cedar Street, New Haven, Conn_____ 1933
Miller, Dayton Clarence, Case School of Applied Science, Cleveland Ohio_ 1921
Miller, George Abram, 1203 West Illinois Street, Urbana, Ill_____ 1921
Millikan, Robert Andrews, California Institute of Technology, Pasadena, Calif_____ 1915
Mitchell, Samuel Alfred, Leander McCormick Observatory, University, Va_____ 1933
Modjeski, Ralph, 121 East Thirty-eighth Street, New York City_____ 1925
Moore, Joseph Haines, Lick Observatory, Mount Hamilton, Calif_____ 1931
Moore, Robert Lee, University of Texas, Austin, Tex_____ 1931
Morgan, Thomas Hunt, California Institute of Technology, Pasadena, Calif_____ 1909
Morse, Harold Marston, E 23 Eliot House, Cambridge, Mass_____ 1932
Moulton, Forest Ray, 327 South La Salle Street, Chicago, Ill_____ 1910

6. Members of the National Academy of Sciences—Continued

Elected

Muller, Hermann Joseph, University of Texas, Austin, Tex_____ 1931
Nichols, Edward Leamington, Cornell University, Ithaca, N. Y_____ 1901
Norris, James Flack, Massachusetts Institute of Technology, Cambridge,
Mass_____ 1934
Northrop, John Howard, Rockefeller Institute for Medical Research,
Princeton, N. J_____ 1934
Novy, Frederick George, University of Michigan, Ann Arbor, Mich_____ 1924
Noyes, Arthur Amos, California Institute of Technology, Pasadena, Calif 1905
Noyes, William Albert, University of Illinois, Urbana, Ill_____ 1910
Opie, Eugene Lindsay, Cornell University Medical School, 1300 York
Avenue, New York City_____ 1923
Osborn, Henry Fairfield, American Museum of Natural History, Seventy-
seventh Street and Central Park West, New York City_____ 1900
Osgood, William Fogg, 1800 Thousand Oaks Boulevard, Berkeley, Calif__ 1904
Osterhout, Winthrop John Vanleuven, Rockefeller Institute for Medical
Research, Sixty-sixth Street and York Avenue, New York City_____ 1919
Palache, Charles, Harvard University, Cambridge, Mass_____ 1934
Parker, George Howard, 16 Berkeley Street, Cambridge, Mass_____ 1913
Pauling, Linus, California Institute of Technology, Pasadena, Calif_____ 1933
Pearl, Raymond, 1901 East Madison Street, Baltimore, Md_____ 1916
Pierce, George Washington, Cruft Laboratory, Harvard University, Cam-
bridge, Mass_____ 1920
Pillsbury, Walter Bowers, University of Michigan, Ann Arbor, Mich____ 1925
Pupin, Michael Idvorsky, Columbia University, New York City_____ 1905
Ransome, Frederick Leslie, California Institute of Technology, Pasadena,
Calif_____ 1914
Reid, Harry Fielding, Johns Hopkins University, Baltimore, Md_____ 1912
Richards, Alfred Newton, University of Pennsylvania, Philadelphia, Pa__ 1927
Richtmyer, Floyd Karker, Rockefeller Hall, Cornell University, Ithaca,
N. Y_____ 1932
Ritt, Joseph Fels, Columbia University, New York City_____ 1933
Rivers, Thomas Milton, Rockefeller Institute for Medical Research, Sixty-
sixth Street and York Avenue, New York City_____ 1934
Robinson, Benjamin Lincoln, Gray Herbarium, Cambridge, Mass_____ 1921
Ross, Frank Elmore, Yerkes Observatory, Williams Bay, Wis_____ 1930
Rous, Francis Peyton, Rockefeller Institute for Medical Research, Sixty-
sixth Street and York Avenue, New York City_____ 1927
Ruedemann, Rudolf, New York State Museum, Albany, N. Y_____ 1928
Russell, Henry Norris, Princeton University, Princeton, N. J_____ 1918
Ryan, Harris Joseph, Stanford University, Stanford University, Calif____ 1920
Sabin, Florence Rena, Rockefeller Institute for Medical Research, Sixty-
sixth Street and York Avenue, New York City_____ 1925
St. John, Charles Edward, Mount Wilson Observatory, Pasadena, Calif__ 1924
Sapir, Edward, Yale University, New Haven, Conn_____ 1934
Saunders, Frederick Albert, Jefferson Physical Laboratory, Cambridge,
Mass_____ 1925
Sauveur, Albert, Harvard University, Cambridge, Mass_____ 1927
Schlesinger, Frank, Yale University Observatory, New Haven, Conn____ 1916
Schuchert, Charles, Peabody Museum, Yale University, New Haven,
Conn_____ 1910
Scott, William Berryman, Princeton University, Princeton, N. J_____ 1906
Seares, Frederick Hanley, Mount Wilson Observatory, Pasadena, Calif__ 1919
Seashore, Carl Emil, State University of Iowa, Iowa City, Iowa_____ 1922
Setchell, William Albert, University of California, Berkeley, Calif_____ 1919
Shaffer, Philip Anderson, Washington University Medical School, St.
Louis, Mo_____ 1928
Shapley, Harlow, Harvard College Observatory, Cambridge, Mass_____ 1924
Sherman, Henry Clapp, Columbia University, New York City_____ 1933
Slater, John Clarke, Massachusetts Institute of Technology, Cambridge,
Mass_____ 1932
Slipher, Vesto Melvin, Lowell Observatory, Flagstaff, Ariz_____ 1921
Smith, Theobald, Rockefeller Institute for Medical Research, Princeton,
N. J_____ 1903
Stakman, Elvin Charles, University of Minnesota, Minneapolis, Minn___ 1934
Stebbins, Joel, Washburn Observatory, Madison, Wis_____ 1920

FOREIGN ASSOCIATES OF THE NATIONAL ACADEMY OF SCIENCES

	Elected
Adams, Frank Dawson, McGill University, Montreal, Canada	1920
Barrois, Charles, Université, 41 rue Pascal, Lille, France	1908
Bjerknes, V. F. K., University, Oslo, Norway	1934
Bohr, Niels, University of Copenhagen, Copenhagen, Denmark	1925
Bower, Frederick Orpen, 2, The Crescent, Ripon, Yorks, England	1929
Brogger, W. C., Universitet, Oslo, Norway	1903
Debye, Peter, Physikalisches Institut der Universitat, Linnéstrasse 5, Leipzig, Germany	1931
de Sitter, Willem, Sterrewacht te Leiden, Leiden, The Netherlands	1929
Deslandres, Henri, Bureau des Longitudes, 21 rue de Téhéran, Paris 8, France	1913
de Vries, Hugo, Lunteren, The Netherlands	1904
Dyson, (Sir) Frank Watson, The Royal Observatory, Greenwich, London, S. E., England	1926
Eddington, (Sir) Arthur Stanley, Observatory, Cambridge, England	1925
Einstein, Albert, Institute for Advanced Study, Princeton, N. J. (U. S. A.)	1922
Forsyth, A. R., Imperial College of Science and Technology, London, England	1907
Hadamard, Jacques, 25 rue Jean Dolent, Paris XIV, France	1926
Hadfield, (Sir) Robert A., 22 Carlton House Terrace, S. W. 1, London, England	1928
Hardy, Godfrey Harold, New College, Oxford, England	1927
Heim, Albert, Zurich, Switzerland	1913
Hertwig, Richard von, Zoologische Institut, University of Munich, Munich, Germany	1929
Hilbert, David, Wilhelm-Weberstrasse 29, Gottingen, Germany	1907
Hopkins, (Sir) Frederick Gowland, University, Cambridge, England	1924
Kustner, Karl Friedrich, Mehlem bei Bonn, Germany	1913
Lacroix, F. Alfred A., 23 rue Jean-Dolent, Paris XIV, France	1920
Larmor, (Sir) Joseph, St. John's College, Cambridge, England	1908
Marconi, (Marchese) Guglielmo, Marconi House, Strand, London, W. C. 2, England	1932
Pavlov, I. P., Institute for Experimental Medicine, Leningrad, U. S. S. R. Russia	1908
Penck, Albrecht, Knesebeckstrasse 48, Berlin W. 15, Germany	1909
Picard, Charles Emile, 25 Quai Conti, Paris (VI), France	1903
Planck, Max, Wangenheimstrasse 21, Berlin-Grunewald, Germany	1926
Prain, (Sir) David, The Well Farm, Warlingham, Surrey, England	1920
Ramon y Cajal, Santiago, University of Madrid, Alfonso XII, n. 62, Madrid, Spain	1920
Robinson, Robert, Dyson Perrins Laboratory, South Parks Road, Oxford, England	1934
Rutherford, (Lord) Ernest, Newnham Cottage, Queen's Road, Cambridge, England	1911
Sabatier, Paul, Allée des Zephyrs, No. 11, Toulouse, France	1927
Schneider, Charles Eugene, 42 rue d'Anjou, Paris, France	1925
Schuster, (Sir) Arthur, Yeldall, Twyford, Berkshire, England	1913
Sherrington, (Sir) Charles Scott, University, Oxford, England	1924
Sommerfeld, Arnold, University of Munich, Munich, Germany	1929
Spemann, Hans, Zoologisches Institut, Freiburg, i. Br. Germany	1925
Stumpf, Carl, Potsdamerstrasse 15, Berlin-Lichterfelde, West, Germany	1927
Thomson, (Sir) Joseph, Trinity Lodge, Cambridge, England	1903
Vallee, Poussin, C. de la, University of Louvain, Louvain, Belgium	1929
Volterra, Vito, Universita, Rome, Italy	1911
Wieland, Heinrich, Chemisches Laboratorium, Bayer. Akademie der Wissenschaften, Arcisstrasse 1, Munich 2 NW, Germany	1932
Willstaetter, Richard, Moehlstrasse 29, Munich O. 27, Germany	1926

7. MEDALISTS OF THE NATIONAL ACADEMY

	Medal	Year		Medal	Year
Abbe, Cleveland [1]	Welfare	1916	Hoover, Herbert Clark	Welfare	1920
Abbot, Charles Greeley	Draper	1910	Huggins, Sir William [1]	Draper	1901
Abel, Othenio [2]	Elliot	1920	Kapteyn, J. C.[1]	Watson	1913
Adams, Walter Sidney	Draper	1918	Keeler, James Edward [1]	Draper	1899
Albert I, Prince of Monaco [1,2]	Agassiz	1918	Langley, Samuel Pierpont [1]	do	1886
Auwers, G. F. J. Arthur [1]	Watson	1891	Leuschner, Armin Otto	Watson	1915
Barnett, Samuel Jackson [1,2]	Comstock	1918	Margerie, Emmanuel de [2]	Thompson	1923
Bather, Francis Arthur [2]	Thompson	1932	Mather, Stephen Tyng [1,2]	Welfare	1930
Beebe, William [2]	Elliot	1918	Merrill, George Perkins [1]	Smith	1922
Bigelow, Henry Bryant	Agassiz	1931	Michelson, Albert Abraham [1]	Draper	1916
Bjerknes, Vilhelm	do	1926	Millikan, Robert Andrews	Comstock	1913
Black, Davidson [1,2]	Elliot	1931	Newton, Hubert Anson [1]	Smith	1888
Bohr, Niels	Barnard	1925	Osborn, Henry Fairfield	Elliot	1929
Bragg, Sir William Henry [2]	do	1914	Park, William Hallock [2]	Welfare	1932
Breuil, Henri [2]	Elliot	1924	Pettersson, Otto Sven [2]	Agassiz	1924
Bridgman, P. W.	Comstock	1933	Pickering, Edward Charles [1]	Draper	1888
Campbell, William Wallace	Draper	1906	Pinchot, Gifford [2]	Welfare	1916
Cannon, Annie Jump [2]	do	1931	Ridgway, Robert [1]	Elliot	1919
Canu, Ferdinand [1,2]	Elliot	1923	Rose, Wickliffe [1,2]	Welfare	1931
Carty, John J.[1]	Carty	1932	Rowland, Henry Augustus [1]	Draper	1890
Chandler, Seth Carlo [1]	Watson	1894	Russell, Henry Norris	do	1922
Chapin, Charles V.[2]	Welfare	1928	Rutherford (Lord) Ernest	Barnard	1909
Chapin, James P.[2]	Elliot	1932	Schmidt, Johannes [2]	Agassiz	1930
Chapman, Frank Michler	do	1917	Schoenfeld, Ed. [1,2]	Watson	1889
Charlier, C. V. L.[2]	Watson	1924	Schuchert, Charles	Thompson	1934
Clarke, John Mason [1]	Thompson	1925	Scott, W. B	do	1930
Coghill, George Ellett [2]	Elliot	1930	Seton, Ernest Thompson [2]	Elliot	1928
Davisson, C. J.	Comstock	1928	Shapley, Harlow	Draper	1926
Dean, Bashford [1,2]	Elliot	1921	Sigsbee, Rear Admiral Charles Dwight, U. S. Navy. [1,2]	Agassiz	1920
Defant, Albert [2]	Agassiz	1932			
de Sitter, Willem	Watson	1929			
Deslandres, Henri	Draper	1913	Slipher, V. M.	Draper	1932
Duane, William	Comstock	1923	Smith, James Perrin [1]	Thompson	1928
Eddington, A. S.	Draper	1924	Stebbins, Joel	Draper	1915
Einstein, Albert	Barnard	1921	Stensio, Erik A: Son [2]	Elliot	1927
Ekman, V. Walfrid [2]	Agassiz	1928	Stiles, Charles Wardell [1]	Welfare	1921
Fabry, Charles [2]	Draper	1919	Stratton, Samuel Wesley [1]	do	1917
Fairchild, David [2]	Welfare	1933	Ulrich, Edward Oscar	Thompson	1930
Fowler, Alfred [2]	Draper	1920	Vogel, Herman Karl [1]	Draper	1893
Gardiner, J. Stanley [2]	Agassiz	1929	Vollmer, August [2]	Welfare	1934
Gill, Sir David [1]	Watson	1899	Walcott, Charles Doolittle [1]	Thompson	1921
Goethals, George Washington.[1,2]	Welfare	1914	Weber, Max [2]	Agassiz	1927
			Wheeler, William Morton	Elliot	1922
Gorgas, William Crawford [1,2]	do	1914	White, David	Thompson	1931
Gould, Benjamin Apthorp [1]	Watson	1887	Do.	Walcott	1934
Gran, Haakon Hasberg [2]	Agassiz	1934	Wilson, Edmund B	Elliot	1925
Hale, George Ellery	Draper	1904	Wright, William Hammond	Draper	1928
Heisenberg, Werner [2]	Barnard	1930	Zeeman, P.[2]	do	1921
Helland-Hansen, Bjorn [2]	Agassiz	1933			
Hjort, Johan [2]	do	1913			

[1] Deceased.
[2] Not member or foreign associate of the academy.

8. PRESIDENTS OF THE ACADEMY

Alexander Dallas Bache	1863–67	Ira Remsen	1907–13
Joseph Henry	1868–78	William Henry Welch	1913–17
William Barton Rogers	1879–82	Charles Doolittle Walcott	1917–23
Othniel Charles Marsh	1883–95	Albert Abraham Michelson	1923–27
Wolcott Gibbs	1895–1900	Thomas Hunt Morgan	1927–31
Alexander Agassiz	1901–7	William Wallace Campbell	1931–

9. DECEASED MEMBERS AND FOREIGN ASSOCIATES

DECEASED MEMBERS

	Date of election	Date of death		Date of election	Date of death
Abbe, Cleveland	1878	Oct. 28, 1916	Armsby, H. P	1920[1]	Oct. 19, 1921
Abbot, Henry L	1872	Oct. 1, 1927	Atkinson, George Francis	1918[1]	Nov. 14, 1918
Agassiz, Alexander	1866	Mar. 27, 1910	Bache, Alexander Dallas	(2)	
Agassiz, Louis	(2)	Dec. 14, 1873	Bailey, Solon Irving	1923	June 5, 1931
Alexander, J. H	(2)	Mar. 2, 1867	Baird, Spencer F	1864	Aug. 19, 1887
Alexander, Stephen	(2)	June 25, 1883	Barker, George F	1876[1]	May 24, 1910
Allen, J. A	1876	Aug. 29, 1921	Barnard, E. E	1911	Feb. 6, 1923

See footnotes at end of table.

9. Deceased Members and Foreign Associates—Continued

DECEASED MEMBERS—Continued

	Date of election	Date of death		Date of election	Date of death
Barnard, F. A. P.	(1 ?)	Apr. 27, 1889	Hadley, James	1872	Nov. 14, 1872
Barnard, J. G.	(?)	May 14, 1882	Hague, Arnold	1885	May 16, 1917
Barrell, Joseph	1919	May 4, 1919	Haldeman, S. S.	1876	Sept. 20, 1880
Bartlett, W. H. C.	(?)	Feb. 11, 1893	Hall, Asaph	1875	Nov. 22, 1907
Becker, George Ferdinand	1901	Apr. 20, 1919	Hall, G. Stanley	1915	Apr. 24, 1924
Beecher, Charles Emerson	1899	Feb. 14, 1904	Hall, James	(?)	Aug. 7, 1898
Bell, A. Graham	1883 1	Aug. 2, 1922	Halsted, W. S.	1917 1	Sept. 7, 1922
Billings, John S.	1883	Mar. 11, 1913	Hastings, C. S.	1889 1	Jan. 29, 1932
Bocher, Maxime	1909 1	Sept. 12, 1918	Hayden, F. V.	1873	Dec. 22, 1887
Boltwood, B. B.	1911	Aug. 14, 1927	Hayford, John F.	1911 1	Mar. 10, 1925
Boss, Lewis	1889	Oct. 5, 1912	Henry, Joseph	(?)	May 13, 1878
Bowditch, Henry P.	1887	Mar. 13, 1911	Hilgard, Eugene W.	1872	Jan. 8, 1916
Branner, J. C.	1905	Mar. 1, 1922	Hilgard, Julius E.	(?)	May 9, 1890
Brewer, William H.	1880	Nov. 2, 1910	Hill, George William	1874	Apr. 16, 1914
Britton, Nathaniel L.	1914 1	June 25, 1934	Hill, Henry B.	1883	Apr. 6, 1903
Brooks, William Keith	1884	Nov. 12, 1908	Hillebrand, W. F.	1908	Feb. 7, 1925
Brown-Sequard, Charles E.	1868	Apr. 2, 1894	Hitchcock, Edward	(?)	Feb. 27, 1864
Brush, George Jarvis	1868	Feb. 6, 1912	Holbrook, J. E.	1868	Sept. 8, 1871
Bumstead, Henry A.	1913	Dec. 31, 1920	Holden, Edward Singleton	1885	Mar. 16, 1914
Burgess, George K.	1922 1	July 2, 1932	Holmes, William H.	1905 1	Apr. 20, 1933
Carty, John J.	1917 1	Dec. 27, 1932	Howe, H. M.	1917	May 14, 1922
Casey, Thomas L.	1890	Mar. 25, 1896	Hubbard, J. S.	(?)	Aug. 16, 1863
Caswell, Alexis	(?)	Jan. 8, 1877	Humphreys, A. A.	(?)	Dec. 27, 1883
Chamberlin, Thomas Chrowder	1903	Nov. 15, 1928	Hunt, T. Sterry	1873	Feb. 12, 1892
Chandler, Charles Frederick	1874	Aug. 25, 1925	Huntington, G. S.	1921 1	Jan. 5, 1927
Chandler, Seth Carlo	1858 1	Dec. 31, 1913	Hyatt, Alpheus	1875	Jan. 15, 1902
Chauvenet, William	(?)	Dec. 13, 1877	Iddings, Joseph P.	1907 1	Sept. 8, 1920
Clark, Henry James	1872	July 1, 1870	James, William	1903 1	Aug. 26, 1910
Clark, William B.	1908	July 27, 1917	Johnson, S. W.	1866	July 21, 1909
Clarke, Frank Wigglesworth	1909	May 23, 1931	Keeler, J. E.	1900	Aug. 12, 1900
Clarke, John M.	1909	May 29, 1925	Kemp, James F.	1911	Nov. 17, 1926
Coffin, James H.	1869	Feb. 6, 1873	King, Clarence	1876	Dec. 24, 1901
Coffin, J. H. C.	(?)	Jan. 8, 1890	Kirtland, Jared P.	1865	Dec. 10, 1877
Comstock, Cyrus B.	1884	May 29, 1910	Lane, J. Homer	1872	May 3, 1880
Comstock, George C.	1890 1	May 11, 1934	Langley, Samuel P.	1876	Feb. 27, 1906
Cook, George H.	1887	Sept. 22, 1889	Lea, Matthew Carey	1892	Mar. 15, 1897
Cooke, Josiah P.	1872	Sept. 3, 1894	Le Conte, John	1878	Apr. 29, 1891
Cope, Edward D.	1872	Apr. 12, 1897	Le Conte, John L.	(?)	Nov. 15, 1883
Coues, Elliott	1877	Dec. 25, 1899	Le Conte, Joseph	1875	July 6, 1901
Coulter, John Merle	1909	Dec. 23, 1928	Leidy, Joseph	(?)	Apr. 30, 1891
Councilman, William T.	1904 1	May 27, 1933	Lesley, J. Peter	(?)	June 1, 1903
Crafts, James M.	1872	June 21, 1917	Lesquereux, Leo	1864	Oct. 25, 1889
Dall, William H.	1897 1	Mar. 27, 1927	Loeb, Jacques	1910	Feb. 11, 1924
Dalton, J. C.	1864	Feb. 2, 1889	Longstreth, Miers F.	(?)	Dec. 27, 1891
Dana, James D.	(?)	Apr. 14, 1895	Loomis, Elias	1873	Aug. 15, 1889
Davidson, George	1874 1	Dec. 2, 1911	Lovering, Joseph	1873	Jan. 18, 1892
Davis, Charles H.	(?)	Feb. 18, 1877	Lusk, Graham	1915 1	July 18, 1932
Davis, William M.	1904 1	Feb. 5, 1934	Lyman, Theodore	1872	Sept. 9, 1897
Draper, Henry	1877	Nov. 20, 1882	Mahan, D. H.	(?)	Sept. 16, 1871
Draper, John W.	1877	Jan. 4, 1882	Mall, Franklin P.	1907	Nov. 17, 1917
Dutton, C. E.	1884 1	Jan. 4, 1912	Marsh, G. P.	1866	July 23, 1882
Eads, James B.	1872	Mar. 8, 1887	Marsh, O. C.	1874 1	Mar. 18, 1899
Edison, Thomas A.	1927	Oct. 18, 1931	Mayer, Alfred M.	1872	July 13, 1897
Eigenmann, Carl H.	1923 1	Apr. 24, 1927	Mayor, A. G.	1916	June 25, 1922
Elkin, W. L.	1895 1	May 30, 1933	Mayo-Smith, Richmond	1890	Nov. 11, 1901
Emmons, Samuel F.	1892	Mar. 28, 1911	Meek, F. B.	1869	Dec. 21, 1876
Englemann, George	(?)	Feb. 4, 1884	Meigs, M. C.	1865	Jan. 2, 1892
Farlow, W. G.	1879	June 3, 1919	Meltzer, Samuel James	1912	Nov. 8, 1920
Ferrel, William	1868	Sept. 18, 1891	Mendenhall, T. C.	1887 1	Mar. 22, 1924
Fewkes, Jesse Walter	1914	May 31, 1930	Merrill, George Perkins	1922 1	Aug. 15, 1929
Forbes, Stephen Alfred	1918	Mar. 13, 1930	Michelson, A. A.	1888 1	May 9, 1931
Fraser, John Fries	(?)	Oct. 12, 1872	Minot, Charles Sedgwick	1897	Nov. 19, 1914
Freeman, John R.	1918 1	Oct. 6, 1932	Mitchell, Henry	1885 1	Dec. 1, 1902
Gabb, William M.	1876	May 30, 1878	Mitchell, Silas Weir	1865	Jan. 4, 1914
Genth, F. A.	1872	Feb. 2, 1893	Moore, E. H.	1901 1	Dec. 30, 1932
Gibbs, Josiah Willard	1879	Apr. 28, 1903	Morgan, Louis H.	1875	Dec. 17, 1881
Gibbs, Wolcott	(?)	Dec. 9, 1908	Morley, E. W.	1897	Feb. 24, 1923
Gilbert, Grove Karl	1883	May 1, 1918	Morse, Edward Sylvester	1876 1	Dec. 20, 1925
Gill, Theodore Nicholas	1873	Sept. 25, 1914	Morse, Harmon N.	1907	Sept. 8, 1920
Gilliss, James Melville	(?)	Feb. 9, 1865	Morton, Henry	1874	May 9, 1902
Gooch, Frank Austin	1897	Aug. 12, 1929	Nef, John Ulric	1904 1	Aug. 13, 1915
Goodale, G. L.	1890	Apr. 15, 1923	Newberry, J. S.	(?)	Dec. 7, 1892
Goode, G. Brown	1888	Sept. 6, 1896	Newcomb, Simon	1869	July 11, 1909
Gould, Augustus A.	(?)	Sept. 15, 1866	Newton, H. A.	(?)	Aug. 12, 1896
Gould, Benjamin A.	(?)	Nov. 26, 1896	Newton, John	1876	May 1, 1895
Gray, Asa	(?)	Jan. 30, 1888	Nichols, Ernest Fox	1908	Apr. 29, 1924
Guyot, Arnold	(?)	Feb. 8, 1884	Norton, William A.	1873	Sept. 21, 1883
			Oliver, James E.	1872	Mar. 27, 1895
			Osborne, Thomas Burr	1910	Jan. 29, 1929
			Packard, A. S.	1872	Feb. 14, 1905

See footnotes at end of table.

5

9. *Deceased members and foreign associates*—Continued

DECEASED MEMBERS—Continued

	Date of election	Date of death		Date of election	Date of death
Peirce, Benjamin [1]	(1 ?)	Oct. 6, 1880	Stimpson, William	1868	May 26, 1872
Peirce, Benjamin Osgood	1906	Jan. 14, 1913	Story, William Edward	1908 1	Apr. 11, 1930
Peirce, Charles S. S.	1877 1	Apr. 20, 1914	Stratton, S. W.	1917 1	Oct. 18, 1931
Penfield, Samuel L.	1900	Aug. 13, 1906	Strong, Theodore	(?)	Feb. 1, 1869
Peters, C. H. F.	1876 1	July 18, 1890	Sullivant, W. S.	1872	Apr. 30, 1873
Pickering, Edward C.	1873	Feb. 3, 1919	Swain, George F.	1923 1	July 1, 1931
Pirsson, Louis V.	1913 1	Dec. 8, 1919	Thaxter, Roland	1912 1	Apr. 22, 1932
Pourtales, L. F.	1873	July 19, 1880	Torrey, John	(?)	Mar. 10, 1873
Powell, John W.	1880	Sept. 23, 1902	Totten, J. G.	(?)	Apr. 22, 1864
Power, Frederick B.	1924 1	Mar. 26, 1927	Trowbridge, Augustus	1919 1	Mar. 14, 1934
Prudden, T. Mitchell	1901	Apr. 10, 1924	Trowbridge, John	1878	Feb. 18, 1923
Pumpelly, Raphael	1872	Aug. 10, 1923	Trowbridge, William P.	1872	Aug. 12, 1892
Putnam, Frederic W.	1885	Aug. 18, 1915	Trumbull, James H.	1872	Aug. 5, 1897
Remsen, Ira	1882	Mar. 4, 1927	Tuckerman, Edward	1868	Mar. 15, 1886
Richards, T. W.	1899 1	Apr. 2, 1928	Van Hise, C. R.	1902	Nov. 19, 1918
Ridgway, Robert	1917	Mar. 25, 1929	Vaughan, Victor Clarence	1915 1	Nov. 21, 1929
Rodgers, John	(?)	May 5, 1882	Verrill, Addison E. [3]	1872	Dec. 10, 1926
Rogers, Fairman	(?)	Aug. 22, 1900	Walcott, Charles D.	1896 1	Feb. 9, 1927
Rogers, Robert E. [10]	(?)	Sept. 6, 1884	Walker, Francis A.	1878	Jan. 5, 1897
Rogers, William A.	1885	Mar. 1, 1898	Warren, G. K.	1876	Aug. 8, 1882
Rogers, William B. [11]	(?)	May 30, 1882	Washburn, E. W.	1932 1	Feb. 6, 1934
Rood, Ogden N.	1865	Nov. 12, 1902	Washington, H. S.	1921 1	Jan. 7, 1934
Rosa, E. B.	1913 1	May 17, 1921	Watson, James C.	1868	Nov. 23, 1880
Rowland, Henry A.	1881	Apr. 16, 1901	Watson, Sereno	1889	Mar. 9, 1892
Royce, Josiah	1906 1	Sept. 14, 1916	Webster, A. G.	1903 1	May 15, 1923
Rutherfurd, Lewis M.	(?)	May 30, 1892	Welch, William H.	1895 1	Apr. 30, 1934
Sabine, Wallace C. W.	1917	Jan. 10, 1919	Wells, Horace L.	1903	Dec. 19, 1924
Sargent, Charles S.	1895	Mar. 22, 1927	Wheeler, Henry Lord	1909 1	Oct. 30, 1914
Saxton, Joseph	(?)	Oct. 26, 1873	White, Charles A.	1889	June 29, 1910
Schott, Charles A.	1872	July 31, 1901	Whitman, C. O.	1895	Dec. 6, 1910
Scudder, Samuel H.	1877	May 17, 1911	Whitney, Josiah D. [4]	(1 ?)	Aug. 19, 1896
Sellers, William	1873 1	Jan. 24, 1905	Whitney, William D. [4]	1865 1	June 29, 1894
Silliman, Benj., Sr.	(?)	Nov. 24, 1864	Wilczynski, E. J. [5]	1919 1	Sept. 14, 1932
Silliman, Benj., Jr.	(?)	Jan. 14, 1885	Williston, Samuel W.	1915	Aug. 30, 1918
Smith, Alexander	1915	Sept. 8, 1922	Winlock, Joseph	(?)	June 11, 1875
Smith, Edgar F.	1899 1	May 3, 1928	Wood, Horatio C.	1879 1	Jan. 3, 1920
Smith, Erwin F.	1913 1	Apr. 6, 1927	Woodward, J. J.	1873	Aug. 17, 1884
Smith, J. Lawrence	1872	Oct. 12, 1883	Woodward, Robert S.	1896 1	June 29, 1924
Smith, James Perrin	1925 1	Jan. 1, 1931	Worthen, A. H.	1872	May 6, 1888
Smith, Sidney Irving [7]	1884	May 6, 1926	Wright, Arthur Williams	1881	Dec. 19, 1915
Sperry, Elmer A.	1925 1	June 16, 1930	Wyman, Jeffries	(?)	Sept. 4, 1874
Squier, George O.	1919 1	Mar. 24, 1934	Young, Charles A.	1872	Jan. 3, 1908

DECEASED FOREIGN ASSOCIATES

Adams, J. C.
Airy, Sir George B.
Argelander, F. W. A.
Arrhenius, S.A.
Auwers, G. F. J. Arthur
Backlund, Oskar
Baer, Karl Ernest von
Baeyer, Adof von
Barrande, Joachin
Bateson, William
Beaumont, L. Elie de
Becquerel, Henri
Berthelot, M. P. E.
Bertrand, J. L. F.
Boltzmann, Ludwig
Bornet, Edouard
Boussingault, J. B. J. D.
Boveri, Theodor
Braun, Alexander
Brewster, Sir David
Bunsen, Robert W.
Burmeister, C. H. C.
Candolle, Alphonse de
Cayley, Arthur
Chasles, Michel
Chevreul, M. E.
Clausius, Rudolph
Cornu, Alfred
Crookes, Sir William
Darboux, Gaston
Darwin, Sir George Howard
Dewar, Sir James
Dove, H. W.
Dumas, J. B.

Ehrlich, Paul
Eijkman, Christian
Engler, Adolph
Faraday, Michael
Fischer, Emil
Geikie, Sir Archibald
Geugenbaur, Karl
Gill, Sir David
Glydém, Hugo
Goebel, K. E. von
Groth, Paul von
Haber, Fritz
Hamilton, Sir Wilam Rowan
Helmholtz, Baron H. von
Hoff, J. H. van't
Hofmann, A. W.
Hooker, Sir Joseph D.
Huggins, Sir William
Huxley, T. H.
Ibañez, Carlos
Janssen, J.
Jordan, M. E. C.
Joule, James P.
Kapteyn, J. C.
Kekulé, August
Kelvin, Lord
Kirchoff, G. R.
Klein, Felix
Koch, Robert
Kölliker, Albert von
Kohlrausch, Frederich
Kossel, Albrecht
Kronecker, Hugo
Lacaze-Duthiers, Henri de

Lankester, Sir E. Ray
Leuckart, Rudolph
Lie, Sophus
Liebig, Justus von
Lister, Lord
Loewy, Maurice
Lorentz, Hendrik Antoon
Ludwig, K. F. W.
Marey, E. J.
Mendeléeff, D. I.
Milne-Edwards, Henri
Moissan, Henri
Murchison, Sir Roderick I.
Murray, Sir John
Onnes, Heike Kamerlingh
Oppolzer, Theodore von
Ostwald, Wilhelm
Owen, Sir Richard
Parsons, Sir Charles Algernon
Pasteur, Louis
Peters, C. A. F.
Pfeffer, Wilhelm
Plana, G. A. A.
Poincaré, Jules Henri
Rammelsberg, C. F.
Ramsey, Sir William
Rayleigh, Lord
Regnault, Victor
Retzius, Gustav
Reymond, Emil Du Bois
Richthofen, F. von
Rosenbusch, Karl Harry Ferdinand
Roux, Wilhelm

9. Deceased members and foreign associates—Continued

DECEASED FOREIGN ASSOCIATES—Continued

Rubner, Max
Sachs, Julius von
Schiaparelli, Giovanni
Seeliger, Hugo R. von
Stas, Jean Servais
Stokes, Sir George G.
Strasburger, Edouard
Struve, Otto von

Suess, Eduard
Sylvester, J. J.
Tisserand, F. F.
Van der Waals, J. D.
Virchow, Rudolph von
Vogel, H. C.
Waldeyer, Wilhelm
Weierstrauss, Karl

Weismann, August
Wöhler, Frederich
Wolf, Max F. J. C.
Wundt, Wilhelm
Würtz, Adolph
Zirkel, Ferdinand
Zittell, K. A. R. von

[1] Biographical Memoirs have not been published.
[2] Charter member, Mar. 3, 1863.
[3] Transferred to roll of members emeriti, 1929.
[4] Transferred to roll of members emeriti, 1932.
[5] Resigned, 1909.
[6] Resigned, 1873.
[7] Transferred to roll of members emeriti in 1908.
[8] Transferred to roll of members emeriti in 1924.
[9] Transferred to roll of members emeriti in 1925.
[10] Dropped 1866, reelected 1875.
[11] Dropped 1866, reelected 1872.

NATIONAL RESEARCH COUNCIL

1. EXECUTIVE ORDER ISSUED BY THE PRESIDENT OF THE UNITED STATES MAY 11, 1918

The National Research Council was organized in 1916 at the request of the President by the National Academy of Sciences, under its congressional charter, as a measure of national preparedness. The work accomplished by the council in organizing research and in securing cooperation of military and civilian agencies in the solution of military problems demonstrates its capacity for larger service. The National Academy of Sciences is therefore requested to perpetuate the National Research Council, the duties of which shall be as follows:

1. In general, to stimulate research in the mathematical, physical, and biological sciences, and in the application of these sciences to engineering, agriculture, medicine, and other useful arts, with the object of increasing knowledge, of strengthening the national defense, and of contributing in other ways to the public welfare.

2. To survey the larger possibilities of science, to formulate comprehensive projects of research, and to develop effective means of utilizing the scientific and technical resources of the country for dealing with these projects.

3. To promote cooperation in research, at home and abroad, in order to secure concentration of effort, minimize duplication, and stimulate progress; but in all cooperative undertakings to give encouragement to individual initiative, as fundamentally important to the advancement of science.

4. To serve as a means of bringing American and foreign investigators into active cooperation with the scientific and technical services of the War and Navy Departments and with those of the civil branches of the Government.

5. To direct the attention of scientific and technical investigators to the present importance of military and industrial problems in connection with the war, and to aid in the solution of these problems by organizing specific researches.

6. To gather and collate scientific and technical information, at home and abroad, in cooperation with governmental and other agencies, and to render such information available to duly accredited persons.

Effective prosectuion of the council's work requires the cordial collaboration of the scientific and technical branches of the Government, both military and civil. To this end representatives of the Government, upon the nomination of the National Academy of Sciences, will be designated by the President as members of the council, as heretofore, and heads of the departments immediately concerned will continue to cooperate in every way that may be required.

WOODROW WILSON

THE WHITE HOUSE, *May 11, 1918.*

(No. 2859)

2. ARTICLES OF ORGANIZATION, NATIONAL RESEARCH COUNCIL

PREAMBLE

The National Academy of Sciences, under the authority conferred upon it by its charter enacted by the Congress, and approved by President Lincoln on March 3, 1863, and pursuant to the request expressed in an Executive order made by President Wilson on May 11, 1918, adopts the following articles of organization for the National Research Council, to replace the organization under which it has operated heretofore.

ARTICLE I. PURPOSE

It shall be the purpose of the National Research Council to promote research in the mathematical, physical, and biological sciences, and in the application of

161

these sciences to engineering, agriculture, medicine, and other useful arts, with the object of increasing knowledge, of strengthening the national defense, and of contributing in other ways to the public welfare, as expressed in the Executive order of May 11, 1918.

ARTICLE II. MEMBERSHIP

SECTION 1. The membership of the National Research Council shall be chosen with the view of rendering the council an effective federatoin of the principal research agencies in the United States concerned with the fields of science and technology named in article I.

SEC. 2. The council shall be composed of—

1. Representatives of national scientific and technical societies.
2. Representatives of the Government, as provided in the Executive order.
3. Representatives of other research organizations and other persons whose aid may advance the objects of the council.

SEC. 3. The membership of the council shall consist specifically of the members of the executive board and the members of the divisions, constituted as provided in articles III and IV.

SEC. 4. Membership in the council shall be limited to citizens of the United States. This, however, shall not be construed as applying to membership in committees, appointed by or acting under the council, whose members are not necessarily members of the council, provided that members not citizens of the United States shall in no case form a majority of any committee.

ARTICLE III. DIVISIONS

SECTION 1. The council shall be organized in divisions of two classes:

A. Divisions dealing with the more general relations and activities of the council.

B. Divisions dealing with special branches of science and technology.

SEC. 2. The divisions of the council shall be as follows:

A. Divisions of general relations:
 I. Division of Federal relations.
 II. Division of foreign relations.
 III. Division of States relations.
 IV. Division of educational relations.

B. Divisions of science and technology:
 V. Division of physical sciences.
 VI. Division of engineering and industrial research.
 VII. Division of chemistry and chemical technology.
 VIII. Division of geology and geography.
 IX. Division of medical sciences.
 X. Division of biology and agriculture.
 XI. Division of anthropology and psychology.

SEC. 3. The number of divisions and the grouping of subjects in article III, section 2, may be modified by the executive board of the National Research Council.

SEC. 4. (a) Each division of general relations shall consist of a chairman, one or more vice chairmen, representatives of national and international organizations, and members at large, appointed as provided in article VI.

(b) There may be an executive committee of each division of general relations, consisting of the chairman and three or more of the members, who shall be chosen by the division at a regular meeting, confirmed by the executive board, and hold office for 1 year terminating on June 30 or, in case of any one or more of such executive committees, on such later date as the chairman of the council may have previously ordered. Between meetings of a division its executive committee shall have power to act on all matters for the division, except those which may be reserved by the division for its own action; but the executive committee shall report all its actions to the division.

SEC. 5. (a) Each division of science and technology shall consist of a chairman and of representatives of such national societies as seem essential for the conduct of the business of the division, appointed as provided in article VI. Members at large, not to exceed three, may also be appointed as provided in article VI. From the membership of the division thus constituted, a smaller group not to exceed 12, shall be designated as executive members, who alone may be reimbursed by the National Research Council for travel expenses incurred in attendance upon meetings of the division.

(b) There may be an executive committee of each division of science and technology, consisting of the chairman and three or more of the executive members, who shall be chosen by the division at a regular meeting, confirmed by the executive board, and hold office for 1 year terminating on June 30 or, in the case of any one or more of such executive committees, on such later date as the chairman of the council may have previously ordered. Between meetings of a division its executive committee shall have power to act on all matters for the division except those which may be reserved by the division for its own action; but the executive committee shall report all its actions to the division.

(c) The terms of office of the chairmen of the divisions of science and technology, other than that of engineering and industrial research, shall be so arranged by the chairman of the council that one-third of these terms expire each year.

SEC. 6. The chairman of each division shall be, ex officio, a member of all committees of the division.

SEC. 7. Actions by the divisions involving matters of policy shall be subject to approval by the executive board.

ARTICLE IV. ADMINISTRATION

SECTION 1. The general officers of the National Research Council shall be a chairman, chosen as provided in article V, section 1; a treasurer (see art. V, sec. 3), and such honorary officers as may be appointed by the council of the National Academy of Sciences, upon nomination by the executive board.

SEC. 2. The affairs of the National Research Council shall be administered by an executive board and its administrative committee. Actions by these bodies involving financial responsibilities or the appointment of general officers must be approved by the council of the National Academy of Sciences, or by the executive committee of the council of the National Academy of Sciences under general authority, or under such special authority as may be conferred on it by the council of the National Academy of Sciences.

SEC. 3. The executive board shall consist of the members of the executive committee of the council of the National Academy of Sciences; the chairman, treasurer, and honorary officers of the National Research Council; the chairmen of the divisions of general relations and of the divisions of science and technology of the National Research Council; the members of the committee on policies; the president or other representative of the American Association for the Advancement of Science; the chairman or other representative of the Engineering Foundation; and six members at large appointed for a term of 3 years, or for an unexpired term in case of vacancy, by the president of the National Academy of Sciences, on recommendation of the executive board. The president of the National Academy of Sciences shall preside at the meetings of the executive board.

SEC. 4. In administrative matters the executive board shall be represented by an administrative committee, which shall consist of the chairman and treasurer of the National Research Council, the president, vice president, and home secretary of the national academy, and the chairmen of the divisions of science and technology of the National Research Council.

SEC. 5. The administrative committee shall have power to act upon all matters except those which may be reserved by the executive board for its own action; but the administrative committee shall report all its actions to the executive board. The administrative committee shall prepare the annual budget for submission to the executive board at its annual meeting.

SEC. 6. (a) There shall also be a committee on policies of the National Research Council. This committee shall be composed of nine members appointed for terms of 3 years by the executive board, preferably so that it may consist largely of persons who have had past experience in the affairs of the National Research Council. The executive board shall appoint the chairman of the committee on policies to serve for 1 year beginning July 1 or until his successor is appointed. The committee shall submit to the executive board recommendations as to general policies.

(b) At the annual meeting of the executive board in 1933, 9 members of the committee on policies shall be appointed; 3 to serve for 1 year, 3 for 2 years, and 3 for 3 years, their respective terms to be determined by lot. Each year thereafter the terms of three members will expire, and their successors, to serve for 3 years each, shall be appointed at the annual meeting of the executive board in that year. The date of expiration of the terms shall be June 30. In case of vacancy the executive board may fill the unexpired term by appointment.

ARTICLE V. APPOINTMENT AND DUTIES OF OFFICERS OF THE RESEARCH COUNCIL

SECTION 1. The chairman of the National Research Council shall be appointed by the executive board, subject to confirmation by the council of the National Academy of Sciences, and shall hold office at the pleasure of the board. The chairman shall be the executive officer of the National Research Council and shall have charge of its general administration. He shall act as chairman of its administrative committee, and shall be, ex officio, a member of all divisions and committees of the council.

SEC. 2. There shall be appointed by the executive board, upon recommendation of the chairman of the National Research Council, an officer with the title of executive secretary of the council, whose duties it shall be to assist the chairman in the administration of the council. He shall attend all meetings of the executive board and of the administrative committee, and act as their secretary, and shall hold office at the pleasure of the board.

SEC. 3. The treasurer of the National Academy of Sciences shall be, ex officio, treasurer of the National Research Council.

SEC. 4. In case of a vacancy in the office of the chairman of the National Research Council, or of the absence or disability of the chairman, an acting chairman may be appointed by the council of the National Academy of Sciences, or by the executive committee of the council of the national academy, upon recommendation of the executive board of the research council or its administrative committee.

ARTICLE VI. NOMINATION AND APPOINTMENT OF OFFICERS AND MEMBERS OF DIVISIONS

SECTION 1. *Divisions of science and technology.*—(a) The chairman of each division shall be nominated to the executive board by the division concerned, with the approval of the administrative committee. The chairman shall be appointed by the executive board at its annual meeting for a term of 3 years.

(b) The national societies to be represented in each of the divisions shall be determined by the division concerned, subject to the approval of the executive board.

(c) The representatives of national societies in each division shall be nominated by the societies, at the request of the chairman of the division, and, after approval by the executive board, shall be appointed by the president of the National Academy of Sciences to membership in the National Research Council for a term of 3 years, and assigned to the division.

(d) Members at large, if any, in each division shall be nominated by the division concerned, with the approval of the executive board, and shall be appointed by the president of the National Academy of Sciences to membership in the National Research Council for a term of 3 years, and assigned to the division.

(e) The executive members in each division shall be designated by the division concerned, subject to the approval of the executive board.

SEC. 2. *Divisions of general relations.*—(a) The officers of each of the divisions of general relations shall be appointed by the executive board to serve for a period of 3 years, except that the foreign secretary of the National Academy of Sciences shall be, ex officio, chairman of the division of foreign relations, and that the appointment of the chairman of the division of Federal relations shall be subject to confirmation by the council of the National Academy of Sciences.

(b) The national and international societies or associations to be represented in each of these divisions shall be determined by the division concerned, subject to the approval of the executive board.

(c) The representatives of such societies or associations shall be nominated by the societies or associations, at the request of the chairman of the division, and, after approval by the executive board, shall be appointed by the president of the National Academy of Sciences to membership in the council for a period of 3 years, and assigned to the division.

(d) Members at large in each division shall be nominated by the division, approved by the executive board, and appointed by the president of the National Academy of Sciences to membership in the council for a period of 3 years, and assigned to the division.

(e) The Government bureaus, civil and military, to be represented in the division of Federal relations shall be determined by the council of the National Academy of Sciences, on recommendation from the executive board of the National Research Council.

(*f*) The representatives of the Government shall be nominated by the president of the National Academy of Sciences, after conference with the secretaries of the departments concerned, and the names of those nominated shall be presented to the President of the United States for designation by him for service with the National Research Council. Each Government representative shall serve during the pleasure of the President of the United States, not to exceed a term of 3 years, and a vacancy from any cause shall be filled for the remainder of the term in the same manner as in the case of the original designation.

SEC. 3. The terms of office of officers and members, unless otherwise provided, shall terminate on June 30 of the year in which their appointments expire.

SEC. 4. Vacancies occurring in the divisions of either class, except as to representatives of the Government, may be filled for the unexpired term by the executive board, upon recommendation of the division concerned, or ad interim by the administrative committee upon similar recommendation.

ARTICLE VII. MEETINGS

SECTION 1. The annual meeting of the executive board shall be held in April in the city of Washington at the time of the meeting of the National Academy of Sciences. Special meetings may be held at other times at the call of the chairman of the National Research Council. A majority of the members of the board shall constitute a quorum for the transaction of business.

SEC. 2. Stated meetings of the administrative committee shall be held in the city of Washington at least five times a year, at such dates as shall be determined by the chairman of the National Research Council. Special meetings may be held at other times on call of the chairman. Five members of the committee shall constitute a quorum for the transaction of business.

SEC. 3. The committee on policies shall hold one stated meeting during the year, preferably in Washington at the time of the annual meeting of the National Academy of Sciences. Special meetings may be held at any time on call of the chairman of the committee. Five members of the committee shall constitute a quorum for the transaction of business.

SEC. 4. Each division of science and technology shall hold at least one stated meeting during the year, at a time to be determined by the chairman of the division in consultation with the chairman of the council. Special meetings may be called at other times by the chairman of the division.

SEC. 5. Meetings of any division of general relations shall be held upon the call of its chairman.

ARTICLE VIII. PUBLICATIONS AND REPORTS

SECTION 1. An annual report on the work of the National Research Council shall be presented by the chairman to the National Academy of Sciences.

SEC. 2. Other publications of the National Research Council may include papers, bulletins, reports, and memoirs, which may appear in the Proceedings or Memoirs of the National Academy of Sciences, in the publications of other societies, in scientific and technical journals, or in a separate series of the National Research Council.

ARTICLE IX. AMENDMENTS

SECTION 1. By action of the National Academy of Sciences, on April 29, 1919, power of amendment of these articles of organization is given to the council of the National Academy of Sciences.

3. BYLAWS

APPROVED APRIL 26, 1933

1. There shall be a publication and Research Information Service, to consist of a director and such other staff as the executive board shall direct. The service shall be under the supervision of a standing committee of the executive board which shall be composed of the chairman and treasurer of the National Research Council, the chairman of the committee on policies, and the director of the service. The functions of the service shall be to cooperate with the divisions of the National Research Council in obtaining required data, to maintain a library of sources, to prepare compilations of general scientific interest, and to edit and superintend the publication of all Bulletins, Reprints, and miscellaneous printed matter issued by the National Research Council. The director of the service shall attend the meetings of the administrative committee, but without vote.

2. The treasurer shall have the assistance of a salaried and bonded officer, the bursar, who shall be chosen by the finance committee of the National Academy of Sciences and be directly responsible to the treasurer.

3. The executive board may create such other salaried officers as are necessary for the transaction of the business of the council.

4. Officers of the council, members of the executive board, and special agents of the council, when authorized to travel on business of the council, may be allowed their necessary expenses.

5. Executive members of the divisions of science and technology and members of the executive committee of any division of general relations, when attending an authorized meeting, may be reimbursed for traveling expenses, or such portion thereof as the division chairman may determine, within the funds made available for that purpose in the budget.

6. The chairman of each division shall direct the administrative and scientific work of the division.

7. In the fiscal year in which the term of office of a chairman of a division expires it shall be his duty to appoint, on or before February 1, a nominating committee of three, chosen from present or former members of the division or from the membership of existing committees of the division, who, in consultation with the chairman of the division and the chairman of the council, shall select an available candidate for the chairmanship for the ensuing term. The name of the candidate shall be reported to the division through its chairman and, if approved by the division, shall be recommended to the executive board at its annual meeting for appointment, as provided in article VI, sections 1 and 2, of the articles of organization.

8. Each division of science and technology is empowered to arrange, in accordance with its special needs, for the selection of the executive members and members at large of the division, and for an executive committee, to be appointed annually, as provided in article III, section 5 (a) and (b), and article VI, section 1 (d) of the articles of organization.

Each division may designate also one of its executive members to act as vice chairman of the division, the term of office to be for 1 year.

9. Following the termination of any regular 3-year period of service the chairman or members of a division shall be eligible for reappointment in the same status only after a lapse of 1 year, except that the executive board may continue the service of a chairman or members for a second period of 3 years, or less, when such action is recommended by the division concerned.

10. An annual honorarium may be paid to the chairman of each division of science and technology and an annual maintenance fund shall be appropriated for the support of the work of each division of the council. The amount of the honorarium and of the maintenance fund of each division shall be determined by the administrative committee, subject to the approval of the executive board and the council of the National Academy of Sciences, or its executive committee.

11. The maintenance fund allotted to each division shall be expended under the authority of the chairman of the division to provide for meetings of the division and its various committees, and other necessary expenses, in accordance with the regulations in force in the council controlling financial expenditures.

12. No member of a committee constituted to administer funds entrusted to the National Research Council shall receive an honorarium or salary from such funds for his services, except in cases specifically authorized in advance by the executive board or its administrative committee, but members of such committees may be reimbursed from the funds for expenses incurred in the work of the committee.

13. Members of special committees organized within any of the divisions must be approved by the administrative committee before official notification of appointment is made by the chairman of the division.

14. Solicitation of funds for the support of projects of a division may be made only after authorization by both the executive board (or its administrative committee) and the council of the National Academy of Sciences (or its executive committee). Such solicitation shall be conducted under the direction of the chairman of the National Research Council acting in conjunction with the chairman of the division concerned.

15. Special funds granted to the National Research Council, other than those for fellowships and grants-in-aid, must be expended in accordance with budgets previously approved by the administrative committee.

16. It shall be the duty of the chairman of each division of the council to submit an annual report of the activities of his division to the chairman of the

council on or before June 30. Interim reports shall be made to the chairman of the council before each stated meeting of the administrative committee.

17. Standing committees of the executive board, unless otherwise provided for, shall be appointed annually by the board at its April meeting, or, in case of need, by the administrative committee at one of its stated meetings.

18. The executive board, at its annual meeting in April, shall appoint a nominating committee of three members to prepare nominations for presentation at the next annual meeting of the board for vacancies in the committee on policies and in the list of members at large of the board, occurring at the end of the fiscal year.

19. Amendments of bylaws may be made by the executive board at any authorized meeting of the board.

20. A publication to be known as the "Bulletin of the National Research Council" shall be established to provide for the publication of materials originating in the work of the council. The Bulletin shall be issued as occasion demands.

21. A series to be known as the "Reprint and Circular Series of the National Research Council" shall provide for the distribution of papers published or printed by or for the National Research Council.

4. ORGANIZATION OF THE COUNCIL, 1933–34

Officers and Executive Board

OFFICERS

Honorary chairman, George E. Hale, honorary director, Mount Wilson Observatory, Carnegie Institution of Washington, Pasadena, Calif.

Honorary vice chairman, William H. Welch,[1] director emeritus, School of Hygiene and Public Health; professor emeritus of the history of medicine, and director emeritus, Institute of the History of Medicine, Johns Hopkins University, Baltimore, Md.

Secretary emeritus, Vernon Kellogg, National Research Council, Washington, D. C.

Chairman, Isaiah Bowman, director, American Geographical Society; National Research Council, Washington, D. C.

Treasurer, Arthur Keith, treasurer, National Academy of Sciences; geologist, United States Geological Survey, Washington, D. C.

Executive secretary, Albert L. Barrows, National Research Council, Washington, D. C.

Bursar, J. H. J. Yule, National Research Council, Washington, D. C.

Chief clerk, C. L. Wade, National Research Council, Washington. D. C.

EXECUTIVE BOARD

Chairman, Isaiah Bowman.

MEMBERS

Honorary chairman, honorary vice chairman, chairman, secretary emeritus, treasurer, and chairmen of divisions of the National Research Council.

Executive committee of the council of the National Academy Sciences

President, W. W. Campbell, president emeritus, University of California, and director emeritus, Lick Observatory; National Academy of Sciences, Washington, D. C.

Vice president, Arthur L. Day, director, Geophysical Laboratory, Carnegie Institution of Washington, 2801 Upton Street, Washington, D. C.

Home secretary, Fred. E. Wright, petrologist, Geophysical Laboratory, Carnegie Institution of Washington, 2801 Upton Street, Washington, D. C.

Treasurer, Arthur Keith.

Chairman of the National Research Council, Isaiah Bowman.

Ross G. Harrison, Sterling professor of biology, and director of the Osborn Zoological Laboratory, Yale University, New Haven, Conn.

Henry Norris Russell, Charles A. Young professor of astronomy, and director of the observatory, Princeton University, Princeton, N. J.

[1] Deceased.

Committee on Policies of the National Research Council

R. A. Millikan, chairman; director, Norman Bridge laboratory of physics, and chairman of the executive council, California Institute of Technology, Pasadena, Calif.

Karl T. Compton, president, Massachusetts Institute of Technology, Cambridge, Mass.

Simon Flexner, director, Rockefeller Institute for Medical Research, Sixty-sixth Street and York Avenue, New York City.

William H. Howell, director emeritus and professor emeritus of physiology, School of Hygiene and Public Health, Johns Hopkins University, Baltimore, Md.

Frank B. Jewett, vice-president, American Telephone & Telegraph Co.; president, Bell Telephone Laboratories, Inc., 195 Broadway, New York City.

Frank R. Lillie, dean of the division of biological sciences, and professor of embryology, University of Chicago, Chicago, Ill.

John C. Merriam, president, Carnegie Institution of Washington, Washington, D. C.

A. A. Noyes, director, Gates Chemical Laboratory, California Institute of Technology, Pasadena, Calif.

Fred. E. Wright, Carnegie Institution of Washington, Washington, D. C.

Representatives of Organizations

President of the American Association for the Advancement of Science, Edward L. Thorndike, professor of education and director of the division of educational psychology of the Institute of Educational Research in Teachers College, Columbia University, New York City.

Chairman of the Engineering Foundation, George W. Fuller,[1] consulting hydraulic and sanitary engineer, 170 Broadway, New York City.

Members at Large

Roger Adams, professor of organic chemistry, University of Illinois, Urbana Ill.

Gano Dunn, president, J. G. White Engineering Corporation, 43 Exchange Place, New York City.

John Johnston, director of research, United States Steel Corporation, Kearney, N. J.

Raymond Pearl, professor of biology, School of Medicine and School of Hygiene and Public Health, Johns Hopkins University, Baltimore, Md.

Oswald Veblen, professor of mathematics, Institute for Advanced Study, Princeton University, Princeton, N. J.

A. F. Woods, director of scientific work, United States Department of Agriculture, Washington, D. C.

ADMINISTRATIVE COMMITTEE

Chairman, Isaiah Bowman; the treasurer of the National Research Council, the president, vice president, and home secretary of the National Academy of Sciences, and the chairmen of the divisions of science and technology of the National Research Council.

COMMITTEES

The chairman of the National Research Council is, ex officio, a member of all divisions and committees of the council.

Committee on grants-in-aid: Chairman, Isaiah Bowman; Francis G. Blake, Arthur Keith, Charles F. Kettering, I. F. Lewis, A. T. Poffenberger, F. K. Richtmyer, W. H. Twenhofel, F. W. Willard; secretary, C. J. West.

Committee on publication and research information service: Chairman, ex officio, Isaiah Bowman; Arthur Keith, ex officio; R. A. Millikan, ex officio; C. J. West, ex officio. Director of publication and Research Information Service, C. J. West.

Committee on building (joint committee with the National Academy of Sciences): Chairman, Gano Dunn; George E. Hale, H. E. Howe, Vernon Kellogg, John C. Merriam, R. A. Millikan, A. A. Noyes, Augustus Trowbridge;[1] Secretary of the committee, Paul Brockett.

Advisory committee on buildings and grounds (joint committee with the National Academy of Sciences): Chairman, Paul Brockett, executive secretary, and custodian of buildings and grounds, National Academy of Sciences, Washington, D. C.; Arthur L. Day, Vernon Kellogg, David White, Fred. E. Wright.

[1] Deceased.

Committee on exhibits (joint committee with the National Academy of Sciences): Chairman, Fred. E. Wright; secretary, Paul Brockett; Isaiah Bowman, Francis G. Blake, L. P. Eisenhart, George E. Hale, Ludvig Hektoen, L. J. Henderson, A. W. Hull, Arthur E. Kennelly, Charles F. Kettering, Elmer P. Kohler, C. K. Leith, I. F. Lewis, C. E. McClung, Elmer D. Merrill, A. T. Poffenberger, F. K. Richtmyer, Harlow Shapley, Joel Stebbins, W. H. Twenhofel, F. W. Willard, R. S. Woodworth.

Executive committee: Chairman, Fred. E. Wright; secretary, Paul Brockett; Arthur L. Day, George E. Hale, Vernon Kellogg, John C. Merriam.

Advisory committee on fellowships: Chairman, ex officio, Isaiah Bowman; Simon Flexner, G. Carl Huber, F. K. Richtmyer, W. J. Robbins, E. B. Wilson.

Committee on patent policy: Chairman, Karl T. Compton; Simon Flexner, Archie Palmer, Joseph Rossman, Robert A. Wilson.

Committee on Policies. (See p. 170.)

TECHNICAL COMMITTEES

Committee on cooperation with Research Corporation: Chairman, F. G. Cottrell, consulting chemist, United States Bureau of Chemistry and Soils, Washington, D. C.; William J. Hale, Maurice Holland.

Committee on publication of excerpts from International Critical Tables: Isaiah Bowman, F. K. Richtmyer, F. W. Willard.

Advisory committee to the American commissioners on Annual Tables of Constants and Numerical Data: Chairman, F. K. Richtmyer, professor of physics and dean of the graduate school, Cornell University, Ithaca, N. Y.; Saul Dushman, Frank B. Jewett, John Johnston, Charles F. Kettering, C. E. K. Mees, Charles L. Parsons. American commissioners, F. K. Richtmyer and C. J. West.

Committee of apparatus makers and users—Executive committee: Chairman, W. D. Collins, chief, Division of Quality of Water, United States Geological Survey, Washington, D. C.; secretary, C. J. West; Lyman J. Briggs, Arthur L. Day, Morris E. Leeds, F. K. Richtmyer, J. M. Roberts.

Executive committee of the American Geophysical Union (representing the American section of the International Geodetic and Geophysical Union): Chairman, W. J. Humphreys, principal meteorologist, in charge of meteorological physics, United States Weather Bureau, Washington, D. C.; vice chairman, Austin H. Clark; secretary, John A. Fleming; H. G. Avers, H. B. Bigelow, William Bowie, C. N. Fenner, W. R. Gregg, D. L. Hazard, N. H. Heck, I. F. Lewis, G. W. Littlehales, H. A. Marmer, R. A. Millikan, Harry Fielding Reid, F. K. Richtmyer, C. S. Scofield, W. H. Twenhofel, Frank Wenner, F. W. Willard.

National committee on instruments and methods of research (to cooperate with similar committee of the International Council of Scientific Unions): C. G. Abbot, F. K. Richtmyer, Fred. E. Wright.

Committee on research publications: Chairman, F. K. Richtmyer; Francis G. Blake, Isaiah Bowman, Davenport Hooker, Arthur B. Lamb, H. C. Parmelee, A. T. Poffenberger, W. H. Twenhofel. Secretary, C. J. West.

REPRESENTATIVES OF THE COUNCIL ON ——

Editorial board of the Proceedings of the National Academy of Sciences: Francis G. Blake, Isaiah Bowman, Charles F. Kettering, I. F. Lewis, A. T. Poffenberger, F. K. Richtmyer, W. H. Twenhofel, F. W. Willard; member of the editorial executive committee, Isaiah Bowman.

Council of the National Parks Association: Vernon Kellogg.

Board of trustees of Science Service: C. G. Abbot, H. E. Howe, Vernon Kellogg.

Divisions of the Council

I. DIVISION OF FEDERAL RELATIONS

Chairman, —— ——.
Vice chairman, Charles F. Marvin.
Secretary, Paul Brockett.

EXECUTIVE COMMITTEE

Chairman, —— ——; vice chairman, Charles F. Marvin; J. R. Mohler, A. M. Stimson.

MEMBERS OF THE DIVISION

Paul Brockett, secretary of the division; executive secretary and custodian of buildings and grounds, National Academy of Sciences, Washington, D. C.

The President of the United States, on the nomination of the National Academy of Sciences. has designated the following representatives of the various departments to act as members of this division.

DEPARTMENT OF STATE

Wilbur J. Carr, Assistant Secretary of State.

DEPARTMENT OF THE TREASURY

A. M. Stimson, Medical Director, Public Health Service.

DEPARTMENT OF WAR

Brig. Gen. Alfred T. Smith, Chief, Military Intelligence Division, United States Army.

Maj. Randolph T. Pendleton, Coast Artillery Corps, United States Army.
Col. Roger Brooke, Medical Corps, United States Army.
Lt. Col. Francis B. Wilby, Corps of Engineers, United States Army.
Col. Charles M. Wesson, Ordnance Department, United States Army.
Maj. Gen. Irving J. Carr, Chief Signal Officer, United States Army.
Maj. Gen. B. D. Foulois, Air Corps, United States Army.
Maj. Gen. Claude E. Brigham, Chief, Chemical Warfare Service, United States Army.

DEPARTMENT OF JUSTICE

———— ————.

POST OFFICE DEPARTMENT

———— ————.

DEPARTMENT OF THE NAVY

Capt. Hayne Ellis, Director of Naval Intelligence, Office of Naval Operations, United States Navy.

Capt. J. H. Hellweg, Superintendent, Naval Observatory, Bureau of Navigation, United States Navy.

Rear Admiral A. L. Parsons, Chief, Bureau of Yards and Docks, United States Navy.

Rear Admiral E. B. Larimer Chief, Bureau of Ordnance, United States Navy.

Rear Admiral Emory S. Land, Chief, Bureau of Construction and Repair, United States Navy.

Rear Admiral Samuel M. Robinson, Chief, Bureau of Engineering, United States Navy.

Rear Admiral Percival E. Rossiter, Chief, Bureau of Medicine and Surgery, United States Navy.

DEPARTMENT OF THE INTERIOR

Elwood Mead, Commissioner, Bureau of Reclamation.
W. C. Mendenhall, Director, Geological Survey.
Harold C. Bryant, Assistant Director, National Park Service.

DEPARTMENT OF AGRICULTURE

Charles F. Marvin, Associate Chief, Weather Bureau.
J. R. Mohler, Chief, Bureau of Animal Industry.
Karl F. Kellerman, Chief, Division of Plant Disease Eradication and Control, Bureau of Entomology.
E. H. Clapp, Assistant Forester in charge of the Branch of Research, Forest Service.
Henry G. Knight, Chief, Bureau of Chemistry and Soils.
Lee A. Strong, Chief, Bureau of Entomology.
———— ————, Bureau of Biological Survey.
Thomas H. MacDonald, Chief, Bureau of Public Roads.
S. H. McCrory, Chief, Bureau of Agricultural Engineering.

DEPARTMENT OF COMMERCE

Joseph A. Hill, Chief Statistician, Statistical Research, Bureau of the Census.
Lyman J. Briggs, Director, National Bureau of Standards.
Frank T. Bell, Commissioner, Bureau of Fisheries.
George R. Putnam, Commissioner, Bureau of Lighthouses.
William Bowie, Chief, Division of Geodesy, Coast and Geodetic Survey.
—————— ——————, Patent Office.
Scott Turner, Director, Bureau of Mines.

DEPARTMENT OF LABOR

Isador Lubin, Commissioner of Labor Statistics.

SMITHSONIAN INSTITUTION

C. G. Abbot, Secretary, Smithsonian Institution.

NATIONAL ADVISORY COMMITTEE FOR AERONAUTICS

J. S. Ames, chairman, National Advisory Committee for Aeronautics; president, Johns Hopkins University, Baltimore, Md.

II. DIVISION OF FOREIGN RELATIONS

Chairman, ex officio, R. A. Millikan.
Vice chairman, Wilbur J. Carr.
Vice chairman, Arthur E. Kennelly.
Secretary, Albert L. Barrows.

EXECUTIVE COMMITTEE

Chairman R. A. Millikan; vice chairmen, Wilbur J. Carr and Arthur E. Kennelly; William Bowie, Lyman J. Briggs, Herbert E. Gregory, George E. Hale, T. Wayland Vaughan.

MEMBERS OF THE DIVISION ·

Ex officio

President of the National Academy of Sciences: W. W. Campbell, president emeritus University of California, and director emeritus Lick Observatory; National Academy of Sciences, Washington, D. C.
Foreign secretary of the National Academy of Sciences: R. A. Millikan, chairman of the division; director, Norman Bridge Laboratory of Physics, and chairman of the executive council, California Institute of Technology, Pasadena, Calif.
Chairman of the National Research Council, the chairmen of all divisions of the council, and the director of the Research Information Service.

Representatives of—

AMERICAN ASSOCIATION FOR THE ADVANCEMENT OF SCIENCE

W. A. Noyes, emeritus professor of chemistry, University of Illinois, Urbana, Ill.

AMERICAN ACADEMY OF ARTS AND SCIENCES

Arthur E. Kennelly, emeritus professor of electrical engineering, Harvard University, Cambridge, Mass.

AMERICAN PHILOSOPHICAL SOCIETY

L. S. Rowe, Director, Pan American Union, Washington, D. C.

DEPARTMENT OF STATE

Wilbur J. Carr, Assistant Secretary of State, Washington, D. C.

DEPARTMENT OF THE NAVY

Capt. Hayne Ellis, Director of Naval Intelligence, Office of Naval Operations, Washington, D. C.

DEPARTMENT OF WAR

Brig. Gen. Alfred T. Smith, Chief, Military Intelligence Division, Washington, D. C.

INTERNATIONAL ASTRONOMICAL UNION

Henry Norris Russell, ex officio, chairman, American section, International Astronomical Union; Charles A. Young professor of astronomy, and director of the observatory, Princeton University, Princeton, N. J.

INTERNATIONAL GEODETIC AND GEOPHYSICAL UNION

Henry B. Bigelow, director, Woods Hole Oceanographic Institute; professor of zoology, and curator of oceanography in the Museum of Comparative Zoology, Harvard University, Cambridge, Mass.

William Bowie, president, Association of Geodesy, International Goedetic and Geophysical Union; Chief, Division of Geodesy, United States Coast and Geodetic Survey, Washington, D. C.

Lyman J. Briggs, director, National Bureau of Standards, Washington, D. C.

John A. Fleming, general secretary, American Geophysical Union; president, Association of Terrestrial Magnetism and Electricity, International Geodetic and Geophysical Union; acting director, department of terrestrial magnetism, Carnegie Institution of Washington, 5241 Broad Branch Road, Washington, D. C.

W. J. Humphreys, chairman, American Geophysical Union; principal meteorologist in charge of meteorological physics, United States Weather Bureau, Washington, D. C.

C. S. Scofield, chairman, section of hydrology, American Geophysical Union; principal agriculturist, United States Bureau of Plant Industry, Washington, D. C.

Thomas G. Thompson, member of the executive committee of the Association on Oceanography, International Geodetic and Geophysical Union; professor of chemistry and director of the oceanographic laboratories, University of Washington, Seattle, Wash.

INTERNATIONAL UNION OF CHEMISTRY

Charles L. Reese, vice president, International Union of Chemistry, 4158 Du Pont Building, Wilmington, Del.

INTERNATIONAL UNION OF PURE AND APPLIED PHYSICS

R. A. Millikan, ex officio, president, International Union of Pure and Applied Physics, and chairman of the American section; director, Norman Bridge Laboratory of Physics; and chairman of the executive council, California Institute of Technology, Pasadena, Calif.

INTERNATIONAL SCIENTIFIC RADIO UNION

Arthur E. Kennelly, emeritus professor of electrical engineering, Harvard University, Cambridge, Mass.

INTERNATIONAL GEOGRAPHICAL UNION

Douglas W. Johnson, chairman, National Committee of the United States, International Geographical Union; professor of physiography, Columbia University, New York City.

INTERNATIONAL BUREAU OF WEIGHTS AND MEASURES

Lyman J. Briggs, Director, National Bureau of Standards, Washington, D. C.

INTERNATIONAL ELECTROTECHNICAL COMMISSION

Clayton H. Sharp, president, United States National Committee of the International Electrotechnical Commission, 294 Fisher Avenue, White Plains, N. Y.

INTERNATIONAL COMMISSION ON ILLUMINATION

E. C. Crittenden, Chief, Electrical Division, and Assistant Director, National Bureau of Standards, Washington, D. C.

Members at Large

P. G. Agnew, secretary, American Standards Association, 29 West Thirty-ninth Street, New York City.

Hugh S. Cumming, Surgeon General, United States Public Health Service, Washington, D. C.

Herbert E. Gregory, director, Bishop Museum of Polynesian Ethnology and Natural History, Honolulu, Hawaii.

George E. Hale, honorary director, Mount Wilson Observatory, Carnegie Institution of Washington, Pasadena, Calif.

Maurice C. Hall, principal zoologist in charge of the Zoological Division, United States Bureau of Animal Industry, Washington, D. C.

John C. Merriam, president, Carnegie Institution of Washington, Washington, D. C.

Elihu Root, 31 Nassau Street, New York City.

Frank Schlesinger, professor of astronomy, and director of the observatory, Yale University, New Haven, Conn.

Walter T. Swingle, principal physiologist in charge of Crop Physiology and Breeding Investigations, United States Bureau of Plant Industry, Washington, D. C.

T. Wayland Vaughan, director, Scripps Institution of Oceanography, La Jolla, Calif.

COMMITTEES

The chairman of the division is, ex officio, a member of all committees of the division.

Committee on Pacific investigations: Chairman, Herbert E. Gregory.

REPRESENTATIVES OF THE NATIONAL RESEARCH COUNCIL ON—

Executive committee of the International Council of Scientific Unions: George E. Hale.

Council of the Pacific Science Association: Herbert E. Gregory.

International Committee on Oceanography of the Pacific, of the Pacific Science Association: T. Wayland Vaughan.

III. DIVISION OF STATES RELATIONS

Chairman, Raymond A. Pearson.
Vice chairman, Albert L. Barrows.

EXECUTIVE COMMITTEE

Chairman, Raymond A. Pearson; vice chairman, Albert L. Barrows; Morris M. Leighton, Jacob G. Lipman, A. R. Mann, Edwin G. Nourse, A. F. Woods, B. Youngblood.

MEMBERS OF THE DIVISION

Raymond A. Pearson, chairman of the division; president, University of Maryland, College Park, Md.

Albert L. Barrows, vice chairman of the division; executive secretary, National Research Council, Washington, D. C.

Representatives of—

DIVISION OF EDUCATIONAL RELATIONS

Vernon Kellogg, secretary emeritus, National Research Council, Washington, D. C.

DIVISION OF PHYSICAL SCIENCES

William Bowie, Chief, Division of Geodesy, United States Coast and Geodetic Survey, Washington, D. C.

DIVISION OF ENGINEERING AND INDUSTRIAL RESEARCH

A. C. Fieldner, Chief Engineer, Experiment Stations Division, United States Bureau of Mines, Washington, D. C.

DIVISION OF CHEMISTRY AND CHEMICAL TECHNOLOGY

Frank C. Whitmore, Dean, School of Chemistry and Physics, Pennsylvania State College, State College, Pa.

DIVISION OF GEOLOGY AND GEOGRAPHY

Edward B. Mathews, professor of mineralogy and petrography, Johns Hopkins University; State geologist of Maryland; director, State weather service, Baltimore, Md.

DIVISION OF MEDICAL SCIENCES

Carl Voegtlin, Chief, Division of Pharmacology, National Institute of Health, Washington, D. C.

DIVISION OF BIOLOGY AND AGRICULTURE

I. F. Lewis, Miller professor of biology and agriculture, University of Virginia, University, Va.

DIVISION OF ANTHROPOLOGY AND PSYCHOLOGY

Carl E. Guthe, director, Museum of Anthropology, University of Michigan, Ann Arbor, Mich.

ASSOCIATION OF AMERICAN STATE GEOLOGISTS

Henry B. Kümmel, director of conservation and development, and State geologist of New Jersey, Trenton, N. J.

SOCIETY OF AMERICAN FORESTERS

F. W. Besley, State forester of Maryland, Baltimore, Md.

Members at Large and Regional Representatives

R. D. Hetzel, president, Pennsylvania State College, State College, Pa.
Morris M. Leighton, chief, Illinois State Geological Survey, Urbana, Ill.
Jacob G. Lipman, dean, College of Agriculture, professor of agriculture, and director, Agricultural Experiment Station, Rutgers University, New Brunswick, N. J.
A. R. Mann, provost, Cornell University, Ithaca, N. Y.
H. W. Mumford, dean, College of Agriculture, and director, Agricultural Experiment Station, University of Illinois, Urbana, Ill.
Edwin G. Nourse, director, Institute of Economics of the Brookings Institution, 744 Jackson Place, Washington, D. C.
T. S. Palmer, biologist, 1939 Biltmore Street, Washington, D. C.
A. F. Woods, Director of Scientific Work, United States Department of Agriculture, Washington, D. C.
B. Youngblood, principal agricultural economist, Office of Experiment Stations, United States Department of Agriculture, Washington, D. C.

IV. DIVISION OF EDUCATIONAL RELATIONS

Chairman, William Charles White.
Secretary, Albert L. Barrows.

EXECUTIVE COMMITTEE

Chairman, William Charles White; Frank Aydelotte, S. P. Capen, C. E. McClung, C. R. Mann, John C. Merriam, H. W. Tyler.

MEMBERS OF THE DIVISION

William Charles White, chairman of the division; chairman, medical research committee, National Tuberculosis Association; pathologist in charge of tuberculosis research, National Institute of Health, Washington, D. C.

Ex Officio

Chairman of the research fellowship board in physics, chemistry, and mathematics, National Research Council: Simon Flexner, director, Rockefeller Institute for Medical Research, Sixty-sixth Street and York Avenue, New York City.

Chairman of the medical fellowship board, National Research Council: G. Carl Huber, dean of the Graduate School, professor of anatomy and director, Anatomical Laboratories, University of Michigan, Ann Arbor, Mich.

Chairman of the board of national research fellowships in the biological sciences, National Research Council: W. J. Robbins, professor of botany and dean of the Graduate School, University of Missouri, Columbia, Mo.

Representatives of—

ASSOCIATION OF LAND-GRANT COLLEGES AND UNIVERSITIES

Raymond A. Pearson, president, University of Maryland, College Park, Md.

AMERICAN ASSOCIATION OF UNIVERSITY PROFESSORS

Marion P. Whitney, emeritus professor of German, Vassar College, 186 Edward Street, New Haven, Conn.

AMERICAN COUNCIL ON EDUCATION

C. R. Mann, director, American Council on Education, 744 Jackson Place, Washington, D. C.

ASSOCIATION OF AMERICAN COLLEGES

Arthur H. Compton, Charles H. Swift distinguished service professor of physics, University of Chicago, Chicago, Ill.

ASSOCIATION OF AMERICAN UNIVERSITIES

Guy S. Ford, professor of history and dean of the Graduate School, University of Minnesota, Minneapolis, Minn.

NATIONAL ASSOCIATION OF STATE UNIVERSITIES

Frank L. McVey, president, University of Kentucky, Lexington, Ky.

UNITED STATES OFFICE OF EDUCATION

Frederick J. Kelly, Chief, Division of Collegiate-Professional Education, Office of Education, United States Department of the Interior, Washington, D. C.

Members at large

Frank Aydelotte, president, Swarthmore College, Swarthmore, Pa.

S. P. Capen, chancelor, University of Buffalo, Buffalo, N. Y.

Herbert E. Hawkes, professor of mathematics and dean of Columbia College, Columbia University, New York City.

C. E. McClung, professor of zoology and director of the Zoological Laboratory, University of Pennsylvania, Philadelphia, Pa.

John C. Merriam, president, Carnegie Institution of Washington, Washington, D. C.

H. W. Tyler, emeritus professor of mathematics, Massachusetts Institute of Technology; consultant in science, Library of Congress, Washington, D. C.

Ernest H. Wilkins, president, Oberlin College, Oberlin, Ohio.

Fernandus Payne, liaison member from the division of biology and agriculture; professor of zoology and dean of the Graduate School, Indiana University, Bloomington, Ind.

V. DIVISION OF PHYSICAL SCIENCES

Chairman, F. K. Richtmyer.
Vice chairman, Henry A. Barton.

EXECUTIVE COMMITTEE

Chairman, F. K. Richtmyer; vice chairman, Henry A. Barton; H. L. Rietz, Henry Norris Russell, P. I. Wold, John Zeleny.

MEMBERS OF THE DIVISION

F. K. Richtmyer, professor of physics and dean of the Graduate School, Cornell University; chairman of the division, National Research Council, Washington, D. C.

Representatives of Societies

AMERICAN ASTRONOMICAL SOCIETY

H. D. Curtis, professor of astronomy and director, Detroit Observatory, University of Michigan, Ann Arbor, Mich.
John A. Miller, professor of astronomy and director, Sproul Observatory, Swarthmore College, Swarthmore, Pa.
Henry Norris Russell, Charles A. Young professor of astronomy and director of the Observatory, Princeton University, Princeton, N. J.

AMERICAN PHYSICAL SOCIETY

J. W. Beams, professor of physics, University of Virginia, University, Va.
Arthur H. Compton, Charles H. Swift distinguished service professor of physics, University of Chicago, Chicago, Ill.
C. J. Davisson, Bell Telephone Laboratories, Inc., 463 West Street, New York City.
L. O. Grondahl, director of research, Union Switch and Signal Co., Swissvale, Pa.
Herbert E. Ives, physicist, Bell Telephone Laboratories, Inc., 463 West Street, New York City.
John Zeleny, professor of physics, Yale University, New Haven, Conn.

AMERICAN MATHEMATICAL SOCIETY

A. B. Coble, professor of mathematics, University of Illinois, Urbana, Ill.
E. R. Hedrick, professor of mathematics, University of California at Los Angeles, Los Angeles, Calif.
R. G. D. Richardson, dean of the Graduate School and professor of mathematics, Brown University, Providence, R. I.

OPTICAL SOCIETY OF AMERICA

Carl L. Bausch, Bausch & Lomb Optical Co., Rochester, N. Y.
L. B. Tuckerman, assistant chief, Division of Mechanics and Sound, National Bureau of Standards, Washington, D. C.
David L. Webster, professor of physics, Stanford University, Stanford University, California.

MATHEMATICAL ASSOCIATION OF AMERICA

H. L. Rietz, professor of mathematics, University of Iowa, Iowa City, Iowa.

ACOUSTICAL SOCIETY OF AMERICA

Harvey Fletcher, acoustical research director, Bell Telephone Laboratories, Inc., 463 West Street, New York City.

AMERICAN INSTITUTE OF PHYSICS

Henry A. Barton, vice-chairman of the division; director, American Institute of Physics, 11 East Thirty-eighth Street, New York City.

Members at large

T. C. Fry, mathematician, Bell Telephone Laboratories, Inc., 463 West Street, New York City.

H. D. Smyth, associate professor of physics, Princeton University, Princeton, N. J.

P. I. Wold, professor of physics, Union College, Schenectady, N. Y.

COMMITTEES

The chairman of the division is, ex officio, a member of all committees of the division.

EXECUTIVE COMMITTEES OF AMERICAN SECTIONS OF INTERNATIONAL UNIONS

International Astronomical Union: Chairman, Henry Norris Russell.

International Union of Pure and Applied Physics: The division of physical sciences acts as the American section of the International Union of Pure and Applied Physics.

International Scientific Radio Union: Chairman, A. E. Kennelly.

ADMINISTRATIVE COMMITTEE

Committee on revolving fund for the publication of mathematical books: Chairman, George D. Birkhoff, professor of mathematics, Harvard University, Cambridge, Mass.

RESEARCH COMMITTEES

Committee on bibliography on orthogonal polynomials: Chairman, J. A. Shohat, assistant professor of mathematics, University of Pennsylvania, Philadelphia, Pa.

Committee on exhibition methods and technique: Chairman, Fay C. Brown, 407 Wilson Lane, Bethesda, Md.

Committee on a glossary of physical terms: Chairman, Le Roy D. Weld, professor of physics, Coe College, Cedar Rapids, Iowa.

Committee on line spectra of the elements: Chairman, Henry Norris Russell.

Committee on methods of measurement of radiation: Chairman, W. E. Forsythe, physicist, Lamp Development Laboratory, National Lamp Works, Nela Park, Cleveland, Ohio.

Committee on numerical integration: Chairman, Albert A. Bennett, professor of mathematics, Brown University, Providence, R. I.

Committee on physical constants: Chairman, Raymond T. Birge, professor of physics, University of California, Berkeley, Calif.

Committee on physics of the earth: Chairman, F. K. Richtmyer, ex officio.

Subsidiary committee on terrestrial magnetism and electricity: Chairman, John A. Fleming, acting director, department of terrestrial magnetism, Carnegie Institution of Washington, 5241 Broad Branch Road, Washington, D. C.

Subsidiary committee on internal constitution of the earth: Chairman, L. H. Adams, physical chemist, Geophysical Laboratory, Carnegie Institution of Washington, 2801 Upton Street, Washington, D. C.

Editorial board of the committee: Chairman, Fred. E. Wright, petrologist, Geophysical Laboratory, Carnegie Institution of Washington, 2801 Upton Street, Washington, D. C.

Committee on rational transformations: Chairman, Virgil Snyder, professor of mathematics, Cornell University, Ithaca, N. Y.

Committee on the relation between physics and the medical sciences: Chairman, F. K. Richtmyer, ex officio.

Subcommittee on receptor organs: Chairman, Charles Sheard, chief, section of physics and biophysical research, Mayo Clinic, Rochester, Minn.

Advisory committee on a Service Institute for Biophysics: Chairman, H. B. Williams, Dalton professor of physiology, College of Physicians and Surgeons, Columbia University, New York City.

Committee on symbols, units, and nomenclature (to cooperate with a similar committee of the International Union of Pure and Applied Physics): Chairman, E. C. Crittenden, Chief, Electrical Division, and assistant director, National Bureau of Standards, Washington, D. C.

VI. DIVISION OF ENGINEERING AND INDUSTRIAL RESEARCH

[Engineering Societies Building, 29 West Thirty-ninth Street, New York City]

Chairman, Charles F. Kettering.
Vice chairman, D. S. Jacobus.
Director, Maurice Holland.
Secretary, William Spraragen.

EXECUTIVE COMMITTEE

Chairman, Charles F. Kettering; vice chairman, D. S. Jacobus; F. O. Clements, Dugald C. Jackson, Frank B. Jewett, John Johnston, Robert Ridgway.

MEMBERS OF THE DIVISION

Charles F. Kettering, chairman of the division; vice president and director, General Motors Corporation; president, General Motors Research Corporation, Detroit, Mich.

Representatives of Societies

AMERICAN SOCIETY OF CIVIL ENGINEERS

George T. Seabury, ex officio, secretary, American Society of Civil Engineers, 29 West Thirty-ninth Street, New York City.
Robert Ridgway, chief engineer, board of transportation, City of New York, New York City.
Edward H. Rockwell, professor of civil engineering and director, department of civil engineering, Lafayette College, Easton, Pa.
Ole Singstad, chief consulting engineer on tunnels, The Port of New York Authority, 80 Eighth Avenue, New York City.
C. J. Tilden, Strathcona professor of engineering mechanics, Yale University, New Haven, Conn.

AMERICAN INSTITUTE OF MINING AND METALLURGICAL ENGINEERS

A. B. Parsons, ex officio, secretary, American Institute of Mining and Metallurgical Engineers, 29 West Thirty-ninth Street, New York City.
John Johnston, director, department of research and technology, United States Steel Corporation, Kearny, N. J.
C. E. MacQuigg, Union Carbide & Carbon Research Corporation, Long Island City, N. Y.
George A. Orrok, consulting engineer, 21 East Fortieth Street, New York City.

AMERICAN SOCIETY OF MECHANICAL ENGINEERS

Calvin W. Rice, ex officio, secretary, American Society of Mechanical Engineers, 29 West Thirty-ninth Street, New York City.
W. D. Ennis, Alexander Crombie Humphreys professor of economic engineering, Stevens Institute of Technology, Hoboken, N. J.
F. M. Farmer, chief engineer, Electrical Testing Laboratories, Eightieth Street and East End Avenue, New York City.
D. S. Jacobus, vice chairman of the division; advisory engineer, Babcock & Wilcox Co., 85 Liberty Street, New York City.
Albert Kingsbury, president, Kingsbury Machine Works, 4314 Tackawanna Street, Philadelphia, Pa.
G. W. Lewis, director of aeronautical research, National Advisory Committee for Aeronautics, Navy Building, Washington, D. C.
W. R. Webster, chairman of the board, Bridgeport Brass Co., Bridgeport, Conn.

AMERICAN INSTITUTE OF ELECTRICAL ENGINEERS

H. H. Henline, ex officio, secretary, American Institute of Electrical Engineers, 29 West Thirty-ninth Street, New York City.
H. P. Charlesworth, assistant chief engineer, American Telephone & Telegraph Co., 195 Broadway, New York City.
L. W. Chubb, director, research laboratories, Westinghouse Electric & Manufacturing Co., East Pittsburgh, Pa.
Dugald C. Jackson, professor of electric power production and distribution, Massachusetts Institute of Technology, Cambridge, Mass.

Frank B. Jewett, vice president, American Telephone & Telegraph Co.; president, Bell Telephone Laboratories, Inc., 195 Broadway, New York City.

Chester W. Rice, assistant to the vice president, General Electric Co., Schenectady, N. Y.

AMERICAN SOCIETY OF REFRIGERATING ENGINEERS

W. J. King, research engineer, General Electric Co., Schenectady, N. Y.

AMERICAN SOCIETY FOR TESTING MATERIALS

F. O. Clements, technical director, research laboratories, General Motors Corporation, Detroit, Mich.

K. G. Mackenzie, consulting chemist, The Texas Co., 135 East Forty-second Street, New York City.

AMERICAN SOCIETY FOR METALS

R. S. Archer, Republic Steel Corporation, One Hundred and Eighteenth Street and Calumet River, Chicago, Ill.

AMERICAN SOCIETY OF HEATING AND VENTILATING ENGINEERS

A. C. Willard, professor of heating and ventilation, University of Illinois, Urbana, Ill.

ILLUMINATING ENGINEERING SOCIETY

W. F. Little, engineer in charge of photometry, Electrical Testing Laboratories, Eightieth Street and East End Avenue, New York City.

WESTERN SOCIETY OF ENGINEERS

William B. Jackson, rate engineer, New York Edison Co., 4 Irving Place, New York City.

SOCIETY OF AUTOMOTIVE ENGINEERS

Grosvenor Hotchkiss, Teleregister Corporation, 60 Hudson Street, New York City.

F. C. Mock, engineer, Bendix Research Corporation, 545 North Arlington Avenue, East Orange, N. J.

AMERICAN WELDING SOCIETY

Henry M. Hobart, consulting engineer, General Electric Co., Schenectady, N. Y.

Members at Large

J. W. Barker, dean, School of Engineering, Columbia University, New York City.

H. C. Parmelee, vice president, McGraw-Hill Publishing Co., 330 West Forty-second Street, New York City.

H. E. Talbott, Jr., chairman of the board, North American Aviation, Inc., 230 Park Avenue, New York City.

COMMITTEES

The chairman of the division is, ex officio, a member of all committees and boards of the division.

Committee on electrical insulation: Chairman, John B. Whitehead, professor of electrical engineering and dean of the engineering faculty, Johns Hopkins University, Baltimore, Md.

Subcommittee on chemistry: Chairman, F. M. Clark, General Electric Co., Pittsfield, Mass.

Subcommittee on physics: Chairman, V. Karapetoff, professor of electrical engineering, Cornell University, Ithaca, N. Y.

Subcommittee on program of research: Chairman, John B. Whitehead.

Committee on heat transmission—Executive committee: Chairman, Willis H. Carrier.

Subcommittee on heat transfer by radiation: Chairman, J. D. Keller, Carnegie Institute of Technology, Schenley Park, Pittsburgh, Pa.

Subcommittee on heat transfer by convection: Chairman, W. H. McAdams, professor of chemical engineering, Massachusetts Institute of Technology, Cambridge, Mass.

Subcommittee on thermal insulation: Chairman, T. Smith Taylor, T. Smith Taylor Laboratories, 45 Grover Lane, Caldwell, N. J.

Subcommittee on nomenclature and definitions: Chairman, E. F. Mueller, physicist, National Bureau of Standards, Washington, D. C.

Committee on industrial lighting: Chairman, Dugald C. Jackson.

REPRESENTATIVES OF THE DIVISION ON—

Committees of the American Society for Testing Materials

Committee A–8 on magnetic analysis: R. L. Sanford, physicist, National Bureau of Standards, Washington, D. C.

Committee for the investigation of sulphur and phosphorus in steel: J. H. Hall, metallurgical engineer, Taylor-Wharton Iron & Steel Co., High Bridge, N. J.

Committee on Ferrous Metals, Advisory to the National Bureau of Standards

Enrique Touceda, consulting engineer, Broadway and Thacher Street, Albany, N. Y.

Sectional Committee on Safety Code for Brakes and Brake Testing of the National Bureau of Standards

S. S. Steinberg, professor of civil engineering, University of Maryland, College Park, Md.

ADVISORY BOARDS TO THE DIVISION OF ENGINEERING AND INDUSTRIAL RESEARCH

AMERICAN BUREAU OF WELDING

[Advisory board on welding research, sponsored by the American Welding Society]

Officers

Director, C. A. Adams.

Committees of the American Bureau of Welding

Committee on structural steel welding: Chairman, Leon S. Moisseiff, consulting engineer, 99 Wall Street, New York City.

Committee on fundamental investigations in welding: Chairman, H. M. Hobart.

HIGHWAY RESEARCH BOARD

Chairman, A. T. Goldbeck, director of the engineering bureau, National Crushed Stone Association, Washington, D. C.

Committees of the Highway Research Board

Committee on curing of concrete pavement slabs: Chairman, F. C. Lang' engineer of tests and inspection, Minnesota Department of Highways, 1246 University Avenue, St. Paul, Minn.

Committee on design: Chairman, A. T. Goldbeck.

Committee on fillers and cushion courses for brick and block pavements: Chairman, J. S. Crandell, professor of highway engineering, University of Illinois, Urbana, Ill.

Committee on use of high elastic limit steel for concrete reinforcement: Chairman, Herbert J. Gilkey, head, theoretical and applied mechanics department, Iowa State College, Ames, Iowa.

Committee on highway finance: Chairman, Thomas H. MacDonald, Chief, United States Bureau of Public Roads, Washington, D. C.

Committee on maintenance: Chairman, B. C. Tiney, maintenance engineer, State Highway Department, Lansing, Mich.

Committee on materials and construction: Chairman, H. S. Mattimore, engineer of tests and materials investigation, State Department of Highways, Harrisburg, Pa.

Committee on correlation of research in mineral aggregates: Chairman, W. J. Emmons, director, Michigan State Highway Laboratory, University of Michigan, Ann Arbor, Mich.

Committee on roadside development (in cooperation with the American Association of State Highway Officials): Chairman, Luther M. Keith, director of roadside development, State Highway Department, Hartford, Conn.

Committee on tractive resistance and allied problems: Chairman, W. E. Lay, professor of mechanical engineering, University of Michigan, Ann Arbor, Mich.

Committee on traffic: Chairman, W. A. Van Duzer, director of vehicles and traffic, District of Columbia, Washington, D. C.

Committee on highway transportation economics: Chairman, R. L. Morrison, professor of highway engineering and highway transport, University of Michigan, Ann Arbor, Mich.

VII. DIVISION OF CHEMISTRY AND CHEMICAL TECHNOLOGY

Chairman, F. W. Willard.

EXECUTIVE COMMITTEE

Chairman, F. W. Willard; Hans T. Clarke, Harry A. Curtis, Edward Mack, Jr., Charles L. Reese.

MEMBERS OF THE DIVISION

F. W. Willard, chairman of the division; executive vice president, Nassau Smelting & Refining Co., 50 Church Street, New York City.

Representatives of Societies

AMERICAN CHEMICAL SOCIETY

Marston T. Bogert, professor of organic chemistry, Columbia University, New York City.

Edward Mack, Jr., professor of physical chemistry, Ohio State University, Columbus, Ohio.

Charles L. Parsons, secretary and business manager, American Chemical Society, Mills Building, Washington, D. C.

Austin M. Patterson, professor of chemistry, Antioch College, Yellow Springs, Ohio.

Edward R. Weidlein, director, Mellon Institute of Industrial Research, Pittsburgh, Pa.

Frank C. Whitmore, dean of the School of Chemistry and Physics, Pennsylvania State College, State College, Pa.

ELECTROCHEMICAL SOCIETY

Paul J. Kruesi, president, Southern Ferro-Alloys Co., Chattanooga, Tenn.

AMERICAN INSTITUTE OF CHEMICAL ENGINEERS

Harry A. Curtis, chief chemical engineer, Tennessee Valley Authority, Ferris Hall, University of Tennessee, Knoxville, Tenn.

AMERICAN CERAMIC SOCIETY

J. C. Hostetter, director of development and research, Corning Glass Works, Corning, N. Y.

Members at Large

Donald H. Andrews, professor of chemistry, Johns Hopkins University, Baltimore, Md.

Hans T. Clarke, professor of biological chemistry, Columbia University, New York City.

Charles L. Reese, ex officio, vice president, International Union of Chemistry, 4158 du Pont Building, Wilmington, Del.

COMMITTEES

The chairman of the division is, ex officio, a member of all committees of the division.

Advisory committee to the National Bureau of Standards on research on the preservation of records: Chairman, F. W. Willard.

Advisory committee to the National Bureau of Standards on corrosion resistance of ferrous pipe materials: ————.

Committee on the publication of an Annual Survey of American Chemistry: Chairman, F. W. Willard.

Committee on the chemistry of colloids: Chairman, Harry B. Weiser, professor of chemistry, Rice Institute, Houston, Tex.

Committee on the construction and equipment of chemical laboratories: Chairman, C. R. Hoover, E. B. Nye professor of chemistry, Wesleyan University, Middletown, Conn. .

Committee on contact catalysis: Chairman, Wilder D. Bancroft, World War memorial professor of physical chemistry, Cornell University, Ithaca, N. Y.

Committee on photochemistry: Chairman, Hugh S. Taylor, David B. Jones. professor of chemistry, Princeton University, Princeton, N. J.

Committee on the preparation and publication of a list of ring systems used in organic chemistry (joint committee with the American Chemical Society); Chairman, Austin M. Patterson.

International Union of Chemistry: The division of chemistry and chemical technology acts as the American section of the International Union of Chemistry.

Representatives of the division in the council of the International Union of Chemistry: Edward Bartow, Claude S. Hudson, John Johnston, Charles L. Parsons, Charles L. Reese, Frank C. Whitmore.

VIII. DIVISION OF GEOLOGY AND GEOGRAPHY

Chairman, W. H. Twenhofel.
Vice chairman, W. L. G. Joerg.

EXECUTIVE COMMITTEE

Chairman, W. H. Twenhofel; vice chairman, W. L. G. Joerg; James Gilluly, R. S. Knappen, Morris M. Leighton.

MEMBERS OF THE DIVISION

Representatives of Societies

GEOLOGICAL SOCIETY OF AMERICA

E. C. Case, professor of historical geology and paleontology, University of Michigan, Ann Arbor, Mich.

E. H. Sellards, professor of geology, University of Texas; director, State Bureau of Economic Geology, Austin, Tex.

MINERALOGICAL SOCIETY OF AMERICA

W. F. Foshag, curator of physical and chemical geology, United States National Museum, Washington, D. C.

PALEONTOLOGICAL SOCIETY

August F. Foerste, associate in paleontology, United States National Museum, Washington, D. C.

ASSOCIATION OF AMERICAN GEOGRAPHERS

Nevin M. Fenneman, professor of geology and geography, University of Cincinnati, Cincinnati, Ohio.

K. C. McMurry, professor of geography, University of Michigan, Ann Arbor, Mich.

AMERICAN GEOGRAPHICAL SOCIETY

W. L. G. Joerg, editor, Research Series, American Geographical Society, Broadway at One Hundred and Fifty-sixth Street, New York City.

SOCIETY OF ECONOMIC GEOLOGISTS

James Gilluly, geologist, United States Geological Survey, Washington, D. C.

AMERICAN ASSOCIATION OF PETROLEUM GEOLOGISTS

R. S. Knappen, geologist, Gypsy Oil Co., Tulsa, Okla.

Members at Large

Mark Jefferson, professor of geography, Michigan State Normal College, Ypsilanti, Mich.

Morris M. Leighton, chief, Illinois State Geological Survey, Urbana, Ill.

W. H. Twenhofel, chairman of the division; professor of geology, University of Wisconsin, Madison, Wis.

COMMITTEES

The chairman of the division is, ex officio, a member of all committees of the division.

Advisory committee to the division: Chairman, W. H. Twenhofel.

National committee of the United States, International Geographical Union: Chairman, Douglas W. Johnson, professor of physiography, Columbia University, New York City.

Committee on Pan American Institute of Geography and History: Chairman, C. H. Birdseye, chief of the division of engraving and printing, United States Geological Survey, Washington, D. C.

Committee on fellowships: Chairman, Arthur Keith, geologist, United States Geological Survey, Washington, D. C.

TECHNICAL COMMITTEES

Committee on accessory minerals of crystalline rocks: Chairman, A. N. Winchell, professor of geology, University of Wisconsin, Madison, Wis.

Committee on aerial photographs: Chairman, C. H. Birdseye.

Committee on batholithic problems: Chairman, Frank F. Grout, professor of geology and mineralogy, University of Minnesota, Minneapolis, Minn.

Committee on Bibliography of Economic Geology: Chairman, Waldemar Lindgren, William Barton Rogers professor of economic geology, Massachusetts Institute of Technology, Cambridge, Mass.

Committee on conservation of the scientific results of drilling: Chairman, Wilbur A. Nelson, professor of geology, University of Virginia, University, Va.

Committee on cooperation with the Bureau of the Census: Chairman, W. L. G. Joerg.

Committee on isostasy: Chairman, William Bowie, chief, Division of Geodesy, United States Coast and Geodetic Survey, Washington, D. C.

Committee on land classification: Chairman, K. C. McMurry.

Committee on the measurement of geological time: Chairman, Alfred C. Lane, Pearson professor of geology and mineralogy, Tufts College, Tufts College, Mass.

Committee on micropaleontology: Chairman, Joseph A. Cushman, director, Cushman Laboratory for Foraminiferal Research, Sharon, Mass.

Committee on paleobotany: Chairman, David White, principal geologist, United States Geological Survey, Washington, D. C.

Committee on processes of ore deposition: Chairman, Edson S. Bastin, professor of economic geology, University of Wisconsin, Madison, Wis.

Committee on sedimentation: Chairman, A. C. Trowbridge, professor of geology, University of Iowa, Iowa City, Iowa.

Committee on State geological surveys: Chairman, Morris M. Leighton, chief, Illinois State Geological Survey, Urbana, Ill.

Committee on stratigraphy: Chairman, Carl O. Dunbar, professor of paleontology and stratigraphy, and curator of invertebrate paleontology, Yale University, New Haven, Conn.

Committee on studies in petroleum geology: Chairman, W. T. Thom, Jr., associate professor of geology, Princeton University, Princeton, N. J.

Committee on tectonics: Chairman, G. R. Mansfield, geologist in charge of areal and nonmetalliferous deposits, United States Geological Survey, Washington, D. C.

REPRESENTATIVES OF THE DIVISION ON—

Advisory council of the Board of Surveys and Maps of the Federal Government: Arthur Keith.

National council of the American Association of Water Well Drillers: O. E. Meinzer.

Committee on the classification of coal of the American Society for Testing Materials: Taisia Stadnichenko.

IX. DIVISION OF MEDICAL SCIENCES

Chairman, Francis G. Blake.
Vice chairman, Ludvig Hektoen.

EXECUTIVE COMMITTEE

Chairman, Francis G. Blake; vice chairman, Ludvig Hektoen; Stanhope Bayne-Jones, Howard T. Karsner, Esmond R. Long, Lewis H. Weed.

MEMBERS OF THE DIVISION

Francis G. Blake, chairman of the division; Sterling professor of medicine, School of Medicine, Yale University; physician in chief, New Haven Hospital, New Haven, Conn.

Representatives of Societies

AMERICAN ASSOCIATION OF ANATOMISTS

Lewis H. Weed, professor of anatomy and director of the School of Medicine, Johns Hopkins University, Baltimore, Md.

AMERICAN ASSOCIATION OF PATHOLOGISTS AND BACTERIOLOGISTS

Howard T. Karsner, professor of pathology and director, Institute of Pathology, Western Reserve University, Cleveland, Ohio.

AMERICAN DENTAL ASSOCIATION

C. T. Messner, 5712 Twenty-third Street, Washington, D. C.

AMERICAN MEDICAL ASSOCIATION

Charles A. Doan, professor and director of medical and surgical research, Ohio State University, Columbus, Ohio.

AMERICAN NEUROLOGICAL ASSOCIATION

Israel Strauss, 116 West Fifty-ninth Street, New York City.

AMERICAN PHYSIOLOGICAL SOCIETY

Walter J. Meek, professor of physiology and assistant dean of the Medical School, University of Wisconsin, Madison, Wis.

AMERICAN PSYCHIATRIC ASSOCIATION

John C. Whitehorn, director of laboratories, McLean Hospital, Waverley, Mass.

AMERICAN ROENTGEN RAY SOCIETY

Merrill C. Sosman, assistant professor of medicine, Harvard Medical School, Boston, Mass.

AMERICAN SOCIETY OF BIOLOGICAL CHEMISTS

Glenn E. Cullen, director of laboratories, Pediatric Research Foundation, and professor of research pediatrics, University of Cincinnati, Cincinnati, Ohio.

AMERICAN SOCIETY FOR CLINICAL INVESTIGATION

Cyrus C. Sturgis, director, Simpson Memorial Institute, and professor of internal medicine, University of Michigan, Ann Arbor, Mich.

AMERICAN SOCIETY FOR EXPERIMENTAL PATHOLOGY

Louise Pearce, associate member, Rockefeller Institute for Medical Research, Sixty-sixth Street and York Avenue, New York City.

AMERICAN SOCIETY FOR PHARMACOLOGY AND EXPERIMENTAL THERAPEUTICS

C. W. Edmunds, professor of materia medica and therapeutics, University of Michigan, Ann Arbor, Mich.

AMERICAN SURGICAL ASSOCIATION

Joseph C. Bloodgood, clinical professor of surgery, Johns Hopkins University, Baltimore, Md.

AMERICAN VETERINARY MEDICAL ASSOCIATION

Charles Murray, professor and head of veterinary investigation, division of veterinary medicine, Iowa State College, Ames, Iowa.

ASSOCIATION OF AMERICAN PHYSICIANS

Warfield T. Longcope, professor of medicine, Johns Hopkins University, Baltimore, Md.

SOCIETY OF AMERICAN BACTERIOLOGISTS

Stanhope Bayne-Jones, professor of bacteriology, and master of Trumbull College, Yale University, New Haven, Conn.

REPRESENTATIVE OF THE DIVISION OF FEDERAL RELATIONS

Col. Roger Brooke, Medical Corps, United States Army, Washington, D. C.

Members at Large

A. J. Carlson, professor of physiology, University of Chicago, Chicago, Ill.

Ludvig Hektoen, director, John McCormick Institute for Infectious Diseases, 637 South Wood Street, Chicago, Ill.

Esmond R. Long, professor of pathology, School of Medicine, and director of the laboratory of the Henry Phipps Institute, University of Pennsylvania, Philadelphia, Pa.

COMMITTEES

The chairman of the division is, ex officio, a member of all committees of the division.

Advisory committee to the division: Stanhope Bayne-Jones, Henry A. Christian, Edmund V. Cowdry, Frederick P. Gay, Ludvig Hektoen, William H. Howell, Raymond Hussey, C. M. Jackson, Howard T. Karsner, George W. McCoy, William Charles White.

Advisory committee on a survey of tropical diseases: Chairman, Frederick P. Gay, professor of bacteriology, College of Physicians and Surgeons, Columbia University, New York City.

Committee on American Registry of Pathology: Chairman, Howard T. Karsner.

Committee on climate and health: Chairman, George C. Shattuck, assistant professor of tropical medicine, Harvard Medical School, Boston, Mass.

Committee on drug addiction: Chairman, William Charles White, chairman, medical research committee, National Tuberculosis Association; pathologist in charge of tuberculosis research, National Institute of Health, Washington, D. C.

Committee for survey of research on gonococcus and gonococcal infections: Chairman, Stanhope Bayne-Jones.

Committee on medical problems of animal parasitology: Chairman, Henry B. Ward, permanent secretary, American Association for the Advancement of Science; emeritus professor of zoology, University of Illinois, Urbana, Ill.

Committee on microbiology of the soil (joint committee with the division of biology and agriculture): Chairman, William Charles White.

Committee on nasal sinuses: Chairman, Edmund V. Cowdry, professor of cytology, School of Medicine, Washington University, St. Louis, Mo.

Committee for research in problems of sex: Chairman, Robert M. Yerkes, professor of psychobiology, Yale University, New Haven, Conn.

X. DIVISION OF BIOLOGY AND AGRICULTURE

Chairman, I. F. Lewis.
Vice chairman, Frank E. Lutz.

EXECUTIVE COMMITTEE

Chairman, I. F. Lewis; vice chairman, Frank E. Lutz; Fernandus Payne, J. H. Bodine, James M. Sherman, E. C. Stakman.

MEMBERS OF DIVISION

I. F. Lewis, chairman of the division; Miller professor of biology and agriculture, University of Virginia, University, Va.

Representatives of Societies

GROUP I.—BOTANICAL SOCIETY OF AMERICA

A. J. Eames, professor of botany, Cornell University, Ithaca, N. Y.

GROUP II.—AMERICAN SOCIETY OF ZOOLOGISTS

J. H. Bodine, professor of zoology, University of Iowa, Iowa City, Iowa.

GROUP III.—AMERICAN SOCIETY OF ANIMAL PRODUCTION, AMERICAN DAIRY SCIENCE ASSOCIATION, AND POULTRY SCIENCE ASSOCIATION

O. E. Reed, Chief, United States Bureau of Dairy Industry, Washington, D. C.

GROUP IV.—AMERICAN SOCIETY OF AGRONOMY, SOCIETY OF AMERICAN FORESTERS, AND AMERICAN SOCIETY FOR HORTICULTURAL SCIENCE

E. N. Munns, senior silviculturist, in charge of the Division of Silvics, United States Forest Service, Washington, D. C.

GROUP V.—AMERICAN PHYTOPATHOLOGICAL SOCIETY AND SOCIETY OF AMERICAN BACTERIOLOGISTS

James M. Sherman, professor of dairy industry, Cornell University, Ithaca, N. Y.

GROUP VI.—AMERICAN GENETIC ASSOCIATION, ECOLOGICAL SOCIETY OF AMERICAN AND GENETICS SOCIETY OF AMERICA

C. E. Leighty, principal agronomist in charge of dry land agricultural investigations, United States Bureau of Plant Industry, Washington, D. C.

GROUP VII.—AMERICAN PHYSIOLOGICAL SOCIETY, PHYSIOLOGICAL SECTION OF THE BOTANICAL SOCIETY OF AMERICA, AND AMERICAN SOCIETY OF BIOLOGICAL CHEMISTS

E. N. Transeau, professor of botany and director of the botanic garden, Ohio State University, Columbus, Ohio.

GROUP VIII.—AMERICAN ASSOCIATION OF ECONOMIC ENTOMOLOGISTS, ENTOMOLOGICAL SOCIETY OF AMERICA, AND AMERICAN SOCIETY OF MAMMALOGISTS

Frank E. Lutz, curator of entomology, American Museum of Natural History, Seventy-seventh Street and Central Park West, New York City.

Members at large

Wallace O. Fenn, professor of physiology, School of Medicine and Dentistry, University of Rochester, Rochester, N. Y.
Fernandus Payne, professor of zoology and dean of the Graduate School, Indiana University, Bloomington, Ind.
E. C. Stakman, professor of plant pathology, University of Minnesota, University Farm, St. Paul, Minn.

COMMITTEES

The chairman of the division is, ex officio, a member of all committees of the division.

Advisory committee to the division: C. E. Allen, L. J. Cole, William Crocker, W. C. Curtis, B. M. Duggar, R. A. Harper, Duncan S. Johnson, L. R. Jones, Vernon Kellogg, Frank R. Lillie, C. E. McClung, Maynard M. Metcalf, Fernandus Payne, Lorande L. Woodruff, A. F. Woods.

Committee on agronomy: Chairman, Richard Bradfield, professor of soils, Ohio State University, Columbus, Ohio.

Committee on animal breeding: Chairman, E. W. Sheets, principal animal husbandman, in charge of the Animal Husbandry Division, United States Bureau of Animal Industry, Washington, D. C.

Committee on animal nutrition: Chairman, Paul E. Howe, senior biological chemist, in charge of nutrition investigations, Animal Husbandry Division, United States Bureau of Animal Industry, Washington, D. C.

Committee on aquiculture: Chairman, J. G. Needham, professor of entomology and limnology, Cornell University, Ithaca, N. Y.

National finance committee on botanical nomenclature: Chairman, A. S. Hitchcock, principal botanist, in charge of systematic agrostology, United States Bureau of Plant Industry, Washington, D. C.

Committee on the effects of radiation on living organisms: Chairman, W. C. Curtis, professor of zoology, University of Missouri, Columbia, Mo.

    Subcommittee on allotment of grants: Chairman, D. H. Tennent, professor of biology, Bryn Mawr College, Bryn Mawr, Pa.

    Subcommittee on survey: Chairman, B. M. Duggar, professor of applied and physiological botany, University of Wisconsin, Madison, Wis.

Committee on the ecology of grasslands in North America: Chairman, V. E. Shelford, professor of zoology, University of Illinois, Urbana, Ill.

Committee on forestry: Chairman, Raphael Zon, director, Lake States Forest Experiment Station, St. Paul, Minn.

Committee on human heredity: Chairman, Charles B. Davenport, director, department of genetics, Carnegie Institution of Washington, Cold Spring Harbor, Long Island, N. Y.

    Subcommittee on family records: Chairman, Ellsworth Huntington, research associate in geography, Yale University, New Haven, Conn.

Committee on infectious abortion (joint committee with the division of medical sciences): Chairman, Karl F. Meyer, professor of bacteriology, and director, Hooper Foundation, University of California, San Francisco, Calif.

Committee on pharmacognosy and pharmaceutical botany: Chairman, Heber W. Youngken, professor of pharmacognosy, Massachusetts College of Pharmacy, Boston, Mass.

Committee on research publications (joint committee with the Union of American Biological Societies): Chairman, Davenport Hooker, professor of anatomy, University of Pittsburgh, Pittsburgh, Pa.

    Subcommittee on permanent organization of editors of biological journals: Chairman, Raymond Pearl, professor of biology. School of Medicine and School of Hygiene and Public Health, Johns Hopkins University, Baltimore, Md.

    Subcommittee on economic and production problems of biological journals: Chairman, Fernandus Payne.

Committee on tropical research: Chairman, W. C. Allee, professor of zoology, University of Chicago, Chicago, Ill.

Committee on wild life: Chairman, John C. Merriam, president, Carnegie Institution of Washington, Washington, D. C.

    Subcommittee on training men for administrative and education work in wild life: Chairman, A. G. Ruthven, president, University of Michigan, Ann Arbor, Mich.

REPRESENTATIVES OF THE DIVISION ON—

Board of trustees of Biological Abstracts: A. F. Blakeslee, J. P. Moore, J. R. Schramm, A. F. Woods.

Institute for Research in Tropical America: I. F. Lewis.

Board of governors of the Crop Protection Institute: E. D. Ball.

Board of review of the Marine Biological Laboratory: Fernandus Payne.

Tropical Plant Research Foundation: R. S. Harper.

XI. DIVISION OF ANTHROPOLOGY AND PSYCHOLOGY

Chairman, A. T. Poffenberger.
Vice chairman, Edward Sapir.

EXECUTIVE COMMITTEE

Chairman, A. T. Poffenberger; vice chairman, Edward Sapir; H. S. Langfeld, F. G. Speck.

MEMBERS OF THE DIVISION

A. T. Poffenberger, chairman of the division; professor of psychology, Columbia University, New York City.

Representatives of Societies

AMERICAN ANTHROPOLOGICAL ASSOCIATION

S. A. Barrett, director, Milwaukee Public Museum, Milwaukee, Wis.

John M. Cooper, professor of anthropology, Catholic University of America, Washington, D. C.

M. J. Herskovits, associate professor of anthropology, Northwestern University, Evanston, Ill.

Edward Sapir, Sterling professor of anthropology, Yale University, New Haven, Conn.

F. G. Speck, professor of anthropology, University of Pennsylvania, Philadelphia, Pa.

Clark Wissler, professor of anthropology, Institute of Human Relations, Yale University; curator of anthropology, American Museum of Natural. History, Seventy-seventh Street and Central Park West, New York City.

AMERICAN PSYCHOLOGICAL ASSOCIATION

John E. Anderson, professor of psychology, and director of the Institute of Child Welfare, University of Minnesota, Minneapolis, Minn.

W. S. Hunter, G. Stanley Hall professor of genetic psychology, Clark University, Worcester, Mass.

Karl S. Lashley, professor of psychology, University of Chicago, Chicago, Ill.

Joseph Peterson, professor of psychology, George Peabody College for Teachers, Nashville, Tenn.

W. B. Pillsbury, professor of psychology, and director of the psychological laboratory, University of Michigan, Ann Arbor, Mich.

Herbert Woodrow, professor of psychology, University of Illinois, Urbana, Ill.

Members at Large

Knight Dunlap, professor of experimental psychology, Johns Hopkins University, Baltimore, Md.

H. S. Langfeld, professor of psychology, and director of psychological laboratory, Princeton University, Princeton, N. J.

M. W. Stirling, Chief, United States Bureau of American Ethnology, Washington, D. C.

COMMITTEES

The chairman of the division is, ex officio, a member of all committees of the division.

Advisory committee on a handbook of South American Indians: Chairman, John M. Cooper.

Committee on problems of auditory deficiency: Chairman, Harvey Fletcher, Research Laboratory, Bell Telephone Laboratories, Inc., 463 West Street, New York City.

Committee on State archeological surveys: Chairman, Carl E. Guthe, director, Museum of Anthropology, University of Michigan, Ann Arbor, Mich.

Subcommittee on the Tennessee Valley: Chairman, M. W. Stirling.

Committee on child development: Chairman, R. S. Woodworth, professor of psychology, Columbia University, New York City.

Subcommittee on selection of child development abstracts and bibliography: Chairman, A. T. Poffenberger.

Committee on psychiatric investigations: Chairman, Madison Bentley, Sage professor of psychology, Cornell University, Ithaca, N. Y.

Committee on the psychology of the highway: Chairman, A. R. Lauer, associate professor of psychology, Iowa State College, Ames, Iowa.
Committee on fellowships: Chairman, A. T. Poffenberger.

REPRESENTATIVES OF THE DIVISION ON—

Public safety advisory committee of the National Safety Council: A. R. Lauer.

5. NATIONAL RESEARCH COUNCIL FELLOWSHIPS

PHYSICS, CHEMISTRY, AND MATHEMATICS

Sums amounting to $1,850,000 have been made available by the Rockefeller Foundation to the National Research Council during the period from May 1, 1919, to June 30, 1935, for the maintenance of a series of research fellowships in physics, chemistry, and mathematics. These funds are administered by a research fellowship board in physics, chemistry, and mathematics appointed by the executive board of the National Research Council. The fellowship board also appoints a number of fellows to work abroad, supported by funds furnished by the Rockefeller Foundation.

Fellowships are awarded to individuals who have demonstrated a high order of ability in research and who have received the Ph.D. degree or equivalent training.

MEMBERS OF THE BOARD

Simon Flexner, chairman, director, Rockefeller Institute for Medical Research, Sixty-sixth Street and York Avenue, New York City.

F. K. Richtmyer, ex officio, secretary, chairman of the division of physical sciences, National Research Council; professor of physics, and dean of the Graduate School, Cornell University, Ithaca, N. Y.

F. W. Willard, ex officio, chairman of the division of chemistry and chemical technology, National Research Council; executive vice president, Nassau Smelting & Refining Co., 50 Church Street, New York City.

Roger Adams, professor of organic chemistry, University of Illinois, Urbana, Ill.

Gilbert A. Bliss, professor of mathematics, University of Chicago, Chicago, Ill.

George D. Birkhoff, professor of mathematics, Harvard University, Cambridge, Mass.

Karl T. Compton, president, Massachusetts Institute of Technology, Cambridge, Mass.

F. G. Keyes, professor of physical chemistry, Massachusetts Institute of Technology, Cambridge, Mass.

Elmer P. Kohler, Abbott and James Lawrence professor of chemistry, Harvard University, Cambridge, Mass.

C. E. Mendenhall, professor of physics, University of Wisconsin, Madison, Wis.

R. A. Millikan, director, Norman Bridge Laboratory of Physics, and chairman of the executive council, California Institute of Technology, Pasadena, Calif.

Oswald Veblen, professor of mathematics, Institute for Advanced Study, Princeton University, Princeton, N. J.

Fellowships for 1933–34 have been awarded to the following persons:

IN PHYSICS

John F. Allen
Norris E. Bradbury
Charles A. Bradley, Jr.
Willoughby M. Cady
Frank G. Dunnington
Robley D. Evans
Alfred B. Focke
Wendell H. Furry
William W. Hansen
George G. Harvey
Norman P. Heydenburg
Montgomery H. Johnson, Jr.
Robert B. King
Franz N. Kurie
Charlton M. Lewis

Gordon L. Locher
Andrew McKellar
Edwin M. McMillan
James H. McMillen
Lyman G. Parratt
Milton S. Plesset [1]
Nathan Rosen
Lynn H. Rumbaugh
Edward W. Samson
George H. Shortley, Jr.
Philip T. Smith
Chester M. Van Atta
John A. Wheeler
Albert E. Whitford
Rolland M. Zabel

[1] Fellows appointed to work abroad.

IN CHEMISTRY

Isador Amdur
Richard S. Bear
William S. Benedict
Richard W. Blue
Alan T. Chapman
Arthur C. Cope
Paul C. Cross
Jacob M. A. DeBruyne
Victor Deitz
Alden J. Deyrup
Raymond M. Fuoss [1]
Edward S. Gilfillan, Jr.
John F. Hicks, Jr.
Ralph R. Hultgren
Wendell F. Jackson

George E. Kimball
Donovan E. Kvalnes
John A. Leermakers
Irving E. Muskat
Melson S. Newman
Richard A. Ogg, Jr.[1]
John L. Oncley
Albert Sherman
Howard A. Smith
Marvin A. Spielman
Robert C. Swain
Nelson R. Trenner
Arthur T. Williamson [1]
Calvert C. Wright
George F. Wright

IN MATHEMATICS

Sherburne F. Barber
Leonard M. Blumenthal
Robert H. Cameron
Joseph L. Doob
Gustav A. Hedlund
Magnus R. Hestenes
Ralph Hull

Ralph D. James [1]
Daniel C. Lewis, Jr.
Edgar R. Lorch
Robert S. Martin
Deane Montgomery
David S. Nathan
Mildred M. Sullivan
Edwin W. Titt

MEDICAL SCIENCES

Funds amounting to $600,000, available over the period from January 1, 1922, to December 31, 1927, have been appropriated to the National Research Council jointly by the General Education Board and the Rockefeller Foundation, and an additional sum of $361,000 for the period from January 1, 1928, to June 30, 1935, has been pledged by the Rockefeller Foundation for the establishment under the division of medical sciences of a series of post-doctorate fellowships in medicine. The administration of these fellowships has been placed in the hands of a medical fellowship board appointed by the executive board of the National Research Council.

Fellowships are awarded to individuals who have demonstrated a high order of ability in research and who have received the Ph. D. or M. D. degree or equivalent training.

MEMBERS OF THE BOARD

G. Carl Huber, chairman, dean of the Graduate School, professor of anatomy, and director of the anatomical laboratories, University of Michigan, Ann Arbor, Mich.

Francis G. Blake, chairman, division of medical sciences, National Research Council; Sterling professor of medicine, School of Medicine, Yale University; physician in chief, New Haven Hospital, New Haven, Conn.

Walter B. Cannon, George Higginson professor of physiology, Harvard Medical School, Boston, Mass.

Evarts A. Graham, Bixby professor of surgery, School of Medicine, Washington University, St. Louis, Mo.

Eugene L. Opie, professor of pathology, Cornell University Medical College; pathologist, New York Hospital, New York City.

[1] Fellows appointed to work abroad.

Fellowships for 1933–34 have been awarded to the following persons:

Caroline C. Bedell	Carl V. Moore, Jr.
Maurice Brodie	James M. Orten
John H. Calhoun	Alwin M. Pappenheimer [1]
Louis H. Cohen	Wesley T. Pommerenke
James K. W. Ferguson [1]	Edgar J. Poth
Earl W. Flosdorf	Boris B. Rubenstein
Smith Freeman	Albert B. Sabin [1]
Louis S. Goodman	Clarence F. Schmidt, Jr.
William G. Gordon	Henry G. Schwartz
Arthur T. Hertig	Robert D. Steihler
Joseph Hughes	Randall L. Thompson
Thomas H. Jukes	William Trager
Champ Lyons	William McC. Tuttle
Edward J. G. McGrath	Arthur J. Vorwald [1]
John J. Miller, Jr.	Julius White

BIOLOGICAL SCIENCES

Sums amounting to $1,188,525 for the period from July 1, 1923, to June 30, 1935, have been made available by the Rockefeller Foundation to the National Research Council for the establishment under the divisions of biology and agriculture and of anthropology and psychology of a series of post-doctorate fellowships in the biological sciences, including zoology, botany, anthropology and psychology, and beginning July 1, 1929, including also fellowships in agriculture and forestry, for the purpose of promoting fundamental research in these subjects. The administration of these fellowships has been placed in the hands of a board of national research fellowships in the biological sciences appointed by the executive board of the National Research Council.

The fellowship board also appoints a number of fellows to work abroad, supported by funds furnished by the Rockefeller Foundation.

Fellowships are awarded to individuals who have demonstrated a high order of ability in research and who have received the Ph. D. degree or equivalent training.

MEMBERS OF THE BOARD

W. J. Robbins, chairman, professor of botany, and dean of the Graduate School, University of Missouri, Columbia, Mo.

I. F. Lewis, ex officio, chairman of the division of biology and agriculture, National Research Council; Miller professor of biology and agriculture, University of Virginia, University, Va.

A. T. Poffenberger, ex officio, chairman of the division of anthropology and psychology, National Research Council; professor of psychology, Columbia University, New York City.

A. M. Banta, professor of biology, Brown University, Providence, R. I.

Madison Bentley, Sage professor of psychology, Cornell University, Ithaca, N. Y.

L. J. Cole, professor of genetics, University of Wisconsin, Madison, Wis.

Max W. Gardner, professor of plant pathology, University of California, Berkeley, Calif.

Carl Hartley, principal pathologist, Division of Forest Pathology, United States Bureau of Plant Industry, Washington, D. C

M. H. Jacobs, professor of general physiology, University of Pennsylvania, Philadelphia, Pa.

E. J. Kraus, professor of botany, University of Chicago, Chicago, Ill.

Robert H. Lowie, professor of anthropology, University of California, Berkeley, Calif.

Joseph Peterson, professor of psychology, George Peabody College for Teachers, Nashville, Tenn.

Edward Sapir, Sterling professor of anthropology, Yale University, New Haven, Conn.

Edmund W. Sinnott, professor of botany, Barnard College, Columbia University, New York City.

D. H. Tennent, professor of biology, Bryn Mawr College, Bryn Mawr, Pa

Fellowships for 1933–34 have been awarded to the following persons:

[1] Fellows appointed to work abroad.

IN AGRICULTURE

Donald C. Boughton
Lester E. Casida
Harold E. Clark
William U. Gardner
Carter M. Harrison

Kenneth W. Neatby [1]
Luther Shaw
William K. Smith
William C. Snyder [1]
Arthur N. Wilcox [1]

IN ANTHROPOLOGY

Walter Dyk
Frederick S. Hulse

Isabel T. Kelly
Carl C. Seltzer.

IN BOTANY

Ernst C. Abbe
Jorgen M. Birkeland [1]
Paul R. Burkholder
David R. Goddard
Roy Graham [1]
Thomas Kerr
Luzern G. Livingston
Gordon Mackinney

Elmer S. Miller
Laurence S. Moyer
Stuart M. Pady
Herbert P. Riley
Richard S. Rosenfels
William H. Tharp
Raymond E. Zirkle

IN FORESTRY

Dow V. Baxter [1]

John Ehrlich [1]

IN PSYCHOLOGY

Edward F. Edelman
Glenn A. Fry
Theodore A. Jackson
Joseph McV. Hunt
Isadore Krechevsky
Robert W. Leeper
Donald B. Lindsley

Lorenz E. Misbach
Joseph E. Morsh
Orval H. Mowrer
Joseph G. Needham
Robert H. Peckham
Kenneth W. Spence
John B. Wolfe

IN ZOOLOGY

Horace A. Barker
Donald H. Barron [1]
Richard M. Bond
Harry G. Day
Hiram B. Glass
George W. D. Hamlett
Robert T. Hill [1]
Charles W. Hooker
Katharine R. Jeffers
Thomas Park

Austin Phelps
Dorothea Rudnick
George K. Smelser
H. Burr Steinbach
Margaret Sumwalt
George W. Taylor
George Wald
Gordon L. Walls
John W. Wells [1]

NATIONAL LIVE STOCK AND MEAT BOARD FELLOWSHIPS

Funds amounting to $52,750 have been appropriated by the National Live Stock and Meat Board for the support, during the years 1924–34, of fellowships for the study of the place of meat in the diet. These fellowships are administered by a special committee appointed by the executive board of the National Research Council and operating under the division of biology and agriculture. In accepting these appropriations, the National Research Council has reserved the right to publish, without restriction, the results obtained under these fellowships.

MEMBERS OF THE COMMITTEE

Paul E. Howe, chairman, senior chemist, in charge of nutrition investigations, Animal Husbandry Division, United States Bureau of Animal Industry, Washington, D. C.

---

[1] Fellows appointed to work abroad.

Anna E. Boller, director, department of nutrition, National Live Stock and Meat Board, 407 South Dearborn Street, Chicago, Ill.

C. Robert Moulton, Institute of American Meat Packers, Chicago, Ill.

H. C. Sherman, Mitchill professor of chemistry, Columbia University, New York City.

During the year 1933–34, with the special consent of the donors, these funds are being used as research grants in the direct support of investigations. Those who are utilizing grants from this fund for the year 1933–34 are as follows:

George O. Burr, University of Minnesota, Minneapolis, Minn.

H. A. Mattell, University of Iowa, Iowa City, Iowa.

6. MEMBERS OF THE NATIONAL RESEARCH COUNCIL, 1933–34

Abbot, C. G., Smithsonian Institution, Washington, D. C.

Adams, Roger, University of Illinois, Urbana, Ill.

Agnew, P. G., American Engineering Standards Association, 29 West Thirty-ninth Street, New York City.

Ames, J. S., Johns Hopkins University, Baltimore, Md.

Anderson, John E., University of Minnesota, Minneapolis, Minn.

Andrews, Donald H., Johns Hopkins University, Baltimore, Md.

Archer, R. S., Republic Steel Corporation, One Hundred and Eighteenth Street and Calumet River, Chicago, Ill.

Aydelotte, Frank, Swarthmore College, Swarthmore, Pa.

Barker, J. W., Columbia University, New York City.

Barrett, S. A., Milwaukee Public Museum, Milwaukee, Wis.

Barrows, Albert L., National Research Council, Washington, D. C.

Barton, Henry A., American Institute of Physics, 11 East Thirty-eighth Street, New York City.

Bausch, Carl L., Bausch & Lomb Optical Co., Rochester, N. Y.

Bayne-Jones, Stanhope, Yale University, New Haven, Conn.

Beams, J. W., University of Virginia, University, Va.

Bell, Frank T., United States Bureau of Fisheries, Washington, D. C.

Besley, F. W., State forester of Maryland, Baltimore, Md.

Bigelow, H. B., Harvard University, Cambridge, Mass.

Blake, Francis G., Yale University, New Haven, Conn.

Bloodgood, Joseph C., Johns Hopkins University, Baltimore, Md.

Bodine, J. H., University of Iowa, Iowa City, Iowa.

Bogert, Marston T., Columbia University, New York City.

Bowie, William, United States Coast and Geodetic Survey, Washington, D. C.

Bowman, Isaiah, American Geographical Society, Broadway at One Hundred and Fifty-sixth Street, New York City.

Briggs, Lyman J., National Bureau of Standards, Washington, D. C.

Brigham, Maj. Gen. Claude E., Chemical Warfare Service, War Department, Washington, D. C.

Brooke, Col. Roger, Medical Corps, War Department, Washington, D. C.

Bryant, Harold C., National Park Service, Washington, D. C.

Campbell, W. W., Lick Observatory, Mount Hamilton, Calif.

Capen, S. P., University of Buffalo, Buffalo, N. Y.

Carlson, A. J., University of Chicago, Chicago, Ill.

Carr, Maj. Gen. Irving J., Chief Signal Officer, War Department, Washington, D. C.

Carr, Wilbur, J., Department of State, Washington, D. C.

Case, E. C., University of Michigan, Ann Arbor, Mich.

Charlesworth, H. P., American Telephone & Telegraph Co., 195 Broadway, New York City.

Chubb, L. W., Westinghouse Electric & Manufacturing Co., East Pittsburgh, Pa.

Clapp, Earle H., United States Forest Service, Washington, D. C.

Clarke, Hans T., Columbia University, New York City.

Clements, F. O., General Motors Research Corporation, Detroit, Mich.

Coble, A. B., University of Illinois, Urbana, Ill.

Compton, Arthur H., University of Chicago, Chicago, Ill.

Compton, Karl T., Massachusetts Institute of Technology, Cambridge, Mass.

Cooper, John M., Catholic University of America, Washington, D. C.

Crittenden, E. C., National Bureau of Standards, Washington, D. C.

Cullem, Glenn E., University of Cincinnati, Cincinnati, Ohio.

Cumming, Hugh S., United States Public Health Service, Washington, D. C.

Curtis, Harry A., Ferris Hall, University of Tennessee, Knoxville, Tenn.

Curtis, Heber D., University of Michigan, Ann Arbor, Mich.

Davisson, C. J., Bell Telephone Laboratories, Inc., 463 West Street, New York City.
Day, A. L., Geophysical Laboratory of the Carnegie Institution of Washington, 2801 Upton Street, Washington, D. C.
Doan, Charles A., Ohio State University, Columbus, Ohio.
Dunlap, Knight, Johns Hopkins University, Baltimore, Md.
Dunn, Gano, J. G. White Engineering Corporation, 43 Exchange Place, New York City.
Eames, A. J., Cornell University, Ithaca, N. Y.
Edmunds, C. W., University of Michigan, Ann Arbor, Mich.
Ellis, Capt. Hayne, Office of Naval Operations, Navy Department, Washington, D. C.
Ennis, W. D., Stevens Institute of Technology, Hoboken, N. J.
Farmer, F. M., Electrical Testing Laboratories, Eightieth Street and East End Avenue, New York City.
Fenn, Wallace O., University of Rochester, Rochester, N. Y.
Fenneman, Nevin M., University of Cincinnati, Cincinnati, Ohio.
Fieldner, A. C., United States Bureau of Mines, Washington, D. C.
Fleming, J. A., Department of Terrestrial Magnesism of the Carnegie Institution of Washington, 5241 Broad Branch Road, Washington, D. C.
Fletcher, Harvey, Bell Telephone Laboratories, Inc., 463 West Street, New York City.
Flexner, Simon, Rockefeller Institute for Medical Research, Sixty-sixth Street and York Avenue, New York City.
Foerste, August F., United States National Museum, Washington, D. C.
Ford, Guy S., University of Minnesota, Minneapolis, Minn.
Foshag, W. F., United States National Museum, Washington, D. C.
Foulois, Maj. Gen. B. D., Air Corps, War Department, Washington, D. C.
Fry, T. C., Bell Telephone Laboratories, Inc., 463 West Street, New York City.
Gilluly, James, United States Geological Survey, Washington, D. C.
Gregory, Herbert E., Bishop Museum, Honolulu, Hawaii.
Grondahl, L. O., Union Switch & Signal Co., Swissvale, Pa.
Guthe, Carl E., University of Michigan, Ann Arbor, Mich.
Hale, George E., Mount Wilson Observatory, Pasadena, Calif.
Hall, Maurice C., United States Bureau of Animal Industry, Washington, D. C.
Harrison, Ross G., Yale University, New Haven, Conn.
Hawkes, Herbert E., Columbia University, New York City.
Hedrick, E. R., University of California at Los Angeles, Los Angeles, Calif.
Hektoen, Ludvig, John McCormick Institute for Infectious Diseases, 637 South Wood Street, Chicago, Ill.
Hellweg, Capt. Julius F., Naval Observatory, Navy Department, Washington, D. C.
Henline, H. H., American Institute of Electrical Engineers, 29 West Thirty-ninth Street, New York City.
Herskovits, M. J., Northwestern University, Evanston, Ill.
Hetzel, R. D., Pennsylvania State College, State College, Pa.
Hill, Joseph A., United States Bureau of the Census, Washington, D. C.
Hobart, Henry M., General Electric Co., Schenectady, N. Y.
Hostetter, J. C., Corning Glass Works, Corning, N. Y.
Hotchkiss, Grosvenor, Teleregister Corporation, 60 Hudson Street, New York City.
Howell, W. H., School of Hygiene and Public Health, Johns Hopkins University, Baltimore, Md.
Huber, G. Carl, University of Michigan, Ann Arbor, Mich.
Humphreys, W. J., United States Weather Bureau, Washington, D. C.
Hunter, W. S., Clark University, Worcester, Mass.
Ives, Herbert E., Bell Telephone Laboratories, Inc., 463 West Street, New York City.
Jackson, Dugald C., Massachusetts Institute of Technology, Cambridge, Mass.
Jackson, William B., New York Edison Co., 4 Irving Place, New York City.
Jacobus, D. S., Babcock & Wilcox Co., 85 Liberty Street, New York City.
Jefferson, Mark, Michigan State Normal College, Ypsilanti, Mich.
Jewett, Frank B., American Telephone & Telegraph Co., 195 Broadway, New York City.
Joerg, W. L. G., American Geographical Society, Broadway at One Hundred and Fifty-sixth Street, New York City.
Johnson, Douglas W., Columbia University, New York City.

Johnston, John, United States Steel Corporation, Kearney, N. J.
Karsner, Howard T., Western Reserve University, Cleveland, Ohio.
Keith, Arthur, United States Geological Survey, Washington, D. C.
Kellerman, Karl F., United States Bureau of Entomology, Washington, D. C.
Kellogg, Vernon, 2305 Bancroft Place, Washington, D. C.
Kelly, Frederick J., United States Office of Education, Washington, D. C.
Kennelly, A. E., Harvard University, Cambridge, Mass.
Kettering, Charles F., General Motors Research Corporation, Detroit, Mich.
King, W. J., General Electric Co., Schenectady, N. Y.
Kingsbury, Albert, Kingsbury Machine Works, Frankford, Philadelphia, Pa.
Kinnan, William A., United States Patent Office, Washington, D. C.
Knappen, R. S., Gypsy Oil Co., Tulsa, Okla.
Knight, Henry G., United States Bureau of Chemistry and Soils, Washington, D. C.
Kreusi, Paul J., Southern Ferro-Alloys Co., Chattanooga, Tenn.
Kümmel, Henry B., State Geologist, Trenton, N. J.
Land, Rear Admiral Emory S., Bureau of Construction and Repair, Navy Department, Washington, D. C.
Langfeld, H. S., Princeton University, Princeton, N. J.
Larimer, Rear Admiral E. B., Bureau of Ordnance, Navy Department, Washington, D. C.
Lashley, Karl S., University of Chicago, Chicago, Ill.
Leighton, Morris M., State Geological Survey, Urbana, Ill.
Leighty, C. E., United States Bureau of Plant Industry, Washington, D. C.
Lewis, G. W., National Advisory Committee for Aeronautics, Washington, D. C.
Lewis, I. F., University of Virginia, University, Va.
Lillie, Frank R., University of Chicago, Chicago, Ill.
Lipman, Jacob G., New Jersey Agricultural Experiment Station, New Brunswick, N. J.
Little, W. F., Electrical Testing Laboratories, Eightieth Street and East End Avenue, New York City.
Long, Esmund R., University of Pennsylvania, Philadelphia, Pa.
Longcope, Warfield T., Johns Hopkins University, Baltimore, Md.
Lubin, Isador, Department of Labor, Washington, D. C.
Lutz, Frank E., American Museum of Natural History, Seventy-seventh Street and Central Park West, New York City.
MacDonald, Thomas H., United States Bureau of Public Roads, Washington, D. C.
Mack, Edward, Jr., Ohio State University, Columbus, Ohio.
Mackenzie, K. G., The Texas Co., 135 East Forty-second Street, New York City.
MacQuigg, C. E., Union Carbide & Carbon Research Corporation, Long Island City, N. Y.
Mann, A. R., Cornell University, Ithaca, N. Y.
Mann, C. R., American Council on Education, 744 Jackson Place, Washington, D. C.
Marvin, Charles F., United States Weather Bureau, Washington, D. C.
Mathews, E. B., Johns Hopkins University, Baltimore, Md.
McClung, C. E., University of Pennsylvania, Philadelphia, Pa.
McCrory, S. H., United States Bureau of Agricultural Engineering, Washington, D. C.
McMurry, K. C., University of Michigan, Ann Arbor, Mich.
McVey, Frank L., University of Kentucky, Lexington, Ky.
Mead, Elwood, United States Bureau of Reclamation, Washington, D. C.
Meek, Walter J., University of Wisconsin, Madison, Wis.
Mendenhall, W. C., United States Geological Survey, Washington, D. C.
Merriam, John C., Carnegie Institution of Washington, Washington, D. C.
Messner, C. T., 5712 Twenty-third Street, Washington, D. C.
Miller, John A., Swarthmore College, Swarthmore, Pa.
Millikan, R. A., California Institute of Technology, Pasadena, Calif.
Mock, F. C., Bendix Research Corporation, East Orange, N. J.
Mohler, J. R., United States Bureau of Animal Industry, Washington, D. C.
Mumford, H. W., University of Illinois, Urbana, Ill.
Munns, E. N., United States Forest Service, Washington, D. C.
Murray, Charles, Iowa State College, Ames, Iowa.
Nourse, Edwin G., Institute of Economics, 744 Jackson Place, Washington, D. C.
Noyes, A. A., California Institute of Technology, Pasadena, Calif.
Noyes, W. A., University of Illinois, Urbana, Ill.

Orrok, George A., 21 East Fortieth Street, New York City.
Palmer, T. S., 1939 Biltmore Street, Washington, D. C.
Parmelee, H. C., McGraw-Hill Publishing Co., 330 West Forty-second Street, New York City.
Parsons, A. B., American Institute of Mining and Metallurgical Engineers, 29 West Thirty-ninth Street, New York City.
Parsons, Rear Admiral A. L., Bureau of Yards and Docks, Navy Department, Washington, D. C.
Parsons, Charles L., American Chemical Society, Mills Building, Washington, D. C.
Patterson, Austin M., Antioch College, Yellow Springs, Ohio.
Payne, Fernandus, Indiana University, Bloomington, Ind.
Pearce, Louise, Rockefeller Institute for Medical Research, Sixty-sixth Street and York Avenue, New York City.
Pearl, Raymond, School of Hygiene and Public Health, Johns Hopkins University, Baltimore, Md.
Pearson, R. A., University of Maryland, College Park, Md.
Pendleton, Maj. Ralph T., Coast Artillery Corps, War Department, Washington, D. C.
Peterson, Joseph, George Peabody College for Teachers, Nashville, Tenn.
Pillsbury, W. B., University of Michigan, Ann Arbor, Mich.
Poffenberger, A. T., Columbia University, New York City.
Putnam, George R., United States Bureau of Lighthouses, Washington, D. C.
Redington, Paul G., United States Bureau of Biological Survey, Washington, D. C.
Reed, O. E., United States Bureau of Dairy Industry, Washington, D. C.
Reese, Charles L., Du Pont Building, Wilmington, Del.
Rice, Calvin W., American Society of Mechanical Engineers, 29 West Thirty-ninth Street, New York City.
Rice, Chester W., General Electric Co., Schenectady, N. Y.
Richardson, R. G. D., Brown University, Providence, R. I.
Richtmyer, F. K., Cornell University, Ithaca, N. Y.
Ridgway, Robert, Board of Transportation, City of New York, New York City.
Rietz, H. L., University of Iowa, Iowa City, Iowa.
Robbins, W. J., University of Missouri, Columbia, Mo.
Robinson, Rear Admiral Samuel M., Bureau of Engineering, Navy Department, Washington, D. C.
Rockwell, Edward H., Lafayette College, Easton, Pa.
Root, Elihu, 31 Nassau Street, New York City.
Rossiter, Rear Admiral Percival E., Bureau of Medicine and Surgery, Navy Department, Washington, D. C.
Rowe, L. S., Pan-American Union, Washington, D. C.
Russell, Henry Norris, Princeton University, Princeton, N. J.
Sapir, Edward, Yale University, New Haven, Conn.
Scofield, C. S., United States Bureau of Plant Industry, Washington, D. C.
Seabury, George T., American Society of Civil Engineers, 29 West Thirty-ninth Street, New York City.
Sellards, E. H., University of Texas, Austin, Tex.
Sharp, Clayton H., 294 Fisher Avenue, White Plains, N. Y.
Sherman, James M., Cornell University, Ithaca, N. Y.
Singsted, Ole, Port of New York Authority, 80 Eighth Avenue, New York City.
Smith, Brig. Gen. Alfred T., Military Intelligence Division, War Department, Washington, D. C.
Smyth, H. D., Princeton University, Princeton, N. J.
Sosman, Merrill C., Harvard Medical School, Boston, Mass.
Speck, F. G., University of Pennsylvania, Philadelphia, Pa.
Stakman, E. C., University Farm, University of Minnesota, St. Paul, Minn.
Stimson, A. M., United States Public Health Service, Washington, D. C.
Stirling, M. W., United States Bureau of American Ethnology, Washington, D. C.
Strauss, Israel, 116 West Fifty-ninth Street, New York City.
Strong, Lee A., United States Bureau of Entomology, Washington, D. C.
Sturgis, Cyrus C., University of Michigan, Ann Arbor, Mich.
Swingle, Walter T., United States Bureau of Plant Industry, Washington, D. C.
Talbott, H. E., Jr., North American Aviation, Inc., 230 Park Avenue, New York City.
Thompson, Thomas G., University of Washington, Seattle, Wash.

Thorndike, Edward L., Teachers College, Columbia University, New York City.
Tilden, C. J., Yale University, New Haven, Conn.
Transeau, E. N., Ohio State University, Columbus, Ohio.
Tuckerman, L. B., National Bureau of Standards, Washington, D. C.
Turner, Scott, United States Bureau of Mines, Washington, D. C.
Twenhofel, W. H., University of Wisconsin, Madison, Wis.
Tyler, H. S., Library of Congress, Washington, D. C.
Vaughan, T. Wayland, Scripps Institution of Oceanography, La Jolla, Calif.
Veblen, Oswald, Institute for Advanced Study, Princeton University, Princeton, N. J.
Voegtlin, Carl, National Institute of Health, Washington, D. C.
Webster, David L., Stanford University, Stanford University, Calif.
Webster, W. R., Bridgeport Brass Co., Bridgeport, Conn.
Weed, Lewis H., Johns Hopkins University, Baltimore, Md.
Weidlein, E. R., Mellon Institute for Industrial Research, Pittsburgh, Pa.
Wesson, Lt. Col. Charles M., Ordnance Department, War Department, Washington, D. C.
White, William Charles, National Institute of Health, Washington, D. C.
Whitehorn, J. C., McLean Hospital, Waverley, Mass.
Whitmore, Frank C., Pennsylvania State College, State College, Pa.
Whitney, Marian P., 186 Edward Street, New Haven, Conn.
Wilby, Lt. Col. Francis B., Corps of Engineers, War Department, Washington, D. C.
Wilkins, Ernest H., Oberlin College, Oberlin, Ohio.
Willard, A. C., University of Illinois, Urbana, Ill.
Willard, F. W., Nassau Smelting & Refining Co., 50 Church Street, New York City.
Wissler, Clark, American Museum of Natural History, Seventy-seventh Street and Central Park West, New York City.
Wold, P. I., Union College, Schnectady, N. Y.
Woodrow, Herbert, University of Illinois, Urbana, Ill.
Woods, A. F., United States Department of Agriculture, Washington, D. C.
Wright, Fred. E., Geophysical Laboratory of the Carnegie Institution of Washington, 2801 Upton Street, Washington, D. C.
Youngblood, B., Office of Experiment Stations, United States Department of Agriculture, Washington, D. C.
Zeleny, John, Yale University, New Haven, Conn.

O

REPORT OF THE
NATIONAL ACADEMY
OF SCIENCES

FISCAL YEAR
1934-1935

REPORT OF THE
NATIONAL ACADEMY
OF SCIENCES

FISCAL YEAR

1934 - 1935

UNITED STATES
GOVERNMENT PRINTING OFFICE
WASHINGTON : 1936

CONTENTS

LETTER OF TRANSMITTAL

NATIONAL ACADEMY OF SCIENCES,
January 24, 1936.

Hon. JOHN N. GARNER,
  President of the United States Senate.

SIR: I have the honor to transmit to you herewith the report of my predecessor, Dr. W. W. Campbell, as president of the National Academy of Sciences, for the fiscal year ended June 30, 1935.

  Yours respectfully,

FRANK R. LILLIE, *President.*

ACT OF INCORPORATION

AN ACT To incorporate the National Academy of Sciences

Be it enacted by the Senate and House of Representatives of the United States of America in Congress assembled, That Louis Agassiz, Massachusetts; J. H. Alexander, Maryland; S. Alexander, New Jersey; A. D. Bache, at large; F. B. Barnard,[1] at large; J. G. Barnard, United States Army, Massachusetts; W. H. C. Bartlett, United States Military Academy, Missouri; U. A. Boyden,[2] Massachusetts; Alexis Caswell, Rhode Island; William Chauvenet, Missouri; J. H. C. Coffin, United States Naval Academy, Maine; J. A. Dahlgren,[2] United States Navy, Pennsylvania; J. D. Dana, Connecticut; Charles H. Davis, United States Navy, Massachusetts; George Englemann, Saint Louis, Missouri; J. F. Frazer, Pennsylvania; Wolcott Gibbs, New York; J. M. Giles,[3] United States Navy, District of Columbia; A. A. Gould, Massachusetts; B. A. Gould, Massachusetts; Asa Gray, Massachusetts; A. Guyot, New Jersey; James Hall, New York; Joseph Henry, at large; J. E. Hilgard, at large, Illinois; Edward Hitchcock, Massachusetts; J. S. Hubbard, United States Naval Observatory, Connecticut; A. A. Humphreys, United States Army, Pennsylvania; J. L. Le Conte, United States Army, Pennsylvania; J. Leidy, Pennsylvania; J. P. Lesley, Pennsylvania; M. F. Longstreth, Pennsylvania; D. H. Mahan, United States Military Academy, Virginia; J. S. Newberry, Ohio; H. A. Newton, Connecticut; Benjamin Peirce, Massachusetts; John Rodgers, United States Navy, Indiana; Fairman Rogers, Pennsylvania; R. E. Rogers, Pennsylvania; W. B. Rogers, Massachusetts; L. M. Rutherfurd, New York; Joseph Saxton, at large; Benjamin Silliman, Connecticut; Benjamin Silliman, junior, Connecticut; Theodore Strong, New Jersey; John Torrey, New York; J. G. Totten, United States Army, Connecticut; Joseph Winlock, United States Nautical Almanac, Kentucky; Jeffries Wyman, Massachusetts; J. D. Whitney, California; their associates and successors duly chosen, are hereby incorporated, constituted, and declared to be a body corporate, by the name of the National Academy of Sciences.

SEC. 2. *And be it further enacted,* That the National Academy of Sciences shall consist of not more than fifty ordinary members, and the said corporation hereby constituted shall have power to make its own organization, including its constitution, bylaws, and rules and regulations; to fill all vacancies created by death, resignation, or otherwise; to provide for the election of foreign and domestic members, the division into classes, and all other matters needful or usual in such institution, and to report the same to Congress.

SEC. 3. *And be it further enacted,* That the National Academy of Sciences shall hold an annual meeting at such place in the United States as may be designated, and the Academy shall, whenever called upon by any department of the Government, investigate, examine, experiment, and report upon any subject of science or art, the actual expense of such investigations, examinations, experiments, and reports to be paid from appropriations which may be made for the purpose, but the Academy shall receive no compensation whatever for any services to the Government of the United States.

GALUSHA A. GROW,
Speaker of the House of Representatives.

SOLOMON FOOTE,
President of the Senate pro tempore.

Approved, March 3, 1863.

ABRAHAM LINCOLN, *President.*

[1] The correct name of this charter member was F. A. P. Barnard.
[2] Declined.
[3] The correct name of this charter member was J. M. Gillis.

AMENDMENTS

AN ACT To amend the act to incorporate the National Academy of Sciences

Be it enacted by the Senate and House of Representatives of the United States of America in Congress assembled, That the act to incorporate the National Academy of Sciences, approved March third, eighteen hundred and sixty-three, be, and the same is hereby, so amended as to remove the limitation of the number of ordinary members of said Academy as provided in said act.

Approved, July 14, 1870.

_____

AN ACT To authorize the National Academy of Sciences to receive and hold trust funds for the promotion of science, and for other purposes

Be it enacted by the Senate and House of Representatives of the United States of America in Congress assembled, That the National Academy of Sciences, incorporated by the act of Congress approved March third, eighteen hundred and sixty-three, and its several supplements be, and the same is hereby, authorized and empowered to receive bequests and donations and hold the same in trust, to be applied by the said Academy in aid of scientific investigations and according to the will of the donors.

Approved, June 20, 1884.

_____

AN ACT To amend the act authorizing the National Academy of Sciences to receive and hold trust funds for the promotion of science, and for other purposes

Be it enacted by the Senate and House of Representatives of the United States of America in Congress assembled, That the act to authorize the National Academy of Sciences to receive and hold trust funds for the promotion of science, and for other purposes, approved June twentieth, eighteen hundred and eighty-four, be, and the same is hereby, amended to read as follows:

"That the National Academy of Sciences, incorporated by the act of Congress approved March third, eighteen hundred and sixty-three, be, and the same is hereby, authorized and empowered to receive by devise, bequest, donation, or otherwise, either real or personal property, and to hold the same absolutely or in trust, and to invest, reinvest, and manage the same in accordance with the provisions of its constitution, and to apply said property and the income arising therefrom to the objects of its creation and according to the instructions of the donors: *Provided, however,* That the Congress may at any time limit the amount of real estate which may be acquired and the length of time the same may be held by said National Academy of Sciences."

SEC. 2. That the right to alter, amend, or repeal this act is hereby expressly reserved.

Approved, May 27, 1914.

ANNUAL REPORT OF THE NATIONAL ACADEMY OF SCIENCES

REVIEW OF THE YEAR 1934-35

The council of the Academy formally requested the president of the Academy to deliver an address at the annual meeting held in the city of Washington in the period April 21-24, 1935. President Campbell spoke as follows:

The Academy's dinner of each year is attended for the first time by many of its recently elected members. It is a safe guess that those new members have an incomplete understanding of the historic reason for the Academy's creation and existence. It was in the middle year of our Great War between the States, the year 1863, that the United States Government, feeling the need of a definite and responsible organization of the scientists of the Nation to which it could go at any time for information and advice on scientific subjects, incorporated and constituted the National Academy of Sciences, by a special act of Congress. This act, in effect the charter of the Academy, is a remarkable document; remarkable in its brevity, its clarity, and, in my opinion, its wisdom.

The first paragraph of the congressional act consists of the statement that 50 American scientists, whose names are recorded in alphabetical order in the act, beginning appropriately with Louis Agassiz, of Harvard, on the Atlantic coast, and ending with "J. D. Whitney, California; their associates and successors duly chosen, are hereby incorporated, constituted, and declared to be a body corporate, by the name of the National Academy of Sciences."

The remaining 15 lines of the printed charter contain 5 specifications, which I shall now quote, and briefly comment upon:

Firstly, "* * * the National Academy of Sciences shall consist of not more than 50 ordinary members." The Congress, in 1870, removed the limitation placed upon the number of ordinary members, and the Academy has itself fixed the limit, for the time being, at 300. The actual number is now 275, of whom 2 are women. There are also 44 foreign associates; that is, honorary members, eminent scientists of other nations.

Secondly, "* * * the National Academy of Sciences shall hold an annual meeting at such place in the United States as may be designated." The Academy's annual meeting is held always in the city of Washington, in the month of April. The Academy holds a stated meeting in the autumn of each year, always at some center of higher education or research activity other than Washington. It met last November in Cleveland. It will meet next November at the University of Virginia.

Thirdly, there is the specification which defines the purpose, apparently the sole purpose, of the Congress in establishing the Academy, namely: "* * * the Academy shall, whenever called upon by any department of the Government, investigate, examine, experiment, and report upon any subject of science or art [meaning the practical arts], the actual expense of such investigations, examinations, experiments, and reports to be paid from appropriations which may be made for the purpose, but the Academy shall receive no compensation whatever for any services to the Government of the United States."

As an unwritten corollary to this specification, I may say, chiefly for the benefit of our newer members, that the American citizen, the American scientist, who accepts election to membership in the Academy tacitly agrees to respond to the Government's call for the study of, and report and advice upon, any subject lying within his field of special interest, and without expectation of financial recompense for his services. In the 72 years of its existence the Academy has complied a great many times with requests from the Government for information and advice, gladly, and as promptly as practicable, on problems exhibiting a wide range of character and magnitude. The Academy, naturally and in accord with the expectations of the Congress in 1863, is uniquely prepared to meet the Government's needs. To describe one recent case in illustration of that fact: When the National Planning Board, operating under the auspices of the Interior Department, on April 24 of last year, formally requested the National Academy of Sciences to advise it concerning "The role of science in national planning", the Academy's report to be made available to the Board well before the close of June, I assigned the duty of conducting as comprehensive a study of the subject as the time limitation would permit, and of preparing the report, to the Academy's standing Committee on Government Relations, consisting of John C. Merriam, Chairman, the President and the Vice President of the Academy, the Chairman of the National Research Council, the chairmen of the Academy's 11 several sections, and the Chairman of the Division of Federal Relations of the Research Council—a committee of 16 members representing, very appropriately in this particular problem, every one of the principal fields in the domain of the physical and the biological sciences. At the same time advantage was taken of the Academy's constitutional provision which says that—"It shall be competent for the president, in special cases, to call in the aid, upon committees, of experts or men of special attainment not members of the Academy," to add to the resources of the committee the valued knowledge, experience, and judgment of 12 distinguished scientists not members of the Academy, and also of 11 additional Academy members; making a total personnel of 39. The committee's report, published in the Academy's annual report for 1933–34, was finished, thanks largely to the chairman's energy and executive ability, and transmitted by the Academy to the Planning Board on June 18, 55 days after the date of the request.

Recalling that the Academy's members number about 275, and that they represent in reasonably normal proportions the several physical sciences and biological sciences, including medicine, psychology and anthropology, a modest application of arithmetical division suggests that the Academy could, in case of emergency call, constitute a full score of committees composed of a dozen Academy members each, without any overlappings of personnel, and without requisitioning its aged members. This is an imaginary "set-up" of committees; it will probably never occur in fact. The Academy's collective membership represents uniquely in the United States a great reservoir of knowledge, experience, and tested judgment on scientific subjects; and much can be said as to the wisdom of the congressional plan that "any department of the Government" may call upon the Academy for information and advice upon questions in any division of the physical sciences and the biological sciences. Academy committees can be, and always have been, constituted each in excellent accord with the nature of the problem involved; and experience has shown that to the Academy's resources in personnel can be added nonmembers whose chief interests and activities have been closely related to the subjects respectively concerned.

It is a universally recognized fact that governments may count upon obtaining the most dependable advice, in general, from institutions which are independent of political considerations and relationships, and whose members have no political interests except those possessed by all good citizens, and no financial or other material concern with the outcome of studies conducted for the Government. I do not know of any other group of citizens of the Republic who are so universally contented with their present lot as are the members of this Academy. Using some ponderous language, I may proudly say that they are all interested in the eternal verities. They have been seeking the truth, as represented by scientific facts and principles, and they have been fairly successful in their quests; otherwise they would not be members of the Academy. Looking in the opposite direction, I regard it as essential to the welfare of the Academy, through the decades and centuries which lie before it, that the Academy be at all times completely free of political elements in its organic and administrative relationships. I think the Congress of 1863, perhaps in response to the advices of some of the wise men who were prospective charter members of the Academy, must have realized the importance of this condition, for,

Fourthly, there is a specification in the Academy's congressional charter which says that the "corporation (i. e., the National Academy of Sciences) hereby constituted shall have power to make its own organization, including its constitution, bylaws, and rules and regulations; to fill all vacancies created by death, resignation, or otherwise; to provide for the election of foreign and domestic members, the division into classes, and all other matters needful or usual in such institution, and"

Fifthly, the specification that the Academy "report the same to Congress."

The charter conditions that the Academy govern itself in all things, and that the Academy receive no compensation whatever for any services to the Government of the United States, are precisely as they should be, as both the fundamental purposes of our institution, and the traditions and experiences of similar institutions in the capital cities of other nations clearly proclaim. In confirmation of these facts, I cannot do better than to quote from the annual address delivered by the president of the Royal Society of London, Sir William Huggins, in the year 1904: The Royal Society—

"asks for no endowment from the state, for it could not tolerate the control from without which follows the acceptance of public money, nor permit of that interference with its internal affairs which, as is seen in some foreign academies, is associated with state endowment. * * * The financial independence of the Royal Society, neither receiving nor wishing to accept state aid for its own private purposes, has enabled the society to give advice and assistance which, both with the Government and with Parliament, have the weight and finality of a wholly disinterested opinion. I (the president of the Royal Society) may quote here the words of a recent letter from His Majesty's Treasury: 'Their lordships have deemed themselves in the past very fortunate in being able to rely, in dealing with scientific questions, upon the aid of the Royal Society, which commands not only the confidence of the scientific world, but also of Parliament.' "

The Royal Society received its royal charter in the year 1662, and it was therefore 242 years old when President Huggins thus spoke. The Royal Society has had long experience, and it is very wise.

I have regarded the charter of the Academy, received by gift of the Congress, as a trust closely approaching the sacred, to be .violated or disregarded at the Academy's peril. In accordance with the specific command of its charter from the Congress, the Academy reports annually to the Congress.

The charter contains one clause which, speaking in a familiar manner, may be interpreted as a blanket provision conferring unspecified powers: "The National Academy of Sciences shall * * * have power * * * to provide for * * * all other matters needful or usual in such institution." It is thereby permitted, and may have been intended by its founders, that the Academy shall be active in encouraging the extension of knowledge in the domain of the physical and the biological sciences, through research and discovery: Firstly, by making a high degree of success in this field of endeavor the principal and essential criterion for election to membership in the Academy; secondly, by the description and the interpretation of research results achieved by its members and other invited scientists, through the medium of papers presented at the Academy's meetings; thirdly, by awarding medals and honoraria to members and nonmembers in recognition of notable research achievements, or for applications of science to the public welfare; fourthly, by making grants of money to members and nonmembers for the support of definite and promising research plans from funds which will have come to the Academy by gifts and bequests; and in yet other ways. These things the National Academy has done with commendable success, as have also the leading academies of sciences in other nations.

In the first three decades of this century, and earlier, there was widespread recognition of the obvious fact that scientific discoveries and their applications were contributing enormously to the physical comforts and the material well-being of the peoples who dwell in what we may call the scientific nations; scientific discovery, directly and indirectly, was responsible, above all other influences combined, for the raising of the standards of living and the lengthening of the average span of human life, in the astonishing degrees we are all aware of. Within the past 3 or 4 years, however, scientific discoveries, and especially the accelerated speed with which such discoveries had recently been made, have been under some degree of suspicion as to their resultant values to the human race. People in great and unaccustomed numbers have been suffering privations, both physical and spiritual, and they have been looking for the sources of their misfortunes. Scientific discoveries, coming too rapidly, have been blamed. However, the accusations have been made more or less irresponsibly, and apparently without basis of serious and comprehensive thought or verified fact, for discoveries in science are but truth uncovered, truth which had been existing and operating a long, long time, though we didn't know it; and we have suffered no harm in suddenly learning about it. It is doubtless true that advances of knowledge in the fields of the various sciences have, through their applications to the affairs of the world, subtracted from the demands for human labor in some of the older industries, but it should be remembered that these applications have to their credit the creation and development of new activities, many and on relatively large scales, which have undoubtedly given employment to greater numbers of both men and women than had been displaced from the earlier activities.

What is quite another thing, the applications of labor-saving machinery in factory and mill, on the farm and elsewhere, have, with apparent reason, been blamed for some of the ills of the world. Early in June 1928, full 16 months before the financial slump of October 1929, I heard an able and well-informed man quote to a small but distinguished audience in New York City the indisputable evidence that in the few years then just passed a great many thousands of workmen, both skilled and unskilled, in mills and factories, had been displaced by labor-saving machines; displaced so rapidly that they failed in large measure to secure other positions; and that already there was much suffering in consequence. The speaker, whom many of you know very well, said in substance to the men before him, many of whose names are as household words to you: "If these conditions can develop and exist in the period of greatest manufacturing activity ever experienced in our country, what will happen when years of economic depression arrive?" "I ask and urge", said the speaker, "that you men of large affairs and wide experience give thought to the great problem which seems to lie ahead of us."

The predicted problem of unemployment and its dire consequences have certainly been with us through the past 5 years. However, the labor-saving machinery under suspicion had but little relation, and much of it absolutely no relation, to recent discoveries in science. For example, we have all seen labor-saving machinery at work in the construction of modern highways and on the farms, which certainly had no relation to recent discoveries in science![1] Rather were the offending machines, with relatively few exceptions, the products of mechanical engineers' and electrical engineers' inventive genius, aroused by the urge of the Great War's abnormal demands and later by the urge of competition, perhaps due in some measure to low wages in other lands and relatively high wages and other conditions at home. I do not pursue the subject further because, in my opinion, it lies almost wholly within the immense and important domain of economics and the social sciences.

There is one superlatively important consequence of discoveries and developments in the physical and the biological sciences which seldom gets any description or discussion in books and newspapers read by people in general. In preceding paragraphs I have been treating of science chiefly in its "bread and butter" aspects. I here refer to the profound influence of scientific discovery, through the decades and the centuries, upon our modes of thought, upon our freedom of speech and freedom of search for the truth, upon our ways of looking at life and life's affairs. The subject is a most tempting one; and if time were abundant, as it is not, I should have liked to develop it; but I must limit myself to a few more or less disconnected illustrations and statements.

Nearly 40 years ago, while on a scientific mission in central India, I camped in a region whose people were suffering from their second successive year of famine. I could not induce any of the emaciated millions of Hindus around us to accept a slice of bread or a can of peaches, because, for reasons attaching to their caste system, all of our food, from their point of view, was unclean in the theological sense, and to eat it would destroy their chances of happiness in the world to come.

The Hindus and the Mohammedans and the other "fatalistic" peoples, with relatively few exceptions, have been falling far behind with respect to what we make bold to call world progress, not because they have been retrograding

[1] After this address was finished, I learned from Time for April 22, pp. 36–38, that a machine for picking cotton, in replacement of human labor, has been invented and subjected to successful test. Time says that "In 7½ hours it gathers as much cotton as a diligent hand-picker gathers in an 11-week season." I doubt if it bears intimate relation to any recent discovery in science, but the subject might easily become one of vast importance, economically and politically.

in the absolute sense but because the other peoples have relatively forged ahead. Their disadvantages have lain less in their failure to profit from the material benefits of applied science than in their holding to the mystical philosophies of old, which are "fatal" to progress. The essence of the philosophy of science is the cause and effect principle. The tenets of the scientific spirit tell us, whenever we are dealing with really serious matters, to "Prove all things; hold fast that which is good."

The year 1859, three-quarters of a century ago, marked an astonishing epoch in the intellectual history of the world; in no previous year had so much been done to liberate the spirit of man. In that year was published the Origin of Species; in that year were discovered the principles of spectroscopy. It is true that many of the ideas on evolution antedated Darwin; but Darwin's systematized and fortified ideas took root, and thenceforward there developed rapidly the hypothesis, and I might almost say the conviction, that the principles of evolution are applicable to nearly all—perhaps all—things: to our ideas on almost any subject; certainly to the religions and the theologies of the earth's peoples; to the earth, in that it is not only very old, and the result of evolutionary processes, but that the earth's surface features and all things upon the earth are changing, more or less slowly evolving, in orderly manner, with the passing of time. Some of the revelations of the spectroscope antedated Kirchhoff; but with the ability to interpret spectroscopic observations of the sun, of the other stars, of the nebulæ, there came rapidly a realization of the unity of the great universe. The earth is not only not flat; it is not the center of the universe; it is just one of the sun's smaller children; our sun itself is just a humble star among the billions of stars in our own stellar system; and there are, at the least, many tens of millions of other stellar systems. These are facts, established at the cost of great labor, and they have influenced and modified our ideas and attitudes most profoundly. No longer do we repeat the old dicta, "We shall never be able to know the chemical composition of the stars"; "The conditions existing in the deep interior of the earth must forever remain unknown"; and many similar beliefs of the last century and earlier.

The dread malady, diphtheria, now comes to a very low percentage of families, but with every comprehending family there resides an inspiring appreciation of the values beyond price which reside in the antitoxin made available by scientific research. Relatively few families have members or friends at sea, but every intelligent family finds mental and spiritual comfort in the knowledge that wireless telegraphy is ever alert to rob the oceans of their most cruel terrors. Our physicists have not yet learned what electricity really is, but I think they hold to the expectation that they or their successors will some day find out what it is. Their discoveries about the constitution of the atoms and the ways of their constituent parts promise to be as marvelous as the modern developments of astronomical knowledge. At any rate, the physicists know much more about electricity than the astronomers do about gravitation. We know something of what gravitation is doing, and of what it will do, but we seem to know nothing about the mechanism of its action, nothing of the technical reason why it exists. Of all the forces known to man, gravitation is marvelous beyond compare. The velocity of light and of electricity, 186,000 miles a second, seems to be a snail's pace in contrast with the effective speed of gravitational action. Pulses of light, emitted by the sun, require 500 seconds for their journey to the earth, whereas the sun's gravitational pull upon the earth, compelling the earth to travel in its elliptic orbit, seems to act instantaneously across the gap of 93 millions of miles. At any rate, the tests of that hypothesis have been many, and not one of them has given or suggested an answer to the contrary. The gravitational action of two bodies upon each other seems not to be affected or modified by the placing or presence of other bodies, no matter how massive, between them. A pebble at my foot at midnight and the farthermost atom of calcium on the far side of the sun are thought to attract each other precisely as they would if the entire body of the earth save that one pebble, and the entire body of the sun save that one calcium atom, were annihilated and nonexistent. The strength of the mutual gravitational pull of two bodies seems not to depend upon their temperatures, their magnetic states, or any other known conditions.

I have mentioned these well-known facts not at all for the information of any single member of this intelligent audience, but to link a few of the many marvelous accomplishments of the past with some of the outstanding mysteries of the present, in illustration of the spirit of science which says that research will proceed in the hope and expectation that with the passing of the centuries and the millennia the greatest of mysteries in our surroundings on the earth and in the universe will one by one be resolved. Why should we not have confidence that many children of today will live to see all infectious and contagious diseases banished from the earth through the discoveries of medical science and the administrations of public-health services? Why should not man aim at an ever more complete comprehension of the universe in which he is living and working? I think we are all in accord with the thesis that the vast body of known truth about our surroundings, as revealed by the ways and the means of the physical and the biological sciences, is incomparably more wonderful and inspiring than the fiction of the most lively imagination and, being idealistic and nonmaterialistic in character, is of the imperishable treasures of the human race.

On nine occasions within the year the Secretary of State requested the confidential advice and recommendations of the Academy on subjects having relationships with fields of science represented by Academy memberships. The president of the Academy, after conference with the chairmen or other members of the sections respectively concerned, complied with these requests as promptly as the geographic distances and other attending conditions permitted. At the close of the year the Secretary of State made formal acknowledgment, in generous terms, of the services rendered by the Academy.

On February 25, 1935, the Honorable Harold L. Ickes, chairman of the National Resources Board, wrote to the president of the Academy as follows:

The National Resources Board, appreciating the helpful assistance given (by the National Academy of Sciences) in connection with the preparation of the report of the National Planning Board (in April–May–June 1934) and in the development of research projects for consideration by the National Resources Board, is desirous of putting the relations between the Board and your organization on a continuing basis. I am writing, therefore, in the hope that you can see your way clear to name three scientists to represent your organization to assist the Resources Board * * * in an advisory and coordinating capacity.

On February 26 the president of the Academy responded as follows:

* * * After conversations in person or by long-distance telephone with all who are directly concerned, and by virtue of the authority conferred upon me by the Academy's constitution, I have had the privilege and honor of appointing the following members of the National Academy of Sciences to assist the National Resources Board in the capacities defined by your letter:

Dr. John C. Merriam, president of the Carnegie Institution of Washington, and chairman of the National Academy's standing Committee on Government Relations;

Dr. Edwin B. Wilson, professor of vital statistics, Harvard (University) School of Public Health; and

Dr. Frank R. Lillie, dean of the division of biological sciences, University of Chicago.

I am asking Dr. Merriam to serve as the chairman of the group of three representatives.

In still other ways the Academy has served the Government within the year.

The stated autumn meeting of the Academy, held in Cleveland, Ohio, in November 1934 and the stated annual meeting held in the city of Washington, in April 1935 were gratifyingly successful. The salient facts in relation to these meetings: as to their scientific programs in original description of new developments and discoveries in the physical and the biological sciences; as to the presentations of five gold medals and one financial honorarium in recognition of notable contributions by their recipients to knowledge in the domain of the sciences or of eminence in the applications of science to the public welfare; as to the making of financial grants in support of many research projects; as to further progress made in studies conducted by Academy committees on scientific subjects at the Government's request; as to the state of the Academy's memberships; as to the state of the Academy's finances and physical properties, etc.; are recorded in later sections of this report.

From the beginning of its life, in 1863, the National Academy of Sciences has always been prepared to fulfill promptly and efficiently the one purpose of the Congress of the United States in establishing the Academy by special act of the Congress, as described on earlier pages. Realizing keenly the Academy's heavy responsibility as an official adviser of the Government on scientific subjects, the president of the Academy made definite efforts in March and April 1933 to acquaint high Government officials with the existence and the one governmental purpose of the Academy. To the council of the Academy assembled in stated session on the evening of April 23, 1933, with 11 of its 12 members in attendance, the president of the Academy described in considerable detail the efforts made up to that date. The council's views were that those efforts were timely, adequate, and all that could be appropriately made.

Conscientiously seeking the most promising types of administrative machinery for rendering this advisory service, in the future as in the past, the officers and members of the Academy in formal session on April 24, 1935, a special committee of the Academy on May 9, 1935, and the executive committee of the Academy's council in stated session on May 11, 1935, took the actions described on pages 27–30 of this report. The purpose and intent of this new action was that when the Academy receives a request for service from any branch or department of the Government, the Committee on Government Relations if practicable to assemble it promptly, otherwise the executive committee of said committee, shall recommend to the president of the Academy, for appointment by the president of the Academy, the membership of a subcommittee of the Committee on Government Relations, this subcommittee to have the duty of rendering the specific service requested by the Government, and be discharged upon the completion of its report on the subject concerned.

A grant of $5,000 made by the Carnegie Corporation of New York, available to apply upon the costs of special administrative services of the Academy, is gratefully acknowledged.

MEETINGS OF THE NATIONAL ACADEMY

The 1934 autumn meeting of the National Academy of Sciences was held in Cleveland, Ohio, on November 19, 20, and 21, 1934, upon invitation by the Case School of Applied Science and the Western Reserve University.

BUSINESS SESSION

Thirty-six members responded to roll call, as follows:

C. G. Abbot	W. D. Harkins	W. R. Miles
Roger Adams	Ross G. Harrison	Dayton O. Miller
W. D. Bancroft	L. J. Henderson	J. F. Norris
F. G. Benedict	H. E. Ives	F. K. Richtmyer
Isaiah Bowman	F. B. Jewett	Rudolf Ruedemann
Vannevar Bush	L. R. Jones	Charles Schuchert
W. W. Campbell	Arthur Keith	Harlow Shapley
A. J. Carlson	C. F. Kettering	H. C. Sherman
J. McKeen Cattell	C. K. Leith	Ambrose Swasey
K. T. Compton	Frank Leverett	Edwin B. Wilson
H. D. Curtis	F. R. Lillie	R. S. Woodworth
William K. Gregory	Ernest Merritt	Fred. E. Wright

PRESIDENT'S ANNOUNCEMENTS

The president of the Academy made the following announcements:

DEATHS SINCE THE APRIL MEETING

Members.—William Henry Welch, born April 8, 1850, elected to the Academy in 1895, died April 30, 1934.

George Cary Comstock, born February 12, 1855, elected to the Academy in 1899, died May 11, 1934.

Nathaniel Lord Britton, born January 15, 1859, elected to the Academy in 1914, died June 25, 1934.

Harris Joseph Ryan, born January 8, 1866, elected to the Academy in 1920, died July 3, 1934.

Berthold Laufer, born October 11, 1874, elected to the Academy in 1930, died September 13, 1934.

Otto Knut Olof Folin, born April 4, 1867, elected to the Academy in 1916, died October 25, 1934.

Foreign associates.—Santiago Ramon y Cajal, University of Madrid, Spain, elected a foreign associate in 1920, died October 17, 1934.

Sir Arthur Schuster, Berkshire, England, elected a foreign associate in 1913, died October 14, 1934.

DELEGATES APPOINTED SINCE THE APRIL MEETING

To the meeting of the International Council of Scientific Unions, Brussels, Belgium, July 9–11, 1934: Edwin Hubble (National Research Council only).

To the International Congress of Geography, Warsaw, Poland, August 23–31, 1934: S. W. Boggs, Isaiah Bowman, Louise A. Boyd, Douglas Johnson, James Gordon Steese, O. D. von Engeln, John J. Wright (National Research Council only).

To the meeting of the International Scientific Radio Union, London, England, September 12–19, 1934: L. A. Briggs, J. H. Dellinger, Lloyd Espenschied, G. C. Gross, R. A. Heising, A. G. Jensen, Harry R. Mimno, H. M. Turner, Karl S. Van Dyke (National Research Council only).

To the inauguration of William Orville Mendenhall as president of Whittier College, Whittier, Calif., September 21, 1934: F. L. Ransome (National Academy of Sciences only).

To the meeting of the International Union of Pure and Applied Physics, London and Cambridge, England, October 1–6, 1934: R. M. Bozorth, Robert B. Brode, A. H. Compton, R. A. Millikan (National Research Council only).

To the inauguration of the Maison de la Chimie, Paris, France, October 19–20, 1934: E. B. Benger (National Research Council only).

TEMPORARY CHAIRMAN OF SECTION OF ENGINEERING

W. F. Durand, appointed to conduct the balloting for nomination of new members and the election of a chairman of the section in succession to A. E. Kennelly, resigned.

MARINE BIOLOGICAL LABORATORY

Committee on Review of Marine Biological Laboratory at Woods Hole: C. R. Stockard, appointed as the Academy representative on the committee during the absence of Thomas Barbour in South Africa.

APPOINTMENTS TO THE TRUST FUND COMMITTEES

Marcellus Hartley fund: J. B. Conant as member, for the period ending with the close of the annual meeting in 1938 (succeeding William H. Welch, deceased).

Marsh fund: W. K. Gregory as chairman, for the period ending with the close of the annual meeting in 1937 (succeeding T. W. Vaughan, resigned). Adolph Knopf as member, for the period ending with the close of the annual meeting in 1936 (succeeding T. W. Vaughan).

John J. Carty fund: H. S. Jennings as member, for the period ending with the annual meeting in 1939 (in place of H. J. Muller, who declined because of absence in Europe).

Charles Doolittle Walcott fund: The Royal Society of London nominated W. D. Lang as its representative on the board of trustees of the Walcott fund, to succeed F. A. Bather, deceased.

Subcommittee on library: C. S. Hudson, chairman for the period ending with the close of the annual meeting in 1937; W. W. Coblentz, vice chairman, 1937; Raymond Pearl, 1936; G. S. Streeter, 1936; and John R. Swanton, 1935.

Two subcommittees of the Committee on Government Relations, in place of the subcommittee already in existence, as follows:

A (physical sciences): J. C. Merriam, chairman; A. W. Hull, E. P. Kohler, C. K. Leith, Joel Stebbins, Edwin B. Wilson, the president, and the home secretary of the Academy.

B (biological sciences): J. C. Merriam, chairman; J. R. Angell, Ludvig Hektoen, Frank R. Lillie, E. D. Merrill, R. S. Woodworth, the president, and the home secretary of the Academy.

HIGHWAY RESEARCH BOARD

In order to carry on effectively the work of the Highway Research Board of the Division of Engineering and Industrial Research of the National Research Council, it is necessary that there be close cooperation of the board and the United States Department of Agriculture. To bring this about, the Bureau of Public Roads of the Department shares with the Research Council the expenses of the work. The cooperative contract was renewed for the year 1934–35. The Department of Agriculture's contribution for the year, paid to the treasurer of the National Academy of Sciences, for expenditure under the authorization of the Academy was $15,000.

REPORTS OF THE TREASURER AND AUDITING COMMITTEE

The annual report of the treasurer of the Academy covering the fiscal year 1933–34 was presented, and upon recommendation by the council of the Academy was accepted for inclusion in the printed annual report of the National Academy of Sciences for that period.

The report of the auditing committee was presented, and upon recommendation by the council of the Academy was accepted for inclusion in the printed annual report of the National Academy of Sciences for the fiscal year 1933–34.

These reports appeared on page 95–125 of the annual report of the National Academy of Sciences for the fiscal year 1933–34.

AMENDMENTS TO THE BYLAWS

The council of the Academy recommended that the first sentence of bylaw III.1 (reading "The annual meeting of the Academy shall begin on the fourth Monday of April") be deleted because it conflicted with article III, section 1, of the constitution which provides: "The Academy shall hold one stated meeting, called the annual meeting, in April of each year in the city of Washington, and another stated meeting, called the autumn meeting, at a place to be determined by the council. The council shall also have power to fix the date of each meeting." The recommendation was approved by the Academy.

JAMES CRAIG WATSON FUND

Consideration was given to the election of a successor to G. C. Comstock, deceased, as one of the three members of the board of trustees of the James Craig Watson fund. The recommendation of the council of the Academy that F. H. Seares be made trustee was approved by the Academy.

The following report from the trustees of the Watson fund was presented:

Your board of trustees of the Watson fund unanimously recommends as follows:

No. 50. A grant of $4,925, expendable over a period of 2 years as follows: $2,125 from October 1, 1934, to June 30, 1935; $2,800 from July 1, 1935, to June 30, 1936. This grant is to be applied by the trustees under the general direction of the chairman and under the direct supervision of Dr. Sophia H. Levy, of the department of mathematics of the University of California, to the development and testing of the perturbations of additional critical cases of minor planets which have a mean motion approximately in the ratio of 2:1 to that of Jupiter.

Four Watson planets of this critical type had previously been successfully completed on the basis of the Berkeley tables (Memoirs, National Academy of Sciences, vol. XIV). Last spring it became possible to test the results on recent observations with the assistance of two expert computers who also had the necessary theoretical training. These workers were paid from Civil Works Administration funds. The differences between theory and observation were less than had been expected. Encouraged by these results, perturbations were then developed and tested with the Berkeley tables for a fifth Watson planet which had previously been investigated with some difficulty by another theory. Although this planet had a critical mean motion near 550″, observations over the unusual interval of 60 years were well represented. It is thus conclusively established that general perturbations may be developed with the Berkeley tables for several hundred planets. (Results published in abstract: Publications of the Astronomical Society of the Pacific, October 1934.)

The American contribution to the international program of investigating the motions of minor planets is the development of general perturbations which shall hold over a long period of time. This has been accomplished under the direction of the chairman for all the Watson planets, and for two planets of the Trojan group by Brown and his disciples. The general objective of these researches is to do away with the prevailing practice of empirically correcting elements from time to time and carrying them forward by special perturbations. The former Civil Works Administration workers, Dr. C. M. Anderson, Jr., and Mrs. Barbara P. Riggs, M. A., are at present voluntary computing ephemerides, inclusively of the perturbations, for the five planets referred to above. These ephemerides are to be furnished to the Berlin Rechen-Institut, which is adopting the American program.

It is proposed to secure the services of Dr. Anderson and Mrs. Riggs for a definite period of time on a salary basis, the former to be paid at the rate of $125 per month and the latter at the rate of $100 per month. The additional $100 per annum requested is for incidental expenses.

This program was under consideration by Professor Comstock during his last illness. The chairman feels assured that death only prevented his written approval.

During the past 3 years the University of California has contributed a total of $4,350 toward the work related to this program.

The condition of the Watson fund on October 31, 1934, was as follows: Invested income, $1,000; uninvested income, $6,087.56; invested capital, $24,475; uninvested capital, $525.

F. E. Ross,
A. O. Leuschner, <i>Chairman.</i></div>

Report accepted and recommendations approved.

HENRY DRAPER FUND

The following telegraphed report from the chairman of the committee on the Henry Draper fund, V. M. Slipher, was presented with the recommendation by the council of the Academy that the recommendation contained therein be approved and that presentation of the medal be made at the coming April meeting:

The Henry Draper committee of the National Academy of Sciences respectfully recommends to the Academy that the Draper gold medal be awarded next April to Dr. J. S. Plaskett, in recognition of his able and consistent labors in stellar radial velocities and related studies energetically pursued for nearly 30 years.

V. M. Slipher, Chairman.

Recommendation approved.

REPORT OF THE COMMITTEE ON LONG-RANGE WEATHER FORECASTING

Due to misunderstanding of arrangements for meeting, it was not possible to bring together the committee on long-range weather forecasting at the time of the annual meeting of the Academy in April 1934. No formal meeting of the committee has been held since that time, but many conferences by the chairman have concerned specifically the question for which this committee was established. As was indicated in the conference on this subject held by the committee at a recent annual meeting of the Academy, the questions under discussion have concerned not so much the specific forecasting as they have related to problems involved in discussion of causes of climatic variation and the possibility that such changes are due to factors in which there is a determinable and cyclic or periodic element.

Effort is being made to bring together the data bearing upon these questions as derived from studies of other institutions in the hope that consideration can be given to this problem before the annual meeting of the Academy in 1935.

John C. Merriam, Chairman.

Report accepted.

Since the annual meeting of the Academy in April 1934 the chairman of the committee has visited the localities at which studies on the relation between research and education in national parks have been conducted under the auspices of the Academy committee. The work being done at Grand Canyon, Crater Lake, and Yosemite has all progressed practically to the point of completion and with the conclusion of studies on a few details these activities will be finished in the next few months.

It is important to note that as related to these studies of education and research there have developed in each of the national parks under consideration a series of researches of the most fundamental type in which noteworthy progress has been made.

JOHN C. MERRIAM, *Chairman.*

Report accepted.

REPORT OF THE COMMITTEE ON GOVERNMENT RELATIONS

Since the date of the annual meeting of the National Academy in April 1934, the Government Relations Committee has been called upon by the president of the Academy to prepare a report on the role of science in national planning, this request having come to the Academy from the chairman of the National Planning Board. The committee was called together on April 28, and a program was laid out for study of this project with a view to making a report which would be available in the early part of June. Although the difficulties in this study were very great, it was possible to prepare a report which was in the hands of the National Planning Board at the time of its meeting on June 18, 1934.[1]

Printed copies of the National Planning Board report have just today been released, including the report on the role of science in national planning, pages 40–53.

Within the period since the annual meeting of the Academy in April 1934, the president of the Academy has approved the development of such organization within the committee as would make possible the meeting of groups in the physical sciences and in the biological sciences for discussion of problems toward the consideration of which the National Academy might reasonably be expected sometime to contribute. Discussion of such problems is already under way with a view to defining the field of study in which the Academy might conceivably be helpful.

JOHN C. MERRIAM, *Chairman.*

Report accepted.

PRESENTATION OF MEDAL

At the dinner of the Academy on November 20, 1934, the Mary Clark Thompson medal and accompanying honorarium of $250 were presented to Charles Schuchert. The award had been approved at the preceding April meeting in recognition of Dr. Schuchert's "important work in the classification and distribution of Paleozoic invertebrates; for the broad perspective, originality, faithfulness of detail, and stimulating philosophy of his contributions to historical geology; and for his outstanding accomplishments in the field of paleogeography." The presentation address prepared by Dr. David White as chairman of the committee on the Mary Clark Thompson fund was read.

---

[1] This report was published in the Annual Report of the National Academy of Sciences for the fiscal year 1933–34, pp. 25–43.

BARNARD MEDAL AWARD

The will of F. A. P. Barnard establishing the Barnard Medal for Meritorious Services to Science, to be awarded by the trustees of Columbia University, stipulated that the National Academy of Sciences shall declare to the trustees of the university every 5 years the name of the person whom the Academy considers most deserving of the medal. At the annual meeting in April 1934 the Academy's committee on the Barnard Medal recommended that the Academy nominate Edwin Hubble for recipient of the medal for the period 1930-35. The Academy, in business session, approved the nomination and forwarded the name to the trustees of Columbia University. The report of the Academy's committee recommending the award read as follows:

The committee on the Barnard Medal, of the National Academy of Sciences, recommends the adoption of the following report for presentation to the trustees of Columbia University:

"The National Academy of Sciences recommends to the trustees of Columbia University that the Barnard Medal, for the 5 years ending January 1, 1935, be awarded to Dr. Edwin Hubble in recognition of his important studies of extra-galactic nebulae.

"Dr. Hubble's work in this field was first devoted to a clarification of the distinction between galactic and extra-galactic nebular objects, and to a classification of the different types of elliptic, spiral, barred-spiral, and irregular nebulae which do occur outside the limits of our own galaxy. This was followed by studies of the apparent diameters and apparent magnitudes of these nebulae, together with investigations of their absolute magnitudes and distances based on the observed magnitudes of the different types of star which can be recognized in the nearer of these objects.

"With the help of precise methods for determining the magnitudes and distances of the nebulae, it then became possible to study their distribution in space. The work of Dr. Hubble has shown a large-scale rough uniformity in the spatial distribution of nebulae out to the twentieth magnitude, the majority of the nebulae being relatively isolated and a small fraction associated in more or less populous clusters. His work has also satisfactorily explained the absence of observed nebulae near the plane of the Milky Way as due to absorbing material, and has shown an increase in nebular counts between the zone of avoidance and the galactic poles which would correspond to the effect of a layer of such material.

"The most striking result of Dr. Hubble's determinations of apparent and absolute magnitudes, however, has been the discovery of a linear relation between the distances of the extra-galactic nebulae and the shift towards the red end of the spectrum, observed in the spectral lines which they emit. This remarkable discovery of a linear relation between red-shift and distance, with its possible interpretation as due to a systematic recessional motion of the nebulae, is of the greatest importance for cosmology. The fact that most of the nearest nebulae do exhibit a red-shift was found by Slipher as early as 1922. Making use of his methods for determining distance it was then shown by Hubble in 1929 that red-shift and distance are approximately proportional out to 2,000,000 parsecs, and it has since been shown by the combined efforts of Hubble and Humason that the relation remains almost exactly linear out to 30,000,000 parsecs.

"It is fair to say that Dr. Hubble's studies of the extra-galactic nebulae provide the greatest contribution that has been made in recent years to our observational knowledge of the large-scale behavior of the universe."

(Signed) W. W. CAMPBELL.
BERGEN DAVIS.
A. A. NOYES.
R. C. TOLMAN.
ARTHUR L. DAY,
Chairman.

SCIENTIFIC SESSIONS

The following papers were presented at the scientific sessions by members of the Academy or persons introduced by members:

MONDAY, NOVEMBER 19, 1934

Christian Nusbaum, Case School of Applied Science (introduced by Dayton C. Miller): An X-ray study of grain-growth in metals produced by heat treatment (illustrated).

F. K. Richtmyer, T. R. Cuykendall, and M. T. Jones, Cornell University: The measurement of the absorption coefficients of X-rays of very short wavelength (illustrated).

R. C. Gibbs and H. M. O'Bryan, Cornell University (introduced by Ernest Merritt): Evaporated surfaces on gratings for the vacuum ultraviolet. (illustrated).

Edward S. Lamar and Karl T. Compton, Massachusetts Institute of Technology: A special theory of cathode sputtering (illustrated).

A. A. Michelson, F. G. Pease, and F. Pearson, Mount Wilson Observatory: Measurement of the velocity of light in a partial vacuum (illustrated).

C. G. Suits, General Electric Co. (introduced by Albert W. Hull): The temperature of the copper arc (illustrated).

William D. Harkins, University of Chicago: The synthesis of light atomic nuclei and the resulting disintegration and emission of gamma rays (illustrated).

W. W. Coblentz, National Bureau of Standards: Biographical Memoir of Edward Bennett Rosa. (Read by title.)

Henry Crew, Northwestern University: Biographical Memoir of Thomas Corwin Mendenhall. (Read by title.)

Ernest P. Lane, Harvard University: Biographical Memoir of Ernest Julius Wilczynski. (Read by title.)

Richard Stevens Burington, Case School of Applied Science (introduced by Arthur B. Coble): On the equivalence of quadrics in m—affine n—space and its relation to the equivalence of 2m-pole networks (illustrated).

J. R. Musselman, Western Reserve University (introduced by Arthur B. Coble): On certain types of hexagons (illustrated).

Harlow Shapley, Harvard College Observatory: Investigations of variable stars (illustrated).

C. G. Abbot, Smithsonian Institution: Energy spectrum measurements of the hotter stars (illustrated).

Otto Struve, Yerkes Observatory (introduced by Edwin B. Frost): The excitation of spectral lines in expanding nebular shells (illustrated).

J. J. Nassau and L. G. Henyey, Case School of Applied Science (introduced by Ambrose Swasey): The Ursa major group (illustrated).

William Bowie, United States Coast and Geodetic Survey: Fundamental geodetic surveys in the United States nearing completion (illustrated).

Robert R. McMath and Robert M. Petrie, University of Michigan (introduced by Heber D. Curtis): Solar prominences recorded by the motion-picture method (illustrated).

A. O. Leuschner, University of California: Elements and general Jupiter perturbations of 10 Watson planets.

Harlow Shapley, Harvard College Observatory: Variation and evolution among the stars (illustrated).

TUESDAY, NOVEMBER 20, 1934

Joseph M. Hayman, Western Reserve University (introduced by A. N. Richards): The presence of creatinine in blood plasma (illustrated).

Carl J. Wiggers, Western Reserve University (introduced by Joseph Erlanger): Further observations on systolic and diastolic coronary flow under natural conditions (illustrated).

A. J. Carlson, University of Chicago: Criteria of alcohol intoxication (illustrated).

Francis G. Benedict and Cornelia Golay Benedict, Nutrition Laboratory, Carnegie Institution: The temperature of the expired air, a hitherto unused physiological and clinical measure (illustrated).

Norman C. Wetzel, Western Reserve University (introduced by A. J. Carlson): Energetics of growth and metabolism in the chick embryo and a calculation of the efficiency of these processes (illustrated).

H. C. Sherman and H. L. Campbell, Columbia University: Rate of growth and length of life (illustrated).

A. H. Hersh, Western Reserve University (introduced by E. G. Conklin): The relative growth function applied to white-eyed mosaics of the bar series of drosophila (illustrated).

Alan R. Moritz, Western Reserve University (introduced by H. Gideon Wells): Arteriolar changes in essential hypertension (illustrated).

William K. Gregory, American Museum of Natural History: On the evolution of the skulls of vertebrates, with special reference to heritable changes in proportional diameters (anisomerism) (illustrated).

T. Wingate Todd, Western Reserve University (introduced by Ales Hrdlicka): Post-natal growth patterns of the primate brain (illustrated).

Torald Sollmann and Nora E. Schreiber, Western Reserve University (introduced by Dayton C. Miller): The fate of mercury in acute bichloride poisoning.

Wilder D. Bancroft, Esther C. Farnham, and John E. Rutzler, Cornell University: Preliminary tests with sodium rhodanate on rabbits and chickens (illustrated).

J. M. Rogoff, University of Chicago (introduced by A. J. Carlson): Present status of the adrenal cortex problem (illustrated).

WEDNESDAY, NOVEMBER 21, 1934

A. C. Seletzky, Case School of Applied Science (introduced by John B. Whitehead): Current and voltage loci of polyphase circuits (illustrated).

Frank Leverett and Donald C. MacLachlan, University of Michigan: Variations in tilt lines in the Huron-Erie district (illustrated).

John C. Merriam, Carnegie Institution of Washington: Nature and extent of tertiary formations immediately following the Columbia lava flows of the Northwest (illustrated).

Charles F. Kettering, General Motors Corporation: Recent developments in Diesel engines (illustrated).

H. M. Boylston, Case School of Applied Science (introduced by Albert Sauveur): Some notes on the ageing of metals.

Robert E. Burk, Western Reserve University (introduced by E. P. Kohler): The significance of the persistence of the crystalline state above the melting point (illustrated).

Eric A. Arnold, Case School of Applied Science (introduced by Roger Adams): The thermal decomposition of ammonia on metallic surfaces.

O. L. Inman, Kettering Foundation, Antioch College (introduced by Charles F. Kettering): The present status of studies on photosynthesis (illustrated).

Paul Rothemund, Kettering Foundation, Antioch College (introduced by Charles F. Kettering): Chlorophyll and the proto-chlorophyll problem (illustrated).

ANNUAL MEETING

The National Academy of Sciences held its annual spring meeting, 1935, in the Academy Building, Washington, D. C., on April 22, 23, and 24, 1935.

BUSINESS SESSION

One hundred and thirteen members were present, as follows:

Abbot, C. G.	Bowman, Isaiah	Conklin, E. G.
Allen, E. T.	Bridgman, P. W.	Cross, Whitman
Barbour, Thomas	Brown, E. W.	Cushing, Harvey
Benedict, F. G.	Campbell, W. W.	Daly, R. A.
Berry, E. W.	Cattell, J. McKeen	Davenport, C. B.
Birkhoff, G. D.	Clark, W. M.	Davis, Bergen
Blakeslee, A. F.	Clinton, G. P.	Davisson, C. J.
Blichfeldt, H. F.	Coblentz, W. W.	Day, A. L.
Boas, Franz	Compton, K. T.	Dodge, B. O.
Bowie, William	Conant, J. B.	DuBois, E. F.

Duggar, B. M.
Durand, W. F.
East, E. M.
Erlanger, Joseph
Fred, E. B.
Gasser, H. S.
Gherardi, B.
Harkins, W. D.
Harper, R. A.
Harrison, R. G.
Henderson, L. J.
Hovgaard, William
Howard, L. O.
Howe, M. A.
Howell, W. H.
Hrdlicka, Ales
Hudson, C. S.
Hull, A. W.
Ives, H. E.
Jacobs, W. A.
Jewett, F. B.
Johnson, D. W.
Kasner, Edward
Keith, Arthur
Kemble, E. C.
Kennelly, A. E.
Keyes, F. G.
Knopf, Adolph

Kofoid, C. A.
Kohler, E. P.
Kraus, C. A.
Kunkel, L. O.
Lawrence, E. O.
Lillie, F. R.
MacCallum, W. G.
McClung, C. E.
McCollum, E. V.
Mason, Max
Mendenhall, W. C.
Merriam, J. C.
Merrill, E. D.
Merritt, Ernest
Miles, W. R.
Miller, D. C.
Millikan, R. A.
Mitchell, S. A.
Morgan, T. H.
Morse, Marston
Norris, J. F.
Northrop, J. H.
Osborn, H. F.
Osterhout, W. J. V.
Palache, Charles
Parker, G. H.
Pauling, Linus
Pearl, Raymond

Reid, H. F.
Richtmyer, F. K.
Rivers, T. M.
Russell, H. N.
Sapir, E.
Shaffer, P. A.
Shapley, Harlow
Slater, J. C.
Slipher, V. M.
Stejneger, Leonhard
Stockard, C. R.
Stratton, G. M.
Streeter, G. L.
Swanton, J. R.
Swasey, Ambrose
Trumpler, R. J.
Vaughan, T. W.
Veblen, Oswald
Webster, D. L.
White, H. S.
Whitehead, J. B.
Wiener, Norbert
Wilson, Edwin B.
Wood, R. W.
Woodworth, R. S.
Wright, Fred. E.
Yerkes, R. M.

PRESIDENT'S ANNOUNCEMENTS

The president of the Academy made the following announcements:

DEATHS SINCE THE AUTUMN MEETING

Members.—Theobald Smith, born July 31, 1859, elected to the Academy in 1908, died December 10, 1934.

David White, born July 1, 1862, elected to the Academy in 1912, died February 7, 1935.

Walter Jones, born April 28, 1865, elected to the Academy in 1918, died February 28, 1935.

William Duane, born February 17, 1872, elected to the Academy in 1920, died March 7, 1935.

Michael Idvorsky Pupin, born October 4, 1858, elected to the Academy in 1905, died March 12, 1935.

Foreign associate.—Willem de Sitter, Sterrewacht te Leiden, Leiden, The Netherlands, elected a foreign associate in 1929, died November 21, 1934.

LETTER FROM THE PRESIDENT OF THE UNITED STATES

The following communication from the President of the United States was read to the Academy by President Campbell, followed by the text of President Campbell's proposed reply:

THE WHITE HOUSE,
Washington, April 22, 1935.

MY DEAR MR. CAMPBELL: As you and your eminent colleagues meet in the seventy-first annual assembly of the National Academy of Sciences, I bid you warm welcome to Washington and express my cordial wish for the greater development and usefulness of the Academy.

The country has every reason to be proud of the record of its scientific men and engineers. In astronomy, medicine, physics, chemistry, geology, and other sciences, and in the progress of engineering in all its branches, the contributions of America have been and still are outstanding in a friendly world rivalry.

It is a matter for thankfulness that among the many sources of world dis-
trust and jealousies, science preserves an ideal of purity, truthfulness, and
mutual good will toward all nations. Not only do cooperative international
scientific projects flourish, but the publications of scientists are received at
face value in all lands, even though they be politically at variance.

The National Academy's charter provides that the Academy shall be ready
at all times to give advice when called upon by any branch of Government.
This privilege has been availed of by Government on many occasions. One of
the most notable was during the Great War when the National Research Council was established by the Academy at President Wilson's call to mobilize the
scientific learning and ability of the country to aid in that great struggle.

I take this opportunity to thank the Academy for the advice and assistance
it has given the administration during the past 2 years, particularly where
problems pertaining to the scientific policies of the Government have arisen.

With renewed congratulations and best wishes, I remain,

    Very sincerely yours,

                       FRANKLIN D. ROOSEVELT.

                  NATIONAL ACADEMY OF SCIENCES,
                        April 22, 1935,

The Honorable the PRESIDENT OF THE UNITED STATES.

MY DEAR MR. PRESIDENT: I have the great pleasure of acknowledging the
receipt of your esteemed communication of today which extends to the members of the National Academy of Sciences a warm welcome to Washington for
the holding of the Academy's annual meeting of 1935, and expresses your
cordial wish for the greater development and usefulness of the Academy.

Your letter was read to the members of the Academy this afternoon at the
opening of the first general assembly of this week's meeting, and I was
requested and instructed to convey to you an expression of the Academy's deep
appreciation of your thoughtful and courteous messages.

I am also requested to assure you that the members of the Academy are
happy in their obligation and privilege of advising the Government of the
United States on subjects within the domain of the physical and the biological
sciences, whenever called upon by any branch or department of the Government for such service, under the wise provision of the Academy's congressional
charter that "the Academy shall receive no compensation whatever for any
services to the Government."

I have the honor to remain, sir,

    Yours respectfully,

                    W. W. CAMPBELL, *President.*

CHANGE IN SECTION AFFILIATION

The president announced that John Howard Northrop had been
transferred from the section of pathology and bacteriology to the
section of physiology and biochemistry at his request and with the
approval of the latter section.

ASSIGNMENT OF BIOGRAPHICAL MEMOIRS

Edward Bennett Rosa, assigned to W. W. Coblentz, and manuscript received.
George Perkins Merrill, assigned to Waldemar Lindgren, and manuscript
received.
Roland Thaxter, assigned to G. P. Clinton, and manuscript received.
John Ripley Freeman, assigned to Vannevar Bush.
Eliakim Hastings Moore, assigned to G. A. Bliss and L. E. Dickson.
William Henry Holmes, assigned to John R. Swanton.
William Lewis Elkin, assigned to Frank Schlesinger.
Edward Wight Washburn, assigned to W. A. Noyes.
Augustus Trowbridge, assigned to K. T. Compton.
William Henry Welch, assigned to Simon Flexner.

George Cary Comstock, assigned to Joel Stebbins.
Nathaniel Lord Britton, assigned to Marshall A. Howe.
Otto Folin, assigned to P. A. Shaffer.
David White, assigned to Charles Schuchert.
William Duane, assigned to P. W. Bridgman.
Walter Jones, assigned to W. Mansfield Clark.

SECTION CHAIRMEN

New chairmen of sections, elected by the sections for a term of 3 years commencing at the close of the annual meeting of 1935:

Section of astronomy.—A. O. Leuschner, to succeed Joel Stebbins.
Section of engineering.—Bancroft Gherardi, to succeed W. F. Durand, who was temporary chairman in succession to A. E. Kennelly (resigned).
Section of chemistry.—C. A. Kraus, to succeed E. P. Kohler.
Section of botany.—A. F. Blakeslee, to succeed E. D. Merrill.
Section of anthropology and psychology.—C. E. Seashore, to succeed R. S. Woodworth.

DELEGATES APPOINTED SINCE THE AUTUMN MEETING

To the opening of the new museum and the centenary celebration of the Geological Survey of Great Britain, London, England, July 1935: Arthur L. Day.

To the third centenary of the Museum National d'Histoire Naturelle, Paris, June 24–29, 1935: L. J. Henderson.

To the triennial meeting of the International Astronomical Union, Paris, July 10 to 17, 1935: W. S. Adams, E. W. Brown, Capt. J. F. Hellweg, W. D. Lambert, A. O. Leuschner, John A. Miller. S. A. Mitchell, Henry Norris Russell, Frank Schlesinger, Frederick Slocum (National Research Council only).

To the extraordinary general assembly of the International Union of Geodesy and Geophysics, Paris, July 18, 1935: W. S. Adams, E. W. Brown, W. D. Lambert, Frank Schlesinger (National Research Council only).

To the Third International Congress of Soil Science, Oxford, England, July 30 to August 7, 1935: Oswald Schreiner (National Research Council only).

To the Sixth International Botanical Congress, Amsterdam, September 2 to 7, 1935; E. D. Merrill, A. F. Blakeslee, B. O. Dodge, D. R. Hoagland, C. E. Allen, W. A. Setchell, E. C. Stakman, H. A. Spoehr, and B. M. Duggar.

TRUST FUND COMMITTEE APPOINTMENTS

J. Lawrence Smith Fund.—F. R. Moulton, to succeed Frank Schlesinger as chairman, for the period ending in 1937. E. W. Brown, to succeed Dr. Schlesinger as member. Term, 5 years.
Cyrus B. Comstock fund.—R. A. Millikan as member and chairman, succeeding Max Mason. Term, 5 years.
Marsh fund.—E. D. Merrill reappointed as member. Term, 5 years.
Murray fund.—T. Wayland Vaughan as member and chairman. Term, 3 years.
Marcellus Hartley fund.—C. A. Kofoid, to succeed Max Mason as member. Term, 3 years.
Mary Clark Thompson fund.—Waldemar Lindgren, to succeed David White as chairman, for the period ending in 1937. E. O. Ulrich, to succeed Dr. White as member. Term, 3 years.
Joseph Henry fund.—C. E. Seashore, to succeed E. L. Thorndike as member. Term, 5 years.
John J. Carty fund.—G. D. Birkhoff, to succeed W. J. V. Osterhout as member. Term, 5 years.

BOARD OF TRUSTEES OF SCIENCE SERVICE

Harlow Shapley was named a representative of the National Academy of Sciences on the board of trustees of Science Service to fill the vacancy caused by the death of David White (to continue until the close of Science Service's annual meeting in 1936) ; and Robert A. Millikan was named to succeed himself, for a period of 3 years.

John C. Merriam, Frank R. Lillie, and Edwin B. Wilson were appointed National Academy of Sciences representatives on the National Resources Board, representation having been requested by the chairman of that board.

TELLERS

A. W. Hull and B. M. Duggar were appointed tellers to count the preference ballots of 1935 on nominations for Academy membership.

COMMITTEE APPOINTMENTS

Nominating committee, appointed by authority of the council of the Academy, to make nominations for president, home secretary, and two members of the council of the Academy, to fill vacancies due to occur on June 30, 1935: Ross G. Harrison, chairman; Arthur L. Day, W. J. V. Osterhout, Edwin B. Wilson, and R. S. Woodworth.

Joint advisory committee on buildings and grounds.—Arthur L. Day and Fred. E. Wright reappointed members in representation of the council of the National Academy (terms coterminous with their respective terms as members of the council); Gano Dunn and F. K. Richtmyer appointed as members in representation of the executive board of the Research Council (terms coterminous with their respective terms as members of the executive board). Former National Research Council representatives on this joint committee were Vernon Kellogg and David White.

Special committee on the operation of buildings and grounds.—Appointed by direction of the council of the Academy: Gano Dunn, chairman; Frank B. Jewett, Clark Wissler.

Auditing committee.—W. C. Mendenhall, chairman; W. W. Coblentz, and G. L. Streeter.

Committee on Biographical Memoirs.—Raymond Pearl, to succeed David White (deceased) as member.

Committee on funds for Academy purposes.—F. R. Lillie as member to succeed William H. Welch (deceased).

COMMITTEES DISCHARGED

Announcement was made of the discharge, by the council, of the following committees: national research fund committee; committee on funds for publication of research; committee on extrasectional memberships.

PROCEEDINGS, MANAGING EDITOR

Announcement was made of the election by the council of the Academy on the preceding evening of Edwin B. Wilson as managing editor of the Proceedings of the National Academy of Sciences, to succeed himself, for the period ending with the autumn meeting in 1936.

DUES

The recommendation of the council that dues for membership in the Academy for the year ending with the annual meeting in 1936 be $10, was approved.

REPORT OF THE FOREIGN SECRETARY

The foreign secretary presented an oral report at the annual meeting in 1935, stating that it was his intention to prepare, at the end of the Academy fiscal year, a report on the work of his office from July 1, 1934, to June 30, 1935, which follows:

During the year the deaths of Santiago Ramon y Cajal, University of Madrid, Spain, Sir Arthur Schuster, Berkshire, England, and Willem de Sitter, Sterrewacht te Leiden, Leiden, The Netherlands, had reduced the number of foreign associates in the fields of zoology and anatomy, physics, and astronomy, respectively. There were elected at the annual meeting two foreign associates from the field of pathology and bacteriology: John Scott Haldane, New College, Oxford University, Oxford, England, and Jules Bordet, Pasteur Institute, Brussels, Belgium. The number of foreign associates in the Academy is limited by the constitution to 50 at any one time, and at the close of the year, there were 43.

In the report of the foreign secretary last year, reference was made to congressional action under consideration authorizing the payment of the American share of the expenses of the International Council of Scientific Unions and affiliated unions each year as it becomes due. This bill is on the calendar of the Senate, having passed the House of Representatives, and it is expected that it will come up for final consideration in the near future. If the bill goes through, to carry out the intent of the authorization, it is expected there will be included in the third deficiency bill an item to cover the American share of the expenses for 1935, as a deficiency item for the fiscal year 1936. The passage of this authorization will make it possible for the Department of State to include regularly, with the authority of Congress, an item in the estimates to cover the payment of the United States' part in the expenses of the International Council of Scientific Unions and affiliated unions. This provision will be appreciated by the scientific men in the United States, as it puts them on an equal footing with the representatives of other scientific bodies in foreign countries at the meetings of these unions, and gives them an opportunity to discuss the subjects brought up, feeling that they do so in their own right.

In connection with international meetings abroad, such as scientific congresses and the meetings of the affiliated unions, the National Academy of Sciences and the National Research Council took part in the following, and appointments of delegates by the president of the Academy were made as indicated.

International Council of Scientific Unions, Brussels, July 9, 1934. Edwin P. Hubble (delegate for the National Research Council).

International Geographical Congress, Warsaw, Poland, August 23-31, 1934. Isaiah Bowman, S. W. Boggs, Louise A. Boyd, Douglas Johnson, J. G. Steese, O. D. von Engeln, John J. Wright (delegates for the National Research Council).

International Scientific Radio Union, London, England, September 12-19, 1934. L. A. Briggs, J. H. Dellinger, Lloyd Espenschied, G. C. Gross, R. A. Heising, A. G. Jensen, Harry R. Mimno, H. M. Turner, Karl S. Van Dyke (delegates for the National Research Council).

Congress of Mathematicians of the Slav Countries, Prague, Czechoslovakia, September 23-28, 1934. Solomon Lefschetz (delegate for the National Academy of Sciences).

International Union of Pure and Applied Physics, London and Cambridge, England, October 1-6, 1934. R. M. Bozorth, Robert B. Brode, A. H. Compton, R. A. Millikan (delegates for the National Research Council).

Inauguration of the Maison de la Chimie, Paris, France, October 19-20, 1934. E. B. Benger (delegate for the National Research Council).

The National Research Council and the National Academy of Sciences will be represented at meetings later this year as follows:

Third Centenary of the Museum National d'Histoire Naturelle, Paris, France, June 24-29, 1935. L. J. Henderson (delegate for the National Academy of Sciences).

International Union of Astronomy, Paris, France, July 10-17, 1935. Ten representatives (delegates for the National Research Council).

International Union of Geodesy and Geophysics, Extraordinary Session, Paris, France, July 1935. Four representatives (delegates for the National Research Council).

To the opening of the New Museum and the Centenary Celebration of the Geological Survey of Great Britain, London, England, July 1935. Arthur L. Day (delegate for the National Academy of Sciences).

Third International Congress of Soil Science, Oxford, England, July 30-August 7, 1935. Oswald Schreiner (delegate for the National Research Council).

(Signed)   T. H. MORGAN,
Foreign Secretary.

REPORT OF THE HOME SECRETARY

During the past year no scientific Memoirs of the National Academy of Sciences have been issued. Of the Biographical Memoirs the second, third, fourth, and fifth memoirs in volume 16 have been published. Seven manuscripts are in hand awaiting printing when further funds become available.

Since the last annual meeting 11 members and 3 foreign associates have died, as follows:

MEMBERS.

William Henry Welch, born April 8, 1850, elected to the Academy in 1895, died April 30, 1934.

George Cary Comstock, born February 12, 1855, elected to the Academy in 1899, died May 11, 1934.

Nathaniel Lord Britton, born January 15, 1859, elected to the Academy in 1914, died June 25, 1934.

Harris Joseph Ryan, born January 8, 1866, elected to the Academy in 1920, died July 3, 1934.

Berthold Laufer, born October 11, 1874, elected to the Academy in 1930, died September 13, 1934.

Otto Folin, born April 4, 1867, elected to the Academy in 1916, died October 25, 1934.

Theobald Smith, born July 31, 1859, elected to the Academy in 1908, died December 10, 1934.

David White, born July 1, 1862, elected to the Academy in 1912, died February 7, 1935.

Walter Jones, born April 28, 1865, elected to the Academy in 1918, died February 28, 1935.

William Dunne, born February 17, 1872, elected to the Academy in 1920, died March 7, 1935.

Michael Idvorsky Pupin, born October 4, 1858, elected to the Academy in 1905, died March 12, 1935.

FOREIGN ASSOCIATES.

Sir Arthur Schuster, Berkshire, England, elected a foreign associate in 1913, died October 14, 1934.

Santiago Ramon y Cajal, University of Madrid, Spain, elected a foreign associate in 1920, died October 17, 1934.

Willem de Sitter, Sterrewacht te Leiden, Leiden, The Netherlands, elected a foreign associate in 1929, died November 21, 1934.

John Howard Northrop has been transferred from the section of pathology and bacteriology to the section of physiology and biochemistry, at his request and with the approval of the latter section.

There are now 274 members, 1 member emeritus, and 42 foreign associates.

FRED. E. WRIGHT, *Home Secretary.*

Report accepted.

REPORT OF THE TREASURER

Attention was called to the annual report of the treasurer for the fiscal year July 1, 1933, to June 30, 1934, as contained in the Annual Report of the National Academy of Sciences for 1933–34, which had just been distributed. The supplementary statement of the treasurer as of December 31, 1934, was presented; it was received for filing.

REPORTS OF TRUST FUNDS

ALEXANDER DALLAS BACHE FUND

At the meetings of the Academy held in April and November 1934, the board of directors of the Bache fund of the National Academy of Sciences made the following grants:

No. 345, for $500, to Dr. Cecilia Payne Gaposchkin, Harvard College Observatory, for the determination of the photographic magnitudes of southern hemisphere stars.

No. 346, for $500, to Dr. H. T. Stetson, Harvard Institute of Geographical Exploration, for investigation of anomalies in radio longitude determinations.

No. 347, for $500, to Dr. Henry B. Ward, University of Illinois, for investigation of the problems of salmon migration.

No. 348, for $400, to Dr. Frank C. Jordan, Allegheny Observatory, for assistance in stellar parallax determinations.

No. 549, for $400, to Dr. T. T. Chen, Yale University, for investigation of the chromosomes of Paramecium in relation to problems of protozoal genetics.

No. 350, for $400, to Dr. D. B. McLaughlin, University of Michigan, for researches on peculiar and variable stellar spectra.

No. 351, for $270, to Dr. Harold Heath, Hopkins Marine Station, Pacific Grove, Calif., for an investigation of the formation of termite castes.

The bursar of the Academy reports $1,125.45 available for grants, as of date of March 31, 1935.

> EDWIN B. WILSON.
> W. J. V. OSTERHOUT.
> HEBER D. CURTIS, *Chairman.*

Report accepted.

JAMES CRAIG WATSON FUND

No report was received from the board of trustees of the James Craig Watson Fund.

HENRY DRAPER FUND

The Henry Draper committee recommended to the Academy at its autumn meeting that it award the Henry Draper medal this year to Dr. John Stanley Plaskett, director of the Dominion Astrophysical Observatory at Victoria, Canada. Dr. Plaskett's consistent and fruitful program of stellar velocity observations, which he conducted with very exceptional skill and energy, and the important conclusions he deduced from his rich observational material have afforded substantial scientific grounds for this award to him. Moreover, our medalist must be credited with outstanding work in another direction. For it was due to his foresight, conviction, and diplomacy that the Canadian Government became persuaded the people of Canada should have a large reflecting telescope, and the great Dominion Astrophysical Observatory, with its excellent 72-inch reflector, stands as a memorial to his vision and steadfastness of purpose. In Dr. Plaskett's hands, this splendid observatory has already developed traditions and has won a high place among the world's leading observatories.

No other disbursements were made by the committee from the Henry Draper fund this year.

> V. M. SLIPHER, *Chairman.*

Report accepted.

J. LAWRENCE SMITH FUND

The condition of the fund on March 31, 1935, is as follows:

Invested income	$1,478.25
Uninvested income	5,490.72
Invested capital	10,000.00

The total assets of the fund are, therefore, $16,968.97.

No appropriations from the fund have been made during the past year, and no appropriation is recommended at this time.

> FRANK SCHLESINGER, *Chairman.*

Report accepted.

BENJAMIN APTHORP GOULD FUND

The directors of the Gould fund of the National Academy of Sciences have the honor to report as follows on the appropriations made from the Gould fund for scientific research during the year April 1, 1934, to March 31, 1935, and on the condition of the fund, as of March 31, 1935:

W. J. Luyten (Apr. 24, 1934)	$250
Benjamin Boss (July 5, 1934)	800
William J. Luyten (Jan. 1, 1935)	250
J. S. Plaskett (Mar. 20, 1935)	300
S. A. Mitchell (Mar. 20, 1935)	500
Total appropriations	2,100

The condition of the Gould fund as of March 31, 1935, was as follows:

Invested capital	$16,702.50
Invested income	1,512.50
Uninvested capital	3,297.50
Uninvested income	14,398.85

HEBER D. CURTIS.
ERNEST W. BROWN.
F. R. MOULTON, *Chairman.*

Report accepted.

WOLCOTT GIBBS FUND

No awards were made from the Wolcott Gibbs fund during the past year.

E. P. KOHLER, *Chairman.*

Report accepted.

CYRUS B. COMSTOCK FUND

The chairman of the committee on the Cyrus B. Comstock fund reported on the financial condition of that fund.

Report accepted.

MARSH FUND

I beg to submit the report of the committee on the Marsh fund for the year 1934 and the recommendations for grants during 1935.

Reports have been received from the grantees of 1934 as follows:

Prof. Douglas Johnson, Columbia University, requested a grant of $100 in order to construct a series of projected profiles in Southern Wisconsin to be used in the study of the correlation of Appalachian erosion surfaces. He reports that the work done on this fund is entirely completed.

Rear Admiral Nares, International Hydrographic Bureau, Monaco, requested a grant of $125 toward the expenses of the employment of assistance in plotting data on ocean depths in charts to be used in a new edition of the General Bathymetric Chart of the Oceans. He reports that the grant was insufficient to pay the salary of a draughtsman and the money has been held, pending the receipt of additional funds. He requests a renewal of the grant.

Dr. Charles B. Read was voted a grant of $225 to enable him to collect fossil plants from the coal fields of Belgium and nearby regions and to study in the museums of that section. This money was not drawn by Dr. Read and no report has been received from him. The grant is therefore still credited to him and is a charge upon the Marsh fund for 1935.

Mr. Albert E. Wood requested a grant of $100 to enable him to pay for illustrations of papers dealing with fossil rodents, especially fossil Heteromyidae and Geomyidae. Four papers have been published by Mr. Wood with the assistance of earlier grants from the Marsh fund and his main paper, containing the illustrations made on the present grant, is now in press and will be published by the Carnegie Museum.

In a letter dated April 3 and received April 8, Dr. C. B. Read, of the Geological Survey, canceled the allotment made to him from the Marsh fund in 1934 and thus released the amount of $225 for distribution.

The bursar of the National Academy of Science reports the uninvested income from the Marsh fund, as of March 31, 1935, as follows:

Uninvested income _____ $1,060.11

The committee on the Marsh fund, therefore, recommends that the following awards be made:

Rear Admiral John D. Nares, renewal of grant_____ $125.00
Dr. L. D. Boonstra, South African Museum, Capetown:
    For completion of work on the fossil mammallike reptiles of South Africa, done chiefly at his own expense, in various museums in Europe and America; endorsed by Henry Fairfield Osborn and Walter Granger_____ 250.00
Mr. Russell M. Logie, Peabody Museum, Yale University:
    For investigation of faunas of Manlius group, New York State; stratigraphy completed and desirable to study faunas collected during that investigation before they are scattered; endorsed by Charles Schuchert, Carl O. Dunbar, Charles K. Swartz_____ 500.00
875.00

Balance_____ 185.11

WILLIAM K. GREGORY, Chairman.

Report accepted and recommendations approved.

MURRAY FUND

The committee on the Murray fund unanimously recommends that the Agassiz medal for the year 1934 be awarded to Dr. Thomas Wayland Vaughan, director of Scripps Institution of Oceanography for his investigations of corals, foraminifera, and submarine deposits, and for his leadership in developing oceanographic activities on the Pacific Coast of America.

DOUGLAS JOHNSON,
CHARLES A. KOFOID,
HENRY B. BIGELOW, Chairman.

Report accepted and recommendation approved.

MARCELLUS HARTLEY FUND

No report was received from the committee on the Marcellus Hartley fund.

DANIEL GIRAUD ELLIOT FUND

No report was received from the committee on the Daniel Giraud Elliot fund.

MARY CLARK THOMPSON FUND

No report was received from the committee on the Mary Clark Thompson fund.

JOSEPH HENRY FUND

The following are abstracts of reports received covering the work done during the past year under the grants from the Joseph Henry fund.

54. Prof. C. E. McClung, University of Pennsylvania, $700 to aid in the collection of Orthopteran material in Japan and elsewhere. This grant was made in 1933, but not reported in 1934 because Dr. McClung was then in Japan. On his return he reported the collection of nearly 2,000 specimens, including many new genera and one entirely new subfamily, and the establishment of direct contacts in Japan, China, the Philippines, Java, and Ceylon which ought in future to yield nearly all the material that is available for work along these lines.

56. Prof. Edward L. Bowles and Mr. Ellis A. Johnson, Massachusetts Institute of Technology, $500 for expenses in their research on fluctuation noise in vacuum tube circuits and amplifiers. This research is an extension of previous work on a group of problems arising from the statistical effects of the thermal agitation of electrons, both in high-resistance conductors and in vacuum tubes, with applications to the theory of these effects and to the

practical uses of such apparatus. The grant has been of great assistance to Professor Bowles and Mr. Johnson in perfecting their equipment and developing instruments of new types required by the unusual sort of changes with time occurring in these fluctuation currents; and this new apparatus will be used in further continuation of these researches.

57. Prof. T. Wayland Vaughan, the Scripps Institution of Oceanography, University of California, $75 for collecting biological material to complete his work on a treatise to be entitled "Handbuch der Paleozoologie." Professor Vaughan reports that he has received some excellent material from France with a part of this grant and he expects to receive the rest during this year.

58. Prof. F. A. Jenkins, University of California, $300 toward a 30,000-line diffraction grating for his researches on band spectra. The grating was made by Prof. R. W. Wood, and Professor Jenkins reports that its revolving power is probably equal to that of any similar grating now in existence.

59. Prof. Simon Freed, University of Chicago, $400 toward an electromagnet for his researches on the magnetic susceptibilities of metals dissolved in liquid ammonia. Professor Freed has as yet made no expenditures from this grant, because to date he has been working on this problem with another magnet purchased with a previous grant from this same fund to Prof. W. D. Harkins. Having obtained important preliminary results with this magnet, he now considers it desirable to build a magnet more powerful than can be made for $400. He is therefore holding this grant pending action on an application for $500 more.

60. Prof. Ernest O. Lawrence, University of California, $400 toward a cathode-ray oscillograph with auxiliary apparatus, to be used for the detection and measurement of various nuclear radiations. This apparatus has been used with great success in determining the kinetic energies of neutrons emitted from various substances, and also in studying atomic disintegrations produced by neutrons. With its aid Professor Lawrence and Dr. Malcom G. Henderson are continuing investigations in this field.

On behalf of the committee on the Joseph Henry fund the following recommendations for grants under this fund are hereby presented to the Academy:

61. $300 to Prof. Simon Freed, of the University of Chicago, toward the expenses of construction of a powerful magnet, on condition that he obtain from other sources the $200 necessary for the completion of this project.

62. $500 to Prof. Francis Bitter, of the Massachusetts Institute of Technology, toward the construction of a coil giving a very intense magnetic field, on condition that he obtain from other sources such extra funds as may be necessary for the completion of this project.

63. $300 to Dr. T. T. Chen, of Yale University, for technical assistance for research on the behavior of chromosomes in Paramecium.

64. $175 to Prof. James J. Brady, of St. Louis University, for the purchase of a vacuum thermopile and low-resistance galvanometer, for researches in the photo-electric effect in thin films.

65. $400 to Prof. G. W. Keitt, of the University of Wisconsin, for technical assistance to finish a research on the nature of parasitism and disease resistance in plants.

66. $300 to Prof. William D. Harkins, of the University of Chicago, toward a radioactive source to be used in the study of artificial radioactivity, on condition that he obtain from other sources, $300 more, as needed for the completion of this project.

67. $250 to Mrs. Elsa G. Allen of Cornell University, for expense of publication of a study of the eastern ground squirrel (Tamias striatus lysteri).

D. L. WEBSTER, *Chairman.*

Report accepted and recommendations approved.

CHARLES DOOLITTLE WALCOTT FUND

No report was received from the directors of the Charles Doolittle Walcott fund.

JOHN J. CARTY FUND

Under the terms of the deed of gift of the John J. Carty fund, a designation of award could be made this year. After a careful review, the committee has, however, decided to make no recommendation for 1935, but to let the matter stand over another year.

The financial status of the John J. Carty medal and award fund on March 31, 1935, as reported by the bursar, was as follows:

Uninvested income _____ $2,309.22
Invested capital_____ 24,742.50
Uninvested capital_____ 257.50

F. B. JEWETT, *Chairman.*

Report accepted.

REPORT ON THE PROCEEDINGS

It is customary at this time to make a report on the Proceedings of the National Academy of Sciences. With the close of the calendar year 1934 we completed the twentieth volume of the Proceedings. There were 154 contributions, making 690 pages. The average length of the contributions was 4.5 pages. The distribution was as follows:

Mathematics	37	Zoology and anatomy	10
Astronomy	9	Botany	5
Physics	21	Genetics	26
Chemistry	11	Physiology and biochemistry	17
Geology and paleontology	7	Pathology and bacteriology	2
Engineering	2	Psychology and anthropology	7

Of the 154 contributions 53 were by members of the Academy, 14 were by National Research Fellows and persons working under research grants from the Academy or Council, and 17 were read before the Academy.

EDWIN B. WILSON, *Managing Editor.*

Report accepted.

REPORT OF COMMITTEE ON OCEANOGRAPHY

The committee on oceanography wishes to state that the reports by Dr. T. Wayland Vaughan on the international status of oceanography, and of Dr. T. G. Thompson on the subject of "Oceanography in Universities", referred to in the last annual report of the committee, are now in an advanced stage of preparation and should be ready for publication during the calendar year. This committee begs to repeat its recommendation of last year that it be continued pending completion of these reports, reserving decision as to the future status of the committee.

F. R. LILLIE, *Chairman.*

Report accepted and recommendation approved.

REPORT OF COMMITTEE ON BIOGRAPHICAL MEMOIRS

During the past year seven manuscripts of Biographical Memoirs have been received. This has kept down the rate of increase of unprepared memoirs. There are now 61 unprepared as compared with 59 last year, and 51 two years ago.

Letters have been sent to all new members of the Academy, elected last year, reminding them of the need of photographs, and photographs have been received from most of them.

Also, letters have been sent to all who are writing memoirs asking for report on progress.

The anthropometric data gathered by Dr. Hrdlicka on the members of the Academy have been analyzed and the results are now about ready for publication.

A. HRDLICKA.
RAYMOND PEARL.
E. L. THORNDIKE.
FRED. E. WRIGHT.
C. B. DAVENPORT, *Chairman.*

Report accepted.

REPORT OF COMMITTEE ON CONSERVATION OF NATIONAL RESOURCES

The committee on conservation of national resources has discussed intensively the responsibilities of the Academy with reference to conservation of resources. There have been informal meetings of other members of the Academy with members of the committee.

The committee is of the opinion that the Academy should give continuing study to the conservation of national resources with a view to aiding either informally or by reply to direct request when the Government desires aid on specific problems.

There have been many informal conferences with Government officials and requests from the Government for aid in study of conservation questions. Some of the problems discussed have been of such a nature that they might, under special circumstances, be considered controversial, and in such cases information has been made available which could be used in attempt to secure solution of questions under consideration.

It is the opinion of the committee that from time to time it will be wise to invite officials of the Government to discuss before the Academy major questions touching national resources insofar as they present problems toward which the thought of the Academy might well be directed.

Considering that there is wisdom in attempting so to organize the activities of the Academy that those functions which concern Government relations be brought together, it is recommended that the committee on conservation of national resources be discharged, and that such activities as relate to conservation of national resources be considered either by appointment of special committees, or through subcommittees of the committee on Government Relations.

JOHN C. MERRIAM, *Chairman.*

Report accepted and recommendations approved.

REPORT OF COMMITTEE ON GOVERNMENT RELATIONS

The following report from the Committee on Government Relations was presented by its chairman, Mr. John C. Merriam:

In addition to general discussion of many problems by subcommittees or informal groups of the Government Relations committee, the whole committee was called together on April 29, 1934, for consideration of the request of the National Planning Board to the National Academy for a report on the role of science in national planning, and the committee also met on April 23, 1935.

The task of preparing a report on the role of science in national planning assigned to the Government Relations committee was carried out by study of special topics by many individual members of the committee and by special reports prepared by other members of the Academy and by a few nonmembers who were specially equipped for rapid assembling of the material desired. A small subcommittee of the Government Relations committee, consisting of Dr. Fred. E. Wright, Dr. E. D. Merrill, and Dr. R. S. Woodworth, digested as much of the data as had been secured in the first 2 weeks and prepared reports which were transmitted to the chairman for use in assembling all of the information obtained.

The whole body of data secured for the role of science report was condensed in the form of a statement under the title "The Role of Science in National Planning", which was transmitted by the president of the Academy to the National Planning Board in time for its meeting in June 1934. With this statement was a group of 30 documents which were copies of original reports forwarded by members of the Academy and others for use in connection with this study. These copies of original documents were transmitted to the Planning Board for its confidential use. The condensed report was for use of the Board in the discretion of the Board and of the President of the United States. The condensed report was released by approval of the President of the United States in printed form on November 16, 1934.

Recognizing the Committee on Government Relations are set up for the purpose of giving consideration to governmental problems which are or may be proper subjects for study of the Academy, it is important to develop such an organization plan as will give the maximum of effectiveness and flexibility to the committee. As originally set up, the Government Relations committee was composed of chairmen of the sections. This plan was put into effect at the time when the Academy set aside a period at each annual meeting which might be used for the discussion by the sections of their special problems either relating to membership or to general questions of the Academy. It was thought that with the chairmen of the sections as members of the Government Relations committee it would be possible from time to time to carry back to the sections certain problems which might require consideration by the experts of the Academy in given fields.

Experience of several years has brought out the difficulties of bringing this committee together for consideration of major questions. The plan has therefore been modified by adding to the committee members at large selected because of their special interest in governmental problems and their availability.

It is suggested that in continuation of the Government Relations committee the representation of sections by their chairmen could be maintained if the number of members at large is increased as this may be deemed desirable in study of special problems.

In order to make possible the discussion of governmental questions without the requirement of too great expenditure of time or loss of time, it is considered desirable that an executive committee of five or preferably seven members selected because of their knowledge of Government problems and because of their availability be appointed. Such an executive committee could be given much of the power of the committee for action between meetings of the whole committee.

It is recommended that instead of standing subcommittees on special subjects under the Committee on Government Relations the committee or the executive committee appoint such special committees from time to time as may be needed for study of special problems, these committees to be discharged when their special tasks are completed.

At the time the Committee on Government Relations was set up it was the expectation that the president of the Academy or the presiding officer would be chairman. There has been variation from this rule to the extent that the person who was presiding officer at the time the committee first met has been continued as chairman of the committee. The Academy may wish to recognize the importance of having the president of the Academy as chairman of the Committee on Government Relations.

In order to continue study of the means of reorganization of the Government Relations committee, it is recommended that a committee be appointed to give careful study to this question and to report to the council of the Academy such changes of the present organization as seem desirable. It is recommended that the committee include those representatives of the Academy who are in closest touch with activities concerning Government relations, these being the president, the vice president, and the home secretary, along with two other members intimately related to the study of Government problems. The present organization will continue until modification is made on the basis of further studies.

JOHN C. MERRIAM, *Chairman.*

It was

Moved, that a special committee, to consist of the president, vice president, and home secretary, together with two additional members, be appointed by the president to study the organization of the Committee on Government Relations and to report to the council of the Academy or its executive committee such changes of the present organization as seem desirable. Adopted.

The president appointed as the additional members of the special committee Mr. John C. Merriam and Mr. Karl T. Compton. It was

Moved, that the original Committee on Government Relations stand as it is constituted until the report of the special committee has been acted on by the council of the Academy or its executive committee. Adopted.

Later, on May 11, 1935, the special committee authorized by the Academy to study the organization of the Committee on Government Relations, presented the following report to the executive committee of the council of the Academy:

The meeting of the special committee authorized by the Academy to study the organization of the Committee on Government Relations, and to report to the council of the Academy such changes of the present organization as seem desirable, was called to order by President Campbell on May 9, 1935, at 10 a. m., in the office of the president and council of the Academy. Present: Messrs. Campbell, K. T. Compton, Day, Merriam, Wright, and, by invitation, President-elect Lillie.

The report of the chairman, John C. Merriam, of the Committee on Government Relations, approved by the National Academy of Sciences in business session on April 24, 1935, was discussed in detail and with special reference to its recommendations. The special committee recommends to the council of the Academy:

(1) That the Committee on Government Relations shall consist of: The president, the vice president, the home secretary, and the chairman or specially elected representative of each of the sections of the National Academy of Sciences; the chairman of the National Research Council; and members at large.

(2) That there shall be an executive committee of at least five members, appointed from the membership of the Committee on Government Relations.

(3) That there shall be subcommittees on general or special subjects, appointed by the President of the Academy on the recommendation of the Committee on Government Relations or of its executive committee; and that the present subcommittees on (a) physical sciences, and (b) biological sciences be discharged.

In view of the importance and range of the Government problems to be considered, it is suggested that each section of the Academy be requested, in the election of its chairman or representative who shall serve as a member of the Committee on Government Relations, to take into consideration the availability and the qualifications of the member for such service.

                    W. W. CAMPBELL, *Chairman.*

After consideration, the following modifications were made:

In recommendation (1): After the expression "the president", insert the following: "who shall serve as chairman,".

In recommendation (2): Following the last word and period "Relations.", add the sentence: "The president shall be chairman of the executive committee."

The last paragraph of the report was amended by the deletion of the words "chairman or" in the phrase "in the election of its chairman or representative" and by the substitution of the following expression for "service." at the end of the report: "service, and therefore that the chairman of each section and its sectional member of the Committee on Government Relations be balloted for separately, with, however, no prohibition of the election of the same member of the section to both offices."

It was—

Moved, that the executive committee approve the recommendations numbered (1), (2), and (3), in the report of the special committee referred to above with the modifications as indicated; this action to go into effect on July 1, 1935. Adopted.

The executive committee of the council of the Academy agreed that the new executive committee of the Committee on Government Relations should be a small one, and favored the recommendation made in the report of the Committee on Government Relations, approved by the Academy on April 24, 1935, that it consist of from five to seven members. It was also the understanding of the executive committee that in accordance with the constitution of the Academy, the vice president, by virtue of his office, shall, in the absence of the president, act as chairmen of the Committee on Government Relations and of its executive committee.

Moved, that the report of the special committee be accepted and, subject to the modifications made by the executive committee, be approved, and that the special committee be discharged. Adopted.

Moved, that the resignation of John C. Merriam, presented in his letter addressed to the president of the Academy dated April 15, 1935, as chairman and member of the Committee on Government Relations, be accepted with expressions of regret and of gratitude for the services he has rendered to the Academy as chairman of the committee during the past 9½ years. Adopted.

The president of the Academy then stated he would at once appoint Frank R. Lillie to serve as chairman of the present Committee on Government Relations in succession to Mr. Merriam, for the period May 11 to July 1, 1935.

REPORT OF COMMITTEE ON LONG-RANGE WEATHER FORECASTING

The committee on long-range weather forecasting was assembled for the purpose of giving consideration to questions that might have to do with the longer cycles in weather or in climate, with a view to determining what values may be available and what types of investigation might well be entered upon to advantage. A symposium covering problems presented before the Academy by the committee in April 1932 has been published and has been the basis of other conferences and investigations at various institutions in the past few years.

Although the committee has not been active through meetings in the past year, a study of the problems to which its attention has been devoted has been carried on vigorously by various institutions.

Within the past year the Carnegie Institution of Washington has defined two groups of investigations bearing upon this question. One is that represented by the study of atmospheric problems relating to weather forecasting, conducted by Dr. V. Bjerknes, this being the continuation of a series of investigations carried on under auspices of the Carnegie Institution for the past 29 years. The second group of problems represents the long-range period or cycle, and has been made the subject of special researches by a group of investigators related in various ways to the tree-ring cycle studies carried on for many years by Dr. A. E. Douglass, of the University of Arizona.

Through cooperation of the University of Arizona, Dr. Douglass has been freed from teaching duties in order that he may devote himself to concentrated study of the climatic aspect of his tree-ring researches. Dr. Douglass has been provided with three assistants and with modest support for his investigations. Other students of the subject, including Dr. J. Bartels, of Eberswalde, Germany, associated with the department of terrestrial magnetism of Carnegie Institution, have taken up study of aspects of the cycle problem related to the work of Dr. Douglass. Statistical examination of the results of Dr. Douglass' work has been taken up by Dr. Dinsmore Alter, of the University of Kansas. In another direction investigations are being conducted in the field of recent climatic changes in the Southwest as they are interpreted both through rainfall record and through succession of phenomena as they are studied by the geologist, palaeontologist, the student of the problem of early man, and the student of the significance of ecological changes represented in the life of the Southwest.

It has been possible also to secure the cooperation of students of cycle researches from the point of view of the mathematical-statistical investigation problem through the cooperation of Dr. E. B. Wilson and from point of view of the investigator of other aspects of the cycle problem as seen through the work of Dr. Wesley C. Mitchell.

The investigations conducted by the Carnegie Institution involve also the checking of various aspects of the study of cyclic changes as they are expressed in astronomical work at Mount Wilson Observatory and through research on magnetic changes under investigation by the department of terrestrial magnetism.

Significant relations of the work centering around the studies of Dr. Douglass are also those expressed in the work of Dr. Abbot, of the Smithsonian Institution, and many other investigators in this country. It is hoped that the impetus given to these researches by the activities of the committee on long-range weather forecasting of the Academy may be important in the furtherance of study on these problems.

It is recommended that the committee be discharged.

JOHN C. MERRIAM, *Chairman.*

Report accepted and recommendation approved.

REPORT OF COMMITTEE ON SCIENTIFIC PROBLEMS OF NATIONAL PARKS

This committee has given its attention over a number of years to investigation of methods by which the great research opportunities of national parks may be turned to advantage through the developing educational system of the parks.

Report has already been made to the Academy concerning the work carried on over many years at the Grand Canyon and culminating in a research program at Yavapai station. The plan worked out at Yavapai station was based upon studies of a considerable group of leading investigators of America and was designed to give opportunity for the visitor to know what are considered the principal elements in the story of the canyon.

As has been pointed out in earlier reports, the studies at the Grand Canyon have led to an extended series of fundamental investigations which have been necessary in order to secure the data needed for an educational program. These researches have included a study of the structure and origin of the oldest rocks in the canyon; an investigation of the nature of the Algonkian, the second series in the Grand Canyon; a study of the fauna of the Cambrian, the earliest period of the third, or uppermost, division of the Grand Canyon; a study of the Devonian and its fauna; a study of the vertebrate fauna of the Hermit and Supai horizons; a descriptions and interpretation of the Coconino sandstone of the upper canyon wall; and a study of the stratigraphy and faunas of the Kaibab, the uppermost member of the canyon wall. These investigations have been supported in part by the National Park Service; they have been further given cooperation of the Geological Survey, the University of Arizona, the University of California, California Institutes of Technology, the Smithsonian Institution, and the Carnegie Institution of Washington. The later investigations have been financed in considerable part by the Carnegie Institution of Washington in cooperation with the National Park Service.

It is important to note that the later investigations of the geology and palaeontology of the Grand Canyon have opened a great field for research which seems scarcely less significant than the whole of the work done up to the present time.

Studies have also been made on means for presentation of the story of the great intrusions of granite which have made possible the development of a canyon with the characteristics of Yosemite. Through cooperation of a considerable group of investigators—representing the Geological Survey, California Institute of Technology, the University of California, and the Carnegie Institution of Washington, a plan has been devised for presenting this story in the simplest possible form. The working out of this plan has involved research in various directions and has emphasized the need for further studies.

At Crater Lake, Oreg., one of the most intensive studies of the committee has been directed toward development of means by which the scientific story of this unique lake could be presented in such relation to the aesthetic values of the lake as to lead the visitor from an interest in the aesthetic features into an appreciation of the story of the nature and origin of the mountain. The plan as worked out has seemed to be extraordinarily successful, both from the scientific point of view and from the point of view of human interest and appreciation on the part of visitors. There has developed a natural trend of interest from appreciation of the color and beauty of the lake into a consideration of the great geological and historical features which have made the lake possible.

The studies at Crater Lake, as in other regions, have demonstrated the great need for continued intensive investigation upon matters which should be touched in any educational program. Several important researches on the geological and biological features of the Crater Lake region have already been carried out, and some have been published. The committee has been urging complete restudy of the geology of the Crater Lake region to follow the excellent study of this area published some years ago by Dr. Diller, of the Geological Survey. Where the attention of the public is directed definitely to a great feature of this nature, it is important that the story be known as fully as possible in order to distinguish between what are scientific facts and what are suppositions. So, for example, it is desirable to have as nearly as possible final judgment regarding late stages in the history of the mountain which produced the crater, in order that there may be a settlement of the question whether the last steps were wholly of the type of a catastrophic or explosive eruption, or whether other factors were involved.

The final steps in study of the Crater Lake problem by the committee involved study of the question as to what makes the water blue, carried out by Dr. Edison Pettit, of Carnegie Institution. Although this question has been asked by various scientific investigations, Dr. Pettit's study furnishes important evidence that the scattering effect is responsible. This paper will be published.

The committee does not plan to hold further meetings, but certain expenditures which have been authorized should be cared for by authority of committee organization, and the committee should, therefore, be allowed to stand during the coming year with the understanding that it be discharged in 1936.

JOHN C. MERRIAM, *Chairman.*

Report accepted and approved.

REPORT ON BUILDINGS AND GROUNDS

During the last 2 or 3 years the development of the part of the city in the vicinity of the Lincoln Memorial has shown the wisdom of the men responsible for the selection of a site for the Academy building. Even the change in the old name of B Street for the north side of the Mall to Constitution Avenue has had its effect, for, from a narrow street, it has assumed the proportions of a boulevard. The completion of the Pharmaceutical Building and of the Public Health Service Building, and the planting of their grounds, has been one more step toward the fruition of the proposed plan that from the Capitol Grounds on the east, to the river on the west, there shall be a great open avenue, with harmonious buildings on the north side and park on the south.

In the widening and repaving of Constitution Avenue, completed last year, the part from Twentieth Street to the river was narrowed on the north side on account of the effect on the architecture and landscaping of the Academy grounds. It is hoped that further widening at this point will not be necessary, as the cost of altering the Academy grounds will be high. The question of widening the avenue was considered in the original plans by the architect after consultation with the Engineers of the Army when the garden wall was placed far enough back, as they thought, to take care of future improvements of this kind. An avenue of the present proportions was not conceived at that time.

In the further beautifying of this section, the square immediately to the east of the Academy grounds has been selected as the building site for the Federal Reserve Board. Competition is now going forward for plans for a structure in harmony with the Academy building, the Public Health Service Building, the Pan American Building, and the Pharmaceutical Building. It is expected that it will be about 6 months before the bids are let, and another 6 months before actual work is started on the building.

The routine work on the Academy building has been continued from day to day, as has the pointing to take care of leaks in the dome and surrounding walls and the northeast elevations of the main building. Painting of the rooms and halls has been continued so that this part of the original program is being carried out.

The good soil on the grounds is more or less of a covering without any depth. Efforts are being made to meet this condition by the use of fertilizers, and this year a little more was added when a carload of hyperhumus was distributed over the grounds, but a carload, considering the whole, does not add very much to the surface in any one place. It is felt that with additions as they can be given, eventually the ground will be in such condition that the plants will want to grow.

The elevator installed at the time of the construction of the building has been run for a short time in the morning and at noon for a number of years. The elevator inspector of the District required that new cables be installed, as the old ones had broken strands, and their elasticity had gone. The replacement of the cables and a few minor repairs was accomplished without interrupting the service for more than 2 or 3 days.

The question of ventilation of the public rooms during meetings has been given study and thought, with the hope that something could be done to relieve a situation that occurs sometimes; that is, when the temperature and humidity outside, as may happen during the April meetings, is higher than that inside. The present ventilating system, the best that could be had when the building was erected, brings in pure air, but at the same time it brings in the heat and humidity from the outside. Air conditioning is the answer, but the cost is prohibitive.

: During the summer a severe storm or cloudburst flooded the streets of. Washington to the extent that traffic was halted, and a great deal of damage was done. The city sewerage system was inadequate, and in the Academy. building the water backed up, flooding the boiler room, and some water came in under the doors in the basement. As the water continued to rise in the boiler room, the fire in the hot-water heater was drawn to prevent damage. The sewer outlets in the basement became geysers, as did those under the drinking fountains on the first floor and the outlets on the roof. Through the force of the water, a hole was blown in a drain pipe inside the wall of the west gallery of the auditorium, threatening the decorations. Repairs were started immediately; the damage required cutting into the wall above the paneling to the drain pipe, and the taking out and replacing of an elbow and a length of pipe. The work was carefully done, so that when completed there was no evidence that anything had happened.

In the heating system, just at the beginning of the season, a leak developed in the main which supplied the east end of the building. This was taken care of through the efforts of a steam fitter working all night. These immediate repairs made it possible to continue heating the rooms without interruption.

Last year the steam coils of the heating boilers were carefully gone over for a general inspection and replacement of needed parts. This year the hot-water boiler received attention. It was dismantled and thoroughly cleaned and overhauled, leaving it in first-class condition. This is the first time this boiler has had attention of this kind since the occupancy of the building by the Academy and Research Council.

During the year plans have been in progress for the construction of a new building for the Interior Department, and the various parts of land from Eighteenth to Nineteenth Streets and from C to D Streets were purchased by the Government. On one of these was a power-distributing station of the Potomac Electric Power Co., which is the only system operating in the District. This necessitated the removal from this vicinity of direct current, the principal kind of electricity used in this part of the city since electrical service was first given many years ago. The company feels that with their main plant miles away in the eastern part of the city, they cannot afford to supply direct current, and that now is the time to change to a three-phase alternating-current system, and plans are being carried forward, looking toward this end. The main equipment in the Academy and Research Council building is, in the most part, fitted for direct current, but at the time the building was erected the company ran special alternating-current cable to take care of such exhibits as require that kind of current, but this is not sufficient to care for all the needs. With the change-over in mind, the lighting equipment has been gone over, looking to the replacement of motors and proper wiring. In addition to the alternating current, the Potomac Electric Power Co. will install a motor generator set for the purpose of giving the Academy direct current for its special needs. It is the purpose of the company to complete this entire work by June 30, 1935. These changes will be made without expense to the Academy.

PAUL BROCKETT,
Custodian, Buildings and Grounds.

Report accepted.

REPORT ON EXHIBITS

The series of exhibits in the Academy and Research Council building, representing fundamentals in scientific discovery and recent progress in scientific research, have continued to be of great interest to the public and to educational institutions. The image of the sun and its spectrum, together with the Foucault pendulum, continue to catch the visitor's eye immediatley on entering the building, with an invitation to investigate further.

To the exhibits of the Bell Telephone Laboratories, illustrating the basic principles of electrical communications, several new pieces of apparatus showing recent developments have been added. They consist of (1) a new oscilloscope, (2) a vacuum-tube exhibit with an operating fluorescent plate tube surrounded by some specimens of tubes, and (3) a demonstration model of the mechanism of the carbon transmitter with meters and an optical system to show completely the action which takes place.

The instruments in the exhibit of the Weather Bureau station have remained intact with the addition of an electrical recording thermograph for recording the outside temperature from the roof. The ultraviolet lamp exhibit and the apparatus for showing the Zeeman effect, which had been loaned to the Century of Progress Exposition in Chicago, were returned; the necessary repairs on these two exhibits have been made and they are again to be placed on exhibition. The Zeeman apparatus was returned to Professor Pfund at Johns Hopkins University, but a new instrument to demonstrate this phenomenon will be constructed in the machine shop of the Academy to take its place. One of the exhibits, lent by the Sperry Gyroscope Co., entitled "See the Earth Turn", consists of a gyroscope which has been running continuously during the day for 6 or 7 years. It was found that the bearings and suspension were out of order, and the company generously had the instrument returned for a thorough overhauling and a replacement of worn parts. In the General Electric Co. exhibits some of the latest products of the work of its research laboratory are shown; it has recently added an important and exceptional exhibit, namely, the sun motor. Four photoelectric cells affected by light in combination generate sufficient current to run a small motor.

Another exhibit returned from the Century of Progress is that of the National Advisory Committee for Aeronautics, with many new pieces of apparatus. Among these are included: Full-scale wind tunnel, control system of an airplane, fuel-spray combustion research exhibit, the progress of aviation (models of 1903, 1917, 1927, and 1933), vertical wind tunnel, measure of air bumps and pressure on wings, why an airplane flys, variable-density wind tunnel, model of Navy C-class airship, and combustion chambers for compression. It is regretted that this material will remain with the Academy and Research Council for a short time only, as it has been ordered by Congress to the San Diego Exposition. For the time being, other exhibits from the Langley Field laboratory will take its place.

The interest shown by the many questions asked by the public, and the desire of visitors to study the exhibits in detail gives assurance that the methods adopted of making it possible for the visitor himself to perform an experiment and to observe the results obtained, are accomplishing the object for which this exhibition was established. During the year there have been 40,811 visitors.

PAUL BROCKETT, *Secretary,*
Joint Committee on Exhibits.

Report accepted.

ELECTIONS

The elections at the annual meeting resulted as follows:

President of the Academy: Frank R. Lillie (succeeding W. W. Campbell). Term, 4 years commencing July 1, 1935.

Home secretary: Fred. E. Wright (succeeding himself). Term, 4 years commencing July 1, 1935.

Members of the council of the Academy for 3 years commencing July 1, 1935: Henry Norris Russell and Ross G. Harrison; each succeeding himself.

New members of the Academy: Norman Levi Bowen, Geophysical Laboratory, Carnegie Institution of Washington, Washington, D. C.; Charles Manning Child, University of Chicago, Chicago, Ill.; George Ellett Coghill, Wistar Institute, Philadelphia, Pa.; James Ewing, Memorial Hospital, New York City; Merritt Lyndon Fernald, Gray Herbarium, Cambridge, Mass.; Harvey Fletcher, Bell Telephone Laboratories, New York City; Ross Aiken Gortner, University Farm, St. Paul, Minn.; Earnest Albert Hooton, Harvard University, Cambridge, Mass.; Jerome Clark Hunsaker, Massachusetts Institute of Technology, Cambridge, Mass.; Walter Samuel Hunter, Clark University, Worcester, Mass.; Dunham Jackson, University of Minnesota, Minneapolis, Minn.; Chester Ray Longwell, Yale University, New Haven, Conn.; Harold Clayton Urey, Columbia University, New York City; and John Hasbrouck Van Vleck, Harvard University, Cambridge, Mass.

New foreign associates of the Academy: John Scott Haldane, New College, Oxford University, Oxford, England, and Jules Bordet, Pasteur Institute, Brussels, Belgium.

(On June 30, 1935, the number of members of the Academy was 286 and the number of foreign associates 43.)

PRESENTATION OF MEDALS

Four gold medals were presented at the dinner of the Academy on Tuesday evening, April 23, 1935, as follows:

Agassiz medal: Awarded to Haakon Hasberg Gran, of the University of Oslo, Oslo, Norway, in recognition of his contributions to knowledge of the factors controlling organic production in the sea. In the absence of Dr. Gran the medal was received for him by the Honorable Wilhelm Munthe de Morgenstierne, the Minister of Norway, for transmission through diplomatic channels. The presentation address, prepared by the chairman of the committee on the Agassiz medal award, Dr. H. B. Bigelow, was read in his absence.

Henry Draper medal: Awarded to John Stanley Plaskett, director of the Dominion Astrophysical Observatory, Victoria, British Columbia, in recognition of his able and consistent labors in stellar radial velocities, and related studies energetically pursued for nearly 30 years. In the absence of Dr. Plaskett the medal was received for him by Dr. Frank Dawson Adams, foreign associate of the Academy from Canada. The presentation address was made by the chairman of the committee on the Draper fund, Dr. V. M. Slipher.

Daniel Giraud Elliot medal and honorarium of $200: Awarded to James P. Chapin, of the American Museum of Natural History, New York City, in recognition of his work entitled, "The Birds of the Belgian Congo," Part I, published as a bulletin of the American Museum of Natural History in 1932. The presentation address, prepared by Dr. F. M. Chapman, was read by Dr. Ross G. Harrison, chairman of the committee on the Elliot fund.

Public Welfare medal: Awarded to August Vollmer, member of the staff of the department of political science, University of California, and during many years chief of police of Berkeley, Calif., in recognition of his application in police administration of scientific methods to crime detection and to crime prevention. The medal was handed to the home secretary for transmission to Mr. Vollmer. The presentation address was made by Dr. Max Mason, member of the committee which recommended the award.

SCIENTIFIC SESSIONS

The scientific sessions for the presentation of papers by members of the Academy or persons introduced by them were well attended. The papers presented were as follows:

MONDAY, APRIL 22, 1935

Francis G. Benedict and Ernest G. Ritzman, nutrition laboratory of the Carnegie Institution of Washington, Boston, Mass., and the New Hampshire Agricultural Experiment Station, Durham, N. H.: Liability of the basal metabolism of the dairy cow (illustrated).

Eugene F. DuBois and James D. Hardy, Russell Sage Institute of Pathology in affiliation with New York Hospital, New York City: Heat losses from the human body (illustrated).

C. A. Kofoid, University of California, Berkeley, Calif.: Some remarkable ciliate Protozoa from the cæcum of the Indian elephant (illustrated).

W. G. MacCallum, Johns Hopkins University, Baltimore, Md.: Diabetes in relation with anterior hypophysis (illustrated).

E. C. MacDowell, department of genetics, Carnegie Institution of Washington, Cold Spring Harbor, N. Y. (introduced by A. F. Blakeslee): Maternal influence upon longevity and upon the incidence of leukemia in mice (illustrated).

Walter R. Miles and K. T. Behanan, Yale University, New Haven, Conn.: Oxygen consumption during Yogic breathing exercises (illustrated).

John H. Northrop and M. Kunitz, Rockefeller Institute for Medical Research, Princeton, N. J.: Isolation from pancreas of a substance which inhibits trypsin digestion and its effect on the activation of trypsin (illustrated).

W. J. V. Osterhout and S. E. Hill, Rockefeller Institute for Medical Research, New York City: Some aspects of anesthesia and irritability (illustrated).

G. H. Parker, Harvard University, Cambridge, Mass: What is a resting state and an active state in chromatophores, particularly Melanophores (illustrated)?

Thomas M. Rivers, Rockefeller Institute for Medical Research, New York City, and T. F. McNair Scott, M. R. C. P., Lond.: Meningitis in man caused by a .filterable virus.

Edward Kasner, Columbia University, New York City: Transformations of differential elements (illustrated).

Marston Morse, Harvard University, Cambridge, Mass.: Four theorems on the envelope of extremals.

Norbert Wiener, Massachusetts Institute of Technology, Cambridge, Mass.: Tauberian gap theorems (illustrated).

S. A. Mitchell, University of Virginia, University, Va.: The shape of the corona and its relation to the sun spot cycle (illustrated).

P. van de Kamp and A. N. Vyssotsky, University of Virginia, University, Va. (introduced by S. A. Mitchell): Analysis of 18,000 proper motions derived at the Leander McCormick Observatory.

Donald H. Menzel, Harvard College Observatory, Cambridge, Mass. (introduced by Harlow Shapley): Recent advances in our knowledge of the solar chromosphere (illustrated).

Robert J. Trumpler, Lick Observatory, Mount Hamilton, Calif.: Observational evidence of an Einstein red shift in class O stars (illustrated).

Frank Schlesinger, Yale University, New Haven, Conn.: Report on the progress of the Yale Zone observations (illustrated).

William Bowie, United States Coast and Geodetic Survey, Washington, D. C.: Science in the United States Coast and Geodetic Survey.

C. R. Stockard, Cornell University Medical College, New York City: New endocrine complexes from recombinations of old breed types (illustrated).

George L. Streeter, department of embryology, Carnegie Institution of Washington, Baltimore, Md.: Significance of the amnion (illustrated).

A. H. Wright, Cornell University, Ithaca, N. Y. (introduced by Leonhard Stejneger): Some rare amphibians and reptiles of the United States (illustrated).

A. F. Blakeslee, A. F. Avery, and A. D. Bergner, department of genetics, Carnegie Institution of Washington, Cold Spring Harbor, N. Y.: A type in datura with extra-chromosomal material which in inheritance resembles a recessive (illustrated).

M. Demerec, department of genetics, Carnegie Institution of Washington, Cold Spring Harbor, N. Y. (introduced by A. F. Blakeslee): Relative importance of various genes to the organism (illustrated).

B. O. Dodge, New York Botanical Garden, New York City: The mechanism of sexual reproduction in Neurospora and Gelasinospora (illustrated).

E. W. Sinnott, Columbia University, New York City (introduced by R. A. Harper): The genetic control of developmental relationships and its bearing on the theory of gene action (illustrated).

Walter T. Swingle, United States Department of Agriculture, Washington, D. C. (introduced by R. A. Harper): Old and new criteria for determining the relationships of higher plants (illustrated).

P. A. Levene and Alexander Rothen, Rockefeller Institute for Medical Research, New York City: Analysis of rotatory dispersion curves of members of homologous series of the type   CH$_3$ (illustrated).

$$H\text{-}C\text{-}(CH_2)_x\ X$$

$$R$$

Linus Pauling, California Institute of Technology, Pasadena, Calif.: The oxygen equilibrium of hemoglobin and its structural interpretation (illustrated).

Philip A. Shaffer, Washington University Medical School, St. Louis, Mo.: A simple factor affecting the velocity of ionic oxidation-reduction reactions in aqueous solutions: equivalence of valence change (illustrated).

W. Harold Smith, National Bureau of Standards, Washington, D. C. (introduced by W. W. Coblentz): Some physical properties of rubber prepared by .fractionation and crystallization (illustrated).

J. A. Stratton, Massachusetts Institute of Technology, Cambridge, Mass. (introduced by John C. Slater): Solutions of the wave equation in spheroidal coordinates (illustrated).

Philip M. Morse, Massachusetts Institute of Technology, Cambridge, Mass. ·(introduced by John C. Slater): Exact solutions of wave diffraction and scattering problems in elliptic and spheroidal coordinates (illustrated).

M. A. Biot, Graduate School of Engineering, Harvard University, Cambridge, Mass. (Introduced by C. A. Adams) : Quadratic wave equation—flood waves in a channel with quadratic friction. Read by title.

Frank B. Jewett, American Telephone & Telegraph Co., New York City: Electrical communications, past, present, and future (illustrated).

TUESDAY, APRIL 23, 1935

R. W. Wood and G. H. Dieke, Johns Hopkins University, Baltimore, Md.: Arc spectra of hydrogen and deuterium (illustrated).

J. A. Bearden, Johns Hopkins University, Baltimore, Md. (introduced by R. W. Wood) : X-ray wave-lengths and the fundamental constants (illustrated).

K. T. Compton and J. C. Boyce, Massachusetts Institute of Technology, Cambridge, Mass.: Spectroscopic investigations in the extreme ultraviolet (illustrated).

William V. Houston, California Institute of Technology, Pasadena, Calif. (introduced by Robert A. Millikan) : A model of atomic nuclei (illustrated).

E. O. Lawrence, E. M. McMillan, and R. L. Thornton, University of California, Berkeley, Calif.: A new type of excitation function for nuclear reactions (illustrated).

Robert A. Millikan and H. Victor Neher, California Institute of Technology, Pasadena, Calif.: Further experiments on the cosmic ray longitude effect (illustrated).

F. D. Murnaghan, Johns Hopkins University, Baltimore, Md. (introduced by Joseph S. Ames) : On the fundamental equations of elasticity with special reference to the behavior of solids and liquids under extreme pressures.

F. K. Richtmyer and E. Ramberg, Cornell University, Ithaca, N. Y.: The width of spectrum lines (illustrated).

Anna W. Pearsall, Hamilton, N. Y. (introduced by F. K. Richtmyer) : Intensities of X-ray satellites (illustrated).

Otto Stern, Carnegie Institute of Technology, Pittsburgh, Pa. (by invitation) : Remarks on the measurement of the magnetic moment of the proton (illustrated).

Henry Fairfield Osborn, American Museum of Natural History, New York City: The ancestral tree of the Proboscidea. Discovery, evolution, migration, and extinction over a 50,000,000-year period (illustrated).

John C. Merriam, Carnegie Institution of Washington, Washington, D. C.: A re iew of evidence relating to status of the problem of antiquity of man in Florida.

Felix Bernstein, Columbia University, New York (introduced by Franz Boas) : The change in the range of accommodation with age and its connection with length of life (illustrated).

Franz Boas, Columbia University, New York City: The tempo of growth of fraternities (illustrated).

Carlyle F. Jacobsen, Yale School of Medicine, New Haven, Conn. (introduced by Robert M. Yerkes) : The neutral basis of memory in primates (illustrated).

Frank H. H. Roberts, Jr., Bureau of American Ethnology, Smithsonian Institution, Washington, D. C. (introduced by John R. Swanton) : A habitation site and workshop attributable to so-called Folsom man (illustrated).

E. Sapir, Yale University, New Haven, Conn.: Event classifications in Navaho, a study in linguistic psychology (illustrated).

G. M. Stratton and Franklin M. Henry, University of California, Berkeley, Calif.: Some reactions of Mongolians and Caucasians in an emotional situation.

L. O. Howard, United States Department of Agriculture, Washington, D. C.: Biographical Memoir of Edward Sylvester Morse. Read by title.

Waldemar Lindgren, Massachusetts Institute of Technology, Cambridge, Mass.: Biographical Memoir of George Perkins Merrill. Read by title.

W. A. Noyes, Urbana, Ill.: Biographical Memoir of Edward Wight Washburn. Read by title.

G. P. Clinton, Connecticut Agricultural Experiment Station, New Haven, Conn.: Biographical Memoir of Roland Thaxter. Read by title.

REPORT OF THE NATIONAL RESEARCH COUNCIL

FOR THE YEAR JULY 1, 1934, TO JUNE 30, 1935

(Prepared in the office of the chairman of the Council with the assistance of the chairmen of divisions of the Council)

The following report is presented to the National Academy of Sciences on the operations of the National Research Council during the fiscal year July 1, 1934, to June 30, 1935.

In addition to work of the Council upon divisional projects, the attention of the Council has been given during the past year to certain general matters deemed to be of major importance in carrying out the purposes of the Council. These include:

(a) The work of the post-doctorate fellowships which have been administered by the Research Council during the past 15 years, and the need for the continuation of the fellowship system;

(b) The results which have been obtained in the support of investigations through individual grants-in-aid during the past 6 years;

(c) The principles which should govern the disposition of patents upon the results of research supported by public trust funds, and a redefinition of the patent policy of the National Research Council;

(d) The recognition of borderlands of research which require knowledge from two or more of the traditional scientific fields, and means for the encouragement of such research.

OFFICERS OF THE NATIONAL RESEARCH COUNCIL, 1935-36

The officers of the Council for the year July 1, 1935, to June 30, 1936, as duly elected, are as follows:

GENERAL OFFICERS

Honorary chairman: George E. Hale, honorary director, Mount Wilson Observatory, Carnegie Institution of Washington, Pasadena, Calif.

Secretary emeritus: Vernon Kellogg, National Research Council, Washington, D. C.

Chairman: Frank R. Lillie, dean emeritus, of the division of biological sciences; Andrew MacLeish distinguished service professor, emeritus, of embryology, University of Chicago; and president, National Academy of Sciences, Washington, D. C.

Treasurer: Arthur Keith, treasurer, National Academy of Sciences, Washington, D. C.

CHAIRMEN OF THE DIVISIONS OF GENERAL RELATIONS

Federal relations: George R. Putnam, former Commissioner, Bureau of Lighthouses, Department of Commerce, Washington, D. C.

Foreign relations: T. H. Morgan, chairman of the division of biology, William G. Kerckhoff laboratories of the biological sciences, California Institute of Technology, Pasadena, Calif.; and foreign secretary, National Academy of Sciences.

States relations: Raymond A. Pearson, former president, University of Maryland, College Park, Md.

Educational relations: William Charles White, chairman, medical research committee, National Tuberculosis Association; pathologist in charge of tuberculosis research, National Institute of Health, Washington, D. C.

CHAIRMEN OF DIVISIONS OF SCIENCE AND TECHNOLOGY

Physical sciences: R. A. Millikan, director, Norman Bridge laboratory of physics, and chairman of the executive council, California Institute of Technology, Pasadena, Calif.

Engineering and industrial research: Charles F. Kettering, vice president and director, General Motors Corporation; president, General Motors Research Corporation, Detroit, Mich.

Chemistry and chemical technology: F. W. Willard, executive vice president, Nassau Smelting & Refining Co., 50 Church Street, New York City.

Geology and geography: Edson S. Bastin, professor of petrology; chairman of the department of geology and paleontology, University of Chicago, Chicago, Ill.

Medical sciences: Francis G. Blake, Sterling professor of medicine, School of Medicine, Yale University, New Haven, Conn.

Biology and agriculture: I. F. Lewis, dean of the university and Miller professor of biology and agriculture, University of Virginia, Charlottesville, Va.

Anthropology and psychology: Edward Sapir, Sterling professor of anthropology and linguistics, and Fellow of Trumbull College, Yale University, New Haven, Conn.

The chairman of the National Research Council has been appointed upon a half-time basis for the past 2 years and this arrangement is to be continued for the coming year. The chairmen of six of the divisions of science and technology are retained on the basis of a modest honorarium and render generously of their time and attention to Council matters, far in excess of any services for which their honoraria may be considered a remuneration. It would be difficult, if not impossible, to carry out the purposes of the National Research Council without the cooperation of the division chairmen in the development of the program of the Council in the several major fields of science.

GENERAL ACTIVITIES OF THE COUNCIL

Fellowships.—During the past year the National Research Council has expended upon post-doctorate fellowships $221,927.73, of which about 8.8 percent was used for administration. (For the distribution of this sum among the three fellowship boards of the Council, see p. 11.) This unusually large proportion for administrative expenses was occasioned in part by the decreased total fund used for fellowships this year and in part by the maintenance of a field secretary for the Research Fellowship Board in Physics, Chemistry, and Mathematics for the purpose of making a special study of the fellowships.

These funds have supported a total of 96 fellows during the greater part of the year. Last year (1933–34) the number of active fellows was 165. For the coming year (1935–36), in view of the restriction of funds, the boards in charge of the fellowship programs have appointed a total of only 60 fellows. (A number of the fellows of the past year had retired from their fellowships before the compilation of the following table as of June 30, 1935, and a considerable number of fellows appointed for the coming year had at that date not undertaken their fellowship work.)

TABLE I.—*National Research Council fellowships as of June 30, 1935*

	Number of fellows active	Number of fellows under appointment (not yet active)	Number of past fellows	Total number of fellows appointed	Total number of applications received
Physical sciences	20	12	427	459	1,489
Medical sciences	2	6	231	239	1,117
Biological sciences	19	22	309	350	1,346
Total	41	40	967	1,048	3,952

The funds which have been expended for these series of fellowships by the Rockefeller Foundation since their establishment in 1919, 1922, and 1923, respectively, have amounted in total as follows (June 30, 1935): Physics, chemistry, and mathematics, $1,782,545.86; medical sciences, $779,914.02; biological sciences, $1,207,165; total, $3,769,624.88. Of this total sum $192,067.84, or about 5.1 percent, was used for administrative expenses. Although not measurable in dollars, the institutions at which these fellows have been located for their fellowship work have contributed extensively to the support of the investigations carried on by the fellows, by providing housing and general laboratory facilities and in many cases by furnishing special apparatus and materials, often at considerable cost.

After operating for periods of from 12 to 15 years there are (as of June 30, 1935) 967 past fellows of these three boards, who, with the 81 now active or under appointment, have been selected from 3,952 applicants as shown in table I above. These National Research fellows were stationed for their fellowship work at about 60 American universities. Two hundred and forty-five of the fellows have studied abroad.

It is clear that past fellows of the Council are taking their places prominently among the scientific leaders of the country. The five awards made under the American Chemical Society for work in pure chemistry, established by Dr. A. C. Langmuir a few years ago, have been given to past fellows of the Council. Of 396 past fellows in the physical sciences, about 73 percent are now engaged in academic work, of whom two-thirds are already of professorial grade. Of the 220 past fellows in the medical sciences, 80 percent are engaged in academic work; and of the 285 past fellows in the biological sciences, about 70 percent.

Repeatedly the outstanding men in science are found to have held National Research fellowships. In the judgment of many leading physicists and chemists the brilliant advances in chemistry made in the United States during the past decade, and perhaps even more strikingly in physics, have been largely due to the opportunity given to superior young men to pursue advanced work in the post-doctoral period. Such results bear out the expectations of the founders of the fellowships that the finding and development of talented young men for scientific leadership means a substantial national gain.

The responsibility for maintaining these fellowships for the preparation of scientific leaders rests upon all agencies alike—the foundations, the universities, technical institutes, industry, and social agencies—that strive to increase national welfare through the elevation of standards of living in which scientific applications play so large a part.

Grants-in-aid.—During the year 1934–35 the National Research Council has made 116 general grants-in-aid of research, totaling $50,359.50, from 250 applications. These grants were distributed according to subject as given in table II.

TABLE II

Grants, 1934–35	Number	Amount
Individual grants:		
Physical sciences	18	$8,375.00
Engineering	1	1,000.00
Chemistry	11	5,902.50
Geology and geography	15	6,300.00
Medical sciences	26	12,600.00
Biological sciences	30	10,547.00
Anthropology and psychology	15	5,635.00
Total for individual grants	116	50,359.50
Grants to divisions of the Council: Conferences	15	5,525.63
Grand total	131	55,885.13

For the past 6 years funds have been contributed to the National Research Council by the Rockefeller Foundation for the support of research through grants-in-aid. The funds now in hand will provide for the continuation of grants through the calendar years 1936 and 1937.

During the 6-year period, 1929–36, 667 grants have been made to 503 individual investigators located in 138 universities and colleges and in a limited number of other educational and research institutions of the United States, including a few to independent investigators. In this way $347,074.31 has been distributed. In addition, $25,562.42 has been used for conferences (of which 41 have been held during this period) and 5 grants, totaling $15,500, have been applied to the support of several programs of coordinated investigations under the sponsorship of the divisions of the Research Council. Altogether, $41,062.42 has been used through 46 appropriations for grants for these general purposes.

The total number of grants made during the period from July 1, 1929, to June 30, 1935, is shown in table III.

TABLE III

Total grants, 1929–35	Number	Amount
Individual grants:		
Physical sciences	97	$54,270.06
Engineering	18	12,560.00
Chemistry	75	43,883.00
Geology and geography	110	55,171.00
Medical sciences	123	67,517.50
Biological sciences	144	64,993.00
Anthropology	53	27,509.75
Psychology	47	21,170.00
Total for individual grants	667	347,074.31
Grants to divisions of the Council:		
Conferences	41	25,562.42
Cooperative projects	5	15,500.00
Total	46	41,062.42
Grand total	713	388,136.73

These are but the gross statistics of grants-in-aid operations. The main result is that the grants are supplying funds in a discriminating way to research projects requiring small-scale support for technical assistance, field work, or instruments. Most of the grants have been of modest amount, averaging $532. The total of published results now amounts to several hundred papers which have appeared in scientific journals.

The larger results coming from the awarding of these grants include the possibility of the continuation of research of grantees at their home institutions, encouragement of the individual through this special form of recognition, and bringing to the fore investigations and investigators of high merit. The support of research by special grants is a long and well-recognized method of fostering creative work, especially in institutions that have no free funds for the support of research or for meeting periods of emergency in their research programs.

Patent policy.—Most of the results from the scientific work sponsored by the National Research Council are of such a character as not to be immediately applicable in industry or for special social purposes. However, occasional cases have arisen in which results of a definite nature have been reached which seem to be directly applicable to commercial development. While the Council has preferred not to become involved in patent procedure and administration, several cases have arisen which have required special consideration. Disposition of these cases has been made in accordance with a general principle expressed in action of the executive board on February 13, 1924, as follows:

Moved, that in the event patentable discoveries are made in the course of work carried on under the auspices of the National Research Council it is expected that the fellows or others, on the approval of the Research Council which will defray the cost, will apply for patents on such discoveries as should be protected in the interests of the public and that such patents will be assigned to the National Research Council, and, further

That the National Research Council hereby declares its intention to dedicate to the use of the public, in such manner as the Research Council may deem most effective, the results of such discoveries as are made in the course of investigations conducted under the auspices of the Research Council.

As the custodian of trust funds intended to support scientific research for public benefit the Council has not wished to profit, even in the bookkeeping sense, from any of its operations. During recent years many other institutions have been studying the same problem. New types of patents have developed, and the patent system has come to be relied upon more and more as a standardizing and controlling agency.

In order to pool the experience of institutions that deal with patent matters, and secure broad and detailed discussion, a conference was held in Washington on March 29, 1935, under the auspices of the Council, with an attendance of 38 representatives from various institutions. As a result of this conference and of further study on the part of a special committee of the Council, the patent policy of the Council has been closely reexamined and a committee has been appointed which will pursue the subject still further in the immediate future and in the light of accumulating experience. Beside safeguarding the interests of the public, the Council desires to secure the full and prompt publication of the results of research, conducted under the auspices of the Council or through its committees and fellows, with provision for the recognition of the rights of cooperating agencies and of special conditions which may indicate the method of treating patentable results case by case.

Out of the discussion of the past year has come the suggestion that a central agency might be established in the United States which could serve universities and research institutions by administering for them such patents as it may seem desirable to take out. More competent and experienced handling of patent cases might result and individual institutions be saved a considerable administrative expense and effort. The results of scientific work would thereby be protected also from socially harmful exploitation.

Biological Abstracts.—Biological Abstracts has been issued since 1926, and by December 1935 the ninth volume will have been completed. Volume VIII for 1934 contained 21,469 items. During the past 8 years references have been published to 188,139 books and articles, most of them with abstracts. A large corps of collaborators, including about 300 sectional and topical editors, has furnished material. Correspondents are located in all the scientifically productive countries of the world. The material abstracted is gleaned from about 5,000 journals. Altogether, a most efficient and far-reaching system has been built up for reporting the content of biological contributions from the whole world with the keenest attention to economies consistent with making a reliable and thorough survey. A typographic format and printing specifications have been developed which have been subsequently adopted by other abstracting journals. A new form of comprehensive index by author, subject, and taxonomic classification has been devised especially adapted to botany, zoology, and the allied sciences, and a means has been provided for the coordination of contributions in the fields of biology to a degree which has never before been attained.

The publication of Biological Abstracts has been sponsored by the Union of American Biological Societies and the funds administered through the National Research Council. The editorial expenses have been met from appropriations made by the Rockefeller Foundation, which now total $698,000. The printing expenses have been met. from subscriptions and a limited amount of advertising.

The production of Biological Abstracts has depended very greatly upon the contribution, made without charge, of the abstracting services of its editors and special reviewers. It is the only large abstracting journal which does not pay honoraria for its abstracts. A system for obtaining authors' abstracts has been put into effect which involves a number of the English language journals both in this country and abroad. A repeated and careful study of printing costs indicates that it is cheaper to print Biological Abstracts for all fields of biology in a single volume than to subdivide the material for issue in sections by special fields. It has been found that individual biologists who have ready access to files of the Abstracts in their institutional libraries are making increasing use of the annual index issues of the Abstracts as an effective key to the literature in their fields.

With the increasing interpendence of science, of which the multiplication of problems in the borderlands involving two or more of the classical disciplines is one indication, the need for a systematic review of related literature has become more and more apparent. The use of biological literature extends far beyond the limits of the special fields of zoology and botany. It is resorted to by both physicists and chemists working upon problems relating to biology, and it is, of course, fundamental in the application of biological knowledge to various branches of medicine and public health. Over 25 percent of the institutional subscriptions to the Abstracts are for medical establishments, and over 16 percent of the individual subscribers are engaged in medical research. The organization of the great mass of literature annually produced in all the fields of biology bears rather directly on the welfare of society.

In the editorial preparation of the Abstracts a system of grading the published papers to be abstracted has made it possible to present abstracts of all the important literature in a given field promptly. A considerable number of papers, however, are necessarily omitted from notice because of limitations of editorial time and printing space. It is estimated that about $7,500 a year will be required to issue the unpublished abstracts accumulated during the past 2 or 3 years.

In the fall of 1934, after several years of operation, the Union of American Biological Societies, with the consent of the Rockefeller Foundation, requested the Division of Biology and Agriculture of the National Research Council to make a study of the need and of the use which biology and the related sciences have for a periodically coordinated review of the literature in these fields and of the degree to which Biological Abstracts is meeting this need. Among the results of this inquiry it seems to be indicated that the younger men and the more active investigators regard Biological Abstracts with high appreciation, while those who are more strongly established in their professions appear to make less use of it. Also, those located at large institutions with extensive libraries seem to find less need for the Abstracts than investigators located at smaller institutions. In sum, 88 percent of those replying to a questionnaire that was designed to test the work of the journal regarded it highly, and most zoologists, botanists, and geneticists who replied rate it as indispensable.

Borderlands in science.—Repeated consideration has been given by the administrative committee to the advancement of research in the borderland between traditional scientific fields. Certain borderlands, such as physical chemistry and biochemistry, are now clearly recognized and well cultivated. Others are plainly in need of cultivation. Geology, geography, and biology, for instance, have relationships of special importance in studies of land use and soil erosion. The growing applications of the physical sciences to medicine indicate the potential contributions of the basic sciences when applied cooperatively in the solution of problems requiring an uncommonly wide range of knowledge of facts, principles, and techniques. The extension of the basic sciences themselves requires ever new inquiry as to the wider applications of scientific knowledge to human affairs. The greatest borderland of all is that between the physical and natural sciences on the one hand and the social sciences on the other. It seems probable that the cultivation of this great borderland will be the distinctive mark of the next epoch of advancement in organized research.

The need for utilizing knowledge from several of the conventional fields of science in the attack upon current scientific problems has been recognized repeatedly in the appointment of fellows by the fellowship boards of the Council. Among the research projects of the divisions of the Council are a number which illustrate the coordination of work in several major fields of science—studies of the effects of certain radiations upon living organisms, sponsored by the Council during the past 6 years; certain phases of the investigations by the committee for research in problems of sex; the preparation of the monographs assembled in "The Physics of the Earth"; the organization of the Washington Biophysical Laboratory; the investigations of the committee on industrial lighting; investigations on the varied causes of deterioration of marine piling; studies pertaining to the measurement of geological time; and a concentrated attack upon drug addiction. A conference on the relationships between physics and chemistry was held by two of the divisions of the Council last year.

The encouragement of research in the borderlands of science seems to involve the specific preparation of men, the coordination of different phases of a cooperative problem of common interest, the application of methods and instruments developed in one line of research to other lines and problems, and free range in the planning of research, untrammeled by traditional restrictions and supported by a broad knowledge and deep understanding of related sciences. The history of science supplies abundant proof that the development of a new technique in one field inevitably opens up unexpected opportunities for progress in other fields.

A paper is about to be published in Science upon "Borderlands in Science" [1] which assembles the discussions, illustrations, and points of view brought forward at successive meetings of the administrative

[1] By Dean F. K. Richtmyer, of Cornell University. Science, vol. 82, pp. 379–382, Oct. 25, 1935.

committee. The comments of readers of the paper are invited as a basis for further discussion and report. While it is felt that interest in borderland problems cannot be stimulated artificially, it is believed that all research agencies would welcome an opportunity to cooperate in the effort to utilize the knowledge and methods of the basic sciences in attacks upon new and varied problems on the frontiers of knowledge.

Cooperation with the National Bureau of Standards.—For a number of years the National Research Council has acted as a disbursing agent for funds contributed by industrial corporations or from other nongovernmental sources for the support of scientific and technical investigations conducted at the National Bureau of Standards. The projects of this nature which have been active in the past year have related to methods of locking screw threads, the fabrication of the structural steel work of buildings, fire resistance of various building materials, the strength of brick walls and columns, thermal properties of liquids used as antifreezing compounds in automobiles, the rating of water current meters, investigations upon the corrosion of pipe due to action of the soil, and problems of refrigeration. An earlier project for the study of the durability of paper and the preservation of records has been reorganized this year into the study of the durability of motion-picture films used for record purposes. Upon the special request of the Bureau the National Research Council has appointed advisory committees for assisting in the development of the program of investigations for certain of these projects. The total sum expended through the National Research Council during the past year for investigations conducted at the Bureau of Standards amounts to $7,936.67.

Other general activities of the Council.—The Council has recently forwarded to the office of the Annual Tables of Constants and Numerical Data in Chemistry, Physics, Biology, and Technology, in Paris, the fourth installment ($2,000) under the 5-year appropriation totaling $18,000 which was made in 1932 by the Rockefeller Foundation toward the editorial expenses of the Annual Tables.

A summary statement reviewing the progress of certain of the major activities of the National Research Council during the year 1933-34 was published in Science (vol. 80, pp. 368-373, Oct. 26, 1934) in the fall of 1934, and a similar statement for 1934-35 [2] is in preparation for early publication.

SCIENCE ADVISORY BOARD

In its work of the past year the Board has continued to utilize the facilities of the National Research Council. The division of engineering and industrial research of the Council, particularly, has cooperated with the Board through relationships between this division and bureaus of the Department of Commerce in matters pertaining to the development of research as a guiding factor in industry, in a scrutiny of the relationships of the patent system to the growth of new industries, and in a special study of means for increasing the safety of ships at sea under conditions of fog and low visibility.

---

[2] Isaiah Bowman, Summary Statement of the Work of the National Research Council, 1934-35. Science, vol. 82, pp. 337-342, Oct. 11, 1935.

At the request of the Board, the division of educational relations of the National Research Council undertook a study of the relationships of Government subsidies made available through the land-grant college system to the progress of higher education in this country. The Board and the Council together, through a joint committee on naval research, have made recommendations for increasing the availability of the scientific resources of the country for the use of the Navy Department. The Board has made considerable use of the general facilities of the administrative offices of the Research Council.

The funds of the Board, provided by the Rockefeller Foundation, have been handled by the treasurer of the National Research Council. A total of $23,871.39 has been expended by the Board during the fiscal year.

This report on the work of the Science Advisory Board during the past year includes only those matters in which the National Research Council has actively cooperated with the Board.

AMERICAN GEOPHYSICAL UNION

The sixteenth annual meeting of the American Geophysical Union was held in Washington on April 25 and 26, 1935, and consisted of one general session of the union as a whole and of sessions of the seven sections into which the union is divided, corresponding to the plan of organization of the International Union of Geodesy and Geophysics. These sessions afforded opportunity for the presentation of papers upon geodesy, seismology, meteorology, terrestrial magnetism and electricity, oceanography, volcanology, and hydrology.

The membership of the American Geophysical Union is now well over 600 and represents a gain of some 230 members during the past year. A membership fee of $2 per annum is charged, which, with a small allotment from the National Research Council and contributions from members and several interested organizations, provides for the expenses of the meetings of the union and for the annual publication of its transactions.

In addition to the preparation and holding of its annual meeting, the American Geophysical Union lends its encouragement and support to the advancement of research in the various fields of geodesy and geophysics. It has cooperated with the division of physical sciences of the Council in the preparation of special bulletins on matters of geophysical research. It aided the application of new geophysical methods and instruments to the study of geological problems of continental genesis and evolution. It has encouraged, also, the making of a seismological survey of a part of the submerged Atlantic shelf of the United States to determine the thickness of the sedimentary covering of this submerged shelf.

During the past year certain changes have been under consideration in the statutes and bylaws of the International Union of Geodesy and Geophysics, which were proposed at the Stockholm meeting of the union in 1930 and provisionally adopted by the union at its Lisbon meeting in 1933. The American Geophysical Union has formulated and transmitted American opinion upon these changes. It was expected that these changes would be acted upon

at an extraordinary meeting of the union appointed to be held in
Paris on July 18, 1935, but the plans for the meeting were canceled
during June. The next meeting of the union will be held in Edinburgh in September, 1936.

The American Geophysical Union provides the principal medium
in the United States by which leaders in research in all branches
of geophysics can be brought together for the discussion of problems
of mutual interest. The publication of its annual transactions presents in consolidated form the current results of research in these
fields and makes these results from the United States available for
the use of investigators abroad.

FINANCES

The total amount of money expended through the National Research Council during the fiscal year 1934–35 was $669,876.55. The
distribution of these expenditures among the major types of activities of the Council, together with a comparison with similar
expenditures of the previous year, is shown as follows:

	1933-34		1934-35	
	Amount	Percentage	Amount	Percentage
Fellowships	$360,238.74	44.4	$226,368.84	33.8
Designated projects	240,775.48	29.7	228,291.97	34.1
Administered funds	112,770.61	13.9	119,721.96	17.9
General maintenance	97,793.48	12.0	95,493.78	14.2
Total	811,578.31	100.0	669,876.55	100.0

The funds disbursed for post-doctorate fellowships during 1934–35
were expended by the three fellowship boards of the Council, as follows:

	Stipends and travel expenses of—		Adminis-trative expenses	Percentage of adminis-tration on total ex-penditures for fellow-ships	Total expendi-tures
	Fellows in the United States	Fellows abroad			
Physics, chemistry, and mathematics	$89,749.49	$5,921.07	$9,784.08	11.2	$105,454.64
Medical sciences	23,103.28	4,583.75	1,665.15	5.7	29,352.18
Biological sciences	68,076.71	12,981.20	6,063.00	6.2	87,120.91
Total	$180,929.48	$23,486.02	17,512.23	7.9	221,927.73

Other fellowship funds were given to the Council by corporations
cooperating with the committee on drug addiction and by the National Live Stock and Meat Board.

Funds for specially designated projects, amounting to $228,291.97
(34.1 percent of the total expenditures of the Council) were contributed from outside sources for the support of research mainly of
a cooperative nature and were expended under the direction of
boards or committees of the Council or cooperating agencies. Of

this sum $8,346.93 (3.6 percent) was contributed from technical or industrial agencies. The following tabulation indicates the amounts expended upon certain of these projects during the years 1933–34 and 1934–35:

	1933–34	1934–35
Grants-in-aid	$52,171.55	$57,754.33
Highway research	17,115.37	18,309.19
Welding research	2,093.74	1,165.28
Research in problems of sex	74,717.42	63,936.13
Research on drug addiction	49,434.46	53,519.92
Effects of radiation on living organisms	21,034.46	20,352.11
Child-development investigations	7,005.40	7,012.41
Other projects	17,203.08	6,242.60
Total	240,775.48	228,291.97

The funds administered by the Council as fiscal agent for other organizations, $119,721.96 (17.9 percent of the total disbursements of the Council for the year), included $84,929.71 for Biological Abstracts; $7,936.87 for 17 projects of investigation conducted at the National Bureau of Standards; $1,966.11 for annual tables; and $23,871.39 for the Science Advisory Board.

Sums derived from sources outside of the Council during 1934–35 and expended for fellowships, for designated research projects, and as fiscal agent amounted to $574,382.77 (85.7 percent of the operating expenditures of the Council). This represents a decrease of $139,-402.06 under the total of similar expenditures for the previous year, and is to be accounted for mainly by a decrease of $133,869.90 in the amount of fellowship funds administered by the Council last year. Of these sums expended during the current year, $17,921.30 (3.1 percent) was contributed by industrial agencies.

The remaining portion of the year's operating expenditures ($95,-493.78) was derived chiefly from the income from the endowment provided by the Carnegie Corporation for the Council. Of this sum $92,694.77 was disbursed under provisions of the general administrative budget of the Council for the current year, and $2,799.01 to meet obligations incurred under previous budgets and for miscellaneous minor purposes. These sums were expended for the general maintenance of the Council, and constitute about one-seventh (14 percent) of the total operating expenditures of the Council for the year. They were used for the general expenses of the divisions and committees of the Council, for salaries, publications, supplies, service charges (exclusive of the general maintenance of the building and grounds), and for similar expenses. The amount spent during the past year for the general administrative expenses of the Council ($95,493.78) is less than the sum spent by the Council for these purposes last year ($97,793.48), although it represents a slightly larger proportion of the total expenditures of the Council for the year (one-seventh against one-eighth).

A detailed statement of the finances of the National Research Council will be found in the report of the treasurer of the National Academy of Sciences and the National Research Council (pp. 38–45).

PUBLICATIONS OF THE NATIONAL RESEARCH COUNCIL

The publications of the National Research Council during the past year have included two papers in its bulletin series. One other paper in this series is now in press. The total number of papers issued in the bulletin series of the Council is now 96 and in the reprint and circular series, 106. Several miscellaneous papers have also been issued this year by the Council.

For a list of the titles of all publications of the Council issued prior to January 1928 see no. 73 of the reprint and circular series. More recent titles are given in the subsequent annual reports of the Council.

The publications of the Council issued during the year July 1, 1934, to June 30, 1935, are as follows:

BULLETIN SERIES

No. 96. Selected Topics in Algebraic Geometry, II. Virgil Snyder, A. H. Black, and L. A. Dye. Pages, 84 (November 1934).

No. 97. A Table of Eisenstein-reduced Positive Ternary Quadratic Forms of Determinant ≤ 200. Burton W. Jones. Pages, 51 (June 1935).

MISCELLANEOUS PUBLICATIONS

Organization and Members, National Research Council, 1934-35. December 1934. Pages, 67.

Annual report, National Research Council, 1933-34. Separate reprint from the Annual Report of the National Academy of Sciences 1933-34. May 1935. Pages, 92.

Transactions of the American Geophysical Union, Fifteenth Annual Meeting, April 26-28, 1934, Washington, D. C., and Berkeley, Calif., June 20-21, 1934. Parts I and II. Pages, 633.

Proceedings, Thirteenth Annual Meeting, Highway Research Board, Washington, D. C., December 7 and 8, 1933. Part II. Curing of Concrete Pavement Slabs. April 1935. Pages, 96.

Proceedings, Fourteenth Annual Meeting, Highway Research Board, Washington, D. C., December 6 and 7, 1934. Part I. Pages, 481.

The National Research Council has also assisted in the publication of the Report of the Science Advisory Board, July 31, 1933, to September 1, 1934. December 1934. Pages, 303.

SALES

The total amount received from sales of Council publications from July 1, 1934, to June 30, 1935, is $2,967.91, of which $1,389.03 has been credited to the rotating fund for the publication of monographs of the division of physical sciences.

DIVISION OF FOREIGN RELATIONS

THOMAS HUNT MORGAN, Chairman

International dues.—With the close of the last session of the Seventy-third Congress in June 1934, an act was passed and was signed by the President authorizing the payment, by appropriation through the Department of State, of the annual share of the United States in the expenses of the International Council of Scientific Unions (formerly known as the International Research Council) and the six affiliated international unions to which the National Research Council had adhered. This authorization was applicable to the payment of these dues for the calendar year 1934, but it was given too late to permit including a corresponding item in the last deficiency bill of the session actually making the appropriation to cover the dues.

A second bill was introduced into the first session of the Seventy-fourth Congress authorizing the payment of these dues in subsequent years as follows:

[H. R. 4901, Public, No. 253, 74th Cong.*]

AN ACT To authorize appropriations to pay the annual share of the United States as an adhering member of the International Council of Scientific Unions and Associated Unions

Be it enacted by the Senate and House of Representatives of the United States of America in Congress assembled, That there is hereby authorized to be appropriated, to be expended under the direction of the Secretary of State, in paying the annual share of the United States as an adhering member of the International Council of Scientific Unions and Associated Unions, including the International Astronomical Union, International Union of Chemistry, International Union of Geodesy ad Geophysics, International Union of Mathematics, International Scientific Radio Union, International Union of Physics, and International Geographical Union, and such other international scientific unions as the Secretary of State may designate, such sum as may be necessary for the payment of such annual share, not to exceed $9,000 in any one year.
Approved, ————.

The international organizations to which the National Research Council now adheres and the dues payable are given in the following tables:

	Statutory amount of dues	Equivalent in United States currency at par for 1932
International Council of Scientific Unions	100 pre-war gold francs	$19.30
International Astronomical Union	3,200 pre-war gold francs	617.60
International Union of Chemistry	$675	675.00
International Union of Geodesy and Geophysics	12,000 Swiss francs	2,316.00
International Scientific Radio Union	800 pre-war gold francs	154.40
International Union of Pure and Applied Physics	1,600 French francs	62.72
International Geographical Union	40 pounds sterling	194.66
Total		4,039.68

The National Research Council now has under consideration the matter of adhering to the International Union of Biological Sciences in which the annual dues amount to 800 Swiss francs.

International scientific meetings abroad.—The National Research Council has been represented at international scientific meetings abroad during the past year as follows:

International Council of Scientific Unions, Brussels, July 9, 1934, by Edwin P. Hubble, astronomer, Mount Wilson Observatory, Pasadena, Calif.
International Geographical Congress, Warsaw, Poland, August 23–31, 1934, by five representatives (see p. 23).
International Scientific Radio Union, London, September 12–19, 1934, by seven representatives (see p. 17).
International Union of Pure and Applied Physics, London, October 1–6, 1934, by four representatives (see p. 17).

————

ently enacted into law, Aug. 7, 1935.

Pacific Science Association.—The foreign relationships of the National Research Council in the Pacific area are represented by the affiliation of the Council with the Pacific Science Association under the auspices of which the series of Pacific science congresses has been held. The last (fifth) congress was held in Victoria and Vancouver, British Columbia, in June 1933. The place and date for the sixth congress in this series have not been determined, but decision in regard to the holding of the next Congress was left by action of the association at the fifth Congress in the hands of a committee of which Dr. H. M. Tory, president, National Research Council of Canada (Ottawa, Canada), is chairman.

In the triennial periods between these congresses the research programs recommended by resolutions adopted at the congresses are carried forward by international committees. The National Research Council is now represented upon three of these international committees, oceanography, seismology, and land utilization and classification, and has appointed American national committees to take charge of its participation in these affairs.

DIVISION OF EDUCATIONAL RELATIONS

WILLIAM CHARLES WHITE, Chairman

The chairman of the division of educational relations, with advice from members of the division and others, undertook for the Science Advisory Board an inquiry into the utilization which is being made of Federal funds appropriated for use by the land-grant colleges. The inquiry was pursued through conferences with a large number of consultants and by a form of questionnaire sent to men in position to have observed the results coming to the welfare of the commonwealth from the use of these funds. The expression of opinion thus obtained was used by the Board as its report on the matter.[4]

DIVISION OF PHYSICAL SCIENCES

F. K. RICHTMYER, Chairman

Monographs.—In the series of monographs now in preparation in the division of physical sciences, two have been published during the past year: A supplementary report of the committee on rational transformations, entitled "Selected Topics in Algebraic Geometry, II", (National Research Council Bulletin No. 96, November 1934, 84 pp.); and a report of the committee on tables of positive ternary quadratic forms, entitled "A Table of Eisenstein-reduced Positive Ternary Quadratic Forms of Determinant $\leqq 200$" (National Research Council Bulletin No. 97, June 1935, 51 pp). Other monographs now in preparation include

> Compilation of line spectra of the elements.
> Review of methods for the measurement of radiation.
> Glossary of physical terms.
> Bibliography of orthogonal polynomials.
> Two bulletins in the Physics of the Earth series; Terrestrial Magnetism and Electricity, and Internal Constitution of the Earth, six monographs having already been published in this series.

---

[4] See appendix 5, Second Report of the Science Advisory Board, pp. 312–315, November 1935.

Altogether, the division has now sponsored the publication of 38 research monographs during the past 12 years. Of these monographs, two have been translated into German, "Theories of Magnetism" (National Research Council Bulletin No. 18, August 1922, 261 pp.) and "Critical Potentials" (National Research Council Bulletin No. 48, September 1924, 135 pp.). Two bulletins have been reprinted, "Radioactivity" (National Research Council Bulletin No. 51, March 1925. Second printing, with additions and corrections March 1929, 203 pp.) and "Molecular Spectra in Gases" (National Research Council Bulletin No. 57, December 1926. Second printing, with supplementary list of references and index, September 1930, 366 pp.). Two monographs have also been reissued in a second or revised edition: "The Quantum Theory" (National Research Council Bulletins No. 5, October 1920, and No. 39, November 1923), and "Algebraic Numbers" (National Research Council Bulletins No. 28, February 1923, and No. 62, February 1928).

Two of these monographs have been published outside of the Research Council's series, "Acoustics of Auditoriums," by F. R. Watson (Journal of the Acoustical Society of America, vol. 2, no. 5, pp. 14-43, 1931); and "Handbook on Mathematical Analysis of Statistics", by H. L. Rietz (Houghton-Mifflin Co., 1924). Arrangements have also been made to publish serially in *Physics* the report on Field Methods for Detecting Unhomogeneities in the Earth's Crust (Physics of the Earth series). In 1924-25 the committee on research methods and technique, F. K. Richtmyer, chairman, published 13 papers in the Journal of the Optical Society of America.

Washington Biophysical Laboratory.—Last year the division of physical sciences effected the organization for a Washington Biophysical Laboratory "to undertake fundamental investigations in quantitative biology and to cooperate with other scientific organizations in the development of instruments and methods of measurement, and in such other ways as will promote research in the fields of quantitative biology", under a board of directors of five members and a secretary who is also to be the director of the laboratory. The first investigations of the institution have been initiated in cooperation with the National Bureau of Standards. During the past winter the director of the laboratory, Dr. Frederick S. Brackett, has been engaged in a series of conferences at a number of universities and industrial laboratories in regard to problems of biophysics and investigations in this field which are under way at these institutions, with view to the future development of a program for this laboratory when funds for its establishment can be obtained.

The results of these conferences indicate that there is need for a central spectroscopic laboratory prepared to obtain, among other data, absorption spectra in the visible ultraviolet and infrared regions, that biological investigators would welcome assistance in the application of controllable radiations, that there are large possibilities for the use of radiations advisedly in medical practice, and that in view of these needs and possibilities there is a growing demand for the development of special equipment in this field.

International Scientific Radio Union.—The National Research Council was represented at the meeting of the International Scientific Radio Union at London, September 12 to 19, 1934, by seven representatives, as follows:

L. A. Briggs, European director of communications, R. C. A. Communications, Inc., London, England.

J. H. Dellinger, chief of the radio section, National Bureau of Standards, Washington, D. C.

Lloyd Espenshied, engineer, Bell Telephone Laboratories, Inc., New York City.

H. A. Reising, radio research engineer, Bell Telephone Laboratories, Inc., New York City.

A. G. Jensen, Bell Telephone Laboratories, Inc., New York City.

Harry R. Mimno, assistant professor of physics and communication engineering, Harvard University, Cambridge, Mass.

H. M. Turner, associate professor of electrical engineering, Yale University, New Haven, Conn.

The next meeting of the Union will be held in Rome in 1937.

The American section of the Union held its annual meeting in Washington on April 26, 1935, for the presentation and discussion of 17 technical papers.

International Union of Pure and Applied Physics.—The National Research Council was also represented at the meeting of the International Union of Pure and Applied Physics, which was held in London between the dates October 1 and 6, 1934, by four delegates, as follows:

R. H. Bozorth, Bell Telephone Laboratories, Inc., New York City.

R. B. Brode, professor of physics, University of California, Berkeley, Calif.

Arthur H. Compton, Charles R. Swift distinguished service professor of physics, University of Chicago, Chicago, Ill.

R. A. Millikan, director, Norman Bridge Laboratory of Physics, and chairman of the executive council, California Institute of Technology, Pasadena, Calif.

This meeting was in the form of an international conference on physics organized under the joint auspices of the Union and of the Physical Society (of England). One of the major matters among the agenda was the presentation and discussion of a conference report from the symbols, units, and nomenclature commission of the Union. The next meeting of the Union will be held in Copenhagen in 1936.

Conference on industrial physics.—Under the joint auspices of the American Institute of Physics and of the division of physical sciences of the National Research Council, a conference on the progress of physics in industry and on the relation of industrial physics to universities and to research in general was held in New York City on December 14, 1934. The conference was attended by some 18 persons representing industries, industrial laboratories, and physics departments of universities. As a result of the discussion, a recommendation was made to the American Institute of Physics that a special committee be appointed to bring about closer cooperation between industry and academic agencies for basic research in physics, by the publication of carefully selected pertinent research material, by the holding of later conferences, and by other means.

DIVISION OF ENGINEERING AND INDUSTRIAL RESEARCH

CHARLES F. KETTERING, Chairman

The urge for the progress of science through research carried on in industrial laboratories for the guidance of commercial development is recognized by the National Research Council as one of the main sources of energy for the advancement of scientific knowledge. The problem of finding means for assisting in these advances through industrial channels and of maintaining the closest possible relationship between research progress in industry and the basic research work of universities is one of the main functions of the division of engineering and industrial research of the National Research Council.

Electrical insulation.—The seventh annual meeting of the committee on electrical insulation was held at the University of Illinois on October 25 and 26, 1934, with an attendance of about ninety. Nineteen technical papers were presented concerning current investigations dealing with the theory and practice of electrical insulation, including the influence of pressure upon the breakdown strength of liquids, the interrelation of mechanical stress and dielectric strength in porcelain, the stability of oils under electrical discharge, and the properties of impregnated paper as employed for the insulation of high-voltage equipment. These papers have subsequently been distributed in planograph form through the courtesy of the Brooklyn Edison Co.

A monograph on dielectric theory of insulation, under the title of "Impregnated Paper Insulation", by Dean J. B. Whitehead of Johns Hopkins University, was published in the spring of 1935.

Heat transmission.—The committee on heat transmission has sponsored the preparation of a treatise on "Thermal Insulation" which is being prepared by Mr. E. C. Rack of the Johns-Manville Corporation for publication during 1935. This volume, together with the previously issued monograph upon "Heat Transmission" by Prof. W. H. McAdams, of the Massachusetts Institute of Technology, issued in 1933, will provide a complete review of present knowledge of the transmission and conservation of heat.

Highway research.—The Highway Research Board held the largest meeting of a series of 14 annual meetings in Washington on December 6 and 7, 1934. The registered attendance was 353 against 313 for the meeting of last year and 277 for the twelfth meeting of the board in 1932. From the program of this meeting 29 papers have been selected for publication in the proceedings of the board, which will be issued during the summer of 1935 (in an edition of 2,000 copies). The proceedings of the thirteenth annual meeting, 1933, were published during August 1934 (Pt. I, 410 pp.; Pt. II, 96 pp.), together with several thousand copies of reprints of certain of the more important papers of that meeting, a report on "Gravel type stabilized surfaces for secondary roads" being especially in demand.

The Highway Research Board also issues monthly, except during August and December, the Highway Research Abstracts (in mimeographed form). These abstracts are distributed to about 190 ~ibers in addition to a considerable distribution to special depositories, and present information in regard to highway investigations not otherwise published as well as synopses of the more important recent contributions in highway research.

In addition to acting as an agency for the exchange of information in regard to investigations upon highway construction and management, the Highway Research Board also serves to coordinate investigations upon certain special problems. The committee on stabilized soil road surfaces is preparing a progress report for early publication dealing particularly with the general theory of soil stabilization and the use of calcium chloride for surface treatment. The uses of common salt and of bituminous materials are also being investigated for this purpose. The Rail Steel Bar Association and the Iowa State Engineering Experiment Station have cooperated with the board in the support of investigations upon the use of high elastic-limit steel for concrete reinforcement. Investigations upon the warping of concrete pavement slabs have been conducted with the cooperation of the Portland Cement Association and several State highway departments. The board has been instrumental in arranging for an extensive investigation upon the economic life of highway surfaces, to be undertaken cooperatively by the Bureau of Public Roads and the Iowa State Engineering Experiment Station. The board has also cooperated with the office of the Federal Coordinator of Transportation in reviewing and commenting upon studies made in that office upon the financing of highway and street construction and has lately undertaken special investigations of the cost of highway construction and maintenance and the economics of highway planning. Reports upon progress in these cooperative investigations will be included in the proceedings of the fourteenth annual meeting of the board.

Hydraulic friction.—In order to provide means in this country for sponsoring the coordination of important studies upon the friction of fluids flowing through pipes, which had been previously carried on by a committee of the World Power Conference discontinued in April 1935, the division has appointed a research committee on hydraulic friction, including the members of the former committee and several others. The attention of the committee of the World Power Conference was directed initially to a study of friction losses of pure fluids in straight pipes and channels and will be extended to studies of the nature of turbulence and friction and to the correlation of empirical findings upon the flow of fluids. In view of the part which fluid flow and fluid friction play in many branches of engineering, including aeronautics, acoustics, hydraulics, metallurgy, oceanography, production of petroleum, heat transfer, etc., the importance of advancing knowledge in this field is very great.

Welding research.—Since 1920 the division of engineering and industrial research in cooperation with the American Welding Society has sponsored the American Bureau of Welding for the encouragement of investigations upon both the theory and practice of welding. With a certain reorganization of the society during the past year and the necessary reduction in the staff of the division on the part of the Research Council, arrangements have been made by the society to carry these investigations forward separately. The National Research Council, however, continues to administer funds for two committees of the bureau, the committee on structural steel welding and the committee on fundamental research in welding.

The committee on fundamental research in welding held its fourth annual conference in New York City on October 2, 1934, during the period of the fall meeting of the American Welding Society and the Metal Congress Exposition, with an attendance of over 40. The object of this committee is to place welding operators in touch with university physicists and metallurgists who can undertake research upon fundamental problems encountered in the fusion of metals in welding, particularly iron and steel. Ten special reports were completed in the fall of 1934 by collaborators with this committee, and the committee is in touch altogether with some 66 research projects relating to welding research in progress in university, governmental, and industrial laboratories.

Science Advisory Board.—The Science Advisory Board has continued to make extensive use of the facilities of the division of engineering and industrial research, particularly with respect to the mutual interests of the division and of bureaus of the Department of Commerce in matters relating to the service of research in industry. Among projects in which the division has particularly cooperated with the Science Advisory Board are a study of the relationships between the patent system and the encouragement of new industries, and investigations upon means for increasing the safety of ships at sea under conditions of fog and low visibility by the more extensive use of radio and other forms of signaling. The division has assisted the Federal Bureau of Investigations in the selection of a group of scientific advisers in matters of crime detection and of technical experts on criminal evidence, and has suggested a number of research laboratories which might be of service to the Bureau in this connection. The division has also cooperated with the Bureau of Foreign and Domestic Commerce in the revision of directions which the Bureau issues to its trade representatives abroad in regard to obtaining information concerning foreign industrial developments which would be of value to industrialists of the United States.

DIVISION OF CHEMISTRY AND CHEMICAL TECHNOLOGY

F. W. WILLARD, Chairman

Annual tables.—At the Eleventh Conference of the International Union of Chemistry, which was held in Madrid (Apr. 5 to 11, 1934), the international committee on the publication of Annual Tables of constants and numerical data of chemistry, physics, biology, and technology made an extensive report indicating that the editorial policy of the Tables was under consideration with a view to certain modifications, and a special subcommittee was appointed to draft resolutions concerning this policy and concerning also the financial support for the Tables for consideration at the next meeting of the union, which is to be held at Lucerne in August 1936. Among recommendations adopted by the conference at Madrid in regard to the Tables, were resolutions looking toward—

(a) The establishment of direct relationships between Annual Tables and the International Bureau of Physical Chemical Standards; and (*b*) The reduction of the volume of material to be included in the Tables after the issuing of volume X, but with provision for furnishing upon request documents referred to in the Tables for which space might not permit publication.

The Council continues to administer installments of the appropriation of $18,000 which the Rockefeller Foundation gave in 1932 over a 5-year period for the support of the Annual Tables. The fourth installment in this series, that for 1935, being $2,000 and the final installment, next year, to be $1,000.

Annual survey of American chemistry.—The editorial responsibility for the Annual Survey of American Chemistry was transferred by action of the division in April 1934, to the Research Information Service of the Council. Volume IX of this series was issued in May 1935, as a volume of 396 pages with 25 chapters contributed by 29 authors (Reinhold Publishing Corporation, New York City, in an edition of 1,000 copies).

Contact catalysis.—The tenth and eleventh annual résumés of research in the field of contact catalysis prepared under the auspices of a committee of the division of chemistry and chemical technology, were published by the Council (in mimeographed form) in a combined volume, in May 1935. The tenth report was prepared by Dr. Guy B. Taylor, of the du Pont Experimental Station, Wilmington, Del.; and the eleventh report by Prof. R. E. Burk, of Western Reserve University.

Isotopes of hydrogen.—The committee on isotopes of hydrogen held its second conference in Cleveland on September 13, 1934, for discussion of the present state of research upon the group of problems relating to the atomic structure of hydrogen and its significance with respect to other elements, preparatory to the further discussion of these problems at the meeting of the American Chemical Society in New York City in April, 1935.

Laboratory construction.—The committee on construction and equipment of chemical laboratories reports noting an increase of activity during the past year in the building of college and university chemical laboratories. Members of the committee have been called upon for advice in several of these instances. A large amount of data relating to the construction of laboratories and to the installation of chemical equipment etc., has been accumulated in the office of the chairman of the committee, Prof. C. R. Hoover, of Connecticut Wesleyan University. An article upon the planning of chemical laboratories, resulting from returns from a questionnaire issued by the committee in the spring of 1934, in regard to construction materials and various plans for laboratory arrangement, was included in the 1935 edition of The American School and University, a yearbook devoted to the design and construction, equipment, utilization, and maintenance of educational buildings and grounds. This article supplements the report entitled "Laboratory Construction and Equipment" published by the Chemical Foundation in 1930.

Preservation of records.—The division of chemistry and chemical technology has continued to advise the National Bureau of Standards in the planning of investigations upon the deterioration of paper and the preservation of records. One of the major purposes of this program of investigation was to obtain a basis of information which would be of guidance particularly to librarians and other custodians of important documents. Toward these investigations the Carnegie Corporation contributed $30,000 during the past 6 years.

With the publication of a report upon The Preservation of Records in Libraries (Library Quarterly, vol. IV, p. 371, July 1934), the Bureau of Standards was of the opinion that these investigations should be turned toward the study of the durability of motion picture films as used for record purposes; and the Carnegie Corporation made a further appropriation of $5,000, in the summer of 1934, which has been used by the Bureau to this end. The advantages of the method of preserving records within small space by means of rolled photographic films or film slides and of extending the scope of such records from written and printed documents, to motion-picture scenes make it highly important to determine the factors governing the durability of films used for these purposes.

DIVISION OF GEOLOGY AND GEOGRAPHY

EDSON S. BASTIN, Chairman

Accessory minerals in crystalline rocks.—A committee on accessory minerals in crystalline rocks has been concerned with the detection of minute quantities of significant minerals by methods of concentration rather than by microscopic study of thin sections. The significance of these so-called accessory minerals lies in the aid they afford in correlating igneous rocks and in determining the derivation of fragments of igneous rocks found in sediments. A number of programs of investigation have been coordinated by this committee, and its annual report presents in review the recent results of these investigations and also a survey of American literature pertaining to this subject.

Batholiths.—The committee on batholithic problems has encouraged research during the past year, particularly upon the geology of Holkham Bay in northern Alaska and of the Portland Canal on the British Columbia border. These localities offer unusually extensive exposures of igneous intrusives and of metamorphic effects.

Among other problems which have suggested themselves to the committee are (*a*) a discussion of the criteria which indicate intrusion occurring after the folding of contiguous strata instead of during or alternating with this folding; (*b*) a comparative study of the degree to which batholiths of different ages conform to the folded or corrugated diameter of their roofs; (*c*) the importance of making seismic tests of large granitic masses to determine the nature of their roots or foundations.

The committee has again issued (in mimeographed form) a review of progress in the United States in research upon batholiths during the past year, together with "Annotations of Selected Papers on the Mechanics of Igneous Invasion" and a compilation of "Comments on Magmatic Stoping."

Bibliography of Economic Geology.—Volume VII of the Annotated Bibliography of Economic Geology was completed with the June, 1935 issue of this journal. The subscriptions made for this project several years ago have yielded a total sum of $19,509.78, to which is to be added certain accumulated interest. Of this sum, a balance of $3,012.73 remains, which will be sufficient to carry the bibliography forward for another year.

The journal is issued in two semiannual parts and contains about 2,500 citations each year, annotated to indicate the principal significance of the articles cited.

Through cooperation with the Geological Society of America, which is publishing a bibliography covering the full range of geological subjects, in exchanging references it is expected that the editorial expense of preparing the Annotated Bibliography of Economic Geology can be reduced to about $2,500 per year, the publication costs being approximately met by subscriptions under a contract with the Economic Geology Publishing Co. Toward the editorial expense of the Annotated Bibliography after the end of the fiscal year 1935–36, the Society of Economic Geologists and the American Association of Petroleum Geologists have offered substantial assistance, with the expectation that other funds may be obtained with which to continue this journal.

The Annotated Bibliography presents the whole of the world literature concerning economic geology, but the limited resources at hand have prevented the inclusion of many pertinent topics of technology and the treatment of geological products closely related to the derivation of raw materials. Soils and mineral resources are considered only in their geological significance. In geophysics, articles are included relating to the discovery and examination of ore deposits.

Cooperation with the Bureau of the Census.—A committee on cooperation with the Bureau of the Census has aided the Bureau in obtaining assistance in the preservation of its early records and has advised the Bureau in planning State maps showing minor civil divisions which have now been made for all of the States, most of them on a scale of 16 miles per inch (approximately 1:1,000,000). The importance of these maps lies in their supplying for the first time an authentic basis for the plotting of diversified census statistics according to these smallest of governmental administrative units. In order to determine, however, the real geographic significance of these statistics it is necessary to know the areas as well as the population of these units. In compiling these small unit maps for New England, a peculiar problem was encountered in that in the New England States the population centers within a town (township) are not recorded separately from the rural population of the same township. For the 1930 census this difficulty has been met by regarding as urban those population centers of more than 2,500 inhabitants, if this concentrated population amounts to more than 50 percent of the total population of the township.

International Geographical Congress.—The National Research Council was represented at the International Geographical Congress held in Warsaw, Poland, between the dates August 23 and 31, 1934, under the auspices of the International Geographical Union, by five representatives, as follows:

S. W. Boggs, geographer, Department of State, Washington, D. C.

Isaiah Bowman, chairman, National Research Council; director, American Geographical Society, New York City.

Louise A. Boyd, arctic explorer, San Francisco, Calif.

Gen. J. G. Steese, United States Army (retired), president, Guajillo Corporation, Tulsa, Okla.

John K. Wright, librarian, American Geographical Society, New York City.

The total attendance at the Congress from countries other than Poland was about 345, including representatives from some 44 countries. An extensive cartographic exhibit was prepared in connection with the Congress, and the National Research Council had arranged earlier in the summer of 1934, for a contribution from the United States, consisting of about 430 items, representing the work of several Federal mapping agencies and nongovernmental geographical institutions. Fifty institutions in 23 countries contributed to this exhibit. The next meeting of the Congress will be held in Amsterdam in 1938. The assembly voted to continue the following commissions:

1. Commission for the study of rural populations and habitats, under the presidency of A. Demangeon.
2. Commission for the study of Pliocene and Pleistocene terraces, under the presidency of Douglas Johnson.
3. Commission for the study of climatic variations, under the honorary presidency of L. de Marchi, and the presidency of H. Arctowski.
4. Commission for the publication of ancient maps, under the presidency of R. Almagià.
5. Commission on aerial phototopography, under the presidency of M. Torroja.
6. Commission for the cartography of Tertiary erosion surfaces, under the presidency of E. de Martonne.

Land classification.—The members of the committee on land classification have cooperated during the year with a corresponding committee of the Science Advisory Board and with the National Resources Board, the Tennessee Valley Authority, and other agencies concerned with the development of the land policy of the Federal Government.

It is increasingly evident that an extensive program of land inventorying and land classification is essential to the successful administration of a national land policy, and the work done to date indicates the need of a better-advised and better-coordinated plan of land study than has been provided up to the present. There is especial need for investigators in this field well trained from the geographical point of view.

Measurement of geologic time.—The objective of the committee on the measurement of geologic time is not so much to make an estimate of the total age of the earth as to provide a chronology for the various rocks and thus to be able to appraise the estimates which have been given for the duration of the various geological periods. The coordination of investigations brought about by this committee during the past year has shown a general accordance of the results obtained from the ratios of thorium-lead and radium-lead to thorium and uranium with those obtained from helium. Because of uncertainties in the analysis of the minute amounts of critical substances found in the rocks, the checking of the results of one method by those obtained by other methods is particularly desirable.

Each year the committee issues (in mimeographed form) a résumé of the research results contributed since the last report by 20 or more collaborators with the committee and also a bibliography of articles published recently, both in this country and abroad, relating to the measurement of geologic time.

Micropaleontology.—The committee on micropaleontology has encouraged the general study of fossil micro-organisms on account of the great significance of the formations of that period and wide interest in them. It now proposes to begin an intensive study of the Eocene with view to a better understanding of the fauna, chiefly Foraminifera and Ostracoda, characteristics of various horizons and the correlation of local names given to forms of wide range. Micropaleontology has been regarded as a new field in which pioneer work is essential in order to coordinate contributions in matters of technique as well as the results of the examinations of material explored and to interpret these results in the light both of their geologic and economic significance. To aid in understanding the trend of research in this field, the committee has recently issued a résumé of recent research work.

Ore deposition.—The attention of the committee on ore deposition upon two general groups of problems, (*a*) the genesis of lead and zinc ores in the Mississippi Valley and (*b*) the zoning of ore deposits in the United States, has led to the definition of three further problems: (1) the relationships of the fundamental sciences of chemistry, physics, physical chemistry, and modern mineralogy to the problems of ore deposition; (2) the relationship between geologic structure and ore deposition; (3) the composition of source magmas in relation to the metals derived from them.

A subcommittee of this committee has in preparation a volume concerning the geology of Mississippi Valley lead and zinc deposits, which is being compiled with the assistance of over 20 collaborators.

Paleobotany.—The report of the committee on paleobotany contains (*a*) an annotated list of contributions, both published and in manuscript, in this field from the United States and (*b*) a bibliography of paleobotany for North America covering the past year, which contains some 67 titles of papers dealing not only with detailed studies of fossil plants but with the light which these fossils throw upon the origin and distribution of plants during early periods and upon environmental factors of those times.

Paleoecology.—The objective of the committee on paleoecology is the assembling of data bearing upon the ecologic or environmental relationships of fossil organisms as convincing data of the importance of the study of paleoecology as a factor bearing upon many other geological problems. The committee has recently compiled a review of literature with reference to the relationships of fossil organisms at all levels to the environment in which they lived.

Structural petrology.—In order to meet an increasing interest in the significance of the microscopic texture and structure of igneous and metamorphic rocks as criteria in interpreting the larger crustal structures, the division organized, last year, a committee on structural petrology. The purpose of this committee is the valuation and clarification of methods of research in this field in order that subsequent work may be as well founded as possible. The committee is preparing a glossary of terms used in structural petrology, with a view to the publication of an annotated glossary later. The committee also plans an examination of the data of grain-fabric analysis.

Committee on petroleum geology.—The committee on petroleum geology was organized in 1923 for the purpose of studying the geological problems connected with oil production. From 1926 to 1931 the main work of the committee consisted in cooperating, through the central petroleum committee of the National Research Council, with the American Petroleum Institute in its 5-year program of fundamental work upon the geology, physics, and chemistry of petroleum. With the completion of this program, and in view of the appointment of the chairman of the research committee of the American Association of Petroleum Geologists as a member of the division, the work of the Research Council's committee has been brought to a close and the committee has not been reappointed for the coming year.

In its final report the committee calls attention (a) to the recent publication of comprehensive articles relating to the anticlinal theory of oil production in America, (b) to progress in the solution of scientific problems relating to the origin and migration of oil, (c) to the achievement of the recent drilling of a well to a depth of more than 12,000 feet, (d) to the trend of petroleum geology away from the geology of the surface structures and toward subsurface and geophysical exploration and the use of new pendulum and gravimeter methods, (e) to the increasing importance accorded to basic geological considerations by those responsible for the formulation of policies and legislation making for oil conservation, (f) to the failure of new oil fields to provide additional reserves sufficient to equal the drain on previously known underground reserves resulting from the past year's production, and (g) to the probability of increased geological activity in the oil industry due to increased use of geophysical methods, the need for paleontologic and petrographic work in subsurface correlation, the need for regional structural and paleographic studies and the importance of geologic factors in the development of governmental and company administrative policies.

Scientific results of drilling.—The movement leading to the appointment of the division's committee on the scientific results of drilling began in the International Drilling Congress, which was held in Bucharest in 1925. This conference forwarded to the Government of the United States a resolution of the Congress bespeaking the support of the oil-producing countries of the world for measures for the conservation of the scientific results of drilling for oil, water, and other purposes, and for the improvement of the methods and equipment for drilling operations. The Congress also recommended the appointment of national committees. The matter was regarded favorably by our Government and was referred to the division of geology and geography.

The committee appointed by this Division has been active in calling attention of drilling agencies in the United States to the importance of preserving the records of their underground operations and has established depositories for records and specimen materials of these operations at seven institutions in the United States. A large amount of material has been accumulated, and attention in petroleum development is being directed more and more to the importance of knowledge in regard to geologic formations and structure within and even below the range of drilling operations.

Sedimentation.—A 2-year report for the committee on sedimentation, reviewing the advances made in this field during the years 1932 to 1934, both in the United States and abroad, will be issued as a Bulletin of the National Research Council in the summer of 1935. The report consists of a series of 15 articles on special problems in this field and refers to about 1,000 articles relating to the study of sediments and sedimentary methods, most of which have appeared during the past biennium.

The committee has also supported several studies by means of research grants from funds derived from the sale of the "Treatise on Sedimentation" (two editions) and of the "Geologic Color Charts". The subjects of these studies during the past year were (*a*) concretions in the Champlain formation of the Connecticut River Valley, (*b*) manganese concretions in Ship Harbor Lake and other lakes in Nova Scotia, and (*c*) the bacterial action in lake-bottom deposits in Wisconsin. The committee has also contributed toward the support of the *Journal of Sedimentary Petrography*.

State geological surveys.—The committee on State geological surveys has continued its study of a general plan for the organization and functions of a State geological survey, whether established as a survey or a department of natural resources or a State bureau of mines, in order to meet increasingly intensified industrial needs. The committee believes that the functions of a State geological service should include (*a*) basic geological studies of the petrology and structure of the rocks of local regions; (*b*) a survey and evaluation of the State's mineral resources such as oil and gas, coal, metals, water, and soils; (*c*) studies of the effective utilization of these materials by obtaining full knowledge of their properties and their adaptation to industrial needs involving both studies of the mineralogy and petrology of raw materials and the technique of their utilization; (*d*) engineering, geologic, and topographic mapping; (*e*) mining and ceramic engineering in those States in which mining is carried on; (*f*) the dissemination of information to the people in regard to the State's mineral resources.

Stratigraphy.—The committee on stratigraphy has proceeded with its plans to prepare a synopsis of North American stratigraphy, both by means of correlation of tables for representative geologic columns and by the preparation of a series of descriptive handbooks for each stratigraphic system. A number of the correlation charts have been drafted and are now being circulated for criticism.

Tectonics.—The principal undertaking of the committee on tectonics during the past year has been the planning of a tectonic map of the United States to be compiled on a scale of 1:2,500,000, corresponding to the scale of the new geologic map of the United States issued by the United States Geological Survey. The map is being compiled in 11 sections, each in charge of a member of the committee in conference with geologists of the regions studied.

Under auspices of this committee, Part II of the "Catalogue of Small-Scale Geologic Maps" is being compiled and will include the maps of Europe, Asia, and Africa. Part I of this catalogue, listing maps for North America and the West Indies, was issued in 1933 (in mimeographed form).

Last year, the former committee on isostasy was merged with the committee on tectonics, and the latter committee now follows the accumulation of data on triangulation and gravity measurements throughout the United States. The United States Coast and Geodetic Survey is the principal agency in this country for the making of gravity measurements, although the results of commercial petroleum reconnaissance are in some cases also available.

DIVISION OF MEDICAL SCIENCES

FRANCIS G. BLAKE, Chairman

American registry of pathology.—The committee on the American registry of pathology notes a marked increase in the number of accessions of case reports and of specimens received this year over the accessions of last year. Most of these accessions are in the form of voluntary contributions, since the committee has no funds for the systematic enlargement of its collections. The Registry of Ophthalmic Pathology now has 12 sets of material available for loan. These are in constant demand. New methods of recording data and of analyzing these records have been adopted with a saving in time. A growing interest in these collections on the part of the medical profession is manifest through the increased number of accessions which are being contributed. The present numerical status of the registry is indicated as follows:

Registry of ophthalmic pathology_____ 4,847
Lymphatic tumor registry_____ 479
Bladder tumor registry_____ 1,161
Registry of dental and oral pathology_____ 260

Animal parasitology.—The committee on medical problems of animal parasitology has sponsored a continuation of studies on schistosomiasis in Puerto Rico and a 3-year program of investigations on *Strongyloides stercoralis*, a parasitic roundworm of the human intestine, both of these studies being carried on under the direction of Dr. E. C. Faust, of the School of Medicine of Tulane University, New Orleans. The work on endamoebiasis, initiated under auspices of the division of medical sciences, has been carried on entirely by funds supplied by Vanderbilt University and by the Rockefeller Foundation, under the direction of Dr. Henry E. Meleny. Important results have been obtained concerning the degrees of virulence shown by different strains of amoebae. The influence of various culture media on strains of amoebae and the effect of diets on the severity of infections in experimental animals are among the important parts of this program of investigation.

Gonococcus research.—During the past year the committee on gonococcus and gonococcal infections has completed the survey of research in progress both in the United States and abroad upon the disease caused by this organism. This study was undertaken 2 years ago in cooperation with the American Social Hygiene Association. A large amount of information has been assembled and has been compiled into a report which is to be published in the *Journal of Syphilis and Venereal Diseases.*

Infectious abortion.—The committee on the study of *Brucella* infections has lent its encouragement to the study of infectious abortion in goats in Utah, and members of the committee have participated in intensive programs for the eradication of infectious abortion in farm animals in several States. Three subcommittees have been appointed: (*a*) On the epidemiology of human *Brucella* infections, (*b*) on the preparation of a program of study on the killing power of blood of animals against the *Brucella* organism, and (*c*) on *Trichomonas* infections in relation to abortion.

Narcotics research.—At the close of its sixth year of work the committee on drug addiction reports that some 295 new alkaloid substances have been produced in the cooperating chemical laboratory at the University of Virginia. These have been sent to be tested for their pharmacological properties to the cooperating physiological laboratory at the University of Michigan. A group of 32 phenanthrene derivatives has been sent to collaborators at St. Louis University for the study of their estrogenic properties. Investigators at New York University have cooperated with the committee in microanalytical studies of many of these substances. Much assistance has been given to the committee's program also by the United States Public Health Service and by the Massachusetts State Department of Public Health and by a number of commercial pharmaceutical manufacturing firms.

The program of the committee during the past year has included a continuation of these chemical and pharmacological studies, but the attention of the committee has been extended to include certain clinical aspects of drug addiction and the possibility that certain of the new substances obtained may prove to be suitable for corrective treatment of drug addicts and for medical purposes in the relief of pain in cases of cancer and of excessive coughing in pulmonary tuberculosis. In addition to the patenting of "desomorphine" (dihydrodesoxymorphine–D) last year, application has been made for patents for 13 other substances, and these patents as issued will be assigned to the Secretary of the Treasury for administration under the Federal narcotics law.

Altogether some 75 articles have been published during the past 6 years upon the results of this work. A special monograph is in preparation by Dr. Lyndon F. Small on the pharmacological aspects of the substances described in his treatise upon "The Chemistry of the Opium Alkaloids" prepared in 1932 (supplement no. 103 to the Public Health Reports, 1932).

Sex research.—Work sponsored by the National Research Council during the past 14 years upon problems of sex has yielded over 700 published papers on the part of a score of investigators who have collaborated in these problems. A total of about $810,000 provided by the Rockefeller Foundation has been expended upon these investigations. Perhaps the most important result of this work is the development during the past decade, at a number of institutions throughout the country, of laboratories competent in personnel and in equipment to carry these and related investigations further.

While continuing to support various studies of the general biology of sex, the committee now purposes to devote its chief efforts to the relatively neglected areas in its field of interest such as neurophysiology, psychobiology, and psychopathology. The program for the coming year will give diminished support to many problems which could be taken up relating to hormones and will devote increased attention to problems of sex behavior and reproductive behavior. Eight projects in next year's program, with allotments totaling about $25,000, will fall within the category of behavior as against four projects in this field last year, involving about half this sum. In the field of hormonal, morphological, and miscellaneous studies relating to the physiology of reproduction, 9 investigations with allotments totaling approximately $40,000 are to be supported instead of 16 as last year. In the third category, that of neurology, two investigations with allotments of $8,000 have been authorized in place of investigations on this subject amounting to $4,000 last year. Altogether, $71,850 has been allocated in the program of the committee for 1935-36 for the use of 18 investigators located at 17 institutions.

A conference was held under the auspices of this committee at Woods Hole, Mass., between the dates August 25 and 30, 1934, and was attended by about 25 members and collaborators with the committee. The object of the conference was a full discussion of the problems and objectives of research upon the biology of sex and the planning of strategic approaches to these problems and of special techniques for this group of investigations.

Survey of tropical diseases.—The results of a survey of the incidence of tropical diseases, which has been made under the auspices of the advisory committee on survey of tropical diseases, have been compiled in a monograph entitled "A Geography of Disease", by Dean Earl B. McKinley, of the School of Medicine of George Washington University, and is now in process of publication as a volume of some 500 pages. The monograph will be published as a supplement to the *American Journal of Tropical Medicine* and will also be distributed separately from the George Washington Press. The report will present in tabular form statistics for a recent representative year of the relative occurrence of the tropical diseases in the countries of the world by diseases and also by countries.

DIVISION OF BIOLOGY AND AGRICULTURE

I. F. LEWIS, Chairman

Among the projects of the division of biology and agriculture, there are several which seem to be of special significance to American biologists. One of these is the maintenance of Biological Abstracts, the situation of which has been presented above. (See p. 6.) Others are the furtherance of research upon the biological effects of radiation, the support of the Barro Colorado Island Laboratory, and the organization of systematic studies upon the natural grasslands of North America and the significance of these grasslands in studies of ecology and of soil erosion.

Aquiculture.—The committee on hydrobiology and aquiculture of the division of biology and agriculture arranged for a program at a special session of the Pittsburgh meeting of the American Association for the Advancement of Science, December 27, at which 17 papers were presented.

The committee has given special attention to means for obtaining employment for young men who have been training themselves for research in hydrobiology and aquiculture but who have found it difficult to make a beginning in their profession. The committee has also taken first steps toward the formation of an American Limnological Society to continue and extend the work begun by the committee.

Barro Colorado Island Laboratory.—The Barro Colorado Island Laboratory was established some 12 years ago on an artificial island in Gatun Lake in the Panama Canal Zone under the auspices of the Institute for Research in Tropical America which in turn was sponsored by an early committee of the Council on phytopathology in the tropics. The laboratory has been supported from year to year by subscriptions in the form of the maintenance of "tables" at the laboratory by a number of educational and research institutions of the United States and by donations from interested persons and fees paid by visiting biologists. Because the laboratory serves as an important station for research on problems of tropical plant and animal life, the division of biology and agriculture has recently appointed a committee to assist in obtaining an endowment for the laboratory.

About 20 American scientists worked at the laboratory during the year ended March 1935, and 26 papers were published during the year by these and others who have made use of the laboratory, bringing the total number of published contributions upon work which has been facilitated by the laboratory up to 265.

Botanical nomenclature.—For several years the interests of American botanists in matters of botanical nomenclature have been represented by the national finance committee on botanical nomenclature of the division of biology and agriculture. This committee has also collected certain funds in this country for the maintenance of an International Committee on Nomenclature which was appointed at the Ithaca meeting of the International Botanical Congress in 1926. With the official publication and general acceptance of the International Rules of Botanical Nomenclature this year, the Council's committee has been discharged.

Conservation of wildlife.—In view of the well-recognized need for the sound management of the wildlife resources of the United States in order to prevent their extinction, and in view also of the movement for recreational use of public lands, the committee on wildlife has felt that the most critical need at present in a program for the conservation of wildlife is a properly trained personnel to undertake the studies by which sound management must be guided and to administer policies of wildlife development as adopted for the public domain. Insofar as certain game animals are concerned a "cropping" practice has been proposed within conservative limits with the double object of maintaining a substantial population of these animals and of providing a source of recreation and food from them. These limits, however, must be based upon a background of broad biological knowledge with constant recognition that each wildlife form is subject to a large number of complicated and variable factors in its environment. During the past year the committee has particularly encouraged the development of curricula at certain institutions for the training of wildlife specialists to meet these needs.

Ecology of grasslands.—The committee on the ecology of grasslands has held two conferences during the past 2 years (Austin, Tex., May 31–June 2, 1933, and Fargo and Dickinson, N. Dak., May 31–June 3, 1935), with the object of planning means for preserving areas of grassland as nearly as possible in their natural condition in different parts of the country. The purpose of these grassland reservations is to keep available places where the complicated ecological factors affecting plants and animals in nature can be systematically observed. These studies are important in building up a knowledge of the reaction of organisms to their natural environment and the conditions under which a balance in nature is maintained. The results of these studies are applicable, not only to philosophical considerations in biology, but also to the maintenance of pasturage and of stocks of game and of wildlife and to the prevention of destructive soil erosion.

Several sites have been selected by the committee in western States and in Canada as desirable observation localities and efforts are being made to have these areas set aside as grassland reservations. A number of papers have been published by members of the committee upon phases of this project and the need for establishing such reservations.

Forestry research.—The committee on forestry research reports that the bibliography of North American forestry has now been completed for the literature which has appeared through 1933.

The committee is also undertaking a survey of forestry research in progress in the United States similar to the review of North American Forestry Research compiled by a committee of the Society of American Foresters and published as a bulletin of the National Research Council (no. 4, August 1920).

Medicinal plants.—The committee on pharmacognosy and pharmaceutical botany has continued to encourage research upon the sources of medicinal plants and their uses. A map of the New England States showing the commercial geographical sources of medicinal plants in that region is nearing completion.

Microbiology of the soil.—The committee on the microbiology of the soil is bringing to a close the program of investigations which it has been carrying on during the past 3 years in cooperation with the New Jersey State Agricultural Experiment Station of studies upon the fate of the organism of tuberculosis and of certain acid-fast bacteria in the soil with the publication of a report which will present the importance of knowledge upon the soil as a harborer of micro-organisms, whether pathogenic or not. The first of a series of papers to be published concerning these investigations is—

C. Rhines. The persistence of avian tubercle bacilli in soil and in association with soil micro-organisms. Journal of Bacteriology, volume 29, pages 299-311, March 1933.

National Live Stock and Meat Board fund.—The National Live Stock and Meat Board appropriated the sum of $2,000 to the National Research Council for the year 1934-35, making a total of $54,750 which this board has given to the Council since 1924 for the support of studies upon the place of meat in the human diet. This fund this year has been used toward the support of three programs of investigation:

(1) The role of fat in nutrition and physiology, at the University of Minnesota;
(2) The nutritional value of animal tissues for growth, reproduction, and lactation, at the University of Iowa; and
(3) Studies in the vitamin C content of meat and meat products, University of Arkansas.

Radiation research.—During the past 6 years the division of biology and agriculture of the Council has administered funds totaling $125,000 which have been contributed by the Commonwealth Fund of New York City and by the General Education Board for the support of investigations upon the effects on living organisms of the radiations of light, x-rays, and radium. For the coming 3-year period the Rockefeller Foundation has appropriated a sum of $75,000 for the continued support of this program. The resources for these studies have also been augmented by funds contributed by industrial corporations and by the generous loan of apparatus and radioactive materials by these firms. About 45 investigators have collaborated in the program of the Council's committee in charge of the use of these resources. The administrative cost of these operations has been about 2½ percent of the funds handled.

About 125 papers have been published upon the results of this work. In addition, the committee has sponsored the preparation of a survey of the present status of research in this field. This report is now in press as a two-volume book, to be issued in the fall of 1935.

During this period there has been a great advance in knowledge of the biological effects of radiation, and especially in the application of radiation techniques to studies of genetics. The use of various forms of radiation in experimentation on plants and animals has disclosed large possibilities for research in the field of genetics and has profoundly influenced the development of theories of the cause and mechanism of evolution. It has been said that had it not been for the application of these new techniques, experimentation in genetics would have reached a stage of stagnation. In another direction recent work on photosynthesis promises a clear understanding of this fundamental process in plant life on which all animal life depends. In this progress the committee of the Council which has been in charge of the use of these funds has had a considerable part. While no new, stupendous results have been achieved under the sponsorship of the committee, much verification has been given to preliminary work and many additions have been made to the body of knowledge in this field with assistance from this committee. A later phase of the work of this committee has been the initiation of investigations upon mitogenetic radiation supported by a preliminary grant of $10,000 from the Rockefeller Foundation.

DIVISION OF ANTHROPOLOGY AND PSYCHOLOGY

EDWARD SAPIR, Chairman

American archaeology.—American archaeology, from the finding of relics of early man in the Americas to studies of cultural remains of Indian tribes which clearly antedate the discovery of the Americas by Europeans, has progressed steadily during recent years. The level of interest and of capacity for scientific work in this field has also risen markedly.

Methods for the systematic examination of archaeological sites have been greatly improved and are being followed more and more thoroughly. In addition to the growth of fascinating material available for study relating to the early inhabitants of Central America, Mexico, and the southwestern part of the United States, which has been sponsored so effectively by special research institutions, the Council's committee on State archaeological surveys has directed its attention toward studies, mainly, of the eastern and central regions of the United States. Conferences held in St. Louis (May 17 and 18, 1929), in Chicago (Apr. 10, 1931), and in Birmingham, Ala. (Dec. 18 to 20, 1932), the publication of directions for archaeological explorations, the issuing of periodic circulars concerning current archaeological work, the publication of annual reviews of North American archaeology (through the *Bulletin of the Pan American Union*), the establishment of a repository for pottery fragments at the University of Michigan, and the impetus given to interest in early Americans by the Tennessee Valley exploration in advance of the building of the Norris and Wheeler Dams, have all served, within recent years, to develop and coordinate work in this field.

With the momentum thus begun, it has seemed possible to solidify this interest in the organization of a Society of American Archaeology, and this has been the principal achievement of the Council's committee during the past year. After preliminary discussion at the meeting of the committee in May 1934, and subsequent correspondence, an organization meeting of the society was held at Pittsburgh on December 28, 1934, and the society now has over 70 members. It is expected that presently the society will take over and expand the activities of the committee.

During the past year the committee on State archaeological surveys has issued its twelfth compilation of brief reports on current archaeological work in North America (Circular No. 18, September 1934), recording the work of 59 organizations and of 63 archaeological expeditions during 1933, and a paper upon "Culture Classification Problems in Middle Western Archaeology" (Circular No. 17, Aug. 8, 1934).

The office of the committee is maintained at the University of Michigan and has been supported by appropriations from the Carnegie Corporation, administered through the Carnegie Institution of Washington. This support has been continued for the coming 2-year period in the amount of $4,500.

Child development.—The principal effort of the committee on child development during the past year has been directed upon continuing the publication of *Child Development Abstracts* (issued bimonthly, with a circulation of about 580 copies), now in its ninth volume, and the initiation of the work of the Society for Research in Child Development, which is to take over and extend the work of the Council's former committee on child development. This committee has been supported since 1926 by funds appropriated by the Laura Spelman Rockefeller Memorial, and later by the General Education Board, $82,925 having been appropriated to the Council for this purpose.

For the initiation of the work of the society the General Education Board has recently appropriated $10,500 to be available for an introductory period of 3 years, and also a sum of $5,000 with which to set up a revolving fund for the publication of monographs in this field.

The first biennial meeting of the society was held in Washington on November 3 and 4, 1934. In addition to the business session, the scientific program consisted of symposia on dental caries, and on prenatal and neonatal care, and of meetings of sections of the society for anthropology, dentistry, education, parent education, nutrition, psychiatry, psychology, public health, and sociology. The membership of the society is now about 300.

Occupational standards.—The division of anthropology and psychology has appointed eight members of a technical committee on occupational classification and standards, who, with eight members appointed by the Social Science Research Council, constitute an independent committee which cooperates with the United States Employment Service. An executive committee of this technical committee has directed the work during the past year of a field and headquarters staff, and analyses have been made of occupations in the industries of cotton textiles, oil production and refining, and of automobile manufacture.

In that part of the committee's program dealing with occupational standards, the following problems have been defined: (a) Restandardization of trade tests for the United States Army (b) new occupational interests tests applicable to skilled and semiskilled jobs rather than professional occupation; (c) improvement of tests for mechanical ability, abstract intelligence, social intelligence, and occupational efficiency; (d) determination of the actual value of the tests used in public employment office procedures; and (e) determination of the combination of effects and test scores that are typical of successful workers in various occupations.

Personality and culture.—A conference for the consideration of the relationships between characteristics of personality in groups of peoples, tribes, or races, and the cultural level of these peoples, was held in New York City on March 2, 1935, and a second meeting of a committee of the division on personality in relation to culture was held in New Haven, Conn., on May 28, 1935. This subject is of special interest as one which offers opportunity for combining the contributions of anthropologists, psychiatrists, and psychologists in cultural studies of human behavior.

Cultural anthropology deals with "impersonal" patterns of behavior viewed historically and geographically, and with little or no concern for individual variations and for the significance of these socially transmitted patterns for personality development in the individual. On the other hand, most psychologists are unconcerned about the profound differences in social background responsible for personality variations that are often naively considered to be due to hereditary causes, or at any rate to types of conditioning that are only remotely, if at all, connected with social determinants. The field of personality seen culturally is therefore indicated as theoretically necessary.

Psychology of the highway.—The work of the committee on the psychology of the highway in recent years has consisted of the development of tests for the drivers of automobiles, and of obtaining data from the public and from cooperating concerns which operate a large number of automobiles in regard to the value and practicability of these tests. During the past year the committee has directed its attention mainly to analyzing and appraising the data already obtained.

It appears from certain of these records that more than half of the accidents in the automobile fleets of the corporations cooperating with the committee are caused by a relatively small number of their drivers. Taking these drivers off the road would very greatly reduce the accident rate. If the same ratios are obtained for the general public, the withdrawal of the licenses of all recognized prone-to-accident drivers should greatly increase the public safety on the highways. Whether a prone-to-accident driver can be brought up by any means to a satisfactory level of reliability, is at present, however, an open question.

Survey of South American Indians.—Three years ago the division of anthropology and psychology considered plans for the compilation of a handbook of South American Indians as a companion volume to the "Handbook of American Indians North of Mexico", which was issued by the Bureau of American Ethnology of the Smithsonian Institution in 1907. During the past year these plans have been taken up anew and have been developed on the basis of a 5-year program n cooperation with the Smithsonian Institution, to be carried out under the direction of the Institution, when the enterprise can be financed.

Psychiatric investigations.—The committee on psychiatric investigations has brought to completion the report upon which it has been engaged for the past 2 years in the publication of a volume entitled "The Problem of Mental Disorder" (McGraw-Hill Co., New York). The book is based on articles written by some 25 recognized authorities upon the relationship of psychiatry to the basic sciences of neurology, pharmacology, endocrinology, serology, general and experimental psychology, clinical psychology, cultural anthropology, and heredity.

RESEARCH INFORMATION SERVICE

C. J. WEST, Director

Census of graduate students in chemistry.—The Research Information Service has compiled the eleventh census of graduate students in chemistry for the academic year 1934–35. The totals for this year give 1,376 candidates for the master's degree, 1,750 candidates for the doctor's degree, and 1,534 faculty members engaged in chemical research in 145 universities and colleges of the United States. These totals show an increase over the figures for the previous year 1933–34 of 74, 29, and 48, respectively. The results of the census will be published in the *Journal of Chemical Education* (vol. 12, no. 7, pp. 339–343, August 1935).

Survey of paper research.—At the request of the Technical Association of the Pulp and Paper Industry, the Research Information Service has made a survey of current investigations in the United States on cellulose pulp and paper. These investigations were found to be in progress mainly in 3 Government departments and 12 universities, colleges, and research institutions. The report upon the survey was published in the *Paper Trade Journal* (vol. 100, Technical Section, pp. 251–262, May 16, 1935). A similar survey is being made for investigations in this field which are in progress in Canada.

Additional activities.—The Research Information Service has also had charge of the editing of volume IX of the Annual Survey of American Chemistry. (See p. 21.) Plans have been completed for the preparation of volume X.

A detailed author and subject index of 98 papers which have appeared in the Bulletin series and the 106 papers which have appeared in the *Reprint and Circular Series* of the Council is nearing completion.

A consolidated history of the work of the divisions and committees of the Council, as an extension of the statement published in National Research Council Reprint and Circular Series No. 106, has been completed for the Research Information Service and four of the technical divisions of the Council.

About 500 entries have been added to the file of the Bibliography of Bibliographies in Chemistry, making over 5,000 references now on hand. These will be published as a third supplement to the Bibliography which was initially issued as Bulletin No. 50, 1925. (See also Bulletin No. 71, 1929, and No. 86, 1932.)

The Research Information Service has had charge of the editing and distribution of most of the publications of the Council which have appeared during the year and of the first report of the Science Advisory Board and of several miscellaneous publications of the Council.

ANNUAL REPORT OF THE TREASURER

July 1, 1934, to June 30, 1935

To the PRESIDENT OF THE NATIONAL ACADEMY OF SCIENCES:

I have the honor to submit the following report as treasurer of the Academy for the year from July 1, 1934, to June 30, 1935, and as treasurer of the National Research Council for the same period. As is customary, the first part of this report concerns the transactions of the National Academy of Sciences, including the general fund and the appropriations under the custodian of buildings and grounds, while the second part covers the accounts of the National Research Council.

NATIONAL ACADEMY OF SCIENCES

Under a contract with the Bank of New York & Trust Co., dated June 29, 1933, the bank has served as custodian of securities of the Academy during the past year.

On June 30, 1935, the securities held by the Academy and by the Research Council were distributed among seven different classes, as follows:

	Book value			
	Held by Academy	Held by Research Council	Total held	Percent of total
I. Bonds of railroads	$704,673.00	$9,003.89	$713,676.89	20.4
II. Bonds of public utility corporations	746,820.00	15,400.00	762,220.00	21.8
III. Bonds of industrial corporations	266,533.75		266,533.75	7.6
IV. Bonds of United States, States, counties, and municipalities	122,980.63	26,195.00	149,175.63	4.2
V. Bonds and notes secured by first mortgage on real estate	530,400.00	35,333.00	565,733.00	16.2
VI. Bonds of foreign governments	138,553.25	15,412.50	153,965.75	4.4
Total bonds	2,509,960.63	101,344.39	2,611,305.02	74.6
VII. Common and preferred stocks of companies	887,316.98		887,316.98	25.4
Total	3,397,277.61	101,344.39	3,498,622.00	100.0

The firm of Loomis, Sayles & Co. has continued to act as financial advisers to the National Academy of Sciences during the year just closed.

The following table indicates the distribution of the investments held by the Academy on June 30, 1935, with reference to bonds and common and preferred stocks:

	Face value	Book value	Market value June 30, 1935
Bonds	$2,558,775.00	$2,509,960.63	$2,345,429.64
Common and preferred stocks having fixed par value	368,250.00	488,499.73	531,602.50
Common and preferred stocks having no par value		398,817.25	500,050.38
Total		3,397,277.61	3,377,082.52

The total income from investments during the past year was $137,185.27, or an average yield of 4.03 percent on the book value of $3,397,277.61, or 4.06 percent on the market value on June 30, 1935, of $3,377,082.52.

The investment reserve fund was designed to absorb losses sustained by the Academy in the sale of bonds. The following shows the operation of this fund during the year just closed:

Overdraft on July 1, 1934_____ $554, 487. 40
    Losses sustained:
        On sale of bonds_____ $48, 514. 99
        Taxes, water rents, and attorneys' fees on
          mortgages foreclosed_____   2, 607. 98

            Gross loss for the year_____ 51, 122. 97
    Profits experienced:
        On sale of bonds_____ $13, 795. 43
        Refunds from receivers and attor-
          neys_____   826. 86
        Transferred from various funds, 5
          percent of income on invest-
          ments _____   6, 861. 62

            Gross profit for the year_____ 21, 483. 91

            Net loss for the year_____ 29, 639. 06

Overdraft on June 30, 1935_____ 584, 126. 46

The total receipts of the Academy during the year from all sources amounted to $152,713.80.

The miscellaneous disbursements amounted to $122,236.41, and payments on grants and medals and honoraria amounted to $12,069.53; total disbursements for the year, $134,305.94.

The consolidated investment fund stands at $252,777.94, the same as shown in the last annual report. Of this amount, the sum of $251,361.25 was invested, and the sum of $1,416.69 was uninvested as of June 30, 1935.

The total expenditures up to June 30, 1935, for acquisition of site amounted to $185,764.50, and for erection and equipment of building for the use of the National Academy of Sciences and the National Research Council, paid from funds received from the Carnegie Corporation of New York, $1,446,879.82, and paid from separate Academy funds, $1,765, making a total for building and site, $1,634,-409.32. In addition to these the sum of $614.57 was expended from Academy funds during the year for equipment of the building, making a total of $9,998.05 for this purpose, the sum of $9,383.48 having been previously spent. The sum of $3,120.18 is held in the building construction fund as of June 30, 1935.

Below is found a list of bonds, now held by the National Academy of Sciences, which are in default:

$136, 000 Kansas City, Fort Scott & Memphis Railway Co. 4-percent refunding mortgage fully guaranteed bonds, due October 1, 1936; last interest paid was October 1, 1932.

  50, 000 Missouri Pacific Railroad Co. 5-percent first and refunding mortgage bonds, series G, due November 1, 1978; last interest paid was November 1, 1932.

  60, 000 Missouri Pacific Railroad Co. 5-percent first and refunding mortgage bonds, series I, due February 1, 1981; last interest paid was February 1, 1933.

$50,000 New Orleans, Texas & Mexico Railway Co. 5½-percent first-mortgage bonds, series A, due April 1, 1954; last interest paid was October 1, 1932.

25,000 Raleigh & Augusta Air Line Railroad Co.-Seaboard Air Line Railway Co., 5-percent first-mortgage, guaranteed, due January 1, 1931; bonds represented by certificates of deposit of the Mercantile Trust Co. of Baltimore; last interest paid was July 1, 1931.

50,000 St. Louis-San Francisco Railway Co. 4½-percent consolidated mortgage bonds, series A, due March 1, 1978; last interest paid was September 1, 1932.

Reference was made in my report last year to the liquidation of the fund known as National Research Fund by returning a pro-rata share to all contributors except one, and during the past year refund has been made to this one contributor, thus closing out the account.

Refunds have also been made during the year as follows from the account known as "Publication fund for research":

To the Rockefeller Foundation_____ $239.66
To the General Education Board_____ 500.00

These refunds represented unexpended and unobligated balances of grants made by these two foundations covering a period of several years to aid in the more prompt publication of worthy research material which otherwise would have remained unpublished for an indefinite period. Many scientific publications participated in these grants.

Some of the mortgages held by the Academy on New York City real estate are still in a somewhat precarious state, although the outlook recently has improved. During the year it was necessary for the Academy to foreclose on two pieces of property, aggregating an investment of $16,000, the Academy taking title in each case. On one piece of property on New York City real estate, the Academy accepted bonds of the Home Owner's Loan Corporation in full satisfaction for principal of $4,500 and accrued interest of $175. One mortgage on Washington, D. C., real estate was renewed for a further term of 3 years at the same rate of interest.

The Carnegie Corporation of New York made a contribution of $5,000 during the year for administrative expenses of the Academy, following two similar contributions for like purposes in recent years.

The General Education Board has made a contribution of $1,731.56 to the fund for oceanographic research, supplementing previous contributions for the same purpose.

TRUST FUNDS OF THE ACADEMY

The trust funds of the Academy, the income of which is administered for specific purposes, are enumerated below. The capital of certain funds has been increased beyond the original gift or bequest by the transfer of accumulated income at the request of the donors or by action of the Academy.

Bache fund: Bequest of Alexander Dallas Bache, a member of the Academy, 1870, to aid researches in physical and natural sciences_____ $60,000.00

Watson fund: Bequest of James C. Watson, a member of the Academy, 1874, for the promotion of astronomical science through the award of the Watson gold medal and grants of money in aid of research_____ 25,000.00

Draper fund: Gift of Mrs. Henry Draper, 1883, in memory of her husband, a former member of the Academy, to found the Henry Draper medal, to be awarded for notable investigations in astronomical physics; the balance of income is applied to aid research in the same science_____ 10,000.00

Smith fund: Gift of Mrs. J. Lawrence Smith, 1884, in memory of her husband, a former member of the Academy, to found the J. Lawrence Smith gold medal, to be awarded for important investigations of meteoric bodies and to assist, by grants of money, researches concerning such objects_____ $10,000.00

Gibbs fund: Established by gift of Wolcott Gibbs, a member of the Academy, 1892, and increased by a bequest of the late Morris Loeb, 1914, for the promotion of researches in chemistry_   5,545.50

Gould fund: Gift of Miss Alice Bache Gould, 1897, in memory of her father, a former member of the Academy, for the promotion of researches in astronomy_____   20,000.00

Comstock fund: Gift of Gen. Cyrus B. Comstock, a member of the Academy, 1907, to promote researches in electricity, magnetism, or radiant energy through the Comstock prize money, to be awarded once in 5 years for notable investigations; the fund is to be increased ultimately to $15,000_____   12,406.02

Marsh fund: Bequest of Othniel Charles Marsh, a member of the Academy, 1909, to promote original research in the natural sciences; to the original bequest of $10,000 the Academy has added interest received from the estate and has authorized the increase of the fund to $20,000 by annual additions from income_____   20,000.00

Murray fund: A gift from the late Sir John Murray, 1911, to found the Alexander Agassiz gold medal, in honor of a former member and president of the Academy, to be awarded for original contribution to the science of oceanography_____   6,000.00

Hartley fund: A gift from Mrs. Helen Hartley Jenkins, 1913–1914, in memory of her father, Marcellus Hartley, to found the medal of the Academy awarded for eminence in the application of science to public welfare_____   1,200.00

Billings fund: Established by the bequest of Mrs. Mary Anna Palmer Draper (Mrs. Henry Draper) of $25,000, in 1915, to support the publication of the Proceedings of the Academy, or for other purposes to be determined by the Academy, seven installments_____   22,313.39

Elliot fund: Gift of Margaret Henderson Elliot, to found the Daniel Giraud Elliot gold medal and honorarium for the most meritorious work in zoology or paleontology published in each year_____   8,000.00

Thompson fund: Gift of Mrs. Mary Clark Thompson, 1919, the income thereof to be applied for a gold medal of appropriate design to be awarded annually by the Academy for the most important services to geology and paleontology, the medal to be known as the Mary Clark Thompson gold medal_____   10,000.00

Joseph Henry fund: The sum of $40,000 was contributed by Fairman Rogers, Joseph Patterson, George W. Childs, and others, as an expression of their respect and esteem for Prof. Joseph Henry. This amount was deposited with the Pennsylvania Co. for Insurance of Lives and Granting Annuities in trust, with authorization to collect the income thereon and to pay over the same to Prof. Joseph Henry during his natural life, and after his death to his wife and daughters, and after the death of the last survivor to "deliver the said fund and the securities in which it shall then be invested to the National Academy of Sciences, to be thenceforward forever held in trust under the name and title of the 'Joseph Henry fund.'" The death of Miss Caroline Henry on Nov. 10, 1920, has removed the last surviving heir of Joseph Henry to the income of the Joseph Henry fund. To assist meritorious investigators, especially in the direction of original research. Amount received by the Academy from the Pennsylvania Co. for Insurance of Lives and Granting Annuities, $39,739.57, to which was added $423.93 from income_____   40,163.50

Walcott fund: Gift of Mrs. Mary Vaux Walcott, 1928, in honor of her husband, a former member and president of the Academy, the income to be used for the award of medals and honoraria to persons, the results of whose published researches, explorations, and discoveries in pre-Cambrian or Cambrian life and history shall be judged most meritorious, the award to be made every 5 years, to be known as the Charles Doolittle Walcott fund _____ $5,000.00

Carnegie endowment fund: By resolution voted Mar. 28, 1919, and amended several times since, the Carnegie Corporation of New York pledged $5,000,000 to the National Academy of Sciences for the purposes of the Academy and the National Research Council, of which $1,450,000 was reserved and paid for the erection of a building, and the remainder, $3,550,000, to be capitalized at such times as the corporation finds convenient in view of its other obligations, the amount remaining in the hands of the corporation to bear interest at the rate of 5 percent per annum, seven installments completing capitalization_____ 3,550,000.00

John J. Carty Medal and Award for the advancement of science: Gift of American Telephone & Telegraph Co., Nov. 13, 1930, in recognition of the distinguished achievements of John J. Carty as a scientist and engineer, and his noteworthy contributions to the advancement of fundamental and applied science, and in appreciation of his great services for many years in developing the art of electrical communication and as a lasting testimonial of the love and esteem in which he is held by his many thousand associates in the Bell System; the income thereof to be used for a gold medal and award, not oftener than once in 2 years, by vote of the National Academy of Sciences, to an individual for noteworthy and distinguished accomplishment in any field of science coming within the scope of the charter of the National Academy of Sciences_____ 25,000.00

In addition to the above-named funds, the Academy holds the following:

    Agassiz fund, bequest of Alexander Agassiz, a member of the Academy, 1910, for the general uses of the Academy____ 50,000.00

    Nealley fund, bequest of George True Nealley, 1925, for the general purposes of the Academy, $20,896.01, less refund November 1926, $1,500, to a creditor of the estate; supplemented by additional sum from the estate, March 1931, $159.54 _____ 19,555.55

Total_____ 3,900,183.96

Accounts with individual funds, July 1, 1934, to June 30, 1935

	General fund		Agassiz fund	
	Income	Capital	Income	Capital
Balance July 1, 1934:				
Cash_____	$10,748.06			
Invested_____	8,242.50			$50,000.00
Receipts:				
Interest on investments:				
Agassiz fund_____	2,763.49			
Nealley fund_____	863.39			
Bonds sold_____	8,242.50			
Annual dues from members_____	1,425.00			
Refunds_____	1.50			
Total_____	32,286.44			50,000.00
Disbursements:				
General expenses_____	5,110.89			
Transfer to investment reserve fund___	181.34			
Fees to financial advisers_____	159.14			
Bonds bought_____	8,242.50			
Balance June 30, 1935:				
Cash_____	9,892.57			
Invested_____	8,700.00			50,000.00
Total_____	32,286.44			50,000.00

Accounts with individual funds, July 1, 1934, to June 30, 1935—Continued

	Bache fund		Billings fund	
	Income	Capital	Income	Capital
Balance July 1, 1934				
Cash	$1,037.10			
Invested		$60,000.00		$22,313.39
Receipts: Interest on investments	2,648.17		$984.98	
Total	3,685.27	60,000.00	984.98	22,313.39
Disbursements:				
Grants	2,395.00			
Office expenses	5.00			
Transfer to investment reserve fund	132.41		49.25	
Fees to financial advisers	122.69		45.57	
Transfer to Academy Proceedings			890.16	
Balance June 30, 1935:				
Cash	1,030.17			
Invested		60,000.00		22,313.39
Total	3,685.27	60,000.00	948.98	22,313.39

	Building construction		Building site	
	Income	Capital	Income	Capital
Balance July 1, 1934:				
Cash	$120.18		$10,895.49	
Invested	3,000.00		7,543.25	
Receipts: Interest on investments			356.40	
Total	3,120.18		18,795.14	
Disbursements:				
Fees to financial advisers			15.42	
Transfer to investment reserve fund			17.82	
Transfer to building site income payable to National Research Council, 1935			6,000.00	
Balance June 30, 1935:				
Cash	3,120.18		5,218.65	
Invested			7,543.25	
Total	3,120.18		18,795.14	

	Carnegie endowment fund		Carnegie Corporation special	
	Income	Capital	Income	Capital
Balance July 1, 1934:				
Cash		$577,825.55	$8,126.54	
Invested		2,972,174.45		
Receipts:				
Interest on investments	$120,417.85			
Bonds sold		878,410.28		
Carnegie Corporation of New York			5,000.00	
Total	120,417.85	4,428,410.28	13,126.54	
Disbursements:				
Bonds bought		878,410.28		
Accrued interest on bonds bought	6,223.34			
Transfer to investment reserve fund	6,020.89			
Taxes, fire and liability insurance, etc., on real estate	2,788.40			
Fees to financial advisers	6,077.51			
Transferred to Carnegie endowment fund, income account, N. R. C., 1934	10,000.00			
Transferred to Carnegie endowment fund, income account, N. R. C., 1935	44,000.00			
Transferred to Carnegie endowment fund, income account, N. A. S., 1934	3,716.28			
Transferred to Carnegie endowment fund, income account, N. A. S., 1935	41,591.43			
Committee on the library			277.10	
Government relations allotment			386.45	
Committee on nominations			60.13	
Clerical expenses			552.96	
Balance June 30, 1935:				
Cash		513,670.89	11,849.90	
Invested		3,036,329.11		
Total	120,417.85	4,428,410.28	13,126.54	

Accounts with individual funds, July 1, 1934, to June 30, 1935—Continued

	John J. Carty Medal and Award		Comstock fund	
	Income	Capital	Income	Capital
Balance July 1, 1934:				
Cash	$1,511.08	$391.25	$2,859.60	$7,337.27
Invested		24,608.75	2,000.00	5,068.75
Receipts:				
Interest on investments	1,145.62		580.83	
Bonds sold		7,166.25	4,000.00	
Total	2,656.70	32,166.25	9,440.43	12,406.02
Disbursements:				
Bonds bought		7,166.25	4,000.00	
Accrued interest on bonds bought			51.71	
Commission on collections			4.34	
Transfer to investment reserve fund	57.28		29.04	
Fees to financial advisers	50.48		14.72	
Balance June 30, 1935:				
Cash	2,548.94	257.50	5,340.62	2,662.27
Invested		24,742.50		9,743.75
Total	2,656.70	32,166.25	9,440.43	12,406.02

	Consolidated fund		Draper fund	
	Income	Capital	Income	Capital
Balance July 1, 1934:				
Cash	$1,213.09	$46,166.69	$1,223.94	
Invested		206,611.25		$10,000.00
Receipts:				
Interest on investments	11,334.47		441.74	
Bonds sold		2,980.00		
Total	12,547.56	255,757.94	1,665.68	10,000.00
Disbursements:				
Bonds bought		2,980.00		
Taxes, etc., on real estate	123.42			
Distribution of consolidated fund	11,154.86			
Transfer to investment reserve fund			22.09	
Fees to financial advisers			20.33	
Medal and medal box			352.52	
Balance June 30, 1935:				
Cash	1,269.28	1,416.69	1,270.74	
Invested		251,361.25		10,000.00
Total	12,547.56	255,757.94	1,665.68	10,000.00

	Elliot fund		Fees to financial advisers	
	Income	Capital	Income	Capital
Balance July 1, 1934:				
Cash	$1,919.92			
Invested		$8,000.00		
Receipts:				
Interest on investments	352.49			
Transferred from various funds			$7,010.62	
Total	2,272.41	8,000.00	7,010.62	
Disbursements:				
Medal and medal box	263.37			
Honorarium	200.00			
Engrossing	20.00			
Fees to financial advisers	16.12			
Transfer to investment reserve fund	17.62			
Payment to Loomis, Sayles & Co			7,010.62	
Balance June 30, 1935:				
Cash	1,755.30			
Invested		8,000.00		
Total	2,272.41	8,000.00	7,010.62	

Accounts with individual funds, July 1, 1934, to June 30, 1935—Continued

	Fund for oceanographic research		Gibbs fund	
	Income	Capital	Income	Capital
Balance July 1, 1934:				
Cash	$5, 882. 57		$1, 700. 34	
Invested			1, 023. 75	$5, 545. 50
Receipts:				
General Education Board	1, 731. 56			
Interest on investments			293. 79	
Refund from Thomas G. Thompson	43. 77			
Royalties	11. 25			
Bonds sold			1, 023. 75	
Total	7, 669. 15		4, 041. 63	5, 545. 50
Disbursements:				
Clerical and office expenses	92. 13			
Travel	491. 90			
Transfer to investment reserve fund			14. 69	
Fees to financial advisers			13. 32	
Bonds bought			1, 023. 75	
Balance June 30, 1935:				
Cash	7, 085. 12		2, 989. 87	
Invested				5, 545. 50
Total	7, 669. 15		4, 041. 63	5, 545. 50

	Gould fund		Grand Canyon project	
	Income	Capital	Income	Capital
Balance July 1, 1934:				
Cash	$13, 258. 98	$4, 797. 50	$24. 19	
Invested	3, 992. 50	15, 202. 50		
Receipts:				
Interest on investments	1, 110. 89			
Bonds sold	3, 980. 00	4, 000. 00		
Total	22, 342. 37	24, 000. 00	24. 19	
Disbursements:				
Bonds bought	3, 980. 00	4, 000. 00		
Taxes on real estate	10. 28			
Grants	2, 030. 00			
Transfer to investment reserve fund	55. 54			
Fees to financial advisers	39. 26			
Balance June 30, 1935:				
Cash	14, 714. 79	3, 297. 50	24. 19	
Invested	1, 512. 50	16, 702. 50		
Total	22, 342. 37	24, 000. 00	24. 19	

	Hale lectureship		Hartley fund	
	Income	Capital	Income	Capital
Balance July 1, 1934:				
Cash	$385. 55		$563. 77	
Invested				$1, 200. 00
Receipts: Interest on investments			52. 43	
Total	385. 55		616. 20	1, 200. 00
Disbursements:				
Medal and medal box			95. 42	
Transfer to investment reserve fund			2. 62	
Fees to financial advisers			2. 10	
Balance June 30, 1935:				
Cash	385. 55		516. 06	
Invested				1, 200. 00
Total	385. 55		616. 20	1, 200. 00

Accounts with individual funds, July 1, 1934, to June 30, 1935—Continued

	Joseph Henry fund		Investment reserve fund	
	Income	Capital	Income	Capital
Balance July 1, 1934:				
Cash	$2.33			
Invested	1,023.75	$40,163.50		
Receipts:				
Bonds sold	1,023.75			
Interest on investments	1,822.01			
Profit on sale of bonds			$13,795.43	
Transferred from various funds			6,861.62	
Refunds from receivers and attorneys on real estate			826.86	
Overdraft June 30, 1935			584,126.46	
Total	3,871.84	40,163.50	605,610.37	
Disbursements:				
Grants	1,463.44			
Transfer to investment reserve fund	91.10			
Fees to financial advisers	84.13			
Loss on sale of bonds			48,514.99	
Taxes, water rents, and attorney's fees			2,607.98	
Bonds bought	1,023.75			
Overdraft July 1, 1934			554,487.40	
Balance June 30, 1935:				
Cash	1,209.42			
Invested		40,163.50		
Total	3,871.84	40,163.50	605,610.37	

	Marsh fund		Murray fund	
	Income	Capital	Income	Capital
Balance July 1, 1934:				
Cash	$374.07		$3,333.61	
Invested		$20,000.00	1,000.00	$6,000.00
Receipts:				
Interest on investments	882.34		318.37	
Bonds sold			2,000.00	
Total	1,256.41	20,000.00	6,651.98	6,000.00
Disbursements:				
Grants	475.00			
Transfer to investment reserve fund	41.12		15.92	
Fees to financial advisers	40.66		14.02	
Medal and medal box			349.56	
Commission on collections			2.15	
Purchase of bonds			2,000.00	
Balance June 30, 1935:				
Cash	696.63		4,270.33	
Invested		20,000.00		6,000.00
Total	1,256.41	20,000.00	6,651.98	6,000.00

	National Academy of Sciences, special		National Parks problems	
	Income	Capital	Income	Capital
Balance July 1, 1934: Cash			$2,605.27	
Receipts:				
Reimbursements	$67,428.43			
Due from National Research Council July 1, 1934	2,000.00			
Total	69,428.43		2,605.27	
Disbursements:				
Expenses of Academy	67,428.43			
Picture of Crater Lake			320.40	
Advance to Ansel F. Hall			400.00	
Miscellaneous expenses			20.00	
Balance June 30, 1935:				
Cash			1,864.87	
Due from National Research Council June 30, 1935	2,000.00			
Total	69,428.43		2,605.27	

Accounts with individual funds, July 1, 1934, to June 30, 1935—Continued

	National Research fund		Nealley fund	
	Income	Capital	Income	Capital
Balance July 1, 1934:				
Cash		$46.94		
Invested				$19,555.55
Total		46.94		19,555.55
Disbursements: Refund to contributor		46.94		
Balance June 30, 1935: Invested				19,555.55
Total		46.94		19,555.55

	Academy Proceedings		Joint Proceedings	
	Income	Capital	Income	Capital
Balance July 1, 1934:				
Cash	$2,850.28		$7,069.53	
Invested	1,995.75			
Receipts:				
Interest on investments	113.41			
Annual dues	1,425.00			
Subscriptions			1,852.96	
Reprints and separates	25.50		1,350.43	
Bonds sold	2,000.00			
Transfer from Billings fund	890.16			
Contribution by National Research Council			2,500.00	
Transfer from Academy Proceedings representing contribution by National Academy of Sciences			2,500.00	
Total	9,300.10		15,272.92	
Disbursements:				
Salary of managing editor			750.00	
Printing and distributing			7,213.94	
Commission on collection	2.14			
Bonds bought	2,000.00			
Expenses:				
Boston office			450.00	
Washington office			263.35	
Transfer from Academy Proceedings representing contribution by National Academy of Sciences	2,500.00			
Transfer to investment reserve fund	5.67			
Fees to financial advisers	4.21			
Balance June 30, 1935:				
Cash	3,792.33		6,595.63	
Invested	995.75			
Total	9,300.10		15,272.92	

	Emergency fund Proceedings		Publication fund for research	
	Income	Capital	Income	Capital
Balance July 1, 1934: Cash	$3,327.79		$739.66	
Receipts				
Total	3,327.79		739.66	
Disbursements—refund:				
Rockefeller Foundation			239.66	
General Education Board			500.00	
Balance June 30, 1935: Cash	3,327.79			
Total	3,327.79		739.66	

Accounts with individual funds, July 1, 1934, to June 30, 1935—Continued

	Scientific publication fund		Smith fund	
	Income	Capital	Income	Capital
Balance July 1, 1934:				
Cash	$1,631.28		$5,065.69	
Invested			1,478.25	$10,000.00
Receipts:				
Refund from Joel Stebbins	49.16			
Royalties	3.08			
Interest on investments			555.79	
Total	1,683.52		7,099.73	10,000.00
Disbursements:				
Transfer to investment reserve fund			26.79	
Fees to financial advisers			23.14	
Balance June 30, 1935:				
Cash	1,683.52		5,571.55	
Invested			1,478.25	10,000.00
Total	1,683.52		7,099.73	10,000.00

	Thompson fund		Walcott fund	
	Income	Capital	Income	Capital
Balance July 1, 1934:				
Cash	$2,728.17	$1,037.50	$98.57	$135.00
Invested		8,962.50		4,865.00
Receipts:				
Interest on investments	445.50		226.91	
Bonds sold		8,962.50		
Total	3,173.67	18,962.50	325.48	5,000.00
Disbursements:				
Bonds bought		8,962.50		
Medal and medal box	631.82			
Honorarium	250.00			
Transfer to investment reserve fund	22.28		11.35	
Fees to financial advisers	18.23		9.81	
Balance June 30, 1935:				
Cash	2,251.34	875.00	304.32	135.00
Invested		9,125.00		4,865.00
Total	3,173.67	18,962.50	325.48	5,000.00

	Watson fund	
	Income	Capital
Balance July 1, 1934:		
Cash	$5,791.21	$525.00
Invested	1,000.00	24,475.00
Receipts:		
Interest on investments	875.97	
Bonds sold		9,096.25
Total	7,667.18	34,096.25
Disbursements:		
Bonds bought		9,096.25
Grants	3,500.00	
Real estate taxes and commissions	21.63	
Transfer to investment reserve fund	43.80	
Fees to financial advisers	51.88	
Balance June 30, 1935:		
Cash	3,049.87	1,821.25
Invested	1,000.00	23,178.75
Total	7,667.18	34,096.25

Statement of assets and liabilities, June 30, 1935

ASSETS

[Securities purchased during the fiscal year 1934-35 are indicated thus (*)]

	Face value	Book value	Market value June 30, 1935
Real estate owned	$144,500.00	$144,500.00	$144,500.00
Mortgage notes, secured by first mortgage on real estate	377,900.00	377,900.00	377,900.00
SECURITIES			
American Telephone & Telegraph Co. 5 percent 30-year collateral-trust gold, due Dec. 1, 1946; nos. 640, 4604, 10927, 29245, 29246, 41419, 42526, 43733, 45849, 47282-47284, 49576, 53149, 58466, 64235-64247, 66042, 67397, 74425, 74513, 74630, 74633; 34 at $1,000 each	34,000.00	35,990.00	36,847.50
American Telephone & Telegraph Co. 5 percent 35-year debenture bonds, due Feb. 1, 1965; nos. M17-939, M19-041, M64-124-M64-135, M64-519, M72-201-M72-203, M72-311-M72-316, M72-324, M75-045-M75-050, M91-899, M91-900, M108-560-M108-562, M115-287-M115-289, M131-196-M131-200, M144-885, M145-413, M145-414; 47 at $1,000 each	47,000.00	51,206.75	52,875.00
Argentine Government loan, 1926, 6 percent external sinking-fund gold, public-works issue of Oct. 1, 1926, due Oct. 1, 1960; nos. M1211-M1213, M1255, M1981, M2342, M3255, M3356, M3816, M3818, M6183, M6537, M8435, M8436, M8605, M10433-M10437, M10902, M10904, M10905, M12793, M15271; 25 at $1,000 each	25,000.00	24,936.25	24,312.50
Baltimore & Ohio R. R. Co.: 5 percent refunding and general mortgage, series A, due Dec. 1, 1995; nos. M30222, M33708, M37053, M58345; 4 at $1,000 each; nos. D1256, D1296; 2 at $500 each	5,000.00	4,526.25	3,350.00
Baltimore & Ohio R. R. Co. 5 percent refunding and general mortgage, series D, due Mar. 1, 2000; nos. M4863-M4892; 30 at $1,000 each	30,000.00	28,650.00	20,175.00
Bell Telephone Co. of Canada 5 percent first-mortgage, series C bonds, due May 1, 1960; nos. CM00084, CM00085, CM00277-CM00279, CM00397, CM00527-CM00529, CM00628, CM00629, CM00719, CM00720, CM00750, CM01453-CM01458, CM02295-CM02298, CM02827, CM03184, CM03192, CM03193, CM06441-CM06445, CM06449, CM06450; 35 at $1,000 each	35,000.00	36,488.75	41,168.75
*Bell Telephone Co. of Pennsylvania 5-percent first and refunding mortgage, series C, due Oct. 1, 1960; nos. M5155-M5164, M15108, M18071, M18340, M20233, M20236, M22774, M22775, M28413, M28414, M30036-M30041; 25 at $1,000 each	25,000.00	30,250.00	31,125.00
*Canadian Pacific Ry. Co. 4-percent perpetual consolidated debentures; nos. G5882, G28256, G37790, G37791, G43142, G43143, G81666-G81668, G87312; 10 at $1,000 each	10,000.00	8,525.00	8,875.00
*Canadian Pacific Ry. equipment trust 5-percent bonds fully guaranteed, due July 1, 1944; nos. 21151-21160, 21319-21368; 60 at $1,000 each	60,000.00	67,200.00	67,050.00
Carolina, Clinchfield & Ohio Ry. 5-percent first and consolidated mortgage gold bonds, series A, due Dec. 15, 1952; nos. M652, M906, M933, M1907, M2231, M2434, M2482, M2483, M2609-M2613, M2732, M2864, M2865, M3731-M3733, M3955, M4052-M4054, M4362, M4436-M4440, M5223, M5804, M5902, M5906, M6349, M6918-M6822, M7031; 40 at $1,000 each; nos. D91, D92, D130-D133, D159, D240-D260, D797, D798; 20 at $500 each	50,000.00	54,210.00	55,000.00
*Chesapeake & Ohio Ry. Co. 5-percent first consolidated-mortgage 50-year bonds, due May 1, 1939; nos. 854, 1080, 1083, 1321 1464, 1465, 3503, 3769, 3770, 4811, 4812, 5030, 5112, 5241, 5603, 6351, 6352, 6421, 7496, 11030, 11093, 11875, 11991, 12005, 13336, 13341, 13930, 14707, 15148, 16133, 16836, 18406, 20082, 20770, 20771, 21015, 21016, 21443, 26336, 26338; 40 at $1,000 each	40,000.00	44,500.00	44,950.00
City of Brisbane, Australia, 5-percent 30-year sinking-fund gold bonds, due Mar. 1, 1957; nos. 3368, 3369, 3418-3422, 3789-3793, 3928-3932, 4400-4402, 4630, 4720, 5376, 5975, 6634, 6638, 7341, 7425, 7472, 7487; 30 at $1,000 each	30,000.00	27,670.00	28,237.50
City of Tacoma, Green River special water fund no. 2, 5 percent, due Oct. 1, 1939; nos. 1508-1511; 4 at $1,000 each	4,000.00	4,140.00	4,295.00
Columbia Gas & Electric Corporation 5-percent debenture bonds, due Jan. 15, 1961; nos. A9157-A9181; 25 at $1,000 each	25,000.00	24,437.50	22,375.00
*Commonwealth Edison Co. 4-percent first mortgage bonds, series F, due Mar. 1, 1981; nos. M1452, M4349, M11255, M23708-M23713, M27982, M27983, M35470, M35471, M39476, M39478, M39479, M46972-M46975; 20 at $1,000 each	20,000.00	20,725.00	20,750.00

Statement of assets and liabilities, June 30, 1935—Continued

ASSETS

[Securities purchased during the fiscal year 1934-35 are indicated thus (*)]

	Face value	Book value	Market value June 30, 1935
SECURITIES—continued			
Consolidated Gas Co. of New York 5¼-percent 20-year debenture bonds, due Feb. 1, 1945; nos. M318, M319, M3214, M3317–M3326, M5236–M5245, M5738–M5740, M9598–M9601, M11397–M11399, M11643–M11646, M16509, M16654, M16671–M16680, M21938, M21940, M22190, M22374–M22376, M23870, M23871, M26142, M27181, M27182, M28852, M28905, M28906, M34787, M35519, M38629, M38630, M40419, M44300, M44803, M47911, M48338; 72 at $1,000 each; nos. D1530, D1531; 2 at $500 each	$73,000.00	$75,200.00	$77,015.00
Cosmos Club, Washington, D. C., 4½-percent bonds, due July 1, 1949; nos. 288, 289, 291, 292, 294, 299, 305, 350; 8 at $1,000 each	8,000.00	8,000.00	6,400.00
Denver & Salt Lake Ry. Co., Moffat Road, 6-percent first-mortgage gold bonds, series A, due Jan. 1, 1950; nos. M1460–M1464, M1467–M1478, M1489, M1490, M1495, M1510, M1779, M1828, M1829, M2463; 25 at $1,000 each	25,000.00	26,250.00	26,375.00
Dominion of Canada 5-percent third war loan 20-year bonds, due Mar. 1, 1937; nos. E02374–E02376, E05443, E05444, E19151, E23763–E23765, E40822, E40823, E178424, E178425, E201852–E201854, E204857–E204863; 23 at $1,000 each	23,000.00	22,108.75	24,581.25
Goodyear Tire & Rubber Co. 5-percent first-mortgage and collateral trust bonds, due May 1, 1957; nos. M2001, M2766, M2779, M2780, M3573, M5965, M12741, M15293, M17623, M19518–M19521, M20721, M23021, M24476, M25063, M25475–M25479, M26848, M30596, M34087, M38695–M38699, M39056–M39068, M42907, M43357, M48568, M48569, M54288–M54297, M54551, M56107; 59 at $1,000 each; nos. D129, D702; 2 at $500 each	60,000.00	56,102.50	63,000.00
Government of the Argentine Nation 6-percent external sinking-fund gold bonds, due Oct. 1, 1959; nos. M5611, M10469, M10470, M18165, M18363–M18365, M19643, M20578, M23810; 10 at $1,000 each	10,000.00	9,957.50	9,725.00
Grand Trunk Ry. Co. of Canada, Canadian National Railways, 6-percent 15-year sinking-fund gold-debenture bonds, guaranteed, due Sept. 1, 1936; nos. M00976–M00978, M01129, M01762, M02855, M03925, M04011, M04589, M09544, M10380, M14578–M14592, M14803, M18462–M18471, M19390, M19391, M19530, M19765, M19891, M20542, M21487, M21539, M22610, M23800, M23699; 48 at $1,000 each; nos. D0139–D0142; 4 at $500 each	50,000.00	53,600.00	52,875.00
Grand Trunk Western Ry. Co. first-mortgage 50-year 4 percent gold, due July 1, 1950; nos. 346, 1141, 1584, 1613, 3060, 3061, 3888, 4304, 5025, 5605, 5606; 11 at $1,000 each; nos. 15, 265, 774, 781, 839, 994, 1019, 1055, 1059, 1104, 1189, 1378, 2141, 2143, 2738, 2884, 2942, 2970, 2976, 3220; 20 at $500 each	21,000.00	16,215.00	19,110.00
Great Northern Ry. Co. 7 percent 15-year general mortgage, series A, due July 1, 1936; nos. M61777–M61782; 6 at $1,000 each; no D3241; 1 at $500; nos. C3291, C3536; 2 at $100 each	6,700.00	6,465.50	6,448.75
*Home Owners' Loan Corporation 2¾ percent, series B, fully guaranteed, due Aug. 1, 1949; nos. M–450319K, M–450320L, M–450321A, M–450322B; 4 at $1,000 each; no. X–189950L; 1 at $500; no. T–743769K; 1 at $100; no. R–201772B; 1 at $50; no. P–216331A; 1 at $25	4,675.00	4,675.00	4,702.76
Inland Steel Co. 4½ percent first-mortgage sinking fund, series A, bonds, due Apr. 1, 1978; nos. 10843, 10844, 11422–11427, 11993, 11994, 12708, 12709, 13051, 15938–15942, 15945–15049, 17002, 17003, 19753, 19754, 22395, 22396, 23426–23428, 25336–25342, 28968; 40 at $1,000 each	40,000.00	34,785.00	42,600.00
*Indianapolis Power & Light Co. 5 percent first mortgage, series A, due Jan. 1, 1957; nos. M31026–M31028, M31160–M31164, M31299, M31300, M31367, M31452–M31455, M31833, M31967–M31970, M32054–M32056, M32058–M32064; 30 at $1,000 each	30,000.00	31,237.50	31,312.50
Kansas City, Fort Scott & Memphis Ry. Co. 4 percent refunding mortgage, fully guaranteed bonds, due Oct. 1, 1936; nos. 32, 756, 1013, 1093, 1418–1421, 1447, 1660, 2326, 2593, 2898, 3546, 4196, 4312, 4348, 4468–4472, 4610, 4621, 4787, 4944, 5096, 5447, 5723, 5930, 5932, 6224–6227, 6802, 6811, 6812, 6906, 7191, 7444, 7449, 7475, 7612, 7640, 7641, 7662, 7933, 7934, 8023–8025, 8027, 8028, 8062, 8222, 8624, 8739, 8880, 8970, 9486, 10936, 11733, 11742, 13082–13084, 13483, 13484, 14113, 14256, 14561, 14562, 14651, 14952, 15186, 15187, 15226, 15946, 16079, 16081–16085, 16207, 16276, 16767, 17281, 18104, 18173, 18177, 18453, 18782, 18783, 18906, 18856, 18947, 19069, 19154, 19655, 19893, 19911, 20178, 20235, 20694, 20891, 21065, 21345, 21346, 21387, 21730, 21850–21899, 22822, 22935, 23065, 23124, 23271, 24023, 24188, 24206, 24221, 24542, 24650, 25215, 25499, 25500; 136 at $1,000 each	136,000.00	79,096.25	46,240.00

Statement of assets and liabilities, June 30, 1935—Continued

ASSETS

[Securities purchased during the fiscal year 1934-35 are indicated thus (*)]

	Face value	Book value	Market value June 30, 1935
SECURITIES—continued			
Kansas City Southern Ry. Co. 5 percent refunding and improvement mortgage bonds, due Apr. 1, 1950; nos. M464, M827, M1139-M1141, M1376, M2142, M4310, M4840, M4861, M7091, M7208, M7902, M9833, M10769, M11350, M12276, M12997, M13816, M14505, M14950, M18955-M18957, M19213, M20178, M20242-M20244, M20401; 30 at $1,000 each	$30,000.00	$15,721.25	$20,100.00
Kingdom of Norway 6 percent 20-year external loan sinking-fund gold bonds, due Aug. 1, 1944: nos. 1620-1624, 3665, 3855, 5317, 5925, 6458-6461, 6532, 6557-6559, 6611, 6612, 6614, 8803, 8804, 8880, 11125-11129, 13165, 13166, 14085, 14812, 14818-14820, 15531, 15532, 15703, 15756, 17285, 17286, 17311, 17771, 19312, 19896, 20871, 22047, 22048, 22122, 23338, 23344; 51 at $1,000 each	51,000.00	53,880.75	54,442.50
Lackawanna & Wyoming Valley R. R. Co. 5 percent first mortgage gold bonds, dated July 1, 1913, due Aug. 1, 1951; nos. M853-M902; 50 at $1,000 each	50,000.00	48,750.00	10,500.00
Liggett & Myers Tobacco Co. 7 percent bonds, due Oct. 1, 1944; nos. 448, 3124-3126, 3957-3959, 4697-4701, 5366-5369, 6701, 6702, 7201, 7218, 7228-7231, 7241, 7242, 7251, 7252, 7294-7300, 7348-7350, 8007, 9195, 9196, 9964, 10285, 11219, 13573, 13763-13766, 15135; 50 at $1,000 each	50,000.00	61,845.00	66,250.00
*P. Lorillard Co. 5 percent debentures, due Aug. 1, 1951; nos. 2479, 2480, 2494, 2585, 2599, 2792-2796, 4625-4627, 5918-5925, 6104, 9366-9368; 25 at $1,000 each	25,000.00	29,000.00	29,156.25
Missouri Pacific R. R. Co. 5 percent first and refunding mortgage gold bonds, series G, dated Nov. 1, 1928, due Nov. 1, 1978; nos. M20326-M20375; 50 at $1,000 each	50,000.00	48,712.50	13,500.00
Missouri Pacific R. R. Co. 5 percent first and refunding mortgage, series I, due Feb. 1, 1981; nos. T252-T256, T7644-T7647, T39855-T39859, T39861-T39863, T43949-T43954; 23 at $1,000 each; nos. M9994, M10757, M10758, M16440-M16442, M18265, M18828, M18829, M23249, M30095, M30444, M30546, M30901-M30905, M30908-M30915, M31587, M33255, M38252, M38253, M39860, M39861, M40437-M40440, M46684; 37 at $1,000 each	60,000.00	31,983.75	16,125.00
National Dairy Products Corporation 5¼ percent gold debenture bonds, due Feb. 1, 1948; nos. M3062, M5146-M5191, M16029, M22546, M33248, M46795, M46796, M67999, M71719, M71720, M72946, M75482, M76643-M76658, M76700, M76701; 70 at $1,000 each	70,000.00	69,171.25	72,800.00
*New England Telephone & Telegraph Co. 5 percent first mortgage 30-year, series A, due June 1, 1952; nos. M1747-M1749, M3207-M3212, M9646, M12599, M12717, M12718, M14782-M14784, M16939, M19086-M19088, M20395-M20397, M24655, M28190, M28191, M29674-M29677, M29913-M29919, M33433, M34448; 39 at $1,000 each; nos. D4, D5; 2 at $500 each	40,000.00	48,400.00	48,900.00
*New Jersey Power & Light Co. 4½ percent first mortgage bonds, due Oct. 1, 1960; nos. M8316-M8339, M9625, M10706, M10735, M10843, M11857, M11869; 30 at $1,000 each	30,000.00	30,975.00	31,200.00
New Orleans, Texas & Mexico Ry. Co. 5½ percent first mortgage gold bonds, series A, due Apr. 1, 1954; nos. M439-M448, M647, M1610, M1765-M1767, M1808-M1810, M3396, M6873, M6874, M6896, M6897, M7999, M8135, M8207, M9643, M9950, M9996, M11059-M11063, M11944-M11948, M12486, M12487, M14131-M14133, M14417, M14418, M16406-M16408; 49 at $1,000 each; nos. D200, D201; 2 at $500 each	50,000.00	51,763.75	14,000.00
*New York Edison Co. 6½ percent first lien and refunding mortgage, series A, due Oct. 1, 1941; nos. M72, M73, M117, M124, M645, M2215, M2828, M3150, M3425-M3427, M3459, M3685, M4002, M4824, M5657, M5866, M10592-M10595, M10622, M12355, M13821, M15396, M15678-M15682, M15862-M15864, M15890, M15891, M17120, M20005, M20852, M20976, M21913, M23096, M23097, M23983, M24774, M25591, M25850, M26064, M28484; 48 at $1,000 each; nos. D486, D806, D1494, D1860; 4 at $500 each	50,000.00	57,187.50	56,230.00
Niagara Falls Power Co. 5 percent first and consolidation mortgage bonds, series A, due July 1, 1959; nos. M4994-M4997, M6157-M6162; 10 at $1,000 each	10,000.00	9,860.00	10,850.00
Niagara Falls Power Co. 6 percent first and consolidation mortgage gold bonds, series AA, due Nov. 1, 1950; nos. M388, M571, M608, M740, M1129, M1843, M2561, M2808, M3072, M4269, M4371, M4501, M4502, M4608, M4682, M4696, M5001, M5007, M5008, M5796, M5881, M6050, M6143, M6855, M6881, M6882, M6907, M6978, M7343, M7359, M7422, M7494, M7542, M7745, M8156, M8157, M8274, M8276, M8335-M8341, M8360, M8689, M8690; 48 at $1,000 each; nos. D162, D180, D260, D378, D1220, D1221, D1229, D1465, D1542, D1701, D1838, D1853; 12 at $500 each	54,000.00	57,860.00	58,050.00

Statement of assets and liabilities, June 30, 1935—Continued

ASSETS

[Securities purchased during the fiscal year 1934-35 are indicated thus (*)]

	Face value	Book value	Market value June 30, 1935
SECURITIES—continued			
North American Co. 5 percent debentures, due Feb. 1, 1961; nos. M505, M1404, M1839-M1847, M3951-M3953, M5801-M5810, M5991, M5992, M7712-M7714, M8286, M11067, M13856, M13996, M14000, M14209, M15222, M15223, M15855, M17286, M17527, M17769, M17770, M17964, M18532, M18571, M19074, M19288, M23252-M23258, M23701, M23730, M23954, M24316, M24317, M24704, M24705, M24943; 60 at $1,000 each	$60,000.00	$49,750.00	$59,550.00
Northern Pacific Ry. Co. 6-percent refunding and improvement mortgage, series B, due July 1, 2047; nos. M3544-M-3547, M26853, M26854, M27750-M27754, M84522-M84525, M103231-M103245; 30 at $1,000 each	30,000.00	30,912.50	30,450.00
Ohio Power Co. 4½-percent first and refunding mortgage, series D, bonds, due June 1, 1956; nos. M3248-M3251, M10226-M10230, M10300, M10301, M12400, M12929, M13457, M13696, M13697, M13751, M20986-M20989, M22690, M22691, M25016-M25020, M25569, M28196, M28197; 31 at $1,000 each	31,000.00	30,293.75	32,705.00
Pacific Telephone & Telegraph Co. 5-percent first mortgage and collateral trust sinking-fund 30-year bonds, stamped, due Jan. 2, 1937; nos. M8660, M9559, M10461-M10465, M10619, M10700, M10824, M11130, M11403, M11404, M11954, M11955, M12083, M12156, M12519; 18 at $1,000 each	18,000.00	18,850.00	19,147.50
Pennsylvania Power & Light Co. 4½-percent first mortgage bonds, due Apr. 1, 1981; nos. 50380-50383; 4 at $1,000 each	4,000.00	3,850.00	4,225.00
*Pennsylvania R. R. Co. 4-percent consolidated mortgage sterling, stamped dollar, due May 1, 1948; nos. 66922, 66951, 67152, 67158, 67952, 67953, 76881, 76963, 77342; 9 at $1,000 each	9,000.00	10,170.00	10,170.00
*Potomac Edison Co. 4½-percent first mortgage, series F, due Apr. 1, 1961; nos. M1005-M1013, M1427, M1791-M1793, M2529-M2534, M2662-M2664, M3776, M3872-M3876, M4137; 29 at $1,000 each; nos. D9, D80; 2 at $500 each	30,000.00	31,637.50	31,800.00
Raleigh & Augusta Air Line R. R. Co., Seaboard Air Line Ry. Co. 5-percent guaranteed first mortgage, due Jan. 1, 1931; nos. 701-725; 25, at $1,000 each	25,000.00	25,000.00	15,000.00
St. Louis-San Francisco Ry. Co. 4½-percent consolidated mortgage gold bonds, series A, due Mar. 1, 1978; nos. M7881-M7895, M14120-M14134, M17108, M17963, M17964, M19029, M25732-M25737, M41182, M41183, M41216, M62420-M62424, M91633, M91634; 50 at $1,000 each	50,000.00	43,850.00	5,062.50
*Sierra & San Francisco Power Co. 5-percent first mortgage 40-year, due Aug. 1, 1949; nos. 509, 857, 858, 3081, 3668, 7121, 7321, 7322, 7324, 7474, 7730, 7827-7832, 7936, 8011, 8086, 8087, 8089, 8091-8095, 8197, 8199, 8403; 30 at $1,000 each	30,000.00	33,225.00	33,525.00
Southern Bell Telephone & Telegraph Co. 30-year first mortgage 5-percent sinking-fund gold, due Jan. 1, 1941; nos. M5845, M6230, M9739, M10618, M11576-M11579, M12369, M13965, M15568-M15570, M19695-M19697, M27301, M30234-M30236; 20 at $1,000 each	20,000.00	20,643.75	21,550.00
Texarkana & Fort Smith Ry. Co. 5½ percent first mortgage guaranteed gold bonds, series A, due Aug. 1, 1950; nos. M101, M102, M754-M763, M1593-M1595, M1739, M1742, M1777-M1779, M2014-M2018, M3001, M3002, M3908-M3910, M5767, M6078, M6482, M6757-M6760, M6912, M8341-M8343, M9299, M9472, M9473, M9629-M9631; 47 at $1,000 each; nos. D102, D103, D186, D202, D237, D264; 6a t $500 each	50,000.00	52,271.25	47,000.00
*Twelve Federal Land Banks 3¼ percent Consolidated Federal Farm Loan bonds, due May 1, 1955; nos. 46140L, 46141A-46146F, 46147H, 46148J-46150L, 46151A; 12 at $1,000 each	12,000.00	12,090.00	12,240.00
Union Oil Co. of California 6 percent 20-year, series A, gold, due May 1, 1942; nos. M140-M142, M661, M662, M1733-M1735, M5231, M6140-M6143, M8726; 14 at $1,000 each; nos. D1026, D1027; 2 at $500 each	15,000.00	15,630.00	17,850.00
United States of America 3¼ percent Treasury bonds, due Oct. 15, 1945; nos. 67226F-67229K, 67230L, 67231A-67239K, 67240L, 67241A; 16 at $1,000 each	16,000.00	16,600.00	17,080.00
United States of America 3¼ percent Treasury notes, series A-1936, due Aug. 1, 1936; nos. 21203-C/21206-F; 4 at $1,000 each; nos. 2994-D, 6859-K; 2 at $5,000 each; nos. 15093-C, 18288-J; 2 at $10,000 each	34,000.00	35,147.50	35,232.50
United States of America 2⅛ percent Treasury notes,* series A-1939, due June 15, 1939; nos. 41779-41783; 5 at $10,000 each	50,000.00	50,328.13	51,796.88
Vicksburg, Shreveport & Pacific R. R. Co. prior lien mortgage 6 percent renewed at 5 percent, gold, due Nov. 1, 1915, extended to Nov. 1, 1940; nos. 561, 661, 794, 982, 1323; 5 at $1,000 each	5,000.00	5,050.00	4,750.00
Total	2,558,775.00	2,509,960.63	2,345,429.64

Statement of assets and liabilities, June 30, 1935—Continued

ASSETS

[Securities purchased during the fiscal year 1934-35 are indicated thus (*)]

	Face value	Book value	Market value June 30, 1935
PREFERRED STOCKS			
*Atchison, Topeka & Santa Fe Ry. Co. preferred, par $100, 200 shares	$20,000.00	$14,685.00	$17,475.00
*Johns-Manville Corporation cumulative 7 percent preferred, par $100, 100 shares	10,000.00	12,415.00	12,300.00
*Tidewater Associated Oil Co. 6 percent cumulative convertible preferred, par $100, 200 shares	20,000.00	16,815.00	19,750.00
*United States Gypsum Co. preferred, par $100, 30 shares	3,000.00	4,417.50	4,575.00
Total preferred stocks	53,000.00	48,332.50	54,100.00
COMMON STOCKS			
American Can Co. common, par $25, 200 shares	5,000.00	18,515.00	27,500.00
Atchison, Topeka & Santa Fe Ry. Co. common, par $100, 300 shares	30,000.00	18,102.50	14,400.00
Atlantic Refining Co. common, par $25, 500 shares	12,500.00	13,272.50	13,062.50
Continental Can Co., Inc., common, par $20, 300 shares (*100 shares received as a stock dividend during 1934–35)	6,000.00	13,335.00	24,675.00
Corn Products Refining Co. common, par $25, 250 shares	6,250.00	21,368.67	18,750.00
E. I. du Pont de Nemours & Co. common, par $20, 300 shares	6,000.00	28,507.50	30,300.00
*Endicott Johnson Corporation common, par $50, 500 shares	25,000.00	30,037.50	32,500.00
General Motors Corporation common, par $10, 700 shares	7,000.00	21,227.50	22,925.00
*Hazel-Atlas Glass Co. common, par $25, 250 shares	6,250.00	24,808.90	26,375.00
National Biscuit Co. common, par $10, 500 shares	5,000.00	27,106.98	15,000.00
Norfolk & Western Railway Co. common, par $100, 160 shares	16,000.00	26,876.90	28,240.00
Northern Pacific Ry. Co. common, par $100, 400 shares	40,000.00	9,650.00	7,850.00
*Owens-Illinois Glass Co. common, par $25, 250 shares	6,250.00	23,058.90	24,625.00
Pennsylvania R. R. Co. common, par $50, 500 shares	25,000.00	15,887.50	11,375.00
*Sherwin-Williams Co. common, par $25, 300 shares	7,500.00	25,556.88	30,150.00
Socony-Vacuum Oil Co., Inc., common, par $15, 1,000 shares	15,000.00	12,525.00	13,000.00
Standard Oil Co. of New Jersey common, par $25, 600 shares	15,000.00	24,077.50	27,975.00
Union Oil Co. of California common, par $25, 500 shares	12,500.00	10,625.00	8,937.50
United States Gypsum Co. common, par $20, 400 shares	8,000.00	17,572.50	22,450.00
United States Smelting, Refining & Mining Co. common, par $50, 200 shares	10,000.00	14,285.00	21,800.00
United States Steel Corporation common, par $100, 400 shares	40,000.00	18,002.50	13,350.00
Westinghouse Electric & Manufacturing Co. common, par $50, 100 shares	5,000.00	4,365.00	5,287.50
F. W. Woolworth Co. common, par $10, 600 shares	6,000.00	26,402.50	36,975.00
Total	315,250.00	440,167.23	477,502.50
Air Reduction Co., Inc., common, no par, 200 shares		20,825.00	28,400.00
*American Chicle Co., common, no par, 300 shares		22,252.50	26,737.50
American Cyanamid Co. B common, no par, 200 shares		2,587.50	4,300.00
American Radiator & Standard Sanitary Corporation common, no par, 1,000 shares		15,462.50	14,625.00
Bethlehem Steel Corporation common, no par, 500 shares		16,937.50	13,375.00
Burroughs Adding Machine Co. common, no par, 824 shares (*24 shares received as a stock dividend during 1934–35)		12,675.00	14,008.00
Caterpillar Tractor Co. common, no par, 800 shares		17,337.50	38,800.00
Columbia Gas & Electric Corporation common, no par, 200 shares		4,100.00	1,450.00
First National Stores, Inc., common, no par, 300 shares		17,236.50	16,500.00
General Electric Co. common, no par, 900 shares		21,055.00	23,062.50
W. T. Grant Co. common, no par, 500 shares		16,575.00	16,750.00
Hercules Powder Co. common, no par, 500 shares		24,290.00	41,500.00
International Business Machines Corporation common, no par, 204 shares (*4 shares received as a stock dividend during 1934–35)		26,471.50	36,108.00
International Nickel Co. of Canada, Ltd., common, no par, 1,000 shares		19,275.00	27,500.00
Johns-Manville Corporation common, no par, 300 shares		14,530.25	15,525.00
Libbey-Owens-Ford Glass Co. common, no par, 700 shares		21,092.50	20,825.00
Otis Elevator Co., common, no par, 100 shares		2,062.50	1,725.00
*Parke, Davis & Co. common, no par, 1,000 shares		36,500.00	44,000.00
J. C. Penney Co. common, no par, 600 shares		27,165.00	44,550.00
*Radio Corporation of America common, no par, 25 shares (received as a stock dividend during 1934–35)		100.00	159.38
Republic Steel Corporation common, no par, 200 shares		3,562.50	2,625.00
Sears, Roebuck & Co. common, no par, 500 shares		20,250.00	21,000.00
Standard Oil Co. of California common, no par, 200 shares		7,920.50	6,800.00

Statement of assets and liabilities, June 30, 1935—Continued

ASSETS

[Securities purchased during the fiscal year 1934-35 are indicated thus (*)]

	Face value	Book value	Market value June 30, 1935
COMMON STOCKS—continued			
Timken Roller Bearing Co. common, no par, 700 shares......	....	$20,092.50	$27,475.00
Union Carbide & Carbon Corporation common, no par, 200 shares..	....	8,455.00	12,250.00
Total..............	....	398,817.25	500,050.38
Total common stocks..	....	838,984.48	977,552.88
Total common and preferred stocks........................	....	887,316.98	1,031,652.88
Total securities, including common and preferred stocks.	....	3,397,277.61	3,377,082.52

SUMMARY

Book value of securities as above, including common and preferred stocks....................		$3,397,277.61
Bank balance June 30, 1935, American Security & Trust Co.: National Academy of Sciences proper..	$40,562.76	
Less amount due Bank of New York & Trust Co...................................	2.75	
		40,560.01
Advanced to National Academy of Sciences, special............................		2,000.00
Income receivable:		
Carnegie endowment fund income account, N. A. S., 1935................		2,174.78
Carnegie endowment fund income account, N. R. C., 1935................		10,000.00
·Property account (buildings and grounds at cost):		
Building...	$1,448,644.82	
Grounds...	185,764.50	
		1,634,409.32
Property account (equipment at cost)..		9,998.05
Total assets..		5,096,419.77

LIABILITIES

	Income	Capital		Income	Capital
General fund:			Fund for oceanographic research, uninvested....	$7,085.12	
Invested.............	$3,700.00	....	Gibbs fund:		
Uninvested..........	9,892.57		Invested.............	....	$5,545.50
Agassiz fund, invested..	....	$50,000.00	Uninvested..........	2,989.87	
Bache fund:			Gould fund:		
Invested.............	....	60,000.00	Invested.............	1,512.50	16,702.50
Uninvested..........	1,030.17		Uninvested..........	14,714.79	3,297.50
Billings fund, invested..	....	22,313.39	Grand Canyon project, uninvested....	24.19	
Building construction fund:			Hale lectureship, uninvested....	385.55	
Invested.............			Hartley fund:		
Uninvested..........	3,120.18		Invested.............	....	1,200.00
Building site fund:			Uninvested..........	516.06	
Invested.............	7,543.25		Joseph Henry fund:		
Uninvested..........	5,218.65		Invested.............	....	40,163.50
Carnegie Corporation, special, uninvested....	11,849.90		Uninvested..........	1,209.42	
Carnegie Endowment Fund:			Investment reserve fund, uninvested....	[1]584,126.46	
Invested.............	....	3,036,329.11	Marsh fund:		
Uninvested..........	....	513,670.89	Invested.............	....	20,000.00
John J. Carty Medal and Award:			Uninvested..........	696.63	
Invested.............	....	24,742.50	Murray fund:		
Uninvested..........	2,548.94	257.50	Invested.............	....	6,000.00
Comstock fund:			Uninvested..........	4,270.33	
Invested.............	....	9,743.75	National Parks problems, uninvested....	1,864.87	
Uninvested..........	5,340.62	2,662.27	National Research fund, uninvested....		
Consolidated fund, uninvested....	1,269.28		Nealley fund, invested....	....	19,555.55
Draper fund:			Proceedings:		
Invested.............	....	10,000.00	Academy account:		
Uninvested..........	1,270.74		Invested.........	995.75	....
Elliot fund:			Uninvested......	3,792.33	....
Invested.............	....	8,000.00			
Uninvested..........	1,755.30				

[1] Debit.

Statement of assets and liabilities June 30, 1935—Continued

LIABILITIES—Continued

	Income	Capital		Income	Capital
Proceedings—Continued. Joint account: Uninvested	$6, 595. 63		Income payable to National Research Council, 1935, uninvested	$10, 000. 00	
Emergency fund: Uninvested	3, 327. 79		Total	[1] 448, 171. 56	$3, 900, 183. 96
Publication fund for research, uninvested			Total income		[1] 448, 171. 56
Scientific publication fund, uninvested	1, 683. 52		Total capital		3, 900, 183. 96
Smith fund:					
Invested	1, 478. 25	$10, 000. 00	Total income and capital		3, 452, 012. 40
Uninvested	5, 571. 55		Capital invested in property		1, 634, 409. 32
Thompson fund:			Capital invested in equipment		9, 998. 05
Invested		9, 125. 00			
Uninvested	2, 251. 34	875. 00	Total liabilities		5, 096, 419. 77
Walcott fund:					
Invested		4, 865. 00	Consolidated investment fund:		
Uninvested	304. 32	135. 00			
Watson fund:			Invested		251, 361. 25
Invested	1, 000. 00	23, 178. 75	Uninvested	1, 269. 28	1, 416. 69
Uninvested	3, 049. 87	1, 821. 25			
Appropriations under custodian of buildings and grounds, uninvested	1, 095. 62		Total	1, 269. 28	252, 777. 94

[1] Debit.

General fund, National Academy of Sciences, from July 1, 1934, to June 30, 1935

RECEIPTS

	Budget July 1, 1934, to June 30, 1935	Actually received July 1, 1934, to June 30, 1935	Budget balance June 30, 1935
Interest on investments:			
Agassiz fund	$2, 500. 00	$2, 763. 49	[1] $263. 49
Nealley fund	750. 00	863. 39	[1] 113. 39
Annual dues from members	1, 325. 00	1, 425. 00	[1] 100. 00
Refund		1. 50	[1] 1. 50
Total	4, 575. 00	5, 053. 38	[1] 478. 38
Balance from previous year	18, 000. 00	18, 990. 56	[1] 990. 56
	22, 575. 00	24, 043. 94	[1] 1, 468. 94

[1] In excess of budget.

DISBURSEMENTS

	Budget July 1, 1934, to June 30, 1935	Actually disbursed July 1, 1934, to June 30, 1935	Budget balance June 30, 1935
Treasurer's office:			
Auditor's fees	$200. 00	$200. 00	
Bond of treasurer	25. 00	25. 00	
Miscellaneous expenses	300. 00	288. 14	$11. 86
Transfer to investment reserve fund, 5 percent of income	375. 00	181. 34	193. 66
Total	900. 00	694. 48	205. 52
Home secretary's office:			
Executive secretary's salary	600. 00	600. 00	
Stationery and miscellaneous office expenses	400. 00	399. 60	.40
Reference books	50. 00	45. 72	4. 28
Binding	50. 00	29. 00	21. 00
Printing, multigraphing and engraving	250. 00	236. 06	13. 94
Express and telegrams	250. 00	178. 50	71. 50
Total	1, 600. 00	1, 488. 88	111. 12

General fund, National Academy of Sciences, from July 1, 1934, to June 30, 1935—
Continued

DISBURSEMENTS—Continued

	Budget July 1, 1934, to June 30, 1935	Actually disbursed July 1, 1934, to June 30, 1935	Budget balance June 30, 1935
Annual meeting	$900.00	$891.65	$8.35
Autumn meeting	500.00	442.13	57.87
Total	1,400.00	1,333.78	66.22
Election of members	350.00	339.80	10.20
Memoirs, editorial	200.00	83.25	116.75
Printing of Biographical Memoirs	900.00	899.67	.33
Current publications, preparation for distribution	150.00	128.16	21.84
Postage, regular	250.00	216.68	33.32
Contingent fund	300.00	73.93	226.07
Library binding	500.00		500.00
Expenses of members attending executive committee of council of the Academy	300.00	192.74	107.26
Total	2,950.00	1,934.23	1,015.77
Total for all	6,850.00	5,451.37	1,398.63
Surplus	15,725.00	18,592.57	
Grand total	22,575.00	24,043.94	

Appropriations under custodian of buildings and grounds, July 1, 1934, to June 30, 1935

RECEIPTS

	Budget July 1, 1934, to June 30, 1935	Actually received July 1, 1934, to June 30, 1935	Budget balance June 30, 1935
From Carnegie endowment fund	$44,667.00	$42,492.22	$2,174.78
Refund	12.00	12.00	
Total	44,679.00	42,504.22	2,174.78

DISBURSEMENTS

	Budget July 1, 1934, to June 30, 1935	Actually disbursed July 1, 1934, to June 30, 1935	Budget balance June 30, 1935
Salaries, office of custodian of buildings and grounds	$6,780.00	$6,780.00	
Salaries, employees, building	23,611.00	23,115.51	$495.49
Coal	1,500.00	1,489.99	10.01
Electricity	1,815.00	1,815.00	
Gas	20.00	9.00	11.00
Contingent fund, maintenance of building	5,922.22	5,840.67	81.55
Maintenance of exhibits	3,537.00	3,234.26	302.74
Total, 1933–37	43,185.22	42,284.43	900.79
Insurance, 1933–37	3,987.56	2,891.94	**1,095.62**
Balance July 1, 1934 .... $471.17			
Appropriated July 1, 1934 .... 1,493.78			
Total 1,964.95			
Expended July 1, 1934, to June 30, 1935 .... 869.33			
Balance June 30, 1935 .... 1,095.62			
Total	47,172.78	45,176.37	1,996.41

Reversions June 30, 1935, amounting to $900.79, have been credited to "Carnegie Endowment Fund, Income Account, N. A. S., 1935."

Condensed statement of receipts and disbursements, National Academy of Sciences, July 1, 1934, to June 30, 1935

RECEIPTS

Balance July 1, 1934, as per last report			$22,154.90
Cash receipts:			
Academy Proceedings:			
Annual dues	$1,425.00		
Reprints and separates	25.50		
		$1,450.50	
Joint Proceedings:			
Subscriptions	1,852.96		
Reprints and separates	1,350.43		
National Research Council	2,500.00		
		5,703.39	
General fund, annual dues		1,425.00	
Bank of New York & Trust Co		97.32	
Carnegie Corporation, special: Contribution by Carnegie Corporation of New York		5,000.00	
Fund for oceanographic research:			
Contribution by General Education Board	$1,731.56		
Royalties	11.25		
Thomas G. Thompson, refunds	43.77		
		1,786.58	
General fund, refund		1.50	
Scientific publication fund:			
Royalties	$3.08		
Joel Stebbins, refund	49.16		
		52.24	
Total income from investments		137,185.27	
Maintenance of exhibits, refund		12.00	
			152,713.80
Total			174,868.70

DISBURSEMENTS

General fund:			
Treasurer's office:			
Auditor's fees	$200.00		
Bond of treasurer	25.00		
Miscellaneous expenses (not including $159.14 fees to financial advisers)	129.00		
		$354.00	
Home secretary's office:			
Executive secretary's salary	600.00		
Stationery and miscellaneous office expenses	399.60		
Reference books	45.72		
Binding	29.00		
Printing, multigraphing, and engraving	236.06		
Express and telegrams	178.50		
		1,488.88	
Annual meeting	891.65		
Autumn meeting	442.13		
Election of members	339.80		
Memoirs, editorial	83.25		
Printing of Biographical Memoirs	899.67		
Current publications, preparation for distribution	128.16		
Postage, regular	216.68		
Contingent fund	73.93		
Expenses of members attending executive meetings of council of the Academy	192.74		
		3,268.01	
			$5,110.89

Condensed statement of receipts and disbursements, National Academy of Sciences, July 1, 1934, to June 30, 1935—Continued

DISBURSEMENTS—Continued

Appropriations for maintenance of buildings and grounds, under custodian of buildings and grounds:

Salaries, office of custodian of buildings and grounds	$6,780.00	
Salaries, employees, building	23,115.51	
Coal	1,489.99	
Electricity	1,815.00	
Gas	9.00	
Contingent fund, maintenance of building	5,840.67	
Maintenance of exhibits	3,234.26	
Insurance, 1933–37	869.33	
		$43,153.76
Fees to financial advisers		7,010.62
To National Research Council for general maintenance expenses		43,812.12
Joint Proceedings:		
Salary, managing editor	$750.00	
Printing and distributing	7,213.94	
Expenses:		
Boston office	450.00	
Washington office	263.35	
		8,677.29
Academy Proceedings:		
Commission on real estate		2.14
Fund for oceanographic research:		
Clerical and office expenses	$92.13	
Travel	491.90	
		584.03
Carnegie Corporation, special:		
Committee on the library	277.10	
Government relations allotment	386.45	
Committee on nominations	60.13	
Clerical expenses	552.96	
		1,276.64
National Parks problems:		
Advance to Ansel F. Hall	400.00	
Picture of Crater Lake	320.40	
Miscellaneous expenses	20.00	
		740.40
National research fund: Refunds to contributors		46.94
Publication fund for research:		
Rockefeller Foundation, refund	$239.66	
General Education Board, refund	500.00	
		739.66
Carnegie Endowment fund: Taxes, insurance, and commissions on real estate		2,788.40
Building site fund income, payable to National Research Council for general maintenance expenses		6,000.00
Consolidated fund, real-estate taxes		123.42
Investment reserve fund: Taxes, water rents, and attorney's fees		2,170.10
Payments from trust and other funds:		
Bache fund:		
Cecilia Payne Gaposchkin, grant	$250.00	
Frank C. Jordan, grant	400.00	
T. T. Chen, grant	600.00	
Dean B. McLaughlin, grant	400.00	
Harold Heath, grant	270.00	
H. T. Stetson, grant	250.00	
Curtis W. Sabrosky, grant	225.00	
Office expenses	5.00	
	$2,400.00	
Comstock fund: Commission on real-estate collections	4.34	
Draper fund: Medal and medal box	352.52	

Condensed statement of receipts and disbursements, National Academy of Sciences, July 1, 1934, to June 30, 1935—Continued

DISBURSEMENTS—Continued

Elliot fund:

James P. Chapin, honorarium	$200.00	
Medal and medal box	263.37	
Engrossing	20.00	
		$483.37

Gould fund:

Harlan T. Stetston, grant	180.00	
Astronomical Journal, grant	800.00	
William J. Luyten, grant	250.00	
S. A. Mitchell, grant	500.00	
Helen Sawyer Hogg, grant	300.00	
Taxes on real estate	10.28	
		2,040.28

Hartley fund: Medal and medal box _____ 95.42

Joseph Henry fund:

F. A. Jenkins, grant	$175.00	
T. Wayland Vaughan, grant	13.44	
Frances Bitter, grant	500.00	
James J. Brady, grant	175.00	
T. T. Chen, grant	300.00	
W. D. Hawkins, grant	300.00	
		1,463.44

Marsh fund:

L. D. Boonstra, grant	250.00	
International Hydrographic Bureau, grant	125.00	
Russell M. Logie, grant	100.00	
		475.00

Murray fund:

Medal and medal box	349.56	
Commission on real-estate collections	2.15	
		351.71

Thompson fund:

Medal and medal box	631.82	
Charles Schuchert, honorarium	250.00	
		881.82

Watson fund:

Taxes and commissions on real estate	21.63	
A. O. Leuschner, grant	3,500.00	
		3,521.63

Total payments from trust and other funds	$12,069.53
Total disbursements	134,305.94
Balance June 30, 1935	40,562.76
Grand total	174,868.70

NATIONAL RESEARCH COUNCIL

The disbursements of the National Research Council, under the authority of the National Academy of Sciences, during the year ended June 30, 1935, amounted to $669,876.55. Interest received on temporary investment amounted to $1,300.35.

The investment reserve fund on June 30, 1935, stood at $750.33, an increase for the year of $368.31.

The book value of securities held by the Council on June 30, 1935, was $101,344.39. The following shows the current interest yield on these bonds, according to the valuation used:

	Amount	Yield
		Percent
Face value of bonds held	$102,333.00	3.24
Book value of bonds held	101,344.39	3.31
Market value, June 30, 1935, of bonds held (including one piece of real estate for $25,000, acquired under foreclosure)	103,171.75	3.25

The receipts from various organizations during the year for investigations to be made in cooperation with the National Bureau of Standards amounted to $11,391.01, compared with $11,375 for similar purposes last year.

During the fiscal year ended June 30, 1935, the activities of the Council were supported by funds from various sources, of which the principal are listed below:

(1) For general maintenance expenses of National Research Council:

From the Carnegie endowment fund	$43,812.12
From the Rockefeller Foundation, emergency grant	20,000.00
From the building site fund, National Academy of Sciences, emergency grant	6,000.00
Total available for year ending June 30, 1935	69,812.12
From the Carnegie Corporation of New York, emergency grant, available for year ending June 30, 1936	30,000.00
Total received	99,812.12

The above contributions were the only ones received for the general support of the National Research Council. The Council has disbursed in addition other funds contributed by a large number of organizations and individuals for specific purposes named by the donors. The diversity of these research projects is indicated by the following list of receipts, which are several times larger than receipts for general maintenance.

(2) From the Rockefeller Foundation:

For National Research fellowships in physics, chemistry, and mathematics, year 1934 (R. F. 29131 and R. F. 31052)	41,053.87
For the same purpose, year 1935 (R. F. 31052)	37,500.00
For the same purpose, year 1936 (R. F. 34169)	150.00
For fellowships in medicine, year 1934 (R. F. 39060 and R. F. 31054)	20,016.56
For the same purpose, year 1935 (R. F. 33041)	15,000.00
For fellowships in the biological sciences, year 1934 (R. F. 29004, R. F. 29005, R. F. 31053)	77,880.26
For the same purpose, year 1935 (R. F. 31053)	27,000.81
For international biological abstracts, year 1934 (R. F. 34005)	38,906.28
For the same purpose, year 1935 (R. F. 34152)	34,449.02
For fellowships in the biological sciences, studying abroad, year 1934 (R. F. 29132)	249.80
For indices of Biological Abstracts, years 1934, 1935 (R. F. 34005)	18,685.01
For sex research fund, 1935	64,485.17
For annual tables	2,000.00
For committee on drug addiction, Rockefeller Foundation, year 1934	24,153.85
For the same purpose, year 1935	26,377.87
For mitogenetic radiation	7,500.00

(2) From the Rockefeller Foundation—Continued.

For research aid fund, year 1934	$30, 000. 00
For the same purpose, years 1935-37	25, 000. 00
Total from the Rockefeller Foundation	490, 408. 50

(3) From the General Education Board, for committee on child development, year 1935 .... 6, 300. 00

(4) From various organizations for the Highway Research Board ... 20, 255. 13

(5) From Navy Department for airships investigation 1, 017. 88

(6) From various organizations for work to be conducted in cooperation with National Bureau of Standards:

For investigations on steel structures	181. 96
For acoustic properties of materials	1, 590. 00
For thermal properties of liquids	2, 209. 32
For fire resistance of materials	500. 00
For current meter investigations	9. 73
For thermal investigations	300. 00
For corrosion-resistance of pipe materials	400. 00
For impermanency of records	5, 000. 00
For soil-corrosion investigations	1, 200. 00
Total	11, 391. 01

(7) From various organizations:

For American Bureau of Welding	1, 113. 75
For committee on electrical insulation, 1935	215. 00
For committee on drug addiction, Squibb fellowships, 1935.	1, 400. 00
For committee on drug addiction, Merck fellowship, 1935.	700. 00
For committee on drug addiction, Mallinckrodt fellowship, 1935	1, 000. 00
For bibliography of economic geology	250. 00
For pharmaceutical researches	25. 00
For National Live Stock and Meat Board fellowships	2, 000. 00
For effects of radiation on living organisms	188. 20
For national intelligence tests	1, 909. 06
For child-development abstracts	1, 471. 30
For royalties, international critical tables	1, 340. 00
For Science Advisory Board	18, 000. 00
Total receipts during the year from all sources	672, 249. 48

Receipts and disbursements, National Research Council, from July 1, 1934, to June 30, 1935

RECEIPTS

Appropriation	Received during year	Previously reported	Transfers and other credits	Budget	Budget balance, June 30, 1935
Rockefeller Foundation:					
National research fellowships (R. F. 29131 and R. F. 31052), 1934	$41, 053. 87	$73, 946. 13	----------	$115, 000. 00	----------
National research fellowships (R. F. 31052), 1935	37, 500. 00	------------	----------	37, 500. 00	----------
National research fellowships (R. F. 34169), 1936	150. 00	------------	----------	50, 000. 00	$49, 850. 00
Research fellowships in medicine (R. F. 29060 and R. F. 31054), 1934	20, 016. 56	19, 983. 44	----------	40, 000. 00	----------
Research fellowships in medicine (R. F. 33041), 1935	15, 000. 00	------------	----------	15, 000. 00	----------
Fellowships in the biological sciences (R. F. 29004, R. F. 29005, R. F. 31053), 1934	77, 880. 26	22, 119. 74	----------	100, 000. 00	----------

Receipts and disbursements, National Research Council, from July 1, 1934, to June 30, 1935—Continued

RECEIPTS—Continued

Appropriation	Received during year	Previously reported	Transfers and other credits	Budget	Budget balance, June 30, 1935
Rockefeller Foundation—Continued.					
Fellowships in the biological sciences (R. F. 31052), 1935	$27,000.81			$37,500.00	$10,499.19
International biological abstracts (R. F. 34005), 1934	38,906.28	$26,092.82	$0.90	65,000.00	
International biological abstracts (R. F. 34152), 1935	34,449.02			65,000.00	30,550.98
Fellowships in the biological sciences, studying abroad (R. F. 29132), 1934	249.80	9,750.20		10,000.00	
Indices of Biological Abstracts (R. F. 34005), 1934–35	18,685.01	1,314.99		20,000.00	
Indices of Biological Abstracts (R. F. 34152), 1935				10,000.00	10,000.00
Sex research fund, 1935	64,485.17		514.83	65,000.00	
Committee on drug addiction, Rockefeller Foundation, 1934	24,153.85	25,864.66		50,018.51	
Committee on drug addiction, Rockefeller Foundation, 1935	26,377.87			26,377.87	
Mitogenetic radiation	7,500.00	2,500.00		10,000.00	
Research aid fund, 1934	30,000.00	20,000.00		50,000.00	
Research aid fund, 1935–37	25,000.00			25,000.00	
Committee on Child Development, General Education Board, 1935	6,300.00			6,300.00	
Rotating fund, physics committees	1,589.03	13,542.10		15,131.13	
Highway research board, 1934	1,250.00	20,672.29		21,922.29	
Highway research board, 1935	19,005.13		4,806.92	23,812.05	
American Bureau of Welding	1,113.75	16,123.13		17,236.88	
Committee on electrical insulation, 1935	215.00			215.00	
Bibliography of economic geology	250.00	31,802.22		32,052.22	
Research fund, committee on sedimentation	158.40	2,325.87		2,484.27	
Committee on drug addiction, Merck fellowship, 1935	700.00			700.00	
Committee on drug addiction, Mallinckrodt fellowship, 1935	1,000.00			1,000.00	
Committee on drug addiction, Squibb fellowships, 1935	1,400.00			1,400.00	
Pharmaceutical researches	25.00	560.00		585.00	
National Live Stock and Meat Board fellowships	2,000.00	46,788.87		48,788.87	
Effects of radiation on living organisms	188.20	131,365.39		131,553.59	
National intelligence tests, 1921	1,909.06	23,351.64		25,260.70	
Child development abstracts	1,471.30	12,013.39		13,484.69	
Navy Department appropriation for airships investigation	1,017.88			1,017.88	
Royalty account, international critical tables	1,340.60	51,280.74		52,621.34	
Annual tables	2,000.00	51,747.61		53,747.61	
Science Advisory Board	18,000.00	32,000.00	25.00	50,025.00	
Investigations on steel structures	181.96	15,895.00		16,076.96	
Acoustic properties of materials	1,590.00	21,662.99		23,252.99	
Thermal properties of liquids	2,209.32	5,663.75		7,873.07	
Fire resistance of materials	500.00	11,690.00		12,190.00	
Current meter investigations	9.73	3,200.00		3,209.73	
Thermal investigations	300.00	1,902.91		2,202.91	
Corrosion-resistance of pipe materials	400.00	2,400.00		2,800.00	
Impermanency of records	5,000.00			5,000.00	
Soil-corrosion investigations	1,200.00			1,200.00	
Carnegie endowment fund	43,812.12		187.88	54,000.00	10,000.00
Rockefeller Foundation, National Research Council, 1935	20,000.00			20,000.00	
Building site fund	6,000.00			6,000.00	
Carnegie Corporation of New York, emergency grant	30,000.00			30,000.00	
Total	660,544.98	697,559.88	5,535.53	1,474,540.56	110,900.17
Interest on bonds	1,300.35				
Miscellaneous receipts	5,474.76				
Reimbursements	4,929.39				
Total receipts	672,249.48				
July 1, 1934, cash in banks	66,581.81				
Grand total	738,831.29				

Receipts and disbursements, National Research Council, from July 1, 1934, to June 30, 1935—Continued

DISBURSEMENTS

Division	Disbursed during year	Previously reported	Reversions and other charges	Budget	Budget balance, June 30, 1935
I. Federal relations:					
General maintenance, 1935			$50.00	$50.00	
II. Foreign relations:					
General maintenance, 1934		$60.00	40.00	100.00	
General maintenance, 1935	$8.05		91.95	100.00	
III. States relations:					
General maintenance, 1935			50.00	50.00	
IV. Educational relations:					
General maintenance, 1935	15.72		84.28	100.00	
Division of educational relations, Commonwealth Fund		7,304.01		8,051.55	$747.54
V. Physical sciences:					
General maintenance, 1935	868.49		45.73	914.22	
Revolving fund for publication of mathematical books		4,180.81		5,374.70	1,193.89
Physics committees, 1932		912.50		1,500.00	587.50
Research fellowships (R. F. 29131 and R. F. 31052) 1934	74,523.51	40,676.49		115,200.00	
Research fellowships (R. F. 31052) 1935	31,131.13			37,500.00	6,368.87
Research fellowships (R. F. 34169) 1936	150.00			50,000.00	49,850.00
Rotating fund, physics committees	1,075.61	8,931.75		15,131.13	5,123.77
VI. Engineering and industrial research:					
General maintenance, 1934	15.86	1,283.14		1,299.00	
General maintenance, 1935	1,119.73		15.21	1,200.00	65.06
Highway research board, 1934		17,115.37	4,806.92	21,922.29	
Highway research board, 1935	18,309.19			23,812.05	5,502.86
American Bureau of Welding	1,113.75	16,123.13		17,236.88	
Structural steel investigation	990.83	15,733.48		22,526.68	5,802.37
Heat transmission	50.00	41,974.54		43,154.77	1,130.23
Fundamental research in welding	51.53	1,825.99		1,950.00	72.48
Committee on electrical insulation, 1935	82.96			215.00	132.04
VII. Chemistry and chemical technology:					
General maintenance, 1934	4.23	1,292.00	3.77	1,300.00	
General maintenance, 1935	765.85		434.15	1,200.00	
VIII. Geology and geography:					
General maintenance, 1934		1,444.00		1,500.00	
General maintenance, 1935	1,456.00		1.34	1,400.00	
Bibliography of economic geology	2,477.56	26,562.14		32,052.22	3,012.73
Research fund, committee on sedimentation	378.30	801.04		2,484.27	1,304.93
International cartographic exhibit, Warsaw	27.55	17.93	104.52	150.00	
Committee on stratigraphy				75.00	75.00
IX. Medical sciences:					
General maintenance, 1935	578.07		621.93	1,200.00	
Sex research fund, 1934	862.02	74,305.61		75,167.63	
Sex research fund, 1935	63,074.11			65,000.00	1,925.89
Fellowships in medicine (R. F. 29060 and R. F. 31054), 1934	15,502.61	24,512.21		40,014.82	
Fellowships in medicine (R. F. 33041), 1935	14,014.39			15,200.00	1,185.61
Committee on drug addiction, Squibb fellowships, 1934	651.08	2,148.92		2,800.00	
Committee on drug addiction, Squibb fellowships, 1935	748.92			1,400.00	651.08
Committee on drug addiction, Rockefeller Foundation, 1934	26,902.01	23,116.50		50,018.51	
Committee on drug addiction, Rockefeller Foundation, 1935	23,517.91			26,377.87	2,859.96
Survey of tropical diseases	10.42	1,901.72		2,503.00	590.86
Committee on drug addiction, Merck fellowship, 1935	700.00			700.00	
Committee on drug addiction, Mallinckrodt fellowship, 1935	1,000.00			1,000.00	
X. Biology and agriculture:					
General maintenance, 1933		1,218.16	100.00	1,318.16	
General maintenance, 1935	1,100.00			1,100.00	
Committee on forestry		7,295.43		10,029.99	2,734.56
Food and nutrition committee		9,219.18		9,675.00	455.82

Receipts and disbursements, National Research Council, from July 1, 1934, to June 30, 1935—Continued

DISBURSEMENTS—Continued

Division	Disbursed during year	Previously reported	Reversions and other charges	Budget	Budget balance, June 30, 1935
X. Biology and agriculture—Continued.					
Fellowships in the biological sciences:					
(R. F. 29004, R. F. 29005, R. F. 31053), 1934	$69,252.46	$31,157.04	----------	$100,409.50	----------
Fellowships in the biological sciences (R. F. 31053), 1935	19,732.44	----------	----------	37,500.00	$17,767.56
National Live Stock and Meat Board Fellowships	1,812.50	45,888.03	----------	48,788.87	1,088.34
Committee on infectious abortion, 1929–30	----------	324.88	$25.12	350.00	----------
National committee on botanical nomenclature	----------	2,973.25	----------	3,060.85	87.60
Pharmaceutical researches	----------	265.16	----------	585.00	319.84
Effects of radiation on living organisms	6,995.75	119,442.80	4,839.71	131,553.59	275.33
Biological abstracts, 1929	7.90	4,992.10	----------	5,000.00	----------
Committee on infectious abortion, Certified Milk Producers' Association	.08	1,499.92	----------	1,500.00	----------
Committee on infectious abortion, Commonwealth Fund, 1931	.36	6,599.64	----------	6,600.00	----------
Committee on research publications, 1932	----------	393.92	206.08	600.00	----------
Fellowships in the biological sciences, studying abroad (R. F. 29132), 1934	249.80	9,750.20	----------	10,000.00	----------
International biological abstracts (R. F. 34005), 1934	33,040.15	31,958.95	.90	65,000.00	----------
International biological abstracts (R. F. 34152), 1935	31,690.84	----------	----------	65,000.00	33,309.16
Indices of biological abstracts (R. F. 34005), 1934–35	17,076.27	2,923.73	----------	20,000.00	----------
Indices of biological abstracts (R. F. 34152), 1935	3,114.55	----------	----------	10,000.00	6,885.45
Mitogenetic radiation	8,593.08	705.20	----------	10,000.00	701.72
Committee on radiation	4,763.28	----------	----------	4,839.71	76.43
XI. Anthropology and Psychology:					
General maintenance, 1934	37.82	1,258.54	6.90	1,303.26	----------
General maintenance, 1935	1,057.86	----------	142.14	1,200.00	----------
National intelligence tests, 1921	183.50	16,842.64	----------	25,260.70	8,234.56
Visual limitations for motorists	376.28	5,285.98	----------	5,662.93	.67
Child development abstracts	712.41	7,967.86	----------	13,484.69	4,804.42
Psychiatric investigations	352.52	6,732.71	----------	10,000.00	2,914.77
Committee on child development, General Education Board, 1935	6,300.00	----------	----------	6,300.00	----------
Tennessee Valley archaeology	264.39	1,735.61	----------	2,000.00	----------
Expenses and supplies, 1934	35.90	3,864.80	----------	3,900.70	----------
Expenses and supplies, 1935	4,116.15	----------	11.55	4,346.27	218.57
New equipment, general, 1934	91.23	208.77	----------	300.00	----------
New equipment, general, 1935	728.24	----------	19.76	885.00	137.00
Salaries, 1935	72,186.00	----------	307.50	72,495.00	1.50
Telephone and telegraph, 1934	227.96	2,277.38	----------	2,505.34	----------
Telephone and telegraph, 1935	2,279.08	----------	636.17	3,165.25	250.00
Executive board:					
General maintenance, 1935	1,208.82	----------	.27	1,209.09	----------
American Geophysical Union: **General** maintenance, 1935	400.00	----------	----------	400.00	----------
Publications and publicity:					
General maintenance, 1932	----------	10,600.00	1,500.00	12,100.00	----------
General maintenance, 1934	2,030.01	2,091.76	183.28	4,305.05	----------
General maintenance, 1935	1,095.59	----------	11.03	1,506.62	400.00
National Academy Proceedings and subscriptions, 1935	2,500.00	----------	----------	2,500.00	----------
International auxiliary language	----------	9,630.02	----------	10,065.00	434.98
International critical tables	----------	327,679.52	7,203.11	335,319.75	437.12
Royalty account, international critical tables	----------	51,280.74	1,340.60	52,621.34	----------
Annual tables	1,966.11	51,659.90	----------	53,747.61	121.60
Auditor's fees, 1934	300.00	----------	----------	300.00	----------
Research aid fund (R. F. 30105)	847.04	98,331.43	----------	101,172.49	1,994.02
Research aid fund (R. F. 32010), 1932–33	4,482.01	53,944.05	----------	60,447.69	2,021.63
Research aid fund (R. F. 32109), 1933	2,203.74	47,473.76	----------	50,080.35	402.85

Receipts and disbursements, National Research Council, from July 1, 1934, to June 30, 1935—Continued

DISBURSEMENTS—Continued

Division	Disbursed during year	Previously reported	Reversions and other charges	Budget	Budget balance, June 30, 1935
Executive board—Continued.					
Research aid fund (R. F. 33121), 1934___	$28,090.00	$18,860.00	_____	$50,000.00	$3,050.00
Research aid fund (R. F. 34172), 1935-37_	22,131.54	_____	_____	25,000.00	2,868.46
Attorney's fees, 1935_____	200.00	_____	$100.00	300.00	_____
Science Advisory Board_____	23,871.39	18,922.10	_____	50,025.00	7,231.51
Navy Department appropriation for airships investigation_____	1,017.88	_____	_____	1,017.88	_____
Problems of refrigeration_____	108.33	_____	_____	984.19	875.86
Methods of locking screw threads_____	634.68	45,280.32	_____	45,915.00	_____
Investigations on steel structures_____	163.35	15,713.09	_____	16,076.96	200.32
Fatigue properties of alclad aluminum_	47.15	1,452.85	_____	1,500.00	_____
Investigation of propeller fans_____	9.73	1,231.27	_____	1,241.00	_____
Concrete and clay investigations_____	93.88	7,006.12	_____	7,100.00	_____
Brick work_____	540.82	459.18	_____	1,000.00	_____
Acoustic properties of materials_____	1,183.34	21,477.21	_____	23,252.99	592.44
Investigation of physics of plumbing systems_____	7.56	2,719.10	_____	3,200.00	473.345
Thermal properties of liquids_____	2,313.11	5,548.08	_____	7,873.07	11.88
Fire resistance of materials_____	644.13	11,530.39	_____	12,190.00	15.48
Properties of volatile liquid fuels_____	3.32	2,796.68	_____	2,800.00	_____
Current meter investigations_____	797.20	352.66	_____	3,209.73	2,059.87
Thermal investigations_____	90.66	1,442.04	_____	2,202.91	670.218
Corrosion-resistance of pipe materials____	768.11	2,031.89	_____	2,800.00	_____
Impermanency of records_____	175.00	_____	_____	5,000.00	4,825.00
Soil-corrosion investigations_____	356.50	_____	_____	1,200.00	843.50
Research information service:					
General maintenance, 1934_____	_____	9,587.50	2.50	9,590.00	_____
General maintenance, 1935_____	614.22	_____	8,529.53	9,395.00	251.25
Investment reserve fund_____	426.69	_____	1,743.17	2,920.19	750.33
Total disbursements_____	669,876.55	1,454,106.82	33,259.12	2,356,220.31	198,977.82
June 30, 1935, cash in banks_____	68,954.74	_____	_____	_____	_____
Grand total_____	738,831.29	_____	_____	_____	_____

National Research Council condensed balance sheet as of June 30, 1935

ASSETS

[Securities purchased during the fiscal year 1934-35 are indicated thus (*)]

	Face value	Book value	Market value June 30, 1935
SECURITIES			
General maintenance fund:			
Mortgage notes secured by first mortgage on real estate_____	$10,333.00	$10,333.00	$10,333.00
Real estate owned 322-324 West 41st St., New York, N. Y._____	25,000.00	25,000.00	25,000.00
*Canadian Pacific Ry. Co. 4-percent perpetual consolidated debentures; nos. G34505, G34506; 2 at $1.000 each_____	2,000.00	1,800.78	1,775.00
Government of the Argentine Nation 6-percent external sinking-fund gold bonds, due June 1, 1959; nos. M16652, M33319-M33322; 5 at $1,000 each_____	5,000.00	5,017.50	4,868.75
Kingdom of Norway 6-percent 20-year external loan sinking-fund gold bonds, due Aug. 1, 1944; nos. 621, 1361, 1362, 16940-16944, 21025, 24896; 10 at $1,000 each_____	10,000.00	10,395.00	10,675.00
Pennsylvania Power & Light Co. 4½-percent first-mortgage bonds, due Apr. 1, 1981; nos. 50364-50379; 16 at $1,000 each_____	16,000.00	15,400.00	16,900.00
*12 Federal land banks 3¼-percent consolidated Federal farm loan bonds, due May 1, 1955; nos. 46152B-46156F, 46157H, 46158J-46160L, 46161A-46166F, 46167H, 46168J, 46170L, 46171A-46176F, 46177H, 46178J; 26 at $1,000 each_____	26,000.00	26,195.00	26,520.00
International critical tables:			
*Canadian Pacific Ry. Co. 4-percent perpetual consolidated debentures: nos. G47151-G47153, G48964, G86931, G88057-G88059; 8 at $1,000 each_____	8,000.00	7,202.11	7,100.00
Total_____	102,333.00	101,344.39	103,171.75

National Research Council condensed balance sheet of June 30, 1935—Con.

SUMMARY

Total book value of securities as above	$101,344.39
Cash in banks June 30, 1935	68,954.74
Due from Bank of New York & Trust Co	5,490.94
Income receivable, as shown under column "Budget balance", receipts, p. 101	110,900.17
National Academy of Sciences, special, advances from various funds	8,000.00
Property account, equipment at cost	33,625.40
Total assets	328,324.64

LIABILITIES

Capital invested in property	$33,625.40
Current liabilities:	
Division appropriations as shown under column "Budget balance", disbursements, p. 104	198,977.82
Unappropriated fund, general	48,518.31
National Academy of Sciences, special	10,000.00
Carnegie Corporation of New York, emergency grant	30,000.00
International critical tables: Canadian Pacific Ry. Co. 4 percent debentures	7,203.11
Total liabilities	328,324.64

July 31, 1935.

ARTHUR KEITH, *Treasurer.*

REPORT OF THE AUDITING COMMITTEE

SEPTEMBER 13, 1935.

Dr. FRANK R. LILLIE,
  President, National Academy of Sciences,
    2101 Constitution Ave., Washington, D. C.

DEAR PRESIDENT LILLIE: Following recent past practice, authorized by section 5, article V, of the bylaws of the Academy, the auditing committee engaged the services of a firm of certified public accountants, William L. Yaeger & Co., to prepare a detailed audit of the treasurer's accounts. This firm, after a systematic examination of the accounts of the treasurer of the Academy and of the Research Council and of all securities, has submitted a report of its findings with exhibits attached. This report is transmitted herewith as a part of the auditing committee's report, for the records of the Academy and the Council.

In compliance with the requirements of the bylaws the accountants have (1) verified the record of receipts and disbursements maintained by the treasurer and the agreement of book and bank balances; (2) examined all securities in the custody of the treasurer and the custodian of securities—the Bank of New York & Trust Co.—and have found them to agree with the treasurer's records and have compared the stated income of such securities with the receipts of record, setting forth the results of this comparison as exhibit B; (3) examined all vouchers covering disbursements for account of the Academy including the National Research Council together with the authority therefor and have compared them with the Treasurer's record of expenditures; and (4) have examined and verified the account of the Academy with each trust fund. They report the books of account well and accurately kept and the securities securely cared for and conveniently filed.

The committee has compared the accountant's report with that of the treasurer and accepts the opinion of the accountants that the treasurer's report correctly sets forth the financial condition of the Academy and the National Research Council and is an accurate statement of financial operations for the fiscal year 1935.

Very respectfully yours,

        W. W. COBLENTZ,
        GEORGE L. STREETER,
        W. C. MENDENHALL, *Chairman,*
    Auditing Committee, National Academy of Sciences, 1935.

NATIONAL ACADEMY OF SCIENCES

1. CONSTITUTION

[As amended and adopted Apr. 17, 1872, and further amended Apr. 20, 1875; Apr. 21, 1881; Apr. 19, 1882; Apr. 18, 1883; Apr. 19, 1888; Apr. 18, 1895; Apr. 20, 1899; Apr. 17, 1902; Apr. 18, 1906; Nov. 20, 1906; Apr. 17, 1907; Nov. 20, 1907; Apr. 20, 1911; Apr. 16, 1912; Apr. 21, 1915; Nov. 11, 1924; Nov. 9, 1925; Oct. 18, 1927; Nov. 18, 1929; Sept. 18, 1930; Apr. 24, 1933]

PREAMBLE

Empowered by the act of incorporation enacted by Congress, and approved by the President of the United States on the 3d day of March, A. D. 1863, and in conformity with amendments to said act approved July 14, 1870, June 20, 1884, and May 27, 1914, the National Academy of Sciences adopts the following amended constitution and bylaws:

ARTICLE I.—OF MEMBERS

SECTION 1. The Academy shall consist of members, members emeriti, and foreign associates. Members must be citizens of the United States.

SEC. 2. Members who, from age or inability to attend the meetings of the Academy, wish to resign the duties of active membership may, at their own request, be transferred to the roll of members emeriti by a vote of the Academy.

SEC. 3. The Academy may elect 50 foreign associates.

SEC. 4. Members emeriti and foreign associates shall have the privilege of attending the meetings and of reading and communicating papers to the Academy, but shall take no part in its business, shall not be subject to its assessments, and shall be entitled to a copy of the publications of the Academy.

ARTICLE II.—OF THE OFFICERS

SECTION 1. The officers of the Academy shall be a president, a vice president, a foreign secretary, a home secretary, and a treasurer, all of whom shall be elected for a term of 4 years, by a majority of votes present, at the annual meeting of the year in which the current terms expire. The date of expiration of the terms of office shall be June 30. In case of a vacancy the election shall be held in the same manner at the meeting when such vacancy occurs or at the next stated meeting thereafter, as the Academy may direct, and shall be for a term expiring on June 30 of the fourth year after that in which the election takes place. A vacancy in the office of treasurer or home secretary may, however, be filled by appointment of the president of the Academy until the next stated meeting of the Academy.

COUNCIL

SEC. 2. The officers of the Academy, together with six members to be elected by the Academy, and the chief executive officer of the National Research Council (provided he be a member of the Academy) shall constitute a council for the transaction of such business as may be assigned to them by the constitution or the Academy.

EXECUTIVE COMMITTEE

SEC. 3. There shall be an executive committee of the council of the Academy, composed of seven members, consisting of the president and vice president of the Academy, the chief executive officer of the National Research Council (provided he be a member of the Academy), the home secretary of the Academy, the treasurer of the Academy, and additional members of the council of the Academy appointed by the president.

Their term as members of the executive committee shall be coterminous with the term of their other office.

Except those powers dealing with nominations to membership in the Academy, the executive committee between the meetings of the council shall have all the powers of the council of the Academy, unless otherwise ordered by the council.

The members of the executive committee of the Academy shall by virtue of their office be members of the executive board of the National Research Council and shall represent the Academy at all its meetings.

The president and home secretary of the Academy shall, respectively, be chairman and secretary of the executive committee.

In the absence of the president and the vice president or home secretary the executive committee may select from among its members a chairman or a secretary pro tem.

The executive committee shall keep regular minutes and shall report all of its proceedings to the council of the Academy for their information.

Unless otherwise ordered by the council of the Academy or the executive committee, the executive committee shall meet once in each calendar month, and a special meeting may be called at any time by authority of the chairman, on reasonable notice.

Four members of the executive committee shall constitute a quorum. Letter ballots shall not be valid unless ratified at a meeting.

CUSTODIAN OF BUILDINGS AND GROUNDS

SEC. 4. On recommendation of the president, the council of the Academy shall appoint a "custodian of buildings and grounds", who, except where otherwise provided in the constitution and bylaws, shall have custody of all buildings, grounds, furniture, and other physical property belonging to the National Academy of Sciences or the National Research Council, or entrusted to their care.

He shall be responsible for and shall manage and administer these under such generic rules as the council of the Academy may make, and shall approve all vouchers for pay rolls and disbursements that come under authorized budget items or are specifically authorized by the council of the Academy for the maintenance and operation of the Academy's and the Research Council's physical property.

He shall hold office at the pleasure of the council of the Academy and shall receive such salary as it may agree and shall give such bond for the faithful performance of his duties as it may require.

He shall prepare and present to the finance committee of the Academy the buildings and grounds division of the general budget.

ADVISORY COMMITTEE ON BUILDINGS AND GROUNDS

· He shall be chairman of a joint advisory committee of five on buildings and grounds, of which two members shall be appointed by the president of the Academy from the Academy council, and two from the executive board of the National Research Council, which committee shall decide, subject to the approval of the council of the Academy, all questions of allocation of space and use of public rooms.

FINANCE COMMITTEE

SEC. 5. There shall be a finance committee, of which the treasurer shall be chairman, consisting of the president of the Academy (or in his absence the vice president), the treasurer, the chief executive officer of the National Research Council (provided he be a member of the Academy), and two other members of the Academy appointed by the president, one of whom shall be a member of the executive board of the National Research Council.

It shall be the duty of the finance committee to provide for the safe custody of all financial resources of the Academy and to determine all matters relating to the purchase and sale of its securities.

It shall be the further duty of the finance committee to prepare and present to the council of the Academy for adoption the "general budget", made up of the three "divisional budgets", of the Academy proper, of the Research Council, and of buildings and grounds, which divisional budgets shall be presented to the finance committee, respectively, by the treasurer, the chief executive officer of the National Research Council, and the custodian of buildings and grounds.

The finance committee shall be empowered to employ competent investment counsel (hereinafter called the financial adviser) to advise with the committee upon the purchase and sale of all securities, mortgages or other investments.

PRESIDENT

SEC. 6. The president of the Academy, or, in case of his absence or inability to act, the vice president, shall preside at the meetings of the Academy, of the Academy council, and of the executive board of the National Research Council; shall name all committees except such as are otherwise especially provided for; shall refer investigations required by the Government of the United States to members especially conversant with the subjects, and report thereon to the Academy at its meeting next ensuing; and, with the council, shall direct the general business of the Academy.

EXPERTS ON COMMITTEES

It shall be competent for the president, in special cases, to call in the aid, upon committees, of experts or men of special attainments not members of the Academy.

GOVERNMENT REQUESTS

The president shall be ex-officio a member of all committees empowered to consider questions referred to the Academy by the Government of the United States.

SECRETARIES

SEC. 7. The foreign and home secretaries shall conduct the correspondence proper to their respective departments, advising with the president and council in cases of doubt, and reporting their action to the Academy at one of the stated meetings in each year.

It shall be the duty of the home secretary to give notice to the members of the place and time of all meetings, of all nominations for membership, and of all proposed amendments to the constitution.

It shall be the duty of the home secretary to keep the minutes of each business and scientific session, and after approval to enter these upon the permanent records of the Academy.

TREASURER

SEC. 8. The treasurer shall attend to all receipts and disbursements of the Academy, giving such bond and furnishing such vouchers as the council may require. He shall collect all dues, assessments, and subscriptions, and keep a set of books showing a full account of receipts and disbursements and the condition of all funds of the Academy. He shall be the custodian of the corporate seal of the Academy.

ADMINISTRATIVE COMMITTEE, NATIONAL RESEARCH COUNCIL

SEC. 9. The president, vice president, home secretary, and treasurer shall be members of the administrative committee of the National Research Council and shall represent the Academy at all its meetings.

ARTICLE III.—OF THE MEETINGS

ACADEMY

SECTION 1. The Academy shall hold one stated meeting, called the annual meeting, in April of each year in the city of Washington, and another stated meeting, called the autumn meeting, at a place to be determined by the council. The council shall also have power to fix the date of each meeting.

Special business meetings of the Academy may be called, by order of eight members of the council, at such place and time as may be designated in the call.

Special scientific meetings of the Academy may be held at times and places to be designated by a majority of the council.

SEC. 2. The names of the members present at each session of a meeting shall be recorded in the minutes, and 20 members shall constitute a quorum for the transaction of business.

SEC. 3. Scientific sessions of the Academy, unless otherwise ordered by a majority of the members present, shall be open to the public; sessions for the transaction of business shall be closed.

COUNCIL OF THE ACADEMY

SEC. 4. Stated meetings of the council shall be held during the stated or special meetings of the Academy, and four members shall constitute a quorum for the transaction of business. Special meetings of the council may be convened at the call of the president and two members of the council or of four members of the council.

DUES IN ARREARS

SEC. 5. No member whose dues are in arrears shall vote at any business meeting of the Academy.

ARTICLE IV.—OF ELECTIONS AND REGULATIONS

SECTION 1. All elections of officers and members shall be by ballot, and each election shall be held separately.

SEC. 2. The time for holding an election of officers shall be fixed by the Academy at least 1 day before the election is held.

COUNCIL OF THE ACADEMY

SEC. 3. The election of six members of the council shall be as follows:

At the annual meeting in April 1907, six members of the council to be elected, of whom two shall serve for 3 years, two for 2 years, and two for 1 year, their respective terms to be determined by lot. Each year thereafter the terms of two members shall expire and their successors, to serve for 3 years, shall be elected at the annual meeting in each year. The date of expiration of the terms shall be June 30.

SECTIONS

SEC. 4. The Academy shall be divided by the council into sections representing the principal branches of scientific research. Each section shall elect its own chairman to serve for 3 years. The chairman shall be responsible to the Academy for the work of his section.

NOMINATIONS

Proposals for nomination to membership may be made in writing by any five members of the Academy and addressed to the home secretary; each such proposal shall be accompanied by a record of the scientific activities of the person proposed and a list of his principal contributions to science, in triplicate; and with a statement as to the sections to which the name proposed shall be submitted for consideration. Such proposals as have been received by the home secretary prior to October 15 shall upon that date be sent by him to the chairman of the sections designated, with a copy of the record and list of contributions.

Nominations to membership in the Academy shall be made in writing and approved by two-thirds of the members voting in a section on the branch of research in which the person nominated is eminent, or by a majority of the council in case there is no section on the subject, or by a majority (however distributed) of the members voting in any two sections. The nomination shall be sent to the home secretary by the chairman of the section before January 1 of the year in which the election is to be held, and each nomination shall be accompanied by a list of the principal contributions of the nominee to science. This list shall be printed by the home secretary for distribution among the members of the Academy.

ELECTION PROCEDURE

SEC. 5. Election of members shall be held at the annual meeting in Washington in the following manner: There shall be two ballots— a preference ballot, which must be transmitted to the home secretary in advance of the annual meeting, and a final ballot, to be taken at the meeting.

PREFERENCE BALLOT

Preference ballot.—From the list of nominees submitted by the home secretary, each member shall select and inscribe on a ballot, to an extent not greater than one-half, nor less than one-third the list, those names which he prefers, as these limits shall be interpreted by the home secretary in his discretion, and announced by him, no weight being attached to the order of the names, and ballots not complying with these requirements being discarded. A list of the nominees shall then be prepared, on which the names shall be entered in the order of the number of votes received by each. In case two or more nominees have the same number of votes on this preference list, the order in which they shall be placed on the list shall be determined by a majority vote of members present.

After the preference list has been made up in the manner stated, the chairman of any section having two or more nominees on the list may, when its first nominee is reached, request the permission of the Academy to interchange the positions (on the preference list) of the nominees of his section, without altering in any way the positions of nominees from other sections. If a majority of the members of the Academy present favor permitting a section to make such interchange of its own nominees, it shall be done before proceeding further with the election.

FINAL BALLOT

A vote shall be taken on the nominee who appears first on the preference list, and he shall be declared elected if he receives two-thirds of the votes cast and not less than 30 votes in all. A vote shall then be taken in similar manner on the nominee standing second on the preference list, and so on until all the nominees on the preference list shall have been acted on, or until 15 nominees shall have been elected, or until the total membership of the Academy shall have reached 300.

ELECTION

. Not more than 15 members shall be elected at one annual meeting.
It shall be in order at any point in the course of an election to move that the election be closed. If two-thirds of those present vote in favor of such motion, it shall prevail and the election shall thereupon terminate.

Before and during elections a discussion of the merits of nominees will be in order.

Sec. 6. Every member elected shall accept his membership, personally or in writing, before the close of the next stated meeting after the date of his election. Otherwise, on proof that the secretary has formally notified him of his election, his name shall not be entered on the roll of members.

FOREIGN ASSOCIATES

Sec. 7. Foreign associates may be nominated by the council and may be elected at the annual meeting by a two-thirds vote of the members present.

CERTIFICATES OF ELECTION

Sec. 8. A diploma, with the corporate seal of the Academy and the signatures of the officers, shall be sent by the appropriate secretary to each member on his acceptance of membership, and to foreign associates on their election.

RESIGNATIONS

Sec. 9. Resignations shall be addressed to the president and acted on by the Academy.

DUES, NONPAYMENT

Sec. 10. Whenever a member has not paid his dues for 4 successive years, the treasurer shall report the fact to the council, which may report the case to the Academy with the recommendation that the person thus in arrears be declared to have forfeited his membership. If this recommendation be approved by two-thirds of the members present, the said person shall no longer be a member of the Academy, and his name shall be dropped from the roll.

ARTICLE V.—OF SCIENTIFIC COMMUNICATIONS, PUBLICATIONS, AND REPORTS

SCIENTIFIC SESSIONS

Section 1. Communications on scientific subjects shall be read at scientific sessions of the Academy, and papers by any member may be read by the author or by any other member, notice of the same having been previously given to the secretary.

Sec. 2. Any member of the Academy may read a paper from a person who is not a member and shall not be considered responsible for the facts or opinions expressed by the author, but shall be held responsible for the propriety of the paper.

Persons who are not members may read papers on invitation of the council or of the committee of arrangements.

PUBLICATIONS

Sec. 3. The Academy may provide for the publication, under the direction of the Council, of Proceedings, scientific Memoirs, Biographical Memoirs, and Reports.

PROCEEDINGS

The Proceedings shall be primarily a medium of first publication for original articles in brief form of permanent scientific value.

MEMOIRS

The scientific Memoirs shall provide opportunity for the publication of longer and more detailed scientific investigations.

The Biographical Memoirs shall contain an appropriate record of the life and work of the deceased members of the Academy.

ANNUAL REPORT

An annual report shall be presented to Congress by the president and shall contain the annual reports of the treasurer and the auditing committee, a suitable summary of the reports of the committees in charge of trust funds, and a record of the activities of the Academy for the fiscal year immediately preceding, and other appropriate matter. This report shall be presented to Congress by the president after authorization by the council. It shall also be presented to the Academy at the annual meeting next following.

TREASURER'S REPORT

The treasurer shall prepare a full report of the financial affairs of the Academy at the end of the fiscal year. This report shall be submitted to the council for approval and afterward presented to the Academy at the next stated meeting. He shall also prepare a supplementary financial statement to December 31 of the ensuing fiscal year for presentation at the annual meeting.

GOVERNMENT REQUESTS

Sec. 4. Propositions for investigations or reports by the Academy shall be submitted to the council for approval, except those requested by the Government of the United States, which shall be acted on by the president, who will in such cases report their results to the Government as soon as obtained and to the Academy at its next following stated meeting.

Sec. 5. The advice of the Academy shall be at all times at the disposition of the Government upon any matter of science or art within its scope.

ARTICLE VI.—OF TRUST FUNDS AND THEIR ADMINISTRATION

TRUSTS

SECTION 1. Devises, bequests, donations, or gifts having for their object the promotion of science or the welfare of the Academy may be accepted by the council for the Academy. Before the acceptance of any such trust the council shall consider the object of the trust and all conditions or specifications attaching thereto. The council shall make a report of its action to the Academy.

MEDALS

SEC. 2. Medals and prizes may be established in accordance with the provisions of trusts or by action of the Academy.

TRUST FUND COMMITTEES

SEC. 3. Unless otherwise provided by the deed of gift, the income of each trust fund shall be applied to the objects of that trust by the action of the Academy on the recommendation of a standing committee on that fund.

ARTICLE VII.—OF ADDITIONS AND AMENDMENTS

Additions and amendments to the constitution shall be made only at a stated meeting of the Academy. Notice of a proposition for such a change must be submitted to the council, which may amend the proposition, and shall report thereon to the Academy. Its report shall be considered by the Academy in committee of the whole for amendment.

The proposition as amended, if adopted in committee of the whole, shall be voted on at the next stated meeting, and if it receives two-thirds of the votes cast it shall be declared adopted.

Absent members may send their votes on pending changes in the constitution to the home secretary in writing, and such votes shall be counted as if the members were present.

2. BYLAWS

[In accordance with a resolution of the Academy, taken at its meeting on Apr. 21, 1915, the bylaws are arranged in groups, and each group is numbered to correspond with the article of the constitution to which it relates]

I

1. The holders of the medal for eminence in the application of science to the public welfare shall be notified, like members, of the meetings of the Academy, and invited to participate in its scientific sessions.

II

1. The proper secretary shall acknowledge all donations made to the Academy, and shall at once report them to the council for its consideration.

2. The home secretary shall keep a record of all grants of money or awards of prizes or medals made from trust funds of the Academy. The record for each grant of money shall include the following items: Name of fund, date and number of the grant, name and address of recipient, amount of grant, and date or dates of payment, purpose of grant, record of report of progress, and resulting publications.

3. The executive secretary, who may be a nonmember of the Academy, shall receive a salary to be fixed by the council.

4. The treasurer shall keep the home secretary informed of all warrants received from directors of trust funds not controlled by the Academy and of the date or dates of payment of all warrants.

GOVERNMENT REQUESTS

5. The treasurer is authorized to defray, when approved by the president, all the proper expenses of committees appointed to make scientific investigations at the request of departments of the Government, and in each case to look to the department requesting the investigation for reimbursement to the Academy.

TREASURER, NATIONAL RESEARCH COUNCIL

6. The treasurer is authorized to act as the treasurer ex officio of the National Research Council.

BURSAR

7. The treasurer shall have the assistance of a salaried and bonded officer, the bursar, who shall be chosen by the finance committee and be directly responsible to the treasurer.

INVESTMENTS

8. All investments and reinvestments of either principal or accumulations of income of the trust and other funds of the Academy shall be made by the treasurer, in accordance with the decisions of the finance committee, in the corporate name of the Academy, in the manner and in the securities designated or specified in the instruments creating the several funds, or in the absence of such designation or specification, in bonds of the United States or of the several States, or in bonds or notes secured by first mortgages on real estate, in investments legal for savings banks under the laws of Massachusetts or New York, or in other securities recommended by the financial adviser.

The treasurer may invest the capital of all trust funds of the Academy which are not required by the instruments creating such funds to be kept separate and distinct, in a consolidated fund, and shall apportion the income received from such consolidated fund among the various funds composing the same in the proportion that each of said funds shall bear to the total amount of funds so invested: *Provided, however,* That the treasurer shall at all times keep accurate accounts showing the amount of each trust fund, the proportion of the income from the consolidated fund to which it is entitled, and the expenses and disbursements properly chargeable to such fund.

The treasurer shall have authority, with the approval of the finance committee, to sell, transfer, convey, and deliver in the corporate name and for the benefit of the Academy any stocks, bonds, or other securities standing in the corporate name.

CUSTODIAN OF SECURITIES

9. On the recommendation of the finance committee, the council shall contract with a bank, trust company, or corresponding fiduciary institution to serve as the custodian of securities, including all of the Academy's personal property in the form of bonds, mortgages, and other securities, to collect the income from them, to protect the Academy in respect to expirations, reissues, and notifications, and to buy or sell securities on the order of the treasurer, as approved by the finance committee.

CONTRACTS

10. No contract shall be binding upon the Academy which has not been first approved by the council.

DUES

11. The assessments required for the support of the Academy shall be fixed by the Academy on the recommendation of the council and shall be payable within the calendar year for which they are assessed.

FINANCE COMMITTEE MEETINGS

12. The finance committee may invite to be present at any of its meetings the chief executive officer of the Research Council, the custodian of buildings and grounds, and the bursar, but they shall not vote.

III

ANNUAL MEETING—DATES AND PROCEDURES

1. At the business sessions of the Academy the order of procedure shall be as follows:

(1) Chair taken by the president, or, in his absence, by the vice president.

(2) Roll of members called by home secretary (first session of the meeting only).

(3) Minutes of the preceding session read and approved.

(4) Stated business.

(5) Reports of president, secretaries, treasurer, and committees.

(6) Business from council.

(7) Other business.

RULES OF ORDER

2. The rules of order of the Academy shall be those of the Senate of the United States, unless otherwise provided by the constitution or bylaws of the Academy.

3. In the absence of any officer, a member shall be chosen to perform his duties temporarily, by a plurality of viva-voce votes, upon open nomination.

DEATHS

4. At each meeting the president shall announce the death of any members since the preceding meeting. As soon as practicable thereafter he shall designate a member to write—or to secure from some other source approved by the president—a biographical notice of each deceased member.

LOCAL COMMITTEE

5. For the annual meeting a local committee of five members, appointed for each meeting, and the home secretary shall constitute the committee of arrangements, of which the home secretary shall be chairman. For the autumn meeting a member of the local group shall be chairman of the local committee, of which the home secretary shall be a member ex officio.

SCIENTIFIC PROGRAM

It shall be the duty of the committee of arrangements to prepare the scientific program for the annual meeting, and for this purpose it shall be empowered to solicit papers from members or others. It shall also be empowered to ascertain the length of time required for reading papers to be presented at the scientific sessions of the Academy and, when it appears advisable, to limit the time to be occupied in their presentation or discussion.

The committee of arrangements shall meet not less than 2 months previous to each meeting. It shall prepare the detailed program of each day and in general shall have charge of all business and scientific arrangements for the meeting for which it is appointed.

PAPERS—TIME LIMIT

6. No paper requiring more than 15 minutes for its presentation shall be accepted unless by invitation of the committee of arrangements.

No speaker shall occupy more than 30 minutes for presentation of papers during the scientific sessions of a single meeting of the Academy, except by invitation of the committee of arrangements.

Time shall not be extended except by vote of the Academy, and then not to exceed 5 minutes. The presiding officer shall warn speakers 2 minutes before the expiration of their time.

The discussion of individual papers shall be limited not to exceed 5 minutes, and the total time for discussion by any one speaker for all scientific sessions in any one meeting shall not exceed 15 minutes, unless approved by the Academy.

In order that adequate opportunity be given for the discussion of papers on the program, the committee of arrangements shall, in making up the program for the scientific sessions, allot not more than 80 percent of the available time of each session to the actual reading of papers.

If the number of papers accepted is too large to be presented in the scientific sessions, provision shall be made for holding two or more sessions simultaneously.

In arranging the program the committee of arrangements shall group the papers as nearly as practicable according to subject.

No paper shall be entered upon the printed program of scientific sessions unless the title is in the hands of the committee of arrangements at least 2 weeks in advance of the meeting. In the event that titles are received later, they shall be placed in order of receipt at the end of the list and read, if there is time. Such supplementary titles shall be conspicuously posted.

IV

SECTIONS

1. The term of service of each chairman of a section shall be 3 years, to date from the closing session of the April meeting next following his election. Chairmen of sections shall be chosen by mail ballot, the member receiving the highest number of votes cast to be deemed elected. It shall be the duty of each retiring chairman to conduct the election of his successor, and to report the results of the election to the home secretary before the April meeting at which his term of service expires. Should any section fail to elect a chairman before November 1, the president is empowered to appoint a temporary chairman to serve until the April meeting next following. No chairman shall be eligible for reelection for two consecutive terms.

NOMINATION BALLOTS

2. The chairman of each section of the Academy shall submit to the members of his section, not later than November 1 of each year, a ballot containing the names of all those persons who received not less than two votes in the nominating ballot of the preceding year, or have been submitted to the chairman by the home secretary, and of any other persons who were newly proposed for consideration on the nominating ballots of the preceding year. Each member of the section shall be expected to return this ballot to the chairman within 2 weeks with his signature and with crosses against the names of those persons whom he is prepared to endorse for nomination. Each member may also write upon the ballot in a place provided for the purpose any new names he desires to have included in the ballot to be submitted to the section in the following years. The vote resulting from this ballot shall be regarded as informal.

The chairman shall then submit to the members of his section a new ballot showing the results of the informal vote; and each member shall be expected to return this ballot to the chairman with his signature and with crosses placed against the names of three persons whom he ju es to be most worthy of nomination. In order to secure an adequate number of nominations, the chairman, when necessary, shall obtain by personal solicitation a fuller vote of his section or shall submit to the section a supplementary formal ballot.

The chairman shall then certify to the home secretary, prior to January 1, the names of all persons who have been voted for on the formal ballots, together with a statement of the number of votes each received and of the number of members voting. Of these, all persons who receive the votes of two-thirds of the members voting in the section in cases voted upon by one section only, or the votes of one-half (however distributed) of the members voting in any two sections in cases voted upon by more than one section, shall be considered nominated.

3. Nominations for membership shall give the full name, residence, and the official positions successively held by the candidate, in addition to the list of his contributions to science required by the constitution.

PREFERENCE BALLOT

4. Preference ballots for the election of members shall be sealed in a blank envelope, which shall be enclosed in another bearing the name of the sender, and which shall be addressed to the home secretary, who shall cause the ballots to be tabulated for use at the election. If in any case it is impossible to determine who cast the ballot, or if the latter contain more or fewer than the number of names provided for in article IV, section 5, of the constitution, the ballot shall be rejected, but minor defects in a ballot shall be disregarded when the intent of the voter is obvious.

5. All discussions of the claims and qualifications of nominees at meetings of the Academy shall be held strictly confidential, and remarks and criticisms then made may be communicated to no person who was not a member of the Academy at the time of the discussion.

V

PROCEEDINGS

1. The publication of the Proceedings shall be under the general charge of the council, which shall have final jurisdiction upon all questions of policy relating thereto.

The National Academy of Sciences and the National Research Council shall cooperate in the publication of the Proceedings, beginning with volume VII.

MEMOIRS

2. Memoirs may be presented at any time to the home secretary, who shall report the date of their reception at the next session; but no Memoir shall be published unless it has been read or presented by title before the Academy.

Before publication all Biographical and scientific Memoirs must be referred to the committe on publication, who may, if they deem best, refer any Memoir to a special committee, appointed by the president, to determine whether the same should be published by the Academy.

3. Memoirs shall date, in the records of the Academy, from the date of their presentation to the Academy, and the order of their presentation shall be so arranged by the secretary that, so far as may be convenient, those upon kindred topics shall follow one another.

4. The annual report of the treasurer shall contain—
(1) A concise statement of the source, object, and amount of all trust funds of the Academy.
(2) A condensed statement of receipts and expenditures.
(3) A statement of assets and liabilities.
(4) Accounts with individual funds.
(5) Such other matter as he considers appropriate.

AUDITING COMMITTEE

5. The accounts of the treasurer shall, between July 1 and August 1 of each year, be audited under the direction of a committee of three members to be appointed by the president at the annual meeting of the Academy. It shall be the duty of the auditing committee to verify the record of receipts and disbursements maintained by the treasurer and the agreement of book and bank balances; to examine all securities in the custody of the treasurer and the custodian of securities and to compare the stated income of such securities with the receipts of record; to examine all vouchers covering disbursements for account of the Academy, including the National Research Council, and the authority therefor, and to compare them with the treasurer's record of expenditures; to examine and verify the account of the Academy with each trust fund. The auditing committee may employ an expert accountant to assist the committee. The reports of the treasurer and auditing committee shall be presented to the Academy at the autumn meeting and shall be published with that of the president to Congress. They shall be distributed to the members in printed form at the annual meeting.

VI

PROPERTY

1. All apparatus and other materials of permanent value purchased with money from any grant from a trust fund shall be the property of the Academy unless specific exception is made in the grant or by subsequent action of the council. Receipts for all such property shall be signed by the grantee and shall be forwarded to the home secretary, who shall file them with the custodian of buildings and grounds. All apparatus and unused material of value acquired in this way shall be delivered to the custodian of buildings and grounds on completion of the investigation for which the grant was made, or at any time on demand of the council, and the custodian of buildings and grounds shall give an appropriate release therefor.
2. A stamp corresponding to the corporate seal of the Academy shall be kept by the secretaries, who shall be responsible for the due markings of all books and other objects to which it is applicable.
Labels or other proper marks of similar device shall be placed upon objects not admitting of the stamp.
3. The fiscal year of the Academy shall end on June 30 of each year.

VII

STANDING COMMITTEES—RESEARCH FUNDS

1. Standing committees of the Academy on trust funds, the income of which is applied to the promotion of research, shall consist of three or five members. In order to secure rotation in office in such committees, when not in conflict with the provisions of the deeds of gift, the term of service on a committee of three members shall be 3 years; on a committee of five members the term shall be 5 years.

2. The annual reports of the committees on research funds shall, so far as the Academy has authority to determine their form, give a current number to each award, stating the name, position, and address of the recipient; the subject of research for which the award is made and the sum awarded; and in later annual reports the status of the work accomplished under each award previously made shall be announced, until the research is completed, when announcement of its completion, and, if published, the title and place of publication shall be stated, and the record of the award shall be reported as closed.

VIII

AMENDMENTS

1. Any bylaw of the Academy may be amended, suspended, or repealed on the written motion of any two members, signed by them, and presented at a stated meeting of the Academy, provided the same shall be approved by a majority of the members present.

3. ORGANIZATION OF THE ACADEMY

JUNE 30, 1935

	Expiration of term
Campbell, W. W., president	June 30, 1935
Day, A. L., vice president	June 30, 1937
Morgan, T. H., foreign secretary	June 30, 1938
Wright, F. E., home secretary	June 30, 1935
Keith, Arthur, treasurer	June 30, 1936

ADDITIONAL MEMBERS OF THE COUNCIL

1932–35:	1933–36:	1934–37:
Harrison, R. G.	Compton, K. T.	Adams, Roger
Russell, H. N.	Cattell, J. McKeen	Jennings, H. S.

1933–35:
Bowman, Isaiah, ex officio, as chairman of the National Research Council.[1]

EXECUTIVE COMMITTEE OF THE COUNCIL

Campbell, W. W. (chairman)	Day, A. L.	Russell, H. N.
Bowman, Isaiah[1]	Harrison, R. G.	Wright, F. E.
	Keith, Arthur	

---

[1] The constitution of the Academy specifies that the chairman of the National Research Council be a member of the council of the Academy and a member of the executive committee of the council of the Academy; provided, he be a member of the Academy.

SECTIONS

1. Mathematics

Coble, A. B. (chairman), 1937
Alexander, J. W.
Bateman, Harry
Bell, E. T.
Birkhoff, G. D.
Blichfeldt, H. F.
Bliss, G. A.

Dickson, L. E.
Eisenhart, L. P.
Evans, G. C.
Jackson, Dunham
Kasner, Edward
Lefschetz, Solomon
Miller, G. A.
Moore, R. L.

Morse, Marston
Osgood, W. F.
Ritt, J. F.
Vandiver, H. S.
Van Vleck, E. B.
Veblen, Oswald
White, H. S.
Wiener, Norbert

2. Astronomy

Leuschner, A. O. (chairman), 1938
Abbot, C. G.
Adams, W. S.
Aitken, R. G.
Anderson, J. A.
Babcock, H. D.
Bowie, William
Brown, E. W.

Campbell, W. W.
Curtis, H. D.
Hale, G. E.
Hubble, E. P.
Merrill, P. W.
Mitchell, S. A.
Moore, J. H.
Moulton, F. R.
Ross, F. E.

Russell, H. N.
Schlesinger, F.
Seares, F. H.
Shapley, Harlow
Slipher, V. M.
Stebbins, Joel
Trumpler, R. J.
Wright, W. H.

3. Physics

Hull, A. W. (chairman), 1936
Ames, J. S.
Barus, Carl
Birge, R. T.
Bridgman, P. W.
Coblentz, W. W.
Compton, A. H.
Compton, K. T.
Coolidge, W. D.
Crew, Henry
Davis, Bergen

Davisson, C. J.
Epstein, P. S.
Hall, E. H.
Ives, H. E.
Kemble, E. C.
Lawrence, E. O.
Lyman, Theodore
Mason, Max
Mendenhall, C. E.
Merritt, Ernest
Miller, D. C.
Millikan, R. A.

Nichols, E. L.
Pierce, G. W.
Richtmyer, F. K.
Saunders, F. A.
Slater, J. C.
Thomson, Elihu
Van Vleck, J. H.
Webster, D. L.
Wilson, Edwin B.
Wood, R. W.

4. Engineering

Gherardi, Bancroft (chairman), 1938
Adams, C. A.
Bush, Vannevar
Dunn, Gano
Durand, W. F.
Emmet, W. L. R.

Fletcher, Harvey
Hoover, Herbert
Hovgaard, William
Hunsaker, J. C.
Jewett, F. B.
Kennelly, A. E.
Kettering, C. F.

Modjeski, Ralph
Sauveur, Albert
Stillwell, L. B.
Swasey, Ambrose
Taylor, D. W.
Whitehead, J. B.

5. Chemistry

Kraus, C. A. (chairman), 1938
Adams, Roger
Bancroft, W. D.
Baxter, G. P.
Bogert, Marston T.
Bray, W. C.
Conant, J. B.
Franklin, E. C.
Gomberg, Moses
Gortner, R. A.

Harkins, W. D.
Hildebrand, J. H.
Hudson, C. S.
Hulett, G. A.
Jacobs, W. A.
Johnson, T. B.
Keyes, F. G.
Kohler, E. P.
Lamb, A. B.
Langmuir, Irving
Levene, P. A. T.

Lewis, G. N.
Lind, S. C.
Michael, Arthur
Norris, J. F.
Noyes, A. A.
Noyes, W. A.
Pauling, Linus
Stieglitz, Julius
Tolman, R. C.
Urey, H. C.
Whitney, W. R.

6. *Geology and Paleontology*

Leith, C. K. (chairman), 1936
Allen, E. T.
Berkey, C. P.
Berry, E. W.
Bowen, N. L.
Bowman, Isaiah
Cross, Whitman
Daly, R. A.
Day, A. L.

Johnson, D. W.
Keith, Arthur
Knopf, Adolph
Lawson, A. C.
Leverett, Frank
Lindgren, Waldemar
Longwell, C. R.
Mendenhall, W. C.
Merriam, J. C.
Osborn, H. F.

Palache, Charles
Ransome, F. L.
Reid, H. F.
Ruedemann, Rudolf
Schuchert, Charles
Scott, W. B.
Ulrich, E. O.
Vaughan, T. W.
Willis, Bailey
Wright, F. E.

7. *Botany*

Blakeslee, A. F. (chairman), 1938
Allen, C. E.
Bailey, I. W.
Bailey, L. H.
Campbell, D. H.
Clinton, G. P.
Dodge, B. O.

Duggar, B. M.
East, E. M.
Emerson, R. A.
Fernald, M. L.
Fred, E. B.
Harper, R. A.
Hoagland, D. R.
Howe, M. A.

Jones, L. R.
Kunkel, L. O.
Merrill, E. D.
Osterhout, W. J. V.
Robinson, B. L.
Setchell, W. A.
Stakman, E. C.
Trelease, William

8. *Zoology and Anatomy*

Stockard, C. R. (temporary chairman), 1936
Barbour, Thomas
Bigelow, H. B.
Calkins, G. N.
Castle, W. E.
Chapman, F. M.
Child, C. M.
Coghill, G. E.
Conklin, E. G.
Davenport, C. B.
Detwiler, S. R.
Donaldson, H. H.

Gregory, W. K.
Harrison, R. G.
Harvey, E. N.
Herrick, C. J.
Howard, L. O.
Jennings, H. S.
Kellogg, Vernon
Kofoid, C. A.
Lillie, F. R.
McClung, C. E.
Mark, E. L.
Morgan, T. H.
Muller, H. J.

Parker, G. H.
Pearl, Raymond
Stejneger, Leonhard
Streeter, G. L.
Sturtevant, A. H.
Tennent, D. H.
Wheeler, W. M.
Wilson, Edmund B.
Wilson, H. V. P.
Woodruff, L. L.
Wright, S. G.

9. *Physiology and Biochemistry*

Henderson, L. J. (chairman), 1936
Abel, J. J.
Benedict, F. G.
Benedict, S. R.
Cannon, W. B.
Carlson, A. J.
Chittenden, R. H.

Clark, W. M.
DuBois, E. F.
Erlanger, Joseph
Evans, H. M.
Gasser, H. S.
Henderson, Yandell
Howell, W. H.
Hunt, Reid

McCollum, E. V.
Mendel, L. B.
Northrop, J. H.
Richards, A. N.
Shaffer, P. A.
Sherman, H. C.
Van Slyke, D. D.

10. *Pathology and Bacteriology*

Hektoen, Ludvig (chairman), 1936
Avery, O. T.
Cole, Rufus
Cushing, Harvey
Dochez, A. R.

Ewing, James
Flexner, Simon
Landsteiner, Karl
MacCallum, W. G.
Novy, F. G.
Opie, E. L.

Rivers, T. M.
Rous, Peyton
Sabin, Florence R.
Wells, H. Gideon
Whipple, G. H.
Zinsser, Hans

11. *Anthropology and Psychology*

Seashore, O. E. (chairman), 1938
Angell, J. R.
Boas, Franz
Boring, E. G.
Breasted, J. H.
Cattell, J. McKeen
Dewey, John
Dodge, Raymond

Hooton, E. A.
Hrdlicka, Ales
Hunter, W. S.
Kroeber, A. L.
Lashley, K. S.
Lowie, R. H.
Merriam, C. H.
Miles, W. R.
Pillsbury, W. B.

Sapir, Edward
Stratton, G. M.
Swanton, J. R.
Terman, L. M.
Thorndike, E. L.
Washburn, Margaret F.
Wissler, Clark
Woodworth, R. S.
Yerkes, R. M.

4. STANDING COMMITTEES OF THE ACADEMY

ALBERT NATIONAL PARK

Yerkes, R. M. (chairman).

Chapman, F. M.

Wissler, Clark.

AUDITING COMMITTEE

Mendenhall, W. C. (chairman).

Coblentz, W. W.

Streeter, G. L.

BIOGRAPHICAL MEMOIRS

Davenport, C. B. (chairman).

Hrdlicka, Ales.
Pearl, Raymond.

Thorndike, E. L.
Wright, F. E.

BUILDING COMMITTEE (ORIGINAL JOINT COMMITTEE OF ACADEMY AND RESEARCH COUNCIL ON CONSTRUCTION)

Dunn, Gano (chairman).
Brockett, Paul (secretary).

Hale, G. E.
Howe, H. E.
Kellogg, Vernon.

Merriam, J. C.
Millikan, R. A.
Noyes, A. A.

BUILDINGS AND GROUNDS ADVISORY COMMITTEE (JOINT COMMITTEE OF ACADEMY AND RESEARCH COUNCIL)

Brockett, Paul (chairman).

Day, A. L.
Dunn, Gano.

Richtmyer, F. K.
Wright, F. E.

CALENDAR

Wright, F. E. (chairman).

Campbell, W. W.
Dunn, Gano.

Millikan, R. A.
Russell, H. N.

EXHIBITS (JOINT COMMITTEE OF ACADEMY AND RESEARCH COUNCIL)

Wright, F. E. (chairman).
Brockett, Paul (secretary).
Hale, G. E. (member at large).

Shapley, Harlow (member at large).
The chairman of each of the sections of the Academy.

The chairman of each of the divisions of the Research Council.

Executive committee on exhibits

Wright, F. E. (chairman).
Brockett, Paul (secretary).

Day, A. L.
Hale, G. E.
Kellogg, Vernon.

Merriam, J. C.

FINANCE COMMITTEE

The treasurer of the Academy, chairman ex officio.

The president of the Academy, ex officio (or in his absence, the vice president).

The chairman of the National Research Council, ex officio.
Abbot, C. G.
Dunn, Gano.

FUNDS FOR ACADEMY PURPOSES

Flexner, Simon (chairman).

Kellogg, Vernon.
Lillie, F. R.

Shapley, Harlow.

GOVERNMENT RELATIONS

Merriam, J. C. (chairman and member until May 11, 1935).
Lillie, F. R. (chairman and member from May 11 to June 30, 1935).
The president of the Academy.

The vice president of the Academy.
The chairman of the Research Council.
The chairman of the division of Federal Relations of the Research Council.

The chairman of each of the sections of the Academy.
Wright, F. E.

Subcommittee A (Physical Sciences)

Merriam, J. C. (chairman).
Hull, A. W.
Kohler, E. P.
Leith, C. K.

Stebbins, Joel.
Wilson, Edwin B.
The president of the Academy.

The home secretary of the Academy.

Subcommittee B (Biological Sciences)

Merriam, J. C. (chairman).
Angell, J. R.
Hektoen, Ludvig.
Lillie, F. R.

Merrill, E. D.
Woodworth, R. S.
The president of the Academy.

The home secretary of the Academy.

LIBRARY

———— ———— (chairman)
Adams, W. S.
Cattell, J. McK.

Compton, K. T.
Harkins, W. D.
Henderson, Yandell

Parker, G. H.
Scott, W. B.
Brockett, Paul

Subcommittee

Hudson, C. S. (chairman), 1937
Coblentz, W. W. (vice chairman), 1937

Pearl, Raymond, 1936
Streeter, G. S., 1936

Swanton, John R., 1935

MEMORIALS (BUSTS, PORTRAITS, AND STATUES)

Breasted, J. H. (chairman)
Angell, J. R.

Cushing, Harvey
Day, A. L.
Dunn, Gano

Hale, G. E.
Merriam, J. C.

OCEANOGRAPHY

Bigelow, H. B. (chairman)
Bowie, William

Conklin, E. G.
Day, A. L.
Duggar, B. M.

Merriam, J. C.
Vaughan, T. W.

5. TRUST FUNDS OF THE ACADEMY

ALEXANDER DALLAS BACHE FUND

[$60,000]

Researches in physical and natural science

Board of directors

Curtis, Heber D. (chair-
man)

Osterhout, W. J. V.

Wilson, Edwin B.

JAMES CRAIG WATSON FUND

[$25,000]

Watson medal and the promotion of astronomical research

Trustees

Leuschner, A. O. (chair-
man)

Ross, F. E.

Seares, F. H.

WATSON MEDAL AWARDS

Gould, B. A., 1887
Schoenfeld, Ed., 1889
Auwers, Arthur, 1891

Chandler, S. C., 1894
Gill, Sir David, 1899
Kapteyn, J. C., 1913

Leuschner, A. O., 1915
Charlier, C. V. L., 1924
de Sitter, Willem, 1929

HENRY DRAPER FUND

[$10,000]

Draper medal and investigations in astronomical physics

Members of the committee

Slipher, V. M. (chair-
man), 1937

Merrill, P. W., 1939
Mitchell, S. A., 1940

Shapley, Harlow, 1936
Stebbins, Joel, 1938

HENRY DRAPER MEDAL AWARDS

Langley, S. P., 1886
Pickering, E. C., 1888
Rowland, H. A., 1890
Vogel, H. K., 1893
Keeler, J. E., 1899
Huggins, Sir Wm., 1901
Hale, George E., 1904
Campbell, W. W., 1906
Abbot, C. G., 1910

Deslandres, H., 1913
Stebbins, Joel, 1915
Michelson, A. A., 1916
Adams, W. S., 1918
Fabry, Charles, 1919
Fowler, Alfred, 1920
Zeeman, Pieter, 1921
Russell, H. N., 1922

Eddington, (Sir) Arthur
Stanley, 1924
Shapley, Harlow, 1926
Wright, William Ham-
mond, 1928
Cannon, Annie Jump, 1931
Slipher, V. M., 1932
Plaskett, John Stanley,
1934

J. LAWRENCE SMITH FUND

[$10,000]

J. Lawrence Smith medal and investigations of meteoric bodies

Members of the committee

Moulton, F. R. (chair-
man), 1937

Abbot, C. G., 1936
Allen, E. T., 1938

Brown, E. W., 1940
Ransome, F. L., 1939

J. LAWRENCE SMITH MEDAL AWARDS

Newton, H. A., 1888   Merrill, George P., 1922

BARNARD MEDAL FOR MERITORIOUS SERVICES TO SCIENCE[*]

Discoveries in physical or astronomical science or novel application of science to
purposes beneficial to the human race

Day, Arthur L. (chair-
man)

Campbell, W. W.
Davis, Bergen

Noyes, A. A.
Tolman, R. C.

BARNARD MEDAL AWARDS

Rutherford, (Lord) Ern-
est, 1909
Bragg, (Sir) William
H., 1914

Einstein, Albert, 1921
Bohr, Niels, 1925

Heisenberg, Werner,
1930
Hubble, Edwin, 1935

BENJAMIN APTHORP GOULD FUND

[$20,000]

Researches in astronomy

Board of directors

Moulton, F. R. (chair-
man)

Brown, E. W.

Curtis, H. D.

WOLCOTT GIBBS FUND

[$5,545.50]

Chemical research

[*] Every 5 years the committee recommends the person whom they consider most deserving of the medal, and upon approval by the Academy the name of the nominee is forwarded
to the trustees of Columbia University, who administer the Barnard medal fund.

Board of directors

Kohler, E. P. (chair-   Baxter, G. P.   Franklin, E. C.
man)

CYRUS B. COMSTOCK FUND

[$12,406.02]

Prize awarded every 5 years for most important discovery or investigation in
electricity, magnetism, and radiant energy, or to aid worthy investigations
in those subjects

Members of the committee

Millikan, R. A. (chair-   Coolidge, W. D., 1939   Compton, A. H., 1938
man), 1940   Crew, Henry, 1937   Miller, D. C., 1936

COMSTOCK PRIZE AWARDS

Millikan, R. A., 1913   Duane, William, 1923   Bridgman, P. W., 1933
Barnett, S. J., 1918   Davisson, C. J., 1928

MARSH FUND

[$20,000]

Original research in the natural sciences

Members of the committee

Gregory, W. K. (chair-   Berry, E. W., 1938   Merrill, E. D., 1940
man), 1937   Knopf, Adolph, 1936   Reid, H. F., 1939

AGASSIZ FUND

[$50,000]

General uses of the Academy

MURRAY FUND

[$6,000]

Agassiz medal for contributions to oceanography

Members of the committee

Vaughan, T. Wayland   Johnson, Douglas, 1936   Kofoid, C. A., 1937
(chairman), 1938

AGASSIZ MEDAL AWARDS

Hjort, Johan, 1913   · Weber, Max, 1927   Defant, Albert, 1932
Albert I, Prince of Mon-   Ekman, Vagn Walfrid,   Helland - Hansen, Bjorn,
aco, 1918   1928   1933
Sigsbee, C. D., 1920   Gardiner, J. Stanley, 1929 Gran, Haakon Hasberg,
Pettersson, Otto Sven,   Schmidt, Johannes, 1930   1934
1924   Bigelow, Henry Bryant,   Vaughan, T. Wayland,
Bjerknes, Vilhelm, 1926   1931   1935

MARCELLUS HARTLEY FUND

[$1,200]

Medal for eminence in the application of science to the public welfare

Members of the committee

Cushing, Harvey (chairman), 1937
Ames, J. S., 1936

Conant, J. B., 1938
Donaldson, H. H., 1936
Hoover, Herbert, 1937

Kofoid, C. A., 1938

PUBLIC WELFARE MEDAL AWARDS

(In memory of Marcellus Hartley)

Goethals. G. W., 1914
Gorgas, W. C., 1914
Abbe, Cleveland, 1916
Pinchot, Gifford, 1916
Stratton, S. W., 1917

Hoover, Herbert, 1920
Stiles, C. W., 1921
Chapin, Charles V., 1928
Mather, Stephen Tyng, 1930

Rose, Wickliffe, 1931
Park, William Hallock, 1932
Fairchild, David, 1933
Vollmer, August, 1934

DANIEL GIRAUD ELLIOT FUND

[$8,000]

Medal and honorarium for most meritorious work in zoology or paleontology published each year

Members of the committee

Harrison, Ross G. (chairman)

Osborn, H. F.

Wheeler, W. M.

DANIEL GIRAUD ELLIOT MEDAL AWARDS

Chapman, F. M., 1917
Beebe, William, 1918
Ridgway, Robert, 1919
Abel, Othenio, 1920
Dean, Bashford, 1921
Wheeler, Wm. Morton, 1922

Canu, Ferdinand, 1923
Breuil, Henri, 1924
Wilson, Edmund B., 1925
Stensiö, Erik A : Son, 1927
Seton, Ernest Thompson, 1928

Osborn, Henry Fairfield, 1929
Coghill, George Ellett, 1930
Black, Davidson, 1931
Chapin, James P., 1932

BILLINGS FUND

[$22,313.39]

For partial support of the Proceedings, or for such other purposes as the Academy may select

MARY CLARK THOMPSON FUND

[$10,000]

Medal for most important services to geology and paleontology

Members of the committee

Lindgren, Waldemar (chairman), 1937

Mendenhall, W. C., 1936

Ulrich, E. O., 1938

MARY CLARK THOMPSON MEDAL AWARDS

Walcott, Charles Doolittle, 1921
Margerie, Emm. de, 1923
Clarke, John Mason, 1925
Smith, James Perrin, 1928

Scott, William Berryman, 1930
Ulrich, Edward Oscar, 1930
White, David, 1931

Bather, Francis Arthur, 1932
Schuchert, Charles, 1934

JOSEPH HENRY FUND

[$40,163.50]

To assist meritorious investigators, especially in the direction of original research

Members of the committee

Webster, D. L. (chairman), 1939	Jones, L. R., 1938 Seashore, C. E., 1940	Taylor, D. W., 1936 Wilson, H. V., 1937

GEORGE TRUE NEALLEY FUND

[$19,555.55]

For the general purposes of the Academy

CHARLES DOOLITTLE WALCOTT FUND

[$5,000]

For stimulation of research in pre-Cambrian or Cambrian life by award of a medal and honorarium

Board of directors

Schucbert, Charles (temporary chairman)	Abbot, C. G.[a] Barrois, Charles[b]	Lang, W. D.[c] Ulrich, E. O.

CHARLES DOOLITTLE WALCOTT MEDAL AWARD

White, David, 1934

JOHN J. CARTY FUND

[$25,000]

Medal and monetary award, not oftener than once in every 2 years, to an individual for noteworthy and distinguished accomplishment in any field of science coming within the scope of the charter of the Academy

Members of the committee

Jewett, F. B. (chairman), 1936	Bancroft, W. D., 1937 Birkhoff, G. D., 1940	Howell, W. H., 1938 Jennings, H. S., 1939

JOHN J. CARTY MEDAL AWARD

Carty, John J., 1932

CARNEGIE ENDOWMENT FUND

[$3,550,000]

For the purposes of the National Academy of Sciences and National Research Council

---

[a] Representing the Smithsonian Institution.
[b] Representing the Institut de France.
[c] Representing the Royal Society of London.

6. MEMBERS OF THE NATIONAL ACADEMY OF SCIENCES

JULY 1, 1935

Abbot, Charles Greeley, Smithsonian Institution, Washington, D. C_____ 1915
Abel, John Jacob, Department of Pharmacology, Johns Hopkins Medical
   School, Baltimore, Md_____ 1912
Adams, Comfort Avery, Harvard Engineering School, Cambridge, Mass___ 1930
Adams, Roger, University of Illinois, Urbana, Ill_____ 1929
Adams, Walter Sydney, Mount Wilson Observatory, Pasadena, Calif_____ 1917
Aitken, Robert Grant, 1109 Spruce St., Berkeley, Calif_____ 1918
Alexander, James Waddell, Princeton, N. J_____ 1930
Allen, Charles Elmer, University of Wisconsin, Madison, Wis_____ 1924
Allen, Eugene Thomas, 1862 Mintwood Pl., Washington, D. C_____ 1930
Ames, Joseph Sweetman. Johns Hopkins University, Baltimore, Md_____ 1909
Anderson, John August, Mount Wilson Observatory, Pasadena, Calif____ 1928
Angell, James Rowland, Yale University, New Haven, Conn_____ 1920
Avery, Oswald Theodore, Rockefeller Institute for Medical Research, 66th
   St. and York Ave., New York City_____ 1933
Babcock, Harold Delos, Mount Wilson Observatory, Pasadena, Calif____ 1933
Bailey, Irving Widmer, Bussey Institution, Forest Hills, Boston 30, Mass_ 1929
Bailey, Liberty Hyde, Ithaca, N. Y_____ 1917
Bancroft, Wilder Dwight, 7 East Ave., Ithaca, N. Y_____ 1920
Barbour, Thomas, Museum of Comparative Zoology, Cambridge, Mass____ 1933
Barus, Carl, Brown University, Providence, R. I_____ 1892
Bateman, Harry, California Institute of Technology, Pasadena, Calif____ 1930
Baxter, Gregory Paul, T. Jefferson Coolidge Jr. Memorial Laboratory,
   Cambridge, Mass_____ 1916
Bell, Eric Temple, California Institute of Technology, Pasadena, Calif___ 1927
Benedict, Francis Gano, Nutrition Laboratory, 29 Vila St., Boston, Mass_ 1914
Benedict, Stanley Rossiter, Cornell University Medical College, 1300
   York Ave., New York City_____ 1924
Berkey, Charles Peter, Department of Geology and Mineralogy, Columbia
   University, New York City_____ 1927
Berry, Edward Wilber, Johns Hopkins University, Baltimore, Md_____ 1922
Bigelow, Henry Bryant, Museum of Comparative Zoology, Harvard Uni-
   versity, Cambridge, Mass_____ 1931
Birge, Raymond Thayer, University of California, Berkeley, Calif_____ 1932
Birkhoff, George David, 984 Memorial Drive, Cambridge, Mass_____ 1918
Blakeslee, Albert Francis, Department of Genetics, Carnegie Institution
   of Washington, Cold Spring Harbor, L. I., N. Y_____ 1929
Blichfeldt, Hans Frederick, Box 875, Stanford University, Calif_____ 1920
Bliss, Gilbert Ames, University of Chicago, Chicago, Ill_____ 1916
Boas, Franz, Columbia University, New York City_____ 1900
Bogert, Marston Taylor, 566 Chandler Laboratories, Columbia University,
   New York City_____ 1916
Boring, Edwin Garrigues, Harvard University, Cambridge, Mass_____ 1932
Bowen, Norman Levi, Geophysical Laboratory, 2801 Upton St., Washing-
   ton, D. C_____ 1935
Bowie, William, U. S. Coast and Geodetic Survey, Washington, D. C___ 1927
Bowman, Isaiah, Johns Hopkins University, Baltimore, Md_____ 1930
Bray, William Crowell, Department of Chemistry, University of Cali-
   fornia, Berkeley, Calif_____ 1924
Breasted, James Henry, The Oriental Institute, University of Chicago,
   Chicago, Ill_____ 1923
Bridgman, Percy Williams, Jefferson Physical Laboratory, Cambridge,
   Mass_____ 1918
Brown, Ernest William, 116 Everit St., New Haven, Conn_____ 1923
Bush, Vannevar, Massachusetts Institute of Technology, Cambridge,
   Mass _____ 1934
Calkins, Gary Nathan, Columbia University, New York City_____ 1919
Campbell, Douglas Houghton, Stanford University, Stanford University,
   Calif_____ 1910
Campbell, William Wallace, 1960 Vallejo St., San Francisco_____ 1902
Cannon, Walter Bradford, Harvard Medical School, 240 Longwood Ave.,
   Boston 17, Mass_____ 1914
Carlson, Anton Julius, University of Chicago, Chicago, Ill_____ 1920
Castle. William Ernest, 186 Payson Rd., Belmont, Mass_____ 1915
Cattell, James McKeen, Garrison, N. Y_____ 1901

6. Members of the National Academy of Sciences—Continued

Elected

Chapman, Frank Michler, American Museum of Natural History, 77th St., and Central Park West, New York City_____ 1921
Child, Charles Manning, University of Chicago, Chicago, Ill_____ 1935
Chittenden, Russell Henry, Sheffield Scientific School, New Haven, Conn___1890
Clark, William Mansfield, Johns Hopkins Medical School, Washington and Monument Sts., Baltimore, Md_____ 1928
Clinton, George Perkins, Connecticut Agricultural Experiment Station, New Haven, Conn_____ 1930
Coble, Arthur Byron, University of Illinois, Urbana, Ill_____ 1924
Coblentz, William Weber, Bureau of Standards, Washington, D. C._____ 1930
Coghill, George Ellett, Fallsington, Bucks County, Pa_____ 1935
Cole, Rufus, Hospital of the Rockefeller Institute, 66th St. and York Ave., New York City_____ 1922
Compton, Arthur Holly, University of Chicago, Chicago Ill_____ 1927
Compton, Karl Taylor, 111 Charles River Rd., Cambridge, Mass_____ 1924
Conant, James Bryant, Harvard University, Cambridge 38, Mass_____ 1929
Conklin, Edwin Grant, Princeton University, Princeton, N. J_____ 1908
Coolidge, William David, General Electric Co., Schnectady, N. Y_____ 1925
Crew, Henry, 620 Library Pl., Evanston, Ill_____ 1909
Cross, Charles Whitman, 101 East Kirke St., Chevy Chase, Md_____ 1908
Curtis, Heber Doust, Observatory, University of Michigan, Ann Arbor, Mich _____ 1919
Cushing, Harvey Williams, Yale Medical School, New Haven, Conn____ 1917
Daly, Reginald Aldworth, Geological Museum, Harvard University, Cambridge, Mass_____ 1925
Davenport, Charles Benedict, Carnegie Institution of Washington, Cold Spring Harbor, Long Island, N. Y_____ 1912
Davis, Bergen, Columbia University, New York City_____ 1929
Davisson, Clinton Joseph, Bell Telephone Laboratories, 463 West St., New York City_____ 1929
Day, Arthur Louis, Geophysical Laboratory, 2801 Upton St., Washington, D. C._____ 1911
Detwiler, Samuel Randall, College of Physicians and Surgeons, 630 West 168th St., New York City_____ 1932
Dewey, John, Columbia University, New York City_____ 1910
Dickson, Leonard Eugene, University of Chicago, Chicago, Ill_____ 1913
Dochez, Alphonse Raymond, Columbia University, Presbyterian Hospital, 620 West 168 St., New York City_____ 1933
Dodge, Bernard Ogilvie, New York Botanical Garden, Bronx Park (Fordham Station), New York City_____ 1933
Dodge, Raymond, Institute of Human Relations, Yale University, New Haven, Conn_____ 1924
Donaldson, Henry Herbert, Wistar Institute of Anatomy, Philadelphia, Pa_____ 1914
DuBois, Eugene Floyd, New York Hospital, 525 East 68th St., New York City_____ 1933
Duggar, Benjamin Minge, Biology Bldg., University of Wisconsin, Madison, Wis_____ 1927
Dunn, Gano, 80 Broad St., New York City_____ 1919
Durand, William Frederick, Stanford University, Stanford University, Calif _____ 1917
East, Edward Murray, Bussey Institution, Forest Hills, Boston 30, Mass_____ 1925
Eisenhart, Luther Pfahler, Princeton, N. J_____ 1922
Emerson, Rollins Adams, Cornell University, Ithaca, N. Y_____ 1927
Emmet, William LeRoy, General Electric Co., Schenectady, N. Y_____ 1921
Epstein, Paul Sophus, 1484 Oakdale St., Pasadena, Calif_____ 1930
Erlanger, Joseph, Washington University School of Medicine, 4580 Scott Ave, St. Louis, Mo_____ 1922
Evans, Griffith Conrad, Department of Mathematics, University of California, Berkeley, Calif_____ 1933
Evans, Herbert McLean, Anatomical Laboratory, University of California, Berkeley, Calif_____ 1927
Ewing, James, Memorial Hospital, New York City_____ 1935
Fernald, Merritt Lyndon, Gray Herbarium, Harvard University, Cam-

6. *Members of the National Academy of Sciences*—Continued

Elected

Fletcher, Harvey, Bell Telephone Laboratories, 463 West St., New York City_____ 1935

Flexner, Simon, Rockefeller Institute for Medical Research, 66th St. and York Ave., New York City_____ 1908

Franklin, Edward Curtis, 662 Mirada, Stanford University, Calif_____ 1914

Fred, Edwin Broun, College of Agriculture, University of Wisconsin, Madison, Wis_____ 1931

Gasser, Herbert Spencer, Rockefeller Institute for Medical Research, 66th St. and York Ave., New York City_____ 1934

Gherardi, Bancroft, 195 Broadway, New York City_____ 1933

Gomberg, Moses, University of Michigan, Ann Arbor, Mich_____ 1914

Gortner, Ross Aiken, University Farm, St. Paul, Minn_____ 1935

Gregory, William King, American Museum of Natural History, 77th St. and Central Park West, New York City_____ 1927

Hale, George Ellery, Mount Wilson Observatory, Pasadena, Calif_____ 1902

Hall, Edwin Herbert, 39 Garden St., Cambridge, Mass_____ 1911

Harkins, William Draper, University of Chicago, Chicago, Ill_____ 1921

Harper, Robert Almer, Columbia University, New York City_____ 1911

Harrison, Ross Granville, Yale University, Osborn Zoological Laboratory, New Haven, Conn_____ 1913

Harvey, Edmund Newton, Princeton University, Princeton, N. J_____ 1934

Hektoen, Ludvig, 637 South Wood St., Chicago, Ill_____ 1918

Henderson, Lawrence Joseph, 4 Willard St., Cambridge, Mass_____ 1919

Henderson, Yandell, Yale University, New Haven, Conn_____ 1923

Herrick, Charles Judson, Department of Anatomy, University of Chicago, Chicago, Ill_____ 1918

Hildebrand, Joel Henry, University of California, Berkeley, Calif_____ 1929

Hoagland, Dennis Robert, University of California, Berkeley, Calif____ 1934

Hooton, Earnest Albert, Peabody Museum, Harvard University, Cambridge, Mass_____ 1935

Hoover, Herbert Clark, Palo Alto, Calif_____ 1922

Hovgaard, William, Hotel Margaret, Columbia Heights, Brooklyn, N. Y. 1929

Howard, Leland Ossian, Bureau of Entomology, U. S. Department of Agriculture, Washington, D. C_____ 1916

Howe, Marshall Avery, New York Botanical Garden, Bronx Park, New York City_____ 1923

Howell, William Henry, 112 St. Dunstan's Road, Baltimore, Md_____ 1905

Hrdlicka, Ales, U. S. National Museum, Washington, D. C_____ 1921

Hubble, Edwin Powell, Mount Wilson Observatory, Pasadena, Calif____ 1927

Hudson, Claude Silbert, National Institute of Health, 25th and E Sts. NW., Washington, D C_____ 1927

Hulett, George Augustus, Princeton University, Princeton, N. J_____ 1922

Hull, Albert Wallace, Research Laboratory, General Electric Co., Schenectady, N. Y_____ 1929

Hunsaker, Jerome Clark, Massachusetts Institute of Technology, Cambridge, Mass_____ 1935

Hunt, Reid, Harvard Medical School, Boston, Mass_____ 1919

Hunter, Walter Samuel, Clark University, Worcester, Mass_____ 1935

Ives, Herbert Eugene, Bell Telephone Laboratories, 463 West St., New York City_____ 1933

Jackson, Dunham, University of Minnesota, Minneapolis, Minn_____ 1935

Jacobs, Walter Abraham, Rockefeller Institute for Medical Research, 66th St. and York Ave., New York City_____ 1932

Jennings, Herbert Spencer, Eastman House, 18 Norham Gardens, Oxford, England _____ 1914

Jewett, Frank Baldwin, American Telephone & Telegraph Co., 195 Broadway, New York City_____ 1918

Johnson, Douglas Wilson, Columbia University, New York City_____ 1932

Johnson, Treat Baldwin, Bethwood, Amity Rd., Bethany, Conn_____ 1919

Jones, Lewis Ralph, University of Wisconsin, Madison, Wis_____ 1920

Kasner, Edward, Columbia University, New York City_____ 1917

Keith, Arthur, U. S. Geological Survey, Washington, D. C_____ 1928

Kellogg, Vernon Lyman, 2305 Bancroft Pl., Washington, D. C_____ 1930

Kemble, Edwin Crawford, Jefferson Physical Laboratory, Harvard University, Cambridge, Mass_____ 1931

6. *Members of the National Academy of Sciences*—Continued

Elected

Kennelly, Arthur Edwin, Harvard University, Cambridge, Mass_____ 1921
Kettering, Charles Franklin, General Motors Corporation, Detroit, Mich__ 1928
Keyes, Frederick George, Massachusetts Institute of Technology, Cambridge, Mass _____ 1930
Knopf, Adolph, Yale University, New Haven, Conn_____ 1931
Kofoid, Charles Atwood, University of California, Berkeley, Calif_____ 1922
Kohler, Elmer Peter, Converse Laboratory, Harvard University, Cambridge, Mass _____ 1920
Kraus, Charles August, Brown University, Providence, R. I_____ 1925
Kroeber, Alfred L., University of California, Berkeley, Calif_____ 1928
Kunkel, Louis Otto, Rockefeller Institute for Medical Research, Princeton, N. J_____ 1932
Lamb, Arthur Becket, Chemical Laboratory, Harvard University, Cambridge, Mass _____ 1924
Landsteiner, Karl, Rockefeller Institute for Medical Research, 66th St. and York Ave., New York City_____ 1932
Langmuir, Irving, General Electric Co., Schenectady, N. Y_____ 1918
Lashley, Karl Spencer, Biological Laboratories, Harvard University, Cambridge, Mass _____ 1930
Lawrence, Ernest Orlando, University of California, Berkeley, Calif____ 1934
Lawson, Andrew Cowper, University of California, Berkeley, Calif_____ 1924
Lefschetz, Solomon, 190 Prospect St., Princeton, N. J_____ 1925
Leith, Charles Kenneth, University of Wisconsin, Madison, Wis_____ 1920
Leuschner, Armin Otto, Students' Observatory, University of California, Berkeley, Calif_____ 1913
Levene, Phoebus Aaron Theodore, Rockefeller Institute for Medical Research, 66th St. and York Ave., New York City_____ 1916
Leverett, Frank, 1724 South University Ave., Ann Arbor, Mich_____ 1929
Lewis, Gilbert Newton, University of California, Berkeley, Calif_____ 1913
Lillie, Frank Rattray, National Academy of Sciences, 2101 Constitution Ave., Washington, D. C_____ 1915
Lind, Samuel Colville, School of Chemistry, University of Minnesota, Minneapolis, Minn_____ 1930
Lindgren, Waldemar, Massachusetts Institute of Technology, Cambridge, Mass _____ 1909
Longwell, Chester Ray, Yale University, New Haven, Conn_____ 1935
Lowie, Robert Harry, University of California, Berkeley, Calif_____ 1931
Lyman, Theodore, Research Laboratory of Physics, Harvard University, Cambridge, Mass_____ 1917
MacCallum, William George, Johns Hopkins Medical School, Baltimore, Md _____ 1921
McClung, Clarence Erwin, University of Pennsylvania, Philadelphia, Pa_ 1920
McCollum, Elmer Verner, School of Hygiene and Public Health, 615 North Wolfe St., Baltimore, Md_____ 1920
Mark, Edward Laurens, 109 Irving St., Cambridge, Mass_____ 1903
Mason, Max, Rockefeller Foundation, 49 West 49th St., New York City__ 1923
Mendel, Lafayette Benedict, Sterling Hall of Medicine, Yale University, 333 Cedar St., New Haven, Conn_____ 1913
Mendenhall, Charles Elwood, Sterling Hall, University of Wisconsin, Madison, Wis_____ 1918
Mendenhall, Walter Curran, U. S. Geological Survey, Washington, D. C__ 1932
Merriam, Clinton Hart, 1919 16th St., Washington, D. C_____ 1902
Merriam, John Campbell, Carnegie Institution of Washington, Washington, D. C_____ 1918
Merrill, Elmer Drew, Gray Herbarium, Cambridge, Mass_____ 1923
Merrill, Paul Willard, Mount Wilson Observatory, Pasadena, Calif_____ 1929
Merritt, Ernest George, Rockefeller Hall, Ithaca, N. Y_____ 1914
Michael, Arthur, 219 Parker St., Newton Center, Mass_____ 1889
Miles, Walter Richard, Institute of Human Relations, 333 Cedar St., New Haven, Conn_____ 1933
Miller, Dayton Clarence, Case School of Applied Science, Cleveland, Ohio_ 1921
Miller, George Abram, 1203 West Illinois St., Urbana, Ill_____ 1921
Millikan, Robert Andrews, California Institute of Technology, Pasadena, Calif _____ 1915

6. Members of the National Academy of Sciences—Continued

Elected

Mitchell, Samuel Alfred, Leander McCormick Observatory, University, Va. 1933
Modjeski, Ralph, 52 Vanderbilt Ave., New York City_____ 1925
Moore, Joseph Haines, Lick Observatory, Mount Hamilton, Calif_____ 1931
Moore, Robert Lee, University of Texas, Austin, Tex_____ 1931
Morgan, Thomas Hunt, California Institute of Technology, Pasadena, Calif _____ 1909
Morse, Harold Marston, Institute for Advanced Study, Princeton, N. J__ 1932
Moulton, Forest Ray, 327 South La Salle St., Chicago, Ill_____ 1910
Muller, Hermann Joseph, University of Texas, Austin, Tex_____ 1931
Nichols, Edward Leamington, Cornell University, Ithaca, N. Y_____ 1901
Norris, James Flack, Massachusetts Institute of Technology, Cambridge, Mass _____ 1934
Northrop, John Howard, Rockefeller Institute for Medical Research, Princeton, N. J_____ 1934
Novy, Frederick George, University of Michigan, Ann Arbor, Mich_____ 1924
Noyes, Arthur Amos, California Institute of Technology, Pasadena, Calif__ 1905
Noyes, William Albert, University of Illinois, Urbana, Ill_____ 1910
Opie, Eugene Lindsay, Cornell University Medical School, 1300 York Ave., New York City_____ 1923
Osborn, Henry Fairfield, American Museum of Natural History, 77th St. and Central Park West, New York City_____ 1900
Osgood, William Fogg, 1800 Thousand Oaks Blvd., Berkeley, Calif_____ 1904
Osterhout, Winthrop John Vanleuven, Rockefeller Institute for Medical Research, 66th St. and York Ave., New York City_____ 1919
Palache, Charles, Harvard University, Cambridge, Mass_____ 1934
Parker, George Howard, 16 Berkeley St., Cambridge, Mass_____ 1913
Pauling, Linus, California Institute of Technology, Pasadena, Calif_____ 1933
Pearl, Raymond, 1901 East Madison St., Baltimore, Md_____ 1916
Pierce, George Washington, Cruft Laboratory, Harvard University, Cambridge, Mass _____ 1920
Pillsbury, Walter Bowers, University of Michigan, Ann Arbor, Mich_____ 1925
Ransome, Frederick Leslie, California Institute of Technology, Pasadena, Calif _____ 1914
Reid, Harry Fielding, Johns Hopkins University, Baltimore, Md_____ 1912
Richards, Alfred Newton, University of Pennsylvania, Philadelphia, Pa___ 1927
Richtmyer, Floyd Karker, Rockefeller Hall, Cornell University, Ithaca, N. Y. _____ 1932
Ritt, Joseph Fels, Columbia University, New York City_____ 1933
Rivers, Thomas Milton, Rockefeller Institute for Medical Research, 66th St. and York Ave., New York City_____ 1934
Robinson, Benjamin Lincoln, Gray Herbarium, Cambridge, Mass_____ 1921
Ross, Frank Elmore, Yerkes Observatory, Williams Bay, Wis_____ 1930
Rous, Francis Peyton, Rockefeller Institute for Medical Research, 66th St. and York Ave., New York City_____ 1927
Ruedemann, Rudolf, New York State Museum, Albany, N. Y_____ 1928
Russell, Henry Norris, Princeton University, Princeton, N. J_____ 1918
Sabin, Florence Rena, Rockefeller Institute for Medical Research, 66th St. and York Ave., New York City_____ 1925
Sapir, Edward, Yale University, New Haven, Conn_____ 1934
Saunders, Frederick Albert, Jefferson Physical Laboratory, Cambridge, Mass _____ 1925
Sauveur, Albert, Harvard University, Cambridge, Mass_____ 1927
Schlesinger, Frank, Yale University Observatory, New Haven, Conn_____ 1916
Schuchert, Charles, Peabody Museum, Yale University, New Haven, Conn _____ 1910
Scott, William Berryman, Princeton University, Princeton, N. J_____ 1906
Seares, Frederick Hanley, Mt. Wilson Observatory, Pasadena, Calif_____ 1919
Seashore, Carl Emil, State University of Iowa, Iowa City, Iowa_____ 1922
Setchell, William Albert, University of California, Berkeley, Calif_____ 1919
Shaffer, Philip Anderson, Washington University Medical School, St. Louis, Mo _____ 1928
Shapley, Harlow, Harvard College Observatory, Cambridge, Mass_____ 1924
Sherman, Henry Clapp, Columbia University, New York City_____ 1933
Slater, John Clarke, Massachusetts Institute of Technology, Cambridge, Mass _____ 1932

6. Members of the National Academy of Sciences—Continued

	Elected
Slipher, Vesto Melvin, Lowell Observatory, Flagstaff, Ariz	1921
Stakman, Elvin Charles, University of Minnesota, Minneapolis, Minn	1934
Stebbins, Joel, Washburn Observatory, Madison, Wis	1920
Stejneger, Leonhard, U. S. National Museum, Washington, D. C	1923
Stieglitz, Julius Oscar, University of Chicago, Chicago, Ill	1911
Stillwell, Lewis Buckley, Elm Road, Princeton, N. J	1921
Stockard, Charles Rupert, Cornell University Medical School, New York City	1922
Stratton, George Malcolm, University of California, Berkeley, Calif	1928
Streeter, George Linius, Department of Embryology, Carnegie Institution, Wolfe and Madison Sts., Baltimore, Md	1931
Sturtevant, Alfred Henry, California Institute of Technology, Pasadena, Calif	1930
Swanton, John Reed, Bureau of American Ethnology, Smithsonian Institution, Washington, D. C	1932
Swasey, Ambrose, 7808 Euclid Ave., Cleveland, Ohio	1922
Taylor, David Watson, 1869 Wyoming Ave., Washington, D. C	1918
Tennent, David Hilt, Bryn Mawr College, Bryn Mawr, Pa	1929
Terman, Lewis Madison, 761 Dolores, Stanford University, Calif	1928
Thomson, Elihu, 22 Monument Ave., Swampscott, Mass	1907
Thorndike, Edward Lee, Teachers College, Columbia University, New York City	1917
Tolman, Richard Chace, California Institute of Technology, Pasadena, Calif	1923
Trelease, William, University of Illinois, Urbana, Ill	1902
Trumpler, Robert Julius, Lick Observatory, Mount Hamilton, Calif	1932
Ulrich, Edward Oscar, U. S. National Museum, Washington, D. C	1917
Urey, Harold Clayton, Columbia University, New York City	1935
Vandiver, Harry Shultz, University of Texas, Austin, Tex	1934
Van Slyke, Donald Dexter, Rockefeller Institute for Medical Research, 66th St. and York Ave., New York City	1921
Van Vleck, Edward Burr, 519 North Pickney St., Madison, Wis	1911
Van Vleck, John Hasbrouck, Harvard University, Cambridge, Mass	1935
Vaughan, Thomas Wayland, Scripps Institution of Oceanography, University of California, La Jolla, Calif	1921
Veblen, Oswald, Princeton University, Princeton, N. J	1919
Washburn, Margaret Floy, Vassar College, Poughkeepsie, N. Y	1931
Webster, David Locke, Physics Department, Room 385, Stanford University, Stanford University, Calif	1923
Wells, Harry Gideon, University of Chicago, Chicago, Ill	1925
Wheeler, William Morton, Institute of Biology, Divinity Ave., Cambridge, Mass	1912
Whipple, George Hoyt, School of Medicine of the University of Rochester, Crittenden Blvd., Rochester, N. Y	1929
White, Henry Seely, Vassar College, Poughkeepsie, N. Y	1915
Whitehead, John Boswell, Johns Hopkins University, Baltimore, Md	1932
Whitney, Willis Rodney, General Electric Co., Schenectady, N. Y	1917
Wiener, Norbert, Massachusetts Institute of Technology, Cambridge, Mass	1934
Willis, Bailey, Box 1365, Stanford University, Calif	1920
Wilson, Edmund Beecher, Columbia University, New York City	1899
Wilson, Edwin Bidwell, 55 Shattuck St., Boston 17, Mass	1919
Wilson, Henry Van Peters, University of North Carolina, Chapel Hill, N. C	1927
Wissler, Clark, American Museum of Natural History, New York City	1929
Wood, Robert Williams, Johns Hopkins University, Baltimore, Md	1912
Woodruff, Lorande Loss, Yale University, New Haven, Conn	1924
Woodworth, Robert Sessions, Columbia University, New York City	1921
Wright, Frederick Eugene, Geophysical Laboratory, 2801 Upton Street, Washington, D. C	1923
Wright, Sewall Green, University of Chicago, Chicago, Ill	1934
Wright, William Hammond, Lick Observatory, Mount Hamilton, Calif	1922
Yerkes, Robert Mearns, Yale School of Medicine, 333 Cedar St., New Haven, Conn	1923
Zinsser, Hans, Harvard Medical School, 240 Longwood Ave., Boston, Mass	1924

MEMBER EMERITUS

Elected

Jackson, Charles Loring, 383 Beacon St., Boston, Mass_____ 1883

FOREIGN ASSOCIATES OF THE NATIONAL ACADEMY OF SCIENCES

Adams, Frank Dawson, McGill University, Montreal, Canada_____ 1920
Barrois, Charles Université, 41 rue Pascal, Lille, France_____ 1908
Bjerknes, V. F. K., University, Oslo, Norway_____ 1934
Bohr, Niels, University of Copenhagen, Copenhagen, Denmark_____ 1925
Bordet, Jules, Pasteur Institute, Rue du Remorquer 28, Brussels, Belgium _____ 1935
Bower, Frederick Orpen, 2, The Crescent, Ripon, Yorks, England_____ 1929
Brogger, W. C., Universitet, Oslo, Norway_____ 1903
Debye, Peter, Physikalisches Institut der Universitat, Linnéstrasse 5, Leipzig, Germany_____ 1931
Deslandres, Henri, Bureau des Longitudes, 21 rue de Téhéran, Paris 8, France_____ 1913
Dyson, Sir Frank Watson, The Royal Observatory, Greenwich, London S. E., England_____ 1926
Eddington, Sir Arthur Stanley, Observatory, Cambridge, England_____ 1925
Einstein, Albert, Institute for Advanced Study, Princeton, N. J. (U. S. A.)_____ 1922
Forsythe, A. R., Imperial College of Science and Technology, London, England _____ 1907
Hadamard, Jacques, 25 rue Dolent, Paris XIV, France_____ 1926
Hadfield, Sir Robert A., 22 Carlton House Terrace, S. W. 1, London, England_____ 1928
Haldane, John Scott, New College, Oxford, England_____ 1935
Hardy, Godfrey Harold, New College, Oxford, England_____ 1927
Helm, Albert, Zurich, Switzerland_____ 1913
Hertwig, Richard von, Zoologisches Institut, University of Munich, Munich, Germany_____ 1929
Hilbert, David, Wilhelm-Weberstrasse 29, Gottingen, Germany_____ 1907
Hopkins, Sir Frederick Gowland, University, Cambridge, England_____ 1924
Kustner, Karl Friedrich, Mehlem bei Bonn, Germany_____ 1913
Lacroix, F. Alfred A., 23 rue Jean-Dolent, Paris XIV, France_____ 1920
Larmor, Sir Joseph, St. John's College, Cambridge, England_____ 1908
Marconi, Marchese Guglielmo, Marconi House, Strand, London, W. C. 2, England _____ 1932
Pavlov, I. P., Institute for Experimental Medicine, Leningrad, U. S. S. R., Russia_____ 1908
Penck, Albrecht, Knesebeckstrasse 48, Berlin W 15, Germany_____ 1900
Picard, Charles Emile, 25 Quai Conti, Paris (VI), France_____ 1903
Planck, Max, Wangenheimstrasse 21, Berlin-Grunewald, Germany_____ 1926
Prain, Sir David, The Well Farm, Warlingham, Surrey, England_____ 1920
Robinson, Robert, Dyson Perrins Laboratory, South Parks Road, Oxford, England_____ 1934
Rutherford, Lord Ernest, Newnham Cottage, Queen's Road, Cambridge, England_____ 1911
Sabatier, Paul, Allée des Zephyrs, No. 11, Toulouse, France_____ 1927
Schneider, Charles Eugene, 42 rue d'Anjou, Paris, France_____ 1925
Sherrington, Sir Charles Scott, "Broomside," Valley Road, Ipswich, England _____ 1924
Sommerfeld, Arnold, University of Munich, Munich, Germany_____ 1929
Spemann. Hans, Zoologisches Institut, Freiburg, i. Br., Germany_____ 1925
Stumpf, Carl, Potsdamerstrasse 15, Berlin-Lichterfelde West, Germany__ 1927
Thomson, Sir Joseph, Trinity Lodge, Cambridge, England_____ 1903
Vallee-Poussin, C. de la, University of Louvain, Louvain, Belgium_____ 1929
Volterra, Vito, Universita, Rome, Italy_____ 1911
Wieland, Heinrich. Chemisches Laboratorium Bayer. Akademie der Wissenschaften. Arcisstrasse 1, Munich 2 NW, Germany_____ 1932
Willstaetter, Richard, Moehlstrasse 29, Munich O. 27, Germany_____ 1926

7. MEDALISTS OF THE NATIONAL ACADEMY

	Medal	Year		Medal	Year
Abbe, Cleveland [1]	Welfare	1916	Hoover, Herbert Clark	Welfare	1920
Abbot, Charles Greeley	Draper	1910	Hubble, Edwin	Barnard	1935
Abel, Othenio [2]	Elliot	1920	Huggins, Sir William [1]	Draper	1901
Adams, Walter Sidney	Draper	1918	Kapteyn, J. C.[1]	Watson	1913
Albert I[er], Prince of Monaco[1][2]	Agassiz	1918	Keeler, James Edward [1]	Draper	1899
Auwers, G. F. J. Arthur [1]	Watson	1891	Langley, Samuel Pierpont [1]	do	1886
Barnett, Samuel Jackson [1]	Comstock	1918	Leuschner, Armin Otto	Watson	1915
Bather, Francis Arthur [2]	Thompson	1932	Margerie, Emmanuel de [2]	Thompson	1923
Beebe, William [2]	Elliot	1918	Mather, Stephen Tyng [1][2]	Welfare	1930
Bigelow, Henry Bryant	Agassiz	1931	Merrill, George Perkins [1]	Smith	1922
Bjerknes, Vilhelm	do	1926	Michelson, Albert Abraham [1]	Draper	1916
Black, Davidson [1][2]	Elliot	1931	Millikan, Robert Andrews	Comstock	1913
Bohr, Niels	Barnard	1925	Newton, Hubert Anson [1]	Smith	1888
Bragg, Sir William Henry [2]	do	1914	Osborn, Henry Fairfield	Elliot	1929
Breuil, Henri [2]	Elliot	1924	Park, William Hallock [2]	Welfare	1932
Bridgman, P. W.	Comstock	1933	Pettersson, Otto Sven [2]	Agassiz	1924
Campbell, William Wallace	Draper	1906	Pickering, Edward Charles [1]	Draper	1888
Cannon, Annie Jump [2]	do	1931	Pinchot, Gifford [2]	Welfare	1916
Canu, Ferdinand [1][2]	Elliot	1923	Plaskett, John Stanley [2]	Draper	1934
Carty, John J.[1]	Carty	1932	Ridgway, Robert [1]	Elliot	1919
Chandler, Seth Carlo [1]	Watson	1894	Rose, Wickliffe [1][2]	Welfare	1931
Chapin, Charles V.[2]	Welfare	1928	Rowland, Henry Augustus [1]	Draper	1890
Chapin, James P.[2]	Elliot	1932	Russell, Henry Norris	do	1922
Chapman, Frank Michler	do	1917	Rutherford (Lord) Ernest	Barnard	1909
Charlier, C. V. L.[2]	Watson	1924	Schmidt, Johannes [2]	Agassiz	1930
Clarke, John Mason [1]	Thompson	1925	Schoenfeld, Ed.[1][2]	Watson	1889
Coghill, George Ellett	Elliot	1930	Schuchert, Charles	Thompson	1934
Davisson, C. J.	Comstock	1928	Scott, W. B.	do	1930
Dean, Bashford [1]	Elliot	1921	Seton, Ernest Thompson [2]	Elliot	1928
Defant, Albert [2]	Agassiz	1932	Shapley, Harlow	Draper	1926
de Sitter, Willem [1]	Watson	1929	Sigsbee, Rear Admiral Charles Dwight, U. S. Navy.[1][2]	Agassiz	1920
Deslandres, Henri	Draper	1913	Slipher, V. M.	Draper	1932
Duane, William [1]	Comstock	1923	Smith, James Perrin [1]	Thompson	1928
Eddington (Sir) Arthur Stanley.	Draper	1924	Stebbins, Joel	Draper	1915
Einstein, Albert	Barnard	1921	Stensio, Erik A: Son [2]	Elliot	1927
Ekman, V. Walfrid [2]	Agassiz	1928	Stiles, Charles Wardell [1]	Welfare	1921
Fabry, Charles [2]	Draper	1919	Stratton, Samuel Wesley [1]	do	1917
Fairchild, David [2]	Welfare	1933	Ulrich, Edward Oscar	Thompson	1930
Fowler, Alfred [2]	Draper	1920	Vaughan, T. Wayland	Agassiz	1935
Gardiner, J. Stanley [2]	Agassiz	1929	Vogel, Herman Karl [1]	Draper	1893
Gill, Sir David [1]	Watson	1899	Vollmer, August [2]	Welfare	1934
Goethals, George Washington.[1][2]	Welfare	1914	Walcott, Charles Doolittle [1]	Thompson	1921
Gorgas, William Crawford [1][2]	do	1914	Weber, Max [2]	Agassiz	1927
Gould, Benjamin Apthorp [1]	Watson	1887	Wheeler, William Morton	Elliot	1922
Gran, Haakon Hasberg [2]	Agassiz	1934	White, David [1]	Thompson	1931
Hale, George Ellery	Draper	1904	Do	Walcott	1934
Heisenberg, Werner [2]	Barnard	1930	Wilson, Edmund B.	Elliot	1925
Helland-Hansen, Bjorn [2]	Agassiz	1933	Wright, William Hammond	Draper	1928
Hjort, Johan [2]	do	1913	Zeeman, P.[2]	do	1921

[1] Deceased.
[2] Not member or foreign associate of the Academy.

8. PRESIDENTS OF THE ACADEMY

Alexander Dallas Bache	1863–67		Ira Remsen	1907–13
Joseph Henry	1868–78		William Henry Welch	1913–17
William Barton Rogers	1879–82		Charles Doolittle Walcott	1917–23
Othniel Charles Marsh	1883–95		Albert Abraham Michelson	1923–27
Wolcott Gibbs	1895–1900		Thomas Hunt Morgan	1927–31
Alexander Agassiz	1901–7		William Wallace Campbell	1931–35

9. DECEASED MEMBERS AND FOREIGN ASSOCIATES

DECEASED MEMBERS

Name	Date of election	Date of death
Abbe, Cleveland	1878[a]	Oct. 28, 1916
Abbot, Henry L	1872	Oct. 1, 1927
Agassiz, Alexander	1866	Mar. 27, 1910
Agassiz, Louis	(2)	Dec. 14, 1873
Alexander, J. H	(2)	Mar. 2, 1867
Alexander, Stephen	(2)	June 25, 1883
Allen, J. A	1876	Aug. 29, 1921
Armsby, H. P	1920[1]	Oct. 19, 1921
Atkinson, George Francis	1918[1]	Nov. 14, 1918
Bache, Alexander Dallas	(2)	Feb. 14, 1867
Bailey, Solon Irving	1923	June 5, 1931
Baird, Spencer F	1864	Aug. 19, 1887
Barker, George F	1873[1]	May 24, 1910
Barnard, E. E	1911	Feb. 6, 1923
Barnard, F. A. P	(1 2)	Apr. 27, 1889
Barnard, J. G	(2)	May 14, 1882
Barrell, Joseph	1919	May 4, 1919
Bartlett, W. H. C	(2)	Feb. 11, 1893
Becker, George Ferdinand	1901	Apr. 20, 1919
Beecher, Charles Emerson	1899	Feb. 14, 1904
Bell, A. Graham	1883[1]	Aug. 2, 1922
Billings, John S	1883	Mar. 11, 1913
Bocher, Maxime	1909[1]	Sept. 12, 1918
Boltwood, B. B	1911	Aug. 14, 1927
Boss, Lewis	1880	Oct. 5, 1912
Bowditch, Henry P	1887	Mar. 13, 1911
Branner, J. C	1905	Mar. 1, 1922
Brewer, William H	1880	Nov. 2, 1910
Britton, Nathaniel L	1914[1]	June 26, 1934
Brooks, William Keith	1884	Nov. 12, 1908
Brown-Sequard, Charles E	1868	Apr. 2, 1894
Brush, George Jarvis	1868	Feb. 6, 1912
Bumstead, Henry A	1913	Dec. 31, 1920
Burgess, George K	1922[1]	July 2, 1932
Carty, John J	1917[1]	Dec. 27, 1932
Casey, Thomas L	1890	Mar. 25, 1896
Caswell, Alexis	(2)	Jan. 8, 1877
Chamberlin, Thomas Chrowder	1903	Nov. 15, 1928
Chandler, Charles Frederick	1874	Aug. 25, 1925
Chandler, Seth Carlo	1888[1]	Dec. 31, 1913
Chauvenet, William	(2)	Dec. 13, 1877
Clark, Henry James	1872	July 1, 1879
Clark, William B	1908	July 27, 1917
Clarke, Frank Wigglesworth	1909	May 23, 1931
Clarke, John M	1909	May 29, 1925
Coffin, James H	1869	Feb. 6, 1873
Coffin, J. H. C	(2)	Jan. 8, 1890
Comstock, Cyrus B	1884	May 29, 1910
Comstock, George C	1899[1]	May 11, 1934
Cook, George H	1887	Sept. 22, 1889
Cooke, Josiah P	1872	Sept. 3, 1894
Cope, Edward D	1872	Apr. 12, 1897
Coues, Elliott	1877	Dec. 25, 1899
Coulter, John Merle	1909	Dec. 23, 1928
Councilman, William T.[1]	1904[1]	May 27, 1933
Crafts, James M	1872	June 21, 1917
Dall, William H	1897[1]	Mar. 27, 1927
Dalton, J. C	1864	Feb. 2, 1889
Dana, E. S	1884[1]	June 16, 1935
Dana, James D	(2)	Apr. 14, 1895
Davidson, George	1874[1]	Dec. 2, 1911
Davis, Charles H	(2)	Feb. 18, 1877
Davis, William M	1904[1]	Feb. 5, 1934
Draper, Henry	1877	Nov. 20, 1882
Draper, John W	1877	Jan. 4, 1882
Duane, William	1920[1]	Mar. 7, 1935
Dutton, C. E	1884[1]	Jan. 4, 1912
Eads, James B	1872	Mar. 8, 1887
Edison, Thomas A	1927	Oct. 18, 1931
Eigenmann, Carl H	1923[1]	Apr. 24, 1927
Elkin, W. L	1895[1]	May 30, 1933
Emmons, Samuel F	1892	Mar. 28, 1911
Englemann, George	(2)	Feb. 4, 1884
Farlow, W. G	1879	June 3, 1919
Ferrel, William	1868	Sept. 18, 1891
Fewkes, Jesse Walter	1914	May 31, 1930
Folin, Otto	1916[1]	Oct. 25, 1934
Forbes, Stephen Alfred	1918	Mar. 13, 1930
Fraser, John Fries	(2)	Oct. 12, 1872
Freeman, John R	1918[1]	Oct. 6, 1932
Frost, Edwin Brant	1908[1]	May 14, 1935
Gabb, William M	1876	May 30, 1878
Genth, F. A	1872	Feb. 2, 1893
Gibbs, Josiah Willard	1879	Apr. 28, 1903
Gibbs, Wolcott	(2)	Dec. 9, 1908
Gilbert, Grove Karl	1883	May 1, 1918
Gill, Theodore Nicholas	1873	Sept. 25, 1914
Gilliss, James Melville	(2)	Feb. 9, 1865
Gooch, Frank Austin	1897	Aug. 12, 1929
Goodale, G. L	1890	Apr. 15, 1923
Goode, G. Brown	1888	Sept. 6, 1896
Gould, Augustus A	(2)	Sept. 15, 1866
Gould, Benjamin A	(2)	Nov. 26, 1896
Gray, Asa	(2)	Jan. 30, 1888
Guyot, Arnold	(2)	Feb. 8, 1884
Hadley, James	1872	Nov. 14, 1872
Hague, Arnold	1885	May 15, 1917
Haldeman, S. S	1876	Sept. 20, 1880
Hall, Asaph	1875	Nov. 22, 1907
Hall, G. Stanley	1915	Apr. 24, 1924
Hall, James	(2)	Aug. 7, 1898
Halsted, W. S	1917[1]	Sept. 7, 1922
Hastings, C. S	1889[1]	Jan. 29, 1932
Hayden, F. V	1873	Dec. 22, 1887
Hayford, John F	1911	Mar. 10, 1925
Henry, Joseph	(2)	May 13, 1878
Hilgard, Eugene W	1872	Jan. 8, 1916
Hilgard, Julius E	(2)	May 9, 1890
Hill, George William	1874	Apr. 16, 1914
Hill, Henry B	1883	Apr. 6, 1903
Hillebrand, W. F	1908	Feb. 7, 1925
Hitchcock, Edward	(2)	Feb. 27, 1864
Holbrook, J. E	1868	Sept. 8, 1871
Holden, Edward Singleton	1885	Mar. 16, 1914
Holmes, William H.[4]	1905[1]	Apr. 20, 1933
Howe, H. M	1917	May 14, 1922
Hubbard, J. S	(2)	Aug. 16, 1863
Humphreys, A. A	(2)	Dec. 27, 1883
Hunt, T. Sterry	1873	Feb. 12, 1892
Huntington, G. S	1924[1]	Jan. 5, 1927
Hyatt, Alpheus	1875	Jan. 15, 1902
Iddings, Joseph P	1907[1]	Sept. 8, 1920
James, William[a]	1903[1]	Aug. 26, 1910
Johnson, S. W	1866	July 21, 1909
Jones, Walter	1918[1]	Feb. 28, 1935
Keeler, J. E	1900	Aug. 12, 1900
Kemp, James F	1911	Nov. 17, 1926
King, Clarence	1876	Dec. 24, 1901
Kirtland, Jared P	1865	Dec. 10, 1877
Lane, J. Homer	1872	May 3, 1880
Langley, Samuel P	1876	Feb. 27, 1906
Laufer, Berthold	1930[1]	Sept. 13, 1934
Lea, Matthew Carey	1892	Mar. 15, 1897
Le Conte, John	1878	Apr. 29, 1891
Le Conte, John L	(2)	Nov. 15, 1883
Le Conte, Joseph	1875	July 6, 1901
Leidy, Joseph	(2)	Apr. 30, 1891
Lesley, J. Peter	(2)	June 1, 1903
Lesquereux, Leo	1864	Oct. 25, 1889
Loeb, Jacques	1910	Feb. 12, 1924
Longstreth, Miers F	(2)	Dec. 27, 1891
Loomis, Elias	1873	Aug. 15, 1889
Lovering, Joseph	1873	Jan. 18, 1892
Lusk, Graham	1915[1]	July 18, 1932
Lyman, Theodore	1872	Sept. 9, 1897
Mahan, D. H	(2)	Sept. 16, 1871
Mall, Franklin P	1907	Nov. 17, 1917
Marsh, G. P	1866	July 23, 1882
Marsh, O. C	1874[1]	Mar. 18, 1899
Mayer, Alfred M	1872	July 13, 1897
Mayor, A. G	1916	June 25, 1922
Mayo-Smith, Richmond	1890	Nov. 11, 1901
Meek, F. B	1869	Dec. 21, 1876

See footnotes at end of table.

9. Deceased Members and Foreign Associates—Continued

DECEASED MEMBERS—Continued

	Date of election	Date of death		Date of election	Date of death
Meigs, M. C.	1865	Jan. 2, 1892	Scudder, Samuel H.	1877	May 17, 1911
Meltzer, Samuel James	1912	Nov. 8, 1920	Sellers, William	1873 [1]	Jan. 24, 1905
Mendenhall, T. C.	1887	Mar. 22, 1924	Silliman, Benj., Sr.	(?)	Nov. 24, 1864
Merrill, George Perkins	1922	Aug. 15, 1929	Silliman, Benj., Jr.	(?)	Jan. 14, 1885
Michelson, A. A.	1888 [1]	May 9, 1931	Smith, Alexander	1915	Sept. 8, 1922
Minot, Charles Sedgwick	1897	Nov. 19, 1914	Smith, Edgar F.	1890 [1]	May 3, 1928
Mitchell, Henry	1885 [1]	Dec. 1, 1902	Smith, Erwin F.	1913 [1]	Apr. 6, 1927
Mitchell, Silas Weir	1865	Jan. 4, 1914	Smith, J. Lawrence	1872	Oct. 12, 1883
Moore, E. H.	1901 [1]	Dec. 30, 1932	Smith, James Perrin	1925 [1]	Jan. 1, 1931
Morgan, Louis H.	1875	Dec. 17, 1881	Smith, Sidney Irving [?]	1884	May 6, 1926
Morley, E. W.	1897	Feb. 24, 1923	Smith, Theobald	1908 [1]	Dec. 10, 1934
Morse, Edward Sylvester	1876	Dec. 20, 1925	Sperry, Elmer A.	1925 [1]	June 16, 1930
Morse, Harmon N.	1907	Sept. 8, 1920	Squier, George O.	1919 [1]	Mar. 24, 1934
Morton, Henry	1874	May 9, 1902	Stimpson, William	1868	May 26, 1872
Nef, John Ulric	1904 [1]	Aug. 13, 1915	Story, William Edward	1908 [1]	Apr. 11, 1930
Newberry, J. S.	(?)	Dec. 7, 1892	Stratton, S. W.	1917 [1]	Oct. 18, 1931
Newcomb, Simon	1869	July 11, 1909	Strong, Theodore	(?)	Feb. 1, 1869
Newton, H. A.	(?)	Aug. 12, 1896	Sullivant, W. S.	1872	Apr. 30, 1873
Newton, John	1876	May 1, 1895	Swain, George F.	1923 [1]	July 1, 1931
Nichols, Ernest Fox	1908	Apr. 29, 1924	Thaxter, Roland	1912 [1]	Apr. 22, 1932
Norton, William A.	1873	Sept. 21, 1883	Torrey, John	(?)	Mar. 10, 1873
Oliver, James E.	1872	Mar. 27, 1895	Totten, J. G.	(?)	Apr. 22, 1864
Osborne, Thomas Burr	1910	Jan. 29, 1929	Trowbridge, Augustus	1919 [1]	Mar. 14, 1934
Packard, A. S.	1872	Feb. 14, 1905	Trowbridge, John	1878	Feb. 18, 1923
Peirce, Benjamin [?]	(1 [?])	Oct. 6, 1880	Trowbridge, William P.	1872	Aug. 12, 1892
Peirce, Benjamin Osgood	1906	Jan. 14, 1914	Trumbull, James H.	1872	Aug. 5, 1897
Peirce, Charles S. S.	1877 [?]	Apr. 20, 1914	Tuckerman, Edward	1868	Mar. 15, 1886
Penfield, Samuel L.	1900	Aug. 13, 1906	Van Hise, C. R.	1902	Nov. 19, 1918
Peters, C. H. F.	1876 [1]	July 18, 1890	Vaughan, Victor Clarence	1915 [1]	Nov. 21, 1929
Pickering, Edward C.	1873	Feb. 3, 1919	Verrill, Addison E. [?]	1872	Dec. 10, 1926
Pirsson, Louis V.	1913 [1]	Dec. 8, 1919	Walcott, Charles D.	1896 [1]	Feb. 9, 1927
Pourtales, L. F.	1873	July 19, 1880	Walker, Francis A.	1878	Jan. 5, 1897
Powell, John W.	1880	Sept. 23, 1902	Warren, G. K.	1876	Aug. 8, 1882
Power, Frederick B.	1924 [1]	Mar. 26, 1927	Washburn, E. W.	1932 [1]	Feb. 6, 1934
Prudden, T. Mitchell	1901	Apr. 10, 1924	Washington, H. S.	1921 [1]	Jan. 7, 1934
Pumpelly, Raphael	1872	Aug. 10, 1923	Watson, James C.	1868	Nov. 23, 1880
Pupin, Michael Idvorsky	1905 [1]	Mar. 12, 1935	Watson, Sereno	1889	Mar. 9, 1892
Putnam, Frederic W.	1885	Aug. 18, 1915	Webster, A. G.	1903 [1]	May 15, 1923
Remsen, Ira	1882	Mar. 4, 1927	Welch, William H.	1895 [1]	Apr. 30, 1934
Richards, T. W.	1899 [1]	Apr. 2, 1928	Wells, Horace L.	1903	Dec. 19, 1924
Ridgway, Robert	1917	Mar. 25, 1929	Wheeler, Henry Lord	1909 [1]	Oct. 30, 1914
Rodgers, John	(?)	May 5, 1882	White, Charles A.	1889	June 29, 1910
Rogers, Fairman	(?)	Aug. 22, 1900	White, David	1912 [1]	Feb. 7, 1935
Rogers, Robert E.[10]	(?)	Sept. 6, 1884	Whitman, C. O.	1895	Dec. 6, 1910
Rogers, William A.	1865	Mar. 1, 1898	Whitney, Josiah D.[?]	(1 [?])	Aug. 19, 1896
Rogers, William B.[11]	(?)	May 30, 1882	Whitney, William D.[?]	1865 [1]	June 29, 1894
Rood, Ogden N.	1865	Nov. 12, 1902	Wilczynski, E. J.[?]	1919	Sept. 14, 1932
Rosa, E. B.	1913	May 17, 1921	Williston, Samuel W.	1915	Aug. 30, 1918
Rowland, Henry A.	1881	Apr. 16, 1901	Winlock, Joseph	(?)	June 11, 1875
Royce, Josiah	1906 [1]	Sept. 14, 1916	Wood, Horatio C.	1879 [1]	Jan. 3, 1920
Rutherfurd, Lewis M.	(?)	May 30, 1892	Woodward, J. J.	1873	Aug. 17, 1884
Ryan, Harris Joseph	1920 [1]	July 3, 1934	Woodward, Robert S.	1896 [1]	June 29, 1924
Sabine, Wallace C. W.	1917	Jan. 10, 1919	Worthen, A. H.	1872	May 6, 1888
St. John, Charles Edward	1924 [1]	Apr. 26, 1935	Wright, Arthur Williams	1881	Dec. 19, 1915
Sargent, Charles S.	1895	Mar. 22, 1927	Wyman, Jeffries	(?)	Sept. 4, 1874
Saxton, Joseph	(?)	Oct. 26, 1873	Young, Charles A.	1872	Jan. 3, 1908
Schott, Charles A.	1872	July 31, 1901			

DECEASED FOREIGN ASSOCIATES

Adams, J. C.
Airy, Sir George B.
Argelander, F. W. A.
Arrhenius, S. A.
Auwers, G. F. J. Arthur
Backlund, Oskar
Baer, Karl Ernest von
Baeyer, Adolf von
Barrande, Joachin
Bateson, William
Beaumont, L. Elie de
Becquerel, Henri
Berthelot, M. P. E.
Bertrand, J. L. F.
Boltzmann, Ludwig
Bornet, Edouard

Boussingault, J. B. J. D.
Boveri, Theodor
Braun, Alexander
Brewster, Sir David
Bunsen, Robert W.
Burmeister, C. H. C.
Candolle, Alphonse de
Cayley, Arthur
Chasles, Michel
Chevreul, M. E.
Clausius, Rudolph
Cornu, Alfred
Crookes, Sir William
Darboux, Gaston
Darwin, Sir George Howard
de Sitter, Willem

de Vries, Hugo
Dewar, Sir James
Dove, H. W.
Dumas, J. B.
Ehrlich, Paul
Eijkman, Christian
Engler, Adolph
Faraday, Michael
Fischer, Emil
Geikie, Sir Archibald
Geugenbaur, Karl
Gill, Sir David
Glydém, Hugo
Goebel, K. E. von
Groth, Paul von
Haber, Fritz

See footnotes at end of table.

9. *Deceased Members and Foreign Associates*—Continued

DECEASED FOREIGN ASSOCIATES—Continued

Hamilton, Sir William Rowan
Helmholtz, Baron H. von
Hoff, J. H. van't
Hofmann, A. W.
Hooker, Sir Joseph D.
Huggins, Sir William
Huxley, T. H.
Ibañez, Carlos
Janssen, J.
Jordan, M. E. C.
Joule, James P.
Kapteyn, J. C.
Kekulé, August
Kelvin, Lord
Kirchoff, G. R.
Klein, Felix
Koch, Robert
Kölliker, Albert von
Kohlrausch, Frederich
Kossel, Albrecht
Kronecker, Hugo
Lacaze-Duthiers, Henri de
Lankester, Sir E. Ray
Leuckart, Rudolph
Lie, Sophus
Liebig, Justus von
Lister, Lord

Loewy, Maurice
Lorentz, Hendrik Antoon
Ludwig, K. F. W.
Marey, E. J.
Mendeléeff, D. I.
Milne-Edwards, Henri
Moissan, Henri
Murchison, Sir Roderick I.
Murray, Sir John
Onnes, Heike Kamerlingh
Oppolzer, Theodore von
Ostwald, Wilhelm
Owen, Sir Richard
Parsons, Sir Charles Algernon
Pasteur, Louis
Peters, C. A. F.
Pfeffer, Wilhelm
Piana, G. A. A.
Poincairé, Jules Henri
Rammelsberg, C. F.
Ramon y Cajal, Santiago
Ramsey, Sir William
Rayleigh, Lord
Regnault, Victor
Retzius, Gustav
Reymond, Emil Du Bois
Richthofen, F. von

Rosenbusch, Karl Harry Ferdi-
  nand
Roux, Wilhelm
Rubner, Max
Sachs, Julius von
Schiaparelli, Giovanni
Schuster, Sir Arthur
Seeliger, Hugo R. von
Stas, Jean Servais
Stokes, Sir George G.
Strasburger, Edouard
Struve, Otto von
Suess, Eduard
Sylvester, J. J.
Tisserand, F. F.
Van der Waals, J. D.
Virchow, Rudolph von
Vogel, H. C.
Waldeyer, Wilhelm
Weierstrauss, Karl
Weismann, August
Wöhler, Frederich
Wolf, Max F. J. C.
Wundt, Wilhelm
Würtz, Adolph
Zirkel, Ferdinand
Zittell, K. A. R. von

[1] Biographical Memoirs have not been published.
[2] Charter member, Mar. 3, 1863.
[3] Transferred to roll of members emeriti, 1929.
[4] Transferred to roll of members emeriti, 1932.
[5] Resigned, 1909.
[6] Resigned, 1873.
[7] Transferred to roll of members emeriti in 1908.
[8] Transferred to roll of members emeriti in 1924.
[9] Transferred to roll of members emeriti in 1925.
[10] Dropped 1866, reelected 1875.
[11] Dropped 1866, reelected 1872.

NATIONAL RESEARCH COUNCIL

1. EXECUTIVE ORDER ISSUED BY THE PRESIDENT OF THE UNITED STATES, MAY 11, 1918

The National Research Council was organized in 1916 at the request of the President by the National Academy of Sciences, under its congressional charter, as a measure of national preparedness. The work accomplished by the Council in organizing research and in securing cooperation of military and civilian agencies in the solution of military problems demonstrates its capacity for larger service. The National Academy of Sciences is therefore requested to perpetuate the National Research Council, the duties of which shall be as follows:

1. In general, to stimulate research in the mathematical, physical, and biological sciences, and in the application of these sciences to engineering, agriculture, medicine, and other useful arts, with the object of increasing knowledge, of strengthening the national defense, and of contributing in other ways to the public welfare.

2. To survey the larger possibilities of science, to formulate comprehensive projects of research, and to develop effective means of utilizing the scientific and technical resources of the country for dealing with these projects.

3. To promote cooperation in research, at home and abroad, in order to secure concentration of effort, minimize duplication, and stimulate progress; but in all cooperative undertakings to give encouragement to individual initiative, as fundamentally important to the advancement of science.

4. To serve as a means of bringing American and foreign investigators into active cooperation with the scientific and technical services of the War and Navy Departments and with those of the civil branches of the Government.

5. To direct the attention of scientific and technical investigators to the present importance of military and industrial problems in connection with the war, and to aid in the solution of these problems by organizing specific researches.

6. To gather and collate scientific and technical information, at home and abroad, in cooperation with governmental and other agencies, and to render such information available to duly accredited persons.

Effective prosecution of the Council's work requires the cordial collaboration of the scientific and technical branches of the Government, both military and civil. To this end representatives of the Government, upon the nomination of the National Academy of Sciences, will be designated by the President as members of the Council, as heretofore, and the heads of the department immediately concerned will continue to cooperate in every way that may be required.

WOODROW WILSON

THE WHITE HOUSE, *May 11, 1918.*

(No. 2859)

2. ARTICLES OF ORGANIZATION, NATIONAL RESEARCH COUNCIL

PREAMBLE

The National Academy of Sciences, under the authority conferred upon it by its charter enacted by the Congress, and approved by President Lincoln on March 3, 1863, and pursuant to the request expressed in an Executive order made by President Wilson on May 11, 1918, adopts the following articles of organization for the National Research Council, to replace the organization under which it has operated heretofore.

ARTICLE I.—PURPOSE

It shall be the purpose of the National Research Council to promote research in the mathematical, physical, and biological sciences, and in the application of these sciences to engineering, agriculture, medicine, and other useful arts, with the object of increasing knowledge, of strengthening the national defense, and of contributing in other ways to the public welfare, as expressed in the Executive order of May 11, 1918.

ARTICLE II.—MEMBERSHIP

SECTION 1. The membership of the National Research Council shall be chosen with the view of rendering the Council an effective federation of the principal research agencies in the United States concerned with the fields of science and technology named in article I.

SEC. 2. The Council shall be composed of—
1. Representatives of national scientific and technical societies.
2. Representatives of the Government, as provided in the Executive order.
3. Representatives of other research organizations and other persons whose aid may advance the objects of the Council.

SEC. 3. The membership of the Council shall consist specifically of the members of the executive board and the members of the divisions, constituted as provided in articles III and IV.

SEC. 4. Membership in the Council shall be limited to citizens of the United States. This, however, shall not be construed as applying to membership in committees, appointed by or acting under the Council, whose members are not necessarily members of the Council, provided that members not citizens of the United States shall in no case form a majority of any committee.

ARTICLE III.—DIVISIONS

SECTION 1. The Council shall be organized in divisions of two classes:
A. Divisions dealing with the more general relations and activities of the Council.
B. Divisions dealing with special branches of science and technology.

SEC. 2. The divisions of the Council shall be as follows:
A. Divisions of general relations:

    I. Division of federal relations.
    II. Division of foreign relations.
    III. Division of States relations.
    IV. Division of educational relations.

B. Divisions of science and technology:

    V. Division of physical sciences.
    VI. Division of engineering and industrial research.
    VII. Division of chemistry and chemical technology.
    VIII. Division of geology and geography.
    IX. Division of medical sciences.
    X. Division of biology and agriculture.
    XI. Division of anthropology and psychology.

SEC. 3. The number of divisions and the grouping of subjects in article III, section 2, may be modified by the executive board of the National Research Council.

SEC. 4. (a) Each division of general relations shall consist of a chairman, one or more vice chairmen, representatives of national and international organizations, and members-at-large, appointed as provided in article VI.

(b) There may be an executive committee of each division of general relations, consisting of the chairman and three or more of the members, who shall be chosen by the division at a regular meeting, confirmed by the executive board, and hold office for 1 year, terminating on June 30, or, in case of any one or more of such executive committees, on such later date as the chairman of the Council may have previously ordered. Between meetings of a division its executive committee shall have power to act on all matters for the division, except those which may be reserved by the division for its own action; but the executive committee shall report all its actions to the division.

Sec. 5 (a) Each division of science and technology shall consist of a chairman and of representatives of such national societies as seem essential for the conduct of the business of the division, appointed as provided in article VI. Members-at-large, not to exceed three, may also be appointed as provided in article VI. From the membership of the division thus constituted, a smaller group, not to exceed 12, shall be designated as executive members who alone may be reimbursed by the National Research Council for travel expenses incurred in attendance upon meetings of the division.

(b) There may be an executive committee of each division of science and technology, consisting of the chairman and three or more of the executive members, who shall be chosen by the division at a regular meeting, confirmed by the executive board, and hold office for 1 year terminating on June 30 or, in the case of any one or more of such executive committees, on such later date as the chairman of the Council may have previously ordered. Between meetings of a division its executive committee shall have power to act on all matters for the division except those which may be reserved by the division for its own action; but the executive committee shall report all its actions to the division.

(c) The terms of office of the chairman of the divisions of science and technology, other than that of engineering and industrial research, shall be so arranged by the chairman of the Council that one-third of these terms expire each year.

Sec. 6. The chairman of each division shall be, ex officio, a member of all committees of the division.

Sec. 7. Actions by the divisions involving matters of policy shall be subject to approval by the executive board.

Article IV.—Administration

Section 1. The general officers of the National Research Council shall be a chairman, chosen as provided in article V, section 1, a treasurer (see art. V, sec. 3), and such honorary officers as may be appointed by the council of the National Academy of Sciences, upon nomination by the executive board.

Sec. 2. The affairs of the National Research Council shall be administered by an executive board and its administrative committee. Actions by these bodies involving financial responsibilities or the appointment of general officers must be approved by the council of the National Academy of Sciences, or by the executive committee of the council of the National Academy of Sciences under general authority, or under such special authority as may be conferred on it by the council of the National Academy of Sciences.

Sec. 3. The executive board shall consist of the members of the executive committee of the council of the National Academy of Sciences; the chairman, treasurer, and honorary officers of the National Research Council; the chairmen of the divisions of general relations and of the divisions of science and technology of the National Research Council; the members of the committee on policies; the president or other representative of the American Association for the Advancement of Science; the chairman or other representative of the Engineering Foundation; and six members-at-large appointed for a term of 3 years, or for an unexpired term in case of vacancy, by the president of the National Academy of Sciences, on recommendation of the executive board. The president of the National Academy of Sciences shall preside at the meetings of the executive board.

Sec. 4. In administrative matters the executive board shall be represented by an administrative committee, which shall consist of the chairman and treasurer of the National Research Council, the president, vice president, and home secretary of the National Academy, and the chairmen of the divisions of science and technology of the National Research Council.

Sec. 5. The administrative committee shall have power to act upon all matters except those which may be reserved by the executive board for its own action; but the administrative committee shall report all its actions to the executive board. The administrative committee shall prepare the annual budget for submission to the executive board at its annual meeting.

Sec. 6. (a) There shall also be a committee on policies of the National Research Council. This committee shall be composed of nine members appointed for terms of 3 years by the executive board, preferably so that it may consist largely of persons who have had past experience in the affairs of the National Research

Council. The executive board shall appoint the chairman of the committee on policies to serve for 1 year beginning July 1, or until his successor is appointed. This committee shall submit to the executive board recommendations as to general policies.

(b) At the annual meeting of the executive board in 1933, nine members of the committee on policies shall be appointed; three to serve for 1 year, three for 2 years, and three for 3 years, their respective terms to be determined by lot. Each year thereafter the terms of three members will expire, and their successors, to serve for 3 years each, shall be appointed at the annual meeting of the executive board in that year. The date of expiration of the terms shall be June 30. In case of vacancy the executive board may fill the unexpired term by appointment.

ARTICLE V.—APPOINTMENT AND DUTIES OF OFFICERS OF THE RESEARCH COUNCIL

SECTION 1. The chairman of the National Research Council shall be appointed by the executive board, subject to confirmation by the council of the National Academy of Sciences, and shall hold office at the pleasure of the board. The chairman shall be the executive officer of the National Research Council and shall have charge of its general administration. He shall act as chairman of its administrative committee, and shall be, ex officio, a member of all divisions and committees of the Council.

SEC. 2. There shall be appointed by the executive board, upon recommendation of the chairman of the National Research Council, an officer with the title of executive secretary of the Council, whose duties it shall be to assist the chairman in the administration of the Council. He shall attend all meetings of the executive board and of the administrative committee, and act as their secretary, and shall hold office at the pleasure of the board.

SEC. 3. The treasurer of the National Academy of Sciences shall be, ex officio, treasurer of the National Research Council.

SEC. 4. In case of a vacancy in the office of the chairman of the National Research Council or of the absence or disability of the chairman, an acting chairman may be appointed by the council of the National Academy of Sciences, or by the executive committee of the council of the National Academy, upon recommendation of the executive board of the Research Council or its administrative committee.

ARTICLE VI.—NOMINATION AND APPOINTMENT OF OFFICERS AND MEMBERS OF DIVISIONS

SECTION 1. *Divisions of science and technology.*—(a) The chairman of each division shall be nominated to the executive board by the division concerned, with the approval of the administrative committee. The chairman shall be appointed by the executive board at its annual meeting for a term of 3 years.

(b) The national societies to be represented in each of the divisions shall be determined by the division concerned, subject to the approval of the executive board.

(c) The representatives of national societies in each division shall be nominated by the societies, at the request of the chairman of the division, and, after approval by the executive board, shall be appointed by the president of the National Academy of Sciences to membership in the National Research Council for a term of 3 years, and assigned to the division.

(d) Members-at-large, if any, in each division shall be nominated by the division concerned, with the approval of the executive board, and shall be appointed by the president of the National Academy of Sciences to membership in the National Research Council for a term of 3 years, and assigned to the division.

(e) The executive members in each division shall be designated by the division concerned, subject to the approval of the executive board.

SEC. 2. *Divisions of general relations.*—(a) The officers of each of the divisions of general relations shall be appointed by the executive board to serve for a period of 3 years, except that the foreign secretary of the National Academy of Sciences shall be, ex officio, chairman of the division of foreign relations, and that the appointment of the chairman of the division of Federal relations shall be subject to confirmation by the council of the National Academy of Sciences.

(b) The national and international societies or associations to be represented in each of these divisions shall be determined by the division concerned, subject to the approval of the executive board.

(c) The representatives of such societies or associations shall be nominated by the societies or associations, at the request of the chairman of the division, and, after approval by the executive board, shall be appointed by the president of the National Academy of Sciences to membership in the Council for a period of 3 years, and assigned to the division.

(d) Members-at-large in each division shall be nominated by the division, approved by the executive board, and appointed by the president of the National Academy of Sciences to membership in the Council for a period of 3 years, and assigned to the division.

(e) The Government bureaus, civil and military, to be represented in the division of Federal relations shall be determined by the council of the National Academy of Sciences, on recommendation from the executive board of the National Research Council.

(f) The representatives of the Government shall be nominated by the president of the National Academy of Sciences, after conference with the secretaries of the departments concerned, and the names of those nominated shall be presented to the President of the United States for designation by him for service with the National Research Council. Each Government representative shall serve during the pleasure of the President of the United States, not to exceed a term of 3 years, and a vacancy from any cause shall be filled for the remainder of the term in the same manner as in the case of the original designation.

SEC. 3. The terms of office of officers and members, unless otherwise provided, shall terminate on June 30 of the year in which their appointments expire.

SEC. 4. Vacancies occurring in the divisions of either class, except as to representatives of the Government, may be filled for the unexpired term by the executive board, upon recommendation of the division concerned, or ad interim by the administrative committee upon similar recommendation.

ARTICLE VII.—MEETINGS

SECTION 1. The annual meeting of the executive board shall be held in April in the city of Washington at the time of the meeting of the National Academy of Sciences. Special meetings may be held at other times at the call of the chairman of the National Research Council. A majority of the members of the board shall constitute a quorum for the transaction of business.

SEC. 2. Stated meetings of the administrative committee shall be held in the city of Washington at least five times a year, at such dates as shall be determined by the chairman of the National Research Council. Special meetings may be held at other times on call of the chairman. Five members of the committee shall constitute a quorum for the transaction of business.

SEC. 3. The committee on policies shall hold one stated meeting during the year, preferably in Washington at the time of the annual meeting of the National Academy of Sciences. Special meetings may be held at any time on call of the chairman of the committee. Five members of the committee shall constitute a quorum for the transaction of business.

SEC. 4. Each division of science and technology shall hold at least one stated meeting during the year, at a time to be determined by the chairman of the division in consultation with the chairman of the Council. Special meetings may be called at other times by the chairman of the division.

SEC. 5. Meetings of any division of general relations shall be held upon the call of its chairman.

ARTICLE VIII.—PUBLICATIONS AND REPORTS

SECTION 1. An annual report on the work of the National Research Council shall be presented by the chairman to the National Academy of Sciences.

SEC. 2. Other publications of the National Research Council may include papers, bulletins, reports, and memoirs, which may appear in the Proceedings or Memoirs of the National Academy of Sciences, in the publications of other societies, in scientific and technical journals, or in a separate series of the National Research Council.

ARTICLE IX—AMENDMENTS

SECTION 1. By action of the National Academy of Sciences, on April 29, 1919, power of amendment of these articles of organization is given to the council of the National Academy of Sciences.

3. BYLAWS

1. There shall be a publication and Research Information Service, to consist of a director and such other staff as the executive board shall direct. The service shall be under the supervision of a standing committee of the executive board which shall be composed of the chairman and treasurer of the National Research Council, the chairman of the committee on policies, and the director of the Service. The functions of the Service shall be to cooperate with the divisions of the National Research Council in obtaining required data, to maintain a library of sources, to prepare compilations of general scientific interest, and to edit and superintend the publication of all bulletins, reprints, and miscellaneous printed matter issued by the National Research Council. The director of the Service shall attend the meetings of the administrative committee, but without vote.

2. The treasurer shall have the assistance of a salaried and bonded officer, the bursar, who shall be chosen by the finance committee of the National Academy of Sciences and be directly responsible to the treasurer.

3. The executive board may create such other salaried officers as are necessary for the transaction of the business of the Council.

4. Officers of the Council, members of the executive board, and special agents of the Council, when authorized to travel on business of the Council, may be allowed their necessary expenses.

5. Executive members of the divisions of science and technology and members of the executive committee of any division of general relations, when attending an authorized meeting, may be reimbursed for traveling expenses, or such portion thereof as the division chairman may determine, within the funds made available for that purpose in the budget.

6. The chairman of each division shall direct the administrative and scientific work of the division.

7. In the fiscal year in which the term of office of a chairman of a division expires it shall be his duty to appoint, on or before February 1, a nominating committee of three, chosen from present or former members of the division or from the membership of existing committees of the division, who, in consultation with the chairman of the division and the chairman of the Council, shall select an available candidate for the chairmanship for the ensuing term. The name of the candidate shall be reported to the division through its chairman and, if approved by the division, shall be recommended to the executive board at its annual meeting for appointment, as provided in article VI, sections 1 and 2, of the articles of organization.

8. Each division of science and technology is empowered to arrange, in accordance with its special needs, for the selection of the executive members and members-at-large of the division, and for an executive committee, to be appointed annually, as provided in article III, section 5 (a) and (b), and article VI, section 1 (d) of the articles of organization.

Each division may designate also one of its executive members to act as vice chairman of the division, the term of office to be for 1 year.

9. Following the termination of any regular 3-year period of service the chairman or members of a division shall be eligible for reappointment in the same status only after a lapse of 1 year, except that the executive board may continue the service of a chairman or members for a second period of 3 years, or less, when such action is recommended by the division concerned.

10. An annual honorarium may be paid to the chairman of each division of science and technology, and an annual maintenance fund shall be appropriated for the support of the work of each division of the Council. The amount of the honorarium and of the maintenance fund of each division shall be determined by the administrative committee, subject to the approval of the executive board and the council of the National Academy of Sciences or its executive committee.

11. The maintenance fund allotted to each division shall be expended under the authority of the chairman of the division to provide for meetings of the

division and its various committees, and other necessary expenses, in accordance with the regulations in force in the Council controlling financial expenditures.

12. No member of a committee constituted to administer funds entrusted to the National Research Council shall receive an honorarium or salary from such funds for his services, except in cases specifically authorized in advance by the executive board or its administrative committee, but members of such committees may be reimbursed from the funds for expenses incurred in the work of the committee.

13. Members of special committees organized within any of the divisions must be approved by the administrative committee before official notification of appointment is made by the chairman of the division.

14. Solicitation of funds for the support of projects of a division may be made only after authorization by both the executive board (or its administrative committee) and the council of the National Academy of Sciences (or its executive committee). Such solicitation shall be conducted under the direction of the chairman of the National Research Council acting in conjunction with the chairman of the division concerned.

15. Special funds granted to the National Research Council, other than those for fellowships and grants-in-aid, must be expended in accordance with budgets previously approved by the administrative committee.

16. It shall be the duty of the chairman of each division of the Council to submit an annual report of the activities of his division to the chairman of the Council on or before June 30. Interim reports shall be made to the chairman of the Council before each stated meeting of the administrative committee.

17. Standing committees of the executive board, unless otherwise provided for, shall be appointed annually by the board at its April meeting, or, in case of need, by the administrative committee at one of its stated meetings.

18. The executive board, at its annual meeting in April, shall appoint a nominating committee of three members to prepare nominations for presentation at the next annual meeting of the board for vacancies in the committee on policies and in the list of members at large of the board, occurring at the end of the fiscal year.

19. Amendments of bylaws may be made by the executive board at any authorized meeting of the board.

20. A publication to be known as the Bulletin of the National Research Council shall be established to provide for the publication of materials originating in the work of the Council. The Bulletin shall be issued as occasion demands.

21. A series to be known as the Reprint and Circular Series of the National Research Council shall provide for the distribution of papers published or printed by or for the National Research Council.

4. ORGANIZATION OF THE COUNCIL, 1934-35

A. Officers and Executive Board

OFFICERS

Honorary chairman, George E. Hale, honorary director, Mount Wilson Observatory, Carnegie Institution of Washington, Pasadena, Calif.

Secretary emeritus, Vernon Kellogg, National Research Council, Washington, D. C.

Chairman, Isaiah Bowman, director, American Geographical Society; National Research Council, Washington, D. C.

Treasurer, Arthur Keith, treasurer, National Academy of Sciences; geologist, United States Geological Survey, Washington, D. C.

Executive secretary, Albert L. Barrows, National Research Council, Washington, D. C.

Bursar, J. H. J. Yule, National Research Council, Washington, D. C.

Chief clerk, C. L. Wade, National Research Council, Washington, D. C.

EXECUTIVE BOARD

Presiding officer, W. W. Campbell, president, National Academy of Sciences; president emeritus, University of California, and director emeritus, Lick Observatory; National Academy of Sciences, Washington, D. C.

MEMBERS

Honorary chairman, chairman, secretary emeritus, treasurer, and chairmen of divisions of the National Research Council.

Executive Committee of the Council of the National Academy of Sciences

W. W. Campbell.

Arthur L. Day, vice president, National Academy of Sciences; director, Geophysical Laboratory, Carnegie Institution of Washington, 2801 Upton Street, Washington, D. C.

Fred. E. Wright, home secretary, National Academy of Sciences; petrologist, Geophysical Laboratory, Carnegie Institution of Washington, 2801 Upton Street, Washington, D. C.

Arthur Keith.

Isaiah Bowman.

Ross G. Harrison, Sterling professor of biology, and director of the Osborn Zoological Laboratory, Yale University, New Haven, Conn.

Henry Norris Russell, Charles A. Young professor of astronomy, and director of the observatory, Princeton University, Princeton, N. J.

Committee on Policies of the National Research Council

R. A. Millikan, chairman, director. Norman Bridge Laboratory of Physics, and chairman of the executive council, California Institute of Technology, Pasadena, Calif.

Walter B. Cannon, George Higginson professor of physiology, Harvard Medical School, Boston, Mass.

Karl T. Compton, president, Massachusetts Institute of Technology, Cambridge, Mass.

Simon Flexner, director, Rockefeller Institute for Medical Research, Sixtysixth Street and York Avenue, New York City.

Frank B. Jewett, vice president, American Telephone & Telegraph Co.; president, Bell Telephone Laboratories, Inc., 195 Broadway, New York City.

A. V. Kidder, chairman, division of historical research, Carnegie Institution of Washington, P. O. Box 71, Andover, Mass.

Frank R. Lillie, dean of the division of biological sciences, and professor of embryology, University of Chicago, Chicago, Ill.

John C. Merriam, president, Carnegie Institution of Washington, Washington, D. C.

A. A. Noyes, director, Gates Chemical Laboratory, California Institute of Technology. Pasadena, Calif.

Representatives of Organizations

President of the American Association for the Advancement of Science, Karl T. Compton.

Representative of the Engineering Foundation, H. P. Charlesworth, assistant chief engineer, American Telephone & Telegraph Co., 195 Broadway, New York City.

Members at Large

Knight Dunlap, professor of experimental psychology, Johns Hopkins University, Baltimore, Md.

Gano Dunn, president, J. G. White Engineering Corporation, 80 Broad Street, New York City.

Nevin M. Fenneman, professor of geology and geography, University of Cincinnati, Cincinnati, Ohio.

John Johnston, director of research, United States Steel Corporation, Kearney, N. J.

Oswald Veblen, professor of mathematics, Institute for Advanced Study, Princeton University, Princeton, N. J.

A. F. Woods, principal pathologist, Bureau of Plant Industry, United States Department of Agriculture, Washington, D. C.

Chairman, Isaiah Bowman; the treasurer of the National Research Council, the president, vice president, and home secretary of the National Academy of Sciences, and the chairmen of the divisions of science and technology of the National Research Council.

COMMITTEES

The chairman of the National Research Council is, ex officio, a member of all divisions and committees of the Council.

Committee on grants-in-aid: Chairman, Isaiah Bowman; Edson S. Bastin, Francis G. Blake, Arthur Keith, Charles F. Kettering, I. F. Lewis, F. K. Richtmyer, Edward Sapir, F. W. Willard. Secretary, C. J. West.

Committee on nominations: Chairman, Arthur L. Day; Karl T. Compton, I. F. Lewis.

Committee on publication and Research Information Service: Chairman, ex officio, Isaiah Bowman; Arthur Keith, ex officio; R. A. Millikan, ex officio; C. J. West, ex officio. Director of publication and Research Information Service, C. J. West.

Committee on building (joint committee with the National Academy of Sciences): Chairman, Gano Dunn; George E. Hale, H. E. Howe, Vernon Kellogg, John C. Merriam, R. A. Millikan, A. A. Noyes. Secretary of the committee, Paul Brockett.

Advisory committee on buildings and grounds (joint committee with the National Academy of Sciences): Chairman, Paul Brockett, executive secretary and custodian of buildings and grounds, National Academy of Sciences, Washington, D. C.; Arthur L. Day, F. K. Richtmyer, Gano Dunn, Fred. E. Wright.

Committee on exhibits (joint committee with the National Academy of Sciences): Chairman, Fred. E. Wright; secretary, Paul Brockett; Edson S. Bastin, Isaiah Bowman, Francis G. Blake, A. B. Coble, George E. Hale, Ludvig Hektoen, L. J. Henderson, A. W. Hull, Arthur E. Kennelly, Charles F. Kettering, Elmer P. Kohler, C. K. Leith, I. F. Lewis, Frank R. Lillie, Elmer D. Merrill, F. K. Richtmyer, Edward Sapir, Harlow Shapley, Joel Stebbins, F. W. Willard, R. S. Woodworth.

Executive committee: Chairman, Fred. E. Wright; secretary, Paul Brockett; Arthur L. Day, George E. Hale, Vernon Kellogg, John C. Merriam.

Advisory committee on fellowships: Chairman, ex officio, Isaiah Bowman; Francis G. Blake, Simon Flexner, F. K. Richtmyer, W. J. Robbins, E. B. Wilson.

Committee on patent policy: Chairman, Karl T. Compton; Simon Flexner, Archie Palmer, Joseph Rossman, Robert E. Wilson.

TECHNICAL COMMITTEES

Committee on cooperation with Research Corporation: Chairman, F. G. Cottrell, consulting chemist, United States Bureau of Chemistry and Soils, Washington, D. C.; William J. Hale, Maurice Holland.

Committee on publication of excerpts from International Critical Tables: Isaiah Bowman, F. K. Richtmyer, F. W. Willard.

Advisory Committee to the American Commissioners on Annual Tables of Constants and Numerical Data: Chairman, F. K. Richtmyer, dean of the Graduate School and professor of physics, Cornell University, Ithaca, N. Y.; Saul Dushman, Frank B. Jewett, John Johnston, Charles F. Kettering, C. E. K. Mees, Charles L. Parsons. American commissioners, F. K. Richtmyer and C. J. West.

Committee of apparatus makers and users—executive committee: Chairman, W. D. Collins, chief, division of quality of water, United States Geological Survey, Washington, D. C.; secretary, C. J. West; Lyman J. Briggs, Arthur L. Day, Morris E. Leeds, F. K. Richtmyer, J. M. Roberts.

Executive committee of the American Geophysical Union (representing the American section of the International Geodetic and Geophysical Union): Chairman, W. J. Humphreys, principal meteorologist, in charge of meteorological physics, United States Weather Bureau, Washington, D. C.; vice chairman, Austin H. Clark; secretary, John A. Fleming; H. G. Avers, Edson S. Bastin, William Bowie, C. N. Fenner, W. R. Gregg, D. L. Hazard, N. H. Heck, H. F.

Johnston, I. F. Lewis, H. A. Marmer, T. H. Morgan, F. K. Richtmyer, C. S. Scofield, Frank Wenner, F. W. Willard.

Advisory committee on instruments and methods of research (to cooperate with a similar committee of the International Council of Scientific Unions): Chairman, Fred. E. Wright; O. G. Abbot, F. K. Richtmyer.

Committee on naval research (joint committee with the Science Advisory Board): Chairman, R. A. Millikan; Francis G. Blake, Isaiah Bowman, Frank B. Jewett, Charles F. Kettering, C. K. Leith, F. K. Richtmyer, F. W. Willard.

Committee on research publications: Chairman, F. K. Richtmyer; Edson S. Bastin, Francis G. Blake, Isaiah Bowman, Davenport Hooker, Arthur B. Lamb, H. C. Parmelee, Edward Sapir. Secretary, C. J. West.

REPRESENTATIVES OF THE COUNCIL ON—

Editorial Board of the Proceedings of the National Academy of Sciences: Edson S. Bastin, Francis G. Blake, Isaiah Bowman, Charles F. Kettering, I. F. Lewis, F. K. Richtmyer, Edward Sapir, F. W. Willard. Member of the editorial executive committee, Isaiah Bowman.

Council of the National Parks Association: Vernon Kellogg.

Board of Trustees of Science Service: C. G. Abbot, Ludvig Hektoen, H. E. Howe.

B. Divisions of the Council

I. DIVISION OF FEDERAL RELATIONS

Chairman, George R. Putnam.
Vice chairman, ——— ———.
Secretary, Paul Brockett.

EXECUTIVE COMMITTEE

Chairman, George R. Putnam; vice chairman, ——— ———; J. R. Mohler, A. M. Stimson.

MEMBERS OF THE DIVISION

Paul Brockett, secretary of the division; executive secretary and custodian of buildings and grounds, National Academy of Sciences, Washington, D. C.

The President of the United States, on the nomination of the National Academy of Sciences, has designated the following representatives of the various departments to act as members of this division.

DEPARTMENT OF STATE

Wilbur J. Carr, Assistant Secretary of State.

DEPARTMENT OF THE TREASURY

A. M. Stimson, Medical Director, Public Health Service.

DEPARTMENT OF WAR

Brig. Gen. Harry E. Knight, General Staff, in charge of military intelligence, United States Army.

Maj. Randolph T. Pendleton, Coast Artillery Corps, United States Army.

Col. Roger Brooke, Medical Corps, United States Army.

Lt. Col. Francis B. Wilby, Corps of Engineers, United States Army.

Col. John E. Munroe, Ordnance Department, United States Army.

Maj. Gen. Irving J. Carr, Chief Signal Officer, United States Army.

Maj. Gen. B. D. Foulois, Air Corps, United States Army.

Maj. Gen. Claude E. Brigham, Chief, Chemical Warfare Service, United States Army.

DEPARTMENT OF JUSTICE

J. Edgar Hoover, Director, Federal Bureau of Investigation.

POST OFFICE DEPARTMENT

Wrightson Chambers, superintendent, Division of Engineering and Research.

DEPARTMENT OF THE NAVY

———— ————, Director of Naval Intelligence, Office of Naval Operations, United States Navy.

Capt. J. F. Hellweg, superintendent, Naval Observatory, Bureau of Navigation, United States Navy.

———— ————, Chief, Bureau of Yards and Docks, United States Navy.

Rear Admiral Harold R. Stark, Chief, Bureau of Ordnance, United States Navy.

Rear Admiral Emory S. Land, Chief, Bureau of Construction and Repair, United States Navy.

Rear Admiral Samuel M. Robinson, Chief, Bureau of Engineering, United States Navy.

Rear Admiral Percival E. Rossiter, Chief, Bureau of Medicine and Surgery, United States Navy.

DEPARTMENT OF THE INTERIOR

Elwood Mead, Commissioner, Bureau of Reclamation.
W. C. Mendenhall, Director, Geological Survey.
Harold C. Bryant, Assistant Director, National Park Service.

DEPARTMENT OF AGRICULTURE

———— ————, Weather Bureau.
J. R. Mohler, Chief, Bureau of Animal Industry.
E. H. Clapp, Assistant Forester, in charge of the Branch of Research, Forest Service.
Henry G. Knight, Chief, Bureau of Chemistry and Soils.
Lee A. Strong, Chief, Bureau of Entomology and Plant Quarantine.
———— ————, Bureau of Biological Survey.
Thomas H. MacDonald, Chief, Bureau of Public Roads.
S. H. McCrory, Chief, Bureau of Agricultural Engineering.

DEPARTMENT OF COMMERCE

Joseph A. Hill, Chief Statistician, Statistical Research, Bureau of the Census.
Lyman J. Briggs, Director, National Bureau of Standards.
Frank T. Bell, Commissioner, Bureau of Fisheries.
George R. Putnam, Commissioner, Bureau of Lighthouses.
William Bowie, Chief, Division of Geodesy, Coast and Geodetic Survey.
Charles H. Pierce, Classification Examiner, Patent Office.
———— ————, Bureau of Mines.

DEPARTMENT OF LABOR

Isador Lubin, Commissioner of Labor Statistics.

SMITHSONIAN INSTITUTION

C. G. Abbot, Secretary, Smithsonian Institution.

NATIONAL ADVISORY COMMITTEE FOR AERONAUTICS

J. S. Ames, Chairman, National Advisory Committee for Aeronautics; president, Johns Hopkins University, Baltimore, Md.

II. DIVISION OF FOREIGN RELATIONS

Chairman, ex officio, T. H. Morgan.
Vice chairman, Wilbur J. Carr.
Vice chairman, Arthur E. Kennelly.
Secretary, Albert L. Barrows.

EXECUTIVE COMMITTEE

Chairman, T. H. Morgan; vice chairmen, Wilbur J. Carr and Arthur E. Kennelly; William Bowie, Lyman J. Briggs, Herbert E. Gregory, George E. Hale, T. Wayland Vaughan.

MEMBERS OF THE DIVISION

Ex officio

President of the National Academy of Sciences: W. W. Campbell, president emeritus, University of California, and director emeritus, Lick Observatory; National Academy of Sciences, Washington, D. C.

Foreign secretary of the National Academy of Sciences: T. H. Morgan, chairman of the division of biology, William G. Kerckhoff laboratories of the biological sciences, California Institute of Technology, Pasadena, Calif.

Chairman of the National Research Council, the chairmen of all divisions of the Council, and the director of the Research Information Service.

Representatives of—

AMERICAN ASSOCIATION FOR THE ADVANCEMENT OF SCIENCE

W. A. Noyes, emeritus professor of chemistry, University of Illinois, Urbana, Ill.

AMERICAN ACADEMY OF ARTS AND SCIENCES

Arthur E. Kennelly, vice chairman of the division; emeritus professor of electrical engineering, Harvard University, Cambridge, Mass.

AMERICAN PHILOSOPHICAL SOCIETY

L. S. Rowe, Director, Pan American Union, Washington, D. C.

DEPARTMENT OF STATE

Wilbur J. Carr, vice chairman of the division; Assistant Secretary of State, Washington, D. C.

DEPARTMENT OF THE NAVY

———— ————, Naval Intelligence, Office of Naval Operations, Washington, D. C.

DEPARTMENT OF WAR

Brig. Gen. Harry E. Knight, General Staff, in charge of Military Intelligence Division, Washington, D. C.

INTERNATIONAL ASTRONOMICAL UNION

Henry Norris Russell, ex officio, chairman, American section, International Astronomical Union; Charles A. Young professor of astronomy and director of the observatory, Princeton University, Princeton, N. J.

INTERNATIONAL GEODETIC AND GEOPHYSICAL UNION

Henry B. Bigelow, director, Woods Hole Oceanographic Institute; professor of zoology and curator of oceanography in the Museum of Comparative Zoology, Harvard University, Cambridge, Mass.

William Bowie, president, Association of Geodesy, International Geodetic and Geophysical Union; Chief, Division of Geodesy, United States Coast and Geodetic Survey, Washington, D. C.

Lyman J. Briggs, Director, National Bureau of Standards, Washington, D. C.

John A. Fleming, general secretary, American Geophysical Union; president, Association of Terrestrial Magnetism and Electricity, International Geodetic and Geophysical Union; acting director, department of terrestrial magnetism, Carnegie Institution of Washington, 5241 Broad Branch Road, Washington, D. C.

W. J. Humphreys, chairman, American Geophysical Union; principal meteorologist in charge of meteorological physics, United States Weather Bureau, Washington, D. C.

C. S. Scofield, chairman, section of hydrology, American Geophysical Union; principal agriculturist, United States Bureau of Plant Industry, Washington, D. C.

Thomas G. Thompson, member of the executive committee of the Association on Oceanography, International Union of Geodesy and Geophysics; professor of chemistry and director of the oceanographic laboratories, University of Washington, Seattle, Wash.

INTERNATIONAL UNION OF CHEMISTRY

Edward Bartow, vice president, International Union of Chemistry; professor of chemistry and head of the department of chemistry and chemical engineering, State University of Iowa, Iowa City, Iowa.

INTERNATIONAL UNION OF PURE AND APPLIED PHYSICS

F. K. Richtmyer, ex-officio, chairman, division of physical sciences, National Research Council; dean of the Graduate School and professor of physics, Cornell University, Ithaca, N. Y.

INTERNATIONAL SCIENTIFIC RADIO UNION

Arthur E. Kennelly, ex-officio, chairman of the American section, International Scientific Radio Union; emeritus professor of electrical engineering, Harvard University, Cambridge, Mass.

INTERNATIONAL GEOGRAPHICAL UNION

Douglas Johnson, chairman, national committee of the United States, International Geographical Union; professor of physiography, Columbia University, New York City.

INTERNATIONAL BUREAU OF WEIGHTS AND MEASURES

Lyman J. Briggs, Director, National Bureau of Standards, Washington, D. C.

INTERNATIONAL ELECTROTECHNICAL COMMISSION

Clayton H. Sharp, president, United States national committee of the International Electrotechnical Commission, 294 Fisher Avenue, White Plains, N. Y.

INTERNATIONAL COMMISSION ON ILLUMINATION

E. C. Crittenden, Chief, Electrical Division, and Assistant Director, National Bureau of Standards, Washington, D. C.

Members at Large

P. G. Agnew, secretary, American Standards Association, 29 West Thirty-ninth Street, New York City.

Hugh S. Cumming, Surgeon General, United States Public Health Service, Washington, D. C.

Herbert E. Gregory, director, Bishop Museum of Polynesian Ethnology and Natural History, Honolulu, Hawaii.

George E. Hale, honorary director, Mount Wilson Observatory, Carnegie Institution of Washington, Pasadena, Calif.

Maurice C. Hall, principal zoologist in charge of the Zoological Division, United States Bureau of Animal Industry, Washington, D. C.

John C. Merriam, president, Carnegie Institution of Washington, Washington, D. C.

Elihu Root, 31 Nassau Street, New York City.

Frank Schlesinger, professor of astronomy and director of the observatory, Yale University, New Haven, Conn.

Walter T. Swingle, principal physiologist in charge of crop physiology and breeding investigations, United States Bureau of Plant Industry, Washington, D. C.

T. Wayland Vaughan, director, Scripps Institution of Oceanography, La Jolla, Calif.

COMMITTEES

The chairman of the division is, ex officio, a member of all committees of the division.

Committee on Pacific Investigations: Chairman, Herbert E. Gregory.

COMMITTEES COOPERATING WITH INTERNATIONAL COMMITTEES OF THE PACIFIC SCIENCE ASSOCIATION

American National Committee on Oceanography of the Pacific: Chairman, T. Wayland Vaughan.

American National Committee on Land Classification and Utilization in the Pacific: Chairman, Carl O. Sauer, professor of geography, University of California, Berkeley, Calif.

American Committee on Pacific Seismology: Chairman, James B. Macelwane, S. J., professor of geophysics and dean of the Graduate School, St. Louis University, St. Louis, Mo.

REPRESENTATIVE OF THE NATIONAL RESEARCH COUNCIL ON—

Council of the Pacific Science Association: Herbert E. Gregory.

III. DIVISION OF STATES RELATIONS

Chairman, Raymond A. Pearson.
Vice chairman, Albert L. Barrows.

EXECUTIVE COMMITTEE

Chairman, Raymond A. Pearson; vice chairman, Albert L. Barrows; Morris M. Leighton, Jacob G. Lipman, A. R. Mann, Edwin G. Nourse, A. F. Woods, B. Youngblood.

MEMBERS OF THE DIVISION

Raymond A. Pearson, chairman of the division; president, University of Maryland, College Park, Md.

Albert L. Barrows, vice chairman of the division; executive secretary, National Research Council, Washington, D. C.

Representatives of—

DIVISION OF EDUCATIONAL RELATIONS

———— ————.

DIVISION OF PHYSICAL SCIENCES

William Bowie, Chief, Division of Geodesy, United States Coast and Geodetic Survey, Washington, D. C.

DIVISION OF ENGINEERING AND INDUSTRIAL RESEARCH

A. C. Fieldner, chief engineer, Experiment Stations Division, United States Bureau of Mines, Washington, D. C.

DIVISION OF CHEMISTRY AND CHEMICAL TECHNOLOGY

Frank C. Whitmore, dean, School of Chemistry and Physics, Pennsylvania State College, State College, Pa.

Chairman of the medical fellowship board, National Research Council. Francis G. Blake, Sterling professor of medicine, School of Medicine, Yale University; physician in chief, New Haven Hospital, New Haven, Conn.

Chairman of the board of national research fellowships in the biological sciences, National Research Council. W. J. Robbins, professor of botany, and dean of the Graduate School, University of Missouri, Columbia, Mo.

Representatives of—

ASSOCIATION OF LAND-GRANT COLLEGES AND UNIVERSITIES

Raymond A. Pearson, president, University of Maryland, College Park, Md.

AMERICAN ASSOCIATION OF UNIVERSITY PROFESSORS

F. K. Richtmyer, dean of the graduate school and professor of physics, Cornell University, Ithaca, N. Y.

AMERICAN COUNCIL ON EDUCATION

C. R. Mann, director emeritus, American Council of Education, 744 Jackson Place, Washington, D. C.

ASSOCIATION OF AMERICAN COLLEGES

Arthur H. Compton, Charles H. Swift distinguished service professor of physics, University of Chicago, Chicago, Ill.

ASSOCIATION OF AMERICAN UNIVERSITIES

———— ————

NATIONAL ASSOCIATION OF STATE UNIVERSITIES

Frank L. McVey, president, University of Kentucky, Lexington, Ky.

UNITED STATES OFFICE OF EDUCATION

Frederick J. Kelly, chief, division of collegiate-professional education, Office of Education, United States Department of the Interior, Washington, D. C.

Members-at-Large

Harry W. Chase, president, New York University, New York City.

James Bryant Conant, president, Harvard University, Cambridge, Mass.

C. E. McClung, professor of zoology and director of the zoological laboratory, University of Pennsylvania, Philadelphia, Pa.

A. R. Mann, provost, Cornell University, Ithaca, N. Y.

John C. Merriam, president, Carnegie Institution of Washington, Washington, D. C.

H. W. Tyler, emeritus professor of mathematics, Massachusetts Institute of Technology; consultant in science, Library of Congress, Washington, D. C.

A. F. Woods, principal pathologist, Bureau of Plant Industry, United States Department of Agriculture, Washington, D. C.

Fernandus Payne, liaison member from the division of biology and agriculture; professor of zoology and dean of the Graduate School, Indiana University, Bloomington, Ind.

V. DIVISION OF PHYSICAL SCIENCES

Chairman, F. K. Richtmyer.
Vice chairman, Henry A. Barton.

EXECUTIVE COMMITTEE

Chairman, F. K. Richtmyer; vice chairman, Henry A. Barton; H. D. Curtis, Herbert E. Ives, H. L. Rietz, P. I. Wold.

MEMBERS OF THE DIVISION

F. K. Richtmyer, dean of the Graduate School, and professor of physics, Cornell University; chairman of the division, National Research Council, Washington, D. C.

Representatives of societies

AMERICAN ASTRONOMICAL SOCIETY

H. D. Curtis, professor of astronomy, and director, Detroit Observatory, University of Michigan, Ann Arbor, Mich.
John A. Miller, professor of astronomy, and director, Sproul Observatory, Swarthmore College, Swarthmore, Pa.
Frederick Slocum, professor of astronomy, and director, Van Vleck Observatory, Wesleyan University, Middletown, Conn.

AMERICAN PHYSICAL SOCIETY

J. W. Beams, professor of physics, University of Virginia, University, Va.
C. J. Davisson, Bell Telephone Laboratories, Inc., 463 West Street, New York City.
L. O. Grondahl, director of research, Union Switch & Signal Co., Swissvale, Pa.
Herbert E. Ives, physicist, Bell Telephone Laboratories, Inc., 463 West Street, New York City.
G. W. Stewart, professor of physics, State University of Iowa, Iowa City, Iowa.
John Zeleny, professor of physics, Yale University, New Haven, Conn.

AMERICAN MATHEMATICAL SOCIETY

A. B. Coble, professor of mathematics, University of Illinois, Urbana, Ill.
Marston Morse, professor of mathematics, Institute for Advanced Study, Princeton University, Princeton, N. J.
R. G. D. Richardson, dean of the Graduate School, and professor of mathematics, Brown University, Providence, R. I.

OPTICAL SOCIETY OF AMERICA

Carl L. Bausch, Bausch & Lomb Optical Co., Rochester, N. Y.
L. B. Tuckerman, Assistant Chief, Division of Mechanics and Sound, National Bureau of Standards, Washington, D. C.
David L. Webster, professor of physics, Stanford University, Stanford University, Calif.

MATHEMATICAL ASSOCIATION OF AMERICA

H. L. Rietz, professor of mathematics, State University of Iowa, Iowa City, Iowa.

ACOUSTICAL SOCIETY OF AMERICA

Harvey Fletcher, acoustical research director, Bell Telephone Laboratories, Inc., 463 West Street, New York City.

AMERICAN INSTITUTE OF PHYSICS

Henry A. Barton, vice chairman of the division; director, American Institute of Physics, 11 East 38th Street, New York City.

Members-at-Large

P. W. Bridgman, Hollis professor of mathematics and natural philosophy, Harvard University, Cambridge, Mass.
H. D. Smyth, associate professor of physics, Princeton University, Princeton, N. J.
P. I. Wold, professor of physics, Union College, Schenectady, N. Y.

COMMITTEES

The chairman of the division is, ex officio, a member of all committees of the division.

EXECUTIVE COMMITTEES OF AMERICAN SECTIONS OF INTERNATIONAL UNIONS

International Astronomical Union: Chairman, Henry Norris Russell, Charles A. Young professor of astronomy, and director of the observatory, Princeton University, Princeton, N. J.

International Union of Pure and Applied Physics: The division of physical sciences acts as the American section of the International Union of Pure and Applied Physics.

International Scientific Radio Union: Chairman, Arthur E. Kennelly.

ADMINISTRATIVE COMMITTEE

Committee on revolving fund for the publication of mathematical books: Chairman, George D. Birkhoff, professor of mathematics, Harvard University, Cambridge, Mass.

RESEARCH COMMITTEES

Committee on bibliography on orthogonal polynomials: Chairman, J. A. Shohat, assistant professor of mathematics, University of Pennsylvania, Philadelphia, Pa.

Committee on Exhibition methods and technique: Chairman, Fay C. Brown, 407 Wilson Lane, Bethesda, Md.

Committee on a glossary of physical terms: Chairman, LeRoy D. Weld, professor of physics, Coe College, Cedar Rapids, Iowa.

Committee on line spectra of the elements: Chairman, Henry Norris Russell.

Committee on methods of measurement of radiation: Chairman, W. E. Forsythe, physicist, lamp development laboratory, National Lamp Works, Nela Park, Cleveland, Ohio.

Committee on physical constants: Chairman, Raymond T. Birge, professor of physics, University of California, Berkeley, Calif.

Committee on physics of the earth: Chairman, F. K. Richtmyer, ex officio.

Subsidiary committee on terrestrial magnetism and electricity: Chairman, John A. Fleming, acting director, department of terrestrial magnetism, Carnegie Institution of Washington, 5241 Broad Branch Road, Washington, D. C.

Subsidiary committee on internal constitution of the earth: Chairman, L. H. Adams, physical chemist, geophysical laboratory, Carnegie Institution of Washington, 2801 Upton Street, Washington, D. C.

Editorial board of the committee: Chairman, Fred. E. Wright, petrologist, geophysical laboratory, Carnegie Institution of Washington, 2801 Upton Street, Washington, D. C.

Committee on the relation between physics and the medical sciences: Chairman, F. K. Richtmyer, ex officio.

Subcommittee on receptor organs: Chairman, Charles Sheard, chief, section of physics and biophysical research, Mayo Clinic, Rochester, Minn.

Advisory committee on a service institute for biophysics: Chairman, H. B. Williams, Dalton professor of physiology, College of Physicians and Surgeons, Columbia University, New York City.

Committee on symbols, units, and nomenclature (to cooperate with a similar committee of the International Union of Pure and Applied Physics): Chairman, E. C. Crittenden, chief, electrical division, and assistant director, National Bureau of Standards, Washington, D. C.

Committee on tables of positive ternary quadratic forms: Chairman, B. W. Jones, assistant professor of mathematics, Cornell University, Ithaca, N. Y.

REPRESENTATIVE OF THE DIVISION ON—

Committee on magnetic and electric magnitudes of the American Standards Association: Leigh Page, professor of theoretical physics, Yale University, New Haven, Conn.

VI. DIVISION OF ENGINEERING AND INDUSTRIAL RESEARCH

[Engineering Societies Building, 29 West 39th St., New York City]

Chairman, Charles F. Kettering.
Vice chairman, D. S. Jacobus.
Director, Maurice Holland.

EXECUTIVE COMMITTEE

Chairman, Charles F. Kettering; vice chairman, D. S. Jacobus; F. O. Clements, W. D. Ennis, Dugald C. Jackson, Frank B. Jewett, John Johnston, Robert Ridgway.

MEMBERS OF THE DIVISION

Charles F. Kettering, chairman of the division; vice president and director, General Motors Corporation; president, General Motors Research Corporation, Detroit, Mich.

Representatives of Societies

AMERICAN SOCIETY OF CIVIL ENGINEERS

George T. Seabury, ex officio, secretary, American Society of Civil Engineers, 29 West Thirty-ninth Street, New York City.
Robert Ridgway, 24 Gramercy Park, New York City.
Edward H. Rockwell, professor of civil engineering and director, division of civil engineering, Lafayette College, Easton, Pa.
Ole Singstad, chief consulting engineer on tunnels, the Port of New York Authority, 80 Eighth Avenue, New York City.

AMERICAN INSTITUTE OF MINING AND METALLURGICAL ENGINEERS

A. B. Parsons, ex officio, secretary, American Institute of Mining and Metallurgical Engineers, 29 West Thirty-ninth Street, New York City.
John Johnston, director, department of research and technology, United States Steel Corporation, Kearney, N. J.
C. E. McQuigg, Union Carbide and Carbon Research Laboratories, Inc., 30 East Forty-second Street, New York City.
H. J. Rose, senior industrial fellow, Mellon Institute of Industrial Research, University of Pittsburgh, Pittsburgh, Pa.

AMERICAN SOCIETY OF MECHANICAL ENGINEERS

C. E. Davies, ex officio, secretary, American Society of Mechanical Engineers, 29 West Thirty-ninth Street, New York City.
W. D. Ennis, Alexander Crombie Humphreys professor of economic engineering, Stevens Institute of Technology, Hoboken, N. J.
F. M. Farmer, chief engineer, Electrical Testing Laboratories, Eightieth Street and East End Avenue, New York City.
D. S. Jacobus, vice chairman of the division; advisory engineer, Babcock & Wilcox Co., 85 Liberty Street, New York City.
W. R. Webster, chairman of the board, Bridgeport Brass Co., Bridgeport, Conn.

AMERICAN INSTITUTE OF ELECTRICAL ENGINEERS

H. H. Henline, ex officio, secretary, American Institute of Electrical Engineers, 29 West Thirty-ninth Street, New York City.
L. W. Chubb, director, Research Laboratories, Westinghouse Electric & Manufacturing Co., East Pittsburgh, Pa.
Dugald C. Jackson, professor of electric power production and distribution, Massachusetts Institute of Technology, Cambridge, Mass.
Chester W. Rice, assistant to the vice president, General Electric Co., Schenectady, N. Y.

AMERICAN SOCIETY OF REFRIGERATING ENGINEERS

W. J. King, research engineer, General Electric Co., Schenectady, N. Y.

AMERICAN SOCIETY FOR TESTING MATERIALS

F. O. Clements, technical director, Research Laboratories, General Motors Corporation, Detroit, Mich.
H. W. Gillett, director, Battelle Memorial Institute, Columbus, Ohio.

AMERICAN SOCIETY FOR METALS

R. S. Archer, Republic Steel Corporation, One Hundred and Eighteenth Street and Calumet River, Chicago, Ill.

AMERICAN SOCIETY OF HEATING AND VENTILATING ENGINEERS

F. E. Giesecke, director, Engineering Experiment Station, Agricultural and Mechanical College of Texas, College Station, Tex.

ILLUMINATING ENGINEERING SOCIETY

W. F. Little, engineer in charge of photometry, Electrical Testing Laboratories, Eightieth Street and East End Avenue, New York City.

WESTERN SOCIETY OF ENGINEERS

William B. Jackson, rate engineer, New York Edison Co., 4 Irving Place, New York City.

SOCIETY OF AUTOMOTIVE ENGINEERS

Grosvenor Hotchkiss, Teleregister Corporation, 60 Hudson Street, New York City.
E. P. Warner, editor, Aviation; assistant to the president, McGraw-Hill Publishing Co., 330 West Forty-second Street, New York City.

AMERICAN WELDING SOCIETY

Henry M. Hobart, consulting engineer, General Electric Co., Schenectady, N. Y.

Members-at-Large

J. W. Barker, dean, School of Engineering, Columbia University, New York City.
Frank B. Jewett, vice president, American Telephone and Telegraph Co.; president, Bell Telephone Laboratories, Inc., 195 Broadway, New York City.
H. C. Parmelee, vice president, McGraw-Hill Publishing Co., 330 West Forty-second Street, New York City.

COMMITTEES

The chairman of the division is, ex officio, a member of all committees and boards of the division.
Committee on electrical insulation: Chairman, John B. Whitehead, professor of electrical engineering, and dean of the engineering faculty, Johns Hopkins University, Baltimore, Md.
    Subcommittee on Chemistry: Chairman, F. M. Clark, General Electric Co., Pittsfield, Mass.
    Subcommittee on physics: Chairman, V. Karapetoff, professor of electrical engineering, Cornell University, Ithaca, N. Y.
    Subcommittee on program of research: Chairman, John B. Whitehead.
Committee on relationships between universities and industry: Chairman, J. W. Barker.
Committee on heat transmission: Chairman, Willis H. Carrier, president, Carrier Engineering Corporation, Newark, N. J.
    Subcommittee on heat transfer by radiation: Chairman, J. D. Keller, Carnegie Institute of Technology, Schenley Park, Pittsburgh, Pa.
    Subcommittee on heat transfer by convection: Chairman, W. H. McAdams, professor of chemical engineering, Massachusetts Institute of Technology, Cambridge, Mass.

Carrier Engineering Corporation, Newark, N. J.—Continued.

Subcommittee on thermal insulation: Chairman, T. Smith Taylor, T. Smith Taylor Laboratories, 45 Grover Lane, Caldwell, N. J.

Subcommittee on nomenclature and definitions: Chairman, E. F. Mueller, physicist, National Bureau of Standards, Washington, D. C.

Committee on industrial lighting: Chairman, Dugald C. Jackson.

REPRESENTATIVES OF THE DIVISION ON—

Committees of the American Society for Testing Materials: Committee A-8 on magnetic analysis; R. L. Sanford, physicist, National Bureau of Standards, Washington, D. C. Committee for the investigation of sulphur and phosphorus in steel: J. H. Hall, metallurgical engineer, Taylor-Wharton Iron & Steel Co., High Bridge, N. J.

Committee on Ferrous Metals, Advisory to the National Bureau of Standards: Enrique Touceda, consulting engineer, Broadway and Thacher Street, Albany, N. Y.

Sectional Committee on Safety Code for Brakes and Brake Testing of the National Bureau of Standards: S. S. Steinberg, professor of civil engineering, University of Maryland, College Park, Md.

AMERICAN BUREAU OF WELDING

[Advisory Board on welding research, sponsored by the American Welding Society]

Director, C. A. Adams, Abbott and James Lawrence professor of engineering, Harvard University, Cambridge, Mass.

COMMITTEES

Committee on structural steel welding: Chairman, Leon S. Moisseiff, consulting engineer, 99 Wall Street, New York City.

Committee on fundamental investigations in welding: Chairman, H. M. Hobart.

HIGHWAY RESEARCH BOARD

Chairman, A. T. Goldbeck, director of the engineering bureau, National Crushed Stone Association, Washington, D. C.

COMMITTEES

Committee on curing of concrete pavement slabs: Chairman, F. C. Lang, engineer of tests and inspection, Minnesota Department of Highways, 1246 University Avenue, St. Paul, Minn.

Committee on design: Chairman, A. T. Goldbeck.

Committee on fillers and cushion courses for brick and block pavements: Chairman, J. S. Crandell, professor of highway engineering, University of Illinois, Urbana, Ill.

Committee on use of high elastic-limit steel for concrete reinforcement: Chairman, Herbert J. Gilkey, head, theoretical and applied mechanics department, Iowa State College, Ames, Iowa.

Committee on highway finance: Chairman, Thomas H. MacDonald, Chief, United States Bureau of Public Roads, Washington, D. C.

Committee on maintenance: Chairman, C. P. Owens, maintenance engineer, State highway department, Jefferson City, Mo.

Committee on materials and construction: Chairman, H. S. Mattimore, engineer of tests and materials investigation, State department of highways, Harrisburg, Pa.

Committee on correlation of research in mineral aggregates: Chairman, W. J. Emmons, associate professor of highway engineering and director, State highway laboratory, University of Michigan, Ann Arbor, Mich.

Committee on roadside development (in cooperation with the American Association of State Highway Officials): Chairman, Luther M. Keith, director of roadside development, State highway department, Hartford, Conn.

Committee on tractive resistance and allied problems: Chairman, W. E. Lay, professor of mechanical engineering, University of Michigan, Ann Arbor, Mich.

Committee on traffic: Chairman, W. A. Van Duzer, director of vehicles and traffic, District of Columbia, Washington, D. C.

Committee on highway transportation economics: Chairman, R. L. Morrison, professor of highway engineering and highway transport, University of Michigan, Ann Arbor, Mich.

VII. DIVISION OF CHEMISTRY AND CHEMICAL TECHNOLOGY

Chairman, F. W. Willard.

EXECUTIVE COMMITTEE

Chairman, F. W. Willard; Hans T. Clarke, Harry A. Curtis, Charles L. Parsons, Harold C. Urey.

MEMBERS OF THE DIVISION

F. W. Willard, chairman of the division; executive vice president, Nassau Smelting & Refining Co., 50 Church Street, New York City.

Representatives of Societies

AMERICAN CHEMICAL SOCIETY

Marston T. Bogert, professor of organic chemistry, Columbia University, New York City.

William Lloyd Evans, professor of chemistry, Ohio State University, Columbus, Ohio.

Charles L. Parsons, secretary and business manager, American Chemical Society, Mills Building, Washington, D. C.

Austin M. Patterson, vice president and professor of chemistry, Antioch College, Yellow Springs, Ohio.

Harold C. Urey, professor of chemistry, Columbia University, New York City.

Edward R. Weidlein, director, Mellon Institute of Industrial Research, Pittsburgh, Pa.

ELECTROCHEMICAL SOCIETY

Hiram S. Lukens, professor of chemistry and director of the Harrison Laboratory, University of Pennsylvania, Philadelphia, Pa.

AMERICAN INSTITUTE OF CHEMICAL ENGINEERS

Harry A. Curtis, chief chemical engineer, Tennessee Valley Authority, Ferris Hall, University of Tennessee, Knoxville, Tenn.

AMERICAN CERAMIC SOCIETY

J. C. Hostetter, director of development and research, Corning Glass Works, Corning, N. Y.

Ex officio

Edward Bartow, vice president, International Union of Chemistry; professor of chemistry and chemical engineering, State University of Iowa, Iowa City, Iowa.

Members-at-Large

Hans T. Clarke, professor of biological chemistry, Columbia University, New York City.

Charles A. Kraus, research professor of chemistry, Brown University, Providence, R. I.

Hobart H. Willard, professor of analytical chemistry, University of Michigan, Ann Arbor, Mich.

COMMITTEES

The chairman of the division is, ex officio, a member of all committees of the division.

Advisory committee on Annual Survey of American Chemistry: Chairman, F. W. Willard.

Advisory committee to the National Bureau of Standards on research on the reproduction of records: Chairman, H. M. Lydenberg, director, New York Public Library, New York City.

Committee on the construction and equipment of chemical laboratories: Chairman, C. R. Hoover; E. B. Nye professor of chemistry, Wesleyan University, Middletown, Conn.

Committee on hydrogen isotopes: Chairman, Harold C. Urey, professor of chemistry, Columbia University, New York City.

Committee on photochemistry: Chairman, Hugh S. Taylor, David B. Jones professor of chemistry, Princeton University, Princeton, N. J.

Committee on the preparation and publication of a list of ring systems used in organic chemistry (joint committee with the American Chemical Society): Chairman, Austin M. Patterson.

International Union of Chemistry: The division of chemistry and chemical technology acts as the American section of the International Union of Chemistry.

VIII. DIVISION OF GEOLOGY AND GEOGRAPHY

Chairman, Edson S. Bastin.
Vice chairman, W. L. G. Joerg.

EXECUTIVE COMMITTEE

Chairman, Edson S. Bastin; vice chairman, W. L. G. Joerg; E. C. Case, Nevin M. Fenneman, Thomas B. Nolan, W. H. Twenhofel.

MEMBERS OF THE DIVISION

Representatives of Societies

GEOLOGICAL SOCIETY OF AMERICA

Donald C. Barton, geologist and geophysicist, Humble Oil & Refining Co., Houston, Tex.

E. C. Case, professor of historical geology and paleontology, University of Michigan, Ann Arbor, Mich.

MINERALOGICAL SOCIETY OF AMERICA

W. F. Foshag, curator of physical and chemical geology, United States National Museum, Washington, D. C.

PALEONTOLOGICAL SOCIETY

August F. Foerste, associate in paleontology, United States National Museum, Washington, D. C.

ASSOCIATION OF AMERICAN GEOGRAPHERS

Nevin M. Fenneman, professor of geology and geography, University of Cincinnati, Cincinnati, Ohio.

C. F. Marbut, Chief, Division of Soil Survey, United States Bureau of Chemistry and Soils, Washington, D. C.

AMERICAN GEOGRAPHICAL SOCIETY

W. L. G. Joerg, vice chairman of the division; editor, research series, American Geographical Society, Broadway at One Hundred and Fifty-sixth Street, New York City.

SOCIETY OF ECONOMIC GEOLOGISTS

Thomas B. Nolan, Associate Geologist, United States Geological Survey, Washington, D. C.

AMERICAN ASSOCIATION OF PETROLEUM GEOLOGISTS

R. S. Knappen, geologist, Gypsy Oil Co., Tulsa, Okla.

Members-at-Large

Edson S. Bastin, chairman of the division; professor of economic geology, University of Chicago, Chicago, Ill.
Mark Jefferson, professor of geography, Michigan State Normal College, Ypsilanti, Mich.
Morris M. Leighton, chief, Illinois State Geological Survey, Urbana, Ill.

COMMITTEES

The chairman of the division is, ex officio, a member of all committees of the division.
Advisory committee to the division: Chairman, Edson S. Bastin.
National committee of the United States, International Geographical Union: Chairman, Douglas W. Johnson, professor of physiography, Columbia University, New York City.
Committee on Pan American Institute of Geography and History: Chairman, C. H. Birdseye, Chief of the Division of Engraving and Printing, United States Geological Survey, Washington, D. C.
Committee on fellowships: Chairman, Arthur Keith, Geologist, United States Geological Survey, Washington, D. C.

TECHNICAL COMMITTEES

Committee on accessory minerals of crystalline rocks: Chairman, A. N. Winchell, professor of geology, University of Wisconsin, Madison, Wis.
Committee on aerial photographs: Chairman, C. H. Birdseye.
Committee on batholithic problems: Chairman, Frank F. Grout, professor of geology and mineralogy, University of Minnesota, Minneapolis, Minn.
Committee on bibliography of economic geology: Chairman, Waldemar Lindgren, professor emeritus of economic geology, Massachusetts Institute of Technology, Cambridge, Mass.
Committee on conservation of the scientific results of drilling: Chairman, Wilbur A. Nelson, professor of geology, University of Virginia, University, Va.
Committee on cooperation with the Bureau of the Census: Chairman, W. L. G. Joerg.
Committee on land classification: Chairman, K. C. McMurry, professor of geography, University of Michigan, Ann Arbor, Mich.
Committee on the measurement of geological time: Chairman, Alfred C. Lane, Pearson professor of geology and mineralogy, Tufts College, Medford, Mass.
Committee on micropaleontology: Chairman, Joseph A. Cushman, director, Cushman Laboratory for Foraminiferal Research, Sharon, Mass.
Committee on paleobotany: Chairman, Roland W. Brown, assistant geologist, United States Geological Survey, Washington, D. C.
Committee on paleoecology: Chairman, W. H. Twenhofel, professor of geology, University of Wisconsin, Madison, Wis.
Committee on petrotectonics: Chairman, James Gilluly, geologist, United States Geological Survey, Washington, D. C.
Committee on processes of ore deposition: Chairman, W. H. Newhouse, associate professor of economic geology, Massachusetts Institute of Technology, Cambridge, Mass.
Committee on sedimentation: Chairman, A. C. Trowbridge, professor of geology, University of Iowa, Iowa City, Iowa.
Committee on State geological surveys: Chairman, Morris M. Leighton, chief, Illinois State Geological Survey, Urbana, Ill.

Committee on stratigraphy: Chairman, Carl O. Dunbar, professor of paleontology and stratigraphy, and curator of invertebrate paleontology, Yale University, New Haven, Conn.

Committee on studies in petroleum geology: Chairman, W. T. Thom, Jr., associate professor of geology, Princeton University, Princeton, N. J.

Committee on tectonics: Chairman, Chester R. Longwell, Henry Barnard Davis professor of geology, Yale University, New Haven, Conn.

REPRESENTATIVES OF THE DIVISION ON—

Advisory Council of the Board of Surveys and Maps of the Federal Government: Arthur Keith.

National Council of the American Association of Water Well Drillers: O. E. Meinzer.

Committee on the classification of coal, of the American Society for Testing Materials: Taisia Stadnichenko.

IX. DIVISION OF MEDICAL SCIENCES

Chairman, Francis G. Blake.
Vice chairman, Howard T. Karsner.

EXECUTIVE COMMITTEE

Chairman, Francis G. Blake; vice chairman, Howard T. Karsner; Glenn E. Cullen, Esmond R. Long, Alfred N. Richards, Lewis H. Weed.

MEMBERS OF THE DIVISION

Francis G. Blake, chairman of the division; Sterling professor of medicine, School of Medicine, Yale University; physician in chief, New Haven Hospital, New Haven, Conn.

Representatives of Societies

AMERICAN ASSOCIATION OF ANATOMISTS

Lewis H. Weed, professor of anatomy and director of the School of Medicine, Johns Hopkins University, Baltimore, Md.

AMERICAN ASSOCIATION OF PATHOLOGISTS AND BACTERIOLOGISTS

Howard T. Karsner, vice chairman of the division; professor of pathology, and director, Institute of Pathology, Western Reserve University, Cleveland, Ohio.

AMERICAN DENTAL ASSOCIATON

O. T. Messner, 5712 Twenty-third Street, Washington, D. O.

AMERICAN MEDICAL ASSOCIATION

Charles A. Doan, professor and director of medical and surgical research, Ohio State University, Columbus, Ohio.

AMERICAN NEUROLOGICAL ASSOCIATION

Israel Strauss, 116 West Fifty-ninth Street, New York City.

AMERICAN PHYSIOLOGICAL SOCIETY

Walter J. Meek, professor of physiology, and assistant dean of the Medical School, University of Wisconsin, Madison, Wis.

AMERICAN PSYCHIATRIC ASSOCIATION

Clifford B. Farr, director of laboratories, department of mental and nervous diseases, Pennsylvania Hospital, Philadelphia, Pa.

AMERICAN ROENTGEN RAY SOCIETY

Merrill C. Sosman, assistant professor of medicine, Harvard Medical School, Boston, Mass.

AMERICAN SOCIETY OF BIOLOGICAL CHEMISTS

Glenn E. Cullen, director of laboratories, Pediatric Research Foundation, and professor of research pediatrics, University of Cincinnati, Cincinnati, Ohio.

AMERICAN SOCIETY FOR CLINICAL INVESTIGATION

John P. Peters, John Slade Ely professor of medicine, Yale University, New Haven, Conn.

AMERICAN SOCIETY FOR EXPERIMENTAL PATHOLOGY

Carl V. Weller, professor of pathology, and director of the pathological laboratories, University of Michigan, Ann Arbor, Mich.

AMERICAN SOCIETY FOR PHARMACOLOGY AND EXPERIMENTAL THERAPEUTICS

C. W. Edmunds, professor of materia medica and therapeutics, University of Michigan, Ann Arbor, Mich.

AMERICAN SURGICAL ASSOCIATION

Joseph C. Bloodgood, clinical professor of surgery, Johns Hopkins University, Baltimore, Md.

AMERICAN VETERINARY MEDICAL ASSOCIATION

Karl F. Meyer, professor of bacteriology, and director of the Hooper Foundation for Medical Research, University of California, San Francisco, Calif.

ASSOCIATION OF AMERICAN PHYSICIANS

Warfield T. Longcope, professor of medicine, Johns Hopkins University, Baltimore, Md.

SOCIETY OF AMERICAN BACTERIOLOGISTS

David John Davis, professor of pathology and bacteriology, and dean of the college of medicine, University of Illinois, Chicago, Ill.

Representative of the Division of Federal Relations

Col. Roger Brooke, Medical Corps, United States Army, Washington, D. C.

Members-at-Large

A. J. Carlson, professor of physiology, University of Chicago, Chicago, Ill.
Esmond R. Long, professor of pathology, School of Medicine, and director, Henry Phipps Institute, University of Pennsylvania, Philadelphia, Pa.
Alfred N. Richards, professor of pharmacology, University of Pennsylvania, Philadelphia, Pa.

COMMITTEES

The chairman of the division is, ex officio, a member of all committees of the division.

Advisory committee to the division: Stanhope Bayne-Jones, Henry A. Christian, Edmund V. Cowdry, Frederick P. Gay, Ludvig Hektoen, William H. Howell, Raymond Hussey, C. M. Jackson, Howard T. Karsner, George W. McCoy, William Charles White.

Advisory committee on a survey of tropical diseases: Chairman, Frederick P. Gay, professor of bacteriology, College of Physicians and Surgeons, Columbia University, New York City.

Committee on American registry of pathology: Chairman, Howard T. Karsner.

Committee on the study of Brucella infections: Chairman, Karl F. Meyer.

Committee on climate and health: Chairman, George C. Shattuck, assistant professor of tropical medicine, Harvard Medical School, Boston, Mass.

Committee on drug addiction: Chairman, William Charles White, chairman, medical research committee, National Tuberculosis Association; pathologist in charge of tuberculosis research, National Institute of Health, Washington, D. C.

Committee for survey of research on gonococcus and gonococcal infections: Chairman, Stanhope Bayne-Jones, professor of bacteriology and master of Trumbull College, Yale University, New Haven, Conn.

Committee on medical problems of animal parasitology: Chairman, Henry B. Ward, permanent secretary, American Association for the Advancement of Science; emeritus professor of zoology, University of Illinois, Urbana, Ill.

Committee on microbiology of the soil (joint committee with the division of biology and agriculture): Chairman, William Charles White.

Committee for research in problems of sex: Chairman, Robert M. Yerkes, professor of psychobiology, Yale University, New Haven, Conn.

X. DIVISION OF BIOLOGY AND AGRICULTURE

Chairman, I. F. Lewis.
Vice chairman, J. H. Bodine.

EXECUTIVE COMMITTEE

Chairman, I. F. Lewis; vice chairman, J. H. Bodine; Wallace O. Fenn, E. N. Munns, Fernandus Payne, E. N. Transeau.

MEMBERS OF THE DIVISION

I. F. Lewis, chairman of the division; dean of the university; and Miller professor of biology and agriculture, University of Virginia, University, Va.

Representatives of Societies

GROUP I.—BOTANICAL SOCIETY OF AMERICA

A. J. Eames, professor of botany, Cornell University, Ithaca, N. Y.

GROUP II.—AMERICAN SOCIETY OF ZOOLOGISTS

J. H. Bodine, professor of zoology, University of Iowa, Iowa City, Iowa.

GROUP III.—AMERICAN SOCIETY OF ANIMAL PRODUCTION, AMERICAN DAIRY SCIENCE ASSOCIATION, POULTRY SCIENCE ASSOCIATION

O. E. Reed, Chief, United States Bureau of Dairy Industry, Washington, D. C.

GROUP IV.—AMERICAN SOCIETY OF AGRONOMY, SOCIETY OF AMERICAN FORESTERS, AMERICAN SOCIETY FOR HORTICULTURAL SCIENCE

E. N. Munns, senior silviculturist, in charge of the Division of Silvics, United States Forest Service, Washington, D. C.

GROUP V.—AMERICAN PHYTOPATHOLOGICAL SOCIETY, SOCIETY OF AMERICAN BACTERIOLOGISTS

H. P. Barss, principal botanist, and associate in experiment station administration, Office of Experiment Stations, United States Department of Agriculture, Washington, D. C.

GROUP VI.—AMERICAN GENETIC ASSOCIATION, ECOLOGICAL SOCIETY OF AMERICA, GENETICS SOCIETY OF AMERICA

Henry Allen Gleason, head curator, New York Botanical Garden, Bronx Park, New York City.

GROUP VII.—AMERICAN PHYSIOLOGICAL SOCIETY, PHYSIOLOGICAL SECTION OF THE BOTANICAL SOCIETY OF AMERICA, AMERICAN SOCIETY OF BIOLOGICAL CHEMISTS

E. N. Transeau, professor of botany and director of the botanic garden, Ohio State University, Columbus, Ohio.

GROUP VIII.—AMERICAN ASSOCIATION OF ECONOMIC ENTOMOLOGISTS, ENTOMOLOGICAL SOCIETY OF AMERICA, AMERICAN SOCIETY OF MAMMALOGISTS

Remington Kellogg, assistant curator of the Division of Mammals, United States National Museum, Washington, D. C.

Members-at-Large

Wallace O. Fenn, professor of physiology, School of Medicine and Dentistry, University of Rochester, Rochester, N. Y.
Fernandus Payne, professor of Zoology and dean of the Graduate School, Indiana University, Bloomington, Ind.
A. H. Wright, professor of zoology, Cornell University, Ithaca, N. Y.

COMMITTEES

The chairman of the division is, ex officio, a member of all committees of the division.

Advisory committee to the division: C. E. Allen, L. J. Cole, William Crocker, W. C. Curtis, B. M. Duggar, R. A. Harper, Duncan S. Johnson, L. R. Jones, Vernon Kellogg, Frank R. Lillie, C. E. McClung, Maynard M. Metcalf, Fernandus Payne, Lorande L. Woodruff, A. F. Woods.

Committee on agronomy: Chairman, Richard Bradfield, professor of soils, Ohio State University, Columbus, Ohio.

Committee on animal nutrition: Chairman, Paul E. Howe, senior chemist, in charge of nutrition investigations, Animal Husbandry Division, United States Bureau of Animal Industry, Washington, D. C.

Subcommittee on the relation of energy metabolism to agriculture: Chairman, Paul E. Howe.

Committee on hydrobiology and aquiculture: Chairman, J. G. Needham, professor of entomology and limnology, Cornell University, Ithaca, N. Y.

National finance committee on botanical nomenclature: Chairman, A. S. Hitchcock, principal botanist, in charge of systematic agrostology, United States Bureau of Plant Industry, Washington, D. C.

Committee on radiation: Chairman, B. M. Duggar, professor of applied and physiological botany, University of Wisconsin, Madison, Wis.

Subcommittee on mitogenetic radiation: Chairman, I. F. Lewis.

Subcommittee on survey: Chairman, B. M. Duggar.

Committee on the ecology of grasslands in North America: Chairman, V. E. Shelford, professor of zoology, University of Illinois, Urbana, Ill.

Committee on forestry: Chairman, Raphael Zon, director, Lake States Forest Experiment Station, St. Paul, Minn.

Committee on human heredity: Chairman, Laurence H. Snyder, associate professor of zoology and entomology, Ohio State University, Columbus, Ohio.

Committee on pharmacognosy and pharmaceutical botany: Chairman, Heber W. Youngken, professor of pharmacognosy, Massachusetts College of Pharmacy, Boston, Mass.

Committee on research publications (joint committee with the Union of American Biological Societies): Chairman, Davenport Hooker, professor of anatomy, University of Pittsburgh, Pittsburgh, Pa.

Subcommittee on economic and production problems of biological journals: Chairman, Davenport Hooker.

Committee on wildlife: Chairman, Aldo Leopold, professor of wildlife management and research director of the arboretum, University of Wisconsin, Madison, Wis.

Subcommittee on training men for administrative and education work in wildlife: Chairman, A. G. Ruthven, president, University of Michigan, Ann Arbor, Mich.

REPRESENTATIVES OF THE DIVISION ON—

Board of trustees of *Biological Abstracts:* A. F. Blakeslee, J. P. Moore, J. R. Schramm, A. F. Woods.
Institute for Research in Tropical America: I. F. Lewis.
Board of governors of the Crop Protection Institute: F. D. Fromme.
Board of review of the Marine Biological Laboratory: Fernandus Payne.
Tropical Plant Research Foundation: R. A. Harper.

XI. DIVISION OF ANTHROPOLOGY AND PSYCHOLOGY

Chairman, Edward Sapir.
Vice chairman, Walter S. Hunter.

EXECUTIVE COMMITTEE

Chairman, Edward Sapir; vice chairman, Walter S. Hunter; John M. Cooper, A. T. Poffenberger.

MEMBERS OF THE DIVISION

Edward Sapir, chairman of the division; Sterling professor of anthropology, Yale University, New Haven, Conn.

Representatives of Societies

AMERICAN ANTHROPOLOGICAL ASSOCIATION

S. A. Barrett, director, Milwaukee Public Museum, Milwaukee, Wis.
John M. Cooper, professor of anthropology, Catholic University of America, Washington, D. C.
M. J. Herskovits, associate professor of anthropology, Northwestern University, Evanston, Ill.
E. A. Hooton, professor of anthropology and curator of somatology in the Peabody Museum, Harvard University, Cambridge, Mass.
Robert Redfield, associate professor of anthropology, University of Chicago, Chicago, Ill.
Frank H. H. Roberts, Jr., archaeologist, Bureau of American Ethnology, Smithsonian Institution, Washington, D. C.
Clark Wissler, professor of anthropology, Institute of Human Relations, Yale University; curator of anthropology, American Museum of Natural History, Seventy-seventh Street and Central Park West, New York City.

AMERICAN PSYCHOLOGICAL ASSOCIATION

J. F. Dashiell, professor of psychology, University of North Carolina, Chapel Hill, N. O.
W. S. Hunter, vice chairman of the division; G. Stanley Hall professor of genetic psychology, Clark University, Worcester, Mass.
Karl S. Lashley, professor of psychology, Harvard University, Cambridge, Mass.
W. R. Miles, professor of psychology, Yale University, New Haven, Conn.
Joseph Peterson, professor of psychology, George Peabody College for Teachers, Nashville, Tenn.
L. L. Thurstone, professor of psychology, University of Chicago, Chicago, Ill.
Herbert Woodrow, professor of psychology, University of Illinois, Urbana, Ill.

Members-at-Large

Knight Dunlap, professor of experimental psychology, Johns Hopkins University, Baltimore, Md.
H. S. Langfeld, professor of psychology, and director of the psychological laboratory, Princeton University, Princeton, N. J.
Leslie Spier, research associate in anthropology, Yale University, New Haven, Conn.

COMMITTEES

The chairman of the division is, ex officio, a member of all committees of the division.

Committee on problems of auditory deficiency: Chairman, Knight Dunlap.

Committee on State archaeological surveys: Chairman, Carl E. Guthe, director, museum of anthropology, University of Michigan, Ann Arbor, Mich.

Subcommittee on the Tennessee Valley: Chairman, M. W. Stirling, Chief, Bureau of American Ethnology, Smithsonian Institution, Washington, D. C.

Committee on child development: Chairman, R. S. Woodworth, professor of psychology, Columbia University, New York City.

Subcommittee on selection of child development abstracts and bibliography: Chairman, Carroll E. Palmer, consultant, office of child hygiene, United States Public Health Service; associate in biostatics, School of Hygiene and Public Health, Johns Hopkins University, Baltimore, Md.

Committee on personality in relation to culture: Chairman, Edward Sapir.

Committee on psychiatric investigations: Chairman, Madison Bentley, Sage professor of psychology, Cornell University, Ithaca, N. Y.

Committee on the psychology of the highway: Chairman, H. M. Johnson, professor of psychology, Graduate School, American University, Washington, D. C.

Subcommittee for the Mid-Western area: Chairman, A. R. Lauer, associate professor of psychology, Iowa State College, Ames, Iowa.

Subcommittee on commercial drivers: Chairman, W. C. Shriver, Chrysler Motor Co., Dayton, Ohio.

Advisory committee on a survey of South American Indians: Chairman, John M. Cooper.

Committee on fellowships: Chairman, Edward Sapir.

REPRESENTATIVES OF THE DIVISION ON—

Technical committee on occupational studies, of the United States Employment Service: Paul S. Achilles, W. V. Bingham, Clark L. Hull, F. J. Keller, L. J. O'Rourke, Donald G. Patterson, A. T. Poffenberger, Morris S. Viteles.

3. NATIONAL RESEARCH COUNCIL FELLOWSHIPS

PHYSICS, CHEMISTRY, AND MATHEMATICS

Sums amounting to $1,987,500 have been made available by the Rockefeller Foundation to the National Research Council during the period from May 1, 1919, to June 30, 1935, for the maintenance of a series of research fellowships in physics, chemistry, and mathematics. These funds are administered by a research fellowship board in physics, chemistry, and mathematics appointed by the executive board of the National Research Council.

Fellowships are awarded to individuals who have demonstrated a high order of ability in research and who have received the Ph. D. degree or equivalent training.

MEMBERS OF THE BOARD

Simon Flexner, chairman, director, Rockefeller Institute for Medical Research, 66th Street and York Avenue, New York City.

F. K. Richtmyer, ex officio, secretary, chairman of the division of physical sciences, National Research Council; dean of the Graduate School, and professor of physics, Cornell University, Ithaca, N. Y.

F. W. Willard, ex officio, chairman of the division of chemistry and chemical technology, National Research Council; executive vice president, Nassau Smelting & Refining Co., 50 Church Street, New York City.

Roger Adams, professor of organic chemistry, University of Illinois, Urbana, Ill.

Gilbert A. Bliss, professor of mathematics, University of Chicago, Chicago, Ill.

George D. Birkhoff, professor of mathematics, Harvard University, Cambridge, Mass.

Karl T. Compton, president, Massachusetts Institute of Technology, Cambridge, Mass.

F. G. Keyes, professor of physical chemistry, Massachusetts Institute of Technology, Cambridge, Mass.

Elmer P. Kohler, Sheldon Emery professor of organic chemistry, Harvard University, Cambridge, Mass.

C. E. Mendenhall, professor of physics, University of Wisconsin, Madison, Wis.

R. A. Millikan, director, Norman Bridge laboratory of physics, and chairman of the executive council, California Institute of Technology, Pasadena, Calif.

Oswald Veblen, professor of mathematics, institute for advanced study, Princeton University, Princeton, N. J.

Fellowships for 1934-35 have been awarded to the following persons:

IN PHYSICS

John F. Allen	Edward B. Jordan, Jr.	Charles H. Shaw
Tom W. Bonner	Franz N. D. Kurie	George H. Shortley, Jr.
Charles A. Bradley, Jr.	Charlton M. Lewis	Edwin A. Uehling
Frederick W. Brown	Andrew McKellar	Chester M. Van Atta
Frank G. Dunnington	James H. McMillen	John A. Wheeler
Norman P. Heydenburg	Lyman G. Parratt	Albert E. Whitford
Robert B. Jacobs	Robert Serber	

IN CHEMISTRY

Manson Benedict	Earl A. Gulbransen	Howard A. Smith
William S. Benedict	Lindsay Helmholz	Marvin A. Spielman
Paul C. Cross	John F. G. Hicks, Jr.	Carsten C. Steffens
Victor Deitz	Ralph R. Hultgren	Nelson R. Trenner
Ludo K. Frevel	George E. Kimball	Hervey H. Voge
Edward S. Gilfillan, Jr.	Earl A. Long	George F. Wright
Robert G. Gould, Jr.	Albert Sherman	

IN MATHEMATICS

Sherburne F. Barber	Daniel C. Lewis, Jr.	Sumner B. Myers
Leonard M. Blumenthal	William T. Martin	David S. Nathan
Robert H. Cameron	Deane Montgomery	Malcolm I. S. Robertson
Ralph Hull	Francis J. Murray	G. Cuthbert Webber

MEDICAL SCIENCES

Funds amounting to $550,000, available over the period from January 1, 1922, to December 31, 1927, have been appropriated to the National Research Council jointly by the General Education Board and the Rockefeller Foundation, and an additional sum of $361,000 for the period from January 1, 1928, to June 30, 1935, has been pledged by the Rockefeller Foundation for the establishment under the division of medical sciences of a series of post-doctorate fellowships in medicine. The administration of these fellowships has been placed in the hands of a medical fellowship board appointed by the executive board of the National Research Council.

Fellowships are awarded to individuals who have demonstrated a high order of ability in research and who have received the Ph. D. or M. D. degree or equivalent training.

MEMBERS OF THE BOARD

Francis G. Blake, chairman, chairman of the division of medical sciences, National Research Council; Sterling professor of medicine, School of Medicine, Yale University; physician-in-chief, New Haven Hospital, New Haven, Conn.

Walter B. Cannon, George Higginson professor of physiology, Harvard Medical School, Boston, Mass.

Evarts A. Graham, Bixby professor of surgery, School of Medicine, Washington University, St. Louis, Mo.

Eugene L. Opie, professor of pathology, Cornell University Medical College; pathologist, New York Hospital, New York City.

Lewis H. Weed, professor of anatomy and director of the School of Medicine, Johns Hopkins University, Baltimore, Md.

Fellowships for 1934–35 have been awarded to the following persons:

Ralph W. Barris	Henry S. Dunning	Myron Prinzmetal
Harold Blumberg	Knox H. Finley[1]	Henry G. Schwartz
Dean A. Clark	Harry B. Friedgood	Robert Tennant
Jack M. Curtis	Benjamin F. Miller	Caroline Bedell Thomas
		William McC. Tuttle

BIOLOGICAL SCIENCES

Sums amounting to $1,276,841.31 for the period from July 1, 1923, to June 30, 1935, have been made available by the Rockefeller Foundation to the National Research Council for the establishment under the divisions of biology and agriculture and of anthropology and psychology of a series of post-doctorate fellowships in the biological sciences, including zoology, botany, anthropology, and psychology, and beginning July 1, 1929, including also fellowships in agriculture and forestry, for the purpose of promoting fundamental research in these subjects. The administration of these fellowships has been placed in the hands of a board of national research fellowships in the biological sciences appointed by the executive board of the National Research Council.

Fellowships are awarded to individuals who have demonstrated a high order of ability in research and who have received the Ph. D. degree or equivalent training.

MEMBERS OF THE BOARD

W. J. Robbins, Chairman, professor of botany, and dean of the Graduate School, University of Missouri, Columbia, Mo.

I. F. Lewis, ex officio, chairman of the division of biology and agriculture, National Research Council; dean of the university, and Miller professor of biology and agriculture, University of Virginia, University, Va.

Edward Sapir, ex officio, chairman of the division of anthropology and psychology, National Research Council; professor of anthropology, Yale University, New Haven, Conn.

A. M. Banta, professor of biology, Brown University, Providence, R. I.

Harvey Carr, professor of psychology, University of Chicago, Chicago, Ill.

L. J. Cole, professor of genetics, University of Wisconsin, Madison, Wis.

R. A. Emerson, professor of plant breeding and geneticist in the Agricultural Experiment Station, Cornell University, Ithaca, N. Y.

Max W. Gardner, professor of plant pathology, University of California, Berkeley, Calif.

Caswell Grave, Rebstock professor of zoology, Washington University, St. Louis, Mo.

Carl Hartley, principal pathologist, division of forest pathology, United States Bureau of Plant Industry, Washington, D. C.

George E. Nichols, professor of botany, and director of the botanical gardens, Yale University, New Haven, Conn.

Joseph Peterson, professor of psychology, George Peabody College for Teachers, Nashville, Tenn.

H. L. Shapiro, associate curator of physical anthropology, American Museum of Natural History, Seventy-seventh Street and Central Park West, New York City.

D. H. Tennent, professor of biology, Bryn Mawr College, Bryn Mawr, Pa.

Fellowships for 1934–35 have been awarded to the following persons:

IN AGRICULTURE

Robert V. Boucher	William U. Gardner	Jay L. Lush[1]
Harold E. Clark	C. M. Harrison	Louis L. Madsen

IN ANTHROPOLOGY

Carolyn Adler	Willard W. Hill	Carl C. Seltzer
Walter Dyk		

---

[1] Fellows appointed to work abroad.

IN BOTANY

Ernst C. Abbe	Harold J. Brodie	Laurence S. Moyer
Kenneth F. Baker	David R. Goddard	Stuart M. Pady
James Bonner[1]	Gordon Mackinney	

IN FORESTRY

Robert F. Chandler, Jr.   Theodore C. Scheffer

IN PSYCHOLOGY

Edward E. Anderson	Donald B. Lindsley	Leon A. Pennington
Sarah C. Dunlap	Edwin B. Newman	Stanley S. Stevens
J. McVicker Hunt		

IN ZOOLOGY

H. Albert Barker	Milan J. Kopac	Frederick J. Stare
William R. Breneman	Walter Alan Mozley[1]	H. Burr Steinbach
Donald P. Costello	Thomas Park	Jacinto Steinhardt[1]
Quentin M. Gelman	Herbert Shapiro	Neal A. Weber
Robert H. Hamilton[1]		

NATIONAL LIVE STOCK AND MEAT BOARD FELLOWSHIPS

Funds amounting to $54,750 have been appropriated by the National Live Stock and Meat Board for the support, during the years 1924-35, of fellowships for the study of the place of meat in the diet. These fellowships are administered by a special committee appointed by the executive board of the National Research Council and operating under the division of biology and agriculture. In accepting these appropriations, the National Research Council has reserved the right to publish, without restriction, the results obtained under these fellowships.

MEMBERS OF THE COMMITTEE

Paul E. Howe, chairman, senior chemist, in charge of nutrition investigations, Animal Husbandry Division, United States Bureau of Animal Industry, Washington, D. C.

Anna E. Boiler, director, department of nutrition, National Live Stock and Meat Board, 407 South Dearborn St., Chicago, Ill.

C. Robert Moulton, Institute of American Meat Packers, Chicago, Ill.

H. C. Sherman, Mitchill professor of chemistry, Columbia University, New York City.

During the year 1934-35, with the special consent of the donors, these funds are being used as research grants in the direct support of investigations. Those who are utilizing grants from this fund for the year 1934-35 are as follows:

George O. Burr, University of Minnesota, Minneapolis, Minn.
Paul L. Day, School of Medicine, University of Arkansas, Little Rock, Ark.
H. A. Mattill, University of Iowa, Iowa City, Iowa.

6. MEMBERS OF THE NATIONAL RESEARCH COUNCIL, 1934-35

Abbot, C. G., Smithsonian Institution, Washington, D. C.
Agnew, P. G., American Standards Association, 29 West Thirty-ninth Street, New York City.
Ames, J. S., Johns Hopkins University, Baltimore, Md.
Archer, R. S., Republic Steel Corporation, One Hundred and Eighteenth Street and Calumet River, Chicago, Ill.
Barker, J. W., Columbia University, New York City.
Barrett, S. A., Milwaukee Public Museum, Milwaukee, Wis.
Barrows, Albert L., National Research Council, Washington, D. C.

---

[1] Fellows appointed to work abroad.

Barss, H. P., Office of Experiment Stations, United States Department of Agriculture, Washington, D. C.

Barton, Donald C., Humble Oil & Refining Co., Houston, Tex.

Barton, Henry A., American Institute of Physics, 11 East Thirty-eighth Street, New York City.

Bartow, Edward, State University of Iowa, Iowa City, Iowa.

Bastin, Edson S., University of Chicago, Chicago, Ill.

Bausch, Carl L., Bausch & Lomb Optical Co., Rochester, N. Y.

Beams, J. W., University of Virginia, University, Va.

Bell, Frank T., Bureau of Fisheries, United States Department of Commerce, Washington, D. C.

Besley, F. W., State Forester of Maryland, Baltimore, Md.

Bigelow, Henry B., Museum of Comparative Zoology, Harvard University, Cambridge, Mass.

Blake, Francis G., School of Medicine, Yale University, New Haven, Conn.

Bloodgood, Joseph C., School of Medicine, Johns Hopkins University, Baltimore, Md.

Bodine, J. H., State University of Iowa, Iowa City, Iowa.

Bogert, Marston T., Columbia University, New York City.

Bowie, William, Coast and Geodetic Survey, United States Department of Commerce, Washington, D. C.

Bowman, Isaiah, National Research Council, Washington, D. C.

Bridgman, P. W., Harvard University, Cambridge, Mass.

Briggs, Lyman J., National Bureau of Standards, Washington, D. C.

Brigham, Maj. Gen. Claude E., Chemical Warfare Service, War Department, Washington, D. C.

Brooke, Col. Roger, Medical Corps, War Department, Washington, D. C.

Bryant, Harold C., National Park Service, Washington, D. C.

Campbell, W. W., National Academy of Sciences, Washington, D. C.

Cannon, W. B., Harvard Medical School, Boston, Mass.

Carlson, A. J., School of Medicine, University of Chicago, Chicago, Ill.

Carr, Maj. Gen. Irving J., Chief Signal Officer, War Department, Washington, D. C.

Carr, Wilbur J., Department of State, Washington, D. C.

Case, E. C., University of Michigan, Ann Arbor, Mich.

Chambers, Wrightson, Post Office Department, Washington, D. C.

Charlesworth, H. P., American Telephone & Telegraph Co., 195 Broadway, New York City.

Chase, Harry W., New York University, New York City.

Chubb, L. W., Westinghouse Electric & Manufacturing Co., East Pittsburgh, Pa.

Clapp, E. H., Forest Service, United States Department of Agriculture, Washington, D. C.

Clarke, Hans T., Columbia University, New York City.

Clements, F. O., General Motors Corporation, Detroit, Mich.

Coble, A. B., University of Illinois, Urbana, Ill.

Compton, Arthur H., University of Chicago, Chicago, Ill.

Compton, Karl T., Massachusetts Institute of Technology, Cambridge, Mass.

Conant, James Bryant, Harvard University, Cambridge, Mass.

Cooper, John M., Catholic University of America, Washington, D. C.

Crittenden, E. C., National Bureau of Standards, Washington, D. C.

Cullen, Glenn E., Children's Hospital, Research Foundation, Cincinnati, Ohio.

Cumming, Hugh S., United States Public Health Service, Washington, D. C.

Curtis, Harry A., Tennessee Valley Authority, care University of Tennessee, Knoxville, Tenn.

Curtis, Heber D., University of Michigan, Ann Arbor, Mich.

Dashiell, J. F., University of North Carolina, Chapel Hill, N. C.

Davies, C. E., American Society of Mechanical Engineers, 29 West Thirty-ninth Street, New York City.

Davis, David John, College of Medicine, University of Illinois, Chicago, Ill.

Davisson, C. J., Bell Telephone Laboratories, Inc., 463 West Street, New York City.

Day, Arthur L., Geophysical Laboratory of the Carnegie Institution of Washington, 2801 Upton Street, Washington, D. C.

Doan, Charles A., Ohio State University, Columbus, Ohio.

Dunlap, Knight, Johns Hopkins University, Baltimore, Md.

Dunn, Gano, J. G. White Engineering Corporation, 80 Broad Street, New York City.

Eames, A. J., Cornell University, Ithaca, N. Y.
Edmunds, C. W., School of Medicine, University of Michigan, Ann Arbor, Mich.
Ennis, W. D., Stevens Institute of Technology, Hoboken, N. J.
Evans, William Lloyd, Ohio State University, Columbus, Ohio.
Farmer, F. M., Electrical Testing Laboratories, Eightieth Street and East End Avenue, New York City.
Farr, Clifford B., Pennsylvania Hospital, Philadelphia, Pa.
Fenn, Wallace O., University of Rochester, Rochester, N. Y.
Fenneman, Nevin M., University of Cincinnati, Cincinnati, Ohio.
Fieldner, A. C., Bureau of Mines, United States Department of the Interior, Washington, D. C.
Fleming, John A., Department of Terrestrial Magnetism of the Carnegie Institution of Washington, 5241 Broad Branch Road, Washington, D. C.
Fletcher, Harvey, Bell Telephone Laboratories, Inc., 463 West Street, New York City.
Flexner, Simon, Rockefeller Institute for Medical Research, Sixty-sixth Street and York Avenue, New York City.
Foerste, August F., United States National Museum, Washington, D. C.
Foshag, W. F., United States National Museum, Washington, D. C.
Foulois, Major General B. D., Air Corps, War Department, Washington, D. C.
Giesecke, F. E., Agricultural and Mechanical College of Texas, College Station, Tex.
Gillett, H. W., Battelle Memorial Institute, Columbus, Ohio.
Gleason, Henry Allen, New York Botanical Garden, Bronx Park, New York City.
Gregory, Herbert E., Bishop Museum of Polynesian Ethnology and Natural History, Honolulu, Hawaii.
Grondahl, L. O., Union Switch and Signal Co., Swissvale, Pa.
Guthe, Carl E., University of Michigan, Ann Arbor, Mich.
Hale, George E., Mount Wilson Observatory, Pasadena, Calif.
Hall, Maurice C., Bureau of Animal Industry, United States Department of Agriculture, Washington, D. C.
Harrison, Ross G., Yale University, New Haven, Conn.
Hellweg, Capt. J. F., Naval Observatory, Navy Department, Washington, D. C.
Henline, H. H., American Institute of Electrical Engineers, 29 West Thirty-ninth Street, New York City.
Herskovits, M. J., Northwestern University, Evanston, Ill.
Hetzel, R. D., Pennsylvania State College, State College, Pa.
Hill, Joseph A., Bureau of the Census, United States Department of Commerce, Washington, D. C.
Hobart, Henry M., General Electric Co., Schenectady, N. Y.
Hooton, E. A., Harvard University, Cambridge, Mass.
Hoover, J. Edgar, Department of Justice, Washington, D. C.
Hostetter, J. C., Corning Glass Works, Corning, N. Y.
Hotchkiss, Grosvenor, Teleregister Corporation, 60 Hudson Street, New York City.
Humphreys, W. J., Weather Bureau, United States Department of Agriculture, Washington, D. C.
Hunter, W. S., Clark University, Worcester, Mass.
Ives, Herbert E., Bell Telephone Laboratories, Inc., 463 West Street, New York City.
Jackson, Dugald C., Massachusetts Institute of Technology, Cambridge, Mass.
Jackson, William B., New York Edison Co., 4 Irving Place, New York City.
Jacobus, D. S., Babcock & Wilcox Co., 85 Liberty Street, New York City.
Jefferson, Mark, Michigan State Normal College, Ypsilanti, Mich.
Jewett, Frank B., American Telephone & Telegraph Co., 195 Broadway, New York City.
Joerg, W. L. G., American Geographical Society, Broadway at One Hundred and Fifty-Sixth Street, New York City.
Johnson, Douglas W., Columbia University, New York City.
Johnston, John, United States Steel Corporation, Kearney, N. J.
Karsner, Howard T., Western Reserve University, Cleveland, Ohio.
Keith, Arthur, Geological Survey, United States Department of the Interior, Washington, D. C.
Kellogg, Remington, United States National Museum, Washington, D. C.
Kellogg, Vernon, 2305 Bancroft Place, Washington, D. C.

Kelly, Frederick J., Office of Education, United States Department of the Interior, Washington, D. C.

Kennelly, Arthur E., Harvard University, Cambridge, Mass.

Kettering, Charles F., General Motors Corporation, Detroit, Mich.

Kidder, A. V., Post Office Drawer 71, Andover, Mass.

King, W. J., General Electric Co., Schenectady, N. Y.

Knappen, R. S., The Gypsy Oil Co., Tulsa, Okla.

Knight, Brigadier General Harry E., General Staff, War Department, Washington, D. C.

Knight, Henry G., Bureau of Chemistry and Soils, United States Department of Agriculture, Washington, D. C.

Kraus, Charles A., Brown University, Providence, R. I.

Kummel, Henry B., State Geologist, Trenton, N. J.

Land, Rear Admiral Emory S., Bureau of Construction and Repair, Navy Department, Washington, D. C.

Langfeld, H. S., Princeton University, Princeton, N. J.

Lashley, Karl S., Harvard University, Cambridge, Mass.

Leighton, Morris M., State Geological Survey, Urbana, Ill.

Lewis, I. F., University of Virginia, University, Va.

Lillie, Frank R., University of Chicago, Chicago, Ill.

Lipman, Jacob G., New Jersey Agricultural Experiment Station, New Brunswick, N. J.

Little, W. F., Electrical Testing Laboratories, Eightieth Street and East End Avenue, New York City.

Long, Esmond R., Henry Phipps Institute, University of Pennsylvania, Philadelphia, Pa.

Longcope, Warfield T., School of Medicine, Johns Hopkins University, Baltimore, Md.

Lubin, Isador, United States Department of Labor, Washington, D. C.

Lukens, Hiram S., University of Pennsylvania, Philadelphia, Pa.

MacDonald, T. H., Bureau of Public Roads, United States Department of Agriculture, Washington, D. C.

MacQuigg, C. E., Union Carbide and Carbon Research Laboratories, 30 East Forty-second Street, New York City.

Mann, A. R., Cornell University, Ithaca, N. Y.

Mann, C. R., American Council on Education, Washington, D. C.

Marbut, C. F., Bureau of Chemistry and Soils, United States Department of Agriculture, Washington, D. C.

Mathews, Edward B., Johns Hopkins University, Baltimore, Md.

McClung, C. E., University of Pennsylvania, Philadelphia, Pa.

McCrory, S. H., Bureau of Agricultural Engineering, United States Department of Agriculture, Washington, D. C.

McVey, Frank L., University of Kentucky, Lexington, Ky.

Mead, Elwood, Reclamation Service, United States Department of the Interior, Washington, D. C.

Meek, Walter J., Medical School, University of Wisconsin, Madison, Wis.

Mendenhall, W. C., Geological Survey, United States Department of the Interior, Washington, D. C.

Merriam, John C., Carnegie Institution of Washington, Washington, D. C.

Messner, C. T., 5712 Twenty-third Street, NW., Washington, D. C.

Meyer, Karl F., Hooper Foundation, University of California, Berkeley, Calif.

Miles, W. R., Yale University, New Haven, Conn.

Miller, John A., Swarthmore College, Swarthmore, Pa.

Millikan, R. A., California Institute of Technology, Pasadena, Calif.

Mohler, J. R., Bureau of Animal Industry, United States Department of Agriculture, Washington, D. C.

Morgan, T. H., California Institute of Technology, Pasadena, Calif.

Morse, Marston, Harvard University, Cambridge, Mass.

Mumford, H. W., University of Illinois, Urbana, Ill.

Munns, E. N., Forest Service, United States Department of Agriculture, Washington, D. C.

Munroe, Col. John E., Ordnance Department, War Department, Washington, D. C.

Nolan, Thomas B., Geological Survey, United States Department of the Interior, Washington, D. C.

Nourse, Edwin G., Institute of Economics, Brookings Institution, Washington, D. C.

Noyes, A. A., California Institute of Technology, Pasadena, Calif.
Noyes, W. A., University of Illinois, Urbana, Ill.
Palmer, T. S., 1939 Biltmore Street, NW., Washington, D. C.
Parmelee, H. C., McGraw-Hill Publishing Co., 330 West Forty-second Street, New York City.
Parsons, A. B., American Institute of Mining and Metallurgical Engineers, 29 West Thirty-ninth Street, New York City.
Parsons, Charles L., American Chemical Society, Mills Building, Washington, D. C.
Patterson, Austin M., Antioch College, Yellow Springs, Ohio.
Payne, Fernandus, Indiana University, Bloomington, Ind.
Pearson, Raymond A., University of Maryland, College Park, Md.
Pendleton, Maj. R. T., Coast Artillery Corps, War Department, Washington, D. C.
Peters, John P., School of Medicine, Yale University, New Haven, Conn.
Peterson, Joseph, George Peabody College for Teachers, Nashville, Tenn.
Pierce, Charles H., Patent Office, United States Department of Commerce, Washington, D. C.
Putnam, George R., Bureau of Lighthouses, United States Department of Commerce, Washington, D. C.
Redfield, Robert, University of Chicago, Chicago, Ill.
Reed, O. E., Bureau of Dairy Industry, United States Department of Agriculture, Washington, D. C.
Rice, Chester W., General Electric Co., Schenectady, N. Y.
Richards, Alfred N., School of Medicine, University of Pennsylvania, Philadelphia, Pa.
Richardson, R. G. D., Brown University, Providence, R. I.
Richtmyer, F. K., Cornell University, Ithaca, N. Y.
Ridgway, Robert, 24 Gramercy Park, New York City.
Rietz, H. L., State University of Iowa, Iowa City, Iowa.
Robbins, W. J., University of Missouri, Columbia, Mo.
Roberts, Frank H. H., Jr., Bureau of American Ethnology, Smithsonian Institution, Washington, D. C.
Robinson, Rear Admiral Samuel M., Bureau of Engineering, Navy Department, Washington, D. C.
Rockwell, Edward H., Lafayette College, Easton, Pa.
Root, Elihu, 31 Nassau Street, New York City.
Rose, H. J., Mellon Institute of Industrial Research, University of Pittsburgh, Pittsburgh, Pa.
Rossiter, Rear Admiral Percival E., Bureau of Medicine and Surgery, Navy Department, Washington, D. C.
Rowe, L. S., Pan American Union, Washington, D. C.
Russell, Henry Norris, Princeton University, Princeton, N. J.
Sapir, Edward, Yale University, New Haven, Conn.
Schlesinger, Frank, Yale University, New Haven, Conn.
Scofield, C. S., Bureau of Plant Industry, United States Department of Agriculture, Washington, D. C.
Seabury, George T., American Society of Civil Engineers, 29 West Thirty-ninth Street, New York City.
Sharp, Clayton H., 294 Fisher Avenue, White Plains, N. J.
Singstad, Ole, Port of New York Authority, 80 Eighth Avenue, New York City.
Slocum, Frederick, Wesleyan University, Middletown, Conn.
Smyth, H. D., Princeton University, Princeton, N. J.
Sosman, Merrill C., Harvard Medical School, Boston, Mass.
Spier, Leslie, Yale University, New Haven, Conn.
Stark, Rear Admiral Harold R., Bureau of Ordnance, Navy Department, Washington, D. C.
Stewart, G. W., State University of Iowa, Iowa City, Iowa.
Stimson, A. M., United States Public Health Service, Washington, D. C.
Strauss, Israel, 118 West Fifty-ninth Street, New York City.
Strong, Lee A., Bureau of Entomology, United States Department of Agriculture, Washington, D. C.
Swingle, Walter T., Bureau of Plant Industry, United States Department of Agriculture, Washington, D. C.
Thompson, Thomas G., University of Washington, Seattle, Wash.
Thurstone, L. L., University of Chicago, Chicago, Ill.
Transeau, E. N., Ohio State University, Columbus, Ohio.

Tuckerman, L. B., National Bureau of Standards, Washington, D. C.
Tyler, H. W., Library of Congress, Washington, D. C.
Urey, Harold C., Columbia University, New York City.
Vaughan, T. Wayland, Scripps Institution of Oceanography, La Jolla, Calif.
Veblen, Oswald, Institute for Advanced Study, Princeton University, Princeton, N. J.
Voegtlin, Carl, National Institute of Health, Washington, D. C.
Warner, E. P., McGraw-Hill Publishing Co., 330 West Forty-second Street, New York City.
Webster, David L., Stanford University, Stanford University, Calif.
Weed, Lewis H., School of Medicine, Johns Hopkins University, Baltimore, Md.
Weidlein, Edward R., Mellon Institute of Industrial Research, University of Pittsburgh, Pittsburgh, Pa.
Weller, Carl V., University of Michigan, Ann Arbor, Mich.
White, William Charles, National Institute of Health, Washington, D. C.
Whitmore, Frank C., Pennsylvania State College, State College, Pa.
Wilby, Lt. Col. Francis B., Corps of Engineers, War Department, Washington, D. C.
Willard, F. W., Nassau Smelting & Refining Co., 50 Church Street, New York City.
Willard, Hobart H., University of Michigan, Ann Arbor, Mich.
Wissler, Clark, American Museum of Natural History, Seventy-seventh Street and Central Park West, New York City.
Wold, P. I., Union College, Schenectady, N. Y.
Woodrow, Herbert, University of Illinois, Urbana, Ill.
Woods, A. F., Bureau of Plant Industry, United States Department of Agriculture, Washington, D. C.
Wright, A. H., Cornell University, Ithaca, N. Y.
Wright, Fred. E., Geophysical Laboratory of the Carnegie Institution of Washington, 2801 Upton Street, Washington, D. C.
Youngblood, B., United States Department of Agriculture, Washington, D. C.
Zeleny, John, Yale University, New Haven, Conn.

O

REPORT OF THE
NATIONAL ACADEMY
OF SCIENCES

FISCAL YEAR
1935-1936

REPORT OF THE
NATIONAL ACADEMY
OF SCIENCES

FISCAL YEAR
1935 - 1936

UNITED STATES
GOVERNMENT PRINTING OFFICE
WASHINGTON : 1937

33

III

LETTER OF TRANSMITTAL

NATIONAL ACADEMY OF SCIENCES,
Washington, D. C., January 11, 1937.

Hon. JOHN N. GARNER,
President of the United States Senate.

SIR: I have the honor to transmit to you herewith the report of the president of the National Academy of Sciences for the fiscal year ended June 30, 1936.

Yours respectfully,

FRANK R. LILLIE, *President.*

ACT OF INCORPORATION

AN ACT To Incorporate the National Academy of Sciences

Be it enacted by the Senate and House of Representatives of the United States of America in Congress assembled, That Louis Agassiz, Massachusetts; J. H. Alexander, Maryland; S. Alexander, New Jersey; A. D. Bache, at large; F. B. Barnard,[1] at large; J. G. Barnard, United States Army, Massachusetts; W. H. C. Bartlett, United States Military Academy, Missouri; U. A. Boyden,[2] Massachusetts; Alexis Caswell, Rhode Island; William Chauvenet, Missouri; J. H. C. Coffin, United States Naval Academy, Maine; J. A. Dahlgren,[3] United States Navy, Pennsylvania; J. D. Dana, Connecticut; Charles H. Davis, United States Navy, Massachusetts; George Englemann, Saint Louis, Missouri; J. F. Frazer, Pennsylvania; Wolcott Gibbs, New York; J. M. Giles,[3] United States Navy, District of Columbia; A. A. Gould, Massachusetts; B. A. Gould, Massachusetts; Asa Gray, Massachusetts; A. Guyot, New Jersey; James Hall, New York; Joseph Henry, at large; J. E. Hilgard, at large, Illinois; Edward Hitchcock, Massachusetts; J. S. Hubbard, United States Naval Observatory, Connecticut; A. A. Humphreys, United States Army, Pennsylvania; J. L. Le Conte, United States Army, Pennsylvania; J. Leidy, Pennsylvania; J. P. Lesley, Pennsylvania; M. F. Longstreth, Pennsylvania; D. H. Mahan, United States Military Academy, Virginia; J. S. Newberry, Ohio; H. A. Newton, Connecticut; Benjamin Peirce, Massachusetts; John Rodgers, United States Navy, Indiana; Fairman Rogers, Pennsylvania; R. E. Rogers, Pennsylvania; W. B. Rogers, Massachusetts; L. M. Rutherfurd, New York; Joseph Saxton, at large; Benjamin Silliman, Connecticut; Benjamin Silliman, junior, Connecticut; Theodore Strong, New Jersey; John Torrey, New York; J. G. Totten, United States Army, Connecticut; Joseph Winlock, United States Nautical Almanac, Kentucky; Jeffries Wyman, Massachusetts; J. D. Whitney, California; their associates and successors duly chosen, are hereby incorporated, constituted, and declared to be a body corporate, by the name of the National Academy of Sciences.

Sec. 2. *And be it further enacted,* That the National Academy of Sciences shall consist of not more than fifty ordinary members, and the said corporation hereby constituted shall have power to make its own organization, including its constitution, bylaws, and rules and regulations; to fill all vacancies created by death, resignation, or otherwise; to provide for the election of foreign and domestic members, the division into classes, and all other matters needful or usual in such institution, and to report the same to Congress.

Sec. 3. *And be it further enacted,* That the National Academy of Sciences shall hold an annual meeting at such place in the United States as may be designated, and the Academy shall, whenever called upon by any department of the Government, investigate, examine, experiment, and report upon any subject of science or art, the actual expense of such investigations, examinations, experiments, and reports to be paid from appropriations which may be made for the purpose, but the Academy shall receive no compensation whatever for any services to the Government of the United States.

GALUSHA A. GROW,
Speaker of the House of Representatives.

SOLOMON FOOTE,
President of the Senate pro tempore.

Approved, March 3, 1863.

ABRAHAM LINCOLN, *President.*

---

[1] The correct name of this charter member was F. A. P. Barnard.
[2] Declined.
[3] The correct name of this charter member was J. M. Gilliss.

AMENDMENTS

AN ACT To amend the act to incorporate the National Academy of Sciences

Be it enacted by the Senate and House of Representatives of the United States of America in Congress assembled, That the act to incorporate the National Academy of Sciences, approved March third, eighteen hundred and sixty-three, be, and the same is hereby, so amended as to remove the limitation of the number of ordinary members of said Academy as provided in said act.

Approved, July 14, 1870.

AN ACT To authorize the National Academy of Sciences to receive and hold trust funds for the promotion of science, and for other purposes

Be it enacted by the Senate and House of Representatives of the United States of America in Congress assembled, That the National Academy of Sciences, incorporated by the act of Congress approved March third, eighteen hundred and sixty-three, and its several supplements be, and the same is hereby, authorized and empowered to receive bequests and donations and hold the same in trust, to be applied by the said Academy in aid of scientific investigations and according to the will of the donors.

Approved, June 20, 1884.

AN ACT To amend the act authorizing the National Academy of Sciences to receive and hold trust funds for the promotion of science, and for other purposes

Be it enacted by the Senate and House of Representatives of the United States of America in Congress assembled, That the act to authorize the National Academy of Sciences to receive and hold trust funds for the promotion of science, and for other purposes, approved June twentieth, eighteen hundred and eighty-four, be, and the same is hereby, amended to read as follows:

"That the National Academy of Sciences, incorporated by the act of Congress approved March third, eighteen hundred and sixty-three, be, and the same is hereby, authorized and empowered to receive by devise, bequest, donation, or otherwise, either real or personal property, and to hold the same absolutely or in trust, and to invest, reinvest, and manage the same in accordance with the provisions of its constitution, and to apply said property and the income arising therefrom to the objects of its creation and according to the instructions of the donors: *Provided, however,* That the Congress may at any time limit the amount of real estate which may be acquired and the length of time the same may be held by said National Academy of Sciences."

SEC. 2. That the right to alter, amend, or repeal this act is hereby expressly reserved.

Approved, May 27, 1914.

ANNUAL REPORT OF THE NATIONAL ACADEMY OF SCIENCES

REVIEW OF THE YEAR 1935-36

The National Academy of Sciences, organized in 1863, brings together by election to membership a selection of the most distinguished men of science of America. In so doing it seeks to confer honor on these men, and to be prepared, according to the obligations of its congressional charter, to advise the Government of the United States on any subject within the field of the natural sciences.

Election to membership is through nomination by members of the 11 sections. Such nominations, if approved by two-thirds vote of the members of the section concerned, are sent to all members of the Academy for consideration and vote by mail as to order of preference; and are finally voted upon at the annual meeting of the Academy in the order determined by the preference ballot. Membership in the Academy is limited by its constitution to 300; at the close of the fiscal year 1935-36 there were 292 members. Not more than 15 members may be elected at any one meeting.

In responding to requests for advice from the departments and independent scientific agencies of the Government, a special committee of qualified men, often including some who are not members of the Academy, is appointed to consider each request and to report back to the Academy. After suitable consideration the report and recommendations of the special committee are transmitted by the president of the Academy to the department of the Government in which the request originated.

The history of the Government relations of the Academy, dating back to the time of President Lincoln, is of much interest. But referring only to recent events, at the time of the Great War the Academy made a special proffer of its services to the Government in 1916, and, at the request of President Wilson, organized the National Research Council as its agency to cooperate with the Council of National Defense. In 1918 President Wilson requested the Academy, in an Executive order, to perpetuate the National Research Council in broader form, but still with special emphasis on Government relations, for which a special Division of Federal Relations was set up.

The Academy further, in 1926, reestablished its own Committee on Government Relations, with emphasis on the general strategy of aid to the Government whether in war or in peace.

During the recent economic depression, on July 31, 1933, the President of the United States appointed a Science Advisory Board for a period of 2 years, "with authority, acting through the machinery and under the jurisdiction of the National Academy of Sciences and the National Research Council", to consider special problems arising in the various Federal departments. Before the termination of its period of appointment it became apparent that the work of the Science Advisory Board could not be completed on time. It also became obvious that the Academy possessed a confusing multiplicity of agencies in its Government relations. Accordingly, the President of the United States extended the appointment of the Science Advisory Board to December 1, 1935, and requested the Academy to set up a single agency of the Academy to deal with these matters thereafter.

The council of the Academy accordingly reorganized its committee on Government relations so as to include the work of the Science Advisory Board under the name of the Government Relations and Science Advisory Committee, and gave to an executive committee of this body full power to act in interim. The president of the Academy was made the chairman of this committee. The President of the United States thereupon sent word to all departments and independent agencies of the Government through the National Resources Committee, calling attention to the availability of its services.

In order to give some idea of the range of subjects that have been considered, the list of existing subcommittees is given as follows:

> Subcommittee on the Weather Bureau.
> Subcommittee on the War and Navy Departments.
> Subcommittee on the relation of the patent system to the stimulation of new industries.
> Subcommittee on signaling for safety at sea.
> Advisory subcommittee on signaling for safety at sea.
> Subcommittee on the design and construction of airships.
> Subcommittee on Biological Abstracts.
> Subcommittee on Bureau of Standards relations.
> Subcommittee on physical types in the American population.
> Subcommittee on soil conservation.

While the business of the Academy and that of the National Research Council for the year is given in detail in the body of this report, there are certain points to which special attention may be called: First, the efforts made by the Academy on behalf of the Research Council for the securing of legislation to provide for the payment of the annual share of the United States in the expenses of the International Council of Scientific Unions and affiliated unions has been consummated; the United States is thus enabled to resume a relation which had been discontinued at the beginning of the depression in 1932, when Congress failed to make appropriation to cover the amount needed. There is still one year (1934) for which the dues have not been paid. It is hoped that an item in one of the deficiency bills will make it possible to provide the amount needed. Progress in advancing knowledge of the natural sciences is promoted by such international organization which brings the nations together for round-table discussion of the scientific problems that concern all and which are continually coming up for consideration.

In the Academy there are a number of small trust funds the income of which is available for grants to assist scientific research workers in carrying on, or completing, some particular piece of work. The amounts that can be granted in this way are small but often of material assistance when most needed. During the year grants in the following subjects were made: Astronomy, $2,065; astrophysics, $500; electricity, $900; biology, $650; entomology, $325; geology and paleontology, $650; zoology, $450; and oceanography, $125. Medals were awarded in the fields of astronomy, biology, and public welfare.

The interest of the members of the Academy in the annual meeting is evidenced by the attendance, each year, of over one-third of the total membership. At the autumn meeting, held at the University of Virginia, the following is a summary of the papers included on the program in the subjects indicated: Zoology, six; physiology, three; anatomy, one; pathology, three; physics, five; biology, one; chemistry, one; medicine, two; psychology, three; paleontology, two; astronomy, six; geology, four; anthropology, two; botany, three; mathematics, three; geodesy, one; and seven Biographical Memoirs of deceased members were presented by title. At the annual meeting there were 45 papers on the program, distributed among the sciences as follows: Mathematics, four; astronomy, four; physics, nine; engineering, one; chemistry, one; meteorology, one; geology, seven; biology, one; botany, two; zoology, one; bacteriology, one; physiology, five; pathology, two; medicine, one; psychology, four; and anthropology, one. Of these papers, 31 were read by Academy members and 14 by nonmembers. In addition, there were four Biographical Memoirs read by title.

At the same meeting two medals were presented: The Agassiz Medal for Oceanography, to T. Wayland Vaughan, in recognition of his investigations of corals, foraminifera, and submarine deposits and for his leadership in developing oceanographic activities on the Pacific coast of America; and the Public Welfare Medal, to F. F. Russell, in recognition of his work on the etiology of yellow fever and of his studies of epidemic areas.

MEETINGS OF THE NATIONAL ACADEMY

AUTUMN MEETING, 1935

The 1935 autumn meeting of the National Academy of Sciences was held in Charlottesville, Va., on November 18, 19, and 20, 1935, upon invitation by the University of Virginia.

BUSINESS SESSION

Forty-nine members responded to the roll call, as follows:

Abbot, C. G.
Bancroft, W. D.
Berry, E. W.
Blakeslee, A. F.
Bowen, N. L.
Bowie, William.
Bowman, Isaiah.
Cattell, J. McKeen.
Compton, Karl T.
Crew, Henry.
Cross, Whitman.
Day, A. L.
Donaldson, H. H.
Fletcher, Harvey.
Harper, R. A.
Harrison, R. G.
Howell, W. H.

Hrdlicka, Ales.
Hull, A. W
Hunsaker, J. C.
Ives, H. E.
Jones, L. R.
Kasner, Edward.
Keith, Arthur.
Kennelly, A. E.
Leuschner, A. O.
Lillie, F. R.
Mendenhall, W. C.
Miles, W. R.
Miller, D. C.
Millikan, R. A.
Mitchell, S. A.
Norris, J. F.
Parker, G. H.

Pearl, Raymond.
Scott, W. B.
Sherman, H. C.
Stockard, C. R.
Streeter, G. L.
Swanton, J. R.
Swasey, Ambrose.
Tennent, D. H.
Urey, H. C.
Veblen, Oswald.
White, H. S.
Wilson, Edwin B.
Wilson, H. V.
Woodworth, R. S.
Wright, F. E.

Frank Dawson Adams, foreign associate, also attended the autumn meeting.

PRESIDENT'S ANNOUNCEMENTS

The president of the Academy made the following announcements:

DEATHS SINCE THE ANNUAL MEETING

Charles Edward St. John, born March 15, 1857, elected to the Academy in 1924, died April 26, 1935.

Edwin Brant Frost, born July 14, 1866, elected to the Academy in 1908, died May 14, 1935.

Edward Salisbury Dana, born November 16, 1849, elected to the Academy in 1884, died June 16, 1935.

Benjamin Lincoln Robinson, born November 8, 1864, elected to the Academy in 1921, died July 27, 1935.

Charles Elwood Mendenhall, born August 1, 1872, elected to the Academy in 1918, died August 18, 1935.

Carl Barus, born February 19, 1856, elected to the Academy in 1892, died September 28, 1935.

Frederick Leslie Ransome, born December 2, 1868, elected to the Academy in 1914, died October 6, 1935.

Charles Loring Jackson (emeritus), born April 4, 1847, elected to the Academy in 1883, died October 28, 1935.

Henry Fairfield Osborn, born August 8, 1857, elected to the Academy in 1900, died November 6, 1935.

Foreign associate.—Hugo de Vries, of Lunteren, the Netherlands, elected a foreign associate in 1904, died May 21, 1935.

Maxime Bocher, assigned to G. D. Birkhoff.
Henry Prentiss Armsby, assigned to S. R. Benedict.
William Stewart Halsted, assigned to W. G. MacCallum and manuscript received.
George Fillmore Swain, assigned to William Hovgaard.
Graham Lusk, assigned to E. F. DuBois.
Harris J. Ryan, assigned to D. L. Webster.
Theobald Smith, assigned to Hans Zinsser.
Charles E. St. John, assigned to W. S. Adams.
Edwin Brant Frost, assigned to G. E. Hale.
Edward Salisbury Dana, assigned to Adolph Knopf.
Benjamin Lincoln Robinson, assigned to M. L. Fernald.
Charles Elwood Mendenhall, assigned to J. H. Van Vleck.
Carl Barus, assigned to C. A. Kraus.

DELEGATES APPOINTED SINCE THE APRIL MEETING

To the Third Centenary of the founding of l'Académie Française, Paris, June 17–20, 1935—L. J. Henderson.
To the Centenary of the Geological Survey of Great Britain, London, July 3–5, 1935—Arthur L. Day.
To the Fifteenth International Congress of Physiology, Leningrad and Moscow, August 9–17, 1935—W. B. Cannon.
To the Twelfth International Congress of Zoology, Lisbon, Portugal, September 14–25, 1935—Leonhard Stejneger, Thomas Barbour, H. S. Jennings, W. M. Wheeler.
To the Nineteenth International Congress of Orientalists, Rome, September 23–29, 1935—James H. Breasted.
To the Second General Assembly of the Pan American Institute of Geography and History, Washington, October 14–19, 1935—William Bowie, Isaiah Bowman, Whitman Cross, Arthur L. Day, W. C. Mendenhall, John C. Merriam, Fred. E. Wright.
To the celebration of the one-hundredth anniversary of the birth of Andrew Carnegie, Dunfermline, Scotland, November 25, 1935—John H. Finley.

TEMPORARY CHAIRMAN OF SECTION OF ZOOLOGY AND ANATOMY

Temporary chairman of section of zoology and anatomy appointed to conduct the present balloting for nominations and the election of a regular chairman (succeeding F. R. Lillie, resigned)—C. R. Stockard; for the period ending at the close of the annual meeting, April 1936.

TRUST FUND COMMITTEE APPOINTMENTS

Henry Draper fund: S. A. Mitchell as member, for the period ending with the annual meeting in 1940 (succeeding R. G. Aitken).
Murray fund: T. Wayland Vaughan as member and chairman, for the period ending with the annual meeting in 1938 (succeeding H. B. Bigelow, who declined reappointment).
J. Lawrence Smith fund: Charles Palache as member, for the period ending with the annual meeting in 1939 (filling the unexpired term of F. L. Ransome, deceased).
Daniel Giraud Elliot fund: W. K. Gregory as member, succeeding H. F. Osborn, deceased.

COMMITTEE APPOINTMENTS

Finance committee: C. G. Abbot and F. B. Jewett, to serve during the fiscal year ending June 30, 1936, with ex officio members: Arthur Keith, treasurer and chairman, and president Lillie.
Library committee: W. D. Harkins as member, succeeding F. R. Lillie, resigned.
Oceanography committee: H. B. Bigelow as member and chairman, succeeding F. R. Lillie, resigned.

Joint advisory committee on buildings and grounds: Edson S. Bastin and I. F. Lewis, succeeding Gano Dunn and F. K. Richtmyer as representatives of the executive board of the National Research Council.

Executive committee of the council of the Academy: Roger Adams (1937), K. T. Compton (1936) and Ross G. Harrison, reappointed (1938).

Committee on Government relations: The president of the Academy, chairman ex officio, F. R. Lillie; the vice president of the Academy, Arthur L. Day; the home secretary of the Academy, F. E. Wright; the chairman or specially elected representative of each of the 11 sections of the Academy, Messrs. A. B. Coble, A. O. Leuschner, A. W. Hull, Bancroft Gherardi, C. A. Kraus, C. K. Leith, A. F. Blakeslee, C. R. Stockard, L. J. Henderson, Ludvig Hektoen, C. E. Seashore. Members at large: Roger Adams, Isaiah Bowman, K. T. Compton, Gano Dunn, Simon Flexner, F. B. Jewett, L. R. Jones, R. A. Millikan, Edwin B. Wilson, G. H. Whipple. Executive committee of the committee on Government relations: The president of the Academy, chairman ex officio (Mr. Lillie), Isaiah Bowman, K. T. Compton, Arthur L. Day, F. B. Jewett, C. K. Leith, R. A. Millikan.

HIGHWAY RESEARCH BOARD

The work of the Highway Research Board, under the Division of Engineering and Industrial Research of the National Research Council, is carried on by cooperation with the Bureau of Public Roads of the Department of Agriculture, which this year renewed the contract for contribution toward the expenses of the Board for the year 1935–36, calling for the payment of $20,000.

REPORTS OF THE TREASURER AND AUDITING COMMITTEE

The annual report of the treasurer of the Academy covering the fiscal year 1934–35 was presented, and upon recommendation by the council of the Academy was accepted for inclusion in the printed annual report of the National Academy of Sciences for that period.

The report of the auditing committee was presented, and upon recommendation by the council of the Academy was accepted for inclusion in the printed annual report of the National Academy of Sciences for the fiscal year 1934–35.

These reports appeared on pages 77–105 of the annual report of the National Academy of Sciences for the fiscal year 1934–35.

MR. MENDEL TRANSFERRED TO ROLL OF MEMBERS EMERITI

The request of Lafayette B. Mendel (elected to the Academy in 1913) that he be transferred to the roll of members emeriti was received and, upon recommendation by the council of the Academy, was approved.

JAMES CRAIG WATSON FUND

The following report from the trustees of the James Craig Watson fund was presented:

The board of trustees recommend that the purposes of grant No. 50, voted at the fall meeting of 1934 (payable to the Watson trustees), be extended so as to include:

Determination of Saturn perturbations and incidental revision of tests based on comparisons of theories with observations.

A new theory of the Watson planet number (132) Aethra. The theory of Hartog, Berlin, reported at the fall meeting of 1934 has since been found to be not as satisfactory as had been anticipated.

A. O. LEUSCHNER, *Chairman.*

Report accepted and recommendation approved.

MARSH FUND

The following report from the committee on the Marsh fund was presented:

The Marsh fund committee has received a satisfactory report of progress from Dr. Harry S. Ladd, who, with Dr. J. E. Hoffmeister and other specialists, is preparing a report on the geology and invertebrate palaeontology of the Lau Islands (eastern Fiji). This important project is being carried on jointly by the University of Rochester and the Bishop Museum. Owing to conditions set forth in a letter from Dr. Ladd, the sum of $400 is needed for the remaining expenses of preparation.

Dr. T. W. Vaughan recommends for favorable consideration the application of Dr. Ladd for $400 for the purpose noted above. The committee' on the Marsh fund therefore endorses the application and recommends to the National Academy of Sciences an appropriation of $400 to Dr. Harry S, Ladd, to be used in completing a comprehensive report on the geology of the Lau Islands.

WILLIAM K. GREGORY, *Chairman.*

Report accepted and recommendation approved.

MARCELLUS HARTLEY FUND

The following report from the committee on the Marcellus Hartley fund was presented:

Under the terms of the Marcellus Hartley fund, providing a medal for eminence in the application of science to public welfare, the committee recommends, first, a dual award; second, that this award be made to Surgeon General Hugh S. Cumming and Dr. F. F. Russell.

HARVEY CUSHING, *Chairman.*

Report accepted and recommendations approved.

MURRAY FUND

The chairman of the Murray fund reported that the financial condition of that fund on October 31, 1935, according to the bursar, was as follows: Invested income, none; uninvested income, $4,068.03; invested capital, $6,000; uninvested capital, none.

Report accepted.

SCIENTIFIC SESSIONS

The following papers were presented at the scientific sessions by members of the Academy or persons introduced by members:

MONDAY, NOVEMBER 18, 1935

C. R. Stockard, Cornell University Medical College, New York City: Giant Skin Growth on Mammals with Normal Sized Skeletons (illustrated).

H. E. Jordan, University of Virginia Medical School (introduced by S. A. Mitchell): The Role of the Lymphocyte in Blood Formation (illustrated).

W. H. Howell, Johns Hopkins Medical School, Baltimore, Md.: The Production of Blood Platelets in the Lungs (illustrated).

Henry H. Donaldson, Wistar Institute of Anatomy, Philadelphia, Pa.: On the Significance of the Numerical Relations of the Fibers in the Spinal Nerves of the Mouse, Rat, Dog, and Man (illustrated).

S. W. Britton and H. Silvette, University of Virginia Medical School (introduced by W. B. Cannon): Cortico-adrenal Inuuences on Sodium and Carbohydrate Metabolism (illustrated).

Raymond Pearl, Johns Hopkins Medical School, Baltimore, Md.; On the Incidence of Tuberculosis Among Offspring of Tuberculosis Parents (illustrated).

D. I. Macht, Baltimore, Md. (introduced by E. V. McCollum): An Experimental and Clinical Study of Cobra Venom as an Analgesic (illustrated).

Alfred Chanutin and Stephan Ludewig, University of Virginia Medical School (introduced by S. A. Mitchell): Experimental Renal Insufficiency Produced by Partial Nephrectomy. Effect of meat diets (illustrated).

Yandell Henderson, Yale University, New Haven, Connecticut: How Cars Go Out of Control: Analysis of the Driver's Reflexes.

W. G. MacCallum, Johns Hopkins Hospital, Baltimore, Md.; Biographical Memoir of William Stewart Halsted. Read by title.

Albert W. Hull, General Electric Co., Schenectady, N. Y.: An Oscillograph with a Memory (illustrated).

J. W. Beams, University of Virginia (introduced by S. A. Mitchell): The Production and Use of High Rotational Speeds (illustrated).

Herbert E. Ives and H. B. Briggs, Bell Telephone Laboratories, New York City: The Optical Constants and Photoelectric Emission of Potassium (illustrated).

A. E. Kennelly, Harvard University, Cambridge, Mass.: The International Adoption of the Giorgi System of M. K. S. units by the International Electrotechnical Commission, June 1935 (illustrated).

Edwin B. Wilson, Harvard University, Cambridge, Mass.: Heights and Weights of 275 Public School Girls in Ten Consecutive Years (illustrated).

L. F. Small, University of Virginia (introduced by Marston T. Bogert): Studies of New Narcotics (illustrated).

H. C. Sherman, Columbia University, New York City: Calcium as a Factor in the Nutritional Improvement of Health (illustrated).

W. R. Miles, Yale University, New Haven, Conn.: An analysis of Color-blindness in 11,000 Museum Visitors (illustrated).

J. G. Dusser de Barenne and W. S. McCulloch, Yale University, New Haven, Conn. (introduced by W. R. Miles): Action Potentials of the Various Layers of the Cerebral Cortex (illustrated).

George H. Meeker, University of Pennsylvania, Philadelphia, Pa.: Biographical Memoir of Edgar Fahs Smith. Read by title.

Harold Clayton Urey, Columbia University, New York City: Varieties of Water and Their Separation.

TUESDAY, NOVEMBER 19, 1935

W. B. Scott, Princeton University, N. J.: The Extinct Giant Ground-Sloths of North and South America (illustrated).

F. E. Wright, Geophysical Laboratory, Carnegie Institution of Washington, Washington, D. C.: The Frequency Distribution of Lunar Craters With Reference to Size (illustrated).

Arthur L. Day, Geophysical Laboratory, Washington, D. C.: The Mechanism of Geysers (illustrated).

E. W. Berry, Johns Hopkins University, Baltimore, Md.: Geological Setting of the Archaeology of Lake Tacarigua, Venezuela (illustrated).

N. L. Bowen, Geophysical Laboratory, Carnegie Institution of Washington, Washington, D. C.: Ferrous Metasilicate in Nature (illustrated).

Joseph K. Roberts, University of Virginia (introduced by Charles P. Berkey): William Barton Rogers and His Contribution to the Geology of Virginia.

R. A. Millikan and H. V. Neher, California Institute of Technology, Pasadena, Calif.: Geographic Distribution of Cosmic Ray Intensities (illustrated).

A. Hrdlička, United States National Museum, Washington, D. C.: Anthropological Excavations on Kodiak Island (illustrated by motion pictures).

M. W. Stirling, Bureau of American Ethnology, Smithsonian Institution (introduced by John R. Swanton): Exploration of a Mound at Belle Glade, Fla. (illustrated).

W. D. Bancroft and J. E. Rutzler, Jr., Cornell University, Ithaca, N. Y.: The Copper Beech and the Sugar Maple (illustrated).

Ross G. Harrison, Yale University, New Haven, Conn.: Relations of Symmetry in the Developing Ear of Amblystoma (illustrated).

D. H. Tennent, Bryn Mawr College, Bryn Mawr, Pa.: The Photodynamic Effects of Vital Dyes on Fertilized Sea Urchin Eggs (illustrated).

G. H. Parker, Harvard University, Cambridge, Mass.: The Earliest Responses of Vertebrate Melanophores (illustrated).

W. A. Kepner, W. C. Gregory, and R. J. Porter, University of Virginia (introduced by E. G. Conklin): The Manipulation of the Nematocysts of Hydra by Microstomum (illustrated).

W. Conway Price, Rockefeller Institute for Medical Research, Princeton, N. J. (introduced by R. A. Harper): Virus Concentration in Relation to Acquired Immunity From Tobacco Ring Spot (illustrated).

A. F. Blakeslee, J. L. Cartledge, and M. J. Murray, Department of Genetics, Carnegie Institution of Washington, Cold Spring Harbor, Long Island, N. Y.; Increased Mutation Rate From Aged Datura Pollen (illustrated).

S. A. Wingard, Virginia Agricultural Experiment Station, Blacksburg, Va. (introduced by R. A. Harper): Studies of the Nature of Rust Resistance in Beans (illustrated).

C. C. Speidel, University of Virginia (introduced by Ross G. Harrison): The Effects of Alcohol on Nerves in Living Frog Tadpoles (illustrated by motion pictures).

WEDNESDAY, NOVEMBER 20, 1935

Edward Kasner, Columbia University, New York City; Conformed Geometry.

G. T. Whyburn, University of Virginia (introduced by S. A. Mitchell): Continuous Transformations on Certain Manifolds.

H. S. Uhler, Yale University, New Haven, Conn. (introduced by F. Schlesinger): On the Computation of −! to 400 Decimal Places, Together With Associated Numbers. Read by title.

C. G. Abbot, Smithsonian Institution, Washington, D. C.: Solar Variation and Weather Studies (illustrated).

William Bowie, United States Coast and Geodetic Survey, Washington, D. C.: The National Mapping Plan of the National Resources Board (illustrated).

F. L. Whipple, T. E. Sterne, and D. Norman, Harvard College Observatory, Cambridge, Mass. (introduced by Harlow Shapley): Prismatic Deviation as a Function of Cosmical Deviation (illustrated).

P. van de Kamp and A. N. Vyssotsky, Leander McCormick Observatory, University, Va. (introduced by S. A. Mitchell): The Proportion of Dwarfs Among Tenth Magnitude Stars (illustrated).

M. L. Humason, Mount Wilson Observatory, Pasadena, Calif. (introduced by W. S. Adams): New Velocities of Extra-Galactic Nebulae (illustrated).

S. A. Mitchell, Leander McCormick Observatory, University, Va.: The Magnitudes of 6,284 Stars in 350 Regions of Long Period Variables (illustrated).

G. A. Bliss and L. E. Dickson, University of Chicago, Chicago, Ill.: Biographical Memoir of Eliakim Hastings Moore. Read by title.

Vannevar Bush, Massachusetts Institute of Technology, Cambridge, Mass.: Biographical Memoir of John Ripley Freeman. Read by title.

Charles Schuchert, Peabody Museum, Yale University, New Haven, Conn.: Biographical Memoir of David White. Read by title.

John R. Swanton, Bureau of American Ethnology, Smithsonian Institution, Washington, D. C.: Biographical Memoir of William Henry Holmes. Read by title.

A. E. Kennelly, Graduate School of Engineering, Harvard University, Cambridge, Mass.: Biographical Memoir of Samuel Wesley Stratton. Read by title.

ANNUAL MEETING

The National Academy of Sciences held its annual spring meeting, 1936, in the Academy Building, Washington, D. C., on April 27, 28, and 29, 1936.

BUSINESS SESSION

One hundred and seventeen members responded to roll call, as follows:

Abbot, C. G.	Barbour, Thomas	Bliss, G. A.
Adams, Roger	Bigelow, H. B.	Boas, Franz
Allen, C. E	Birkhoff, G. D.	Bowen, N. L.
Allen, E. T.	Blakeslee, A. F.	Bowie, William

Bridgman, P. W.
Brown, E. W.
Bush, Vannevar
Campbell, D. H.
Cannon, W. B.
Castle, W. E.
Cattell, J. McKeen
Clark, W. M.
Clinton, G. P.
Coble, A. B.
Coblentz, W. W.
Compton, A. H.
Compton, K. T.
Conant, J. B.
Conklin, E. G.
Cross, Whitman
Curtis, H. D.
Davenport, C. B.
Davis, Bergen
Day, A. L.
Dodge, B. O.
Duggar, B. M.
Durand, W. F.
East, E. M.
Fletcher, Harvey
Flexner, Simon
Gasser, H. S.
Hall, E. H.
Harper, R. A.
Harrison, R. G.
Harvey, E. N.
Hektoen, Ludvig
Henderson, L. J.
Hooton, E. A.
Hovgaard, William

Howard, L. O.
Howe, M. A.
Howell, W. H.
Hrdlicka, Ales
Hudson, C. S.
Hull, A. W.
Hunsaker, J. C.
Hunter, W. S.
Ives, H. E.
Jackson, Dunham
Johnson, Douglas
Jones, L. R.
Kasner, Edward
Keith, Arthur
Kemble, Edwin C.
Keyes, F. G.
Kraus, C. A.
Kunkel, L. O.
Langmuir, Irving
Lawrence, E. O.
Leith, C. K.
Leuschner, A. O.
Levene, P. A.
Lillie, F. R.
Longwell, C. R.
McClung, C. E.
Mark, E. L.
Mason, Max
Mendenhall, W. C.
Merrill, E. D.
Merritt, Ernest
Miles, W. R.
Miller, D. C.
Millikan, R. A.
Mitchell, S. A.

Morse, Marston
Norris, J. F.
Noyes, W. A.
Osterhout, W. J. V.
Pauling, Linus
Pearl, Raymond
Pillsbury, W. B.
Richtmyer, F. K.
Ritt, J. F.
Russell, H. N.
Sabin, Florence R.
Sauveur, Albert
Schlesinger, Frank
Seashore, C. E.
Sherman, H. C.
Slater, John C.
Stakman, E. C.
Stebbins, Joel
Stejneger, Leonhard
Stockard, C. R.
Streeter, G. L.
Swanton, J. R.
Swasey, Ambrose
Thorndike, E. L.
Urey, Harold C.
Van Vleck, E. B.
Van Vleck, J. H.
Vaughan, T. W.
Veblen, Oswald
Washburn, Margaret F.
Wilson, Edwin B.
Wood, R. W.
Woodworth, R. S.
Wright, F. E.
Yerkes, R. M.

PRESIDENT'S ANNOUNCEMENTS

DEATHS SINCE THE AUTUMN MEETING

Members

James Henry Breasted, born August 27, 1865, elected to the Academy in 1923, died December 2, 1935.
Lafayette Benedict Mendel (emeritus), born February 5, 1872, elected to the Academy in 1913, died December 9, 1935.

Foreign associates

I. P. Pavlov, of Leningrad, Union of Soviet Socialist Republics, elected a foreign associate in 1908, died February 27, 1936.
John Scott Haldane, of Oxford, England, elected a foreign associate in 1935, died March 14-15 (midnight), 1936.

BIOGRAPHIES ASSIGNED SINCE THE AUTUMN MEETING

Berthold Laufer, assigned to K. S. Latourette, nonmember.
Charles Loring Jackson, assigned to Frank C. Whitmore, nonmember.
James Henry Breasted, assigned to John A. Wilson, nonmember.
Lafayette Benedict Mendel, assigned to Russell H. Chittenden.

DELEGATES APPOINTED SINCE THE AUTUMN MEETING

To the inauguration of Arthur A. O'Leary, S. J., as president of Georgetown University, Washington, D. C., November 23, 1935, Arthur Keith.

To the Charter Day exercises of the University of California, San Francisco, Calif., March 23, 1936, W. W. Campbell.

To the International Congress of Mathematicians, Oslo, Norway, July 13 to 18, 1936, George D. Birkhoff, H. F. Blichfeldt, L. P. Eisenhart, Solomon Lefschetz, Oswald Veblen, Norbert Wiener, Harry Bateman.

To the International Union of Chemistry, Lucerne, Switzerland, August 16–22, 1936, Roger Adams, Edward Bartow, Frederick Bates, Wallace R. Brode, Emma P. Carr, E. J. Crane, John B. Ekeley, Gustavus J. Esselen, Colin G. Fink, Ross A. Gortner, J. C. Hostetter, James F. Norris, Austin M. Patterson, Charles L. Reese, Atherton Seidell, Alexander Silverman, Robert E. Swain.

To the Sixth General Assembly of the International Union of Geodesy and Geophysics, Edinburgh, Scotland, September 17 to 26, 1936, Harry Bateman, Lloyd V. Berkner, William Bowie, James E. Church, E. G. Conklin, Arthur L. Day, Carl Elges, Richard M. Field, John A. Fleming, Frank Goldstone, Lawrence M. Gould, Beno Gutenberg, Harry D. Harradon, Nicholas H. Heck, Paul R. Heyl, William H. Hobbs, Columbus Iselin, Walter D. Lambert, Rev. Father J. Joseph Lynch, S. J., James B. Macelwane, Oscar E. Mainzer, William J. Peters, William C. Repetti, Roger Revelle, Harlan T. Stetson, Lt. Elliott B. Strauss, U. S. N., William T. Thom, Jr., Lt. P. W. Thompson, U. S. A., Thomas G. Thompson, Clinton L. Utterback, T. Wayland Vaughan, Richard H. Weitman, H. O. Wentworth, Oliver R. Wulf.

To the tercentenary celebration of Harvard University, Cambridge, Mass., September 16, 17, and 18, 1936, Frank R. Lillie.

To the Third World Power Conference, Washington, D. C., September 7 to 12, 1936, Gano Dunn and C. F. Kettering on the part of the Academy; W. F. Durand and Frank B. Jewett on the part of the Research Council.

SECTION CHAIRMEN

New chairmen of sections, elected by the sections for a term of 3 years commencing at the close of the present annual meeting:

Section of physics.—Max Mason to succeed A. W. Hull.

Section of geology and paleontology.—W. C. Mendenhall, to succeed C. K. Leith.

Section of zoology and anatomy.—C. R. Stockard, who has been serving as temporary chairman, elected as the regular chairman.

Section of physiology and biochemistry.—W. Mansfield Clark, to succeed L. J. Henderson.

Section of pathology and bacteriology.—Simon Flexner, to succeed Ludvig Hektoen.

TRUST FUND COMMITTEE APPOINTMENTS

Alexander Dallas Bache fund.—Edwin B. Wilson elected chairman to succeed Heber D. Curtis (resigned); Charles R. Stockard elected to succeed Mr. Curtis as member.

Henry Draper fund.—W. S. Adams, to succeed Harlow Shapley as member. Term, 5 years.

J. Lawrence Smith fund.—R. J. Trumpler, to succeed C. G. Abbot as member. Term, 5 years.

Cyrus B. Comstock fund.—C. J. Davisson, to succeed D. C. Miller as member. Term, 5 years.

Marsh fund.—C. R. Longwell, to succeed Adolph Knopf as member. Term, 5 years.

Murray fund.—Arthur L. Day, to succeed Douglas Johnson as member. Term, 3 years.

Marcellus Hartley fund.—A. W. Hull, to succeed J. S. Ames as member. Max Mason to succeed H. H. Donaldson as member. Terms, 3 years.

Mary Clark Thompson fund.—W. C. Mendenhall, to succeed himself as member. Term, 3 years.

Joseph Henry fund.—Vannevar Bush to succeed D. W. Taylor as member. Term, 5 years.

Charles Doolittle Walcott fund.—T. Wayland Vaughan selected by the president and council to succeed Charles Schuchert (resigned) as member and temporary chairman.

John J. Carty fund.—F. B. Jewett to succeed himself as chairman. Term, 5 years.

Nominating committee, appointed by authority of the executive committee of the council of the Academy to nominate a treasurer and two members of the council of the Academy to fill vacancies occurring June 30, 1936—C. G. Abbot, chairman; Simon Flexner; and Edwin B. Wilson.

Tellers to count the preference ballots on nominations of new members—A. F. Blakeslee and C. B. Davenport.

Auditing committee.—C. S. Hudson, chairman; N. L. Bowen; and W. H. Howell.

Government Relations and Science Advisory Committee.—The sections of the Academy have elected the following persons to serve as their representatives on the Government Relations and Science Advisory Committee, commencing at the close of the present annual meeting, the term of each representative to be coterminous with that of the chairman of his section, as indicated:

Mathematics, Oswald Veblen (1937).
Astronomy, A. O. Leuschner (1938).
Physics, Edwin B. Wilson (1939).
Engineering, Bancroft Gherardi (1938).
Chemistry, Roger Adams (1938).
Geology and paleontology, Isaiah Bowman (1939).
Zoology and anatomy, C. R. Stockard (1939).
Botany, A. F. Blakeslee (1938).
Physiology and biochemistry, A. J. Carlson (1939).
Pathology and bacteriology, Simon Flexner (1939).
Anthropology and psychology, C. E. Seashore (1938).

BOARD OF TRUSTEES OF SCIENCE SERVICE

Harlow Shapley was nominated by the executive committee of the council of the Academy to succeed himself as one of the three representatives of the Academy on the board of Trustees of Science Service for a period of 3 years.

HEALTH COMMITTEE OF THE LEAGUE OF NATIONS

W. H. Howell was appointed by authority of the council of the Academy to serve as the representative of the Academy, without vote, on the advisory commission for technical studies of the health committee of the League of Nations, the work of the commission to be carried on by correspondence.

AUTUMN MEETING

To be held in Chicago at the University of Chicago, November 16, 17, and 18, 1936. Committee on arrangements: A. H. Compton, W. D. Harkins, A. J. Carlson, F. R. Moulton, C. J. Herrick; additional members, Henry Crew, of Northwestern University; Roger Adams, of the University of Illinois; and C. K. Leith, of the University of Wisconsin.

PROCEEDINGS, MANAGING EDITOR

Announcement was made of the election, by the council of the Academy on the preceding evening, of Edwin B. Wilson as managing editor of the Proceedings of the National Academy of Sciences, to succeed himself, for the period ending with the autumn meeting in 1937.

DUES

The recommendation of the council that dues for membership in the Academy for the year ending with the annual meeting in 1937 be $10 was approved.

AMENDMENTS TO THE CONSTITUTION

The following proposed amendments to the constitution (which had been approved by the committee of the whole at the autumn meeting in 1935 and recommended for approval by the Academy in business session at this annual meeting) were adopted:

ART. II, SEC. 5. Substitute for the word "two" the words "two as abov.. t

ERRATUM SLIP

Report of the National Academy of Sciences for the Fiscal Year
1935-1936

(Insert opposite Page 13)

Page 13—Under AMENDMENTS TO THE CONSTITUTION, Art. IV Sec. 4. In the material blocked out as being deleted by amendment the fol‐ lowing was included through an oversight:

Nominations to membership in the Academy shall be made in writing and approved by two-thirds of the members voting in a section on the branch of research in which the person nominated is eminent, or by a majority of the council in case there is no section on the subject, or by a majority (however distributed) of the members voting in any two sections. The nomination shall be sent to the home secretary by the chairman of the section before January 1 of the year in which the elec‐ tion is to be held, and each nomination shall be accompanied by a list of the principal contributions of the nominee to science. This list shall be printed by the home secretary for distribution among the members of the Academy.

Please note that the above-quoted passages remain in full force and effect as the second paragraph of Art. IV Sec. 4 of the Constitution.

F. E. WRIGHT,
Home Secretary.

May 24, 1937.

AMENDMENTS TO THE BYLAWS

The committee on revision of the constitution and bylaws presented recommendations for amendment of the bylaws. These were con‐ sidered and amended on the floor, resulting in their adoption as follows:

IV:2. (1) Intersectional: Proposals for nomination to membership may be made in writing by any five members of the Academy and addressed to the home secretary; each such proposal shall be accompanied by a record of the scientific activities of the person proposed and by a list of his principal contributions to science, in triplicate; and with a statement as to the sections to which the name proposed shall be submitted for consideration. Such proposals as have been received by the home secretary prior to October 1 shall upon that date be sent by him to the chairman of each section designated, with a copy of the record and list of contributions.

(2) Sectional: Proposals for nomination to membership shall be in writing and shall be sent to the chairman of the section not later than October 1. The proposal for nomination of any individual will be accepted for consideration by the section only if it is accompanied by a list of titles and references of the more important published scientific articles of the individual and by a factual summary not over 250 words in length, of his accomplishments.

Each section chairman shall edit material thus received, and, at the time of the informal ballot, distribute it, together with the material from the home secretary, relative to intersectional proposals, to the members of the section. The home secretary's office, if called upon, will assist the chairman of the sections in the multigraphing of this material.

Each chairman shall keep a record of the names listed on the informal ballot and shall strike from the lists those names which were on the list in the previous year and received less than two votes on the informal ballot or had been on the list for 3 consecutive years without receiving in any one of these years on the informal ballot so many as one-fourth of the votes cast (counting the votes according to the number of members in the section who vote and not by the number of persons on the list for whom they vote). The home secretary shall keep a record of the votes on the informal ballots in the case of those persons proposed to two or more sections of the Academy and shall cause such names to be stricken from the lists of all sections if in 3 consecutive years there be no two sections in which the number of votes cast for the proposed nominee exceeds one-sixth of the votes cast in those sections except in case the number should be as many as one-fourth of the votes cast in one section, in which case the proposal should be considered thenceforth as a proposal in that section only. No proposal for nomination which is thus stricken from the list of the informal ballot shall be considered by the section (or sections) unless again proposed for nomination in the appropriate manner in a subsequent year.

NOMINATION BALLOTS

IV:3. The chairman of each section of the Academy shall submit to the members of his section not later than November 1 of each year an informal ballot containing, in alphabetical order and without indications of rank on ballots of the previous year, the names of all those persons who received not less than two votes in the informal ballot of the preceding year and not less than one-fourth of the votes on the informal ballot in at least 1 of the preceding 3 years in the case of names in the list for 3 years or have been continued on the list by the home secretary or have been added to the list by him or have been newly proposed for consideration in accordance with the procedure above defined. Each member of the section shall be expected to return his ballot to the chairman within 2 weeks, with his signature and with crosses against the names of those persons whom he is prepared to endorse for nomination. The vote resulting from this ballot shall be regarded as informal.

The chairman shall then submit to the members of his section a new ballot showing the results of the informal vote; and each member shall be expected to return this ballot to the chairman, with his signature and with crosses placed against names of three persons whom he judges to be worthy of nomination.

In order to secure an adequate number of nominations, the chairman, when necessary, shall obtain by personal solicitation a fuller vote of his section or shall submit to the section a supplementary formal ballot.

The chairman shall then certify to the home secretary, prior to January 1, the names of all persons who have been voted for on the formal ballots, together with a statement of the number of votes each candidate received and of the number of members voting. Of these all persons who receive the votes of two-thirds of the members voting in the section in cases voted upon by one section only, or the votes of one-half (however distributed) of the members voting in any two sections in cases voted upon by more than one section, shall be considered nominated.

A properly edited statement of the accomplishments of each individual nominated to the Academy by the sections shall be sent by the section chairmen to the home secretary, along with the nominations of the section. These statements, together with summaries pertaining to those persons nominated intersectionally or nominated by the council, shall be reproduced and distributed to the members of the Academy at the time of the preference ballot.

Persons nominated to the Academy and rejected by the Academy at the ensuing election may not be further considered by the sections until they have again been proposed for nomination in the appropriate manner in a subsequent year. Persons nominated but not voted upon by the Academy shall without further action be presented to the Academy upon the preference ballot of the next following year; but, if again not voted upon, the nominations shall lapse and not be considered except when renewed in the regular order.

REPORT OF THE FOREIGN SECRETARY

The growing international interest in scientific research and in science in general through international cooperation leads one to feel that the fundamentals of science are being recognized as a basis upon which the future depends. That this must have been the thought of those who had to do with the early framing of the Academy is shown in the resolution of Mr. Gould, presented in response to the request of the foreign secretary for instructions regarding notices to foreign societies, recorded in the minutes of 1864, which read:

"*Resolved*, That the foreign secretary be requested to notify foreign national scientific academies and societies of the organization of this Academy and ask their cooperation.

"That the Academy approve the views of the foreign secretary as just expressed by him and empower him to use his discretion in carrying out the principles of selection."

While the constitution of the Academy provided for 50 foreign associates, just as it does today, the number has never reached the limit, and according to the bylaws in 1863 not more than 10 foreign associates shall be elected at any one meeting. The first list, elected January 1864, comprised Sir William Rowan Hamilton, Karl Ernst Von Baer, Michael Faraday, J. B. Elie de Beaumont, Sir David Brewster, G. A. A. Plana, Robert Bunsen, F. W. A. Argelander, Michel Chasles, and Henri Milne-Edwards. Since that meeting, and including the first 10, there have been elected to the Academy 171 foreign associates. The number on the roll today is 41, divided among the sciences as recognized in the sections of the Academy as follows: Mathematics, eight; astronomy, four; physics, seven; engineering, three; chemistry, four; geology and paleontology, seven; botany, two; zoology and anatomy, two; physiology and pathology, three; anthropology and psychology, one. Three foreign associates died since the last annual meeting: Hugo de Vries, of Lunteren, The Netherlands; I. P. Pavlov, of Leningrad, Union of Soviet Socialist Republics; and John Scott Haldane, of Oxford, England.

In last year's report I referred to the International Council of Scientific Unions and affiliated unions and the appropriation by the Government of funds to pay the American share in the expenses of those bodies. The authorization bill which was pending at the close of the year was later passed by both Houses of Congress and became a law. Immediately upon passage, an item was included in the first deficiency bill of the last Congress, at the request of the Department of State, to cover the unpaid share of expenses for 1935. These were paid on the approval of the bill. Those for 1936 and future payments will be taken care of automatically by the continuing authorization. There still remains to be paid the amount for 1934, and while there was special authorization for this and a request made for an appropriation to cover the amount, Congress has not up to this time approved the appropriation. It is hoped that further effort can be made to cover the period for 1934.

At the request of the Department of State, delegates have been suggested to the Department of State and appointments have been made on behalf of the Academy. Invitations received by the National Academy of Sciences have also been given attention. The bodies receiving favorable consideration were as follows:

International Congress of Mathematicians, Oslo, Norway, July 13–18, 1936.

Fifteenth International Congress of Physiology, Leningrad and Moscow, Union of Soviet Socialist Republics, August 9–17, 1935.

International Union of Chemistry. Lucerne, Switzerland, August 16-22, 1936.
Third World Power Conference, Washington, D. C., September 7-12, 1936.
Twelfth International Congress of Zoology, Lisbon, Portugal, September 14-25, 1935.
Sixth General Assembly of the International Union of Geodesy and Geophysics, Edinburgh, Scotland, September 17-26, 1936.
Nineteenth International Congress of Orientalists, Rome, Italy, September 23-29, 1935.
Second General Assembly of the Pan American Institute of Geography and History, Washington, D. C., October 14-19, 1935.
One hundredth anniversary of the birth of Andrew Carnegie, Dunfermline, Scotland, November 25, 1935.

T. H. MORGAN, Foreign Secretary.

Report accepted.

REPORT OF THE HOME SECRETARY

During the past year six Biographical Memoirs have been published. These were issued as the sixth, seventh, and eighth memoirs of volume XVI, and the first, second, and third memoirs of volume XVII. Thirteen manuscripts are in hand awaiting printing when funds become available.

No scientific Memoirs have been published for several years.

Since the last annual meeting nine members and two members emeriti have died:

Charles Edward St. John, born March 15, 1857, elected to the Academy in 1924, died April 26, 1935.

Edwin Brant Frost, born July 14, 1866, elected to the Academy in 1908, died May 14, 1935.

Edward Salisbury Dana, born November 16, 1849, elected to the Academy in 1884, died June 16, 1935.

Benjamin Lincoln Robinson, born November 8, 1864, elected to the Academy in 1921, died July 27, 1935.

Charles Elwood Mendenhall, born August 1, 1872, elected to the Academy in 1918, died August 18, 1935.

Carl Barus, born February 19, 1856, elected to the Academy in 1892, died September 28, 1935.

Frederick Leslie Ransome, born December 2, 1868, elected to the Academy in 1914, died October 6, 1935.

Charles Loring Jackson (emeritus), born April 4, 1847, elected to the Academy in 1883, died October 28, 1935.

Henry Fairfield Osborn, born August 8, 1857, elected to the Academy in 1900, died November 6, 1935.

James Henry Breasted, born August 27, 1865, elected to the Academy in 1923, died December 2, 1935.

Lafayette Benedict Mendel (emeritus), born February 5, 1872, elected to the Academy in 1913, died December 9, 1935.

Three foreign associates have died since the last annual meeting:

Hugo de Vries, of Lunteren, the Netherlands, elected a foreign associate in 1904, died May 21, 1935.

I. P. Pavlov, of Leningrad, Union of Soviet Socialist Republics, elected a foreign associate in 1908, died February 27, 1936.

John Scott Haldane, of Oxford, England, elected a foreign associate in 1935, died March 14-15 (midnight), 1936.

There are now 277 [1] members and 41 foreign associates.

FRED. E. WRIGHT, Home Secretary.

Report accepted.

REPORT OF THE TREASURER

Attention was called to the annual report of the treasurer for the fiscal year July 1, 1934, to June 30, 1935, as contained in the Annual Report of the National Academy of Sciences for 1934-35, which had

---

[1] Gilbert Newton Lewis resigned in December 1934, and is not included in this number.

just been distributed. The supplementary statement of the treasurer as of December 31, 1935, was presented and received for filing.

Report accepted.

Two reports were received from the board of trustees of the James Craig Watson fund, as follows:

The will of James Craig Watson (1838–80) contains the following provision: "It is my wish that the Academy may, if it shall seem proper, provide for a gold medal of the value of $100, to be awarded, with a further gratuity of $100, from time to time, to the person in any country who shall make any astronomical discovery or produce any astronomical work worthy of special reward as contributing to our science."
The trustees of the James Craig Watson fund unanimously recommend that the Watson medal be awarded to Ernest William Brown, of Yale University, in recognition of his outstanding contributions, mainly in the field of gravitational theory in the solar system. For biographical data in regard to Mr. Brown reference is made to American Men of Science.
Among his most outstanding contributions are his well-known lunar theory and its constant perfection. In this connection his work on secular accelerations deserves particular mention. Among theories which have been attempted for the motion of the minor planets of the Trojan group, that of Brown is the most outstanding as regards originality and elegance of treatment, and the most perfect in its representation of observed motion. He has made important contributions in the field of general planetary theory, and in the general theory of resonance, and in its application to the solar system. The general theory of the 8th satellite of Jupiter on which he is still engaged already is recognized as an achievement of the highest order. His recent papers dealing with Fourier's series and the development of the perturbative functions mark a new epoch in the theory of general perturbations. Special mention may be made here of his rapid methods for calculating the constant part and the coefficient of any periodic term in the disturbing function and his expansion of the constant term to any order. Of greatest importance also are his demonstration of the effect of the attraction of the moon on the rate of the Shortt clock and of the moon as a time piece in general, intimately connected with his theory of the variable rate of the rotation of the earth.
Inspection of the list of his publications (to 1923) in Poggendorff's Worterbuch is evidence of his wide range of scientific contributions. During the past 12 years his contributions, included in some 70 papers, cover even a wider range and are of growing importance.

All this work culminated in 1933 in a volume of 300 pages replete with original work on planetary motion, published in conjunction with Clarence A. Shook. It is the most up-to-date and scientific presentation of one of the most difficult fields of science.

A. O. LEUSCHNER, Chairman.

Report accepted and recommendation approved.

Your board of trustees of the Watson fund unanimously recommends as follows:

Grant no. 51.—A grant of $200 to Dr. Wallace J. Eckert of Columbia University in support of the determination of accurate special perturbations and orbits of 16 minor planets selected by Dr. Dirk Brouwer of Yale University in Astronomical Journal No. 1022, in connection with an investigation of systematic errors in star places. The observational part of the program is being carried out at the Yale University Observatory under the direction of Dr. Frank Schlesinger. The grant is intended for the purchase of tabulating cards for use in calculating the perturbations by the punch card method, described in Astronomical Journal No. 1034, and now being successfully applied at Columbia University.

Grant no. 50.—A supplementary grant of $1,500 for continuation of the theoretical and numerical study of perturbations as approved by the Academy at the fall meetings of 1934 and 1935, for the salary, July 1, 1936 to June 30, 1937, of Research Associate Dr. Claude M. Anderson, Jr., who has participated in the work with eminent success for over 2 years. A like amount for a check computer and incidental expenses is being requested from the research board of the University of California.

Perfection of the perturbations of certain Watson planets of the Hecuba group has become imperative on account of recently discovered periodic discrepancies between theory, based on the Berkeley Tables, and observations. Errors of theory or of computation are not involved, but the situation calls for inclusion of additional terms in the theories of individual planets and probably also for extension of the Tables. These recommendations are in line with the objectives of Watson as stated in his will.

The trustees report that the work during the past 2 years on the very difficult Hecuba group has been most timely and eminently successful, not only in prediction, except for the periodic variations, which are now being controlled, but also in bringing to light more clearly the characteristics of the motion of planets of the Hecuba group. Publication of the final Memoir is being deferred until the extensions referred to above shall have been made. The total number of planets of the Hecuba group treated by the Berkeley Tables so far, is 14. The planets selected were such as to provide the most critical tests of our theory.

With reference to (132) Aethra, inclusion of which for the first time in the program was authorized at the fall meeting, 1935, the trustees report that Dr. Paul Herget has voluntarily undertaken development of perturbations by Hansen's method. Grant no. 50 has been drawn on for this purpose to the limited extent of only about $20 so far, for check computing. It is hoped that the new theory now being developed by Herget will prove successful.

The condition of the Watson fund on March 31, 1936, was as follows:

Invested income	$1,000.00
Uninvested income	2,219.84
Invested capital	24,575.00
Uninvested capital	425.00

A. O. LEUSCHNER,
Chairman.
F. E. Ross.
F. H. SEARES.

Report accepted and recommendations approved.

DRAPER FUND

The Draper committee recommends that the National Academy make from the Henry Draper fund two grants:

I. A grant of $300 to Messrs. Theodore E. Sterne and Richard E. Leary, of Harvard College Observatory, to enable them to continue their important work developing more effective means for the measurement of the radiation from the stars; and

II. A grant in same amount to Dr. Frank E. Ross, Yerkes Observatory, to be used in aiding the early publication of more of his splendid photographs of the Milky Way. This is with the understanding that the Yerkes Observatory provide—or there be secured from some other sources—an equal amount to aid in the publication of this important photographic record of the Milky Way. It will be recalled that the publication of the first group of these photographs was aided by a grant from this Academy a couple years ago.

It is hoped these two small grants will receive the approval of the Academy.

V. M. SLIPHER, *Chairman.*

Report accepted and recommendations approved.

J. LAWRENCE SMITH FUND

The committee during the year ended March 31, 1936, did not recommend the awarding of a medal for original investigations of meteoric bodies or the making of a grant for aid in investigation of meteoric bodies, the two purposes for which the fund was established.

The condition of the J. Lawrence Smith fund as of April 1, 1936, was as follows:

Invested capital_____ $10,000.00
Invested income_____ 995.75
Uninvested income _____ 6,487.36

C. G. ABBOT,
E. T. ALLEN,
ERNEST W. BROWN,
CHARLES PALACHE,
F. R. MOULTON,
Chairman.

Report accepted.

GOULD FUND

The directors of the Gould fund of the National Academy of Sciences have the honor to report as follows:

Grants made during the year April 1, 1935, to March 31, 1936:

To Frank Schlesinger, Yale University (June 17, 1935), for part payment of a wide-angle camera_____ $765
To the Lick Observatory (Jan. 16, 1936), for assistance in determining the solar parallax from photographs of Eros in 1931_____ 500
To S. A. Mitchell, Leander McCormick Observatory, Virginia (Feb. 25, 1936), for aid in the reduction of photographic parallax and proper motion plates_____ 500

The condition of the Gould fund as of March 31, 1936, was as follows:

Invested capital_____ $19,471.25
Invested income_____ 1,512.50
Uninvested capital_____ 528.75
Uninvested income_____ 14,788.48

HEBER D. CURTIS,
ERNEST W. BROWN,
F. R. MOULTON, *Chairman.*

Report accepted.

WOLCOTT GIBBS FUND

The directors of the Gibbs fund made a grant of $300 to Prof. Arthur C. Cope, of Bryn Mawr College, for the purchase of a centrifuge. The state of the fund as of March 31, 1936 was as follows:

Uninvested income_____ $2,894.02
Invested capital_____ 5,545.50

E. P. KOHLER, *Chairman.*

Report accepted.

MARSH FUND

I beg to submit the report of the committee on the Marsh fund for the year 1935 and the recommendations for grants during 1936.

Reports have been received from the grantees of 1935 as follows:

1. Dr. L. D. Boonstra, of the South African Museum, Capetown, received a grant of $250 for the completion of work on the fossil mammal-like reptiles of South Africa.

Dr. Boonstra reports that his grant was used in studying the deinocephalian material from South Africa preserved in the American Museum, in working out the fossils from the matrix and in the preparation of two papers now in press: (1) On Some Features of the Cranial Morphology of the Tapinocephalid Deinocephalians, in which certain skulls, hitherto described only in external features, are figured in dorsal, lateral, palatal, and occipital surfaces in addition to a description of the brain case; (2) On the Cranial Morphology of Some Titanosuchid Deinocephalians, a critical account of the morphological features of these skulls.

2. Russell M. Logie, of the Peabody Museum, Yale University, received a grant of $500 for investigation of the faunas of the Manlius group, New York.

Mr. Logie reports that owing to illness and the necessity of doing other work at the same time, only a small part of his time could be given to his problem. The work done to date on the Cobleskill and Decker Ferry sections of the Manlius group is summarized as follows: A general rearrangement of collections has been made into definite horizons and a biologic arrangement, as far as possible, within each horizon; preparation of specimens from these sections has been begun, the fossils identified and classified as they were worked out; one collecting trip was made to secure further material from certain areas; no photographic work has yet been done. Mr. Logie's report includes a faunal list of all specimens identified by him to date, comprising about 53 species. Mr. Logie holds a balance of $458.75 unexpended and is continuing work on the problem.

3. Vice Admiral John D. Nares, of the International Hydrographic Bureau, Monaco, received a grant of $125 for work on a new edition of the General Bathymetric Chart of the Oceans.

Admiral Nares reports that the grants of 1934, 1935 ($125 each) were used in employing a draftsman for plotting charts of ocean depths obtained in soundings taken by the International Hydrographic Bureau in many ocean areas. The third edition of the Bathymetric Chart of the Oceans is now in preparation. Two sheets and one supplementary sheet, covering three areas of the Atlantic Ocean, have already been issued (1935, 1936), partly financed by these grants, and three other sheets are in preparation, to be issued in 1936, 1937.

4. Dr. Harry S. Ladd, of the United States National Museum, Washington, received a grant of $400 for the completion of a comprehensive report on the geology of the Lau Islands.

Dr. Ladd's grant was made in November 1935, and consequently his report covers only about 4 months of work. The Lauan report is continuing, and the several collaborators engaged in this work report satisfactory progress to Dr. Ladd. At the time of writing there was an unexpended balance of $292.78, which will be used to cover expenses of drafting and section cutting.

In regard to new grants for 1936, the committee recommends that the following awards be made:

1. Dr. William C. Darrah, of the Palaeobotanical Laboratory, Harvard University, for comparative study of reproductive structures of Paleozoic plants (application endorsed by Prof. E. D. Merrill) _____ $250.00
2. Vice Admiral John D. Nares, International Hydrographic Bureau, Monaco, for work in plotting depths in ocean areas for the third edition of the General Bathymetric Chart of the Oceans_____ 125.00
3. Dr. Albert E. Wood, Cape May Courthouse, N. J., for continuation of studies on the fossil Heteromyidae and other rodent families. A monograph, On the Evolution and Relationship of the Heteromyid Rodents, has been published by the Carnegie Museum (Annals, XXIV, 73-262). The work contains 157 figures, all made on earlier grants from the Marsh fund, as well as illustrations for two other papers now

in press. Several other papers on allied subjects have been published by the American Museum. Application endorsed by Profs. W. B. Scott and William K. Gregory-- $250.00

Total_____ 625.00

Uninvested income available for grants, Mar. 31, 1936_____ 636.47
Amount recommended for grants_____ 625.00

Balance_____ 11.47

WILLIAM K. GREGORY, *Chairman.*

Report accepted and recommendations approved.

MURRAY FUND

The committee on the Murray fund unanimously recommends that the Agassiz medal for the year 1935 be awarded to Dr. Martin Knudsen, professor of physics, in the University of Copenhagen, for his various contributions to oceanography, including his report on the hydrography of the Danish "Ingolf" Expedition, published in 1898; the preparation of his hydrographic tables published by the International Council for the Exploration of the Sea; his inauguration of standard sea water distributed to other oceanographic institutions by the International Council for the Exploration of the Sea; his invention or improvement of the designs of oceanographic instruments; and his leadership in the development of precise methods in the study of physical oceanography.

Martin Knudsen was born on the island of Funen, Denmark, February 15, 1871; student, University of Copenhagen, 1890–96; honorary doctor of philosophy, University of Lund, Sweden; professor of physics, University of Copenhagen, since 1912; rector of the university, 1927–28; hydrographer of the "Ingolf" Expedition to Iceland and Greenland waters, 1895–96; director of the Danish Hydrographical Investigations since 1902; Danish delegate to the International Council for the Study of the Sea since 1902 (hydrographical assistant to the Bureau since 1902, hydrographical consultant since 1925, vice president of the council since 1933, member of the Hydrographical Committee of the Council since 1902, chairman since 1925), since 1908 charged with the preparation of standard water for chlorine titrations; member, Royal Danish Academy of Sciences, since 1909 (secretary, since 1917); vice president, International Union of Pure and Applied Physics, since 1923; president, International Association of Physical Oceanography, since 1930; member, Société Géographique de la Finlande, Kungl. Fysiografiska Sällskapet, Lund, Kgl. Gesellschaft der Wissenschaften zu Göttingen, Preussische Akademie der Wissenschaften, Finska Vetenskaps-Societeten, Royal Institution of Great Britain, Kungl. Vetenskaps Societeten, Upsala, Det norske Vitenskaps-Akademi; honorary member, Danish Geographical Society.

Author of more than 40 papers on oceanographic subjects, extending over a period of more than 30 years.

DOUGLAS JOHNSON,
CHARLES A. KOFOID,
T. WAYLAND VAUGHAN,
Chairman.

Report accepted and recommendation approved.

MARCELLUS HARTLEY FUND

No report was received from the committee on the Marcellus Hartley fund.

DANIEL GIRAUD ELLIOT FUND

No report was received from the committee on the Daniel Giraud Elliot fund.

MARY CLARK THOMPSON FUND

, I beg to submit herewith my report on the Mary Clark Thompson fund of the National Academy. Last year I was appointed chairman of the committee. to replace David White who had just died. Later on in 1935 another member of the committee, Dr. F. L. Ransome, passed away, leaving myself as chairman, Dr. E. O. Ulrich and Dr. W. C. Mendenhall as the remaining members. The committee has agreed that under the present conditions it would be better to pass up the distribution of a medal or honorarium until next year.

Mr. J. Herbert J. Yule, the bursar, writes me that the condition of the fund on March 31, 1936, was as follows:

Total uninvested income	$2, 604. 22
Invested capital	9, 125. 00
Uninvested capital	875. 00

There is therefore no reason why the award could not be determined upon, but in the present condition of the committee we think it best to recommend deferring the matter until 1937.

W. C. MENDENHALL,
E. O. ULRICH,
WALDEMAR LINDGREN,
Chairman.

Report accepted.

JOSEPH HENRY FUND

The following are abstracts of reports received covering the work done during the past year under grants from the Joseph Henry fund:

61. Prof. Simon Freed, of the University of Chicago, $300 toward the expenses of the construction of a powerful magnet. This project has been delayed, but will be undertaken this summer.

62. Prof. Francis Bitter, of the Massachusetts Institute of Technology, $500 toward the construction of a coil giving a very intense magnetic field. This coil has been constructed and installed and is found capable of giving a field of 120,000 gauss over a space 3 c.c. in diameter.

63. Dr. T. T. Chen, of Yale University, $300 for technical assistance for research on the behavior of chromosomes in paramecium. Dr. Chen reports observations and conclusions on a large array of phenomena occurring during fission, endomixis, and conjugation.

64. Prof. James J. Brady, of St. Louis University, $175 for apparatus for researches on the photoelectric effect in thin films. The apparatus has been purchased and Professor Brady is now making progress in researches with it.

65. Prof. G. W. Keitt, of the University of Wisconsin, $400 for technical assistance to finish a research on the nature of parasitism and disease resistance in plants. Professor Keitt reports that with the aid of this grant he has finished the cytological studies for this work and is now preparing a paper.

66. Prof. William D. Harkins, of the University of Chicago, $300 toward a radioactive source to be used in a study of artificial radioactivity. No report has been received on this project.

67. Mrs. Elsa G. Allen, of Cornell University, $250 for expense of publication of a study of the eastern ground squirrel. This paper is now practically completed and will be published shortly.

D. L. WEBSTER,
Chairman.

This report was supplemented by the following recommendations for new grants, presented for the committee by Mr. L. R. Jones, acting chairman in the absence of Chairman Webster:

To Prof. Francis Bitter, Massachusetts Institute of Technology, Cambridge, Mass.: For researches on electrical resistance and applied properties of metals, $900.

To Dr. T. T. Chen, Yale University, New Haven, Conn.: For researches on chromosomes of paramecium, $200.

To Dr. W. W. Coblentz, United States Bureau of Standards, Washington, D. C.: For researches on solar radiations at high altitudes, $500.

Report accepted and recommendations approved.

CHARLES DOOLITTLE WALCOTT FUND

No report was received from the directors of the Charles Doolittle Walcott fund.

JOHN J. CARTY FUND

The committee on the John J. Carty Medal and Award for the Advancement of Science, consisting of Wilder D. Bancroft, George D. Birkhoff, William H. Howell, H. S. Jennings, and Frank B. Jewett, chairman, has considered the matter of this medal and award and recommends to the Academy that the gold medal with the bronze replicas and the diploma, together with the remainder of the accumulated income, as provided for in the deed of gift, be this year bestowed upon Dr. Edmund Beecher Wilson, of Columbia University. If this recommendation is accepted, it will be the second award of the Carty Medal, the first having been in 1932, at which time it was awarded to General Carty, himself.

In recent years, Professor Wilson has stood preeminent in the field of zoology, and the influence he has had on two generations of biologists is of a very high order. His individual researches on experimental embryology are classical, and his papers on cytology have been fundamental. His great book, The Cell in Development and Inheritance, has perhaps influenced subsequent biological thought more than any other book produced in this country.

In arriving at its present decision to recommend Professor Wilson, the committee has been guided by the terms of the Deed of Gift, which as they relate to the recipient's qualifications read as follows: "The award may be either for specific accomplishment in some field of science, or for general service in the advancement of fundamental and applied science."

In view of his outstanding contributions, the committee has no hesitancy in suggesting that Professor Wilson's selection is appropriate both as to "specific accomplishment" and "general service" and we, its members, believe that every consideration points to him as one eminently qualified to receive the Carty Medal.

F. B. JEWETT, *Chairman.*

Report accepted and recommendation approved.

REPORT ON THE PROCEEDINGS

It is customary at this time to make a report on the Proceedings of the National Academy of Sciences. With the close of the calendar year 1935 we completed the twenty-first volume of the Proceedings. There were 151 contributions making 692 pages. The average length of the contributions was 4.58 pages. The distribution was as follows:

Mathematics	48	Zoology and anatomy	16
Astronomy	4	Botany	5
Physics	15	Genetics	30
Chemistry	5	Physiology and biochemistry	8
Geology and paleontology	12	Pathology and bacteriology	1
Engineering	3	Psychology and anthropology	4

Of the 151 contributions 52 were by members of the Academy, 7 were by National Research Fellows and persons working under research grants from the Academy or Council and 14 were read before the Academy.

EDWIN B. WILSON, *Managing Editor.*

Report accepted.

REPORT OF COMMITTEE ON BIOGRAPHICAL MEMOIRS

During the past calendar year (1935) 15 manuscripts of Biographical Memoirs have been received. There remain 50 memoirs assigned, but not as yet prepared. This is 11 less unprepared memoirs than we reported last year. Memoirs for 11 persons have not yet (April 1936) been assigned, including 2 who died in the nineteenth century, 2 who died in the second decade of this century, 3 in the third decade.

Letters have been sent to all members of the Academy who have not hitherto deposited biographical materials, asking them to do so.

A. HRDLICKA.
RAYMOND PEARL.
E. L. THORNDIKE.
F. E. WRIGHT.
C. B. DAVENPORT, <i>Chairman.</i>

Report accepted.

GOVERNMENT RELATIONS AND SCIENCE ADVISORY COMMITTEE

In 1925 at the meeting of the Academy in Madison, Wis., provision was made for the organization of a Committee on Government Relations of the National Academy of Sciences "to study the relation of the Academy to greater problems as set up by the Government." Dr. John C. Merriam became chairman, and throughout the work of the committee up to the annual meeting in 1935 the committee functioned under his leadership. On July 31, 1933, the President of the United States under an Executive order created the Science Advisory Board, with members of the Academy appointed for 2 years, "with authority, acting through the machinery and under the jurisdiction of the National Academy of Sciences and the National Research Council to appoint committees to deal with specific problems in the various departments." At the annual meeting in 1935 a report from the Committee on Government Relations recommending reorganization of that committee was approved, and a special committee for this purpose was appointed to report to the council of the Academy or its executive committee.

Upon report from the special committee on May 11, 1935, the executive committee of the council of the Academy adopted the following organization of the Committee on Government Relations:

(1) That the Committee on Government Relations shall consist of: The president, who shall serve as chairman, the vice president, the home secretary, and the chairman or specially elected representative of each of the sections of the National Academy of Sciences; the chairman of the National Research Council; and members at large.

(2) That there shall be an executive committee of at least five members, appointed from the membership of the Committee on Government Relations. The president shall be chairman of the executive committee.

(3) That there shall be subcommittees on general or special subjects, appointed by the president of the Academy on the recommendation of the Committee on Government Relations or its executive committee; and that the present subcommittees on (a) physical sciences, and (b) biological sciences be discharged.

The retiring president of the Academy left the appointment of the members-at-large and of the executive committee to the incoming president.

On July 15, 1935, the President of the United States communicated with the president of the Academy requesting that the Academy provide some single agency, board, or committee which could carry on the work of the National Academy of Sciences, the National Research Council, and the Science Advisory Board in their relations to the Government. In order to provide time for such action, at the suggestion of the chairman of the Science Advisory Board and the president of the Academy, the President of the United States continued the Science Advisory Board by an Executive order from July 31 to December 1, 1935.

The first meeting of the new Government Relations Committee was held on November 19, 1935, in Munroe Hall, University of Virginia, Charlottesville, Va., at 2 p. m. The actions taken then consisted in the appointment of the members-at-large of the Committee on Government Relations and the appointment of the executive committee of six members with the understanding that other members would be added later as necessity arose. The following subcommittees of the Science Advisory Board were taken over: On the Weather Bureau, on the War and Navy Departments, on the relations of the patent system to the stimulation of new industries, on signaling for safety at sea, on the design and construction of airships, and on Biological Abstracts.

At a special meeting of the council of the Academy held on November 30, 1935, the name of the Government Relations Committee was changed to Government Relations and Science Advisory Committee.

The executive committee of the Government Relations and Science Advisory Committee held its first meeting on January 19, 1936, in the National Academy of Sciences Building, Washington. Among the actions taken at that time was the making of the minutes of the Science Advisory Board from July 31, 1933, to December 1, 1935, a part of the records of the Government Relations and Science Advisory Committee. With this action the taking over of the functions of the Science Advisory Board was completed.

On December 26 President Roosevelt sent a further communication acknowledging receipt of a communication from the president of the Academy on December 6, which gave the organization of the Government Relations and Science Advisory Committee and stated that he had asked the National Resources Committee to circulate a memorandum to the scientific agencies of the Federal Government calling attention to the fact that the National Academy of Sciences had set up the Government Relations and Science Advisory Committee, which would include in its program the unfinished work of the Science Advisory Board, and requesting the agencies to send all pertinent communications relating to Government scientific research addressed to the Academy. At the same time he called attention to the President's National Resources Committee and its Advisory Science Committee for the consideration of broader long-time scientific problems of natural and human resources.

The activities of the executive committee of the Government Relations and Science Advisory Committee since that time include:

(1) Approval of the report of the subcommittee on Biological Abstracts for transmission to the Secretary of Agriculture.

(2) At the request of the Secretary of the Navy appointment of a subcommittee to study certain special problems.

(3) Approval of the report of the subcommittee on design and construction of airships (W. F. Durand, chairman), and forwarding to the Secretary of Navy.

(4) Approval of the action of the administrative committee of the National Research Council in appointing the executive committee of the Government Relations and Science Advisory Committee as a committee of the National Research Council for the purpose of correlation.

(5) Appointment of an advisory subcommittee on research in soil conservation at the request of the Secretary of Agriculture.

(6) Consideration of a communication from Mr. Delano, vice chairman of the National Resources Committee, dated March 6, requesting advice on matters of interest to the National Resources Committee and needed for the purpose of its report, and authorization for appointment of a subcommittee to deal with the first question presented, namely, on the extent of physical variation in the population of this country and regarding distribution of physical types. A subcommittee on the status of metallurgical research was also authorized and is under consideration. The third question, on problems in the field of technology, has been referred for advice to the members of the Academy sections on physics, chemistry, and engineering.

FRANK R. LILLIE, *Chairman.*

Report accepted.

COMMITTEE ON THE CALENDAR

The chairman of the committee on the calendar, Mr. F. E. Wright, reported that his committee had considered a communication from Dr. A. E. Kennelly which had been referred to his committee by the executive committee of the council of the Academy on February 11, 1936, and that the committee had reported 3 to 2 against endorsement to the council of the Academy of any form of change in the calendar at the present time. It was further reported that the council of the Academy at its meeting on Sunday, April 26, 1936, had been informed of the committee's action and that the council thereupon approved the following resolution and recommended it for adoption by the Academy, which would rescind the Academy's action favoring adoption of the 13-month calendar which had been taken at the business session on April 23, 1928:

Whereas none of the schemes for calendar reform at present advocated can be practicable before 1950:

Resolved, That the council of the Academy deems it inadvisable for the Academy to endorse any of the proposed plans at the present time.

After consideration and discussion the Academy adopted the following resolution:

Resolved, That the Academy deems it inadvisable for the Academy to endorse any of the proposed plans for calendar reform at the present time and hereby rescinds its action of April 23, 1928, when the 13-month calendar was approved.

Adopted.

REPORT ON BUILDINGS AND GROUNDS

During the past year there have been many comments on the beauty of the Academy-Research Council Building. The copper roof, the bronze panels, and the trim of the doors and windows have acquired just the right tint of green to go with the mellowing walls to make a perfect setting. This is apparent from Constitution Avenue but the view from the Lincoln Memorial gives a perspective which makes the picture as it should be seen.

Perhaps no greater compliment could be paid to the architect, Mr. Goodhue, and the members of the Academy who approved the plans than the fact that the new buildings at the west end of Constitution Avenue have been designed to harmonize with the architecture of the Academy Building.

During the last 12 years the building has required no major repairs, and the stone in the building proper has not weathered. The exceptional winter, when the thermometer ranged near zero for 2 months, opened many joints on the front and it is expected that the worst of these can be taken care of this spring. In the two airwells the expansion and contraction in the brick work created one or two leaks which are receiving immediate attention.

It is too early to tell what effect the freezing weather has had on the trees, plants, and shrubs in the grounds. On the pools there was ice to the depth of 6 to 7 inches. To avoid the forcing of the walls a rectangular hole was broken in the center of the ice every morning to take care of the expansion. The marble trim of the pools suffered in the loosening of joints and in some cases the cracking of the marble.

The availability of stone workers in the District on account of building operations, especially the new Interior and Federal Reserve Buildings now being erected, may delay the repair work on the pools to some extent.

In last year's report reference was made to the change-over of the main electrical system in the building from direct current to alternating current. This work was completed by fall. At considerable expense the Potomac Electric Power Co. replaced wiring, switches, motors, fans, and grinding machines with all new equipments. This was fortunate for the Academy because some of the wiring and the motors had seen considerable service. The recently installed cabinets and switches are of the latest safety type. To avoid possible break-down, duplicate power lines were run into the building, but only one set is in use while the other is ready in an emergency.

To take care of the Academy's needs for direct current two generator sets were installed. The smaller one of 5 kilovolt-amperes capacity will be all that is needed ordinarily in connection with the exhibits and the larger of 25 kilovolt-amperes capacity will furnish current for the projection machines, etc. Two Tungar chargers for the charging of batteries supplying current to the more delicate instruments were also installed by the company. All of this work was done and the material was supplied without expense to the Academy except for superintendence and work getting things ready.

When the heating plant was installed the layout of the pipes in the basement had to be changed in order to give headroom. This was successfully done but in a few places there has been some noise. An experimental check valve was installed which has been very successful and the same scheme will be carried out in other places where trouble has been noted. No repairs to the boilers have been necessary with the exception of a new damper regulator requested by the insurance inspector.

Sun and dampness have affected the shades for darkening the auditorium and it has been necessary to purchase a new set.

The replacement of the electric water cooler on the second floor was necessary. The company furnished the most modern type and gave a liberal allowance so that the cost of the new machine was reasonable.

The building was fortunate during the recent rising of the Potomac River in that it was not in the flooded area. The staff was ready for any emergency and kept close watch each day and night to care for the building and its contents should the necessity arise.

PAUL·BROCKETT,
Custodian, Buildings and Grounds.

Report accepted.

REPORT ON EXHIBITS

The object in maintaining the exhibits is to give to the public an opportunity to understand, through visual methods, the fundamentals as well as recent advances in the natural sciences. That this is accomplished is evidenced by the number who come for the purposes of study. While the labels are prepared so that the individual can find his way about leisurely, special consideration is given to classes that come for the purposes of study. There were many of the latter throughout the year.

The story of communication as told by the exhibit of the Bell Telephone Laboratories, from the fundamentals in electricity to the telephone, has a fascination for the students of that subject. The four new exhibits installed at the time of the last meeting of the Academy have been an added attraction as they show the latest developments in the telephone transmitter, the oscillograph, making the effects of the human voice visible, and the vacuum tube amplifier.

The National Advisory Committee for Aeronautics, which from time to time makes changes in the material from its laboratory to show the latest results of their research work in aeronautics, has this year placed in the series four new exhibits: Models of the latest types of wing; models of recent types of hulls and floats and a series of planes visualizing the progress of aviation, from the Wright machine of 1903, the Curtiss machine of 1917, the Ryan monoplane of 1927 (the type used by Lindbergh), to the Northrop "Delta" of 1933, a low-wing cabin monoplane with cowling over the air-cooled engine, developed by the National Advisory Committee for Aeronautics.

From the laboratories of the General Electric Co., four new working models were added: (1) Demonstrating the magnetic power of the new material, alnico, where the magnetic power of this new alloy is shown in two instruments; (2) an instrument to measure, by means of the colors of very thin films, caused by interference of light waves deflected from the outer and inner surfaces of soap-bubble films, the thickness of the film, whereby the thickness of the film determines the color; (3) a spectroscope, to study light and ultraviolet radiation, transmitted through quartz prisms thrown on a screen through quartz glass, pyrex glass, and plain glass, at the will of the observer, makes it possible for the visitor to visualize the transparency of these media in viewing the spectrum of the mercury arc; (4) a sunlight motor of fractional horsepower, operated by light converted into electric energy produced by four photoelectric cells. This device works continuously when the instrument is set in the sunlight; to make it available, however, to the public at all times, it is necessary to use artificial light through the pressure of a button. It is expected that other exhibits from the laboratories of this company will be in place before the annual meeting.

In the southeast exhibit room there is a painting of the spectrum, artificially lighted. Efforts have been made to secure a painting of the phenomenon of the aurora borealis, or northern lights, for study. Recently there has been conceived a plan to construct an apparatus to show one of these magnificent displays from the beginning to the finish. There is promise of success.

In connection with the presentation of papers, a study has been made for a method of warning a speaker, without embarrassment, that his allotted time is almost at an end; also when it is finished. A lighted bronze sign on the rostrum table, divided into two compartments, having on one side the words "two minutes" with a white light, and on the other the word "stop" with red light, was thought of and was constructed by a sign maker. To operate this automatically by means of setting an electric clock was part of the problem. The instrument maker, after some study, worked out a combination of cams and switches, in combination with an electric clock, and produced an instrument that is exactly what was wanted. Now the presiding officer turns a dial to the number of minutes assigned when the speaker starts to present his paper, and the warning is flashed when the time allotted to the speaker is reached.

The numbers of classes and schools who take advantage of the facilities for study here continue to increase. The total number of visitors for the year was 62,621.

PAUL BROCKETT,
Secretary, Committee on Exhibits.

Report accepted.

ELECTIONS

The elections at the annual meeting resulted as follows:

Treasurer: Arthur Keith (reelected for a term of 4 years, commencing July 1, 1936).

New members of the council of the Academy: Simon Flexner and John Boswell Whitehead (succeeding K. T. Compton and J. McKeen Cattell) for 3 years, commencing July 1, 1936.

New members of the Academy: Leo Hendrik Baekeland, Bakelite Corporation, New York City; Eliot Blackwelder, Stanford University, Palo Alto, Calif.; Ira Sprague Bowen, California Institute of Technology, Pasadena, Calif.; Wallace Hume Carothers, E. I. du Pont de Nemours & Co., Wilmington, Del.; Alexander Forbes, Harvard University, Cambridge, Mass.; William Francis Giauque, University of California, Berkeley, Calif.; Clark Leonard Hull, Institute of Human Relations, Yale University, New Haven, Conn.; Edwin Oakes Jordan, University of Chicago, Chicago, Ill.; Alfred Vincent Kidder, division of historical research, Carnegie Institution of Washington, Washington, D. C.; Warren Harmon Lewis, department of embryology, Carnegie Institution of Washington, Baltimore, Md.; Robert Sanderson Mulliken, University of Chicago, Chicago. Ill.; William Cumming Rose, University of Illinois, Urbana, Ill.; Edmund Ware Sinnott, Columbia University, New York City; Joseph Leonard Walsh, Harvard University, Cambridge, Mass.; Orville Wright, 15 North Broadway, Dayton, Ohio.

PRESENTATION OF MEDALS

Two gold medals were presented at the dinner of the Academy on Tuesday evening, April 28, 1936: The Agassiz Medal for Oceanography, which had been awarded to T. Wayland Vaughan, of the Scripps Institution of Oceanography, of the University of California, La Jolla, Calif., in recognition of his investigations of corals, foraminifera, and submarine deposits, and for his leadership in developing oceanographic activities on the Pacific coast of America; and the Public Welfare Medal, which had been awarded to Dr. F. F. Russell, former director of the International Health Division of the Rockefeller Foundation and at present lecturer in preventive medicine and hygiene and epidemiology at Harvard University, in recognition of his work on the etiology of yellow fever and studies of epidemic areas.

SCIENTIFIC SESSIONS

The scientific sessions for the presentation of papers by members of the Academy or persons introduced by them were well attended. The papers presented were as follows:

MONDAY, APRIL 27, 1936

William Hovgaard, Brooklyn, N. Y.: Torsion of rectangular tubes (illustrated)

Edward Kasner, Columbia University, New York City: Conformal and equilong symmetry (illustrated).

Marston Morse, Institute for Advanced Study, Princeton, N. J.: Abstract Equilibrium Theory (illustrated).

George D. Birkhoff. Cambridge, Mass.: On the Problem of Stability in Dynamics.

Dunham Jackson, University of Minnesota, Minneapolis, Minn.: Problems of Closest Approximation in Two Variables (illustrated).

Fred L. Mohler, National Bureau of Standards, Washington, D. C. (introduced by W. W. Coblentz): Equilibrium Between Excitation and Ionization in a High Pressure Discharge (illustrated).

Allan C. G. Mitchell, New York University, New York City (introduced by S. A. Mitchell): Scattering of Slow Neutrons (illustrated).

E. O. Lawrence and J. M. Cork, University of California, Berkeley, Calif.: The Transmutation of Platinum by Deutrons (illustrated).

George R. Harrison, Massachusetts Institute of Technology, Cambridge, Mass. (introduced by K. T. Compton): Systematic Determination of Wave Lengths and Intensities of the Spectral Lines of the Chemical Elements (illustrated).

Robley D. Evans, Massachusetts Institute of Technology, Cambridge, Mass. (introduced by John C. Slater): New Radioactivity Detection Technique Applied to the Study of Radium Poisoning (illustrated).

Albert W. Hull, General Electric Company, Schenectady, N. Y.: Changing Direct Current to Alternating Current by Means of Thyratrons (illustrated).

R. A. Millikan, H. V. Neher, and Serge Korff, California Institute of Technology, Pasadena, Calif.: Cosmic Rays at High Altitudes on Two Sides of the World in the Equatorial Belt (illustrated).

C. G. Abbot, Smithsonian Institution, Washington, D. C.: Preliminary Study of Temperature Effects of Short Solar Fluctuations (illustrated).

Dinsmore Alter, Griffith Observatory, Los Angeles, Calif. (introduced by Robert J. Trumpler): Periodogram Analysis of Rainfall of the Pacific Coast (illustrated).

A. O. Leuschner, Sophia H. Levy, Claude M. Anderson, Barbara P. Riggs, University of California, Berkeley, Calif.: Periodic Departures of the Motion of Minor Planets of the Hecuba Group From Prediction With the Berkeley Tables of Perturbations (illustrated).

Frederick H. Seares, Mount Wilson Observatory, Carnegie Institution of Washington, Pasadena, Calif.: Selective Absorption of Starlight by Interstellar Clouds (illustrated).

Charles P. Olivier, University of Pennsylvania, Philadelphia, Pa. (introduced by Frank Schlesinger): Results of the Yale Photographic Meteor Work, 1893–1909.

Francis P. Shepard, University of Illinois, Urbana, Ill. (introduced by William Bowie): The Underlying Causes of Submarine Canyons (illustrated).

Douglas Johnson and Robert E. Bates, Columbia University, New York City: Correlation of Erosion Surfaces in Southwestern Wisconsin (illustrated).

N. L. Bowen and J. F. Schairer, Geophysical Laboratory, Carnegie Institution of Washington, Washington, D. C.: The System, Albite-Fayalite (illustrated).

T. Wayland Vaughan, the Scripps Institution of Oceanography, La Jolla, Calif.: Stolon-Systems of Communication Between the Equatorial Chambers of Orbitoidal Foraminifera (illustrated).

William D. Urry, Massachusetts Institute of Technology, Cambridge, Mass. (introduced by F. G. Keyes): The Helium Method Applied to Pre-Cambrian Chronology Problems (illustrated).

H. N. Russell, R. J. Lang, A. S. King, and R. B. King, Princeton University, Princeton, N. J.: Recent Progress in the Analysis of Rare-Earth Spectra.

R. W. Wood, Johns Hopkins University, Baltimore, Md.: Some New Effects Obtained With High Explosives (illustrated).

Arthur L. Day, Geophysical Laboratory, Carnegie Institution of Washington, Washington, D. C.: The Hot Spring Problem in Yellowstone Park (illustrated).

TUESDAY, APRIL 28, 1936

Harry H. Laughlin, Department of Genetics, Carnegie Institution of Washington, Cold Spring Harbor, Long Island, N. Y. (introduced by A. F. Blakeslee): The Quantitative Index of Resemblance in Geographic Distribution (illustrated).

B. O. Dodge, New York Botanical Garden, New York City: Interspecific Hybrids Involving Factors for Ascus Abortion (illustrated).

A. F. Blakeslee, A. G. Avery, and A. D. Bergner, Department of Genetics, Carnegie Institution of Washington, Cold Spring Harbor, Long Island, N. Y.: A Method of Isolating Tertiary $2n+1$ Forms in Datura From Prime Types by Use of Double Half Chromosomes (illustrated).

Sven Hörstadius, University of Stockholm, Stockholm, Sweden (introduced by Ross G. Harrison): Sea-Urchin Larvae With Cytoplasm of One Species and Nucleus of Another (illustrated).

Francis G. Benedict and John M. Bruhn, Nutrition Laboratory, Carnegie Institution of Washington, Boston, Mass., and the Yale Laboratories of Primate Biology, Inc., Orange Park, Fla.: Chimpanzee Metabolism. Read by title.

Francis G. Benedict and Robert C. Lee, Nutrition Laboratory, Carnegie Institution of Washington, Boston, Mass.: Studies on the Body Temperatures of Elephants (illustrated). Read by title.

Florence R. Sabin, the Rockefeller Institute for Medical Research, New York City: Development of the Cells of the Blood and Bone Marrow in the Rabbit (illustrated).

Simon Flexner, the Rockefeller Institute for Medical Research, New York City: Second Attacks and Reinfection in Poliomyelitis.

John W. M. Bunker and Robert S. Harris, Massachusetts Institute of Technology, Cambridge, Mass. (introduced by V. Bush): Effectiveness of Various Wave Lengths of Ultraviolet Light in Experimental Rickets (illustrated).

David I. Macht and Raymond E. Gardner, Johns Hopkins University, and Pharmacological Research Laboratory of Hyson, Westcott & Dunning, Inc., Baltimore, Md. (introduced by D. H. Tennent): Phytopharmacological Reactions of Normal, Toxic, and Atoxic Blood Sera (illustrated).

E. Newton Harvey, Alfred L. Loomis, and Garret Hobart, Princeton University, Princeton, N. J., and the Loomis Laboratory, Tuxedo Park, N. Y.: Electrical Potentials From the Human Brain (illustrated).

Charles B. Davenport and William Drager, Department of Genetics, Carnegie Institution of Washington, Cold Spring Harbor, Long Island, N. Y.: Growth Curve of Infants (illustrated).

P. A. Levene and Alexandre Rothen, Rockefeller Institute for Medical Research, New York City: The Absolute Configurations of Carbinols of the Type

$$H-\overset{\displaystyle R_1}{\underset{\displaystyle R_2}{C}}-(CH_2)_nX \text{ (illustrated).}$$

Linus Pauling and Charles D. Coryell, California Institute of Technology, Pasadena, Calif.: The Magnetic Properties and Structure of Hemoglobin and Related Substances.

Robert M. Yerkes and James H. Elder, Yale Laboratories of Primate Biology, Inc., New Haven, Conn.: The Sexual and Reproductive Cycles of Chimpanzee (illustrated).

Henry W. Nissen and Meredith P. Crawford, Yale Laboratories of Primate Biology, Inc., New Haven, Conn. (introduced by Robert M. Yerkes): Altruism and Cooperation Among Chimpanzees (illustrated).

William A. Hunt, Connecticut College for Women, New London, Conn., and Carney Landis, New York State Psychiatric Institute, New York City (introduced by R. S. Woodworth): The Startle Pattern (illustrated).

W. B. Pillsbury, University of Michigan, Ann Arbor, Mich.: Body Type and Success in College (illustrated).

Carl E. Seashore, State University of Iowa, Iowa City, Iowa: The Psychology of a Musical Ornament.

Franz Boas, Columbia University, New York City: The Effects of American Environment on Immigrants and Their Descendants (illustrated).

Hans Zinsser, Harvard Medical School, Boston, Mass.: Biographical Memoir of Theobald Smith. Read by title.

M. L. Fernald, Gray Herbarium, Harvard University, Cambridge, Mass.: Biographical Memoir of Benjamin Lincoln Robinson. Read by title.

William Hovgaard, Brooklyn, N. Y.: Biographical Memoir of George Fillmore Swain. Read by title.

P. W. Bridgman, Harvard University, Cambridge, Mass.: Biographical Memoir of William Duane. Read by title.

REPORT OF THE NATIONAL RESEARCH COUNCIL

FOR THE YEAR JULY 1, 1935, TO JUNE 30, 1936

(Prepared in the office of the chairman of the Council with the asssitance of the chairmen of divisions of the Council)

The following report is presented to the National Academy of Sciences by the National Research Council upon the activities of the Council during the fiscal year July 1, 1935, to June 30, 1936.

OFFICERS OF THE NATIONAL RESEARCH COUNCIL, 1936–37

The officers, members, and committees of the Council for the current year, 1935–36, are given in an appendix to this report (p. 147).

The officers of the Council for the ensuing year July 1, 1936, to June 30, 1937, are as follows:

GENERAL OFFICERS

Honorary chairman: George E. Hale, honorary director, Mount Wilson Observatory, Carnegie Institution of Washington, Pasadena, Calif.

Secretary emeritus: Vernon Kellogg, National Research Council, Washington, D. C.

Chairman: Ludvig Hektoen, director, John McCormick Institute for Infectious Diseases, 629 South Wood Street, Chicago, Ill.

Treasurer: Arthur Keith, treasurer, National Academy of Sciences, Washington, D. C.

CHAIRMEN OF THE DIVISIONS OF GENERAL RELATIONS

Federal relations: George R. Putnam, former Commissioner, Bureau of Lighthouses, Department of Commerce, Washington, D. C.

Foreign relations: T. H. Morgan, chairman of the division of biology, William G. Kerckhoff Laboratories of the Biological Sciences, California Institute of Technology, Pasadena, Calif.; and foreign secretary, National Academy of Sciences.

States relations: Raymond A. Pearson, special assistant to the administrator, Resettlement Administration, Washington, D. C.

Educational relations: William Charles White, chairman, medical research committee, National Tuberculosis Association; pathologist in charge of tuberculosis research, National Institute of Health, Washington, D. C.

CHAIRMEN OF DIVISIONS OF SCIENCE AND TECHNOLOGY

Physical sciences: R. A. Millikan, director, Norman Bridge Laboratory of Physics, and chairman of the executive council, California Institute of Technology, Pasadena, Calif.

Engineering and industrial research: Vannevar Bush, vice president of the institute, and dean of the graduate school, Massachusetts Institute of Technology, Cambridge, Mass.

Chemistry and chemical technology: Herbert R. Moody, professor of chemistry and director of the chemical laboratories, College of the City of New York, New York City.

Geology and geography: Edson S. Bastin, professor of petrology; chairman of the department of geology and paleontology, University of Chicago, Chicago, Ill.

Medical sciences: Esmond R. Long, professor of pathology, School of Medicine, and director, Henry Phipps Institute, University of Pennsylvania, Philadelphia, Pa.

Biology and agriculture: R. E. Coker, professor of zoology, and chairman of the division of natural sciences, University of North Carolina, Chapel Hill, N. C.

Anthropology and psychology: W. S. Hunter, professor of psychology and director of the psychological laboratory, Brown University, Providence, R. I.

The chairman of the National Research Council for the past 3 years has been appointed upon a half-time basis and this arrangement is to be continued for the coming year. During the past year the chairman of the Council has also been the president of the National Academy of Sciences. The chairmen of six of the divisions of science and technology are retained on the basis of modest honoraria which by no means compensate them as salary for the time and attention which they devote to the affairs of the Council. The chairman of the seventh technical division and the chairmen of the divisions of general relations of the Council serve without honoraria or other compensation. The generous services of these chairmen of divisions makes it possible to carry out one of the two principal features of the original plan for the National Research Council which was, through its division chairmen, to offer a certain leadership in the encouragement of scientific research. The other major feature on which the Council is founded is the representation in its membership of the national societies of science and technology in this country so that the interests and support of these societies can in a measure be coordinated as may seem desirable from time to time. This relationship is carried out through the representation of 83 societies in the membership of the divisions of the Council.

GENERAL ACTIVITIES OF THE COUNCIL

The past year completes the twentieth year of operation of the National Research Council since its organization by the National Academy of Sciences in the summer of 1916 after the Academy had offered its services to the Federal Government in the interests of national security. Since the termination of the World War the Research Council has endeavored to serve the interests of scientific research in this country as a mechanism of coordination operated by American scientific men themselves in relation to academic, industrial, and governmental interests in science. It is clear that the Council has little, if any, effectiveness apart from the use which these men may make of the facilities of such relationships under the auspices and coordinated support which it offers.

The major activities of the Council are of a continuing nature from year to year, and the advancement of these undertakings during the period covered by this report is outlined in the following pages.

Significant among new developments is a special understanding reached with the Rockefeller Foundation with respect to the support of certain central purposes of the Council and also the relationship effected between the Council and the Government Relations and Science Advisory Committee of the National Academy with respect to cooperation with the Federal Government. Special recent attention has also been given to the matter of abstracting and documentation of scientific literature.

Government relations.—The charter of the National Academy of Sciences provides among other things that "* * * the Academy shall, whenever called upon by any department of the Government, investigate, examine, experiment, and report upon any subject of science or art * * *." In order to be better prepared to meet these responsibilities, a Government Relations Committee was set up in the National Academy of Sciences in 1925.

The Executive order by President Wilson in 1918 requesting the Academy of Sciences to perpetuate the National Research Council also strongly emphasized Government relations and pointed to the duty of scientific men to cooperate actively with the scientific and technical services of the various departments of the National Government.

From 1933 to the end of 1935 the National Research Council cooperated closely with the Science Advisory Board which was set up under Executive order of President Roosevelt "acting through the machinery and under the jurisdiction of the National Academy of Sciences and the National Research Council to appoint committees to deal with specific problems in the various departments." The important work of this Board under the chairmanship of Dr. Karl T. Compton is well known, and is recorded in its published reports.

With the expiration of the period of appointment of the Science Advisory Board, December 1, 1935, its functions were combined with those of the Government Relations Committee of the Academy in a new committee known as the Government Relations and Science Advisory Committee related both to the Academy and the Council. This committee, which centralizes the Federal relations of Academy and Council, is composed of 24 members with a smaller internal executive committee comprising a majority of the members of the Science Advisory Board; it has taken over certain continuing committees of the latter, and has appointed other committees on request of Government departments.

Among these enterprises are the appointment of advisory committees to the Weather Bureau, to the National Bureau of Standards and to the Soil Conservation Service, certain assistance to the Navy Department, a study of the relationship of the United States patent system to the stimulation of new industries, the improvement of means for signaling for safety at sea, particularly in cases of fog, and means for the comprehensive abstracting of scientific literature in the field of biology. A report of a committee of the Science Advisory Board completed last July for the Navy Department on the design and construction of airships definitely recommended further experimentation in the construction of lighter-than-air aircraft with view to the successful development of this method of transportation.

The National Academy of Sciences is also represented on the science committee of the National Resources Committee operating under Executive order of President Roosevelt; and through this relationship is brought into contact with problems of general national importance, in which the outlook and resources of science are assuming increasing significance.

Fellowships.—In the administration of the post-doctorate fellowships of the National Research Council, which have been supported to a very generous extent by the Rockefeller Foundation during the past 16 years, the Council feels that it has reached a stage of transition. The experimental period for these fellowships has been passed. They have demonstrated in repeated cases their value in providing opportunity for the development of research leadership. It is equally clear also that the present times do not require the maintenance of so large a number of these fellows as seemed advisable in the initial stages of the enterprise, and the number of these fellowships has been progressively decreased in the course of 4 years from 165 fellows in 1933-34 to 96 in 1934-35, 60 for 1935-36, and 49 under appointment for the coming year, 1936-37.

It is evident, however, that such fellowships as these have a most important place in the American educational system, at least in the present generation, and that the opportunities afforded by these fellowships for a year or two or three of advanced experience in research must in some way be continued. It can hardly be urged too strongly that the future progress of research in this country depends upon the bringing up of new leaders and preparing them to push out as far as possible into the frontiers of knowledge during the early years of their careers. With this in view the question of the proper basis of support for such fellowships has been given earnest consideration in the Council during the past 2 years by the members of the three fellowship boards (representing the fields of the physical-chemical sciences, of medicine, and of the biological sciences). It is evident also that the responsibility for providing this special training for selected advanced students upon entering on their research careers does not devolve solely on any single institution or foundation indefinitely. The matter has already been discussed with organizations and institutions for higher education in regard to the responsibility of universities for supporting education at this additional level from now on and in increasing degree. In addition to university responsibility for these fellowships, there is opportunity for the establishment of a permanent endowment for the advancement of scientific knowledge through the training of personnel which in the current decade would appear to be through the support of post-doctorate fellowships but which at a later time may more properly be by other means to be determined in the light of later conditions.

Matters of administration of these fellowships have also concerned the Council during the past year, including the size of stipend in relation to living costs and other attractive professional openings, the method of selecting fellows, and reduction in the cost of administration, but the main consideration has been the realization that American science at this period needs these fellowships and that they ought by some plan to be continued.

For the coordination of policies of its three fellowship boards the Council has maintained since 1932 an advisory committee on fellowships composed of the chairman of the Council, of a representative from each of the three fellowship boards and of two additional members-at-large. This committee held its sixth meeting in New York on January 11, 1936, from which suggestions were offered for the consideration of the fellowship boards looking toward the consolidation at least of the boards representing the physical and the biological sciences into a single board, for the sake of economy of administration, among other reasons, in view of the reduction of the amount of the fellowship funds to be administered in the future through the National Research Council.

The following tables give certain statistics covering the operation of these fellowships:

TABLE I. *National Research Council post-doctorate fellowships as of May 31, 1936*

	Number of fellows active in United States and abroad	Number of fellows under appointment (not yet active)	Number of past fellows	Total number of fellows appointed	Total number of applications received	Period of operations (years)
Physical sciences	27	11	432	470	1,564	17
Medical sciences	7	7	232	246	1,159	13
Biological sciences	22	18	328	368	1,414	12
Total	56	36	992	1,084	4,137	

TABLE II.—*Fellowship Expenditures, July 1, 1935, to June 30, 1936*

	Expended for stipends and travel of fellows [1]		Total expenditures for stipends and travel of fellows in United States and abroad	Administrative expenses	Total expenditures	Percetage of administrative expenditures on total expenditures
	In United States	Abroad				
Physical sciences	$46,171.64	$1,296.64	$47,468.28	$4,675.47	$52,143.75	8.98
Medical sciences	9,142.93	3,644.74	12,787.67	1,592.10	14,379.77	11.07
Biological sciences	34,523.82	13,145.94	47,669.76	4,913.16	52,582.92	9.34
Total	89,838.39	18,087.32	107,925.71	11,180.73	119,106.44	9.39

[1] Including an occasional allowance for laboratory fees or materials.

Grants-in-aid.—For the past 7 years the National Research Council has had the administration of special funds (also provided by the Rockefeller Foundation) for the support of research through individual research grants of modest amounts. This has been a useful aid to research in the United States but, again, it can hardly be urged that any single agency should commit its funds indefinitely to the support of any one form of activity. The funds which the Council has had lately for use in general research grants will be discontinued before the close of the next year.

The statistics for the number of grants made during the past year and for the total number of grants since 1929 are given in the following tables. The cost of administering these funds during the past 7 years has been about 3 percent of the total of funds used, in addition to certain supervision and general office facilities which the Council has been able to provide.

TABLE III.—*Grants-in-aid awarded during 1935–36*

Grants, 1935–36	Number	Amount
Individual grants:		
Physical sciences	10	$4,087
Chemistry	6	3,300
Geology and geography	10	3,405
Medical sciences	10	5,600
Biological sciences	12	3,517
Anthropology and psychology	12	6,615
Total for individual grants	60	26,524
Grants to divisions of the Council: Conferences	12	4,490
Grant total	72	31,014

TABLE IV.—*Total grants-in-aid, awarded 1929–36 (July 1, 1929–June 30, 1936)*

Total grants, 1929–36	Number	Amount
Individual grants:		
Physical sciences	107	$61,157.06
Engineering	18	12,560.00
Chemistry	81	47,183.00
Geology and geography	120	56,576.00
Medical sciences	134	73,617.50
Biological sciences	155	68,510.00
Anthropology	58	31,349.75
Psychology	54	23,945.00
Total for individual grants	727	376,898.31
Grants to divisions of the Council:		
Conferences	50	28,752.42
Cooperative projects	5	13,500.00
Total for divisional projects	55	42,252.42
Grand total	782	419,150.73

The immediate result coming from these grants-in-aid is that a number of individual pieces of research work has been furthered by furnishing technical assistance, apparatus and instruments, supplies, and funds for field expenses. A large number of published papers has followed. But the larger results coming from the awarding of these grants include the possibility of continuation of support for the research work of grantees by their home institutions, the encouragement of individuals through this special form of recognition, and bringing to the fore investigations and investigators of high merit. In many cases there are later results of a less tangible nature due to the encouragement given to individual investigators and the stimulus afforded to institutions for the increased support of research on the part of their faculty members, which also justify the use of a certain amount of money nationally in this way.

Integration of the sciences.—Doctor Bowman, in his summary statement of the work of the National Research Council for 1934–35, referred to the consideration which had been given by the administrative committee to borderlands·between the traditional scientific fields. This consideration has led to the formation of an interdivisional committee on borderlands in science between the divisions of physics, chemistry, and geology. A similar committee in the biological sciences, if formed, would integrate numerous overlapping interests between biology, psychology and anthropology, and the medical sciences.

These should be promising aids to the integrating functions with reference to the natural sciences, which it is the business of the National Research Council to exercise. The present time is an age of integration in which the functional, as contrasted with the purely logical, aspects of science are coming to the fore. There is an insistent urge to utilize all scientific. knowledge obtainable for the public welfare in the innumerable ways now open for the application of knowledge in industry, in governmental administration, in public welfare, and in other relationships of our social order. Such problems do not accommodate themselves to the limits of the traditional fields of learning. They invade several fields at once and demand contributions frequently from a varied group of scientific men. Integration of knowledge from different sources brought to bear upon a single social purpose or end, is characteristic of the present scientific situation.

The committee on borderland fields between geology, chemistry, and physics, which was appointed by the Council in the spring of 1936, met in Washington on June 5, with all but 2 of its 15 members present. At this meeting the major objectives of the committee were agreed upon as follows: (1) The stimulation of research in borderland fields between chemistry, physics, and geology; (2) the preparation of a list of research projects in these fields; (3) the appraisal as far as possible of the significance of the various projects listed; (4) the consideration of the facilities available at different localities for various types of research; and (5) the consideration of the means of instigating and of carrying on a given project.

A large number of projects was recognized as invading the principal fields of chemistry, physics, and geology which were classified in 16 groups to facilitate their consideration, as follows: (1) Radioactivity and its bearing on geologic problems; (2) the investigation of systems consisting only of volatiles; (3) the investigation of volatile systems in contact with liquids or solids at various temperatures and pressures; (4) phase equilibria in solid-liquid systems; (5) colloids in geologic problems; (6) the physical chemistry of replacement; (7) new methods of the quantitative analysis of geologic materials; (8) analytical chemical investigations of geologic materials; (9) fundamental constants of minerals and rocks; (10) the experimental approach to stress conditions under which minerals form; (11) rock deformation; (12) hydrodynamics; (13) volcanology; (14) the application of geophysical field methods to some geologic problems; (15) seismological problems; and (16) miscellaneous problems.

The committee also made two definite recommendations relating to (*a*) the completion of a revision, now in preparation, of James D.

Dana's System of Mineralogy; and (*b*) the publication of data on the bulk densities of many rocks which have already been analyzed.

Annual Tables.—With the current year the Council has transmitted to the Paris office of the Annual Tables of Constants and Numerical Data in Chemistry, Physics, Biology, and Technology the last installment of the appropriation of $18,000 made by the Rockefeller Foundation in 1932 for the support of these Tables.

The international committee in charge of the publication of the Annual Tables under the joint auspices of the International Council of Scientific Unions and the International Union of Chemistry is making a vigorous effort to increase its resources and to bring the publication of the Tables down to date. The adequate support of these Tables requires subsidization with considerable funds in addition to the sale of the volumes. In the United States the advisory committee to the American commissioners has undertaken without guaranteeing any definite fund to solicit sums which it is hoped will amount to about $13,000 per year from pledges to cover a 5-year period.

Abstracting and documentation of scientific literature.—Since its early years the National Research Council has been concerned with the problem of making the rapidly increasing volume of scientific literature more readily available through the development of methods of abstracting and documentation. In 1919 the Research Information Service of the Council sponsored a special study of a system of analytical abstracting adapted particularly to the physical sciences, and in 1920 prepared a list of "Periodical Bibliographies and Abstracts for the Scientific and Technical Journals of the World" (N. R. C. Bulletin No. 3, June 1920, pages 131–154). An exhaustive study was made in 1922 of the fields covered by the abstracting journals of the world at that time. Special suggestions adaptable to the abstracting of anthropological literature were published by the Council in its Reprint and Circular Series, No. 56 (July 1924).

The Council was represented in an international conference to consider the future of the International Catalogue of Scientific Literature which was held in London on September 28 and 29, 1920, and held a conference in Washington on April 24, 1922, to discuss the future activities of the Concilium Bibliographicum, and on March 31, 1923, for the further consideration of abstracting and bibliographical methods.

From 1921 to 1925 the Council contributed support to the editing of Botanical Abstracts and encouraged the expanding of Botanical Abstracts into Biological Abstracts under the auspices of the Union of American Biological Societies. The first number of Biological Abstracts appeared in December 1926. The funds provided by the Rockefeller Foundation for the support of Biological Abstracts during the ensuing 10-year period have been administered through the Research Council. The division of anthropology and psychology of the Council assisted the American Psychological Association in establishing Psychological Abstracts in 1927, and through its committee on child development began the publication of Child Development Abstracts in the same year. The Highway Research Board has issued an abstracting serial since 1931, entitled "Highway Research Abstracts" (in mimeographed form).

In 1928 the division of anthropology and psychology held a conference of editors and business managers of anthropological and psychological journals for a discussion of the need for publication outlet in these fields in the United States and other editing and publication problems. This division has also prepared an index to the first 40 volumes of American Anthropology.

In 1924 a plan was proposed for a journal of geological abstracts which it was not possible to carry out, but in 1929 the Annotated Bibliography of Economic Geology was established under the auspices of a committee of the division of geology and geography of the Council.

In the field of chemistry the National Research Council has cooperated with Chemical Abstracts in the preparation of four editions of the list of periodicals abstracted by Chemical Abstracts. The Council has also published three Bulletins (No. 50, 1925; No. 71, 1929; No. 86, 1932) as successive compilations of a "Bibliography of Bibliographies on Chemistry and Chemical Technology", also a classified list of published bibliographies in physics (Bulletin No. 47, 1924), a bibliography for geology (Bulletin No. 36, 1923), for psychology (Bulletin No. 65, 1928), and other special bibliographies.

A conference of editors of biological publications was held in Washington on January 16, 1932, under the auspices of the division of biology and agriculture of the Council for the discussion of problems of financing biological publications, of printing specifications, and the preparation of articles for publication.

During the past year an additional conference was held in Washington (Dec. 9 and 10, 1935) for a discussion of the special financial situation of Biological Abstracts and the rapid growth of scientific literature of late years and the effect which new methods of scientific publication may have upon the problem of documentation. The conference was attended by about 35 members, including editors of abstracting journals, librarians, publishers, and others. The objectives considered were the place and function of abstracting and indexing in scientific literature, the form and content of abstracts and the use of analytical indexes, the fundamental delimitation of fields and their relation to specific subjects, the methodology of abstracting and indexing, and means for the reproduction and distribution of abstracts. As a result of this conference a standing committee of the National Research Council was appointed "to represent the various scientific divisions of the Council with instructions to prepare and present a long-time program looking toward the effective support of abstracting agencies in the several fields of science."

Biological Abstracts.—The National Research Council has continued to administer the editorial funds provided by the Rockefeller Foundation for Biological Abstracts. Volume IX, for 1935, of the Abstracts contained references, in most cases accompanied by an abstract, to 20,597 bibliographic items. Indexes are now available for all of the previous volumes except volume V, for which the index is now in preparation.

It is to be regretted that funds have not been found as yet with which to carry on Biological Abstracts after the current calendar year. In the discussion of the general abstracting problems at the conference on abstracting which was held by the Council last December, and in the considerations before the standing committee on abstracting and documentation of scientific literature appointed as a result of this conference, the standards set by Biological Abstracts and the service of the Abstracts in providing a review of biological literature of the world and in integrating in a measure the many diverse fields of the biological sciences and their overreaching into chemistry and physics, have been continually in view, and the consequent needs of this journal for further financial support. The Science Advisory Board also, at the special request of the Secretary of Agriculture last summer, appointed a committee to consider possible sources of further support for Biological Abstracts in view of the need for a reviewing journal for biological literature in several of the bureaus of that Department.

Material for volume XI of Biological Abstracts is already in hand, and drastic economies by the editorial staff have made possible the issuance of the 1937 volume. Unless further financial support is found, however, this will be the concluding volume.

During the past introductory period of 10 years the contributions from the Rockefeller Foundation, which at no time felt that it should undertake the permanent support of this enterprise, have amounted to $773,000 (including certain funds which will remain available to permit the completion of volume X of the Abstracts and its index).

Cooperation with the National Bureau of Standards.—The National Research Council has continued to act as disbursing agent for funds contributed by industrial corporations and from other nongovernmental sources for the support of special investigations carried on at the National Bureau of Standards. These investigations during the past year have related to fire resistance of various building materials, fabrication of structural steel work of buildings, the thermal properties of liquid materials used as antifreezing compounds, characteristics of chromel-alumel thermocouples, acoustic properties of materials, corrosion of pipe due to action of the soil, problems of refrigeration, and the development of spark plugs for use in aviation. The Council has also continued to cooperate with the Bureau in a special advisory capacity, through the division of chemistry and chemical technology, in investigations upon the stability of filmslides for use in the preservation of records.

The total sum expended through the National Research Council during the past year for these nine problems of investigation conducted at the Bureau of Standards amounts to $12,620.16.

Central purposes or functions.—Whatever may be accomplished by the divisions of science and technology in their respective fields certain central functions can be served only by the Council as a whole. Finance and administration is one on which all other functions depend. This granted, the main central function is to provide the auspices under which the scientific men of the country may meet to consider the promotion of research broadly, or in special fields. Out of this all else will flow. Provision must, of course, be made for the meetings of the various administrative bodies. But, quite apart from that, the budget of the Council must make provision for rather frequent conferences of a nonadministrative kind. Funds for this purpose have been set aside for a series of years, and it is hoped that it may be possible to increase the funds devoted to this purpose. A second central function in which the Academy and Council cooperate is the maintenance of appropriate Government relations referred to above. This also requires special budgetary provision. A third central function is the support of special international scientific undertakings, in which the National Research Council should be able to cooperate.

In providing funds to augment those derived from the Council's endowment for administrative and central purposes, grateful acknowledgment is made to the Carnegie Corporation of New York and to the Rockefeller Foundation for their aid in tiding the Council over a period of reduced income in addition to their other large contributions to the Council.

Summary statement.—A summary statement of the more important activities of the National Research Council during the fiscal year 1935–36, prepared by the chairman of the Council, Dr. Frank R. Lillie, was published in Science, September 28, 1936 (vol. 84, pp. 278–283).

AMERICAN GEOPHYSICAL UNION

The seventeenth annual meeting of the American Geophysical Union was held in Washington, D. C., on April 30 and May 1, 1936. The scientific session of the general assembly consisted of a symposium on recent trends in geophysical research, including the presentation of papers upon the following subjects: The Place of Geodesy in Geophysical Research, Recent Developments in the Geophysical Study of Oceanic Basins, Trends in Seismological Research, and Recent Progress in the Physical Interpretation of Synoptic Weather Charts. Sessions of the seven sections of the Union, each section representing a special field of interest in the organization of the Union as a whole, afforded opportunity for the presentation of papers and discussion of more specialized subjects. A feature of the meeting was a series of exhibits by maps and models (1) to depict the "basement complex" of the older metamorphic rocks underlying the portion of the United States extending from the Atlantic coast westward to include the Rocky Mountains, with the sedimentary formations of more recent geological periods removed; and (2) to show how this "basement complex" affects the areal distribution of surface sediments, local gravity and magnetic variations, and regional variations in crustal temperatures. Four technical resolutions were adopted relating to topographic mapping, radio time signals, oceanographic observations, and hydrographic surveys.

A Pacific coast meeting of the Section on Hydrology of the Union was held at Pasadena, Calif., January 31 and February 1, 1936. One of the four sessions of this meeting was devoted to a joint meeting with the Western Interstate Snow Survey Conference, at which eight papers were presented relating to the coordination and standardization of snow-surveying and its methods.

The papers presented at the sessions of the April meeting in Washington, over 130, together with those presented at the meeting in Pasadena last January, are to be published in the annual *Transactions* of the Union (Pts. I and II, July 1936, 563 pages).

During the past year the American Geophysical Union has continued to lend cooperation to the division of physical sciences in the preparation of its series of monographs on the Physics of the Earth.

The American Geophysical Union will be represented at the Sixth General Assembly of the International Union of Geodesy and Geophysics, which is to be held at Edinburgh, Scotland, between the dates September 17 and 26, 1936, by a delegation of 33 representatives. This will be one of the largest delegations ever appointed by the National Research Council to attend an international meeting abroad.

The total membership of the Union on May 1, 1936, was 769, a gain of 156 members during the past year.

FINANCES

The total amount of money expended through the National Research Council during the fiscal year 1935–36 (exclusive of the purchase of temporary securities) was $523,831.64. The following table gives the distribution of these expenses among the major types of activities of the Council in comparison with those of the previous year:

TABLE V.—*Classified Expenditures of the National Research Council July 1, 1935, to June 30, 1936*

	1934–35		1935–36	
	Amount	Percentage	Amount	Percentage
Fellowships	$226,368.84	33.8	$123,579.80	23.6
Designated project funds	228,291.97	34.1	228,846.22	43.7
Administered funds	119,721.96	17.9	75,160.99	14.3
General maintenance	95,493.78	14.2	96,244.63	18.4
Total	669,876.55	100.0	523,831.64	100.0

The distribution of the expenditures for post-doctorate fellowships is given in table II, page 35. In addition to $119,106.44 expended for post-doctorate fellowships, other special fellowship funds have been expended in connection with investigations upon drug addiction amounting during the year to $3,099.08.

Funds amounting to $228,846.22, which is about the same amount as corresponding funds for the previous year (1934–35), were contributed from outside sources for the support of special research projects of the Council. These projects are mainly of a cooperative nature and include some of the larger current undertakings of the Council, such as programs of investigation for research in problems of sex, the chemistry and physiology of narcotic drugs, the biological effects of radiation, and highway construction and operation, and are all in charge of committees or boards of the Council or cooperating agencies. Of this sum ($228,846.22) $7,225.26 (3.1 percent) was contributed from industrial and technical sources.

TABLE VI.—*Specially designated project funds*

	1934–35	1935–36
Grants-in-aid	$57,754.33	$43,790.36
Highway research	18,309.19	26,522.12
Research in problems of sex	63,936.13	73,345.01
Research on drug addiction	53,519.92	50,590.00
Effects of radiation on living organisms	20,352.11	24,438.95
Child development investigations	7,012.41	(¹)
Bibliography of Economic Geology	2,477.35	2,795.82
Other projects	4,930.53	7,363.96
Total	228,291.97	228,846.22

¹ See table VII.

The National Research Council also administers certain funds placed in its hands for the support of investigations conducted by Government bureaus or other agencies in the technical programs of which the Council has no part, its responsibility being limited only to the administration of these funds on the order of the controlling body. In several instances these agencies have been organizations resulting from movements initiated by the National Research Council. Among operations of this nature the Council has also handled funds since 1927 for the support of special investigations carried on at the National Bureau of Standards in accordance with the system of research associates which the Bureau has been authorized to recognize in its operations. The Council has also administered funds provided by the Rockefeller Foundation for the editorial work of Biological Abstracts; funds contributed by the Foundation toward the support of the Annual Tables of Constants and Numerical Data, which are published in Paris; funds for the Science Advisory Board, and those also for the newly organized Society for Research in Child Development, which has taken over the direction of activities formerly conducted by the Council's committee on child development. These administered funds this year are $44,560.97 less than those of last year, a decrease to be accounted for mainly in the reduction of funds for the Biological Abstracts and in the termination of activities of the Science Advisory Board.

TABLE VII.—*Funds administered as fiscal agent*

	1934–35	1935–36
Biological Abstracts	$84,929.71	$43,472.23
Investigations conducted by the National Bureau of Standards	7,936.87	12,620.16
Annual Tables of Constants and Numerical Data	1,966.11	492.35
Science Advisory Board	23,871.39	7,231.51
Society for Research in Child Development	(¹)	5,405.64
Other projects	1,017.88	5,939.10
Total	119,721.96	75,160.99

¹ See table VI.

The funds used for the administrative expenses of the Council ($96,244.63) were derived largely from the income from the endowment of the Council provided by the Carnegie Corporation of New

York but were augmented by certain special appropriations from the Carnegie Corporation and from the Rockefeller Foundation for this purpose. Of this sum $94,812.67 was disbursed under the provisions of the general administrative budget of the Council for the current year (set up as $98,855), and $1,431.96 was expended to meet deferred obligations incurred under previous budgets and for miscellaneous minor purposes. These administrative expenditures this year amount to $750.85 more than those of last year and constitute about two-elevenths of the total expenditures of the Council in comparison with expenses for administrative purposes of about one-seventh of the total expenditures of the Council last year, due to the decrease of $146,044.91 in the total expenditures of the Council for the current year. The administrative expenses include the general expenses of the divisions and committees of the Council, executive and clerical salaries, publications, supplies, service costs (exclusive of the general maintenance of the building and grounds) and similar charges.

The National Research Council met the payment of 1 percent on its salary roll imposed by the District of Columbia Unemployment Compensation Act (making payments totaling $409.89) from January 1 to June 22, 1936, when an amendment to the act became effective exempting scientific organizations, among others, from the provisions of this act.

A detailed statement of the finances of the National Research Council will be found in the report of the treasurer of the National Academy of Sciences and National Research Council (p. 97).

PUBLICATIONS OF THE NATIONAL RESEARCH COUNCIL

During the past year one paper has been issued in the Bulletin series of the National Research Council and one in the Reprint and Circular series, in addition to several miscellaneous publications.

BULLETIN SERIES

No. 98. Report of the Committee on Sedimentation, 1932–34. Prepared under the auspices of the Division of Geology and Geography, National Research Council. July 1935. Pages, 246.

REPRINT AND CIRCULAR SERIES

No. 107. Industrial Prospecting. C. F. Kettering. December 1935. Pages, 3.

MISCELLANEOUS PUBLICATIONS

Organization and Members, 1935–36. January 1936. Pages, 68.
Annual Report, National Research Council, 1934–35. Separate reprint from the Annual Report of the National Academy of Sciences, 1934–35. May 1936. Pages, 82.
Transactions of the American Geophysical Union, Sixteenth Annual Meeting, April 25 and 26, 1935, Washington, D. C. Parts I and II. Pages, 530.

PUBLICATIONS OF THE HIGHWAY RESEARCH BOARD OF THE DIVISION OF ENGINEERING AND INDUSTRIAL RESEARCH

Proceedings, Fifteenth Annual Meeting. December 4–6, 1935. Washington, D. C. Pages, 394.

Organization, Aims and Activities. December 1935. Pages, 16.
Progress Report of Project Committee on Stabilized Soil Road Surfaces. August 1935. Pages, 38.
Progress Report of Project Committee on Stabilized Soil Road Surfaces. June 1936. Pages, 23.
Highway Research Abstracts. Nos. 1–10, 1935–36 (monthly, except December and August).

The Council has also assisted in the publication of the Second Report of the Science Advisory Board, covering the period from September 1, 1934, to October 31, 1935, 494 pages (December 1935).

SALES

Receipts from sales of publications of the National Research Council from July 1, 1935, to June 30, 1936, have amounted to $2,097.10, of which $1,224.55, under authorization of the Council effective since 1931, has been credited to the rotating fund for the publication of reports of committees of the division of physical sciences.

DIVISIONS OF GENERAL RELATIONS

The National Research Council has in its organization four divisions of general relations, representing the interests of the Council in the research work of the Federal Government, the international relationships of science, the course of research in State scientific agencies, and the relation of research to teaching, especially in institutions of higher education.

Of these divisions of general relationships, the division of Federal relations is maintained in order to bring together a body of about 40 representatives of agencies of the Federal Government designated by the President to cooperate with the National Research Council under the provisions of the Executive order of President Wilson of 1918.

The division of foreign relations also brings together representatives of agencies in the United States which have a specific interest in scientific affairs abroad or a connection with international scientific organizations. · (For this division a special report follows.)

The executive committees of the divisions of States relations and of educational relations have both held meetings recently to consider means whereby the relationships which these two divisions are intended to cover might be the more clearly defined in the organization of the National Research Council and with increased effectiveness. Recommendations from these two divisions to this end are now before the Council for consideration.

DIVISION OF FOREIGN RELATIONS

THOMAS HUNT MORGAN, Chairman; WILBUR J. CARR and FRANK SCHLESINGER, Vice Chairmen

International dues.—It is gratifying to be able to report that the matter of the payment of the dues from the United States in the International Council of Scientific Unions and the seven international unions to which the National Research Council now adheres is in a favorable situation. These dues have been paid for the calendar year 1935 under special congressional authorization (Public, No. 371, 73d Cong., June 16, 1934). By a similar act passed last summer (Public, No. 253, 74th Cong., Aug. 7, 1935) continuing authority has been established for the payment of these dues by the State Department up to a sum not to exceed $9,000 in any one year. Steps are being taken under this authorization to arrange for the payment this fall of these obligations for the calendar year 1936. Provision still remains to be made for the payment of these dues for the year 1934, and it is hoped that this can be accomplished presently, completely meeting the financial obligations of the United States toward these important international organizations.

For the year 1935 the National Research Council paid from its own funds the dues in the International Union of Biological Sciences (800 Swiss francs at a cost of $265.04), since this was the first year of the adherence of the Council to this Union and arrangements had not yet been completed to include this item with the other governmental payments. It is believed, however, that for subsequent years the dues in this Union can be recognized under the now existing authorization for governmental payments.

TABLE VIII.—*International organizations to which the National Research Council has adhered*

[Gold franc equals $0.3267 (Swiss franc); French franc equals $0.0663 (as of July 1, 1936)]

	Statutory assessment	Current exchange
International Council of Scientific Unions	100 gold francs	$32.67
International Astronomical Union	2,400 gold francs	784.08
International Union of Chemistry	$675	675.00
International Union of Geodesy and Geophysics	12,000 Swiss gold francs	3,920.40
International Scientific Radio Union	800 gold francs	261.36
International Union of Pure and Applied Physics	1,600 French francs	106.08
International Geographical Union	3,200 French francs	212.16
International Union of the Biological Sciences	800 Swiss francs	261.36
		6,253.11

International scientific meeting.—The National Research Council was represented by 10 delegates at the Fifth General Assembly of the International Astronomical Union which was held in Paris between the dates July 10 to 17, 1935.

Pacific Science Association.—The National Research Council is now cooperating with three international technical committees of the Pacific Science Association through the appointment of American national committees under the division of foreign relations. These are: Committee on oceanography of the Pacific, committee on Pacific seismology, committee on land classification and utilization of the Pacific.

Plans have not yet been determined for holding the Sixth Pacific Science Congress, but are in the hands of a hold-over committee which was appointed at the Fifth Congress held in Victoria and Vancouver, June 1-14, 1933, and of which Maj. Gen. A. G. L. McNaughton, president of the National Research Council of Canada, is chairman.

Divisions of Science and Technology

DIVISION OF PHYSICAL SCIENCES

R. A. Millikan, Chairman; Henry A. Barton, Vice Chairman

International Astronomical Union.—The Fifth General Assembly of the International Astronomical Union was held in Paris, July 10 to 17, 1935, and was attended by 26 American astronomers, among whom the following had been appointed as representatives of the National Research Council:

Henry Norris Russell, Charles A. Young professor of astronomy and director of the observatory, Princeton University, Princeton, N. J.

W. S. Adams, director, Mount Wilson Observatory of the Carnegie Institution of Washington, Pasadena, Calif.

E. W. Brown, professor of mathematics, Yale University, New Haven, Conn.

Capt. J. F. Hellweg, superintendent of the Naval Observatory, Department of the Navy, Washington, D. C.

Walter D. Lambert, geodesist, Coast and Geodetic Survey, United States Department of Commerce, Washington, D. C.

A. O. Leuschner, professor of astronomy and director of the students' observatory, University of California, Berkeley, Calif.

John A. Miller, professor of astronomy and director of the Sproul Observatory, Swarthmore College, Swarthmore, Pa.

S. A. Mitchell, director, Leander McCormick Observatory, University of Virginia, University, Va.

Frank Schlesinger, director, Yale University Observatory, New Haven, Conn.

Frederick Slocum, professor of astronomy and director of the Van Vleck Observatory, Wesleyan University, Middletown, Conn.

Of the 32 technical committees of the Union which reported at this meeting, 11 are in charge of American astronomers as chairmen. The report of the meeting, issued in the spring of 1936, comprises a volume of some 240 pages.

International Scientific Radio Union.—The American Section of the International Scientific Radio Union held its annual meeting in Washington on May 1, 1936, jointly with the Institute of Radio Engineers for the presentation and discussion of 18 technical papers.

International Union of Pure and Applied Physics.—The committee on symbols, units, and nomenclature of the International Union of Pure and Applied Physics has formulated a report which has been circulated in the United States for comment upon the important recommendations which it contains relating to the permeability ratio of magnetic induction to magnetizing force.

Advisory Council on Applied Physics.—The division of physical sciences has lent its support to the organization of an advisory council on applied physics organized last fall under the auspices of the American Institute of Physics. The first meeting of the council was held at Pittsburgh on November 16 in conjunction with an open conference on applied physics sponsored by the University of Pittsburgh. The objective of this advisory council is to encourage the interest already shown by industrial corporations in the teaching of physics in colleges and universities and to bring university research in physics and progress in physical research under industrial stimulus more closely together.

Glossary of physical terms.—The committee in charge of the compilation of a glossary of physical terms has brought the preparation of this glossary since its undertaking in 1934 to a point at which further items to be added will consist mainly of terms recently introduced into physics. Over 60 consulting physicists have contributed to this compilation and the glossary now contains over 5,100 terms. It remains to include certain new terms, to omit for the sake of economy in printing those items which seem to be clearly understood in practice, to edit the whole in preparation for publication, and to add a number of standard tables of physical constants. The division of physical sciences believes that this can now be done under the personal editorship of the committee chairman without the necessity of retaining the committee in the organization of the Council and the committee will not be continued after this year.

Measurement of radiation.—A monograph on "The Measurement of Radiation", prepared last year by Dr. W. E. Forsythe, of the National Lamp Works, Cleveland, Ohio, has been completed and will be published as a report of the division's committee on measurement of radiation. This is one of the first monographs of the division to be published commercially, most of the others having been issued through the Bulletin Series of the Council.

Hydrology.—Following upon a recommendation from the American Geophysical Union in 1935, the division of physical sciences has organized this spring a new subcommittee under its committee on the physics of the earth to prepare a monograph on hydrology to serve as an authentic source-book of scientific information upon the problems of fresh-water supply and distribution on account of the great importance of the application of this information to national problems of water resources.

This monograph, as now planned, will consist of some 15 chapters relating to problems of precipitation and evaporation, snow sheets and glacier formation, lakes and streams, transpiration from vegetation, soil moisture, ground water and artesian conditions, floods and droughts, methods of stream gaging and estimating river flow, and the relation of run-off to erosion and transportation of soil material.

Line spectra of the elements.—The committee on line spectra of the elements has been engaged for several years in assembling and coordinating the results of spectrographic work contributed by a number of investigators in different institutions to produce eventually a comprehensive compendium of data (to be published in the form of a series of monographs) concerning the spectra of the elemental substances. While this work has been stimulated from the astronomical point of view, it is believed that it will have many other applications.

Washington Biophysical Institute.—The Washington Biophysical Institute (formerly designated as the Washington Biophysical Laboratory) formulated last fall a 5-year program of research upon two special problems: (a) the   otoc emistry of water and of simple aqueous systems, particularly in relation to ultra-violet light, in cooperation with the National Bureau of Standards; and (b) the photochemistry of pure steroles in relation to monochromatic irradiation, in cooperation with the Cold Spring Harbor Laboratory on Long Island. Due to the untimely death of Dr. R. G. Harris, director of the Cold Spring Harbor Laboratory, it has not been possible to carry out this program.

The institute is also giving attention to plans for research upon the photosensitivity exhibited by living organisms, such as the so-called photodynamic diseases of mammals. Such investigations as these require the construction of special monochromatic illuminators and spectroscopic apparatus and it is the development of such equipment which the institute regards as one of its main functions.

DIVISION OF ENGINEERING AND INDUSTRIAL RESEARCH

CHARLES F. KETTERING, Chairman; VANNEVAR BUSH and D. S. JACOBUS, Vice Chairmen; MAURICE HOLLAND, Director.

Research laboratory tour.—The division of engineering and industrial research organized last fall its third research laboratory tour. Two previous trips of this nature had been arranged in 1930 and 1931. The trip of last fall (Oct. 20–26) was attended by about 55 industrial and financial executives from many sections of the country and included visits at laboratories of the following companies:

General Electric Co., Schenectady, N. Y.
Eastman Kodak Co., Rochester, N. Y.
B. F. Goodrich Co., Akron, Ohio.
Gulf Refining Co., Pittsburgh, Pa.
Mellon Institute, Pittsburgh, Pa.
Bell Telephone Laboratories, New York City.

Highway research board.—The highway research board of the Council, which is in close cooperation with the Bureau of Public Roads, represents a method by which the Research Council offers continuing assistance to the Federal Government in effecting a certain coordination of nongovernmental research agencies, such as the State highway commissions, engineering departments in universities, and a number of industrial corporations which are concerned with aspects of the planning, building, and maintenance of highways during this period when motor transport is dominant. The board now has contacts with all of the State highway agencies and with some 35 technical and commercial associations and organizations of national scope. Its numerous committees represent various problems of highway finance, transportation economics, design, materials and construction, maintenance, traffic flow and regulation, highway safety, and soils investigations, from the point of view of the highway engineer and administrator.

The program of the board has been enlarged during the past year to include systematic studies of highway financing, costs of providing highway service, and the economic relationships of highways of various types to the progress of the communities which they serve.

The fifteenth annual meeting of the board was held in Washington, D. C., December 5 and 6, with an attendance of about 378 delegates representing State highway departments, bureaus of the Federal Government, college and university engineering departments, national societies and commissions, and commercial interests. A large number of papers was presented at this meeting, mainly the results of activities of the committees of the board. Of these papers about 35 have been published in the proceedings of the meeting (in a volume of some 394 pages).

The board issues a monthly serial (except for August and December) entitled "Highway Research Abstracts" (in mimeographed form in an edition of 1,000 copies), which presents advance information of important research ′n progress in this field and digests of articles published in various places which ought to be made widely available.

Two reports of the project committee on stabilized road surfaces have been issued relating to the building of low-cost dirt roads by means of proper grading, the use of proper fillers, and treatment with binding materials such as clay in correct proportions and inexpensive artificial binders such as calcium chloride and salt. The board also published last winter a prospectus of its organization and activities in a pamphlet of 16 pages.

Electrical insulation.—The growth of the committee on electrical insulation is an example of one mode of operation of the National Research Council. Beginning as a small committee of the division of engineering and industrial research about 9 years ago, this committee has arranged each year for a symposium on the results of current investigations on dielectrics. At these symposia some 15 or 20 papers are ordinarily offered for discussion, and of late years the meetings of the committee, held in various industrial centers in the northeastern States, often in conjunction with other meetings of electrical engineers, have attracted large attendance. The eighth meeting of the committee was held last fall at Pittsfield, Mass., under the host auspices of the General Electric Co., October 17 and 18, 1935, with an attendance of about 76. Reports of these meetings are manifolded inexpensively and are circulated among electrical engineers both in the United States and to a considerable extent abroad, and the separate papers are also published in the technical and scientific journals.

The committee now contains an active group of about 90 members and an even larger number of additional correspondents. It has become an effective agency for the encouragement of research in this field, for the exchange of information on current developments, and for the stimulation of new research on matters brought out in discussion at its annual conferences.

Hydraulic friction.—The purpose which the committee on hydraulic friction has set for itself is to review theoretical and experimental studies of hydraulic friction for the flow of homogeneous fluids in straight pipes without joints or bends and in straight open channels of simple geometrical and constant cross-sections for conditions showing negligible effect of compressibility.

The committee now has in preparation a report upon the present status of research on turbulence as related to fluid friction with application to the flow problems encountered by civil and mechanical engineers.

Heat transmission.—The committee on heat transmission has made arrangements for the completion by Dr. B. Townshend, of the Johns-Manville Research Laboratories, Manville, N. J., of the monograph on insulation which was begun some years ago under sponsorship of this committee. It is expected that the monograph will be completed in the fall of 1936 and that it will be published commercially.

Universities and industry.—Opportunity was afforded last December to extend the series of conferences on the relationships between universities and industry by discussions which were held in Los

Angeles, Seattle, and Boulder. Colo., for consideration of the contacts between engineering departments in the educational institutions of these regions with industrial development in the vicinity. The first conference of this series was held in Chicago, April 29, 1933. The objective of these conferences is to bring out the nature of the research in progress at educational institutions which would be of interest to various industries in their vicinity and to discuss the facilities of these institutions for undertaking certain types of industrial research and ways in which local industry might avail itself of these resources; also the conditions under which investigations upon industrial problems might be taken up at educational institutions, such as the teaching load of faculty members, satisfactory understandings with neighboring consulting laboratories, the control, publication, and patenting of results, advertising announcements, and the disposition of fees tendered for the research services of faculty members. These discussions are in fact similar to those in which the National Research Council has cooperated with the American Institute of Physics in the consideration of means for more closely relating the interests of research in physics in the universities with physical research in industrial organizations.

World Power Conference.—Much of the attention of the office of the division of engineering and industrial research during the spring and summer of 1936 was given to the assistance of the American National Committee for the Third World Power Conference in preparation for the conference which is to be held in Washington, D. C., September 7 to 12, 1936, in conjunction with the Second Congress of the International Commission on Large Dams. The principal service which is being rendered by the division in these preparations is in connection with the organizaton of tours to be conducted both before and after the week of the conference to enable attendants at the conference to visit industrial centers and localities of power development in the United States.

Annual meeting.—The annual meeting of the division of engineering and industrial research was held in the Engineers Club, in New York City, on the evening of May 4, 1936. Dr. Frank B. Jewett presented a statement concerning the activities of the Science Advisory Board, and reports were also given from several of the research committees of the division.

DIVISION OF CHEMISTRY AND CHEMICAL TECHNOLOGY

F. W. WILLARD, Chairman

International Union of Chemistry.—A delegation of six councilors and nine delegates from the United States was appointed early in the year to the Twelfth Conference of the International Union of Chemistry which will be held in Lucerne, Switzerland, between the dates August 16 and 22, 1936. It is customary also for a considerable number of other chemists from the countries adhering to the union to attend its meetings in addition to the official representatives.

Annual Survey of American Chemistry.—The tenth volume of the Annual Survey of American Chemistry, prepared under the auspices of the division of chemistry and chemical technology and edited by the Research Information Service of the Council, was published last May (by the Reinhold Publishing Co., New York City). This volume of 487 pages reviews the contributions of American chemists during the calendar year 1935 in a series of 25 chapters contributed by 32 authors. Twelve of these chapters were devoted to subjects of industrial chemistry although presenting a different range of topics from those of the previous volume, according to the editorial plan for dealing with certain subjects only every second or third year.

Chemical laboratories.—The work of the committee on construction and equipment of chemical laboratories, which resulted, under the former leadership of Father Coyle of Georgetown University, in the publication in 1930 of a volume entitled "The Construction and Equipment of Chemical Laboratories", has been continued under the chairmanship of Prof. C. R. Hoover, of the department of chemistry of Connecticut Wesleyan University. Professor Hoover has assembled a large amount of information concerning construction plans and materials for chemical laboratories and special equipment and furnishings, which he is ready to make available on request from those who are engaged in the erection of chemical laboratories. His collection of information is coming to be, from the point of view of the chemist who is to use the laboratory, a valuable adjunct to the planning of the architect and of the engineer in the construction of these buildings. During the past year information has been supplied to about 20 institutions, several of them high schools, for the construction of new laboratories or the remodeling of old structures. A number of new materials and improved methods of construction have been tested and recommendations have been furnished to builders or makers of laboratory equipment.

Isotopes of hydrogen.—The committee on isotopes of hydrogen served in important ways in cooperation with the American Chemical Society after its appointment in 1934 to coordinate the work of the many investigators in the United States who had turned their attention to this new development in the field of chemistry. Research on this subject, however, rather quickly established its contacts with related investigations and soon became well supported and coordinated with other branches of chemistry. This development has made it appear unnecessary to continue the division's committee on isotopes of hydrogen after this year, and the committee has been discharged.

Photochemistry.—The committee on photochemistry is preparing its third report, which will summarize the present status of research in this field in a way comparable with the two previous reports which this committee had issued in 1928 and 1930 (National Research Council Reprint and Circular Series, Nos. 81 and 96). It is believed that such a report will be especially opportune at this time in order to review recent contributions which have been made concerning band spectra and dissociation spectra and their relations to photochemistry, particularly in the field of polyatomic molecules.

Preservation of records.—For some years the division of chemistry and chemical technology has maintained an advisory committee to the National Bureau of Standards on the preservation of records, which has worked with the Bureau in connection with an extensive program of investigations relating to the durability of papers and means for the preservation of printed and written records. These investigations have been supported since 1931 by appropriations from the Carnegie Corporation now totaling $35,000. Among results coming from the work conducted prior to this year are data concerning the causes of deterioration of books, and atmospheric and other conditions to be met in libraries in order to prevent undue deterioration. During the past year these investigations have been directed toward the durability of film-slides used for record purposes through accelerated aging tests and the development of specifications for the manufacture of stable film-slides and for their preservation in storage and in use, on account of the increasing utilization of film for record as well as for projection purposes. A report recently prepared for the Carnegie Corporation by the National Bureau of Standards says of the problem that—

> Because of the complexity of the combined film base and photographic emulsion, and the present dearth of knowledge relative to this problem, it can be only partly solved within 1 year. A similar study should be made of sound-recording materials. Improved cameras and photographic emulsions are needed for reproduction of records contained on discolored or rough papers. And, finally, the present reading devices for the film records are not entirely satisfactory, and effort should be made to improve them also.

Ring systems.—The committee on ring systems in inorganic chemistry has continued its work of compiling formulas and analytical diagrams of the chemical constitution of organic substances. It is estimated that the report now in preparation is about three-fourths complete. It already contains descriptions for some 3,200 ring systems.

DIVISION OF GEOLOGY AND GEOGRAPHY

EDSON S. BASTIN, Chairman; W. L. G. JOERG, Vice Chairman

In addition to the regular work of its committees, summarized below, the work of the division of geology and geography during the past year has been marked especially by three movements: The organization of a joint committee on borderland problems with the divisions of chemistry and chemical technology and of physical sciences of the Council (see pp. 37–38); the reorganization of the committee on the scientific results of drilling; and the distribution of the reports of several of the committees of the division. These reports have been mimeographed, in some cases in editions of several hundred copies. A small charge is made for the reports sufficient to cover the postage.

Accessory minerals of crystalline rocks.—The committee on accessory minerals of crystalline rocks has again prepared an annual summary (mimeographed) digesting the principal papers published in the United States and abroad relating to the accessory minerals found in rocks. It is by means of certain characteristic minerals occurring in minute quantities in sedimentary rocks that it has been found that in many cases the materials of these rocks can be traced to their origins in older metamorphic or igneous formations and that the relationships of certain rocks can be compared.

The committee has now been in operation for about 5 years, and in its successive reports has abstracted over 200 articles. During this period a marked increase in the number of American contributions has been noted over that of the previous 5-year period. Much of the increased attention to this subject on the part of American geologists and mineralogists is believed to be due to the work of this committee.

Among other features which the scrutiny of this subject has brought out are the need for uniform methods of study of these minerals and a clearer understanding of what constitute "accessory" minerals themselves. The criterion of occurrence in such small quantities as to be susceptible of study only by methods of concentration rather than in thin rock sections is regarded as an artificial distinction and inconclusive.

Bibliography of Economic Geology.—With the completion of volume VIII of the Annotated Bibliography of Economic Geology with the issue for July 1936 (presenting 2,617 items), the management of this publication will be transferred to the Society of Economic Geologists. The Bibliography was established in 1928 under the auspices of a committee of the division of geology and geography. Subscriptions made by about 170 institutions, societies, and individuals during the early years of the undertaking, which were increased by interest on the funds invested, have amounted to $21,528.55 and have been sufficient to provide for the editorial work of the Bibliography until June 30, 1936. A small balance remaining will be transferred as of that date to the society, and the Bibliography will continue to be published as heretofore by the Economic Geology Publishing Co. It is expected that receipts from the sale of the journal will approximately pay for its printing and distribution. In addition to the Society of Economic Geologists, the Geological Society of America and the American Association of Petroleum Geologists are also supporting the work.

Cooperation with the Bureau of the Census.—The original object of the committee on cooperation with the Bureau of the Census, which was organized about 1924, was to define the boundaries of the major physiographic provinces of the United States in terms of the nearest corresponding boundaries of minor civil divisions so that population and other statistics reported by the Bureau of the Census according to these administrative units might be grouped by natural divisions and possible correlations be made evident. This original objective has been broadened into a program which, in general, addresses itself to the problem of reconstructing the natural distributional pattern of various elements represented in the statistics, mainly population and agricultural data. In this connection the committee last year took up the question of the determination of the areas of minor civil divisions in order to make possible the calculation of distributional densities of various kinds. The committee also advocated the special enumeration of unincorporated population centers, especially in New England, in order to differentiate the more accurately between rural and urban districts.

International Geographical Union.—In cooperation with the American Geographical Society of New York, the National Committee for the United States of the International Geographical Union has furnished the Union with a list of American geographers and others in the United States professionally interested in geography, and also with a list of university departments of geography, Federal and State bureaus, museums, libraries, and other institutions concerned with geographical matters for the use of the Union in connection with plans for its seventh meeting, which will be held in Amsterdam in 1938.

Land classification.—The committee on land classification was reorganized last year and has devoted itself to the utilization of aerial photography as an aid in geographical work in general and also to problems of land classification, with special reference to the use of aerial photographs in areal classification studies in northern Michigan and the Tennessee Valley as a basis for land surveys and investigations of types of land areas. The committee also has in preparation a Handbook on the Georgraphical Interpretation of Air Photographs. Special use will be made in this handbook of photographs and data available for northern Michigan and for the Tennessee Valley.

Measurement of geologic time.—The committee on the measurement of geologic time has again issued (in mimeographed form) a report summarizing the contributions made during the past year to the study of the determination of geologic time, especially by the measurement of atomic disintegration in certain critical elements found in the older rocks. In the present report the method of calculating the present ages of these rocks by the helium ratio and the lead ratio and other methods were discussed. A special conference on this subject was held in Boston on September 17, 1935, with an attendance of about 30.

Micropaleontology.—The efforts of the committee on micropaleontology have been devoted during the past 2 years to encouraging detailed studies of the microfaunas of the Eocene formations of the North American Continent and the West Indian region, with special attention to fully describing the faunas of certain critical or type localities. In this the committee is in touch with the work of some 35 micropaleontologists in the United States. With respect to the older Paleozoic formations, it is becoming apparent that microfossils are less rare in the formations of that period than had been supposed. Consequently, the range of usefulness of microfossils as indicators of horizon limits and other determinations is likely to be greatly increased by studies of the microfaunas of these older rocks in addition to corresponding studies of more recent microfossils.

Millionth map of Hispanic America.—A special feature of the annual meeting of the division of geology and geography on May 2, 1936, was the exhibition of 60 sheets, which had then been finished, of the map of Hispanic America on the scale of 1:1,000,000. The remaining sheets in the full series of 102 maps will be issued later this year. This enterprise for mapping all of the territory from the southern border of the United States to Cape Horn, on a uniform scale, was undertaken by the American Geographical Society in 1920. The National Research Council lent encouragement to the plan and made a small contribution toward the publication of the Catalog of Maps of South America (4 vols., 1930–32) which constituted the major source material for the production of the atlas.

The project has cost about $400,000, which was raised by the American Geographical Society, and has required 15 years for its completion, with a staff of 10 or more compilers and draftsmen during most of this time. These maps are comparable with the map of the world on a scale of 1:1,000,000, which is being compiled for

European countries by the commission for the International Map of the World, which has its headquarters in Southampton, England.

Ore deposition.—The committee on ore deposition has encouraged the undertaking of three new projects during the year:

1. Laboratory investigations of the two-component volatile system of carbon dioxide and water under varying pressures in equilibrium with a silicate melt at a constant temperature of 1000°, supported by a grant of $3,500 from the Penrose fund of the Geological Society of America and carried on at the Geophysical Laboratory of the Carnegie Institution of Washington.

2. Field studies of the fracturing of limestone and dolomite and the relation of mineralization to selective fracturing.

3. Studies of the influence of structure in local mineralization as a factor in ore deposition through the comparison of data contributed by geologists and mining engineers with respect to detailed studies of structure and of the occurrence of ores in certain districts.

Earlier studies sponsored by the committee are culminating in the preparation of summary reports upon the genesis of the lead-zinc ores of the Mississippi Valley through the cooperation of a number of geologists familiar with the geology and mineralogy of that region.

Committee on paleobotany.—The committee on palebotany has compiled its usual annual bibliography of published and unpublished work on American paleobotany (for distribution in mimeographed form). This bibliography, with brief digests of a number of the articles cited, constitutes a review of the year's contributions in this field (Apr. 1, 1935, to Apr. 1, 1936).

Five American paleobotanists attended the Sixth International Botanical Congress n Amsterdam, September 2 to 7, and also the Second Congress for Carboniferous Stratigraphy which was held at Heerlen, Netherlands, September 9 to 12.

Paleoecology.—The committee on paleoecology has proceeded on the principle that the occurrence of fossils in the rocks can only be correctly interpreted in the light of ecological conditions which presumably corresponded to those in the environment of similar organisms today and that knowledge of these conditions is essential to the correct interpretation of stratigraphic relationships. The report of the committee for this year contains statements concerning the paleoecology of five groups: the vertebrates, arthropods, trilobites, sponges, and paleozoic plants, as well as a general discussion of the relationships of organisms and their environment.

Pan American Institute of Geography and History.—In view of the advice which the National Research Council has given to the State Department in the past concerning relationships of the United States with the Pan American Institute of Geography and History, a recommendation is reported from the Secretary of State to the President (February 1935) that—

Membership of the United States in the institute would be desirable as the institute will provide an international agency for the collection, coordination, and dissemination of geographical and historical information which will be of value to numerous organs of the Government of the United States, scientific organizations, educational institutions, and interested scholars.

This recommendation was in accordance with the majority opinion of the committee of this division which considered this matter.

The second general assembly of the Institute was held in Washington, D. C., October 14 to 19, 1935, in buildings of the Pan American Union, the Carnegie Institution of Washington, and the National

Geographic Society. Funds for the expenses of this meeting were provided through the State Department, and Congress has taken action authorizing the payment by the United States to the Institute of the sum of $10,000 annually toward the maintenance of the Institute. The next general assembly of the Institute has been announced for Lima, Peru, in 1938.

Aerial photographs.—The interests of the committee on land classification are closely related to those of the committee on aerial photographs in the development of techniques for aerial surveying. The latter committee has given much consideration to means for collecting land photographs and making them generally available in The National Archives, as has been done in Canada through a Canadian national library of aerial photographs, and the committee has lent its support to recommendations made by the American Society of Photogrammetry to this end.

Scientific results of drilling.—The interest of the division of geology and geography in the preservation of the scientific results of drilling goes back to recommendations adopted by the International Drilling Congress at Bucharest in 1925, urging the various governments represented to take steps for the preservation of the data obtainable from the drilling of wells for water and oil. In the fall of 1926 two conferences were held by the division to consider the nature, amount, and distribution of drilling data, and the best means for the conservation of these data. These conferences brought out (1) the importance of this body of information relating to the surface layers of the earth's crust to be had from drilled wells which are often the only means for obtaining any definite knowledge of these structures; (2) the large mass of data which should be available from the extensive drilling operations then in progress (involving the annual expenditure of approximately $25,000,000 for water wells and $625,000,000 for oil wells); and (3) the regrettable fact that much of this information is being lost or only imperfectly and inaccurately preserved. It was suggested that simple instructions to the well driller would greatly improve the scientific value of his records, although the collection of records and materials from drilling operations and their preparation for successful scientific study would require extensive cooperation and facilities.

During the next 8 years the committee which this division of the Council organized sponsored the establishment of seven depositories for drilling records, of which five are still functioning, three of these as adjuncts of State geological surveys. The difficulty, however, in obtaining the large funds necessary for the proper preservation of this material, on account of its bulkiness and weight and the large number of wells being drilled, made it seem that further efforts in this direction on the part of the division's committee were ineffective, and the work of the committee was temporarily discontinued.

After careful study of the whole situation the committee was reconstituted in the autumn of 1935 with new personnel and objectives. The present aim of this committee is to educate the general body of well drillers in the need for the preservation of drilling records and to encourage State geological surveys as the logical depositories for these records, in addition to certain universities, to undertake the systematic preservation of logs and of selected rock samples from wells.   The work of the committee is, therefore, almost wholly the coordination of support on the part of drilling concerns, oil companies, State geological surveys, and other agencies in the careful selection and systematic preservation of significant materials of this nature as the basis of important geological studies.

The committee held a meeting at Tulsa, Okla., at the time of the meeting of the American Association of Petroleum Geologists, March 21, 1936, at which opinion was expressed in favor of—

1. State geological surveys and similar agencies, together with the departments of geology in certain universities, as favorable depositories for the results of well drilling, a single national depository being regarded as quite impractical on account of the great mass of material to be preserved and the frequent local significance of this material.

2. Standardization by the State geological surveys of methods of preserving well cuttings, cores, and logs within their respective States.

3. The desirability of cataloging the materials preserved by the several State geological surveys.

4. The importance of selectively preserving such materials and records now in the hands of oil companies as can be made publicly available.

5. The desire of the Research Council's committee to give such advice and support as it can to this work and assistance in the coordination of the efforts of all groups concerned.

Committee on sedimentation.—The committee on sedimentation was reorganized this year with view to directing special attention to investigations upon unconsolidated recent sediments along seacoasts and in lake bottoms.   The previous work of the committee had been devoted mainly to the study of indurated sediments and culminated in the publication of a "Treatise on Sedimentation" (first edition, 1926; second edition, 1932).

The committee now has in preparation for publication a series of papers upon the character and mode of deposition of unconsolidated sediments.

Among other projects of the committee are the preparation of a series of papers on the terminology and classification of sediments, the listing of student theses relating to sedimentation (whether published or unpublished), and the support of two research programs: (1) a chemical study of lake sediments; and (2) the development of a practical bottom sampler capable of taking cores several feet in length.   The report of the committee for the biennium 1932–34 was published in September 1935 as Bulletin no. 98 of the Council and contained papers contributed by 15 authors in this field. Several additional papers are presented in the mimeographed report covering the work of the committee for the past year.

State geological surveys.—On account of the change in industrial and educational conditions in the United States since the establishment of many of the State geological surveys during the latter part of the last century, the committee on State geological surveys, after having published a descriptive report upon these surveys (National Research Council Bulletin No. 88, November 1932) is now engaged upon a study of the present objectives of these surveys with respect to basic geological and geographical studies and the interpretation of results of these studies in economic terms applicable to the ultimate development of industries and the conservation of natural resources.

Stratigraphy.—The committee on stratigraphy has been engaged upon the compilation of a series of 12 correlation charts for the geological columns in significant localities of the North American continent so as to make possible the correlation of various formations on the geological time scale. The chart for the Silurian formations, two charts for Tertiary formations, and the chart for Cretaceous formations, in the Gulf and Atlantic provinces, have been completed and plans for their publication are now under consideration. A series of descriptive handbooks to accompany these charts is also in preparation.

Structural petrology.—The committee on structural petrology was organized 2 years ago in order to effect a comparison of several methods and techniques of study of the mechanism of igneous intrusions. A glossary of terms used for studies in structural petrology was first undertaken and is now nearly completed. Descriptions of specific methods of study in this field have been prepared for publication and also a comparison of the principal theories advanced for rock deformations. The committee is in search of a particular metamorphic area or igneous mass which would be suitable for the application of these several methods of study in a strictly comparable way in order to determine the specific usefulness of the several methods.

Tectonics.—The committee on tectonics has been engaged upon the preparation of a tectonic map of the United States to represent the structural features of the earth's crust for this part of the North American continent. The map is being drawn on a scale of 1:2,500,-000, corresponding to the scale of the new geological map of the United States issued in 1933 by the United States Geological Survey, and is being compiled in 11 sections, each of which is in charge of one or two members of the committee who are working in conference with other geologists familiar with the regions covered. The first section of the map was completed this spring.

DIVISION OF MEDICAL SCIENCES

FRANCIS G. BLAKE, Chairman; HOWARD T. KARSNER, Vice Chairman

American Registry of Pathology.—The collections of the American Registry of Pathology in the Army Medical Museum are steadily increasing and cover at present the following materials, the section for otolaryngic pathology having been added this year at the request of the Academy of Ophthalmology and Otolaryngology:

Ophthalmic pathology	accessions	5,262
Lymphatic tumors	cases	548
Bladder tumors	do	1,342
Oral and dental	do	694
Otolaryngic pathology	do	550

The Registry is becoming more and more valuable as a collection of case histories and materials relating to cancer and other types of tumors. Two papers upon the materials in these collections have been published during the past year as follows:

Wilder, Helenor Campbell. An Improved Technique for Silver Impregnation of Reticulum Fibers. American Journal of Pathology. Volume XI. September 1935, pages 817–819.

Callender, G. R. and Wilder, Helenor Campbell. Melanoma of the Choroid: The Prognostic Significance of Argyrophil Fibers. American Journal of Cancer. Volume XXV, no. 2, October 1935.

And two papers were presented before the American Urological Association as follows:

Cancer of the Bladder: A Study of the Five-Year End Results in 658 Epithelial Tumors of the Bladder in the Carcinoma Registry of the American Urological Association. Russell S. Ferguson and committee.

Grading of Bladder Tumors. Major Raymond O. Dart and committee.

Endocrinology.—At the request of the John and Mary R. Markle Foundation, the division of medical sciences has appointed a committee to advise the Foundation in regard to the desirability of devoting funds to the support of research on the physiology and pathology of the endocrine glands. This committee held a meeting in New York on May 27 for the purpose of planning a summarizing report of current research and the nature and direction of opportunities for future investigations in this field.

Infectious abortion.—Under the auspices of the committee on infectious abortion a form of report blank has been prepared to serve as a guide in the epidemiologic study of human *Brucella* infections and a "research program for the study of both natural and acquired immunity to *Brucella* infections with special reference to the killing power of blood and the development of practical means to determine differences in degrees of resistance" has also been formulated by a subcommittee. While this latter program is more extensive than that which any one institution can be expected to support, various parts of it are under investigation in a number of cooperating institutions.

The subcommittee on the relationship of *Trichomonas* infection to abortion has also drawn up a program of several problems of research to be suggested to investigators in this field.

Microbiology of the soil.—During the latter part of the year 1934–35 three papers were published as follows relating to work sponsored by the committee on the microbiology of the soil (a joint committee with the division of biology and agriculture):

Rhines, Chester:

The Persistence of Avian Tubercle Bacillin in Soil and in Association with Soil Micro-organisms. Journal of Bacteriology. Volume 29, March 1935, pages 299–311.

The Longevity of Tubercle Bacilli in Sewage and Stream-Water. American Review of Tuberculosis. Volume XXXI, April 1935, pages 493–497.

The Relationship of Soil Protozoa to Tubercle Bacilli. Journal of Bacteriology. Volume 29, April 1935, pages 369–381.

With the publication of these papers the work of the committee has been brought to a close.

Narcotics research.—The Council's committee on drug addiction has been engaged for the past 7 years in a study of the chemistry of narcotic alkaloids and the physiological reactions of these substances for the purpose of obtaining precise knowledge upon the composition of these drugs and their effects in medical practice and in addiction cases supported by funds provided for this purpose by the Rockefeller Foundation. A strong laboratory has been created at the University of Virginia for analytical and synthetic studies of this group of chemicals. Another strong group has been built up at the University of

Michigan for pharmacological studies of substances produced by this chemical laboratory. Up to this time about 300 new alkaloids have been prepared, the more promising of which have been fully tested physiologically with interesting and useful results in regard to several of the new substances as leading possibly to the production of more controllable and more beneficial drugs than opium and its derivatives. Several of these substances have been or are being patented in the interests of control and the patents issued have been presented to the United States Government in the person of the Secretary of the Treasury for administration.

A group of 32 phenanthrene derivatives has been sent to collaborators in St. Louis University for the study of the estrogenic properties for these substances, an unexpected development in the chemical analysis of these derivatives.

Much assistance has been given to the committee's program also by the United States Public Health Service, by the Massachusetts State Department of Public Health, and by a number of commercial pharmaceutical manufacturing firms. The latter phases of the committee's work while continuing the basic studies of the chemistry of narcotic alkaloids have included also certain clinical studies of drug addiction and the possibility that certain of the new substances obtained may prove to be suitable for corrective treatment of drug addicts and for other medical purposes, such as the relief of pain in cases of cancer and of excessive coughing in pulmonary tuberculosis. Probably the most interesting conclusion from the attempt to correlate the relation of the physical structure of chemical substances to physiological action in animals and man is that narcotics may be arranged in series from dihydrodesoxymorphine-D to pseudo-codeine in their relation to addiction.

All the clinical work in connection with the study is being carried out by the United States Public Health Service Division of Mental Hygiene at the new narcotic farm at Lexington, Ky., and at the State hospitals of Massachusetts under the direction of the Department of Public Health.

The committee has been greatly aided in studying the underlying principles of narcotic drugs in relation to drug addiction by other universities and departments of the Federal Government.

The comprehensive book "The Chemistry of the Opium Alkaloids" prepared by Dr. Lyndon F. Small and published by the Public Health Service (Supplement No. 103 to the Public Health Reports, 1932, 375 pp.) forms a base line for all studies in this field and permission has been granted for its translation into Japanese. Requests for translation into German and another language are pending. A companion volume upon the pharmacology of morphine derivatives is now in preparation.

Research on gonococcus.—The report of the committee for survey of research on gonococcus and gonococcal infections, which has cooperated on this project during the last 3 years with the American Social Hygiene Association, has been published as a supplement to the American Journal of Syphilis, Gonorrhea, and Venereal Diseases (vol. 1, Apr. 1, 1936, 179 pp., with a bibliography of over 500 items). This report is a comprehensive survey and analysis of most of the papers on the gonococcus and gonococcal infection published in the

United States and abroad during the period 1930–34 with reviews of the more important earlier papers and of certain papers issued in 1935. The report concludes with recommendations and comments from the committee relating to the programs of research now in progress in this field. The report has been widely distributed, copies having been sent to about 2,500 subscribers to the Journal and 450 copies to individual investigators in this field, to directors of medical laboratories and officials of public health organizations.

Research in problems of sex.—One of the most important projects undertaken by the National Research Council in the field of the medical sciences is the program which the committee for research in problems of sex has been conducting for over 14 years and which has been supported by appropriations from the Rockefeller Foundation now amounting to $965,000.

During the early years of these investigations the studies of collaborators with the committee were devoted largely to phases of the physiology of sex in man and in a number of the lower animals. It is felt by the committee that with the strong emphasis which has been placed in medical science on the endocrinological aspects of sex rather than on the phenomena of sex behavior and reproduction, the attention of the committee should be turned to the neural instead of the hormonal controls in sex phenomena. Accordingly, in recent years, increasing attention has been given by the committee to the psychology and psychobiology of sex. Altogether over 760 papers have resulted from this work at the hands of some 66 collaborators in many institutions of the United States. During the past year the committee has had at its disposal a sum of $77,000 from which $72,050 was allotted in grants for 18 projects located at 16 institutions. The program of the committee is to be continued next year on approximately the same scale as during the past year.

Early last January a conference of the committee and several of its collaborators was held in St. Louis to plan for the revision of the book entitled "Sex and Internal Secretions", prepared under the auspices of the committee in 1932 by Dr. Edgar Allen, of the Yale University Medical School. The first edition of this book is to be revised later with prospect of publication next year.

While these results mean a definite contribution in this branch of science, not the least valuable of the results obtained through this undertaking is the development of a score or more of competent centers for research in this field and the application of large resources to research on these problems in addition to the grants made by the committee.

Survey of tropical diseases.—The report upon the survey of the incidence of tropical diseases which was made in 1934 and 1935 under the auspices of the advisory committee on a survey of tropical diseases has been published as a monograph entitled "A Geography of Disease", prepared by Dean E. B. McKinley, dean of the School of Medicine of George Washington University. The report appeared as a supplement to the October 1935 issue of the American Journal of Tropical Medicine and has also been distributed separately as a publication from the George Washington University Press (495 pp.). The report presents in tabular form statistics for representative recent years of the relative occurrence of tropical diseases in countries throughout the world, compiled according to types of diseases and also according to countries.

DIVISION OF BIOLOGY AND AGRICULTURE

I. F. LEWIS, Chairman; R. E. COKER, Vice Chairman

Committee on animal nutrition.—A conference on energy metabolism and the energy requirements and food utilization of farm animals was held at Pennsylvania State College June 14–15, 1935, under the auspices of the committee on animal nutrition (with an attendance of about 25). The report of this conference has been mimeographed for distribution. The objective of the discussion is outlined from the following statement of the chairman of the committee:

Studies of energy, energy metabolism, and efficiency of feed utilization have a relationship to agriculture in establishing:

(a) Fundamental concepts of the energy requirements of animals of different ages, sexes, and conditions of production, including work.

(b) Fundamentals of the utilization of feed, the nutritive elements in feed and the interrelation of the various feedstuffs.

(c) The characteristics of animals.

Aquiculture.—The activities of the committee on aquiculture, which the division of biology and agriculture has maintained for the past 12 years, have led this year to the organization of the Limnological Society of America with a charter membership of over 200. The initial meeting of the society was held in St. Louis in December at the time of the meeting of the American Association for the Advancement of Science. The functions of the former committee on aquiculture will be taken over and extended by the society and the committee has been discontinued. The society has at once been affiliated with the division.

Barro Colorado Island Laboratory.—In the twelfth annual report of the Director of the Barro Colorado Island Laboratory, attention is again called to the desirability of permanently endowing this station in the Panama Canal Zone for field study in tropical biology. The laboratory is at present supported by fees for tables maintained by seven educational and research institutions of the United States and by the fees of visiting scientists and special contributions. The laboratory has been operated on a narrow margin within its total current receipts, which amounted last year to $7,112.88. These receipts include a substantial increase in the charges paid by those who have worked at the laboratory during the year.

About 40 scientists, including several from Europe, have visited the laboratory in the course of the year besides a large number of other visitors. The laboratory is especially well located for study of ants and termites and tropical birds and serves advantageously as a base for expeditions to other parts of the Canal Zone and the Isthmus of Panama. A careful set of meteorological records is kept at the laboratory which go back now for a period of 11 years. Twenty papers have been published this year on scientific work done at the laboratory, bringing the total number of these papers up to 285.

Ecology of grasslands.—The committee on the ecology of grasslands of North America has continued its efforts to have set aside for scientific study certain grassland areas in Nebraska, Texas, Saskatchewan, Oklahoma, Arizona, Iowa, and Illinois. The object of these reservations is to provide natural opportunities for the training of investigators and teachers and permanent material for research upon the natural life-conditions and relationships of the plants and animals peculiar to the formerly extensive grassland areas of the United States.

Endorsements.—In response to a special request in the spring of 1936, the division of biology and agriculture has given advice concerning conditions of permanency for the Baldwin Bird Research Laboratory. The division has also been requested recently to appoint a special committee to advise in regard to the future development of the Cold Spring Harbor Biological Laboratory, in addition to advice given to the laboratory upon certain phases of its program in 1930.

In past years this division of the Council has been called upon several times for advice concerning research institutions or other scientific undertakings, as for example:

Marine Biological Laboratory at Woods Hole (1919).
Mulford Biological Expedition to South America (1920).
American Institute of Baking (1920).
Glacier Bay National Park (1924).
Mount Desert Island Biological Station (1925).
Bermuda Biological Station (1926).
Graduate School of Tropical Agriculture (1928).
Highlands Museum and Biological Laboratory, North Carolina (1931).
Rocky Mountain Biological Station (1932).
Site for tropical experiment station and school of tropical agriculture (1932).

Forestry.—In view of the extensive discussion of forestry problems in late years, the committee on forestry of the division of biology and agriculture has regarded it as timely to "review again the scope of intrinsic merit of present-day forestry research and the degree to which it meets present-day needs."

To this end data have been systematically brought together concerning the status of research now in progress by all forestry agencies of the United States. These reports are now nearly complete for most sections of the country and are being studied with a view to making the information in them available publicly in a way which will point out clearly the directions in which forestry research should move and bring about increased coordination of effort among research men and forest administrators.

Human heredity.—The committee on human heredity has been concerned in an advisory way with several matters relating to the application of knowledge of heredity to human conditions, including the establishment of state family research bureaus, the legal recognition of blood tests in certain cases of illegitimacy, in criminal cases, and in civil suits, the incorporation of courses on medical genetics into the curricula of medical schools, heredity studies of dental caries, the systematic life-time study of twins from both the genetic and therapeutic standpoints, and the collection of sex linkage data.

Medicinal plants.—The committee on pharmacognosy and pharmaceutical botany reports with regret the death of Dr. W. W. Eggleston, of the Bureau of Plant Industry, who has been engaged for some years in the compilation of a drug plant map of New England.. This work will be carried on by Mr. A. F. Sievers, of the same Bureau. Data have been collected for a census of drug plants of the southeastern portion of New York State and the northeastern section of New Jersey, looking toward the completion of a drug plant survey of the Eastern States.

Member societies.—Three new societies have accepted invitations for affiliation with the division: The Limnological Society of America, the Mycological Society of America, and the American Society of Plant Physiologists, thus making a total of 22 societies now affiliated with the division.

National Live Stock and Meat Board fund.—A committee of the division of biology and agriculture has continued to administer a fund, this year, of $1,000 for the support of investigations conducted at the University of Minnesota upon the role of fat in nutrition and in physiology.

Radiation research.—The committee on radiation, which has been encouraging coordinated research upon the biological effects of ultra-violet light, X-rays, and radium emanations during the past 7 years, has entered this year upon a new chapter of activity supported by a grant of $75,000 from the Rockfeller Foundation which will be available for the 3-year period beginning July 1, 1935. From the allotment under this appropriation for use this year, 19 grants, totaling $16,050, have been made to collaborators with the committee. Thirty-two chapters have been published during the year on the results of these and earlier projects supported by the committee. A portion of the allotment of the appropriation for this year, not to exceed $7,500, has been used for exploring the possibilities of mitogenetic radiation through investigations conducted at the University of Wisconsin under the direction of the committee. A résumé of present knowledge of this subject, together with the addition of the results of recent work by the author, Dr. Alexander Hollaender, was published last fall in a paper entitled "Some Phases of Mitogenetic Ray Phenomena" (Journal of the Optical Society of America, Vol. XXV, No. 9, September 1935, pp. 270–286). A more complete report covering the results of an unusually well controlled series of experiments in this difficult field during the past year has been issued in mimeographed form for distribution and criticism, and will be published later.

A two-volume book, "The Biological Effects of Radiation", which has been in preparation by the committee for some years as a critical and comprehensive review of knowledge in this field was published last spring (by the McGraw-Hill Book Co., 1,343 pages). Its 43 chapters were contributed by 46 collaborating authors under the editorial supervision of Dr. B. M. Duggar.

The plans of the committee for the coming year include commitments for grants for the support of 23 projects, of which 5 are in continuation of previous studies sponsored by the committee, totaling $21,815. Several of these projects are directed toward obtaining a broader basis of quantitative data relating to the biological effects of radiation and also toward studies of fundamental physiological and developmental responses of cells and tissues, metabolism in the broadest sense, significant biological products, and relevant absorption and emission spectroscopy. Attention will also be given to the development of physical apparatus adapted to making careful measurements of radiation and at the same time suitable for work with biological material. During the past 7 years the committee has aided in the work of about 50 collaborators and from this work about 127 publications have been issued.

The committee has thus had a considerable part in the introduction and adaptation for biological research of the new techniques of physics which have opened up large new areas for investigation, particularly with respect to genetics.

Wildlife conservation.—The past year has been marked with respect to the interests of wildlife by two special events. One of these was the acceptance by the Bureau of Biological Survey of a sum of about $80,000 contributed by industrial corporations to be devoted to setting up a series of wildlife research units in land-grant colleges not previously engaged in such work. The Council's committee on wildlife has advised the Bureau in regard to the manner of initiation of these projects.

The second event was the holding of a large national wildlife conference in Washington, D. C., at the call of the President, February 3–7, 1936. This committee has also advised with the Wild Life Institute which was organized as one of the results of this conference. For next year the committee has been reorganized as the committee on wildlife and nature reserves in order to enable it to undertake as an additional objective the formulation of a program for the scientific selection of natural areas to be kept inviolate and to assist in arranging for the reservation of these areas and the competent administration of them.

DIVISION OF ANTHROPOLOGY AND PSYCHOLOGY

EDWARD SAPIR, Chairman; WALTER S. HUNTER, Vice Chairman

American archaeology.—The committtee on State archaeological surveys of the division of anthropology and psychology has continued to give encouragement to the surveys of archaeological remains in portions of the Tennessee Valley which it is expected may soon be inundated in the course of the construction of several large dams in that region, extending the reconnaissance which was undertaken 2 years ago. This work has been carried on with the assistance of Federal and State relief agencies and appropriations from the Carnegie Corporation of New York and later by a grant from the National Research Council. These latter grants have been used as a coordinating fund to meet expenses which could not be covered by funds from governmental sources.

The Tennessee River Valley was the habitat in prehistoric time of many tribes, who used its great bottom lands and its many islands as sites on which to build large villages. The wealth of evidence of prehistoric occupancy by many different peoples is everywhere apparent. This area undoubtedly exceeds in archaeological importance any other like area in the southeastern United States.

A conference was held in Indianapolis under the auspices of the committee between the dates December 6 and 8, 1935, for the discussion of archaeological problems relating to the early inhabitants of the wooded portions of the northern part of the Mississippi and Ohio Valleys and the Great Lakes region (attendance 18). One of the most important of these matters is the organization of present knowledge of the cultural relationships of the aboriginal people which occupied this region and the coordination of current investigations. Other problems are the definition of the characteristic determinants for cultural levels, the completion of systems of nomenclature for pottery relics, stone artifacts and other materials, and the definition of group terms for application to various races of these peoples.

Three numbers in the series of circulars issued occasionally by the committee have been sent out during the year: No. 19, May 27, 1935, calling attention to items of archaeological interest on the program of the sessions of section H (anthropology) at the meeting of the American Association for the Advancement of Science at Minneapolis last June; No. 20, October 1935, concerning a request for cooperation in establishing a laboratory and information center for archaeo- and ethno-conchology at Tulane University, New Orleans; and No. 21, January 14, 1936, a similar request for cooperation in establishing a center for the collection of copper artifacts at the Montana School of Mines, Butte.

The thirteenth annual report on Archaeological Field Work in North America during 1934, in the series which, of late years, the chairman of this committee has customarily prepared, was published in the first issue of American Antiquity. Previous annual accounts had been published in the American Archaeology Series of the Pan American Union, that for 1931, 1932, and 1933 appearing in No. 7 of that series.

The committee on State archaeological surveys has also been fostering the development of a Society for American Archaeology which was organized in December 1934, and now has a membership of about 430. The society has undertaken the publication of a quarterly journal, American Antiquity, the first number of which was distributed in July 1935. The fourth number just issued completes the first volume of about 325 pages. The first meeting of the society was held at Andover, Mass., on December 29, 1935, in conjunction with the annual meeting of the American Folk-Lore Society.

While it is expected that the Society for American Archaeology will presently take over and extend the activities which this committee of the Council has been sponsoring, the committee will be continued for a time and has received from the Carnegie Corporation of New York a third and final grant, in this instance of $4,500, for its support. This fund is administered through the Carnegie Institution of Washington. The headquarters of the committee continue to be located at the University of Michigan.

Auditory deficiency.—The committee on auditory deficiency has sponsored a study leading to the construction of performance tests of intelligence for young deaf children. The tests are based on a variety of material appealing to the interests of young children which can be molded into suitable form as a measure of intelligence. The tests as first approved are now undergoing further study and selection looking toward their standardization.

Child development.—This year marks the transition to independent status of the program of encouragement of research in child development which the National Research Council has carried on for several years supported by funds provided by the Laura Spelman Rockefeller Memorial and later by the General Education Board. The Council's connection with this work began with the organization of its committee on child welfare research in 1920 which has been termed the committee on child development since 1924. Between 1925 and 1933, four conferences were held for the discussion of the organization and course of research in this field. A full-time director for the committee was maintained between the years 1926 and 1929 and in order to aid in the development of a trained personnel for research on child development problems a series of post-graduate scholarships (under which 116 appointments were made) and a series of postdoctoral fellowships (under which 14 appointments were made) were maintained for several years by the memorial. An abstract journal in this field, Child Development Abstracts and Bibliography, now in its tenth volume, was established by the committee, and numerous research projects have been encouraged. Interest in this field developed rapidly and at a conference held in Chicago on June 24, 1933, the committee brought about the organization of a Society for Research in Child Development.

During the past year this society, with a membership of over 300, has taken over most of the responsibilities of the Council's committee. The office of the committee and the society still continues to be in the National Academy-Research Council Building and the Council is administering for the society an appropriation of $10,500 provided by the General Education Board for an introductory period of 3 years beginning January 1, 1936, and a grant of $5,000 for inaugurating a series of monographs.

The society will continue to publish Child Development Abstracts and Bibliography (issued in planograph form in an edition of 800 copies). The first number of the monograph series appeared last November and contained a paper by Dr. Nancy Bayley upon "The Development of Motor Abilities During the First Three Years." The society has also taken over from the Williams & Wilkins Co., in Baltimore, the editing and publishing of the quarterly journal, Child Development.

The first meeting of the society was held on November 3 and 4, 1934, and the second biennial meeting will be held, also in Washington, D. C., October 30–November 1, 1936. Regional meetings in the intervening 2-year period have been held in Los Angeles, Chicago, and New Haven.

The total of funds administered by the Council for this work received from the Laura Spelman Rockefeller Memorial and the General Education Board since 1926, including the appropriation available during the next 2 years, is $98,425. In addition to this sum, the memorial devoted large funds to the support of the scholarships and fellowships appointed by the committee during the period from 1926 to 1929.

The whole movement is an example of the successful development of a new field in science through the stimulation of interest in an important subject and the coordination of support among workers in this field until a stage has been reached at which the movement can proceed on a self-supporting basis. It is an example also of another area in science in which contributions from several of the major disciplines are applied toward a group of newly recognized important problems.

Directory of anthropologists.—The office of the division has been engaged during the year in the compilation of a world directory of anthropologists including over 1,750 names.

Laboratory of Anthropology at Santa Fe, N. Mex.—The Council was invited last February to name a representative member on a committee to examine the Laboratory of Anthropology at Santa Fe, N. Mex. This laboratory has been in existence for some 6 years. Being left without a director, due to resignation of the former incumbent, the board of trustees to the advisory board of the laboratory felt it desirable to study the situation of the laboratory and its policies to the end that it might most effectively carry out the purposes for which it was founded. In response to this request the Council nominated Prof. Leslie Spier, of Yale University, for appointment by the trustees on this examining committee.

The importance of the work of this laboratory is becoming increasingly appreciated from the realization that anthropological knowledge is of basic significance not only in connection with policies of the Government for dealing with the remnants of aboriginal peoples within the borders of the United States, but also in consideration of social conditions, problems of acquired cultures, and certain aspects of technology and fine arts and of fields of human biology. The laboratory at Santa Fe is regarded as in a peculiarly favorable situation to contribute to the study of these problems.

Occupational studies.—Since the division of anthropology and psychology was asked to nominate eight members of the technical committee for occupational classification and standards set up by the United States Employment Office, together with a similar group to be nominated by the Social Science Research Council, the division has retained an interest in the work of this technical committee.

The program of the committee has covered two general projects, namely, job analysis and worker analysis. The first is an attempt to classify jobs in functional units rather than upon the basis of superficial description; and the second is an attempt to discover and to measure the worker's ability to perform these functional units.

Job analyses have been in progress in the cotton textile, automobile, building construction, lumber, hotel, furniture, and certain retail industries, with working centers in 12 cities. Descriptions have been published for the first two, and descriptions for the third are in press. An attempt is being made to discover common factors in various jobs, with the expectation that they may be grouped eventually into families having similar functional units.

Department store jobs have been selected for worker analysis because of the number of persons engaged, and the favorable opportunity for research. Both selling and nonselling activities are included in the study. This work is being done in five cities at present.

Personality and culture.—The committee on personality in relation to culture has considered a program for training cultural anthropologists in personality studies by means of psychoanalytic techniques through a series of fellowships in preparation for work upon personality problems of different cultural levels. The committee has also prepared the preliminary draft of a "Handbook to Psychological Leads for Ethnological Field Workers" which has been distributed in mimeographed form for criticism. It is hoped that this handbook may eventually be of use to ethnologists in their field studies of individual and racial differences in cultural phenomena.

Psychology of the highway.—The committee on the psychology of the highway has continued to encourage studies of the national problem of highway safety through an examination of plans for the study of the performance of drivers and of prognostic tests for drivers. The subcommittee on commercial drivers has reviewed the accident experience of four large fleet operating companies which have contributed the records of some 2,000 drivers during the period from 1928 to 1936. The examination of these records—

has defined more and more closely a relatively small group of drivers who regularly and habitually have a large proportion of all the accidents which accrue to the company's drivers in any given period.

From these observations two sets of problems arise:

(1) Is it feasible, independently of their accident records, to distinguish these accident-prone drivers from their fellows; and (2) if these drivers should be eliminated, what will happen (a) if they are replaced by drivers selected at random; and (b) if they are replaced by drivers selected according to the results of some set of prognostic tests?

Thus far the best prognostic tests that have been reported remove only about one-sixth of the standard error in estimating driving ability which attends the mere guess that each individual has the average driving skill of the group. This is not enough of an improvement to warrant the installation of elaborate tests. Reliance upon the accident history of drivers is expensive but it leads to almost certain results. The records of one of these cooperating companies during the past 8 years indicate that a policy of eliminating those drivers who have had the largest number of accidents per year, replacing them with men selected at random, has reduced the number of accidents per year to about 22 percent of those formerly encountered.

These results point with increasing clearness to the conclusion that it may be possible to eliminate a large fraction, perhaps one-third, of all accidents, minor and fatal, on the public highways each year by taking off the road this small percentage of the general drivers who have had most of the accidents during the previous year.

The chairman of the Middle West subcommittee of the committee on the psychology of the highway has studied these problems in that region through the use of the traveling testing laboratory equipped 3 years ago and through other studies of the effects of manual handicaps, visual factors in space perception and reaction time in relation to driving.

Annual meeting.—At an evening session of the annual meeting of the division which was held in Washington, D. C., on April 26, 1936, two special papers were presented:

Quantitative Measures of Developmental Processes Manifested in Infant Behavior Patterns, by Dr. Myrtle B. McGraw, of the Normal Child Development Clinic, Columbia Medical Center, New York City.

The Pitcairn Islanders, by Prof. H. L. Shapiro, American Museum of Natural H[---] [---] York City.

RESEARCH INFORMATION SERVICE

C. J. WEST, *Director*

Fellowships and scholarships in industry.—The Research Information Service has this year repeated the survey of fellowships and scholarships which are supported at American universities by industrial corporations during the current academic year, and in February published a list of 275 such positions maintained by 85 firms (Industrial and Engineering Chemistry, news edition, Vol. 14, Feb. 20, 1936, pp. 67-69). About 25 firms which have supported positions of this sort in years past have not continued them during this year. Subsequently a list of 20 additional fellowships and scholarships was compiled from later returns (Industrial and Engineering Chemistry, news edition, Vol. 14, May 20, 1936, p. 202), making a total of 295 positions reported to the Council in response to its inquiry this year, a larger number than has been reported for any previous year.

List of Doctoral Dissertations.—The second consolidated annual list of "Doctoral Dissertations Accepted by American Universities during the Academic Year 1934–35" was issued last fall by the H. W. Wilson Co., having been compiled by the Association of Research Libraries in cooperation with the National Research Council and the American Council of Learned Societies with the contribution of certain support. The total number of doctor's degrees given by American universities in all subjects for the academic year 1934–35 was 2,649, and for the previous year (1933–34) 2,620. Of these, 1,534 were granted in 1934–35 in the sciences, and 1,550 in the previous year (28 sciences being recognized). The total number of institutions reporting in this compilation is 85. This consolidated list continues the statistics which the National Research Council has compiled for doctorates in the sciences since 1920, and will be continued for the current year 1935–36 under the same arrangements.

Census of graduate students in chemistry.—The twelfth census of "Graduate Students in Chemistry", prepared by the Research Information Service this spring, shows 1,411 research students registered for the master's degree in chemistry, 1,748 candidates for the doctor's degree, and 1,607 faculty members carrying on research in departments of chemistry in the 142 American colleges and universities reporting (Journal of Chemical Education, Vol. 13, July 1936, pp. 339–343). The tables for the current year compare with those for previous years as follows:

	Census year					
	Twelfth, 1935–36	Eleventh, 1934–35	Tenth, 1933–34	Eighth, 1931–32	Seventh, 1930–31	Fifth, 1928–29
Reporting institutions	142	144	141	142	137	137
Candidates for master's degree	1,411	1,376	1,302	1,596	1,376	970
Candidates for doctor's degree	1,748	1,750	1,721	1,665	1,419	1,101
Total students	3,159	3,126	3,023	3,261	2,795	2,071
Faculty members	1,607	1,534	1,421	1,392	1,401	1,089

List of chemical periodicals.—In cooperation with Chemical Abstracts the Research Information Service has also prepared a fourth location list of periodicals abstracted by Chemical Abstracts. This revision has been made in this way at 5-year intervals since 1920. Some 256 libraries of the United States, the Hawaiian Islands, and Canada have cooperated in checking the location of about 2.500 chemical and other scientific periodicals containing chemical articles. The list is to be published by Chemical Abstracts as a part of one of its regular issues and also as a separate.

Bibliography of Pulp and Paper Making.—As a cooperating project with the Technical Association of the Paper and Pulp Industry the Research Information Service has completed this year a "Bibliography of Pulp and Paper Making for the Period 1929 to 1935" in extension of the bibliography on this subject from 1900 to 1928 which was compiled by Dr. C. J. West in 1929 (982 pages). The new bibliography contains over 12,000 references and was published last fall by the Lockwood Trade Journal Co. (803 pages) for the Technical Association.

Review of current research on pulp and paper.—The review of current research on pulp and paper in the Government and university laboratories of the United States, which was prepared by the Research Information Service last year (published in the Paper Trade Journal, Vol. 100, May 16, 1935, pp. 41–52) has been extended to include current research on pulp and paper in the Government and university laboratories of Canada (published in the Paper Trade Journal, Vol. 101, No. 7, Aug. 15, 1935, pp. 36–42).

International Critical Tables book fund.—This year the first income has been received for the Research Information Service from the investment of funds remaining on hand upon the completion of the International Critical Tables. This residue, by action of the executive board of the Council (June 13, 1933) upon recommendation of the trustees of the Tables, was set up as "a capital sum to be applied toward the revision of the International Critical Tables or the preparation of additional volumes of the Tables", but with the provision that the income from this sum as invested be made "available to the Research Information Service for the purchase of reference books, subscriptions to scientific publications, and other source materials."

The investments of this fund now represent $7,060 (book value), and are yielding about $300 per year. In addition, there is on hand an uninvested balance of 1,804.23 derived from royalties upon the sale of the Tables received since the first investment of these funds.

Editorial assistance.—In addition to the issuing of compilations such as those mentioned above, the Research Information Service has also assisted in editing a number of other publications with which the National Research Council has been connected, including the Second Report of the Science Advisory Board; the "Geography of Diseases", published under the auspices of the committee on tropical diseases of the division of medical sciences; and volume X of the Annual Survey of American Chemistry, published under joint auspices with the division of chemistry and chemical technology of the Council.

Discontinuance of the Research Information Service.—It is to be recorded that the Research Information Service was ordered discontinued as of June 30, 1936, by action of the administrative committee of the Council on June 6, in accordance with action of the executive board on April 29, 1936, and after this step had been under consideration by the Council since the meeting of the board on April 28, 1935, and had been given special consideration by the administrative committee at its meeting on April 4, 1936.

This action admittedly was taken with regret but was done on account of the necessity of reducing the budget of the Council in view of diminished income during recent years, and because it was felt that such reference and informational work as the Council can carry on is not more than that which is ordinarily provided with usual library reference facilities and does not assume the proportions of a general or extensive research informational service. The purely library functions of the former Research Information Service will be continued and it is hoped that it can be arranged to continue also by various means a number of the special compilations which have been issued through the Council in the past.

ANNUAL REPORT OF THE TREASURER

JULY 1, 1935, TO JUNE 30, 1936

To the PRESIDENT OF THE NATIONAL ACADEMY OF SCIENCES:

I have the honor to submit the following report as treasurer of the Academy for the year from July 1, 1935, to June 30, 1936, and as treasurer of the National Research Council for the same period. Following the usual procedure, the first part of this report covers the transactions of the National Academy of Sciences, including the general fund and the appropriations under the custodian of buildings and grounds, and the second part covers the accounts of the National Research Council.

NATIONAL ACADEMY OF SCIENCES

Under a contract dated June 29, 1933, the Bank of New York & Trust Co. has served as custodian of securities of the Academy during the past year.

The following have served as financial advisers of the Academy during the year just closed: The firm of Loomis, Sayles & Co., from July 1, 1935, to October 31, 1935; and Mr. Joseph Stanley-Brown, from November 1, 1935, to June 30, 1936.

On June 30, 1936, the securities held by the Academy and by the Research Council were distributed as follows:

	Book value			
	Held by Academy	Held by Research Council	Total held	Percent of total
I. Bonds of railroads	$1,612,463.75	$38,543.75	$1,651,007.50	43.8
II. Bonds of public utility corporations	581,000.00	15,400.00	596,400.00	15.8
III. Bonds of industrial corporations	50,250.00		50,250.00	1.3
IV. Bonds of United States, States, counties, and municipalities		26,195.00	26,195.00	.7
V. Bonds and notes secured by first mortgage on real estate	529,900.00	35,333.00	565,233.00	15.0
VI. Bonds of foreign governments	34,893.75	15,412.50	50,306.25	1.3
Total bonds	2,808,507.50	130,884.25	2,939,391.75	77.9
VII. Common and preferred stocks of companies	832,981.43		832,981.43	22.1
Total	3,641,488.93	130,884.25	3,772,373.18	100.0

The following table indicates the distribution of the investments held by the Academy on June 30, 1936, with reference to bonds and common and preferred stocks:

	Face value	Book value	Market value June 30, 1936
Bonds	$2,952,900	$2,808,507.50	$2,707,367.50
Common and preferred stocks having fixed par value	369,700	6,869.93	632,518.12
Common and preferred stocks having no par value		316,111.50	478,887.50
Total		3,641,498.93	3,818,773.12

The total income from investments during the past year was $161,153.70, less $17,791.31 accrued interest on bonds bought, making a net income of $143,362.39, or an average yield of 3.94 percent on the book value of $3,641,488.93, or 3.76 percent on the market value on June 30, 1936, of $3,818,773.12.

The investment reserve fund was designed to absorb losses sustained by the Academy in the sale of bonds. The following shows the operation of this fund during the year just closed:

Overdraft on July 1, 1935		$584,126. 46
Profits on sale of bonds	$227,283. 43	
Less losses on sale of bonds	8,365. 03	
Net profit on sale of bonds	218,918. 40	
Transferred from various funds, 5 percent of income on investments	7,940. 56	
Additions to the fund	226,858. 96	
Transfer to Bache fund, income adjustment	$212. 88	
Transfer to Comstock fund, income adjustment	671. 92	
Deductions from the fund	884. 80	
Net additions for year		225,974. 16
Overdraft on June 30, 1936		358,152. 30

The net profit shown above has been reinvested in income-producing securities.

During the year the original wills and deeds of trust pertaining to all the trust funds of the Academy have been carefully considered by an attorney employed by the Academy for that purpose, and his written opinions secured thereon, as a result of which the Bache fund, carried for many years as a part of the consolidated investment fund, has been segregated from that fund and is now carried as a separate fund on the Academy books; and three funds—John J. Carty Medal and Award fund, Thompson fund, and Walcott fund—hitherto carried as independent funds, have been merged as parts of the consolidated investment fund. In segregating the Bache fund it was necessary to make an adjustment amounting to $212.88, which was charged to the investment reserve fund.

In accordance also with the opinion of the attorney, the account of the Comstock fund was restated, resulting in an adjustment of $671.92, which was likewise charged to the investment reserve fund.

The total receipts of the Academy during the year from all sources amounted to $179,134.47.

The miscellaneous disbursements amounted to $177,044.02, and payments on grants, medals, and honoraria, amounted to $12,143.15; total disbursements for the year $189,187.17.

The consolidated investment fund has been decreased by $60,000 by the segregation of the Bache fund, now carried as an independent fund; and has been increased by the merger with it of the John J. Carty Medal and Award fund, $25,000, Thompson fund, $10,000, and Walcott fund, $5,000; total $40,000, making a net decrease of $20,000 in the consolidated investment fund, which on June 30, 1936, stands at $232,777.94. Of this amount, $232,666.45 was invested, and $111.49 was uninvested.

The total expenditures up to June 30, 1936, for acquisition of site amounted to $185,764.50, and for erection and equipment of building for the use of the National Academy of Sciences and the National Research Council, paid from funds received from the Carnegie Corporation of New York, $1,446,879.82 and paid from separate Academy funds, $1,765, making a total for building and site, $1,634,409.32. In addition to these the sum of $896.88 was expended from Academy funds during the year for the equipment of the building, making a total of $10,894.93 for this purpose, the sum of $9,998.05 having been previously spent. The sum of $3,120.18 is held in the building construction fund as of June 30, 1936.

Below is found a list of bonds, now held by the National Academy of Sciences, which are in default:

Kansas City, Fort Scott & Memphis Ry. Co. 4-percent refunding mortgage fully guaranteed bonds, due Oct. 1, 1936; last interest paid was Oct. 1, 1932	$136,000
Missouri Pacific R. R. Co. 5-percent first and refunding mortgage bonds series G, due Nov. 1, 1978; last interest paid was Nov. 1, 1932	50,000
Missouri Pacific R. R. Co. 5-percent first and refunding mortgage bonds, series I, due Feb. 1, 1981; last interest paid was Feb. 1, 1933	60,000
New Orleans, Texas & Mexico Ry. Co. 5½-percent first-mortgage, Series A, due April 1, 1954; last interest paid was Oct. 1, 1932; bonds represented by certificates of deposit of the Chase National Bank of New York	50,000
Raleigh & Augusta Air Line R. R. Co.-Seaboard Air Line Ry. Co. 5-percent first-mortgage, guaranteed, due Jan. 1, 1931; bonds represented by certificates of deposit of the Mercantile Trust Co. of Baltimore; last interest paid was Jan. 1, 1932	25,000
St. Louis-San Francisco Ry. Co. 4½-percent consolidated mortgage bonds, series A, due Mar. 1, 1978; last interest paid was Sept. 1, 1932	50,000
Total	371,000

The amount of annual interest not now being paid on above bonds is $17,190.

There has been some improvement during the year in the situation affecting mortgages held by the Academy on New York City real estate, but there is still much cause for real concern. During the year it was necessary for the Academy to foreclose on one piece of property, involving an investment of $9,500, on which the Academy took title. Foreclosure has been resorted to only as a last resort to protect the investment already made. On another mortgage a curtail of $500 on the principal was received.

TRUST FUNDS OF THE ACADEMY

The trust funds of the Academy, the income of which is administered for specific purposes, are enumerated below. The capital of certain funds has been increased beyond the original gift or bequest by the transfer of accumulated income at the request of the donors or by action of the Academy.

Bache fund: Bequest of Alexander Dallas Bache, a member of the Academy, 1870, to aid researches in physical and natural sciences	$60,000.00
Watson fund: Bequest of James C. Watson, a member of the Academy, 1874, for the promotion of astronomical science	

through the award of the Watson gold medal and grants of money in aid of research_____ $25,000.00

Draper fund: Gift of Mrs. Henry Draper, 1883, in memory of her husband, a former member of the Academy, to found the Henry Draper medal, to be awarded for notable investigations in astronomical physics; the balance of income is applied to aid research in the same science_____ 10,000.00

Smith fund: Gift of Mrs. J. Lawrence Smith, 1884, in memory of her husband, a former member of the Academy, to found the J. Lawrence Smith gold medal, to be awarded for important investigations of meteoric bodies and to assist, by grants of money, researches concerning such objects_____ 10,000.00

Gibbs fund; Established by gift of Wolcott Gibbs, a member of the Academy, 1892, and increased by a bequest of the late Morris Loeb, 1914, for the promotion of researches in chemistry_____ 5,545.50

Gould fund: Gift of Miss Alice Bache Gould, 1897, in memory of her father, a former member of the Academy, for the promotion of researches in astronomy_____ 20,000.00

Comstock fund: Gift of Gen. Cyrus B. Comstock, a member of the Academy, 1907, to promote researches in electricity, magnetism, or radiant energy through the Comstock prize money, to be awarded once in 5 years for notable investigations; the fund is to be increased ultimately to $15,000_____ 12,406.02

Marsh fund: Bequest of Othniel Charles Marsh, a member of the Academy, 1909, to promote original research in the natural sciences; to the original bequest of $10,000 the Academy has added interest received from the estate and has authorized the increase of the fund to $20,000 by annual additions from income_____ 20,000.00

Murray fund: A gift from the late Sir John Murray, 1911, to found the Alexander Agassiz gold medal, in honor of a former member and president of the Academy, to be awarded for original contribution to the science of oceanography_____ 6,000.00

Hartley fund: A gift from Mrs. Helen Hartley Jenkins, 1913–14, in memory of her father, Marcellus Hartley, to found the medal of the Academy awarded for eminence in the application of science to public welfare_____ 1,200.00

Billings fund: Established by the bequest of Mrs. Mary Anna Palmer Draper (Mrs. Henry Draper) of $25,000, in 1915, to support the publication of the Proceedings of the Academy or for other purposes to be determined by the Academy, 7 installments_____ 22,313.39

Elliot fund: Gift of Margaret Henderson Elliot, to found the Daniel Giraud Elliot gold medal and honorarium for the most meritorious work in zoology or paleontology published in each year _____ 8,000.00

Thompson fund: Gift of Mrs. Mary Clark Thompson, 1919, the income thereof to be applied for a gold medal of appropriate design to be awarded annually by the Academy for the most important services to geology and paleontology, the medal to be known as the Mary Clark Thompson gold medal_____ 10,000.00

Joseph Henry fund: The sum of $40,000 was contributed by Fairman Rogers, Joseph Patterson, George W. Childs, and others, as an expression of their respect and esteem for Prof. Joseph Henry. This amount was deposited with the Pennsylvania Co. for Insurance of Lives and Granting Annuities in trust, with authorization to collect the income thereon and to pay over the same to Prof. Joseph Henry during his natural life, and after his death to his wife and daughters, and after the death of the last survivor to "deliver the said fund and the securities in which it shall then be invested to the National Academy of Sciences, to be thenceforward forever held in trust under the name and title of the 'Joseph Henry fund.'" The death of Miss Caroline Henry on Nov. 10, 1920, has removed the last surviving heir of Joseph Henry to the income of the Joseph

Henry fund. To assist meritorious investigators, especially in the direction of original research. Amount received by the Academy from the Pennsylvania Co. for Insurance of Lives and Granting Annuities, $39,739.57 to which was added $423.93 from income_____ $40,163.50

Walcott fund: Gift of Mrs. Mary Vaux Walcott, 1928, in honor of her husband, a former member and president of the Academy, the income to be used for the award of medals and honoraria to persons, the result of whose published researches, explorations, and discoveries in pre-Cambrian or Cambrian life and history shall be judged most meritorious, the award to be made every . 5 years, to be known as the "Charles Doolittle Walcott fund"___ 5,000.00

Carnegie endowment fund: By resolution voted Mar. 28, 1919, and amended several times since, the Carnegie Corporation of New York pledged $5,000,000 to the National Academy of Sciences for the purposes of the Academy and the National Research Council, of which $1,450,000 was reserved and paid for the erection of a building, and the remainder, $3,550,000, to be capitalized at such times as the corporation finds convenient in view of its other obligations, the amount remaining in the hands of the corporation to bear interest at the rate of 5 percent per annum; 7 installments completing capitalization_____ 3,550,000.00

John J. Carty Medal and Award for the advancement of science: Gift of American Telephone & Telegraph Co., Nov. 13, 1930, in recognition of the distinguished achievements of John J. Carty as a scientist and engineer, and his noteworthy contributions to the advancement of fundamental and applied science, and in appreciation of his great services for many years in developing the art of electrical communication and as a lasting testimonial of the love and esteem in which he is held by his many thousand associates in the Bell System: the income thereof to be used for a gold medal and award, not oftener than once in 2 years, by vote of the National Academy of Sciences, to an individual for noteworthy and distinguished accomplishment in any field of science coming within the scope of the charter of the National Academy of Sciences_____ 25,000.00

In addition to the above-named funds, the Academy holds the following:

Agassiz fund, bequest of Alexander Agassiz, a member of the Academy, 1910, for the general uses of the Academy_____ 50,000.00

Nealley fund, bequest of George True Nealley, 1925, for the general purposes of the Academy, $20,896.01, less refund November 1926, $1,500, to a creditor of the estate; supplemented by additional sum from the estate, March 1931, $159.54_____ 19,555.55

Total_____ 3,900,183.96

Accounts with individual funds, July 1, 1935, to June 30, 1936

	General fund		Agassiz fund	
	Income	Capital	Income	Capital
Balance July 1, 1935:				
Cash	$9,892.57			
Invested	8,700.00			$50,000.00
Receipts:				
Interest on investments:				
Agassiz fund	3,015.16			
Nealley fund	1,011.80			
Bonds sold	14,600.00			
Annual dues from members	1,380.00			
Refund	4.00			
Total	38,603.53			50,000.00
Disbursements:				
General expenses	4,520.35			
Transfer to investment reserve fund	201.35			
Fees to financial advisers	149.39			
Bonds bought	14,600.00			
Accrued interest on **bonds bought**	187.50			
Balance June 30, 1936:				
Cash	7,419.94			
Invested	11,525.00			50,000.00
Total	38,603.53			50,000.00

	Bache fund		Billings fund	
	Income	Capital	Income	Capital
Balance July 1, 1935:				
Cash	$1,030.17			
Invested		$60,000.00		$22,313.39
Receipts:				
Interest on investments	4,155.56		$1,154.29	
Transferred from consolidated fund capital		60,000.00		
Bonds sold		**1,120.63**		
Transferred from investment reserve fund—				
adjustment	212.88			
Refund	32.50			
Total	5,431.11	121,120.63	1,154.29	$22,313.39
Disbursements:				
Grants	3,170.00			
Office expenses	2.71			
Bonds bought		61,120.63		
Accrued interest **on bonds bought**	332.04			
Transfer to investment reserve fund	**207.78**		57.71	
Fees to financial advisers	112.06		43.55	
Transfer to academy Proceedings			1,053.03	
Balance June 30, 1936:				
Cash	**1,606.52**	147.63		
Invested		59,852.37		22,313.39
Total	5,431.11	121,120.63	1,154.29	22,313.39

Accounts with individual funds, July 1, 1935, to June 30, 1936—Continued

	Building construction		Building site	
	Income	Capital	Income	Capital
Balance July 1, 1935:				
Cash	$3,120.18		$5,218.65	
Invested			7,543.25	
Receipts:				
Interest on investments			356.40	
Total	3,120.18		13,118.30	
Disbursements:				
Fees to financial advisers			18.67	
Transfer to investment reserve fund			17.82	
Balance June 30, 1936:				
Cash	3,120.18		5,538.56	
Invested			7,543.25	
Total	3,120.18		13,118.30	

	Carnegie endowment fund		Carnegie Corporation special	
	Income	Capital	Income	Capital
Balance July 1, 1935:				
Cash		$513,670.89	$11,849.90	
Invested		3,036,329.11		
Receipts:				
Interest on investments	$139,604.33			
Bonds sold		1,681,911.62		
Total	139,604.33	5,231,911.62	11,849.90	
Disbursements:				
Government relations			99.34	
Library			11.00	
Attorney's fees for examining deeds of trust			500.00	
Members of Academy council attending special meetings			58.32	
Transfer to D. C. unemployment compensation tax, 1936			140.13	
Bonds bought		1,681,911.62		
Accrued interest on bonds bought	15,416.91			
Transfer to investment reserve fund	6,980.22			
Fees to financial advisers	5,365.85			
Taxes, fire and liability insurance, etc., on real estate	5,466.57			
Transferred to Carnegie endowment fund, income account, N. R. C., 1935	10,000.00			
Transferred to Carnegie endowment fund, income account, N. R. C., 1936	33,646.33			
Transferred to Carnegie endowment fund, income account, N. A. S., 1935	2,174.78			
Transferred to Carnegie endowment fund, income account, N. A. S., 1936	43,640.12			
Balance, June 30, 1936:				
Cash	16,913.55	239,423.61	11,041.11	
Invested		3,260,571.39		
Total	139,604.33	5,231,911.62	11,849.90	

Accounts with individual funds, July 1, 1935, to June 30, 1936—Continued

	John J. Carty Medal and Award		Comstock fund	
	Income	Capital	Income	Capital
Balance, July 1, 1935:				
Cash	$2,548.94	$257.50	$5,340.62	$2,652.27
Invested		24,742.50		9,743.75
Receipts:				
Interest on investments	1,376.34		505.35	
Bonds sold		39,513.75		9,743.75
Transfer from investment reserve fund adjustment			671.92	
Total	3,925.28	64,513.75	6,517.89	22,149.77
Disbursements:				
Bonds bought		14,513.75		9,743.75
Transferred to consolidated fund, capital		25,000.00		
Fees to financial advisers	43.55		6.00	
Transfer to investment reserve fund	68.82			
Accrued interest on bonds bought			84.81	
Balance, June 30, 1936:				
Cash	3,812.91		6,427.08	78.52
Invested		25,000.00		12,327.50
Total	3,925.28	64,513.75	6,517.89	22,149.77

	Consolidated fund		Draper fund	
	Income	Capital	Income	Capital
Balance, July 1, 1935:				
Cash	$1,269.28	$1,416.69	$1,270.74	
Invested		251,361.25		$10,000.00
Receipts:				
Interest on investments	15,821.92		517.67	
Bonds sold		184,733.63		
Transfer from John J. Carty Medal and Award, capital		25,000.00		
Transfer from Walcott fund, capital		5,000.00		
Transfer from Thompson fund, capital		10,000.00		
Total	17,091.20	477,511.57	1,788.41	10,000.00
Disbursements:				
Bonds bought		184,733.63		
Accrued interest on bonds bought	2,261.65			
Distribution of consolidated fund capital	13,072.42			
Taxes, etc., on real estate	393.36			
Grants			600.00	
Transfer to investment reserve fund			25.88	
Fees to financial advisers			18.67	
Transfer to Bache fund, capital		60,000.00		
Balance June 30, 1936:				
Cash	1,363.77	111.49	1,143.86	
Invested		232,666.45		10,000.00
Total	17,091.20	477,511.57	1,788.41	10,000.00

Accounts with individual funds, July 1, 1935, to June 30, 1936—Continued

	D. C. unemployment compensation tax, 1936		Electric current change-over	
	Income	Capital	Income	Capital
Balance July 1, 1935				
Receipts:				
Transfer from Carnegie Corporation, special	$140.13			
Reimbursement from Potomac Electric Power Co			$8,769.00	
Total	140.13		8,769.00	
Disbursements:				
D. C. Unemployment Compensation Board, tax on salaries	140.13			
New electrical equipment			8,769.00	
Total	140.13		8,769.00	

	Elliot fund		Fees to financial advisers	
	Income	Capital	Income	Capital
Balance July 1, 1935:				
Cash	$1,755.30			
Invested		$8,000.00		
Receipts:				
Interest on investments	413.08			
Transfer from various funds			$6,211.65	
Total	2,168.38	8,000.00	6,211.65	
Disbursements:				
Transfer to investment reserve fund	20.65			
Fees to financial advisers	12.44			
Loomis, Sayles & Co			2,000.86	
Joseph Stanley-Brown			4,210.79	
Balance June 30, 1936:				
Cash	2,135.29			
Invested		8,000.00		
Total	$2,168.38	8,000.00	6,211.65	

	Fund for oceanographic research		Gibbs fund	
	Income	Capital	Income	Capital
Balance July 1, 1935:				
Cash	$7,085.12		$2,989.87	
Invested				$5,545.50
Receipts:				
Sale of "Oceanography"	11.25			
Interest on investments			286.28	
Total	7,096.37		3,276.15	5,545.50
Disbursements:				
Expenses of T. Wayland Vaughan	105.48			
Grants			300.00	
Transfer to investment reserve fund			14.31	
Fees to financial advisers			12.44	
Balance June 30, 1936:				
Cash	6,990.89		2,949.40	
Invested				5,545.50
Total	7,096.37		3,276.15	5,545.50

Accounts with individual funds, July 1, 1935, to June 30, 1936—Continued

	Gould fund		Grand Canyon project	
	Income	Capital	Income	Capital
Balance July 1, 1935:				
Cash	$14,714.79	$3,297.50	$24.19	
Invested	1,512.50	16,702.50		
Receipts:				
Interest on investments	1,020.11			
Bonds sold		6,007.50		
Total	17,247.40	26,007.50	24.19	
Disbursements:				
Grants	1,934.50			
Bonds bought		6,007.50		
Accrued interest on bonds bought	161.54			
Taxes, etc., on real estate	35.46			
Transfer to investment reserve fund	56.01			
Fees to financial advisers	37.33			
Balance June 30, 1936:				
Cash	8,467.56	477.50	24.19	
Invested	6,555.00	19,522.50		
Total	17,247.40	26,007.50	24.19	

	Hale lectureship		Hartley fund	
	Income	Capital	Income	Capital
Balance July 1, 1935:				
Cash	$385.55		$516.06	
Invested				$1,200.00
Receipts:				
Interest on investments			61.45	
Total	385.55		577.51	1,200.00
Disbursements:				
Medals and medal boxes			193.88	
Transfer to investment reserve fund			3.07	
Balance June 30, 1936:				
Cash	385.55		380.56	
Invested				1,200.00
Total	385.55		577.51	1,200.00

	Joseph Henry fund		Investment reserve fund	
	Income	Capital	Income	Capital
Balance July 1, 1935:				
Cash	$1,209.42			
Invested		$40,163.50		
Receipts:				
Interest on investments	2,077.21			
Profit on sale of bonds			$227,283.43	
Transferred from various funds			7,940.56	
Overdraft June 30, 1936			358,152.30	
Total	3,286.63	40,163.50	593,376.29	
Disbursements:				
Grants	2,236.56			
Transfer to investment reserve fund	103.86			
Fees to financial advisers	68.45			
Loss on sale of bonds			8,365.03	
Transfer to Bache fund, income adjustment			212.88	
Transfer to Comstock fund, income adjustment			671.92	
Overdraft July 1, 1935			584,126.46	
Balance June 30, 1936:				
Cash	877.76			
Invested		40,163.50		
Total	3,286.63	40,163.50	593,376.29	

Accounts with individual funds, July 1, 1935, to June 30, 1936—Continued

	Marsh fund		Murray fund	
	Income	Capital	Income	Capital
Balance July 1, 1935:				
Cash	$696.63		$4,270.33	
Invested		$20,000.00		$6,000.00
Receipts:				
Interest on investments	1,034.03		309.82	
Total	1,730.66	20,000.00	4,580.15	6,000.00
Disbursements:				
Grants	1,425.00			
Medals and medal boxes			304.82	
Transfer to investment reserve fund	51.70		15.49	
Fees to financial advisers	37.33		12.44	
Balance June 30, 1936:				
Cash	216.63		4,247.40	
Invested		20,000.00		6,000.00
Total	1,730.66	20,000.00	4,580.15	6,000.00

	National Academy of Sciences, special		National Parks problems	
	Income	Capital	Income	Capital
Balance July 1, 1935:				
Cash			$1,864.87	
Receipts:				
Reimbursements	$71,483.50			
Due from National Research Council July 1, 1935	2,000.00			
Total	73,483.50		1,864.87	
Disbursements:				
Expenses of Academy	71,483.50			
Painting of Crater Lake			150.00	
Miscellaneous expenses			110.66	
Balance June 30, 1936:				
Cash			1,604.21	
Due from National Research Council June 30, 1936	2,000.00			
Total	73,483.50		1,864.87	

	Nealley fund		Emergency fund Proceedings	
	Income	Capital	Income	Capital
Balance July 1, 1935:				
Cash			$3,327.79	
Invested		$19,555.55		
Total		19,555.55	3,327.79	
Balance June 30, 1936:				
Cash			3,327.79	
Invested		19,555.55		
Total		19,555.55	3,327.79	

Accounts with individual funds, July 1, 1935, to June 30, 1936—Continued

	Academy Proceedings		Joint Proceedings	
	Income	Capital	Income	Capital
Balance July 1, 1935:				
Cash	$3,792.33		$6,595.62	
Invested	996.75			
Receipts:				
Interest on investments	59.40			
Annual dues	1,380.00			
Subscriptions			1,920.77	
Reprints and separates	113.25		1,692.80	
Transfer from Billings fund	1,053.03			
Contribution by National Research Council			2,500.00	
Transfer from Academy Proceedings representing contribution by National Academy of Sciences			2,500.00	
Transfer from National Parks problems for reprints			4.04	
Total	7,393.76		15,213.23	
Disbursements:				
Salary of managing editor			750.00	
Printing and distributing			7,651.11	
Expenses:				
Boston office			460.00	
Washington office			209.83	
Transfer from Academy Proceedings representing contribution by National Academy of Sciences	2,500.00			
Transfer to investment reserve fund	2.97			
Balance June 30, 1936:				
Cash	3,895.04		6,142.39	
Invested	996.75			
Total	7,393.76		15,213.23	

	Scientific publication fund		Smith fund	
	Income	Capital	Income	Capital
Balance July 1, 1935:				
Cash	$1,683.52		$5,571.55	
Invested			1,478.25	$10,000.00
Receipts:				
Interest on investments			610.28	
Bonds sold			482.50	
Royalties on Oceanography	3.12			
Total	1,686.64		8,142.58	10,000.00
Disbursements:				
Bonds bought			482.50	
Accrued interest on bonds bought			29.25	
Grant			450.00	
Transfer to investment reserve fund			30.51	
Fees to financial advisers			18.67	
Balance June 30, 1936:				
Cash	$1,686.64		$3,008.40	
Invested			4,123.25	10,000.00
Total	1,686.64		8,142.56	10,000.00

Accounts with individual funds, July 1, 1935, to June 30, 1936—Continued

	Thompson fund		Walcott fund	
	Income	Capital	Income	Capital
Balance July 1, 1935:				
Cash	$2,251.34	$875.00	$304.32	$135.00
Invested		9,125.00		4,865.00
Receipts:				
Interest on investments	459.07		311.43	
Bonds sold		18,250.00		9,865.00
Total	2,710.41	28,250.00	615.75	14,865.00
Disbursements:				
Bonds bought		8,250.00		4,865.00
Transfer to consolidated fund, capital		10,000.00		5,000.00
Accrued interest on bonds bought			80.56	
Transfer to investment reserve fund	22.95		15.57	
Fees to financial advisers	18.67		12.44	
Balance June 30, 1936:				
Cash	2,668.79		507.18	
Invested		10,000.00		5,000.00
Total	2,710.41	28,250.00	615.75	14,865.00

	Watson fund	
	Income	Capital
Balance July 1, 1935:		
Cash	$3,049.87	$1,821.25
Invested	1,000.00	23,178.75
Receipts:		
Interest on investments	877.79	
Bonds sold		15,963.53
Total	4,927.66	40,963.53
Disbursements:		
Grant	1,425.00	
Bonds bought		15,963.53
Accrued interest on bonds bought	50.11	
Taxes and commissions on real estate	65.22	
Transfer to investment reserve fund	43.89	
Fees to financial advisers	43.55	
Balance June 30, 1936:		
Cash	2,299.89	193.53
Invested	1,000.00	24,806.47
Total	4,927.66	40,963.53

Statement of assets and liabilities, June 30, 1936

ASSETS

[Securities purchased during the fiscal year 1935-36 are indicated thus (*)]

	Face value	Book value	Market value June 30, 1936
Real estate owned	$154,000.00	$154,000.00	$154,000.00
Mortgage notes, secured by first mortgage on real estate	367,900.00	367,900.00	367,900.00
SECURITIES			
American Telephone & Telegraph Co. 5-percent 35-year debenture bonds due Feb. 1, 1965: Nos. M17-939, M19-041, M64-124-M64-135, M64-519, M72-201-M72-203, M72-311-M72-316, M72-324, M75-045-M75-050, M91-899, M91-900, M108-560-M108-562, M115-287-M115-289, M131-196-M131-200, M144-885, M145-413, M145-414 (47, at $1,000 each)	47,000.00	51,208.75	53,227.50
Argentine Government Loan, 1926, 6-percent external sinking-fund gold, public-works issue of Oct. 1, 1926, due Oct. 1, 1960: Nos. M1211-M1213, M1255, M1981, M2342, M3255, M3356, M3816, M3818, M6183, M6537, M8435, M8436, M8605, M10433-M10437, M10902, M10904, M10905, M12793, M15271 (25, at $1,000 each)	25,000.00	24,936.25	25,187.50
*Atlantic Coast Line R. R. Co. 4-percent first consolidated mortgage 50-year bonds, due July 1, 1952: Nos. 44251-44280, 44284-44299, 49136-49139 (50, at $1,000 each)	50,000.00	48,375.00	48,250.00
Baltimore & Ohio R. R. Co. 5-percent refunding and general mortgage, series A, due Dec. 1, 1995: Nos. *M1494, *M1844, *M3376, *M5138, *M5382, *M7519, *M7996, *M9020, *M11535, *M17752, *M17753, *M18061, *M19333, *M19334, *M26419, M30222, *M33707, M33708, *M34174, *M34175, *M34202, *M35387, *M35680, *M35920, *M36568, *M36854, M37053, *M37253, *M38333, *M38459, *M38460, *M40594, *M42486, *M44032, *M45782, *M47157, *M47899, *M48251, *M48252, *M48255-*M48262, *M48273, *M48274, *M48779, *M148780, *M48837, *M52228, *M52748, *M52756, *M52952, *M52994, *M53730, *M56285, *M56286, *M57654-*M57660, *M58155, M58345 (69, at $1,000 each); nos. D1256, D1298(2, at $500 each)	70,000.00	57,238.75	59,850.00
Baltimore & Ohio R. R. Co. 5-percent refunding and general mortgage, series D, due Mar. 1, 2000: Nos. M4863-M4892 (30, at $1,000 each)	30,000.00	28,650.00	25,275.00
Bell Telephone Co. of Canada 5-percent first mortgage, series C, bonds due May 1, 1960: Nos. CM00084, CM00085, CM00277-CM00279, CM00397, CM00527-CM00529, CM00628, CM00629, CM00719, CM00750, CM01453-CM01458, CM02295-CM02298, CM02827, CM03184, CM03192, CM03193, CM06441-CM06445, CM06449, CM06450 (35, at $1,000 each)	35,000.00	36,488.75	42,962.50
Canadian Pacific Ry. Co. 4 percent perpetual consolidated debentures: Nos. G5882, G28256, G37790, G37791, G43142, G43143, G81666-G81668, G87312 (10, at $1,000 each)	10,000.00	8,525.00	9,475.00
*Central Illinois Public Service Co. 4½-percent first mortgage, series F, due Dec. 1, 1967: Nos. M99, M1159, M1352, M1353, M1742, M2514, M3006-M3010, M4564, M4565, M4050, M5085-M5088, M5292, M7468, M9671, M12536, M14255, M14383, M18524, M18525, M18527, M19609, M21746, M21747, M25019, M25020, M25022, M25322, M25323, M25519-M25521, M26041, M26252-M26254, M26339, M26340, M26366, M26926, M26927, M27087, M27349, M27836 (50, at $1,000 each)	50,000.00	49,556.25	50,250.00
*Central Pacific Railway Co. 5-percent 35-year bonds, fully guaranteed, due Aug. 1, 1960: Nos. M927, M935, M1586, M1687-M1690, M4371, M4373, M5512-M5514, M6423-M6427, M7871, M7872, M8369, M9516, M10127-M10129, M10547, M10548, M12788, M13272, M13341, M13477, M14970-M14973, M19550, M19753, M20144, M21557, M22401-M22405, M23086-M23095, M23882, M24354, M25010-M25014, M26094, M26095, M26465, M26643, M28040, M28466, M29550, M29551, M29544, M30545, M30693, M30694, M32978, M33159-M33173, M33277, M33278, M33612, M34012, M34438, M35849, M36674, M36981, M36982, M37052 (99, at $1,000 each); nos. D887, D888 (2, at $500 each)	100,000.00	92,067.50	100,500.00
*Cleveland, Cincinnati, Chicago & St. Louis Ry. Co. 5-percent refunding and improvement mortgage, series D, due July 1, 1963: Nos. M15, M22, M98, M128, M129, M291-M293, M298-M300, M1470, M1571, M1723, M1724, M1913, M2334, M2701, M2886, M2887, M3158, M3433, M3436, M3984, M6129-M6131, M6155-M6159, M6192-M6196, M6323-M6328, M6414, M6415, M6616-M6620, M6949, M6950, M7003, M8118, M8739-M8746, M8751-M8753, M9604, M9606-M9608, M9797-M9800, M9834, M10377-M10379, M10381, M11442, M10542, M10543, M10545, M10626, M11975, M12124, M12341, M13127, M13593, M13807, M13808, M14156, M15571, M15772, M18582, M18768, M19632-M19636 (100, at $1,000 each)	100,000.00	93,351.25	101,750.00

Statement of assets and liabilities, June 30, 1936—Continued

ASSETS—Continued

[Securities purchased during the fiscal year 1935–36 are indicated thus (*)]

	Face value	Book value	Marketvalue June 30, 1936
SECURITIES—continued			
Columbia Gas & Electric Corporation 5-percent debenture bonds, due Jan. 15, 1961: Nos. A9157–A9181, *A33237–*A33261 (50, at $1,000 each)	$50,000.00	$49,093.75	$52,375.00
Cosmos Club, Washington, D. C., 4½-percent bonds, due July 1, 1949: Nos. 288, 289, 291, 292, 294, 299, 305, 350 (8, at $1,000 each)	8,000.00	8,000.00	8,000.00
Government of the Argentine Nation 6-percent external sinking fund gold bonds, due Oct. 1, 1959: Nos. M5611, M10469, M10470, M18165, M18363–M18365, M19643, M20578, M23810 (10, at $1,000 each)	10,000.00	9,957.50	10,075.00
*Great Northern Railway Co. 5-percent general mortgage, series C, due Jan. 1, 1973: Nos. M997–M1000, M1633, M1640, M2384, M2798–M2800, M3138–M3141, M4540, M4761, M4762, M4945–M4952, M5430, M5475, M5476, M6377, M6380, M6381, M6588, M7005, M10158, M10175, M10430, M10834, M11758–M11760, M13302–M13306, M14301, M14517–M14520 (50, at $1,000 each)	50,000.00	51,071.25	54,750.00
*Great Northern Ry. Co. 4½-percent general mortgage, series D, due July 1, 1976: Nos. M7891, M7892, M9067, M10973, M11227, M11676–M11685, M11934, M12895, M12910–M12934, M13730, M13731, M13860–M13865 (50, at $1,000 each)	50,000.00	50,437.50	51,500.00
*Illinois Central R. R. Co. 4-percent refunding mortgage, due Nov. 1, 1955: Nos. 1884, 10985, 10986, 12888, 13435, 13436, 14214, 14653–14655, 14781–14791, 14842–14854, 19859–19863, 19874–19876, 22558–22562, 23431–23434, 28682–28688, 28773–28780, 30991–31015, 33092–33096, 33104–33107 (106, at $1,000 each)	100,000.00	87,187.50	84,875.00
*Illinois Power & Light Corporation 5-percent first and refunding mortgage, series C, due Dec. 1, 1956: Nos. CM5436–CM5440, CM9374, CM10635, CM11774–CM11778, CM12086, CM12165–CM12167, CM12286, CM12850–CM12855, CM15804, CM23872 (25, at $1,000 each)	25,000.00	25,062.50	25,000.00
Indianapolis Power & Light Co. 5-percent first mortgage, series A, due Jan. 1, 1957: Nos. M31026–M31028, M31160–M31164, M31299, M31300, M31367, M31452–M31455, M31833, M31967–M31970, M32054–M32056, M32058–M32064 (30, at $1,000 each)	30,000.00	31,237.50	31,762.50
Kansas City, Fort Scott & Memphis Ry. Co. 4-percent refunding mortgage, fully guaranteed, due Oct. 1, 1936; Nos. 32, 756, 1013, 1093, 1418–1421, 1447, 1660, 2326, 2593, 2898, 3546, 4196, 4312, 4348, 4468–4472, 4610, 4621, 4787, 4944, 5096, 5447, 5728, 5930, 5932, 6224–6227, 6802, 6811, 6812, 6906, 7191, 7444, 7449, 7475, 7612, 7640, 7641, 7662, 7933, 7934, 8023–8025, 8027, 8028, 8062, 8222, 8624, 8739, 8880, 8970, 9486, 10936, 11733, 11742, 13082–13084, 13483, 13484, 14113, 14256, 14561, 14562, 14651, 14952, 15186, 15187, 15226, 15946, 16079, 16081–16085, 16207, 16276, 16767, 17281, 18104, 18173, 18177, 18453, 18782, 18783, 18906, 18856, 18947, 19060, 19154, 19655, 19893, 19911, 20178, 20235, 20694, 20891, 21065, 21345, 21346, 21387, 21730, 21880–21889, 22822, 22935, 23065, 23124, 23271, 24023, 24188, 24206, 24221, 24542, 24650, 25215, 25499, 25500 (136, at $1,000 each)	136,000.00	79,096.25	61,200.00
Lackawanna & Wyoming Valley R. R. Co. 5 percent first-mortgage gold bonds, dated July 1, 1913, due Aug. 1, 1951; Nos. M853–M902 (50, at $1,000 each)	50,000.00	48,750.00	13,500.00
*Louisville & Nashville R. R. Co. 4-percent first and refunding mortgage, series D, due Apr. 1, 2003: Nos. Temporary TM3646, TM4903–TM4907, TM6128–TM6132, TM6265, TM8052, TM8905, TM8900, TM9228–TM9237 (25, at $1,000 each)	25,000.00	26,062.50	25,500.00
*Michigan Central R. R. Co. 4½-percent refunding and improvement mortgage, series C, due Jan. 1, 1979: Nos. M2598, M2624–M2629, M2914–M2918, M2924, M2925, M2969–M2977, M2979–M2982, M2989–M3018, M5038, M5039, M7118–M7120, M8761–M8766, M10472–M10479, M10790–M10793, M10840–M10859 (100, at $1,000 each)	100,000.00	101,687.50	104,250.00
Missouri Pacific R. R. Co. 5-percent first and refunding mortgage gold bonds, series G, dated Nov. 1, 1928, due Nov. 1, 1978: Nos. M20326–M20375 (50, at $1,000 each)	50,000.00	48,712.50	15,750.00
Missouri Pacific R. R. Co. 5-percent first and refunding mortgage, series I, due Feb. 1, 1931: Nos. M9994, M10757, M10758, M15428–M15450, M16440–M16442, M18265, M18828, M18829, M23249, M30095, M30444, M30546, M30901–M30905, M30906–M30915, M31587, M33255, M38252, M38253, M39860, M39861, M40437–M40440, M46664 (60, at $1,000 each)	60,000.00	31,983.75	18,900.00
*National Dairy Products Corporation 3¼-percent debentures, due May 1, 1951: Nos. M17660–M17709 (50, at $1,000 each)	50,000.00	50,250.00	52,250.00

Statement of assets and liabilities, June 30, 1936—Continued

ASSETS—Continued

[Securities purchased during the fiscal year 1935-36 are indicated thus (*)]

	Face value	Book value	Market value June 30, 1936
SECURITIES—continued			
New Jersey Power & Light Co. 4½-percent first-mortgage bonds, due Oct. 1, 1960: Nos. M8316-M8339, M9625, M10706, M10735, M10843, M11857, M11869 (30, at $1,000 each)	$30,000.00	$30,975.00	$31,875.00
New Orleans, Texas & Mexico Ry. Co. 5½-percent first-mortgage gold bonds, series A, due Apr. 1, 1954: Nos. M439-M448, M647, M1610, M1765-M1767, M1808-M1810, M3396, M6873, M6874, M6896, M6897, M7099, M8135, M8207, M9643, M9950, M9996, M11059-M11063, M11944-M11948, M12486, M12487, M14131-M14133, M14417, M14418, M16406-M16408 (49, at $1,000 each); nos. D200, D201; 2, at $500 each	50,000.00	51,763.75	20,000.00
*New York Central R. R. Co. 4-percent consolidation mortgage, series A, due Feb. 1, 1998: Nos. 174, 175, 881, 3006, 3007, 3338, 3357, 4598, 4696, 4697, 4930, 4931, 5007-5010, 6951, 11025, 11275, 13509, 14244-14253, 15158, 15957, 17891, 18132, 18625-18627, 19737, 19738, 23781-23783, 23796-23800, 23815-23817, 23837-23842, 26402, 35837-35840, 36218-36220, 38251, 38481, 45422-45429, 45437-45440, 45442, 45661-45666, 45935, 47287, 51585-51594, 52383, 59373, 67761 (100, at $1,000 each)	100,000.00	91,187.50	96,000.00
*New York Central R. R. Co. 4½-percent refunding and improvement mortgage, series A, due Oct. 1, 2013: Nos. 71303-71309, 71324-71327, 102836-102849 (25, at $1,000 each)	25,000.00	21,906.25	21,625.00
*New York, Chicago & St. Louis R. R. Co., 4½-percent refunding mortgage, series C, due Sept. 1, 1978: Nos. M1212, M1213, M1388, M1496, M4071, M4262, M9766, M12891-M12895, M13756, M17785-M17787, M19970, M20178, M24744, M30336, M36549, M37475, M45006, M51497, M59532 (25, at $1,000 each)	25,000.00	22,250.00	22,062.50
North American Co. 5-percent debentures, due Feb. 1, 1961: Nos. M505, M1404, M1839-M1847, M3951-M3953, M5801-M5810, M5991, M5992, M7712-M7714, M8296, M11067, M13855, M13996, M14000, M14209, M15223, M15855, M17286, M17527, M17769, M17770, M17964, M18532, M18571, M19074, M19288, M23252-M23256, M23701, M23730, M23954, M24316, M24317, M24704, M24705, M24943 (60, at $1,000 each)	60,000.00	49,750.00	63,825.00
*Northern Indiana Public Service Co., 4½-percent first and refunding mortgage, series E, due Dec. 1, 1970: Nos. M3341-M3350, M4410, M4659, M4830, M5448-M5450, M5583, M5585, M5611, M5639, M5948, M7061-M7085, M8327, M10034, M10035, M12284 (50, at $1,000 each)	50,000.00	50,463.75	51,750.00
*Northern Pacific Ry. Co., 5-percent refunding and improvement, series C, due July 1, 2047: Nos. M7471-M7488, M7496 (19, at $1,000 each)	19,000.00	18,667.50	20,448.75
*Northern Pacific Ry. Co. 5-percent refunding and improvement, series D, due July 1, 2047: No. 6054 (1, at $1,000)	1,000.00	982.50	1,072.50
*Northern Pacific Ry. Co. 4½-percent refunding and improvement mortgage, series A, due July 1, 2047: Nos. M1535, M1543, M1731-M1746, M2745-M2750, M4111, M6230, M9839, M9840, M9844, M9845, M9874, M9889, M9890, M11335, M11336, M11879, M11981-M11983, M12241, M12281, M12919, M13425, M13767, M13768, M16139-M16143 (50, at $1,000 each)	50,000.00	51,130.00	51,500.00
*Penn Central Light & Power Co. 4½-percent first mortgage, due Nov. 1, 1977: Nos. M2119, M3002, M3010, M3818, M8830-M3833, M5147-M5149, M5350, M5351, M7064, M9051, M9317, M11877, M13260, M13892, M15125, M15154, M15705-M15709, M16569, M16853, M18536-M18539, M18733, M19765, M19861, M19862, M20184, M20185, M21209, M21637-M21639, M21818 (44, at $1,000 each); nos. D55, D267-D269, D690, D713, D767, D927-D929, D953, D954 (12, at $500 each)	50,000.00	50,638.75	52,125.00
*Pennsylvania Railroad Co. 4½-percent 40-year debentures, due Apr. 1, 1970: Nos. 7625-7628, 8670, 15107, 16747, 19428, 20386, 28115, 30074, 30075, 30772, 34941, 38154-38163, 41003-41052, 51958 (75, at $1,000 each)	75,000.00	75,802.50	77,625.00
*Pennsylvania R. R. Co. 3¾-percent general mortgage, series C, due Apr. 1, 1970: Nos. 2477-2501 (25, at $1,000 each)	25,000.00	25,593.75	25,343.75
*Pere Marquette Ry. Co. 5-percent refunding and general mortgage, series A, due July 1, 1956: Nos. M21, M22, M1216, M1332, M5176, M8410-M8425, M8753, M8845, M10606-M10609, M10614, M10615, M11230-M11232, M11272, M11543, M14313, M16352, M17420, M19519, M20043, M27406, M27407, M28317, M29070, M29072, M29073, M29244, M30084, M32849, M32850 (50, at $1,000 each)	50,000.00	51,423.75	52,125.00

Statement of assets and liabilities, June 30, 1936—Continued

ASSETS—Continued

[Securities purchased during the fiscal year 1935–36 are indicated thus (*)]

	Face value	Book value	Market value June 30, 1936
SECURITIES—continued			
*Pere Marquette Ry. Co. 4½-percent first mortgage, series C, due Mar. 1, 1980; Nos. M2241–M2250, M5206, M5220–M5223, M5226–M5235, M5801–M5805, M5831–M5850, M10751–M10775 (75, at $1,000 each)	$75,000.00	$74,468.75	$74,718.75
Potomac Edison Co. 4½-percent first mortgage, series F, due Apr. 1, 1961; Nos. M1005–M1013, M1427, M1791–M1793, M2529–M2534, M2662–M2664, M3776, M3872–M3876, M4137 (29, at $1,000 each); nos. D9, D80 (2, at $500 each)	30,000.00	31,637.50	32,100.00
Raleigh & Augusta Air Line R. R. Co.–Seaboard Air Line Ry. Co. 5-percent guaranteed first mortgage, due Jan. 1, 1931; Nos. 701–725 (25 at $1,000 each)	25,000.00	25,000.00	16,000.00
*Reading Co. 4-percent Jersey Central collateral, due Apr. 1, 1951; Nos. 1864–1866, 2853, 2855, 4257, 6766, 7309, 7599, 9111–9113, 9399, 9400, 14836, 17677, 18459–18467 (25, at $1,000 each)	25,000.00	24,967.50	25,000.00
St. Louis-San Francisco Ry. Co. 4½-percent consolidated mortgage gold bonds, series A ,due Mar. 1, 1978: Nos. M7881–M7895, M14120–M14134, M17108, M17963, M17964, M19029, M25732–M25737, M41182, M41183, M41216, M62420–M62424, M91633, M91634 (50, at $1,000 each)	50,000.00	43,850.00	9,500.00
*Southern Pacific Co. 4½-percent 40 year, due Mar. 1, 1968: Nos. 8705, 14695, 14697,14973–14975, 15806–15813, 15815–15817, 15819, 15821–15827 (25, at $1,000 each)	25,000.00	22,750.00	22,500.00
*Southern Pacific R. R. Co. 4-percent first refunding mortgage, fully guaranteed, due Jan. 1, 1955: Nos. M313, M3165, M3820, M17397, M17516–M17518, M20575, M21725, M24721, M24722, M31383–M31386, M32176, M32177, M38177–M38179, M44597, M45985,M51575 ,M53760, M61776, M67525, M68611, M70225, M73973, M79399, M82433, M82435, M84344, M95451, M95452, M100116, M100117, M100123–M100125, M102503, M112593–M112595, M125232, M125233, M128554Z, M128555Z, M135824 ,M135825 (50,at $1,000 each)	50,000.00	48,906.25	52,812.50
*Southwestern Light & Power Co. 5-percent first mortgage, series A, due Feb. 1, 1957: Nos. M503–M505, M768, M780, M1474, M1475, M2731, M3182, M4310–M4312, M4474, M4732, M5043, M6224, M6225, M6280 (18, at $1,000 each); nos. D225, D229, D681, D684 (4, at $500 each)	20,000.00	20,282.50	20,725.00
Texarkana & Fort Smith Ry. Co. 5½-percent first-mortgage guaranteed gold bonds, series A, due Aug. 1, 1950: Nos. M101, M102, M754–M763, M1593–M1595, M1739, M1742, M1777–M1779, M2014–M2018, M3001, M3002, M3908–M3910, M5767, M6078, M6482, M6757–M6760, M6912, M8341–M8343, M9299, M9472, M9473, M9629–M9631 (47, at $1,000 each); Nos. D102, D103, D186, D202, D237, D264 (6, at $500 each)	50,000.00	52,271.25	52,437.50
*Texas Electric Service Co. 5-percent first mortgage, due July 1, 1960: Nos. M30506–M30530 (25, at $1,000 each)	25,000.00	25,625.00	25,968.75
*Texas & Pacific Ry. Co. 5-percent general and refunding mortgage, series C, due Apr. 1, 1979: Nos. 1047–1050, 1337, 1340, 1406–1415, 1587, 1599, 1755, 1757, 1906, 7397, 7399, 8852–8856, 8797, 9501, 10206, 10207, 10646, 10939–10943, 11501, 11551, 11583, 11585–11587, 11589, 11764, 12256, 13278, 13383, 13434, 13435, 13791, 13830, 15707, 15749, 16708, 16853, 16854, 18585, 18644, 19039, 19149–19152, 19325–19328, 19367, 19368, 19574, 19576, 19951, 19952 (75, at $1,000 each)	75,000.00	75,046.25	78,281.25
*Texas & Pacific Ry. Co. 5-percent general and refunding mortgage, series D, due Dec. 1, 1980: Nos. 1365, 1366, 1369, 3001–3003, 3182, 5316–5325, 5980, 12251–12256, 12972 (25, at $1,000 each)	25,000.00	25,000.00	26,156.25
*Tide Water Power Co. 5-percent first mortgage, series A, due Feb. 1, 1979: Nos. M51, M53, M54, M973, M1375, M2901, M2204–M3210, M3585,M3932–M3941, M4582, M5033–M5035, M5981, M5982 (30, at $1,000 each)	30,000.00	30,230.00	30,375.00
Vicksburg, Shreveport & Pacific R. R. Co. prior-lien mortgage 6-percent renewed at 5-percent gold, due Nov. 1, 1915, extended to Nov. 1, 1940: Nos. 561, 661, 794, 962, 1323 (5, at $1,000 each)	5,000.00	5,050.00	5,100.00
Total	2,952,900.00	2,806,507.50	2,707,357.50

Statement of assets and liabilities, June 30, 1936—Continued

ASSETS—Continued

[Securities purchased during the fiscal year 1935–36 are indicated thus (*)]

	Face value	Book value	Market value June 30, 1936
PREFERRED STOCKS			
Atchison, Topeka & Santa Fe Ry. Co. preferred, par $100, 200 shares	$20,000.00	$14,685.00	$20,525.00
Tidewater Associated Oil Co. 6-percent cumulative convertible preferred, par $100, 200 shares	20,000.00	16,815.00	21,050.00
Total	40,000.00	31,500.00	41,575.00
*Commercial Investment Trust Corporation convertible preference $4.25 stock, series of 1935, no par, 400 shares	....	41,025.00	45,200.00
Total preferred stocks	....	72,525.00	* 86,775.00
COMMON STOCKS			
American Can Co. common, par $25, 200 shares	5,000.00	18,515.00	26,100.00
American Cyanamid Co. B common, par $10, 500 shares (*300 shares purchased during 1935–36)	5,000.00	11,557.50	17,000.00
*American Telephone & Telegraph Co. common, par $100, 500 shares	50,000.00	86,625.00	83,750.0
Atchison, Topeka & Santa Fe Ry. Co. common, par $100, 300 shares	30,000.00	18,102.50	22,800.00
Continental Can Co., Inc., common, par $20, 320 shares (*20 share purchased during 1935–36)	6,400.00	14,535.00	24,480.00
Corn Products Refining Co. common, par $25, 250 shares	6,250.00	21,368.67	19,906.25
E. I. du Pont de Nemours & Co. common, par $20, 300 shares	6,000.00	23,507.50	44,850.00
Endicott Johnson Corporation common, par $50, 500 shares	25,000.00	30,037.50	31,000.00
General Motors Corporation common, par $10, 1,005 shares (*300 shares purchased and *5 shares received as a stock dividend during 1935–36)	10,050.00	37,705.00	66,706.87
Hazel-Atlas Glass Co. common, par $25, 500 shares (*250 shares purchased during 1935–36)	12,500.00	53,180.30	54,250.00
National Biscuit Co. common, par $10, 500 shares	5,000.00	27,106.98	17,687.50
Norfolk & Western Ry. Co., common, par $100, 160 shares	16,000.00	26,876.90	40,800.00
Northern Pacific Ry. Co. common, par $100, 400 shares	40,000.00	9,650.00	11,200.00
Pennsylvania R. R. Co. common, par $50, 500 shares	25,000.00	15,887.50	15,625.00
Socony-Vacuum Oil Co., Inc., common, par $15, 500 shares	7,500.00	6,262.50	6,500.00
Standard Oil Co. of New Jersey common, par $25, 500 shares	12,500.00	20,064.58	29,500.00
Union Oil Co. of California common, par $25, 500 shares	12,500.00	10,625.00	11,000.00
United States Smelting, Refining & Mining Co. common, par $50, 200 shares	10,000.00	14,285.00	17,100.00
United States Steel Corporation common, par $100, 400 shares	40,000.00	18,002.50	24,000.00
F. W. Woolworth Co. common, par $10, 500 shares	5,000.00	21,475.00	26,687.50
Total	329,700.00	485,369.93	590,943.12
Air Reduction Co., Inc., common, no par, 300 shares (100 shares exchanged for *300 shares during 1935–36)	....	10,412.50	20,550.00
American Chicle Co. common, no par, 300 shares	....	22,252.50	27,450.00
*Briggs Manufacturing Co. common, no par, 500 shares	....	30,212.50	25,375.00
Burroughs Adding Machine Co. common, no par, 500 shares	....	7,691.14	12,687.50
Caterpillar Tractor Co. common, no par, 1,000 shares (*200 shares purchased during 1935–36)	....	28,522.50	76,500.00
Columbia Gas & Electric Corporation common, no par, 200 shares	....	4,100.00	3,800.00
First National Stores, Inc., common, no par, 300 shares	....	17,236.50	14,175.00
General Electric Co. common, no par, 1,000 shares (*100 shares purchased during 1935–36)	....	24,732.50	37,500.00
Hercules Powder Co. common, no par, 300 shares	....	14,596.25	32,400.00
Libbey-Owens-Ford Glass Co. common, no par, 500 shares	....	15,066.07	28,500.00
*Loew's, Inc., common, no par, 500 shares	....	24,950.00	24,312.50
Parke, Davis & Co. common, no par, 500 shares	....	18,076.54	20,750.00
J. C. Penney Co. common, no par, 500 shares	....	22,637.50	42,687.50
Sears, Roebuck & Co. common, no par, 500 shares	....	20,250.00	37,000.00
Timken Roller Bearing Co. common, no par, 500 shares	....	14,350.00	30,000.00
Total	....	275,086.50	433,687.50
Total common stocks	....	760,456.43	1,024,630.62
Total common and preferred stocks	....	832,981.43	1,111,405.62
Total securities, including common and preferred stocks	....	3,641,488.93	3,818,773.12

Statement of assets and liabilities, June 30, 1936—Continued

SUMMARY

Book value of securities as above, including common and preferred stocks	$3,641,488.93
Bank balance June 30, 1936:	
American Security & Trust Co.: National Academy of Sciences proper	30,510.06
Bank of New York & Trust Co	11,738.62
Advanced to National Academy of Sciences, special	2,000.00
Property account (buildings and grounds at cost):	
Building	$1,448,644.82
Grounds	185,764.50
	1,634,409.32
Property account (equipment at cost)	10,894.93
Total assets	**5,331,041.86**

LIABILITIES

	Income	Capital		Income	Capital
General fund:			Marsh fund:		
Invested	$11,525.00		Invested		$20,000.00
Uninvested	7,419.94		Uninvested	$216.63	
Agassiz fund, invested		$50,000.00	Murray fund:		
Nealley fund, invested		19,555.55	Invested		6,000.00
Bache fund:			Uninvested	4,247.40	
Invested		59,852.37	National Parks problems,		
Uninvested	1,606.52	147.63	uninvested	1,604.21	
Billings fund, invested		22,313.39	Academy Proceedings:		
Building construction			Invested	995.75	
fund, uninvested	3,120.18		Uninvested	3,895.04	
Building site fund:			Joint Proceedings, unin-		
Invested	7,543.25		vested	6,142.39	
Uninvested	5,538.56		Emergency fund Proceed-		
Carnegie Corporation,			ings, uninvested	3,327.79	
special, uninvested	11,041.11		Scientific publication		
Carnegie endowment			fund, uninvested	1,686.04	
fund:			Smith fund:		
Invested		3,260,571.39	Invested	4,123.25	10,000.00
Uninvested	16,913.55	289,428.61	Uninvested	3,008.40	
John J. Carty Medal and			Thompson fund:		
Award:			Invested		10,000.00
Invested		25,000.00	Uninvested	2,868.79	
Uninvested	3,812.91		Walcott fund:		
Comstock fund:			Invested		5,000.00
Invested		12,327.50	Uninvested	507.18	
Uninvested	6,427.08	78.52	Watson fund:		
Consolidated fund, unin-			Invested	1,000.00	24,806.47
vested	1,363.77		Uninvested	2,299.89	193.53
Draper fund:			Appropriations under		
Invested		10,000.00	custodian of buildings		
Uninvested	1,143.86		and grounds, unin-		
Elliot fund:			vested	1,780.66	
Invested		8,000.00		[1]214,446.35	3,900,183.96
Uninvested	2,135.29				
Fund for oceanographic			Total income		[1]214,446.53
research, uninvested	6,990.89		Total capital		3,900,183.96
Gibbs fund:			Total income and		
Invested		5,545.50	capital		3,685,737.61
Uninvested	2,049.40		Capital invested in		
Gould fund:			property		1,634,409.32
Invested	6,555.00	19,522.50	Capital invested in		
Uninvested	8,467.56	477.50	equipment		10,894.93
Grand Canyon project,			Total liabilities		5,331,041.86
uninvested	24.19				
Hale lectureship, unin-				Income	Capital
vested	385.55				
Hartley fund:			Consolidated investment		
Invested		1,200.00	fund:		
Uninvested	380.56		Invested		232,666.54
Joseph Henry fund:			Uninvested	1,363.77	111.49
Invested		40,163.50	Total	1,363.77	232,777.04
Uninvested	877.76				
Investment reserve fund,					
uninvested	[1]358,152.30				

[1] Debit.

General fund, National Academy of Sciences, from July 1, 1935, to June 30, 1936

RECEIPTS

	Budget, July 1, 1935 to June 30, 1936	Actually received, July 1, 1935 to June 30, 1936	Budget balance, June 30, 1936
Interest on investments:			
Agassiz fund	$2,500.00	$3,015.16	[1] $515.16
Nealley fund	750.00	1,011.80	[1] 261.80
Annual dues from members	1,375.00	1,380.00	[1] 5.00
Refund		4.00	[1] 4.00
Total	4,625.00	5,410.96	[1] 785.96
Balance from previous year	16,500.00	18,592.57	[1] 2,092.57
Total	21,125.00	24,003.53	[1] 2,878.53

DISBURSEMENTS

	Budget, July 1, 1935 to June 30, 1936	Actually disbursed, July 1, 1935 to June 30, 1936	Budget balance, June 30, 1936
Treasurer's office:			
Auditor's fees	$200.00	$200.00	
Bond of treasurer	25.00	25.00	
Miscellaneous expenses	500.00	277.96	$222.04
Transfer to investment reserve fund, 5 percent of income	375.00	201.35	173.65
Total	1,100.00	704.31	395.69
Home secretary's office:			
Executive secretary's salary	600.00	600.00	
Stationery and miscellaneous office expenses	400.00	397.69	2.31
Reference books	50.00	42.35	7.65
Binding	50.00		50.00
Printing, multigraphing, and engraving	250.00	190.47	59.53
Express and telegrams	150.00	79.26	70.74
Total	1,500.00	1,309.77	190.23
Annual meeting	900.00	775.40	124.60
Autumn meeting	500.00	226.98	273.02
Total	1,400.00	1,002.38	397.62
Election of members	350.00	322.85	27.15
Memoirs, editorial	200.00	79.00	121.00
Printing of Biographical Memoirs	900.00	899.35	.65
Current publications, preparation for distribution	150.00	105.36	44.64
Postage, regular	250.00	250.00	
Contingent fund	400.00	23.65	376.35
Library binding	500.00		500.00
Expenses of members attending executive committee of council of the Academy	300.00	174.42	125.58
Total	3,050.00	1,854.63	1,195.37
Accrued interest on bonds bought		187.50	[1] 187.50
Total for all	7,050.00	5,058.59	1,991.41
Surplus	14,075.00	18,944.94	
Grand total	21,125.00	24,003.53	

[1] In excess of budget.

Appropriations under custodian of buildings and grounds, July 1, 1935, to June 30, 1936

RECEIPTS

	Budget July 1, 1935, to June 30, 1936	Actually received July 1, 1935, to June 30, 1936	Budget balance June 30, 1936
From Carnegie endowment fund	$44,667.00	$44,667.00	
From Carnegie endowment fund for previous year	2,174.78	2,174.78	
Total	46,841.78	46,841.78	

Appropriations under custodian of buildings and grounds, July 1, 1935, to June 30, 1936—Continued

DISBURSEMENTS

	Budget July 1, 1935 to June 30, 1936	Actually disbursed, July 1, 1935 to June 30, 1936	Budget balance, June 30, 1936
Salaries, office of custodian of buildings and grounds	$6,780.00	$6,780.00	
Salaries, employees, building	23,210.00	23,179.61	$30.39
Coal	1,500.00	1,425.61	74.39
Electricity	1,815.00	1,773.79	41.21
Gas	20.00	9.00	11.00
Contingent fund, maintenance of building	5,923.22	5,510.39	412.83
Maintenance of exhibits	3,925.00	3,467.94	457.06
Total	43,173.22	42,146.34	1,026.88
Insurance, 1933–37	1,493.78	828.74	1,760.66

Balance July 1, 1935	$1,095.62
Appropriated July 1, 1935	1,493.78
	2,589.40
Expended July 1, 1935, to June 30, 1936	828.74
Balance June 30, 1936	1,760.66

	Budget	Actually disbursed	Budget balance
Total	44,667.00	42,975.08	2,787.54

NOTE.—Reversions June 30, 1936, amounting to $1,026.88, have been credited to "Carnegie endowment fund, N. A. S., 1936."

Condensed statement of receipts and disbursements, National Academy of Sciences, July 1, 1935, to June 30, 1936

RECEIPTS

Balance July 1, 1935, as per last report			$40,562.76
Cash receipts:			
Academy Proceedings:			
Annual dues	$1,380.00		
Reprints and separates	113.25		
		$1,493.25	
Joint Proceedings:			
Subscriptions	1,920.77		
Reprints and separates	1,692.89		
National Research Council	2,500.00		
		6,113.66	
General fund:			
Annual dues	1,380.00		
Refund	4.00		
		1,384.00	
Electric current change over: From Potomac Electric Power Co		8,769.00	
Fund for oceanographic research: Sale of Oceanography		11.25	
Scientific publication fund: Royalties on Oceanography		3.12	
Total income from investments		161,153.70	
Bache fund: E. R. Becker, refund		32.50	
Cash sale of bonds, Home Owners Loan Corporation		173.99	
			179,134.47
Total			219,697.23

DISBURSEMENTS

General fund:		
Treasurer's office:		
Auditor's fees	$200.00	
Bond of treasurer	25.00	
Miscellaneous expenses (not including $149.39 fees to financial advisers)	128.57	
		$353.57

DISBURSEMENTS—continued

General fund—Continued.
  Home secretary's office:

Executive secretary's salary	$600.00	
Stationery and miscellaneous office expenses	397.69	
Reference books	42.35	
Binding		
Printing, multigraphing, and engraving	190.47	
Express and telegrams	79.26	
		$1,309.77
Annual meeting	775.40	
Autumn meeting	226.98	
Election of members	322.85	
Memoirs, editorial	79.00	
Printing of Biographical Memoirs	899.35	
Current publications, preparation for distribution	105.36	
Postage, regular	250.00	
Contingent fund	23.65	
Expenses of members attending executive meetings of council of the Academy	174.42	
		2,857.01
		$4,520.35

Appropriations for maintenance of buildings and grounds, under custodian of buildings and grounds:		
Salaries, office of custodian of buildings and grounds	6,780.00	
Salaries, employees, building	23,179.61	
Coal	1,425.61	
Electricity	1,773.79	
Gas	9.00	
Contingent fund, maintenance of building	5,510.39	
Maintenance of exhibits	3,467.94	
Insurance, 1933–37	828.74	
		42,975.08
Fees to financial advisers		6,211.65
To National Research Council for general maintenance expenses		43,466.18
Joint Proceedings:		
Salary, managing editor	$750.00	
Printing and distributing	7,651.11	
Expenses:		
Boston office	460.00	
Washington office	209.83	
		9,070.94
Fund for oceanographic research: Expenses of T. Wayland Vaughan		105.48
Carnegie Corporation, special:		
Committee on the library	$11.00	
Government relations allotment	99.34	
Attorney's fees for examining deeds of trust	500.00	
Expenses of members of Academy council attending special meetings	58.32	
		668.66
D. C. unemployment compensation tax:		
Tax on Academy salaries		140.13
National Parks problems:		
Painting of Crater Lake	$150.00	
Miscellaneous expenses	106.62	
		256.62
Carnegie endowment fund: Taxes, insurance, and commissions on real estate		5,466.57
Consolidated fund: Real-estate taxes		393.36
Advance for purchase of bonds		55,000.00
Electric current change-over: Purchase of new electrical equipment		8,769.00

DISBURSEMENTS—continued

Payments from trust and other funds:

Bache fund:

Hudson Hoagland, grant	$450.00	
Barnard Burks, grant	100.00	
Eric Ponder, grant	1,000.00	
Malcolm Dale, grant	600.00	
Demarest Davenport, grant	300.00	
Robert R. McMath, grant	720.00	
Miscellaneous expenses	2.71	
		$3,172.71

Draper fund:

Theodore E. Sterne, grant	300.00	
Frank E. Ross, grant	300.00	
		600.00
Gibbs fund: A. C. Cope, grant		300.00

Gould fund:

Real-estate taxes, commissions, and repairs	$35.46	
Harlan T. Stetson, grant	169.50	
University of California, grant	500.00	
S. A. Mitchell, grant	500.00	
Frank Schlesinger, grant	765.00	
		1,969.96
Hartley fund: Medals and medal boxes		193.88

Joseph Henry fund:

G. W. Keitt, grant	$400.00	
F. A. Jenkins, grant	125.00	
Simon Freed, grant	300.00	
M. G. Rutten, grant	61.56	
Elsa G. Allen, grant	250.00	
T. T. Chen, grant	200.00	
Francis Bitter, grant	900.00	
		2,236.56

Marsh fund:

Russell M. Logie, grants	400.00	
Harry S. Ladd, grant	400.00	
William C. Darrah, grant	250.00	
Albert Elmer Wood, grant	250.00	
International Hydrographic Bureau, grant	125.00	
		1,425.00
Murray fund: Medals and medal boxes		304.82
Smith fund: Thomas C. Poulter, grant		450.00

Watson fund:

A. O. Leuschner, grant	$1,425.00	
Real estate taxes and commissions	65.22	
		1,490.22
Total payments from trust and other funds		$12,143.15

Total disbursements	189,187.17
Balance June 30, 1936	30,510.06
Grand total	219,697.23

NATIONAL RESEARCH COUNCIL

The disbursements of the National Research Council, under the authority of the National Academy of Sciences, during the year ended June 30, 1936, amounted to $565,831.64. Interest received on temporary investment amounted to $2,170.40.

The investment reserve fund on June 30, 1936, stood at $1,404.20, an increase for the year of $653.87.

The book value of securities held by the Council on June 30, 1936, was $130,884.25. The following shows the current interest yield on these bonds, according to the valuation used:

	Amount	Yield percent
Face value of bonds held	$137,333.00	3.53
Book value of bonds held	130,884.25	3.71
Market value, June 30, 1936, of bonds held (including 1 piece of real estate for $25,000, acquired under foreclosure)	137,840.50	3.52

The receipts from various organizations during the year for investigations to be made in cooperation with the National Bureau of Standards amounted to $9,193.33.

During the fiscal year ended June 30, 1936, the activities of the Council were supported by funds from various sources of which the principal are listed below:

(1) For general maintenance expenses of the National Research Council:

    From the Carnegie endowment fund $43,466.18
    From the Rockefeller Foundation, 1936 10,000.00
    From the Carnegie Corporation of New York, emergency grant, 1936 (received during the previous fiscal year) 30,000.00

        Total available for year ending June 30, 1936 83,466.18

    The Carnegie Corporation of New York has made an emergency grant of $30,000 to be available for the fiscal year 1937, and this amount was received during the past fiscal year.

    The above contributions were the only ones received for the general support of the National Research Council. The Council has disbursed in addition other funds contributed by a large number of organizations and individuals for specific purposes named by the donors. The diversity of these research projects is indicated by the following list of receipts, which are several times larger than receipts for general maintenance.

(2) From the Rockefeller Foundation:

    For National Research fellowships in physics, chemistry, and mathematics, year 1936 (R. F. 34169) 49,573.90
    For fellowships in medicine, year 1936 (R. F. 34164) 15,866.85
    For fellowships in the biological sciences, year 1935 (R. F. 31053) 10,499.19
    For the same purpose, year 1936 (R. F. 34169) 46,315.82
    For international biological abstracts, year 1935 (R. F. 34152) 28,248.74
    For the same purpose, years 1935–37 (R. F. 35123) 3,640.97
    For indices of Biological Abstracts, year 1935 (R. F. 34152) 10,000.00
    For sex-research fund, year 1936 71,573.79
    For committee on drug addiction, Rockefeller Foundation, year 1935 23,622.13
    For the same purpose, year 1936 27,169.98
    For committee on radiation, year 1936 24,399.13
    For research aid fund years 1932–33 6,000.00
    For the same purpose, years 1935–37 36,000.00
    For annual tables 1,000.00
    For central purposes, National Research Council, Rockefeller Foundation, years 1936–37 35,000.00

        Total from the Rockefeller Foundation 388,910.50

(3) From the General Education Board:

Monographs in child development, 1936_____	$1,500.00
Child Development Society, General Education Board, 1936__	1,750.00

Total from the General Education Board_____ 3,250.00

(4) From various organizations for the Highway Research Board___ 26,324.38

(5) From Navy Department for airships investigation_____ 5,939.10

(6) From various organizations for work to be conducted in cooperation with National Bureau of Standards:

For problems of refrigeration_____	403.33
For acoustic properties of materials_____	225.00
For thermal properties of liquids_____	1,065.00
For fire resistance of materials_____	2,500.00
For thermal investigations_____	850.00
For ignition research_____	4,150.00

Total_____ 9,193.33

(7) From various organizations:

For bibliography of economic geology_____	505.00
For research fund, committee on sedimentation_____	123.85
For survey of tropical diseases_____	2,415.38
For committee on drug addiction, Squibb fellowships, 1936__	1,400.00
For committee on drug addiction, Merck fellowship, 1936____	700.00
For committee on drug addiction, Mallinckrodt fellowship, 1936 _____	1,000.00
For committee on endocrinology_____	2,000.00
For National Live Stock and Meat Board fellowships_____	1,000.00
For national intelligence tests_____	863.36
For child development abstracts_____	1,937.58
For royalties, International Critical Tables_____	1,224.00

Total receipts during the year from all sources_____ 541,073.62

Receipts and disbursements, National Research Council, from July 1, 1935, to June 30, 1936

RECEIPTS

Appropriation	Received during year	Previously reported	Transfers and other credits	Budget	Budget balance June 30, 1936
Rockefeller Foundation:					
National research fellowships (R. F. 34169) 1936_____	$49,573.90	$150.00	_____	$50,000.00	$276.10
Research fellowships in medicine (R. F. 34164) 1936_____	15,866.85	_____	_____	20,000.00	4,133.15
Fellowships in the biological sciences (R. F. 31053) 1935_____	10,499.19	27,000.81	_____	37,500.00	_____
Fellowships in the biological sciences (R. F. 34169) 1936_____	46,315.82	_____	_____	50,000.00	3,684.18
International Biological Abstracts (R. F. 34152) 1935_____	28,248.74	34,449.02	_____	65,000.00	2,302.24
International biological abstracts (R. F. 35123) 1935–37_____	3,640.97	_____	_____	40,000.00	36,359.03
Indices of Biological Abstracts (R. F. 34152) 1935_____	10,000.00	_____	_____	10,000.00	_____
Sex research fund, 1936_____	71,573.79	_____	$1,925.89	73,499.68	_____
Committee on drug addiction, Rockefeller Foundation, 1935_____	23,622.13	26,377.87	_____	50,000.00	_____
Committee on drug addiction, Rockefeller Foundation, 1936_____	27,169.98	_____	_____	27,169.98	_____
Committee on radiation, 1936_____	24,399.13	_____	_____	24,399.13	_____
Research aid fund (R. F. 32010) 1932–33__	6,000.00	60,447.69	_____	66,447.69	_____
Research aid fund (R. F. 34172) 1935–37__	36,000.00	25,000.00	102.07	61,102.07	_____
Central purposes of National Research Council, Rockefeller Foundation, 1936–37_____	35,000.00	_____	4,702.55	39,702.55	_____

Receipts and disbursements, National Research Council, from July 1, 1935, to June 30, 1936—Continued

RECEIPTS—Continued

Appropriation	Received during year	Previously reported	Transfers and other credits	Budget	Budget balance June 30, 1936
General Education Board:					
Monographs in child development, 1936..	$1,500.00	....	....	$1,500.00	....
Child Development Society, General Education Board, 1936..............	1,750.00	....	....	1,750.00	....
Rotating fund, physics committees...........	1,224.55	$15,131.13	....	16,355.68	....
Highway Research Board, 1935.............	1,250.00	23,812.05	....	25,062.05	....
Highway Research Board, 1936.............	24,074.38	....	$6,752.86	30,827.24	....
Bibliography of economic geology...........	505.00	32,052.22	....	32,557.22	....
Research fund, committee on sedimentation..	123.85	2,484.27	....	2,608.12	....
Committee on drug addiction, Squibb fellowships, 1936...................	1,400.00	....	....	1,400.00	....
Survey of tropical diseases................	2,415.38	2,503.00	....	4,918.38	....
Committee on drug addiction, Merck fellowship, 1936....................	700.00	....	....	700.00	....
Committee on drug addiction, Mallinckrodt fellowship, 1936................	1,000.00	....	....	1,000.00	....
Committee on endocrinology.............	2,000.00	....	....	2,000.00	....
National Live Stock and Meat Board fellowships...................	1,000.00	48,788.87	....	49,788.87	....
National intelligence tests, 1921..........	863.36	25,260.70	....	26,124.06	....
Child development abstracts.............	1,937.58	13,484.69	....	15,422.27	....
International Critical Tables.............	143.11	335,319.75	1,224.00	336,686.86	....
Royalty account, International Critical Tables.....................	1,224.00	52,621.34	....	53,845.34	....
Annual tables......................	1,000.00	53,747.61	....	54,747.61	....
Navy Department appropriation for air-ships investigation..............	5,939.10	1,017.88	....	6,956.98	....
Problems of refrigeration.............	403.33	984.19	....	1,387.52	....
Acoustic properties of materials.........	225.00	23,252.99	....	23,477.99	....
Thermal properties of liquids...........	1,065.00	7,873.07	....	8,938.07	....
Fire resistance of materials.............	2,500.00	12,190.00	....	14,690.00	....
Thermal investigations...............	850.00	2,202.91	....	3,052.91	....
Ignition research....................	4,150.00	....	....	4,150.00	....
Carnegie endowment fund.............	43,466.18	....	180.15	43,646.33	....
Rockefeller Foundation, National Research Council, 1936..................	10,000.00	....	....	10,000.00	....
Carnegie Corporation of New York, emergency grant, 1937.............	30,000.00	....	....	30,000.00	....
Total............................	530,620.32	826,152.06	14,887.52	1,418,414.60	$46,754.70
Sale of bonds.......................	388.55	....	....	....	....
Interest on bonds....................	2,170.40	....	....	....	....
Miscellaneous receipts...............	3,677.83	....	....	....	....
Reimbursements....................	4,216.52	....	....	....	....
Total receipts...................	541,073.62	....	....	....	....
July 1, 1935, cash in banks..............	68,954.74	....	....	....	....
Grand total.....................	610,028.36	....	....	....	....

DISBURSEMENTS

Division	Disbursed during year	Previously reported	Reversions and other charges	Budget	Budget balance June 30, 1936
I. Federal relations:					
General maintenance, 1936........	....	....	$50.00	$50.00	....
II. Foreign relations:					
General maintenance, 1936........	$61.89	....	38.11	100.00	....
Annual dues, International Union of Biological Sciences, 1936......	265.04	....	9.96	275.00	....
III. States relations:					
General maintenance, 1936........	....	....	50.00	50.00	....
IV. Educational relations:					
General maintenance, 1936........	13.34	....	86.66	100.00	....
Division of educational relations, Commonwealth Fund...........	....	$7,304.01	....	8,051.55	$747.54

Receipts and disbursements, National Research Council, from July 1, 1935, to June 30, 1936—Continued

DISBURSEMENTS—Continued

Division	Disbursed during year	Previously reported	Reversions and other charges	Budget	Budget balance June 30, 1936
V. Physical sciences:					
General maintenance, 1936	$422.32		$427.18	$900.00	$50.50
Revolving fund for publication of mathematical books		$4,180.81		5,623.12	1,442.31
Physics committees, 1932		912.50		1,500.00	587.50
Research fellowships (R. F. 31053) 1935	6,368.87	31,131.13		37,500.00	
Research fellowships (R. F. 34169) 1936	45,774.88	150.00		50,102.76	4,177.88
Rotating fund, physics committees	603.04	10,007.36		16,355.63	5,745.28
VI. Engineering and industrial research:					
General maintenance, 1935	57.92	1,134.94	7.14	1,200.00	
General maintenance, 1936	1,653.79		1.79	1,701.85	46.27
Highway Research Board, 1935		18,309.10		25,062.05	
Highway Research Board, 1936	26,522.12		5,752.66	30,827.24	4,305.12
Structural steel investigation	1,312.31	16,724.31		22,526.68	4,490.06
Heat transmission	59.48	42,024.54		43,154.77	1,073.75
Fundamental research in welding	72.48	1,877.52		1,950.00	
Committee on electrical insulation, 1935	62.35	82.96		215.00	69.69
VII. Chemistry and chemical technology:					
General maintenance, 1936	975.74		224.26	1,200.00	
VIII. Geology and geography:					
General maintenance, 1936	1,399.95		.05	1,460.00	
Bibliography of economic geology	2,795.82	29,039.49		32,557.22	721.91
Research fund, committee on sedimentation	532.00	1,179.34		2,608.12	896.78
Committee on stratigraphy	28.22			75.00	46.78
IX. Medical sciences:					
General maintenance, 1936	662.51		537.49	1,200.00	
Sex research fund, 1935	376.25	63,074.11	1,925.89	65,376.25	
Sex research fund, 1936	72,968.76			73,499.68	530.92
Fellowships in Medicine (R. F. 33041) 1935	1,231.44	14,014.39		15,245.83	
Fellowships in medicine (R. F. 34164) 1936	13,147.61			20,000.00	6,852.39
Committee on drug addiction, Squibb fellowships, 1935	651.08	748.92		1,400.00	
Committee on drug addiction, Squibb fellowships, 1936	748.00			1,400.00	652.00
Committee on drug addiction, Rockefeller Foundation, 1935	26,482.09	23,517.91		50,000.00	
Committee on drug addiction, Rockefeller Foundation, 1936	24,107.91			27,169.98	3,062.07
Survey of tropical diseases	3,006.24	1,912.14		4,918.38	
Committee on drug addiction, Merck fellowship, 1936	700.00			700.00	
Committee on drug addiction, Mallinckrodt fellowship, 1936	1,000.00			1,000.00	
Committee on endocrinology	87.31			2,000.00	1,912.69
X. Biology and agriculture:					
General maintenance, 1936	797.77		55.98	1,103.75	250.00
Committee on forestry	57.86	7,295.43		10,029.99	2,676.71
Food and nutrition committee		9,219.18		9,675.00	455.82
Fellowships in the biological sciences (R. F. 31053) 1935	18,022.56	19,732.44		37,755.00	
Fellowships in the biological sciences (R. F. 34169) 1936	34,560.36			50,077.50	15,517.14
National Live Stock and Meat Board fellowships	1,375.00	47,700.53		49,788.87	713.34
International biological abstracts (R. F. 34152) 1935	32,240.31	31,690.84		65,000.00	1,068.85
International biological abstracts (R. F. 35123) 1936–37	4,346.47			40,000.00	35,653.53
National committee on botanical nomenclature	87.00	2,973.25		3,060.85	
Pharmaceutical researches	42.31	265.16		585.00	277.53
Effects of radiation on living organisms	275.33	131,278.26		131,553.59	
Indices of Biological Abstracts (R. F. 34152) 1935	6,885.45	3,114.55		10,000.00	
Mitogenetic radiation (R. F. 33108)	701.72	9,298.28		10,000.00	
Committee on radiation	76.43	4,763.28		4,839.71	
Committee on radiation (R. F. 35095) 1936	23,385.47			24,399.13	1,013.66

Receipts and disbursements, National Research Council, from July 1, 1935, to June 30, 1936—Continued

DISBURSEMENTS—Continued

Division	Disbursed during year	Previously reported	Reversions and other charges	Budget	Budget balance June 30, 1936
XI. Anthropology and psychology:					
General maintenance, 1936	$1,053.68		$146.32	$1,200.00	
National intelligence tests, 1921		$17,026.14	1,000.00	26,124.06	$8,097.92
Visual limitations for motorists	.67	5,662.26		5,662.93	
Child development abstracts	3,785.74	8,680.27		15,422.27	2,956.26
Psychiatric investigations	1,010.00	7,085.23		10,000.00	1,904.77
Monographs in child development, General Education Board, 1936				1,500.00	1,500.00
Child Development Society, General Education Board, 1936	1,619.90			1,750.00	130.10
Field handbook of individual differences	100.00			1,000.00	900.00
Expenses and supplies, 1935	216.61	4,127.70	1.96	4,346.27	
Expenses and supplies, 1936	3,566.91		424.82	4,257.25	265.52
New equipment, general, 1935	131.41	748.00	5.59	885.00	
New equipment, general, 1936	210.38		289.62	500.00	
Salaries, 1935	1.50	72,493.50		72,495.00	
Salaries, 1936	74,721.72		713.03	75,440.00	5.25
Telephone and telegraph, 1935	140.87	2,915.25		3,256.63	
Telephone and telegraph, 1936	1,807.20		571.33	2,628.53	250.00
Executive board:					
General maintenance, 1936	1,631.52		9.66	1,641.18	
American Geophysical Union, general maintenance, 1936	400.00			400.00	
Publications and publicity:					
General maintenance, 1935	400.00	1,106.62		1,506.62	
General maintenance, 1936	830.23	2,167.56		3,000.00	2.21
National Academy Proceedings and subscriptions, 1936	2,500.00			2,500.00	
International auxiliary language		9,630.02		10,065.00	434.98
International Critical Tables		334,882.63		336,686.86	1,804.23
Royalty account, International Critical Tables		52,621.34	1,224.00	53,845.34	
Annual tables	492.35	53,626.01		54,747.61	629.25
Auditor's fees, 1935	300.00			300.00	
Research aid fund	1,995.23	99,178.47		101,173.70	
Research aid fund, 1932–33	5,540.73	58,426.06		66,447.69	2,480.90
Research aid fund, 1933	402.85	49,677.50		50,080.35	
Research aid fund, 1934	3,112.62	46,950.00		50,062.62	
Research aid fund, 1935–37	32,738.93	22,131.54		61,102.07	6,231.60
Attorney's fees, 1936	200.00		100.00	300.00	
Science Advisory Board	7,231.51	42,793.49		50,025.00	
Navy department appropriation for airships investigation	5,939.10	1,017.88		6,956.98	
D. C. unemployment compensation tax, 1936	409.89		60.00	564.34	94.45
Research aid funds, refunds				142.39	142.39
Conferences, special studies and committees organized by National Research Council, 1936–37	797.45		4,702.55	5,500.00	
Problems of refrigeration	563.32	108.33		1,387.52	715.87
Investigations on steel structures	200.52	15,876.44		16,076.96	
Impermanency of records	3,080.05	175.00		5,000.00	1,744.95
Acoustic properties of materials	437.33	22,660.55		23,477.99	380.11
Investigation of physics of plumbing systems	80.15	2,726.66		3,200.00	393.19
Thermal properties of liquids	310.86	7,861.19		8,938.07	766.02
Fire resistance of materials	1,463.30	12,174.52		14,690.00	1,052.18
Current meter investigations	1,591.90	1,149.86		3,209.73	467.97
Thermal investigations	20.61	1,532.70		3,052.91	1,499.60
Soil corrosion investigation	843.50	356.50		1,200.00	
Ignition reserach	4,028.62			4,150.00	121.38
Research Information Service:					
General maintenance, 1935	183.65	9,143.75	57.60	9,395.00	10.00
General maintenance, 1936	591.83		8,524.67	9,130.50	14.00
Book fund, research information service	142.26			173.69	31.43
Investment reserve fund	2.35		532.61	1,939.16	1,404.20
Total	523,831.64	1,501,369.74	28,731.64	2,185,431.77	131,498.75
Purchase of bonds	42,000.00				
Total disbursements	565,831.64				
June 30, 1936, cash in banks	44,196.72				
Grand total	610,028.36				

National Research Council condensed balance sheet as of June 30, 1936

ASSETS

[Securities purchased during the fiscal year 1935-36 are indicated thus (*)]

Securities	Face value	Book value	Market value June 30, 1936
General maintenance fund:			
Mortgage notes secured by first mortgage on real estate..........	$10,333.00	$10,333.00	$10,333.00
Real estate owned 322-324 West 41st St., New York, N. Y......	25,000.00	25,000.00	25,000.00
*Baltimore & Ohio Railroad Co., 5 percent refunding and general mortgage, series A, due Dec. 1, 1995; Nos. M362, M8185, M24349, M37088, M45801; 5 at $1,000 each..................	5,000.00	3,800.00	4,275.00
Canadian Pacific Railway Co., 4 percent perpetual consolidated debentures; Nos. G34505, G34506; 2 at $1,000 each...............	2,000.00	1,765.00	1,895.00
Government of the Argentine Nation, 6 percent external sinking-fund gold bonds, due June 1, 1959; Nos. M16652, M33319-M33322; 5 at $1,000 each.................................	5,000.00	5,017.50	5,037.50
Kingdom of Norway, 6 percent, 20-year external loan sinking fund gold bonds, due Aug. 1, 1944; nos. 621, 1361, 1362, 16940-16944, 21025, 24896; 10 at $1,000 each..................	10,000.00	10,395.00	10,662.50
*New York Central Railroad Co., 4 percent, consolidated mortgage, series A, due Feb. 1, 1998; Nos. 38525-38528, 45379, 45380, 45387-45405; 25 at $1,000 each..................	25,000.00	21,343.75	24,000.00
Pennsylvania Power & Light Co., 4½ percent first mortgage bonds, due Apr. 1, 1981; nos. 50364-50379; 16 at $1,000 each......	16,000.00	15,400.00	17,180.00
*Southern Railway Co., 5 percent first consolidated mortgage, due July 1, 1994; Nos. 50909-50913; 5 at $1,000 each..........	5,000.00	4,575.00	5,162.50
Twelve Federal Land Banks 3¼ percent consolidated Federal farm loan bonds, due May 1, 1955; Nos. 46152B-46156F, 46157H, 46158J-46160L, 46161A-46166F, 46167H, 46168J, 46170L, 46171A-46176F, 46177H, 46178J; 26 at $1,000 each..................	26,000.00	26,195.00	26,715.00
International Critical Tables:			
Canadian Pacific Railway Co., 4 percent perpetual consolidated debentures; Nos. G47151-G47153, G48954, G86931, G88057-G88059; 8 at $1,000 each.............................	8,000.00	7,060.00	7,580.00
Total..	137,333.00	130,884.25	137,840.50

SUMMARY

Total book value of securities as above.. $130,884.25
Cash in banks June 30, 1936.. 44,196.72
Due from Bank of New York & Trust Co.. 16,895.81
Income receivable as shown under column "Budget balance"—receipts, page 100........ 46,754.70
National Academy of Sciences, special, advances from various funds.................. 8,000.00
Property account—equipment at cost... 34,047.18

Total assets... 280,778.66

LIABILITIES

Capital invested in property... $34,047.18
Current liabilities:
Division appropriations as shown under column "Budget balance"—disbursements, page 102.. 131,498.75
Unappropriated fund, general... 33,970.18
National Academy of Sciences, special... 10,000.00
Carnegie Corporation of New York—emergency grant, 1937......................... 30,000.00
International Critical Tables: Canadian Pacific Railway Co., 4 percent debentures...... 7,060.00
Central purposes of the National Research Council, Rockefeller Foundation, 1936-37..... 34,202.55

Total liabilities... 280,778.66

JULY 31, 1936.

A'RTHUR KEITH, *Treasurer.*

REPORT OF THE AUDITING COMMITTEE

SEPTEMBER 28, 1936.

Dr. FRANK R. LILLIE,
President, National Academy of Sciences, Washington, D. C.

DEAR PRESIDENT LILLIE: Following recent past practice authorized by section 5, article V, of the bylaws of the Academy, the auditing committee engaged the services of a firm of certified public accountants, William L. Yaeger & Co., to prepare a detailed audit of the treasurer's accounts. This firm, after a systematic examination of the accounts of the treasurer of the Academy and of the

Research Council and of all securities, has submitted a report of its findings, with exhibits attached. This report is transmitted herewith as a part of the auditing committee's report for the records of the Academy and the Council.

The accountants summarize their report as follows:

"Pursuant to agreement, we have during the month of July audited the accounts of the treasurer of the National Academy of Sciences and the accounts of the treasurer of the National Research Council.

"We have verified the record of receipts and disbursements maintained by the treasurer and the agreement of book and bank balances.

"We have examined all securities in the custody of the treasurer and the custodian of securities, the Bank of New York & Trust Co., and found them to agree with the book records and the exhibit B attached hereto.

"We have compared the stated income of such securities with the receipts of record and have set forth the result on exhibit B.

"We have examined all vouchers covering disbursements for account of the Academy, including the National Research Council, together with the authority therefor, and have compared them with the treasurer's record of expenditures.

"We have examined and verified the account of the Academy with each trust fund.

"We found the books of account well and accurately kept and the securities in charge of the trustee conveniently filed as well as securely cared for.

"All information requested by your auditors was promptly and courteously furnished.

"We have examined the report presented by the treasurer and found it to agree with the books and with the exhibits submitted herewith."

The committee accepts the opinion of the accountants that the treasurer's report correctly sets forth the financial condition of the Academy and the National Research Council and is an accurate statement of financial operations for the fiscal year 1936.

Very truly yours,

N. L. BOWEN.
W. H. HOWELL.
C. S. HUDSON, *Chairman.*

NATIONAL ACADEMY OF SCIENCES

1. CONSTITUTION

[As amended and adopted Apr. 17, 1872, and further amended Apr. 20, 1875; Apr. 21, 1881; Apr. 19, 1882; Apr. 18, 1883; Apr. 19, 1888; Apr. 18, 1895; Apr. 20, 1899; Apr. 17, 1902; Apr. 18, 1906; Nov. 20, 1906; Apr. 17, 1907; Nov. 20, 1907; Apr. 20, 1911; Apr. 16, 1912; Apr. 21, 1915; Nov. 11, 1924; Nov. 9, 1925; Oct. 18, 1927; Nov. 18, 1929; Sept. 18, 1930; Apr. 24, 1933; Apr. 27, 1936]

PREAMBLE

Empowered by the act of incorporation enacted by Congress, and approved by the President of the United States on the 3d day of March, A. D. 1863, and in conformity with amendments to said act approved July 14, 1870, June 20, 1884, and May 27, 1914, the National Academy of Sciences adopts the following amended constitution and bylaws:

ARTICLE I.—OF MEMBERS

SECTION 1. The Academy shall consist of members, members emeriti, and foreign associates. Members must be citizens of the United States.

SEC. 2. Members who, from age or inability to attend the meetings of the Academy, wish to resign the duties of active membership may, at their own request, be transferred to the roll of members emeriti by a vote of the Academy.

SEC. 3. The Academy may elect 50 foreign associates.

SEC. 4. Members emeriti and foreign associates shall have the privilege of attending the meetings and of reading and communicating papers to the Academy, but shall take no part in its business, shall not be subject to its assessments, and shall be entitled to a copy of the publications of the Academy.

ARTICLE II.—OF THE OFFICERS

SECTION 1. The officers of the Academy shall be a president, a vice president, a foreign secretary, a home secretary, and a treasurer, all of whom shall be elected for a term of 4 years, by a majority of votes present, at the annual meeting of the year in which the current terms expire. The date of expiration of the terms of office shall be June 30. In case of a vacancy the election shall be held in the same manner at the meeting when such vacancy occurs or at the next stated meeting thereafter, as the Academy may direct, and shall be for a term expiring on June 30 of the fourth year after that in which the election takes place. A vacancy in the office of treasurer or home secretary may, however, be filled by appointment of the president of the Academy until the next stated meeting of the Academy.

COUNCIL

SEC. 2. The·officers of the Academy, together with six members to be elected by the Academy, and the chief executive officer of the National Research Council (provided he be a member of the Academy) shall constitute a council for the transaction of such business as may be assigned to them by the constitution or the Academy. .

EXECUTIVE COMMITTEE

SEC. 3. There shall be an executive committee of the council of the Academy, composed of seven members, consisting of the president and vice president of the Academy, the chief executive officer of the National Research Council (provided he be a member of the Academy), the home secretary of the Academy, the treasurer of the Academy, and additional members of the council of the Academy appointed by the president.

Their term as members of the executive committee shall be coterminous with the term of their other office.

Except those powers dealing with nominations to membership in the Academy, the executive committee between the meetings of the council shall have all the powers of the council of the Academy, unless otherwise ordered by the council.

The members of the executive committee of the Academy shall by virtue of their office be members of the executive board of the National Research Council and shall represent the Academy at all its meetings.

The president and home secretary of the Academy shall, respectively, be chairman and secretary of the executive committee.

In the absence of the president and the vice president or home secretary the executive committee may select from among its members a chairman or a secretary pro tem.

The executive committee shall keep regular minutes and shall report all of its proceedings to the council of the Academy for their information.

Unless otherwise ordered by the council of the Academy or the executive committee, the executive committee shall meet once in each calendar month, and a special meeting may be called at any time by authority of the chairman, on reasonable notice.

Four members of the executive committee shall constitute a quorum. Letter ballots shall not be valid unless ratified at a meeting.

CUSTODIAN OF BUILDINGS AND GROUNDS

SEC. 4. On recommendation of the president, the council of the Academy shall appoint a "custodian of buildings and grounds", who, except where otherwise provided in the constitution and bylaws, shall have custody of all buildings, grounds, furniture, and other physical property belonging to the National Academy of Sciences or the National Research Council, or entrusted to their care.

He shall be responsible for and shall manage and administer these under such generic rules as the council of the Academy may make. and shall approve all vouchers for pay rolls and disbursements that come under authorized budget items or are specifically authorized by the council of the Academy for the maintenance and operation of the Academy's and the Research Council's physical property.

He shall hold office at the pleasure of the council of the Academy and shall receive such salary as it may agree and shall give such bond for the faithful performance of his duties as it may require.

He shall prepare and present to the finance committee of the Academy the buildings and grounds division of the general budget.

ADVISORY COMMITTEE ON BUILDINGS AND GROUNDS

He shall be chairman of a joint advisory committee of five on buildings and grounds, of which two members shall be appointed by the president of the Academy from the Academy council, and two from the executive board of the National Research Council, which committee shall decide, subject to the approval of the council of the Academy, all questions of allocation of space and use of public rooms.

FINANCE COMMITTEE

SEC. 5. There shall be a finance committee, of which the treasurer shall be chairman, consisting of the president of the Academy (or in his absence the vice president), the treasurer, the chief executive officer of the National Research Council (provided he be a member of the Academy), and two or three other members of the Academy appointed by the president, one of whom shall be a member of the executive board of the National Research Council.

It shall be the duty of the finance committee to provide for the safe custody of all financial resources of the Academy and to determine all matters relating to the purchase and sale of its securities.

It shall be the further duty of the finance committee to prepare and present to the council of the Academy for adoption the "general budget", made up of the three "divisional budgets", of the Academy proper, of the Research Council, and of buildings and grounds, which divisional budgets shall be presented to the finance committee, respectively, by the treasurer, the chief executive officer of the National Research Council, and the custodian of buildings and grounds.

The finance committee shall be empowered to employ competent investment counsel (hereinafter called the financial adviser) to advise with the committee upon the purchase and sale of all securities, mortgages, or other investments.

PRESIDENT

SEC. 6. The president of the Academy, or, in case of his absence or inability to act, the vice president, shall preside at the meetings of the Academy, of the Academy council, and of the executive board of the National Research Council; shall name all committees except such as are otherwise especially provided for; shall refer investigations required by the Government of the United States to members especially conversant with the subjects, and report thereon to the Academy at its meeting next ensuing; and, with the council, shall direct the general business of the Academy.

EXPERTS ON COMMITTEES

It shall be competent for the president, in special cases, to call in the aid, upon committees, of experts or men of special attainments not members of the Academy.

GOVERNMENT REQUESTS

The president shall be ex-officio a member of all committees empowered to consider questions referred to the Academy by the Government of the United States.

SECRETARIES

SEC. 7. The foreign and home secretaries shall conduct the correspondence proper to their respective departments, advising with the president and council in cases of doubt, and reporting their action to the Academy at one of the stated meetings in each year.

It shall be the duty of the home secretary to give notice to the members of the place and time of all meetings, of all nominations for membership, and of all proposed amendments to the constitution.

It shall be the duty of the home secretary to keep the minutes of each business and scientific session, and after approval to enter these upon the permanent records of the Academy.

TREASURER

SEC. 8. The treasurer shall attend to all receipts and disbursements of the Academy, giving such bond and furnishing such vouchers as the council may require. He shall collect all dues, assessments, and subscriptions, and keep a set of books showing a full account of receipts and disbursements and the condition of all funds of the Academy. He shall be the custodian of the corporate seal of the Academy.

ADMINISTRATIVE COMMITTEE, NATIONAL RESEARCH COUNCIL

SEC. 9. The president, vice president, home secretary, and treasurer shall be members of the administrative committee of the National Research Council and shall represent the Academy at all its meetings.

ARTICLE III.—OF THE MEETINGS

ACADEMY

SECTION 1. The Academy shall hold one stated meeting, called the annual meeting, in April of each year in the city of Washington, and another stated meeting, called the autumn meeting, at a place to be determined by the council. The council shall also have power to fix the date of each meeting.

Special business meetings of the Academy may be called, by order of eight members of the council, at such place and time as may be designated in the call.

Special scientific meetings of the Academy may be held at times and places to be designated by a majority of the council.

SEC. 2. The names of the members present at each session of a meeting shall be recorded in the minutes and 20 members shall constitute a quorum for the transaction of business.

SEC. 3. Scientific sessions of the Academy, unless otherwise ordered by a majority of the members present, shall be open to the public; sessions for the transaction of business shall be closed.

COUNCIL OF THE ACADEMY

SEC. 4. Stated meetings of the council shall be held during the stated or special meetings of the Academy, and four members shall constitute a quorum for the transaction of business. Special meetings of the council may be convened at the call of the president and two members of the council or of four members of the council.

DUES IN ARREARS

SEC. 5. No member whose dues are in arrears shall vote at any business meeting of the Academy.

ARTICLE IV.—OF ELECTIONS AND REGULATIONS

SECTION 1. All elections of officers and members shall be by ballot, and each election shall be held separately.

SEC. 2. The time for holding an election of officers shall be fixed by the Academy at least 1 day before the election is held.

COUNCIL OF THE ACADEMY

SEC. 3. The election of six members of the council shall be as follows:

At the annual meeting in April 1907, six members of the council to be elected, of whom two shall serve for 3 years, two for 2 years, and two for 1 year, their respective terms to be determined by lot. Each year thereafter the terms of two members shall expire and their successors, to serve for 3 years, shall be elected at the annual meeting in each year. The date of expiration of the terms shall be June 30.

SECTIONS

SEC. 4. The Academy shall be divided by the council into sections representing the principal branches of scientific research. Each section shall elect its own chairman to serve for 3 years. The chairman shall be responsible to the Academy for the work of his section.

ELECTION PROCEDURE

SEC. 5. Election of members shall be held at the annual meeting in Washington in the following manner: There shall be two ballots— a preference ballot, which must be transmitted to the home secretary in advance of the annual meeting, and a final ballot, to be taken at the meeting.

Preference ballot.—From the list of nominees submitted by the home secretary, each member shall select and inscribe on a ballot, to an extent not greater than one-half, nor less than one-third the list, those names which he prefers, as these limits shall be interpreted by the home secretary in his discretion, and announced by him, no weight being attached to the order of the names, and ballots not complying with these requirements being discarded. A list of the nominees shall then be prepared, on which the names shall be entered in the order of the number of votes received by each. In case two or more nominees have the same number of votes on this preference list, the order in which they shall be placed on the list shall be determined by a majority vote of members present.

After the preference list has been made up in the manner stated, the chairman of any section having two or more nominees on the list may, when its first nominee is reached, request the permission of the Academy to interchange the positions (on the preference list) of the nominees of his section, without altering in any way the positions of nominees from other sections. If a majority of the members of the Academy present favor permitting a section to make such interchange of its own nominees, it shall be done before proceeding further with the e ection.

FINAL BALLOT

A vote shall be taken on the nominee who appears first on the preference list, and he shall be declared elected if he receives two-thirds of the votes cast and not less than 30 votes in all. A vote shall then be taken in similar manner on the nominee standing second on the preference list, and so on until all the nominees on the preference list shall have been acted on, or until 15 nominees shall have been elected, or until the total membership of the Academy shall have reached 300, or until the Academy shall terminate the election by vote as provided below. In voting the final ballot, members shall inscribe on the ballot the name of the nominee with either *yes* or *no* or *blank*, and only ballots thus inscribed shall be counted. Members appointed as tellers must vote before counting the ballots.

ELECTION

Not more than 15 members shall be elected at one annual meeting.

It shall be in order at any point in the course of an election to move that the election be closed. If two-thirds of those present vote in favor of such motion, it shall prevail and the election shall thereupon terminate.

Before and during elections a discussion of the merits of nominees will be in order.

SEC. 6. Every member elected shall accept his membership, personally or in writing, before the close of the next stated meeting after the date of his election. Otherwise, on proof that the secretary has formally notified him of his election, his name shall not be entered on the roll of members.

FOREIGN ASSOCIATES

SEC. 7. Foreign associates may be nominated by the council and may be elected at the annual meeting by a two-thirds vote of the members present.

CERTIFICATES OF ELECTION

SEC. 8. A diploma, with the corporate seal of the Academy and the signatures of the officers, shall be sent by the appropriate secretary to each member on his acceptance of membership, and to foreign associates on their election.

RESIGNATIONS

SEC. 9. Resignations shall be addressed to the president and acted on by the Academy.

DUES, NONPAYMENT

SEC. 10. Whenever a member has not paid his dues for 4 successive years, the treasurer shall report the fact to the council, which may report the case to the Academy with the recommendation that the person thus in arrears be declared to have forfeited his membership. If this recommendation be approved by two-thirds of the members present, the said person shall no longer be a member of the Academy, and his name shall be dropped from the roll.

ARTICLE V. — OF SCIENTIFIC COMMUNICATIONS, PUBLICATIONS, AND REPORTS

SCIENTIFIC SESSIONS

SECTION 1. Communications on scientific subjects shall be read at scientific sessions of the Academy, and papers by any member may be read by the author or by any other member, notice of the same having been previously given to the secretary.

SEC. 2. Any member of the Academy may read a paper from a person who is not a member and shall not be considered responsible for the facts or opinions expressed by the author, but shall be held responsible for the propriety of the paper.

Persons who are not members may read papers on invitation of the council or of the committee on arrangements.

PUBLICATIONS

SEC. 3. The Academy may provide for the publication, under the direction of the council, of Proceedings, scientific Memoirs, Biographical Memoirs, and Reports.

PROCEEDINGS

The Proceedings shall be primarily a medium of first publication for original articles in brief form of permanent scientific value.

MEMOIRS

The scientific Memoirs shall provide opportunity for the publication of longer and more detailed scientific investigations.

The Biographical Memoirs shall contain an appropriate record of the life and work of the deceased members of the Academy.

ANNUAL REPORT

An annual report shall be presented to Congress by the president and shall contain the annual reports of the treasurer and the auditing committee, a suitable summary of the reports of the committees in charge of trust funds, and a record of the activities of the Academy for the fiscal year immediately preceding, and other appropriate matter. This report shall be presented to Congress by the president after authorization by the council. It shall also be presented to the Academy at the annual meeting next following.

TREASURER'S REPORT

The treasurer shall prepare a full report of the financial affairs of the Academy at the end of the fiscal year. This report shall be submitted to the council for approval and afterward presented to the Academy at the next stated meeting. He shall also prepare a supplementary financial statement to December 31 of the ensuing fiscal year for presentation at the annual meeting.

GOVERNMENT REQUESTS

SEC. 4. Propositions for investigations or reports by the Academy shall be submitted to the council for approval, except those requested by the Government of the United States, which shall be acted on by the president, who will in such cases report their results to the Government as soon as obtained and to the Academy at its next following stated meeting.

SEC. 5. The advice of the Academy shall be at all times at the disposition of the Government upon any matter of science or art within its scope.

ARTICLE VI.—OF TRUST FUNDS AND THEIR ADMINISTRATION

TRUSTS

SECTION 1. Devises, bequests, donations, or gifts having for their object the promotion of science or the welfare of the Academy may be accepted by the council for the Academy. Before the acceptance of any such trust the council shall consider the object of the trust and all conditions or specifications attaching thereto. The council shall make a report of its action to the Academy.

MEDALS

SEC. 2. Medals and prizes may be established in accordance with the provisions of trusts or by action of the Academy.

Sec. 3. Unless otherwise provided by the deed of gift, the income of each trust fund shall be applied to the objects of that trust by the action of the Academy on the recommendation of a standing committee on that fund.

Article VII.—Of Additions and Amendments

Additions and amendments to the constitution shall be made only at a stated meeting of the Academy. Notice of a proposition for such a change must be submitted to the council, which may amend the proposition, and shall report thereon to the Academy. Its report shall be considered by the Academy in committee of the whole for amendment.

The proposition as amended, if adopted in committee of the whole, shall be voted on at the next stated meeting; and if it receives two-thirds of the votes cast it shall be declared adopted.

Absent members may send their votes on pending changes in the constitution to the home secretary in writing, and such votes shall be counted as if the members were present.

2. BYLAWS

[In accordance with a resolution of the Academy, taken at its meeting on Apr. 21, 1915, the bylaws are arranged in groups, and each group is numbered to correspond with the article of the constitution to which it relates]

I

1. The holders of the medal for eminence in the application of science to the public welfare shall be notified, like members, of the meetings of the Academy, and invited to participate in its scientific sessions.

II

1. The proper secretary shall acknowledge all donations made to the Academy, and shall at once report them to the council for its consideration.

2. The home secretary shall keep a record of all grants of money or awards of prizes or medals made from trust funds of the Academy. The record for each grant of money shall include the following items: Name of fund, date and number of the grant, name and address of recipient, amount of grant, and date or dates of payment, purpose of grant, record of report of progress, and resulting publications.

3. The executive secretary, who may be a nonmember of the Academy, shall receive a salary to be fixed by the council.

4. The treasurer shall keep the home secretary informed of all warrants received from directors of trust funds not controlled by the Academy and of the date or dates of payment of all warrants.

GOVERNMENT REQUESTS

5. The treasurer is authorized to defray, when approved by the president, all the proper expenses of committees appointed to make

scientific investigations at the request of departments of the Government, and in each case to look to the department requesting the investigation for reimbursement to the Academy.

TREASURER, NATIONAL RESEARCH COUNCIL

6. The treasurer is authorized to act as the treasurer ex officio of the National Research Council.

BURSAR

7. The treasurer shall have the assistance of a salaried and bonded officer, the bursar, who shall be chosen by the finance committee and be directly responsible to the treasurer.

INVESTMENTS

8. All investments and reinvestments of either principal or accumulations of income of the trust and other funds of the Academy shall be made by the treasurer, in accordance with the decisions of the finance committee, in the corporate name of the Academy, in the manner and in the securities designated or specified in the instruments creating the several funds, or in the absence of such designation or specification, in bonds of the United States or of the several States, or in bonds or notes secured by first mortgages on real estate, in investments legal for savings banks under the laws of Massachusetts or New York, or in other securities recommended by the financial adviser.

The treasurer may invest the capital of all trust funds of the Academy which are not required by the instruments creating such funds to be kept separate and distinct, in a consolidated fund, and shall apportion the income received from such consolidated fund among the various funds composing the same in the proportion that each of said funds shall bear to the total amount of funds so invested: *Provided, however,* That the treasurer shall at all times keep accurate accounts showing the amount of each trust fund, the proportion of the income from the consolidated fund to which it is entitled, and the expenses and disbursements properly chargeable to such fund.

The treasurer shall have authority, with the approval of the finance committee, to sell, transfer, convey, and deliver in the corporate name and for the benefit of the Academy any stocks, bonds, or other securities standing in the corporate name.

CUSTODIAN OF SECURITIES

9. On the recommendation of the finance committee, the council shall contract with a bank, trust company, or corresponding fiduciary institution to serve as the custodian of securities, including all of the Academy's personal property in the form of bonds, mortgages, and other securities, to collect the income from them, to protect the Academy in respect to expirations, reissues, and notifications, and to buy or sell securities on the order of the treasurer, as approved by the finance committee.

CONTRACTS

10. No contract shall be binding upon the Academy which has not been first approved by the council.

DUES

11. The assessments required for the support of the Academy shall be fixed by the Academy on the recommendation of the council and shall be payable within the calendar year for which they are assessed.

FINANCE COMMITTEE MEETINGS

12. The finance committee may invite to be present at any of its meetings the chief executive officer of the Research Council, the custodian of buildings and grounds, and the bursar, but they shall not vote.

III

ANNUAL MEETING—DATES AND PROCEDURES

1. At the business sessions of the Academy the order of procedure shall be as follows:

(1) Chair taken by the president, or, in his absence, by the vice president.

(2) Roll of members called by home secretary (first session of the meeting only).

(3) Minutes of the preceding session read and approved.

(4) Stated business.

(5) Reports of president, secretaries, treasurer, and committees

(6) Business from council.

(7) Other business.

RULES OF ORDER

2. The rules of order of the Academy shall be those of the Senate of the United States, unless otherwise provided by the constitution or bylaws of the Academy.

·3. In the absence of any officer, a member shall be chosen to perform his duties temporarily, by a plurality of viva-voce votes, upon open nomination.

DEATHS

4. At each meeting the president shall announce the death of any members since the preceding meeting. As soon as practicable thereafter he shall designate a member to write—or to secure from some other source approved by the president—a biographical notice of each deceased member:

COMMITTEE ON ARRANGEMENTS

5. For the annual meeting a local committee [1] of five members, appointed for each meeting, and the home secretary shall constitute the committee on arrangements, of which the home secretary shall be

---

[1] At the business session on November 18, 1936, this by-law was amended by deleting the word "local" so that the name of the committee will be "committee on arrangements."

chairman. For the autumn meeting a member of the local group shall be chairman of the local committee, of which the home secretary shall be a member ex officio.

SCIENTIFIC PROGRAM

It shall be the duty of the committee on arrangements to prepare the scientific program for the annual meeting, and for this purpose it shall be empowered to solicit papers from members or others. It shall also be empowered to ascertain the length of time required for reading papers to be presented at the scientific sessions of the Academy and, when it appears advisable, to limit the time to be occupied in their presentation or discussion.

The committee on arrangeemnts shall meet not less than 2 months previous to each meeting. It shall prepare the detailed program of each day and in general shall have charge of all business and scientific arrangements for the meeting for which it is appointed.

PAPERS—TIME LIMIT

6. No paper requiring more than 15 minutes for its presentation shall be accepted unless by invitation of the committee on arrangements.

No speaker shall occupy more than 30 minutes for presentation of papers during the scientific sessions of a single meeting of the Academy, except by invitation of the committee on arrangements.

Time shall not be extended except by vote of the Academy, and then not to exceed 5 minutes. The presiding officer shall warn speakers 2 minutes before the expiration of their time.

The discussion of individual papers shall be limited not to exceed 5 minutes, and the total time for discussion by any one speaker for all scientific sessions in any one meeting shall not exceed 15 minutes, unless approved by the Academy.

In order that adequate opportunity be given for the discussion of pabers on the program, the committee on arrangements shall, in making up the program for the scientific sessions, allot not more than 80 percent of the available time of each session to the actual reading of papers.

If the number of papers accepted is too large to be presented in the scientific sessions, provision shall be made for holding two or more sessions simultaneously.

In arranging the program the committee on arrangements shall group the papers as nearly as practicable according to subject.

No paper shall be entered upon the printed program of scientific sessions unless the title is in the hands of the committee on arrangements at least 2 weeks in advance of the meeting. In the event that titles are received later, they shall be placed in order of receipt at the end of the list and read, if there is time. Such supplementary titles shall be conspicuously posted.

IV

SECTIONS

1. The term of service of each chairman of a section shall be 3 years, to date from the closing session of the April meeting next fol-

lowing his election. Chairmen of sections shall be chosen by mail ballot, the member receiving the highest number of votes cast to be deemed elected. It shall be the duty of each retiring chairman to conduct the election of his successor, and to report the results of the election to the home secretary before the April meeting at which his term of service expires. Should any section fail to elect a chairman before November 1, the president is empowered to appoint a temporary chairman to serve until the April meeting next following. No chairman shall be eligible for reelection for two consecutive terms.

PROPOSALS FOR NOMINATION

2. (1) Intersectional: Proposals for nomination to membership may be made in writing by any five members of the Academy and addressed to the home secretary; each such proposal shall be accompanied by a record of the scientific activities of the person proposed and by a list of his principal contributions to science, in triplicate; and with a statement as to the sections to which the name proposed shall be submitted for consideration. Such proposals as have been received by the home secretary prior to October 1 shall upon that date be sent by him to the chairman of each section designated, with a copy of the record and list of contributions.

(2) Sectional: Proposals for nomination to membership shall be in writing and shall be sent to the chairman of the section not later than October 1. The proposal for nomination of any individual will be accepted for consideration by the section only if it is accompanied by a list of titles and references of the more important published scientific articles of the individual and by a factual summary not over 250 words in length, of his accomplishments.

Each section chairman shall edit material thus received and, at the time of the informal ballot, distribute it together with the material from the home secretary, relative to intersectional proposals, to the members of the section. The home secretary's office, if called upon, will assist the chairmen of the sections in the multigraphing of this material.

Each chairman shall keep a record of the names listed on the informal ballot and shall strike from the lists those names which were on the list in the previous year and received less than 2 votes on the informal ballot or had been on the list for 3 consecutive years without receiving in any one of these years on the informal ballot so many as one-fourth of the votes cast (counting the votes according to the number of members in the section who vote and not by the number of persons on the list for whom they vote). The home secretary shall keep a record of the votes on the informal ballots in the case of those persons proposed to two or more sections of the Academy and shall cause such names to be stricken from the lists of all sections if in three consecutive years there be no two sections in which the number of votes cast for the proposed nominee exceeds one-sixth of the votes cast in those sections except in case the number should be as many as one-fourth of the votes cast in one section in which case the proposal should be considered thenceforth as a proposal in that section only. No proposal for nomination which is thus stricken from the list of the informal ballot shall be considered by the section (or sections) unless again proposed for nomination in the appropriate manner in a subsequent year.

NOMINATION BALLOTS

3. The chairman of each section of the Academy shall submit to the members of his section not later than November 1 of each year an informal ballot containing, in alphabetical order and without indications of rank on ballots of the previous year, the names of all those persons who received not less than two votes in the informal ballot of the preceding year and not less than one-fourth of the votes on the informal ballot in at least one of the preceding three years in the case of names in the list for three years or have been continued on the list by the home secretary or have been added to the list by him or have been newly proposed for consideration in accordance with the procedure above defined. Each member of the section shall be expected to return his ballot to the chairman within two weeks, with his signature and with crosses against the names of those persons whom he is prepared to endorse for nomination. The vote resulting from this ballot shall be regarded as informal.

The chairman shall then submit to the members of his section a new ballot showing the results of the informal vote; and each member shall be expected to return this ballot to the chairman with his signature and with crosses placed against names of three persons whom he judges to be worthy of nomination.

In order to secure an adequate number of nominations, the chairman, when necessary, shall obtain by personal solicitation a fuller vote of his section or shall submit to the section a supplementary formal ballot.

The chairman shall then certify to the home secretary, prior to January 1, the names of all persons who have been voted for on the formal ballots together with a statement of the number of votes each candidate received and of the number of members voting. Of these all persons who receive the votes of two-thirds of the members voting in the section in cases voted upon by one section only, or the votes of one-half (however distributed) of the members voting in any two sections in cases voted upon by more than one section shall be considered nominated.

A properly edited statement of the accomplishments of each individual nominated to the Academy by the sections shall be sent by the section chairmen to the home secretary along with the nominations of the section. These statements together with summaries pertaining to those persons nominated intersectionally or nominated by the council shall be reproduced and distributed to the members of the Academy at the time of the preference ballot.

Persons nominated to the Academy and rejected by the Academy at the ensuing election may not be further considered by the sections until they have again been proposed for nomination in the appropriate manner in a subsequent year. Persons nominated but not voted upon by the Academy shall without further action be presented to the Academy upon the preference ballot of the next following year; but, if again not voted upon, the nominations shall lapse and not be considered except when renewed in the regular order.

4. Preference ballots for the election of members shall be sealed in a blank envelope, which shall be enclosed in another bearing the name of the sender, and which shall be addressed to the home secretary, who shall cause the ballots to be tabulated for use at the election. If in any case it is impossible to determine who cast the ballot, or if the latter contain more or fewer than the number of names provided for in article IV, section 5, of the constitution, the ballot shall be rejected, but minor defects in a ballot shall be disregarded when the intent of the voter is obvious.

5. All discussions of the claims and qualifications of nominees at meetings of the Academy shall be held strictly confidential, and remarks and criticisms then made may be communicated to no person who was not a member of the Academy at the time of the discussion.

V

PROCEEDINGS

1. The publication of the Proceedings shall be under the general charge of the council, which shall have final jurisdiction upon all questions of policy relating thereto.

The National Academy of Sciences and the National Research Council shall cooperate in the publication of the Proceedings, beginning with volume VII.

MEMOIRS

2. Memoirs may be presented at any time to the home secretary, who shall report the date of their reception at the next session; but no Memoir shall be published unless it has been read or presented by title before the Academy.

Before publication all Biographical and scientific Memoirs must be referred to the committee on publication, who may, if they deem best, refer any Memoir to a special committee, appointed by the president, to determine whether the same should be published by the Academy.

3. Memoirs shall date, in the records of the Academy, from the date of their presentation to the Academy, and the order of their presentation shall be so arranged by the secretary that, so far as may be convenient, those upon kindred topics shall follow one another.

TREASURER'S REPORT

4. The annual report of the treasurer shall contain—

(1) A concise statement of the source, object, and amount of all trust funds of the Academy.

(2) A condensed statement of receipts and expenditures.

(3) A statement of assets and liabilities.

(4) Accounts with individual funds.

(5) Such other matter as he considers appropriate.

AUDITING COMMITTEE

5. The accounts of the treasurer shall, between July 1 and August 1 of each year, be audited under the direction of a committee of three

members to be appointed by the president at the annual meeting of the Academy. It shall be the duty of the auditing committee to verify the record of receipts and disbursements maintained by the treasurer, and the agreement of book and bank balances; to examine all securities in the custody of the treasurer and the custodian of securities and to compare the stated income of such securities with the receipts of record; to examine all vouchers covering disbursements for account of the Academy, including the National Research Council, and the authority therefor, and to compare them with the treasurer's record of expenditures; to examine and verify the account of the Academy with each trust fund. The auditing committee may employ an expert accountant to assist the committee. The reports of the treasurer and auditing committee shall be presented to the Academy at the autumn meeting and shall be published with that of the president to Congress. They shall be distributed to the members in printed form at the annual meeting.

VI

PROPERTY

1. All apparatus and other materials of permanent value purchased with money from any grant from a trust fund shall be the property of the Academy unless specific exception is made in the grant or by subsequent action of the council. Receipts for all such property shall be signed by the grantee and shall be forwarded to the home secretary, who shall file them with the custodian of buildings and grounds. All apparatus and unused material of value acquired in this way shall be delivered to the custodian of buildings and grounds on completion of the investigation for which the grant was made, or at any time on demand of the council, and the custodian of buildings and grounds shall give an appropriate release therefor.

2. A stamp corresponding to the corporate seal of the Academy shall be kept by the secretaries, who shall be responsible for the due markings of all books and other objects to which it is applicable.

Labels or other proper marks of similar device shall be placed upon objects not admitting of the stamp.

3. The fiscal year of the Academy shall end on June 30 of each year.

VII

STANDING COMMITTEES—RESEARCH FUNDS

1. Standing committees of the Academy on trust funds, the income of which is applied to the promotion of research, shall consist of 3 or 5 members. In order to secure rotation in office in such committees, when not in conflict with the provisions of the deeds of gift, the term of service on a committee of 3 members shall be 3 years; on a committee of five members the term shall be 5 years.

2. The annual reports of the committees on research funds shall, so far as the Academy has authority to determine their form, give a current number to each award, stating the name, position, and address of the recipient; the subject of research for which the award is made

and the sum awarded; and in later annual reports the status of the work accomplished under each award previously made shall be announced, until the research is completed, when announcement of its completion, and, if published, the title and place of publication shall be stated, and the record of the award shall be reported as closed.

VIII

AMENDMENTS

1. Any bylaw of the Academy may be amended, suspended, or repealed on the written motion of any two members, signed by them, and presented at a stated meeting of the Academy, provided the same shall be approved by a majority of the members present.

3. ORGANIZATION OF THE ACADEMY

JULY 1, 1936

	Expiration of term
Lillie, F. R., president	June 30, 1939
Day, A. L., vice president	June 30, 1937
Morgan, T. H., foreign secretary	June 30, 1938
Wright, F. E., home secretary	June 30, 1939
Keith, Arthur, treasurer	June 30, 1940

ADDITIONAL MEMBERS OF THE COUNCIL

1934–37:	1935–38:	1936–39:
Adams, Roger.	Harrison, R. G.	Flexner, Simon.
Jennings, H. S.	Russell, H. N.	Whitehead, J. B.
	1936–37 Hektoen, Ludvig [1]	

EXECUTIVE COMMITTEE OF THE COUNCIL

Lillie, F. R. (chairman).	Harrison, R. G.	Keith, Arthur.
Adams, Roger.	Hektoen, Ludvig. [1]	Wright, F. E.
Day, A. L.		

SECTIONS

1. Mathematics

Coble, A. B. (chairman), 1937.	Eisenhart, L. P.	Ritt, J. F.
Alexander, J. W.	Evans, G. C.	Vandiver, H. S.
Bateman, Harry.	Jackson, Dunham.	Van Vleck, E. B.
Bell, E. T.	Kasner, Edward.	Veblen, Oswald.
Birkhoff, G. D.	Lefschetz, Solomon.	Walsh, J. L.
Blichfeldt, H. F.	Miller, G. A.	Weiner, Norbert.
Bliss, G. A.	Moore, R. L.	White, H. S.
Dickson, L. E.	Morse, Marston.	
	Osgood, W. F.	

2. Astronomy

Leuschner, A. O. (chairman), 1938.	Brown, E. W.	Ross, F. E.
Abbot, C. G.	Campbell W. W.	Russell, H. N.
Adams, W. S.	Curtis, H. D.	Schlesinger, F.
Aitken, R. G.	Hale, G. E.	Seares, F. H.
Anderson, J. A.	Hubble, E. P.	Shapley, Harlow.
Babcock, H. D.	Merrill, P. W.	Slipher, V. M.
Bowen, I. S.	Mitchell, S. A.	Stebbins, Joel.
Bowie, William.	Moore, J. H.	Trumpler, R. J.
	Moulton, F. R.	Wright, W. H.

[1] The constitution of the Academy provides that the chairman of the National Research Council be a member of the council of the Academy and also a member of the executive committee of the council of the Academy, provided he be a member of the Academy.

3. *Physics*

Mason, Max (chairman), 1939.
Ames, J. S.
Birge, R. T.
Bridgman, P. W.
Coblentz, W. W.
Compton, A. H.
Compton, K. T.
Coolidge, W. D.
Crew, Henry.
Davis, Bergen.

Davisson, C. J.
Epstein, P. S.
Hall, E. H.
Hull, A. W.
Ives, H. E.
Kemble, E. C.
Lawrence, E. O.
Lyman, Theodore.
Merritt, Ernest.
Miller, D. C.
Millikan, R. A.

Mulliken, R. S.
Nichols, E. L.
Pierce, G. W.
Richtmyer, F. K.
Saunders, F. A.
Slater, J. C.
Thomson, Elihu.
Van Vleck, J. H.
Webster, D. L.
Wilson, Edwin B.
Wood, R. W.

4. *Engineering*

Gherardi, Bancroft (chairman), 1938.
Adams, C. A.
Baekeland, L. H.
Bush, Vannevar.
Dunn, Gano.
Durand, W. F.
Emmet, W. L. R.

Fletcher, Harvey.
Hoover, Herbert.
Hovgaard, William.
Hunsaker, J. C.
Jewett, F. B.
Kennelly, A. E.
Kettering, C. F.
Modjeski, Ralph.

Sauveur, Albert.
Stillwell, L. B.
Swasey, Ambrose.
Taylor, D. W.
Whitehead, J. B.
Wright, Orville.

5. *Chemistry*

Kraus, C. A. (chairman) 1938.
Adams, Roger.
Bancroft, W. D.
Baxter, G. P.
Bogert, Marston T.
Bray, W. C.
Carothers, W. H.
Conant, J. B.
Franklin, E. C.
Glauque, W. F.

Gomberg, Moses.
Gortner, R. A.
Harkins, W. D.
Hildebrand, J. H.
Hudson, C. S.
Hulett, G. A.
Jacobs, W. A.
Johnson, T. B.
Keyes, F. G.
Kohler, E. P.
Lamb, A. B.

Langmuir, Irving.
Levene, P. A. T.
Lind, S. C.
Michael, Arthur.
Norris, J. F.
Noyes, W. A.
Pauling, Linus.
Stieglitz, Julius.
Tolman, R. C.
Urey, H. C.
Whitney, W. R.

6. *Geology and Paleontology*

Mendenhall, W. C. (chairman), 1939
Allen, E. T.
Berkey, C. P.
Berry, E. W.
Blackwelder, Eliot
Bowen, N. L.
Bowman, Isaiah
Cross, Whitman
Daly, R. A.

Day, A. L.
Johnson, D. W.
Keith, Arthur
Knopf, Adolph
Lawson, A. G.
Leith, C. K.
Leverett, Frank
Lindgren, Waldemar
Longwell, C. R.
Merriam, J. C.

Palache, Charles
Reid, H. F.
Ruedemann, Rudolf
Schuchert, Charles
Scott, W. B.
Ulrich, E. O.
Vaughan, T. W.
Willis, Bailey
Wright, F. E.

7. *Botany*

Blakeslee, A. F. (chairman), 1938
Allen, C. E.
Bailey, I. W.
Bailey, L. H.
Campbell, D. H.
Clinton, G. P.
Dodge, B. O.

Duggar, B. M.
East, E. M.
Emerson, R. A.
Fernald, M. L.
Fred, E. B.
Harper, R. A.
Hoagland, D. R.
Howe, M. A.

Jones, L. R.
Kunkel, L. O.
Merrill, E. D.
Osterhout, W. J. V.
Setchell, W. A.
Sinnott, E. W.
Stakman, E. C.
Trelease, William

8. *Zoology and Anatomy*

Stockard, C. R. (chairman), 1939
Barbour, Thomas
Bigelow, H. B.
Calkins, G. N.
Castle, W. E.
Chapman, F. M.
Child, C. M.
Coghill, G. E.
Conklin, E. G.
Davenport, C. B.
Detwiler, S. R.
Donaldson, H. H.

Gregory, W. K.
Harrison, R. G.
Harvey, E. N.
Herrick, C. J.
Howard, L. O.
Jennings, H. S.
Kellogg, Vernon
Kofoid, C. A.
Lewis, W. H.
Lillie, F. R.
McClung, C. E.
Mark, E. L.
Morgan, T. H.

Muller, H. J.
Parker, G. H.
Pearl, Raymond
Stejneger, Leonhard
Streeter, G. L.
Sturtevant, A. H.
Tennent, D. H.
Wheeler, W. M.
Wilson, Edmund B.
Wilson, H. V. P.
Woodruff, L. L.
Wright, S. G.

9. *Physiology and Biochemistry*

Clark, W. M. (chairman), 1939.
Abel, J. J.
Benedict, F. G.
Benedict, S. R.
Cannon, W. B.
Carlson, A. J.
Chittenden, R. H.

DuBois, E. F.
Erlanger, Joseph.
Evans, H. M.
Forbes, Alexander.
Gasser, H. S.
Henderson, L. J.
Henderson, Yandell.
Howell, W. H.

Hunt, Reid.
McCollum, E. V.
Northrop, J. H.
Richards, A. N.
Rose, W. C.
Shaffer, P. A.
Sherman, H. C.
Van Slyke, D. D.

10. *Pathology and Bacteriology*

Flexner, Simon (chairman), 1939.
Avery, O. T.
Cole, Rufus.
Cushing, Harvey.
Dochez, A. R.
Ewing, James.

Hektoen, Ludvig.
Jordan, E. O.
Landsteiner, Karl.
MacCallum, W. G.
Novy, F. G.
Opie, E. L.
Rivers, T. M.

Rous, Peyton.
Sabin, Florence R.
Wells, H. Gideon.
Whipple, G. H.
Zinsser, Hans.

11. *Anthropology and Psychology*

Seashore, C. E. (chairman), 1938.
Angell, J. R.
Boas, Franz.
Boring, E. G.
Cattell, J. McKeen.
Dewey, John.
Dodge, Raymond.
Hooton, E. A.
Hrdlicka, Ales.

Hull, C. L.
Hunter, W. S.
Kidder, A. V.
Kroeber, A. L.
Lashley, K. S.
Lowie, R. H.
Merriam, C. H.
Miles, W. R.
Pillsbury, W. B.

Sapir, Edward.
Stratton, G. M.
Swanton, J. R.
Terman, L. M.
Thorndike, E. L.
Washburn, Margaret E.
Wissler, Clark.
Woodworth, R. S.
Yerkes, R. M.

4. STANDING COMMITTEES OF THE ACADEMY

ALBERT NATIONAL PARK

Yerkes, R. M. (chairman).
Chapman, F. M.
Wissler, Clark.

AUDITING COMMITTEE

Hudson, C. S. (chairman).
Bowen, N. L.
Howell, W. H.

BIOGRAPHICAL MEMOIRS

Davenport, C. B. (chairman).
Hrdlicka, Ales.
Pearl, Raymond.
Thorndike E. L.
Wright, F. E.

BUILDINGS AND GROUNDS ADVISORY COMMITTEE (JOINT COMMITTEE OF ACADEMY AND RESEARCH COUNCIL)

Brockett, Paul (chairman).	Bastin, E. S.	Lewis, I. F.
	Day, A. L.	Wright, F. E.

CALENDAR

Wright, F. E. (chairman).	Campbell, W. W.	Millikan, R. A.
	Dunn, Gano.	Russell, H. N.

EXHIBITS (JOINT COMMITTEE OF ACADEMY AND RESEARCH COUNCIL)

Wright, F. E. (chairman).
Brockett, Paul (secretary).
Hale, G. E. (member at large).

Shapley, Harlow (member at large).
The chairman of each of the sections of the Academy.

The chairman of each of the divisions of the Research Council.

Executive committee on exhibits

Wright, F. E. (chairman).
Brockett, Paul (secretary).

Day, A. L.
Hale, G. E.
Kellogg, Vernon.

Merriam, J. C.

FINANCE COMMITTEE

The treasurer of the Academy, chairman ex officio.

The president of the Academy, ex officio (or in his absence, the vice president).

The chairman of the National Research Council, ex officio.
Abbot, C. G.
Jewett, F. B.

FUNDS FOR ACADEMY PURPOSES

Flexner, Simon (chairman).	Kellogg, Vernon.	Shapley, Harlow.
	Lillie, F. R.	

GOVERNMENT RELATIONS AND SCIENCE ADVISORY COMMITTEE

The president of the Academy, chairman ex officio (F. R. Lillie, 1939).
The vice president of the Academy (A. L. Day, 1937).
The home secretary of the Academy (F. E. Wright, 1939).
The Chairman or specially elected representative of each Section of the Academy, as follows:

Mathematics	Oswald Veblen, 1937.
Astronomy	A. O. Leuschner, 1938.
Physics	Edwin B. Wilson, 1939.
Engineering	Bancroft Gherardi, 1938.
Chemistry	Roger Adams, 1938.
Geology and Paleontology	Isaiah Bowman, 1939.
Botany	A. F. Blakeslee, 1938.
Zoology and Anatomy	C. R. Stockard, 1939.
Physiology and Biochemistry	A. J. Carlson, 1939.
Pathology and Bacteriology	Simon Flexner, 1939.
Anthropology and Psychology	C. E. Seashore, 1938.

The Chairman of the National Research Council (July 1, 1936, to June 30, 1937, Ludvig Hektoen).
Members at large, as follows:

K. T. Compton (1938).	L. R. Jones (1939).	R. A. Millikan (1937).
Gano Dunn (1939).	C. K. Leith (1939).	G. H. Whipple (1937).
F. B. Jewett (1939).		

Executive committee of Government Relations and Science Advisory Committee

F. R. Lillie (chairman ex officio)	K. T. Compton	L. R. Jones
Roger Adams	A. L. Day	C. K. Leith
Isaiah Bowman	Gano Dunn	R. A. Millikan
	F. B. Jewett	G. H. Whipple

LIBRARY

Hudson, C. S. (chairman). Compton, K. T. Parker, G. H.
Adams, W. S. Harkins, W. D. Scott, W. B.
Cattell, J. McK. Henderson, Yandell. Brockett, Paul.

Subcommittee

Hudson, C. S. (chair- Pearl, Raymond. Swanton, John R.
man). Streeter, G. S.
Coblentz, W. W. (vice
chairman).

MEMORIALS (BUSTS, PORTRAITS, AND STATUES)

---------------- (chair- Cushing, Harvey Hale, G. E.
man). Day, A. L. Merriam, J. C.
Angell, J. R. Dunn, Gano.

OCEANOGRAPHY

Bigelow, H. B. (chair- Conklin, E. G. Merriam, J. C.
man). Day, A. L. Vaughan, T. W.
Bowie, William. Duggar, B. M.

PROCEEDINGS, EDITORIAL BOARD

Blake, F. G. Henderson, L. J. Richtmyer, F. K.
Day, A. L. Jewett, F. B. Sapir, Edward.
Dunn, Gano. Kettering, C. F. Schlesinger, Frank.
Eisenhart, L. P. Lewis, I. F. Wheeler, W. M.
Harrison, R. G. Morgan, T. H. Willard, F. W.
Hektoen, Ludvig. Osterhout, W. J. V. Wright, F. E.

PUBLICATIONS OF THE ACADEMY

The president The home secretary Conklin, E. G.

REVISION OF THE CONSTITUTION

Wilson, Edwin B. (chair- Day, A. L. Merriam, J. C.
man) Dunn, Gano Morgan, T. H.

SCIENTIFIC PROBLEMS OF NATIONAL PARKS

Merriam, J. C. (chairman) Whiting, Frederic Allen Wright, F. E.

WEIGHTS, MEASURES, AND COINAGE

Kennelly, A. E. (chair- Baxter, G. P. Wood, R. W.
man) Bowie, William
Ames, J. S. Mendenhall, C. E.

5. TRUST FUNDS OF THE ACADEMY

ALEXANDER DALLAS BACHE FUND

[$60,000]

Researches in physical and natural science

Board of directors

Wilson, Edwin B., chair- Osterhout, W. J. V. Stockard, C. R.
man.

JAMES CRAIG WATSON FUND

[$25,000]

Watson medal and the promotion of astronomical research

Trustees

Leuschner, A. O., chair-　　Ross, F. E.　　　　　　　　Seares, F. H.
man.

WATSON MEDAL AWARDS

Gould, B. A., 1887　　　　Chandler, S. C., 1894　　Leuschner, A. O., 1915
Schoenfeld, Ed., 1889　　Gill, Sir David, 1899　　Charlier, C. V. L., 1924
Auwers, Arthur, 1891　　Kapteyn, J. C., 1913　　de Sitter, Willem, 1929

HENRY DRAPER FUND

[$10,000]

Draper medal and investigations in astronomical physics

MEMBERS OF THE COMMITTEE

Slipher, V. M., chairman　Adams, W. S. (1941)　　Mitchell, S. A. (1940)
　(1937)　　　　　　　　　Merrill, P. W. (1939)　Stebbins, Joel (1938)

HENRY DRAPER MEDAL AWARDS

Langley, S. P., 1886　　　Deslandres, H., 1913　　Eddingtion, Sir Arthur
Pickering, E. C., 1888　　Stebbins, Joel, 1915　　　Stanley, 1924
Rowland, H. A., 1890　　Michelson, A. A., 1916　Shapley, Harlow, 1926
Vogel, H. K., 1893　　　Adams, W. S., 1918　　Wright, William Ham-
Keeler, J. E., 1899　　　Fabry, Charles, 1919　　　mond, 1928
Huggins, Sir Wm., 1901　Fowler, Alfred, 1920　　Cannon, Annie Jump, 1931
Hale, George E., 1904　　Zeeman, Pieter, 1921　　Slipher, V. M., 1932
Campbell, W. W., 1906　　Russell, H. N., 1922　　Plaskett, John Stanley,
Abbot, C. G., 1910　　　　　　　　　　　　　　　1934

J. LAWRENCE SMITH FUND

[$10,000] .

J. Lawrence Smith medal and investigations of meteoric bodies

Members of the committee

Moulton, F. R., chairman　Allen, E. T. (1938)　　Palache, Charles (1939)
　(1937)　　　　　　　　　Brown, E. W. (1940)　Trumpler, R. J. (1941)

J. LAWRENCE SMITH MEDAL AWARDS

Newton, H. A., 1888　　　　　　　　　Merrill, George P., 1922

BARNARD MEDAL FOR MERITORIOUS SERVICES TO SCIENCE [*]

Discoveries in physical or astronomical science or novel application of science
to purposes beneficial to the human race

Members of the committee

Whitney, W. R., chair-　Campbell, W. W.　　　Day, Arthur L.
　man　　　　　　　　Davis, Bergen　　　　Tolman, R. C.

---

[*] Every 5 years the committee recommends the person whom they consider most
deserving of the medal, and upon approval by the Academy, the name of the nominee is
forwarded to the trustees of Columbia University, who administer the Barnard medal fund.

BARNARD MEDAL AWARDS

Rutherford, Baron; Ern- Einstein, Albert, 1921 Heisenberg, Werner, 1930
est Rutherford, 1909 Bohr, Niels, 1925 Hubble, Edwin, 1935
Bragg, Sir William H.,
1914

BENJAMIN APTHORP GOULD FUND

[$20,000]

Researches in astronomy

Board of directors

Moulton, F. R., chairman Brown, E. W. Curtis, H. D.

WOLCOTT GIBBS FUND

[$5,545.50]

Chemical research

Board of directors

Kohler, E. P., chairman Baxter, G. P. Franklin, E. C.

CYRUS B. COMSTOCK FUND

[$12,406.02]

Prize awarded every 5 years for most important discovery or investigation in
electricity, magnetism, and radiant energy, or to aid worthy investigations
in those subjects

Members of the committee

Millikan, R. A., chairman Compton, A. H. (1938) Crew, Henry (1937)
(1940) Coolidge, W. D. (1939) Davisson, C. J. (1941)

COMSTOCK PRIZE AWARDS

Millikan, R. A., 1913. Duane, William, 1923. Bridgman, P. W., 1933.
Barnett, S. J., 1918. Davisson, C. J., 1928.

MARSH FUND

[$20,000]

Original research in the natural sciences

Members of the committee

Gregory, W. K., chairman Berry, E. W. (1938) Merrill, E. D. (1940)
(1937) . Longwell, C. R. (1041) Reid, H. F. (1939)

AGASSIZ FUND

[$50,000]

General uses of the Academy

MURRAY FUND

[$6,000]

Agassiz medal for contributions to oceanography

Members of the committee

Vaughan, T. Wayland, chairman (1938)

Day, A. L. (1939)

Kofoid, C. A. (1937)

AGASSIZ MEDAL AWARDS

Hjort, Johan, 1913.
Albert I, Prince of Monaco, 1918.
Sigsbee, C. D., 1920.
Pettersson, Otto Spen, 1924.
Bjerknes, Vilhelm, 1926.

Weber, Max, 1927.
Ekman, Vagn Walfrid, 1928.
Gardiner, J. Stanley, 1929.
Schmidt, Johannes, 1930.
Bigelow, Henry Bryant, 1931.

Defant, Albert, 1932.
Helland-Hansen, Bjorn, 1933.
Gran, Haakon Hasberg, 1934.
Vaughan, T. Wayland, 1935.

MARCELLUS HARTLEY FUND

[$1,200]

Medal for eminence in the application of science to the public welfare

Members of the committee

Cushing, Harvey, chairman (1937)
Conant, J. B. (1938)

Hoover, Herbert (1937)
Hull, A. W. (1939)

Kofoid, C. A. (1938)
Mason, Max (1939)

PUBLIC WELFARE MEDAL AWARDS

(In memory of Marcellus Hartley)

Goethals, G. W. 1914.
Gorgas, W. C., 1914.
Abbe, Cleveland, 1916.
Pinchot, Gifford, 1916.
Stratton, S. W., 1917.
Hoover, Herbert, 1920.

Stiles, C. W., 1921.
Chapin, Charles V., 1928.
Mather, Stephen Tyng, 1930.
Rose, Wickliffe, 1931.

Park, William Hallock, 1932.
Fairchild, David, 1933.
Vollmer, August, 1934.
Russell, F. F., 1935.

DANIEL GIRAUD ELLIOT FUND

[$8,000]

Medal and honorarium for most meritorious work in zoology or paleontology published each year

Members of the committee

Harrison, Ross G., chairman

Gregory, W. K.

Wheeler, W. M.

DANIEL GIRAUD ELLIOT MEDAL AWARDS

Chapman, F. M., 1917
Beebe, William, 1918
Ridgeway, Robert, 1919
Abel, Othenio, 1920
Dean, Bashford, 1921
Wheeler, Wm. Morton, 1922

Canu, Ferdinand. 1923
Breuil, Henri, 1924
Wilson, Edmund B., 1925
Stensiö, Erik A: Son, 1927
Seton, Ernest Thompson, 1928

Osborn, Henry Fairfield 1929
Coghill, George Ellett, 1930
Black, Davidson, 1931.
Chapin, James P., 1932

BILLINGS FUND

[$22,313.39]

For partial support of the Proceedings, or for such other purposes as the Academy may select

MARY CLARK THOMPSON FUND

[$10,000]

Medal for most important services to geology and paleontology

Members of the committee

Lindgren, Waldemar, chairman (1937)　Mendenhall, W. C. (1939)　Ulrich, E. O. (1938)

MARY CLARK THOMPSON MEDAL AWARDS

Walcott, Charles Doolittle, 1921　Scott, William Berryman, 1930　Bather, Francis Arthur, 1932

Margerie, Emm. de, 1923　Ulrich, Edward Oscar, 1930　Schucbert, Charles, 1934

Clarke, John Mason, 1925

Smith, James Perrin, 1928　White, David, 1931

JOSEPH HENRY FUND

[$40,163.50]

To assist meritorious investigators, especially in the direction of original research

Members of the committee

Webster, D. L., chairman (1939)　Bush, Vannevar (1941)　Seashore, C. E. (1940)

Jones, L. R. (1938)　Wilson, H. V. (1937)

GEORGE TRUE NEALLEY FUND

[$19,555.55]

For the general purposes of the Academy

CHARLES DOOLITTLE WALCOTT FUND

[$5,000]

For stimulation of research in pre-Cambrian or Cambrian life by award of a medal and honorarium

Board of directors

Vaughan, T. W., temporary chairman

Abbot, C. G.[a]

Barrois, Charles[b]

Lang, W. D.[c]

Ulrich, E. O.

CHARLES DOOLITTLE WALCOTT MEDAL AWARD

White, David, 1934

JOHN J. CARTY FUND

[$25,000]

Medal and monetary award, not oftener than once in every 2 years, to an individual for noteworthy and distinguished accomplishment in any field of science coming within the scope of the charter of the Academy

---

[a] Representing the Smithsonian Institution.
[b] Representing the Institut de France.
[c] Representing the Royal Society of London.

JOHN J. CARTY MEDAL AWARD

Carty, John J., 1932

CARNEGIE ENDOWMENT FUND

[$3,550,000]

For the purposes of the National Academy of Sciences and National Research Council

6. MEMBERS OF THE NATIONAL ACADEMY OF SCIENCES

JULY 1, 1936

Elected

Abbot, Charles Greeley, Smithsonian Institution, Washington, D. C.____ 1915
Abel, John Jacob, Laboratory for Endocrine Research, Johns Hopkins
   Medical School, Baltimore, Md_____ 1912
Adams, Comfort Avery, The Eward G. Budd Manufacturing Co., Phila-
   delphia, Pa_____ 1930
Adams, Roger, University of Illinois, Urbana, Ill_____ 1929
Adams, Walter Sydney, Mount Wilson Observatory, Pasadena, Calif.____ 1917
Aitken, Robert Grant, 1109 Spruce St., Berkeley,. Calif_____ 1918
Alexander, James Waddell, Princeton. N. J_____ 1930
Allen, Charles Elmer, University of Wisconsin, Madison, Wis_____ 1924
Allen, Eugene Thomas, 1862 Mintwood Pl., Washington, D. C_____ 1930
Ames, Joseph Sweetman, Johns Hopkins University, Baltimore, Md.___ 1909
Anderson, John August, Mount Wilson Observatory, Pasadena, Calif__ 1928
Angell, James Rowland, Yale University, New Haven, Conn_____ 1920
Avery, Oswald Theodore, Rockefeller Institute for Medical Research,
   66th St. and York Ave., New York City_____ 1933
Babcock, Harold Delos, Mount Wilson Observatory, Pasadena, Calif__ 1933
Baekeland, Leo Hendrik, Bakelite Corporation, 247 Park Ave., New
   York City_____ 1936
Bailey, Irving Widmer, Biological Laboratories, Harvard University,
   Cambridge, Mass_____ 1929
Bailey, Liberty Hyde, Ithaca, N. Y_____ 1917
Bancroft, Wilder Dwight, 7 East Ave., Ithaca, N. Y_____ 1920
Barbour, Thomas, Museum of Comparative Zoology, Cambridge, Mass____ 1933
Bateman, Harry, California Institute of Technology, Pasadena, Calif____ 1930
Baxter, Gregory Paul, T. Jefferson Coolidge, Jr., Memorial Laboratory,
   Cambridge, Mass _____ 1916
Bell, Eric Temple, California Institute of Technology, Pasadena, Calif____ 1927
Benedict, Francis Gano, Nutrition Laboratory, 29 Vila St., Boston, Mass__ 1914
Benedict, Stanley Rossiter, Cornell University Medical College, 1300 York
   Ave., New York City_____ 1924
Berkey, Charles Peter, Department of Geology and Mineralogy, Columbia
   University, New York City_____ 1927
Berry, Edward Wilber, Johns Hopkins University, Baltimore, Md_____ 1922
Bigelow, Henry Bryant, Museum of Comparative Zoology, Harvard Univer-
   sity, Cambridge, Mass_____ 1931
Birge, Raymond Thayer, University of California, Berkeley, Calif_____ 1932
Birkhoff, George David, 984 Memorial Drive, Cambridge, Mass_____ 1918
Blackwelder, Eliot, P. O. Box N, Stanford University, Calif_____ 1936
Blakeslee, Albert Francis, Department of Genetics, Carnegie Institution
   of Washington, Cold Spring Harbor, Long Island. N. Y_____ 1929
Blichfeldt, Hans Frederick, Box 875, Stanford University, Calif_____ 1920
Bliss, Gilbert Ames, University of Chicago, Chicago, Ill_____ 1916
Boas, Franz, Columbia University, New York City_____ 1900
Bogert, Marston Taylor, 566 Chandler Laboratories, Columbia University,
   New York City_____ 1916
Boring, Edwin Garrigues, Harvard University, Cambridge, Mass_____ 1932
Bowen, Ira Sprague, California Institute of Technology, Pasadena, Calif__ 1936

Elected

Bowen, Norman Levi, Geophysical Laboratory, 2801 Upton St., Washington, D. C_____ 1935

Bowie, William, United States Coast and Geodetic Survey, Washington, D. C._____ 1927

Bowman, Isaiah, Johns Hopkins University, Baltimore, Md_____ 1930

Bray, William Crowell, Department of Chemistry, University of California, Berkeley, Calif_____ 1924

Bridgman, Percy Williams, Jefferson Physical Laboratory, Cambridge, Mass_____ 1918

Brown, Ernest William, Yale Observatory, Prospect St., New Haven, Conn. 1923

Bush, Vannevar, Massachusetts Institute of Technology, Cambridge, Mass_____ 1934

Calkins, Gary Nathan, Columbia University, New York City_____ 1919

Campbell, Douglas Houghton, Stanford University, Stanford Universtiy, Calif_____ 1910

Campbell, William Wallace, 1980 Vallejo St., San Francisco, Calif_____ 1902

Cannon, Walter Bradford, Harvard Medical School, 25 Shattuck St., Boston 17, Mass_____ 1914

Carlson, Anton Julius, University of Chicago, Chicago, Ill_____ 1920

Carothers, Wallace Hume, E. I. duPont de Nemours & Co., Wilmington, Del_____ 1936

Castle, William Ernest, Hilgard Hall, University of California, Berkeley, Calif_____ 1915

Cattell, James McKeen, Garrison, N. Y._____ 1901

Chapman, Frank Michler, American Museum of Natural History, 77th St. and Central Park West, New York City_____ 1921

Child, Charles Manning, University of Chicago, Chicago, Ill_____ 1935

Chittenden, Russell Henry, Sheffield Scientific School, New Haven, Conn. 1890

Clark, William Mansfield, Johns Hopkins Medical School, Washington and Monument Streets, Baltimore, Md_____ 1928

Clinton, George Perkins, Connecticut Agricultural Experiment Station, New Haven, Conn._____ 1930

Coble, Arthur Byron, University of Illinois, Urbana, Ill_____ 1924

Coblentz, William Weber, Bureau of Standards, Washington, D. C._____ 1930

Coghill, George Ellett, 409 E. Union Street, Gainesville, Fla_____ 1935

Cole, Rufus, Hospital of the Rockefeller Institute, 66th St. and York Avenue, New York City_____ 1922

Compton, Arthur Holly, University of Chicago, Chicago, Ill_____ 1927

Compton, Karl Taylor, 111 Charles River Road, Cambridge, Mass_____ 1924

Conant, James Bryant, Harvard University, Cambridge 38, Mass_____ 1929

Conklin, Edwin Grant, Princeton University, Princeton, N. J_____ 1908

Coolidge, William David, General Electric Co., Schenectady, N. Y_____ 1925

Crew, Henry, 620 Library Place, Evanston, Ill_____ 1909

Cross, Charles Whitman, 101 East Kirke St., Chevy Chase, Md_____ 1908

Curtis, Heber Doust, Observatory, University of Michigan, Ann Arbor, Mich_____ 1919

Cushing, Harvey Williams, Yale School of Medicine, New Haven, Conn. 1917

Daly, Reginald Aldworth, Geological Museum, Harvard University, Cambridge, Mass_____ 1925

Davenport, Charles Benedict, Carnegie Institution of Washington, Cold Spring Harbor, L. I., N. Y._____ 1912

Davis, Bergen, Columbia University, New York City_____ 1929

Davisson, Clinton Joseph, Bell Telephone Laboratories, 463 West St., New York City_____ 1929

Day, Arthur Louis, Geophysical Laboratory, 2801 Upton St., Washington, D. C._____ 1911

Detwiler, Samuel Randall, College of Physicians and Surgeons, 630 West 168th St., New York City_____ 1932

Dewey, John, Columbia University, New York City_____ 1910

Dickson, Leonard Eugene, University of Chicago, Chicago, Ill_____ 1913

Dochez, Alphonse Raymond, Columbia University, Presbyterian Hospital, 620 West 168th St., New York City_____ 1933

Dodge, Bernard Ogilvie, New York Botanical Garden, Bronx Park (Fordham Station), New York City_____ 1933

Dodge, Raymond, Tryon, N. C._____ 1924

Elected

Donaldson, Henry Herbert, Wistar Institute of Anatomy and Biology, Philadelphia, Pa_____ 1914

DuBois, Eugene Floyd, New York Hospital, 525 East 68th St., New York City_____ 1933

Duggar, Benjamin Minge, Biology Building, University of Wisconsin, Madison, Wis_____ 1927

Dunn, Gano, 80 Broad St., New York City_____ 1919

Durand, William Frederick, Stanford University, Stanford University, Calif_____ 1917

East, Edward Murray, Biological Laboratories, Harvard University, Cambridge, Mass_____ 1925

Eisenhart, Luther Pfahler, Princeton, N. J_____ 1922

Emerson, Rollins Adams, Cornell University, Ithaca, N. Y_____ 1927

Emmet, William Le Roy, General Electric Co., Schenectady, N. Y_____ 1921

Epstein, Paul Sophus, 1484 Oakdale St., Pasadena, Calif_____ 1930

Erlanger, Joseph, Washington University School of Medicine, 4580 Scott Ave., St. Louis, Mo_____ 1922

Evans, Griffith Conrad, Department of Mathematics, University of California, Berkeley, Calif_____ 1933

Evans, Herbert McLean, Institute of Experimental Biology, University of California, Berkeley, Calif_____ 1927

Ewing, James, Memorial Hospital. New York City_____ 1935

Fernald, Merritt Lyndon, Gray Herbarium, Harvard University, Cambridge, Mass_____ 1935

Fletcher, Harvey, Bell Telephone Laboratories, 463 West St., New York City _____ 1935

Flexner, Simon, Rockefeller Institute for Medical Research, 66th St. and York Ave., New York City_____ 1908

Forbes, Alexander, Harvard Medical School, Boston, Mass_____ 1936

Franklin, Edward Curtis, 662 Mirada, Stanford University, Calif_____ 1914

Fred, Edwin Broun, College of Agriculture, University of Wisconsin, Madison, Wis_____ 1931

Gasser, Herbert Spencer, Rockefeller Institute for Medical Research, 66th St. and York Ave., New York City_____ 1934

Gherardi, Bancroft, 195 Broadway, New York City_____ 1933

Giauque, William Francis, University of California, Berkeley, Calif_____ 1936

Gomberg, Moses, University of Michigan, Ann Arbor, Mich_____ 1914

Gortner, Ross Aiken, University Farm, St. Paul, Minn_____ 1935

Gregory, William King, American Museum of Natural History, 77th St. and Central Park West, New York City_____ 1927

Hale, George Ellery, Mount Wilson Observatory, Pasadena, Calif_____ 1902

Hall, Edwin Herbert, 39 Garden St., Cambridge, Mass_____ 1911

Harkins, William Draper, University of Chicago, Chicago, Ill_____ 1921

Harper, Robert Almer, Columbia University, New York City_____ 1911

Harrison, Ross Granville, Yale University, Osborn Zoological Laboratory, New Haven, Conn_____ 1913

Harvey, Edmund Newton, Princeton University, Princeton, N. J_____ 1934

Hektoen, Ludvig, 637 South Wood St., Chicago, Ill_____ 1918

Henderson, Lawrence Joseph, Morgan Hall, Soldiers Field, Boston, Mass__ 1919

Henderson, Yandell, Yale University, New Haven, Conn_____ 1923

Herrick, Charles Judson, Department of Anatomy, University of Chicago, Chicago, Ill_____ 1918

Hildebrand, Joel Henry, Gilman Hall, University of California, Berkeley, Calif _____ 1929

Hoagland, Dennis Robert, 3048 Life Sciences Bldg., University of California, Berkeley, Calif_____ 1934

Hooton, Earnest Albert, Peabody Museum, Harvard University, Cambridge, Mass_____ 1935

Hoover, Herbert Clark, Palo Alto, Calif_____ 1922

Hovgaard, William, Hotel Margaret, Columbia Heights, Brooklyn, N. Y__ 1929

Howard, Leland Ossian, Bureau of Entomology, United States Department of Agriculture, Washington, D. C_____ 1916

Howe, Marshall Avery, New York Botanical Garden, Bronx Park, New York City_____ 1923

Howell, William Henry, 112 St. Dunstan's Road, Baltimore, Md_____ 1905

Hrdlicka, Ales, United States National Museum, Washington, D. C_____ 1921

Elected

Hubble, Edwin Powell, Mount Wilson Observatory, Pasadena, Calif____ 1927
Hudson, Claude Silbert, National Institute of Health, 25th and E Sts., Washington, D. C.____ 1927
Hulett, George Augustus, Princeton University, Princeton, N. J._____ 1922
Hull, Albert Wallace, Research Laboratory, General Electric Co., Schenectady, N. Y.____ 1929
Hull, Clark Leonard, Institute of Human Relations, Yale University, 333 Cedar St., New Haven, Conn.____ 1936
Hunsaker, Jerome Clark, Massachusetts Institute of Technology, Cambridge, Mass.____ 1935
Hunt, Reid, Harvard Medical School, Boston, Mass.____ 1919
Hunter, Walter Samuel, Brown University, Providence, R. I.____ 1935
Ives, Herbert Eugene, Bell Telephone Laboratories, 463 West St., New York City____ 1933
Jackson, Dunham, University of Minnesota, Minneapolis, Minn.____ 1935
Jacobs, Walter Abraham, Rockefeller Institute for Medical Research, 66th Street and York Ave., New York City____ 1932
Jennings, Herbert Spencer, Johns Hopkins University, Baltimore, Md.____ 1914
Jewett, Frank Baldwin, American Telephone & Telegraph Co., 195 Broadway, New York City____ 1918
Johnson, Douglas Wilson, Columbia University, New York City____ 1932
Johnson, Treat Baldwin, Bethwood, Amity Road, Bethany, Conn.____ 1919
Jones, Lewis Ralph, University of Wisconsin, Madison, Wis.____ 1920
Jordan, Edwin Oakes, University of Chicago, Chicago, Ill.____ 1936
Kasner, Edward, Columbia University, New York City____ 1917
Keith, Arthur, United States Geological Survey, Washington, D. C.____ 1928
Kellogg, Vernon Lyman, 2305 Bancroft Place, Washington, D. C.____ 1930
Kemble, Edwin Crawford, Jefferson Physical Laboratory, Harvard University, Cambridge, Mass.____ 1931
Kennelly, Arthur Edwin, Harvard University, Cambridge, Mass.____ 1921
Kettering, Charles Franklin, General Motors Corporation, Detroit, Mich.____ 1928
Keyes, Frederick George, Massachusetts Institute of Technology, Cambridge, Mass.____ 1930
Kidder, Alfred Vincent, The Red House, Beverly Farms, Mass.____ 1936
Knopf, Adolph, Yale University, New Haven, Conn.____ 1931
Kofoid, Charles Atwood, University of California, Berkeley, Calif.____ 1922
Kohler, Elmer Peter, Converse Memorial Laboratory, Harvard University, Frisbie Place, Cambridge, Mass.____ 1920
Kraus, Charles August, Brown University, Providence, R. I.____ 1925
Kroeber, Alfred L., University of California, Berkeley, Calif.____ 1928
Kunkel, Louis Otto, Rockefeller Institute for Medical Research, Princeton, N. J.____ 1932
Lamb, Arthur Becket, Chemical Laboratory, Harvard University, Cambridge, Mass.____ 1024
Landsteiner, Karl, Rockefeller Institute for Medical Research, 66th \ St. and York Ave., New York City____ 1932
Langmuir, Irving, General Electric Co., Schenectady, N. Y.____ 1918
Lashley, Karl Spencer, Biological Laboratories, Harvard University, Cambridge, Mass.____ 1930
Lawrence, Ernest Orlando, University of California, Berkeley, Calif.____ 1934
Lawson, Andrew Cowper, University of California, Berkeley, Calif.____ 1924
Lefschetz, Solomon, 190 Prospect St., Princeton, N. J.____ 1925
Leith, Charles Kenneth, University of Wisconsin, Madison, Wis.____ 1920
Leuschner, Armin Otto, Students' Observatory, University of California, Berkeley, Calif.____ 1913
Levene, Phoebus Aaron Theodore, Rockefeller Institute for Medical Research, 66th St. and York Ave., New York City____ 1916
Leverett, Frank, 1724 South University Ave., Ann Arbor, Mich.____ 1929
Lewis, Warren Harmon, Department of Embryology, Carnegie Institution of Washington, Wolfe and Madison Sts., Baltimore, Md.____ 1936
Lillie, Frank Rattray, National Academy of Sciences, 2101 Constitution Ave., Washington, D. C.____ 1015
Lind, Samuel Colville, School of Chemistry, University of Minnesota, Minneapolis, Minn.____ 1930
Lindgren, Waldemar, Massachusetts Institute of Technology, Cambridge, Mass.____ 1909

Elected

Longwell, Chester Ray, Kirtland Hall, Yale University, New Haven, Conn_____ 1935
Lowie, Robert Harry, University of California, Berkeley, Calif_____ 1931
Lyman, Theodore, Research Laboratory of Physics, Harvard University, Cambridge, Mass _____ 1917
MacCallum, William George, Department of Pathology, Johns Hopkins University, 1833 East Monument St., Baltimore, Md_____ 1921
McClung, Clarence Erwin, University of Pennsylvania, Philadelphia, Pa__ 1920
McCollum, Elmer Verner, School of Hygiene and Public Health, 615 North Wolfe St., Baltimore, Md_____ 1920
Mark, Edward Laurens, 109 Irving St., Cambridge, Mass_____ 1903
Mason, Max, California Institute of Technology, Pasadena, Calif_____ 1923
Mendenhall, Walter Curran, U. S. Geological Survey, Washington, D. C___ 1932
Merriam, Clinton Hart, 1919 16th St., Washington, D. C_____ 1902
Merriam, John Campbell, Carnegie Institution of Washington, Washington, D. C_____ 1918
Merrill, Elmer Drew, Gray Herbarium, Cambridge, Mass_____ 1923
Merrill, Paul Willard, Mount Wilson Observatory, Pasadena, Calif_____ 1929
Merritt, Ernest George, 1 Grove Pl., Ithaca, N. Y_____ 1914
Michael, Arthur, 219 Parker St., Newton Center, Mass_____ 1889
Miles, Walter Richard, Yale University, 333 Cedar St., New Haven, Conn_ 1933
Miller, Dayton Clarence, Case School of Applied Science, Cleveland, Ohio _____ 1921
Miller, George Abram, 1203 West Illinois St., Urbana, Ill_____ 1921
Millikan, Robert Andrews, California Institute of Technology, Pasadena, Calif_____ 1915
Mitchell, Samuel Alfred, Leander McCormick Observatory, University, Va_ 1933
Modjeski, Ralph, 52 Vanderbilt Ave., New York City_____ 1925
Moore, Joseph Haines, Lick Observatory, Mount Hamilton, Calif_____ 1931
Moore, Robert Lee, University of Texas, Austin, Tex_____ 1931
Morgan, Thomas Hunt, California Institute of Technology, Pasadena, Calif_____ 1909
Morse, Harold Marston, Institute for Advanced Study, Princeton, N. J____ 1932
Moulton, Forest Ray, 327 South La Salle St., Chicago, Ill_____ 1910
Muller, Hermann Joseph, Russian Academy of Sciences, Moscow, Union of Soviet Socialist Republics_____ 1931
Mulliken, Robert Sanderson, University of Chicago, Chicago, Ill_____ 1936
Nichols, Edward Leamington, Cornell University, Ithaca, N. Y_____ 1901
Norris, James Flack, Massachusetts Institute of Technology, Cambridge, Mass_____ 1934
Northrop, John Howard, Rockefeller Institute for Medical Research, Princeton, N. J_____ 1934
Novy, Frederick George, 721 Forest Ave., Ann Arbor, Mich_____ 1924
Noyes, William Albert, University of Illinois, Urbana, Ill_____ 1910
Opie, Eugene Lindsay, Cornell University Medical School, 1300 York Ave., New York City _____ 1923
Osgood, William Fogg, 1800 Thousand Oaks Blvd., Berkeley, Calif_____ 1904
Osterhout, Winthrop John Vanleuven, Rockefeller Institute for Medical Research, 66th St. and York Ave., New York City_____ 1919
Palache, Charles, Harvard University, Cambridge, Mass_____ 1934
Parker, George Howard, 16 Berkeley St., Cambridge, Mass_____ 1913
Pauling, Linus, California Institute of Technology, Pasadena, Calif_____ 1933
Pearl, Raymond, 1901 East Madison St., Baltimore, Md_____ 1916
Pierce, George Washington, Cruft Laboratory, Harvard University, Cambridge, Mass_____ 1920
Pillsbury, Walter Bowers, University of Michigan, Ann Arbor, Mich_____ 1925
Reid, Harry Fielding, Johns Hopkins University, Baltimore, Md_____ 1912
Richards, Alfred Newton, University of Pennsylvania, Philadelphia, Pa__ 1927
Richtmyer, Floyd Karker, Rockefeller Hall, Cornell University, Ithaca, N. Y_____ 1932
Ritt, Joseph Fels, Columbia University, New York City_____ 1933
Rivers, Thomas Milton, Rockefeller Institute for Medical Research, 66th St. and York Ave., New York City_____ 1934
Rose, William Cumming, University of Illinois, Urbana, Ill_____ 1936
Ross, Frank Elmore, Mount Wilson Observatory, Pasadena, Calif_____ 1930

Elected

Rous, Francis Peyton, Rockefeller Institute for Medical Research, 66th
St. and York Ave., New York City_____ 1927
Ruedemann, Rudolph, New York State Museum, Albany, N. Y._____ 1928
Russell, Henry Norris, Princeton University, Princeton, N. J._____ 1918
Sabin, Florence Rena, Rockefeller Institute for Medical Research, 66th
St. and York Ave., New York City_____ 1925
Sapir, Edward, Yale University, New Haven, Conn._____ 1934
Saunders, Frederick Albert, Jefferson Physical Laboratory, Cambridge,
Mass._____ 1925
Sauveur, Albert, Harvard University, Cambridge, Mass._____ 1927
Schlesinger, Frank, Yale University Observatory, New Haven, Conn.____ 1916
Schuchert, Charles, Peabody Museum, Yale University, New Haven, Conn. 1910
Scott, William Berryman, Princeton University, Princeton, N. J._____ 1906
Seares, Frederick Hanley, Mount Wilson Observatory, Pasadena, Calif.___ 1919
Seashore, Carl Emil, State University of Iowa, Iowa City, Iowa_____ 1922
Setchell, William Albert, University of California, Berkeley, Calif._____ 1919
Shaffer, Philip Anderson, Washington University Medical School, St.
Louis, Mo._____ 1928
Shapley, Harlow, Harvard College Observatory, Cambridge, Mass._____ 1924
Sherman, Henry Clapp, Columbia University, New York City_____ 1933
Sinnott, Edmund Ware, Columbia University, New York City_____ 1936
Slater, John Clarke, Massachusetts Institute of Technology, Cambridge,
Mass._____ 1932
Slipher, Vesto Melvin, Lowell Observatory, Flagstaff, Ariz._____ 1921
Stakman, Elvin Charles, University Farm, St. Paul, Minn._____ 1934
Stebbins, Joel, Washburn Observatory, Madison, Wis._____ 1920
Stejneger, Leonhard, United States National Museum, Washington, D. C. 1923
Stieglitz, Julius Oscar, University of Chicago, Chicago, Ill._____ 1911
Stillwell, Lewis Buckley, Elm Road, Princeton, N. J._____ 1921
Stockard, Charles Rupert, Cornell University Medical School, 1300 York
Ave., New York City_____ 1922
Stratton, George Malcolm, University of California, Berkeley, Calif.____ 1928
Streeter, George Linius, Department of Embryology, Carnegie Institution,
Wolfe and Madison Sts., Baltimore, Md._____ 1931
Sturtevant, Alfred Henry, California Institute of Technology, Pasadena,
Calif._____ 1930
Swanton, John Reed, Bureau of American Ethnology, Smithsonian Insti-
tution, Washington, D. C._____ 1932
Swasey, Ambrose, 7808 Euclid Ave., Cleveland, Ohio_____ 1922
Taylor, David Watson, 1869 Wyoming Ave., Washington, D. C._____ 1918
Tennent, David Hilt, Bryn Mawr College, Bryn Mawr, Pa._____ 1929
Terman, Lewis Madison, 761 Dolores, Stanford University, Calif._____ 1928
Thomson, Elihu, 22 Monument Ave., Swampscott, Mass._____ 1907
Thorndike, Edward Lee, Teachers College, Columbia University, New
York City_____ 1917
Tolman, Richard Chace, California Institute of Technology, Pasadena,
Calif._____ 1923
Trelease, William, University of Illinois, Urbana, Ill._____ 1902
Trumpler, Robert Julius, Lick Observatory, Mount Hamilton, Calif.____ 1932
Ulrich, Edward Oscar, United States National Museum, Washington,
D. C._____ 1917
Urey, Harold Clayton, Columbia University, New York City_____ 1935
Vandiver, Harry Shultz, University of Texas, Austin, Tex._____ 1934
Van Slyke, Donald Dexter, Rockefeller Institute for Medical Research,
66th St. and York Ave., New York City_____ 1921
Van Vleck, Edward Burr, 519 N. Pickney St., Madison, Wis._____ 1911
Van Vleck, John Hasbrouck, Harvard University, Cambridge, Mass.____ 1935
Vaughan, Thomas Wayland, 3333 P St., Washington, D. C._____ 1921
Veblen, Oswald, The Institute for Advanced Study, Fine Hall, Prince-
ton, N. J._____ 1919
Walsh, Joseph Leonard, Harvard University, Cambridge, Mass._____ 1936
Washburn, Margaret Floy, Vassar College, Poughkeepsie, N. Y._____ 1931
Webster, David Locke, Physics Department, Room 385, Stanford Uni-
versity, Stanford University, Calif._____ 1923

Elected

Wells, Harry Gideon, University of Chicago, Chicago, Ill_____ 1925
Wheeler, William Morton, Institute of Biology, Divinity Ave., Cambridge,
    Mass _____ 1912
Whipple, George Hoyt, School of Medicine of the University of Rochester,
    Crittenden Blvd., Rochester, N. Y_____ 1929
White, Henry Seely, Vassar College, Poughkeepsie, N. Y_____ 1915
Whitehead, John Boswell, Johns Hopkins University, Baltimore, Md__ 1932
Whitney, Willis Rodney, General Electric Co., Schenectady, N. Y_____ 1917
Wiener, Norbert, Massachusetts Institute of Technology, Cambridge,
    Mass _____ 1934
Willis, Bailey, Box 1365, Stanford University, Calif_____ 1920
Wilson, Edmund Beecher, Columbia University, New York City_____ 1899
Wilson, Edwin Bidwell, 55 Shattuck St., Boston 17, Mass_____ 1919
Wilson, Henry Van Peters, University of North Carolina, Chapel Hill,
    N. C_____ 1927
Wissler, Clark, American Museum of Natural History, New York City__ 1929
Wood, Robert Williams, Johns Hopkins University, Baltimore, Md_____ 1912
Woodruff, Lorande Loss, Yale University, New Haven, Conn_____ 1924
Woodworth, Robert Sessions, Columbia University, New York City_____ 1921
Wright, Frederick Eugene, Geophysical Laboratory, 2801 Upton St.,
    Washington, D. C_____ 1923
Wright, Orville, 15 N. Broadway, Dayton, Ohio_____ 1936
Wright, Sewall Green, University of Chicago, Chicago, Ill_____ 1934
Wright, William Hammond, Lick Observatory, Mount Hamilton, Calif__ 1922
Yerkes, Robert Mearns, Yale School of Medicine, 333 Cedar St., New
    Haven, Conn_____ 1923
Zinsser, Hans, Harvard Medical School, 240 Longwood Ave., Boston,
    Mass _____ 1924

FOREIGN ASSOCIATES OF THE NATIONAL ACADEMY OF SCIENCES

July 1, 1936

Adams, Frank Dawson, McGill University, Montreal, Canada_____ 1920
Barrois, Charles, Université, 41 rue Pascal, Lille, France_____ 1908
Bjerknes, V. F. K., University, Oslo, Norway_____ 1934
Bohr, Niels, University of Copenhagen, Copenhagen, Denmark_____ 1925
Bordet, Jules, Pasteur Institute, Rue du Remorqueur, 28, Brussels, Bel-
    gium_____ 1935
Bower, Frederick Orpen, 2, The Crescent, Ripon, Yorks, England_____ 1929
Brogger, W. C., Universitet, Oslo, Norway_____ 1903
Debye, Peter, Physikalisches Institut der Universitat, Linnestrasse 5,
    Leipzig, Germany_____ 1931
Deslandres, Henri, Bureau des Longitudes, 21 rue de Téhéran, Paris 8,
    France _____ 1913
Dyson, Sir Frank Watson, 27, Westcombe Park Road, Blackheath, London
    S. E. 3, England_____ 1926
Eddington, Sir Arthur Stanley, Observatory, Cambridge, England_____ 1925
Einstein, Albert, Institute for Advanced Study, Princeton, N. J.
    (U. S. A.)_____ 1922
Forsyth, A. R., Imperial College of Science and Technology, London,
    England_____ 1907
Hadamard, Jacques, 25 rue Jean-Dolent, Paris XIV, France_____ 1926
Hadfield, Sir Robert A., 22 Carlton House Terrace, S. W. 1, London,
    England_____ 1928
Hardy, Godfrey Harold, New College, Oxford, England_____ 1927
Heim, Albert, Zurich, Switzerland_____ 1913
Hertwig, Richard, Zoologisches Institut, Louisenstrasse 14, Munich,
    Germany _____ 1929
Hilbert, David, Wilhelm-Weberstrasse 29, Gottingen, Germany_____ 1907
Hopkins, Sir Frederick Gowland, University, Cambridge, England_____ 1924
Kustner, Karl Friedrich, Mehlem bei Bonn, Germany_____ 1913
Lacroix, F. Alfred A., 23 rue Jean-Dolent, Paris XIV, France_____ 1920
Larmor, Sir Joseph, St. John's College, Cambridge, England_____ 1908
Marconi, Marchese Guglielmo, 11, Via Condotti, Rome, Italy_____ 1932
Penck, Albrecht, Knesebeckstrasse 48, Berlin, W. 15, Germany_____ 1909
Picard, Charles Emile, 25 Quai Conti, Paris (VI), France_____ 1903

Elected

Planck, Max, Wangenheimstrasse 21, Berlin-Grunewald, Germany_____ 1926
Prain, Sir David, The Well Farm, Warlingham, Surrey, England_____ 1920
Robinson, Robert, Dyson Perrins Laboratory, South Parks Road, Oxford, England_____ 1934
Rutherford, Baron ; Ernest Rutherford, Newnham Cottage, Queen's Road, Cambridge, England_____ 1911
Sabatier, Paul, Allée des Zephyrs, No. 11, Toulouse, France_____ 1927
Schneider, Charles Eugène, 42 rue d'Anjou, Paris, France_____ 1925
Sherrington, Sir Charles Scott, "Broomside", Valley Road, Ipswich, England _____ 1924
Sommerfeld, Arnold, University of Munich, Munich, Germany_____ 1929
Spemann, Hans, Zoologisches Institut, Freiburg, i. Br., Germany_____ 1925
Stumpf, Carl, Potsdamerstrasse 15, Berlin-Lichterfelde West, Germany__ 1927
Thomson, Sir Joseph, Trinity Lodge, Cambridge, England_____ 1903
Vallee-Poussin, C. de la, University of Louvain, Louvain, Belgium_____ 1929
Volterra, Vito, Via in Lucina 17, Rome, Italy_____ 1911
Wieland, Heinrich. Chemisches Laboratorium Bayer. Akademie der Wissenschaften, Sophienstrasse 10, Munich, 2 NW., Germany_____ 1932
Willstaetter, Richard, Moehlstrasse 29, Munich, O. 27, Germany_____ 1926

7. MEDALISTS OF THE NATIONAL ACADEMY

	Medal	Year		Medal	Year
Abbe, Cleveland [1]_____	Welfare_____	1916	Hubble, Edwin_____	Barnard_____	1935
Abbot, Charles Greeley_____	Draper_____	1910	Huggins, Sir William [1]_____	Draper_____	1901
Abel, Othenio [3]_____	Elliot_____	1920	Kapteyn, J. C.[1]_____	Watson_____	1913
Adams, Walter Sidney_____ __	Draper_____	1918	Keeler, James Edward [1]_____	Draper_____	1899
Albert I[er], Prince of Monaco[1] [3]	Agassiz_____	1918	Langley, Samuel Pierpont [1]___	____do_____	1886
Auwers, G. F. J. Arthur [1]____	Watson_____	1891	Leuschner, Armin Otto_____	Watson_____	1915
Barnett, Samuel Jackson [1]___	Comstock____	1918	Margerie, Emmanuel de [3]____	Thompson__	1923
Bather, Francis Arthur [1]_____	Thompson__	1932	Mather, Stephen Tyng [1] [1]___	Welfare_____	1930
Beebe, William [3]_____	Elliot____ __	1918	Merrill, George Perkins [1]____	Smith_____	1922
Bigelow, Henry Bryant____ __	Agassiz_____	1931	Michelson, Albert Abraham [1]__	Draper_____	1916
Bjerknes, Vilhelm [1] [3]_____	____do_____	1926	Millikan, Robert Andrews___	Comstock___	1913
Black, Davidson [1] [3]_____	Elliot_____	1931	Newton, Hubert Anson [1]____	Smith_____	1888
Bohr, Niels_____	Barnard_____	1925	Osborn, Henry Fairfield [1]____	Elliot_____	1929
Bragg, Sir William Henry [3]__	____do_____	1914	Park, William Hallock [3]_____	Welfare_____	1932
Breuil, Henri [3]_____	Elliot_____	1924	Pettersson, Otto Sven [3]_____	Agassiz_____	1924
Bridgman, P. W_____	Comstock____	1933	Pickering, Edward Charles [1]__	Draper_____	1888
Campbell, William Wallace__	Draper_____	1906	Pinchot, Gifford [3]_____	Welfare_____	1916
Cannon, Annie Jump [3]_____	____do_____	1931	Plaskett, John Stanley [3]_____	Draper_____	1934
Canu, Ferdinand [1] [3]_____	Elliot_____	1923	Ridgway, Robert [1]_____	Elliot_____	1919
Carty, John J. [1]_____	Carty_____	1932	Rose, Wickliffe [1] [3]_____	Welfare_____	1931
Chandler, Seth Carlo [1]_____	Watson_____	1894	Rowland, Henry Augustus [1]___	Draper_____	1890
Chapin, Charles V.[1]_____	Welfare_____	1928	Russell, F. F.[3]_____	Welfare_____	1935
Chapin, James P.[1]_____	Elliot_____	1932	Russell, Henry Norris_____	Draper_____	1922
Chapman, Frank Michler_____	____do_____	1917	Rutherford Baron; Ernest	Barnard_____	1909
Charlier, C. V. L.[3]_____	Watson_____	1924	Rutherford		
Clarke, John Mason [1]_____	Thompson__	1925	Schmidt, Johannes [3]_____	Agassiz_____	1930
Coghill, George Ellett_____	Elliot_____	1930	Shoenfeld, Ed. [1] [3]_____	Watson_____	1889
Davisson, C. J_____	Comstock____	1928	Schuchert, Charles_____	Thompson__	1934
Dean, Bashford [1] [1]_____	Elliot_____	1921	Scott, W. B_____	____do_____	1930
Defant, Albert [3]_____	Agassiz_____	1932	Seton, Ernest Thompson [3]____	Elliot_____	1928
de Sitter, Willem [1]_____	Watson_____	1920	Shapley, Harlow_____	Draper_____	1926
Deslandres, Henri_____	Draper_____	1913	Sigsbee, Rear Admiral	Agassiz_____	1920
Duane, William [1]_____	Comstock____	1923	Charles Dwight, U. S.		
Eddington, Sir Arthur Stanley.	Draper_____	1924	Navy.[1] [3]		
			Slipher, V. M_____	Draper_____	1932
Einstein, Albert_____	Barnard_____	1921	Smith, James Perrin [1]_____	Thompson__	1928
Ekman, V. Walfrid [3]_____	Agassiz_____	1928	Stebbins, Joel_____	Draper_____	1915
Fabry, Charles [3]_____	Draper_____	1919	Stensio, Erik A: Son [3]_____	Elliot_____	1927
Fairchild, David [3]_____	Welfare_____	1933	Stiles, Charles Wardell [1]_____	Welfare_____	1921
Fowler, Alfred [3]_____	Draper_____	1920	Stratton, Samuel Wesley [1]___	____do_____	1917
Gardiner, J. Stanley [3]_____	Agassiz_____	1929	Ulrich, Edward Oscar_____	Thompson__	1930
Gill, Sir David [1]_____	Watson_____	1899	Vaughan, T. Wayland_____	Agassiz_____	1935
Goethals, George Washington.[1] [3]	Welfare_____	1914	Vogel, Herman Karl [1]_____	Draper_____	1893
			Vollmer, August [1]_____	Welfare_____	1934
Gorgas, William Crawford [1] [1]	____do_____	1914	Walcott, Charles Doolittle [1]__	Thompson__	1921
Gould, Benjamin Apthorp [1]_	Watson_____	1887	Weber, Max [3]_____	Agassiz_____	1927
Gran, Haakon Hasberg [1]____	Agassiz_____	1934	Wheeler, William Morton____	Elliot_____	1922
Hale, George Ellery_____	Draper_____	1904	White, David [1]_____	Thompson__	1931
Heisenberg, Werner [3]_____	Barnard_____	1930	Do_____	Walcott____	1934
Helland-Hansen, Bjorn [3]____	Agassiz_____	1933	Wilson, Edmund B_____	Elliot_____	1925
Hjort, Johan [3]_____	____do_____	1913	Wright, William Hammond___	Draper_____	1928
Hoover, Herbert Clark_____	Welfare_____	1920	Zeeman, P.[3]_____	____do_____	1921

8. PRESIDENTS OF THE ACADEMY

Alexander Dallas Bache	1863-67	William Henry Welch	1913-17
Joseph Henry	1868-78	Charles Doolittle Walcott	1917-23
William Barton Rogers	1879-82	Albert Abraham Michelson	1923-27
Othniel Charles Marsh	1883-95	Thomas Hunt Morgan	1927-31
Wolcott Gibbs	1895-1900	William Wallace Campbell	1931-35
Alexander Agassiz	1901-7	Frank Rattray Lillie	1935-
Ira Remsen	1907-13		

9. DECEASED MEMBERS AND FOREIGN ASSOCIATES

DECEASED MEMBERS

	Date of election	Date of death		Date of election	Date of death
Abbe, Cleveland	1878 a	Oct. 28, 1916	Draper, John W	1877	Jan. 4, 1882
Abbot, Henry L	1872	Oct. 1, 1927	Duane, William	1920 1	Mar. 7, 1935
Agassiz, Alexander	1866	Mar. 27, 1910	Dutton, C. E	1884 1	Jan. 4, 1912
Agassiz, Louis	(1)	Dec. 14, 1873	Eads, James B	1872	Mar. 8, 1887
Alexander, J. H	(1)	Mar. 2, 1867	Edison, Thomas A	1927	Oct. 18, 1931
Alexander, Stephen	(1)	June 25, 1883	Eigenmann, Carl H	1923 1	Apr. 24, 1927
Allen, J. A	1876	Aug. 29, 1921	Elkin, W. L	1895 1	May 30, 1933
Armsby, H. P	1920 1	Oct. 19, 1921	Emmons, Samuel F	1892	Mar. 28, 1911
Atkinson, George Francis	1918 1	Nov. 14, 1918	Engelmann, George	(1)	Feb. 4, 1884
Bache, Alexander Dallas	(1)	Feb. 14, 1867	Farlow, W. G	1879	June 3, 1919
Bailey, Solon Irving	1923	June 5, 1931	Ferrel, William	1868	Sept. 18, 1891
Baird, Spencer F	1864	Aug. 19, 1887	Fewkes, Jesse Walter	1914	May 31, 1930
Barker, George F	1876 1	May 24, 1910	Folin, Otto	1916 1	Oct. 25, 1934
Barnard, E. E	1911	Feb. 6, 1923	Forbes, Stephen Alfred	1918	Mar. 13, 1930
Barnard, F. A. P	(1 1)	Apr. 27, 1889	Fraser, John Fries	(1)	Oct. 12, 1872
Barnard, J. G	(1)	May 24, 1882	Freeman, John R	1918 1	Oct. 6, 1932
Barrell, Joseph	1919	May 4, 1919	Frost, Edwin Brant	1908 1	May 14, 1935
Bartlett, W. H. C	(1)	Feb. 11, 1893	Gabb, William M	1876	May 30, 1878
Barus, Carl	1892 1	Sept. 28, 1935	Genth, F. A	1872	Feb. 2, 1893
Becker, George Ferdinand	1901	Apr. 20, 1919	Gibbs, Josiah Willard		Apr. 28, 1903
Beecher, Charles Emerson	1899	Feb. 14, 1904	Gibbs, Wolcott		Dec. 9, 1908
Bell, A. Graham	1883 1	Aug. 2, 1922	Gilbert, Grove Karl		May 1, 1918
Billings, John S	1883	Mar. 11, 1913	Gill, Theodore Nicholas		Sept. 25, 1914
Bocher, Maxime	1909 1	Sept. 12, 1918	Gilliss, James Melville		Feb. 9, 1865
Boltwood, B. B	1911	Aug. 14, 1927	Gooch, Frank Austin		Aug. 12, 1929
Boss, Lewis	1889	Oct. 5, 1912	Goodale, G. L		Apr. 15, 1923
Bowditch, Henry P	1887	Mar. 13, 1911	Goode, G. Brown		Sept. 6, 1896
Branner, J. C	1905	Mar. 1, 1922	Gould, Augustus A		Sept. 15, 1866
Breasted, James Henry	1923 1	Dec. 2, 1935	Gould, Benjamin A		Nov. 26, 1896
Brewer, William H	1880	Nov. 2, 1910	Gray, Asa		Jan. 30, 1888
Britton, Nathaniel L	1914 1	June 25, 1934	Guyot, Arnold		Feb. 8, 1884
Brooks, William Keith	1884	Nov. 12, 1908	Hadley, James		Nov. 14, 1872
Brown-Sequard, Charles E	1868	Apr. 2, 1891	Hague, Arnold		May 15, 1917
Brush, George Jarvis	1868	Feb. 6, 1912	Haldeman, S. S		Sept. 20, 1880
Bumstead, Henry A	1913	Dec. 31, 1920	Hall, Asaph		Nov. 22, 1907
Burgess, George K	1922 1	July 2, 1932	Hall, G. Stanley		24, 1924
Carty, John J	1917 1	Dec. 27, 1932	Hall, James		7, 1898
Casey, Thomas L	1890	Mar. 25, 1896	Halsted, W. S		7, 1922
Caswell, Alexis	(1)	Jan. 8, 1877	Hastings, C. S		29, 1932
Chamberlin, Thomas Chrowder	1903	Nov. 15, 1928	Hayden, F. V		22, 1887
			Hayford, John F		10, 1925
Chandler, Charles Frederick	1874	Aug. 25, 1925	Henry, Joseph		13, 1878
Chandler, Seth Carlo	1888 1	Dec. 31, 1913	Hilgard, Eugene W		8, 1916
Chauvenet, William	(1)	Dec. 13, 1877	Hilgard, Julius E		9, 1890
Clark, Henry James	1872	July 1, 1879	Hill, George William		16, 1914
Clark, William B	1908	July 27, 1917	Hill, Henry B		6, 1903
Clarke, Frank Wigglesworth	1909	May 23, 1931	Hillebrand, W. F		7, 1925
Clarke, John M	1909	May 29, 1925	Hitchcock, Edward		27, 1864
Coffin, James H	1869	Feb. 6, 1873	Holbrook, J. E		8, 1871
Coffin, J. H. C	(1)	Jan. 8, 1890	Holden, Edward Singleton		16, 1914
Comstock, Cyrus B	1884	May 29, 1910	Holmes, William H		20, 1933
Comstock, George C	1899 1	May 11, 1934	Howe, H. M		14, 1922
Cook, George H	1887	Sept. 22, 1889	Hubbard, J. S		16, 1863
Cooke, Josiah P	1872	Sept. 3, 1894	Humphreys, A. A		27, 1883
Cope, Edward D	1872	Apr. 12, 1897	Hunt, T. Sterry		
Coues, Elliott	1877	Dec. 25, 1899	Huntington, G. S		5,
Coulter, John Merle	1909	Dec. 23, 1928	Hyatt, Alpheus		15,
Councilman, William T	1904 1	May 27, 1933	Iddings, Joseph P		8,
Crafts, James M	1872	June 21, 1917	Jackson, Charles Loring		28,
Dall, William H	1897 1	Mar. 27, 1927	James, William		26,
Dalton, J. C	1864	Feb. 2, 1889	Johnson, S. W		21,
Dana, E. S	1884 1	June 16, 1935	Jones, Walter		28,
Dana, James D	(1)	Apr. 14, 1895	Keeler, J. E		12,
Davidson, George	1874 1	Dec. 2, 1911	Kemp, James F		17,
Davis, Charles H	(1)	Feb. 18, 1877	King, Clarence		24, 1901
Davis, William M	1904 1	Feb. 5, 1934	Kirtland, Jared P		10, 1877
Draper, Henry	1877	Nov. 20, 1882	Lane, J. Homer		3, 1880
			Langley, Samuel P		27, 1906
			Laufer, Berthold		13, 1934

For footnotes see end of table.

DECEASED MEMBERS—Continued

Name	Date of election	Date of death	Name	Date of election	Date of death
Lea, Matthew Carey	1892	Mar. 15, 1897	Rogers, William A.	1885	Mar. 1, 1898
Le Conte, John	1878	Apr. 29, 1891	Rogers, William B.[10]	(?)	May 30, 1882
Le Conte, John L.	(?)	Nov. 15, 1883	Rood, Ogden N.	1865	Nov. 12, 1902
Le Conte, Joseph	1875	July 6, 1901	Rosa, E. B.	1913	May 17, 1921
Leidy, Joseph	(?)	Apr. 30, 1891	Rowland, Henry A.	1881	Apr. 16, 1901
Lesley, J. Peter	(?)	June 1, 1903	Royce, Josiah	1906 1	Sept. 14, 1916
Lesquereux, Leo	1864	Oct. 25, 1889	Rutherfurd, Lewis M.	(?)	May 30, 1892
Loeb, Jacques	1910	Feb. 12, 1924	Ryan, Harris Joseph	1920 1	July 3, 1934
Longstreth, Miers F.	(?)	Dec. 27, 1891	Sabine, Wallace C. W.	1917	Jan. 10, 1919
Loomis, Elias	1873	Aug. 15, 1889	St. John, Charles Edward	1924 1	Apr. 26, 1935
Lovering, Joseph	1873	Jan. 18, 1892	Sargent, Charles S.	1895	Mar. 22, 1927
Lusk, Graham	1915 1	July 18, 1932	Saxton, Joseph	(?)	Oct. 26, 1873
Lyman, Theodore	1872	Sept. 9, 1897	Schott, Charles A.	1872	July 31, 1901
Mahan, D. H.	(?)	Sept. 16, 1871	Scudder, Samuel H.	1877	May 17, 1911
Mell, Franklin P.	1907	Nov. 17, 1917	Sellers, William	1873 1	Jan. 24, 1905
Marsh, G. P.	1866	July 23, 1882	Silliman, Benj., Sr.	(?)	Nov. 24, 1864
Marsh, O. C.	1874 1	Mar. 18, 1899	Silliman, Benj., Jr.	(?)	Jan. 14, 1885
Mayer, Alfred M.	1872	July 13, 1897	Smith, Alexander	1915	Sept. 8, 1922
Mayor, A. G.	1916	June 25, 1922	Smith, Edgar F.	1899 1	May 3, 1928
Mayo-Smith, Richmond	1890	Nov. 11, 1901	Smith, Erwin F.	1913 1	Apr. 6, 1927
Meek, F. B.	1869	Dec. 21, 1876	Smith, J. Lawrence	1872	Oct. 12, 1883
Meigs, M. C.	1865	Jan. 2, 1892	Smith, James Perrin	1925 1	Jan. 1, 1931
Meltzer, Samuel James	1912	Nov. 8, 1920	Smith, Sidney Irving [11]	1884	May 6, 1926
Mendel, Lafayette B.	1913 17	Dec. 9, 1935	Smith, Theobald	1908 1	Dec. 10, 1934
Mendenhall, Charles Elwood	1918 1	Aug. 18, 1935	Sperry, Elmer A.	1925 1	June 16, 1930
Mendenhall, T. C.	1887	Mar. 22, 1924	Squier, George O.	1919 1	Mar. 24, 1934
Merrill, George Perkins	1922	Aug. 15, 1929	Stimpson, William	1868	May 26, 1872
Michelson, A. A.	1888 1	May 9, 1931	Story, William Edward	1908 1	Apr. 11, 1930
Minot, Charles Sedgwick	1897	Nov. 19, 1914	Stratton, S. W.	1917 1	Oct. 18, 1931
Mitchell, Henry	1885 1	Dec. 1, 1902	Strong, Theodore	(?)	Feb. 1, 1869
Mitchell, Silas Weir	1865	Jan. 4, 1914	Sullivant, W. S.	1872	Apr. 30, 1873
Moore, E. H.	1901 1	Dec. 30, 1932	Swain, George F.	1923 1	July 1, 1931
Morgan, Louis H.	1875	Dec. 17, 1881	Thaxter, Roland	1912	Apr. 22, 1932
Morley, E. W.	1897	Feb. 24, 1923	Torrey, John	(?)	Mar. 10, 1873
Morse, Edward Sylvester	1876	Dec. 20, 1925	Totten, J. G.	(1)	Apr. 22, 1864
Morse, Harmon N.	1907	Sept. 8, 1920	Trowbridge, Augustus	1919 1	Mar. 14, 1934
Morton, Henry	1874	May 9, 1902	Trowbridge, John	1878	Feb. 18, 1923
Nef, John Ulric	1904 1	Aug. 13, 1915	Trowbridge, William P.	1872	Aug. 12, 1892
Newberry, J. S.	(?)	Dec. 7, 1892	Trumbull, James H.	1872	Aug. 5, 1897
Newcomb, Simon	1869	July 11, 1909	Tuckerman, Edward	1868	Mar. 15, 1886
Newton, H. A.	(?)	Aug. 12, 1896	Van Hise, C. R.	1902	Nov. 19, 1918
Newton, John	1870	May 1, 1895	Vaughan, Victor Clarence	1915 1	Nov. 21, 1929
Nichols, Ernest Fox	1908	Apr. 29, 1924	Verrill, Addison E.[12]	1872	Dec. 10, 1926
Norton, William A.	1873	Sept. 21, 1883	Walcott, Charles D.	1896 1	Feb. 9, 1927
Oliver, James E.	1872	Mar. 27, 1895	Walker, Francis A.	1878	Jan. 5, 1897
Osborn, Henry Fairfield	1900 1	Nov. 6, 1935	Warren, G. K.	1876	Aug. 8, 1882
Osborne, Thomas Burr	1910	Jan. 29, 1929	Washburn, E. W.	1932 1	Feb. 6, 1934
Packard, A. S.	1872	Feb. 14, 1906 5	Washington, H. S.	1921 1	Jan. 7, 1934
Peirce, Benjamin	(1 2)	Oct. 6, 1880	Watson, James C.	1868	Nov. 23, 1880
Peirce, Benjamin Osgood	1906	Jan. 14, 1914	Watson, Sereno	1889	Mar. 9, 1892
Peirce, Charles S. S.	1877 1	Apr. 20, 1914	Webster, A. G.	1903 1	May 15, 1923
Penfield, Samuel L.	1900	Aug. 13, 1906	Welch, William H.	1895 1	Apr. 30, 1934
Peters, C. H. F.	1876 1	July 18, 1890	Wells, Horace L.	1903	Dec. 19, 1924
Pickering, Edward C.	1873	Feb. 3, 1919	Wheeler, Henry Lord	1909 1	Oct. 30, 1914
Pirsson, Louis V.	1913 1	Dec. 8, 1919	White, Charles A.	1889	June 29, 1910
Pourtales, L. F.	1873	July 19, 1880	White, David	1912 1	Feb. 7, 1935
Powell, John W.	1880	Sept. 23, 1902	Whitman, C. O.	1895	Dec. 6, 1910
Power, Frederick B.	1924 1	Mar. 26, 1927	Whitney, Josiah D.	(1 2)	Aug. 19, 1896
Prudden, T. Mitchell	1901	Apr. 10, 1924	Whitney, William D.	1865 1	June 29, 1894
Pumpelly, Raphael	1872	Aug. 10, 1923	Wilczynski, E. J.[13]	1919	Sept. 14, 1932
Pupin, Michael Idvorsky	1905 1	Mar. 12, 1935	Williston, Samuel W.	1915	Aug. 30, 1918
Putnam, Frederic W.	1885	Aug. 18, 1915	Winlock, Joseph	(?)	June 11, 1875
Ransome, F. L.	1914 1	Oct. 6, 1935	Wood, Horatio C.	1879 1	Jan. 3, 1920
Remsen, Ira	1882	Mar. 4, 1927	Woodward, J. J.	1873	Aug. 17, 1884
Richards, T. W.	1899 1	Apr. 2, 1928	Woodward, Robert S.	1896 1	June 29, 1924
Ridgway, Robert	1917	Mar. 25, 1929	Worthen, A. H.	1872	May 6, 1888
Robinson, B. L.	1921 1	July 27, 1935	Wright, Arthur Williams	1881	Dec. 19, 1915
Rodgers, John	(?)	May 5, 1882	Wyman, Jeffries	(?)	Sept. 4, 1874
Rogers, Fairman	(?)	Aug. 22, 1900	Young, Charles A.	1872	Jan. 3, 1908
Rogers, Robert E.	(?)	Sept. 6, 1884			

1 Biographical Memoirs have not been published.
2 Charter member, Mar. 3, 1863.
3 Transferred to roll of members emeriti, 1929.
4 Transferred to roll of members emeriti, 1932.
5 Transferred to roll of members emeriti in 1933.
6 Resigned, 1909.
7 Transferred to roll of members emeriti in 1935.

8 Resigned, 1873.
9 Dropped 1866, reelected 1875.
10 Dropped 1866, reelected 1872.
11 Transferred to roll of members emeriti in 1908.
12 Transferred to roll of members emeriti in 1924.
13 Transferred to roll of members emeriti in 1925.

DECEASED FOREIGN ASSOCIATES

Adams, J. C.
Airy, Sir George B.
Argelander, F. W. A.
Arrhenius, S. A.
Auwers, G. F. J. Arthur
Backlund, Oskar
Baer, Karl Ernest von
Baeyer, Adolf von
Barrande, Joachin
Bateson, William
Beaumont, L. Elie de
Becquerel, Henri
Berthelot, M. P. E.
Bertrand, J. L. F.
Boltzmann, Ludwig
Bornet, Edouard
Boussingault, J. B. J. D.
Boveri, Theodor
Braun, Alexander
Brewster, Sir David
Bunsen, Robert W.
Burmeister, C. H. C.
Candolle, Alphonse de
Cayley, Arthur
Chasles, Michel
Chevreul, M. E.
Clausius, Rudolph
Cornu, Alfred
Crookes, Sir William
Darboux, Gaston
Darwin, Sir George Howard
de Sitter, Willem
de Vries, Hugo
Dewar, Sir James
Dove, H. W.
Dumas, J. B.
Ehrlich, Paul
Eijkman, Christian
Engler, Adolph
Faraday, Michael
Fischer, Emil
Geikie, Sir Archibald
Gegenbaur, Karl
Gill, Sir David
Glydém, Hugo

Goebel, K. E. von
Groth, Paul von
Haber, Fritz
Haldane, John Scott
Hamilton, Sir William Rowan
Helmholtz, Baron H. von
Hoff, J. H. van't
Hofmann, A. W.
Hooker, Sir Joseph D.
Huggins, Sir William
Huxley, T. H.
Ibañez, Carlos
Janssen, J.
Jordan, M. E. C.
Joule, James P.
Kapteyn, J. C.
Kekulé, August
Kelvin, Lord
Kirchoff, G. R.
Klein, Felix
Koch, Robert
Kölliker, Albert von
Kohlrausch, Frederich
Kossel, Albrecht
Kronecker, Hugo
Lacaze-Duthiers, Henri de
Lankester, Sir E. Ray
Leuckart, Rudolph
Lie, Sophus
Liebig, Justus von
Lister, Lord
Loewy, Maurice
Lorentz, Hendrik Antoon
Ludwig, K. F. W.
Marey, E. J.
Mendeléeff, D. I.
Milne-Edwards, Henri
Moissan, Henri
Murchison, Sir Roderick I.
Murray, Sir John
Onnes, Heike Kamerlingh
Oppolzer, Theodore von
Ostwald, Wilhelm
Owen, Sir Richard

Parsons, Sir Charles Algernon
Pasteur, Louis
Pavlov, I. P.
Peters, C. A. F.
Pfeffer, Wilhelm
Plana, G. A. A.
Poincaire, Jules Henri
Rammelsberg, C. F.
Ramon y Cajal, Santiago
Ramsey, Sir William
Rayleigh, Lord
Regnault, Victor
Retzius, Gustav
Reymond, Emil Du Bois
Richthofen, F. von
Rosenbusch, Karl Harry Ferdinand
Roux, Wilhelm
Rubner, Max
Sachs, Julius von
Schiaparelli, Giovanni
Schuster, Sir Arthur
Seeliger, Hugo R. von
Stas, Jean Servais
Stokes, Sir George G.
Strasburger, Edouard
Struve, Otto von
Suess, Eduard
Sylvester, J. J.
Tisserand, F. F.
Van der Waals, J. D.
Virchow, Rudolph von
Vogel, H. C.
Waldeyer, Wilhelm
Weierstrauss, Karl
Weismann, August
Wöhler, Frederich
Wolf, Max F. J. C.
Wundt, Wilhelm
Würtz, Adolph
Zirkel, Ferdinand
Zittell, K. A. R. von

NATIONAL RESEARCH COUNCIL

1. EXECUTIVE ORDER ISSUED BY THE PRESIDENT OF THE UNITED STATES MAY 11, 1918

The National Research Council was organized in 1916 at the request of the President by the National Academy of Sciences, under its congressional charter, as a measure of national preparedness. The work accomplished by the Council in organizing research and in securing cooperation of military and civilian agencies in the solution of military problems demonstrates its capacity for larger service. The National Academy of Sciences is therefore requested to perpetuate the National Research Council, the duties of which shall be as follows:

1. In general, to stimulate research in the mathematical, physical, and biological sciences, and in the application of these sciences to engineering, agriculture, medicine, and other useful arts, with the object of increasing knowledge, of strengthening the national defense, and of contributing in other ways to the public welfare.

2. To survey the larger possibilities of science, to formulate comprehensive projects of research, and to develop effective means of utilizing the scientific and technical resources of the country for dealing with these projects.

3. To promote cooperation in research, at home and abroad, in order to secure concentration of effort, minimize duplication, and stimulate progress; but in all cooperative undertakings to give encouragement to individual initiative, as fundamentally important to the advancement of science.

4. To serve as a means of bringing American and foreign investigators into active cooperation with the scientific and technical services of the War and Navy Departments and with those of the civil branches of the Government.

5. To direct the attention of scientific and technical investigators to. the present importance of military and industrial problems in connection with the war, and to aid in the solution of these problems by organizing specific researches.

6. To gather and collate scientific and technical information, at home and abroad, in cooperation with governmental and other agencies, and to render such information available to duly accredited persons.

Effective prosecution of the Council's work requires the cordial collaboration of the scientific and technical branches of the Government, both military and civil. To this end representatives of the Government, upon the nomination of the National Academy of Sciences, will be designated by the President as members of the Council, as heretofore, and the heads of the departments immediately concerned will continue to cooperate in every way that may be required.

WOODROW WILSON.

THE WHITE HOUSE, *May 11, 1918.*

· [No. 2859]
·

2. ARTICLES OF ORGANIZATION, NATIONAL RESEARCH COUNCIL

PREAMBLE

The National Academy of Sciences, under the authority conferred upon it by its charter enacted by the Congress, and approved by President Lincoln on March 3, 1863, and pursuant to the request expressed in an Executive order made by President Wilson on May 11, 1918, adopts the following articles of organization for the National Research Council, to replace the organization under which it has operated heretofore.

ARTICLE I.—PURPOSE

It shall be the purpose of the National Research Council to promote research in the mathematical, physical, and biological sciences, and in the application of these sciences to engineering, agriculture, medicine, and other useful arts, with the object of increasing knowledge, of strengthening the national defense, and of contributing in other ways to the public welfare, as expressed in the Executive order of May 11, 1918.

ARTICLE II.—MEMBERSHIP

SECTION 1. The membership of the National Research Council shall be chosen with the view of rendering the Council an effective federation of the principal research agencies in the United States concerned with the fields of science and technology named in article I.

SEC. 2. The Council shall be composed of—
1. Representatives of national scientific and technical societies.
2. Representatives of the Government, as provided in the Executive order.
3. Representatives of other research organizations and other persons whose aid may advance the objects of the Council.

SEC. 3. The membership of the Council shall consist specifically of the members of the executive board and the members of the divisions, constituted as provided in articles III and IV.

SEC. 4. Membership in the Council shall be limited to citizens of the United States. This, however, shall not be construed as applying to membership in committees, appointed by or acting under the Council, whose members are not necessarily members of the Council, provided that members not citizens of the United States shall in no case form a majority of any committee.

ARTICLE III.—DIVISIONS

SECTION 1. The Council shall be organized in divisions of two classes:

    A. Divisions dealing with the more general relations and activities of the Council.
    B. Divisions dealing with special branches of science and technology.

SEC. 2. The Divisions of the Council shall be as follows:

    A. Divisions of general relations:

        I. Division of Federal relations.
        II. Division of foreign relations.
        III. Division of States relations.
        IV. Division of educational relations.

    B. Divisions of science and technology:

        V. Division of physical sciences.
        VI. Division of engineering and industrial research.
        VII. Division of chemistry and chemical technology.
        VIII. Division of geology and geography.
        IX. Division of medical sciences.
        X. Division of biology and agriculture.
        XI. Division of anthropology and psychology.

SEC. 3. The number of divisions and the grouping of subjects in article III, section 2, may be modified by the executive board of the National Research Council.

SEC. 4 (a). Each division of general relations shall consist of a chairman, one or more vice chairmen, representatives of national and international organizations, and members at large, appointed as provided in article VI.

(b). There may be an executive committee of each division of general relations, consisting of the chairman and three or more of the members, who shall be chosen by the division at a regular meeting, confirmed by the executive board, and hold office for one year terminating on June 30th or in case of any one or more of such executive committees, on such later date as the chairman of the Council may have previously ordered. Between meetings of a division its executive committee shall have power to act on all matters for the division, except those which may be reserved by the division for its own action; but the executive committee shall report all its actions to the division.

SEC. 5 (a). Each division of science and technology shall consist of a chairman and of representatives of such national societies as seem essential for the conduct of the business of the division, appointed as provided in article VI. Members at large, not to exceed three, may also be appointed as provided in article VI. From the membership of the division thus constituted, a smaller group, not to exceed twelve, shall be designated as executive members who alone may be reimbursed by the National Research Council ʹfor travel expenses incurred in attendance upon meetings of the division.

(b). There may be an executive committee of each division of science and technology, consisting of the chairman and three or more of the executive members, who shall be chosen by the division at a regular meeting, confirmed by the executive board, and hold office for 1 year terminating on June 30 or, in the case of any one or more of such executive committees, on such later date as the chairman of the Council may have previously ordered. Between meetings of a division its executive committee shall have power to act on all matters for the division except those which may be reserved by the division for its own action; but the executive committee shall report all its actions to the division.

(c). The terms of office of the chairmen of the divisions of science and technology, other than that of engineering and industrial research, shall be so arranged by the chairman of the Council that one-third of these terms expire each year.

SEC. 6. The chairman of each division shall be, ex officio, a member of all committees of the division.

SEC. 7. Actions by the divisions involving matters of policy shall be subject to approval by the executive board.

ARTICLE IV.—ADMINISTRATION

SECTION 1. The general officers of the National Research Council shall be a chairman, chosen as provided in article V, section 1, a treasurer (see art. V, sec. 3), and such honorary officers as may be appointed by the council of the National Academy of Sciences, upon nomination by the executive board.

SEC. 2. The affairs of the National Research Council shall be administered by an executive board and its administrative committee. Actions by these bodies involving financial responsibilities or the appointment of general officers must be approved by the council of the National Academy of Sciences, or by the executive committee of the council of the National Academy of Sciences under general authority, or under such special authority as may be conferred on it by the council of the National Academy of Sciences.

SEC. 3. The executive board shall consist of the members of the executive committee of the council of the National Academy of Sciences; the chairman, treasurer, and honorary officers of the National Research Council; the chairmen of the divisions of general relations and of the divisions of science and technology of the National Research Council; the members of the committee on policies; the president or other representative of the American Association for the Advancement of Science; the chairman or other representative of the Engineering Foundation, and six members at large appointed for a term of 3 years, or for an unexpired term in case of vacancy, by the president of the National Academy of Sciences, on recommendation of the executive board. The president of the National Academy of Sciences shall preside at the meetings of the executive board.

SEC. 4. In administrative matters the executive board shall be represented by an administrative committee, which shall consist of the chairman and treasurer of the .National Research Council, the president, vice president, and home secretary of the National Academy, and the chairmen of the divisions of science and technology of the National Research Council.

SEC. 5. The administrative committee shall have power to act upon all matters except those which may be reserved by the executive board for its own action; but the administrative committee shall report all its actions to the executive board. The administrative committee shall prepare the annual budget for submission to the executive board at its annual meeting.

SEC. 6. (a) There shall also be a committee on policies of the National Research Council. This committee shall be composed of nine members appointed for terms of 3 years by the executive board, preferably so that it may consist largely of persons who have had past experience in the affairs of the National Research Council. The executive board shall appoint the chairman of the committee on policies to serve for 1 year beginning July 1 or until his successor is appointed. This committee shall submit to the executive board recommendations as to general policies.

(b) At the annual meeting of the executive board in 1933, nine members of the committee on policies shall be appointed; three to serve for 1 year, three for 2 years, and three for 3 years, their respective terms to be determined by lot. Each year thereafter the terms of three members will expire, and their successors, to serve for 3 years each, shall be appointed at the annual meeting of the executive board in that year. The date of expiration of the terms shall be June 30. In case of vacancy the executive board may fill the unexpired term by appointment.

ARTICLE V.—APPOINTMENT AND DUTIES OF OFFICERS OF THE RESEARCH COUNCIL

SECTION 1. The chairman of the National Research Council shall be appointed by the executive board, subject to confirmation by the council of the National Academy of Sciences, and shall hold office at the pleasure of the board. The chairman shall be the executive officer of the National Research Council and shall have charge of its general administration. He shall act as chairman of its administrative committee, and shall be, ex officio, a member of all divisions and committees of the Council.

SEC. 2. There shall be appointed by the executive board, upon recommendation of the chairman of the National Research Council, an officer with the title of executive secretary of the Council, whose duties it shall be to assist the chairman in the administration of the Council. He shall attend all meetings of the executive board and of the administrative committee, and act as their secretary, and shall hold office at the pleasure of the board.

SEC. 3. The treasurer of the National Academy of Sciences shall be, ex officio, treasurer of the National Research Council.

SEC. 4. In case of a vacancy in the office of the chairman of the National Research Council or of the absence or disability of the chairman an acting chairman may be appointed by the council of the National Academy of Sciences, or by the executive committee of the council of the National Academy, upon recommendation of the executive board of the Research Council or its administrative committee.

ARTICLE VI.—NOMINATION AND APPOINTMENT OF OFFICERS AND MEMBERS OF DIVISIONS

SECTION 1. *Divisions of Science and Technology.*—(a) The chairman of each division shall be nominated to the executive board by the division concerned, with the approval of the administrative committee. The chairman shall be appointed by the executive board at its annual meeting for a term of 3 years.

(b) The national societies to be represented in each of the divisions shall be determined by the division concerned, subject to the approval of the executive board.

(c) The representatives of national societies in each division shall be nominated by the societies, at the request of the chairman of the division, and, after approval by the executive board, shall be appointed by the president of the National Academy of Sciences to membership in the National Research Council for a term of 3 years, and assigned to the division.

(d) Members at large, if any, in each division shall be nominated by the division concerned, with the approval of the executive board, and shall be appointed by the president of the National Academy of Sciences to membership in the National Research Council for a term of 3 years, and assigned to the division.

(e) The executive members in each division shall be designated by the division concerned, subject to the approval of the executive board.

SEC. 2. *Divisions of general relations.*—(a) The officers of each of the divisions of general relations shall be appointed by the executive board to serve for a period of 3 years, except that the foreign secretary of the National Academy of Sciences shall be, ex officio, chairman of the division of foreign relations, and that the appointment of the chairman of the division of Federal relations shall be subject to confirmation by the council of the National Academy of Sciences.

(b) The national and international societies or associations to be represented in each of these divisions shall be determined by the division concerned, subject

(c) The representatives of such societies or associations shall be nominated by the societies or associations, at the request of the chairman of the division, and, after approval by the executive board, shall be appointed by the president of the National Academy of Sciences to membership in the Council for a period of 3 years, and assigned to the division.

(d) Members at large in each division shall be nominated by the division, approved by the executive board, and appointed by the president of the National Academy of Sciences to membership in the Council for a period of 3 years, and assigned to the division.

(e) The Government bureaus, civil and military, to be represented in the division of Federal relations shall be determined by the council of the National Academy of Sciences, on recommendation from the executive board of the National Research Council.

(f) The representatives of the Government shall be nominated by the president of the National Academy of Sciences, after conference with the secretaries of the departments concerned, and the names of those nominated shall be presented to the President of the United States for designation by him for service with the National Research Council. Each Government representative shall serve during the pleasure of the President of the United States, not to exceed a term of 3 years, and a vacancy from any cause shall be filled for the remainder of the term in the same manner as in the case of the original designation.

SEC. 3. The terms of office of officers and members, unless otherwise provided, shall terminate on June 30 of the year in which their appointments expire.

SEC. 4. Vacancies occurring in the divisions of either class, except as to representatives of the Government, may be filled for the unexpired term by the executive board, upon recommendation of the division concerned, or ad interim by the administrative committee upon similar recommendation.

ARTICLE VII.—MEETINGS

SECTION 1. The annual meeting of the executive board shall be held in April in the city of Washington at the time of the meeting of the National Academy of Sciences. Special meetings may be held at other times at the call of the chairman of the National Research Council. A majority of the members of the board shall constitute a quorum for the transaction of business.

SEC. 2. Stated meetings of the administrative committee shall be held in the city of Washington at least five times a year, at such dates as shall be determined by the chairman of the National Research Council. Special meetings may be held at other times on call of the chairman. Five members of the committee shall constitute a quorum for the transaction of business.

SEC. 3. The committee on policies shall hold one stated meeting during the year, preferably in Washington at the time of the annual meeting of the National Academy of Sciences. Special meetings may be held at any time on call of the chairman of the committee. Five members of the committee shall constitute a quorum for the transaction of business.

SEC. 4. Each division of science and technology shall hold at least one stated meeting during the year, at a time to be determined by the chairman of the division in consultation with the chairman of the Council. Special meetings may be called at other times by the chairman of the division.

SEC. 5. Meetings of any division of general relations shall be held upon the call of its chairman.

ARTICLE VIII.—PUBLICATIONS AND REPORTS

SECTION 1. An annual report on the work of the National Research Council shall be presented by the chairman to the National Academy of Sciences.

SEC. 2. Other publications of the National Research Council may include papers, bulletins, reports, and memoirs, which may appear in the Proceedings or Memoirs of the National Academy of Sciences, in the publications of other societies, in scientific and technical journals, or in a separate series of the National Research Council.

ARTICLE IX.—AMENDMENTS

SECTION 1. By action of the National Academy of Sciences, on April 29, 1919, power of amendment of these articles of organization is given to the council of the National Academy of Sciences.

3. BYLAWS

APPROVED APRIL 26, 1933

1. There shall be a Publication and Research Information Service, to consist of a director and such other staff as the executive board shall direct. The Service shall be under the supervision of a standing committee of the executive board which shall be composed of the chairman and treasurer of the National Research Council, the chairman of the committee on policies, and the director of the Service. The functions of the Service shall be to cooperate with the divisions of the National Research Council in obtaining required data, to maintain a library of sources, to prepare compilations of general scientific interest, and to edit and superintend the publication of all bulletins, reprints, and miscellaneous printed matter issued by the National Research Council. The director of the Service shall attend the meetings of the administrative committee, but without vote.

2. The treasurer shall have the assistance of a salaried and bonded officer, the bursar, who shall be chosen by the finance committee of the National Academy of Sciences and be directly responsible to the treasurer.

3. The executive board may create such other salaried officers as are necessary for the transaction of the business of the Council.

4. Officers of the Council, members of the executive board, and special agents of the Council, when authorized to travel on business of the Council, may be allowed their necessary expenses.

5. Executive members of the divisions of science and technology and members of the executive committee of any division of general relations, when attending an authorized meeting, may be reimbursed for traveling expenses, or such portion thereof as the division chairman may determine, within the funds made available for that purpose in the budget.

6. The chairman of each division shall direct the administrative and scientific work of the division.

7. In the fiscal year in which the term of office of a chairman of a division expires it shall be his duty to appoint, on or before February 1, a nominating committee of three, chosen from present or former members of the division or from the membership of existing committees of the division, who, in consultation with the chairman of the division and the chairman of the Council, shall select an available candidate for the chairmanship for the ensuing term. The name of the candidate shall be reported to the division through its chairman and, if approved by the division, shall be recommended to the executive board at its annual meeting for appointment, as provided in article VI, sections 1 and 2, of the articles of organization.

8. Each division of science and technology is empowered to arrange, in accordance with its special needs, for the selection of the executive members and members-at-large of the division, and for an executive committee, to be appointed annually, as provided in article III, section 5 (a) and (b), and article VI, section 1 (d) of the articles of organization.

Each division may designate also one of its executive members to act as vice chairman of the division, the term of office to be for 1 year.

9. Following the termination of any regular 3-year period of service the chairman or members of a division shall be eligible for reappointment in the same status only after a lapse of 1 year, except that the Executive Board may continue the service of a chairman or members for a second period of 3 years, or less, when such action is recommended by the division concerned.

10. An annual honorarium may be paid to the chairman of each division of science and technology and an annual maintenance fund shall be appropriated for the support of the work of each division of the Council. The amount of the honorarium and of the maintenance fund of each division shall be determined by the administrative committee, subject to the approval of the executive board and the council of the National Academy of Sciences or its executive committee.

11. The maintenance fund allotted to each division shall be expended under the authority of the chairman of the division to provide for meetings of the division and its various committees, and other necessary expenses, in accordance with the regulations in force in the Council controlling financial expenditures.

12. No member of a committee constituted to administer funds entrusted to the National Research Council shall receive an honorarium or salary from such funds for his services, except in cases specifically authorized in advance by the

executive board or its administrative committee, but members of such committees may be reimbursed from the funds for expenses incurred in the work of the committee.

13. Members of special committees organized within any of the divisions must be approved by the administrative committee before official notification of appointment is made by the chairman of the division.

14. Solicitation of funds for the support of projects of a division may be made only after authorization by both the executive board (or its administrative committee) and the council of the National Academy of Sciences (or its executive committee). Such solicitation shall be conducted under the direction of the chairman of the National Research Council acting in conjunction with the chairman of the division concerned.

15. Special funds granted to the National Research Council, other than those for fellowships and grants-in-aid, must be expended in accordance with budgets previously approved by the administrative committee.

16. It shall be the duty of the chairman of each division of the Council to submit an annual report of the activities of his division to the chairman of the Council on or before June 30. Interim reports shall be made to the chairman of the Council before each stated meeting of the administrative committee.

17. Standing committees of the executive board, unless otherwise provided for, shall be appointed annually by the board at its April meeting, or, in case of need, by the administrative committee at one of its stated meetings.

18. The executive board, at its annual meeting in April, shall appoint a nominating committee of three members to prepare nominations for presentation at the next annual meeting of the board for vacancies in the committee on policies and in the list of members at large of the board, occurring at the end of the fiscal year.

19. Amendments of bylaws may be made by the executive board at any authorized meeting of the board.

20. A publication to be known as the Bulletin of the National Research Council shall be established to provide for the publication of materials originating in the work of the Council. The Bulletin shall be issued as occasion demands.

21. A series to be known as the Reprint and Circular Series of the National Research Council shall provide for the distribution of papers published or printed by or for the National Research Council.

4. ORGANIZATION OF THE NATIONAL RESEARCH COUNCIL, 1935-36

A. Officers and Executive Board

OFFICERS

Honorary chairman, George E. Hale, honorary director, Mount Wilson Observatory, Carnegie Institution of Washington, Pasadena, Calif.

Secretary emeritus, Vernon Kellogg, National Research Council, Washington, D. C.

Chairman, Frank R. Lillie, dean emeritus, of the division of biological sciences, and Andrew MacLeish distinguished service professor of embryology, emeritus, University of Chicago; and president, National Academy of Sciences, Washington, D. C.

Treasurer, Arthur Keith, treasurer, National Academy of Sciences; geologist, United States Geological Survey, Washington, D. C.

Executive secretary, Albert L. Barrows, National Research Council, Washington, D. C.

Bursar, J. H. J. Yule, National Research Council, Washington, D. C.

Chief clerk, C. L. Wade, National Research Council, Washington, D. C.

EXECUTIVE BOARD

Presiding officer, Frank R. Lillie, president, National Academy of Sciences, ex officio.

MEMBERS, EX OFFICIO

Honorary chairman, chairman, secretary emeritus, and treasurer of the National Research Council.

Executive committee of the Council of the National Academy of Sciences

Frank R. Lillie.
Arthur L. Day, vice president, National Academy of Sciences; director, Geophysical Laboratory, Carnegie Institution of Washington, 2801 Upton Street, Washington, D. C.
Fred. E. Wright, home secretary, National Academy of Sciences; petrologist, Geophysical Laboratory, Carnegie Institution of Washington, 2801 Upton Street, Washington, D. C.
Arthur Keith.
Roger Adams, professor of organic chemistry, University of Illinois, Urbana, Ill.
Ross G. Harrison, Sterling professor of biology, and director of the Osborn Zoological Laboratory, Yale University, New Haven, Conn.

Committee on Policies of the National Research Council

R. A. Millikan, chairman, director, Norman Bridge Laboratory of Physics; and chairman of the executive council, California Institute of Technology, Pasadena, Calif.
Isaiah Bowman, president, Johns Hopkins University, Baltimore, Md.
Walter B. Cannon, George Higginson professor of physiology, Harvard Medical School, Boston, Mass.
Karl T. Compton, president, Massachusetts Institute of Technology, Cambridge, Mass.
Simon Flexner, director emeritus, Rockefeller Institute for Medical Research, Sixty-sixth Street and York Avenue, New York City.
Frank B. Jewett, vice president, American Telephone & Telegraph Co.; president, Bell Telephone Laboratories, Inc., 195 Broadway, New York City.
A. V. Kidder, chairman, division of historical research, Carnegie Institution of Washington, P. O. Box 71, Andover, Mass.
John C. Merriam, president, Carnegie Institution of Washington, Washington, D. C.
A. A. Noyes,[1] director, Gates Chemical Laboratory, California Institute of Technology, Pasadena, Calif.

Representatives of organizations

· President of the American Association for the Advancement of Science, Edwin G. Conklin, Henry Fairfield Osborn professor of biology, emeritus, Princeton University, Princeton, N. J.
Representative of the Engineering Foundation, H. P. Charlesworth, assistant chief engineer, American Telephone & Telegraph Co., 195 Broadway, New York City.

Chairmen of the Divisions of the National Research Council

Members-at-Large

W. C. Curtis, professor of zoology, University of Missouri, Columbia Mo.
Knight Dunlap, professor of psychology, University of California at Los Angeles, Los Angeles, Calif.
Nevin M. Fenneman, professor of geology and geography, University of Cincinnati, Cincinnati, Ohio.
John Johnston, director of research, United States Steel Corporation, Kearney, N. J.
Oswald Veblen, professor of mathematics, Institute for Advanced Study, Princeton University, Princeton, N. J.
F. W. Willard, executive vice president, Nassau Smelting & Refining Co., 50 Church street, New York City.

ADMINISTRATIVE COMMITTEE

Chairman, Frank R. Lillie; the treasurer of the National Research Council; the president, vice president, and home secretary of the National Academy of Sciences; and the chairmen of the divisions of science and technology of the National Research Council.

---

[1] Deceased.

COMMITTEES

(The chairman of the National Research Council is, ex officio, a member of all divisions and committees of the Council)

Government Relations and Science Advisory Committee: Chairman, Frank R. Lillie; Roger Adams, Isaiah Bowman, Karl T. Compton, Arthur L. Day, Gano Dunn, Fran B. Jewett, L. R. Jones, C. K. Leith, R. A. Millikan, George H. Whipple.   k

Committee on grants-in-aid: Chairman, Frank R. Lillie; Edson S. Bastin, Francis G. Blake, Arthur Keith, Charles F. Kettering, I. F. Lewis, R. A. Millikan, Edward Sapir, F. W. Willard; secretary, C. J. West.

Committee on nominations: Chairman, Nevin M. Fenneman; Frank B. Jewett, F. W. Willard.

Committee on publication and research information service: Chairman, ex officio, Frank R. Lillie; Arthur Keith, ex officio; R. A. Millikan, ex officio; C. J. West, ex officio. Director of publication and research information service, C. J. West.

Committee on building (joint committee with the National Academy of Sciences): Chairman, Gano Dunn; George E. Hale, H. E. Howe, Vernon Kellogg, John C. Merriam, R. A. Millikan, A. A. Noyes. Secretary of the committee, Paul Brockett.

Advisory committee on buildings and grounds (joint committee with the National Academy of Sciences): Chairman, Paul Brockett, executive secretary and custodian of buildings and grounds, National Academy of Sciences, Washington, D. C.; Edson S. Bastin, Arthur L. Day, I. F. Lewis, Fred. E. Wright.

Committee on exhibits (joint committee with the National Academy of Sciences): Chairman, Fred. E. Wright; secretary, Paul Brockett; Edson S. Bastin, Francis G. Blake, A. F. Blakeslee, A. B. Coble, Bancroft Gherardi, George E. Hale, Ludvig Hektoen, L. J. Henderson, A. W. Hull, Charles F. Kettering, Charles A. Kraus, C. K. Leith, A. O. Leuschner, I. F. Lewis, Frank R. Lillie, R. A. Millikan, Edward Sapir, C. E. Seashore, Harlow Shapley, C. R. Stockard, F. W. Willard.

Executive committee: Chairman, Fred. E. Wright; secretary, Paul Brockett; Arthur L. Day, George E. Hale, Vernon Kellogg, John C. Merriam.

Advisory committee on fellowships: Chairman, ex officio, Frank R. Lillie; Francis G. Blake, Simon Flexner, F. K. Richtmyer, W. J. Robbins, E. B. Wilson.

Committee on patent policy: Chairman, F. W. Willard; George W. McCoy, Archie Palmer, Alfred Stengel, Robert E. Wilson.

TECHNICAL COMMITTEES

Committee on abstracting and documentation of scientific literature: Chairman, I. F. Lewis; A. Parker Hitchens, L. R. Jones, C. E. McClung, Austin M. Patterson, George B. Pegram, J. B. Reeside, Jr.

Committee on cooperation with Research Corporation: Chairman, F. G. Cottrell, consulting chemist, United States Bureau of Chemistry and Soils, Washington, D. C.; William J. Hale, Maurice Holland.

Committee on publication of excerpts from International Critical Tables: Chairman, F. K. Richtmyer, dean of the graduate school and professor of physics, Cornell University, Ithaca, N. Y.; C. J. West, F. W. Willard.

Advisory committee to the American commissioners on Annual Tables of Constants and Numerical Data: Chairman, F. K. Richtmyer, dean of the graduate school and professor of physics, Cornell University, Ithaca, N. Y.; Edward Bartow, Lyman J. Briggs, Karl T. Compton, Saul Dushman, Frank B. Jewett, John Johnston, Charles F. Kettering, G. N. Lewis, S. C. Lind, C. E. K. Mees, R. A. Millikan, Harlow Shapley, C. M. A. Stine, F. W. Sullivan, Jr., John F. Thompson, C. J. West, F. W. Willard. American commissioners, F. K. Richtmyer and C. J. West.

Committee of apparatus makers and users—executive committee: Chairman, W. D. Collins, Chief, Division of Quality of Water, United States Geological Survey, Washington, D. C.; secretary, C. J. West; Lyman J. Briggs, Arthur L. Day, Morris E. Leeds, F. K. Richtmyer, J. M. Roberts.

Executive committee of the American Geophysical Union (representing the American section of the International Geodetic and Geophysical Union): Chairman, N. H. Heck, Chief, Division of Terrestrial Magnetism and Seismology, United States Coast and Geodetic Survey, Washington, D. C.; vice chairman,

R. H. Field; secretary, John A. Fleming; E. T. Allen, Edison S. Bastin, William Bowie, Charles F. Brooks, Austin H. Clark, C. L. Garner, O. H. Gish, W. R. Gregg, D. L. Hazard, C. O. Iselin, H. F. Johnson, F. W. Lee, I. F. Lewis, R. A. Millikan, T. H. Morgan, C. S. Scofield, P. C. Whitney, F. W. Willard.

Advisory committee on instruments and methods of research (to cooperate with a similar committee of the International Council of Scientific Unions): Chairman, Fred. E. Wright; C. G. Abbot, F. K. Richtmyer.

Committee on naval research: Chairman, R. A. Millikan; Francis G. Blake, Isaiah Bowman, Frank B. Jewett, Charles F. Kettering, C. K. Leith, F. W. Willard.

Committee on research publications: Chairman, F. K. Richtmyer; Edson S. Bastin, Francis G. Blake, Davenport Hooker, Arthur B. Lamb, Frank R. Lillie, H. C. Parmelee, Edward Sapir. Secretary, C. J. West.

REPRESENTATIVES OF THE COUNCIL ON—

Editorial board of the Proceedings of the National Academy of Sciences: Edson S. Bastin, Francis G. Blake, Charles F. Kettering, I. F. Lewis, Frank R. Lillie, R. A. Millikan, Edward Sapir, F. W. Willard. Member of the editorial executive committee, Frank R. Lillie.

Council of the National Parks Association: Vernon Kellogg.

Board of trustees of Science Service: C. G. Abbot, H. E. Howe, Ludvig Hektoen.

B. Divisions of General Relations

I. DIVISION OF FEDERAL RELATIONS

Chairman, George R. Putnam.
Vice chairman, Wilbur J. Carr.
Secretary, Paul Brockett.

EXECUTIVE COMMITTEE

Chairman, George R. Putnam; vice chairman, Wilbur J. Carr; C. G. Abbot, Lyman J. Briggs, J. R. Mohler, A. M. Stimson.

MEMBERS OF THE DIVISION

The President of the United States, on the nomination of the National Academy of Sciences, has designated the following representatives of the various departments to act as members of this division:

DEPARTMENT OF STATE

Wilbur J. Carr, Assistant Secretary of State.

DEPARTMENT OF THE TREASURY

A. M. Stimson, Medical Director, Public Health Service.

DEPARTMENT OF WAR

Col. Francis H. Lincoln, General Staff, in charge of Military Intelligence, United States Army.
Maj. Randolph T. Pendleton, Coast Artillery Corps, United States Army.
Lt. Col. E. R. Gentry, Medical Corps, United States Army.
Col. Warren T. Hannum, Corps of Engineers, United States Army.
Col. John E. Munroe, Ordnance Department, United States Army.
Maj. Gen. James B. Allison, Chief Signal Officer, United States Army.
Maj. Gen. Oscar Westover, Air Corps, United States Army.
Maj. Gen. Claude E. Brigham, Chief, Chemical Warfare Service, United States Army.

DEPARTMENT OF JUSTICE

J. Edgar Hoover, Director of Investigations.

Wrightson Chambers, superintendent, Division of Engineering and Research.

DEPARTMENT OF THE NAVY

Capt. S. C. Hooper, technical assistant to the Chief of Naval Operations, United States Navy.

—— ——, Intelligence Division, Office of Naval Operations, United State Navy.

Capt. J. F. Hellweg, Superintendent, Naval Observatory, Bureau of Navigation, United States Navy.

Rear Admiral N. M. Smith, Chief, Bureau of Yards and Docks, United States Navy.

Rear Admiral Harold R. Stark, Chief, Bureau of Ordnance, United States Navy.

Rear Admiral Emory S. Land, Chief, Bureau of Construction and Repair, United States Navy.

Rear Admiral Harold G. Bowen, Chief, Bureau of Engineering, United States Navy.

Rear Admiral Percival S. Rossiter, Chief, Bureau of Medicine and Surgery, United States Navy.

DEPARTMENT OF THE INTERIOR

Elwood Mead,[1] Commissioner, Bureau of Reclamation.

W. C. Mendenhall, Director, Geological Survey.

Harold C. Bryant, Assistant Director, National Park Service.

DEPARTMENT OF AGRICULTURE

—— ——, Weather Bureau.

J. R. Mohler, Chief, Bureau of Animal Industry.

E. H. Clapp, Assistant Forester, in charge of the Branch of Research, Forest Service.

Henry G. Knight, Chief, Bureau of Chemistry and Soils.

Lee A. Strong, Chief, Bureau of Entomology and Plant Quarantine.

—— ——, Bureau of Biological Survey.

Thomas H. MacDonald, Chief, Bureau of Public Roads.

S. H. McCrory, Chief, Bureau of Agricultural Engineering.

DEPARTMENT OF COMMERCE

Joseph A. Hill, Chief Statistician, Statistical Research, Bureau of the Census.

Lyman J. Briggs, Director, National Bureau of Standards.

Frank T. Bell, Commissioner, Bureau of Fisheries.

George R. Putnam, Bureau of Lighthouses.

William Bowie, Chief, Division of Geodesy, Coast and Geodetic Survey.

Charles H. Pierce, classification examiner, Patent Office.

—— ——, Bureau of Mines.

DEPARTMENT OF LABOR

Isador Lubin, Commissioner of Labor Statistics.

SMITHSONIAN INSTITUTION

C. G. Abbot, Secretary, Smithsonian Institution.

NATIONAL ADVISORY COMMITTEE FOR AERONAUTICS

J. S. Ames, chairman, National Advisory Committee for Aeronautics; president, emeritus, Johns Hopkins University, Baltimore, Md.

Secretary of the division: Paul Brockett, executive secretary, and custodian of buildings and grounds, National Academy of Sciences, Washington, D. C.

---

[1] Deceased.

II. DIVISION OF FOREIGN RELATIONS

Chairman, ex officio, T. H. Morgan.
Vice chairman, Wilbur J. Carr.
Vice chairman, Frank Schlesinger.
Secretary, Albert L. Barrows.

EXECUTIVE COMMITTEE

Chairman, T. H. Morgan; vice chairmen, Wilbur J. Carr and Frank Schlesinger; William Bowie, Edward Bartow, George E. Hale, L. S. Rowe.

MEMBERS OF THE DIVISION

Ex officio

President of the National Academy of Sciences: Frank R. Lillie, dean, emeritus, of the division of biological sciences, and Andrew MacLeish distinguished-service professor of embryology, emeritus, University of Chicago.

Foreign secretary of the National Academy of Sciences: T. H. Morgan, chairman of the division of biology, William G. Kerckhoff laboratories of the biological sciences, California Institute of Technology, Pasadena, Calif.

Chairman of the National Research Council, the chairmen of all divisions of the Council, and the director of the Research Information Service.

Representatives of—

AMERICAN ASSOCIATION FOR THE ADVANCEMENT OF SCIENCE

W. A. Noyes, emeritus professor of chemistry, University of Illinois, Urbana, Ill.

AMERICAN ACADEMY OF ARTS AND SCIENCES

Arthur E. Kennelly, emeritus professor of electrical engineering, Harvard University, Cambridge, Mass.

AMERICAN PHILOSOPHICAL SOCIETY

L. S. Rowe, director, Pan American Union, Washington, D. C.

DEPARTMENT OF STATE

Wilbur J. Carr, vice chairman of the division, Assistant Secretary of State, Washington, D. C.

DEPARTMENT OF THE NAVY

———— ————.

DEPARTMENT OF WAR

Brig. Gen. Harry E. Knight, General Staff, in charge of Military Intelligence, Washington, D. C.

INTERNATIONAL ASTRONOMICAL UNION

Henry Norris Russell, ex officio, chairman, American section, International Astronomical Union; Charles A. Young professor of astronomy and director of the observatory, Princeton University, Princeton, N. J.

INTERNATIONAL GEODETIC AND GEOPHYSICAL UNION

Henry B. Bigelow, director, Woods Hole Oceanographic Institute; professor of zoology and curator of oceanography in the Museum of Comparative Zoology, Harvard University, Cambridge, Mass.

William Bowie, president, International Geodetic and Geophysical Union; Chief, Division of Geodesy, United States Coast and Geodetic Survey, Washington, D. C.

Lyman J. Briggs, Director, National Bureau of Standards, Washington, D. C.

John A . Fleming, general secretary, American Geophysical Union; president, Association of Terrestrial Magnetism and Electricity, International Geodetic and Geophysical Union; acting director, department of terrestrial magnetism, Carnegie Institution of Washington, 5241 Broad Branch Road, Washington, D. C.

N. H. Heck, chairman, American Geophysical Union; Chief, Division of Terrestrial Magnetism and Seismology, United States Coast and Geodetic Survey, Washington, D. C.

C. S. Scofield, chairman, section of hydrology, American Geophysical Union; principal agriculturist, United States Bureau of Plant Industry, Washington, D. C.

Thomas G. Thompson, member of the executive committee of the Association on Oceanography, International Union of Geodesy and Geophysics; professor of chemistry and director of the oceanographic laboratories, University of Washington, Seattle, Wash.

INTERNATIONAL UNION OF CHEMISTRY

Edward Bartow, vice president, International Union of Chemistry; professor of chemistry and head of the department of chemistry and chemical engineering, State University of Iowa, Iowa City, Iowa.

INTERNATIONAL UNION OF PURE AND APPLIED PHYSICS

R. A. Millikan, ex officio, chairman, division of physical sciences, National Research Council; director, Norman Bridge Laboratory of Physics, and chairman of the executive council, California Institute of Technology, Pasadena, Calif.

INTERNATIONAL SCIENTIFIC RADIO UNION

Arthur E. Kennelly, ex officio, chairman of the American section, International Scientific Radio Union; emeritus professor of electrical engineering, Harvard University, Cambridge, Mass.

INTERNATIONAL GEOGRAPHICAL UNION

Douglas Johnson, chairman, national committee of the United States, International Geographical Union; professor of physiography, Columbia University, New York City.

INTERNATIONAL BUREAU OF WEIGHTS AND MEASURES

Lyman J. Briggs, Director, National Bureau of Standards, Washington, D. C.

INTERNATIONAL ELECTROTECHNICAL COMMISSION

Clayton H. Sharp, president, United States national committee of the International Electrotechnical Commission, 294 Fisher Avenue, White Plains, New York.

INTERNATIONAL COMMISSION ON ILLUMINATION

E. C. Crittenden, Chief, Electrical Division, and Assistant Director, National Bureau of Standards, Washington, D. C.

Members-at-Large

C. G. Abbot, secretary, Smithsonian Institution, Washington, D. C.

P. G. Agnew, secretary, American Standards Association, 29 West Thirty-ninth Street, New York City.

Arthur H. Compton, Charles H. Swift distinguished service professor of physics, University of Chicago, Chicago, Ill.

John W. Finch, director, United States Bureau of Mines, Washington, D. C.

Herbert E. Gregory, director, Bishop Museum of Polynesian Ethnology and Natural History, Honolulu, Hawaii.

George E. Hale, honorary director, Mount Wilson Observatory, Carnegie Institution of Washington, Pasadena, Calif.

C. E. McClung, professor of zoology, and director of the zoological laboratory, University of Pennsylvania, Philadelphia, Pa.

Elihu Root, 31 Nassau Street, New York City.

· Frank Schlesinger, vice chairman of the division, professor of astronomy, and director of the observatory, Yale University, New Haven, Conn.

COMMITTEES

The chairman of the division is, ex officio, a member of all committees of the division.

Committee on Pacific Investigations: Chairman, Herbert E. Gregory.

COMMITTEES COOPERATING WITH INTERNATIONAL COMMITTEES OF THE PACIFIC SCIENCE ASSOCIATION

American National Committee on Oceanography of the Pacific: Chairman, Thomas G. Thompson.

American National Committee on Land Classification and Utilization in the Pacific: Chairman, Carl O. Sauer, professor of geography, University of California, Berkeley, Calif.

American Committee on Pacific Seismology: Chairman, James B. Macelwane. S. J., professor of geophysics and dean of the graduate school, St. Louis University, St. Louis, Mo.

REPRESENTATIVE OF THE NATIONAL RESEARCH COUNCIL ON—

Council of the Pacific Science Association: Herbert E. Gregory.

III. DIVISION OF STATES RELATIONS

Chairman, Raymond A. Pearson.
Vice chairman, Albert L. Barrows.

EXECUTIVE COMMITTEE

Chairman, Raymond A. Pearson; vice chairman, Albert L. Barrows; Morris M. Leighton, Jacob G. Lipman, A. R. Mann, Edwin G. Nourse, A. F. Woods, B. Youngblood.

MEMBERS OF THE DIVISION

Raymond A. Pearson, chairman of the division; Special Assistant to the Administrator, United States Resettlement Administration, Washington, D. C.

Albert L. Barrows, vice chairman of the division; executive secretary, National Research Council, Washington, D. C.

Representatives of—

DIVISION OF EDUCATIONAL RELATIONS

———— ————.

DIVISION OF PHYSICAL SCIENCES

William Bowie, Chief, Division of Geodesy, United States Coast and Geodetic Survey, Washington, D. C.

DIVISION OF ENGINEERING AND INDUSTRIAL RESEARCH

A. C. Fieldner, chief engineer, Experiment Stations Division, United States Bureau of Mines, Washington, D. C.

DIVISION OF CHEMISTRY AND CHEMICAL TECHNOLOGY

Frank C. Whitmore, dean, school of chemistry and physics, Pennsylvania State College, State College, Pa.

DIVISION OF GEOLOGY AND GEOGRAPHY

⁻rd B. Mathews. rofessor of mineralo ˌ d trogra by Johns Honkina

DIVISION OF MEDICAL SCIENCES

Carl Voegtlin, chief, division of pharmacology, National Institute of Health, Washington, D. C.

DIVISION OF BIOLOGY AND AGRICULTURE

I. F. Lewis, dean of the university, and Miller professor of biology and agriculture, University of Virginia, University, Va.

DIVISION OF ANTHROPOLOGY AND PSYCHOLOGY

Carl E. Guthe, director, Museum of Anthropology, University of Michigan, Ann Arbor, Mich.

ASSOCIATION OF AMERICAN STATE GEOLOGISTS

Henry B. Kummel, director of conservation and development, and State geologist of New Jersey, Trenton, N. J.

SOCIETY OF AMERICAN FORESTERS

F. W. Besley, State forester of Maryland, Baltimore, Md.

Members-at-Large and Regional Representatives

R. D. Hetzel, president, Pennsylvania State College, State College, Pa.

Morris M. Leighton, chief, Illinois State Geological Survey, Urbana, Ill.

Jacob G. Lipman, dean, college of agriculture, professor of agriculture, and director, agricultural experiment station, Rutgers University, New Brunswick, N. J.

A. R. Mann, provost, Cornell University, Ithaca, N. Y.

H. W. Mumford, dean, college of agriculture, and director, agricultural experiment station, University of Illinois, Urbana, Ill.

Edwin G. Nourse, director, Institute of Economics of the Brookings Institution, 744 Jackson Place, Washington, D. C.

T. S. Palmer, biologist, 1939 Biltmore Street, N. W., Washington, D. C.

A. F. Woods, principal pathologist, Bureau of Plant Industry, United States Department of Agriculture, Washington, D. C.

B. Youngblood, principal agricultural economist, Office of Experiment Stations, United States Department of Agriculture, Washington, D. C.

IV. DIVISION OF EDUCATIONAL RELATIONS

Chairman, William Charles White.
Secretary, Albert L. Barrows.

EXECUTIVE COMMITTEES

Chairman, William Charles White; Harry W. Chase, C. E. McClung, A. R. Mann, C. R. Mann, John C. Merriam, A. F. Woods.

MEMBERS OF THE DIVISION

William Charles White, chairman of the division; chairman, medical research committee, National Tuberculosis Association; pathologist in charge of tuberculosis research, National Institute of Health, Washington, D. C.

Ex officio

Chairman of the research fellowship board in physics, chemistry, and mathematics, National Research Council. Simon Flexner, director, emeritus, Rockefeller Institute for Medical Research, Sixty-sixth Street and York Avenue, New York City.

Chairman of the medical fellowship board, National Research Council, Francis G. Blake, Sterling professor of medicine, Yale University; physician in chief, New Haven Hospital, New Haven, Conn.

Chairman of the board of national research fellowships in the biological sciences, National Research Council. W. J. Robbins, professor of botany, and dean of the graduate school, University of Missouri, Columbia, Mo.

Representatives of—

ASSOCIATION OF LAND-GRANT COLLEGES AND UNIVERSITIES

Raymond A. Pearson, Special Assistant to the Administrator, United States Resettlement Administration, Washington, D. C.

AMERICAN ASSOCIATION OF UNIVERSITY PROFESSORS

F. K. Richtmyer, dean of the graduate school, and professor of physics, Cornell University, Ithaca, N. Y.

AMERICAN COUNCIL ON EDUCATION

C. R. Mann, director emeritus, American Council on Education, 744 Jackson Place, Washington, D. C.

ASSOCIATION OF AMERICAN COLLEGES

Arthur H. Compton, Charles H. Swift distinguished service professor of physics, University of Chicago, Chicago, Ill.

ASSOCIATION OF AMERICAN UNIVERSITIES

———— ————.

NATIONAL ASSOCIATION OF STATE UNIVERSITIES

Frank L. McVey, president, University of Kentucky, Lexington, Ky.

UNITED STATES OFFICE OF EDUCATION

Frederick J. Kelly, chief, division of collegiate-professional education. Office of Education, United States Department of the Interior, Washington, D. C.

Members-at-Large

Harry W. Chase, president, New York University, New York City.
James Bryant Conant, president, Harvard University, Cambridge, Mass.
C. E. McClung, professor of zoology, and director of the zoological laboratory, University of Pennsylvania, Philadelphia, Pa.
A. R. Mann, provost, Cornell University, Ithaca, N. Y.
John C. Merriam, president, Carnegie Institution of Washington, Washington, D. C.
H. W. Tyler, Emeritus professor of mathematics, Massachusetts Institute of Technology; consultant in science, Library of Congress, Washington, D. C.
A. F. Woods, principal pathologist, Bureau of Plant Industry, United States Department of Agriculture, Washington, D. C.
Fernandus Payne, liaison member from the division of biology and agriculture; professor of zoology, and dean of the graduate school, Indiana University, Bloomington, Ind.

C. Divisions of Science and Technology

V. DIVISION OF PHYSICAL SCIENCES

Chairman, R. A. Millikan.
Vice chairman, Henry A. Barton.

EXECUTIVE COMMITTEE

Chairman, R. A. Millikan; vice chairman, Henry A. Barton; Herbert E. Ives, Marston Morse, F. K. Richtmyer, Frederick Slocum, G. W. Stewart, P. I. Wold.

MEMBERS OF THE DIVISION

R. A. Millikan, chairman of the division; director of the Norman Bridge Laboratory of Physics, and chairman of the executive council, California Institute of Technology, Pasadena, Calif.

Representatives of Societies

AMERICAN ASTRONOMICAL SOCIETY

John A. Miller, professor of astronomy, and director, Sproul Observatory, Swarthmore College, Swarthmore, Pa.

Herbert R. Morgan, astronomer, United States Naval Observatory, Washington, D. C.

Frederick Slocum, professor of astronomy, and director of the Van Vleck Observatory, Wesleyan University, Middletown, Conn.

AMERICAN PHYSICAL SOCIETY

W. G. Cady, Foss professor of physics, Wesleyan University, Middletown, Conn.

Lee A. du Bridge, professor of physics, University of Rochester, Rochester, N. Y.

L. O. Grondahl, director of research, Union Switch & Signal Co., Swissvale, Pa.

Herbert E. Ives, physicist, Bell Telephone Laboratories, Inc., 463 West Street, New York City.

G. W. Stewart, professor of physics, State University of Iowa, Iowa City, Iowa.

John Zeleny, professor of physics, Yale University, New Haven, Conn.

AMERICAN MATHEMATICAL SOCIETY

Marston Morse, professor of mathematics, Institute for Advanced Study, Princeton University, Princeton, N. J.

R. G. D. Richardson, dean of the graduate school, and professor of mathematics, Brown University, Providence, R. I.

J. H. Van Vleck, associate professor of mathematical physics, Harvard University, Cambridge, Mass.

OPTICAL SOCIETY OF AMERICA

Carl L. Bausch, Bausch & Lomb Optical Co., Rochester, N. Y.

L. B. Tuckerman, assistant chief, Division of Mechanics and Sound, National Bureau of Standards, Washington, D. C.

David L. Webster, professor of physics, Stanford University, Stanford, Calif.

MATHEMATICAL ASSOCIATION OF AMERICA

W. R. Longley, Richard M. Colgate professor of mathematics, Yale University, New Haven, Conn.

ACOUSTICAL SOCIETY OF AMERICA

Harvey Fletcher, acoustical research director, Bell Telephone Laboratories, Inc., 463 West Street, New York City.

AMERICAN INSTITUTE OF PHYSICS

Henry A. Barton, vice chairman of the division; director, American Institute of Physics, 175 Fifth Avenue, New York City.

Members-at-Large

P. W. Bridgman, Hollis professor of mathematics and natural philosophy, Harvard University, Cambridge, Mass.

F. K. Richtmyer, dean of the graduate school, and professor of physics, Cornell University, Ithaca, N. Y.

P. I. Wold, professor of physics, Union College, Schenectady, N. Y.

The chairman of the division is, ex officio, a member of all committees of the division.

Chairman, Charles F. Kettering; vice-chairmen, Vannevar Bush and D. S. Jacobus; F. O. Clements, E. S. Fickes, Dugald C. Jackson, Frank B. Jewett, C. E. MacQuigg, H. A. Poillon, Ole Singstad.

MEMBERS OF THE DIVISION

Charles F. Kettering, chairman of the division; vice president and director, General Motors Corporation; president, General Motors Research Corporation, Detroit, Mich.

Representatives of Societies

AMERICAN SOCIETY OF CIVIL ENGINEERS

George T. Seabury, ex officio, secretary, American Society of Civil Engineers, 29 West Thirty-ninth Street, New York City.
John H. Gregory, professor of civil and sanitary engineering, Johns Hopkins University, Baltimore, Md.
George L. Lucas, engineer of inspection, the Port of New York Authority, 111 Eighth Avenue, New York City.
Ole Singstad, chief consulting engineer on tunnels, the Port of New York Authority, 80 Eighth Avenue, New York City.

AMERICAN INSTITUTE OF MINING AND METALLURGICAL ENGINEERS

A. B. Parsons, ex officio, secretary, American Institute of Mining and Metallurgical Engineers, 29 West Thirty-ninth Street, New York City.
Edwin S. Fickes, senior vice-president, Aluminum Co. of America, 801 Gulf Building, Pittsburgh, Pa.
C. E. MacQuigg, Union Carbide & Carbon Research Laboratories, Inc., 30 East Forty-second Street, New York City.
H. J. Rose, senior industrial fellow, Mellon Institute of Industrial Research, University of Pittsburgh, Pittsburgh, Pa.

AMERICAN SOCIETY OF MECHANICAL ENGINEERS

C. E. Davies, ex officio, secretary, American Society of Mechanical Engineers, 29 West Thirty-ninth Street, New York City.
F. M. Farmer, chief engineer, Electrical Testing Laboratories, Eightieth Street and East End Avenue, New York City.
Bert Houghton, 1274 East Twenty-third Street, Brooklyn, N. Y.
D. S. Jacobus, vice chairman of the division; advisory engineer, Babcock & Wilcox Co., 85 Liberty Street, New York City.

AMERICAN INSTITUTE OF ELECTRICAL ENGINEERS

H. H. Henline, ex officio, secretary, American Institute of Electrical Engineers, 29 West Thirty-ninth Street, New York City.
Vannevar Bush, vice chairman of the division; vice president of the institute, and dean of the graduate school, Massachusetts Institute of Technology, Cambridge, Mass.
L. W. Chubb, director, research laboratories, Westinghouse Electric & Manufacturing Co., East Pittsburgh, Pa.
Dugald C. Jackson, professor emeritus of electric power production and distribution, and honorary lecturer in the department of electrical engineering, Massachusetts Institute of Technology, Cambridge, Mass.
John B. Whitehead, dean of the engineering faculty, and professor of electrical engineering, Johns Hopkins University, Baltimore, Md.

AMERICAN SOCIETY OF REFRIGERATING ENGINEERS

W. J. King, research engineer, General Electric Co., Schenectady, N. Y.

AMERICAN SOCIETY FOR TESTING MATERIALS

F. O. Clements, technical director, research laboratories, General Motors Corporation, Detroit, Mich.

H. W. Gillett, director of research, Battelle Memorial Institute, Columbus, Ohio.

AMERICAN SOCIETY FOR METALS

R. S. Archer, 10951 Longwood Drive, Chicago, Ill.

AMERICAN SOCIETY OF HEATING AND VENTILATING ENGINEERS

F. E. Giesecke, engineering experiment station, Agricultural & Mechanical College of Texas, College Station, Tex.

ILLUMINATING ENGINEERING SOCIETY

W. F. Little, engineer in charge of photometry, Electrical Testing Laboratories, Eightieth Street and East End Avenue, New York City.

WESTERN SOCIETY OF ENGINEERS

William B. Jackson, electrical engineer, Broadview, Cheshire, Mass.

SOCIETY OF AUTOMOTIVE ENGINEERS

Carl Breer, executive engineer, Chrysler Corporation, 341 Massachusetts Avenue, Detroit, Mich.

E. P. Warner, editor, Aviation; assistant to the president, McGraw-Hill Publishing Co., 330 West Forty-second Street, New York City.

AMERICAN WELDING SOCIETY

Henry M. Hobart, consulting engineer, General Electric Co., Schenectady, N. Y.

Members-at-Large

J. W. Barker, dean, School of Engineering, Columbia University, New York City.

Frank B. Jewett, vice president, American Telephone & Telegraph Co.; president, Bell Telephone Laboratories, Inc., 195 Broadway, New York City.

Howard Poillon, president, Research Corporation, 405 Lexington Avenue, New York City.

COMMITTEES

The chairman of the division is, ex officio, a member of all committees and boards of the division.

Committee on electrical insulation: Chairman, John B. Whitehead.

Subcommittee on chemistry: Chairman, F. M. Clark, General Electric Co., Pittsfield, Mass.

Subcommittee on physics: Chairman, Wheeler P. Davey, research professor of physics and chemistry, Pennsylvania State College, State College, Pa.

Subcommittee on program of research: Chairman, John B. Whitehead.

Committee on relationships between universities and industry: Chairman, J. W. Barker.

Committee for research on hydraulic friction: Chairman, Theodor von Karman, professor of aeronautics, and director, Daniel Guggenheim Laboratory, California Institute of Technology, Pasadena, Calif.

Committee on heat transmission, executive committee: Chairman, Willis H. Carrier, president, Carrier Engineering Corporation, Newark, N. J.

Subcommittee on heat transfer by radiation: Chairman, J. D. Keller, Carnegie Institute of Technology, Schenley Park, Pittsburgh, Pa.

Subcommittee on heat transfer by convection: Chairman, W. H. McAdams, professor of chemical engineering, Massachusetts Institute of Technology, Cambridge, Mass.

Subcommittee on thermal insulation: Chairman, T. Smith Taylor, T. Smith Taylor Laboratories, 45 Grover Lane, Caldwell, N. J.

Subcommittee on nomenclature and definitions: Chairman, E. F. Mueller, physicist, National Bureau of Standards, Washington, D. C.

Committee on industrial lighting: Chairman, Dugald C. Jackson.

REPRESENTATIVES OF THE DIVISION ON—

COMMITTEES OF THE AMERICAN SOCIETY FOR TESTING MATERIALS

Committee A–8 on magnetic analysis: R. L. Sanford, physicist, National Bureau of Standards, Washington, D. C.

Committee for the investigation of sulphur and phosphorus in steel: J. H. Hall, metallurgical engineer, Taylor-Wharton Iron & Steel Co., High Bridge, N. J.

Committee on ferrous metals, advisory to the National Bureau of Standards: Enrique Touceda, consulting engineer, Broadway and Thacher Street, Albany, N. Y.

Sectional committee on safety code for brakes and brake testing of the National Bureau of Standards: S. S. Steinberg, professor of civil engineering, University of Maryland, College Park, Md.

HIGHWAY RESEARCH BOARD

Chairman, A. T. Goldbeck, director of the engineering bureau, National Crushed Stone Association, Washington, D. C.

COMMITTEES

Department of highway finance and administration: Chairman, Thomas H. MacDonald, Chief, United States Bureau of Public Roads, Washington, D. C.

Department of highway transportation economics: Chairman, R. L. Morrison, professor of highway engineering and highway transport, University of Michigan, Ann Arbor, Mich.

Project committee on tractive resistance and allied problems: Chairman, W. E. Lay, professor of mechanical engineering, University of Michigan, Ann Arbor, Mich.

Project committee on cost of motor vehicle operation: Chairman, E. W. James, Chief, Division of Highway Transport, United States Bureau of Public Roads, Washington, D. C.

Project committee on economic life of pavements: Chairman, Anson Marston, senior dean of engineering, Iowa State College, Ames, Iowa.

Department of highway design: Chairman, A. T. Goldbeck.

Project committee on roadside development (in cooperation with the American Association of State Highway Officials): Chairman, Luther M. Keith, director of roadside development, State Highway Department, Hartford, Conn.

Project committee on use of high elastic limit steel for concrete reinforcement: Chairman, Herbert J. Gilkey, head, theoretical and applied mechanics department, Iowa State College, Ames, Iowa.

Project committee on pavement joints: Chairman, J. W. Kushing, research and testing engineer, Michigan Highway Department, Lansing, Mich.

Project committee on antiskid properties of road surfaces: Chairman, George E. Martin, consulting engineer, general tarvia department, the Barrett Co., New York City.

Project committee on highway guard rails: Chairman, F. V. Reagel, engineer of materials, Missouri Highway Department, Jefferson City, Mo.

Project committee on design of flexible type road surfaces: Chairman, A. C. Benkelman, United States Bureau of Public Roads, Washington, D. C.

Project committee on sight distance: (Chairman not yet appointed.)

Project committee on relation of curvature to speed: Chairman, C. N. Conner, United States Bureau of Public Roads, Washington, D. C.

Department of materials and construction: Chairman, C. H. Scholer, construction materials engineer, Engineering Experiment Station, Manhattan, Kans.

Project committee on the effect of freezing and thawing on concrete containing cement of different compositions: Chairman, H. S. Mattimore, engineer of tests and materials investigations, State Department of Highways, Harrisburg, Pa.

Project committee on volume changes in concrete: Chairman, C. H. Scholer.

Project committee on correlation of research in mineral aggregates: Chairman, W. J. Emmons, associate professor of highway engineering, University of Michigan, Ann Arbor, Mich.

Project committee on curing of concrete pavement slabs: Chairman, F. C. Lang, engineer of tests and inspection, Minnesota department of highways, 1246 University Avenue, St. Paul, Minn.

Project committee on fillers and cushion courses for brick and block pavements: Chairman, J. S. Crandell, professor of highway engineering, University of Illinois, Urbana, Ill.

Department of maintenance: Chairman, C. P. Owens, maintenance engineer, State Highway Department, Jefferson City, Mo.

Project committee on maintenance costs: Chairman, H. K. Bishop, Chief, Division of Construction, United States Bureau of Public Roads, Washington, D. C.

Project committee on maintenance of cracks and expansion joints in concrete pavements: Chairman, W. H. Root, maintenance engineer, Iowa State Highway commission, Ames, Iowa.

Project committee on warping of concrete pavement slabs: Chairman, C. P. Owens, maintenance engineer, Missouri Highway Department, Jefferson City, Mo.

Department of traffic: Chairman, C. J. Tilden, professor of engineering mechanics, Yale University, New Haven, Conn.

Project committee on traffic capacity: Chairman, A. N. Johnson, dean, College of Engineering, University of Maryland, College Park, Md.

Project committee on traffic survey methods and forms: Chairman, J. G. McKay, director, Cleveland Highway Research Bureau, Cleveland, Ohio.

Project committee on vehicle and highway mechanics as related to traffic: Chairman, H. C. Dickinson, Chief, Heat and Power Division, National Bureau of Standards, Washington, D. C.

Project committee on traffic regulations in municipalities: Chairman, W. S. Canning, engineering director, Keystone Automobile Club, Philadelphia, Pa.

Department of soils investigations: Chairman, C. A. Hogentogler, senior highway engineer, United States Bureau of Public Roads, Washington, D. C.

Project committee on stabilized roads: Chairman, C. A. Hogentogler.

VII. DIVISION OF CHEMISTRY AND CHEMICAL TECHNOLOGY

Chairman, F. W. Willard.

EXECUTIVE COMMITTEE

Chairman, F. W. Willard; E. K. Bolton, Charles L. Parsons, Austin M. Patterson, Harold C. Urey.

MEMBERS OF THE DIVISION

F. W. Willard, chairman of the division; executive vice president, Nassau Smelting & Refining Co., 50 Church Street, New York City.

Representatives of Societies

AMERICAN CHEMICAL SOCIETY

E. K. Bolton, chemical director, E. I du Pont de Nemours & Co., Wilmington, Del.

E. J. Crane, editor, Chemical Abstracts, Ohio State University, Columbus, Ohio.

William Lloyd Evans, professor of chemistry, Ohio State University, Columbus, Ohio.

Charles L. Parsons, secretary and business manager, American Chemical Society, Mills Building, Washington, D. C.

Harold C. Urey, professor of chemistry, Columbia University, New York City.

Edward R. Weidlein, director, Mellon Institute of Industrial Research, Pittsburgh, Pa.

Hiram S. Lukens, professor of chemistry, and director of the Harrison Laboratory, University of Pennsylvania, Philadelphia, Pa.

AMERICAN INSTITUTE OF CHEMICAL ENGINEERS

Ellery L. Wilson, vice president, director, and general superintendent, Rumford Chemical Works, Providence, R. I.

AMERICAN CERAMIC SOCIETY

J. C. Hostetter, director of development and research, Corning Glass Works, Corning, N. Y.

Ex officio

Edward Bartow, vice president, International Union of Chemistry; professor of chemistry, and head of the department of chemistry and chemical engineering, State University of Iowa, Iowa City, Iowa.

Members-at-Large

Charles A. Kraus, research professor of chemistry, Brown University, Providence, R. I.

Austin M. Patterson, vice president and professor of chemistry, Antioch College, Yellow Springs, Ohio.

Hobart H. Willard, professor of analytical chemistry, University of Michigan, Ann Arbor, Mich.

Ross A. Gortner, liaison member from the division of biology and agriculture; professor of agricultural biochemistry, University of Minnesota, University Farm, St. Paul, Minn.

COMMITTEES

The chairman of the division is, ex officio, a member of all committees of the division.

Advisory committee on Annual Survey of American chemistry: Chairman, F. W. Willard.

Advisory committee to the National Bureau of Standards on research on the reproduction of records: Chairman, H. M. Lydenberg, director, New York Public Library, New York City.

Committee on the chemistry of colloids: Chairman, Harry B. Weiser, professor of chemistry and dean, Rice Institute, Houston, Tex.

Committee on the construction and equipment of chemical laboratories: Chairman, C. R. Hoover; L. B. Nye professor of chemistry, Wesleyan University, Middltown, Conn.

Committee on hydrogen isotopes: Chairman, Harold C. Urey, professor of chemistry, Columbia University, New York City.

Committee on photochemistry: Chairman, Hugh S. Taylor, David B. Jones professor of chemistry, Princeton University, Princeton, N. J.

Committee on the preparation and publication of a list of ring systems used in organic chemistry (joint committee with the American Chemical Society): Chairman, Austin M. Patterson.

International Union of Chemistry: The division of chemistry and chemical technology acts as the American section of the International Union of Chemistry.

VIII. DIVISION OF GEOLOGY AND GEOGRAPHY

Chairman, Edson S. Bastin.
Vice chairman, W. L. G. Joerg.

EXECUTIVE COMMITTEE

Chairman, Edson S. Bastin; vice chairman, W. L. G. Joerg; A. F. Buddington, Charles Butts, W. F. Foshag, Robert S. Platt.

MEMBERS OF THE DIVISION

Representatives of Societies

GEOLOGICAL SOCIETY OF AMERICA

Donald C. Barton, geologist and geophysicist, Humble Oil & Refining Co., Houston, Tex.
A. F. Buddington, professor of geology, Princeton University; Princeton, N. J.

MINERALOGICAL SOCIETY OF AMERICA

W. F. Foshag, curator of physical and chemical geology, United States National Museum, Washington, D. C.

PALEONTOLOGICAL SOCIETY

Charles Butts, geologist, 1808 Kenyon Street, NW., Washington, D. C.

ASSOCIATION OF AMERICAN GEOGRAPHERS

Frank E. Williams, professor of geography, Wharton School of Commerce and Finance, University of Pennsylvania, Philadelphia, Pa.
Robert S. Platt, associate professor of geography, University of Chicago, Chicago, Ill.

AMERICAN GEOGRAPHICAL SOCIETY

W. L. G. Joerg, vice chairman of the division; editor, Research Series, American Geographical Society, Broadway at One Hundred and Fifty-sixth Street, New York City.

SOCIETY OF ECONOMIC GEOLOGISTS

Thomas B. Nolan, associate geologist, United States Geological Survey, Washington, D. C.

AMERICAN ASSOCIATION OF PETROLEUM GEOLOGISTS

F. H. Labee, chief geologist, Sun Oil Co., Dallas, Tex.

Members-at-Large

Florence Bascom, geologist, care of United States Geological Survey, Washington, D. C.
Edson S. Bastin, chairman of the division; professor of economic geology, University of Chicago, Chicago, Ill.
Ellsworth Huntington, research associate in geography, Yale University, New Haven, Conn.

COMMITTEES

The chairman of the division is, ex officio, a member of all committees of the division.
Advisory committee to the division: Chairman, Edson S. Bastin.
National committee of the United States, International Geographical Union: Chairman, Douglas Johnson, professor of physiography, Columbia University, New York City.
Committee on Pan American Institute of Geography and History: Chairman, C. H. Birdseye, Chief of the Division of Engraving and Printing, United States Geological Survey, Washington, D. C.
Committee on fellowships: Chairman, Arthur Keith, geologist, United States Geological Survey, Washington, D. C.

TECHNICAL COMMITTEES

Committee on accessory minerals of crystalline rocks: Chairman, A. N. Winchell, professor of geology, University of Wisconsin, Madison, Wis.

Committee on aerial photographs: Chairman, C. H. Birdseye.

Committee on Bibliography of Economic Geology: Chairman, Waldemar Lindgren, professor emeritus of economic geology, Massachusetts Institute of Technology, Cambridge, Mass.

Committee on conservation of scientific results of drilling: Chairman, Allen C. Tester, assistant professor of geology, State University of Iowa; assistant State geologist, Iowa City, Iowa.

Committee on cooperation with the Bureau of Census: Chairman, W. L. G. Joerg.

Committee on land classification: Chairman, K. C. McMurry, professor of geography, University of Michigan, Ann Arbor, Mich.

Committee on the measurement of geological time: Chairman, Alfred C. Lane, Pearson professor of geology and mineralogy, Tufts College, Tufts College, Mass.

Committee on micropaleontology: Chairman, Joseph A. Cushman, director, Cushman Laboratory for Foraminiferal Research, Sharon, Mass.

Committee on paleobotany: Chairman, Roland W. Brown, assistant geologist, United States Geological Survey, Washington, D. C.

Committee on paleoecology: Chairman, W. H. Twenhofel, professor of geology, University of Wisconsin, Madison, Wis.

Committee on processes of ore deposition: Chairman, W. H. Newhouse, associate professor of economic geology, Massachusetts Institute of Technology, Cambridge, Mass.

Committee on sedimentation: Chairman, Parker D. Trask, associate geologist, United States Geological Survey, Washington, D. C.

Committee on State geological surveys: Chairman, Morris M. Leighton, Chief, Illinois State Geological Survey, Urbana, Ill.

Committee on stratigraphy: Chairman, Carl O. Dunbar, professor of paleontology and stratigraphy, and curator of invertebrate paleontology, Yale University, New Haven, Conn.

Committee on structural petrology: Chairman, T. S. Lovering, associate professor of geology, University of Michigan, Ann Arbor, Mich.

Committee on tectonics: Chairman, Chester R. Longwell, Henry Barnard Davis professor of geology, Yale University, New Haven, Conn.

REPRESENTATIVES OF THE DIVISION ON—

Advisory council of the Board of Surveys and Maps of the Federal Government: George W. Stose.

National council of the American Association of Water Well Drillers: O. E. Meinzer.

Committee on the classification of coal of the American Society for Testing Materials: Taisia Stadnichenko.

IX. DIVISION OF MEDICAL SCIENCES

Chairman, Francis G. Blake.
Vice chairman, Howard T. Karsner.

EXECUTIVE COMMITTEE

Chairman, Francis G. Blake; vice chairman, Howard T. Karsner; Philip Bard, George W. Corner, Glenn E. Cullen, Esmond R. Long.

MEMBERS OF THE DIVISION

Francis G. Blake, chairman of the division; Sterling professor of medicine, School of Medicine, Yale University; physician in chief, New Haven Hospital, New Haven, Conn.

Representatives of Societies

AMERICAN ASSOCIATION OF ANATOMISTS

Lewis H. Weed, professor of anatomy and director of the School of Medicine, Johns Hopkins University, Baltimore, Md.

AMERICAN ASSOCIATION OF PATHOLOGISTS AND BACTERIOLOGISTS

Howard T. Karsner, vice chairman of the division; professor of pathology and director, Institute of Pathology, Western Reserve University, Cleveland, Ohio.

AMERICAN DENTAL ASSOCIATION

C. T. Messner, 5712 Twenty-third Street, Washington, D. C.

AMERICAN MEDICAL ASSOCIATION

L. R. Thompson, Assistant Surgeon General, United States Public Health Service, Washington, D. C.

AMERICAN NEUROLOGICAL ASSOCIATION

Walter Freeman, 1726 I Street, NW., Washington, D. C.

AMERICAN PHYSIOLOGICAL SOCIETY

Philip Bard, professor of physiology, School of Medicine, Johns Hopkins University, Baltimore, Md.

AMERICAN PSYCHIATRIC ASSOCIATION

Clifford B. Farr, director of laboratories, Department of Mental and Nervous Diseases, Pennsylvania Hospital, Philadelphia, Pa.

AMERICAN ROENTGEN RAY SOCIETY

Merrill C. Sosman, assistant professor of medicine, Harvard Medical School, Boston, Mass.

AMERICAN SOCIETY OF BIOLOGICAL CHEMISTS

Glenn E. Cullen, director of laboratories, Pediatric Research Foundation, and professor of research pediatrics, University of Cincinnati, Cincinnati, Ohio.

AMERICAN SOCIETY FOR CLINICAL INVESTIGATION

John P. Peters, John Slade Ely professor of medicine, Yale University, New Haven, Conn.

AMERICAN SOCIETY FOR EXPERIMENTAL PATHOLOGY

Carl V. Weller, professor of pathology, and director of the pathological laboratories, University of Michigan, Ann Arbor, Mich.

AMERICAN SOCIETY FOR PHARMACOLOGY AND EXPERIMENTAL THERAPEUTICS

C. W. Edmunds, professor of materia medica and therapeutics, University of Michigan, Ann Arbor, Mich.

AMERICAN SURGICAL ASSOCIATION

Harvey B. Stone, associate professor of surgery, School of Medicine, Johns Hopkins University, Baltimore, Md.

AMERICAN VETERINARY MEDICAL ASSOCIATION

Karl F. Meyer, professor of bacteriology, and director of the Hooper Foundation for Medical Research, University of California, San Francisco, Calif.

ASSOCIATION OF AMERICAN PHYSICIANS

O. H. Perry Pepper, professor of clinical medicine, School of Medicine, University of Pennsylvania, Philadelphia, Pa.

David John Davis, professor of pathology and bacteriology, and dean of the College of Medicine, University of Illinois, Chicago, Ill.

Representative of the Division of Federal Relations

Lt. Col. E. R. Gentry, Medical Corps, United States Army, Washington, D. C.

Members-at-Large

George W. Corner, professor of anatomy, School of Medicine, University of Rochester, Rochester, N. Y.

Esmond R. Long, professor of pathology, School of Medicine, and director, Henry Phipps Institute, University of Pennsylvania, Philadelphia, Pa.

Alfred N. Richards, professor of pharmacology, University of Pennsylvania, Philadelphia, Pa.

COMMITTEES

The chairman of the division is, ex officio, a member of all committees of the division.

Advisory committee to the division: Stanhope Bayne-Jones, Henry A. Christian, Edmund V. Cowdry, Frederick P. Gay, Ludvig Hektoen, William H. Howell, Raymond Hussey, C. M. Jackson, Howard T. Karsner, George W. McCoy, William Charles White.

Committee on American registry of pathology: Chairman, Howard T. Karsner.

Committee on the study of brucella infections: Chairman, Karl F. Meyer.

Committee on drug addiction: Chairman, William Charles White, chairman, medical research committee, National Tuberculosis Association; pathologist in charge of tuberculosis research, National Institute of Health, Washington, D. C.

Committee for survey of research on gonococcus and gonococcal infections: Chairman, Stanhope Bayne-Jones, dean of the School of Medicine, professor of bacteriology, and master of Trumbull College, Yale University, New Haven, Conn.

Committee on medical problems of animal parasitology: Chairman, Henry B. Ward, permanent secretary, American Association for the Advancement of Science; emeritus professor of zoology, University of Illinois, Urbana, Ill.

Committee on microbiology of the soil (joint committee with the Division of Biology and Agriculture): Chairman, William Charles White.

Committee for research in problems of sex: Chairman, Robert M. Yerkes, professor of psychobiology, Yale University, New Haven, Conn.

X. DIVISION OF BIOLOGY AND AGRICULTURE

Chairman, I. F. Lewis.
Vice chairman, R. E. Coker.

EXECUTIVE COMMITTEE

Chairman, I. . Lewis; vice chairman, R. E. Coker; Fernadus Payne, E. N. Transeau, A. H. Wright.

MEMBERS OF THE DIVISION

I. F. Lewis, chairman of the division, dean of the University, and Miller professor of biology and agriculture, University of Virginia, University, Va.

Representatives of Societies

GROUP I. BOTANICAL SOCIETY OF AMERICA

Elmer D. Merrill, administrator of botanical collections, Gray Herbarium, Harvard University, Cambridge, Mass.

GROUP II. AMERICAN SOCIETY OF ZOOLOGISTS

L. V. Heilbrunn, associate professor of zoology, University of Pennsylvania, Philadelphia, Pa.

GROUP III. AMERICAN SOCIETY OF ANIMAL PRODUCTION, AMERICAN DAIRY SCIENCE ASSOCIATION, POULTRY SCIENCE ASSOCIATION

O. E. Reed, chief, United States Bureau of Dairy Industry, Washington, D. C.

GROUP IV. AMERICAN SOCIETY OF AGRONOMY, SOCIETY OF AMERICAN FORESTERS, AMERICAN SOCIETY FOR HORTICULTURAL SCIENCE

E. C. Auchter, principal horticulturist, United States Bureau of Plant Industry, Washington, D. C.

GROUP V. AMERICAN PHYTOPATHOLOGICAL SOCIETY, SOCIETY OF AMERICAN BACTERIOLOGISTS

H. P. Barss, principal botanist, and associate in experiment station administration, Office of Experiment Stations, United States Department of Agriculture, Washington, D. C.

GROUP VI. AMERICAN GENETIC ASSOCIATION, ECOLOGICAL SOCIETY OF AMERICA, GENETICS SOCIETY OF AMERICA

Henry Allen Gleason, head curator, New York Botanical Garden, Bronx Park, New York City.

GROUP VII. AMERICAN PHYSIOLOGICAL SOCIETY, PHYSIOLOGICAL SECTION OF THE BOTANICAL SOCIETY OF AMERICA, AMERICAN SOCIETY OF BIOLOGICAL CHEMISTS

E. N. Transeau, professor of botany and director of the botanic garden, Ohio State University, Columbus, Ohio.

GROUP VIII. AMERICAN ASSOCIATION OF ECONOMIC ENTOMOLOGISTS, ENTOMOLOGICAL SOCIETY OF AMERICA, AMERICAN SOCIETY OF MAMMALOGISTS

Remington Kellogg, assistant curator of the division of mammals, United States National Museum, Washington, D. C.

Members-at-Large

R. E. Coker, professor of zoology, University of North Carolina, Chapel Hill, N. C.
Fernandus Payne, professor of zoology and dean of the graduate school, Indiana University, Bloomington, Ind.
A. H. Wright, professor of zoology, Cornell University, Ithaca, N. Y.

Committees

The chairman of the division is, ex officio, a member of all committees of the division.

Advisory committee to the division: C. E. Allen, L. J. Cole, William Crocker, W. C. Curtis, B. M. Duggar, R. A. Harper, Duncan S. Johnson, L. R. Jones, Vernon Kellogg, Frank R. Lillie, C. E. McClung, Maynard M. Metcalf, Fernandus Payne, Lorande L. Woodruff, A. F. Woods.

Committee on agronomy: Chairman, Richard Bradfield, professor of soils, Ohio State University, Columbus, Ohio.

Committee on animal nutrition: Chairman, Paul E. Howe, senior chemist, in charge of nutrition investigations, Animal Husbandry Division, United States Bureau of Animal Industry, Washington, D. C.

Committee on the ecology of grasslands in North America: Chairman, V. E. Shelford, professor of zoology, University of Illinois, Urbana, Ill.

Committee on forestry: Chairman, Raphael Zon, director, Lake States Forest Experiment Station, St. Paul, Minn.

Committee on human heredity: Chairman, Laurence H. Snyder, associate professor of zoology and entomology, Ohio State University, Columbus, Ohio.

Committee on hydrobiology and aquiculture: Chairman, J. G. Needham, professor of entomology and limnology, Cornell University, Ithaca, N. Y.

Committee on pharmacognosy and pharmaceutical botany: Chairman, Heber W. Youngken, professor of pharmacognosy, Massachusetts College of Pharmacy, Boston, Mass.

Committee on radiation: Chairman, B. M. Duggar, professor of applied and physiological botany, University of Wisconsin, Madison, Wis.

Subcommittee on mitogenetic radiation: Chairman, I. F. Lewis.

Subcommittee on survey: Chairman, B. M. Duggar.

Committee on wild-life: Chairman, Aldo Leopold, professor of wild-life management and research director of the arboretum, University of Wisconsin, Madison, Wis.

Subcommittee on training men for administrative and education work in wild-life: Chairman, A. G. Ruthven, president, University of Michigan, Ann Arbor, Mich.

REPRESENTATIVES OF THE DIVISION ON—

Board of trustees of Biological Abstracts: A. F. Blakeslee, C. E. McClung, J. R. Schramm, A. F. Woods.

Board of governors of the Crop Protection Institute: Remington Kellogg.

XI. DIVISION OF ANTHROPOLOGY AND PSYCHOLOGY

Chairman, Edward Sapir.
Vice chairman, Walter S. Hunter.

EXECUTIVE COMMITTEE

Chairman, Edward Sapir; vice chairman, Walter S. Hunter; Clark L. Hull, J. R. Swanton.

MEMBERS OF THE DIVISION

Edward Sapir, chairman of the division, Sterling professor of anthropology, Yale University, New Haven, Conn.

Representatives of Societies

AMERICAN ANTHROPOLOGICAL ASSOCIATION

S. A. Barrett, director, Milwaukee Public Museum, Milwaukee, Wis.

Ruth Benedict, assistant professor of anthropology, Columbia University, New York City.

M. J. Herskovits, associate professor of anthropology, Northwestern University, Evanston, Ill.

E. A. Hooton, professor of anthropology and curator of somatology in the Peabody Museum, Harvard University, Cambridge, Mass.

Robert Redfield, associate professor of anthropology, University of Chicago, Chicago, Ill.

Frank H. H. Roberts, Jr., archaeologist, Bureau of American Ethnology, Smithsonian Institution, Washington, D. C.

H. L. Shapiro, associate curator of physical anthropology, American Museum of Natural History, New York City.

William Duncan Strong, senior ethnologist, Bureau of American Ethnology, Smithsonian Institution, Washington, D. C.

AMERICAN PSYCHOLOGICAL ASSOCIATION

J. F. Dashiell, professor of psychology, University of North Carolina, Chapel Hill, N. C.

Clark L. Hull, professor of psychology, Yale University, New Haven, Conn.

W. S. Hunter, vice chairman of the division; G. Stanley Hall professor of genetic psychology, Clark University, Worcester, Mass.

W. R. Miles, professor of psychology, Yale University, New Haven, Conn.

Donald G. Paterson, professor of psychology, University of Minnesota, Minneapolis, Minn.

L. L. Thurstone, professor of psychology, University of Chicago, Chicago, Ill.

Herbert Woodrow, professor of psychology, University of Illinois, Urbana, Ill.
R. S. Woodworth, professor of psychology, Columbia University, New York City.

Members-at-Large

H. S. Langfeld, professor of psychology, and director of the psychological laboratory, Princeton University, Princeton, N. J.
Leslie Spier, research associate in anthropology, Yale University, New Haven, Conn.
J. R. Swanton, ethnologist, Bureau of American Ethnology, Smithsonian Institution, Washington, D. C.

COMMITTEES

The chairman of the division is, ex officio, a member of all committees of the division.
Committee on problems of auditory deficiency: Chairman, Knight Dunlap, professor of psychology, University of California at Los Angeles, Los Angeles, Calif.
Committee on State archaeological surveys: Chairman, Carl E. Guthe, director, Museum of Anthropology, University of Michigan, Ann Arbor, Mich.
Committee on child development: Chairman, R. S. Woodworth, professor of psychology, Columbia University, New York City.
 Subcommittee on selection of child development abstracts and bibliography: Chairman, Carroll E. Palmer, consultant, office of child hygiene, United States Public Health Service; associate in biostatics, School of Hygiene and Public Health, Johns Hopkins University, Baltimore, Md.
Committee on personality in relation to culture: Chairman, Edward Sapir.
 Subcommittee on the preparation of a handbook of psychological leads for ethnological field work: Chairman, A. Irving Hallowell, professor of anthropology, University of Pennsylvania, Philadelphia, Pa.
 Subcommittee on training fellowships: Chairman, Harry Stack Sullivan, psychiatrist, 60 East Forty-second Street, New York City.
 Subcommittee on agenda: Chairman, Mark A. May, professor of psychology, Yale University, New Haven, Conn.
Committee on the psychology of the highway: Chairman, H. M. Johnson, professor of psychology, American University, Washington, D. C.
 Subcommittee for the midwestern area: Chairman, A. R. Lauer, associate professor of psychology, Iowa State College, Ames, Iowa.
 Subcommittee on commercial drivers: Chairman, W. C. Shriver, Chrysler Motor Co., Dayton, Ohio.
Committee on a survey of South American Indians: Chairman, John M. Cooper, professor of anthropology, Catholic University of America, Washington, D. C.
 Executive subcommittee: Chairman, John M. Cooper.
Committee on fellowships: Chairman, Edward Sapir.

REPRESENTATIVES OF THE DIVISION ON—]

Technical committee on occupational studies of the United States employment service; Paul S. Achilles, W. V. Bingham, Clark L. Hull, F. J. Keller, L. J. O'Rourke, Donald G. Paterson, A. T. Poffenberger, Morris S. Viteles.

5. NATIONAL RESEARCH COUNCIL FELLOWSHIPS

PHYSICS, CHEMISTRY, AND MATHEMATICS

Sums amounting to $2,075,000 have been made available by the Rockefeller Foundation to the National Research Council during the period from May 1, 1919, to June 30, 1937, for the maintenance of a series of research fellowships in physics, chemistry, and mathematics. These funds are administered by a research-fellowship board in physics, chemistry, and mathematics appointed by the executive board of the National Research Council.

Fellowships are awarded to individuals who have demonstrated a high order of ability in research and who have received the degree of doctor of philosophy or equivalent training.

MEMBERS OF THE BOARD

Simon Flexner, chairman, director emeritus, Rockefeller Institute for Medical Research, Sixty-sixth Street and York Avenue, New York City.

F. K. Richtmyer, secretary, dean of the Graduate School, and professor of physics, Cornell University, Ithaca, N. Y.

Roger Adams, professor of organic chemistry, University of Illinois, Urbana, Ill.

Gilbert A. Bliss, professor of mathematics, University of Chicago, Chicago, Ill.

George D. Birkhoff, professor of mathematics, Harvard University, Cambridge, Mass.

Karl T. Compton, president, Massachusetts Institute of Technology, Cambridge, Mass.

F. G. Keyes, professor of physical chemistry, Massachusetts Institute of Technology, Cambridge, Mass.

Elmer P. Kohler, Sheldon Emery professor of organic chemistry, Harvard University, Cambridge, Mass.

R. A. Millikan, chairman, division of physical sciences, National Research Council; director, Norman Bridge laboratory of physics and chairman of the executive council, California Institute of Technology, Pasadena, Calif.

John T. Tate, professor of physics, University of Minnesota, Minneapolis, Minn.

Oswald Veblen, professor of mathematics, Institute for Advanced Study, Princeton University, Princeton, N. J.

F. W. Willard, ex-officio, chairman of the division of chemistry and chemical technology, National Research Council; executive vice president, Nassau Smelting & Refining Co., 50 Church Street, New York City.

Fellowships for 1935–36 have been awarded to the following persons:

IN PHYSICS

Walter E. Albertson.
Tom W. Bonner.
Robert B. Jacobs.
Edward B. Jordan, Jr.

Arnold T. Nordsieck.
Robert Serber.
Charles H. Shaw.

Edwin A. Uehling.
Stanley N. Van Voorhis.
Milton G. White.

IN CHEMISTRY

Manson Benedict.
Lyman G. Bonner.
Ludo K. Frevel.
Robert G. Gould, Jr.

Lindsay Helmholz.
Donald E. Hull.
Gilbert W. King.
Earl A. Long.

Harry F. Miller.
Hervey H. Voge.
Frank H. Westheimer.

IN MATHEMATICS

James A. Clarkson.
Norman Levinson.
William T. Martin.

Francis J. Murray.
Sumner B. Myers.

John B. Rosser.
G. Cuthbert Webber.

MEDICAL SCIENCES

Funds amounting to $550,000, available over the period from January 1, 1922, to December 31, 1927, have been appropriated to the National Research Council, jointly by the General Education Board and the Rockefeller Foundation, and an additional sum of $401,000 for the period from January 1, 1928, to June 30, 1937, has been pledged by the Rockefeller Foundation for the establishment under the division of medical sciences of a series of post-doctorate fellowships in medicine. The administration of these fellowships has been placed in the hands of a medical fellowship board appointed by the executive board of the National Research Council.

Fellowships are awarded to individuals who have demonstrated a high order of ability in research and who have received the degree of doctor of philosophy or doctor of medicine or equivalent training.

MEMBERS OF THE BOARD

Francis G. Blake, chairman; chairman of the division of medical sciences, National Research Council; Sterling professor of medicine, School of Medicine, Yale University; physician in chief, New Haven Hospital, New Haven, Conn.

Walter B. Cannon, George Higginson professor of physiology, Harvard Medical School, Boston, Mass.

Evarts A. Graham, Bixby professor of surgery, School of Medicine, Washington University, St. Louis, Mo.

Eugene L. Opie, professor of pathology, Cornell University Medical College; pathologist, New York Hospital, New York City.

Lewis H. Weed, professor of anatomy and director of the School of Medicine, Johns Hopkins University, Baltimore, Md.

Fellowships for 1935-36 have been awarded to the following persons:

Oscar E. Bloch, Jr.	Samuel Gurin.	E. Byron Riegel.
Berry Campbell.	Benjamin F. Miller.	Morris F. Shaffer.
Windsor Cutting.		

BIOLOGICAL SCIENCES

Sums amounting to $1,364,344.31 for the period from July 1, 1923, to June 30, 1937, have been made available by the Rockefeller Foundation to the National Research Council for the establishment under the divisions of biology and agriculture and of anthropology and psychology of a series of postdoctorate fellowships in the biological sciences, including zoology, botany, anthropology, and psychology, and beginning July 1, 1929, including also fellowships in agriculture and forestry, for the purpose of promoting fundamental research in these subjects. The administration of these fellowships has been placed in the hands of a board of national research fellowships in the biological sciences appointed by the executive board of the National Research Council.

Fellowships are awarded to individuals who have demonstrated a high order of ability in research and who have received the degree of doctor of philosophy or equivalent training.

MEMBERS OF THE BOARD

W. J. Robbins, chairman, professor of botany and dean of the Graduate School, University of Missouri, Columbia, Mo.

I. F. Lewis, ex officio, chairman of the division of biology and agriculture, National Research Council; dean of the University and Miller professor of biology and agriculture, University of Virginia, University, Va.

Edward Sapir, ex officio, chairman of the division of anthropology and psychology, National Research Council; professor of anthropology, Yale University, New Haven, Conn.

A. M. Banta, professor of biology, Brown University, Providence, R. I.

Harvey Carr, professor of psychology, University of Chicago, Chicago, Ill.

L. J. Cole, professor of genetics, University of Wisconsin, Madison, Wis.

R. A. Emerson, professor of plant breeding and geneticist in the Agricultural Experiment Station, Cornell University, Ithaca, N. Y.

Max W. Gardner, professor of plant pathology, University of California, Berkeley, Calif.

Caswell Grave, Rebstock professor of zoology, Washington University, St. Louis, Mo.

Carl Hartley, principal pathologist, division of forest pathology, United States Bureau of Plant Industry, Washington, D. C.

Clark L. Hull, professor of psychology, Yale University, New Haven, Conn.

George E. Nichols, professor of botany and director of the botanical gardens, Yale University, New Haven, Conn.

H. L. Shapiro, associate curator of physical anthropology, American Museum of Natural History, Seventy-seventh Street and Central Park West, New York City.

D. H. Tennent, professor of biology, Bryn Mawr College, Bryn Mawr, Pa.

Fellowships for 1935–36 have been awarded to the following persons:

IN AGRICULTURE

Lyman A. Dean[1] William R. Graham	Hugo W. Nilson	Harland G. Wood

IN ANTHROPOLOGY

Helen L. Dawson[1]	Cora Dubois	Charles F. Voegelin

IN BOTANY

Walter S. Flory, Jr. Winslow R. Hatch	Harold N. Moldenke[1]	Donald P. Rogers

IN FORESTRY

William Clark Bramble[1]
James W. Johnston, Jr.[1]

IN PSYCHOLOGY

Glen Finch	Ward C. Halstead	Edward H. Kemp

IN ZOOLOGY

Henry Alver Bess Donald R. Charles	Frances Sue Dorris Graham Phillips DuShane	Richard M. Eakin[1] Benjamin R. Speicher

NATIONAL LIVE STOCK AND MEAT BOARD FELLOWSHIPS

Funds amounting to $55,750 have been appropriated by the National Live Stock and Meat Board for the support, during the years 1924–36, of fellowships for the study of the place of meat in the diet. These fellowships are administered by a special committee appointed by the executive board of the National Research Council and operating under the division of biology and agriculture. In accepting these appropriations, the National Research Council has reserved the right to publish, without restriction, the results obtained under these fellowships.

MEMBERS OF THE COMMITTEE

Paul E. Howe, chairman, senior chemist, in charge of nutrition investigations, Animal Husbandry Division, United States Bureau of Animal Industry, Washington, D. C.

Anna E. Boller, director, department of nutrition, National Live Stock and Meat Board, 407 South Dearborn Street, Chicago, Ill.

C. Robert Moulton, 628 Garrett Place, Evanston, Ill.

H. C. Sherman, Mitchill professor of chemistry, Columbia University, New York City.

During the year 1935–36. with the special consent of the donors, these funds are being used as research grants in the direct support of investigations. A grant from this fund for the year 1935–36 has been awarded as follows:

George O. Burr, University of Minnesota, Minneapolis, Minn.

6. MEMBERS OF THE NATIONAL RESEARCH COUNCIL, 1935–36

Abbot, C. G., Smithsonian Institution, Washington, D. C.

Adams, Roger, University of Illinois, Urbana, Ill.

Agnew, P. G., American Standards Association, 29 West Thirty-ninth Street, New York City.

Allison, Maj. Gen. James B., chief signal officer, War Department, Washington, D. C.

---

[1] Fellows appointed to work abroad.

Ames, Joseph S., Johns Hopkins University, Baltimore, Md.
Archer, R. S., 10951 Longwood Drive, Chicago, Ill.
Auchter, E. C., United States Bureau of Plant Industry, Washington, D. C.
Bard, Philip, School of Medicine, Johns Hopkins University, Baltimore, Md.
Barker, J. W., Columbia University, New York City.
Barrett, S. A., Milwaukee Public Museum, Milwaukee, Wis.
Barrows, Albert L., National Research Council, Washington, D. C.
Barss, H. P., Office of Experiment Stations, United States Department of Agriculture, Washington, D. C.
Barton, Donald C., Humble Oil & Refining Co., Houston, Tex.
Barton, Henry A., American Institute of Physics, 175 Fifth Avenue, New York City.
Bartow, Edward, State University of Iowa, Iowa City, Iowa.
Bascom, Florence, care of United States Geological Survey, Washington, D. C.
Bastin, Edson S., University of Chicago, Chicago, Ill.
Bausch, Carl L., Bausch & Lomb Optical Co., Rochester, N. Y.
Bell, Frank T., United States Bureau of Fisheries, Washington, D. C.
Benedict, Ruth, Columbia University, New York City.
Besley, F. W., State forester of Maryland, Baltimore, Md.
Bigelow, H. B., Member of Comparative Zoology, Harvard University, Cambridge, Mass.
Blake, Francis G., School of Medicine, Yale University, New Haven, Conn.
Bolton, E. K., E. I. du Pont de Nemours & Co., Wilmington, Del.
Bowie, William, United States Coast and Geodetic Survey, Washington, D. C.
Bowman, Isaiah, Johns Hopkins University, Baltimore Md.
Breer, Carl, Chrysler Corporation, Detroit, Mich.
Bridgman, P. W., Harvard University, Cambridge, Mass.
Briggs, Lyman J., National Bureau of Standards, Washington, D. C.
Brigham, Maj. Gen. Claude E., Chemical Warfare Service, War Department, Washington, D. C.
Bryant, Harold C., National Park Service, Washington, D. C.
Buddington, A. F., Princeton University, Princeton, N. J.
Bush, Vannevar, Massachusetts Institute of Technology, Cambridge, Mass.
Butts, Charles, United States Geological Survey, Washington, D. C.
Cady, W. G., Wesleyan University, Middletown, Conn.
Cannon, W. B., Harvard Medical School, Boston, Mass.
Carr, Wilbur J., Department of State, Washington, D. C.
Chambers, Wrightson, Post Office Department, Washington, D. C.
Charlesworth, H. P., American Telephone & Telegraph Co., 195 Broadway, New York City.
Chase, Harry W., New York University, New York City.
Chubb, L. W., Westinghouse Electric & Manufacturing Co., East Pittsburgh, Pa.
Clapp, E. H. United States Forest Service, Washington, D. C.
Clements, F. O., General Motors Research Corporation, Detroit, Mich.
Coker, R. E., University of North Carolina, Chapel Hill. N. C.
Compton, Arthur H., University of Chicago, Chicago, Ill.
Compton, Karl T., Massachusetts Institute of Technology, Cambridge, Mass.
Conant, James Bryant, Harvard University, Cambridge, Mass.
Corner, George W., School of Medicine, University of Rochester, Rochester, N. Y.
Crane, E. J., Chemical Abstracts, Ohio State University, Columbus, Ohio.
Crittenden, E. C., National Bureau of Standards, Washington, D. C.
Cullen, Glenn E., Children's Hospital, Research Foundation, Cincinnati, Ohio.
Curtis, W. C., University of Missouri, Columbia, Mo.
Dashiell, J. F., University of North Carolina, Chapel Hill, N. C.
Davies, C. E., American Society of Mechanical Engineers, 29 West Thirty-ninth St., New York City.
Davis, David John, College of Medicine, University of Illinois, Chicago, Ill.
Day, Arthur L., Geophysical Laboratory, Carnegie Institution of Washington, 2801 Upton Street, Washington, D. C.
DuBridge, Lee A., University of Rochester, Rochester, N. Y.
Dunlap, Knight, University of California at Los Angeles, Los Angeles, Calif.
Edmunds, C. W., School of Medicine, University of Michigan, Ann Arbor, Mich.
Evans, William Lloyd, Ohio State University, Columbus, Ohio.
Farmer, F. M., Electrical Testing Laboratories, Eightieth Street and East End Avenue, New York City.
Farr, Clifford B., Pennsylvania Hospital, Philadelphia, Pa.

Fenneman, Nevin M., University of Cincinnati, Cincinnati, Ohio.
Fickes, Edwin S., Aluminum Co. of America, Pittsburgh, Pa.
Fieldner, A. C., United States Bureau of Mines, Washington, D. C.
Finch, John W., United States Bureau of Mines, Washington, D. C.
Fleming, John A., department of terrestrial magnetism, Carnegie Institution of Washington, 5241 Broad Branch Road, Washington, D. C.
Fletcher, Harvey, Bell Telephone Laboratories, Inc., 463 West Street, New York City.
Flexner, Simon, Rockefeller Institute for Medical Research, New York City.
Foshag, W. F., United States National Museum, Washington, D. C.
Foulois, Maj. Gen. B. D., Air Corps, War Department, Washington, D. C.
Freeman, Walter, 1726 I Street, NW., Washington, D. C.
Gentry, Lt. Col. E. R., Medical Corps, War Department, Washington, D. C.
Giesecke, F. E., Agricultural and Mechanical College of Texas, College Station, Tex.
Gillett, H. W., Battelle Memorial Institute, Columbus, Ohio.
Gleason, Henry Allen, New York Botanical Garden, Bronx Park, New York City.
Gortner, Ross A., University of Minnesota Farm, St. Paul, Minn.
Gregory, Herbert E., Bishop Museum of Polynesian Ethnology and Natural History, Honolulu, Hawaii.
Gregory, John H., Johns Hopkins University, Baltimore, Md.
Grondahl, L. O., Union Switch & Signal Co., Swissvale, Pa.
Guthe, Carl E., University of Michigan, Ann Arbor, Mich.
Hale, George E., Mount Wilson Observatory, Pasadena, Calif.
Hannum, Col. Warren T., Corps of Engineers, War Department, Washington, D. C.
Harrison, Ross G., Osborn Zoological Laboratories, Yale University, New Haven, Conn.
Heck, Capt. N. H., United States Coast and Goedetic Survey, Washington, D. C.
Hellbrunn, L. V., University of Pennsylvania, Philadelphia, Pa.
Hellweg, Capt. J. F., United States Naval Observatory, Washington, D. C.
Henline, H. H., American Institute of Electrical Engineers, 29 West Thirty-ninth Street, New York City.
Herskovits, M. J., Northwestern·University, Evanston, Ill.
Hetzel, R. D., Pennsylvania State College, State College, Pa.
Hill, Joseph A., United States Bureau of the Census, Washington, D. C.
Hobart, Henry M., General Electric Co., Schenectady, N. Y.
Hooper, Capt. S. C., Office of the Chief of Naval Operations, Navy Department Washington, D. C.
Hooton, E. A., Peabody Museum. Harvard University, Cambridge, Mass.
Hoover, J. Edgar, Department of Justice, Washington, D. C.
Hostetter, J. C., Corning Glass Works, Corning, N. Y.
Houghton, Bert, Brooklyn Edison Co., Brooklyn, N. Y.
Hull, Clark L., Yale University, New Haven, Conn.
Hunter, W. S., Clark University, Worcester, Mass.
Huntington, Ellsworth, Yale University, New Haven, Conn.
Ives, Herbert E., Bell Telephone Laboratories, Inc., 463 West Street, New York City.
Jackson, Dougald C., Massachusetts Institute of Technology, Cambridge, Mass.
Jackson, William B., New York Edison Co., 1 Irving Place, New York City.
Jacobus, D. S., Babcock & Wilcox Co., 85 Liberty Street, New York City.
Jewett, Frank B., American Telephone & Telegraph Co., 195 Broadway, New York City.
Joerg, W. L. G., American Geographical Society, Broadway at One Hundred Fifty-sixth Street, New York City.
Johnson, Douglas, Columbia University, New York City.
Johnston, John, United States Steel Corporation, Kearney, N. J.
Karsner, Howard T., Pathological Laboratory, Western Reserve University, Cleveland, Ohio.
Keith, Arthur, United States Geological Survey, Washington, D. C.
Kellogg, Remington, United States National Museum, Washington, D. C.
Kellogg, Vernon, National Research Council, Washington, D. C.
Kelly, Frederick J., United States Office of Education, Washington, D. C.
Kennelly, Arthur E., Harvard University, Cambridge, Mass.

Kettering, Charles F., General Motors Research Corporation, Detroit, Mich.
Kidder, A. V., Post Office Drawer 71, Andover, Mass.
King, W. J., General Electric Co., Schenectady, N. Y.
Knight, Brig. Gen. Harry E., Intelligence Division, War Department, Washington, D. C.
Knight, Henry G., United States Bureau of Chemistry and Soils, Washington, D. C.
Kraus, Charles A., Brown University, Providence, R. I.
Kummel, Henry B., State Geologist, Trenton, N. J.
Lahee, F. H., Sun Oil Co., Dallas, Tex.
Land, Rear Admiral Emory S., Bureau of Construction and Repair, Navy Department, Washington, D. C.
Langfeld, H. S., Psychological Laboratory, Princeton University, Princeton, N. J.
Leighton, Morris M., Illinois State Geological Survey, Urbana, Ill.
Lewis, I. F., University of Virginia, University, Va.
Lillie, Frank R., National Research Council, Washington, D. C.
Lincoln, Col. Francis M., Intelligence Division, General Staff, War Department, Washington, D. C.
Lipman, Jacob G., Agricultural Experiment Station, New Brunswick, N. J.
Little, W. F., Electrical Testing Laboratories, Eightieth Street and East End Avenue, New York City.
Long, Esmond R., Henry Phipps Institute, Philadelphia, Pa.
Longley, W. R., Yale University, New Haven, Conn.
Lubin, Isador, United States Bureau of Labor Statistics, Washington, D. C.
Lucas, George L., The Port of New York Authority, 111 Eighth Avenue, New York City.
Lukens, Hiram S., University of Pennsylvania, Philadelphia, Pa.
MacDonald, Thomas H., United States Bureau of Public Roads, Washington, D. C.
MacQuigg, C. E., Union Carbide and Carbon Research Laboratories, 30 East Forty-second Street, New York City.
Mann, A. R., Cornell University, Ithaca, N. Y.
Mann, C. R., American Council on Education, Washington, D. C.
Mathews, Edward B., Johns Hopkins University, Baltimore, Md.
McClung, C. E., Zoological Laboratories, University of Pennsylvania, Philadelphia, Pa.
McCrory, S. H., United States Bureau of Agricultural Engineering, Washington, D. C.
McVey, Frank L., University of Kentucky, Lexington, Ky.
Mendenhall, W. C., United States Geological Survey, Washington, D. C.
Merriam, John C., Carnegie Institution of Washington, Washington, D. C.
Merrill, Elmer D., Gray Herbarium, Harvard University, Cambridge, Mass.
Messner, C. T., 5712 Twenty-third Street, Washington, D. C.
Meyer, Karl F., Hooper Foundation, University of California, Berkeley, Calif.
Miles, W. R., Yale University, New Haven, Conn.
Miller, John A., Sproul Observatory, Swarthmore College, Swarthmore, Pa.
Millikan, R. A., California Institute of Technology, Pasadena, Calif.
Mohler, J. R., United States Bureau of Animal Industry, Washington, D. C.
Morgan, Herbert R., United States Naval Observatory, Washington, D. C.
Morgan, T. H., Kerckhoff Laboratories of the Biological Sciences, California Institute of Technology, Pasadena, Calif.
Morse, Marston, Institute for Advanced Study, Princeton University, Princeton, N. J.
Mumford, H. W., University of Illinois, Urbana, Ill.
Munroe, Col. John E., Ordnance Department, War Department, Washington, D. C.
Nolan, Thomas B., United States Geological Survey, Washington, D. C.
Nourse, Edwin G., Institute of Economics, Brookings Institution, Washington, D. C.
Noyes, W. A., University of Illinois, Urbana, Ill.
Palmer, T. S., 1939 Biltmore Street, Washington, D. C.
Parsons, A. B., American Institute of Mining and Metallurgical Engineers, 29 West Thirty-ninth Street, New York City.
Parsons, Charles L., American Chemical Society, Mills Building, Washington, D. C.

Paterson, Donald G., University of Minnesota, Minneapolis, Minn.
Patterson, Austin M., Antioch College, Yellow Springs, Ohio.
Payne, Fernandus, Indiana University, Bloomington, Ind.
Pearson, Raymond A., Resettlement Administration, Washington, D. C.
Pendleton, Maj. Randolph T., Coast Artillery Corps, War Department, Washington, D. C.
Pepper, G. H. Perry, School of Medicine, University of Pennsylvania, Philadelphia, Pa.
Peters, John P., School of Medicine, Yale University, New Haven, Conn.
Pierce, Charles H., United States Patent Office, Washington, D. C.
Platt, Robert S., University of Chicago, Chicago, Ill.
Poillon, Howard, Research Corporation, 408 Lexington Avenue, New York City.
Putnam, George R., United States Bureau of Lighthouses, Washington, D. C.
Redfield, Robert, University of Chicago, Chicago, Ill.
Reed, O. E., United States Bureau of Dairy Industry, Washington, D. C.
Richards, Alfred N., School of Medicine, University of Pennsylvania, Philadelphia, Pa.
Richardson, R. G. D., Brown University, Providence, R. I.
Richtmyer, F. K., Cornell University, Ithaca, N. Y.
Robbins, W. J., University of Missouri, Columbia, Mo.
Roberts, Frank H. H., Bureau of American Ethnology, Smithsonian Institution, Washington, D. C.
Robinson, Rear Admiral Samuel M., Bureau of Engineering, Navy Deartment, Washington, D. C.
Root, Elihu, 31 Nassau Street, New York City.
Rose, H. J., Mellon Institute of Industrial Research, Pittsburgh, Pa.
Rossiter, Rear Admiral Percival E., Bureau of Medicine and Surgery, Navy Department, Washington, D. C.
Rowe, L. S., Pan American Union, Washington, D. C.
Russell, Henry Norris, Princeton University Observatory, Princeton, N. J.
Sapir, Edward, Yale University, New Haven, Conn.
Schlesinger, Frank, Yale University Observatory, New Haven, Conn.
Scofield, C. S., United States Bureau of Plant Industry, Washington, D. C.
Seabury, George W., American Society of Civil Engineers, 29 West Thirty-ninth Street, New York City.
Shapiro, H. L., American Museum of Natural History, New York City.
Sharp, Clayton H., 294 Fisher Avenue, White Plains, N. Y.
Singstad, Ole, Port of New York Authority, 80 Eighth Avenue, New York City.
Slocum, Frederick, Van Vleck Observatory, Wesleyan University, Middletown, Conn.
Sosman, Merrill C., Harvard Medical School, Boston, Mass.
Spier, Leslie, Yale University, New Haven, Conn.
Stark, Rear Admiral Harold R., Bureau of Ordnance, Navy Department, Washington, D. C.
Stewart, George W., University of Iowa, Iowa City, Iowa.
Stimson, A. M., United States Public Health Service, Washington, D. C.
Strong, Lee A., United States Bureau of Entomology, Washington, D. C.
Strong, William Duncan, Bureau of American Ethnology, Smithsonian Institution, Washington, D. C.
Swanton, John R., Bureau of American Ethnology, Smithsonian Institution, Washington, D. C.
Stone, Harvey B., School of Medicine, Johns Hopkins University, Baltimore, Md.
Thompson, L. R., United States Public Health Service, Washington, D. C.
Thompson, Thomas G., Oceanographic Laboratories, University of Washington, Seattle, Wash.
Thurstone, L. L., University of Chicago, Chicago, Ill.
Transeau, E. N., Ohio State University, Columbus, Ohio.
Tuckerman, L. B., National Bureau of Standards, Washington, D. C.
Tyler, H. W., Library of Congress, Washington, D. C.
Urey, Harold C., Columbia University, New York City.
Van Vleck, J. H., Harvard University, Cambridge, Mass.
Veblen, Oswald, Institute for Advanced Study, Princeton University, Princeton, N. J.
Voegtlin, Carl, National Institute of Health, Washington, D. C.
Warner, E. P., McGraw-Hill Publishing Co., 330 West Forty-second Street, New York City.

Webster, David L., Stanford University, Stanford University, Calif.
Weed, Lewis H., School of Medicine, Johns Hopkins University, Baltimore, Md.
Weidlein, Edward R., Mellon Institute of Industrial Research, Pittsburgh, Pa.
Weller, Carl V., Pathological Laboratories, University of Michigan, Ann Arbor, . Mich.
White, William Charles, National Institute of Health, Washington, D. C.
Whitehead, John B., Johns Hopkins University, Baltimore, Md.
Whitmore, Frank C., Pennsylvania State College, State College, Pa.
Willard, F. W., Nassau Smelting and Refining Company, 50 Church Street, New York City.
Willard, Hobart H., University of Michigan, Ann Arbor, Mich.
Wilson, Ellery L., Rumford Chemical Works, Providence, R. I.
Wold, P. I., Union College, Schenectady, N. Y.
Woodrow, Herbert, University of Illinois, Urbana, Ill.
Woods, A. F., United States Bureau of Plant Industry, Washington, D. C.
Wright, A. H., Cornell University, Ithaca, N. Y.
Wright, Fred. E., Geophysical Laboratory, Carnegie Institution of Washington, 2801 Upton Street, Washington, D. C.
Woodworth, R. S., Columbia University, New York City.
Youngblood, B., Office of Experiment Stations, United States Department of Agriculture, Washington, D. C.
Zeleny, John, Yale University, New Haven, Conn.

O

REPORT OF THE
NATIONAL ACADEMY
OF SCIENCES

FISCAL YEAR
1936-1937

REPORT OF THE
NATIONAL ACADEMY
OF SCIENCES

FISCAL YEAR
1936–1937

UNITED STATES
GOVERNMENT PRINTING OFFICE
WASHINGTON : 1938

CONTENTS

LETTER OF TRANSMITTAL

NATIONAL ACADEMY OF SCIENCES,
Washington, D. C., January 8, 1938.

Hon. JOHN N. GARNER,
President of the United States Senate.

SIR: I have the honor to transmit to you herewith the report of the president of the National Academy of Sciences for the fiscal year ended June 30, 1937.

Yours respectfully,

FRANK R. LILLIE, President.

ACT OF INCORPORATION

AN ACT To incorporate the National Academy of Sciences

Be it enacted by the Senate and House of Representatives of the United States of America in Congress assembled, That Louis Agassiz, Massachusetts; J. H. Alexander, Maryland; S. Alexander, New Jersey; A. D. Bache, at large; F. B. Barnard,[1] at large; J. G. Barnard, United States Army, Massachusetts; W. H. C. Bartlett, United States Military Academy, Missouri; U. A. Boyden,[2] Massachusetts; Alexis Caswell, Rhode Island; William Chauvenet, Missouri; J. H. C. Coffin, United States Naval Academy, Maine; J. A. Dahlgren,[2] United States Navy, Pennsylvania; J. D. Dana, Connecticut; Charles H. Davis, United States Navy, Massachusetts; George Englemann, Saint Louis, Missouri; J. F. Frazer, Pennsylvania; Wolcott Gibbs, New York; J. M. Giles,[3] United States Navy, District of Columbia; A. A. Gould, Massachusetts; B. A. Gould, Massachusetts; Asa Gray, Massachusetts; A. Guyot, New Jersey; James Hall, New York; Joseph Henry, at large; J. E. Hilgard, at large, Illinois; Edward Hitchcock, Massachusetts; J. S. Hubbard, United States Naval Observatory, Connecticut; A. A. Humphreys, United States Army, Pennsylvania; J. L. Le Conte, United States Army, Pennsylvania; J. Leidy, Pennsylvania; J. P. Lesley, Pennsylvania; M. F. Longstreth, Pennsylvania; D. H. Mahan, United States Military Academy, Virginia; J. S. Newberry, Ohio; H. A. Newton, Connecticut; Benjamin Peirce, Massachusetts; John Rodgers, United States Navy, Indiana; Fairman Rogers, Pennsylvania; R. E. Rogers, Pennsylvania; W. B. Rogers, Massachusetts; L. M. Rutherfurd, New York; Joseph Saxton, at large; Benjamin Silliman, Connecticut; Benjamin Silliman, junior, Connecticut; Theodore Strong, New Jersey; John Torrey, New York; J. G. Totten, United States Army, Connecticut; Joseph Winlock, United States Nautical Almanac, Kentucky; Jeffries Wyman, Massachusetts; J. D. Whitney, California; their associates and successors duly chosen, are hereby incorporated, constituted, and declared to be a body corporate, by the name of the National Academy of Sciences.

SEC. 2. *And be it further enacted,* That the National Academy of Sciences shall consist of not more than fifty ordinary members, and the said corporation hereby constituted shall have power to make its own organization, including its constitution, bylaws, and rules and regulations; to fill all vacancies created by death, resignation, or otherwise; to provide for the election of foreign and domestic members, the division into classes, and all other matters needful or usual in such institution, and to report the same to Congress.

SEC. 3. *And be it further enacted,* That the National Academy of Sciences shall hold an annual meeting at such place in the United States as may be designated, and the Academy shall, whenever called upon by any department of the Government, investigate, examine, experiment, and report upon any subject of science or art, the actual expense of such investigations, examinations, experiments, and reports to be paid from appropriations which may be made for the purpose, but the Academy shall receive no compensation whatever for any services to the Government of the United States.

GALUSHA A. GROW,
Speaker of the House of Representatives.

SOLOMON FOOTE,
President of the Senate pro tempore.

Approved, March 3, 1863.
ABRAHAM LINCOLN, *President.*

---

[1] The correct name of this charter member was F. A. P. Barnard.
[2] Declined.
[3] The correct name of this charter member was J. M. Gilliss.

AMENDMENTS

AN ACT To amend the act to incorporate the National Academy of Sciences

Be it enacted by the Senate and House of Representatives of the United States of America in Congress assembled, That the act to incorporate the National Academy of Sciences, approved March third, eighteen hundred and sixty-three, be, and the same is hereby, so amended as to remove the limitation of the number of ordinary members of said Academy as provided in said act.

Approved, July 14, 1870.

AN ACT To authorize the National Academy of Sciences to receive and hold trust funds for the promotion of science, and for other purposes

Be it enacted by the Senate and House of Representatives of the United States of America in Congress assembled, That the National Academy of Sciences, incorporated by the act of Congress approved March third, eighteen hundred and sixty-three, and its several supplements be, and the same is hereby, authorized and empowered to receive bequests and donations and hold the same in trust, to be applied by the said Academy in aid of scientific investigations and according to the will of the donors.

Approved, June 20, 1884.

AN ACT To amend the act authorizing the National Academy of Sciences to receive and hold trust funds for the promotion of science, and for other purposes

Be it enacted by the Senate and House of Representatives of the United States of America in Congress assembled, That the act to authorize the National Academy of Sciences to receive and hold trust funds for the promotion of science, and for other purposes, approved June twentieth, eighteen hundred and eighty-four, be, and the same is hereby, amended to read as follows:

"That the National Academy of Sciences, incorporated by the act of Congress approved March third, eighteen hundred and sixty-three, be, and the same is hereby, authorized and empowered to receive by devise, bequest, donation, or otherwise, either real or personal property, and to hold the same absolutely or in trust, and to invest, reinvest, and manage the same in accordance with the provisions of its constitution, and to apply said property and the income arising therefrom to the objects of its creation and according to the instructions of the donors: *Provided, however,* That the Congress may at any time limit the amount of real estate which may be acquired and the length of time the same may be held by said National Academy of Sciences."

SEC. 2. That the right to alter, amend, or repeal this act is hereby expressly reserved.

Approved, May 27, 1914.

ANNUAL REPORT OF THE NATIONAL ACADEMY OF SCIENCES

REVIEW OF THE YEAR 1936–37

The progress of science throughout the world during 1936 and 1937 has been in marked contrast to the confusion in international political affairs. Science has, on the whole, remained truly international. There has been a universal effort to advance knowledge, and its common possession by the peoples of the world, in spite of some interference with liberty of research in certain places. There has been rapid progress in the association and cooperation of scientific men with economic development, and the application of the results of science to problems of government, whether technical or social. There has been no time in the history of the world when the importance of utilization of scientific knowledge for the good of the Nation has been more evident. In these times of international rivalry the nation that is backward in its scientific personnel and equipment is in danger, with reference both to progress and its own ultimate freedom.

In the following report of the National Academy of Sciences, special attention is directed to the included report of its agency, the National Research Council, and reference is made to this report for many of the most important activities of the whole organization.

Among the numerous activities of the parent body, the National Academy of Sciences, a few are selected for special comment.

About 10 years ago the relative backwardness of the United States in the study of oceanography was strongly impressed on certain members of the Academy, and a committee was appointed to study the place of the United States in a world-wide program of oceanography. The ocean which bounds our shores is a source of wealth and a means of communication, both national and international. A thorough understanding of the laws that govern the ocean and which control its production of food and other marine products is obviously of great national importance.

The program of studies that occupied the committee received financial support for its investigation from private sources on a generous scale. The results of the work of this committee have been presented in a report by Henry B. Bigelow, entitled "Oceanography: Its scope, problems, and economic importance," published in 1931; and the manuscript of a second report, "International Aspects of Oceanography: Oceanographic data and provisions for oceanographic research," by T. Wayland Vaughan, was completed at the close of this year and made ready for the printer. Its publication may be expected early in the coming fall. In addition to this, the committee, during its

1

active period, presented recommendations to the Rockefeller Foundation, which made provision for the establishment and endowment of the Woods Hole Oceanographic Institution; the Bermuda Biological Station for Research was aided and endowed; and, on the Pacific coast the University of Washington Oceanographic Laboratories were set up and a new building was provided for the Scripps Institution of Oceanography of the University of California. These acts of the Foundation enable the United States to take a greater part in the world-wide program. At the same time greater interest in oceanography in the Federal agencies has been manifested, viz., in the Navy, the Coast and Geodetic Survey, the Bureau of Fisheries, and the ice patrol of the Coast Guard—and the advance of oceanographic research throughout the country has been stimulated.

In the Academy's relations to the Government through its Government Relations and Science Advisory Committee, several problems have been considered. Perhaps the most important is the report on the technical phases of the loss of the *Macon* and the general review of airship design and construction for the Navy Department. A report with recommendations has been completed and presented to the Secretary of the Navy.

The subcommittee on the Weather Bureau reports that upper air stations, looking to the use of air-mass methods for forecasting, have been introduced on its recommendation.

The subcommittee available for consultation by the Department of the Navy feels that the group of 50 young scientists, given reserve commissions in the Navy upon recommendation by the subcommittee, will be of real service in advancing the work of that Department.

Early in the year a request from the Department of Agriculture for appointment of a committee to review the Department's research program on toxic properties of materials used for controlling destruction of food by fungi, insects, and other pests, was considered and referred to a special committee. The committee's report with recommendations was transmitted to the Secretary of Agriculture, and the suggestions made have been carried out by the Department.

International relations in scientific research receive the constant attention of the Academy and the National Research Council. The Academy has a foreign secretary who is also chairman of the division of foreign relations of the National Research Council. By correspondence and by visits, contact is maintained with foreign scientific bodies and academies. On invitation, nominations are made to the Department of State for advice and recommendation as to the desirability of accepting invitations from foreign governments to participate in international scientific congresses; and suggestions are also made to the Department of State as to suitable persons to represent the Government of the United States at such congresses without expense to the Department. Special arrangements for interchange of lecturers and of courtesies to visiting members are being made between the Royal Society of Great Britain and the National Academy of Sciences, which were still pending at the date of this report and which will be dealt with more fully in a subsequent report.

The income from the small trust funds of the Academy has been used, to the extent of $5,820, to aid research problems being carried on by individuals. The grants included observations and study of meteors, publication of observations of meteors secured at Little America and other stations in Antarctica, completing a survey of the Haviland (Kans.) meteor crater and surrounding region, to collect vertebrate material from the Lake Pennsylvania beds of the Upper Cisco and Lower Wichita groups of Texas, to purchase a supply of retene for use in the synthesis of materials that induce cancer, and for researches on magneto-chemical problems.

The medal provided by the Mary Clark Thompson fund was awarded to Amadeus William Grabau, professor of paleontology in the National University of China, Peking, and chief paleontologist to the Chinese Geological Survey, for his distinguished record in paleontology and stratigraphic geology.

The medal provided by the Henry Draper fund was awarded to C. E. Kenneth Mees, in recognition of his outstanding researches in photographic processes.

The Agassiz Medal, provided by the Murray fund, was awarded to Edgar Johnson Allen for his personal researches on marine biology.

The medal provided by the Marcellus Hartley fund for application of science to the public welfare was awarded to Willis R. Whitney for his outstanding work in the fundamentals of scientific research for the public good.

The award provided by the Charles B. Comstock fund was awarded to Ernest O. Lawrence for development of the cyclotron and the results in the field of the transmutation of the elements which have been obtained with the aid of this new technique.

The Academy held two business sessions—one, the autumn meeting in Chicago in November, and the other, the annual meeting in Washington in April. At the same time scientific sessions were held. At the autumn meeting 93 papers were presented, distributed as follows:

Mathematics, 3; astronomy, 4; physics, 9; chemistry, 13; geology, 1; paleobotany, 3; genetics, 4; botany, 1; mycology, 1; anatomy, 2; entomology, 1; zoology, 6; biochemistry, 6; physiology, 19; bacteriology, 4; medicine, 6; pathology, 3; pharmacology, 4; psychology, 3.

At the annual meeting 43 papers were listed on the program, distributed as follows:

Mathematics, 3; physics, 7; chemistry, 3; crystallography, 1; paleontology, 1; oceanography, 2; genetics, 6; pathology, 1; physiology, 4; embryology, 2; biochemistry, 3; psychology, 2; anthropology, 2; biographical memoirs, 6. Members of the Academy read 29 papers; nonmembers, 14 papers.

In the National Research Council, consideration was given, among other matters, to the administration of fellowships, grants-in-aid, scientific aids to learning, borderland problems in science, international relationships, film-slide investigations, highway research, endocrinology, sex research, drug addiction, and radiation research. Details of these studies will be found in the formal report of the Council to the Academy on pages 29 to 64.

MEETINGS OF THE NATIONAL ACADEMY

AUTUMN MEETING, 1936

The 1936 autumn meeting of the National Academy of Sciences was held in Chicago, Ill., on November 16, 17, and 18, 1936, upon invitation by the University of Chicago.

BUSINESS SESSION

Thirty-nine members responded to roll call, as follows:

Adams, C. A.
Blakeslee, A. F.
Bliss, G. A.
Bowen, N. L.
Campbell, D. H.
Carlson, A. J.
Cattell, J. McK.
Child, C. M.
Coble, A. B.
Compton, A. H.
Crew, Henry
Duggar, B. M.
Gasser, H. S.

Gortner, R. A.
Gregory, W. K.
Harrison, R. G.
Hektoen, Ludvig
Herrick, C. J.
Hudson, C. S.
Jackson, Dunham
Jewett, F. B.
Keith, Arthur
Kidder, A. V.
Lillie, F. R.
Lind, S. C.
Moulton, F. R.

Mulliken, R. S.
Noyes, W. A.
Rose, W. C.
Scott, W. B.
Seashore, C. E.
Shaffer, P. A.
Slipher, V. M.
Stakman, E. C.
Stebbins, Joel
Stieglitz, Julius
Van Vleck, E. B.
Wells, H. Gideon
Wright, F. E.

PRESIDENT'S ANNOUNCEMENTS

The president of the Academy made the following announcements:

DEATHS SINCE THE ANNUAL MEETING

Arthur Amos Noyes, born September 13, 1866, elected to the Academy in 1905, died June 3, 1936.

Edwin Oakes Jordan, born July 28, 1866, elected to the Academy in April 1936, died September 2, 1936.

COMMITTEE APPOINTMENTS SINCE THE ANNUAL MEETING

Committee on the Barnard Medal for Meritorious Services to Science.—W. R. Whitney as chairman to succeed Arthur L. Day (resigned). Dr. Day will remain a member of the committee, thus filling the vacancy caused by the death of Dr. A. A. Noyes.

Joint committee on buildings and grounds.—Ludvig Hektoen, to succeed I. F. Lewis as one of the representatives of the Research Council. (Dr. Lewis' appointment expired when he ceased to be a member of the executive board of the Research Council.)

Joint committee on exhibits.—Ludvig Hektoen as a member of the executive committee, to succeed Vernon Kellogg.

Government Relations and Science Advisory Committee.—C. K. Leith as a member at large, succeeding Isaiah Bowman who is now on the committee as representative of the section of geology and paleontology. (Dr. Leith had hitherto been on the committee as representative of that section.)

Committee on arrangements for the annual meeting to be held in Washington, April 26 to 28, 1937: F. E. Wright, chairman ex officio; E. T. Allen, N. L. Bowen, W. M. Clark, W. W. Coblentz, C. S. Hudson.

To the centenary of the Geological Survey of Pennsylvania, Harrisburg, Pa., June 12 and 13, 1936: W. C. Mendenhall.

To the fiftieth anniversary of the founding of Sigma Xi, Ithaca, N. Y., June 19 and 20, 1936: E. G. Conklin, W. F. Durand, and F. R. Lillie.

To the inauguration of Grover C. Dillman as president of the Michigan College of Mining and Technology, Houghton, Mich., August 6, 1936: Heber D. Curtis.

To the ceremonies in connection with the presentation of a bust of Lord Kelvin to the Smithsonian Institution by the English-Speaking Union, Washington, October 8, 1936; F. E. Wright.

HIGHWAY RESEARCH BOARD

The work of the Highway Research Board, under the division of engineering and industrial research of the National Research Council, is carried on by cooperation with the Bureau of Public Roads of the Department of Agriculture, which renewed the contract for contribution toward the expenses of the Board for the year 1936–37, calling for the payment of $20,000. Under a separate, special agreement with the Department of Agriculture this year, the Highway Research Board conducted investigations concerning highway safety, these investigations being financed to an extent of not more than $75,000 under the terms of that contract.

REPORTS OF THE TREASURER AND AUDITING COMMITTEE

The annual report of the treasurer of the Academy covering the fiscal year 1935–36 was presented, and upon recommendation by the council of the Academy was accepted for inclusion in the printed annual report of the National Academy of Sciences for that period.

The report of the auditing committee was presented, and upon recommendation by the council of the Academy was accepted for inclusion in the printed annual report of the National Academy of Sciences for the fiscal year 1935–36.

These reports appeared on pages 75–104 of the annual report of the National Academy of Sciences for the fiscal year 1935–36.

AMENDMENTS TO THE BYLAWS

Upon recommendation by the council of the Academy the bylaws were amended as follows:

Change bylaw III.5 to read:

"COMMITTEE ON ARRANGEMENTS

"5. For the annual meeting a committee of five members, appointed for each meeting, and the home secretary shall constitute the committee on arrangements, of which the home secretary shall be chairman. For the autumn meeting a member of the local group shall be chairman of the committee on arrangements, of which the home secretary shall be a member ex officio."

In bylaw III.5, under "Scientific program" change, in the first and second paragraphs, the designation "committee of arrangements" to read "committee on arrangements."

In bylaw III.6 change, in paragraphs 1, 2, 5, 7, and 8, the designation "committee of arrangements" to read, "committee on arrangements."

Amendments adopted.

RESIGNATION OF GILBERT N. LEWIS

The resignation of Mr. Gilbert N. Lewis from membership in the Academ   left over from the 1935 annual meeting   w   presented for consideration, and on recommendation from the council of the Academy was accepted with regret, as of the date of the resignation, December 29, 1934.

TRANSFER OF RAYMOND DODGE TO ROLL OF MEMBERS EMERITI

The request of Mr. Raymond Dodge to be transferred to the roll of members emeriti was granted upon recommendation by the council of the Academy.

RESIGNATION OF FOREIGN SECRETARY AND ELECTION OF SUCCESSOR

The resignation of Mr. Thomas Hunt Morgan as foreign secretary of the Academy, owing to distance from Washington, was accepted with regret. The nominating committee, which had been asked to submit the name of a successor, nominated Mr. Lawrence Joseph Henderson, and Mr. Henderson was duly elected to the office for a term of 4 years ending June 30, 1940.

HENRY DRAPER FUND

The committee on the Henry Draper fund presented the following recommendation:

Nov. 10, 1936.

The Draper Committee recommends that the National Academy of Sciences award the Henry Draper Medal to Dr. C. E. Kenneth Mees for his fruitful investigations in photographic processes which have given emulsions sensitive to red and infrared of the spectrum and made possible recent great advance in knowledge of this highly important region of the radiant energy of the stars.

V. M. Slipher, *Chairman.*

Recommendation approved.

J. LAWRENCE SMITH FUND

Two recommendations were presented from the committee on the J. Lawrence Smith fund, as follows:

The committee of the J. Lawrence Smith fund of the National Academy of Sciences recommends that a grant of $450 be made from the fund to Dr. Thomas C. Poulter, second in command of the Byrd Antarctic Expedition, and in charge of the scientific work of the expedition, for the purpose of tabulating and putting in form for publication observations of meteors secured at Little America and other stations in Antarctica. There are 7,000 of these observations, and in addition 23,000 observations made elsewhere in the world in cooperation with Dr. Poulter's work.

By unanimous action, the committee of the J. Lawrence Smith fund recommends a grant of $400 to Dr. Harlow Shapley, of Harvard College Observatory, for the purpose of paying in part for the reduction of observations of meteors secured by the Harvard-Cornell Meteor Expedition to Arizona a few years ago. The proposed computations will be carried out under the direction of Dr. Opik, in Tartu, Estonia.

C. G. Abbot.
E. T. Allen.
Ernest W. Brown.
Charles Palache.
F. R. Moulton, *Chairman.*

Recommendations approved.

37878—38——2

MARY CLARK THOMPSON FUND

On April 6, 1936, it was recommended that the Mary Clark Thompson award of the National Academy be deferred until 1937.

After consultation through correspondence the committee met on May 2 and decided to recommend that the recipient of this award be Dr. Amadeus William Grabau, born in Cedarburg, Wis., on January 9, 1870, later teaching in the Massachusetts Institute of Technology, Harvard, and Columbia, and at present professor at the National University of Peking and chief paleontologist of the Chinese Geological Survey.

Previous medalists include C. D. Walcott, E. de Margerie, J. Perrin Smith, John M. Clarke, William B. Scott, E. O. Ulrich, David White, and F. A. Bather. The committee feels that the long and distinguished record of Professor Grabau in paleontology and stratigraphic geology fully entitles him to this distinction. The committee recommends that, if convenient, the award be made at the coming fall meeting of the Academy, and also that an honorarium of an amount to be determined later should be granted. Our bursar, Mr. 'J. Herbert J. Yule, writes under date of April 3, 1936, that the uninvested capital of the Mary Clark Thompson fund is $875.

The committee would be glad if you would kindly inform it whether a more detailed statement of the life and activities of Professor Grabau is required. The recommendation for conferring the award at the next meeting is based on the fact that Professor Grabau has for some time been in poor health and is conducting his scientific work under very considerable physical difficulties.

W. C. MENDENHALL.
E. O. ULRICH.
WALDEMAR LINDGREN, *Chairman.*

Recommendations approved.

PRESENTATION OF MEDALS

The Public Welfare Medal for 1935, which had been awarded to Gen. Hugh S. Cumming at the previous autumn meeting, in recognition of his work in the Public Health Service, was presented to him during the dinner of the Academy on Tuesday evening, November 17.

The John J. Carty Award for the Advancement of Science, which had been voted to Edmund Beecher Wilson at the annual meeting in April 1936, in recognition of his distinguished accomplishments in the field of zoology and the influence he has had on two generations of zoologists, was received for him by Mr. Ross G. Harrison, as Mr. Wilson was unable to attend the dinner. The award, consisting of a gold medal, certificate, and monetary award of $3,000, was later presented to Mr. Wilson at a small private luncheon in New York.

SCIENTIFIC SESSIONS

The following papers were presented at the scientific sessions by members of the Academy or persons introduced by members:

MONDAY, NOVEMBER 16, 1936

G. A. Bliss, University of Chicago: Some Recent Advances in the Theory of the Calculus of Variations.

L. E. Dickson, University of Chicago: Remarkable Results in Additive Number Theory.

Dunham Jackson, University of Minnesota: Polynomial Approximation on a Curve of the Fourth Degree.

A. E. Whitford and G. E. Kron, University of Wisconsin (introduced by Joel Stebbins): Photoelectric Guiding of Astronomical Telescopes.

Joel Stebbins and Albert E. Whitford, Mount Wilson Observatory and University of Wisconsin: The Colors of Stars in a Region in Sagittarius.

G. P. Kuiper, Yerkes Observatory, University of Chicago (introduced by F. R. Moulton): The Empirical Mass Luminosity Relation.

George W. Moffitt, Yerkes Observatory, University of Chicago (introduced by F. R. Moulton): The 82-Inch Reflector of the McDonald Observatory.

Robert R. McMath and Edison Pettit, University of Michigan (introduced by Heber D. Curtis): Solar Activity Recorded by the Motion-Picture Method at the McMath-Hulburt Observatory of the University of Michigan (illustrated by motion pictures).

F. E. Wright, Carnegie Institution of Washington, D. C.: A Projection Method for Ascertaining the Heights, Shapes, and Dimensions of the Surface Features of the Moon.

E. M. K. Gelling, University of Chicago (introduced by A. J. Carlson): The Pituitary Gland of Whales.

F. A. Hartman, G. W. Thorn, Helen R. Garbutt, and F. A. Hitchcock, Ohio State University (introduced by C. M. Child): The Effect of Cortin Upon Renal Excretion and Balance of Electrolytes in the Human Being.

J. M. Rogoff, University of Chicago (introduced by A. J. Carlson): The Adrenals in Diabetes.

David Duncan, T. F. Galligher, and F. C. Koch, University of Chicago (introduced by F. R. Lillie): The Character of the Estrus-Inhibiting Substance in Testis-Tissue Extracts.

A. C. Ivy, Northwestern University (introduced by Ludvig Hektoen): Enterogastrone: Proof of the Existence and Methods of Assay.

F. C. McLean and W. Bloom, University of Chicago (introduced by A. J. Carlson): Mode of Action of Parathyroid Extract in Bone.

M. B. Visscher, University of Minnesota (introduced by F. R. Lillie): The Mechanical Efficiency of the Heart as a Measure of Its Fitness.

S. W. Ranson, Northwestern University (introduced by C. J. Herrick): The Regulation of Body Temperature by the Hypothalamus.

Emil Witschi, University of Iowa (introduced by F. R. Lillie): The Role of Stimulative and Inhibitive Induction in the Development of Primary and Secondary Sex Characters.

Arthur H. Compton, University of Chicago: Effect of Galactic Rotation on Cosmic Rays.

Gregory Breit, University of Wisconsin (introduced by A. H. Compton): Approximately Relativistic Equations for Nuclear Particles.

William D. Harkins, University of Chicago: The Intermediate Product in Nuclear Reactions, and Disintegration in Steps (by title).

G. E. M. Jauncey, Washington University (introduced by Joseph Erlanger): Anisotropy in the Atomic Vibrations of Zinc Crystals as Revealed by the Scattering of X-rays.

W. H. Zachariasen, University of Chicago (introduced by A. H. Compton): Constitution of the Borates.

Henry G. Gale, University of Chicago (introduced by A. H. Compton): The Ruling and Testing of Diffraction Gratings.

Simon Freed and Raymond Mesirow, University of Chicago (introduced by W. D. Harkins): Absorption Spectra of the Rare Earths in Crystals.

Robert S. Mulliken, University of Chicago: Electronic Structures of Molecules.

T. F. Young, University of Chicago (introduced by W. D. Harkins): A Comparison of Differential Heats of Dilution With the Predictions of the Theory of Debye and Hückel.

John C. Ballar, Jr., E. H. Huffman, and A. R. Wreath, University of Illinois (introduced by W. A. Noyes): Configuration Changes in the Reactions of Complex Inorganic Compounds.

L. F. Audrieth and C. Slobutsky, University of Illinois (introduced by W. A. Noyes): Catalytic Effect of Ammonium Salts on the Ammonolysis of Diethylmalonate in Liquid Ammonia.

A. F. Blakeslee, Station for Experimental Evolution, Cold Spring Harbor, N. Y., A. D. Bergner, and A. G. Avery: Distribution of Chromosomal Prime Types in Datura Stramonium.

Lillian S. Eichelberger, University of Chicago (introduced by H. Gideon Wells): The Effect of Dehydration on the Exchange of Salt and Water Between Muscle and Blood.

Henry N. Harkins, University of Chicago (introduced by W. D. Harkins): Plasmaphoresis, Plasma Exudation, and Traumatic Shock.

S. Slight, University of Chicago (introduced by H. Gideon Wells): Respiratory Phenomena in a Case of Dementia Praecox.

J. C. Walker, University of Wisconsin (introduced by L. R. Jones): The Nature of Disease Resistance in Plants.

W. H. Taliaferro and M. P. Sarles, University of Chicago (introduced by F. R. Lillie): Mechanism of Immunity to Nippostrongylus Muris, the Intestinal Nematode of the Rat.

M. R. Irwin and L. J. Cole, University of Wisconsin (introduced by Ludvig Hektoen): Immuno-genetic Studies on Species Relationships.

Oram C. Woolpert and N. Paul Hudson, Ohio State University (introduced by H. Gideon Wells): The Relative Susceptibility of the Mammalian Fetus to Infectious Agents.

William King Gregory, American Museum of Natural History, New York City: Transformation of Organic Designs, Paleontologic Aspects of Organic Evolution.

TUESDAY, NOVEMBER 17, 1936

H. I. Schlesinger, University of Chicago (introduced by W. D. Harkins): Problems in the Chemistry of Boron Hydrides as Illustrated by the Newly Discovered Compounds B_3H_7N and BH_3CO.

C. S. Hudson and Ernest L. Jackson, National Institute of Health, Washington, D. C.: A New Method of Determining the Ring Structures of Glycosides.

W. B. Scott, Princeton University: A New and Problematical Catlike Fossil From the Eocene.

C. O. Rosendahl, University of Minnesota (introduced by A. J. Carlson): Contribution to the Knowledge of Pleistocene Vegetation in Minnesota.

A. C. Noé, University of Chicago (introduced by F. R. Lillie): Paleobotanical Research in the University of Chicago. (By title.)

Normal C. Fassett, University of Wisconsin (introduced by L. R. Jones): Preglacial Plant Relics in the Driftless Area.

C. F. Kettering, General Motors Research Corporation: Objectives of Chlorophyll Research.

V. M. Albers and H. V. Knorr, Antioch College (introduced by C. F. Kettering): The Absorption Spectra of Solutions of Pure Chlorophyll and of Chloroplasts in Living Cells.

Paul Rothemund, Antioch College (introduced by C. F. Kettering): Recent Advances in the Chemistry of Chlorophyll.

Ondess L. Inman, Antioch College (introduced by C. F. Kettering): The Ratios of Chlorophyll a and b and the Mechanism of Photosynthesis.

T. R. Hogness, F. P. Zschelle, Jr., A. E. Sidwell, Jr., and E. S. G. Barron, University of Chicago (introduced by W. D. Harkins): Spectroscopic Analysis of Hemochromogens: The Ferriheme Hydroxide-Cyanide Equilibrium.

George L. Clark, University of Illinois (introduced by W. A. Noyes): X-ray Studies of the Structures of Biological Materials.

Philip A. Schaffer, Washington University Medical School: Slow Ionic Oxidation-Reduction Reactions (Their Mechanism and Catalysis).

O. H. Robertson, University of Chicago (introduced by F. R. Lillie): The Role of the Macrophage in the Mechanism of Recovery From Experimental Lobar Pneumonia in the Dog.

Felix Saunders and S. A. Koser, University of Chicago (introduced by H. Gideon Wells): Some Chemical Properties of an Essential Growth Factor for Pathogenic Bacteria.

C. P. Miller, University of Chicago (introduced by Ludvig Hektoen): Experimental Meningococcal Infection.

H. Close Hesseltine, University of Chicago (introduced by A. J. Carlson): A Study of Genital Mycosis.

Wm. J. Dieckmann, University of Chicago (introduced by F. R. Lillie): Blood Volume Changes in Eclampsia.

F. L. Adair, M. E. Davis, and Sarah H. Pearl, University of Chicago (introduced by A. J. Carlson): A Study of the Action of Some Oxytocics, Especially Ergonovine, on the Postpartum Uterus.

Arthur L. Tatum, University of Wisconsin (introduced by A. J. Carlson): Some Relationships Between Structure and Function of Organic Arsenicals in Experimental Chemotherapy.

Martin H. Hanke, University of Chicago (introduced by A. J. Carlson) : The Acid-Base and Energy Metabolism of the Stomach and Pancreas.

J. H. Bodine, University of Iowa (introduced by C. E. Seashore) : Active and Blocked Embryonic Cells—Some Phases of Their Physiology.

Carl Cori and G. T. Cori, Washington University (introduced by Joseph Erlanger) : The Formation and Fermentation of Hexosemonophosphate in Muscle.

Carl E. Seashore, University of Iowa: The Scientific Analysis of Piano Performance.

Joseph Tiffin, University of Iowa (introduced by C. E. Seashore) : Strobo-scopic Studies of the Human Vocal Cords.

C. G. Loosli, University of Chicago (introduced by C. J. Herrick) : Histo-logical Studies of the Respiratory Portion of the Mammalian Lungs.

Helen T. Graham and Lorente de No, Washington University (introduced by Joseph Erlanger) : Transmission of Successive Impulses Across Synapses.

R. W. Gerard, University of Chicago (introduced by A. J. Carlson) : Poten-tials in the Frog's Nervous System.

G. W. Bartelmez, University of Chicago (introduced by C. J. Herrick) : Some Effects of Histologic Procedures on Cells.

N. D. Hoerr, University of Chicago (introduced by C. J. Herrick) : The Se-cretion of Hydrochloric Acid in the Stomach as Revealed by the Freezing-Drying Method.

L. R. Dragstedt, University of Chicago (introduced by A. J. Carlson) : A New Pancreas Hormone.

J. Bronfenbrenner, Washington University (introduced by Joseph Erlanger) : The Mechanism of the Lytic Action of Bacteriophage.

Bengt Hamilton, University of Chicago (introduced by H. Gideon Wells) : The Antirachitic Effect of Tartrate and Citrate.

A. E. Emerson, University of Chicago (introduced by C. M. Child) : Termite Nests—A Study of the Phylogeny of Behavior.

Alfred C. Kinsey, Indiana University (introduced by C. M. Child) : An Evo-lutionary Analysis of Insular and Continental Species.

Wm. F. Petersen, University of Illinois (introduced by F. R. Lillie) : Mete-orological Environment and Organic Differentiation.

Charles Huggins, University of Chicago (introduced by F. R. Lillie) : The Laws Governing the Distribution of Bone Marrow in the Extremities in Mammals.

N. Kleitman and S. Titelbaum, University of Chicago (introduced by A. J. Carlson) : Establishment of Diurnal Temperature Curve in the Child.

A. G. Bills, University of Chicago (introduced by C. J. Herrick) : A Study of Certain Fatigue Symptoms in Mental Work.

L. J. Stadler and G. F. Sprague, University of Missouri (introduced by Sewall Wright) : Contrasts in the Genetic Effects of Ultraviolet Radiation and X-rays.

Paul Weiss, University of Chicago (introduced by C. J. Herrick) : The Reality of Neurofibrils in the Living Ganglion Cell and Nerve Fiber.

R. A. Brink, University of Wisconsin (introduced by Sewall Wright) : The Physiological Basis of Heterosis.

E. S. G. Barron, University of Chicago (introduced by H. G. Wells) : Oxida-tion-Reduction Potentials of Hemoglobins.

E. C. Stakman, University of Minnesota: Variation in Ustilago Zeae.

J. T. Buchholz, University of Illinois (introduced by William Trelease) : Seed Cone Development in Sequoia Gigantea.

R. M. Fraps, University of Chicago (introduced by C. M. Child) : Reaction Gradients and Pigmentation Thresholds in Feathers.

Gordon H. Scott, Washington University (introduced by Joseph Erlanger) : Spectrographic Analysis of Pure Samples of Cytoplasm and of Nuclei From Liver Cells.

D. H. Peterson, T. F. Galligher, and F. C. Koch, University of Chicago (intro-duced by J. Stieglitz) : The Conjugated Form of Male Sex Hormone in Human Urine.

W. C. Allee and Gertrude Evans, University of Chicago (introduced by C. M. Child) : Some Effects of Numbers Present on the Rate of First Cleavage in Arbacia.

G. P. DuShane, University of Chicago (introduced by C. M. Child) : Some Derivatives of the Neural Folds in Amphibian Embryos: Pigment Cells, Spinal Ganglia, and Rohon-Beard Cells.

W. W. Swanson and Vivian Iob, University of Chicago (introduced by A. J. Carlson) : Correlation of Mineral Growth and Body Growth in the Young Rat.

H. H. Newman, University of Chicago (introduced by F. R. Lillie) : Studies of Correlations Between Measured Mental and Physical Differences in Identical Twins Reared Apart and Rated Differences in the Environment.

F. W. Schlutz and Helen Oldham, University of Chicago (introduced by A. J. Carlson) : The Utilization of Organic and Inorganic Iron in Early Infancy.

Katsuji Kato, University of Chicago (introduced by C. J. Herrick) : The Histology of Bone Marrow in Cobalt Polycythemia.

E. Jacobson, University of Chicago (introduced by A. J. Carlson) : The Influence of Tension and Relaxation on Blood Pressure.

A. Alving and W. Gordon, University of Chicago (introduced by H. Gideon Wells) : Studies on the Renal Excretion Ratio and Reabsorption of Urea in the Dog.

ANNUAL MEETING, 1937

The National Academy of Sciences held its annual spring meeting, 1937, in the Academy Building, Washington, D. C., on April 26, 27, and 28, 1937.

BUSINESS SESSION

One hundred and thirty-two members responded to roll call, as follows:

Abbot, C. G.	Gherardi, Bancroft	Miles, W. R.
Adams, Roger	Gortner, R. A.	Miller, D. C.
Allen, C. E.	Hall, E. H.	Millikan, R. A.
Allen, E. T.	Harkins, W. D.	Morse, Marston
Bailey, L. H.	Harper, R. A.	Moulton, F. R.
Barbour, Thomas	Harrison, R. G.	Norris, J. F.
Benedict, F. G.	Harvey, E. N.	Novy, F. G.
Berry, E. W.	Hektoen, Ludvig	Noyes, W. A.
Bigelow, H. B.	Henderson, L. J.	Ople, E. L.
Birkhoff, G. D.	Henderson, Yandell	Osterhout, W. J. V.
Blakeslee, A. F.	Hovgaard, William	Pillsbury, W. B.
Bliss, G. A.	Howard, L. O.	Reid, H. F.
Bogert, Marston T.	Howell, W. H.	Ritt, J. F.
Boring, E. G.	Hrdlička, Aleš	Rivers, T. M.
Bowen, N. L.	Hudson, C. S.	Rose, W. C.
Bowman, Isaiah	Hull, A. W.	Rous, Peyton
Bridgman, P. W.	Hull, C. L.	Ruedemann, Rudolf
Brown, E. W.	Hunsaker, J. C.	Saunders, F. A.
Bush, Vannevar	Hunter, W. S.	Sauveur, Albert
Cattell, J. McKeen	Ives, H. E.	Schlesinger, Frank
Clark, W. M.	Jennings, H. S.	Seashore, C. E.
Clinton, G. P.	Jewett, F. B.	Shapley, Harlow
Coble, A. B.	Johnson, Douglas	Sinnott, E. W.
Coblentz, W. W.	Jones, L. R.	Stakman, E. C.
Compton, A. H.	Kasner, Edward	Stejneger, Leonhard
Compton, K. T.	Keith, Arthur	Stockard, C. R.
Conant, J. B.	Kraus, C. A.	Streeter, G. L.
Conklin, E. G.	Kroeber, A. L.	Swasey, Ambrose
Cross, Whitman	Kunkel, L. O.	Thorndike, E. L.
Cushing, Harvey	Lefschetz, Solomon	Urey, H. C.
Davenport, C. B.	Leuschner, A. O.	Van Vleck, J. H.
Davis, Bergen	Levene, P. A.	Vaughan, T. W.
Davisson, C. J.	Lewis, W. H.	Veblen, Oswald
Dodge, B. O.	Lillie, F. R.	Walsh, J. L.
Duggar, B. M.	Lind, S. C.	Whipple, G. H.
Dunn, Gano	Lindgren, Waldemar	White, H. S.
Durand, W. F.	Longwell, C. R.	Whitehead, J. B.
Emerson, R. A.	MacCallum, W. G.	Wiener, Norbert
Erlanger, Joseph	McClung, C. E.	Wilson, Edwin B.
Fletcher, Harvey	Mason, Max	Wood, R. W.
Flexner, Simon	Mendenhall, W. C.	Woodruff, L. L.
Forbes, Alexander	Merriam, J. C.	Wright, F. E.
Fred E. B.	Merrill. E. D.	Wright. Sewall

DEATHS SINCE THE AUTUMN MEETING

Members

Stanley Rossiter Benedict, born March 17, 1884, elected to the Academy in 1924, died December 21, 1936.

Marshall Avery Howe, born June 6, 1867, elected to the Academy in 1923, died December 24, 1936.

Julius Oscar Stieglitz, born May 26, 1867, elected to the Academy in 1911, died January 10, 1937.

Edward Curtis Franklin, born March 1, 1862, elected to the Academy in 1914, died February 4, 1937.

Elihu Thomson, born March 29, 1853, elected to the Academy in 1907, died March 13, 1937.

William Morton Wheeler, born March 19, 1865, elected to the Academy in 1912, died April 19, 1937.

Foreign associates

Karl Friedrich Kustner, of Germany, elected a foreign associate in 1913, died October 15, 1936.

Carl Stumpf, of Germany, elected a foreign associate in 1927, died December 25, 1936.

BIOGRAPHIES ASSIGNED SINCE THE AUTUMN MEETING

Othniel C. Marsh, assigned to Charles Schuchert.
William Edward Story, assigned to R. C. Archibald.
Nathaniel Lord Britton, assigned to E. D. Merrill.
Harris Joseph Ryan, reassigned to W. F. Durand.
Henry Fairfield Osborn, assigned to W. K. Gregory.
Arthur Amos Noyes, assigned to Linus Pauling.
Edward Curtis Franklin, assigned to C. A. Kraus.
Edwin Oakes Jordan, assigned to Ludvig Hektoen.
Stanley Rossiter Benedict, assigned to E. V. McCollum.
Marshall Avery Howe, assigned to W. A. Setchell.
Julius Oscar Stieglitz, assigned to W. A. Noyes.
Elihu Thomson, assigned to Karl T. Compton.

DELEGATES APPOINTED SINCE THE AUTUMN MEETING

To the centenary celebration of the founding of Mount Holyoke College, South Hadley, Mass., May 7 and 8, 1937: Margaret Floy Washburn.

To the meeting of the International Council of Scientific Unions, London, April 27–May 4, 1937: L. W. Hackett, W. B. Donham, and W. A. Noyes, Jr.

SECTION OF MATHEMATICS

G. C. Evans elected by the section as chairman (succeeding A. B. Coble) for 3 years commencing at the close of this meeting. G. A. Bliss elected representative of the section to serve on the Government Relations and Science Advisory Committee (succeeding Oswald Veblen) for the same period.

COMMITTEE APPOINTMENTS

Government Relations and Science Advisory Committee.—G. H. Whipple and R. A. Millikan, both reappointed members-at-large, for 3 years ending June 30, 1940.

Nominating committee to nominate a vice president and two members of the council of the Academy.—C. G. Abbot, chairman; Simon Flexner, and Edwin B. Wilson.

Tellers to count the preference ballot on nominations to membership in the Academy.—C. B. Davenport and A. W. Hull.

Auditing committee.—William Bowie, chairman; T. Wayland Vaughan, and W. Mansfield Clark.

Henry Draper fund.—Joel Stebbins to succeed V. M. Slipher as chairman, for the remainder of his term of membership, ending April 1938. Edwin Hubble to succeed Dr. Slipher as a member of the committee; term, 5 years.

J. Lawrence Smith fund.—E. T. Allen to succeed F. R. Moulton as chairman, for the remainder of his term of membership, ending April 1938. J. A. Anderson to succeed Mr. Moulton as a member of the committee; term, 5 years.

Cyrus B. Comstock fund.—Dayton C. Miller to succeed Henry Crew as a member of the committee; term, 5 years.

Marsh fund.—W. K. Gregory reappointed as chairman; term, 5 years.

Murray fund.—E. G. Conklin to succeed C. A. Kofoid as a member of the committee; term, 3 years.

Marcellus Hartley fund.—A. W. Hull to succeed Harvey Cushing as chairman of the committee for the period ending April 1939; Mr. Cushing to remain a member of the committee for a further term of 3 years. Herbert Hoover reappointed as a member of the committee; term, 3 years.

Mary Clark Thompson fund.—W. C. Mendenhall to succeed Waldemar Lindgren as chairman, for the period ending in April 1939. C. K. Leith to succeed Mr. Lindgren as a member of the committee; term, 3 years.

Joseph Henry fund.—L. R. Jones to succeed D. L. Webster (resigned) as chairman, for the remainder of his term of membership, ending April 1938. F. K. Richtmyer to succeed Mr. Webster as a member of the committee, for the period ending in April 1939. G. L. Streeter to succeed H. V. Wilson as a member of the committee; term, 5 years.

John J. Carty fund.—J. B. Conant to succeed W. D. Bancroft as a member of the committee; term, 5 years.

PROCEEDINGS, MANAGING EDITOR

Announcement was made of the election, by the council of the Academy on the preceding evening, of Edwin B. Wilson as managing editor of the Proceedings of the National Academy of Sciences, to succeed himself, for the period ending with the autumn meeting in 1938.

DUES

The recommendation of the council that dues for membership in the Academy for the year ending with the annual meeting in 1938 be $10 was approved.

AMENDMENT OF THE CONSTITUTION

Consideration was given to the proposed amendment of article IV, section 5, fourth paragraph, of the constitution, to increase the limit of membership to 350 instead of 300, as reported favorably by the committee of the whole at the meeting on November 16, 1936. After discussion and defeat of a motion to table the proposal, it was voted to adopt the amendment, increasing the limit of membership to 350. Adopted.

REPORT OF THE FOREIGN SECRETARY

As foreign secretary of the National Academy of Sciences, I have the honor to make the following report for the year 1936–37:

At the autumn meeting of the Academy the resignation of Mr. Thomas Hunt Morgan as foreign secretary was presented to the Academy and the present secretary was then elected to succeed him. Mr. Morgan's retirement must be a source of regret to all his colleagues, for it is a serious loss to the Academy.

Thereupon I assumed the duties of carrying on the foreign correspondence of the Academy, of consulting with the sections of the Academy and proposing to the council nominations of foreign associates, and of advising the president in the choice of delegates of the Academy and of other representatives to academic and scientific gatherings and festivities in foreign countries.

Immediately after the November meeting the question of nominations of foreign associates was examined and I hope that the council will be able to present nominations at the present meeting.

Addresses of congratulation have been sent to the University of Athens on the occasion of its centenary and to the Deutsche Akademie der Naturforscher of Halle which is celebrating its two hundred and fiftieth year.

Delegates have been appointed to the meeting of the International Council of Scientific Unions to be held in London April 27–May 4, 1937. Attention has also been given to the choice of American representatives at the following meetings:

Congress on Corrosion by Sea Water, Academie Mediterraneenne, Monte Carlo, March 25–28, 1937.

Fifth International Commission of Agricultural Industries, Scheveningen, Netherlands, July 12–17, 1937.

Seventeenth International Geological Congress, Moscow, July 20–29, 1937.

Congress to celebrate the tricentennial anniversary of Descartes' "Discourse on Method," Paris, August 1–6, 1937.

Eighth International Congress of Historical Sciences, Switzerland, August 28–September 4, 1938.

Thirteenth International Congress of Sociology, Paris, September 2–5, 1937.

Seventeenth International Congress of Anthropology and Archaeology, Bucharest, September 1937.

Fifth Commission of International Society of Soil Science, Madrid, September 1937.

Eleventh International Congress of Psychology, Paris, July 25–31, 1937.

L. J. HENDERSON, *Foreign Secretary.*

Report accepted.

REPORT OF THE HOME SECRETARY

Since the last annual meeting, volume 16 of the Biographical Memoirs has been published in bound form, ten biographies have been issued as parts of volume 17; one more biography is in press for that volume, and six biographies are in press for volume 18. Seven manuscripts are awaiting publication when funds become available.

Eight members have died since the last annual meeting:

Arthur Amos Noyes, born September 13, 1866, elected to the Academy in 1905, died June 3, 1936.

Edwin Oakes Jordan, born July 28, 1866, elected to the Academy in April 1936, died September 2, 1936.

Stanley Rossiter Benedict, born March 17, 1884, elected to the Academy in 1924, died December 21, 1936.

Marshall Avery Howe, born June 6, 1867, elected to the Academy in 1923, died December 24, 1936.

Julius Oscar Stieglitz, born May 26, 1867, elected to the Academy in 1911, died January 10, 1937.

Edward Curtis Franklin, born March 1, 1862, elected to the Academy in 1914, died February 4, 1937.

Elihu Thomson, born March 29, 1853, elected to the Academy in 1907, died March 13, 1937.

William Morton Wheeler, born March 19, 1865, elected to the Academy in 1912, died April 19, 1937.

Two foreign associates have died:

Karl Friedrich Kustner, of Germany, elected a foreign associate in 1913, died October 15, 1936.

Carl Stumpf, of Germany, elected a foreign associate in 1927, died December 29, 1936.

Raymond Dodge was transferred, at his request, in November 1936, to the roll of members emeriti.

There are now 283 members, 1 member emeritus, and 39 foreign associates.

F. E. WRIGHT, *Home Secretary.*

Report accepted.

REPORT OF THE TREASURER

Attention was called to the annual report of the treasurer for the fiscal year July 1, 1935, to June 30, 1936, as contained in the Annual

Report of the National Academy of Sciences for 1935–36, which had just been distributed. A supplementary statement of the treasurer as of December 31, 1936, was presented and received for filing.

ALEXANDER DALLAS BACHE FUND

During the past year the board of directors of the Alexander Dallas Bache fund of the National Academy of Sciences made the following grants:

No. 356, for $1,000, to Dr. Eric Ponder, Cold Spring Harbor Biological Laboratory. For a study of the effects of narcotics and similar substances on the electrical changes in heart muscle.

No. 357, for $600, to Dr. Malcolm Dole, Northwestern University. For investigations on the atomic weight of oxygen in the air and in carbonate rocks.

No. 358, for $300, to Mr. Demorest Davenport, Biological Laboratory, Harvard University. For taxonomic and genetic studies of the genus Coenonympha (Lepidoptera).

No. 359, for $720, to Mr. Robert R. McMath, McMath-Hulbert Observatory, Lake Angelus, Mich. For a special Bell and Howard precision gate mechanism for solar motion picture work on prominences with the new solar tower.

No. 360, for $250, to Prof. Frank M. Hull, for studies collating fossil and recent genera of the syrphidae.

The bursar of the Academy reports $3,689.26 as available for grants as of the date of March 18, 1937.

W. J. V. OSTERHOUT.
CHARLES R. STOCKARD.
EDWIN B. WILSON, *Chairman.*

Report accepted.

JAMES CRAIG WATSON FUND

Your board of trustees of the Watson fund unanimously recommends as follows:

Grant No. 52.—A grant of $90 to Mr. L. Peltier of Delphos, Ohio, to enable him to acquire sections 1 and 2 of the Franklin-Adams charts. The charts are to be used for rough positions of newly found objects and in a regular program of estimates of magnitudes.

Mr. Peltier is an amateur astronomer who has to his credit several discoveries, particularly of new comets, and it seems appropriate for the Academy to give him encouragement.

Grant No. 50.—The report on the work of applying and testing the Berkeley Tables, etc., is being deferred until the autumn meeting. Much progress has been made and the results are highly satisfactory. It is of interest that after independent tests the Berlin Rechen-Institut has adopted the Berkeley Tables for ephemeris computation of planets of the Hecuba group and has added a member to its staff for that purpose.

The condition of the Watson fund on March 31, 1937, was as follows:

Invested income	$1,000.00
Uninvested income	1,158.62
Invested capital	24,533.97
Univested capital	466.03

F. E. ROSS.
F. H. SEARES.
A. O. LEUSCHNER, *Chairman.*

Report accepted and recommendation approved.

HENRY DRAPER FUND

In November the Draper committee recommended that the Academy award its Henry Draper Medal to Dr. C. E. Kenneth Mees, director of the research laboratory of the Eastman Kodak Co., in recognition of his outstanding researches in photographic processes. For more than a quarter of a century Dr. Mees has continued his investigations which have resulted in most fruitful developments in emulsions, especially those sensitive to the long wave lengths of the spectrum that have been vitally instrumental in important advances in certain astronomical researches.

During the present year no grants have been made from this fund.

> W. S. Adams,
> Paul W. Merrill,
> S. A. Mitchell,
> Joel Stebbins,
> V. M. Slipher, *Chairman.*

Report accepted.

J. LAWRENCE SMITH FUND

Two reports were presented from the committee on the J. Lawrence Smith fund, as follows:

APRIL 5, 1937.

The committee on the J. Lawrence Smith fund of the National Academy of Sciences has the honor to report as follows:

During the year ended March 31, 1937, the following recommendations were made for grants to aid in investigating meteoric bodies:

To Thomas C. Poulter (April 1936) for the purpose of tabulating and preparing for publication observations of meteors secured in Antarctica---- $450
To Harlow Shapley (July 1936) to pay in part for reduction of meteor observations secured by Harvard-Cornell Meteor Expedition to Arizona; computations to be carried out by Dr. Opik in Tartu, Estonia--------- 400

No recommendation was made during the year ended March 31, 1937, for the awarding of a medal for original investigations of meteoric bodies.

The condition of the J. Lawrence Smith fund as of March 31, 1937, was as follows:

Invested capital	$10,000.00
Invested income	4,123.25
Uninvested income	3,080.30

> F. R. Moulton, *Chairman.*

Report accepted.

APRIL 9, 1937.

The committee of the J. Lawrence Smith fund of the National Academy of Sciences recommends a grant of $800 to Mr. H. H. Nininger, 1955 Fairfax Street, Denver, Colo., to assist him in completing a survey of the Haviland, Kans., meteor crater and surrounding region.

> F. R. Moulton, *Chairman.*

Recommendation approved.

BENJAMIN APTHORP GOULD FUND

The directors of the Gould fund of the National Academy of Sciences have the honor to report as follows:

Grant made during the year April 1, 1936, to March 31, 1937:

To Jan Schilt, Columbia University, New York, for determining the photographic magnitudes of all the Gesellschaft stars between declinations +30° and +50° (Dec. 3, 1936) -------------------------------- $500

The condition of the Gould fund as of March 31, 1937, was as follows:

Invested capital	$19,948.00
Invested income	10,247.65
Total invested capital and income	30,195.65
Uninvested capital	52.00
Uninvested income	5,581.01
Total uninvested capital and income	5,633.01

> Heber D. Curtis.
> Ernest W. Brown.
> F. R. Moulton, *Chairman.*

ted.

Since their last report the directors of the Gibbs fund have made two grants: One of $210 to Prof. Henry E. Bent, of the University of Missouri, for the purchase of optical equipment, and the other of $150 to Dr. C. E. Teeter, of the Cambridge School of Liberal Arts, for the purchase of electrical apparatus.

The condition of the fund as of March 31, 1937, was as follows:

Uninvested income_____ $2,797.24
Invested capital_____ 5,545.50

E. P. KOHLER, *Chairman.*

Report accepted.

I beg to submit the report of the committee on the Marsh fund for the year 1936 and also the recommendations for grants during 1937.

I. *Reports on grants made in 1936*

(1) The International Hydrographic Bureau received $125 for work on the third edition of the General Bathymetric Chart of the Oceans.

The International Hydrographic Bureau reports, through the secretary general, G. Spicer Simson, that the work on the third edition of the chart was continued, part of which was published in Special Publication No. 30, part A_1 (North Atlantic Ocean), and part A_1 (South Atlantic Ocean) by the International Hydrographic Bureau in May 1935, and March 1936, respectively. Sheet B_1 will be published shortly. This covers soundings from the parallel of 46°40′ N. to that of 72° N.

A supplementary sheet annexed to sheet A_1 permits the examination as a whole of the bathymetry of the South Atlantic Ocean as far to the southward as the limit of the main sheet and to the meridian of Cape Agulhas. This will be incorporated in the third editions of sheets AIV and A'IV when they are published. The preparation of sheet AIV is nearing completion.

The additional (temporary) draughtsman paid partially from the grant from the Marsh fund is still being employed plotting deep-sea soundings for the Bathymetric Chart, and this has considerably expedited the preparation of the new edition of the various sheets of this chart.

(2) Dr. Albert E. Wood received a grant of $250 for work on the fossil Heteromyidae and other fossil rodents.

During the past year Dr. Wood has published a detailed analysis of the rodent and lagemorph fossils that he collected in the Cuyama beds of California. A paper discussing fossil rodents from the Siwalik beds of India has been completed and accepted for publication. A second paper on additional material from these beds has been begun.

These several studies have added to our knowledge of the late Miocene or early Pliocene rabbits and heteromyids and describe a number of new forms from the Siwaliks.

Dr. Wood reports that he still has a balance of $34.85 of his grant, which will be used in the continuance of his studies on the same material.

(3) Dr. William C. Darrah received $250 from the Marsh fund for the purpose of comparative studies of the reproductive structures of Paleozoic plants.

Dr. Darrah reports that he was able to make two collecting trips and collected more than 40 fruiting specimens, of which 30 will be described and figured within the next year. These will add materially to our knowledge of Paleozoic plant phylogeny.

A paper entitled "Codonotheca and Crossotheca: Polleniferous Structures of Pteridosperms" is now in press. Another paper dealing with spores and spore-bearing parts of ferns and their allies is in preparation.

Two preliminary reports were presented at the meetings of the American Association for the Advancement of Science, which were briefly reviewed in Science, February 5, 1937.

Dr. Darrah reports a cash balance of $24.85, which will be used to complete the series of photographs for publication.

II. *New application for grant*

(1) Dr. Alfred S. Romer of Harvard University has made application for a grant of $225 to enable him to send Mr. L. I. Price of his department to collect vertebrate material from the late Pennsylvania beds of the Upper Cisco and Lower Wichita groups of Texas.

Dr. Romer stresses the desirability of making a collection of tetrapod material from these beds, which appear to have been overlooked in other expeditions to this locality. He strongly endorses Mr. Price as an experienced and careful collector.

This application has been recommended by all members of the committee on the Marsh fund.

III. *Renewal of grant*

(1) A renewal of the grant for $125 to the International Hydrographic Bureau is tentatively reserved, pending delayed correspondence with the secretary-general. N. B. This has been confirmed by cable. Grant approved by committee.

Summary

Uninvested income from the Marsh fund, Mar. 31, 1937		$966.57
Application A. S. Romer	$225.00	
Renewal Hydrographic Bureau	125.00	
Total		350.00
Balance		616.57

WILLIAM K. GREGORY, *Chairman.*

Report accepted and recommendations approved.

CYRUS B. COMSTOCK FUND

The committee on the Cyrus B. Comstock fund recommends that the Comstock prize be awarded, for the 5-year period 1933–38, to E. O. Lawrence for the development of the cyclotron and the results in the field of the transmutation of the elements which have been obtained with the aid of this new technique.

In addition, the committee recommends that the amount of the prize for this award be $2,500 and that presentation be made at the autumn meeting in 1937.

ROBERT A. MILLIKAN, *Chairman.*

Report accepted and recommendations approved.

Earlier in the year the committee on the Comstock fund had recommended, and the executive committee of the council of the Academy had approved, the suggestion that the treasurer of the Academy be directed to transfer from the income of that fund a sufficient amount to maintain the value of the capital of the fund at the limit of $15,000 set by the donor, Cyrus B. Comstock, in the deed of gift establishing the Comstock fund.

MURRAY FUND

The committee on the Murray fund unanimously recommends that the Agassiz Medal for the year 1937 be awarded to Dr. E. J. Allen, director emeritus of the Plymouth Laboratory of the Marine Biological Association of the United Kingdom, for his personal researches on marine biology, and the great influence which he has exerted on the study of marine organisms in their relation to the marine environment. The following is a brief biographical sketch and some of Dr. Allen's honors:

"ALLEN, Edgar Johnson, D. Sc. (Lond.); Hon. LL. D. (Edin.); F. R. S. 1914; Foreign Member, Royal Academy of Denmark; Secretary of the Marine Biological Association of the United Kingdom and Director of the Plymouth Laboratory, 1895–1936; President, Devonshire Association, 1916; Hansen Memorial

Medal and Prize, Copenhagen, 1923; Linnean Gold Medal, 1926; Darwin Medal of the Royal Society, 1936; *b.* 1866; *s.* of late Rev. Richard Allen. *Educ.:* Kingswood School; Yorkshire College, Leeds; University of Berlin; University College, London. Sherbrooke Scholarship, 1900."

An appraisal of Dr. Allen's personal scientific work and of his influence on the development of marine biology was prepared for the use of the committee on the Murray fund by one of Dr. Allen's British colleagues, Dr. G. P. Bidder, who did not know what use would be made of his statement. It is as follows:

"Allen succeeded to the direction of a great stone building mounted on the cliffs of a sewage-polluted estuary in 1895; it was universally regarded a 'white elephant,' impossible to keep up on its small income of £1,800 a year. He turned the laboratory into a highly efficient machine for research, many times more work being published from it in his first 5 years than in the former 10 years of its existence. He managed to fill its tables and to attract zoologists of independent means, he insensibly and tactfully guiding their research. In 1902 the English Government decided to join in the international exploration of the North Sea and Allen was asked to take charge of the investigations; these were a splendid success, remaining in his hands until the Government started a Scientific Division of the Ministry of Fisheries of their own in 1910. Allen was invited to be head of this, but he preferred to remain at his laboratory with an income about one-third of what he could have received as a Government servant.

"After the war Allen arranged his staff as a team, allotting to each his place and line of research. More money was obtained and the Plymouth Laboratory now ranks as one of the great laboratories of the world.

"Allen's studies of *Nitschia* and artificial sea water started an altogether new line of research, making us appreciate that we knew very little about sea water as a biological environment. This is the basis of most of the marine work under Allen's direction—studies on the inorganic elements in sea water and on the plankton and sunlight; everywhere we see physiological experimentation to understand what this means. The broad plan of campaign is Allen's, the strategy and tactics his, the arrangement of his plan and duty to each man as well. In much of the work of Plymouth, Allen's name should really appear as a joint author."

ARTHUR L. DAY.
CHARLES A. KOFOID.
T. WAYLAND VAUGHAN, *Chairman.*

Report accepted and recommendation approved.

MARCELLUS HARTLEY FUND

I wish to inform you that the committee on the Marcellus Hartley fund out of seven candidates that had been proposed favor the nomination of Willis R. Whitney to receive the next award of the Public Welfare Medal, for his outstanding work in the fundamentals of scientific research for the public good.

HARVEY CUSHING, *Chairman.*

Report accepted and recommendation approved.

DANIEL GIRAUD ELLIOT FUND

No report was received from the committee on the Daniel Giraud Elliot fund.

MARY CLARK THOMPSON FUND

No report was received from the committee on the Mary Clark Thompson fund.

JOSEPH HENRY FUND

The following are abstracts of reports received covering the work done during the past year under grants from the Joseph Henry fund:

68. Prof. Francis Bitter, of the Massachusetts Institute of Technology, $900, to continue work on his apparatus for producing a very intense magnetic field.

Construction and tests have proved that the apparatus works as expected, and auxiliary apparatus is under construction for a variety of researches with this strong field. Expenditures to date have come to $431.06, leaving a balance of $468.94 to be spent within the coming year.

69. Dr. T. T. Chen, of Johns Hopkins University, $200, for researches on chromosomes of paramecium. His report shows progress along many lines and a considerable program for the future, with the expenditure of $22.65 to date, leaving a balance of $177.35.

70. Dr. W. W. Coblentz, of the Bureau of Standards, $500, to continue his investigation of ultraviolet solar radiation at high altitudes. This work has been delayed, so that no expenditure has been made to date, but it is being resumed this spring.

D. L. WEBSTER,
Acting Chairman.

The recommendations for new grants were presented by Dr. L. R. Jones, chairman of the committee:

To Prof. Marston T. Bogert, department of chemistry, Columbia University, $250 for the purchase of a supply of retene for use in the synthesis of carcinogenic materials.

To Dr. P. W. Selwood, department of chemistry, Northwestern University, $500 for hiring part-time technical assistants in researches on magneto-chemical problems.

Report accepted and recommendations approved.

CHARLES DOOLITTLE WALCOTT FUND

No report was received from the directors of the Charles Doolittle Walcott fund.

JOHN J. CARTY FUND

No report was received from the committee on the John J. Carty fund as the Carty medal is recommended for award only biannually, in accordance with the deed of gift.

REPORT ON THE PROCEEDINGS

It is customary at this time to make a report on the Proceedings of the National Academy of Sciences. With the close of the calendar year 1936 we completed the twenty-second volume of the Proceedings. There were 148 contributions, making 721 pages. The average length of the contributions was 4.87 pages. The distribution was as follows:

Mathematics	35	Genetics	18
Astronomy	10	Zoology and anatomy	14
Physics and engineering	13	Physiology and biochemistry	21
Chemistry	6	Bacteriology and pathology	3
Geology and paleontology	9	Anthropology and psychology	8
Botany	11		

Of the 148 contributions 45 were by members of the Academy, 9 were by National Research fellows and persons working under research grants from the Academy, and 15 were read before the Academy.

It may be observed that the proportion of contributions in the fields of the physical sciences is less than the proportionate number of members of the Academy in those fields.

EDWIN B. WILSON,
Managing Editor.

Report accepted.

REPORT OF COMMITTEE ON BIOGRAPHICAL MEMOIRS

During the past year 14 manuscripts of Biographical Memoirs have been received. There remain 47 memoirs assigned but not yet prepared. This number is nine less than that reported last year. Memoirs for 12 persons have not yet been assigned.

Letters have been sent to all members of the Academy who have undertaken to write Biographical Memoirs (41 persons), and replies have been received from 25 indicating various stages of progress.

In the latter part of December letters were sent to all members of the Academy who had not deposited photographs in the personnel file. The result was very gratifying, since the executive secretary's office reports the receipt of a large number of photographs during January and February. There still remain 56 members of the Academy who have not deposited photographs.

The committee has carefully examined Dr. Hrdlička's report on anthropometry of Academy members, which was referred to it for the purpose, and is recommending the report, as critically revised by him, for publication by the Academy.

> A. HRDLIČKA.
> RAYMOND PEARL.
> E. L. THORNDIKE.
> F. E. WRIGHT.
> C. B. DAVENPORT, *Chairman.*

Report accepted.

GOVERNMENT RELATIONS AND SCIENCE ADVISORY COMMITTEE

In the last report of the chairman of the Government Relations and Science Advisory Committee, a sketch was given of the history and affiliations of the committee with the National Academy of Sciences and the United States Government, and a résumé of its activities up to that time. Since that report was presented, a second report from the subcommittee on airships has been received and transmitted to the Secretary of the Navy. It is understood that the findings of this subcommittee and the material presented are of value to the Department.

A first report of another subcommittee to study certain special problems has been presented to the Secretary of the Navy, and a letter has come, expressing appreciation.

During the early part of the summer, a request came to the Academy from the Secretary of Agriculture, asking for advice on the research program of the Department of Agriculture relating to toxic properties of substances used in or on food. A subcommittee of the Government Relations and Science Advisory Committee was appointed. This subcommittee met in Washington during the latter part of December for a 2-day conference, the members spending a large part of their time in the laboratories of the Food and Drug Administration studying the methods and facilities. A report was completed, and on February 11, 1937, transmitted to the Secretary of Agriculture, who wrote a note of appreciation, in which he asked the Academy to continue the committee for purposes of consultation. The Food and Drug Administration has already taken steps to carry out the suggestions presented.

Other requests from agencies of the Government are now under consideration by the committee.

> FRANK R. LILLIE, *Chairman.*

Report accepted.

COMMITTEE ON OCEANOGRAPHY

The chairman of the committee on oceanography, Mr. Bigelow, presented an oral report which was accepted.

REPORT ON BUILDINGS AND GROUNDS

The recent development of the triangular section of northwest Washington from Pennsylvania Avenue on the north to the basin and river on the south has for many years occupied the minds of those planning the city's future. While it was conceived that something must be done when the Lincoln Memorial was placed where it is, that other structures of equal importance and beauty must follow, it was many years before B Street, now Constitution Avenue, became more than an ill-paved narrow thoroughfare. Now it is a broad avenue worthy of a great city.

With the completion of the Federal Reserve Building and the new Department of the Interior this year there are left two other projected developments: One, the Pan American Annex; and the other, the use of the Naval Hospital grounds. From Seventeenth Street the buildings already erected on the north side of Constitution Avenue are the Pan American, the new Department of the Interior, the Public Health, the Federal Reserve, the National Academy of Sciences, and the Pharmaceutical. The Naval Hospital is now a group of small buildings, and is to the west of the Pharmaceutical Building. The area just north of the Academy Building, facing the C Street side, has been suggested as a place for the new War and Navy Department Building. It will occupy, if the suggestion is carried through, the ground from C Street on the south to Virginia Avenue on the north, and from Twenty-first Street on the east to Twenty-third Street on the west. Final approval, authorization, and money are still to be provided. In connection with the Academy grounds there has been some concern that the further widening of Constitution Avenue would necessitate the moving in of the curb line some 8 feet and continuing the walks as in front of the Public Health and the Pharmaceutical Buildings. If this plan is carried out it will affect the pools in front of the Academy Building; the lowest one near the street will have to be eliminated. Should this happen the whole architectural effect of the building would be altered but there is much doubt today whether it will ever be done.

The grounds have received thought and study, especially the approach from Constitution Avenue where the pools and walks have been constructed on made ground. For this reason the foundation for the pavement and the pools is not all that could be asked for. With the severe winter of a year ago, the trim of the pools parted at the joints, and some of the marble disintegrated. The cost of these repairs is large, and they have not been pushed as funds were not adequate; it is hoped that part of next year's funds will be made available for their repair.

Some replacements have been made in the planting and the lawns have become a problem to eliminate crab grass and the weeds. Efforts will be made during the coming summer and fall to put them in proper condition.

The joints in the facade of the building, and the stones of the terrace, have stood up well during the 13 years since the building was erected, but they now require attention to prevent moisture from getting in and freezing next winter. The matter is being taken up, and it is expected that it will be attended to before cold weather.

Small matters have been cared for, such as the request of the fire marshal of the District of Columbia that certain rewiring be done in the basement of the building, and the suggestion of the fire-insurance companies for the addition of fire extinguishers and the use of fireproof cloth on the ventilating conduits. These have all been attended to, and it is expected that they will have a bearing on the rates for fire insurance when the time comes for a renewal of the policies.

The cleaning of the building requires much time, as 60,000 visitors bring in dust and dirt which must be removed. Five hundred visitors counted before 10 o'clock on a damp morning may necessitate the cleaning of the exhibition halls over again. During meetings the halls and rooms have to be cleaned two or three times a day.

Dampness still seeps through some of the walls on the second floor and two rooms have required repainting for this reason. The contractor, at his own suggestion and expense, repainted the long hall on the second floor as the painting did not hold up as it should. Stairway walls soil quickly, and, as there is a limit to the washing, they had to be repainted this year.

The heating plant is functioning as it should, and no special repairs have been necessary. We are still using soft coal as it was originally planned we should, and it is hoped that those who have to do with the administration of the new smoke law will allow us to continue.

Meetings, including those of the Academy and its committees, and those of the National Research Council and its affiliated bodies, for discussion of scientific research matters, have been held in the building.

At this time, with the exceptions mentioned above, the building and grounds are in excellent condition.

PAUL BROCKETT,
Custodian, Buildings and Grounds.

Report accepted.

37878—38——3

REPORT ON EXHIBITS

To have exhibits from which the layman can gain knowledge of the phenomena of nature has been the aim of many groups in America, especially in Washington, since the beginning of the last century. To interest the visitor to the extent of wanting to know more about natural phenomena has been the thought; that is, to incite interest in an understanding way. Two innovations in the education of the public through the museum idea during the last half century have had great influence. The first was Dr. Langley's idea of a children's museum in the Smithsonian Institution where a room was set aside for animals, birds, and other objects written about in children's books. Simple labels told the story and over the door was the legend "Knowledge begins with wonder." The idea was immediately adopted by other museums in various places. The second was Dr. Hale's suggestion that in the Academy Building there should be live exhibits demonstrating fundamental experiments resulting from scientific research that were the foundation of important developments. Further, he felt that the latest results from laboratories devoting their time to scientific research and the application of their results to our everyday comfort were equally important. This idea for the benefit of the younger generation and of older people worked out so well in the Academy Building that it has since been studied at home and abroad; there are now many other places where the public can perform the experiments and produce the phenomena of the early masters in research to awaken their interest in scientific research.

The question of labels clear to the public has been under consideration since the inception of the exhibit idea, but no matter how great the effort they have not been satisfactory. Mr. Gifford Pinchot, formerly Chief of the Forestry Service and later Governor of Pennsylvania, has appreciated the situation and is lending his thought in the way of valuable suggestions as a layman.

During the year no new exhibits have been added, but the care of what we have and of keeping the material in working condition has fully occupied the time of the instrument maker. In checking over the instruments, he sees some way of presenting the whole or a part of an exhibit to bring about a better understanding of the objectives to be reached. To cite an instance, the rail interferometer had a vibration that should not have been there. It was located by him in the base which was an I beam; that is, in working the experiment the base was bent as well as the rail when pressure was applied. By supporting the flanges of the I beam with ribs the vibration was eliminated.

In the exhibit of the Bell Telephone Laboratories every effort is made by the laboratories to have the material up to date and in good working order. Members of the staff come to Washington to assist in keeping it in the best working condition.

The National Advisory Committee for Aeronautics expects to add in the near future to their present exhibits many new working models showing the latest achievements. They have been hampered in doing this by the necessity of contributing to the Government part in expositions throughout the country.

The General Electric Co. is preparing new material to illustrate better some of the experiments shown, and hopes to have them completed and new models in place before the annual meeting of the Academy this year.

The celebration of the one-hundredth anniversary of the inauguration of the present American patent system took place during last November. One part of the program consisted of a demonstration of the latest application of the scientific results of commercial laboratories to modern development in various fields. These demonstrations were held at the request of Mr. Kettering, a member of the Academy, in the auditorium of the building.

The constant watching of the exhibits and keeping them in working condition is due to the painstaking efforts of Mr. Frank H. Schloer, the instrument maker, whose knowledge of how they should work and the phenomena they should show is an asset.

The popularity of the exhibition series continues, as is shown by the number of visitors, 57,283, for the year.

PAUL BROCKETT,
Secretary, Committee on Exhibits.

Report accepted.

ELECTIONS

The elections at the annual meeting resulted as follows:

Vice president of the Academy: Arthur L. Day, reelected for a further term of 4 years, ending June 30, 1941.

Two members of the council of the Academy, term 3 years commencing July 1, 1937: H. S. Jennings (succeeding himself) and Oswald Veblen (succeeding Roger Adams).

Foreign associate: August Krogh, zoologist; professor of zoophysiology, Copenhagen University, Copenhagen, Denmark.

New members: Calvin Blackman Bridges, California Institute of Technology, Pasadena, Calif.; Oliver Ellsworth Buckley, Bell Telephone Laboratories, New York City; Arthur Jeffery Dempster, University of Chicago, Chicago, Ill.; Ernest William Goodpasture, Vanderbilt University, Nashville, Tenn.; Carl Gottfried Hartman, department of embryology, Carnegie Institution of Washington, Baltimore, Md.; Donnel Foster Hewett, United States Geological Survey, Washington, D. C.; Leo Loeb, Washington University, St. Louis, Mo.; Duncan Arthur MacInnes, Rockefeller Institute for Medical Research, New York City; George Richards Minot, Boston City Hospital, Boston, Mass.; John von Neumann, Institute for Advanced Study, Princeton, N. J.; Seth Barnes Nicholson, Mount Wilson Observatory, Pasadena, Calif.; Otto Struve, Yerkes Observatory, Williams Bay, Wis.; Francis Bertody Sumner, Scripps Institution of Oceanography, La Jolla, Calif.; Charles Thom, United States Department of Agriculture, Washington, D. C.; and Edward Chace Tolman, University of California, Berkeley, Calif.

PRESENTATION OF MEDALS

Four gold medals were presented at the dinner of the Academy on Tuesday evening, April 27, 1937: The James Craig Watson medal and accompanying honorarium of $100 which had been awarded to Ernest William Brown, Yale University Observatory, New Haven, Conn., in recognition of his outstanding contributions to astronomical science, mainly in the field of gravitational theory in the solar system; the Henry Draper medal, awarded to C. E. Kenneth Mees, of the Eastman Kodak Co., Rochester, N. Y., in recognition of his investigations in photographic processes which have given emulsions sensitive to the red and infrared of the spectrum and made possible the recent great advance in the knowledge of this highly important region of the radiant energy of the stars; the Agassiz medal for oceanography, which had been awarded to Martin Knudsen, of the University of Copenhagen, Copenhagen, Denmark, in recognition of his contributions to that field of scientific research, including his report on the hydrography of the Danish "Ingolf" expedition published in 1898, the preparation of his hydrographic tables published by the International Council for the Exploration of the Sea, his inauguration of standard sea water distributed to other oceanographic institutions by the International Council for the Exploration of the Sea, his invention or improvement of the designs of oceanographic instruments, and his leadership in the development of precise methods in the study of physical oceanography; and the Mary Clark Thompson medal with accompanying honorarium of $250, awarded to Amadeus William Grabau, of the National University of Peking, Peiping, China, in recognition of his long and distinguished record in paleontology and stratigraphic geology. Owing to the inability of the recipients to be present, the Agassiz Medal was received for Mr. Knudsen by the minister of Denmark, for transmission to him through diplomatic channels, and the Thompson medal was received for Mr. Grabau by his wife, Mary Antin Grabau, in his behalf.

SCIENTIFIC SESSIONS

The scientific sessions for the presentation of papers by members of the Academy or persons introduced by them were well attended. The papers presented were as follows:

MONDAY, APRIL 26, 1937

G. H. Parker, Harvard University, Cambridge, Mass.: A Catalog of Neurohumors.

Warren H. Lewis, Department of Embryology, Carnegie Institution of Washington, Wolfe and Madison Streets, Baltimore, Md.: Pinocytosis—Drinking by Cells (illustrated).

G. L. Streeter, E. A. Park, and Deborah Jackson, Department of Embryology, Carnegie Institution of Washington, Wolfe and Madison Streets, Baltimore, Md.: Hereditary Vulnerability to Dietary Defects in the Development of Bone (illustrated).

Sewall Wright, University of Chicago, Chicago, Ill.: The Distribution of Gene Frequencies in Populations (illustrated).

Simon Flexner, Rockefeller Institute for Medical Research, New York City: Immunity and Reinfection in Experimental Poliomyelitis (illustrated).

George W. Corner, the University of Rochester, School of Medicine and Dentistry, Rochester, N. Y. (introduced by George H. Whipple): Experimental Menstruation (illustrated).

Francis G. Benedict and Robert C. Lee, Nutrition Laboratory, Carnegie Institution of Washington, 29 Vila Street, Boston, Mass.: Body Fat as a Factor in Heat Production (illustrated).

Henry Gray Barbour, Yale Medical School, New Haven, Conn. (introduced by Yandell Henderson): Sympathomimetic Influence of Deuterium Oxide (illustrated).

Howard W. Haggard and Leon A. Greenberg, Yale University, New Haven, Conn. (introduced by Yandell Henderson): The Effects of Alcohol as Influenced by Blood Sugar (illustrated).

Oscar Schotté, Amherst College, Amherst, Mass. (introduced by Ross G. Harrison): Embryonic Induction in Regenerating Tissue (illustrated).

H. U. Sverdrup, Scripps Institution of Oceanography, University of California, La Jolla, Calif. (introduced by T. Wayland Vaughan): On the Evaporation From the Oceans (illustrated).

Columbus Iselin, Woods Hole Oceanographic Institution, Woods Hole, Mass. (introduced by Henry B. Bigelow): How Deep Do Ocean Currents Flow? (illustrated).

Rudolf Ruedemann, New York State Museum, Albany, N. Y.: Plankton and Radiolarian Ooze in Paleozoic Formations of New York (illustrated).

Norbert Wiener and Norman Levinson, Massachusetts Institute of Technology, Cambridge, Mass.: Random Waring's Theorems.

Marston Morse, Institute for Advanced Study, Princeton, N. J.: Lower Reducibility of Functions (illustrated).

Edward Kasner, Columbia University, New York City: Trihornometry: A New Chapter in Geometry (illustrated).

Ross Aiken Gortner and Henry B. Bull, Division of Agricultural Biochemistry, University of Minnesota, Sr. Paul, Minn.: Electrokinetics XIX. Interfacial Energy and Molecular Structure of Organic Compounds V. The Electric Moment of an Al_2O_3; Benzene-Nitrobenzene Interface (illustrated).

P. A. Levene and Alexandre Rothen, Rockefeller Institute for Medical Research, New York City: Mechanism of the Reaction of Substitution and Walden Inversion (illustrated).

G. H. Whipple, University of Rochester, Rochester, N. Y.: The Romance of Hemoglobin (illustrated).

TUESDAY, APRIL 27, 1937

Harold D. Babcock, Mount Wilson Observatory, Carnegie Institution of Washington, Pasadena, Calif.: Internuclear Distance in Oxygen Molecules

L. H. Germer and K. H. Storks, Bell Telephone Laboratories, Inc., New York City (introduced by Frank B. Jewett): The Structure of Langmuir-Blodgett Films of Stearic Acid (illustrated).

I. S. Bowen, R. A. Millikan, and H. V. Neher, California Institute of Technology, Pasadena, Calif.: The Influence of the Earth's Magnetic Field on Cosmic Ray Intensities up to the Top of the Atmosphere (illustrated).

M. S. Vallarta, Massachusetts Institute of Technology, Cambridge, Mass. (introduced by Arthur H. Compton): Cosmic Rays and the Magnetic Moment of the Sun (illustrated).

M. A. Tuve, L. R. Hafstad, and N. P. Heydenburg, Department of Terrestrial Magnetism, Carnegie Institution of Washington, Washington, D. C. (introduced by W. W. Coblentz): The Structural Forces of Atomic Nuclei.

A. G. McNish, Department of Terrestrial Magnetism, Carnegie Institution of Washington, Washington, D. C. (introduced by F. E. Wright): Terrestrial Effects Accompanying Several Bright Chromospheric Eruptions (illustrated).

J. G. Trump and R. J. Van de Graaff, Massachusetts Institute of Technology, Cambridge, Mass. (introduced by Karl T. Compton): Million-volt Direct-Current X-ray Generator for the Huntington Memorial Hospital (illustrated).

R. W. Wood, Johns Hopkins University, Baltimore, Md.: Unique Crystallization Phenomena of Protocatechuic Acid. Motion pictures of automotive crystals.

Herbert E. Ives, Bell Telephone Laboratories, Inc., New York City: The Measurement of Light Signals on Moving Bodies by Transported Rods and Clocks (illustrated).

M. Demerec, Department of Genetics, Carnegie Institution of Washington, Cold Spring Harbor, N. Y. (introduced by A. F. Blakeslee): Differences in Mutability in Various Wild-Type Lines of Drosophila Melanogaster (illustrated).

Albert F. Blakeslee, Amos G. Avery, and A. Dorothy Bergner, Department of Genetics, Carnegie Institution of Washington, Cold Spring Harbor, N. Y.: Bud Sports in Datura Due to Elimination to Specific Chromosomes (illustrated).

E. C. MacDowell, J. S. Potter, and M. J. Taylor, Department of Genetics, Carnegie Institution of Washington, Cold Spring Harbor, N. Y. (introduced by A. F. Blakeslee): A Treatment of Hosts Having Opposite Effects on Leukemic Cells of High and Low Virulence (illustrated).

Edmund W. Sinnott, Columbia University, New York City: A Developmental Analysis of the Relation Between Cell Size and Fruit Size in the Cucurbitaceae (illustrated).

E. Newton Harvey, Alfred L. Loomis, and Garret A. Hobart, III, Princeton University, Princeton, N. J., and Loomis Laboratory, Tuxedo Park, New York: Cerebral Processes During Sleep as Studied by Human Brain Potentials (illustrated).

Robley D. Evans, Massachusetts Institute of Technology, Cambridge, Mass. (introduced by K. T. Compton): Elimination of Radium Impurities From the Blood Stream (illustrated).

Walter R. Miles, Institute of Human Relations, Yale University, New Haven, Conn.: Changes in Respiratory Pattern Associated with Different Types of Vocalization (illustrated).

Edward L. Thorndike, Teachers College, Columbia University, New York City: Individual Differences in Communities (illustrated).

Aleš Hrdlička, United States National Museum, Washington, D. C.: Observations and Measurements on the Members of the National Academy of Sciences. (Read by title.)

Charles B. Davenport, Department of Genetics, Carnegie Institution of Washington, Cold Spring Harbor, N. Y.: Biographical Memoir of George Davidson. (Read by title.)

Karl T. Compton, Massachusetts Institute of Technology, Cambridge, Mass.: Biographical Memoir of Agustus Trowbridge. (Read by title.)

Aleš Hrdlička, United States National Museum, Washington, D. C.: Biographical Memoir of George Sumner Huntington. (Read by title.)

Walter S. Adams, Mount Wilson Observatory, Carnegie Institution of Washington, Pasadena, Calif.: Biographical Memoir of Charles Edward St. John. (Read by title.)

Leonhard Stejneger, United States National Museum, Washington, D. C.: Biographical Memoir of Carl H. Eigenmann. (Read by title.)

Joseph S. Ames, Johns Hopkins University, Baltimore, Md.: Biographical Memoir of Arthur Gordon Webster. (Read by title.)

REPORT OF THE NATIONAL RESEARCH COUNCIL

FOR THE YEAR JULY 1, 1936, TO JUNE 30, 1937

(Prepared in the office of the chairman of the Council, with the assistance of the chairmen of the divisions of the Council)

The following report is presented to the National Academy of Sciences by the National Research Council upon the activities of the Council during the fiscal year July 1, 1936, to June 30, 1937.

OFFICERS OF THE NATIONAL RESEARCH COUNCIL, 1937–38

The officers, members, and committees of the Council for the current year, 1936–37, are given in an appendix to this report (pp. 138–168).

The elected officers of the Council for the ensuing year, July 1, 1937, to June 30, 1938, are as follows:

GENERAL OFFICERS

Honorary chairman: George E. Hale, honorary director, Mount Wilson Observatory, Carnegie Institution of Washington, Pasadena, Calif.

Chairman: Ludvig Hektoen, director, John McCormick Institute for Infectious Diseases, 629 South Wood Street, Chicago, Ill.

Treasurer: Arthur Keith, treasurer, National Academy of Sciences, Washington, D. C.

CHAIRMEN OF THE DIVISIONS OF GENERAL RELATIONS

Federal relations: Lyman J. Briggs, director, National Bureau of Standards, Washington, D. C.

Foreign relations: L. J. Henderson, Abbott and James Lawrence professor of chemistry, Harvard University, Boston, Mass.

Educational relations: William Charles White, chairman, medical research committee, National Tuberculosis Association; pathologist in charge of tuberculosis research, National Institute of Health, Washington, D. C.

CHAIRMEN OF DIVISIONS OF SCIENCE AND TECHNOLOGY

Physical sciences: Luther P. Eisenhart, professor of mathematics and dean of the graduate school, Princeton University, Princeton, N. J.

Engineering and industrial research: Vannevar Bush, vice president of the institute and dean of the graduate school, Massachusetts Institute of Technology, Cambridge, Mass.

Chemistry and chemical technology: Herbert R. Moody, professor of chemistry and director of the chemical laboratories, College of the City of New York, New York City.

Geology and geography: Chester R. Longwell, Henry Barnard Davis professor of geology, Yale University, New Haven, Conn.

Medical sciences: Esmond R. Long, professor of pathology, school of medicine, and director, Henry Phipps Institute, University of Pennsylvania, Philadelphia, Pa.

Biology and agriculture: R. E. Coker, professor of zoology and chairman of the division of natural sciences, University of North Carolina, Chapel Hill, N. C.

Anthropology and psychology: W. S. Hunter, professor of psychology and director of the psychological laboratory, Brown University, Providence, R. I.

ORGANIZATION

The organization of the National Research Council during the past year has remained about the same as it has been since the reorganization of the Council which became effective July 1, 1933. The Council contains 240 members associated with its 11 divisions and its executive board. Of these, 113 are representatives nominated by 83 societies and research institutions which are affiliated with the Council through representative membership; 38 are Government representatives designated by the President as members of the Council in accordance with the Executive order of President Wilson (May 11, 1918) ; 53 are elective members at large; and 36 are members ex officio or on other formal bases.

Besides these, the committee members include about 785 additional names, and there is a body of about 625 past members to whom the Council still turns on occasion for advice and assistance.

The Council has had on its calendar for the past year some 80 projects, large and small and of varying nature and significance. Each of these projects has been in charge of a committee or a supervising board and a group of subcommittees. Of these projects, nine were initiated during the year; six projects have been brought to termination.

A number of the Council's undertakings have been continued for the past 10 or 15 years, or even longer, and their programs have become well known in the fields of work represented.

GENERAL ACTIVITIES OF THE COUNCIL

Fellowships.—This year has marked a change in the method of administration for the post-doctorate fellowships of the National Research Council which have been supported since 1919 by funds provided by the Rockefeller Foundation. In order to effect economies of administration, and to more closely integrate also a fellowship interest of the Council, the advisory committee on fellowships at its meeting in New York on October 10, 1936, recommended that the former national research fellowship board in physics, chemistry, and mathematics, and the board of national research fellowships n the biological sciences be combined into a single board. This new board was subsequently appointed by the executive board of the Council as a body of five members, and in the spring of 1937 assumed charge of the selection of fellows to be appointed in the fields represented by the two former fellowship boards and by special arrangement with the Rockefeller Foundation in the fields of geology, paleontology, and physical geography as well. The medical fellowship board, however, also of five members, is continued as formerly. In the selection of fellows the new board will be assisted by special standing committees in the five technical divisions of the Council concerned, and these committees have been appointed so as to conserve the experience of the Council in the administration of fellowships by including in their membership a number of the members of the two former fellowship boards.

Last spring the fellowship applications considered totaled 162 by the national research fellowships board in the natural sciences and 58 by the medical fellowship board. From these the two boards made 14 reappointments and 35 new appointments for the academic year 1937–38. Of these appointments, after deducting resignations and postponements, the total number in the medical sciences is 13 and in the other sciences 32. The prospect is that somewhat fewer appointments can be made for the following year, but the Council looks forward to the continuation of a considerable number of fellowships each year.

There are now over 1,100 past fellows of the Council. Of these about one-quarter used their fellowships for study abroad and have returned to the United States. Over three-quarters of all the past fellows are engaged in educational and research institutions. About five-eighths of those engaged in academic work are already of professorial grade, and some of the students of these past fellows are beginning to apply for fellowships. A number of past fellows of the Council have been recognized as outstanding scientific men through subsequent fellowship and research appointments and through the receipt of prizes and awards.

TABLE I.—*National Research Council postdoctorate fellowships, as of May 31, 1937*

	Number of fellows active in United States and abroad	Number of new fellows under appointment (not yet active)	Number of past fellows	Total number of fellows appointed [1]	Number of applications considered, spring of 1937	Total number of new applications received	Period of operations (years)
Physical sciences	15	14	454	483	56	1,632	18
Medical sciences	9	10	237	256	58	1,217	15
Biological sciences	19	11	350	409	79	1,496	13
Total	43	35	1,041	1,148	193	4,345	

[1] Including appointees who resigned before entering upon fellowship work.

TABLE II.—*Fellowship expenditures, July 1, 1936, to June 30, 1937*

	Expended for stipends and travel of fellows		Total expenditures for stipends and travel of fellows in United States and abroad	Administrative expenses	Total expenditures	Percentage of administrative expenditures on total expenditures
	In United States	Abroad				
Physical sciences	$28,697.47	$315.55	$29,013.02	[1] $3,197.89	$32,210.91	9.92
Medical sciences	17,428.31	508.33	17,936.64	1,859.23	19,795.87	9.34
Biological sciences	31,405.43	7,981.59	39,387.02	2,288.54	41,675.56	5.49
Total	77,531.21	8,805.47	86,336.68	7,345.66	93,682.34	7.83

[1] Including administrative expenses of the new board, representing both physical and biological sciences, since January 1937.

Grants-in-aid.—The system of general grants-in-aid of research which the Council has maintained for the past 8 years upon funds supplied by the Rockefeller Foundation will be terminated with the current year, except that in the medical sciences there remains a sum of a few thousand dollars which will be available for the support of resear_ch on medical problems until the end of the calendar year 1937.

From these appropriations, 762 grants have been made for the individual support of research in sums averaging less than $600 each. About $30,000 has also been used for conferences during the period and $13,500 for certain cooperative projects of the Council.

It is felt that this fund has served many useful purposes in meeting certain needs which were almost of the nature of an emergency in augmenting and capitalizing other research resources so as to accomplish additional progress, in bridging gaps in which research projects might have lapsed or the interest of an investigator might have languished, and in lending assistance and encouragement to investigators by calling attention to the merit or promise of their work. However, a number of other funds from which grants-in-aid of research may be made are now available through other organizations, and in general the funds available for the support of research in this way are both larger than ever before and better known than formerly.

TABLE III.—*Grants-in-aid awarded during 1936–37*

Grants, 1936–37	Number	Amount
Individual grants:		
Physical sciences	3	$800.00
Chemistry	3	900.00
Geology and geography	7	1,345.00
Medical sciences	14	6,866.00
Biological sciences	5	1,400.00
Anthropology and psychology	3	900.00
Total for individual grants	35	12,211.00

TABLE IV.—*Total grants-in-aid, awarded 1929–37*

Total grants July 1, 1929–June 30, 1937	Number	Amount
Individual grants:		
Physical sciences	110	$61,957.06
Engineering	18	12,560.00
Chemistry	84	48,083.00
Geology and geography	127	59,921.00
Medical sciences	148	60,483.50
Biological sciences	160	69,910.00
Anthropology	60	32,040.75
Psychology	55	24,145.00
Total for individual grants	762	389,109.31
Grants to divisions of the Council:		
Conferences	50	28,752.42
Cooperative projects	5	13,500.00
Total grants to divisions	55	42,252.42
Grand total	817	431,361.73

Patent policy.—Under its general policy of dedicating to the use of the public in such manner as may seem to be most effective the results from research work sponsored by the Council, the Council has met a number of situations for which a solution has been reached by various means in accordance with indications of attendant conditions and usually by the assignment of the interests of the Council to other institutions whose administrative policies are substantially parallel to those of the National Research Council in this respect. It has been apparent in several of these cases that new factors are entering into the relationships of science to the public which affect the uses to be made of results of the research, particularly those which impinge directly upon the public welfare, as do many of the research developments in the field of medicine. In connection with the production of certain new narcotic drugs arising from work of the Council's committee on drug addiction, it has become clear that the manufacture of these drugs ought to be controlled for the protection of the public and to facilitate the enforcement of national laws. The only method available for the necessary control over the manufacture and use of these drugs is by patenting them. An arrangement was therefore effected to meet this situation by consultation between the committee and representatives of several governmental agencies concerned, at a conference on February 10, 1937, by which patents on certain of these substances, which come under the Federal narcotic laws, are assigned on issuance to the Government, thus providing a control over them in this country. In order to extend this control abroad, the Research Corporation of New York, at the request of the Council, applied for patents on these substances in several other countries.

There are also certain substances which are being developed by the committee on drug addiction which do not fall under the jurisdiction of narcotic laws but which, nevertheless, ought to be controlled as to standard and distribution in the interests of the public. Patenting these substances appears to be the only recourse and the Council plans to arrange to assign to the Research Corporation, or another suitable agency, patents on such substances as should thus be controlled.

Borderland problems.—For the past 2 years the Council has been interested in the development of certain borderland problems lying "in between" the regular disciplines in the major fields of science, or requiring for their solution combined contributions from two or more of the traditional disciplines. Two movements for the coordination of borderland research have resulted. One of these is represented by two conferences (in Washington, D. C., June 5 and Dec. 4 and 5, 1936) held by an interdivisional committee of the divisions of geology and geography, chemistry and chemical technology, and physical sciences for the consideration of problems in the field of geology on which attack must be made by means of the methods of physics and chemistry. Several lists of borderland problems have been combined relating to phase equilibrium, the deposition of minerals in the colloid state, radio activity, differential pressures, the physical constants of geological materials, rock deformation, hydrodynamics, and geophysics. A statement of these problems recently published in Science (April 9, 1937, pp. 361–362) invites advice and comment as to the further development of these problems, as well as suggestions as to the location of facilities which can be brought to bear upon them. It is planned later to publish a more extensive report defining the status of a number of the problems as starting points for further investigations. A study has also been published of the problems common to the fields of physical geology, stratigraphy, paleontology, and geography, which seem to have a particularly important hearing at this time.

Resulting directly from these discussions two committees have been appointed by the division of geology and geography, one on density currents which is to prepare plans for studying the movement of masses of water of varying density and burden of sediment, and the other a committee on the preparation of a handbook of physical constants of geological materials.

The second general subject for borderland discussions was represented by a conference (January 23, 1937, in Philadelphia) for the consideration of problems involving the life sciences (medicine, biology, anthropology, and psychology) by an interdivisional committee representing the divisions of medical sciences, of biology and agriculture, and of anthropology and psychology. A number of research topics of broad interest were suggested at this conference including (1) experimental neuroses with a critical scientific study of the basis of psychoanalysis; (2) ageing as an involution process; (3) endocrines, hormones, and auxones in relation to human life; (4) certain aspects of cellular physiology; (5) the genetics of pathogenic organisms in relation to pathological change and resistance, and in relation also to genetic factors in the infected host; (6) aërial dissemination of pathogenic organisms and of allergens; (7) problems of parasitology in animals and man; and (8) education by means of training fellowships in sciences related to the particular science in which a prospective fellow may have been initially trained.

Several of these problems have been taken up for consideration by the three life science divisions of the Research Council and the results which are being obtained in connection with them are referred to later in this report (see pages 56, 59 and 62).

The problem of ageing is one that was already under consideration by the Union of American Biological Societies and was more fully developed at a conference held by the union at Woods Hole June 24–26, 1937. Matters of ageing are also involved among other interests of a committee on cellular physiology appointed by the division of biology and agriculture this spring.

Scientific aids to learning.—Among the projects of the Council newly undertaken is a study of the adaptation of certain modern scientific developments as aids to learning, not only in the formal educational system of the schools and universities, but for purposes of adult education and for the reliable information of the public at large. Among these possibilities are the utilization of the radio both for schoolroom use and for public broadcasting; motion-pictures, with special reference to classroom instruction, field and laboratory observations, and other uses; television; increased utilization of the phonograph in educational work, and improved forms of documentation.

During the past 400 or 500 years the dissemination of knowledge has been mainly dependent upon the printed page, which in turn was a tremendous gain over the written and spoken word to which education as well as all forms of communication had previously been limited. The educational possibilities of these newer developments in science and technology seem to be almost immeasurable in the extension of the uses which have been made of printing. The adaptation of these mechanical devices, however, for the imparting of knowledge successfully and without waste seems to require thoroughgoing studies of the characteristics of these inventions, of their relationship to social usages and of the perceptive processes of the human mind.

Supported by funds from the Carnegie Corporation, the National Research Council has appointed a committee on scientific aids to learning, which has taken offices in New York City and which, with the assistance of a director on full time, will attempt to clarify the bases for the educational utilization of these scientific and technological aids and to formulate a program of investigations leading to their suitable and more extended use.

Patent Office centennial.—At the special request of the Secretary of Commerce, the facilities of the National Academy-Research Council Building were made available for a centennial celebration of the American patent system, which was held on November 23, 1936, under auspices of a national committee appointed by the Secretary. The celebration consisted of a morning session at which four addresses were presented reviewing the contributions which the patent system has made to the progress of American science and invention, and with prospect to the future; and of an afternoon session at which a number of recent scientific developments were demonstrated which may come later to be adapted to industrial uses.

Cooperation with the National Bureau of Standards.—Since 1927 the National Research Council has served as a fiscal agent to hold and disburse funds contributed by industrial corporations and other nongovernmental agencies for the support of special investigations to be carried on at the National Bureau of Standards in accordance with the system maintained at the Bureau for aiding industry in research by receiving research associates to work at the Bureau in cooperation with it and under its direction. These investigations during the past year have related to the following projects: Fire resistance of various building materials; properties of liquids, as antifreeze compounds in automobiles; characteristics of chromel-alumel thermocouples; acoustic properties of building materials; the development of special spark plugs for use in aviation; the physics of plumbing systems, and the chemical and physical properties of wire. The Council has also continued to cooperate with the Bureau in a special advisory capacity through the division of chemistry and chemical technology in investigations upon the stability of photographic film used for record purposes (see . 50). The total sum expended through the Council during 1936-37 for these projects was $13,606.16.

Abstracting and documentation.—Since the conference on abstracting and documentation which was held by the National Research Council on December 9, and 10, 1935, the Council has maintained a committee to engage upon studies of means for improving facilities for the publication and distribution of scientific literature, including especially the abstracting of the literature of the various fields of science. Believing that the major difficulty at present in the dissemination of scientific knowledge through publication is in the cost of printing, the committee has undertaken a study of the costs of publishing scientific periodicals with view to preparing a handbook of information concerning effective and economic forms and styles of printing, and the utilization of new processes of manifolding.

The Research Council has also had interest in the organization of the American Documentation Institute under the auspices of Science Service. This institute is encouraging especially the use of film both for record purposes and also as a new mode of publication suited · to limited distribution at moderate cost of articles and data which it will not be necessary to distribute by more expensive methods of printing.

Biological Abstracts.—With the most careful husbanding of funds remaining in the last appropriation made for the Biological Abstracts by the Rockefeller Foundation, and with aid from the Works Progress Administration and other sources, and with generous effort on the part of its editorial staff, Biological Abstracts has been continued during the past year, concluding volume X with 22,787 references and entering upon volume XI. The highly integrated indexes of all of the annual volumes thus far issued have now been completed (except that for volume V, which is now in press). A number of biological societies have made contributions toward the support of the Abstracts on the basis of voluntary or mandatory membership assessments or by treasury grants, and the editors of most of the American biological journals have cooperated in arranging to provide authors' abstracts of articles published by them. Biological Abstracts continues to receive the volunteer services of its numerous section editors and reviewers, which is indicative of the wide appreciation of the value of this journal. The trustees of the Abstracts are continuing their efforts to obtain additional permanent funds from other sources to provide for the continuation of this journal.

Annual Tables.—During the summer of 1936 the American Commissioners for the Annual Tables of Constants and Numerical Data, supported by an enlarged advisory committee, undertook the solicitation of funds to be contributed from the United States toward the annual expenses of editing and publishing these Tables. A gratifying return was received from the initial solicitation, but it was not possible to meet the full amount that it was hoped could be obtained.

At a meeting in Lucerne on August 20, 1936, of the Commission on Annual Tables of the International Union of Chemistry, the American Commissioners were represented by Dr. J. C. Hostetter, formerly director of development and research of the Corning Glass Works, and by Dr. Edward Bartow, professor of chemistry, University of Iowa. At this meeting Dr Charles Marie, whose vision and energy have created the Annual Tables and who had served as editor of the Tables for 27 years, resigned from active editorial connection. He was at once made honorary secretary general of the Tables and in this capacity is a member of the organization in the Union which is responsible for the Tables. In his place Dr. N. Thon was appointed editor-in-chief of the Tables and Dr. Pierre Auger, secretary-general, and a board of managers was appointed to supervise the editing and publishing of the Tables. A single International Commission, to which the board of managers is to report, also was set up to take the place of two parallel organizations which had previously been in existence under the Union in connection with the Tables. On this new Commission each of the countries contributing to the support of the Tables is to be represented by a delegate.

Certain items of editorial policy for the Tables also were adopted at the Lucerne meeting, including the issuing of the annual volume not later than November of each year, the continuation of the publication of the Tables in English and in French (as has been done since 1925), the addition of an alphabetic index of properties and a general index for chemical substances, and a policy for making the Tables more critically discriminative than previously in the data presented through reference to an increased number of scientific atuhorities.

At the Madrid meeting of the International Union of Chemistry in 1934 a grant of 150,000 francs was made to the Tables in order to bring them up to date (for 1935) through the publication of volume XI, and this volume is now being prepared.

The National Research Council has paid over on order of the Paris office of the Tables the last installment ($1,000) in the appropriation of $18,000 made by the Rockefeller Foundation in 1932 toward the support of Annual Tables.

Central purposes fund.—The central purposes fund provided for the Council by the Rockefeller Foundation, has been used in part to augment the general administrative resources of the Council, in part for the expenses of the Government Relations and Science Advisory Committee of the National Academy of Sciences, which is also a committee of the National Research Council, and in part for conferences. The fund is also available for the support of participation in certain international relationships of science. Allotments from this year's conference portion of the central purposes fund have been as follows:

Conference on borderland problems in physics, chemistry, and geology, Washington, D. C., December 4–5, 1936.
Conference on problems of parasitology, Philadelphia, January 2, 1937.
Conference on borderland problems in the life sciences, Philadelphia, January 23, 1937.
Conference on patent problems of the committee on drug addiction, Washington, D. C., February 10, 1937.
Meeting of the committee on the ethnological utilization of motion pictures, Chicago, March 6, 1937.
Meeting of the committee on a handbook of physical constants of geological materials, Washington, D. C., April 16, 1937.
Conference on experimental neuroses, Washington, D. C., April 17–18, 1937.
Meeting of the committee on problems of neurotic behavior, New Haven, Conn., June 12–13, 1937.
Meeting of the committee on the ecology of grasslands in North America, Scotts Bluff, Nebr., June 18–19, 1937.
Meetings of the committee on syphilis, Washington, D. C., July 17 and September 18, 1937.

Library.—On account of necessary economies the National Research Council last year reduced the activities of its former research information service to those mainly of a reference library for the purpose of providing the Council with information upon movements with which it may be connected, to meet so far as its facilities permit requests for sources of scientific data, and to refer to competent advisers technical and scientific questions which may be received. The resources of the library consist mainly of general reference works and source books in the sciences, of abstract journals, directories, compilations of data, and other materials serving to orient the Council in regard to scientific organizations and relationships.

During the past year the librarian has been engaged in a compilation of the third edition of the Handbook of Scientific and Technical Societies of the United States and Canada, in cooperation with the National Research Council of Canada, which will be published in the fall of 1937. This compilation will include 930 organizations for the United States and its dependencies and 143 for Canada.

The librarian has also assembled certain data concerning the achievement of past fellows of the Council and has assisted in the solicitation of funds for the Annual Tables and has revised the list of international scientific congresses held since 1930.

By special arrangement made on recommendation of the trustees of the International Critical Tables upon the completion of the publication of these Tables the Council retains the balance remaining from royalties for the sale of the Tables as an invested fund the income from which is used for the purchase of books and periodicals for the Council's library. The greater part of the royalties from the sale of these Tables was used to complete the editorial work upon them, but the balance remaining, together with royalties subsequently received, amounts (as of June 30, 1937) to $10,538.58, of which $10,037.22 has been productively invested. From the income from the funds invested the sum of $144.63 was spent during the year to increase the reference materials of the library.

Summary statement.—Through the courtesy of Science a brief Summary Statement of the Activities of the National Research Council, 1936-37, has been prepared and published (Science, vol. 86, pp. 315-320, October 8, 1937), outlining the major undertakings of the Council during the past year.

AMERICAN GEOPHYSICAL UNION

The American Geophysical Union held its eighteenth meeting in Washington on April 28, 29, and 30, 1937, and a regional meeting at Denver, Colo., between the dates June 21 and 26 in conjunction with the summer meeting of the American Association for the Advancement of Science for the Section of Hydrology and the South Continental Divide Snow-survey Conference.

The Union was established in 1919 as the American Section of the International Union of Geodesy and Geophysics to promote the study of problems relating to the figure and physics of the earth. The executive committee of the American Geophysical Union is a committee of the executive board of the National Research Council. During the past year the membership of the Union has increased to 928, a gain of about 160 since the previous meeting. This membership is divided into seven sections relating to geodesy, seismology, meteorology, terrestrial magnetism and electricity, oceanography, volcanology, and hydrology, corresponding to sections of the International Union of Geodesy and Geophysics. Thirty-three members of the American Geophysical Union attended the Seventh Triennial Assembly of the International Union at Edinburgh, Scotland, September 17 to 26, 1936. The American delegation presented the invitation of the American Geophysical Union to the International Union to hold its next meeting in Washington, D. C., in 1939, and this invitation has been accepted.

The papers presented at the meeting of the American Geophysical Union have been published in the Transactions of the Union (2 volumes, 663 pages), and an abbreviated account of the meeting will be found in Science (vol. 86, pp. 102–104, July 13, 1937).

At the meeting in April 1937, special resolutions were adopted expressing appreciation to the Smithsonian Institution and the United States Geological Survey for cooperation in projects promoted by the Union; to the Navy Department for the continuation of the system of radio time signals issued by the Bureau of Navigation and for the organization of the third expedition for the study of gravity at sea from September 1936 to January 1937; to the American Telephone & Telegraph Co. for the loan of a crystal chronometer for use on this gravimetric expedition, and to the American Philosophical Society for a grant of funds to aid the expedition. Another resolution endorsed the establishment of the seismological observatory at Pennsylvania State College. Other resolutions commended the eastern section of the Seismological Society of America upon the formation of a committee on amateur seismology, the Blue Hill Meteorological Observatory of Harvard University for its projected 5-year program of research (of great importance on account of its bearing upon safety in flight), and a number of Government agencies for preserving invaluable hydrological records.

FINANCES

The total amount of money expended through the National Research Council during the fiscal year 1936–37 (exclusive of the purchase of temporary securities) was $474,284.43. The following table gives the distribution of these expenses among the major types of activities of the Council in comparison with those of the previous year:

TABLE V.—*Classified expenditures of the National Research Council July 1, 1936, to June 30, 1937*

	1935–36		1936–37	
	Amount	Percentage	Amount	Percentage
Fellowships [1]	$123,579.80	23.6	$97,505.59	20.6
Designated project funds	228,844.22	43.7	241,166.53	50.8
Administered funds	75,160.09	14.3	45,377.57	9.6
General maintenance	96,244.63	18.4	90,234.74	19.0
Total	523,831.64	100.0	474,284.43	100.0

[1] Because of slight variations in accounting procedure these figures differ somewhat from those given in the report of the treasurer of the Council.

The distribution of the expenditures for post-doctorate fellowships is given in table II, page 31. In addition to $94,280.59 expended for post-doctorate fellowships, other special fellowship funds have been expended in connection with investigations upon drug addiction amounting during the year to $3,100.

37878—38——4

Funds amounting to $241,166.53, which are somewhat in excess of corresponding funds for the previous year (1935–36), were contributed from outside sources for the support of special research projects of the Council. These projects are mainly of a cooperative nature and include some of the larger current undertakings of the Council, such as programs of investigation in problems of sex, the chemistry and physiology of narcotic drugs, the biological effects of radiation, and highway construction and operation, and are all in charge of committees or boards of the Council or cooperating agencies. Of this sum, $6,487.26 (2.7 percent) was contributed from industrial and technical sources.

TABLE VI.—*Specially designated project funds, expenditures*

	1935–36	1936–37
Grants-in-aid	$43,790.36	$15,060.74
Highway research	26,522.12	64,427.70
Research in problems of sex	73,345.01	70,442.53
Research on drug addiction	50,590.00	50,799.77
Effects of radiation on living organisms	24,438.95	24,040.59
Conferences		7,243.07
Other projects	10,159.78	9,152.13
Total	228,846.22	241,166.53

The National Research Council also administers certain funds placed in its hands for the support of investigations conducted by Government bureaus or other agencies in the technical programs of which the Council has no part, its responsibility being limited only to the administration of these funds on the order of the controlling body. In several instances these agencies have been organizations resulting from movements initiated by the National Research Council. Among operations of this nature the Council has also handled funds since 1927 for the support of special investigations carried on at the National Bureau of Standards in accordance with the system of research associates which the Bureau has been authorized to recognize in its operations. The Council has also administered funds provided by the Rockefeller Foundation for the editorial work of Biological Abstracts; funds contributed by the Foundation toward the support of the Annual Tables of Constants and Numerical Data, which are published in Paris, and funds also for the Society for Research in Child Development.

TABLE VII.—*Funds administered as fiscal agent, expenditures*

	1935–36	1936–37
Biological Abstracts	$43,472.23	$23,308.30
Investigations conducted by the National Bureau of Standards	12,620.16	13,606.16
Annual Tables of Constants and Numerical Data	492.35	752.15
Science Advisory Board	7,231.51	
Society for Research in Child Development	5,405.64	7,710.96
Other projects	5,939.10	
Total	75,160.99	45,377.57

The funds used for the administrative expenses of the Council ($90,234.74) were derived largely from the income from the endowment of the Council provided by the Carnegie Corporation of New York but were augmented by certain special appropriations from the Carnegie Corporation and from the Rockefeller Foundation for this purpose. Of this sum, $89,733.10 was disbursed under the provisions of the general administrative budget of the Council for the current year (set up as $100,450) and $501.64 was expended to meet deferred obligations incurred under previous budgets and for miscellaneous minor purposes. These administrative expenditures this year amount to $6,009.89 less than those of last year and constitute somewhat less than one-fifth of the total expenditures of the Council in comparison with expenses for administrative purposes of about two-elevenths of the total expenditures of the Council last year. The administrative expenses include the general expenses of the divisions and committees of the Council, executive and clerical salaries, publications, supplies, service costs (exclusive of the general maintenance of the building and grounds), and similar charges.

A detailed statement of the finances of the National Research Council will be found in the report of the treasurer of the National Academy of Sciences and National Research Council (pp. 87 to 93).

PUBLICATIONS OF THE NATIONAL RESEARCH COUNCIL

During the year one paper has been issued and one is in press in the Bulletin series of the National Research Council, and several miscellaneous publications have been issued.

BULLETIN SERIES

No. 99. Mineral Nutrition of Farm Animals. H. H. Mitchell and F. J. McClure. Prepared under the auspices of the Division of Biology and Agriculture, National Research Council. April 1937. Pages, 135.

No. 100. An Experimental Study of the Problem of Mitogenetic Radiation. Alexander Hollaender and Walter D. Claus. Prepared under the auspices of the Division of Biology and Agriculture, National Research Council. In press.

MISCELLANEOUS PUBLICATIONS

Organization and Members, 1936–37. December 1936. Pages, 67.

Annual Report, National Research Council, 1935–36. Separate reprint from the Annual Report of the National Academy of Sciences, 1935–36. June 1937. Pages, 88.

Transactions of the American Geophysical Union, Seventeenth Annual Meeting, April 30 and May 1 and 2, 1936, Washington, D. C. Parts I and II. Pages, 563.

PUBLICATIONS OF THE HIGHWAY RESEARCH BOARD OF THE DIVISION OF ENGINEERING AND INDUSTRIAL RESEARCH

Proceedings, Sixteenth Annual Meeting, November 18–20, 1936, Washington, D. C. Pages, 390.

Highway Research Abstracts. Nos. 32–42, 1936–37 (monthly, except December and August).

Progress Report of Project Committee on Roadside Development. June 1937. Pages, 86 (mimeographed).

SALES

Receipts from sales of publications of the National Research Council from July 1, 1936 to June 30, 1937 have amounted to $1,994.08, of which $1,049.97, under authorization of the Council effective since 1931, has been credited to the rotating fund for the publication of reports of committees of the division of physical sciences, and $195.57, by special action of the Administrative Committee of the National Research Council, has been credited to the committee on animal nutrition of the division of biology and agriculture.

DIVISIONS OF GENERAL RELATIONS

In addition to its contacts with the Federal Government through the Government Relations and Science Advisory Committee of the National Academy of Sciences, which has also been made a committee of the National Research Council, and through other direct relations between divisions of the Council and scientific bureaus of the Government, the Research Council maintains in its organization a Division of Federal Relations composed of representatives nominated by the National Academy in consultation with the governmental departments and designated for this service by the President in accordance with the Executive order of May 11, 1918, for the purpose of providing effective cooperation between the Council and the Government. This body holds itself in readiness to consider general matters relating to the scientific interests of the Government and is an earnest of the desire of the Council to be of aid to the Government in any way in which its facilities will serve.

Until this year the Council has also maintained a division of states relations to represent the interest of the Council in the progress of research in State scientific agencies aside from the State colleges and universities. During the war the Council had numerous contacts with various State agencies. This division of the Council conducted in its early years a number of studies upon conditions affecting the course of research in State governmental agencies and published several reports upon these studies. In later years, however, the interests of science in State agencies have come to be represented more adequately by other means than had been possible through this division of the Council. After prolonged consideration, therefore, the executive board at its meeting on April 28, 1937, upon recommendation of the executive committee of the division of states relations, took action to discontinue this division at the close of the year. It has been noted, however, that at any time when it may appear that the National Research Council should give attention again to this group of relationships a committee of the Council can at once be appointed to do so directly or to develop plans for giving these relationships renewed consideration.

A division of educational relations is also maintained by the Council to represent its interests in the welfare of research in institutions of higher education, an interest which is based upon the inseparable connection between research and teaching. This division includes in its membership representatives of a number of the college and university organizations of the country.

DIVISION OF FOREIGN RELATIONS

L. J. HENDERSON, Chairman, ex officio
WILBUR J. CARR and FRANK SCHLESINGER, Vice Chairman

International dues.—For the past 2 years, 1935 and 1936, the dues of the United States in the International Council of Scientific Unions and in the seven international unions to which the National Research Council has adhered, have been paid by the Government through the Department of State, and provision has been made for the payment of these dues for 1937. These obligations amount in total, on the present basis of foreign exchange at par, to about $6,000. The unions utilize these funds mainly for current administrative expenses, for publications, and for the expenses of their meetings, which are held triennially except that of the International Union of Chemistry which meets biennially. These funds are not used for the travel expenses of national representatives attending meetings of the unions, and the representatives of the United States pay their expenses personally or from allowances from their institutions. The International Astronomical Union and the International Union of Geodesy and Geophysics also make grants from their funds for the support of cooperative international research undertakings.

Representatives at international scientific meetings.—The National Research Council was represented at international scientific meetings abroad during the past year as follows:

Twelfth Conference of International Union of Chemistry, Lucerne, Switzerland, August 16 to 22; by six councillors and nine delegates.

Sixth General Assembly of the International Union of Geodesy and Geophysics, Edinburgh, September 17 to 25, 1936; by 33 representatives.

The Sixteenth Congress of Industrial Chemistry which had been announced to meet in Barcelona from October 18 to 24, 1936, was indefinitely postponed. The Research Council has also appointed 10 representatives to attend the Seventeenth International Geological Congress, which is to convene in Moscow and Leningrad July 20 to 29, 1937.

The Council also participated in the preparations for the Third World Power Conference and other international conferences held in Washington in September 1936. (See p. 48.)

International Council of Scientific Unions.—The meeting of the International Council of Scientific Unions in London, April 26 to May 4, 1936, was held under auspices of the Royal Society. It was attended by 98 representatives of seven of the unions affiliated with the International Council and of 20 of the countries adhering to it. The National Research Council was represented by three delegates:

Dean Wallace B. Donham, Graduate School of Business Administration, Harvard University, Boston, Mass.

Dr. Lewis W. Hackett, Rockefeller Foundation, 49 West Forty-ninth Street, New York City.

Prof. W. A. Noyes, Jr., Brown University, Providence, R. I.

At this meeting a notable step was taken after several years of negotiation looking toward cooperation between the International Council of Scientific Unions and the Intellectual Cooperation Organization of the League of Nations, and this arrangement is to be considered with view to confirmation at a joint meeting of the Executive Committee of the International Council with the Scientific Experts Committee of the Intellectual Cooperation Organization to be held in Paris on July 9 and 10, 1937.

Under this arrangement the International Council of Scientific Unions is to act as an advisory agency to the Intellectual Cooperation Organization of the League. The Intellectual Cooperation Organization is to consult the International Council on all scientific questions referred to it, and the council is, in turn, to advise with the Intellectual Cooperation Organization upon all international questions affecting the organization of scientific work. A representative of each body will attend the major meetings of the other body. The International Council is to appoint committees in accordance with its usual procedures to study questions on which these two bodies are to collaborate. The manner in which practical work to be carried out is to be determined in each case by mutual agreement, with the International Council remaining free to take such steps as it considers appropriate in any case in which the Intellectual Cooperation Organization does not act. The executive organs of the Intellectual Cooperation Organization will provide the secretariat for technical committees appointed under this agreement and will, to a certain limit, meet the cost of committee meetings. Through the relationships between the International Council of Scientific Unions and the several international unions in special fields, facilities are thus provided for cooperation between these unions also and the Intellectual Cooperation Organization of the League.

Scientific work in the Pacific area.—The committee on Pacific investigations has been in touch with the Hold-Over Committee of the Fifth Pacific Science Congress in regard to the formulation of plans for holding the sixth congress in this series. It has not been found possible, however, to make definite arrangements for the time and place of the next meeting. Meanwhile the commitee has been active in the encouragement of certain investigations on scientific problems pertaining to the Pacific region, especially in the field of ethnology.

The Council also has appointed three American committees to cooperate with international committees under auspices of the Pacific Science Association in the fields of oceanography, of land classification and utilization in the Pacific, and of seismology.

DIVISIONS OF SCIENCE AND TECHNOLOGY

DIVISION OF PHYSICAL SCIENCES

R. A. MILLIKAN, Chairman; HENRY A. BARTON, Vice Chairman

Publications.—The principal contribution of the division of physical sciences has been the publication of monographic treatises in fields of current research. Of these, 45 have now been published, most of them in the Bulletin series of the Council. Two of these have been translated into European languages, and several have been reissued or revised. Last fall a reserve stock of the monograph on Oceanography (N. R. C. Bulletin No. 85, July 1932), which is a part of the series constituting the comprehensive treatise on The Physics of the Earth was prepared for distribution. An additional number in this se·   ·strial Magnetism and Electricity, is now in preparation;

also a monograph on Hydrology, and a second monograph on Meteorology to replace an earlier publication on this subject (Bulletin No. 79, 1931).

Among other publications sponsored by this division, but not published by the Council, is a treatise on Measurement of Radiant Energy by Dr. W. E. Forsythe (McGraw Hill Book Co., Inc., June 1937, 452 pages). A Glossary of Physical Terms, the preparation of which was begun some years ago by a committee of the division, discharged last year, is also in press (McGraw Hill Book Co., Inc.), containing definitions for some 3,250 technical terms of physics and related sciences, having been completed by the former chairman of the committee, Prof. LeRoy D. Weld, of Coe College, Cedar Rapids, Iowa.

Other undertakings in progress are the preparation of a Bibliography of Mathematical Tables and Aids to Computation (including both instruments and tables), and a Bibliography of Orthogonal Polynomials of about 1,500 titles.

Completion of the treatise on line spectra of the elements which has been in progress for several years has been delayed on account of lack of observational data upon the remote ultraviolet and infrared regions of the spectrum for many substances. The completion of this work would be facilitated by the adaptation of bolometric technique to the study of line spectra with a special application to the spectra of alkaline earths.

Washington Biophysical Institute.—This year it has been possible to carry into effect a plan proposed in 1933 for the encouragement of quantitative studies in biology and upon the significance of physical phenomena in life and work for the development of special apparatus for aiding such studies involving also the adaptation of methods and instruments of research in the physical sciences for use in biological investigations. To this end the Washington Biophysical Institute was set up under auspices of the division of physical sciences and the trustees of the institute are regarded as a committee of the division. The initiation of operations by the institute was delayed, however, until last winter when the Rockefeller Foundation appropriated $75,000 to the Council for this purpose over a 5-year period. The active work of the institute was started in April 1937 with the cooperation of the National Bureau of Standards and the National Institute of Health, and is being directed first toward the development of special apparatus including a near-infrared recording spectrometer with glass prisms, a salt prism, infrared spectrograph and auxiliary equipment for use with the standard ultraviolet spectrograph in quantitative absorption analyses.

American Section, International Scientific Radio Union.—The American Section of the International Scientific Radio Union held its annual meeting in Washington, D. C., on April 30, 1937, in conjunction with the Institute of Radio Engineers for the presentation and discussion of some 28 technical papers (attendance about 190). The next (sixth) meeting of the International Union will be held in Rome in September 1938.

DIVISION OF ENGINEERING AND INDUSTRIAL RESEARCH

VANNEVAR BUSH, Chairman
HOWARD A. POILLON, Vice Chairman and MAURICE HOLLAND, Director

(Office: Room 801, Engineering Societies Bldg., 29 West 39th St., New York City)

Electrical insulation.—The ninth annual conference of the committee on electrical insulation was held at the Massachusetts Institute of Technology on November 5, 6, and 7, 1936, with a registered attendance of about 76. The three technical sessions were devoted to discussions of physical and chemical theories of dielectrics, the oxidation and stability of insulating fluids, and new insulating methods and their applications. Most of the 26 papers presented at this meeting have been published in technical engineering and physical journals. The annual report of the chairman of the committee has usually taken the form of a brief, comprehensive review of the more important contributions made during the year in experimental research upon dielectrics and insulation. (The report for the ninth meeting, Recent Progress in Dielectric Research has been published in Electrical Engineering, vol. 55; pp. 1180–1185; November 1936. Abstracts of these papers are issued in planograph form.)

Two subcommittees of the main committee reporting the chemical and physical aspects of electrical insulation have each held two meetings during the year, and a third committee is in charge of plans for bringing out, from time to time, monographic reports in this field in a series in which four numbers have now been issued.

The next conference of the committee will be held in New York City November 4 and 5, 1937, under the host auspices of the Consolidated Edison Co.

European laboratories tour.—Under auspices of the division of engineering and industrial research of the Council a special tour was arranged this summer to enable industrial and financial executives of the United States to visit government, university, and industrial laboratories in European countries. The party contained about 25 members and sailed from New York on the S. S. *Normandie* on May 18, 1937 and disbanded at Heidelberg on June 29. About 40 laboratories were visited in three European countries. The visits were arranged through the courtesy of the Department of Scientific and Industrial Research in England, the Verein Deutscher Ingenieure in Germany, and the Under Secretary of Scientific Research in France. The preparations for the tour were greatly aided in the United States by a number of commercial and industrial organizations.

Members of the tour have returned impressed by the strong momentum of scientific research in Germany under the stimulus of governmental directive and national esprit, the close and successful relations between the government and industry in England in matters of research, and the significance of the recent establishment of the office of Under Secretary for Scientific Research in the Department of Foreign Affairs in France and of the initial appropriation of 10,000,000 francs·for the support of research under the supervision of this new office of the Government.

Highway research board.—Since 1921 the National Research Council has been under contract with the Bureau of Public Roads to render services in the encouragement and coordination of research in the highway field. For this purpose the Council maintains a highway research board which has numerous contacts with State highway commissions, with engineering departments in educational institutions, and with corporations dealing in highway construction materials and road-making machinery.

The sixteenth annual meeting of the board was held in Washington, D. C., on November 19 and 20, 1936, with a total registered attendance of 415 from various sections of the country and with delegations from Canada and from Mexico. The attendance included representatives of State highway commissions and agencies of the Federal Government, engineering schools, and university departments, and automotive and other agencies. Committee reports and research papers were presented at this meeting relating to highway design, materials and construction, highway maintenance, highway finance and administration, highway transportation economics, traffic surveys, and traffic control, and roadside development (jointly with the American Association of State Highway Officials). A special symposium was included upon soil stability as the basis for durable road construction. The report of this meeting has been published in the proceedings of the board (390 pages). The board continues to issue the Highway Research Abstracts (10 monthly numbers per year).

In addition to the encouragement of research work on highway planning and construction the board received a request last winter from the Bureau of Public Roads to undertake a study of highway safety on special funds provided by the Bureau for this purpose. These studies as a whole are to include: (1) The compilation of a digest of existing information relating to research on automobile driving, (2) studies of accident records of drivers, (3) methods of identifying the reckless drivers, (4) tests for drivers both of known and of unknown accident history, (5) analysis of records of serious accidents, (6) analysis of the utility of the technical data which are taken immediately at the time and place of accidents, and (7) methods of accident reporting.

In meeting this request the board has received generous cooperation from a number of State highway and police organizations in making their accident records available for study. In June 1937, the board presented a report to the Bureau of Public Roads dealing particularly with (1) the lack of uniformity in State motor-vehicle laws as a contributing cause to highway accidents, (2) the characteristics and habits of automobile drivers and means for identifying dangerous drivers, and (3) improved methods of reporting accidents needed for the study of the cause and prevention of accidents. These highway safety studies will be continued during the coming year and will include especially analyses of accident records and driver test ratings for 2 previous years with view to determining accident causes and the value of driver tests in identifying dangerous drivers, and also a study of highway speeds and their relation to various highway warning signs and signals and the part which speed plays in causing highway accidents.

Bartlett award.—During 1931 a group of men active in highway construction wishing to establish a mark of recognition of high achievement in the field of highway research, construction, and management, and wishing also to perpetuate the spirit of friendship and helpfulness which Mr. George S. Bartlett had brought into his work in the highway field, established by subscription a fund, the income from which is used for the annual presentation of a plaque known as the George S. Bartlett award.

The award is conferred annually upon an individual who has made an outstanding contribution to highway progress, the recipient being selected by a board of award composed of a representative from the American Association of State Highway Officials, from the American Road Builders' Association, and from the highway research board of the National Research Council. The recipients of the award have been:

1931, Thomas H. MacDonald, chief, U. S. Bureau of Public Roads;
1932, Arthur N. Johnson, dean of the College of Engineering, University of Maryland;
1933, James H. MacDonald, former commissioner of the Connecticut State Highway Department;
1934, Frank F. Rogers, former commissioner of the Michigan State Highway Department;
1935, Edward N. Hines, vice chairman, Wayne County Road Commission, Detroit, Mich.;
1936, Thomas R. Agg, dean, division of engineering, Iowa State College of Agriculture and Mechanic Arts.

Hydraulic friction.—The program which the committee on hydraulic friction set up last year has been necessarily modified by rapid advances in this field and by the publication of recent contributions of investigators upon the mechanism of turbulent flow and by other publications introducing certain new concepts which will cause revision of the former plans of the committee for the publication of a monograph on the present status of knowledge of hydraulic friction. The related problem of turbulence in the atmosphere is also demanding attention in connection with the program which the committee is following.

Phosphorus and sulphur in steel.—The committee on the effects of phosphorus and sulphur in steel of the American Society for Testing Materials, in which the division of engineering and industrial research has maintained a representative member for some years, has submitted its final report to the society and has accordingly been discharged. The work of this committee covered three investigations upon "residual" sulphur in steel, one on "added" sulphur, and one on the effects of phosphorus in steel.

World Power Conference.—During the greater part of the year preceding the Third World Power Conference which was held in Washington, D. C. between the dates September 7 and 12, 1936, the office of the division lent its assistance to the preparations for this Conference, particularly in arranging tours before and after the Conference to enable its members to visit important industrial centers and localities of power development in the eastern part of the United States. About 500 visitors and members of the Congress participated in these tours. During the same period a meeting was also held in Washington of the International Commission on Large Dams, and an International Conference on Letter Symbols of Heat and Thermodynamics in New York City.

The National Research Council was also one of the agencies invited by the Government to cooperate in supporting the Conference on up-stream engineering which was held in Washington, September 22-23, 1936.

DIVISION OF CHEMISTRY AND CHEMICAL TECHNOLOGY

HERBERT R. MOODY, Chairman

International Union of Chemistry.—The National Research Council was represented by a full delegation of six councillors and nine delegates as follows, at the Twelfth Conference of the International Union of Chemistry at Lucerne, Switzerland, August 16 to 22, 1936:

Councillors.—Edward Bartow, vice president of the Union, professor of chemistry and head of the department of chemistry and chemical engineering, State University of Iowa, Iowa City, Iowa; Roger Adams, professor of organic chemistry, University of Illinois, Urbana, Ill.; Gustavus J. Esselen, president, Gustavus J. Esselen, Inc., 857 Boylston Street, Boston, Mass.; J. Clyde Hostetter, vice president, Hartford-Empire Co., Hartford, Conn.; Austin M. Patterson, professor of chemistry and vice president, Antioch College, Yellow Springs, Ohio; Robert E. Swain, professor of chemistry, Stanford University, Stanford, University, Calif.

Delegates.—Frederick J. Bates, principal physicist, National Bureau of Standards, Washington, D. C.; Wallace R. Brode, associate professor of chemistry, Ohio State University, Columbus, Ohio; Emma P. Carr, professor of chemistry, Mount Holyoke College, South Hadley, Mass.; John B. Ekeley, professor of chemistry and head of the department of chemistry, University of Colorado, Boulder, Colo.; Colin G. Fink, professor of chemical engineering, Columbia University, New York City; James F. Norris, professor of organic chemistry, Massachusetts Institute of Technology, Cambridge, Mass.; Atherton Seidell, chemist, National Institute of Health, Washington, D. C.; Alexander Silverman, professor of chemistry, University of Pittsburgh, Pittsburgh, Pa.; Charles L. Reese, Wilmington, Del., was unable to be present and his place was taken informally by Adolph Zimmerli, consulting chemical engineer, New Brunswick, N. J.

Nineteen of the twenty-seven countries adhering to the union were represented at this conference. It was impossible for a Spanish delegation to be present. At the meeting of the union authorization was given to make it possible for alternates to represent the regular national members of various commissions of the union at meetings at which these regular representatives are unable to be present. The Thirteenth Conference of the Union and the Tenth International Congress of Pure and Applied Chemistry will be held in Rome, May 15 to 21, 1938.

Colloid chemistry.—The committee on colloid chemistry has cooperated with the colloid division of the American Chemical Society in arranging for the fourteenth colloid symposium which was held at the University of Minnesota, June 10 and 11, and at the Mayo Foundation at Rochester on June 12, 1937 (attendance about 275). Some 30 papers were presented for discussion, most of which will be published in the October and November 1937 issues of the Journal of Physical Chemistry. The fifteenth symposium will be held at the Massachusetts Institute of Technology, Cambridge, June 9 to 11, 1938.

Construction and equipment of chemical laboratories.—The committee on construction and equipment of chemical laboratories has been active (1) in giving general advice to laboratory builders through interviews and by making available the large number of plans and the data which have been assembled in the office of the chairman of the committee, and (2) by arranging for the testing of special materials, furnishings, and technical equipment for laboratory use.

Low-temperature scales.—The committee on low-temperature scales has compiled a list of problems in this field on which research would be desirable. The committee is studying upon the harmonization of several different scales now in use in the lower temperature ranges looking toward the possible development of a generally acceptable new scale. In its work the committee is in close cooperation with the thermometric committee of the International Institute of Refrigeration.

New committees.—The division has appointed new committees on research in cellulose and allied substances, on the application of X-rays to chemistry and chemical technology, and on the application of mathematics to chemistry.

Photochemistry.—The committee on photochemistry now has in preparation its third report summarizing the status of research in this field. The two previous reports were published in the Reprint and Circular Series of the Council No. 81, 1928; No. 96, 1930.

Reproduction of records.—The work conducted for several years at the National Bureau of Standards which has been supported by grants from the Carnegie Corporation and for which this division of the Council has maintained an advisory committee, changed in character last year after certain definite results had been reached in regard to the optimum conditions for the storage of library materials, and investigations were undertaken upon the deterioration of photographic film which is being used more and more for record purposes. This work has been further supported by contributions from several industrial corporations and by cooperation with certain Government bureaus.

The results of work thus far indicate that while nitrate film is both highly combustible and subject to deterioration, acetate film may be expected to be even more durable than the best record papers if preserved under optimum conditions of 50 percent relative humidity and a temperature range of from 70° to 80° F.

The program for these investigations for the coming year will include work upon the effects of light on film, the stability of new kinds of film, preservative and protective treatments to prevent the damage of film by scratching, the effects of contaminated atmosphere on film in storage, expansion and contraction of film, accelerated ageing tests, and the requirements for fine-grained emulsions.

The rapidly increasing use of film for record purposes in libraries and by record agencies of many kinds intensifies the importance of these investigations. In this connection may be mentioned also the interest which the Research Council has had in the organization of the American Documentation Institute under the auspices of Science Service, which is to develop further the use of film for various types of recording and publication.

Ring systems.—The manuscript of the Catalogue of Ring Systems now contains data on about 3,700 systems and is estimated to be approximately 80 percent complete. Spiro systems will also be included in this compendium.

EDSON S. BASTIN, Chairman; ROBERT S. PLATT, Vice Chairman

The work of the division of geology and geography last year, in addition to the activities of its regular committees, was marked by the culmination of a survey which the chairman of the division had been conducting in order to ascertain what American geologists regard as the most important geological problems for investigation at the present time. In this review the comments of some 300 geologists and geographers were requested, and their replies in regard to physical geography, stratigraphy, and paleontology and economic geology have been issued by the division as one of its special publications. Among subjects for research which were suggested were problems relating to the pre-Cambrian which constitutes a very large part of the geological record, certain of the broader problems of metamorphism and dolomitization, which, though one of the most general of geological phenomena, is still only imperfectly understood.

The year has been marked also by cooperation with other major fields of science in the study of borderland problems of geology, physics, and chemistry. (See p. 33.) The conference with representatives of the fields of physics and chemistry has yielded a number of important results looking toward the preparation of a Handbook of Physical Constants of Geological Materials and the undertaking of a new program of investigation on density currents, and has left with the division a number of additional problems for further consideration.

The reports of a number of the committees of the division have been mimeographed for general distribution each year, and constitute a periodical exchange of recent progress in the fields represented.

Accessory minerals.—In its sixth annual report the committee on accessory minerals of crystalline rocks has emphasized the results of recent methods used in studying accessory minerals, particularly magnetic methods which are applicable to pre-Cambrian rocks of the Lake Superior region. The minerals termed "accessory" are not usually present in crystalline rocks in amounts greater than 5 percent, and some minerals which are quite characteristic of recognized types of rock may occur in amounts less than 5 percent. It is, therefore, not the actual amount of accessory minerals present but rather the nature of exceptional minerals found in certain crystallines in addition to those expected according to the usual formulas which is significant. These additional minerals may often be used to trace the source of sediments or the correlation of various formations. Moreover it is likely that these accessory minerals crystallize first in the process of crystallization and that they may contain rare elements which may be constant in a given intrusive and constitute a reliable characteristic for recognition and for comparison with other rocks. The committee has attached to its report its usual abstract bibliography of current literature in this field.

Cooperation with the Bureau of the Census.—The committee on cooperation with the Bureau of the Census has continued to offer its assistance in the geologic shaping and interpretation of various statistics gathered and published by the Bureau, and in this connection has lately been concerned with "(1) the problem of State maps showing the boundaries of minor civil divisions; (2) the determination of the areas of minor civil divisions of the counties; and (3) the separate enumeration of unincorporated population centers." Partly as a result of the committee's advice, the Bureau has undertaken to develop these projects. The committee is advising further in the publication of a new Statistical Atlas of the United States for the 1940 census, including a large-scale population map, to continue the series of these atlases which have been issued for several decades up to 1920. It is believed that a current atlas will be of distinct value to the Government in view of the attention which is being given to present problems of resettlement, regional planning, conservation, and population movements.

Density currents.—One of the new projects undertaken by the division this year arising from the consideration of borderland problems of physics, chemistry, and geology is a study of the behavior of density currents in bodies of water. By such currents is meant the movement of currents without mixing through or over another body of water of different density by reason of temperature, salt content, or silt content. The problem has its applications in studies of the passage of silt-laden waters through reservoirs or at the confluence of rivers or in the meeting of fresh water with tidewater. The problem can also be extended to include similar movements of bodies of air or of the flow of any fluid in relation to another fluid. The first function of this committee will be to determine what data in field and laboratory work are pertinent to the solution of these problems, and then to arrange for obtaining these data for locations favorable for study, and to suggest appropriate programs of research.

Areas of international concern.—Believing that many international problems have their origin in geographic conditions which are susceptible of clarification by systematic research, the division has appointed a committee on research in areas of international concern. The objective of this committee will be to attempt to define critical problems of international moment in such terms that definite research contributions may be made upon them. Such problems, for instance, are found arising in connection with international boundary zones, corridors for access to the sea and other transportation routes, sources of supply for important raw materials of commerce and industry, areas of colonization and settlement, lines of communication, adjacent regions of poorly balanced resources, and similar matters.

International Geographical Union.—The next International Geographic Congress will be held in Amsterdam July 18 to 28, 1938, under the auspices of the International Geographical Union. In the program of this Congress sections will be organized representing cartography, physical geography, oceanography, human geography, economic geography, colonial geography, historical geography, and the history of geography, geographic landscapes, and methodology and education in geography.

Land classification.—The committee on land classification has been engaged in promoting the use of air photographs as aids in geographical fieldwork and in studying the possibility of making arrangements for the use in geographical research of air photographs with the assistance of several Federal and other agencies.

Measurement of geologic time.—The committee on measurement of geologic time has been engaged for several years in studying the bearing which the rate of atomic decomposition of certain elements found in radioactive minerals may have upon the age of the rocks containing these minerals. At the present stage of knowledge of geology, physics, and chemistry, this committee feels that a better indication of age can be obtained from this source than from other suggested criteria, such as the relative proportions of oxygen or hydrogen isotopes in the waters of minerals, astronomical considerations, nonglacial varves, the development of enamel ridges of molars of proboscidians, or core samples from sediments from the ocean bottom, etc., although all these criteria throw light upon the general problem of the age of the earth. The committee's attention has been turned toward finding and reducing the probable error of age determinations made from the helium ratio and the lead ratio. Such a committee as this constitutes in effect a seminar at large with members and correspondents both in the United States and abroad, and the annual reports of the committee (mimeographed) present résumés of advances in this field.

Micropaleontology.—The work fostered by the committee on micropaleontology has received a great stimulus during the past year in the development of means for taking specimens of deposits on the ocean floor by core-sampling devices, penetrating under favorable conditions 10 feet or more into these deposits. Interpreted on the basis of knowledge of the microplankton today, particularly the Foraminifera, these samples throw much light upon the methods and rates of sedimentation, and the characteristics of the micro fauna and flora of prehistoric seas. It is evident, however, that further studies of living plankton are necessary for the full interpretation of paleontologic material. The committee serves to summarize contributions from many sources upon the paleontological relationships of micro-organisms which require special methods of study but which are valuable in the recognition and correlation of geological horizons.

Ore deposition.—The committee on ore deposition has in preparation a volume on the genesis of lead and zinc ores in the Mississippi Valley and the significant geologic features of these deposits. The committee is also peparing a symposium on the influence of structural geological features on ore deposition.

Paleobotany.—The committee on paleobotany serves in the nature of an extended seminar for advanced workers in this field. A bibliography of current literature is published each year, and the committee promotes the contribution of papers for the programs of meetings of societies which include paleobotany among their interests.

The committee reports that an agreement was reached in the Second International Congress for the Study of Stratigraphy of Carboniferous Rocks, which was held at Heerland, the Netherlands, September 9 to 12, 1935, on an international standard nomenclature of coal petrography in order to harmonize discrepancies in the use of names in different countries (Nomenclature of Coal Petrography; Fuel in Science and Practice, London, vol. 15, January 1936, pp. 14 and 15).

Paleoecology.—Continuing its plan of previous years the committee on paleoecology has encouraged studies of the ecological relationships of various paleoecological groups, including ·Mollusca, Brachiopoda, Cephalopoda, and Protozoa. In addition to reviews of the ecology of Porifera, Arthropoda, Trilobata, Vertebrata, and Paleozoic plants contributed in earlier years, there remains to be treated the relationships of the Echinoderms, Bryozoa, and Coelenterata. The committee feels, however, that with the publication of these summaries much of its original purpose will have been accomplished in bringing stratigraphers, paleontologists, and teachers of geology to appreciate the importance of the ecology of life forms in interpreting sedimentary structures, and the committee has, therefore, requested that it be discontinued.

Physical constants of geological materials.—One of the results of the conferences held last year for the consideration of borderland problems in geology, chemistry, and physics was the organization of an interdivisional committee for the preparation of a Handbook of Physical Constants of Geological Materials. The purpose of this handbook will be to present critically selected physical data concerning the materials with which geologists deal, including average analyses of typical rocks, coefficients of thermal expansion and of compressibility for rocks, minerals, and glasses, velocities of wave propagation, strength and plastic deformation of rocks, specific heats of minerals, melting points, density and viscosity of plastic materials, thermal conductivity, magnetic characteristics, radio activity, and ageing.

Scientific results of drilling.—A year ago a new group was appointed by this division to promote contributions to the subsurface geology of the United States through the preservation and study of records of well drilling both for oil and for water. The program of the committee has been to acquaint organizations and individuals concerned with drilling with the practical and scientific value of the systematic preservation of subsurface materials and records from all types of drilling projects. The most difficult problem connected with this work, however, is the collecting and storing of samples obtained from wells, which are bulky and heavy.

In order to ascertain what provision is made for collecting and studying well samples, the committee has issued a questionnaire to all of the State gelogical surveys and similar bodies, and much information has also been received from oil companies and well-drilling associations. Seventeen States now furnish well drillers with containers in which to return sample cuttings from wells, and 23 States provide facilities for the permanent storage of samples and drilling records. The bureau of economic geology in Texas, for example, has now collected 1,250,000 well samples. The Illinois Geological Survey has preserved 1,370 sets of well data. Missouri, Kansas, Nebraska, Iowa, Michigan, Pennsylvania, New Jersey, and Georgia are among other States which systematically preserve well materials. Several large oil companies maintain warehouses for the preservation of the materials from their wells. In addition to the actual specimens from wells, the committee recognizes that drilling logs and records of geophysical prospecting, the flow of ground waters, and other chemical and physical data are all valuable in contributing to the knowledge of subsurface conditions.

Sedimentation.—The work of the committee on sedimentation has been directed during the past year mainly toward the preparation of a symposium on recent sediments for which some 40 papers have been invited, to be supported by bibliographies and later published. In the annual report of the committee, which summarizes as previously the advances in this field during the year, special attention has been given to the sedimentation studies of the Soil Conservation Service. The subcommittee on terminology has issued its report for fine-grained rocks. Two special research projects have been supported during the year upon funds derived from the sale of Treatise on Sedimentation (two editions), and geological color charts—the organic constituents of Lake Monona in Wisconsin, and the development of a coring device for procuring sedimentary samples from deep waters. Mr. F. M. Varney and Mr. Lowell Redwine, who have developed this device at the University of California at Los Angeles, have received substantial assistance also from other sources, and in view of the possible commercial utilization of this device, they have patented it. They have, however, agreed to permit the unrestricted use of the apparatus for scientific research work not undertaken for profit.

During the year royalty payments amounting to $164.80 have been received on the sale of the second edition of the Treatise on Sedimentation. The total funds received from royalties on the sale of the first edition (published in 1926) were $1,718.95, and of the second edition (published in 1932) $876, making a total of $2,594.95. Of this amount $867.38 was expended for editorial work, mainly in connection with the preparation of the second edition. The balance, augmented by sale of the color chart, published in 1928, has been used for projects of sedimentation research and for the preparation of reports. The cash balance of the committee's funds as of June 30, 1937, was $811.18.

Stratigraphy.—The committee on stratigraphy has completed 4 more of the series of 12 charts projected for the collection of geological formations of various regions of the United States in addition to those completed last year, and has encouraged investigations upon certain problems arising in the course of the compilation of these charts. The charts now ready for publication include one for the Silurian and two for the Tertiary, the Cretaceous chart for the Atlantic and Gulf coasts, and the chart for the Cambrian, Ordovician, Pennsylvanian, and Permian. A series of descriptive handbooks to accompany these charts is also in preparation.

Structural petrology.—The committee on structural petrology has realized the need for additional fieldwork and experimentation in order to provide the data which may serve to harmonize various views in this field and has urged the further development of this work. For the time being, however, the committee has been discontinued, after publishing (in mimeographed form) a selective and annotated bibliography.

Tectonics.—The results of the work of the members of the committee on tectonics have been discussed at two meetings of the committee during the year. The committee is gratified over the issuing by other agencies of several tectonic maps of limited areas of the United States, as indicating a growing interest in maps that represent the structure of the earth's crust and a demand for such maps.

Relationships of the division of geology and geography.—Among other relationships the division of geology and geography is represented on the advisory council of the Federal Board of Surveys and Maps, on the advisory council of the American Association of Water Well Drillers, and on the committee on classification of coal of the American Society for Testing Materials, and is in correspondence with Prof. U. S. Grant, of the University of California at Los Angeles, in regard to investigations of the shore line of California.

The American Shore and Beach Preservation Association, which was founded in 1926 with assistance from a committee of this division in conjunction with several other agencies, held its tenth annual meeting in Washington on December 14, 1936.

DIVISION OF MEDICAL SCIENCES

ESMOND R. LONG, Chairman; HOWARD T. KARSNER, Vice Chairman

American registry of pathology.—The American registry of pathology, established in 1931, is a collection of correlated case histories and pathological specimens for certain diseases showing not only their diagnostic characteristics but also the response of these diseases to various types of treatment. The collection is located in the Army Medical Museum in Washington, D. C., and is supported by sponsorship and by appropriations from a number of medical societies. The data and specimens collected are analyzed and preserved so as to make them readily available for study by practicing physicians and surgeons, and by medical investigators, and a number of sets of illustrative material have been prepared for loan purposes. The registry is under the general sponsorship of the division of the medical sciences, but each section of the registry is in the particular charge of a special advisory committee appointed by the affiliated society or societies immediately concerned.

On account of limited resources the registry has been obliged to select only certain diseases for specialization, including at first certain types of tumors, particularly those of the eye, mouth, larynx, bladder, and lymph glands.

The total number of specimens now contained in the registry is as follows:

Ophthalmic pathology	5,832
Lymphatic tumors	639
Bladder tumors	1,400
Oral and dental pathology	483
Otolaryngic pathology	604

During 1936 two registry exhibits were sent to medical meetings as follows:

History of the Ophthalmoscope and the study set and catalog of Otolaryngic Pathology, to the meeting of the American Academy of Ophthalmology and Otolaryngology in October.

Grading of Epithelial Tumors of the Urinary Bladder, to the meeting of the American Urological Association in May.

Borderland problems.—The division of medical sciences also participated in the conference on borderland problems of the life sciences, held in Philadelphia on January 23, 1937 (see p. 34), and jointly with other divisions of the Council is supporting the development of special interests arising from the discussion at this conference, including problems of cellular physiology, aerial dissemination of pathogens and allergens, genetics of pathogenic organisms, parasitology of animals and man, and experimental neuroses (see pp. 33, 59, and 62).

Drug addiction.—The investigations undertaken 8 years ago upon the chemistry and pharmacology of narcotic drugs as a contribution toward a solution for the narcotic problem have been carried forward vigorously during the past year upon continued support from the Rockefeller Foundation. This work has been conducted under the direction of a committee of the division of medical sciences, in cooperation with the United States Public Health Service, the department of chemistry at the University of Virginia, the department of pharmacology at the University of Michigan, and with the aid of several hospitals for the treatment of malignant diseases, tuberculosis, and drug addiction. Through the Department of State the committee is also in touch with developments abroad relating to the control of narcotics as represented through the Central Permanent Committee on Opium of the League of Nations.

A large number of new drugs having chemical structure similar to that of morphine have been produced and their physiological properties have been studied. These are mainly derivatives of morphine, although a number of them have been synthesized from phenanthrene and other bases, and some seem to have unexpected relationships to estrogenic substances. Several of the more promising substances thus produced have been studied clinically to determine their analgesic potency and their habit-forming properties.

Most gratifying in connection with these investigations has been the generous cooperation of agencies in the Federal and in State Governments, and of manufacturers of pharmaceutics as a demonstration that such cooperation is possible and can lead successfully to results which are not obtainable in any other way. Not the least valuable of the results from this work has been the strong impetus which has been given to the advancement of narcotic chemistry in this country, to the training of chemists in this field, and to the improvement of standards for measuring the effects of narcotics and depressants. The participation of the committee on drug addiction in the development of the patent policy of the council this year has been mentioned elsewhere in this report. (See p. 32.)

Endocrinology.—Last year the John and Mary R. Markle Foundation of New York requested the National Research Council to prepare a report upon the status of research in endocrinology and the prospect for promising further investigation in this field. A special committee of the Council drew up a comprehensive and significant report entitled "An Appraisal of Endocrinology," which was printed by the foundation for a limited distribution. On the basis of this report the foundation has made an appropriation to the Council of $100,000 for the support of research in United States and Canada over a period of 3 years. The first grants from this fund will be made in the fall of the academic year 1937–38.

Parasitology.—As one of the results of the conference on borderland problems in the life sciences (see p. 34), the former committee on medical problems of animal parasitology has been reorganized as the committee on medical problems common to animals and man, the former committee being retained in an advisory capacity. The new committee is cooperating with the United States Public Health Service in a study of the incidence of trichinosis in this country and upon research on a purified antigen for the treatment of trichinosis. Plans have been made in cooperation also with the American Association of Pathologists and Bacteriologists and the American Society of Clinical Pathologists for obtaining specimens of this disease from various parts of the country for study.

Sex research.—The committee for research in problems of sex has continued with strong momentum the program of research which it has been carrying forward for the past 16 years supported on funds provided by the Rockefeller Foundation. For the past year this program has considered 21 projects conducted by collaborators at 16 institutions upon grants totaling $71,030. For the coming year grants aggregating $66,900 have been made to 17 groups of investigators located at 14 institutions. Many of these collaborators have been associated with the committee for several years. The work of several former collaborators with the committee is now being supported directly by the Rockefeller Foundation or by other means.

Very great advances have been made in this subject during the period covered by the work of the Council's committee. Not the least of the contributions in this advance which the committee may have assisted in making is felt to be the development at a score of institutions about the country of strong centers for research in this field. The collaborators with the committee have themselves published about 928 papers during this time. A second edition is now being prepared of the volume compiled for the committee in 1932 by Dr. Edgar Allen, of Yale University, entitled "Sex and Internal Secretions." The new edition will present the contributions of some 26 collaborators.

Among other medical research agencies there seems to be none which is performing the primary function of this committee in aiding and guiding the development of research in this important field. In this work the committee is following a definite program, and while it accepts applications for grants for the support of research on the phenomena of sex, the policy of the committee is to take the initiative in shaping a continuing program according to trends and opportunities for research in this and in supporting fields, and to make its decisions as to grants in favor of work which can be built into this program. While in its earlier years the attention of the committee was directed mainly toward the physiological phenomena of sex and studies of the sex hormones, more recently, with the great impetus which endocrinology has now acquired, it has seemed expedient for the committee to turn its efforts toward the less well developed neural and psychological aspects of these problems.

Syphilis.—The National Research Council is participating in the current movement for control of syphilis by establishing a committee to cooperate with the United States Public Health Service in an evaluation of the many antisyphilitic drugs, and in the improvement of standards for testing these drugs. As a first step in this direction a conference has been planned for the summer of 1937 under auspices of this committee with representatives of firms manufacturing antisyphilitic drugs with view to finding with their aid a way out of the present chaotic condition attending the handling and distribution of these drugs through the adoption of organized and safe standards of the testing of arsenicals and other preparations to be used in the treatment of this disease.

DIVISION OF BIOLOGY AND AGRICULTURE

R. E. COKER, Chairman; H. P. BARSS, Vice Chairman

Aerial dissemination of pathogens and allergens.—The committee on aerial dissemination of pathogens and allergens, in which the division of medical sciences of the Council and the division of anthropology and psychology are also interested as well as the division of biology and agriculture, is developing a program of investigations for the "comprehensive study of aerial dissemination of fungus spores causing spread of plant diseases, the widespread scattering of pollen and subsequent production of undesirable hybrids, the relation of upper-air-borne pollen to allergic troubles, and the possibility of the use of knowledge of upper-air-borne spores and pollen as indices of mass movements of air." The utilization of airplanes for the purpose of collecting specimens from the upper air makes this new field of exploration possible, and commercial airplane companies and bureaus of the Government have generously cooperated in the initiation of this work.

Animal nutrition.—The committee on animal nutrition has sponsored the publication last year of a monograph entitled "Mineral Nutrition of Farm Animals," by Dr. H. H. Mitchell, of the University of Illinois, and Dr. F. J. McClure, formerly of Pennsylvania State College, in the Bulletin series of the Council (No. 99, April 1937, 135 pp., with a bibliography of 571 references). This monograph summarizes present knowledge of this field and of the application of this knowledge to the feeding of animals.

Borderland problems.—The division of biology and agriculture jointly with the division of medical sciences and the division of anthropology and psychology is concerned in the development of interest in problems of cellular physiology, of the genetics of pathogenic organisms, and of experimental neuroses, as well as in the problems of aerobiology to which previous allusion has been made, and with the division of medical sciences with problems relating to parasites common to animals and man. (See pp. 33, 56, and 62.)

Cold Spring Harbor Laboratory.—The division of biology and agriculture has been requested on several occasions to give advice in regard to the organization of certain research institutions, and this year was requested to advise the trustees of the Cold Spring Harbor Laboratory on Long Island, N. Y., in regard to the development of the laboratory. A special committee appointed in the spring of 1936 prepared a detailed report with recommendations for the further development of this important research center in biology.

Ecology of grasslands.—The objective of the committee on ecology of grasslands of North America is the reservation of a sufficient number of grassland areas under suitable control to make possible the utilization of these areas for studies of the ecology of plants and animals characteristic of such areas under their natural conditions. The purposes in maintaining these areas are (1) to preserve natural materials available for study relating to grassland plant and animal association, and (2) to serve as the basis for studies of the conservative uses that can properly be made of such areas, and of steps to be taken to restore areas in which the natural cover has been destroyed. The importance of this appears from the fact that "about 40 percent of the surface of the earth is or was grassland, and that with the development of civilization and modern agriculture, a very considerable part of the natural grassland area has been subjected to drastic change with virtually no investigation or thought of the full consequence that might ensue." This committee has held several meetings in recent years in the Great Plains States for a critical examination of areas that might be considered for permanent reservation.

Forestry.—The committee on forestry has undertaken a survey of forestry research in the United States in various types of agencies with view to providing data to determine how completely the research now in progress is supplying the technical information as a whole which is needed for the sound management of forest lands in this country. The survey should indicate also the directions in which forestry research should be further pressed.

Member societies.—The American Society of Parasitologists has accepted membership in this division this year on the basis of group representation followed by the division, thus making 22 biological societies affiliated with this division of the council.

Pharmacognosy and pharmaceutical botany.—The survey of the distribution of native medicinal plants which has been undertaken by the committee on pharmacognosy and pharmaceutical botany has not yet been completed, but a preliminary report upon "A survey of wild medicinal plants of the United States: Their distribution and abundance" with distribution maps has been issued (mimeographed). This preliminary report shows that the natural production of many essential drugs is not sufficient to supply the demand in the United States. The committee has also pointed out that many medicinal drug plants now imported from abroad could be grown in this country, and urges experimentation in this direction and also in the direction of improvement by selective breeding of the yield and the quality of drugs from native and imported plants.

Preservation of natural conditions.—The interest of the division of biology and agriculture in the conservation of wildlife has been represented for many years by an early committee on wildlife, which later became a committtee on wildlife and nature reserves, and which was changed in name last year to the committee on the preservation of natural conditions (which is concerned with the preservation of primeval areas and of native plant and animal life). This committee has considered a wide variety of matters relating to the preservation of the natural plant and animal resources of the United States, and has made recommendations in regard to them to agencies concerned. The committee has prepared a prospectus relating to the need for the reservation of certain areas in primeval condition, and to the importance of planning for the preservation of native plant and animal species, and has established relationships by correspondence with many organizations in the United States concerned with the conservation of wildlife and natural conditions.

Radiation.—The committee on radiation for the past 8 years has been encouraging research upon the biological effects of various types of radiation (X-rays, ultraviolet light, infrared rays, radium emanations, etc.). It has been gratified in having been able to bring to bear in this field resources not only of appropriations from certain of the foundations, but also the loan or donation of apparatus and supplies, representing in the aggregate large amounts, from a number of instrument makers and manufacturers. These have been made available to collaborators at universities and research institutions, but in doing so the committee has followed the policy of not attempting to furnish continuing support of a given program of investigation indefinitely, but rather of expecting that institutional provision will be made for the continuation of promising programs of investigation after initial assistance from the committee.

From a fund of $75,000 provided by the Rockefeller Foundation for the 3-year period ending June 30, 1938, the committee on radiation made grants this year totaling $22,515 to 22 individual investigators, and has allocated certain funds for the purchase of instruments and apparatus for its collaborators and arranged for the loan of apparatus and radioactive materials. Twenty grants, totaling $21,635, have been appropriated to investigators in this field for the coming year (1937–38). "The program is designed to support projects directed primarily toward obtaining a broader basis of quantitative data in this field, i. e., studies along such lines as the fundamental physiological and developmental responses of cells and tissues, metabolism in the broadest sense, significant biological projects, relevant absorption and emission spectroscopy."

The subcommittee of this committee on mitogenetic radiation now has in press (as N. R. C. Bulletin No. 100, 96 pp.) a report entitled "An Experimental Study of the Problem of Mitogenetic Radiation," by Dr. Alexander Hollaender and Dr. Walter D. Claus. This report gives the results of work which has been sponsored by this subcommittee for the past 2 years in addition to previous interests of the committee in this portion of the total field of radiation. The conclusion from the present study is in general that present methods fail to demonstrate positively the existence of mitogenetic emanations, and that further productive work in this field must depend upon the development of more sensitive instruments and perhaps new methods of approach.

Barro Colorado Island Laboratory.—The annual report of the director of the Barro Colorado Island Laboratory for the year ending February 28, 1937, indicates that the work of the laboratory has been proceeding with undiminished momentum. About 35 scientists visited the island last year in addition to a large number of other interested travelers. The equipment of the laboratory is increasing gradually, two new launches having been added during the year but there are still many needs to be met in order to make possible the best utilization of the island as a tropical biological station. The total disbursements for the laboratory for the past year were $7,400.24.

Crop Protection Institute.—The Crop Protection Institute established in 1926 under auspices of the National Research Council is now related to the council only through the appointment of one of its trustees by the council. For the calendar year 1936 the institute sponsored 16 projects of investigation on insecticides, and published 8 bulletins in the institute series.

DIVISION OF ANTHROPOLOGY AND PSYCHOLOGY

WALTER S. HUNTER, Chairman; J. R. SWANTON, Vice Chairman

Child development research.—The committee on child development confines its activities to cooperating with the Society for Research in Child Development. This society held its second biennial meeting in Washington between the dates October 30 and November 1, 1936. In the program of these meetings it is intended to obliterate for the time being the lines between the several sciences which support the study of child development, and to effect a synthesis of the contributions of these sciences upon the single objective of coming to understand better the process of growth and development of the child. The program of the meeting last fall consisted mainly of symposia on the following topics: Prenatal behavior, the development and care of the primary teeth, promising leads for research, problems of adolescence, on the child's development as a field of research, longitudinal studies (of continuing observations of the same child), preparations and methods of child development studies, and the organism as a whole. Sectional meetings were held for the discussion of problems of adjustment and personality, community health, dentistry, nutrition, the physiology and environment of child growth, and social and cultural environment.

The society now has about 450 members. Its offices are with the National Research Council in Washington. It publishes two journals, Child Development Abstracts and Child Development, for the latter of which the society took over the management last year, and also a series of technical monographs in which six numbers were issued during the past year and several more are in preparation.

Ethnological utilization of motion pictures.—A committee on ethnological utilization of motion pictures was established a year ago in order (1) to make technical information available to anthropologists and psychologists in regard to various forms of recording and of motion-picture instruments, (2) to serve as a clearing agency in arranging for the collection of valid ethnological material, and (3) to provide for the compilation of lists of commercial films known to contain ethnological data of scientific value.

Experimental neuroses.—Following the discussion at the meeting in Philadelphia on January 23, 1937, of the interdivisional committee on borderland problems of the life sciences (see p. 34) the division of anthropology and psychology arranged for a special conference in Washington on April 17 and 18 to consider problems of experimental neurosis and allied questions. The conference was attended by about 28 psychologists, physiologists, psychiatrists, and biologists, and recommended that a permanent committee of the division be set up to continue the consideration of the organization of research in this field. This committee has been appointed. The conference further recommended the holding of similar conferences annually and the preparation of surveys and reviews of portions of the total field and consideration of the possible establishment of a journal for the experimental approach to the study of neurosis. In this subject the divisions of medical sciences and of biology and agriculture are also interested.

Among other topics suggested by the conference for study were: heart reactions in patients as compared with those of normal persons, comparison of memory in adults with that of children, psychodynamic endocrinopathies, anxiety states, correlation studies of experimental neurosis in animals and in human beings, bisexuality, functional sterility, disturbances of the vegetative functions in comparison with daily emotional states, environment analysis of individual psychoneurotic patients, effects of social strata and of milieu upon special forms of neurotic behavior.

Another group of questions proposed involved (1) the study of the normal population of children as well as of the more restricted groups found in clinics and in hospitals; (2) the study of behavior problems, developmentally as well as through retrospect; (3) excitatory and inhibitory responses; (4) the increase in psychological precision; (5) the inertia of ignorance and resistance to change; and (6) the conditions which favor the persistence of neurotic states developing from psychogenic causes.

A third group of suggestions were (1) that psychoanalytic studies should be analyzed from the point of view of experimental psychology; (2) that a thorough practical training in both experimental and clinical psychology is essential; and (3) that a journal on experimental neuroses would be desirable. The subjects of insulin therapy and the relationship between endocrinology and psychoanalytic findings, the effects of cultural restrictions on the child, and the necessity for supplementing psychological studies by sociological studies were also suggested.

The division of anthropology and psychology is interested, with other divisions of the Council, in other matters discussed at the life-sciences conference, including problems of cellular physiology, the genetics of pathogenic organisms, and problems of aërobiology. (See pp. 33, 56, and 59.)

International Directory of Anthropologists.—With the cooperation of the American Anthropological Association, the division is publishing (in mimeographed form) an International Directory of Anthropologists (with bibliographies) which has been compiled in the office of the division. The directory contains some 1,950 names, of which about 600 are from the United States.

Laboratory of Anthropology at Santa Fe.—The advisory council to the board of trustees of the Laboratory of Anthropology at Santa Fe, N. Mex., on which the division of anthropology and psychology nominated a member last year to serve with members similarly nominated by the American Council of Learned Societies and by the Social Science Research Council, presented a report to the trustees last October containing certain suggestions which it is hoped will enable this well-equipped laboratory to become increasingly valuable as a center for research in American anthropology. A particular need of the laboratory for additional funds has already been partially met.

Personality in relation to culture.—The committee on personality in relation to culture reports that through a subcommittee preliminary drafts of parts of a Handbook of Psychological Leads for Ethnological Field Workers have been prepared and circulated (in mimeographed form) for criticism and discussion before final publication.

Psychology of the highway.—The committee on the psychology of the highway has cooperated closely with the highway research board in the studies undertaken by the board on human causes of highway accidents. (See p. 47.) It has assisted in arranging for a critical review of published reports on methods of detecting and handling accident-prone drivers, for an experimental study of the validity of certain sets of tests proposed for the diagnosis of accident-prone drivers, for an analysis of the accident records of one-tenth of the general drivers of Connecticut who were licensed in each of the years 1931-36, for a special age census of licensed drivers and drivers involved in fatal accidents in Connecticut in each of the years 1932-36, and for an analysis of the contributing factors in 1,715 fatal accidents which occurred in 1936. The analysis of the facts disclosed two classes of drivers which contained an excessively large proportion of accident-prone individuals. These classes are, respectively, those drivers who are now younger than 25 years, and those drivers who have had many previous accidents. The committee believes that additional work needs to be done to show (1) how drivers' histories can be obtained and used to best advantage, (2) what can be done to use the present tests of driving skills to best advantage and to develop them further, and (3) how to evaluate the effects of fatigue on driving performance. The midwestern subcommittee of this committee has continued its studies on the relation of scores on driver tests to sex and age.

State archeological surveys.—The committee on State archeological surveys reports that the publication of news items in American Antiquity, the journal of the Society for American Archeology (now in its third volume), makes it unnecessary to continue the compilation of the review of Archeological Field Work in North America which has heretofore been prepared and published in the Bulletin of the Pan American Union. The last summary published in the Bulletin was that for 1934. Similarly, notices in American Antiquity have taken place of the series of mimeographed circulars previously issued by the committee. The committee, however, has distributed a report of the conference on archeology which was held at Indianapolis, December 6, 7, and 8, 1935.

In view of the development of the Society for American Archeology the committee on State archeological surveys, founded by the National Research Council in 1920, will be discontinued after this year. The second annual meeting of the society was held in Washington, December 29, 1936. Its membership is now about 640.

The interests of the division in archeological exploration in the Tennessee Valley area will, however, be continued through a committee on Tennessee Valley archeology which, as a subcommittee of the committee on State archeological surveys, has cooperated with the Bureau of American Ethnology in arranging for the exploration of three new basins in the Tennessee Valley in which dams are being erected: Chickamauga Basin, the Gunthersville Basin, and the Pickwick Basin. This work has been aided by two grants from the National Research Council totaling $1,500, which have been used to coordinate the work of the cooperating agencies and to meet special expenses that could not be charged against Government funds, thus making it possible to maintain a continuous program of exploration in accordance with Government regulations.

ANNUAL REPORT OF THE TREASURER

JULY 1, 1936, TO JUNE 30, 1937

To the President of the National Academy of Sciences:

I have the honor to submit the following report as treasurer of the Academy for the year from July 1, 1936, to June 30, 1937, and as treasurer of the National Research Council for the same period. As is customary, the first part of this report covers the transactions of the National Academy of Sciences, including the general fund, and the appropriations under the custodian of buildings and grounds, and the second part covers the accounts of the National Research Council.

NATIONAL ACADEMY OF SCIENCES

Under a contract dated June 29, 1933, the Bank of New York & Trust Co. has continued to serve as custodian of securities of the Academy during the past year. Mr. Joseph Stanley-Brown has continued to serve as financial adviser of the Academy during the year just closed.

On June 30, 1937, the securities held by the Academy and by the Research Council were distributed as follows:

	Book value			
	Held by Academy	Held by Research Council	Total held	Percent of total
I. Bonds of railroads	$1,846,806.25	$111,127.52	$1,957,933.77	48.9
II. Bonds of public utility corporations	449,778.75		449,778.75	11.2
III. Bonds of industrial corporations	24,437.50		24,437.50	.6
IV. Bonds of United States, States, counties, and municipalities				
V. Bonds and notes secured by first mortgage on real estate	527,400.00	35,333.00	562,733.00	14.1
VI. Bonds of foreign governments	67,750.00	20,369.72	88,119.72	2.2
Total bonds	2,916,172.50	166,830.24	3,083,002.74	77.1
VII. Common and preferred stocks of companies	917,571.52		917,571.52	22.9
Total	3,833,744.02	166,830.24	4,000,574.26	100.0

The following table indicates the distribution of the investments held by the Academy on June 30, 1937, with reference to bonds and common and preferred stocks:

	Face value	Book value	Market value June 30, 1937
Bonds	$3,077,400.00	$2,916,172.50	$2,671,600.00
Common and preferred stocks having fixed par value	365,450.00	543,288.83	602,063.75
Common and preferred stocks having no par value		374,282.69	506,175.00
Total		3,833,744.02	3,779,838.75

The total income from investments during the past year was $187,-142.07, less $8,958.72 accrued interest on bonds bought, making a net income of $178,183.35, or an average yield of 4.64 percent on the book value of $3,833,744.02, or 4.74 percent on the market value on June 30, 1937, of $3,779,838.75.

The investment reserve fund was designed to absorb losses sustained by the Academy in the sale of bonds. The following shows the operation of this fund during the year just closed:

Overdraft on July 1, 1936		$358,152.30
Profits on sale of bonds	$133,352.88	
Interest on investments	4.95	
Less losses on sale of bonds		
Net profits on sale of bonds and interest	133,357.83	
Transferred from various funds, 5 percent of income on investments	9,266.27	
Additions to the fund for year		142,624.10
Overdraft on June 30, 1937		215,528.20

When Mr. Joseph Stanley-Brown became the financial adviser of the Academy on November 1, 1935, the overdraft in this fund amounted to $583,522.03, which has now been reduced to $215,528.20, an improvement of $367,993.83 during the 20 months he has supervised the investments of the Academy. This net profit has been reinvested in income-producing securities. During the same period the book value of the investments of the Academy has increased $463,-006.41, from $3,370,737.61 to $3,833,744.02, and the market value of investments has increased $286,305.68, from $3,493,533.07 to $3,779,838.75.

The capital of the Comstock fund during the year has been increased to $15,000.00 from $12,406.02, a difference of $2,593.98, of which $194.20 was due to profit on sale of bonds and $2,399.78 was transferred from income to capital. The fund now stands at the amount indicated by the donor of the fund.

The total receipts of the Academy during the year from all sources amounted to $199,340.76.

The miscellaneous disbursements amounted to $196,804.16, and payments on grants, medals, and honoraria, amounted to $12,233.84; total disbursements for the year $208,038.00.

The consolidated investment fund on June 30, 1937, stands at $232,777.94, the same as for the previous year. Of this amount, $232,408.69 was invested and $369.25 was uninvested.

The total expenditures up to June 30, 1937, for acquisition of site amounted to $185,764.50, and for erection and equipment of building for the use of the National Academy of Sciences and the National Research Council, paid from funds received from the Carnegie Corporation of New York, $1,446,879.82, and paid from separate Academy funds, $1,765.00, making a total for building and site, $1,-634,409.32. In addition to these, the sum of $1,169.43 was expended from Academy funds during the year for the equipment of the building, making a total of $12,064.36 for this purpose, the sum of $10,894.93 having been previously spent. The sum of $3,120.18 is held in the building construction fund as of June 30, 1937.

Below is found a list of bonds, now held by the National Academy of Sciences, which are in default:

Kansas City, Fort Scott & Memphis Railway Co. 4-percent refunding mortgage fully guaranteed bonds, due Oct. 1, 1936; last interest paid was Oct. 1, 1932_____ $136,000

Missouri Pacific R. R. Co. 5-percent first and refunding mortgage bonds, series G, due Nov. 1, 1978; last interest paid was Nov. 1, 1932_____ 50,000

Missouri Pacific R. R. Co. 5-percent first and refunding mortgage bonds, series I, due Feb. 1, 1981; last interest paid was Feb. 1, 1933_____ 60,000

New Orleans, Texas & Mexico Railway Co. 5½-percent first-mortgage bonds, due Apr. 1, 1954; last interest paid was Apr. 1, 1933; bonds represented by certificates of deposit of the Chase National Bank of New York_____ 50,000

Raleigh & Augusta Air Line R. R. Co.-Seaboard Air Line Railway Co. 5-percent first-mortgage guaranteed, due Jan. 1, 1931; last interest paid was July 1, 1932, bonds represented by certificates of deposit of the Mercantile Trust Co. of Baltimore_____ 25,000

St. Louis-San Francisco Railway Co. 4½-percent consolidated mortgage bonds, series A, due Mar. 1, 1978; last interest paid was Sept. 1, 1932_____ 50,000

Total _____ 371,000

The amount of annual interest not now being paid on above bonds is $17,190.

During the year $1,500 has been curtailed from one mortgage held by the Academy; and two reductions of $500 each have been made on another mortgage. Otherwise the condition of real-estate mortgages remains unsatisfactory.

TRUST FUNDS OF THE ACADEMY

The trust funds of the Academy, the income of which is administered for specific purposes, are enumerated below. The capital of certain funds has been increased beyond the original gift or bequest by the transfer of accumulated income at the request of the donors or by action of the Academy.

Bache fund: Bequest of Alexander Dallas Bache, a member of the Academy, 1870, to aid researches in physical and natural sciences _____ $60,000.00

Watson fund: Bequest of James C. Watson, a member of the Academy, 1874, for the promotion of astronomical science through the award of the Watson gold medal and grants of money in aid of research_____ 25,000.00

Draper fund: Gift of Mrs. Henry Draper, 1883, in memory of her husband, a former member of the Academy, to found the Henry Draper medal, to be awarded for notable investigations in astronomical physics; the balance of income is applied to aid research in the same science_____ 10,000.00

Smith fund: Gift of Mrs. J. Lawrence Smith, 1884, in memory of her husband, a former member of the Academy, to found the J. Lawrence Smith gold medal, to be awarded for important investigations of meteoric bodies and to assist, by grants of money, researches concerning such objects_____ 10,000.00

Gibbs fund: Established by gift of Wolcott Gibbs, a member of the Academy, 1892, and increased by a bequest of the late Morris Loeb, 1914, for the promotion of researches in chemistry_____ 5,545.50

Gould fund: Gift of Miss Alice Bache Gould, 1897, in memory of her father, a former member of the Academy, for the promotion of researches in astronomy_____ 20,000.00

Comstock fund: Gift of Gen. Cyrus B. Comstock, a member of the Academy, 1907, to promote researches in electricity, magnetism, or radiant energy through the Comstock prize money, to be awarded once in 5 years for notable investigations; the fund has been increased from $12,406.02 to $15,000 by profit from sale of bonds and by transfer from income to capital_____ $15,000.00

Marsh fund: Bequest of Othniel Charles Marsh, a member of the Academy, 1909, to promote original research in the natural sciences; to the original bequest of $10,000 the Academy has added interest received from the estate and has authorized the increase of the fund to $20,000 by annual additions from income _____ 20,000.00

Murray fund: A gift from the late Sir John Murray, 1911, to found the Alexander Agassiz gold medal, in honor of a former member and president of the Academy, to be awarded for original contribution to the science of oceanography_____ 6,000.00

Hartley fund: A gift from Mrs. Helen Hartley Jenkins, 1913–14, in memory of her father, Marcellus Hartley, to found the medal of the Academy awarded for eminence in the application of science to public welfare_____ 1,200.00

Billings fund: Established by the bequest of Mrs. Mary Anna Palmer Draper (Mrs. Henry Draper) of $25,000, in 1915, to support the publication of the Proceedings of the Academy or for other purposes to be determined by the Academy, 7 installments_ 22,313.39

Elliot fund: Gift of Margaret Henderson Elliot, to found the Daniel Giraud Elliot gold medal and honorarium for the most meritorious work in zoology or paleontology published in each year_____ 8,000.00

Thompson fund: Gift of Mrs. Mary Clark Thompson, 1919, the income thereof to be applied for a gold medal of appropriate design to be awarded annually by the Academy for the most important services to geology and paleontology, the medal to be known as the Mary Clark Thompson gold medal_____ 10,000.00

Joseph Henry fund: The sum of $40,000 was contributed by Fairman Rogers, Joseph Patterson, George W. Childs, and others, as an expression of their respect and esteem for Prof. Joseph Henry. This amount was deposited with the Pennsylvania Co. for Insurance of Lives and Granting Annuities in trust, with authorization to collect the income thereon and to pay over the same to Prof. Joseph Henry during his natural life, and after his death to his wife and daughters, and after the death of the last survivor to "deliver the said fund and the securities in which it shall then be invested to the National Academy of Sciences, to be thenceforward forever held in trust under the name and title of the 'Joseph Henry fund.'" The death of Miss Caroline Henry on Nov. 10, 1920, has removed the last surviving heir of Joseph Henry to the income of the Joseph Henry fund. To assist meritorious investigators, especially in the direction of original research. Amount received by the Academy from the Pennsylvania Co. for Insurance of Lives and Granting Annuities, $39,739.57, to which was added $423.92 from income_____ 40,163.50

Walcott fund: Gift of Mrs. Mary Vaux Walcott, 1928, in honor of her husband, a former member and president of the Academy, the income to be used for the award of medals and honoraria to persons, the results of whose published researches, explorations, and discoveries in pre-Cambrian or Cambrian life and history shall be judged most meritorious, the award to be made every 5 years, to be known as the "Charles Doolittle Walcott fund"_____ 5,000.00

Carnegie endowment fund: By resolution voted Mar. 28, 1919, and amended several times since, the Carnegie Corporation of New York pledged $5,000,000 to the National Academy of Sciences for the purposes of the Academy and the National Research Council, of which $1,450,000 was reserved and paid for the erection of a building, and the remainder, $3,550,000, to be capitalized at such times as the corporation finds convenient in view of of its other obligations, the amount remaining in the hands of the corporation to bear interest at the rate of 5 percent per annum, 7 installments completing capitalization_____ $3,550,000.00

John J. Carty Medal and Award for the advancement of science: Gift of American Telephone & Telegraph Co., Nov. 13, 1930, in recognition of the distinguished achievements of John J. Carty as a scientist and engineer, and his noteworthy contributions to the advancement of fundamental and applied science, and in appreciation of his great services for many years in developing the art of electrical communication and as a lasting testimonial of the love and esteem in which he is held by his many thousand associates in the Bell System; the income thereof to be used for a gold medal and award, not oftener than once in 2 years, by vote of the National Academy of Sciences, to an individual for noteworthy and distinguished accomplishment in any field of science coming within the scope of the charter of the National Academy of Sciences_____ 25,000.00

In addition to the above-named funds, the Academy holds the following:

Agassiz fund, bequest of Alexander Agassiz, a member of the Academy, 1910, for the general uses of the Academy_____ 50,000.00

Nealley fund, bequest of George True Nealley, 1925, for the general purposes of the Academy, $20,896.01, less refund November 1926, $1,500, to a creditor of the estate; supplemented by additional sum from the estate, March 1931, $159.54_____ 19,555.55

Total _____ 3,902,777.94

Accounts with individual funds, July 1, 1936, to June 30, 1937

	General fund		Agassiz fund	
	Income	Capital	Income	Capital
Balance July 1, 1936:				
Cash_____	$7,419.94			
Invested_____	11,525.00			$50,000.00
Receipts:				
Interest on investments:				
Agassiz fund_____	3,101.73			
Nealley fund_____	1,014.33			
Annual dues from members_____	1,440.00			
Bonds sold_____	1,790.00			
Total_____	26,291.00			50,000.00
Disbursements:				
General expenses_____	5,909.91			
Transfer to investment reserve fund____	205.81			
Fees to financial advisers_____	129.97			
Bonds bought_____	1,790.00			
Accrued interest on bonds bought____	3.33			
Balance June 30, 1937:				
Cash_____	4,936.98			
Invested_____	13,315.00			50,000.00
Total_____	26,291.00			50,000.00

Accounts with individual funds, July 1, 1936, to June 30, 1937—Continued

	Bache fund		Billings fund	
	Income	Capital	Income	Capital
Balance July 1, 1936:				
Cash	$1,606.52	$147.63		
Invested		59,852.37		$22,313.39
Receipts:				
Interest on investments	3,235.69		$1,156.85	
Refunds	392.77			
Bonds sold		10,541.87		
Total	5,234.98	70,541.87	1,156.85	22,313.39
Disbursements:				
Grants	2,365.00			
Office expenses	8.25			
Bonds bought		10,541.87		
Accrued interest on bonds bought	3.33			
Transfer to academy proceedings			1,061.87	
Transfer to investment reserve fund	161.78		57.84	
Fees to financial advisers	99.03		37.14	
Balance June 30, 1937:				
Cash	2,592.59	622.00		
Invested		59,378.00		22,313.39
Total	5,234.98	70,541.87	1,156.85	22,313.39

	Building construction		Building site	
	Income	Capital	Income	Capital
Balance July 1, 1936:				
Cash	$3,120.18		$5,538.56	
Invested			7,543.25	
Receipts:				
Interest on investments			421.91	
Bonds sold			7,543.25	
Total	3,120.18		21,046.97	
Disbursements:				
Bonds bought			7,543.25	
Accrued interest on bonds bought			35.83	
Fees to financial advisers			12.38	
Transfer to investment reserve fund			21.10	
Balance June 30, 1937:				
Cash	3,120.18		4,967.69	
Invested			8,486.75	
Total	3,120.18		21,046.97	

Accounts with individual funds, July 1, 1936, to June 30, 1937—Continued

	Carnegie endowment fund		Carnegie Corporation special	
	Income	Capital	Income	Capital
Balance July 1, 1936:				
Cash	$16,913.55	$289,428.61	$11,041.11	
Invested		3,260,571.39		
Receipts:				
Interest on investments	166,049.96			
Bonds sold		944,190.81		
Total	182,963.51	4,494,190.81	11,041.11	
Disbursements·				
Government relations			7.00	
Clerical assistance			443.33	
Printing of biographical memoirs			1,000.00	
Transfer to D. C. unemployment compensation tax, 1936			19.92	
Bonds bought		944,190.81		
Accrued interest on bonds bought	7,964.16			
Transfer to investment reserve fund	8,302.50			
Fees to financial advisers	5,359.92			
Taxes, fire and liability insurance, etc., on real estate	5,914.79			
Transferred to Carnegie endowment fund, income account, N. R. C., 1937	62,990.75			
Transferred to Carnegie endowment fund, income account, N. A. of S., 1937	45,284.03			
Balance June 30, 1937:				
Cash	47,147.36	105,840.29	9,570.86	
Invested		3,444,159.71		
Total	182,963.51	4,494,190.81	11,041.11	

	John J. Carty Medal and Award		Comstock fund	
	Income	Capital	Income	Capital
Balance July 1, 1936:				
Cash	$3,812.91		$6,427.08	$78.52
Invested		$25,000.00		12,327.50
Receipts:				
Interest on investments	1,236.40		860.23	
Sale of bonds			5,880.00	8,207.50
Profit on sale of bonds			1,129.70	194.20
Transfer from income to capital				2,399.78
Total	5,049.31	25,000.00	14,297.01	23,207.50
Disbursements:				
Honorarium	3,000.00			
Medal and engrossing	269.14			
Fees to financial advisers	43.32			
Transfer to investment reserve fund	61.82			
Bonds bought			5,880.00	8,207.50
Accrued interest on bonds bought			155.13	
Transfer from income to capital			2,399.78	
Balance June 30, 1937:				
Cash	1,675.03		4,604.60	492.50
Invested		25,000.00	1,257.50	14,507.50
Total	5,049.31	25,000.00	14,297.01	23,207.50

Accounts with individual funds, July 1, 1936, to June 30, 1937—Continued

	Consolidated fund		Draper fund	
	Income	Capital	Income	Capital
Balance July 1, 1936:				
Cash	$1, 363. 77	$111. 49	$1, 143. 86	
Invested		232, 666. 45		$10, 000. 00
Receipts:				
Interest on investments	12, 930. 53		519. 24	
Bonds sold		49, 334. 38		
Total	14, 294. 30	282, 112. 32	1, 663. 10	10, 000. 00
Disbursements:				
Bonds bought		49, 334. 38		
Accrued interest on bonds bought	492. 10			
Distribution of consolidated fund	11, 978. 83			
Taxes, etc., on real estate	266. 48			
Medal and medal boxes			366. 70	
Fees to financial advisers			18. 57	
Transfer to investment reserve fund			25. 96	
Balance June 30, 1937:				
Cash	1, 556. 89	369. 25	1, 251. 87	
Invested		232, 408. 69		10, 000. 00
Total	14, 294. 30	282, 112. 32	1, 663. 10	10, 000. 00

	D. C. unemployment compensation tax, 1936		Elliot fund	
	Income	Capital	Income	Capital
Balance July 1, 1936:				
Cash			$2, 135. 29	
Invested				$8, 000. 00
Receipts:				
Interest on investments			415. 39	
Transfer from Carnegie Corporation, special	$19. 92			
Total	19. 92		2, 550. 68	8, 000. 00
Disbursements:				
D. C. Unemployment Compensation Board, tax on salaries	19. 92			
Fees to financial advisers			12. 38	
Transfer to investment reserve fund			20. 77	
Balance June 30, 1937:				
Cash			2, 517. 53	
Invested				8, 000. 00
Total	19. 92		2, 550. 68	8, 000. 00

	Fees to financial advisers		Fund for oceanographic research	
	Income	Capital	Income	Capital
Balance July 1, 1936: Cash			$6, 990. 89	
Receipts:				
Transfer from various funds	$6, 189. 28			
Sale of "Oceanography"			22. 50	
Total	6, 189. 28		7, 013. 39	
Disbursements:				
Fees to Joseph Stanley—Brown	6, 189. 28			
Clerical assistance			450. 00	
Stationery			23. 10	
Cartographic work			589. 40	
Miscellaneous expenses			86. 26	
Balance June 30, 1937: Cash			5, 864. 63	
Total	6, 189. 28		7, 013. 39	

Accounts with individual funds, July 1, 1936, to June 30, 1937—Continued

	Gibbs fund		Gould fund	
	Income	Capital	Income	Capital
Balance July 1, 1936:				
Cash..........	$2,949.40	....	$3,467.56	$477.50
Invested..........	....	$5,545.59	6,555.00	19,522.50
Receipts:				
Interest on investments..............	287.47	....	1,595.13	....
Bonds sold..........	....	....	1,012.50	8,927.50
Total..........	3,236.87	5,545.50	17,630.19	28,927.50
Disbursements:				
Grants..........	360.00	....	1,000.00	....
Fees to financial advisers..........	12.38	....	43.32	....
Transfer to investment reserve fund..........	14.37	....	79.76	....
Bonds bought..........	....	....	1,012.50	8,927.50
Accrued interest on bonds bought..........	....	....	115.00	....
Taxes, etc., on real estate..........	....	....	24.91	....
Balance June 30, 1937:				
Cash..........	2,850.12	....	5,107.05	22.00
Invested..........	....	5,545.50	10,247.65	19,978.00
Total..........	3,236.87	5,545.50	17,630.19	28,927.50

	Grand Canyon project		Hale lectureship	
	Income	Capital	Income	Capital
Balance July 1, 1936:				
Cash..........	$24.19	....	$385.55	....
Total..........	24.19	....	385.55	....
Balance June 30, 1937:				
Cash..........	24.19	....	385.55	....
Total..........	24.19	....	385.55	....

	Hartley fund		Joseph Henry fund	
	Income	Capital	Income	Capital
Balance July 1, 1936:				
Cash..........	$380.56	....	$877.76	....
Invested..........	....	$1,200.00	....	$40,163.50
Receipts:				
Interest on investments..........	61.60	....	2,083.05	....
W. W. Coblentz—refund of grant..........	....	....	450.00	....
Total..........	442.16	1,200.00	3,410.81	40,163.50
Disbursements:				
Medal box..........	10.00	....	....	....
Grants..........	....	....	700.00	....
Fees to financial advisers..........	....	....	68.08	....
Transfer to investment reserve fund..........	3.08	....	104.15	....
Balance June 30, 1937:				
Cash..........	429.08	....	2,538.58	....
Invested..........	....	1,200.00	....	40,163.50
Total..........	442.16	1,200.00	3,410.81	40,163.50

Accounts with individual funds, July 1, 1936, to June 30, 1937—Continued

	Investment reserve fund		Marsh fund	
	Income	Capital	Income	Capital
Balance July 1, 1936:				
Cash			$216.63	
Invested				$20,000.00
Receipts:				
Interest on investments	$4.95		1,037.84	
Profit on sale of bonds	133,352.88			
Transfer from various funds	9,266.27			
Overdraft June 30, 1937	215,528.20			
Total	358,152.30		1,253.97	20,000.00
Disbursements:				
Grants			350.00	
Fees to financial advisers			30.95	
Transfer to investment reserve fund			51.87	
Overdraft July 1, 1936	358,152.30			
Balance June 30, 1937:				
Cash			821.15	
Invested				20,000.00
Total	358,152.30		1,253.97	20,000.00

	Murray fund		National Academy of Sciences, special	
	Income	Capital	Income	Capital
Balance, July 1, 1936:				
Cash	$4,247.40			
Invested		$6,000.00		
Receipts:				
Interest on investments	311.52			
Reimbursements			$76,314.74	
Due from National Research Council July 1, 1936			2,000.00	
Total	4,558.92	6,000.00	78,314.74	
Disbursements:				
Medal and medal boxes	311.74			
Fees to financial advisers	12.38			
Transfer to investment reserve fund	15.58			
Reimbursements			76,314.74	
Balance, June 30, 1937:				
Cash	4,219.22			
Invested		6,000.00		
Due from National Research Council June 30, 1937			2,000.00	
Total	4,558.92	6,000.00	78,314.74	

	National Parks problems		Navy Department—ship stabilization	
	Income	Capital	Income	Capital
Balance, July 1, 1936:				
Cash	$1,604.21			
Receipts:				
Navy Department			$1,970.26	
Adjustment			23.50	
Total	1,604.21		1,993.76	
Disbursements:				
Advance to Howell Williams	100.00			
Expenses of investigation			1,970.26	
Adjustment			23.50	
Balance June 30, 1937:				
Cash	1,504.21			
Total	1,604.21		1,993.76	

Accounts with individual funds, July 1, 1936, to June 30, 1937—Continued

	Nealley fund		Emergency fund Proceedings	
	Income	Capital	Income	Capital
Balance July 1, 1936:				
Cash			$3,327.79	
Invested		$19,555.55		
Total		19,555.55	3,327.79	
Balance June 30, 1937:				
Cash			3,327.79	
Invested		19,555.55		
Total		19,555.55	3,327.79	

	Academy Proceedings		Joint Proceedings	
	Income	Capital	Income	Capital
Balance July 1, 1936:				
Cash	$3,895.04		$6,142.39	
Invested	995.75			
Receipts:				
Interest on investments	63.03			
Annual dues	1,440.00			
Subscriptions			1,982.23	
Reprints and separates	59.55		1,770.45	
Transfer from Billings fund	1,061.87			
Contribution by National Research Council			2,500.00	
Transfer from Academy proceedings representing contribution by National Academy of Sciences			2,500.00	
Bonds sold	995.75			
Total	8,510.99		14,895.07	
Disbursements:				
Salary of managing editor			750.00	
Printing and distributing			7,412.50	
Expenses:				
Boston office			440.00	
Washington office			242.45	
Transfer from Academy proceedings representing contribution by National Academy of Sciences	2,500.00			
Transfer to investment reserve fund	3.15			
Bonds bought	995.75			
Balance June 30, 1937:				
Cash	5,012.09		6,050.12	
Total	8,510.99		14,895.07	

Accounts with individual funds, July 1, 1936, to June 30, 1937—Continued

	Scientific publication fund		Smith fund	
	Income	Capital	Income	Capital
Balance July 1, 1936:				
Cash	$1,686.64		$3,008.40	
Invested			4,123.25	$10,000.00
Receipts:				
Royalties on "Oceanography"	7.50			
Interest on investments			715.93	
Bonds sold			995.75	
Total	1,694.14		8,843.33	
Disbursements:				
Grant			400.00	
Bonds bought			995.75	
Accrued interest on bonds bought			1.67	
Fees to financial advisers			24.76	
Transfer to investment reserve fund			35.80	
Balance June 30, 1937:				
Cash	1,694.14		3,362.85	
Invested			4,022.50	10,000.00
Total	1,694.14		8,843.33	10,000.00

	Thompson fund		Walcott fund	
	Income	Capital	Income	Capital
Balance July 1, 1936:				
Cash	$2,668.79		$507.18	
Invested		$10,000.00		$5,000.00
Receipts:				
Interest on investments	495.02		247.51	
Total	3,163.81	10,000.00	754.69	5,000.00
Disbursements:				
Honorarium	250.00			
Medal and medal boxes	671.40			
Fees to financial advisers	18.57		6.19	
Transfer to investment reserve fund	24.75		12.38	
Balance June 30, 1937:				
Cash	2,199.09		736.12	
Invested		10,000.00		5,000.00
Total	3,163.81	10,000.00	754.69	5,000.00

	Watson fund	
	Income	Capital
Balance July 1, 1936:		
Cash	$2,299.89	$193.53
Invested	1,000.00	24,806.47
Receipts:		
Interest on investments	1,276.09	
Bonds sold	895.00	14,451.25
Total	5,470.98	39,451.25
Disbursements:		
Grants	1,600.00	
Medal and medal boxes	302.62	
Bonds bought	895.00	14,451.25
Accrued interest on bonds bought	183.17	
Taxes, etc., on real estate	44.09	
Fees to financial advisers	43.32	
Transfer to investment reserve fund	63.80	
Balance June 30, 1937:		
Cash	243.99	892.28
Invested	1,895.00	24,107.72
Total	5,470.98	39,451.25

Statement of assets and liabilities, June 30, 1937

ASSETS

[Securities purchased during the fiscal year 1936-37 are indicated thus (*)]

	Face Value	Book Value	Market Value June 30, 1937
Real estate owned	$154,000.00	$154,000.00	$154,000.00
Mortgage notes, secured by first mortgage on real estate	365,400.00	365,400.00	365,400.00
SECURITIES			
*Argentine Republic 4-percent sinking-fund external loan due Apr. 15, 1972; Nos. temporary TM11063-TM11112, TM-28001-TM28025; 75, at $1,000 each	75,000.00	67,750.00	68,906.25
*Atlantic Coast Line Railroad Co. 4½-percent general unified mortgage 50-year, series A, due June 1, 1964; Nos. 3219, 3220, 3676, 3753-3755, 4622, 5309, 5407, 5464, 8727, 8728, 8730, 8732, 8744, 9305, 9306, 9477-9479, 9487, 9488, 9602, 9914, 10585, 10916, 11634-11636, 12324, 12325, 13182, 13915-13918, 14582, 14643, 15437, 15438, 15446, 15447, 18328-18333, 18727, 18728, 19485-19489, 20101, 20121, 22214, 22458, 22791-22795, 23285-23287, 23455-23457, 23990, 24059-24062, 24344-24346, 25329-25331, 25825, 25892-25894, 29604, 29605, 29626, 29627, 29740-29744, 30175, 30176, 30504, 32824, 32837, 32995; 100, at $1,000 each	100,000.00	97,073.75	87,500.00
Baltimore & Ohio R. R. Co. 5-percent refunding and general mortgage, series A, due Dec. 1, 1995; Nos. M1494, M1844, M3376, M5138, M5382, M7519, M7996, M9020, M11535, M17752, M17753, M18061, M19333, M19334, M26419, M30222, M33707, M33708, M34174, M34175, M34202, M35387, M35680, M35920, M36568, M36854, M37053, M37253, M38333, M38459, M38460, M40594, M42486, M44032, M45782, M47157, M47899, M48251, M48252, M48255-M48262, M48273, M48274, M48779, M48780, M48837, M52228, M52748, M52756, M52952, M52994, M53730, M56285, M56286, M57654-M57660, M58155, M58345; 69, at $1,000 each; Nos. D1256, D1298; 2, at $500 each	70,000.00	57,238.75	54,425.00
Baltimore & Ohio R. R. Co. 5-percent refunding and general mortgage, series D, due Mar. 1, 2000; Nos. M4863-M4892; 30, at $1,000 each	30,000.00	28,650.00	23,100.00
Canadian Pacific Ry. Co. 4-percent perpetual consolidated debentures; Nos. O5882, O25561, O28256, *O31802, O37790, O37791, *O43047, O43142, O43143, *O45550, O81686-O81668, O87312; 14, at $1,000 each	14,000.00	12,415.00	13,177.50
Central Illinois Public Service Co. 4¼-percent mortgage, series F, due Dec. 1, 1967; Nos. M99, M1159, M1352, M1353, *M1706, M1742, M2514, M3006-M3010, *M3919, M4564, M4565, M4950, M5085-M5068, M5292, *M6981, M7468, *M8002-*M8005, M9671, *M9938, *M11477, M12536, *M13193, M14255, M14383, *M18295-*M18297, *M18299, *M18305-*M18309, M18524, M18525, M18527, M19609, M21746, M21747, *M24212-*M24216, M25019, M25020, M25022, M25322, M25323, M25519-M25321, M26041, M26252-M26254, M26339, M26340, M26366, M26926, M26927, M27087, M27349, M27836; 74, at $1,000 each; Nos. *D2386, *D3217; 2, at $500 each	75,000.00	74,185.00	72,093.75
Central Pacific Ry. Co. 5-percent 35-year bonds, fully guaranteed, due Aug. 1, 1960; Nos. M927, M935, M1586, M1687-M1690, M4371, M4373, M5512-M5514, M6423-M6427, M7871, M7872, M8369, M9516, M10127-M10129, M10547, M10548, M12788, M13272, M13341, M13477, M14970-M14973, M19550, M19753, M20144, M21527, M22401-M22405, M23086-M23095, M23882, M24354, M25010-M25014, M26094, M26095, M26465, M26643, M28040, M28466, M29550, M29751, M29544, M30545, M30693, M30694, M32878, M32978, M33159-M33173, M33277, M33278, M33612, M34012, M34438, M35849, M36674, M36981, M36982, M37052; 99, at $1,000 each; Nos. D887, D888; 2, at $500 each	100,000.00	92,067.50	95,000.00
*Cleveland, Cincinnati, Chicago & St. Louis Ry. Co. 4½-percent refunding and improvement mortgage, due July 1, 1977; Nos. M585-M589, M689-M693, M4294, M4818, M7306, M8739, M12210, M13151, M13152, M13184, M15774-M15776, M15984-M15987, M17570, M17846, M18749, M19107, M19109, M19111, M19112, M20012, M20021, M21069-M21071, M21170, M21271, M22817, M23846, M23996, M24386, M25340, M25345, M25346, M27393, M27705, M28211-M28218, M28251-M28255, M30029, M31164-M31168, M31198-M32024, M33203, M34191, M35847, M42488, M43326, M43361; 100, at $1,000 each	100,000.00	96,107.50	91,000.00
Columbia Gas & Electric Corporation 5-percent debenture bonds, due Jan. 15, 1961; Nos. A9157-A9181, A33237-A33261; 50, at $1,000 each	50,000.00	49,093.75	48,750.00
Cosmos Club, Washington, D. C., 4½-percent bonds, due July 1, 1949; Nos. 288, 289, 291, 292, 294, 299, 305, 350; 8, at $1,000 each	8,000.00	8,000.00	8,000.00

Statement of assets and liabilities, June 30, 1937—Continued

ASSETS—Continued

[Securities purchased during the fiscal year 1936–37 are indicated thus· (*)]

	Face value	Book value	Market value June 30, 1937
SECURITIES—continued			
*Erie R. R. Co. 4-percent prior lien secured by first consolidated mortgage deed, due Jan. 1, 1996; Nos. 907, 3299, 5171–5181, 5186–5195, 6490, 13058, 13059, 13069–13075, 13091–13094, 13700, 16005, 17424, 26693, 27779, 27780, 28134, 29118, 34191, 34671–34674; 50, at $1,000 each	$50,000.00	$49,875.00	$49,125.00
Great Northern Ry. Co. 5-percent general mortgage, series C, due Jan. 1, 1973; Nos. M997–M1000, M1633, M1640, M2384, M2796–M2800, M3138–M3141, M4540, M4761, M4762, M4945–M4952, M5430, M5475, M5476, M6377, M6380, M6381, M6588, M7005, M10158, M10175, M10430, M10834, M11758–M11760, M13302–M13306, M14301, M14517–M14520; 50, at $1,000 each.	50,000.00	51,071.25	55,187.50
Great Northern Ry. Co. 4½-percent general mortgage, series D, due July 1, 1976; Nos. M7891, M7892, M9067, M10973, M11227, M11676–M11685, M11934, M12895, M12910–M12934, M13730, M13731, M13860–M13865; 50, at $1,000 each	50,000.00	50,437.50	52,250.00
Illinois Central R. R. Co. 4-percent refunding mortgage, due Nov. 1, 1955; Nos. 1884, 10985, 10986, 12888, 13435, 13436, 14214, 14653–14655, 14781–14791, 14842–14854, 19859–19863, 19874–19876, 22558–22562, 23431–23434, 28682–28688, 28773–28780, 30991–31015, 33092–33096, 33104–33107; 100, at $1,000 each.	100,000.00	87,187.50	82,500.00
Illinois Power & Light Corporation 5-percent first and refunding mortgage, series C, due Dec. 1, 1956; Nos. CM5436–CM5440, *CM8905, CM9374, CM10635, CM11774–CM11778, CM12086, CM12165–CM12167, CM12286, CM12850–CM12855, CM15804, *CM19366, *CM22098, *CM22127, *CM23148, CM23872, *CM24459, *CM24833, *CM25202, *CM26437, *CM26438, *CM27319, *CM28678, *CM30459, *CM31827, *CM31828, *CM32560, *CM32946, *CM33452, *CM33453, *CM34136, *CM36286, *CM36287, *CM37727, *CM38475, *CM38494; 50, at $1,000 each	50,000.00	50,737.50	45,875.00
Kansas City, Fort Scott & Memphis Ry. Co. 4-percent refunding mortgage, fully guaranteed, due Oct. 1, 1936; Nos. 32, 756, 1013, 1093, 1418–1421, 1447, 1660, 2326, 2593, 2898, 3546, 4196, 4312, 4348, 4468–4472, 4610, 4621, 4787, 4944, 5096, 5447, 5728, 5930, 5932, 6224–6227, 6802, 6811, 6812, 6906, 7191, 7444, 7449, 7475, 7612, 7640, 7641, 7662, 7933, 7934, 8023–8025, 8027, 8028, 8062, 8222, 8624, 8739, 8880, 8970, 9486, 10936, 11733, 11742, 13082–13084, 13483, 13484, 14113, 14256, 14561, 14562, 14651, 14952, 15186, 15187, 15226, 15946, 16079, 16081–16085, 16207, 16276, 16767, 17281, 18104, 18173, 18177, 18453, 18782, 18783, 18806, 18856, 18947, 19069, 19154, 19655, 19893, 19911, 20178, 20235, 20694, 20891, 21065, 21345, 21346, 21387, 21730, 21880–21889, 22922, 22935, 23065, 23124, 23271, 24023, 24188, 24206, 24221, 24542, 24650, 25215, 25499, 25500; 136, at $1,000 each	136,000.00	79,096.25	59,840.00
Lackawanna & Wyoming Valley R. R. Co. 5-percent first-mortgage gold bonds, dated July 1, 1913, due Aug. 1, 1951; Nos. M853–M902; 50, at $1,000 each	50,000.00	48,750.00	10,000.00
Louisville & Nashville R. R. Co. 4 percent first and refunding mortgage, series D, due Apr. 1, 2003; Nos. M363–M387, 25, at $1,000 each	25,000.00	26,062.50	24,250.00
*Louisville & Nashville R. R. Co. 3¾ percent first and refunding mortgage, series E, due Apr. 1, 2003; Nos. M2538–M2547; 10, at $1,000 each	10,000.00	9,800.00	9,125.00
Missouri Pacific R. R. Co. 5 percent first and refunding mortgage gold bonds, series G, dated Nov. 1, 1928, due Nov. 1, 1978; Nos. M20326–M20375; 50, at $1,000 each	50,000.00	48,712.50	16,250.00
Missouri Pacific R. R. Co. 5 percent first and refunding mortgage, series I, due Feb. 1, 1981; Nos. M9994, M10757, M10758, M15428–M15450, M16440–M16442, M18265, M18828, M18829, M23249, M30095, M30444, M30546, M30901–M30905, M30908–M30915, M31587, M33255, M38252, M38253, M39860, M39861, M40137–M40140, M46664; 60, at $1,000 each	60,000.00	31,963.75	19,950.00
*New Orleans Terminal Co. 4 percent first mortgage 50-year, series A, fully guaranteed, due July 1, 1953; Nos. 3685, 11941–11961, 12106, 12107, 12149; 25, at $1,000 each	25,000.00	22,968.75	22,937.50
New Orleans, Texas & Mexico Ry. Co. 5½-percent first-mortgage gold bonds, series A, due Apr. 1, 1954; Nos. M439–M448, M647, M1610, M1765–M1767, M1808–M1810, M3396, M6873, M6874, M6896, M6897, M7099, M8135, M8207, M9643, M9950, M9996, M11059–M11063, M11944–M11948, M12486, M12487, M14131–M14133, M14417, M14418, M16406–M16408; 49, at $1,000 each; Nos. D200, D201; 2, at $500 each	50,000.00	51,763.75	26,937.50

Statement of assets and liabilities, June 30, 1937—Continued

ASSETS—Continued

[Securities purchased during the fiscal year 1936–37 are indicated thus (*)]

	Face value	Book value	Market value June 30, 1937
SECURITIES—continued			
New York Central R. R. Co. 4½ percent refunding and improvement mortgage, series A, due Oct. 1, 2013; Nos. *406, *1936–*1939, *10846, *18463, *25479, *25480, *28926–*28950, *30209, *38789, *38791, *44245, *45520, *49639–*49642, *51241, *57861, *57863, *59733, *59734, *60651–*60675, *62213, *62265, *62591, *63670–*63674, *65567, *66411, 71303–71309, 71324–71327, *71966, *72989, *72990, *77550, *79505, *79506, *79663, *81578, *82069, *86004, *89422, *94611, *96265, *96266, *102702, 102836–102849, *104070, *104060–*104062, *104840, *105882, *108975, *108960; 131, at $1,000 each	$131,000.00	$119,893.75	$113,315.00
*New York Central & Hudson River R. R. Co. 4½-percent refunding and improvement mortgage, series A, due Oct. 1, 2013; Nos. 246, 1160, 1162, 5761, 9031, 9635, 18532–18534, 20149, 23550, 25713, 27986, 32566, 32567, 32677, 36124–36126; 19, at $1,000 each	19,000.00	17,918.75	16,530.00
New York, Chicago & St. Louis R. R. Co. 4½-percent refunding mortgage, series C, due Sept. 1, 1978; Nos. M1212, M1213, M1388, M1496, *M3083, *M3084, M4071, M4262, *M7326, *M8316, *M9026, *M9652, M9766, *M10611, *M11474, *M11997, *M12329, *M12552, M12891–M12895, *M13686, M13756, *M14377, *M14497, *M16499, *M17579, M17785–M17787, *M18086, *M18087, *M18090, *M18777, *M19405, *M19539, M19970, *M20083, *M20090, M20173, *M20498, *M22758, *M22826, M24744, *M25857, *M26052, *M26422, *M27575, *M28036, *M28141–*M28145, *M28289, *M28577, *M29755, *M30248–*M30250, M30336, *M31740, *M33723, *M34033–*M34035, M36549, *M37223, *M37370, M37475, *M37896, *M38033, *M38470, *M39114, *M39819, *M40208, *M41080, *M44670, *M45004, *M45005, M45006, *M45426–*M45428, *M46833, *M47023, *M47334, *M49681, *M50930, *M50931, M51497, *M52144, *M52174, *M52175, *M53221, *M53276, *M56512, M59532; 100, at $1,000 each	100,000.00	89,281.25	83,500.00
Northern Indiana Public Service Co. 4½-percent first and refunding mortgage, series E, due Dec. 1, 1970; Nos. *M722–*M724, *M1194–*M1198, *M1633, *M1904–*M1906, *M2679, *M2749, M3341–M3350, M4410, M4659, *M4686, *M4771, *M4772, *M4793, *M4794, M4830, M5448–M5450, M5584, M5585, M5611, M5639, *M5866–*M5868, M5948, M7061–M7065, M8327, *M9216, *M9411, M10034, M10035, *M10041, M12284; 75, at $1,000 each	75,000.00	74,526.25	72,750.00
Northern Pacific Ry. Co. 4½-percent refunding and improvement mortgage, series A, due July 1, 2047; Nos. M1535, M1536, M1731–M1746, M2745–M2750, M4111, M6230, *M9683, *M9684, M9839, M9840, M9844, M9845, M9874, M9889, M9890, M11335, M11336, M11879, M11981–M11983, M12241, M12281, *M12285–*M12332, M12919, M13425, M13767, M13768, M16139–M16143; 100, at $1,000 each	100,000.00	100,435.00	95,250.00
Penn Central Light & Power Co. 4½-percent first mortgage, due Nov. 1, 1977; Nos. M2119, M3002, M3010, M3818, M3830–M3833, M5147–M5149, M5350, M5351, M5840, M7064, M9051, M9317, M11877, M13260, M13892, M15125, M15154, M15705–M15709, M16569, M16853, M18536–M18539, M18733, M19765, M19861, M19862, M20184, M20185, M21200, M21637–M21639, M21818; 44 at $1,000 each; Nos. D56, D267–D269, D690, D713, D767, D927–D929, D953, D954; 12, at $500 each	50,000.00	50,638.75	45,500.00
Pennsylvania R. R. Co. 4½-percent 40-year debentures, due Apr. 1, 1970; Nos. 7625–7628, 8670, 15107, 16747, 19428, 20386, 28115, 30074, 30075, 30772, 34941, 38154–38163, 41003–41052, 51958; 75, at $1,000 each	75,000.00	75,802.50	75,468.75
Pennsylvania R. R. Co. 3¾-percent general mortgage, series C, due Apr. 1, 1970; Ncs. 2477–2501; 25, at $1,000 each	25,000.00	25,593.75	24,875.00
*Pennsylvania R. R. Co. 3¼-percent 15-year convertible debentures, due Apr. 1, 1952; Nos. TM3185–TM3188, TM34003, TM34004, TM35210–TM35223, TM36865–TM36869; 25, at $1,000 each	25,000.00	27,201.25	26,312.50
Pere Marquette Ry. Co. 5-percent refunding and general mortgage, series A, due July 1, 1956; Nos. M21, M22, M2116, M1332, M5176, M8410–M8425, M8753, M8845, M9429, M10606–M10609, M10614, M10615, M11230–M11232, M11272, M11543, M14313, M16352, M17420, M19519, M20043, M27406, M27407, M28317, M29070, M29072, M29073, M29244, M30086, M32849, M32850; 50, at $1,000 each	50,000.00	51,423.75	50,000.00
Pere Marquette Ry. Co. 4½-percent first mortgage, series C, due Mar. 1, 1980; Nos. M2241–M2250, M5200, M5220–M5223, M5228–M5235, M5801–M5805, M5831–M5850, M10751–M10775; 75, at $1,000 each	75,000.00	74,468.75	68,250.00

Statement of assets and liabilities, June 30, 1937—Continued

ASSETS—Continued

[Securities purchased during the fiscal year 1936–37 are indicated thus (*)]

	Face value	Book value	Market value June 30, 1937
SECURITIES—continued			
Raleigh & Augusta Air Line R. R. Co.-Seaboard Air Line Ry. Co. 5-percent guaranteed first mortgage, due Jan. 1, 1931; Nos. 701–725: 25, at $1,000 each	$25,000.00	$25,000.00	$21,250.00
Reading Co. 4-percent Jersey Central collateral, due Apr. 1, 1951; Nos. 1864–1866, 2853, 2855, 4257, 6766, 7309, 7589, 9111–9113, 9399, 9400, 14836, 17677, 18459–18467; 25, at $1,000 each	25,000.00	24,967.50	24,093.75
*Republic Steel Corporation 4½-percent general mortgage, series C, due Nov. 1, 1956; Nos. CM8536, CM8537, CM8978, CM8979, CM13414, CM13415, CM13499–CM13502, CM13514–CM13523, CM15021, CM15022, CM20948, CM20949, CM23496; 25, at $1,000 each	25,000.00	24,437.50	24,062.50
St. Louis-San Francisco Ry. Co. 4½-percent consolidated mortgage gold bonds, series A, due Mar. 1, 1978; Nos. M7881–M7895, M14120–M14134, M17108, M17963, M17964, M19029, M25732, M25737, M41182, M41183, M41216, M62420–M62424, M91633, M91634; 50, at $1,000 each	50,000.00	43,850.00	10,250.00
Southern Pacific Co. 4½-percent 40 year, due Mar. 1, 1968; Nos. 8705, 14695, 14697, 14973–14975, 15806–15813, 15815–15817, 15819, 15821–15827: 25, at $1,000 each	25,000.00	22,750.00	21,062.50
*Southern Pacific Co. 4½-percent 50 year, due May 1, 1981; Nos. 3014, 3016–3018, 6426, 8783, 10466, 13435, 15081–15685, 18047, 19331, 32810, 32814, 33595, 33644, 40031, 40032, 42583, 42092, 42974, 48620; 25, at $1,000 each	25,000.00	23,781.25	20,812.50
*Southern Pacific Co. 4½-percent Oregon Lines first mortgage, series A, due Mar 1, 1977; Nos. 5417, 5418, 5422, 6068–6075, 29642–29644, 31263–31274, 32663–32666, 36519, 42195–42197, 51577–51581, 53660, 56612, 58211, 58404, 58405, 59517–59519, 59522–59524; 50, at $1,000 each	50,000.00	49,841.25	46,625.00
Southwestern Light & Power Co. 5-percent first mortgage, series A, due Feb. 1, 1957; Nos. *M365, *M366, M503–M505, M768, M780, M1474, M1475, M2731, M3182, *M3900, *M3920, M4310–M4312, M4615, M4732, M5043, *M6057, M6224, M6225, M6280; 23, at $1,000 each; Nos. D225, D229, D681, D684; 4, at $500 each	25,000.00	25,497.50	25,625.00
Texarkana & Fort Smith Ry. Co. 5½-percent first-mortgage guaranteed gold bonds, series A, due Aug. 1, 1950: Nos. M101, M102, M754–M763, M1593–M1595, M1739, M1742, M1777–M1779, M2014–M2018, M3001, M7002, M3908–M3910, M5767, M6078, M6482, M6757–M6760, M6912, M8341–M8343, M9299, M9472, M9473, M9629–M9631; 47, at $1,000 each; Nos. D102, D103, D186, D202, D237, D264; 6, at $500 each	50,000.00	52,271.25	52,375.00
Texas Electric Service Co. 5-percent first mortgage, due July 1, 1960; Nos. M30506–M30530; 25, at $1,000 each	25,000.00	25,625.00	24,875.00
Texas & Pacific Ry. Co. 5 percent general and refunding mortgage, series C, due Apr. 1, 1979; Nos. 1047–1050, 1337, 1340, 1406–1415, 1587, 1599, 1755, 1757, 1906, 7397, 7399, 8852–8856, 8797, 9501, 10206, 10207, 10646, 10939–10943, 11501, 11581, 11583, 11585–11587, 11589, 11764, 12256, 13278, 13383, 13434, 13435, 13791, 13830, 15707, 15749, 16708, 16853, 16854, 18585, 18644, 19039, 19149–19152, 19325–19328, 19367, 19368, 19574, 19576, 19951, 19952; 75, at $1,000 each	75,000.00	75,046.25	75,375.00
Texas & Pacific Ry. Co. 5-percent general and refunding mortgage, series D, due Dec. 1, 1980; Nos. 1365, 1366, 1369, 3001–3003, 3182, 5316–5325, 5980, 12251–12256, 12972; 25, at $1,000 each	25,000.00	25,000.00	25,000.00
Tide Water Power Co. 5-percent first mortgage, series A, due Feb. 1, 1979; Nos. M51, M53, M54, *M65, *M909–*M912, M973, M1375, *M2356, *M2551, *M2810, M2901, *M3113, *M3114, M3204–M3210, *M3317, *M3344, M3585, M3932–M3941, *M4242, *M4441, M4582, *M4668, *M4951–*M4955, M5033–M5035, M5981, M5982; 50, at $1,000 each	50,000.00	50,725.00	45,125.00
Vicksburg, Shreveport & Pacific R. R. Co. prior-lien mortgage 6 percent, renewed at 5-percent gold, due Nov. 1, 1915, extended to Nov. 1, 1940; Nos. 561, 661, 794, 982, 1323; 5, at $1,000 each	5,000.00	5,050.00	5,300.00
*West Shore R. R. Co. 4 percent first mortgage, fully guaranteed, due Jan. 1, 2361; Nos. 1017,·1467, 1609, 3349, 3476, 4053, 14432, 14834, 14952, 15491, 15595, 15599, 20737, 21434, 24777, 24819, 27046, 27047, 31159, 31836, 31837, 33045, 33716, 33895, 34968; 25, at $1,000 each	25,000.00	24,718.75	22,437.50
Total	3,077,400.00	2,916,172.50	2,671,600.00

Statement of assets and liabilities, June 30, 1937—Continued

ASSETS—Continued

[Securities purchased during the fiscal year 1936–37 are indicated thus (*)]

	Face value	Book value	Market Value June 30, 1937
PREFERRED STOCKS			
Atchison, Topeka & Santa Fe Ry. Co. preferred, par $100, 200 shares	$20,000.00	$14,685.00	$18,600.00
*Caterpillar Tractor Co. preferred, par $100, 20 shares	2,000.00	2,003.75	2,100.00
*North American Co. 6 percent cumulative preferred, par $50, 500 shares	25,000.00	28,125.00	26,125.00
Total	47,000.00	44,813.75	46,825.00
*Tide Water Associated Oil Co. $4.50 cumulative convertible preferred, no par, 200 shares		16,815.00	19,000.00
Total preferred stocks	47,000.00	61,628.75	65,825.00
COMMON STOCK			
American Can Co. common, par $25, 200 shares	5,000.00	18,515.00	19,200.00
American Cyanamid Co. "B" common, par $10, 500 shares	5,000.00	11,557.50	15,062.50
American Telephone & Telegraph Co. common, par $100, 500 shares	50,000.00	86,625.00	83,375.00
Atchison, Topeka & Santa Fe Ry. Co. common, par $100, 300 shares	30,000.00	18,102.50	23,025.00
Continental Can Co., Inc., common, par $20, 320 shares	6,400.00	14,535.00	16,640.00
Corn Products Refining Co. common, par $25, 500 shares. (*250 shares purchased during 1936–37)	12,500.00	39,733.82	30,750.00
E. I. du Pont de Nemours & Co. common, par $20, 300 shares	6,000.00	23,507.50	45,900.00
Endicott Johnson Corporation common, par $50, 500 shares	25,000.00	30,037.50	27,500.00
General Motors Corporation common, par $10, 1,005 shares	10,050.00	37,705.00	49,496.25
Hazel-Atlas Glass Co., common, par $25, 500 shares	12,500.00	53,180.30	50,500.00
National Biscuit Co. common, par $10, 500 shares	5,000.00	27,196.98	11,750.00
Norfolk & Western Ry. Co. common, par $100, 160 shares	16,000.00	26,876.90	38,240.00
Pennsylvania R. R. Co. common, par $50, 500 shares	25,000.00	15,887.50	18,000.00
*Southern Pacific Co. common, par $100, 500 shares	50,000.00	21,250.00	21,687.50
Standard Oil Co. of New Jersey common, par $25, 500 shares	12,500.00	20,064.58	32,750.00
Union Oil Co. of California common, par $25, 500 shares	12,500.00	10,625.00	11,750.00
United States Smelting, Refining & Mining Co. common, par $50, 200 shares			16,800.00
United States Steel Corporation common, par $100, 200 shares	20,000.00	7,405.00	19,875.00
F. W. Woolworth Co. common, par $10, 500 shares	5,000.00	21,475.00	22,937.50
	318,450.00	498,475.03	555,238.75
		10,412.50	20,850.00
		30,212.50	20,187.50
par,			
		26,462.50	10,187.50
Caterpillar Tractor Co. common, no par, 500 shares		14,261.25	45,000.00
Columbia Gas & Electric Corporation common, no par, 300 shares. (*100 shares purchased during 1936–37)		6,212.50	3,337.50
*Commercial Investment Trust Corporation common, no par, 500 shares		43,725.00	32,000.00
*Consolidated Edison Co. of New York, Inc., common, no par, 500 shares		21,087.50	16,625.00
First National Stores, Inc., common, no par, 300 shares		17,236.50	12,000.00
General Electric Co. common, no par, 1,000 shares		24,732.50	52,875.00
Hercules Powder Co. common, no par, 300 shares		14,596.25	44,400.00
Libbey-Owens-Ford Glass Co. common, no par, 300 shares		9,039.65	18,000.00
Loew's, Inc., common, no par, 500 shares		24,950.00	37,562.50
*National Dairy Products Corporation common, no par, 500 shares		12,450.00	9,437.50
Parke, Davis & Co. common, no par, 500 shares		18,076.54	18,500.00
J. C. Penney Co. common, no par, 500 shares		22,637.50	42,750.00
*Phillips Petroleum Co. common, no par, 500 shares		23,175.00	27,062.50
Sears, Roebuck & Co. common, no par, 550 shares (*50 shares purchased during 1936–37)		23,850.00	48,400.00
Timken Roller Bearing Co. common, no par, 500 shares		14,350.00	28,000.00
Total		357,467.69	487,175.00
Total common stocks		855,942.77	1,042,413.75
Total common and preferred stocks		917,571.52	1,108,238.75
Total securities, including common and preferred stocks		3,833,744.02	3,779,838.75

Statement of assets and liabilities, June 30, 1937—Continued

SUMMARY

Book value of securities as above, including common and preferred stocks		$3,833,744.02
Bank balance June 30, 1937:		
American Security & Trust Co.: National Academy of Sciences proper		21,812.82
Bank of New York & Trust Co.		201.59
Advanced to National Academy of Sciences, special		2,000.00
Property account (buildings and grounds at cost):		
Building	$1,448,644.82	
Grounds	185,764.50	
		1,634,409.32
Property account (equipment at cost)		12,064.36
Total assets		5,504,232.11

LIABILITIES

	Income	Capital		Income	Capital
General fund:			Murray fund:		
Invested	$13,315.00		Invested		$6,000.00
Uninvested	4,936.98		Uninvested	$4,219.22	
Agassiz fund, invested		$50,000.00	National Parks problems, uninvested	1,504.21	
Nealley fund, invested		19,555.55	Academy proceedings, uninvested	5,012.09	
Bache fund:			Joint proceedings, uninvested	6,050.12	
Invested		59,378.00	Emergency-fund proceedings, uninvested	3,327.79	
Uninvested	2,692.69	622.09	Scientific publication fund, uninvested	1,694.14	
Billings fund, invested		22,313.39	Smith fund:		
Building-construction fund, uninvested	3,120.18		Invested	4,022.50	10,000.00
Building-site fund:			Uninvested	3,362.85	
Invested	8,466.75		Thompson fund:		
Uninvested	4,997.60		Invested		10,000.00
Carnegie Corporation, special uninvested	0,570.86		Uninvested	2,190.09	
Carnegie endowment fund:			Walcott fund:		
Invested		3,444,159.71	Invested		5,000.00
Uninvested	47,147.36	105,840.29	Uninvested	736.12	
John J. Carty Medal and Award:			Watson fund:		
Invested		25,000.00	Invested	1,895.00	24,107.72
Uninvested	1,675.03		Uninvested	213.99	592.28
Comstock fund:			Appropriations under custodian of buildings and grounds, uninvested	992.77	
Invested	1,257.50	14,597.50			
Uninvested	4,604.60	492.50			
Consolidated fund, uninvested	1,556.59		Total	¹45,019.51	3,902,777.94
Draper fund:					
Invested		10,000.00	Total income		¹45,019.51
Uninvested	1,251.87		Total capital		3,902,777.94
Elliot fund:					
Invested		8,000.00	Total income and capital		3,857,758.43
Uninvested	2,517.53		Capital invested in property		1,634,409.32
Fund for oceanographic research, uninvested	5,864.63		Capital invested in equipment		12,064.36
Gibbs fund:			Total liabilities		5,504,232.11
Invested		5,545.50			
Uninvested	2,850.12				
Gould fund:			Consolidated investment fund:	Income	Capital
Invested	10,247.65	19,978.00	Invested		232,408.69
Uninvested	5,107.05	22.00	Uninvested	1,556.89	369.25
Grand Canyon project, uninvested	24.19		Total	1,556.89	232,777.94
Hale lectureship, uninvested	385.55				
Hartley fund:					
Invested		1,200.00			
Uninvested	429.03				
Joseph Henry fund:					
Invested		40,163.50			
Uninvested	2,538.53				
Investment reserve fund, uninvested	¹215,528.20				
Marsh fund:					
Invested		20,000.00			
Uninvested	821.15				

¹ Debit.

General fund, National Academy of Sciences from July 1, 1936, to June 30, 1937

RECEIPTS

	Budget July 1, 1936, to June 30, 1937	Actually received July 1, 1936, to June 30, 1937	Budget balance June 30, 1937
Interest on investments:			
Agassiz fund	$2,500.00	$3,101.73	[1] $601.73
Nealley fund	750.00	1,014.33	[1] 264.33
Annual dues from members	1,375.00	1,440.00	[1] 65.00
Total	4,625.00	5,556.06	[1] 931.06
Balance from previous year	15,000.00	18,944.94	[1] 3,944.94
Total	19,625.00	24,501.00	[1] 4,876.00

DISBURSEMENTS

	Budget July 1, 1936, to June 30, 1937	Actually disbursed July 1, 1936, to June 30, 1937	Budget balance June 30, 1937
Treasurer's office:			
Auditor's fees	$200.00	$200.00	----------
Bond of treasurer	25.00	25.00	----------
Miscellaneous expenses	500.00	251.80	$248.20
Transfer to investment reserve fund, 5 percent of income	375.00	205.81	169.19
Total	1,100.00	682.61	417.39
Home secretary's office:			
Executive secretary's salary	600.00	600.00	----------
Stationery and miscellaneous office expenses	400.00	400.00	----------
Reference books	50.00	33.70	16.30
Binding	50.00	46.25	3.75
Printing, multigraphing, and engraving	250.00	212.45	37.55
Express and telegrams	150.00	44.94	105.06
Total	1,500.00	1,337.34	162.66
Annual meeting	900.00	755.08	144.92
Autumn meeting	400.00	262.12	137.88
Total	1,300.00	1,017.20	282.80
Election of members	450.00	439.99	10.01
Memoirs, editorial	200.00	**151.25**	48.75
Printing of Biographical Memoirs	2,000.00	1,919.00	81.00
Current publications, preparation for distribution	150.00	150.00	----------
Postage, regular	250.00	250.00	----------
Contingent fund	400.00	131.95	268.05
Library fund	500.00	12.75	487.25
Expenses of members attending executive committee of council of the Academy	300.00	153.60	**146.40**
Total	4,250.00	3,208.54	1,041.46
Accrued interest on bonds bought	----------	3.33	[1] 3.33
Total for all	8,150.00	6,249.02	1,900.98
Surplus	11,475.00	18,251.98	
Grand total	19,625.00	24,501.00	----------

[1] In excess of Budget.

Appropriations under custodian of buildings and grounds, July 1, 1936, to June 30, 1937

RECEIPTS

	Budget July 1, 1936 to June 30, 1937	Actually received July 1, 1936 to June 30, 1937	Budget balance June 30, 1937
From Carnegie endowment fund	$45,284.03	$45,284.03	

DISBURSEMENTS

	Budget July 1, 1936 to June 30, 1937	Actually disbursed July 1, 1936 to June 30, 1937	Budget balance June 30, 1937
Salaries, office of custodian of buildings and grounds	$6,780.00	$6,780.00	
Salaries, employees, building	23,210.00	23,169.23	$40.77
Total disbursements ... $23,183.48			
Less reimbursements ... 14.25			
Net disbursements ... 23,169.23			
Coal	1,500.00	1,493.91	6.09
Electricity	1,815.00	1,815.00	
Gas	20.00	9.00	11.00
Contingent fund, maintenance of building	5,923.22	5,749.08	¹ 174.14
Maintenance of exhibits	3,925.00	3,558.89	366.11
Total	43,173.22	42,575.11	598.11
Insurance, 1933-37	2,534.78	3,602.49	¹ 813.63
Balance, July 1, 1936 ... $1,760.66			
Appropriated:			
July 1, 1936 ... 1,493.78			
May 14, 1937 ... 1,041.00			
2,534.78			
Reimbursement, Aug. 19, 1936 ... 125.68			
Total ... 4,421.12			
Expended July 1, 1936, to June 30, 1937 ... 3,602.49			
Balance, June 30, 1937 ... 818.63			
Total	45,708.00	46,177.60	1,416.74

¹ Not reverted.

˙ Reversions, June 30, 1937, amounting to $423.97, have been credited to Carnegie endowment fund, N. A. S., 1937."

Condensed statement of receipts and disbursements, National Academy of Sciences, July 1, 1936, to June 30, 1937

RECEIPTS

Balance July 1, 1936, as per last report _____ $30,510.06
Cash receipts:
    Academy Proceedings:
        Annual dues _____ $1,440.00
        Reprints and separates _____ 59.55
                       $1,499.55
    Joint Proceedings:
        Subscriptions _____ 1,982.23
        Reprints and separates _____ 1,770.45
        National Research Council _____ 2,500.00
                       6,252.68
    General fund: Annual dues _____ 1,440.00
    Bache fund:
        Frank M. Hull, refund of grant _____ $250.00
        Elmer Hutchinson and T. H. Osgood
          refund of grant _____ 142.77
                       392.77

Condensed statement of receipts and disbursements, National Academy of Sciences, July 1, 1936, to June 30, 1937—Continued

RECEIPTS—continued

Cash receipts—Continued.

Fund for oceanographic research: Sale of "Oceanography"	$22.50	
Joseph Henry fund: W. W. Coblentz, refund of grant	450.00	
Scientific publication fund: Royalties on "Oceanography"	7.50	
Total income from investments	187,142.07	
Navy Department-ship stabilization:		
From Navy Department	$1,970.26	
From adjustment	23.50	
		1,993.76
Salaries, employees, building 1937, refund		14.25
Insurance, 1933–38: Refund on premium		125.68
		$199,340.76

Total	229,850.82

DISBURSEMENTS

General fund:

Treasurer's office:			
Auditor's fees	$200.00		
Bond of treasurer	25.00		
Miscellaneous expenses (not including $129.97 fees to financial advisers)	121.83		
		$346.83	
Home secretary's office:			
Executive secretary's salary	600.00		
Stationery and miscellaneous office expenses	400.00		
Reference books	33.70		
Binding	46.25		
Printing, multigraphing, and engraving	212.45		
Express and telegrams	44.94		
		1,337.34	
Annual meeting	755.08		
Autumn meeting	262.12		
Election of members	439.99		
Memoirs, editorial	151.25		
Printing of Biographical Memoirs	1,919.00		
Current publications, preparation for distribution	150.00		
Postage, regular	250.00		
Contingent fund	131.95		
Library binding	12.75		
Expenses of members attending executive meetings of council of the Academy	153.60		
		4,225.74	
			$5,909.91
Appropriation for maintenance of building and grounds, under custodian of buildings and grounds:			
Salaries, office of custodian of buildings and grounds	6,780.00		
Salaries, employees, building	23,183.48		
Coal	1,493.91		
Electricity	1,815.00		
Gas	9.00		
Contingent fund, maintenance of building	5,749.08		
Maintenance of exhibits	3,558.89		
Insurance, 1933–37	3,602.49		
			46,191.85

Condensed statement of receipts and disbursements, National Academy of Sciences, July 1, 1936, to June 30, 1937—Continued

DISBURSEMENTS—continued

Fees to financial advisers		$6,189.28
To National Research Council for general maintenance expenses		62,774.13
Navy Department, ship stabilization:		
Expenses of investigation	$1,970.26	
Adjustment	23.50	
		1,993.76
Joint Proceedings:		
Salary, managing editor	750.00	
Printing and distributing	7,412.50	
Expenses:		
Boston office	440.00	
Washington office	242.45	
		8,844.95
Fund for oceanographic research:		
Clerical assistance	450.00	
Stationery	23.10	
Cartographic work	589.40	
Miscellaneous expenses	86.26	
		1,148.76
Carnegie Corporation, special:		
Government relations	7.00	
Clerical assistance	443.33	
Printing of Biographical Memoirs	1,000.00	
		1,450.33
D. C. unemployment compensation tax: Tax on Academy salaries		19.92
Advance for purchase of bonds		55,000.00
Carnegie endowment fund: Taxes, fire and liability insurance, etc., on real estate		5,914.79
Consolidated fund: Real-estate taxes, repairs, etc., on real estate		266.48
National Parks problems: Advance to Howell Williams		100.00
Payments from trust and other funds:		
Bache fund:		
Frank M. Hull, grant	$550.00	
Michael Heidelberger, grant	500.00	
Clyde E. Keeler, grant	500.00	
Harlow B. Mills, grant	265.00	
George D. Snell, grant	200.00	
G. Evelyn Hutchinson, grant	350.00	
Stationery	8.25	
		$2,373.25
John J. Carty Medal and Award:		
Edmund Beecher Wilson, honorarium	3,000.00	
Medal and engrossing	269.14	
		3,269.14
Draper fund: Medal and medal boxes		366.70
Gibbs fund:		
C. E. Teeter, Jr., grant	$150.00	
Henry E. Best, grant	210.00	
		360.00
Gould fund:		
Jan Schilt, grant	500.00	
W. J. Luyten, grant	500.00	
Real-estate taxes, commissions, and repairs	24.91	
		1,024.91
Hartley fund: Medal box		10.00
Joseph Henry fund:		
W. W. Coblentz, grant	$450.00	
Marston T. Bogert, grant	250.00	
		700.00

Condensed statement of receipts and disbursements, National Academy of Sciences, July 1, 1936, to June 30, 1937—Continued

DISBURSEMENTS—continued

Payments from trust and other funds—Continued.
Marsh fund:

Alfred S. Romer, grant	$225.00	
International Hydrographic Bureau, grant	125.00	
		$350.00
Murray fund: Medal and medal boxes		311.74
Smith fund: Harlow Shapley, grant		400.00
Thompson fund:		
Amadeus William Grabau, honorarium	$250.00	
Medal and medal box	671.40	
		921.40
Watson fund:		
A. O. Leuschner, grant	1,500.00	
W. J. Eckert, grant	200.00	
Ernest W. Brown, grant	100.00	
Medal and medal boxes	302.62	
Taxes, repairs, commission on real estate	44.08	
		2,146.70

Total payments from trust and other funds	$12,233.84
Total disbursements	208,038.00
Balance June 30, 1937	21,812.82
Total	229,850.82

NATIONAL RESEARCH COUNCIL

The disbursements of the National Research Council, under the authority of the National Academy of Sciences, during the year ended June 30, 1937, amounted to $489,834.44. Interest received on temporary investment amounted to $3,090.64.

The investment reserve fund on June 30, 1937, stood at $6,915.83, an increase of $5,511.63 for the year.

The book value of securities held by the Council on June 30, 1937, was $166,830.24, an increase of $35,945.99 for the year. The following shows the current interest yield on these bonds, according to the valuation used:

	Amount	Yield (percent)
Face value of bonds held	$175,333.00	3.12
Book value of bonds held	166,830.24	3.27
Market value, June 30, 1937, of bonds held (including one piece of real estate for $25,000, acquired under foreclosure)	164,576.75	3.32

The receipts from various organizations during the year for investigations to be made in cooperation with the National Bureau of Standards amounted to $11,598.82.

During the fiscal year ended June 30, 1937, the activities of the Council were supported by funds from various sources of which the principal are listed below:

(1) For general maintenance expenses of the National Research Council:

From the Carnegie endowment fund_____ $62,774.13

From Central purposes of the National Research Council, Rockefeller Foundation, 1936–37_____ 15,000.00

From the Carnegie Corporation of New York—emergency grant, 1937 (received during the previous fiscal year)___ 30,000.00

Total available for year ending June 30, 1937_____ 107,774.13

The Carnegie Corporation of New York has made an emergency grant of $12,000 to be available for the fiscal year 1938, and this amount was received during the past fiscal year.

The above contributions were the only ones received for the general support of the National Research Council. The council has disbursed in addition other funds contributed by a large number of organizations and individuals for specific purposes named by the donors. The diversity of these research projects is indicated by the following list of receipts which are several times larger than receipts for general maintenance:

(2) From the Rockefeller Foundation:

For national research fellowships in physics, chemistry, and mathematics, year 1936 (R. F. 34169)_____ 276.10

For the same purpose, year 1937 (R. F. 35037)_____ 37,500.00

For fellowships in medicine, year 1936 (R. F. 34164)_____ 4,133.15

For the same purpose, year 1937 (R. F. 35036)_____ 11,411.17

For fellowships in the biological sciences, year 1936 (R. F. 34169)_____ 3,684.18

For the same purpose, year 1937 (R. F. 35037)_____ 27,379.61

For international biological abstracts, year 1935 (R. F. 34152)_____ 2,302.24

For the same purpose, year 1935–37 (R. F. 35123)_____ 21,251.11

For sex research fund, year 1937_____ 71,718.71

For committee on drug addiction, Rockefeller Foundation, year 1936_____ 22,830.02

For the same purpose, year 1937_____ 27,303.54

For committee on radiation, year 1937_____ 26,150.29

For research aid fund, years 1932–33_____ 3,000.00

For the same purpose, years 1935–37_____ 9,000.00

For Washington Biophysical Institute, year 1937 (R. F. 37020)_____ 5,000.00

Total from the Rockefeller Foundation_____ 272,940.12

(3) From the General Education Board:

Child Development Society, General Education Board, 1936_ 1,750.00

Child Development Society, General Education Board, 1937_ 1,750.00

Monographs in Child Development, 1937_____ 2,215.00

Total from the General Education Board_____ 5,715.00

(4) From various organizations for the highway-research board__ 67,013.37

(5) From Navy Department for airships investigation_____ 2,035.80

(6) From Carnegie Corporation of New York for Scientific Aids to Learning, 1938_____ 10,000.00

(7) From various organizations for work to be conducted in cooperation with National Bureau of Standards:

For thermal investigations	$400. 00
For acoustic properties of materials	525. 00
For thermal properties of liquids	3, 589. 80
For fire resistance of materials	1, 217. 35
For ignition research	2, 750. 00
For impermanency of records	1, 450. 00
For physical and chemical properties of wire	1, 666. 67
Total	11, 598. 82

(8) From various organizations:

For research fund, committee on sedimentation	176. 75
For committee on drug addiction, Squibb fellowships, 1937	1, 400. 00
For committee on drug addiction, Merck fellowship, 1937	700. 00
For committee on drug addiction, Mallinckrodt fellowship, 1937	1, 000. 00
For food and nutrition committee	195. 57
For national intelligence tests	900. 65
For child-development abstracts	2, 494. 32
For royalties, International Critical Tables	1, 686. 00
For Annual Tables	250. 00
Total receipts during the year from all sources	465, 543. 41

Receipts and disbursements, National Research Council, from July 1, 1936, to June 30, 1937

RECEIPTS

Appropriation	Received during year	Previously reported	Transfers and other credits	Budget	Budget balance June 30, 1937
Rockefeller Foundation:					
National research fellowships (R. F. 34169) 1936	$276. 10	$49, 723. 90		$50, 000. 00	
National research fellowships (R. F. 35037) 1937	37, 500. 00			37, 500. 00	
Research fellowships in medicine (R. F. 34164) 1936	4, 133. 15	15, 866. 85		20, 000. 00	
Research fellowships in medicine (R. F. 35036) 1937	11, 411. 17			20, 000. 00	$8, 588. 83
Fellowships in the biological sciences (R. F. 34169) 1936	3, 684. 18	46, 315. 82		50, 000. 00	
Fellowships in the biological sciences (R. F. 35037) 1937	27, 379. 61			37, 500. 00	10, 120. 39
International biological abstracts (R. F. 34152) 1935	2, 302. 24	62, 697. 76		65, 000. 00	
International biological abstracts (R. F. 35123) 1935–37	21, 251. 11	3, 640. 97		40, 000. 00	15, 107. 92
Sex research fund, 1937	71, 718. 71		$530. 92	72, 249. 63	
Committee on drug addiction, Rockefeller Foundation, 1936	22, 830. 02	27, 169. 98		50, 000. 00	
Committee on drug addiction, Rockefeller Foundation, 1937	27, 303. 54			27, 303. 54	
Committee on radiation, 1937	26, 150. 29		1, 458. 50	27, 608. 79	
Research aid fund, 1932–33	3, 000. 00	66, 447. 69		69, 447. 69	
Research aid fund, 1935–37	9, 000. 00	61, 102. 07	113. 58	70, 215. 65	
Washington Biophysical Institute (R. F. 37020) 1937	5, 000. 00			5, 000. 00	
General Education Board:					
Child Development Society, 1936	1, 750. 00	1, 750. 00		3, 500. 00	
Child Development Society, 1937	1, 750. 00			1, 750. 00	
Monographs in Child Development, 1937	2, 215. 00			2, 215. 00	
Rotating fund, physics committees	1, 049. 97	16, 355. 69		17, 405. 65	
Highway Research Board, 1936	1, 666. 67	30, 827. 24		32, 493. 91	
Highway Research Board, 1937	20, 728. 92		5, 964. 35	26, 693. 27	

Receipts and disbursements, National Research Council, from July 1, 1936, to June 30, 1937—Continued

RECEIPTS—continued

Appropriation	Received during year	Previously reported	Transfers and other credits	Budget	Budget balance June 30, 1937
Safety research project, 1937	$14,617.78			$14,617.78	
Research fund, committee on sedimentation	176.75	$2,608.12		2,784.87	
Committee on drug addiction, Squib fellowships, 1937	1,400.00			1,400.00	
Committee on drug addiction, Merck fellowship, 1937	700.00			700.00	
Committee on drug addiction, Mallinckrodt fellowship, 1937	1,000.00			1,000.00	
Food and nutrition committee	195.57	9,675.00		9,870.57	
Pharmaceutical researches	25.00	585.00		610.00	
National intelligence tests, 1921	900.65	26,124.06		27,024.71	
Child development abstracts	2,494.32	15,422.27		17,916.59	
Royalty account, International Critical Tables	1,686.00	53,845.34		55,531.34	
International Critical Tables	8.60	336,686.86	$2,637.25	339,332.71	
Annual Tables	250.00	54,747.61		54,997.61	
Navy Department appropriation for airships investigation	2,035.80	6,956.98		8,992.78	
Thermal investigations	400.00	3,052.91		3,452.91	
Acoustic properties of materials	525.00	23,477.99		24,002.99	
Thermal properties of liquids	3,589.80	8,938.07		12,527.87	
Fire resistance of materials	1,217.35	14,690.00		15,907.35	
Ignition research	2,750.00	4,150.00		6,900.00	
Impermanency of records	1,450.00	5,000.00		6,450.00	
Physical and chemical properties of wire	1,666.67			1,666.67	
Scientific aids to learning, 1938	10,000.00			10,000.00	
Carnegie endowment fund	62,774.13		216.63	62,990.76	
Carnegie Corporation of New York, emergency grant, 1938	12,000.00			12,000.00	
Total	453,964.10	947,858.17	10,921.23	1,446,560.63	$33,817.14
Sale of bonds	95.39				
Interest on bonds	3,090.64				
Miscellaneous receipts	5,045.24				
Reimbursements	3,348.04				
Total receipts	465,543.41				
July 1, 1936, cash in banks	44,196.72				
Grand total	509,740.13				

DISBURSEMENTS

Divisions	Disbursed during year	Previously reported	Reversions and other charges	Budget	Budget balance June 30, 1937
I. Federal relations:					
General maintenance, 1937			$50.00	$50.00	
II. Foreign relations:					
General maintenance, 1937	$50.78			50.78	
IV. Educational relations:					
General maintenance, 1937	15.14		34.86	50.00	
Division of educational relations, Commonwealth Fund	747.54	$7,304.01		8,051.55	
V. Physical sciences:					
General maintenance, 1936	50.50	849.50		900.00	
General maintenance, 1937	398.83		805.17	1,200.00	
Revolving fund for publication of mathematical books		4,180.81		5,913.91	$1,733.10
Physics committees, 1932		912.50		1,500.00	587.50
Research fellowships (R. F. 34169), 1936	4,177.83	45,924.83		50,102.76	
Research fellowships (R. F. 35037), 1937	28,061.53			37,528.50	9,466.97
Rotating fund, physics committees	377.92	10,610.40		17,405.65	6,417.33
Washington Biophysical Institute (R. F. 37020), 1937	525.31			5,000.00	4,474.69

Receipts and disbursements, National Research Council, from July 1, 1936, to June 30, 1937—Continued

DISBURSEMENTS—continued

Divisions	Disbursed during year	Previously reported	Reversions and other charges	Budget	Budget balance June 30, 1937
VI. Engineering and industrial research:					
General maintenance, 1936....	$24.27	$1,655.58	$22.00	$1,701.	....
General maintenance, 1937....	1,600.00			1,600.	....
Highway Research Board, 1936.	7.44	26,522.12	5,964.35	32,493.	....
Highway Research Board, 1937.	20,662.11	....		26,693.	$6,031.15
Structural Steel Investigation..	2,376.42	18,036.62		22,520.	2,113.64
Heat transmission.............	50.00	42,081.02	....	43,154.86	1,023.75
Committee on electrical insulation, 1935.................	66.78	145.31		215.00	2.91
Safety research project, 1937...	43,758.15	....		44,617.78	859.63
VII. Chemistry and chemical technology:					
General maintenance, 1937......	1,050.85	....	149.15	1,200.00	....
VIII. Geology and geography:					
General maintenance, 1937.....	1,490.06	....	9.94	1,500.00	....
Bibliography of economic geology....................	721.91	31,835.31	....	32,557.22	....
Research fund, committee on sedimentation...........	262.35	1,711.34		2,784.87	811.18
Committee on stratigraphy...	46.78	28.22		75.00	....
IX. Medical Sciences:					
General maintenance, 1937.....	367.81		832.19	1,200.00	....
Sex research fund, 1936........	348.16	72,968.76	530.92	73,847.84	....
Sex research fund, 1937........	70,094.37	....		72,249.63	2,155.26
Fellowships in medicine (R. F. 34164) 1936...............	6,852.39	13,147.61	....	20,000.00	....
Fellowships in medicine (R. F. 35036) 1937...............	12,943.48	....		20,000.00	7,056.52
Committee on drug addiction, Squibb fellowships, 1936.....	652.00	748.00		1,400.00	....
Committee on drug addiction, Squibb fellowships, 1937....	748.00	....		1,400.00	652.00
Committee on drug addiction, Rockefeller Foundation, 1936	25,892.09	24,107.91		50,000.00	....
Committee on drug addiction, Rockefeller Foundation, 1937	24,907.68	....		27,303.54	2,395.86
Committee on drug addiction, Merck fellowship, 1937.......	700.00			700.00	....
Committee on drug addiction, Mallinckrodt fellowship, 1937	1,000.00	....		1,000.00	....
Committee on endocrinology...	392.40	87.31		2,000.00	1,520.29
X. Biology and agriculture:					
General maintenance, 1936.....	....	853.75	250.00	1,103.	....
General maintenance, 1937.....	727.55	....	472.45	1,200.	....
Committee on forestry.........	....	7,353.28		10,029.99	2,676.71
Food and nutrition committee.	455.01	9,219.18	....	9,870.57	196.38
Fellowships in the biological sciences (R. F. 34169) 1936..	15,546.80	34,560.36		50,107.16	....
Fellowships in the biological sciences (R. F. 35037) 1937..	26,698.51	....		37,530.00	10,831.49
National Livestock and Meat Board fellowships............	125.00	49,075.53		49,788.87	588.34
International biological abstracts (R. F. 34152), 1935....	1,068.85	63,931.15		65,000.00	....
International biological abstracts (R. F. 35123), 1935-37..	22,239.45	4,346.47		40,000.00	13,414.08
Pharmaceutical researches.....	6.57	307.47	....	610.00	295.96
Committee on radiation, 1936..	154.93	23,385.47	858.73	24,399.13	....
Committee on radiation, 1937..	23,885.66	....		27,608.79	3,723.13
XI. Anthropology and psychology:					
General maintenance, 1937.....	792.39	....	343.61	$1,200.00	64.00
National intelligence tests, 1921....................	1,150.00	18,026.14	....	27,024.71	7,848.57
Child development abstracts..	2,234.42	12,466.01	....	17,916.59	3,216.16
Psychiatric investigations......	....	8,095.23		10,000.00	1,904.77
Monographs in child development, General Education Board, 1936..............	1,500.00	....		1,500.00	....
Monographs in child development, General Education Board, 1937..............	402.32			2,215.00	1,812.68
Child Development Society, General Education Board, 1936.........................	1,880.10	1,619.90	....	3,500.00	....

Receipts and disbursements, National Research Council, from July 1, 1936, to June 30, 1937—Continued

DISBURSEMENTS—continued

Divisions	Disbursed during year	Previously reported	Reversions and other charges	Budget	Budget balance June 30, 1937
XI.—Continued.					
Child Development Society, General Education Board, 1937	$1,694.12			$1,750.00	$55.88
Field Handbook of Individual Differences	100.00	$100.00		1,000.00	800.00
Expenses and supplies, 1936	279.05	3,991.73	$16.47	4,287.25	
Expenses and supplies, 1937	2,903.10		997.82	3,961.52	60.60
New equipment, general, 1937	231.05		111.58	500.00	157.37
Salaries, 1936	5.25	75,434.75		75,440.00	
Salaries, 1937	70,282.17		1,16.83	71,400.00	
Telephone and telegraph, 1936	140.36	2,378.53	159.00	2,677.89	
Telephone and telegraph, 1937	1,869.27		552.11	2,671.38	250.00
Executive Board:					
General maintenance, 1937	1,168.75		323.75	1,502.50	10.00
American Geophysical Union, general maintenance, 1937	400.00			400.00	
Publications and publicity:					
General maintenance, 1936	2.21	2,997.79		3,000.00	
General maintenance, 1937	1,256.12		43.88	2,500.00	1,200.00
National Academy Proceedings and Subscriptions, 1937	2,500.00			2,500.00	
International Auxiliary Language	434.98	9,630.02		10,065.00	
International Critical Tables		334,882.63	3,948.72	339,332.71	501.36
Royalty account, International Critical Tables		53,845.34	1,686.00	55,531.34	
Annual Tables	752.15	54,118.36		54,997.61	127.10
Auditor's fees, 1936	300.00			300.00	
Research aid fund, 1932–33	739.08	63,966.79		69,447.69	4,741.82
Research aid fund, 1935–37	14,321.66	54,870.47		70,215.65	1,023.52
Attorney's fees, 1937				300.00	300.00
Navy Department appropriation for airships investigation	2,035.80	6,956.98		8,992.78	
D. C. unemployment-compensation tax, 1936	68.10	469.89	54.94	592.93	
D. C. unemployment-compensation tax, 1937			1,000.00	1,000.00	
Research aid funds, refunds				169.06	169.06
Conferences, special studies, and committees organized by N. R. C., 1937	7,243.07		5,256.93	12,500.00	
Advisory Committee on Annual Tables	149.90		.10	150.00	
Retirement fund, 1937				2,700.00	2,700.00
Scientific aids to learning, 1938				10,000.00	10,000.00
Problems of refrigeration		671.65		1,387.52	715.87
Impermanency of records	2,269.73	3,255.05		6,450.00	925.22
Acoustic properties of materials	484.53	23,097.88		24,002.99	420.58
Investigation of physics of plumbing systems	4.20	2,806.81		3,200.00	388.99
Thermal properties of liquids	3,627.69	8,172.05		12,527.87	728.13
Fire resistance of materials	1,790.21	13,637.82		15,907.35	479.32
Current-meter investigations	226.44	2,741.76		3,209.73	241.53
Thermal investigations	1,349.03	1,558.31		3,452.91	550.57
Ignition research	2,854.33	4,028.62		6,900.00	17.05
Physical and chemical properties of wire	1,000.00			1,666.67	666.67
Research information service:					
General maintenance, 1935	3.00	9,385.00	7.00	9,395.00	
General maintenance, 1936	10.35	9,116.50	3.65	9,130.50	
Book fund, research information service	197.03	142.26	2.80	332.09	
Reference library service:					
General maintenance, 1937	555.72		3,781.53	4,380.00	42.75
Book fund, reference library service	144.63			207.63	63.00
Investment reserve fund	667.86		1,003.34	8,587.03	6,915.83
Total	474,284.43	1,278,349.14	30,441.82	1,911,201.67	128,126.28
Purchase of bonds	15,550.01				
Total disbursements	489,834.44				
June 30, 1937, cash in banks	19,905.69				
Grand total	509,740.13				

National Research Council condensed balance sheet as of June 30, 1937

ASSETS

[Securities purchased during the fiscal year 1936-37 are indicated thus *]

Securities	Face value	Book value	Market value June 30, 1937
General maintenance fund:			
Mortgage notes secured by first mortgage on real estate..........	$10,333.00	$10,333.00	$10,333.00
Real estate owned at 322-324 West 41st St., New York. N. Y....	25,000.00	25,000.00	25,000.00
*Atlantic Coast Line Railroad Co., 4½-percent general unified mortgage, 50-year, series A, due June 1, 1964; Nos. 4423, 4427, 4595, 4596, 22491, 22492, 32448; 10 at $1,000 each................	10,000.00	9,496.25	8,750.00
Baltimore & Ohio Railroad Co. 5-percent refunding and general mortgage, series A, due Dec. 1, 1995; Nos. M362, *M3622, *M3785, M8185, M24349, M37088, M45801, *M46230, *M46684, *M58513; 10 at $1,000 each_____	10,000.00	8,272.92	7,775.00
Canadian Pacific Railway Co. 4-percent perpetual consolidated debentures; Nos. *G1602, *G4285, *G7655-*G7659, *G12782, *G15407, *G19782, G34505, G34506, *G76347, *G81995-*G81997; 16 at $1,000 each_____	16,000.00	15,100.00	15,060.00
Cleveland, Cincinnati, Chicago & St. Louis Railway Co. 4½-percent refunding and improvement mortgage, series E due July 1, 1977; Nos. 13182, M29886-M29890, M35311, M35312, M39404, M39405; 10 at $1,000 each_____	10,000.00	9,764.38	9,100.00
*Great Northern Railway Co. 3¾-percent general mortgage. Series L, due Jan. 1, 1967, Nos. M24490-M24519; 30 at $1,000 each _____	30,000.00	28,858.96	28,350.00
Kingdom of Norway 6-percent 20-year external loan sinking fund gold bonds, due Aug. 1, 1944; Nos. 621, 1361, 1362, 16941-16944, 21025, 24896; 9 at $1,000 each_____	9,000.00	9,357.50	9,517.50
*Kingdom of Norway 4½-percent 29-year sinking fund external loan, due Apr. 1, 1965; Nos. M4514-M4516, M7924-M7928, M11934; 9 at $1,000 each_____	9,000.00	9,007.50	9,180.00
*New York Central and Hudson River Railroad Co. 4½-percent refunding and improvement mortgage, series A, due Oct. 1, 2013; Nos. 8476-8500; 25 at $1,000 each_____	25,000.00	22,559.38	21,625.00
*Southern Pacific Co. 4½-percent 50-year, due May 1, 1981; Nos. 1757, 1758, 10328, 14265, 14266; 5 at $1,000 each_____	5,000.00	4,468.13	4,162.50
Southern Railway Co. 5-percent first consolidated mortgage, due July 1, 1994; Nos. 50909-50913; 5 at $1,000 each............	5,000.00	4,575.00	5,212.50
International Critical Tables:			
Canadian Pacific Railway Co. 4-percent perpetual consolidated debentures; Nos. *G13794, G47151-G47153, G48954, G86931, G88057-G88059; 9 at $1,000 each_____	9,000.00	8,032.50	8,471.25
*Kingdom of Norway 4½-percent 29-year sinking fund external loan, due Apr. 1, 1965; Nos. M162, M11935; 2 at $1,000 each.....	2,000.00	2,004.72	2,040.00
Total_____	175,333.00	166,830.24	164,576.75

SUMMARY

Total book value of securities as above_____	$166,830.24
Cash in banks June 30, 1937_____	19,905.69
Due from Bank of New York & Trust Co._____	41.34
Income receivable as shown under column "Budget balance"—receipts—p. 90.	33,817.14
National Academy of Sciences, special, advance from various funds._____	8,000.00
Property account, equipment at cost._____	34,261.13
Total assets_____	262,855.54

LIABILITIES

Capital invested in property_____		34,261.13
Current liabilities:		
Division appropriations as shown under column "Budget balance"—disbursements—p. 92.		128,126.28
Unappropriated fund, general_____		56,474.37
National Academy of Sciences, special_____		10,000.00
Carnegie Corporation of New York—emergency grant, 1938.		12,000.00
General purposes of the National Research Council, Rockefeller Foundation 1936-37......		11,956.54
International Critical Tables:		
Canadian Pacific Railway Co. 4-percent debentures...........................	$8,032.50	
Kingdom of Norway 4½-percent bonds, 1965....................................	2,004.72	
		10,037.22
Total liabilities_____		262,855.54

JULY 31, 1937.

ARTHUR KEITH,
Treasurer.

REPORT OF THE AUDITING COMMITTEE

SEPTEMBER 20, 1937.

Dr. FRANK R. LILLIE,
  President, National Academy of Sciences,
                Washington, D. C.

DEAR PRESIDENT LILLIE: Following recent past practice authorized by section 5, article V, of the bylaws of the National Academy of Sciences, the auditing committee engaged the services of a firm of certified public accountants, William L. Yaeger & Co., to prepare a detailed audit of the treasurer's accounts. This firm, after a systematic examination of the accounts of the treasurer of the Academy and of the National Research Council and of all securities, has submitted a report of its findings, with exhibits attached. This report covers all of the requirements in the bylaws cited above, which are as follows:

"5. The accounts of the treasurer shall, between July 1 and August 1 of each year, be audited * * *. It shall be the duty of the auditing committee to verify the record of receipts and disbursements maintained by the treasurer and the agreement of book and bank balances; to examine all securities in the custody of the treasurer and the custodian of securities and to compare the stated income of such securities with the receipts of record; to examine all vouchers covering disbursements for account of the Academy, including the National Research Council, and the authority therefor, and to compare them with the treasurer's record of expenditures; to examine and verify the account of the Academy with each trust fund. * * *."

The committee accepts the report of the accountants and also their opinion that the treasurer's report correctly sets forth the financial condition of the National Academy of Sciences and the National Research Council and is an accurate statement of financial operations for the fiscal year 1937.

There is a further paragraph attached to the report of the accountants which the committee feels should be quoted here for the information of members of the Academy:

"The deficit in the investment reserve fund of the Academy was again reduced and the Academy is to be congratulated on the efficiency of its financial advisers. On July 1, 1935, the deficit was $584,126.46, due to depreciated values of investments held. This was reduced in the fiscal year ended June 30, 1936, by $225,974.16, leaving a deficit of $358,152.30 as at July 1, 1936. During the fiscal year just ended this deficit was reduced by $142,624.10 and the deficit as at July 1, 1937, is $215,528.20. New income-paying securities were purchased with the net proceeds."

Very truly yours,

W. MANSFIELD CLARK,
T. WAYLAND VAUGHAN,
WILLIAM BOWIE, *Chairman.*

NATIONAL ACADEMY OF SCIENCES

1. CONSTITUTION

[As amended and adopted Apr. 17, 1872, and further amended Apr. 20, 1875; Apr. 21, 1881; Apr. 19, 1882; Apr. 18, 1883; Apr. 19, 1888; Apr. 18, 1895; Apr. 20, 1899; Apr. 17, 1902; Apr. 18, 1906; Nov. 20, 1906; Apr. 17, 1907; Nov. 20, 1907; Apr. 20, 1911; Apr. 16, 1912; Apr. 21, 1915; Nov. 11, 1924; Nov. 9, 1925; Oct. 18, 1927; Nov. 18, 1929; Sept. 18, 1930; Apr. 24, 1933; Apr. 27, 1936; Apr. 28, 1937]

Preamble

Empowered by the act of incorporation enacted by Congress, and approved by the President of the United States on the 3d day of March, A. D. 1863, and in conformity with amendments to said act approved July 14, 1870, June 20, 1884, and May 27, 1914, the National Academy of Sciences adopts the following amended constitution and bylaws:

Article I.—Of Members

Section 1. The Academy shall consist of members, members emeriti, and foreign associates. Members must be citizens of the United States.

Sec. 2. Members who, from age or inability to attend the meetings of the Academy, wish to resign the duties of active membership may, at their own request, be transferred to the roll of members emeriti by a vote of the Academy.

Sec. 3. The Academy may elect 50 foreign associates.

Sec. 4. Members emeriti and foreign associates shall have the privilege of attending the meetings and of reading and communicating papers to the Academy, but shall take no part in its business, shall not be subject to its assessments, and shall be entitled to a copy of the publications of the Academy.

Article II.—Of the Officers

Section 1. The officers of the Academy shall be a president, a vice president, a foreign secretary, a home secretary, and a treasurer, all of whom shall be elected for a term of 4 years, by a majority of votes present, at the annual meeting of the year in which the current terms expire. The date of expiration of the terms of office shall be June 30. In case of a vacancy the election shall be held in the same manner at the meeting when such vacancy occurs or at the next stated meeting thereafter, as the Academy may direct, and shall be for a term expiring on June 30 of the fourth year after that in which the election takes place. A vacancy in the office of treasurer or home secretary may, however, be filled by appointment of the president of the Academy until the next stated meeting of the Academy.

95

COUNCIL

SEC. 2. The officers of the Academy, together with six members to be elected by the Academy, and the chief executive officer of the National Research Council (provided he be a member of the Academy) shall constitute a council for the transaction of such business as may be assigned to them by the constitution or the Academy.

EXECUTIVE COMMITTEE

SEC. 3. There shall be an executive committee of the council of the Academy, composed of seven members, consisting of the president and vice president of the Academy, the chief executive officer of the National Research Council (provided he be a member of the Academy), the home secretary of the Academy, the treasurer of the Academy, and additional members of the council of the Academy appointed by the president.

Their term as members of the executive committee shall be coterminous with the term of their other office.

Except those powers dealing with nominations to membership in the Academy, the executive committee between the meetings of the council shall have all the powers of the council of the Academy, unless otherwise ordered by the council.

The members of the executive committee of the Academy shall by virtue of their office be members of the executive board of the National Research Council and shall represent the Academy at all its meetings.

The president and home secretary of the Academy shall, respectively, be chairman and secretary of the executive committee.

In the absence of the president and the vice president or home secretary the executive committee may select from among its members a chairman or a secretary pro tem.

The executive committee shall keep regular minutes and shall report all of its proceedings to the council of the Academy for their information.

Unless otherwise ordered by the council of the Academy or the executive committee, the executive committee shall meet once in each calendar month, and a special meeting may be called at any time by authority of the chairman, on reasonable notice.

Four members of the executive committee shall constitute a quorum. Letter ballots shall not be valid unless ratified at a meeting.

CUSTODIAN OF BUILDINGS AND GROUNDS

SEC. 4. On recommendation of the president, the council of the Academy shall appoint a "custodian of buildings and grounds," who, except where otherwise provided in the constitution and bylaws, shall have custody of all buildings, grounds, furniture, and other physical property belonging to the National Academy of Sciences or the National Research Council, or entrusted to their care.

He shall be responsible for and shall manage and administer these under such generic rules as the council of the Academy may make, and shall approve all vouchers for pay rolls and disbursements that come under authorized budget items or are specifically authorized by the council of the Academy for the maintenance and operation of the Academy's and the Research Council's physical property.

He shall hold office at the pleasure of the council of the Academy and shall receive such salary as it may agree and shall give such bond for the faithful performance of his duties as it may require.

He shall prepare and present to the finance committee of the Academy the buildings and grounds division of the general budget.

ADVISORY COMMITTEE ON BUILDINGS AND GROUNDS

He shall be chairman of a joint advisory committee of five on buildings and grounds, of which two members shall be appointed by the president of the Academy from the Academy council, and two from the executive board of the National Research Council, which committee shall decide, subject to the approval of the council of the Academy, all questions of allocation of space and use of public rooms.

FINANCE COMMITTEE

SEC. 5. There shall be a finance committee, of which the treasurer shall be chairman, consisting of the president of the Academy (or in his absence the vice president), the treasurer, the chief executive officer of the National Research Council (provided he be a member of the Academy), and two or three other members of the Academy appointed by the president, one of whom shall be a member of the executive board of the National Research Council.

It shall be the duty of the finance committee to provide for the safe custody of all financial resources of the Academy and to determine all matters relating to the purchase and sale of its securities.

It shall be the further duty of the finance committee to prepare and present to the council of the Academy for adoption the "general budget," made up of the three "divisional budgets," of the Academy proper, of the Research Council, and of buildings and grounds, which divisional budgets shall be presented to the finance committee, respectively, by the treasurer, the chief executive officer of the National Research Council, and the custodian of buildings and grounds.

The finance committee shall be empowered to employ competent investment counsel (hereinafter called the financial adviser) to advise with the committee upon the purchase and sale of all securities, mortgages, or other investments.

PRESIDENT

SEC. 6. The president of the Academy, or, in case of his absence or inability to act, the vice president, shall preside at the meetings of the Academy, of the Academy council, and of the executive board of the National Research Council; shall name all committees except such as are otherwise especially provided for; shall refer investigations required by the Government of the United States to members especially conversant with the subjects, and report thereon to the Academy at its meeting next ensuing; and, with the council, shall direct the general business of the Academy.

EXPERTS ON COMMITTEES

It shall be competent for the president, in special cases, to call in the aid, upon committees, of experts or men of special attainments not members of the Academy.

GOVERNMENT REQUESTS

The president shall be ex-officio a member of all committees empowered to consider questions referred to the Academy by the Government of the United States.

SECRETARIES

SEC. 7. The foreign and home secretaries shall conduct the correspondence proper to their respective departments, advising with the president and council in cases of doubt, and reporting their action to the Academy at one of the stated meetings in each year.

It shall be the duty of the home secretary to give notice to the members of the place and time of all meetings, of all nominations for membership, and of all proposed amendments to the constitution.

It shall be the duty of the home secretary to keep the minutes of each business and scientific session, and after approval to enter these upon the permanent records of the Academy.

TREASURER

SEC. 8. The treasurer shall attend to all receipts and disbursements of the Academy, giving such bond and furnishing such vouchers as the council may require. He shall collect all dues, assessments, and subscriptions, and keep a set of books showing a full account of receipts and disbursements and the condition of all funds of the Academy. He shall be the custodian of the corporate seal of the Academy.

ADMINISTRATIVE COMMITTEE, NATIONAL RESEARCH COUNCIL

SEC. 9. The president, vice president, home secretary, and treasurer shall be members of the administrative committee of the National Research Council and shall represent the Academy at all its meetings.

ARTICLE III.—OF THE MEETINGS

ACADEMY

SECTION 1. The Academy shall hold one stated meeting, called the annual meeting, in April of each year in the city of Washington, and another stated meeting, called the autumn meeting, at a place to be determined by the council. The council shall also have power to fix the date of each meeting.

Special business meetings of the Academy may be called, by order of eight members of the council, at such place and time as may be designated in the call.

Special scientific meetings of the Academy may be held at times and places to be designated by a majority of the council.

Sec. 2. The names of the members present at each session of a meeting shall be recorded in the minutes and 20 members shall constitute a quorum for the transaction of business.

Sec. 3. Scientific sessions of the Academy, unless otherwise ordered by a majority of the members present, shall be open to the public; sessions for the transaction of business shall be closed.

COUNCIL OF THE ACADEMY

Sec. 4. Stated meetings of the council shall be held during the stated or special meetings of the Academy, and four members shall constitute a quorum for the transaction of business. Special meetings of the council may be convened at the call of the president and two members of the council or of four members of the council.

DUES IN ARREARS

Sec. 5. No member whose dues are in arrears shall vote at any business meeting of the Academy.

ARTICLE IV.—OF ELECTIONS AND REGULATIONS

Section 1. All elections of officers and members shall be by ballot, and each election shall be held separately.

Sec. 2. The time for holding an election of officers shall be fixed by the Academy at least 1 day before the election is held.

COUNCIL OF THE ACADEMY

Sec. 3. The election of six members of the council shall be as follows:

At the annual meeting in April 1907, six members of the council to be elected, of whom two shall serve for 3 years, two for 2 years, and two for 1 year, their respective terms to be determined by lot. Each year thereafter the terms of two members shall expire and their successors, to serve for 3 years, shall be elected at the annual meeting in each year. The date of expiration of the terms shall be June 30.

SECTIONS

Sec. 4. The Academy shall be divided by the council into sections representing the principal branches of scientific research. Each section shall elect its own chairman to serve for 3 years. The chairman shall be responsible to the Academy for the work of his section.

NOMINATIONS

Nominations to membership in the Academy shall be made in writing and approved by two-thirds of the members voting in a section on the branch of research in which the person nominated is eminent, or by a majority of the council in case there is no section on the subject, or by a majority (however distributed) of the members voting in any two sections. The nomination shall be sent to the home secretary by the chairman of the section before January 1 of the year in which the election is to be held, and each nomination shall be accompanied by a list of the principal contributions of the nominee to science. This list shall be printed by the home secretary for distribution among the members of the Academy.

ELECTION PROCEDURE

SEC. 5. Election of members shall be held at the annual meeting in Washington in the following manner: There shall be two ballots— a preference ballot, which must be transmitted to the home secretary in advance of the annual meeting, and a final ballot, to be taken at the meeting.

PREFERENCE BALLOT

Preference ballot.—From the list of nominees submitted by the home secretary, each member shall select and inscribe on a ballot, to an extent not greater than one-half, nor less than one-third the list, those names which he prefers, as these limits shall be interpreted by the home secretary in his discretion, and announced by him, no weight being attached to the order of the names, and ballots not complying with these requirements being discarded. A list of the nominees shall then be prepared, on which the names shall be entered in the order of the number of votes received by each. In case two or more nominees have the same number of votes on this preference list, the order in which they shall be placed on the list shall be determined by a majority vote of members present.

After the preference list has been made up in the manner stated, the chairman of any section having two or more nominees on the list may, when its first nominee is reached, request the permission of the Academy to interchange the positions (on the preference list) of the nominees of his section, without altering in any way the positions of nominees from other sections. If a majority of the members of the Academy present favor permitting a section to make such interchange of its own nominees, it shall be done before proceeding further with the election.

FINAL BALLOT

A vote shall be taken on the nominee who appears first on the preference list, and he shall be declared elected if he receives two-thirds of the votes cast and not less than 30 votes in all. A vote shall then be taken in similar manner on the nominee standing second on the preference list, and so on until all the nominees on the preference list shall have been acted on, or until 15 nominees shall have been elected, or until the total membership of the Academy shall have reached 350, or until the Academy shall terminate the election by vote as provided below. In voting the final ballot, members shall inscribe on the ballot the name of the nominee with either *yes* or *no* or *blank*, and only ballots thus inscribed shall be counted. Members appointed as tellers must vote before counting the ballots.

ELECTION

Not more than 15 members shall be elected at one annual meeting.

It shall be in order at any point in the course of an election to move that the election be closed. If two-thirds of those present vote in favor of such motion, it shall prevail and the election shall thereupon terminate.

Before and during elections a discussion of the merits of nominees will be in order.

SEC. 6. Every member elected shall accept his membership, personally or in writing, before the close of the next stated meeting after the date of his election. Otherwise, on proof that the secretary has formally notified him of his election, his name shall not be entered on the roll of members.

FOREIGN ASSOCIATES

SEC. 7. Foreign associates may be nominated by the council and may be elected at the annual meeting by a two-thirds vote of the members present.

CERTIFICATES OF ELECTION

SEC. 8. A diploma, with the corporate seal of the Academy and the signatures of the officers, shall be sent by the appropriate secretary to each member on his acceptance of membership, and to foreign associates on their election.

RESIGNATIONS

SEC. 9. Resignations shall be addressed to the president and acted on by the Academy.

DUES, NONPAYMENT

SEC. 10. Whenever a member has not paid his dues for 4 successive years, the treasurer shall report the fact to the council, which may report the case to the Academy with the recommendation that the person thus in arrears be declared to have forfeited his membership. If this recommendation be approved by two-thirds of the members present, the said person shall no longer be a member of the Academy, and his name shall be dropped from the roll.

ARTICLE V.—OF SCIENTIFIC COMMUNICATIONS, PUBLICATIONS, AND REPORTS

SCIENTIFIC SESSIONS

SECTION 1. Communications on scientific subjects shall be read at scientific sessions of the Academy, and papers by any member may be read by the author or by any other member, notice of the same having been previously given to the secretary.

SEC. 2. Any member of the Academy may read a paper from a person who is not a member and shall not be considered responsible for the facts or opinions expressed by the author, but shall be held responsible for the propriety of the paper.

Persons who are not members may read papers on invitation of the council or of the committee on arrangements.

PUBLICATIONS

Sec. 3. The Academy may provide for the publication, under the direction of the council, of Proceedings, scientific Memoirs, Biographical Memoirs, and Reports.

PROCEEDINGS

The Proceedings shall be primarily a medium of first publication for original articles in brief form of permanent scientific value.

MEMOIRS

The scientific Memoirs shall provide opportunity for the publication of longer and more detailed scientific investigations.

The Biographical Memoirs shall contain an appropriate record of the life and work of the deceased members of the Academy.

ANNUAL REPORT

An annual report shall be presented to Congress by the president and shall contain the annual reports of the treasurer and the auditing committee, a suitable summary of the reports of the committees in charge of trust funds, and a record of the activities of the Academy for the fiscal year immediately preceding, and other appropriate matter. This report shall be presented to Congress by the president after authorization by the council. It shall also be presented to the Academy at the annual meeting next following.

TREASURER'S REPORT

The treasurer shall prepare a full report of the financial affairs of the Academy at the end of the fiscal year. This report shall be submitted to the council for approval and afterward presented to the Academy at the next stated meeting. He shall also prepare a supplementary financial statement to December 31 of the ensuing fiscal year for presentation at the annual meeting.

GOVERNMENT REQUESTS

Sec. 4. Propositions for investigations or reports by the Academy shall be submitted to the council for approval, except those requested by the Government of the United States, which shall be acted on by the president, who will in such cases report their results to the Government as soon as obtained and to the Academy at its next following stated meeting.

Sec. 5. The advice of the Academy shall be at all times at the disposition of the Government upon any matter of science or art within its scope.

ARTICLE VI.—OF TRUST FUNDS AND THEIR ADMINISTRATION

TRUSTS

SECTION 1. Devises, bequests, donations, or gifts having for their object the promotion of science or the welfare of the Academy may be accepted by the council for the Academy. Before the acceptance of any such trust the council shall consider the object of the trust and all conditions or specifications attaching thereto. The council shall make a report of its action to the Academy.

MEDALS

SEC. 2. Medals and prizes may be established in accordance with the provisions of trusts or by action of the Academy.

TRUST FUND COMMITTEES

SEC. 3. Unless otherwise provided by the deed of gift, the income of each trust fund shall be applied to the objects of that trust by the action of the Academy on the recommendation of a standing committee on that fund.

ARTICLE VII.—OF ADDITIONS AND AMENDMENTS

Additions and amendments to the constitution shall be made only at a stated meeting of the Academy. Notice of a proposition for such a change must be submitted to the council, which may amend the proposition, and shall report thereon to the Academy. Its report shall be considered by the Academy in committee of the whole for amendment.

The proposition as amended, if adopted in committee of the whole, shall be voted on at the next stated meeting, and if it receives two-thirds of the votes cast it shall be declared adopted.

Absent members may send their votes on pending changes in the constitution to the home secretary in writing, and such votes shall be counted as if the members were present.

2. BYLAWS

[In accordance with a resolution of the Academy, taken at its meeting on Apr. 21, 1915, the bylaws are arranged in groups, and each group is numbered to correspond with the article of the constitution to which it relates]

I

1. The holders of the medal for eminence in the application of science to the public welfare shall be notified, like members, of the meetings of the Academy, and invited to participate in its scientific sessions.

II

1. The proper secretary shall acknowledge all donations made to the Academy, and shall at once report them to the council for its consideration.

2. The home secretary shall keep a record of all grants of money or awards of prizes or medals made from trust funds of the Academy. The record for each grant of money shall include the following items: Name of fund, date and number of the grant, name and address of recipient, amount of grant, and date or dates of payment, purpose of grant, record of report of progress, and resulting publications.

3. The executive secretary, who may be a nonmember of the Academy, shall receive a salary to be fixed by the council.

4. The treasurer shall keep the home secretary informed of all warrants received from directors of trust funds not controlled by the Academy and of the date or dates of payment of all warrants.

GOVERNMENT REQUESTS

5. The treasurer is authorized to defray, when approved by the president, all the proper expenses of committees appointed to make scientific investigations at the request of departments of the Government, and in each case to look to the department requesting the investigation for reimbursement to the Academy.

TREASURER, NATIONAL RESEARCH COUNCIL

6. The treasurer is authorized to act as the treasurer ex officio of the National Research Council.

BURSAR

7. The treasurer shall have the assistance of a salaried and bonded officer, the bursar, who shall be chosen by the finance committee and be directly responsible to the treasurer.

INVESTMENTS

8. All investments and reinvestments of either principal or accumulations of income of the trust and other funds of the Academy shall be made by the treasurer, in accordance with the decisions of the finance committee, in the corporate name of the Academy, in the manner and in the securities designated or specified in the instruments creating the several funds, or in the absence of such designation or specification, in bonds of the United States or of the several States, or in bonds or notes secured by first mortgages on real estate, in investments legal for savings banks under the laws of Massachusetts or New York, or in other securities recommended by the financial adviser.

The treasurer may invest the capital of all trust funds of the Academy which are not required by the instruments creating such funds to be kept separate and distinct, in a consolidated fund, and shall apportion the income received from such consolidated fund among the various funds composing the same in the proportion that each of said funds shall bear to the total amount of funds so invested: *Provided, however,* That the treasurer shall at all times keep accurate accounts showing the amount of each trust fund, the proportion of the income from the consolidated fund to which it is entitled, and the expenses and disbursements properly chargeable to such fund.

The treasurer shall have authority, with the approval of the finance committee, to sell, transfer, convey, and deliver in the corporate name and for the benefit of the Academy any stocks, bonds, or other securities standing in the corporate name.

CUSTODIAN OF SECURITIES

9. On the recommendation of the finance committee, the council shall contract with a bank, trust company, or corresponding fiduciary institution to serve as the custodian of securities, including all of the Academy's personal property in the form of bonds, mortgages, and other securities, to collect the income from them, to protect the Academy in respect to expirations, reissues, and notifications, and to buy or sell securities on the order of the treasurer, as approved by the finance committee.

CONTRACTS

10. No contract shall be binding upon the Academy which has not been first approved by the council.

DUES

11. The assessments required for the support of the Academy shall be fixed by the Academy on the recommendation of the council and shall be payable within the calendar year for which they are assessed.

FINANCE COMMITTEE MEETINGS

12. The finance committee may invite to be present at any of its meetings the chief executive officer of the Research Council, the custodian of buildings and grounds, and the bursar, but they shall not vote.

III

ANNUAL MEETING—DATES AND PROCEDURES

1. At the business sessions of the Academy the order of procedure shall be as follows:

(1) Chair taken by the president, or, in his absence, by the vice president.

(2) Roll of members called by home secretary (first session of the meeting only).

(3) Minutes of the preceding session read and approved.

(4) Stated business.

(5) Reports of president, secretaries, treasurer, and committees.

(6) Business from council.

(7) Other business.

RULES OF ORDER

2. The rules of order of the Academy shall be those of the Senate of the United States, unless otherwise provided by the constitution or bylaws of the Academy.

3. In the absence of any officer, a member shall be chosen to perform his duties temporarily, by a plurality of viva-voce votes, upon open nomination.

DEATHS

4. At each meeting the president shall announce the death of any members since the preceding meeting. As soon as practicable thereafter he shall designate a member to write—or to secure from some other source approved by the president—a biographical notice of each deceased member.

COMMITTEE ON ARRANGEMENTS

5. For the annual meeting a committee of five members, appointed for each meeting, and the home secretary shall constitute the committee on arrangements, of which the home secretary shall be chairman. For the autumn meeting a member of the local group shall be chairman of the committee on arrangements, of which the home secretary shall be a member ex officio.

SCIENTIFIC PROGRAM

It shall be the duty of the committee on arrangements to prepare the scientific program for the annual meeting, and for this purpose it shall be empowered to solicit papers from members or others. It shall also be empowered to ascertain the length of time required for reading papers to be presented at the scientific sessions of the Academy and, when it appears advisable, to limit the time to be occupied in their presentation or discussion.

The committee on arrangements shall meet not less than 2 months previous to each meeting. It shall prepare the detailed program of each day and in general shall have charge of all business and scientific arrangements for the meeting for which it is appointed.

PAPERS—TIME LIMIT

6. No paper requiring more than 15 minutes for its presentation shall be accepted unless by invitation of the committee on arrangements.

No speaker shall occupy more than 30 minutes for presentation of papers during the scientific sessions of a single meeting of the Academy, except by invitation of the committee on arrangements.

Time shall not be extended except by vote of the Academy, and then not to exceed 5 minutes. The presiding officer shall warn speakers 2 minutes before the expiration of their time.

The discussion of individual papers shall be limited not to exceed 5 minutes, and the total time for discussion by any one speaker for all scientific sessions in any one meeting shall not exceed 15 minutes, unless approved by the Academy.

In order that adequate opportunity be given for the discussion of papers on the program, the committee on arrangements shall, in making up the program for the scientific sessions, allot not more than 80 percent of the available time of each session to the actual reading of papers.

If the number of papers accepted is too large to be presented in the scientific sessions, provision shall be made for holding two or more sessions simultaneously.

In arranging the program the committee on arrangements shall group the papers as nearly as practicable according to subject.

No paper shall be entered upon the printed program of scientific sessions unless the title is in the hands of the committee on arrangements at least 2 weeks in advance of the meeting. In the event that titles are received later, they shall be placed in order of receipt at the end of the list and read, if there is time. Such supplementary titles shall be conspicuously posted.

IV

SECTIONS

1. The term of service of each chairman of a section shall be 3 years, to date from the closing session of the April meeting next following his election. Chairmen of sections shall be chosen by mail ballot, the member receiving the highest number of votes cast to be deemed elected. It shall be the duty of each retiring chairman to conduct the election of his successor, and to report the results of the election to the home secretary before the April meeting at which his term of service expires. Should any section fail to elect a chairman before November 1, the president is empowered to appoint a temporary chairman to serve until the April meeting next following. No chairman shall be eligible for reelection for two consecutive terms.

PROPOSALS FOR NOMINATION

2. (1) Intersectional: Proposals for nomination to membership may be made in writing by any five members of the Academy and addressed to the home secretary; each such proposal shall be accompanied by a record of the scientific activities of the person proposed and by a list of his principal contributions to science, in triplicate; and with a statement as to the sections to which the name proposed shall be submitted for consideration. Such proposals as have been received by the home secretary prior to October 1 shall upon that date be sent by him to the chairman of each section designated, with a copy of the record and list of contributions.

(2) Sectional: Proposals for nomination to membership shall be in writing and shall be sent to the chairman of the section not later than October 1. The proposal for nomination of any individual will be accepted for consideration by the section only if it is accompanied by a list of titles and references of the more important published scientific articles of the individual and by a factual summary, not over 250 words in length, of his accomplishments.

Each section chairman shall edit material thus received and, at the time of the informal ballot, distribute it together with the material from the home secretary, relative to intersectional proposals, to the members of the section. The home secretary's office, if called upon, will assist the chairmen of the sections in the multigraphing of this material.

Each chairman shall keep a record of the names listed on the informal ballot and shall strike from the lists those names which were on the list in the previous year and received less than 2 votes on the informal ballot or had been on the list for 3 consecutive years without receiving in any one of these years on the informal ballot so many as one-fourth of the votes cast (counting the votes according to the number of members in the section who vote and not by the number of persons on the list for whom they vote). The home secretary shall keep a record of the votes on the informal ballots in the case of those persons proposed to two or more sections of the Academy and shall cause such names to be stricken from the lists of all sections if in three consecutive years there be no two sections in which the number of votes cast for the proposed nominee exceeds one-sixth of the votes cast in those sections except in case the number should be as many as one-fourth of the votes cast in one section, in which case the proposal should be considered thenceforth as a proposal in that section only. No proposal for nomination which is thus stricken from the list of the informal ballot shall be considered by the section (or sections) unless again proposed for nomination in the appropriate manner in a subsequent year.

NOMINATION BALLOTS

3. The chairman of each section of the Academy shall submit to the members of his section not later than November 1 of each year an informal ballot containing, in alphabetical order and without indications of rank on ballots of the previous year, the names of all those persons who received not less than two votes in the informal ballot of the preceding year and not less than one-fourth of the votes on the informal ballot in at least one of the preceding three years in the case of names in the list for three years or have been continued on the list by the home secretary or have been added to the list by him or have been newly proposed for consideration in accordance with the procedure above defined. Each member of the section shall be expected to return his ballot to the chairman within two weeks, with his signature and with crosses against the names of those persons whom he is prepared to endorse for nomination. The vote resulting from this ballot shall be regarded as informal.

The chairman shall then submit to the members of his section a new ballot showing the results of the informal vote; and each member shall be expected to return this ballot to the chairman with his signature and with crosses placed against names of three persons whom he judges to be worthy of nomination.

In order to secure an adequate number of nominations, the chairman, when necessary, shall obtain by personal solicitation a fuller vote of his section or shall submit to the section a supplementary formal ballot.

The chairman shall then certify to the home secretary, prior to January 1, the names of all persons who have been voted for on the formal ballots together with a statement of the number of votes each candidate received and of the number of members voting. Of these all persons who receive the votes of two-thirds of the members voting in the section in cases voted upon by one section only, or the votes of one-half (however distributed) of the members voting in any two sections in cases voted upon by more than one section shall be considered nominated

A properly edited statement of the accomplishments of each individual nominated to the Academy by the sections shall be sent by the section chairmen to the home secretary along with the nominations of the section. These statements together with summaries pertaining to those persons nominated intersectionally or nominated by the council shall be reproduced and distributed to the members of the Academy at the time of the preference ballot.

Persons nominated to the Academy and rejected by the Academy at the ensuing election may not be further considered by the sections until they have again been proposed for nomination in the appropriate manner in a subsequent year. Persons nominated but not voted upon by the Academy shall without further action be presented to the Academy upon the preference ballot of the next following year; but, if again not voted upon, the nominations shall lapse and not be considered except when renewed in the regular order.

PREFERENCE BALLOT

4. Preference ballots for the election of members shall be sealed in a blank envelope, which shall be enclosed in another bearing the name of the sender, and which shall be addressed to the home secretary, who shall cause the ballots to be tabulated for use at the election. If in any case it is impossible to determine who cast the ballot, or if the latter contain more or fewer than the number of names provided for in article IV, section 5, of the constitution, the ballot shall be rejected, but minor defects in a ballot shall be disregarded when the intent of the voter is obvious.

5. All discussions of the claims and qualifications of nominees at meetings of the Academy shall be held strictly confidential, and remarks and criticisms then made may be communicated to no person who was not a member of the Academy at the time of the discussion.

V

PROCEEDINGS

1. The publication of the Proceedings shall be under the general charge of the council, which shall have final jurisdiction upon all questions of policy relating thereto.

The National Academy of Sciences and the National Research Council shall cooperate in the publication of the Proceedings, beginning with volume VII.

MEMOIRS

2. Memoirs may be presented at any time to the home secretary, who shall report the date of their reception at the next session; but no Memoir shall be published unless it has been read or presented by title before the Academy.

Before publication all Biographical and scientific Memoirs must be referred to the committee on publication, who may, if they deem best, refer any Memoir to a special committee, appointed by the president, to determine whether the same should be published by the Academy.

3. Memoirs shall date, in thé records of the Academy, from the -date of their presentation to the Academy, and the order of their presentation shall be so arranged by the secretary that, so far as may be convenient, those upon kindred topics shall follow one another.

TREASURER'S REPORT

4. The annual report of the treasurer shall contain—
(1) A concise statement of the source, object, and amount of all trust funds of the Academy.
(2) A condensed statement of receipts and expenditures.
(3) A statement of assets and liabilities.
(4) Accounts with individual funds.
(5) Such other matter as he considers appropriate.

AUDITING COMMITTEE

5. The accounts of the treasurer shall, between July 1 and August 1 of each year, be audited under the direction of a committee of three members to be appointed by the president at the annual meeting of the Academy. It shall be the duty of the auditing committee to verify the record of receipts and disbursements maintained by the treasurer and the agreement of book and bank balances; to examine all securities in the custody of the treasurer and the custodian of securities and to compare the stated income of such sécurities with the receipts of record; to examine all vouchers covering disbursements for account of the Academy, including the National Research Council, and the authority therefor, and to compare them with the treasurer's record of expenditures; to examine and verify the account of the Academy with each trust fund. The auditing committee may employ an expert accountant to assist the committee. The reports of the treasurer and auditing committee shall be presented to the Academy at the autumn meeting and shall be published with that of the president to Congress. They shall be distributed to the members in printed form at the annual meeting.

VI

PROPERTY

1. All apparatus and other materials of permanent value purchased with money from any grant from a trust fund shall be the property of the Academy unless specific exception is made in the grant or by subsequent action of the council. Receipts for all such property shall be signed by the grantee and shall be forwarded to the home secretary, who shall file them with the custodian of buildings and grounds. All apparatus and unused material of value acquired in this way shall be delivered to the custodian of buildings and grounds on completion of the investigation for which the grant was made, or at any time on demand of the council, and the custodian of buildings and grounds shall give an appropriate release therefor.
2. A stamp corresponding to the corporate seal of the Academy shall be kept by the secretaries, who shall be responsible for the due markings of all books and other objects to which it is applicable.

Labels or other proper marks of similar device shall be placed upon objects not admitting of the stamp.

3. The fiscal year of the Academy shall end on June 30 of each year.

VII

STANDING COMMITTEES—RESEARCH FUNDS

1. Standing committees of the Academy on trust funds, the income of which is applied to the promotion of research, shall consist of 3 or 5 members. In order to secure rotation in office in such committees, when not in conflict with the provisions of the deeds of gift, the term of service on a committee of 3 members shall be 3 years; on a committee of five members the term shall be 5 years.

2. The annual reports of the committees on research funds shall, so far as the Academy has authority to determine their form, give a current number to each award, stating the name, position, and address of the recipient; the subject of research for which the award is made and the sum awarded; and in later annual reports the status of the work accomplished under each award previously made shall be announced, until the research is completed, when announcement of its completion, and, if published, the title and place of publication shall be stated, and the record of the award shall be reported as closed.

VIII

AMENDMENTS

1. Any bylaw of the Academy may be amended, suspended, or repealed on the written motion of any two members, signed by them, and presented at a stated meeting of the Academy, provided the same shall be approved by a majority of the members present.

3. ORGANIZATION OF THE ACADEMY

JULY 1, 1937

	Expiration of term
Lillie, F. R., president	June 30, 1939
Day, A. L., vice president	June 30, 1941
Henderson, L. J., foreign secretary	June 30, 1940
Wright, F. E. home secretary	June 30, 1939
Keith, Arthur, treasurer	June 30, 1940

ADDITIONAL MEMBERS OF THE COUNCIL

1935–38:	1936–39:	1937–40:
Harrison, R. G.	Flexner, Simon.	Jennings, H. S.
Russell, H. N.	Whitehead, J. B.	Veblen, Oswald.

1937–38: Hektoen, Ludvig.[1]

EXECUTIVE COMMITTEE OF THE COUNCIL

Lillie, F. R., chairman.	Hektoen, Ludvig.[1]	Wright, F. E.
Day, A. L.	Keith, Arthur.	
Harrison, R. G.	Whitehead, J. B.	

[1] The constitution of the Academy provides that the chairman of the National Research Council be a member of the council of the Academy and also a member of the executive committee of the council of the Academy, provided he be a member of the Academy.

SECTIONS

1. *Mathematics*

Evans, G. C., chairman, 1940.
Alexander, J. W.
Bateman, Harry.
Bell, E. T.
Birkhoff, G. D.
Blichfeldt, H. F.
Bliss, G. A.
Coble, A. B.

Dickson, L. E.
Eisenhart, L. P.
Jackson, Dunham.
Kasner, Edward.
Lefschetz, Solomon.
Miller, G. A.
Moore, R. L.
Morse, Marston.
Neumann, J. von.

Osgood, W. F.
Ritt, J. F.
Vandiver, H. S.
Van Vleck, E. B.
Veblen, Oswald.
Walsh, J. L.
White, H. S.
Wiener, Norbert.

2. *Astronomy*

Leuschner, A. O., chairman, 1938.
Abbot, C. G.
Adams, W. S.
Aitken, R. G.
Anderson, J. A.
Babcock, H. D.
Bowen, I. S.
Bowie, William.
Brown, E. W.

Campbell, W. W.
Curtis, H. D.
Hale, G. E.
Hubble, E. P.
Merrill, P. W.
Mitchell, S. A.
Moore, J. H.
Moulton, F. R.
Nicholson, S. B.
Ross, F. E.

Russell, H. N.
Schlesinger, F.
Seares, F. H.
Shapley, Harlow.
Slipher, V. M.
Stebbins, Joel.
Struve, Otto.
Trumpler, R. J.
Wright, W. H.

3. *Physics*

Mason, Max, chairman, 1939.
Ames, J. S.
Birge, R. T.
Bridgman, P. W.
Coblentz, W. W.
Compton, A. H.
Compton, K. T.
Coolidge, W. D.
Crew, Henry.
Davis, Bergen.

Davisson, C. J.
Dempster, A. J.
Epstein, P. S.
Hall, E. H.
Hull, A. W.
Ives, H. E.
Kemble, E. C.
Lawrence, E. O.
Lyman, Theodore.
Merritt, Ernest.
Miller, D. C.

Millikan, R. A.
Mulliken, R. S.
Nichols, E. L.
Pierce, G. W.
Richtmyer, F. K.
Saunders, F. A.
Slater, J. C.
Van Vleck, J. H.
Webster, D. L.
Wilson, Edwin B.
Wood, R. W.

4. *Engineering*

Gherardi, Bancroft, chairman, 1938.
Adams, C. A.
Baekeland, L. H.
Buckley, O. E.
Bush, Vannevar.
Dunn, Gano.
Durand, W. F.

Emmet, W. L. R.
Fletcher, Harvey.
Hoover, Herbert.
Hovgaard, William.
Hunsaker, J. C.
Jewett, F. B.
Kennelly, A. E.
Kettering, C. F.

Modjeski, Ralph.
Sauveur, Albert.
Stillwell, L. B.
Taylor, D. W.
Whitehead, J. B.
Wright, Orville.

5. *Chemistry*

Kraus, C. A., chairman, 1938.
Adams, Roger.
Bancroft, W. D.
Baxter, G. P.
Bogert, Marston T.
Bray, W. C.
Conant, J. B.
Giauque, W. F.
Gomberg, Moses.
Gortner, R. A.

Harkins, W. D.
Hildebrand, J. H.
Hudson, C. S.
Hulett, G. A.
Jacobs, W. A.
Johnson, T. B.
Keyes, F. G.
Kohler, E. P.
Lamb, A. B.
Langmuir, Irving.
Levene, P. A. T.

Lind, S. C.
MacInnes, D. A.
Michael, Arthur.
Norris, J. F.
Noyes, W. A.
Pauling, Linus.
Tolman, R. C.
Urey, H. C.
Whitney, W. R.

6. *Geology and Paleontology*

Mendenhall, W. C., chairman, 1939.
Allen, E. T.
Berkey, C. P.
Berry, E. W.
Blackwelder, Eliot.
Bowen, N. L.
Bowman, Isaiah.
Cross, Whitman.
Daly, R. A.

Day, A. L.
Hewett, D. F.
Johnson, D. W.
Keith, Arthur.
Knopf, Adolph.
Lawson, A. C.
Leith, C. K.
Leverett, Frank.
Lindgren, Waldemar.
Longwell, C. R.

Merriam, J. C.
Palache, Charles.
Reid, H. F.
Ruedemann, Rudolf.
Schuebert, Charles.
Scott, W. B.
Ulrich, E. O.
Vaughan, T. W.
Willis, Bailey.
Wright, F. E.

7. *Botany*

Blakeslee, A. F., chairman, 1938.
Allen, C. E.
Bailey, I. W.
Bailey, L. H.
Campbell, D. H.
Clinton, G. P.
Dodge, B. O.

Duggar, B. M.
East, E. M.
Emerson, R. A.
Fernald, M. L.
Fred, E. B.
Harper, R. A.
Hoagland, D. R.
Jones, L. R.

Kunkel, L. O.
Merrill, E. D.
Osterhout, W. J. V.
Setchell, W. A.
Sinnott, E. W.
Stakman, E. C.
Thom, Charles
Trelease, William.

8. *Zoology and Anatomy*

Stockard, C. R., chairman, 1939.
Barbour, Thomas.
Bigelow, H. B.
Bridges, C. B.
Calkins, G. N.
Castle, W. E.
Chapman, F. M.
Child, C. M.
Coghill, G. E.
Conklin, E. G.
Davenport, C. B.
Detwiler, S. R.
Donaldson, H. H.

Gregory, W. K.
Harrison, R. G.
Hartman, C. G.
Harvey, E. N.
Herrick, C. J.
Howard, L. O.
Jennings, H. S.
Kellogg, Vernon.
Kofoid, C. A.
Lewis, W. H.
Lillie, F. R.
McClung, C. E.
Mark, E. L.
Morgan, T. H.

Muller, H. J.
Parker, G. H.
Pearl, Raymond.
Stejneger, Leonhard.
Streeter, G. L.
Sturtevant, A. H.
Sumner, F. B.
Tennent, D. H.
Wilson, Edmund B.
Wilson, H. V. P.
Woodruff, L. L.
Wright, S. G.

9. *Physiology and Biochemistry*

Clark, W. M., chairman, 1939.
Abel, J. J.
Benedict, F. G.
Cannon, W. B.
Carlson, A. J.
Chittenden, R. H.
DuBois, E. F.

Erlanger, Joseph.
Evans, H. M.
Forbes, Alexander.
Gasser, H. S.
Henderson, L. J.
Henderson, Yandell.
Howell, W. H.
Hunt, Reid.

McCollum, E. V.
Northrop, J. H.
Richards, A. N.
Rose, W. C.
Shaffer, P. A.
Sherman, H. C.
Van Slyke, D. D.

10. *Pathology and Bacteriology*

Flexner, Simon, chairman, 1939.
Avery, O. T.
Cole, Rufus.
Cushing, Harvey.
Dochez, A. R.
Ewing, James.

Goodpasture, E. W.
Hektoen, Ludvig.
Landsteiner, Karl.
Loeb, Leo.
MacCallum, W. G.
Minot, G. R.
Novy, F. G.

Ople, E. L.
Rivers, T. M.
Rous, Peyton.
Sabin, Florence R.
Wells, H. Gideon.
Whipple, G. H.
Zinsser, Hans.

11. *Anthropology and Psychology*

Seashore, C. E., chairman, 1938.
Angell, J. R.
Boas, Franz.
Boring, E. G.
Cattell, J. McKeen.
Dewey, John.
Hooton, E. A.
Hrdlička, Aleš.
Hull, C. L.

Hunter, W. S.
Kidder, A. V.
Kroeber, A. L.
Lashley, K. S.
Lowie, R. H.
Merriam, C. H.
Miles, W. R.
Pillsbury, W. B.
Sapir, Edward.
Stratton, G. M.

Swanton, J. R.
Terman, L. M.
Thorndike, E. L.
Tolman, E. C.
Washburn, Margaret F.
Wissler, Clark.
Woodworth, R. S.
Yerkes, R. M.

4. STANDING COMMITTEES OF THE ACADEMY

ALBERT NATIONAL PARK

Yerkes, R. M., chairman.   Chapman, F. M.   Wissler, Clark.

AUDITING COMMITTEE

Bowie, William, chairman.   Clark, W. M.   Vaughan, T. W.

BIOGRAPHICAL MEMOIRS

Davenport, C. B., chairman.
Hrdlička, Aleš.

Pearl, Raymond.
Thorndike, E. L.

Wright, F. E.

BUILDINGS AND GROUNDS ADVISORY COMMITTEE (JOINT COMMITTEE OF ACADEMY AND RESEARCH COUNCIL)

Brockett, Paul, chairman.
Coker, R. E.

Day, A. L.
Hektoen, Ludvig.

Wright, F. E.

CALENDAR

Wright, F. E., chairman.
Campbell, W. W.

Dunn, Gano.
Millikan, R. A.

Russell, H. N.

EXHIBITS (JOINT COMMITTEE OF ACADEMY AND RESEARCH COUNCIL)

Wright, F. E., chairman.
Brockett, Paul, secretary.
Hale, G. E., member at large.

Shapley, Harlow, member at large.
The chairman of each of the sections of the Academy.

The chairman of each of the divisions of the Research Council.

Executive committee on exhibits

Wright, F. E., chairman.
Brockett, Paul, secretary.

Day, A. L.
Hale, G. E.

Hektoen, Ludvig.
Merriam, J. C.

FINANCE COMMITTEE

The treasurer of the Academy, chairman ex officio (Arthur Keith).
The president of the Academy, ex officio (F. R. Lillie).

The chairman of the National Research Council, ex officio (Ludvig Hektoen).

Abbot, C. G.
Day, A. L.
Jewett, F. B.

FUNDS FOR ACADEMY PURPOSES

Flexner, Simon, chairman.

Kellogg, Vernon.
Lillie, F. R.

Shapley, Harlow.

GOVERNMENT RELATIONS AND SCIENCE ADVISORY COMMITTEE

The president of the Academy, chairman ex officio (F. R. Lillie, 1939).
The vice president of the Academy (A. L. Day, 1941).
The home secretary of the Academy (F. E. Wright, 1939).
The chairman or specially elected representative of each section of the Academy, as follows:

Mathematics ------------------------------------ Bliss, G. A., 1940.
Astronomy -------------------------------------- Leuschner, A. O., 1938.
Physics --- Wilson, Edwin B., 1939.
Engineering ------------------------------------ Gherardi, Bancroft, 1938.
Chemistry -------------------------------------- Adams, Roger, 1938.
Geology and Paleontology ---------------------- Bowman, Isaiah, 1939.
Botany --- Blakeslee, A. F., 1938.
Zoology and Anatomy -------------------------- Stockard, C. R., 1939.
Physiology and Biochemistry ------------------ Carlson, A. J., 1939.
Pathology and Bacteriology -------------------- Flexner, Simon, 1939.
Anthropology and Psychology ------------------ Seashore, C. E., 1938.

The chairman of the National Research Council (Ludvig Hektoen, 1938).
Members-at-large, as follows:

Bush, Vannevar, 1939.   Jewett, F. B., 1939.   Millikan, R. A., 1940.
Compton, K. T., 1938.   Jones, L. R., 1939.   Whipple, G. H., 1940.
Dunn, Gano, 1939.   Leith, C. K., 1939.

Executive committee of Government Relations and Science Advisory Committee

Lillie, F. R., chairman ex   Compton, K. T.   Leith, C. K.
  officio.   Day, A. L.   Millikan, R. A.
Adams, Roger.   Dunn, Gano.   Whipple, G. H.
Bowman, Isaiah.   Jewett, F. B.
Bush, Vannevar.   Jones, L. R.

LIBRARY

Hudson, C. S., chairman.   Compton, K. T.   Parker, G. H.
Adams, W. S.   Harkins, W. D.   Scott, W. B.
Cattell, J. McK.   Henderson, Yandell.   Brockett, Paul.

Subcommittee

Hudson, C. S., chairman.   Pearl, Raymond.   Swanton, J. R.
Coblentz, W. W., vice   Streeter, G. S.
  chairman.

MEMORIALS (BUSTS, PORTRAITS, AND STATUES)

--------------, chairman.   Day, A. L.   Merriam, J. C.
Angell, J. R.   Dunn, Gano.
Cushing, Harvey.   Hale, G. E.

OCEANOGRAPHY

Bigelow, H. B., chairman.   Day, A. L.   Vaughan, T. W.
Bowie, William.   Duggar, B. M.
Conklin, E. G.   Merriam, J. C.

PROCEEDINGS, EDITORIAL BOARD

Bastin, E. S.   Henderson, L. J.   Moody, H. R.
Bush, V.   Hunter, W. S.   Osterhout, W. J. V.
Coker, R. E.   Jewett, F. B.   Richtmyer, F. K.
Day, A. L.   Lamb, A. B.   Seares, F. H.
Eisenhart, L. P.   Long, E. R.   Wright, F. E.
Harrison, R. G.   Miles, W. R.
Hektoen, L.   Millikan, R. A.

PUBLICATIONS OF THE ACADEMY

The president of the Academy (F. R. Lillie).
The home secretary of the Academy (F. E. Wright).
Conklin, E. G.

REVISION OF THE CONSTITUTION

Wilson, Edwin B., chair-
man.

Day, A. L.
Dunn, Gano.

Merriam, J. C.
Morgan, T. H.

SCIENTIFIC PROBLEMS OF NATIONAL PARKS

Merriam, J. C., chairman.   Whiting, Frederic Allen.   Wright, F. E.

WEIGHTS, MEASURES, AND COINAGE

Kennelly, A. E., chairman.
Ames, J. S.

Baxter, G. P.
Bowie, William.

Wood, R. W.

5. TRUST FUNDS OF THE ACADEMY

ALEXANDER DALLAS BACHE FUND

[$60,000]

Researches in physical and natural science

Board of directors

Wilson, Edwin B.,
chairman.

Osterhout, W. J. V.

Stockard, C. R.

JAMES CRAIG WATSON FUND

[$25,000]

Watson medal and the promotion of astronomical research

Trustees

Leuschner, A. O.,
chairman.

Ross, F. E.

Seares, F. H.

WATSON MEDAL AWARDS

Gould. B. A., 1887.
Schoenfeld, Ed., 1889.
Auwers, Arthur, 1891.
Chandler, S. C., 1894.

Gill. Sir David, 1899.
Kapteyn, J. C., 1913.
Leuschner, A. O., 1915.
Charlier, C. V. L., 1924.

de Sitter, Willem, 1929.
Brown, Ernest William,
1936.

HENRY DRAPER FUND

[$10,000]

Draper medal and investigations in astronomical physics

Members of the committee

Stebbins, Joel, chairman,
1938.

Adams, W. S., 1941.
Hubble, Edwin, 1942.

Merrill, P. W., 1939.
Mitchell, S. A., 1940.

HENRY DRAPER MEDAL AWARDS

Langley, S. P., 1886.
Pickering, E. C., 1888.
Rowland, H. A., 1890.
Vogel, H. K., 1893.
Keeler, J. E., 1899.
Huggins, Sir Wm., 1901.
Hale, George E., 1904.
Campbell, W. W., 1906.
Abbot, C. G., 1910.
Deslandres, H., 1913.

Stebbins, Joel, 1915.
Michelson, A. A., 1916.
Adams, W. S., 1918.
Fabry, Charles, 1919.
Fowler, Alfred, 1920.
Zeeman, Pieter, 1921.
Russell, H. N., 1922.
Eddington, Sir Arthur Stanley, 1924.
Shapley, Harlow, 1926.

Wright, William Hammond, 1928.
Cannon, Annie Jump, 1931.
Slipher, V. M., 1932.
Plaskett, John Stanley, 1934.
Mees, C. E. Kenneth, 1936.

J. LAWRENCE SMITH FUND

[$10,000]

J. Lawrence Smith medal and investigations of meteoric bodies

Members of the committee

Allen, E. T., chairman, 1938.

Anderson, J. A., 1942.
Brown, E. W., 1940.

Palache, Charles, 1939.
Trumpler, R. J., 1941.

J. LAWRENCE SMITH MEDAL AWARDS

Newton, H. A., 1888.

Merrill, George P., 1922.

BARNARD MEDAL FOR MERITORIOUS SERVICES TO SCIENCE[2]

Discoveries in physical or astronomical science or novel application of science to purposes beneficial to the human race

Members of the committee

Whitney, W. R., chairman.
Campbell, W. W.

Davis, Bergen.
Day, Arthur L.

Tolman, R. C.

BARNARD MEDAL AWARDS

Rutherford, Baron; Ernest Rutherford, 1909.

Bragg, Sir William H., 1914.
Einstein, Albert, 1921.

Bohr, Neils, 1925.
Heisenberg, Werner, 1930.
Hubble, Edwin, 1935.

BENJAMIN APTHORP GOULD FUND

[$20,000]

Researches in astronomy

Board of directors

Moulton, F. R., chairman.

Brown, E. W.

Curtis, H. D.

WOLCOTT GIBBS FUND

[$5,545.50]

Chemical research

Board of directors

Kohler, E. P., chairman.

Baxter, G. P.

———————————

[2] Every 5 years the committee recommends the person whom they consider most deserving of the medal, and upon approval by the Academy, the name of the nominee is forwarded to the trustees of Columbia University, who administer the Barnard medal fund.

CYRUS B. COMSTOCK FUND

[$12,406.02]

Prize awarded every 5 years for most important discovery or investigation in electricity, magnetism, and radiant energy, or to aid worthy investigations in those subjects

Members of the committee

Millikan, R. A., chairman, 1940.	Coolidge, W. D., 1939. Compton, A. H., 1938.	Davisson, C. J., 1941. Miller, D. C., 1942.

COMSTOCK PRIZE AWARDS

Millikan, R. A., 1913. Barnett, S. J., 1918.	Duane, William, 1923. Davisson, C. J., 1928.	Bridgman, P. W., 1933.

MARSH FUND

[$20,000]

Original research in the natural sciences

Members of the committee

Gregory, W. K., chairman, 1942.	Berry, E. W., 1938. Longwell, C. R., 1941.	Merrill, E. D., 1940. Reid, H. F., 1939.

AGASSIZ FUND

[$50,000]

General uses of the Academy

MURRAY FUND

[$6,000]

Agassiz medal for contributions to oceanography

Members of the committee

Vaughan, T. Wayland, chairman, 1938.	Conklin, E. G., 1940.	Day, A. L., 1939.

AGASSIZ MEDAL AWARDS

Hjort, Johan, 1913. Albert I, Prince of Monaco, 1918. Sigsbee, C. D., 1920. Pettersson, Otto Sven, 1924. Bjerknes, Vilhelm, 1926. Weber, Max, 1927.	Ekman, Vagn Walfrid, 1928. Gardiner, J. Stanley, 1929. Schmidt, Johannes, 1930. Bigelow, Henry Bryant, 1931. Defant, Albert, 1932.	Helland-Hansen, Bjorn, 1933. Gran, Haakon Hasberg, 1934. Vaughan, T. Wayland, 1935. Knudsen, Martin, 1936.

MARCELLUS HARTLEY FUND

[$1,200]

Medal for eminence in the application of science to the public welfare

Members of the committee

Hull, A. W., chairman, 1939. Conant, J. B., 1938.	Cushing, Harvey, 1940. Hoover, Herbert, 1940.	Kofoid, C. A., 1938. Mason, Max, 1939.

PUBLIC WELFARE MEDAL AWARDS

(In memory of Marcellus Hartley)

Goethals, G. W., 1914.
Gorgas, W. C., 1914.
Abbe, Cleveland, 1916.
Pinchot, Gifford, 1916.
Stratton, S. W., 1917.
Hoover, Herbert, 1920.

Stiles, C. W., 1921.
Chapin, Charles V., 1928.
Mather, Stephen Tyng, 1930.
Rose, Wickliffe, 1931.

Park, William Hallock, 1932.
Fairchild, David, 1933.
Vollmer, August, 1934.
Russell, F. F., 1935.
Cumming, Hugh S., 1935.

DANIEL GIRAUD ELLIOT FUND

[$8,000]

Medal and honorarium for most meritorious work in zoology or paleontology published each year

Members of the committee

Harrison, Ross G., chairman

Gregory, W. K.

————————

DANIEL GIRAUD ELLIOT MEDAL AWARDS

Chapman, F. M., 1917.
Beebe, William, 1918.
Ridgway, Robert, 1919.
Abel, Othenio, 1920.
Dean, Bashford, 1921.
Wheeler, Wm. Morton, 1922.

Canu, Ferdinand, 1923.
Breuil, Henri, 1924.
Wilson, Edmund B., 1925.
Stensiö, Erik A.: Son, 1927.
Seton, Ernest Thompson, 1928.

Osborn, Henry Fairfield, 1929.
Coghill, George Ellett, 1930.
Black, Davidson, 1931.
Chapin, James P., 1932.

BILLINGS FUND

[$22,313.39]

For partial support of the Proceedings, or for such other purposes as the Academy may select

MARY CLARK THOMPSON FUND

[$10,000]

Medal for most important services to geology and paleontology

Members of the committee

Mendenhall, W. C., chairman, 1939.

Leith, C. K., 1940.

Ulrich, E. O., 1938.

MARY CLARK THOMPSON MEDAL AWARDS

Walcott, Charles Doolittle, 1921.
Margerie, Emm. de, 1923.
Clarke, John Mason, 1925.
Smith, James Perrin, 1928.

Scott, William Berryman, 1930.
Ulrich, Edward Oscar, 1930.
White, David, 1931.

Bather, Francis Arthur, 1932.
Schuchert, Charles, 1934.
Grabau, Amadeus William, 1936.

JOSEPH HENRY FUND

[$40,163.50]

To assist meritorious investigators, especially in the direction of original research

37878—38——9

Members of the committee

Jones, L. R., chairman, · Richtmyer, F. K., 1939. Streeter, G. L., 1942.
1938. Seashore, C. E., 1940.
Bush, Vannevar, 1941.

GEORGE TRUE NEALLEY FUND

[$19,555.55]

For the general purposes of the Academy

CHARLES DOOLITTLE WALCOTT FUND

[$5,000]

For stimulation of research in pre-Cambrian or Cambrian life by award of a medal and honorarium every 5 years

Board of directors

Vaughan, T. W., temporary chairman. Lang, W. D. (representing the Royal
Abbot, C. G. (representing the Smith- Society of London).
sonian Institution). Ulrich, E. O.
Barrois, Charles (representing the Institut de France).

CHARLES DOOLITTLE WALCOTT MEDAL AWARD

White, David, 1934

JOHN J. CARTY FUND

[$25,000]

Medal and monetary award, not oftener than once in every 2 years, to an individual for noteworthy and distinguished accomplishment in any field of science coming within the scope of the charter of the Academy

Members of the committee

Jewett, F. B., chairman, Birkhoff, G. D., 1940. Howell, W. H., 1938.
1941. Conant, J. B., 1942. Jennings, H. S., 1939.

JOHN J. CARTY MEDAL AWARDS

Carty, John J., 1932. Wilson, Edmund Beecher, 1936.

CARNEGIE ENDOWMENT FUND

[$3,550,000]

For the purposes of the National Academy of Sciences and National Research Council

6. MEMBERS OF THE NATIONAL ACADEMY OF SCIENCES

JULY 1, 1937

Elected

Abbot, Charles Greeley, Smithsonian Institution, Washington, D. C____ 1915
Abel, John Jacob, Laboratory for Endocrine Research, Johns Hopkins
Medical School, Baltimore, Md_____ 1912
Adams, Comfort Avery, The Edward G. Budd Manufacturing Co., Phila-
delphia, Pa_____ 1930
Adams, Roger, University of Illinois, Urbana, Ill_____ 1929
Adams, Walter Sydney, Mount Wilson Observatory, Pasadena, Calif____ 1917
Aitken, Robert Grant, 1109 Spruce St., Berkeley, Calif_____ 1918
Alexander, James Waddell, Princeton, N. J_____ 1930

6. Members of the National Academy of Science—continued

Elected

Allen, Charles Elmer, University of Wisconsin, Madison, Wis_____ 1924
Allen, Eugene Thomas, 1862 Mintwood Pl., Washington, D. C_____ 1930
Ames, Joseph Sweetman, 2 Charlcote Pl., Guilford, Baltimore, Md_____ 1909
Anderson, John August, Mount Wilson Observatory, Pasadena, Calif_____ 1928
Angell, James Rowland, Yale University, New Haven, Conn_____ 1920
Avery, Oswald Theodore, Rockefeller Institute for Medical Research, 66th
  St. and York Ave., New York City_____ 1933
Babcock, Harold Delos, Mount Wilson Observatory, Pasadena, Calif_____ 1933
Baekeland, Leo Hendrik, Bakelite Corporation, 247 Park Ave., New
  York City_____ 1936
Bailey, Irving Widmer, Biological Laboratories, Harvard University, Cam-
  bridge, Mass_____ 1929
Bailey, Liberty Hyde, Bailey Hortorium, Ithaca, N. Y_____ 1917
Bancroft, Wilder Dwight, 7 East Ave., Ithaca, N. Y_____ 1920
Barbour, Thomas, Museum of Comparative Zoology, Cambridge, Mass___ 1933
Bateman, Harry, California Institute of Technology, Pasadena, Calif_____ 1930
Baxter, Gregory Paul, T. Jefferson Coolidge, Jr., Memorial Laboratory,
  Cambridge, Mass_____ 1916
Bell, Eric Temple, California Institute of Technology, Pasadena, Calif____ 1927
Benedict, Francis Gano, Machiasport, Maine_____ 1914
Berkey, Charles Peter, Department of Geology and Mineralogy, Columbia
  University, New York City_____ 1927
Berry, Edward Wilber, Johns Hopkins University, Baltimore, Md_____ 1922
Bigelow, Henry Bryant, Museum of Comparative Zoology, Harvard Uni-
  versity, Cambridge, Mass_____ 1931
Birge, Raymond Thayer, University of California, Berkeley, Calif_____ 1932
Birkhoff, George David, 984 Memorial Drive, Cambridge, Mass_____ 1918
Blackwelder, Eliot, P. O. Box N, Stanford University, Calif_____ 1936
Blakeslee, Albert Francis, Department of Genetics, Carnegie Institution of
  Washington, Cold Spring Harbor, L. I., N. Y_____ 1929
Blichfeldt, Hans Frederik, Box 875, Stanford University, Calif_____ 1920 •
Bliss, Gilbert Ames, University of Chicago, Chicago, Ill_____ 1916
Boas, Franz, Columbia University, New York City_____ 1900
Bogert, Marston Taylor, 566 Chandler Laboratories, Columbia University,
  New York City_____ 1916
Boring, Edwin Garrigues, Harvard University, Cambridge, Mass_____ 1932
Bowen, Ira Sprague, California Institute of Technology, Pasadena, Calif__ 1936
Bowen, Norman Levi, Rosenwald Hall, University of Chicago, Chicago, Ill__ 1935
Bowie, William, 2900 Connecticut Ave., Washington, D. C_____ 1927
Bowman, Isaiah, Johns Hopkins University, Baltimore, Md_____ 1930
Bray, William Crowell, Department of Chemistry, University of Cali-
  fornia, Berkeley, Calif_____ 1924
Bridges, Calvin Blackman, California Institute of Technology, Pasadena,
  Calif_____ 1937
Bridgman, Percy Williams, Research Laboratory of Physics, Harvard Uni-
  versity, Cambridge, Mass_____ 1918
Brown, Ernest William, Yale Observatory, Prospect St., New Haven, Conn. 1923
Buckley, Oliver Ellsworth, Bell Telephone Laboratories, 463 West St.,
  New York City_____ 1937
Bush, Vannevar, Massachusetts Institute of Technology, Cambridge, Mass. 1934
Calkins, Gary Nathan, Columbia University, New York City_____ 1919
Campbell, Douglas Houghton, Stanford University, Stanford University,
  Calif_____ 1910
Campbell, William Wallace, 1980 Vallejo St., San Francisco, Calif_____ 1902
Cannon, Walter Bradford, Harvard Medical School, 25 Shattuck St.,
  Boston 17, Mass_____ 1914
Carlson, Anton Julius, University of Chicago, Chicago, Ill_____ 1920
Castle, William Ernest, Hilgard Hall, University of California, Berkeley,
  Calif_____ 1915
Cattell, James McKeen, Garrison, N. Y_____ 1901
Chapman, Frank Michler, American Museum of Natural History, 77th
  St. and Central Park West, New York City_____ 1921
Child, Charles Manning, Jordan Hall, Stanford University, Stanford
  University, Calif. _____ 1935
Chittenden, Russell Henry, Sheffield Scientific School, New Haven, Conn. 1890

6. Members of the National Academy of Sciences—Continued

Elected

Clark, William Mansfield. Johns Hopkins Medical School, Washington and Monument Streets, Baltimore, Md._____ 1928
Clinton, George Perkins, Connecticut Agricultural Experiment Station, New Haven, Conn._____ 1930
Coble, Arthur Byron, University of Illinois, Urbana, Ill._____ 1924
Coblentz, William Weber, Bureau of Standards, Washington, D. C._____ 1930
Coghill, George Ellett, Rural Route No. 2, Gainesville, Fla._____ 1935
Cole, Rufus, Mt. Kisco, N. Y._____ 1922
Compton, Arthur Holly, University of Chicago, Chicago, Ill._____ 1927
Compton, Karl Taylor, 111 Charles River Rd., Cambridge, Mass._____ 1924
Conant, James Bryant, Harvard University, Cambridge 38, Mass._____ 1929
Conklin, Edwin Grant, Princeton University, Princeton, N. J._____ 1908
Coolidge, William David, General Electric Co., Schenectady, N. Y._____ 1925
Crew, Henry, 620 Library Pl., Evanston, Ill._____ 1909
Cross, Charles Whitman, 101 East Kirke St., Chevy Chase, Md._____ 1908
Curtis, Heber Doust, Observatory, University of Michigan, Ann Arbor, Mich._____ 1919
Cushing, Harvey Williams, Yale School of Medicine, New Haven, Conn.___ 1917
Daly, Reginald Aldworth, Geological Museum, Harvard University, Cambridge, Mass._____ 1925
Davenport, Charles Benedict, Carnegie Institution of Washington, Cold Spring Harbor, L. I., N. Y._____ 1912
Davis, Bergen, Columbia University, New York City_____ 1929
Davisson, Clinton Joseph, Bell Telephone Laboratories, 463 West St., New York City_____ 1929
Day, Arthur Louis, 1565 Old Georgetown Rd., Bethesda, Md._____ 1911
Dempster, Arthur Jeffery, University of Chicago, Chicago, Ill._____ 1937
Detwiler, Samuel Randall, College of Physicians and Surgeons, 630 West 168th St., New York City_____ 1932
Dewey, John, Columbia University, New York City_____ 1910
Dickson, Leonard Eugene, University of Chicago, Chicago, Ill._____ 1913
Docbez, Alphonse Raymond, Columbia University, Presbyterian Hospital, 620 West 168th St., New York City_____ 1933
Dodge, Bernard Ogilvie, New York Botanical Garden, Bronx Park (Fordham Station), New York City_____ 1933
Donaldson, Henry Herbert, Wistar Institute of Anatomy and Biology, Philadelphia, Pa._____ 1914
DuBois, Eugene Floyd, New York Hospital, 525 East 68th St., New York City_____ 1933
Duggar, Benjamin Minge, Biology Bldg., University of Wisconsin, Madison, Wis._____ 1927
Dunn, Gano, 80 Broad St., New York City_____ 1919
Durand, William Frederick, Stanford University, Stanford University, Calif._____ 1917
East, Edward Murray, Biological Laboratories, Harvard University, Cambridge, Mass._____ 1925
Eisenhart, Luther Pfahler, Princeton, N. J._____ 1922
Emerson, Rollins Adams, Cornell University, Ithaca, N. Y._____ 1927
Emmet, William Le Roy, General Electric Co., Schenectady, N. Y._____ 1921
Epstein, Paul Sophus, 1484 Oakdale St., Pasadena, Calif._____ 1930
Erlanger, Joseph, Washington University School of Medicine, 4580 Scott Ave., St. Louis, Mo._____ 1922
Evans, Griffith Conrad, Department of Mathematics, University of California, Berkeley, Calif._____ 1933
Evans Herbert McLean, Institute of Experimental Biology, University of California, Berkeley, Calif._____ 1927
Ewing, James, Memorial Hospital, 2 West 106th St., New York City_____ 1935
Fernald, Merritt Lyndon, Gray Herbarium, Harvard University, Cambridge, Mass._____ 1935
Fletcher, Harvey, Bell Telephone Laboratories, 463 West St., New York City _____ 1935
Flexner, Simon, Rockefeller Institute for Medical Research, 66th St. and York Ave., New York City_____ 1908
Forbes, Alexander, Harvard Medical School, Boston, Mass._____ 1936
Fred, Edwin Broun. College of Agriculture, University of Wisconsin, Madison, Wis._____ 1931

Elected

Gasser, Herbert Spencer, Rockefeller Institute for Medical Research, 66th
St. and York Ave., New York City_____ 1934
Gherardi, Bancroft, 195 Broadway, New York City_____ 1933
Giauque, William Francis, University of California, Berkeley, Calif_____ 1936
Gomberg, Moses, University of Michigan, Ann Arbor, Mich_____ 1914
Goodpasture, Ernest William, Vanderbilt University, Nashville, Tenn_____ 1937
Gortner, Ross Aiken, University Farm, St. Paul, Minn_____ 1935
Gregory, William King, American Museum of Natural History, 77th St.
and Central Park West, New York City_____ 1927
Hale, George Ellery, Mount Wilson Observatory, Pasadena, Calif_____ 1902
Hall, Edwin Herbert, 39 Garden St., Cambridge, Mass_____ 1911
Harkins, William Draper, University of Chicago, Chicago, Ill_____ 1921
Harper, Robert Almer, Columbia University, New York City_____ 1911
Harrison, Ross Granville, Yale University, Osborn Zoological Laboratory,
New Haven, Conn_____ 1913
Hartman, Carl Gottfried, Department of Embryology, Carnegie Institution
of Washington, Wolfe and Madison Sts., Baltimore, Md_____ 1937
Harvey, Edmund Newton, Princeton University, Princeton, N. J_____ 1934
Hektoen, Ludvig, Mayflower Apts., Washington, D. C_____ 1918
Henderson, Lawrence Joseph, Morgan Hall, Soldiers Field, Boston, Mass__ 1919
Henderson, Yandell, Yale University, New Haven, Conn_____ 1923
Herrick, Charles Judson, Department of Anatomy, University of Chicago,
Chicago, Ill_____ 1918
Hewett, Donnel Foster, U. S. Geological Survey, Washington, D. C_____ 1937
Hildebrand, Joel Henry, Gilman Hall, University of California, Berkeley,
Calif_____ 1929
Hoagland, Dennis Robert, 3048 Life Sciences Bldg., University of Califor-
nia, Berkeley, Calif_____ 1934
Hooton, Earnest Albert, Peabody Museum, Harvard University, Cambridge,
Mass_____ 1935
Hoover, Herbert Clark, Palo Alto, Calif_____ 1922
Hovgaard, William, Hotel Margaret, Columbia Heights, Brooklyn, N. Y___ 1929
Howard, Leland Ossian, Bureau of Entomology, U. S. Department of Agri-
culture, Washington, D. C_____ 1916
Howell, William Henry, 112 St. Dunstan's Rd., Baltimore, Md_____ 1905
Hrdlička, Aleš, U. S. National Museum, Washington, D. C_____ 1921
Hubble, Edwin Powell, Mount Wilson Observatory, Pasadena, Calif_____ 1927
Hudson, Claude Silbert, National Institute of Health, 25th and E Sts.,
Washington, D. C_____ 1927
Hulett, George Augustus, Princeton University, Princeton, N. J_____ 1922
Hull, Albert Wallace, Research Laboratory, General Electric Co., Schenec-
tady, N. Y_____ 1929
Hull, Clark Leonard, Institute of Human Relations, Yale University, 333
Cedar St., New Haven, Conn_____ 1936
Hunsaker, Jerome Clark, Massachusetts Institute of Technology, Cam-
bridge, Mass_____ 1935
Hunt, Reid, Harvard Medical School, Boston, Mass_____ 1919
Hunter, Walter Samuel, Brown University, Providence, R. I_____ 1935
Ives, Herbert Eugene, Bell Telephone Laboratories, 463 West St., New York
City _____ 1933
Jackson, Dunham, University of Minnesota, Minneapolis, Minn_____ 1935
Jacobs, Walter Abraham, Rockefeller Institute for Medical Research, 66th
St. and York Ave., New York City_____ 1932
Jennings, Herbert Spencer, Johns Hopkins University, Baltimore, Md_____ 1914
Jewett, Frank Baldwin, American Telephone & Telegraph Co., 195 Broad-
way, New York City_____ 1918
Johnson, Douglas Wilson, Columbia University, New York City_____ 1932
Johnson, Treat Baldwin, Bethwood, Amity Road, Bethany, Conn_____ 1919
Jones, Lewis Ralph, University of Wisconsin, Madison, Wis_____ 1920
Kasner, Edward, Columbia University, New York City_____ 1917
Keith, Arthur, United States Geological Survey, Washington, D. C_____ 1928
Kellogg, Vernon Lyman, 2305 Bancroft Pl., Washington, D. C_____ 1930
Kemble, Edwin Crawford, The Physics Laboratories, Harvard University,
Cambridge, Mass_____ 1931
Kennelly, Arthur Edwin, Harvard University, Cambridge, Mass_____ 1921
Kettering, Charles Franklin, General Motors Corporation, Detroit, Mich__ 1928

Elected

Keyes, Frederick George, Massachusetts Institute of Technology, Cambridge, Mass_____ 1930
Kidder, Alfred Vincent, The Red House, Beverly Farms, Mass_____ 1936
Knopf, Adolph, Yale University, New Haven, Conn_____ 1931
Kofold, Charles Atwood, University of California, Berkeley, Calif_____ 1922
Kohler, Elmer Peter, Converse Memorial Laboratory, Harvard University, Frisbie Place, Cambridge, Mass_____ 1920
Kraus, Charles August, Brown University, Providence, R. I_____ 1925
Kroeber, Alfred L., University of California, Berkeley, Calif_____ 1928
Kunkel, Louis Otto, Rockefeller Institute for Medical Research, Princeton, N. J_____ 1932
Lamb, Arthur Becket, Chemical Laboratory, Harvard University, Cambridge, Mass_____ 1924
Landsteiner, Karl, Rockefeller Institute for Medical Research, 66th St. and York Ave., New York City_____ 1932
Langmuir, Irving, General Electric Co., Schenectady, N. Y_____ 1918
Lashley, Karl Spencer, Biological Laboratories, Harvard University, Cambridge, Mass_____ 1930
Lawrence, Ernest Orlando, University of California, Berkeley, Calif_____ 1934
Lawson, Andrew Cowper, University of California, Berkeley, Calif_____ 1924
Lefschetz, Solomon, 129 Broadmead St., Princeton, N. J_____ 1925
Leith, Charles Kenneth, University of Wisconsin, Madison, Wis_____ 1920
Leuschner, Armin Otto, Students' Observatory, University of California, Berkeley, Calif_____ 1913
Levene, Phoebus Aaron Theodor♂, Rockefeller Institute for Medical Research, 66th St. and York Ave., New York City_____ 1916
Leverett, Frank, 1724 South University Ave., Ann Arbor, Mich._____ 1929
Lewis, Warren Harmon, Department of Embryology, Carnegie Institution of Washington, Wolfe and Madison Sts., Baltimore, Md_____ 1936
Lillie, Frank Rattray, National Academy of Sciences, 2101 Constitution Ave., Washington, D. C_____ 1915·
Lind, Samuel Colville, School of Chemistry, University of Minnesota, Minneapolis, Minn_____ 1930
Lindgren, Waldemar, Massachusetts Institute of Technology, Cambridge, Mass _____ 1909
Loch, Leo, Washington University School of Medicine, St. Louis, Mo_____ 1937
Longwell, Chester Ray, Kirtland Hall, Yale University, New Haven, Conn. 1935
Lowie, Robert Harry, University of California, Berkeley, Calif_____ 1931
Lyman, Theodore, Research Laboratory of Physics, Harvard University, Cambridge, Mass_____ 1917
MacCallum, William George, Department of Pathology, Johns Hopkins University, 1833 East Monument St., Baltimore, Md_____ 1921
McClung, Clarence Erwin, University of Pennsylvania, Philadelphia, Pa__ 1920
McCollum, Elmer Verner, School of Hygiene and Public Health, 615 North Wolfe St., Baltimore, Md_____ 1920
MacInnes, Duncan Arthur, Rockefeller Institute for Medical Research, 66th St. and York Ave., New York City_____ 1937
Mark, Edward Laurens, 109 Irving St., Cambridge, Mass_____ 1903
Mason, Max, California Institute of Technology, Pasadena, Calif_____ 1923
Mendenhall, Walter Curran, United States Geological Survey, Washington, D. C_____ 1932
Merriam, Clinton Hart, 1919 16th St., Washington, D. C_____ 1902
Merriam, John Campbell, Carnegie Institution of Washington, Washington, D. C_____ 1918
Merrill, Elmer Drew, Arnold Arboretum, Jamaica Plain, Mass_____ 1923
Merrill, Paul Willard, Mount Wilson Observatory, Pasadena, Calif_____ 1929
Merritt, Ernest George, 1 Grove Pl., Ithaca, N. Y_____ 1914
Michael, Arthur, 219 Parker St., Newton Center, Mass_____ 1889
Miles, Walter Richard, Yale University, 333 Cedar St., New Haven, Conn. 1933
Miller, Dayton Clarence, Case School of Applied Science, Cleveland, Ohio. 1921
Miller, George Abram, 1203 West Illinois St., Urbana, Ill_____ 1921
Millikan, Robert Andrews, California Institute of Technology, Pasadena, Calif_____ 1915
Minot, George Richards, Thorndike Memorial Laboratory, Boston City Hospital, Boston, Mass_____ 1937
Mitchell, Samuel Alfred, Leander McCormick Observatory, University, Va. 1933

_. Members of the National Academy of Sciences—Continued

Elected

Modjeski, Ralph, ___ Middle Rd., Santa Barbara, Calif_____ 1925
Moore, Joseph Haines, Lick Observatory, Mount Hamilton, Calif_____ 1931
Moore, Robert Lee, University of Texas, Austin, Tex_____ 1931
Morgan, Thomas Hunt, California Institute of Technology, Pasadena,
    Calif _____ 1909
Morse, Harold Marston, Institute for Advanced Study, Princeton, N. J___ 1932
Moulton, Forest Ray, Smithsonian Institution, Washington, D. C_____ 1910
Moulton, Forest Ray, Smithsonian Institution, Washington, D. C_____ 1910
Mulliken, Robert Sanderson, University of Chicago, Chicago, _____ 1936
Neumann, John von, Institute for Advanced Study, Princeton, N. J_____ 1937
Nichols, Edward Leamington, Cornell University, Ithaca, N. Y_____ 1901
Nicholson, Seth Barnes, Mount Wilson Observatory, Pasadena, Calif_____ 1937
Norris, James Flack, Massachusetts Institute of Technology, Cambridge,
    Mass_____ 1934
Northrop, John Howard. Rockefeller Institute for Medical Research,
    Princeton, N. J_____ 1934
Novy, Frederick George, 721 Forest Ave., Ann Arbor, Mich_____ 1924
Noyes, William Albert, University of Illinois, Urbana, _____ 1910
Opie, Eugene Lindsay, Cornell University Medical School, 1300 York Ave.,
    New York City_____ 1923
Osgood, William Fogg, __ Dorset Rd., Belmont Mass_____ 1904
Osterhout, Winthrop John Vanleuven, Rockefeller Institute for Medical
    Research, 66th St. and York Ave., New York City_____ 1919
Palache, Charles, Harvard University, Cambridge, Mass_____ 1934
Parker, George Howard, __ Berkeley St., Cambridge, Mass_____ 1913
Pauling, Linus, California Institute of Technology, Pasadena, Calif_____ 1933
Pearl, Raymond, 1901 East Madison St., Baltimore, Md_____ 1916
Pierce, George Washington, Cruft Laboratory, Harvard University, Cam-
    bridge, Mass_____ 1920
Pillsbury, Walter Bowers, University of Michigan, Ann Arbor, Mich_____ 1925
Reid, Harry Fielding, Johns Hopkins University, Baltimore, Md_____ 1912
Richards, Alfred Newton, University of Pennsylvania, Philadelphia, Pa__ 1927
Richtmyer, Floyd Karker, Rockefeller Hall, Cornell University, Ithaca,
    N. Y_____ 1932
Ritt, Joseph Fels, Columbia University, New York City_____ 1933
Rivers, Thomas Milton, Rockefeller Institute for Medical Research, 66th
    St. and York Ave., New York City_____ 1934
Rose, William Cumming, University of Illinois, Urbana, _____ 1936
Ross, Frank Elmore, Mount Wilson Observatory, Pasadena, Calif_____ 1930
Rous, Francis Peyton, Rockefeller Institute for Medical Research, 66th
    St. and York Ave., New York City_____1927
Ruedemann, Rudolph, New York State Museum, Albany, N. Y_____ 1928
Russell, Henry Norris, Princeton University, Princeton, N. J_____ 1918
Sabin, Florence Rena, Rockefeller Institute for Medical Research, 66th
    St. and York Ave., New York City_____ 1925
Sapir, Edward, Yale University, New Haven, Conn_____ 1934
Saunders, Frederick Albert, Jefferson Physical Laboratory, Cambridge,
    Mass_____ 1925
Sauveur, Albert, Harvard University, Cambridge, Mass_____ 1927
Schlesinger, Frank, Yale University Observatory, New Haven, Conn_____ 1916
Schuchert, Charles, Peabody Museum, Yale University, New Haven, Conn_ 1910
Scott, William Berryman, Princeton University, Princeton, N. J_____ 1906
Seares, Frederick Hanley, Mount Wilson Observatory, Pasadena, Calif___ 1919
Seashore, Carl Emil, State University of Iowa, Iowa City, Iowa_____ 1922
Setchell, William Albert, University of California, Berkeley, Calif_____ 1919
Shaffer, Philip Anderson, Washington University Medical School, St. Louis,
    Mo _____ 1928
Shapley, Harlow, Harvard College Observatory, Cambridge, Mass_____ 1924
Sherman, Henry Clapp, Columbia University, New York City_____ 1933
Sinnott, Edmund Ware, Columbia University, New York City_____ 1936
Slater, John Clarke, Massachusetts Institute of Technology, Cambridge,
    Mass_____ 1932
Slipher, Vesto Melvin, Lowell Observatory, Flagstaff, Ariz_____ 1921
Stakman, Elvin Charles, University Farm, St. Paul, Minn_____ 1934

Members of the National Academy of Sciences—Continued

Elected

Stebbins, Joel, Washburn Observatory, Madison, Wis_____ 1920
Stejneger, Leonhard, United States National Museum, Washington, D. C__ 1923
Stillwell, Lewis Buckley, Elm Rd., Princeton, N. J_____ 1921
Stockard, Charles Rupert, Cornell University Medical School, 1300 York
  Ave., New York City_____ 1922
Stratton, George Malcolm, University of California, Berkeley, Calif_____ 1928
Streeter, George Linius, Department of Embryology, Carnegie Institution
  of Washington, Wolfe and Madison Sts., Baltimore, Md_____ 1931
Struve, Otto, Yerkes Observatory, Williams Bay, Wis_____ 1937
Sturtevant, Alfred Henry, California Institute of Technology, Pasadena,
  Calif_____ 1930
Sumner, Francis Bertody, Scripps Institution of Oceanography, La Jolla,
  Calif_____ 1937
Swanton, John Reed, Bureau of American Ethnology, Smithsonian Institu-
  tion, Washington, D. C_____ 1932
Taylor, David Watson, care of Navy Department, Washington, D. C_____ 1918
Tennent, David Hilt, Bryn Mawr College, Bryn Mawr, Pa_____ 1929
Terman, Lewis Madison, 761 Dolores, Stanford University, Calif_____ 1928
Thom, Charles, United States Department of Agriculture, Washington,
  D. C_____ 1937
Thorndike, Edward Lee, Teachers College, Columbia University, New York
  City _____ 1917
Tolman, Edward Chace, University of California, Berkeley, Calif_____ 1937
Tolman, Richard Chace, California Institute of Technology, Pasadena,
  Calif _____ 1923
Trelease, William, University of Illinois, Urbana, _____ 1902
Trumpler, Robert Julius, Lick Observatory, Mount Hamilton, Calif_____ 1932
Ulrich, Edward Oscar, United States National Museum, Washington, D. C_ 1917
Urey, Harold Clayton, Columbia University, New York City_____ 1935
Vandiver, Harry Schultz, University of Texas, Austin, Tex_____ 1934
Van Slyke, Donald Dexter, Rockefeller Institute for Medical Research,
  66th St. and York Ave., New York City_____ 1921
Van Vleck, Edward Burr, 519 North Pickney St., Madison, Wis_____ 1911
Van Vleck, John Hasbrouck, Harvard University, Cambridge, Mass_____ 1935
Vaughan, Thomas Wayland, 3333 P St., Washington, D. C_____ 1921
Veblen, Oswald, The Institute for Advanced Study, Fine Hall, Princeton,
  N. J_____ 1919
Walsh, Joseph Leonard, Harvard University, Cambridge, Mass_____ 1936
Washburn, Margaret Floy, Vassar College, Poughkeepsie, N. Y_____ 1931
Webster, David Locke, Physics Department, Room 385, Stanford Univer-
  sity, Stanford University, California_____ 1923
Wells, Harry Gideon, University of Chicago, Chicago, _____ 1925
Whipple, George Hoyt, School of Medicine of the University of Rochester,
  Crittenden Blvd., Rochester, N. Y_____ 1929
White, Henry Seely, Vassar College, Poughkeepsie, N. Y_____ 1915
Whitehead, John Boswell, Johns Hopkins University, Baltimore, Md_____ 1932
Whitney, Willis Rodney, General Electric Co., Schenectady, N. Y_____ 1917
Wiener, Norbert, Massachusetts Institute of Technology, Cambridge, Mass_ 1934
Willis, Bailey, Box 1365, Stanford University, California_____ 1920
Wilson, Edmund Beecher, Columbia University, New York City_____ 1899
Wilson, Edwin Bidwell, _ Shattuck St., Boston , Mass_____ 1919
Wilson, Henry Van Peters, University of North Carolina, Chapel Hill,
  N. C_____ 1927
Wissler, Clark, American Museum of Natural History, New York City____ 1929
Wood, Robert Williams, Johns Hopkins University, Baltimore, Md_____ 1912
Woodruff, Lorande Loss, Yale University, New Haven, Conn_____ 1924
Woodworth, Robert Sessions, Columbia University, New York City_____ 1921
Wright, Frederick Eugene, Geophysical Laboratory, 2801 Upton St., Wash-
  ington, D. C_____ 1923
Wright, Orville, _ North Broadway, Dayton, Ohio_____ 1936
Wright, Sewall Green, University of Chicago, Chicago, _____ 1934
Wright, William Hammond, Lick Observatory, Mount Hamilton, Calif____ 1922
Yerkes, Robert Mearns, Yale School of Medicine, 333 Cedar St., New
  Haven, Conn_____ 1923
Zinsser, Hans, Harvard Medical School, 240 Longwood Ave., Boston, Mass_ 1924

_. Members of the National Academy of Sciences—Continued
MEMBER EMERITUS

	Elected
Dodge, Raymond, Tryon, N. C._____	1924

FOREIGN ASSOCIATES OF THE NATIONAL ACADEMY OF SCIENCES

July _, 1937

Adams, Frank Dawson, McGill University, Montreal, Canada_____ 1920
Barrois, Charles, Université, __ rue Pascal, Lille, France_____ 1908
Bjerknes, V. F. K., University, Oslo, Norway_____ 1934
Bohr, Niels, University of Copenhagen, Copenhagen, Denmark_____ 1925
Bordet, Jules, Pasteur Institute, Rue du Remorqueur, , Brussels, Belgium_____ 1935
Bower, Frederick Orpen, , The Crescent, Ripon, Yorks, England_____ 1929
Brogger, W. C., Universitet, Oslo, Norway_____ 1903
Debye, Peter, Physikalisches Institut der Universitat, Linnestrasse , Leipzig, Germany_____ 1931
Deslandres, Henri, Bureau des Longitudes, __ rue de Téhéran, Paris , France_____ 1913
Dyson, Sir Frank Watson, , Westcombe Park Road, Blackheath, London S. E. , England_____ 1928
Eddington, Sir Arthur Stanley, Observatory, Cambridge, England_____ 1925
Einstein, Albert, Institute for Advanced Study, Princeton, N. J., U. S. A. 1922
Forsyth, A. R., Imperial College of Science and Technology, London, England _____ 1907
Hadamard, Jacques, __ rue Emile Faguet, Paris XIV, France_____ 1926
Hadfield, Sir Robert A, __ Carlton House Terrace, S. W. , London, England_____ 1928
Hardy, Godfrey Harold, Trinity College, Cambridge, England_____ 1927
Helm, Albert, Zurich, Switzerland_____ 1913
Hertwig, Richard, Zoologisches Institut, Louisenstrasse , Munich, Germany _____ 1929
Hilbert, David, Wilhelm-Weberstrasse , Gottingen, Germany_____ 1907
Hopkins, Sir Frederick Gowland, University, Cambridge, England_____ 1924
Krogh, August, Universitetets Zoofysiologiske Laboratorium, Juliane Marles Vej , Copenhagen, Denmark_____ 1937
Lacroix, F. Alfred A., __ rue Jean-Dolent, Paris XIV, France_____ 1920
Larmor, Sir Joseph, St. John's College, Cambridge, England_____ 1908
Marconi, Marchese Guglielmo, , Via Condotti, Rome, Italy_____ 1932
Penck, Albrecht, Knesebeckstrasse __, Berlin, W. __, Germany_____ 1909
Picard, Charles Emile, __ Quai Conti, Paris (VI), France_____ 1903
Planck, Max, Wangenheimstrasse , Berlin-Grunewald, Germany_____ 1926
Prain, Sir David, The Well Farm, Warlingham, Surrey, England_____ 1920
Robinson, Robert, Dyson Perrins Laboratory, South Parks Rd., Oxford, England _____ 1934
Rutherford, Baron: Ernest Rutherford, Newham Cottage, Queen's Rd., Cambridge, England_____ 1911
Sabatier, Paul, Allée des Zephyrs, No. , Toulouse. France_____ 1927
Schneider, Charles Eugène, __ rue d'Anjou, Paris, France_____ 1925
Sherrington, Sir Charles Scott, "Broomside," Valley Rd., Ipswich, England_ 1924
Sommerfeld, Arnold, University of Munich, Munich, Germany_____ 1929
Spemann, Hans, Zoologisches Institut, Freiburg, . Br., Germany_____ 1925
Thomson, Sir Joseph, Trinity Lodge, Cambridge, England_____ 1903
Vallee-Poussin, C. de la, University of Louvain, Louvain, Belgium_____ 1929
Volterra, Vito, Via in Lucina __, Rome, Italy_____ 1911
Wieland, Heinrich, Chemisches Laboratorium Bayer. Akademie der Wissenschaften. Sophienstrasse , Munich _ N. W., Germany_____ 1932
Willstaetter, Richard, Moehlstrasse _ , Munich O. _ , Germany_____ 1926

7. MEDALISTS OF THE NATIONAL ACADEMY

Name	Medal	Year
Abbe, Cleveland [1]	Welfare	1916
Abbot, Charles Greeley	Draper	1910
Abel, Othenio [2]	Elliot	1920
Adams, Walter Sidney	Draper	1918
Albert Ier, Prince of Monaco [1,2]	Agassiz	1918
Anwers, O. F. J. Arthur [1]	Watson	1891
Barnett, Samuel Jackson [2]	Comstock	1918
Bather, Francis Arthur [2]	Thompson	1932
Beebe, William [2]	Elliot	1918
Bigelow, Henry Bryant	Agassiz	1931
Bjerknes, Vilhelm	do	1926
Black, Davidson [1,2]	Elliot	1931
Bohr, Niels	Barnard	1925
Bragg, Sir William Henry [2]	do	1914
Breuil, Henri [2]	Elliot	1924
Bridgman, P. W	Comstock	1933
Brown, Ernest William	Watson	1936
Campbell, William Wallace	Draper	1906
Cannon, Annie Jump [2]	do	1931
Canu, Ferdinand [1,2]	Elliot	1923
Carty, John J.[1]	Carty	1932
Chandler, Seth Carlo [1]	Watson	1894
Chapin, Charles V.[2]	Welfare	1928
Chapin, James P.[2]	Elliot	1932
Chapman, Frank Michler	do	1917
Charlier, C. V. L.[2]	Watson	1924
Clarke, John Mason [1]	Thompson	1925
Coghill, George Ellett	Elliot	1930
Cumming, Hugh S.[2]	Welfare	1935
Davisson, C. J	Comstock	1928
Dean, Bashford [1,2]	Elliot	1921
Defant, Albert [2]	Agassiz	1932
de Sitter, Willem [1]	Watson	1929
Deslandres, Henri	Draper	1913
Duane, William [1]	Comstock	1923
Eddington, Sir Arthur Stanley	Draper	1924
Einstein, Albert	Barnard	1921
Ekman, V. Walfrid [2]	Agassiz	1928
Fabry, Charles [2]	Draper	1919
Fairchild, David [2]	Welfare	1933
Fowler, Alfred [2]	Draper	1930
Gardiner, J. Stanley [2]	Agassiz	1929
Gill, Sir David [1]	Watson	1899
Goethals, George Washington.[1,2]	Welfare	1914
Gorgas, William Crawford [1,2]	do	1914
Gould, Benjamin Apthorp [1]	Watson	1887
Graham, Amadeus William [2]	Thompson	1966
Gran, Haakon Hasberg [2]	Agassiz	1934
Hale, George Ellery	Draper	1904
Heisenberg, Werner [2]	Barnard	1930
Helland-Hansen, Bjorn [2]	Agassiz	1933
Hjort, Johan [2]	do	1913
Hoover, Herbert Clark	Welfare	1920
Hubble, Edwin	Barnard	1935
Huggins, Sir William [1]	Draper	1901
Kapteyn, J. C.[2]	Watson	1913
Keeler, James Edward [1]	Draper	1899
Knudson, Martin [2]	Agassiz	1936
Langley, Samuel Pierpont [1]	Draper	1886
Leuschner, Armin Otto	Watson	1915
Margerie, Emmanuel de [2]	Thompson	1923
Mather, Stephen Tyng [1,2]	Welfare	1930
Mees, C. E. Kenneth [2]	Draper	1936
Merrill, George Perkins [1]	Smith	1922
Michelson, Albert Abraham [1]	Draper	1916
Millikan, Robert Andrews	Comstock	1913
Newton, Hubert Anson [1]	Smith	1888
Osborn, Henry Fairfield [1]	Elliot	1929
Park, William Hallock [2]	Welfare	1932
Pettersson, Otto Sven [2]	Agassiz	1924
Pickering, Edward Charles [1]	Draper	1888
Pinchot, Gifford [2]	Welfare	1916
Plaskett, John Stanley [2]	Draper	1934
Ridgway, Robert [1]	Elliot	1919
Rose, Wickliffe [1,2]	Welfare	1931
Rowland, Henry Augustus [1]	Draper	1890
Russell, F. F.[2]	Welfare	1935
Russell, Henry Norris	Draper	1922
Rutherford Baron; Ernest Rutherford	Barnard	1909
Schmidt, Johannes [2]	Agassiz	1930
Shoenfeld, Ed.[2,2]	Watson	1889
Schuchert, Charles	Thompson	1934
Scott, W. B	do	1930
Seton, Ernest Thompson [2]	Elliot	1928
Shapley, Harlow	Draper	1926
Sigsbee, Rear Admiral Charles Dwight, U. S. Navy.[1]	Agassiz	1920
Slipher, V. M	Draper	1932
Smith, James Perrin [1]	Thompson	1928
Stebbins, Joel	Draper	1915
Stensiö, Erik A: Son [2]	Elliot	1927
Stiles, Charles Wardell [2]	Welfare	1921
Stratton, Samuel Wesley [1]	do	1917
Ulrich, Edward Oscar	Thompson	1930
Vaughan, T. Wayland	Agassiz	1935
Vogel, Herman Karl [1]	Draper	1893
Vollmer, August [2]	Welfare	1934
Walcott, Charles Doolittle [1]	Thompson	1921
Weber, Max [2]	Agassiz	1927
Wheeler, William Morton [1]	Elliot	1922
White, David [1]	Thompson	1931
Do	Walcott	1934
Wilson, Edmund B	Elliot	1925
Do	Carty	1936
Wright, William Hammond	Draper	1928
Zeeman, P.[2]	do	1921

[1] Deceased.
[2] Not member or foreign associate of the Academy.

8. PRESIDENTS OF THE ACADEMY

Alexander Dallas Bache	1863-67		William Henry Welch	1913-17
Joseph Henry	1868-78		Charles Doolittle Walcott	1917-23
William Barton Rogers	1879-82		Albert Abraham Michelson	1923-27
Othniel Charles Marsh	1883-95		Thomas Hunt Morgan	1927-31
Wolcott Gibbs	1895-1900		William Wallace Campbell	1931-35
Alexander Agassiz	1901-7		Frank Rattray Lillie	1935-
Ira Remsen	1907-13			

9. DECEASED MEMBERS AND FOREIGN ASSOCIATES

DECEASED MEMBERS

	Date of election	Date of death		Date of election	Date of death
Abbe, Cleveland	1878	Oct. 28, 1916	Englemann, George	(?)	Feb. 4, 1884
Abbot, Henry L	1872	Oct. 1, 1927	Farlow, W. G	1879	June 3, 1919
Agassiz, Alexander	1866	Mar. 27, 1910	Ferrel, William	1868	Sept. 18, 1891
Agassiz, Louis	(?)	Dec. 14, 1873	Fewkes, Jesse Walter	1914	May 31, 1930
Alexander, J. H	(?)	Mar. 2, 1867	Folin, Otto	1916 ¹	Oct. 25, 1934
Alexander, Stephen	(?)	June 25, 1883	Forbes, Stephen Alfred	1918	Mar. 13, 1930
Allen, J. A	1876	Aug. 29, 1921	Franklin, E. C	1914 ¹	Feb. 4, 1937
Armsby, H. P	1920 ¹	Oct. 19, 1921	Frazer, John Fries	(?)	Oct. 12, 1872
Atkinson, George Francis	1918 ¹	Nov. 14, 1918	Freeman, John R	1918	Oct. 6, 1932
Bache, Alexander Dallas	(?)	Feb. 14, 1867	Frost, Edwin Brant	1908 ¹	May 14, 1935
Bailey, Solon Irving	1923	June 5, 1931	Gabb, William M	1876	May 30, 1878
Baird, Spencer F	1864	Aug. 19, 1887	Genth, F. A	1872	Feb. 2, 1893
Barker, George F	1876 ¹	May 24, 1910	Gibbs, Josiah Willard	1879	Apr. 28, 1903
Barnard, E. E	1911	Feb. 6, 1923	Gibbs, Wolcott	(?)	Dec. 9, 1908
Barnard, F. A. P	(¹ ¹)	Apr. 27, 1889	Gilbert, Grove Karl	1883	May 1, 1918
Barnard, J. G	(?)	May 14, 1882	Gill, Theodore Nicholas	1873	Sept. 25, 1914
Barrell, Joseph	1910	May 4, 1919	Gilliss, James Melville	(?)	Feb. 9, 1865
Bartlett, W. H. C	(?)	Feb. 11, 1893	Gooch, Frank Austin	1897	Aug. 12, 1929
Barus, Carl	1892 ¹	Sept. 28, 1935	Goodale, G. L	1890	Apr. 15, 1923
Becker, George Ferdinand	1901	Apr. 20, 1919	Goode, G. Brown	1888	Sept. 6, 1896
Beecher, Charles Emerson	1899	Feb. 14, 1904	Gould, Augustus A	(?)	Sept. 15, 1866
Bell, A. Graham	1883 ¹	Aug. 2, 1922	Gould, Benjamin A	(?)	Nov. 26, 1896
Benedict, Stanley Rossiter	1924 ¹	Dec. 21, 1936	Gray, Asa	(?)	Jan. 30, 1888
Billings, John S	1883	Mar. 11, 1913	Guyot, Arnold	(?)	Feb. 8, 1884
Bocher, Maxime	1909 ¹	Sept. 12, 1918	Hadley, James	1872	Nov. 14, 1872
Boltwood, B. B	1911	Aug. 14, 1927	Hague, Arnold	1885	May 15, 1917
Boss, Lewis	1889	Oct. 5, 1912	Haldeman, S. S	1876	Sept. 20, 1880
Bowditch, Henry P	1887	Mar. 13, 1911	Hall, Asaph	1875	Nov. 22, 1907
Branner, J. C	1905	Mar. 1, 1922	Hall, G. Stanley	1915	Apr. 24, 1924
Breasted, James Henry	1923	Dec. 2, 1935	Hall, James	(?)	Aug. 7, 1898
Brewer, William H	1880	Nov. 2, 1910	Halsted, W. S	1917	Sept. 7, 1922
Britton, Nathaniel L	1914 ¹	June 25, 1934	Hastings, C. S	1889 ¹	Jan. 29, 1932
Brooks, William Keith	1884	Nov. 12, 1908	Hayden, F. V	1873	Dec. 22, 1887
Brown-Sequard, Charles E	1868	Apr. 2, 1894	Hayford, John F	1911	Mar. 10, 1925
Brush, George Jarvis	1868	Feb. 6, 1912	Henry, Joseph	(?)	May 13, 1878
Bumstead, Henry A	1913	Dec. 31, 1920	Hilgard, Eugene W	1872	Jan. 8, 1916
Burgess, George K	1922 ¹	July 2, 1932	Hilgard, Julius E	(?)	May 9, 1890
Carothers, Wallace H	1936 ¹	Apr. 29, 1937	Hill, George William	1874	Apr. 16, 1914
Carty, John J	1917	Dec. 27, 1932	Hill, Henry B	1883	Apr. 6, 1903
Casey, Thomas L	1890	Mar. 25, 1896	Hillebrand, W. F	1908	Feb. 7, 1925
Caswell, Alexis	(?)	Jan. 8, 1877	Hitchcock, Edward	(?)	Feb. 27, 1864
Chamberlin, Thomas Chrowder	1903	Nov. 15, 1928	Holbrook, J. E	1868	Sept. 8, 1871
Chandler, Charles Frederick	1874	Aug. 25, 1925	Holden, Edward Singleton	1885	Mar. 16, 1914
Chandler, Seth Carlo	1888 ¹	Dec. 31, 1913	Holmes, William H.⁴	1905	Apr. 20, 1933
Chauvenet, William	(?)	Dec. 13, 1877	Howe, H. M	1917	May 14, 1922
Clark, Henry James	1872	July 1, 1879	Howe, Marshall Avery	1923 ¹	Dec. 24, 1936
Clark, William B	1908	July 27, 1913	Hubbard, J. S	(?)	Aug. 16, 1863
Clarke, Frank Wigglesworth	1900	May 23, 1931	Humphreys, A. A	(?)	Dec. 27, 1883
Clarke, John M	1909	May 29, 1925	Hunt, T. Sterry	1873	Feb. 12, 1892
Coffin, James H	1869	Feb. 6, 1873	Huntington, G. S	1924	Jan. 5, 1927
Coffin, J. H. C	(?)	Jan. 8, 1890	Hyatt, Alpheus	1875	Jan. 15, 1902
Comstock, Cyrus B	1884	May 29, 1910	Iddings, Joseph P	1907 ¹	Sept. 8, 1920
Comstock, George C	1899 ¹	May 11, 1934	Jackson, Charles Loring	1883 ¹	Oct. 28, 1935
Cook, George H	1887	Sept. 22, 1889	James, William	1903 ¹	Aug. 26, 1910
Cooke, Josiah P	1872	Sept. 3, 1894	Johnson, S. W	1866	July 21, 1909
Cope, Edward D	1872	Apr. 12, 1897	Jones, Walter	1918 ¹	Feb. 28, 1935
Coues, Elliott	1877	Dec. 25, 1899	Jordan, Edwin Oakes	1936 ¹	Sept. 2, 1936
Coulter, John Merle	1909	Dec. 23, 1928	Keeler, J. E	1900	Aug. 12, 1900
Councilman, William T.⁴	1904	May 27, 1933	Kemp, James F	1911	Nov. 17, 1926
Crafts, James M	1872	June 21, 1917	King, Clarence	1876	Dec. 24, 1901
Dall, William H	1897 ¹	Mar. 27, 1927	Kirtland, Jared P	1865	Dec. 10, 1877
Dalton, J. C	1864	Feb. 2, 1889	Lane, J. Homer	1872	May 3, 1880
Dana, E. S	1884	June 16, 1935	Langley, Samuel P	1876	Feb. 27, 1906
Dana, James D	(?)	Apr. 14, 1895	Laufer, Berthold	1930	Sept. 13, 1934
Davidson, George	1874	Dec. 2, 1911	Lea, Matthew Carey	1892	Mar. 15, 1897
Davis, Charles H	(?)	Feb. 18, 1877	Le Conte, John	1878	Apr. 29, 1891
Davis, William M	1904 ¹	Feb. 5, 1934	Le Conte, John L	(?)	Nov. 15, 1883
Draper, Henry	1877	Nov. 20, 1882	Le Conte, Joseph	1875	July 6, 1901
Draper, John W	1877	Jan. 4, 1882	Leidy, Joseph	(?)	Apr. 30, 1891
Duane, William	1920	Mar. 7, 1935	Lesley, J. Peter	(?)	June 1, 1903
Dutton, C. E	1884 ¹	Jan. 4, 1912	Lesquereux, Leo	1864	Oct. 25, 1889
Eads, James B	1872	Mar. 8, 1887	Loeb, Jacques	1910	Feb. 12, 1924
Edison, Thomas A	1927	Oct. 18, 1931	Longstreth, Miers F	(?)	Dec. 27, 1891
Eigenmann, Carl H	1923	Apr. 24, 1927	Loomis, Elias	1873	Aug. 15, 1889
Elkin, W. L	1895	May 30, 1933	Lovering, Joseph	1873	Jan. 18, 1892
Emmons, Samuel F	1892	Mar. 28, 1911	Lusk, Graham	1915 ¹	July 18, 1932
			Lyman, Theodore	1872	Sept. 9, 1897
			Mahan, D. H	(?)	Sept. 16, 1871
			Mall, Franklin P	1907	Nov. 17, 1917

See footnotes at end of table.

9. Deceased members and foreign associates—Continued

DECEASED MEMBERS—continued

Name	Date of election	Date of death	Name	Date of election	Date of death
Marsh, G. P.	1866	July 23, 1882	Sabine, Wallace C. W.	1917	Jan. 10, 1919
Marsh, O. C.	1874 [1]	Mar. 18, 1899	St. John, Charles Edward	1924	Apr. 26, 1935
Mayer, Alfred M.	1872	July 13, 1897	Sargent, Charles S.	1895	Mar. 22, 1927
Mayor, A. G.	1916	June 25, 1922	Saxton, Joseph	(2)	Oct. 26, 1873
Mayo-Smith, Richmond	1890	Nov. 11, 1901	Schott, Charles A.	1872	July 31, 1901
Meek, F. B.	1869	Dec. 21, 1876	Scudder, Samuel H.	1877	May 17, 1911
Meigs, M. C.	1865	Jan. 2, 1892	Sellers, William	1873 [1]	Jan. 24, 1905
Meltzer, Samuel James	1912	Nov. 8, 1920	Silliman, Benj., Sr.	(2)	Nov. 24, 1864
Mendel, Lafayette B.[?]	1913	Dec. 9, 1935	Silliman, Benj., Jr.	(3)	Jan. 14, 1885
Mendenhall, Charles Elwood	1918	Aug. 18, 1935	Smith, Alexander	1915	Sept. 8, 1922
Mendenhall, T. C.	1887	Mar. 22, 1924	Smith, Edgar F.	1899	May 3, 1928
Merrill, George Perkins	1922	Aug. 15, 1929	Smith, Erwin F.	1913 [1]	Apr. 6, 1927
Michelson, A. A.	1888 [1]	May 9, 1931	Smith, J. Lawrence	1872	Oct. 12, 1883
Minot, Charles Sedgwick	1897	Nov. 19, 1914	Smith, James Perrin	1925 [1]	Jan. 1, 1931
Mitchell, Henry	1885 [1]	Dec. 1, 1902	Smith, Sidney Irving [?]	1884	May 6, 1926
Mitchell, Silas Weir	1865	Jan. 4, 1914	Smith, Theobald	1908	Dec. 10, 1934
Moore, E. H.	1901	Dec. 30, 1932	Sperry, Elmer A.	1925 [1]	June 16, 1930
Morgan, Louis H.	1875	Dec. 17, 1881	Squier, George O.	1919 [1]	Mar. 24, 1934
Morley, E. W.	1897	Feb. 24, 1923	Stieglitz, Julius Oscar	1911 [1]	Jan. 10, 1937
Morse, Edward Sylvester	1876	Dec. 20, 1925	Stimpson, William	1868	May 26, 1872
Morse, Harmon N.	1907	Sept. 8, 1920	Story, William Edward	1908 [1]	Apr. 11, 1930
Morton, Henry	1874	May 9, 1902	Stratton, S. W.	1917	Oct. 18, 1931
Nef, John Ulric	1904 [1]	Aug. 13, 1915	Strong, Theodore	(?)	Feb. 1, 1869
Newberry, J. S.	(?)	Dec. 7, 1892	Sullivant, W. S.	1872	Apr. 30, 1873
Newcomb, Simon	1869	July 11, 1909	Swain, George F.	1923	July 1, 1931
Newton, H. A.	(?)	Aug. 12, 1896	Swasey, Ambrose	1922 [1]	June 15, 1937
Newton, John	1876	May 1, 1895	Thaxter, Roland	1912	Apr. 22, 1932
Nichols, Ernest Fox	1908	Apr. 29, 1924	Thomson, Elihu	1907 [1]	Mar. 13, 1937
Norton, William A.	1873	Sept. 21, 1883	Torrey, John	(2)	Mar. 10, 1873
Noyes, Arthur Amos	1905 [1]	June 3, 1936	Totten, J. G.	(3)	Apr. 22, 1864
Oliver, James E.	1872	Mar. 27, 1895	Trowbridge, Augustus	1919	Mar. 14, 1934
Osborn, Henry Fairfield	1900 [1]	Nov. 6, 1935	Trowbridge, John	1878	Feb. 18, 1923
Osborne, Thomas Burr	1910	Jan. 29, 1929	Trowbridge, William P.	1872	Aug. 12, 1892
Packard, A. S.	1872	Feb. 14, 1900[5]	Trumbull, James H.	1872	Aug. 5, 1897
Peirce, Benjamin [3]	(1 3)	Oct. 6, 1880	Tuckerman, Edward	1868	Mar. 15, 1886
Peirce, Benjamin Osgood	1906	Jan. 14, 1914[4]	Van Hise, C. R.	1902	Nov. 19, 1918
Peirce, Charles S. S.	1877[3]	Apr. 20, 1914	Vaughan, Victor Clarence	1915 [1]	Nov. 21, 1929
Penfield, Samuel L.	1900	Aug. 12, 1906	Verrill, Addison E.[11]	1872	Dec. 10, 1926
Peters, C. H. F.	1876 [1]	July 18, 1890	Walcott, Charles D.	1896 [1]	Feb. 9, 1927
Pickering, Edward C.	1873	Feb. 3, 1919	Walker, Francis A.	1878	Jan. 5, 1897
Pirsson, Louis V.	1913 [1]	Dec. 8, 1919	Warren, G. K.	1876	Aug. 8, 1882
Pourtales, L. F.	1873	July 19, 1880	Washburn, E. W.	1932	Feb. 6, 1934
Powell, John W.	1880	Sept. 23, 1902	Washington, H. S.	1921 [1]	Jan. 7, 1934
Power, Frederick B.	1924 [1]	Mar. 26, 1927	Watson, James C.	1868	Nov. 23, 1880
Prudden, T. Mitchell	1901	Apr. 10, 1924	Watson, Sereno	1889	Mar. 9, 1892
Pumpelly, Raphael	1872	Aug. 10, 1923	Webster, A. G.	1903	May 15, 1923
Pupin, Michael Idvorsky	1905 [1]	Mar. 12, 1935	Welch, William H.	1895 [1]	Apr. 30, 1934
Putnam, Frederic W.	1885	Aug. 18, 1915	Wells, Horace L.	1903	Dec. 19, 1924
Ransome, F. L.	1914 [1]	Oct. 6, 1935	Wheeler, Henry Lord	1909 [1]	Oct. 30, 1914
Reusen, Ira	1882	Mar. 4, 1927	Wheeler, William Morton	1912 [1]	Apr. 19, 1937
Richards, T. W.	1899 [1]	Apr. 2, 1928	White, Charles A.	1889	June 29, 1910
Ridgway, Robert	1917	Mar. 25, 1929	White, David	1912	Feb. 7, 1935
Robinson, B. L.	1921	July 27, 1935	Whitman, C. O.	1895	Dec. 6, 1910
Rodgers, John	(?)	May 5, 1882	Whitney, Josiah D.[5]	(1 ?)	Aug. 19, 1896
Rogers, Fairman	(?)	Aug. 22, 1900	Whitney, William D.[5]	1865 [1]	June 29, 1894
Rogers, Robert E.[?]	(?)	Sept. 6, 1884	Wilczynski, E. J.[13]	1919	Sept 14, 1932
Rogers, William A.	1885	Mar. 1, 1898	Williston, Samuel W.	1915	Aug. 30, 1918
Rogers, William B.[10]	(?)	May 30, 1882	Winlock, Joseph	(2)	June 11, 1875
Rood, Ogden N.	1865[?]	Nov. 12, 1902	Wood, Horatio C.	1879 [1]	Jan. 3, 1920
Rosa, E. B.	1913	May 17, 1921	Woodward, J. J.	1873	Aug. 17, 1884
Rowland, Henry A.	1881	Apr. 16, 1901	Woodward, Robert S.	1896 [1]	June 29, 1924
Royce, Josiah	1906 [1]	Sept. 14, 1916	Worthen, A. H.	1872	May 6, 1888
Rutherford, Lewis M.	(?)	May 30, 1892	Wright, Arthur Williams	1881	Dec. 19, 1915
Ryan, Harris Joseph	1920 [1]	July 3, 1934	Wyman, Jeffries	(2) [1]	Sept. 4, 1874
			Young, Charles A.	1872	Jan. 3, 1908

1 Biographical Memoirs have not been published.
2 Charter member, Mar. 3, 1863.
3 Transferred to roll of members emeriti, 1929.
4 Transferred to roll of members emeriti, 1932.
5 Transferred to roll of members emeriti in 1933.
6 Resigned, 1909.
7 Transferred to roll of members emeriti in 1935.
8 Resigned, 1873.
9 Dropped 1866, reelected 1875.
10 Dropped 1866, reelected 1872.
11 Transferred to roll of members emeriti in 1908.
12 Transferred to roll of members emeriti in 1924.
13 Transferred to roll of members emeriti in 1925.

9. Deceased members and foreign associates—Continued

DECEASED FOREIGN ASSOCIATES

Adams, J. C.
Airy, Sir George B.
Argelander, F. W. A.
Arrhenius, S. A.
Auwers, G. F. J. Arthur
Backlund, Oskar
Baer, Karl Ernest von
Baeyer, Adolf von
Barrande, Joachin
Bateson, William
Beaumont, L. Elie de
Becquerel, Henri
Berthelot, M. P. E.
Bertrand, J. L. F.
Boltzmann, Ludwig
Bornet, Edouard
Boussingault, J. B. J. D.
Boveri, Theodor
Braun, Alexander
Brewster, Sir David
Bunsen, Robert W.
Burmeister, C. H. C.
Candollie, Alphonse de
Cayley, Arthur
Chasles, Michel
Chevreul, M. E.
Clausius, Rudolph
Cornu, Alfred
Crookes, Sir William
Darboux, Gaston
Darwin, Sir George Howard
de Sitter, Willem
de Vries, Hugo
Dewar, Sir James
Dove, H. W.
Dumas, J. B.
Ehrlich, Paul
Eijkman, Christian
Engler, Adolph
Faraday, Michael
Fischer, Emil
Geikie, Sir Archibald
Gengenbaur, Karl
Gill, Sir David
Glydém, Hugo

Goebel, K. E. von
Groth, Paul von
Haber, Fritz
Haldane, John Scott
Hamilton, Sir William Rowan
Helmholtz, Baron H. von
Hoff, J. H. van't
Hofmann, A. W.
Hooker, Sir Joseph D.
Huggins, Sir William
Huxley, T. H.
Ibañez, Carlos
Janssen, J.
Jordan, M. E. C.
Joule, James P.
Kapteyn, J. C.
Kekulé, August
Kelvin, Lord
Kirchoff, G. R.
Klein, Felix
Koch, Robert
Kölliker, Albert von
Kohlrausch, Frederick
Kossel, Albrecht
Kronecker, Hugo
Kustner, Karl Friedrich
Lacaze-Duthiers, Henri de
Lankester, Sir E. Ray
Leuckart, Rudolph
Lie, Sophus
Liebig, Justus von
Lister, Lord
Loewy, Maurice
Lorentz, Hendrik Antoon
Ludwig, K. F. W.
Marey, E. J.
Mendeléeff, D. I.
Milne-Edwards, Henri
Moissan, Henri
Murchison, Sir Roderick I.
Murray, Sir John
Onnes, Heike Kamerlingh
Oppolzer, Theodore von
Ostwald, Wilhelm
Owen, Sir Richard

Parsons, Sir Charles Algernon
Pasteur, Louis
Pavlov, I. P.
Peters, C. A. F.
Pfeffer, Wilhelm
Plana, G. A. A.
Poincaire, Jules Henri
Rammelsberg, C. F.
Ramon y Cajal, Santiago
Ramsey, Sir William
Rayleigh, Lord
Regnault, Victor
Retzius, Gustav
Reymond, Emil Du Bois
Richthofen, F. von
Rosenbusch, Karl Harry Ferdinand
Roux, Wilhelm
Rubner, Max
Sachs, Julius von
Schiaparelli, Giovanni
Schuster, Sir Arthur
Seelinger, Hugo R. von
Stas, Jean Servais
Stokes, Sir George G.
Strasburger, Edouard
Struve, Otto von
Stumpf, Carl
Suess, Eduard
Sylvester, J. J.
Tisserand, F. F.
Van der Waals, J. D.
Virchow, Rudolph von
Vogel, H. C.
Waldeyer, Wilhelm
Weierstrauss, Karl
Weismann, August
Wöhler, Frederick
Wolf, Max F. J. C.
Wundt, Wilhelm
Würtz, Adolph
Zirkel, Ferdinand
Zittell, K. A. R. von

NATIONAL RESEARCH COUNCIL .

1. EXECUTIVE ORDER ISSUED BY THE PRESIDENT OF THE UNITED STATES MAY 11, 1918

The National Research Council was organized in 1916 at the request of the President by the National Academy of Sciences, under its congressional charter, as a measure of national preparedness. The work accomplished by the Council in organizing research and in securing cooperation of military and civilian agencies in the solution of military problems demonstrates its capacity for larger service. The National Academy of Sciences is therefore requested to perpetuate the National Research Council, the duties of which shall be as follows:

1. In general, to stimulate research in the mathematical, physical, and biological sciences, and in the application of these sciences to engineering, agriculture, medicine, and other useful arts, with the object of increasing knowledge, of strengthening the national defense, and of contributing in other ways to the public welfare.

2. To survey the larger possibilities of science, to formulate comprehensive projects of research, and to develop effective means of utilizing the scientific and technical resources of the country for dealing with these projects.

3. To promote cooperation in research, at home and abroad, in order to secure concentration of effort, minimize duplication, and stimulate progress; but in all cooperative undertakings to give encouragement to individual initiative, as fundamentally important to the advancement of science.

4. To serve as a means of bringing American and foreign investigators into active cooperation with the scientific and technical services of the War and Navy Departments and with those of the civil branches of the Government.

5. To direct the attention of scientific and technical investigators to the present importance of military and industrial problems in connection with the war, and to aid in the solution of these problems by organizing specific researches.

6. To gather and collate scientific and technical information, at home and abroad, in cooperation with governmental and other agencies, and to render such information available to duly accredited persons.

Effective prosecution of the Council's work requires the cordial collaboration of the scientific and technical branches of the Government, both military and civil. To this end representatives of the Government, upon the nomination of the National Academy of Sciences, will be designated by the President as members of the Council, as heretofore, and the heads of the departments immediately concerned will continue to cooperate in every way that may be required.

WOODROW WILSON.

THE WHITE HOUSE, *May 11, 1918.*

[No. 2859]

2. ARTICLES OF ORGANIZATION, NATIONAL RESEARCH COUNCIL

PREAMBLE

The National Academy of Sciences, under the authority conferred upon it by its charter enacted by the Congress, and approved by President Lincoln on March 3, 1863, and pursuant to the request expressed in an Executive order made by President Wilson on May 11, 1918, adopts the following articles of organization for the National Research Council, to replace the organization under which it has operated heretofore.

ARTICLE I.—PURPOSE

It shall be the purpose of the National Research Council to promote research in the mathematical, physical, and biological sciences, and in the application of these sciences to engineering, agriculture, medicine, and other useful arts, with the object of increasing knowledge, of strengthening the national defense, and of contributing in other ways to the public welfare, as expressed in the Executive order of May 11, 1918.

ARTICLE II.—MEMBERSHIP

SECTION 1. The membership of the National Research Council shall be chosen with the view of rendering the Council an effective federation of the principal research agencies in the United States concerned with the fields of science and technology named in article I.

SEC. 2. The Council shall be composed of—

1. Representatives of national scientific and technical societies.
2. Representatives of the Government, as provided in the Executive order.
3. Representatives of other research organizations and other persons whose aid may advance the objects of the Council.

SEC. 3. The membership of the Council shall consist specifically of the members of the executive board and the members of the divisions, constituted as provided in articles III and IV.

SEC. 4. Membership in the Council shall be limited to citizens of the United States. This, however, shall not be construed as applying to membership in committees, appointed by or acting under the Council, whose members are not necessarily members of the Council, provided that members not citizens of the United States shall in no case form a majority of any committee.

ARTICLE III.—DIVISIONS

SECTION 1. The Council shall be organized in divisions of two classes:

  A. Divisions dealing with the more general relations and activities of the Council.

  B. Divisions dealing with special branches of science and technology.

SEC. 2. The divisions of the Council shall be as follows:

  A. Divisions of general relations:

    I. Division of Federal relations.

    II. Division of foreign relations.

    III. Division of educational relations.

  B. Divisions of science and technology:

    IV. Division of physical sciences.

    V. Division of engineering and industrial research.

    VI. Division of chemistry and chemical technology.

    VII. Division of geology and geography.

    VIII. Division of medical sciences.

    IX. Division of biology and agriculture.

    X. Division of anthropology and psychology.

SEC. 3. The number of divisions and the grouping of subjects in article III, section 2, may be modified by the executive board of the National Research Council.

SEC. 4 (a). Each division of general relations shall consist of a chairman, one or more vice chairmen, representatives of national and international organizations, and members at large, appointed as provided in article VI.

(b). There may be an executive committee of each division of general relations, consisting of the chairman and three or more of the members, who shall be chosen by the division at a regular meeting, confirmed by the executive board, and hold office for 1 year terminating on June 30 or, in case of any one or more of such executive committees, on such later date as the chairman of the Council may have previously ordered. Between meetings of a division its executive committee shall have power to act on all matters for the division, except those which may be reserved by the division for its own action; but the executive committee shall report all its actions to the division.

SEC. 5. (a) Each division of science and technology shall consist of a chairman and of representatives of such national societies as seem essential for the conduct of the business of the division, appointed as provided in article VI. Members at large, not to exceed three, may also be appointed as provided in article VI. From the membership of the division thus constituted, a smaller group, not to exceed 12, shall be designated as executive members who alone may be reimbursed by the National Research Council for travel expenses incurred in attendance upon meetings of the division.

(b) There may be an executive committee of each division of science and technology, consisting of the chairman and three or more of the executive members, who shall be chosen by the division at a regular meeting, confirmed by the executive board, and hold office for one year terminating on June 30 or, in the case of any one or more of such executive committees, on such later date as the chairman of the Council may have previously ordered. Between meetings of a division its executive committee shall have power to act on all matters for the division except those which may be reserved by the division for its own action; but the executive committee shall report all its actions to the division.

(c) The terms of office of the chairmen of the divisions of science and technology, other than that of engineering and industrial research, shall be so arranged by the chairman of the Council that one-third of these terms expire each year.

Sec. 6. The chairman of each division shall be, ex officio, a member of all committees of the division.

Sec. 7. Actions by the divisions involving matters of policy shall be subject to approval by the executive board.

ARTICLE IV.—ADMINISTRATION

SECTION 1. The general officers of the National Research Council shall be a chairman, chosen as provided in article V, section 1, a treasurer (see art. V, sec. 3), and such honorary officers as may be appointed by the council of the National Academy of Sciences, upon nomination by the executive board.

Sec. 2. The affairs of the National Research Council shall be administered by an executive board and its administrative committee. Actions by these bodies involving financial responsibilities or the appointment of general officers must be approved by the council of the National Academy of Sciences, or by the executive committee of the council of the National Academy of Sciences under general authority, or under such special authority as may be conferred on it by the council of the National Academy of Sciences.

Sec. 3. The executive board shall consist of the members of the executive committee of the council of the National Academy of Sciences; the chairman, treasurer, and honorary officers of the National Research Council; the chairmen of the divisions of general relations and of the divisions of science and technology of the National Research Council; the members of the committee on policies; the president or other representative of the American Association for the Advancement of Science; the chairman or other representative of the Engineering Foundation; and six members at large appointed for a term of 3 years, or for an unexpired term in case of vacancy, by the president of the National Academy of Sciences, on recommendation of the executive board. The president of the National Academy of Sciences shall preside at the meetings of the executive board.

Sec. 4. In administrative matters the executive board shall be represented by an administrative committee, which shall consist of the chairman and treasurer of the National Research Council, the president, vice president, and home secretary of the National Academy, and the chairman of the divisions of science and technology of the National Research Council.

Sec. 5. The administrative committee shall have power to act upon all matters except those which may be reserved by the executive board for its own action; but the administrative committee shall report all its actions to the executive board. The administrative committee shall prepare the annual budget for submission to the executive board at its annual meeting.

Sec. 6. (a) There shall also be a committee on policies of the National Research Council. This committee shall be composed of nine members appointed for terms of 3 years by the executive board, preferably so that it may consist largely of persons who have had past experience in the affairs of the National Research Council. The executive board shall appoint the chairman of the committee on policies to serve for 1 year beginning July 1 or until his successor is appointed. This committee shall submit to the executive board recommendations as to general policies.

(b) At the annual meeting of the executive board in 1933 nine members of the committee on policies shall be appointed; three to serve for 1 year, three for

2 years, and three for 3 years, their respective terms to be determined by lot. Each year thereafter the terms of three members will expire,. and their successors, to serve for 3 years each, shall be appointed at the annual meeting of the executive board in that year. The date of expiration of the terms shall be June 30. In case of vacancy the executive board may fill the unexpired term by appointment.

ARTICLE V.—APPOINTMENT AND DUTIES OF OFFICERS OF THE RESEARCH COUNCIL

SECTION 1. The chairman of the National Research Council shall be appointed by the executive board, subject to confirmation by the council of the National Academy of Sciences, and shall hold office at the pleasure of the board. The chairman shall be the executive officer of the National Research Council and shall have charge of its general administration. He shall act as chairman of its administrative committee, and shall be, ex officio, a member of all divisions and committees of the Council.

SEC. 2. There shall be appointed by the executive board, upon recommendation of the chairman of the National Research Council, an officer with the title of executive secretary of the Council, whose duties it shall be to assist the chairman in the administration of the Council. He shall attend all meetings of the executive board and of the administrative committee, and act as their secretary, and shall hold office at the pleasure of the board.

SEC. 3. The treasurer of the National Academy of Sciences shall be, ex officio, treasurer of the National Research Council.

SEC. 4. In case of a vacancy in the office of the chairman of the National Research Council or of the absence or disability of the chairman an acting chairman may be appointed by the council of the National Academy of Sciences, or by the executive committee of the council of the National Academy, upon recommendation of the executive board of the Research Council or its administrative committee.

ARTICLE VI.—NOMINATION AND APPOINTMENT OF OFFICERS AND MEMBERS OF DIVISIONS

SECTION 1. *Divisions of Science and Technology.*—(a) The chairman of each division shall be nominated to the executive board by the division concerned, with the approval of the administrative committee. The chairman shall be appointed by the executive board at its annual meeting for a term of 3 years.

(b) The national societies to be represented in each of the divisions shall be determined by the division concerned, subject to the approval of the executive board.

(c) The representatives of national societies in each division shall be nominated by the societies, at the request of the chairman of the division, and, after approval by the executive board, shall be appointed by the president of the National Academy of Sciences to membership in the National Research Council for a term of 3 years and assigned to the division.

(d) Members at large, if any, in each division shall be nominated by the division concerned, with the approval of the executive board, and shall be appointed by the president of the National Academy of Sciences to membership in the National Research Council for a term of 3 years, and assigned to the division.

(e) The executive members in each division shall be designated by the division concerned, subject to the approval of the executive board.

SEC. 2. *Divisions of general relations.*—(a) The officers of each of the divisions of general relations shall be appointed by the executive board to serve for a period of 3 years, except that the foreign secretary of the National Academy of Sciences shall be, ex officio, chairman of the division of foreign relations, and that the appointment of the chairman of the division of Federal relations shall be subject to confirmation by the council of the National Academy of Sciences.

(b) The national and international societies or associations to be represented in each of these divisions shall be determined by the division concerned, subject to the approval of the executive board.

(c) The representatives of such societies or associations shall be nominated by the societies or associations, at the request of the chairman of the division, and, after approval by the executive board, shall be appointed by the president of the National Academy of Sciences to membership in the Council for a period of 3 years, and assigned to the division.

(d) Members at large in each division shall be nominated by the division, approved by the executive board, and appointed by the president of the National Academy of Sciences to membership in the Council for a period of 3 years, and assigned to the division.

(e) The Government bureaus, civil and military, to be represented in the division of Federal relations shall be determined by the council of the National Academy of Sciences, on recommendation from the executive board of the National Research Council.

(f) The representatives of the Government shall be nominated by the president of the National Academy of Sciences, after conference with the secretaries of the departments concerned, and the names of those nominated shall be presented to the President of the United States for designation by him for service with the National Research Council. Each Government representative shall serve during the pleasure of the President of the United States, not to exceed a term of 3 years, and a vacancy from any cause shall be filled for the remainder of the term in the same manner as in the case of the original designation.

SEC. 3. The terms of office of officers and members, unless otherwise provided, shall terminate on June 30 of the year in which their appointments expire.

SEC. 4. Vacancies occurring in the divisions of either class, except as to representatives of the Government, may be filled for the unexpired term by the executive board, upon recommendation of the division concerned, or ad interim by the administrative committee upon similar recommendation.

ARTICLE VII.—MEETINGS

SECTION 1. The annual meeting of the executive board shall be held in April in the city of Washington at the time of the meeting of the National Academy of Sciences. Special meetings may be held at other times at the call of the chairman of the National Research Council. A majority of the members of the board shall constitute a quorum for the transaction of business.

SEC. 2. Stated meetings of the administrative committee shall be held in the city of Washington at least five times a year, at such dates as shall be determined by the chairman of the National Research Council. Special meetings may be held at other times on call of the chairman. Five members of the committee shall constitute a quorum for the transaction of business.

SEC. 3. The committee on policies shall hold one stated meeting during the year, preferably in Washington at the time of the annual meeting of the National Academy of Sciences. Special meetings may be held at any time on call of the chairman of the committee. Five members of the committee shall constitute a quorum for the transaction of business.

SEC. 4. Each division of science and technology shall hold at least one stated meeting during the year, at a time to be determined by the chairman of the division in consultation with the chairman of the Council. Special meetings may be called at other times by the chairman of the division.

SEC. 5. Meetings of any division of general relations shall be held upon the call of its chairman.

ARTICLE VIII.—PUBLICATIONS AND REPORTS

SECTION 1. An annual report on the work of the National Research Council shall be presented by the chairman to the National Academy of Sciences.

SEC. 2. Other publications of the National Research Council may include papers, bulletins, reports, and memoirs, which may appear in the Proceedings or Memoirs of the National Academy of Sciences, in the publications of other societies, in scientific and technical journals, or in a separate series of the National Research Council.

ARTICLE IX.—AMENDMENTS

SECTION 1. By action of the National Academy of Sciences, on April 29, 1919, power of amendment of these articles of organization is given to the council of the National Academy of Sciences.

Adopted February 14, 1933.

3. BYLAWS

1. The treasurer shall have the assistance of a salaried and bonded officer, the bursar, who shall be chosen by the finance committee of the National Academy of Sciences and be directly responsible to the treasurer.

2. The executive board may create such other salaried officers as are necessary for the transaction of the business of the Council.

3. Officers of the Council, members of the executive board, and special agents of the Council, when authorized to travel on business of the Council, may be allowed their necessary expenses.

4. Executive members of the divisions of science and technology and members of the executive committee of any division of general relations, when attending an authorized meeting, may be reimbursed for traveling expenses, or such portion thereof as the division chairman may determine, within the funds made available for that purpose in the budget.

5. The chairman of each division shall direct the administrative and scientific work of the division.

6. In the fiscal year in which the term of office of a chairman of a division expires it shall be his duty to appoint, on or before February 1, a nominating committee of three, chosen from present or former members of the division or from the membership of existing committees of the division, who, in consultation with the chairman of the division and the chairman of the Council, shall select an available candidate for the chairmanship for the ensuing term. The name of the candidate shall be reported to the division through its chairman and, if approved by the division, shall be recommended to the executive board at its annual meeting for appointment, as provided in article VI, sections 1 and 2, of the articles of organization.

7. Each division of science and technology is empowered to arrange, in accordance with its special needs, for the selection of the executive members and members at large of the division, and for an executive committee, to be appointed annually, as provided in article III, section 5 (a) and (b), and article VI, section 1 (d) of the articles of organization.

Each division may designate also one of its executive members to act as vice chairman of the division, the term of office to be for 1 year.

8. Following the termination of any regular 3-year period of service the chairman or members of a division shall be eligible for reappointment in the same status only after a lapse of 1 year, except that the executive board may continue the service of a chairman or members for a second period of 3 years, or less, when such action is recommended by the division concerned.

9. An annual honorarium may be paid to the chairman of each division of science and technology and an annual maintenance fund shall be appropriated for the support of the work of each division of the Council. The amount of the honorarium and of the maintenance fund of each division shall be determined by the administrative committee, subject to the approval of the executive board and the council of the National Academy of Sciences or its executive committee.

10. The maintenance fund allotted to each division shall be expended under the authority of the chairman of the division to provide for meetings of the division and its various committees, and other necessary expenses, in accordance with the regulations in force in the Council controlling financial expenditures.

11. No member of a committee constituted to administer funds entrusted to the National Research Council shall receive an honorarium or salary from such funds for his services, except in cases specifically authorized in advance by the executive board or its administrative committee, but members of such committees may be reimbursed from the funds for expenses incurred in the work of the committee.

12. Members of special committees organized within any of the divisions must be approved by the administrative committee before official notification of appointment is made by the chairman of the division.

13. Solicitation of funds for the support of projects of a division may be made only after authorization by both the executive board (or its administrative committee) and the council of the National Academy of Sciences (or its executive committee). Such solicitation shall be conducted under the direction of the chairman of the National Research Council acting in conjunction with the chairman of the division concerned.

14. Special funds granted to the National Research Council, other than those for fellowships and grants-in-aid, must be expended in accordance with budgets previously approved by the administrative committee.

15. It shall be the duty of the chairman of each division of the Council to submit an annual report of the activities of his division to the chairman of the Council on or before June 30. Interim reports shall be made to the chairman of the Council before each stated meeting of the administrative committee.

16. Standing committees of the executive board, unless otherwise provided for, shall be appointed annually by the board at its April meeting, or, in case of need, by the administrative committee at one of its stated meetings.

17. The executive board, at its annual meeting in April, shall appoint a nominating committee of three members to prepare nominations for presentation at the next annual meeting of the board for vacancies in the committee on policies and in the list of members at large of the board, occurring at the end of the fiscal year.

18. Amendments of bylaws may be made by the executive board at any authorized meeting of the board.

19. A publication to be known as the Bulletin of the National Research Council shall be established to provide for the publication of materials originating in the work of the Council. The Bulletin shall be issued as occasion demands.

20. A series to be known as the Reprint and Circular Series of the National Research Council shall provide for the distribution of papers published or printed by or for the National Research Council.

Adopted April 26, 1933.

4. ORGANIZATION OF THE NATIONAL RESEARCH COUNCIL, 1936-37

A. Officers and Executive Board

OFFICERS

Honorary chairman, George E. Hale, honorary director, Mount Wilson Observatory, Carnegie Institution of Washington, Pasadena, Calif.

Secretary emeritus, Vernon Kellogg, National Research Council, Washington, D. C.

Chairman, Ludvig Hektoen, director, John McCormick Institute for Infectious Diseases, 629 South Wood Street, Chicago, Ill.

Treasurer, Arthur Keith, treasurer, National Academy of Sciences, geologist, 2210 Twentieth Street NW., Washington, D. C.

Executive secretary, Albert L. Barrows, National Research Council, Washington, D. C.

Bursar, J. H. J. Yule, National Research Council, Washington, D. C.

Chief clerk, C. L. Wade, National Research Council, Washington, D. C.

EXECUTIVE BOARD

Presiding officer, Frank R. Lillie, president, National Academy of Sciences, ex officio.

MEMBERS, EX OFFICIO

Honorary chairman, chairman, secretary emeritus, and treasurer of the National Research Council.

Chairmen of the Divisions of the National Research Council.

Executive Committee of the Council of the National Academy of Sciences

Frank R. Lillie, president, National Academy of Sciences; dean emeritus, of the division of biological sciences, and Andrew MacLeish, distinguished service professor of embryology, emeritus, University of Chicago, Chicago, Ill.

Arthur L. Day, vice president, National Academy of Sciences; research associate, Carnegie Institution of Washington, Washington, D. C.

Ludvig Hektoen.

Fred. E. Wright, home secretary, National Academy of Sciences; petrologist, geophysical laboratory, Carnegie Institution of Washington, 2801 Upton Street, Washington, D. C.

Arthur Keith.

Roger Adams, professor of organic chemistry, University of Illinois, Urbana, Ill.

Ross G. Harrison, Sterling professor of biology and director of the Osborn Zoological Laboratory, Yale University, New Haven, Conn.

Committee on Policies of the National Research Council

R. A. Millikan, chairman, director, Norman Bridge Laboratory of Physics, and chairman of the executive council, California Institute of Technology, Pasadena, Calif.

Isaiah Bowman, president, Johns Hopkins University, Baltimore, Md.

Walter B. Cannon, George Higginson professor of physiology, Harvard Medical School, Boston, Mass.

Karl T. Compton, president, Massachusetts Institute of Technology, Cambridge, Mass.

Gano Dunn, president, J. G. White Engineering Corporation, 80 Broad Street, New York City.

Simon Flexner, director emeritus, Rockefeller Institute for Medical Research, Sixty-sixth Street and York Avenue, New York City.

Frank B. Jewett, vice president, American Telephone & Telegraph Co.; president, Bell Telephone Laboratories, Inc., 195 Broadway, New York City.

A. V. Kidder, chairman, division of historical research, Carnegie Institution of Washington, The Red House, Beverly Farms, Mass.

REPRESENTATIVES OF ORGANIZATIONS

President of the American Association for the Advancement of Science. George D. Birkhoff, Perkins professor of mathematics and dean of the faculties of arts and sciences, Harvard University, Cambridge, Mass.

Representative of the Engineering Foundation, F. M. Farmer, chief engineer, Electrical Testing Laboratories, Eightieth Street and East End Avenue, New York City.

MEMBERS AT LARGE

Gilbert A. Bliss, professor of mathematics, University of Chicago, Chicago, Ill.

W. C. Curtis, professor of zoology, University of Missouri, Columbia, Mo.

Knight Dunlap, professor of psychology, University of California at Los Angeles, Los Angeles, Calif.

Nevin M. Fenneman, professor of geology and geography, University of Cincinnati, Cincinnati, Ohio.

Oswald Veblen, professor of mathematics, Institute for Advanced Study, Princeton University, Princeton, N. J.

F. W. Willard, president, Nassau Smelting & Refining Co., 50 Church Street, New York City.

ADMINISTRATIVE COMMITTEE

Chairman, Ludvig Hektoen; the treasurer of the National Research Council, the president, vice president, and home secretary of the National Academy of Sciences, and the chairmen of the divisions of science and technology of the National Research Council.

COMMITTEES

(The chairman of the National Research Council is, ex officio, a member of all divisions and committees of the Council)

Government relations and science advisory committee: Chairman, Frank R. Lillie; Roger Adams, Isaiah Bowman, Karl T. Compton, Arthur L. Day, Gano Dunn, Ludvig Hektoen, Frank B. Jewett, L. R. Jones, C. K. Leith, R. A. Millikan, George H. Whipple.

Committee on nominations: Chairman, R. A. Millikan; Isaiah Bowman, Frank R. Lillie.

Committee on publication and library: Chairman, Ludvig Hektoen; Henry A. Barton, Walter S. Hunter, H. R. Moody.

Advisory committee on buildings and grounds (joint committee with the National Academy of Science): Chairman, Paul Brockett, executive secretary, and custodian of buildings and grounds, National Academy of Sciences, Washington, D. C.; Edson S. Bastin, Arthur L. Day, Ludvig Hektoen, Fred. E. Wright.

Committee on exhibits (joint committee with the National Academy of Sciences): Chairman, Fred. E. Wright; secretary, Paul Brockett; Edson S. Bastin, A. F. Blakeslee, Vannevar Bush, W. M. Clark, A. B. Coble, R. E. Coker, Simon Flexner, Bancroft Gherardi, George E. Hale, Ludvig Hektoen, Walter S. Hunter, Charles A. Kraus, A. O. Leuschner, Esmond R. Long, Max Mason, W. C. Mendenhall, R. A. Millikan, H. R. Moody, C. E. Seashore, Harlow Shapley, C. R. Stockard.

Executive committee: Chairman, Fred. E. Wright; secretary, Paul Brockett; Arthur L. Day, George E. Hale, Ludvig Hektoen, John C. Merriam.

Advisory committee on fellowships: Chairman, ex officio, Ludvig Hektoen; Francis G. Blake, ex officio, Simon Flexner, ex officio, F. K. Richtmyer, W. J. Robbins, ex officio, E. B. Wilson.

Committee on patent policy: Chairman, F. W. Willard; George W. McCoy, Archie Palmer, Alfred Stengel, Robert E. Wilson.

TECHNICAL COMMITTEES

Committee on abstracting and documentation of scientific literature: Chairman, I. F. Lewis, dean of the university, and Miller professor of biology and agriculture, University of Virginia, University, Va.; A. Parker Hitchens, L. R. Jones, C. E. McClung, George B. Pegram, Austin M. Patterson, J. B. Reeside, Jr.

Committee on cooperation with the Research Corporation: Chairman, F. G. Cottrell, president, Research Associates, Inc., 3400 Nebraska Avenue, Washington, D. C.; William J. Hale, Maurice Holland.

Committee on scientific aids to learning: Chairman, James B. Conant, president, Harvard University, Cambridge, Mass.; secretary, Bethuel M. Webster; Vannevar Bush, Frank B. Jewett, Ben D. Wood. Irvin Stewart, director.

Committee on publication of excerpts from International Critical Tables: Chairman, F. K. Richtmyer, dean of the Graduate School and professor of physics, Cornell University, Ithaca, N. Y.; Henry A. Barton, H. R. Moody.

Advisory committee to the American commissioners on Annual Tables of Constants and Numerical Data: Chairman, F. K. Richtmyer; Edward Bartow, L. J. Briggs, Karl T. Compton, Saul Dushman, Frank B. Jewett, John Johnston, Charles F. Kettering, G. N. Lewis, S. C. Lind, C. E. K. Mees, R. A. Millikan, H. R. Moody, Harlow Shapley, C. M. A. Stine, F. W. Sullivan, Jr., John F. Thompson. C. J. West, F. W. Willard. American commissioners, F. K. Richtmyer and C. J. West.

Committee of apparatus makers and users—executive committee: Chairman, W. D. Collins, Chief Division of Quality of Water, United States Geological Survey, Washington, D. C.; Lyman J. Briggs, Arthur L. Day, Morris E. Leeds, F. K. Richtmyer, J. M. Roberts, C. J. West.

Executive committee of the American Geophysical Union (representing the American section of the International Union of Geodesy and Geophysics): Chairman, N. H. Heck, Chief, Division of Terrestrial Magnetism and Seismology, United States Coast and Geodetic Survey, Washington, D. C.; vice chairman, R. H. Field; secretary, John A. Fleming; E. T. Allen, Edson S. Bastin, William Bowie, Charles F. Brooks, Austin H. Clark, R. E. Coker, C. L. Garner, R. E. Gibson, O. H. Gish, W. R. Gregg, H. D. Harradon, L. J. Henderson, F. W. Lee, R. A. Millikan, H. R. Moody, L. K. Sherman, Thomas G. Thompson, P. C. Whitney.

Committee on relationships with the War and Navy Departments: Chairman, R. A. Millikan; Isaiah Bowman, Vannevar Bush, W. F. Durand, Frank B. Jewett, C. K. Leith, H. R. Moody.

REPRESENTATIVES OF THE COUNCIL ON—

Editorial board of the Proceedings of the National Academy of Sciences: Edson S. Bastin, Vannevar Bush, R. E. Coker, Ludvig Hektoen, Walter S. Hunter, Esmond R. Long, R. A. Millikan, H. R. Moody. Member of the editorial executive committee, Ludvig Hektoen.

Council of the National Parks Association: Vernon Kellogg.

Board of trustees of Science Service: C. G. Abbot, H. E. Howe, Ludvig Hektoen.

B. DIVISIONS OF GENERAL RELATIONS

I. DIVISION OF FEDERAL RELATIONS

Chairman, George R. Putnam.
Vice chairman, Wilbur J. Carr.
Secretary, Paul Brockett.

EXECUTIVE COMMITTEE

Chairman, George R. Putnam; vice chairman, Wilbur J. Carr; C. G. Abbot, Lyman J. Briggs, J. R. Mohler, A. M. Stimson.

MEMBERS OF THE DIVISION

The President of the United States, on the nomination of the National Academy of Sciences, has designated the following representatives of the various Departments to act as members of this division:

DEPARTMENT OF STATE

Wilbur J. Carr, Assistant Secretary of State.

DEPARTMENT OF THE TREASURY

A. M. Stimson, Medical Director, Public Health Service.

DEPARTMENT OF WAR

Col. Francis H. Lincoln, General Staff, in charge of Military Intelligence, United States Army.
————— —————, Coast Artillery Corps, United States Army.
Lt. Col. E. R. Gentry, Medical Corps, United States Army.
Col. Warren T. Hannum, Corps of Engineers, United States Army.
Col. John E. Munroe, Ordnance Department, United States Army.
Maj. Gen. James B. Allison, Chief Signal Officer, United States Army.
Maj. Gen. Oscar Westover, Air Corps, United States Army.
Maj. Gen. Claude E. Brigham, Chief, Chemical Warfare Service, United States Army.

DEPARTMENT OF JUSTICE

J. Edgar Hoover, Director of Investigations.

POST OFFICE DEPARTMENT

Wrightson Chambers, Superintendent, Division of Engineering and Research.

DEPARTMENT OF THE NAVY

Capt. S. C. Hooper, Technical Assistant to the Chief of Naval Operations, United States Navy.
————— —————, Intelligence Division, Office of Naval Operations, United States Navy.
Capt. J. F. Hellweg, Superintendent, Naval Observatory, Bureau of Navigation, United States Navy.
Rear Admiral N. M. Smith, Chief, Bureau of Yards and Docks, United States Navy.
Rear Admiral Harold R. Stark, Chief, Bureau of Ordnance, United States Navy.
Rear Admiral Emory S. Land, Chief, Bureau of Construction and Repair, United States Navy.
Rear Admiral Harold G. Bowen, Chief, Bureau of Engineering, United States Navy.
Rear Admiral Percival S. Rossiter, Chief, Bureau of Medicine and Surgery, United States Navy.

DEPARTMENT OF THE INTERIOR

———— ————, Bureau of Reclamation.
W. C. Mendenhall, Director, Geological Survey.
Harold C. Bryant, Assistant Director, National Park Service.
John W. Finch, Director, Bureau of Mines.

DEPARTMENT OF AGRICULTURE

W. R. Gregg, Chief, Weather Bureau.
J. R. Mohler, Chief, Bureau of Animal Industry.
E. H. Clapp, Associate Chief, Forest Service.
Henry G. Knight, Chief, Bureau of Chemistry and Soils.
Lee A. Strong, Chief, Bureau of Entomology and Plant Quarantine.
Ira N. Gabrielson, Chief, Bureau of Biological Survey.
Thomas H. MacDonald, Chief, Bureau of Public Roads.
S. H. McCrory, Chief, Bureau of Agricultural Engineering.

DEPARTMENT OF COMMERCE

Joseph A. Hill, Chief Statistician, Statistical Research, Bureau of the Census.
Lyman J. Briggs, Director, National Bureau of Standards.
Frank T. Bell, Commissioner, Bureau of Fisheries.
George R. Putnam, Bureau of Lighthouses.
———— ———— ————, Coast and Geodetic Survey.
Charles H. Pierce, Classification Examiner, Patent Office.

DEPARTMENT OF LABOR

Isador Lubin, Commissioner of Labor Statistics.

SMITHSONIAN INSTITUTION

C. G. Abbot, Secretary, Smithsonian Institution.

NATIONAL ADVISORY COMMITTEE FOR AERONAUTICS

J. S. Ames, Chairman, National Advisory Committee for Aeronautics; president, emeritus, Johns Hopkins University, Baltimore, Md.

Secretary of the division, Paul Brockett, executive secretary, and custodian of buildings and grounds, National Academy of Sciences, Washington, D. C.

II. DIVISION OF FOREIGN RELATIONS

Chairman, ex officio, L. J. Henderson.
Vice chairman, Wilbur J. Carr.
Vice chairman, Frank Schlesinger.
Secretary, Albert L. Barrows.

EXECUTIVE COMMITTEE

Chairman, L. J. Henderson; vice chairmen, Wilbur J. Carr and Frank Schlesinger; William Bowie, Edward Bartow, George E. Hale, L. S. Rowe.

MEMBERS OF THE DIVISION

Ex Officio

President of the National Academy of Sciences, Frank R. Lillie, dean, emeritus, of the division of biological sciences, and Andrew MacLeish distinguished service professor of embryology, emeritus, University of Chicago, Chicago, Ill.
Foreign secretary of the National Academy of Sciences, L. J. Henderson, Abbott and James Lawrence professor of chemistry, Harvard University, Cambridge, Mass.
Chairman of the National Research Council and the chairmen of all divisions of the Council.

Representatives of—

AMERICAN ASSOCIATION FOR THE ADVANCEMENT OF SCIENCE

W. A. Noyes, emeritus professor of chemistry, University of Illinois, Urbana, Ill.

AMERICAN ACADEMY OF ARTS AND SCIENCES

Arthur E. Kennelly, emeritus professor of electrical engineering, Harvard University, Cambridge, Mass.

AMERICAN PHILOSOPHICAL SOCIETY

L. S. Rowe, director, Pan American Union, Washington, D. C.

DEPARTMENT OF STATE

Wilbur J. Carr, vice chairman of the division; Assistant Secretary of State, Washington, D. C.

DEPARTMENT OF THE NAVY

————— ————.

DEPARTMENT OF WAR

Col. Francis H. Lincoln, General Staff, in charge of Military Intelligence, United States Army.

INTERNATIONAL ASTRONOMICAL UNION

Henry Norris Russell, ex officio, chairman, American section, International Astronomical Union; Charles A. Young professor of astronomy and director of the observatory, Princeton University, Princeton, N. J.

INTERNATIONAL GEODETIC AND GEOPHYSICAL UNION

Henry B. Bigelow, director, Woods Hole Oceanographic Institute; professor of zoology and curator of oceanography in the Museum of Comparative Zoology, Harvard University, Cambridge, Mass.

William Bowie, president, International Geodetic and Geophysical Union; 2900 Connecticut Avenue, Washington, D. C.

Lyman J. Briggs, director, National Bureau of Standards, Washington, D. C.

John A. Fleming, general secretary, American Geophysical Union; president, Association of Terrestrial Magnetism and Electricity, International Geodetic and Geophysical Union; acting director, department of terrestrial magnetism, Carnegie Institution of Washington, 5241 Broad Branch Road, Washington, D. C.

N. H. Heck, chairman, American Geophysical Union; chief, division of terrestrial magnetism and seismology, United States Coast and Geodetic Survey, Washington, D. C.

L. K. Sherman, chairman, section of hydrology, American Geophysical Union; president, Randolph-Perkins Co., National Bank Building, Chicago, Ill.

Thomas G. Thompson, chairman, section on oceanography, American Geophysical Union; professor of chemistry and director of the oceanographic laboratories, University of Washington, Seattle, Wash.

INTERNATIONAL UNION OF CHEMISTRY

Edward Bartow, vice president, International Union of Chemistry; professor of chemistry and head of the department of chemistry and chemical engineering, State University of Iowa, Iowa City, Iowa.

INTERNATIONAL UNION OF PURE AND APPLIED PHYSICS

R. A. Millikan, ex officio, chairman, division of physical sciences, National Research Council; director, Norman Bridge Laboratory of Physics, and chairman of the executive council, California Institute of Technology, Pasadena, Calif.

INTERNATIONAL SCIENTIFIC RADIO UNION

Arthur E. Kennelly, ex officio, chairman of the American section, International Scientific Radio Union; emeritus professor of electrical engineering, Harvard University, Cambridge, Mass.

INTERNATIONAL GEOGRAPHICAL UNION

Douglas Johnson, chairman, National Committee of the United States, International Geographical Union; professor of pysiography, Columbia University, New York City.

INTERNATIONAL BUREAU OF WEIGHTS AND MEASURES

Lyman J. Briggs, director, National Bureau of Standards, Washington, D. C.

INTERNATIONAL ELECTROTECHNICAL COMMISSION

Clayton H. Sharp, president, United States National Committee of the International Electrotechnical Commission, 294 Fisher Avenue, White Plains, N. Y.

INTERNATIONAL COMMISSION ON ILLUMINATION

E. C. Crittenden, chief, electrical division, and assistant director, National Bureau of Standards, Washington, D. C.

Members at Large

C. G. Abbot, secretary, Smithsonian Institution, Washington, D. C.

P. G. Agnew, secretary, American Standards Association, 29 West Thirty-ninth Street, New York City.

Arthur H. Compton, Charles H. Swift distinguished service professor of physics, University of Chicago, Chicago, Ill.

John W. Finch, director, United States Bureau of Mines, Washington, D. C.

Herbert E. Gregory, emeritus professor of geology, Yale University; emeritus director, Bishop Museum of Polynesian Ethnology and Natural History, Honolulu, Hawaii.

George E. Hale, honorary director, Mount Wilson Observatory, Carnegie Institution of Washington, Pasadena, Calif.

C. E. McClung, professor of zoology, and director of the zoological laboratory, University of Pennsylvania, Philadelphia, Pa.

Frank Schlesinger, vice chairman of the division; professor of astronomy, and director of the observatory, Yale University, New Haven, Conn.

COMMITTEES

The chairman of the division is, ex officio, a member of all committees of the division.

Committee on Pacific investigations: Chairman, Herbert E. Gregory.

COMMITTEES COOPERATING WITH INTERNATIONAL COMMITTEES OF THE PACIFIC SCIENCE ASSOCIATION

American National Committee on Oceanography of the Pacific: Chairman, Thomas G. Thompson.

American National Committee on Land Classification and Utilization in the Pacific: Chairman, Carl O. Sauer; professor of geography, University of California, Berkeley, Calif.

American committee on Pacific Seismology: Chairman, James B. Macelwane, S. J.; professor of geophysics and dean of the graduate school, St. Louis University, St. Louis, Mo.

REPRESENTATIVE OF THE NATIONAL RESEARCH COUNCIL ON—

Council of the Pacific Science Association: Herbert E. Gregory.

III. DIVISION OF STATES RELATIONS

Chairman, Raymond A. Pearson.
Vice chairman, Albert L. Barrows.

EXECUTIVE COMMITTEE

Chairman, Raymond A. Pearson; vice chairman, Albert L. Barrows; Morris M. Leighton, Jacob G. Lipman, A. R. Mann, Edwin G. Nourse, A. F. Woods, B. Youngblood.

MEMBERS OF THE DIVISION

Raymond A. Pearson, chairman of the division; special assistant to the Administrator, Resettlement Administration, Washington, D. C.

Albert L. Barrows, vice chairman of the division; executive secretary, National Research Council, Washington, D. C.

Representatives of—

DIVISION OF EDUCATIONAL RELATIONS

——— ———.

DIVISION OF PHYSICAL SCIENCES

William Bowie, 2900 Connecticut Avenue, Washington, D. C.

DIVISION OF ENGINEERING AND INDUSTRIAL RESEARCH

A. C. Fieldner, chief engineer, Experiment Stations Division, United States Bureau of Mines, Washington, D. C.

DIVISION OF CHEMISTRY AND CHEMICAL TECHNOLOGY

Frank C. Whitmore, dean, School of Chemistry and Physics, Pennsylvania State College, State College, Pa.

DIVISION OF GEOLOGY AND GEOGRAPHY

Edward B. Mathews, professor of mineralogy and petrography, Johns Hopkins University; State geologist of Maryland; director, State weather service, Baltimore, Md.

DIVISION OF MEDICAL SCIENCES

Carl Voegtlin, Chief, division of pharmacology, National Institute of Health, Washington, D. C.

DIVISION OF BIOLOGY AND AGRICULTURE

I. F. Lewis, dean of the university, and Miller professor of biology and agriculture, University of Virginia, University, Va.

DIVISION OF ANTHROPOLOGY AND PSYCHOLOGY

Carl E. Guthe, director of museums, University of Michigan, Ann Arbor, Mich.

ASSOCIATION OF AMERICAN STATE GEOLOGISTS

Henry B. Kummel, director of conservation and development, and State geologist of New Jersey, Trenton, N. J.

SOCIETY OF AMERICAN FORESTERS

F. W. Besley, State forester of Maryland, Baltimore, Md.

Members at Large and Regional Representatives

R. D. Hetzel, president, Pennsylvania State College, State College, Pa.

Morris M. Leighton, chief, Illinois State Geological Survey, Urbana, Ill.

Jacob G. Lipman, dean, College of Agriculture, professor of agriculture, and director, agricultural experiment station, Rutgers University, New Brunswick, N. J.

A. R. Mann, provost, Cornell University, Ithaca, N. Y.

H. W. Mumford, dean, College of Agriculture, and director, agricultural experiment station, University of Illinois, Urbana, Ill.

Edwin G. Nourse, director, Institute of Economics of the Brookings Institution, 744 Jackson Place, Washington, D. C.

T. S. Palmer, biologist, 1939 Biltmore Street NW., Washington, D. C.

A. F. Woods, principal pathologist, Bureau of Plant Industry, United States Department of Agriculture, Washington, D. C.

B. Youngblood, principal agricultural economist, Office of Experiment Stations, United States Department of Agriculture, Washington, D. C.

IV. DIVISION OF EDUCATIONAL RELATIONS

Chairman, William Charles White.
Secretary, Albert L. Barrows.

EXECUTIVE COMMITTEE

Chairman, William Charles White; Harry W. Chase, C. E. McClung, A. R. Mann, C. R. Mann, John C. Merriam, A. F. Woods.

MEMBERS OF THE DIVISION

William Charles White, chairman of the division; chairman, medical-research committee, National Tuberculosis Association; pathologist in charge of tuberculosis research, National Institute of Health, Washington, D. C.

Ex officio

Chairman of the Medical Fellowship Board, National Research Council, Francis G. Blake, Sterling professor of medicine, Yale University; physician in chief, New Haven Hospital, New Haven, Conn.

Representatives of—

ASSOCIATION OF LAND-GRANT COLLEGES AND UNIVERSITIES

Raymond A. Pearson, special assistant to the Administrator, Resettlement Administration, Washington, D. C.

AMERICAN ASSOCIATION OF UNIVERSITY PROFESSORS

F. K. Richtmyer, dean of the graduate school, and professor of physics, Cornell University, Ithaca, N. Y.

AMERICAN COUNCIL ON EDUCATION

C. R. Mann, director emeritus, American Council on Education, 744 Jackson Place, Washington, D. C.

ASSOCIATION OF AMERICAN COLLEGES

Arthur H. Compton, Charles H. Swift distinguished service professor of physics, University of Chicago, Chicago, Ill.

ASSOCIATION OF AMERICAN UNIVERSITIES

NATIONAL ASSOCIATION OF STATE UNIVERSITIES

Frank L. McVey, president, University of Kentucky, Lexington, Ky.

UNITED STATES OFFICE OF EDUCATION

Frederick J. Kelly, Chief, division of collegiate-professional education, Office of Education, United States Department of the Interior, Washington, D. C.

Members at Large

Harry W. Chase, president, New York University, New York City.
James Bryant Conant, president, Harvard University, Cambridge, Mass.
C. E. McClung, professor of zoology, and director of the zoological laboratory, University of Pennsylvania, Philadelphia, Pa.
A. R. Mann, provost, Cornell University, Ithaca, N. Y.
John C. Merriam, president, Carnegie Institution of Washington, Washington, D. C.
H. W. Tyler, emeritus professor of mathematics, Massachusetts Institute of Technology; consultant in science, Library of Congress, Washington, D. C.
A. F. Woods, principal pathologist, Bureau of Plant Industry, United States Department of Agriculture, Washington, D. C.

Fernandus Payne, liaison member from the division of biology and agriculture; professor of zoology, and dean of the graduate school, Indiana University, Bloomington, Ind.

C. DIVISIONS OF SCIENCE AND TECHNOLOGY

V. DIVISION OF PHYSICAL SCIENCES

Chairman, R. A. Millikan.
Vice chairman, Henry A. Barton.

EXECUTIVE COMMITTEE

Chairman, R. A. Millikan; vice chairman, Henry A. Barton; Harvey Fletcher, Marston Morse, F. K. Richtmyer, Frederick Slocum, G. W. Stewart, L. B. Tuckerman.

MEMBERS OF THE DIVISION

R. A. Millikan, chairman of the division; director of the Norman Bridge laboratory of physics, and chairman of the executive council, California Institute of Technology, Pasadena, Calif.

Representatives of Societies

AMERICAN ASTRONOMICAL SOCIETY

R. G. Aitken, director emeritus, Lick Observatory, University of California, Berkeley, Calif.
Herbert R. Morgan, astronomer, United States Naval Observatory, Washington, D. C.
Frederick Slocum, professor of astronomy, and director of the Van Vleck Observatory, Wesleyan University, Middletown, Conn.

AMERICAN PHYSICAL SOCIETY

Detlev W. Bronk, director, Johnson Foundation, University of Pennsylvania, Philadelphia, Pa.
W. G. Cady, Foss professor of physics, Wesleyan University, Middletown, Conn.
Lee A. du Bridge, professor of physics, University of Rochester, Rochester, N. Y.
Saul Dushman, assistant director of research, General Electric Co., Schenectady, N. Y.
G. W. Stewart, professor of physics, State University of Iowa, Iowa City, Iowa.
John Zeleny, professor of physics, Yale University, New Haven, Conn.

AMERICAN MATHEMATICAL SOCIETY

Thornton C. Fry, research engineer, Bell Telephone Laboratories, Inc., 463 West Street, New York City.

Marston Morse, professor of mathematics, Institute for Advanced Study, Princeton University, Princeton, N. J.

J. H. Van Vleck, associate professor of mathematical physics, Harvard University, Cambridge, Mass.

OPTICAL SOCIETY OF AMERICA

Carl L. Bausch, Bausch & Lomb Optical Co., Rochester, N. Y.

L. B. Tuckerman, assistant chief, division of mechanics and sound, National Bureau of Standards, Washington, D. C.

David L. Webster, professor of physics, Stanford University, Stanford University, Calif.

MATHEMATICAL ASSOCIATION OF AMERICA

W. R. Longley, Richard M. Colgate professor of mathematics, Yale University, New Haven, Conn.

ACOUSTICAL SOCIETY OF AMERICA

Harvey Fletcher, acoustical research director, Bell Telephone Laboratories, Inc., 463 West Street, New York City.

AMERICAN INSTITUTE OF PHYSICS

Henry A. Barton, vice chairman of the division; director, American Institute of Physics, 175 Fifth Avenue, New York City.

Members at Large

P. W. Bridgman, Hollis professor of mathematics and natural philosophy, Harvard University, Cambridge, Mass.

F. K. Richtmyer, dean of the graduate school, and professor of physics, Cornell University, Ithaca, N. Y.

Warren Weaver, director for the natural sciences, Rockefeller Foundation, 49 West Forty-ninth Street, New York City.

COMMITTEES

The chairman of the division is, ex officio, a member of all committees of the division.

EXECUTIVE COMMITTEES OF AMERICAN SECTIONS OF INTERNATIONAL UNIONS

International Astronomical Union: Chairman, Henry Norris Russell, Charles A. Young professor of astronomy, and director of the observatory, Princeton University, Princeton, N. J.

International Union of Pure and Applied Physics: The division of physical sciences acts as the American section of the International Union of Pure and Applied Physics.

International Scientific Radio Union: Chairman, Arthur E. Kennelly.

ADMINISTRATIVE COMMITTEE

Committee on revolving fund for the publication of mathematical books: Chairman, Solomon Lefschetz, professor of mathematics, Princeton University, Princeton, N. J.

RESEARCH COMMITTEES

Committee on bibliography of mathematical tables and aids to computation: Chairman, Albert A. Bennett, professor of mathematics, Brown University, Providence, R. I.

Committee on bibliography on orthogonal polynomials: Chairman, J. A. Shohat, assistant professor of mathematics, University of Pennsylvania, Philadelphia, Pa.

Committee on line spectra of the elements: Chairman, Henry Norris Russell.

Committee on methods of measurement of radiation: Chairman, W. E. Forsythe, physicist, lamp development laboratory, National Lamp Works, Nela Park, Cleveland, Ohio.

Committee on physical constants: Chairman, Raymond T. Birge, professor of physics, University of California, Berkeley, Calif.

Committee on physics of the earth: Chairman, R. A. Millikan, ex officio.

Subsidiary committee on hydrology: Chairman, O. E. Meinzer, geologist in charge of the division of ground water, United States Geological Survey, Washington, D. C.

Subsidiary committee on terrestrial magnetism and electricity: Chairman, John A. Fleming, acting director, department of terrestrial magnetism, Carnegie Institution of Washington, 5241 Broad Branch Road, Washington, D. C.

Subsidiary committee on internal constitution of the earth: Chairman, L. H. Adams, physical chemist, geophysical laboratory, Carnegie Institution of Washington, 2801 Upton Street, Washington, D. C.

Editorial board of the committee: Chairman, Fred. E. Wright, petrologist, geophysical laboratory, Carnegie Institution of Washington, 2801 Upton Street, Washington, D. C.

Board of directors of the Washington Biophysical Institute: Chairman, Lyman J. Briggs, director, National Bureau of Standards, Washington, D. C.

REPRESENTATIVE OF THE DIVISION ON—

Committee on electric and magnetic magnitudes of the American Standards Association: Leigh Page, professor of theoretical physics, Yale University, New Haven, Conn.

VI. DIVISION OF ENGINEERING AND INDUSTRIAL RESEARCH

[Engineering Societies Bldg., 29 West 39th St., New York City]

Chairman, Vannevar Bush.
Vice chairman, Howard A. Poillon.
Director, Maurice Holland.

EXECUTIVE COMMITTEE

Chairman, Vannevar Bush; vice chairman, Howard A. Poillon; Carl Breer, F. O. Clements, Galen H. Clevenger, Edwin S. Fickes, R. C. H. Heck, Frank B. Jewett, Fred Lavis, F. T. Llewellyn.

MEMBERS OF THE DIVISION

Representatives of Societies

AMERICAN SOCIETY OF CIVIL ENGINEERS

George T. Seabury, ex officio, secretary, American Society of Civil Engineers, 29 West Thirty-ninth Street, New York City.

Inge M. Lyse, research associate professor of engineering materials, Lehigh University, Bethlehem, Pa.

Fred Lavis, consulting engineer, 30 Broad Street, New York City.

George L. Lucas, engineer of inspection, the Port of New York Authority, 111 Eighth Avenue, New York City.

AMERICAN INSTITUTE OF MINING AND METALLURGICAL ENGINEERS

A. B. Parsons, ex officio, secretary, American Institute of Mining and Metallurgical Engineers, 29 West Thirty-ninth Street, New York City.

Galen H. Clevenger, consulting metallurgist, 67 Sheffield Road, Newtonville, Mass.

Edwin S. Fickes, senior vice president, Aluminum Co. of America, 801 Gulf Building, Pittsburgh, Pa.

H. J. Rose, senior industrial fellow, Mellon Institute of Industrial Research, University of Pittsburgh, Pittsburg, Pa.

AMERICAN SOCIETY OF MECHANICAL ENGINEERS

C. E. Davies, ex officio, secretary, American Society of Mechanical Engineers, 29 West Thirty-ninth Street, New York City.
R. C. H. Heck, professor of mechanical engineering, Rutgers University, New Brunswick, N. J.
Bert Houghton, 1274 East Twenty-third Street, Brooklyn, N. Y.
W. Trinks, professor of mechanical engineering, Carnegie Institute of Technology, Pittsburgh, Pa.

AMERICAN INSTITUTE OF ELECTRICAL ENGINEERS

H. H. Henline, ex officio, secretary, American Institute of Electrical Engineers, 29 West Thirty-ninth Street, New York City.
Vannevar Bush, chairman of the division; vice president of the institute, and dean of the graduate school, Massachusetts Institute of Technology, Cambridge, Mass.
Everett S. Lee, engineer, general engineering laboratory, General Electric Co., Schenectady, N. Y.
John B. Whitehead, dean of the engineering faculty and professor of electrical engineering, Johns Hopkins University, Baltimore, Md.

AMERICAN SOCIETY OF REFRIGERATING ENGINEERS

W. J. King, research engineer, General Electric Co., Schenectady, N. Y.

AMERICAN SOCIETY FOR TESTING MATERIALS

F. O. Clements, technical director, research laboratories, General Motors Corporation, Detroit, Mich.
H. W. Gillett, director, Battelle Memorial Institute, Columbus, Ohio.

AMERICAN SOCIETY FOR METALS

R. S. Archer, chief metallurgist, Republic Steel Corporation, One Hundred and Eighteenth Street and Calumet River, Chicago, Ill.

AMERICAN SOCIETY OF HEATING AND VENTILATING ENGINEERS

F. E. Giesecke, director, engineering experiment station, Agricultural and Mechanical College of Texas, College Station, Tex.

ILLUMINATING ENGINEERING SOCIETY

C. L. Powell, supervising engineer, incandescent lamp department, General Electric Co., 570 Lexington Avenue, New York City.

WESTERN SOCIETY OF ENGINEERS

William B. Jackson, electrical engineer, Broadview, Cheshire, Mass.

SOCIETY OF AUTOMOTIVE ENGINEERS

Carl Breer, executive engineer, Chrysler Corporation, 341 Massachusetts Avenue, Detroit, Mich.
E. P. Warner, consulting aeronautical engineer, Harvard Club, 27 West Forty-fourth Street, New York City.

AMERICAN WELDING SOCIETY

F. T. Llewellyn, research engineer, United States Steel Corporation, 71 Broadway, New York City.

Members at large

Jerome C. Hunsaker, professor in charge of the department of mechanical engineering; in charge of the course in aeronautical engineering, Massachusetts Institute of Technology, Cambridge, Mass.

Frank B. Jewett, vice president, American Telephone & Telegraph Co.; president, Bell Telephone Laboratories, Inc., 195 Broadway, New York City.

Howard A. Poillon, vice chairman of the division; president, Research Corporation, 405 Lexington Avenue, New York City.

COMMITTEES

The chairman of the division is, ex officio, a member of all committees and boards of the division.

Committee on electrical insulation: Chairman, John B. Whitehead.

Subcommittee on program of research: Chairman, John B. Whitehead.

Subcommittee on chemistry: Chairman, F. M. Clark, General Electric Co., Pittsfield, Mass.

Subcommittee on physics: Chairman, Wheeler P. Davey, research professor of physics and chemistry, Pennsylvania State College, State College, Pa.

Committee on relationships between universities and industry: Chairman, J. W. Barker, dean, school of engineering, Columbia University, New York City.

Committee for research on hydraulic friction: Chairman, Theodor von Karman, professor of aeronautics, and director, Daniel Guggenheim Laboratory, California Institute of Technology, Pasadena, Calif.

Committee on heat transmission—executive committee: Chairman, Willis H. Carrier, president, Carrier Engineering Corporation, Newark, N. J.

Subcommittee on heat transfer by radiation: Chairman, J. D. Keller, Carnegie Institute of Technology, Schenley Park, Pittsburgh, Pa.

Subcommittee on heat transfer by convection: Chairman, W. H. McAdams, professor of chemical engineering, Massachusetts Institute of Technology, Cambridge, Mass.

Subcommittee on thermal insulation: Chairman, T. Smith Taylor, professor of physics, Washington and Jefferson College, Washington, Pa.

Subcommittee on nomenclature and definitions: Chairman, E. F. Mueller, physicist, National Bureau of Standards, Washington, D. C.

REPRESENTATIVES OF THE DIVISION ON—

Committee A-8 on magnetic analysis of the American Society for Testing Materials: R. L. Sanford, physicist, National Bureau of Standards, Washington, D. C.

Committee on ferrous metals, advisory to the National Bureau of Standards: Enrique Touceda, consulting engineer, Broadway and Thacher Street, Albany, N. Y.

Sectional committee on safety code for brakes and brake testing of the National Bureau of Standards: S. S. Steinberg, professor of civil engineering, University of Maryland, College Park, Md.

HIGHWAY RESEARCH BOARD

Chairman, H. C. Dickinson, chief, heat and power division, National Bureau of Standards, Washington, D. C.

COMMITTEES

Department of highway finance and administration: Chairman, Thomas H. MacDonald, Chief, United States Bureau of Public Roads, Washington, D. C.

Department of highway transportation economics: Chairman, R. L. Morrison, professor of highway engineering and highway transport, University of Michigan, Ann Arbor, Mich.

Project committee on tractive resistance and allied problems: Chairman, W. E. Lay, professor of mechanical engineering, University of Michigan, Ann Arbor, Mich.

Project committee on cost of motor-vehicle operation: Chairman, E. W. James, Chief, Division of Highway Transport, United States Bureau of Public Roads, Washington, D. C.

Project committee on economic life of pavements: Chairman, Anson Marston, senior dean of engineering, Iowa State College, Ames, Iowa.

Project committee on economic highway planning: Chairman, R. A. Moyer, associate professor of civil engineering, Iowa State College, Ames, Iowa.

Department of highway design: Chairman, C. N. Conner, United States Bureau of Public Roads, Washington, D. C.

Project committee on roadside development (in cooperation with the American Association of State Highway Officials): Chairman, H. J. Neale, landscape engineer, Department of Highways, Richmond, Va.

Project committee on use of high elastic limit steel for concrete reinforcement: Chairman, Herbert J. Gilkey, head, theoretical and applied mechanics department, Iowa State College, Ames, Iowa.

Project committee on pavement joints: Chairman, J. W. Kushing, research and testing engineer, Michigan Highway Department, Lansing, Mich.

Project committee on antiskid properties of road surfaces: Chairman, George E. Martin, consulting engineer, general tarvia department, the Barrett Co., New York City.

Project committee on highway guard rails: Chairman, F. V. Reagel, engineer of materials, Missouri Highway Department, Jefferson City, Mo.

Project committee on design of flexible type road surfaces: Chairman, A. C. Benkelman, United States Bureau of Public Roads, Washington, D. C.

Project committee on sight distances: Chairman not yet appointed.

Project committee on relation of curvature to speed: Chairman, C. N. Conner, United States Bureau of Public Roads, Washington, D. C.

Department of materials and construction: Chairman, C. H. Scholer, construction materials engineer, engineering experiment station, Manhattan, Kans.

Project committee on durability of concrete as affected by the cement: Chairman, H. S. Mattimore, engineer of tests and materials investigations, Department of Highways, Harrisburg, Pa.

Project committee on volume changes in concrete; Chairman, C. H. Scholer.

Project committee on methods of handling and placing concrete in highway construction: Chairman, F. H. Jackson, senior engineer of tests, United States Bureau of Public Roads, Washington, D. C.

Project committee on correlation of research in mineral aggregates: Chairman, R. R. Litehiser, chief engineer, bureau of tests, State highway testing laboratory, Ohio State University, Columbus, Ohio.

Project committee on characteristics of asphalt: Chairman, T. E. Kelly, chief, Division of Tests, United States Bureau of Public Roads, Washington, D. C.

Project committee on curing of concrete pavement slabs: Chairman, F. C. Lang, engineer of tests and inspection, Minnesota Department of Highways, 1246 University Avenue, St. Paul, Minn.

Project committee on development of highway construction equipment (joint committee with the American Road Builders' Association): Chairman, H. F. Clemmer, engineer of materials and tests, Division of Materials, District of Columbia, Washington, D. C.

Project committee on fillers and cushion courses for brick and block pavements: Chairman, J. S. Crandell, professor of highway engineering, University of Illinois, Urbana, Ill.

Department of maintenance: Chairman, C. W. McClain, engineer of maintenance, Indiana State Highway Commission, Indianapolis, Ind.

Project committee on maintenance costs: Chairman, H. K. Bishop, chief, Division of Construction, United States Bureau of Public Roads, Washington, D. C.

Project committee on maintenance of cracks and expansion joints in concrete pavements: Chairman, W. H. Root, maintenance engineer, Iowa State Highway Commission, Ames, Iowa.

Project committee on distortion of pavements: Chairman, C. W. McClain.

Department of traffic: Chairman, C. J. Tilden, professor of engineering mechanics, Yale University, New Haven, Conn.

Project committee on traffic capacity: Chairman, A. N. Johnson, dean, college of engineering, University of Maryland, College Park, Md.

Project committee on traffic-survey methods and forms: Chairman, J. G. McKay, director, Cleveland Highway Research Bureau, Cleveland, Ohio.

Project committee on vehicle and highway mechanics as related to traffic: Chairman, H. C. Dickinson, chief, Heat and Power Division, National Bureau of Standards, Washington, D. C.

Project committee on traffic regulations in municipalities: Chairman, W. S. Canning, engineering director, Keystone Automobile Club, Philadelphia, Pa.

Department of soils investigations: Chairman, C. A. Hogentogler, senior highway engineer, United States Bureau of Public Roads, Washington, D. C.

Project committee on standardization of nomenclature and definitions: Chairman, H. F. Clemmer.

Project committee on what information is desired by a practicing engineer: Chairman, A. L. Gemeny, senior structural engineer, United States Bureau of Public Roads, Washington, D. C.

Project committee on methods of exploring, surveying, and sampling soils for highway purposes: Chairman, Frederick J. Converse, assistant professor of civil engineering, California Institute of Technology, Pasadena, Calif.

Project committee on methods of determining in place the physical characteristics of foundation and subgrade soils: Chairman, W. S. Housel, assistant professor of civil engineering, University of Michigan, Ann Arbor, Mich.

Project committee on methods of testing disturbed soils and the application of the results in practice: Chairman, H. S. Mattimore, engineer of tests and materials investigation, Department of Highways, Harrisburg, Pa.

Project committee on laboratory determinations of the properties of foundation soils in their natural state, and the application of test data in practice: Chairman, Arthur Casagrande, assistant professor of civil engineering, Harvard University, Cambridge, Mass.

Project committee on methods of compaction for control and construction and their effect upon the properties of soils for highway purposes: Chairman, R. R. Philippe, United States Engineer Office, Zanesville, Ohio.

Project committee on practical design of drainage for highways and airports exclusive of bridges and culverts: Chairman, W. J. Schlick, drainage engineer, research staff, Iowa State College, Ames, Iowa.

Project committee on the effect of disturbing the natural structure of a soil on its supporting power: Chairman, H. F. Clemmer.

Project committee on testing equipment and apparatus: Chairman, C. A. Hogentogler.

Project committee on stress distribution in earth masses ((a) load due to own weight, (b) load through pavements, (c) external loads on foundations); Chairman, D. P. Krynine, research associate in soil mechanics, Yale University, New Haven, Conn.

Project committee on physico-chemical testing of soils and the application of the results in practice: Chairman, Hans Winterkorn, research assistant professor of soils, University of Missouri, Columbia, Mo.

Project committee on stabilized roads: Chairman, C. A. Hogentogler.

VII. DIVISION OF CHEMISTRY AND CHEMICAL TECHNOLOGY

Chairman, Herbert R. Moody.

EXECUTIVE COMMITTEE

Chairman, Herbert R. Moody; E. K. Bolton, J. C. Hostetter, Harold C. Urey, Hobart H. Willard.

MEMBERS OF THE DIVISION

Herbert R. Moody, chairman of the division; professor of chemistry and director of the chemical laboratories, College of the City of New York, New York City.

Representatives of Societies

AMERICAN CHEMICAL SOCIETY

E. K. Bolton, chemical director, E. I. du Pont de Nemours & Co., Wilmington, Del.

E. J. Crane, editor, Chemical Abstracts, Ohio State University, Columbus, Ohio.

Gustavus J. Esselen, president and director, Gustavus Esselen, Inc., 857 Boylston Street, Boston, Mass.

William Lloyd Evans, professor of chemistry, Ohio State University, Columbus, Ohio.

Harold C. Urey, professor of chemistry, Columbia University, New York City.

F. W. Willard, president, Nassau Smelting & Refining Co., 50 Church Street, New York City.

ELECTROCHEMICAL SOCIETY

Hiram S. Lukens, professor of chemistry and director of the Harrison Laboratory, University of Pennsylvania, Philadelphia, Pa.

AMERICAN INSTITUTE OF CHEMICAL ENGINEERS

Ellery L. Wilson, vice president, director, and general superintendent, Rumford Chemical Works, Providence, R. I.

AMERICAN CERAMIC SOCIETY

J. C. Hostetter, vice president, Hartford-Empire Co., Hartford, Conn.

Ex Officio

Edward Bartow, vice president, International Union of Chemistry; professor of chemistry, and head of the department of chemistry and chemical engineering, State University of Iowa, Iowa City, Iowa.

Members at Large

Charles A. Kraus, research professor of chemistry, Brown University, Providence, R. I.

Austin M. Patterson, vice president and professor of chemistry, Antioch College, Yellow Springs, Ohio.

Hobart H. Willard, professor of analytical chemistry, University of Michigan, Ann Arbor, Mich.

Ross A. Gortner, liaison member from the division of biology and agriculture; professor of agricultural biochemistry, University of Minnesota, University Farm, St. Paul, Minn.

COMMITTEES

The chairman of the division is, ex officio, a member of all committees of the division.

Advisory committee to the National Bureau of Standards on research on the reproduction of records: Chairman, H. M. Lydenberg, director, New York Public Library, New York City.

Committee on the application of mathematics to chemistry: Chairman, Harold C. Urey.

Committee on colloid science: Chairman, Harry B. Weiser, professor of chemistry and dean, Rice Institute, Houston, Tex.

Committee on construction and equipment of chemical laboratories: Chairman, O. R. Hoover, E. B. Nye professor of chemistry, Wesleyan University, Middletown, Conn.

Committee on low-temperature scales: Chairman, F. 'G. Brickwedde, Chief, Cryogenic Laboratory, National Bureau of Standards, Washington, D. C.

Committee on photochemistry: Chairman, Hugh S. Taylor, David B. Jones professor of chemistry, Princeton University, Princeton, N. J.

Committee on the preparation and publication of a list of ring systems used in organic chemistry (joint committee with the American Chemical Society): Chairman, Austin M. Patterson.

International Union of Chemistry: The division of chemistry and chemical technology acts as the American section of the International Union of Chemistry.

VIII. DIVISION OF GEOLOGY AND GEOGRAPHY

Chairman, Edson S. Bastin.
Vice chairman, Robert S. Platt.

EXECUTIVE COMMITTEE

Chairman, Edson S. Bastin; vice chairman, Robert S. Platt; Donald C. Barton, Florence Bascom, F. H. Lahee, Frank E. Williams.

MEMBERS OF THE DIVISION

Representatives of Societies

GEOLOGICAL SOCIETY OF AMERICA

Donald C. Barton, geologist and geophysicist, Humble Oil & Refining Co., Houston, Tex.
A. F. Buddington, professor of geology, Princeton University, Princeton, N. J.

MINERALOGICAL SOCIETY OF AMERICA

J. F. Schairer, physical chemist, research staff, geophysical laboratory, Carnegie Institution of Washington, 2801 Upton Street, Washington, D. C.

PALEONTOLOGICAL SOCIETY

Charles Butts, geologist, 1808 Kenyon Street NW., Washington, D. C.

ASSOCIATION OF AMERICAN GEOGRAPHERS

Robert S. Platt, associate professor of geography, University of Chicago, Chicago, Ill.
Frank E. Williams, professor of geography, Wharton School of Commerce and Finance, University of Pennsylvania, Philadelphia, Pa.

AMERICAN GEOGRAPHICAL SOCIETY

John K. Wright, librarian, American Geographical Society, Broadway at One Hundred and Fifty-sixth Street, New York City.

SOCIETY OF ECONOMIC GEOLOGISTS

Thomas B. Nolan, associate geologist, United States Geological Survey, Washington, D. C.

AMERICAN CERAMIC SOCIETY

Ross C. Purdy, consulting ceramic engineer, 2525 North High Street, Columbus, Ohio.

AMERICAN ASSOCIATION OF PETROLEUM GEOLOGISTS

F. H. Lahee, chief geologist, Sun Oil Co., Dallas, Tex.

Members at Large

Florence Bascom, geologist, care of United States Geological Survey, Washington, D. C.
Edson S. Bastin, chairman of the division; professor of economic geology, University of Chicago, Chicago, Ill.
L. F. Thomas, associate professor of geography, Washington University, St. Louis, Mo.

COMMITTEES

The chairman of the division is, ex officio, a member of all committees of the division.

Advisory committee to the division: Chairman, Edson S. Bastin.

National committee of the United States, International Geographical Union: Chairman, Douglas Johnson, professor of physiography, Columbia University, New York City.

Committee on fellowships: Chairman, Arthur Keith, geologist, 2210 Twentieth Street NW., Washington, D. C.

TECHNICAL COMMITTEES

Committee on accessory minerals of crystalline rocks: Chairman, A. N. Winchell, professor of geology, University of Wisconsin, Madison, Wis.

Committee on the conservation of scientific results of drilling: Chairman, Allen C. Tester, assistant State geologist; assistant professor of geology, State University of Iowa, Iowa City, Iowa.

Committee on cooperation with the Bureau of the Census: Chairman, John K. Wright.

Committee on geographic classification of surface configuration: Chairman, V. C. Finch, professor of geography, University of Wisconsin, Madison, Wis.

Committee on land classification: Chairman, K. C. McMurry, professor of geography, University of Michigan, Ann Arbor, Mich.

Committee on the measurement of geological time: Chairman, Alfred C. Lane, emeritus professor of geology and mineralogy, Tufts College; 22 Arlington Street, Cambridge, Mass.

Committee on micropaleontology: Chairman, Joseph A. Cushman, director, Cushman Laboratory for Foraminiferal Research, Sharon, Mass.

Committee on paleobotany: Chairman, Roland W. Brown, associate geologist, United States Geological Survey, Washington, D. C.

Committee on paleoecology: Chairman, W. H. Twenhofel, professor of geology, University of Wisconsin, Madison, Wis.

Committee on the preparation of a handbook of physical constants of geological materials: Chairman, Francis Birch, research associate in geophysics, Harvard University, Cambridge, Mass.

Committee on processes of ore deposition: Chairman, W. H. Newhouse, associate professor of economic geology, Massachusetts Institute of Technology, Cambridge, Mass.

Committee on research in areas of international concern: Chairman, Derwent Whittlesey, associate professor of geography, Harvard University, Cambridge, Mass.

Committee on sedimentation: Chairman, Parker D. Trask, associate geologist, United States Geological Survey, Washington, D. C.

Committee on stratigraphy: Chairman, Carl O. Dunbar, professor of paleontology and stratigraphy, and curator of invertebrate paleontology, Yale University, New Haven, Conn.

Committee on structural petrology: Chairman, T. S. Lovering, associate professor of geology, University of Michigan, Ann Arbor, Mich.

Committee on tectonics: Chairman, Chester R. Longwell, Henry Barnard David professor of geology, Yale University, New Haven, Conn.

Correspondent on shoreline investigations in California: U. S. Grant, 4th, associate professor of geology, University of California at Los Angeles, Los Angeles, Calif.

Interdivisional committee on borderlands in science—physics, chemistry, and geology: Chairman, T. S. Lovering.

REPRESENTATIVES OF THE DIVISION ON—

Advisory council of the Board of Surveys and Maps of the Federal Government: George W. Stose.

National council of the American Association of Water Well Drillers: O. E. Meinzer and, ex officio, Allen C. Tester.

Committee on the classification of coal, of the American Society for Testing Materials: Taisia Stadnichenko.

IX. DIVISION OF MEDICAL SCIENCES

Chairman, Esmond R. Long.
Vice chairman, Howard T. Karsner.

EXECUTIVE COMMITTEE

Chairman, Esmond R. Long; vice chairman, Howard T. Karsner; Philip Bard, Earl B. McKinley, L. R. Thompson, D. Wright Wilson.

MEMBERS OF THE DIVISION

Esmond R. Long, chairman of the division; professor of pathology, School of Medicine, and director, Henry Phipps Institute, University of Pennsylvania, Philadelphia, Pa.

Representatives of Societies

AMERICAN ACADEMY OF TROPICAL MEDICINE

E. E. Tyzzer, George Fabyan professor of comparative pathology, Harvard Medical School, Boston, Mass.

AMERICAN ASSOCIATION OF ANATOMISTS

Lewis H. Weed, professor of anatomy, and director of the School of Medicine, Johns Hopkins University, Baltimore, Md.

AMERICAN ASSOCIATION OF PATHOLOGISTS AND BACTERIOLOGISTS

Earl B. McKinley, dean, George Washington University School of Medicine, Washington, D. C.

AMERICAN DENTAL ASSOCIATION

P. C. Lowery, chairman, research committee, American Dental Association; practicing dentist, Lowery Building, Detroit, Mich.

AMERICAN MEDICAL ASSOCIATION

L. R. Thompson, director, National Institute of Health, Washington, D. C.

AMERICAN NEUROLOGICAL ASSOCIATION

Walter Freeman, 1726 Eye Street NW., Washington, D. C.

AMERICAN PHYSIOLOGICAL SOCIETY

Philip Bard, professor of physiology, School of Medicine, Johns Hopkins University, Baltimore, Md.

AMERICAN PSYCHIATRIC ASSOCIATION

Clifford B. Farr, director of laboratories, department of mental and nervous diseases, Pennsylvania Hospital, Philadelphia, Pa.

AMERICAN ROENTGEN RAY SOCIETY

Henry J. Walton, professor of roentgenology, University of Maryland School of Medicine, Baltimore, Md.

AMERICAN SOCIETY OF BIOLOGICAL CHEMISTS

D. Wright Wilson, Benjamin Rush professor of physiological chemistry, University of Pennsylvania, Philadelphia, Pa.

AMERICAN SOCIETY FOR CLINICAL INVESTIGATION

John P. Peters, John Slade Ely professor of medicine, Yale University, New Haven, Conn.

AMERICAN SOCIETY FOR EXPERIMENTAL PATHOLOGY

Carl V. Weller, professor of pathology, and director of the pathological laboratories, University of Michigan, Ann Arbor, Mich.

AMERICAN SOCIETY FOR PHARMACOLOGY AND EXPERIMENTAL THERAPEUTICS

William DeB. MacNider, Kenan research professor of pharmacology, University of North Carolina, Chapel Hill, N. C.

AMERICAN SURGICAL ASSOCIATION

Harvey B. Stone, associate professor of surgery, School of Medicine, Johns Hopkins University, Baltimore, Md.

AMERICAN VETERINARY MEDICAL ASSOCIATION

Karl F. Meyer, professor of bacteriology, and director of the Hooper Foundation for Medical Research, University of California, San Francisco, Calif.   .

ASSOCIATION OF AMERICAN PHYSICIANS

O. H. Perry Pepper, professor of clinical medicine, School of Medicine, University of Pennsylvania, Philadelphia, Pa.

SOCIETY OF AMERICAN BACTERIOLOGISTS.

David John Davis, professor of pathology and bacteriology, and dean of the College of Medicine, University of Illinois, Chicago, Ill.

Representative of the Division of Federal Relations

Lt. Col. E. R. Gentry, Medical Corps, United States Army, Washington, D. C.

Members at Large

George W. Corner, professor of anatomy, School of Medicine, University of Rochester, Rochester, N. Y.

Howard T. Karsner, vice chairman of the division; professor of pathology and director, Institute of Pathology, Western Reserve University, Cleveland, Ohio.

Alfred N. Richards, professor of pharmacology, University of Pennsylvania, Philadelphia, Pa.

COMMITTEES

The chairman of the division is, ex officio, a member of all committees of the division.

Advisory committee to the division: Stanhope Bayne-Jones, Francis G. Blake, Henry A. Christian, Edmund V. Cowdry, Frederick P. Gay, Ludvig Hektoen, William H. Howell, Raymond Hussey, C. M. Jackson, Howard T. Karsner, George W. McCoy, William Charles White.

Advisory committee on research in endocrinology: Chairman, W. B. Cannon, George Higginson professor of physiology, Harvard Medical School, Boston, Mass.

Committee on American registry of pathology: Chairman, Howard T. Karsner.

Committee on the study of brucella infections: Chairman, Karl F. Meyer.

Committee on drug addiction: Chairman, William Charles White, chairman, medical research committee, National Tuberculosis Association; pathologist in charge of tuberculosis research, National Institute of Health, Washington, D. C.

Committee on medical problems of animal parasitology: Chairman, Henry B. Ward, permanent secretary, American Association for the Advancement of Science; emeritus professor of zoology, University of Illinois, Urbana, Ill.

Committee for research in problems of sex: Chairman, Robert M. Yerkes, professor of psychobiology, Yale University, New Haven, Conn.

Committee on syphilis: Chairman, Esmond R. Long. .

X. DIVISION OF BIOLOGY AND AGRICULTURE

Chairman, R. E. Coker.
Vice chairman, H. P. Barss.

EXECUTIVE COMMITTEE

Chairman, R. E. Coker; vice chairman, H. P. Barss; Ivey F. Lewis, E. C. Stakman, A. H. Wright.

MEMBERS OF THE DIVISION

R. E. Coker, chairman of the division; professor of zoology, and chairman of the division of natural sciences, University of North Carolina, Chapel Hill, N. C.

Representatives of Societies

GROUP I. BOTANICAL SOCIETY OF AMERICA

Elmer D. Merrill, administrator of botanical collections, Gray Herbarium, Harvard University, Cambridge, Mass.

GROUP II. AMERICAN SOCIETY OF ZOOLOGISTS

L. V. Hellbrunn, associate professor of zoology, University of Pennsylvania, Philadelphia, Pa.

GROUP III. AMERICAN SOCIETY OF ANIMAL PRODUCTION, AMERICAN DAIRY SCIENCE ASSOCIATION, POULTRY SCIENCE ASSOCIATION

Morley A. Jull, head of the poultry department, Extension Service, University of Maryland, College Park, Md.

GROUP IV. AMERICAN SOCIETY OF AGRONOMY, SOCIETY OF AMERICAN FORESTERS, AMERICAN SOCIETY FOR HORTICULTURAL SCIENCE

E. C. Auchter, principal horticulturist, United States Bureau of Plant Industry, Washington, D. C.

GROUP V. AMERICAN PHYTOPATHOLOGICAL SOCIETY, MYCOLOGICAL SOCIETY OF AMERICA, SOCIETY OF AMERICAN BACTERIOLOGISTS

H. P. Barss, vice chairman of the division; principal botanist, and associate in experiment station administration, Office of Experiment Stations, United States Department of Agriculture, Washington, D. C.

GROUP VI. AMERICAN GENETIC ASSOCIATION, ECOLOGICAL SOCIETY OF AMERICA, GENETICS SOCIETY OF AMERICA, LIMNOLOGICAL SOCIETY OF AMERICA

Henry Allen Gleason, head curator, New York Botanical Garden, Bronx Park, New York City.

GROUP VII. AMERICAN PHYSIOLOGICAL SOCIETY, PHYSIOLOGICAL SECTION OF THE BOTANICAL SOCIETY OF AMERCA, AMERICAN SOCIETY OF BIOLOGICAL CHEMISTS, AMERICAN SOCIETY OF PLANT PHYSIOLOGISTS

McKeen Cattell, associate professor of pharmacology, Cornell University Medical College, New York City.

GROUP VIII. AMERICAN ASSOCIATION OF ECONOMIC ENTOMOLOGISTS, ENTOMOLOGICAL SOCIETY OF AMERICA, AMERICAN SOCIETY OF MAMMALOGISTS

Remington Kellogg, assistant curator of the division of mammals, United States National Museum, Washington, D. C.

Members at Large

I. F. Lewis, dean of the university, and Miller professor of biology and agri-culture, University of Virginia, University, Va.

E. C. Stakman, professor of plant pathology, University of Minnesota, Minne-apolis, Minn.

A. H. Wright, professor of zoology, Cornell University, Ithaca, N. Y.

COMMITTEES

The chairman of the division is, ex officio, a member of all committees of the division.

Advisory committee to the division: C. E. Allen, L. J. Cole, William Crocker, W. C. Curtis, B. M. Duggar, R. A. Harper, Duncan S. Johnson, L. R. Jones, Vernon Kellogg, I. F. Lewis, Frank R. Lillie, C. E. McClung, Maynard M. Met-calf, Fernandus Payne, Lorande L. Woodruff, A. F. Woods.

Committee on agronomy: Chairman, Richard Bradfield, professor of soils, Ohio State University, Columbus, Ohio.

Committee on animal nutrition: Chairman, Paul E. Howe, Chief, Animal Nutrition Division, United States Bureau of Animal Industry, Washington, D. C.

Committee on the ecology of grasslands of North America: Chairman, F. E. Shelford, professor of zoology, University of Illinois, Urbana, Ill.

Committee on forestry: Chairman, Raphael Zon, director, Lake States Forest Experiment Station, St. Paul, Minn.

Committee on human heredity: Chairman, Laurence H. Snyder, associate professor of zoology and entomology, Ohio State University, Columbus, Ohio.

Committee on National Live Stock and Meat Board fellowships: Chairman, Paul E. Howe.

Committee on pharmacognosy and pharmaceutical botany: chairman, Heber W. Youngken, professor of pharmacognosy, Massachusetts College of Pharmacy, Boston, Mass.

Committee on the preservation of natural conditions: Chairman, H. E. Anthony, curator of mammalogy, American Museum of Natural History, Seventy-seventh Street and Central Park West, New York City.

Committee on research publications: Chairman, H. A. Gleason, head curator, New York Botanical Garden, Bronx Park, New York City.

Committee on radiation: Chairman, B. M. Duggar, professor of applied and physiological botany, University of Wisconsin, Madison, Wis.

REPRESENTATIVES OF THE DIVISION ON—

Board of trustees of Biological Abstracts: A. F. Blakeslee, C. E. McClung, J. R. Schramm, A. F. Woods.

Board of governors of the Crop Protection Institute: Remington Kellogg.

XI. DIVISION OF ANTHROPOLOGY AND PSYCHOLOGY

Chairman, Walter S. Hunter.
Vice chairman, J. R. Swanton.

EXECUTIVE COMMITTEE

Chairman, Walter S. Hunter; vice chairman, J. R. Swanton; Carl E. Guthe, Walter R. Miles, Edward Sapir.

MEMBERS OF THE DIVISION

Walter S. Hunter, chairman of the division; professor of psychology and director of the psychological laboratory, Brown University, Providence, R. I.

Representatives of Societies

AMERICAN ANTHROPOLOGICAL ASSOCIATION

Ruth Benedict, assistant professor of anthropology, Columbia University, New York City.

John M. Cooper, professor of anthropology, Catholic University of America, Washington, D. C.

Carl E. Guthe, director of museums, University of Michigan, Ann Arbor, Mich.

E. A. Hooton, professor of anthropolgy and curator of somatology in the Peabody Museum, Harvard University, Cambridge, Mass.

Robert Redfield, associate professor of anthropology, University of Chicago, Chicago, Ill.

Frank H. H. Roberts, Jr., archeologist, Bureau of American Ethnology, Smithsonian Institution, Washington, D. C.

H. L. Shapiro, associate curator of physical anthropolgy, American Museum of Natural History, New York City.

Herbert J. Spinden, Brooklyn Institute of Arts and Sciences, Brooklyn, N. Y.

William Duncan Strong, senior ethnologist, Bureau of American Ethnology, Smithsonian Institution, Washington, D. C.

AMERICAN PSYCHOLOGICAL ASSOCIATION

Edwin G. Boring, professor of psychology and director of the psychological laboratory, Harvard University, Cambridge, Mass.

Leonard Carmichael, professor of psychology and director of the psychological laboratory, University of Rochester, Rochester, N. Y.

J. F. Dashiell, professor of psychology, University of North Carolina, Chapel Hill, N. C.

Clark L. Hull, professor of psychology. Yale University, New Haven, Conn.

W. R. Miles, professor of psychology, Yale University, New Haven, Conn.

Donald G. Paterson, professor of psychology, University of Minnesota, Minneapolis, Minn.

L. L. Thurstone, professor of psychology, University of Chicago, Chicago, Ill.

Edward C. Tolman, professor of psychology, University of California, Berkeley, Calif.

R. S. Woodworth, professor of psychology, Columbia University, New York City.

Members at Large

Leslie Spier, research associate in anthropology, Yale University, New Haven, Conn.

J. R. Swanton, ethnologist, Bureau of American Ethnology, Smithsonian Institution, Washington, D. C.

E. G. Wever, professor of psychology, Princeton University, Princeton, N. J.

COMMITTEES

The chairman of the division is, ex officio, a member of all committees of the division.

Committee on problems of auditory deficiency: Chairman, Knight Dunlap, professor of psychology, University of California at Los Angeles, Los Angeles, Calif.

Committee on State Archaeological Surveys: Chairman, Carl E. Guthe.

Subcommittee on the Tennessee Valley: Chairman, M. W. Stirling, Chief, Bureau of American Ethnology, Smithsonian Institution, Washington, D. C.

Committee on child development: Chairman, R. S. Woodworth, professor of psychology, Columbia University, New York City.

Committee on personality in relation to culture: Chairman, W. Lloyd Warner, associate professor of anthropology and sociology, University of Chicago, Chicago, Ill.

Subcommittee on the preparation of a handbook of psychological leads for ethnological field work: Chairman, A. Irving Hallowell, professor of anthropology, University of Pennsylvania, Philadelphia, Pa.

Subcommittee on training fellowships: Chairman, Harry Stack Sullivan, psychiatrist, 60 East Forty-second Street, New York City.

Subcommittee on agenda: Chairman, Mark A. May, professor of psychology, Yale University, New Haven, Conn.

Committee on the psychology of the highway: Chairman, H. M. Johnson, research associate on the safety research project, Highway Research Board, National Research Council, Washington, D. C.

Subcommittee for the midwestern area: Chairman, A. R. Lauer, associate professor of psychology, Iowa State College, Ames, Iowa.

Subcommittee on commercial drivers: Chairman, W. C. Shriver, 400 Pennsylvania Avenue, Towson, Md.

Committee on ethnological utilization of motion pictures: Chairman, M. J. Herskovits, professor of anthropology, Northwestern University, Evanston, Ill.

Committee on problems of neurotic behavior: Chairman, W. R. Miles, professor of psychology, Yale University, New Haven, Conn.

Committee on a survey of South American Indians: Chairman, John M. Cooper, professor of anthropology, Catholic University of America, Washington, D. C.

Executive subcommittee: Chairman, John M. Cooper.

5. NATIONAL RESEARCH FELLOWSHIPS

The National Research Council has been entrusted by the Rockefeller Foundation with appropriations to provide for a limited number of postdoctorate fellowships for the purpose of promoting fundamental research in science primarily in educational and research institutions of the United States. These fellowships are awarded to persons who have demonstrated a high order of ability in research for the purpose of enabling them to obtain additional experience in research at institutions which make adequate provision for effective prosecution of research. Applicants are eligible for appointment who are citizens of the United States or of Canada and, as a rule, who are under 35 years of age and who have had training equivalent to that represented by the doctor's degree.

The usual initial stipend is from $1,600 to $2,000 per annum. Under special conditions fellows may be appointed for study abroad.

NATURAL SCIENCES

Fellowships in the following subjects are administered by the national research fellowship board in the natural sciences: Physics, astronomy, chemistry, mathematics, geology, paleontology, physical geography, botany, zoology, agriculture, forestry, anthropology, and psychology.

MEMBERS OF THE BOARD

Ludvig Hektoen, ex officio, chairman of the National Research Council; director, John McCormick Institute for Infectious Diseases, 629 South Wood Street, Chicago, Ill., secretary.

Roger Adams, professor of organic chemistry, University of Illinois, Urbana, Ill.

Isaiah Bowman, president, Johns Hopkins University, Baltimore, Md.

Frank R. Lillie, dean emeritus of the division of biological sciences, and Andrew Macleish distinguished service professor emeritus of embryology, University of Chicago, Chicago, Ill.

Max Mason, vice chairman of the observatory council and member of the executive council, California Institute of Technology, Pasadena, Calif.

Fellowships for 1936-37 have been awarded to the following persons:

IN PHYSICS

Walter E. Albertson	Arnold T. Nordsieck	Milton G. White
Emil J. Konopinski	Stanley N. Van Voorhis	Hubert J. Yearian
Alfred O. C. Nier		

IN CHEMISTRY

David E. Adelson	Lyman G. Bonner	Richard C. Lord, Jr.
John Y. Beach	Gilbert W. King	

IN MATHEMATICS

Daniel M. Dribin	Nathan Jacobson	Charles B. Tompkins, II
Aaron Fialkow	Norman Levinson	

IN AGRICULTURE

Arthur B. Chapman	Herbert E. Longenecker[1]

---

[1] Fellows appointed to work abroad.

IN ANTHROPOLOGY

Walter B. Cline[1]   Frederica de Laguna   David G. Mandelbaum[1]

IN BOTANY

Lindsay M. Black   John I. Shafer, Jr.   Folke K. Skoog

IN PSYCHOLOGY

Wilfred J. Bragden   Edwin E. Ghiselli   Lorrin A. Riggs
Quin F. Curtis

IN ZOOLOGY

John B. Buck   Lester Ingle   Hobart M. Smith
Llewellyn T. Evans   Jeanne F. Manery   Maurice Whittinghill
Herschel T. Gier   Paul A. Nicoll

MEDICAL SCIENCES

Fellowships in the medical sciences are administered by the medical fellowship board.

MEMBERS OF THE BOARD

Francis G. Blake, chairman; Sterling professor of medicine, School of Medicine, Yale University; physician in chief, New Haven Hospital, New Haven, Conn.

Walter B. Cannon, George Higginson professor of physiology, Harvard Medical School, Boston, Mass.

Evarts A. Graham, Bixby professor of surgery, School of Medicine, Washington University, St. Louis, Mo.

Esmond R. Long, ex officio, chairman, division of medical sciences, National Research Council; professor of pathology, School of Medicine, and director, Henry Phipps Institute, University of Pennsylvania, Philadelphia, Pa.

Eugene L. Opie, professor of pathology, Cornell University Medical College; pathologist, New York Hospital, New York City.

Lewis H. Weed, professor of anatomy, and director of the School of Medicine, Johns Hopkins University, Baltimore, Md.

Fellowships for 1936–37 have been awarded to the following persons:

Berry Campbell   Wade H. Marshall   Florindo A. Simeone
Robert S. Dow   Anderson Nettleship   James W. Ward
Samuel Gurin   Byron Riegel
Kathel B. Kerr   Reginald A. Shipley

6. MEMBERS OF THE NATIONAL RESEARCH COUNCIL, 1936–37

Abbot, C. G., Smithsonian Institution, Washington, D. C.
Adams, Roger, University of Illinois, Urbana, Ill.
Agnew, P. G., American Standards Association, 29 West Thirty-ninth Street, New York City.
Aitken, R. G., Lick Observatory, University of California, Berkeley, Calif.
Allison, Maj. Gen. James B., Signal Corps, War Department, Washington, D. C.
Ames, Joseph S., Johns Hopkins University, Baltimore, Md.
Archer, R. S., 10951 Longwood Drive, Chicago, Ill.
Auchter, E. C., United States Bureau of Plant Industry, Washington, D. C.
Bard, Philip, School of Medicine, Johns Hopkins University, Baltimore, Md.
Barrows, Albert L., National Research Council, Washington, D. C.
Barss, H. P., Office of Experiment Stations, United States Department of Agriculture, Washington, D. C.
Barton, Donald C., Humble Oil & Refining Co., Houston, Tex.
Barton, Henry A., American Institute of Physics, 175 Fifth Avenue, New York City.

---

[1] Fellows appointed to work abroad.

Bartow, Edward, State University of Iowa, Iowa City, Iowa.
Bascom, Florence, care of United States Geological Survey, Washington, D. C.
Bastin, Edson S., University of Chicago, Chicago, Ill.
Bausch, Carl L., Bausch & Lomb Optical Co., Rochester, N. Y.
Bell, Frank T., United States Bureau of Fisheries, Washington, D. C.
Benedict, Ruth, Columbia University, New York City.
Besley, F. W., State forester of Maryland, Baltimore, Md.
Bigelow, H. B., Harvard University, Cambridge, Mass.
Blake, Francis G., School of Medicine, Yale University, New Haven, Conn.
Bliss, Gilbert A., University of Chicago, Chicago, Ill.
Bolton, E. K., E. I. du Pont de Nemours & Co., Wilmington, Del.
Boring, Edwin G., Harvard University, Cambridge, Mass.
Bowie, William, 2900 Connecticut Avenue, Washington, D. C.
Bowman, Isaiah, Johns Hopkins University, Baltimore, Md.
Breer, Carl, Chrysler Corporation, Detroit, Mich.
Bridgman, P. W., Harvard University, Cambridge, Mass.
Briggs, Lyman J., National Bureau of Standards, Washington, D. C.
Brigham, Maj. Gen. Claude E., Chemical Warfare Service, War Department, Washington, D. C.
Bronk, Detlev W., University of Pennsylvania Hospital, Philadelphia, Pa.
Bryant, Harold C., National Park Service, Washington, D. C.
Buddington, A. F., Princeton University, Princeton, N. J.
Bush, Vannevar, Massachusetts Institute of Technology, Cambridge, Mass.
Butts, Charles, United States Geological Survey, Washington, D. C.
Birkhoff, George D., Harvard University, Cambridge, Mass.
Cady, W. G., Wesleyan University, Middletown, Conn.
Cannon, W. B., Harvard Medical School, Boston, Mass.
Carmichael, Leonard, University of Rochester, Rochester, N. Y.
Carr, Wilbur J., Department of State, Washington, D. C.
Cattell, McKeen, Cornell University Medical College, New York City.
Chambers, Wrightson, Post Office Department, Washington, D. C.
Chase, Harry W., New York University, New York City.
Clapp, E. H., United States Forest Service, Washington, D. C.
Clements, F. O., General Motors Corporation, Detroit, Mich.
Clevenger, Galen H., 67 Sheffield Road, Newtonville, Mass.
Coker, R. E., University of North Carolina, Chapel Hill, N. C.
Compton, Arthur H., University of Chicago, Chicago, Ill.
Compton, Karl T., Massachusetts Institute of Technology, Cambridge, Mass.
Conant, James B., Harvard University, Cambridge, Mass.
Cooper, John M., Catholic University of America, Washington, D. C.
Corner, George W., University of Rochester, Rochester, N. Y.
Crane, E. J., Ohio State University, Columbus, Ohio.
Crittenden, E. C., National Bureau of Standards, Washington, D. C.
Curtis, W. C., University of Missouri, Columbia, Mo.
Dashiell, J. F., University of North Carolina, Chapel Hill, N. C.
Davies, C. E., American Society of Mechanical Engineers, 29 West Thirty-ninth Street, New York City.
Davis, David John, College of Medicine, University of Illinois, Chicago, Ill.
Day, Arthur L., Carnegie Institution of Washington, Washington, D. C.
DuBridge, Lee A., University of Rochester, Rochester, N. Y.
Dunlap, Knight, University of California at Los Angeles, Los Angeles, Calif.
Dunn, Gano, J. G. White Engineering Corporation, 80 Broad Street, New York City.
Dushman, Saul, General Electric Co., Schenectady, N. Y.
Esselen, Gustavus J., 857 Boylston Street, Boston, Mass.
Evans, William Lloyd, Ohio State University, Columbus, Ohio.
Farmer, F. M., Electrical Testing Laboratories, Eightieth Street and East End Avenue, New York City.
Farr, Clifford B., Pennsylvania Hospital, Philadelphia, Pa.
Fenneman, Nevin M., University of Cincinnati, Cincinnati, Ohio.
Fickes, Edwin S., Aluminum Co. of America, Pittsburgh, Pa.
Fieldner, A. C., United States Bureau of Mines, Washington, D. C.
Finch, John W., United States Bureau of Mines, Washington, D. C.

Fleming, John A., department of terrestrial magnetism, Carnegie Institution of Washington, 2801 Upton Street, Washington, D. C.

Fletcher, Harvey, Bell Telephone Laboratories, Inc., 463 West Street, New York City.

Flexner, Simon, Rockefeller Institute for Medical Research, Sixty-sixth Street and York Avenue, New York City.

Freeman, Walter, 1726 Eye Street NW., Washington, D. C.

Fry, Thornton C., Bell Telephone Laboratories, Inc., 463 West Street, New York City.

Gabrielson, Ira N., United States Bureau of Biological Survey, Washington, D. C.

Gentry, Lt. Col. E. R., Medical Corps, War Department, Washington, D. C.

Giesecke, F. E., Agricultural and Mechanical College of Texas, College Station, Tex.

Gillett, H. W., Battelle Memorial Institute, Columbus, Ohio.

Gleason, Henry Allen, New York Botanical Garden, Bronx Park, New York City.

Gortner, Ross A., University Farm, University of Minnesota, St. Paul, Minn.

Gregg, W. R., United States Weather Bureau, Washington, D. C.

Gregory, Herbert E., Bishop Museum of Polynesian Ethnology and Natural History, Honolulu, Hawaii.

Gregory, John H., Johns Hopkins University, Baltimore, Md.

Guthe, Carl E., University of Michigan, Ann Arbor, Mich.

Hale, George E., Mount Wilson Observatory, Pasadena, Calif.

Hannum, Col. Warren T., Corps of Engineers, War Department, Washington, D. C.

Harrison, Ross G., Yale University, New Haven, Conn.

Heck, N. H., United States Coast and Geodetic Survey, Washington, D. C.

Heck, R. C. H., Rutgers University, New Brunswick, N. J.

Heilbrunn, L. V., University of Pennsylvania, Philadelphia, Pa.

Hektoen, Ludvig, John McCormick Institute for Infectious Diseases, 629 South Wood Street, Chicago, Ill.

Hellweg, Capt. F., United States Naval Observatory, Washington, D. C.

Henderson, L. J., Harvard University, Cambridge, Mass.

Henline, H. H., American Institute of Electrical Engineers, 29 West Thirty-ninth Street, New York City.

Hetzel, R. D., Pennsylvania State College, State College, Pa.

Hill, Joseph A., United States Bureau of the Census, Washington, D. C.

Hooper, Capt., S. C., Office of the Chief of Naval Operations, Navy Department, Washington, D. C.

Hooton, E. A., Harvard University, Cambridge, Mass.

Hoover, J. Edgar, United States Department of Justice, Washington, D. C.

Hostetter, J. C., Hartford-Empire Co., Hartford, Conn.

Houghton, Bert, 1274 East Twenty-third Street, Brooklyn, N. Y.

Hull, Clark L., Yale University, New Haven, Conn.

Hunsaker, Jerome C., Massachusetts Institute of Technology, Cambridge, Mass.

Hunter, Walter S., Brown University, Providence, R. I.

Jackson, William B, Broadview, Cheshire, Mass.

Jewett, Frank B., American Telephone & Telegraph Co., 195 Broadway, New York City.

Johnson, Douglas, Columbia University, New York City.

Johnston, John, United States Steel Corporation, Kearney, N. J.

Jull, Morley A., University of Maryland, College Park, Md.

Karsner, Howard T., Western Reserve University, Cleveland, Ohio.

Keith, Arthur, 2210 Twentieth St., N. W., Washington, D. C.

Kellogg, Remington, United States National Museum, Washington, D. C.

Kellogg, Vernon, National Research Council, Washington, D. C.

Kelly, Fred J., United States Office of Education, Washington, D. C.

Kennelly, Arthur E., Harvard University, Cambridge, Mass.

Kidder, A. V., Beverly Farms, Mass.

King, W. J., General Electric Co., Schenectady, N. Y.

Knight, Henry G., United States Bureau of Chemistry and Soils, Washington, D. C.

Kraus, Charles A., Brown University, Providence, R. I.
Kummel, Henry B., State geologist, Trenton, N. J.
Labee, F. H., Sun Oil Co., Dallas, Tex.
Land, Rear Admiral Emory S., Bureau of Construction and Repair, Navy Department, Washington, D. C.
Lavis, Fred, 30 Broad Street, New York City.
Lee, Everett S., General Electric Co., Schenectady, N. Y.
Leighton, Morris M., Illinois State Geological Survey, Urbana, Ill.
Lewis, I. F., University of Virginia, University, Va.
Lillie, Frank R., 5801 Kenwood Avenue, Chicago, Ill.
Lincoln, Col. Francis H., General Staff, War Department, Washington, D. C.
Lipman, Jacob G., State agricultural experiment station, New Brunswick, N. J.
Llewellyn, F. T., United States Steel Corporation, 71 Broadway, New York City.
Long, Esmond R., Henry Phipps Institute, Seventh and Lombard Streets, Philadelphia, Pa.
Longley, W. R., Yale University, New Haven, Conn.
Lowery, P. C., Lowery Building, Detroit, Mich.
Lubin, Isador, United States Department of Labor, Washington, D. C.
Lucas, George L., Port of New York Authority, 111 Eighth Avenue, New York City.
Lukens, Hiram S., University of Pennsylvania, Philadelphia, Pa.
McClung, C. E., University of Pennsylvania, Philadelphia, Pa.
McCrory, S. H., United States Bureau of Agricultural Engineering, Washington, D. C.
McKinley, Earl B., School of Medicine, George Washington University, Washington, D. C.
McVey, Frank L., University of Kentucky, Lexington, Ky.
MacDonald, T. H., United States Bureau of Public Roads, Washington, D. C.
MacNider, William DeB., University of North Carolina, Chapel Hill, N. C.
Mann, A. R., Cornell University, Ithaca, N. Y.
Mann, C. R., American Council on Education, 744 Jackson Place, Washington, D. C.
Mathews, Edward B., Johns Hopkins University, Baltimore, Md.
Mendenhall, W. C., United States Geological Survey, Washington, D. C.
Merriam, John C., Carnegie Institution of Washington, Washington, D. C.
Merrill, Elmer D., Harvard University, Cambridge, Mass.
Meyer, Karl F., University of California, Berkeley, Calif.
Miles, W. R., Yale University, New Haven, Conn.
Millikan, R. A., California Institute of Technology, Pasadena, Calif.
Mohler, J. R., United States Bureau of Animal Industry, Washington, D. C.
Moody, Herbert R., College of the City of New York, New York City.
Morgan, Herbert R., United States Naval Observatory, Washington, D. C.
Morse, Marston, Institute for Advanced Study, Princeton University, Princeton, N. J.
Mumford, H. W., University of Illinois, Urbana, Ill.
Munroe, Col. John E., Ordnance Department, War Department, Washington, D. C.
Nolan, Thomas B., United States Geological Survey, Washington, D. C.
Nourse, Edwin G., Institute of Economics, 744 Jackson Place, Washington, D. C.
Noyes, W. A., University of Illinois, Urbana, Ill.
Palmer, T. S., 1939 Biltmore Street NW., Washington, D. C.
Parsons, A. B., American Institute of Mining and Metallurgical Engineers, 29 West Thirty-ninth Street, New York City.
Patterson, Donald G., University of Minnesota, Minneapolis, Minn.
Patterson, Austin M., Antioch College, Yellow Springs, Ohio.
Payne, Fernandus, Indiana University, Bloomington, Ind.
Pearson, Raymond A., Resettlement Administration, Washington, D. C.
Pendleton, Maj. Randolph T., Coast Artillery Corps, War Department, Washington, D. C.
Pepper, O. H. Perry, School of Medicine, University of Pennsylvania, Philadelphia, Pa.
Peters, John P., Yale Medical School, New Haven, Conn.

Pierce, Charles H., United States Patent Office, Washington, D. C.
Platt, Robert S., University of Chicago, Chicago, Ill.
Poillon, Howard, Research Corporation, 403 Lexington Avenue, New York City.
Powell, C. L., General Electric Co., 570 Lexington Avenue, New York City.
Purdy, Ross C., 2525 North High Street, Columbus, Ohio.
Putnam, George R., United States Bureau of Lighthouses, Washington, D. C.
Redfield, Robert, University of Chicago, Chicago, Ill.
Richards, Alfred N., School of Medicine, University of Pennsylvania, Philadelphia, Pa.
Richtmyer, F. K., Cornell University, Ithaca, N. Y.
Robbins, W. J., University of Missouri, Columbia, Mo.
Roberts, Frank H. H., Jr., Bureau of American Ethnology, Washington, D. C.
Rose, H. J., Mellon Institute of Industrial Research, Pittsburgh, Pa.
Rossiter, Rear Admiral Percival E., Bureau of Medicine and Surgery, Navy Department, Washington, D. C.
Rowe, L. S., Pan American Union, Washington, D. C.
Russell, Henry Norris, Princeton University Observatory, Princeton, N. J.
Schairer, J. F., geophysical laboratory, Carnegie Institution of Washington, 2801 Upton Street, Washington, D. C.
Schlesinger, Frank, Yale University Observatory, New Haven, Conn.
Scofield, C. S., United States Bureau of Plant Industry, Washington, D. C.
Seabury, George W., American Society of Civil Engineers, 29 West Thirty-ninth Street, New York City.
Shapiro, H. L., American Museum of Natural History, Seventy-seventh Street and Central Park West, New York City.
Sharp, Clayton H., 294 Fisher Avenue, White Plains, N. Y.
Sherman, L. K., Randolph-Perkins Co., National Bank Building, Chicago, Ill.
Slocum, Frederick, Van Vleck Observatory, Wesleyan University, Middletown, Conn.
Spier, Leslie, Yale University, New Haven, Conn.
Spinden, Herbert J., Brooklyn Institute of Arts and Sciences, Brooklyn, N. Y.
Stakman, E. C., University of Wisconsin, Madison, Wis.
Stark, Rear Admiral Harold R., Bureau of Ordnance, Navy Department, Washington, D. C.
Stewart, G. W., University of Iowa, Iowa City, Iowa.
Stimson, A. M., United States Public Health Service, Washington, D. C.
Stone, Harvey B., School of Medicine, Johns Hopkins University, Baltimore, Md.
Strong, Lee A., United States Bureau of Entomology, Washington, D. C.
Strong, William Duncan, Bureau of American Ethnology, Washington, D. C.
Swanton, John R., Bureau of American Ethnology, Washington, D. C.
Thomas, L. F., Washington University, St. Louis, Mo.
Thompson, L. R., United States Public Health Service, Washington, D. C.
Thompson, Thomas G., University of Washington, Seattle, Wash.
Thurstone, L. L., University of Chicago, Chicago, Ill.
Tolman, Edward C., University of California, Berkeley, Calif.
Trinks, W. C. L., Carnegie Institute of Technology, Pittsburgh, Pa.
Tuckerman, L. B., National Bureau of Standards, Washington, D. C.
Tyler, H. W., Library of Congress, Washington, D. C.
Tyzzer, E. E., Harvard Medical School, Boston, Mass.
Urey, Harold C., Columbia University, New York City.
Van Vleck, J. H., Harvard University, Cambridge, Mass.
Veblen, Oswald, Institute for Advanced Study, Princeton University, Princeton, N. J.
Voegtlin, Carl, National Institute of Health, Washington, D. C.
Walton, Henry J., School of Medicine, University of Maryland, Baltimore, Md.
Warner, E. P., care of Harvard Club, 27 West Forty-second Street, New York City.
Weaver, Warren, Rockefeller Foundation, 49 West Forty-ninth Street, New York City.
Webster, David L., Stanford University, Stanford University, Calif.
Weed, Lewis H., School of Medicine, Johns Hopkins University, Baltimore, Md.
Weller, Carl V., University of Michigan, Ann Arbor, Mich.
Wever, L. C., Princeton University, Princeton, N. J.
White, William Charles, National Institute of Health, Washington, D. C.

Whitehead, John B., Johns Hopkins University, Baltimore, Md.
Whitmore, Frank C., Pennsylvania State College, State College, Pa.
Willard, F. W., Nassau Smelting & Refining Co., 50 Church Street, New York City.
Willard, Hobart H., University of Michigan, Ann Arbor, Mich.
Williams, Frank E., University of Pennsylvania, Philadelphia, Pa.
Wilson, D. Wright, University of Pennsylvania, Philadelphia, Pa.
Wilson, Ellery L., Rumford Chemical Works, Providence, R. I.
Woods, A. F., United States Bureau of Plant Industry. Washington, D. C.
Woodworth, Robert S., Columbia University, New York City.
Wright, A. H., State College of Agriculture, Cornell University, Ithaca, N. Y.
Wright, Fred. E., geophysical laboratory, Carnegie Institution of Washington, 2801 Upton Street, Washington, D. C.
Wright, John K., American Geographical Society, Broadway at One Hundred and Fifty-sixth Street, New York City.
Youngblood, B., United States Department of Agriculture, Washington, D. C.
Zeleny, John, Yale University, New Haven, Conn.

O